**Problem 8-10** Allowance for Uncollectible Accounts, $3,750
**Problem 8-11** Required Balance in Allowance Account, $2,785
**Problem 8-1A** Note C—Maturity Value, $15,300
**Problem 8-2A** Total Interest Revenue, $1,198.05
**Problem 8-3A** Required Balance in Allowance Account, $2,000
**Problem 8-4A** Required Balance in Allowance Account, $14,197
**Problem 8-5A** Net Accounts Receivable in Requirement 2, $103,204

*Chapter 9*

**Exercise 9-1** Cost of Goods Sold, $90,000
**Exercise 9-2** 19X5 Net Income Overstated, $5,000
**Exercise 9-3** No Key Figure
**Exercise 9-4** Net Income for 19X3, $14,000
**Exercise 9-5** Ending Inventory per Books, $4,450
**Exercise 9-6** Ending Inventory for Requirement 1, $2,700
**Exercise 9-7** Ending Inventory for Requirement 1, $23,060
**Exercise 9-8** Ending Inventory by Items, $15,920
**Exercise 9-9** Cost of Goods Sold, $68,240
**Exercise 9-10** Estimated Ending Inventory at Retail, $25,000
**Problem 9-1** Net Income, $90,000
**Problem 9-2** Ending Inventory Using FIFO, $24,200
**Problem 9-3** No Key Figure
**Problem 9-4** Net Income, $39,300
**Problem 9-5** Ending Inventory Using Periodic, $6,595
**Problem 9-6** Ending Inventory Using FIFO, $14,050
**Problem 9-7** No Key Figure
**Problem 9-8** Inventory Valuation Using Total Inventory, $10,741
**Problem 9-9** No Key Figure
**Problem 9-10** Cost of Goods Sold, $334,320
**Problem 9-11** Net Income, $55,227
**Problem 9-12** Cost of Goods Available for Sale, $641,400
**Problem 9-13** Net Income, $15,055
**Problem 9-1A** Cost of Goods Available for Sale Under Alternative A, $7,030
**Problem 9-2A** Gross Margin, $12,000
**Problem 9-3A** Cost of Goods Available for Sale, $25,200
**Problem 9-4A** Gross Margin Percentage, 42%
**Problem 9-5A** Ending Inventory at Cost in Case 2, $88.00

*Chapter 10*

**Exercise 10-1** No Key Figure
**Exercise 10-2** Cost Apportioned to Land, $80,000
**Exercise 10-3** Cost Apportioned to Land, $96,000
**Exercise 10-4** 19X7—Sum-of-the-Years' -Digits Method, $3,400
**Exercise 10-5** No Key Figure
**Exercise 10-6** 19X4—Depreciation Expense, $5,400
**Exercise 10-7** No Key Figure
**Problem 10-1** Machinery, $29,640
**Problem 10-2** 19X6—Double-declining Balance Methods, $7,690 (rounded)
**Problem 10-3** Depreciation Expense, $795,500
**Problem 10-4** 19X5—Depreciation Expense, $6,840
**Problem 10-5** Year 3—Depreciation Expense—Sum-of-the-Years' -Digits Method, $24,000
**Problem 10-6** No Key Figure
**Problem 10-7** 19X2—Depreciation Expense—Machine B, $8,333 (Rounded)
**Problem 10-8** 19X7—Corrected Net Income, $22,640
**Problem 10-9** 19X3—Depreciation Expense—Machine, $5,000
**Problem 10-1A** 19X2—Depreciation Expense—Double-declining Balance Method, $1,901
**Problem 10-2A** Depreciation Expense, $56,000
**Problem 10-3A** 19X6—Depreciation Expense—Sum-of-the-Years' -Digits Method, $10,000
**Problem 10-4A** Revised Depreciation Expense, $11,000

*Chapter 11*

**Exercise 11-1** 2a. Loss on Disposal, $6,500
**Exercise 11-2** Loss on Disposal, $2,000
**Exercise 11-3** Cash Credited for, $3,000
**Exercise 11-4** Mine Amortization $9 per Ton
**Exercise 11-5** Patent Amortization, $11,400
**Exercise 11-6** Dewdrops above Average Earnings, $15,000
**Problem 11-1** Machine B—Gain on Disposal, $750
**Problem 11-2** Part 4 Loss on Disposal, $2,000
**Problem 11-3** Part 2 Carrying Value, $7,400,000
**Problem 11-4** Franchise Amortization, $4,200
**Problem 11-5** Part 2—15%
**Problem 11-6** Part 3—Oil Field, $16,920,000
**Problem 11-7** Mine Depletion, $90,000
**Problem 11-8** 2d. Loss on Disposal, $8,000
**Problem 11-9** Part 3—Cash Credited for, $44,000
**Problem 11-1A** 2c. Gain on Disposal, $300
**Problem 11-2A** No Key Figure
**Problem 11-3A** Ore Mine—Depletion per Ton, $55.50
**Problem 11-4A** Average Net Income, $29,900
**Problem 11-5A** Carrying Value of Natural Resources, $250,000

*Chapter 12*

**Exercise 12-1** Sept. 1, Interest Expense, $375
**Exercise 12-2** Dec. 31, Interest Expense, $250
**Exercise 12-3** Dec. 31, Interest Expense, $1,800
**Exercise 12-4** Sales Tax Payable, $50,136
**Exercise 12-5** Jan. 31, Product Warranty Liability, $9,000
**Exercise 12-6** Net Earnings, $310.24
**Exercise 12-7** Payroll Tax Expense, $9,590
**Exercise 12-8** Net Earnings, $455.60
**Problem 12-1** Dec. 31, Interest Payable, $2,000
**Problem 12-2** Total Current Liabilities, $142,100
**Problem 12-3** Sales Tax Payable, $6,800
**Problem 12-4** February 28, Property Tax Expense, $1,860
**Problem 12-5** Part 3—Credit Balance of $55
**Problem 12-6** Gross Earnings, $560
**Problem 12-7** Total Payroll Expense, $28,730
**Problem 12-8** Payroll Tax Expense, $135.10
**Problem 12-9** Total Net Pay (All Employees) $2,073.50
**Problem 12-10** Total Current Liabilities, $228,668
**Problem 12-1A** Total Current Liabilities, $92,130
**Problem 12-2A** Excise Tax Payable, $8,925
**Problem 12-3A** March 31, Property Tax Expense, $1,808
**Problem 12-4A** Part 3—Credit Balance of $283
**Problem 12-5A** Federal Unemployment Taxes Payable, $3,240
**Problem 12-6A** Payroll Tax Expense, $122.40

*Chapter 13*

**Exercise 13-1** Cross Capital, $15,300
**Exercise 13-2** Part 2—Kriss, $10,000
**Exercise 13-3** Part B—Stokes Capital, $11,455
**Exercise 13-4** Part 3—Marion Capital, $48,000
**Exercise 13-5** Part 2—Shorter Capital Debit, $5,000
**Exercise 13-6** Part 2—Gomez Capital Debit, $7,500
**Exercise 13-7** Part 2—Lane Capital Credit, $3,000
**Problem 13-1** Part 2C—Fuentes, $13,100
**Problem 13-2** Part 1C—Beamer Capital Credit, $11,200
**Problem 13-3** Part 2—Best's Capital Balance, $54,200
**Problem 13-4** Part 4—Tabor Capital Credit, $30,000
**Problem 13-5** Part 4—Danza Capital Credit, $3,000
**Problem 13-6** Part 5—Carson Capital Balance, $21,000
**Problem 13-7** Part 2—Lee Capital Debit, $4,400
**Problem 13-8** Part 1B—Cash Distribution to Ames, $78,000
**Problem 13-9** Part 4—Harris Capital Credit, $13,360
**Problem 13-1A** Part 2C—David, $16,640
**Problem 13-2A** Part 1D—Acker Capital Credit, $12,200
**Problem 13-3A** Part 5—Tucker Capital Debit, $6,000
**Problem 13-4A** Part 4—Eden Capital Credit, $2,000
**Problem 13-5A** Part 4B—Frey Capital Debit, $43,000

*Chapter 14*

**Exercise 14-1** Part 3—Paid in Capital in Excess of Stated Value, $600,000
**Exercise 14-2** No Key Figure
**Exercise 14-3** Total Contributed Capital, $1,030,000
**Exercise 14-4** 19X3, Preferred Dividend per Share, $15
**Exercise 14-5** No Key Figure
**Exercise 14-6** Part 4, $6 per Share
**Exercise 14-7** No Key Figure
**Exercise 14-8** Common Stockholders' Equity, $2,050,000
**Problem 14-1** Total Contributed Capital, $1,232,000
**Problem 14-2** Total Contributed Capital, $885,000
**Problem 14-3** Part 1—19X6—Common $2.25 per Share
**Problem 14-4** No Key Figure
**Problem 14-5** Part 5, $48 per Share
**Problem 14-6** Part 2, Common $15.90 per Share
**Problem 14-7** Part 3, Preferred $6.00 per Share
**Problem 14-8** Total Stockholders' Equity, $1,397,200
**Problem 14-9** Part 3, Preferred $55 per share
**Problem 14-1A** Total Stockholders' Equity, $686,200
**Problem 14-2A** Part 2, Preferred $15.00 per Share
**Problem 14-3A** No Key Figure
**Problem 14-4A** Part 5, $22 per Share
**Problem 14-5A** Part 2, Preferred $120.00 per Share

*Chapter 15*

**Exercise 15-1** Total Stockholders' Equity, $1,450,000
**Exercise 15-2** Total Stockholders' Equity, $1,272,000
**Exercise 15-3** No Key Figure
**Exercise 15-4** Retained Earnings, December 31, 19X6, $936,000
**Exercise 15-5** Stock Dividends, $140,000
**Exercise 15-6** Net Income, $186,000
**Exercise 15-7** Weighted Average Number of Shares Outstanding, 250,000
**Exercise 15-8** Primary Earnings per Common Share, $4.06
**Problem 15-1** Retained Earnings, December 31, 19X6, $317,800
**Problem 15-2** Total Stockholders' Equity, $1,837,500

# *PRINCIPLES OF ACCOUNTING*

# PRINCIPLES OF ACCOUNTING

*John R. Cerepak*
Fairleigh Dickinson University

*Donald H. Taylor*
University of Arkansas

The first printing of *Principles of Accounting* included the most recent material dealing with The Tax Reform Act of 1986.

Now in this important second printing, we have added a new appendix on the proposed *Statement of Cash Flows* and general updating of *Chapter 18: Statement of Changes in Financial Position.*

*Prentice-Hall, Inc., Englewood Cliffs, New Jersey 07632*

*Library of Congress Cataloging-in-Publication Data*

CEREPAK, JOHN R.
Principles of accounting.

Includes index.
1. Accounting. I. Taylor, Donald H.
II. Title.
HF5635.C436 1987 657 86-20488
ISBN 0-13-700956-9

Editorial/production supervision: Pamela Wilder
Interior and cover design: Jayne Conte
Manufacturing buyer: Ray Keating
Cover photo by Geoff Cove—The Image Bank



Printed in the United States of America

10 9 8 7 6 5 4 3

ISBN 0-13-700956-9 01

Prentice-Hall International (UK) Limited, *London*
Prentice-Hall of Australia Pty. Limited, *Sydney*
Prentice-Hall Canada Inc., *Toronto*
Prentice-Hall Hispanoamericana, S.A., *Mexico*
Prentice-Hall of India Private Limited, *New Delhi*
Prentice-Hall of Japan, Inc., *Tokyo*
Prentice-Hall of Southeast Asia Pte. Ltd., *Singapore*
Editora Prentice-Hall do Brasil, Ltda., *Rio de Janeiro*

*To my parents for their support and understanding, and to Carole for her encouragement and inspiration — John Cerepak*

*To Rosetta, Mike, and Tim, and to my parents, George and Ethel — Don Taylor*

# CONTENTS

## 5 Accounting for a Merchandising Company 152



## 6 Accounting Systems—Manual and Automated 191



# Part Two
# ACCOUNTING FOR ASSETS AND CURRENT LIABILITIES

## 7 Internal Control and Control of Cash 235

## 10 Plant and Equipment: Acquisition and Depreciation 349



## 11 Plant and Equipment: Disposals, Natural Resources, and Intangibles 379



## 12 Current Liabilities and Payroll Accounting 409

# Part Three
## ACCOUNTING FOR PARTNERSHIPS AND CORPORATIONS

# Part Five
# MANAGERIAL ACCOUNTING FOR DECISION MAKING

## 21 Accounting for Manufacturing Companies 783



## 22 Cost Accounting Systems 806



## 23 Cost-Volume-Profit Analysis 843

# PREFACE

A principles of accounting text should be a learning aid that shows students how to formulate accounting information and how to use it in the business world. Such a book should fully explain and illustrate how business transactions are recorded, summarized, classified, reported, and interpreted, and the underlying theory that supports the accounting techniques. If the book accomplishes this purpose, the students will have an understanding of accounting that will enable them to pursue their chosen careers successfully, whether these careers are in accounting or in another related field.

We believe that this text uniquely accomplishes these goals by providing material that states its objectives, shows how these objectives are accomplished, and provides many means for self-assessment by the students of their learning progress. For example, each chapter contains special features designed to aid and measure the students' learning, such as:

Clearly stated learning objectives, uniquely divided into questions that the students should be able to answer when they have completed the chapter, and accounting functions that the students should be able to perform when they have completed the chapter.

Marginal comments that summarize key points and show how the learning objectives are being accomplished. These marginal comments are keyed to the learning objectives in each chapter.

Material that is selected and sequenced according to our own classroom experiences and suggestions from reviewers, editors, and students.

A clear and balanced presentation of subject matter that is relevant to a principles of accounting text.

Numerical and graphical illustrations and exhibits that relate closely to the narrative explanations. All the illustrations and exhibits are purposely kept simple without sacrificing substance.

A highlight problem that covers one or more key chapter concepts and provides an immediate self assessment of the students' learning progress. The answers to these highlight problems are contained in Appendix A.

An end-of-chapter glossary that clearly defines key terms used in the body of the chapter. These key terms are put in boldface when they first appear in the chapter.

Review questions (keyed to the learning objectives) that allow the students to "track" the material through the chapter and reinforce their learning of key concepts.

Analytical questions (keyed to the learning objectives) that allow students to reason out the "whys" as well as the "hows" of concepts presented in the chapter. The chapter material provides the basis for answers to these questions but does not usually provide the direct answers.

Impact analysis questions (keyed to the learning objectives) that allow the students to think about the impact that errors, alternatives, and events have on financial statements and other financial data. These questions enable students to understand the relationship between properly recorded transactions and reliable financial information.

Exercises (keyed to the learning objectives) that allow the students to test their understanding of chapter material with short, and sometimes thought-provoking, simulations.

Problems (keyed to the learning objectives) that allow the students to test their understanding of chapter material with a wide variety of short, medium, long, straightforward, and complex simulations.

Alternate problems (keyed to the learning objectives) that allow the students to reinforce their understanding of chapter material with similar problems but different data combinations and numbers.

When students use this book, they will have a comprehensive, well-illustrated, and easy-to-read learning aid that enables them to

Ascertain the objectives of each chapter.

Follow the chapter material and determine how these objectives are met

Assess their learning progress through a wide variety of definitions, questions, exercises, and problems.

The book is divided into five parts, each of which is described below.

Part One (The Introduction and Chapters 1–6) illustrates in step-by-step manner the basic accounting process and shows how this process develops information needed to assess the operational performance and financial status of the company. This part includes chapters on (1) Financial Statements and the Accounting Equation, (2) Recording Business Transactions, (3) Adjusting the Accounts and Preparing Financial Statements, (4) Completing the Accounting Cycle, (5) Accounting for a Merchandising Company, and (6) Accounting Systems—Manual and Automated.

Part Two (Chapters 7–12) examines how various assets and liabilities are accounted for and how (as well as why) their values are determined. This part includes chapters on (7) Internal Control and the Control of Cash, (8) Notes and Accounts Receivable, (9) Inventories and Cost of Goods Sold, (10) Plant and Equipment: Acquisition and Depreciation, (11) Plant and Equipment: Disposals, Natural Resources, and Intangibles, and (12) Current Liabilities and Payroll Accounting.

Part Three (Chapters 13–17) discusses various aspects of accounting for business entities organized as partnerships and corporations. This part includes chapters on (13) Partnerships, (14) Corporations: Organization and Contributed Equity, (15) Corporations: Retained Earnings, Dividends, Treasury Stock, and Income Reporting, (16) Long-Term Liabilities, and (17) Investments in Corporate Securities.

Part Four (Chapters 18–20) covers specialized financial accounting topics such as financial statement analysis and interpretation, comprehensive discussions of accounting principles and practices, and price-level changes. This part includes chapters on (18) Statement of Changes in Financial Position, (19) Financial Statement Analysis, and (20) Accounting Principles and the Effects of Changing Prices.

Part Five (Chapters 21–28) contains discussions and illustrations of managerial accounting topics and income taxes and their effect on business decisions.

This part includes chapters on (21) Accounting for Manufacturing Companies, (22) Cost Accounting Systems, (23) Cost-Volume-Profit Analysis, (24) Budgeting—Static and Flexible, (25) Standard Costs, (26) Responsibility Accounting and Decentralization Concepts, (27) Capital Budgeting, and (28) Income Taxes and Business Decisions.

## SUPPLEMENTARY MATERIAL

The supplementary materials for *Principles of Accounting* provides a variety of useful tools for both student and instructor. Together they form a total teaching system for the instructor and a total learning system for the student.

### For the Instructor

INSTRUCTOR'S LECTURE MANUAL The lecture guide, prepared by Margot Norwood and Robbie Sheffy, both of Tarrant County Junior College, is organized according to the learning objectives in the text. In addition to detailed lecture notes, lecture outlines, and teaching transparencies, this manual includes grids of assignment material, lists of suggested assignments for both in-class illustrations and homework, and estimated time of completion and level of difficulty grids for all exercises, problems, and alternate problems.

TRANSPARENCIES Available in 2 sets, one covering chapters 1–12 and the other covering chapters 13–28, these include a number of teaching transparencies to enhance your lecture as well as transparencies of worked-out solutions to all the exercises, problems, and alternate problems in the text.

TEST BANK The test bank, prepared by Charles Cheetham of the County College of Morris, contains approximately 1900 questions, exercises, and problems that thoroughly cover the concepts and principles presented in the text. A grid is provided that categorizes the testing material by topic and learning objective. A master answer key follows each chapter's test material in which the questions are labeled as factual or conceptual and are categorized by level of difficulty and estimated time of completion.

ACHIEVEMENT TESTS Three alternative series of Achievement Tests are available in quantity to adopters. Each series includes 10 tests plus a mid-term and final exam.

SOLUTIONS MANUAL Available in two volumes, one for chapters 1–13 and another for chapters 13–28, this manual provides complete answers and worked-out solutions for all the end-of-chapter assignment material. Detailed calculations are included in the solutions where needed. Also included are estimates of time of completion and level of difficulty charts for all exercises, problems, and alternate problems.

### Computer Software for the Instructor

FLOPPY DISK TESTING SERVICE All items from the Test Bank are available on a set of floppy disks for use on an Apple II, IIe, II+, or IBM PC. This service is free to adopters and allows the instructor to access and print questions from the Test Bank on campus. You may add your own questions to the disks. Answer keys are also provided.

**THE PRENTICE-HALL TELEPHONE TEST PREPARATION SERVICE** This service provides instructors with computer-composed, professionally-typed tests consisting of items selected from the Test Bank. Using a service "master" (supplied upon adoption of the text), the instructor simply selects the numbers of the items wanted on the exam master from the Test Bank. Instructors may either write the numbers on the order form or they may call them in on our *toll free* number: (800) 526-0485. Within 24 hours of receiving the order, Prentice-Hall will mail the exam master numbered sequentially along with an answer key.

**GRADE BOOK/CLASS RECORD FILE** This item allows instructors to keep class records, compute class statistics, average grades, print graphs, sort by student name or grade, and more. These disks are available free to adopters. They are available for both Apple and IBM computers.

## For the Student

**STUDY GUIDES** The study guides, prepared by Timothy D. Miller of El Camino College, are available in two volumes, one for chapters 1–13 and one for chapters 13–28. These guides are meant to be used side-by-side with *Principles of Accounting* and are designed to help the student learn the text material as quickly and completely as possible. Included are chapter outlines, summaries of chapter highlights, selected key terms in simplified English, and matching, completion, true/false, and multiple choice questions with answers.

**WORKING PAPERS** Two volumes of working papers, one for chapters 1–13 and one for chapters 13–28, are available on which students can work the solutions to the exercises, problems, and alternate problems in the text.

Note that chapter 13 is included in both volumes to increase flexibility in course design.

**PRACTICE SETS** Four practice sets are available for use with *Principles of Accounting.*

*Practice Set #1. M.L. Gordon, Attorney-at-Law,* covers the accounting cycle for a sole-proprietorship-service business for a one month period. This practice set is designed for use after chapter 4. It should require approximately 10 hours to complete.

*Practice Set #2. Modern Clothes Company* covers the complete accounting cycle for a sole-proprietorship-merchandising business including the use of special journals, petty cash, and bad debt procedures. This practice set may be used after chapter 8. It should require approximately 15 hours to complete.

*Practice Set #3. The Diversified Corporation* covers the accounting transactions for a small, publicly held corporation. The transactions reflect the material in chapters 14–18 of the textbook and the preparation of corporate financial statements. This practice set may be used upon completion of chapter 19. It should require approximately 15 hours to complete.

*Practice Set #4. The Custom Furniture Company* covers the accounting cycle for a manufacturing company, using a job order costing system. The transactions are comprehensive and cover a one-month period. This practice set may be used after chapter 22. It should require approximately 15 hours to complete.

A separate solutions manual is available for all four practice sets.

### Computer Software for the Student

**COMPUTERIZED PRACTICE SETS** Two computerized practice sets accompany *Principles of Accounting.* One covers a sole proprietorship-merchandising business and one covers a corporation. Both are designed for use on microcomputers and are available for both the Apple and IBM computers. A separate solutions manual is available for each of these practice sets.

**COMPUTERIZED TUTORIALS** This unique supplement is available in two volumes, one covering chapters 1–13 and one covering chapters 14–27, for IBM computers. This supplement is designed so that the student can obtain reinforcement of the concepts and principles covered in the text and in the classroom. The tutorials are completely user-friendly and require no prior knowledge of computers.

**THE TWIN®/LOTUS 1-2-3® TEMPLATES FOR SELECTED PROBLEMS** This supplement, prepared by Loren K. Waldman of Franklin University, provides 56 problem templates for selected problems in the text and requires no prior experience with LOTUS 1-2-3. Two problems in each chapter are designated with the symbol of a floppy disk to indicate that these problems can also be solved on the computer. The disks are available *free* to adopters with a license for duplication for your students.

## ACKNOWLEDGMENTS

We would like to thank the following people for their suggestions and comments and for their other aid in developing the manuscript of this book.

Larry J. Anderson, Des Moines Area Community College
Herman R. Andress, Santa Fe Community College
Albert J. Arsenault, Hillsborough Community College
Harry Baggett, Diablo Valley College
Edward J. Banas, Jr., Northern Virginia Community College, Woodbridge Campus
John B. Barrack, University of Georgia
Martin E. Batross, Franklin University
George E. Bennett, Camden County College
Francis A. Bird, University of Richmond
David Bourque, Middlesex Community College
Norma Brown, University of Arkansas
Lloyd J. Buckwell, Jr., Indiana University Northwest
David Buehlmann, University of Nebraska at Omaha
David Byrd, Southwest Missouri State
Sandra Byrd, Southwest Missouri State
Carmela C. Caputo, Empire State College
Eric Carlsen, Kean College of New Jersey
Gyan Chandra, Miami University
Charles Cheetham, County College of Morris
Pauline L. Corn, Virginia Polytechnic Institute and State University
Sharon Cotton, Schoolcraft College
Janet Daniels, University of Hartford
Chris Geels, University of Arkansas

Eva S. Green, University of District of Columbia
Nancy T. Chilson Grzesik, National Education Corporation
Nabil Hassan, Wright State University
Arthur S. Hirshfield, Bronx Community College
George C. Holdren, University of Nebraska—Lincoln
Jean Marie B. Hudson, Lamar University
Fred A. Jacobs, Georgia State University
Jane Kelley, Richland College
Michael Layne, Nassau Community College
Albert Y. Lew, Wright State University
Emily Miklis, Cuyahoga Community College
John Minch, Cabrillo College
Linda Moore, University of Arkansas
Sarah Palmer, Wright State University
Laurie W. Pant, Boston College
Vincent Pelletier, College of DuPage
Larry Peterson, County College of Morris
Robert Ripley, San Diego City College
Nathan Schmukler, Long Island University/C.W. Post Campus
Bill Schwartz, Temple University
Eun Shim, Rutgers University
Ben Shlaes, Des Moines Area Community College
Joel Siegel, Queens College
Sammie L. Smith, Stephen F. Austin State University
Charles A. Spector, State University of New York, Oswego
Christian Vanden Assem, Fairleigh Dickinson University
Dieter H. Weiss, Ferris State College
R.R. Wennagel, College of the Mainland

For his help during various stages of this project we would particularly like to thank Robert Lentz. His creativeness will not go unnoticed and for that we are appreciative.

A special acknowledgment goes to Professor Lou Gilles for his extremely diligent work in reviewing the exercises and problems and their solutions.

We give a special thanks to Julie Collins, Assistant Professor at the University of Oklahoma, for her help in developing the tax material in the text.

We would also like to thank the many people on the Prentice-Hall staff who guided and supported us throughout the development of the text. To Pamela Wilder we express our sincere appreciation for the expert attention that effectively guided this book through the production process. To Nancy McDermott our thanks for her outstanding support in the development of this book and its many supplements. And a very special thanks to Julie Warner, our editor. Her ability, enthusiasm, and commitment to this book will be long remembered and deeply appreciated.

We would like to acknowledge the support of Ernst & Whinney, who examined all the examples, exercises, problems, and solutions to ensure that we are technically and mathematically accurate in our presentation of these materials.

Ernst & Whinney

153 East 53rd Street
New York, New York 10022

212/888-9100

Prentice-Hall, Inc.
Englewood Cliffs, New Jersey

We have examined, for technical correctness and mathematical accuracy, the examples, exercises, and problems included in the First Edition of Principles of Accounting, by Cerepak and Taylor, together with the related solutions included in the accompanying Solutions Manual. Our examination was made in accordance with standards established by the American Institute of Certified Public Accountants and, accordingly, included such procedures as we considered necessary in the circumstances.

In our opinion, all examples, exercises, problems, and related solutions in the textbook and manual referred to above are technically correct and mathematically accurate.

Ernst & Whinney

New York, New York
October 23, 1986

# PRINCIPLES OF ACCOUNTING

# *Introduction: Accounting – A Source of Financial Information*

### *Learning Objectives*

When you complete this Introduction you will be able to answer the following questions:

a. What is accounting?
b. Who needs accounting information—and why?
c. Who supplies accounting information—and how?
d. What standards must accounting information meet to be useful?

*a. Accounting is a service activity that provides useful financial information about an identifiable entity*

What is accounting? Speaking formally, **accounting** is a service activity designed to measure, process, and communicate financial information about an identifiable entity that is useful in making decisions. The key word in this definition is "useful." Accounting provides information that is intended to be *useful*—information that people can use in making decisions.

When we understand how accounting information is used, we will be able to understand why accounting procedures are performed in the ways that they are.

## WHO NEEDS ACCOUNTING INFORMATION—AND WHY?

*b. Accounting information is needed by people whose decisions have a financial impact*

Who needs accounting information? Anyone who

Files an income tax return
Applies for a bank loan or credit card
Plans to make investments
Owns or manages a business

—or, in other words, anyone who makes decisions that have a financial impact.

*b. Those who pay or collect taxes want appropriate information*

The Internal Revenue Service requires individuals and businesses to file annual income tax returns as a means of determining their federal tax liability. Tax information closely parallels accounting information and for most businesses is generated by the company's accounting system.

*b. Lenders want to minimize risk of loss*

Bankers, creditors (those who advance money or goods or services to a business against a promise of future payment), and suppliers use accounting information to assess the risks involved in making loans or granting credit. Here accounting information is used to make a business decision concerning a person's or company's debt-paying ability.

*b. Investors want to achieve their investment goals*

Investors and potential investors in a business enterprise are interested in achieving a gain and avoiding a loss on their investment. They need accounting information that is useful in evaluating the company's past performance and current status in order to make projections about its future performance and status.

*b. Managers need answers to specific questions about the firm's activities and status*

Managers—those individuals involved in directing the operations of the business—need accounting information to answer specific questions, such as the following:

- **a.** What resources does the company own or control?
- **b.** How much cash is available in the bank?
- **c.** How much do customers owe the company? Are customers' accounts being collected on a timely basis?
- **d.** What products are on hand and which ones should be purchased or produced?
- **e.** How much does the company owe to outsiders? Are supplies being paid for on a timely basis?
- **f.** How much does the company earn? Are the reported earnings considered adequate?
- **g.** Are product-selling prices appropriate? Should any be increased or decreased?

## WHO SUPPLIES ACCOUNTING INFORMATION—AND HOW?

All of us as private citizens supply accounting information on a small scale when we file a tax return, apply for a loan or credit card, or make a budget. Many people who operate small businesses keep their own accounts and thus supply their own accounting information.

As their financial affairs and situations become more complicated, however, people and businesses turn to professional accountants for help. These professionals are of three major kinds:

Public accountants
Private accountants
Government and other nonprofit organization accountants

## Public Accountants

*c. Public accountants offer services to the public for a fee*

**Public accountants** are individuals who offer their professional services to the public for a fee. Like attorneys or physicians, they may operate alone or may be associated with others in a partnership or corporation. Like attorneys or physicians, too, public accountants must have a license to practice. Licenses are granted by the individual states, and the requirements for licensing differ from state to state. You can obtain information on the requirements in your own state from the state board of accountancy.

*c. They are licensed as either PAs or CPAs*

Professional accountants are licensed to practice at one of two levels: Public Accountant (PA) or **Certified Public Accountant (CPA).** As an educational background for PAs, some states require only a high school diploma; others require at least two years of college. For CPAs, most states require two or more years of college—often a four-year college degree—plus, in some cases, several years of public accounting experience.

All candidates for the CPA designation must take the CPA examination prepared and graded by the American Institute of Certified Public Accountants (AICPA); since 1952 this exam has been the standard in every state. The CPA exam comprises five sections—two on accounting practice and one each on accounting theory, auditing, and business law—administered over the course of three days, a total of $19\frac{1}{2}$ hours.

*c. They serve the public by attesting, reporting, and advising*

The services of public accountants have been described in general terms as (1) *attesting,* (2) *reporting,* and (3) *advising.* These general functions are embodied in more specific services such as financial auditing, preparation of tax returns, and advice to management.

*c. Financial auditing attests to the fairness of a company's financial statements*

AUDITING (Attesting) The principal service offered by large public accounting firms is financial auditing. An audit is conducted by the firm's partners (owners) and its professional employees, who are independent of the company being audited. The purpose of a financial audit is to gather sufficient and competent evidence to express an opinion as to the fairness of the financial statements prepared by the company's management. In making a financial audit the auditor examines the company's accounting system, gathers evidence from its accounting records, and obtains information from sources both within and outside the firm.

An audit serves society by adding credibility to the company's financial statements.

The strong influence of public opinion, the requirements of stock exchanges, and the needs of agencies such as the Securities and Exchange Commission (SEC) and the Interstate Commerce Commission (ICC) make it necessary for corporations that issue their securities to the public to have their financial statements audited by certified public accountants.

*c. Tax services (reporting) attempt to minimize a client's taxes*

TAX SERVICES (Reporting) Public accountants are often hired to prepare federal and state income tax returns. The accountant's specialized knowledge and experience are called upon to ensure that the minimum amount of taxes will be paid without violating the law.

Because of high tax rates and complex tax laws, a public accountant is often needed to aid in tax planning, the purpose of which is to determine what the tax effect of future business decisions will be. A tax planner may be able to time the business decision so as to achieve the most favorable tax effect on the company or person.

*c. Management advisory services (advising) help management set up accounting systems, budgets, and so forth*

MANAGEMENT ADVISORY SERVICES (Advising) Management advisory services include (1) the design and installation of an accounting system, (2) budget preparation, (3) cash flow analysis, (4) recommendations for inventory levels, (5) suggestions for controlling costs, (6) statistical surveys, (7) financial planning, and (8) advice concerning mergers, acquisitions, and sales of entire businesses. The providing of such services is an area of rapid growth. Most of the large public accounting firms have their own management advisory services department. In some cases, businesses employ the same public accounting firm to perform both audit and management services engagements.

*c. Most major U.S. corporations are audited by one of the "Big Eight" accounting firms*

THE "BIG EIGHT" The size of public accounting firms ranges from large international firms with hundreds of partners to small firms with one or two partners. The eight largest accounting firms (listed below) are international in scope. They are known in the accounting profession as the **Big Eight** and audit most U.S. corporations that sell their securities to the public.

The Big Eight U.S. Accounting Firms

| FIRMS (IN ALPHABETICAL ORDER) | AMONG THEIR CLIENTS |
|---|---|
| Arthur Andersen & Co. | ITT, Texaco |
| Arthur Young & Company | Mobil, Lockheed |
| Coopers & Lybrand | AT&T, Ford |
| Deloitte Haskins & Sells | General Motors, A&P |
| Ernst & Whinney | Coca-Cola, McDonnell Douglas |
| Peat, Marwick, Mitchell & Co. | General Electric, Xerox |
| Price Waterhouse | Exxon, IBM |
| Touche Ross & Co. | Chrysler, Sears |

## Private Accountants

*c. Private accountants are employees of business enterprises*

An accountant employed by a single business enterprise or nonprofit organization is called a **private accountant,** or ***industrial accountant.*** A small business may employ only one or a few private accountants. On the other hand, a large business may employ a staff of several hundred accountants working under the supervision of a chief accounting officer, often called the *controller.* The controller's major responsibility is to provide a reporting system that produces financial information (including financial statements) used by the company and required by laws and regulations. Some private accountants are CPAs who choose to work in industry rather than practice public accounting. Others are **Certified Management Accountants (CMAs),** who pass a rigorous examination prepared and graded by the *Institute of Management Accounting of the National Association of Accountants (NAA),* an organization of accountants working in private industry.

*c. Private accountants often specialize in particular aspects of accounting*

Accountants employed in private industry do a variety of work and often specialize in particular aspects of accounting such as those described in the next few paragraphs.

*General accounting* embodies the overall responsibility for recording a company's transactions and events and for preparing its periodic financial statements.

*Cost accounting* involves (among other things) the collecting and evaluating of data on the cost of a given product, manufacturing process, or service. The purpose is to determine and control the cost of producing specific products and services.

*Budgeting* involves the preparing of a monetary plan of business activities for some future period of time. The objective is to forecast the results of financial activities before these activities take place.

*Internal auditing* is a review and evaluation process. Most large companies have a staff of internal auditors whose primary responsibilities include making sure that efficient operational procedures are used and that established management policies are being followed. By passing an examination and providing evidence of experience, an internal auditor may earn the title **Certified Internal Auditor (CIA),** a designation granted by the *Institute of Internal Auditors.*

### Government and Other Nonprofit Organization Accountants

*c. Accountants are employed by government and other nonprofit organizations*

Accountants in government and other nonprofit organizations perform services similar to those performed by public and private accountants. For example, accountants employed by local, state, and federal governments review and audit payroll, sales, and income tax returns filed each year. Governmental agencies such as the federal tax-levying agency known as the **Internal Revenue Service (IRS)** employ accountants to review and audit income tax returns filed by individuals and corporations. The IRS is responsible for the enforcement of the United States tax laws and the collection of income tax.

The **Securities and Exchange Commission (SEC)** uses accountants to check and review the financial reports of corporations that offer their securities to the public. Other federal governmental agencies that use accountants in a variety of specialized areas are (1) the *General Accounting Office (GAO)*, (2) the *Federal Communications Commission (FCC)*, and (3) the *Interstate Commerce Commission (ICC)*.

There are many nonprofit organizations, such as hospitals, churches, charitable foundations, and educational institutions, that need to employ accountants. Although these organizations do not operate for profit, they are concerned with the efficient allocation of their resources, and they use accounting information as an aid in making decisions pertaining to allocations.

## BOOKKEEPING AND ACCOUNTING

It is important that you clearly understand the distinction between bookkeeping and accounting early in your study of accounting. Bookkeeping is an aspect of the accounting process. It primarily involves recording business data and keeping the financial records of an organization. The work is usually repetitive, routine, and clerical in nature. Accounting, on the other hand, involves much more complex activities, as we mentioned in the preceding paragraphs. To do the work of a professional accountant requires several years of education just to achieve the expected level of knowledge. Accountants are also expected to possess analytical skills and to exercise good judgment.

## STANDARDS THAT ACCOUNTING INFORMATION MUST MEET TO BE USEFUL

*d. Accounting information, to be useful, must be*
*available when needed*
*verifiable*
*consistent*
*unbiased*

To be useful as an aid in decision making, accounting information must be developed with uniform and acceptable standards. In particular, accounting information must be

Available on a timely basis
Verifiable
Free of bias and inconsistencies

To produce such financial information, accountants rely on a body of principles and standards that have developed over time. These are the product of the thought of generations of professional accountants working with the problems that confronted them daily. These principles and standards for compiling, organizing, and reporting financial information are known as **generally accepted accounting principles (GAAP).** Collectively they provide the framework for measuring and reporting business transactions.

*d. To meet these standards, accountants rely on generally accepted accounting principles (GAAP)*

These principles and standards are accepted ways of doing things—not laws of nature such as those developed in the natural sciences. Generally accepted accounting principles are simply "ground rules" or "guides to action," and they may change over time as better ways are found or as new situations are encountered. Individual accounting principles are discussed later in the book as they relate to specific topics.

*d. Generally accepted accounting principles are influenced by authoritative groups: AICPA, FASB, SEC*

A number of authoritative groups have added their influence to the establishment of generally accepted accounting principles. These groups include the American Institute of Certified Public Accountants (AICPA), the Financial Accounting Standards Board (FASB), and the Securities and Exchange Commission (SEC).

The **American Institute of Certified Public Accountants (AICPA)** is a professional organization of certified public accountants. Its members are generally engaged in the practice of public accounting or are employed by industry, government, or academic institutions. For many years the AICPA developed the principles and standards used by most accountants. The AICPA still exerts its influence in the standard-setting process.

The **Financial Accounting Standards Board (FASB)** is the body that now sets standards in the private sector of the accounting profession. The FASB is not part of the AICPA; it is an independent body consisting of seven full-time members representing public accounting, industry, government, and accounting education. With the help of a large research staff, the FASB has issued numerous *Statements of Financial Accounting Standards.* These standards represent the major body of generally accepted accounting principles.

The ***Securities and Exchange Commission (SEC)*** is a federal governmental agency that has the legal authority to establish and enforce accounting practices for companies that trade their securities in interstate commerce. Rather than using its legal authority to establish accounting principles and practices independently, the SEC has closely monitored the work of the FASB. Often the SEC adopts, and occasionally modifies, the recommendations of the FASB.

## GLOSSARY OF KEY TERMS

**Accounting.** A service activity for measuring, processing, and communicating financial information about an identifiable entity that is useful in making economic decisions.

**American Institute of Certified Public Accountants (AICPA).** A professional organization of CPAs, most of whom are engaged in the practice of public accounting or are employed by private industry, governmental agencies, or academic institutions.

**"Big Eight."** The eight largest public accounting firms in the United States.

**Certified Internal Auditor (CIA).** An accountant who has passed a professional examination, has met all other requirements, and has been granted the designation Certified Internal Auditor by the *Institute of Internal Auditors.*

**Certified Management Accountant (CMA).** An accountant who has passed a professional examination, has met all other requirements, and has been granted the designation Certified Management Accountant by the *Institute of Management Accounting of the National Association of Accountants.*

**Certified Public Accountant (CPA).** An accountant who has passed the CPA examination, has met all other state requirements, and has been licensed by a state to practice public accounting as a CPA in that state.

**Financial Accounting Standards Board (FASB).** The body that sets standards in the private sector of the accounting profession.

**Generally Accepted Accounting Principles (GAAP).** Principles and standards for compiling, organizing, and reporting financial information. A more comprehensive definition of generally accepted accounting principles will be developed and discussed later in this book.

**Internal Revenue Service (IRS).** A governmental agency responsible for the enforcement of the United States tax laws and the collection of the income tax.

**Private accountants.** Individuals who practice accounting as employees of a business firm or nonprofit organization.

**Public accountants.** Individuals who practice accounting by offering services to the public on a fee basis.

**Securities and Exchange Commission (SEC).** A federal governmental agency that has the legal power for determining the generally accepted accounting principles for companies whose securities are traded in interstate commerce.

## REVIEW QUESTIONS

*Review Questions throughout the book will help you confirm your mastery of the chapter material. These questions are in the same sequence as the material that has been presented in the chapter.*

*The bracketed abbreviations on the right side of the page identify the Learning Objectives to which the question is related. For example, [LOa] refers to Learning Objective a.*

1. What is accounting? [LOa]
2. Describe the types of accounting information needed by
   a. Managers of businesses
   b. Investors and potential investors in a business
   c. Creditors of a company [LOb]
3. Describe the jobs performed by
   a. Public accountants
   b. Private accountants
   c. Government accountants [LOc]
4. Name the three attributes that accounting information must possess to be useful. [LOd]
5. What is the name given to the principles and standards for compiling, organizing, and reporting financial statement information? [LOd]
6. Name and describe three authoritative groups that have added their influence to the establishment of generally accepted accounting principles. [LOd]

# 1 Financial Statements and the Accounting Equation

## *Learning Objectives*

When you complete this chapter you will be able to

1. Answer the following questions:
   a. What are the four basic functions in the accounting activity?
   b. What are the purposes and the main sections of the income statement? The balance sheet? The capital statement?
   c. What principles and assumptions does each of these statements embody?
   d. What is the accounting equation? What is its purpose?
2. Perform the following accounting functions:
   a. Prepare an income statement.
   b. Prepare a balance sheet.
   c. Analyze a business transaction and describe its effects on the elements of the accounting equation.

*1a. The accounting activity has four basic functions:*
*1. Observe and select business transactions*
*2. Record the transactions*
*3. Classify and summarize for reports*
*4. Interpret the reports*

Accounting, as we learned in the Introduction, is a service activity that provides financial information useful in making decisions. This activity, as developed by generations of accountants, involves four basic functions:

1. *Observe* and *select* those occurrences that give evidence of being a business activity measurable in monetary terms. Examples are the purchase and sale of goods and services, salary payments to company employees, and the purchase of equipment. These activities are known as *business transactions.*
2. *Record* a transaction so that it becomes a part of the company's permanent accounting records. This recording can be done in writing or with mechanical or electronic equipment.
3. *Classify* and *summarize* the recorded business transactions.
   a. Classifying transactions requires grouping them into specific categories. For example, the grouping of receipts and payments of cash is important because it develops information about the company's cash position at a point in time.
   b. Summarizing transactions requires organizing information into a form suitable for reporting to managers, creditors, investors, or other users of accounting information.
4. *Interpret* the contents of the reported information. Accountants are often called upon to discuss the meaning of items presented in the reports, the relationship between certain figures within the reports, and the limitations of the information presented.

It is in steps 3 and 4, where reports are produced and interpreted, that accounting fulfills its purpose as a source of useful information. These reports are called *financial statements.* "Financial statement" is a term for a document that has a good deal of meaning and excitement for the people to whom it relates. We can understand this meaning and excitement when we look more closely into financial statements and see exactly what they communicate.

## BASIC FINANCIAL STATEMENTS

**Financial statements** are periodic reports that are the primary outputs of the accounting process. They communicate accounting information, primarily financial in nature, to management and other parties that use the information in decision making. Three principal financial statements are the income statement, balance sheet, and capital statement.

### The Income Statement

*1b. The income statement shows the company's operating results*

A primary objective of every business firm is to earn a net income, or "profit." The purpose of the **income statement** is to show the company's operating results in terms of net income for a period of time. A basic income statement for a professional tutoring service, Tutorial Associates, is illustrated in Exhibit 1 – 1 on page 10. The statement was prepared by the firm's owner, Carol Cornell.

*1b,2a. The income statement has three main elements: revenues, expenses, and net income (or net loss)*

WHAT THE INCOME STATEMENT INCLUDES Carol's statement includes three elements common to all income statements.

**Revenues** are the inflow of cash or other resources received from customers or clients, which resulted from the sales of merchandise or the rendering of services, or from investments.

**Expenses** are the cost of the goods and services consumed in the process of generating revenue.

EXHIBIT 1–1

TUTORIAL ASSOCIATES
Income Statement
For the Month Ended October 31, 19X2

| | | |
|---|---|---|
| Revenues: | | |
| Fees Earned | $8,600 | |
| Interest Earned | 20 | |
| Total Revenues | | $8,620 |
| Expenses: | | |
| Wages Expense | $4,300 | |
| Rent Expense | 800 | |
| Advertising Expense | 840 | |
| Telephone Expense | 60 | |
| Utilities Expense | 120 | |
| Total Expenses | | 6,120 |
| Net Income | | $2,500 |

**Net income** (or **net loss**) is the amount by which total revenues exceed (or are exceeded by) total expenses.

Note that the heading of the income statement identifies

1. The name of the company (Tutorial Associates)
2. The name of the statement (Income Statement)
3. The period of time covered (For the Month Ended October 31, 19X2), called the **accounting period**

The time period covered is critical when we are analyzing amounts reported on the statement. Certain users, for example, might consider net income of $2,500 inadequate if the statement covered a full year but acceptable if it covered a quarter (three consecutive months of a given year).

Note that the various items of revenue and expense are represented on the Tutorial Associates Income Statement by very simple titles: Fees Earned, Interest Earned, Wages Expense, and so on.

Fees Earned represents amounts earned for the tutoring of students (430 hours of service delivered by the firm at $20 per hour, 430 × $20 = $8,600).

Interest Earned refers to the interest received on the firm's money that has been deposited in a local bank. This figure was provided by the October bank statement mailed to Carol.

Wages Expense represents expenses incurred for college students who are recruited and trained by Tutorial Associates to provide professional-quality tutoring. The tutors are paid $10 per hour (430 hours of tutoring × $10 per hour = Wages Expense of $4,300).

Carol's other expenses are typical of most businesses and are self-explanatory.

*1c. The income statement embodies two assumptions:* **business entity** *and* **time period**

INCOME STATEMENT ASSUMPTIONS Two basic assumptions are evident from the income statement: the **business entity assumption** and the **time period assumption.**

### The Business Entity Assumption

For accounting purposes, a business is considered to be and is treated as a separate entity apart from its owner or owners and all other entities.

Thus the income statement for Tutorial Associates (illustrated in Exhibit 1–1) includes only the revenue and expense transactions of the business entity known as Tutorial Associates. The personal revenue and expense transactions of its owner (Carol Cornell) are not included because they are viewed as belonging to another accounting entity.

During October, for example, Carol might have sold a coin collection that she bought as an investment years earlier. These might be considered business activities, but they are not those of the business entity Tutorial Associates, and so they are excluded from that entity's income statement.

Business entities are usually organized as sole proprietorships, partnerships, or corporations. A **sole proprietorship** is a business owned by an individual, as Tutorial Associates is. A ***partnership*** is a business owned by two or more individuals that operates according to an agreement made among those individuals. A ***corporation*** is a business entity formed under the incorporation laws of an individual state or the federal government. Its owners are called *stockholders* or *shareholders* because their ownership interests are represented by shares of the corporation's stock.

This text discusses and illustrates accounting practices and procedures for each of these widely used forms of business organization. We begin here with the simplest form—the sole proprietorship.

**The Time Period Assumption**

For financial reporting purposes, the operating life of a business entity can be divided into specific time periods, generally of equal length, such as one month, three months (quarterly), and one year (annually).

Thus the income statement for Tutorial Associates reports the revenues earned and the expenses incurred by the firm during the month of October. Tutorial Associates' next income statement might cover a two-month period ending November 30 or a three-month period ending December 31. It is common practice for firms to prepare income statements that cover monthly periods, quarterly periods, and annual periods.

## The Balance Sheet

***1b. The balance sheet shows a firm's financial position***

The **balance sheet,** sometimes called the **statement of financial position,** is a financial statement that lists a company's assets, liabilities, and owner's equity on a given date. Its purpose is to show the financial position of the business at that date. Presented in Exhibit 1–2 on page 12 is a balance sheet showing the financial position of Tutorial Associates on October 31, 19X2, which is the last day of the month covered by the income statement in Exhibit 1–1.

Note that the heading of the balance sheet identifies

1. The name of the company (TUTORIAL ASSOCIATES)
2. The name of the statement (Balance Sheet)
3. The date of the balance sheet (October 31, 19X2)

***1b,2b. The body of the balance sheet has three main sections: assets, liabilities, and owner's equity***

Below the heading is the body of the balance sheet, which consists of three separate sections for assets, liabilities, and owner's equity. These three elements are discussed below.

ASSETS ON THE BALANCE SHEET **Assets** are economic resources that a business entity owns or controls. They result from past transactions or events and are expected to benefit the entity's future operations. Some assets include such

EXHIBIT 1–2

TUTORIAL ASSOCIATES
Balance Sheet
October 31, 19X2

| *Assets* | | *Liabilities* | |
|---|---|---|---|
| Cash | $ 5,500 | Accounts Payable | $ 1,000 |
| Accounts Receivable | 2,200 | Salaries Payable | 400 |
| Land | 6,000 | Notes Payable | 20,000 |
| Building | 61,000 | Mortgage Payable | 40,000 |
| Office Equipment | 3,200 | Total Liabilities | 61,400 |
| | | *Owner's Equity* | |
| | | Carol Cornell, Capital | 16,500 |
| Total Assets | $77,900 | Total Liabilities and Owner's Equity | $77,900 |

items as cash and **accounts receivable** (amounts owed to the business by its customers for goods and services sold to them on credit). Other assets include items such as *inventories* (goods held for sale by a business), land, buildings, and equipment. Assets may also include rights such as those granted by a patent, franchise, or copyright.

Under "Assets" on the Tutorial Associates balance sheet, the first item listed is Cash ($5,500). This is the balance in the firm's bank account or accounts.

Accounts receivable ($2,200) is the total amount owed to Tutorial Associates by its clients (for 110 hours of tutoring at $20 an hour).

Land ($6,000) and Building ($61,000) represent a small office building that Carol Cornell purchased. She decided that investing in property was better than paying rent.

Office Equipment ($3,200) consists of desks, chairs, typewriters, filing cabinets, and similar equipment that Carol purchased from an office equipment dealer.

*1c. The balance sheet embodies the* **cost principle**

**PRINCIPLES AND AN ASSUMPTION THE BALANCE SHEET EMBODIES ABOUT ASSETS** An important principle to be observed when preparing the balance sheet is the **cost principle.**

### The Cost Principle

Resources and services purchased by a business are initially entered in the accounting records at their cost.

*Cost* is the exchange price agreed upon by the parties who make the exchange. For example, the land purchased by Tutorial Associates cost $6,000, and this amount should be used when entering the transaction in the accounting records—even if Carol considered the land to be worth more than $6,000 when it was purchased. This September the tax assessor estimated the market value of the land as $7,000. Carol will nevertheless continue to report this asset on the balance sheet at its original acquisition cost (often called *historical cost*). Accountants have two good reasons for initially recording and for continuing to report certain assets at their historical cost: the **going concern assumption** and the **objectivity principle.**

*1c. The cost principle is supported by the* **going concern assumption** *and the* **objectivity principle**

### The Going Concern Assumption

A business will continue to operate for an indefinite period of time unless there is specific evidence to the contrary.

Certain assets such as land, buildings, and equipment are acquired for use and not for resale. In fact if these assets were sold, the company's activities would be seriously disrupted and curtailed. Since a company's balance sheet is prepared on the assumption that the company will continue to operate for a long period of time, showing the assets not intended for resale at an amount representing their estimated market value is not pertinent and is of little use to the users of the balance sheet.

**The Objectivity Principle**

Accounting information must be free of bias and subject to verification by an independent party knowledgeable in accounting.

Thus the price established in an exchange transaction by two independent parties represents *objective* evidence concerning the cost of an asset or service acquired.

Showing land, buildings, equipment, and many other assets on the balance sheet at their current market value or current replacement cost would require appraisals, opinions, estimates, or judgments, resulting in information that might be too subjective to be useful. Although we will soon see that appraisals, opinions, estimates, and judgments must frequently be used when compiling amounts for financial statements, both preparers and users of the statements believe that the information reported should be as factual and objective as possible.

LIABILITIES ON THE BALANCE SHEET **Liabilities** are the obligations or debts that the business must pay in money or services at some time in the future. Examples are

Amounts owed to persons or companies (called **creditors**) for goods and services bought on credit (called **accounts payable**)

Amounts owed on borrowed money such as loans and notes payable (a **note payable** is evidenced by a written promise to pay another party a definite sum of money at some future determinable date)

Salaries and wages owed to employees (salaries payable)

Taxes owed to the government (taxes payable)

Interest payable

Long-term debt such as mortgages payable

Under "Liabilities" on the Tutorial Associates balance sheet, the first item listed is Accounts Payable ($1,000). This is the amount still owed to an office equipment dealer for the typewriters and filing cabinets.

Salaries Payable ($400) represents two weeks' pay earned by a part-time secretary as of October 31. The check for these earnings will be written out and given to the employee on November 1.

Notes Payable ($20,000) represents an amount borrowed by Carol to make the down payment on the building purchased.

Mortgage Payable ($40,000) represents the balance due on the mortgage loan Carol obtained to purchase the land and building.

LISTING ASSETS AND LIABILITIES ON THE BALANCE SHEET Cash is generally the first asset listed on a balance sheet. Listed next are the assets that are reasonably expected to be converted into cash in the near future or used up while operating the business. Next are the company's more permanent assets, such as land, building, and equipment.

Liabilities are usually listed in the order in which they come due. For example, short-term liabilities, such as accounts payable and salaries payable, are listed before long-term debt, such as mortgage payable.

OWNER'S EQUITY ON THE BALANCE SHEET **Owner's equity,** sometimes called **capital** or **residual equity,** represents the interest (or claims) of the owner or owners in the assets of the business. In terms of dollar amount it is equal to the company's **net assets**—that is, total assets minus total liabilities. Another way to view the concept of owner's equity is to recognize that the total assets of a business are always equal to the total claims against those assets held by creditors (liabilities) and the owners (owner's equity). Thus for any company, its total assets will be equal to its total liabilities plus its owner's equity. Because the claims of creditors take legal precedence, the owner's equity is considered a residual claim on assets. If a company sells all of its assets, the company's owner or owners are entitled to the cash remaining after creditors' claims have been paid in full.

By presenting a few simple examples we may be able to enhance the meaning of owner's equity.

If you decided to go into business and took $30,000 out of your personal bank account to start the firm, your balance sheet information would be as follows:

| *Assets* | | *Liabilities* | |
|---|---|---|---|
| Cash | $30,000 | (None) | |
| | | *Owner's Equity* | |
| | | Capital | $30,000 |
| Total Assets | $30,000 | Total Liabilities and Owner's Equity | $30,000 |

Note that the company has total assets of $30,000, and since there are no liabilities, there are no creditors' claims on those assets. The difference between the assets and the creditors' claims on the assets (the liabilities) represents the owner's claims on the assets. This is your owner's equity. In the early part of the text we will use the owner's name and the word "capital" when referring to the equity of the owner. Later, alternative terminology will be substituted.

Assume that the next thing you did was to borrow $10,000 from a bank. Your balance sheet information would now be as follows:

| *Assets* | | *Liabilities* | |
|---|---|---|---|
| Cash | $40,000 | Note Payable | $10,000 |
| | | *Owner's Equity* | |
| | | Capital | 30,000 |
| Total Assets | $40,000 | Total Liabilities and Owner's Equity | $40,000 |

It is apparent that the total assets of the company increased by $10,000 as a result of borrowing that amount from the bank. There is also an increase in the company's liabilities for that same amount, but your owner's equity is unchanged. The owner's equity in a company is not increased when the company's assets are increased by incurring liabilities. In this case, the bank is now a creditor having a $10,000 claim on the company's assets, and the total assets of the company ($40,000) are equal to the total claims against the assets by creditors ($10,000) and owners ($30,000).

How then does the amount representing owner's equity change? It could change during a period of time as a result of the following:

1. Additional investments of cash or other assets by the owner. Whenever an owner takes cash or some other personal asset and transfers it to (invests it in) the business, his or her owner's equity will increase. Since the transfer causes the company's assets to increase without changing its liabilities, the owner's equity increases. (This source of owner's equity is further discussed and illustrated in a later section of this chapter.)
2. Withdrawals of cash or other assets by the owner (sometimes called **owner's withdrawals**). The owner of a sole proprietorship has the right to withdraw (remove) cash or any other asset from the business for his or her personal use. Since such a withdrawal reduces the company's assets but does not reduce its liabilities, the owner's equity will decrease. (This cause of a decrease in owner's equity is illustrated later in this chapter.)
3. Net income. When the revenues earned exceed the expenses incurred during a given period of time, the difference is the net income for the period. Revenues result in an increase in owner's equity and expenses result in a decrease in owner's equity. Consequently, when revenues exceed expenses, the difference between the two, net income, represents a net increase in owner's equity. (This cause of an increase in owner's equity will be analyzed in Chapter 2.)
4. Net loss. When the expenses incurred for a given period of time exceed the revenues earned for that period, a net loss has been incurred. Similar to net income but opposite in effect, a net loss represents a decrease in owner's equity.

## The Capital Statement

The purpose of the **capital statement** is to disclose the reasons for the changes in owner's equity that occurred during the period. By examining the capital statement for Tutorial Associates shown in Exhibit 1–3, we see that the equity of its owner, Carol Cornell, has increased from $14,700 (the amount shown as capital at the beginning of the period) to $16,500 (the amount shown as capital at the end of the period). We can also see that two factors were responsible for the change, or net increase, that occurred in capital during the period: (1) net income—the excess of revenues over expenses—of $2,500, and (2) withdrawal of $700 made by the company's owner for her personal use during the period.

By explaining the changes that have occurred in owner's equity during a period of time, the capital statement serves as a connecting link between the balance sheet and the income statement.

*EXHIBIT 1–3*

TUTORIAL ASSOCIATES
Capital Statement
For the Month Ended October 31, 19X2

| | | |
|---|---|---|
| Carol Cornell, Capital—October 1, 19X2 | | $14,700 |
| Net income for the month | $2,500 | |
| Less withdrawals | 700 | |
| Increase in capital | | 1,800 |
| Carol Cornell, Capital—October 31, 19X2 | | $16,500 |

### Relationship of the Three Statements

Although they provide different types of financial information, the three financial statements described above are designed to be interrelated. The income statement interrelates with the capital statement by providing the dollar amount of net income or net loss needed for the capital statement. The capital statement interrelates with the balance sheet by providing the owner's capital amount at the end of a period, a figure displayed in the owner's equity section of the balance sheet.

### The Statement of Changes in Financial Position

We must take note here of another important financial statement: the ***statement of changes in financial position.*** For the moment, we simply point out that the statement summarizes a company's financing and investing activities (showing where it obtained funds and how it used them). We will postpone further discussion of this statement until Chapter 18.

Much of accounting deals with the preparation of the four statements described above and with the ways of analyzing and using the financial information they provide.

## THE ACCOUNTING EQUATION

*1d. The accounting equation states that Assets = Liabilities + Owner's Equity*

The balance sheet shown earlier is a formal presentation of the elements of the **accounting equation.** These elements are assets, liabilities, and owner's equity, which the balance sheet presents in the following form:

Assets = Liabilities + Owner's Equity

The equality of assets with the claims of the creditors and the owner shown on the balance sheet of Tutorial Associates (Exhibit 1 – 2) can be expressed in equation form as follows:

| Assets | = Liabilities | + Owner's Equity |
|---|---|---|
| \$77,900 | = \$61,400 | + \$16,500 |

By transposing the Liabilities term in the equation, we show that owner's equity is considered to be a residual claim. The equation is then expressed as follows:

| Assets | − Liabilities | = Owner's Equity |
|---|---|---|
| \$77,900 | − \$61,400 | = \$16,500 |

## EFFECTS OF BUSINESS TRANSACTIONS ON THE ACCOUNTING EQUATION

A **business transaction** is an economic event or activity that affects the financial position of a business entity and must be recorded. Some examples of transactions (with which you are familiar from our Tutorial Associates illustration) are

Purchasing office equipment from a dealer for \$3,200
Borrowing \$40,000 from a bank
Incurring \$400 in salary liability to an employee

*1d,2c. The accounting equation provides a basis for analyzing and recording business transactions*

Business transactions affect the elements in the accounting equation. Every transaction, no matter how simple or complex, can be stated in terms of its effect on one or more of these three elements.

## Analysis of the Effects of Transactions—Illustrated

We will now consider a sequence of eight common business transactions to illustrate their effect on the accounting equation. Keep in mind right from the start that although the transaction will affect one or more elements of the equation, after each transaction the total assets will equal the sum of the total liabilities and owner's equity. We will show in the illustrations that the balance of the accounting equation (and of the balance sheet) is maintained before and after each transaction.

**TRANSACTION 1—INVESTMENT BY OWNER** Stuart Hill, a recent college graduate who worked two years with Tutorial Associates, decides to start a tutoring service in a town in his home state. He starts his business by taking $25,000 of his personal money and depositing it in a bank account in the name of his new firm, Elite Tutors.

We analyze the effects of this transaction on the elements of the accounting equation as follows: The asset Cash is increased by $25,000. Since the money comes from the owner, the company incurs no liabilities. The equity of the owner, recorded as "S. Hill, Capital," is increased by $25,000.

| Assets | = Liabilities | + Owner's Equity |
|---|---|---|
| Cash | None | S. Hill, Capital |
| +25,000 | | +25,000 |

After this transaction has been recorded, the company's first balance sheet appears as follows (where for simplicity we have omitted the date):

ELITE TUTORS

Balance Sheet

| *Assets* | | *Liabilities* | |
|---|---|---|---|
| Cash | $25,000 | (None) | |
| | | *Owner's Equity* | |
| | | S. Hill, Capital | $25,000 |
| Total Assets | $25,000 | Total Liabilities and Owner's Equity | $25,000 |

**TRANSACTION 2—PURCHASE OF AN ASSET FOR CASH** Stuart finds a suitable location for an office and purchases the land and building. The agreed-upon price is $17,000—$5,000 for the land and $12,000 for the building. Stuart pays for the property in full by writing a check for $17,000.

What are the effects of this transaction? The asset Cash is decreased by $17,000. The asset Land is increased by $5,000. The asset Building is increased by $12,000.

| Assets | | | = Liabilities + Owner's Equity |
|---|---|---|---|
| Cash | Land | Building | |
| −17,000 | +5,000 | +12,000 | |

Note that this transaction changes the amounts of three different kinds of assets (three separate items in the Assets section of the balance sheet), but the total amount of assets remains the same. In other words, the transaction changes the *composition* of the firm's assets.

After this transaction has been recorded, the balance sheet appears as follows (the amounts changed by the transaction are shown in color):

ELITE TUTORS
Balance Sheet

| *Assets* | | *Liabilities* | |
|---|---|---|---|
| Cash | $ 8,000 | (None) | |
| Land | 5,000 | *Owner's Equity* | |
| Building | 12,000 | S. Hill, Capital | $25,000 |
| Total Assets | $25,000 | Total Liabilities and Owner's Equity | $25,000 |

**TRANSACTION 3—PURCHASE OF AN ASSET AND INCURRENCE OF A LIABILITY** By reading the classified ads and following up his leads promptly, Stuart is able to buy some used office equipment from a business that is liquidating its resources. The cost of the equipment is $10,000. Stuart's payment consists of a promise to pay $2,000 within a week and the balance of $8,000 within 120 days.

What are the effects of this transaction? The asset Office Equipment is increased by $10,000. The liability Accounts Payable is increased by $10,000.

| Assets | = Liabilities + Owner's Equity |
|---|---|
| Office Equipment | Accounts Payable |
| +10,000 | +10,000 |

After this transaction has been recorded, the balance sheet appears as follows:

ELITE TUTORS
Balance Sheet

| *Assets* | | *Liabilities* | |
|---|---|---|---|
| Cash | $ 8,000 | Accounts Payable | $10,000 |
| Office Equipment | 10,000 | *Owner's Equity* | |
| Land | 5,000 | S. Hill, Capital | 25,000 |
| Building | 12,000 | Total Liabilities and | |
| Total Assets | $35,000 | Owner's Equity | $35,000 |

**TRANSACTION 4—SALE OF AN ASSET FOR CASH** Stuart finds that the land he has purchased is more than he needs for the operation of his business. Rather than pay property tax on it, as well as tie up money he could put to better use in other ways, he subdivides the land and sells the unneeded portion (40% of the total area) for cash at its cost of $2,000 (40% of $5,000).

What are the effects of this transaction? The asset Cash is increased by $2,000. The asset Land is decreased by $2,000.

| Assets | | = Liabilities + Owner's Equity |
|---|---|---|
| Cash | Land | |
| +2,000 | −2,000 | |

After this transaction has been recorded, the balance sheet appears as follows:

ELITE TUTORS
Balance Sheet

| *Assets* | | *Liabilities* | |
|---|---|---|---|
| Cash | $10,000 | Accounts Payable | $10,000 |
| Office Equipment | 10,000 | *Owner's Equity* | |
| Land | 3,000 | S. Hill, Capital | 25,000 |
| Building | 12,000 | Total Liabilities and | |
| Total Assets | $35,000 | Owner's Equity | $35,000 |

TRANSACTION 5—SALE OF AN ASSET ON CREDIT Stuart finds that he does not need the video camera and display system that was among the assets he purchased to operate the business, so he decides to sell it. The video equipment cost Elite Tutors $3,000, and its value on the used-equipment market is $3,500. Because the public relations firm that wants to buy it is next door, and Stuart wants to be a good neighbor, he sells the video system at its cost. The buyer agrees to pay half the amount within five days and the balance within ninety days.

What are the effects of this transaction? The asset Accounts Receivable is increased by $3,000. The asset Office Equipment is decreased by $3,000.

| Assets | | = Liabilities + Owner's Equity |
|---|---|---|
| Accounts Receivable | Office Equipment | |
| +3,000 | −3,000 | |

After this transaction has been recorded, the balance sheet appears as follows:

ELITE TUTORS
Balance Sheet

| *Assets* | | *Liabilities* | |
|---|---|---|---|
| Cash | $10,000 | Accounts Payable | $10,000 |
| Accounts Receivable | 3,000 | | |
| Office Equipment | 7,000 | *Owner's Equity* | |
| Land | 3,000 | S. Hill, Capital | 25,000 |
| Building | 12,000 | Total Liabilities and | |
| Total Assets | $35,000 | Owner's Equity | $35,000 |

**TRANSACTION 6—COLLECTION OF ACCOUNTS RECEIVABLE** Elite Tutors receives a $1,500 check from the public relations firm that purchased the video system, as agreed.

What are the effects of this transaction? The asset Cash is increased by $1,500. The asset Accounts Receivable is decreased by $1,500.

| Assets | | = Liabilities + Owner's Equity |
|---|---|---|
| Cash | Accounts Receivable | |
| +1,500 | −1,500 | |

After this transaction has been recorded, the balance sheet appears as follows:

ELITE TUTORS
Balance Sheet

| *Assets* | | *Liabilities* | |
|---|---|---|---|
| Cash | $11,500 | Accounts Payable | $10,000 |
| Accounts Receivable | 1,500 | | |
| Office Equipment | 7,000 | *Owner's Equity* | |
| Land | 3,000 | S. Hill, Capital | 25,000 |
| Building | 12,000 | Total Liabilities and | |
| Total Assets | $35,000 | Owner's Equity | $35,000 |

**TRANSACTION 7—PAYMENT OF A LIABILITY** As promised, Elite Tutors makes its first payment of $2,000 owed on the office equipment purchased in Transaction 3.

What are the effects of this transaction? The asset Cash is decreased by $2,000. The liability Accounts Payable is decreased by $2,000.

| Assets | = Liabilities + Owner's Equity |
|---|---|
| Cash | Accounts Payable |
| −2,000 | −2,000 |

After this transaction has been recorded, the balance sheet appears as follows:

ELITE TUTORS
Balance Sheet

| *Assets* | | *Liabilities* | |
|---|---|---|---|
| Cash | $ 9,500 | Accounts Payable | $ 8,000 |
| Accounts Receivable | 1,500 | | |
| Office Equipment | 7,000 | *Owner's Equity* | |
| Land | 3,000 | S. Hill, Capital | 25,000 |
| Building | 12,000 | Total Liabilities and | |
| Total Assets | $33,000 | Owner's Equity | $33,000 |

**TRANSACTION 8—WITHDRAWAL BY OWNER** Stuart Hill withdraws $1,000 from the bank account of Elite Tutors to use for his personal activities.

What are the effects of this transaction? It reduces in equal amounts both Assets and Owner's Equity. Thus both Cash and S. Hill, Capital, are reduced by $1,000.

| Assets | = Liabilities + | Owner's Equity |
|---|---|---|
| Cash | | S. Hill, Capital |
| −1,000 | | −1,000 |

After this transaction has been recorded, the balance sheet appears as follows:

ELITE TUTORS
Balance Sheet

| *Assets* | | *Liabilities* | |
|---|---|---|---|
| Cash | $ 8,500 | Accounts Payable | $ 8,000 |
| Accounts Receivable | 1,500 | | |
| Office Equipment | 7,000 | *Owner's Equity* | |
| Land | 3,000 | S. Hill, Capital | 24,000 |
| Building | 12,000 | Total Liabilities and | |
| Total Assets | $32,000 | Owner's Equity | $32,000 |

## SUMMARY ANALYSIS OF TRANSACTIONS

The eight transactions we have just discussed are summarized in Exhibit 1–4 on page 22. This display emphasizes that a balance sheet is a detailed presentation of the accounting equation.

As you review the display, note that after each transaction the equality between total assets and total liabilities plus owner's equity is maintained. The totals at the bottom of the display correspond to the last balance sheet prepared for Elite Tutors.

## A NOTE ON HIGHLIGHT PROBLEMS

Each chapter in this text includes a problem that highlights one or more key concepts explained in the chapter. Solving a Highlight Problem is easier and quicker than solving a Summary Problem (testing *all* key concepts), and it gives you an immediate test of your understanding of the chapter material. If you are not sure of your solution, review the chapter to clarify the concepts. When you are sure that you have solved the problem, compare your answers with the Solution Guide in Appendix A. A correct solution will be encouraging, giving you reinforcement and confidence, and will motivate you to proceed to new material. If you find that your solution is not correct, study the Solution Guide, then return to the Highlight Problem and rework it until you can produce the correct solution without looking at the Solution Guide.

## HIGHLIGHT PROBLEM

Jerry Garamond, who owns Jerry's Game Gallery, wants to borrow some money from a bank to renovate his rather old premises. He already has a mortgage and owes money on account,

*EXHIBIT 1–4*

ELITE TUTORS
Summary Analysis of Transactions

| | | ASSETS | | | | | = | LIABILITIES | + | OWNER'S EQUITY |
|---|---|---|---|---|---|---|---|---|---|---|
| NO. | DESCRIPTION OF TRANSACTION | CASH | ACCOUNTS RECEIVABLE | OFFICE EQUIPMENT | LAND | BUILDING | | ACCOUNTS PAYABLE | | S. HILL, CAPITAL |
| | Balances at beginning | -0- | -0- | -0- | -0- | -0- | = | -0- | | -0- |
| 1 | Investment of cash by the owner | +25,000 | | | | | | | | +25,000 |
| 2 | Purchase of land and building for cash | −17,000 | | | +5,000 | +12,000 | | | | |
| 3 | Purchase of office equipment on account | | | +10,000 | | | | +10,000 | | |
| 4 | Sale of land at cost for cash | + 2,000 | | | −2,000 | | | | | |
| 5 | Sale of office equipment at cost on account | | +3,000 | − 3,000 | | | | | | |
| 6 | Collection on account | + 1,500 | −1,500 | | | | | | | |
| 7 | Payment on account | − 2,000 | | | | | | − 2,000 | | |
| 8 | Withdrawal of cash by the owner | − 1,000 | | | | | | | | − 1,000 |
| | Balance at end | 8,500 | +1,500 | + 7,000 | +3,000 | +12,000 | = | 8,000 | + | 24,000 |
| | | | | 32,000 | | | = | 8,000 | + | 24,000 |

and he wonders whether he is "up to his neck in debt." He shows you an index card on which he has penciled the following items:

| | |
|---|---|
| Cash | $12,000 |
| Accounts receivable | 31,000 |
| Building | 40,000 |
| Equipment | 27,000 |
| Accounts payable | 18,000 |
| Mortgage payable | 25,000 |

and he asks you, "What is my company's financial position—how do I stand?"

Required:
Prepare a balance sheet for Jerry's Game Gallery.

## GLOSSARY OF KEY TERMS

**Accounting equation.** An algebraic expression of the balance sheet: Assets = Liabilities + Owner's Equity.

**Accounting period.** The period of time covered by an income statement. Generally a year, a quarter of a year, or a month.

**Accounts payable.** Amounts owed to creditors for goods or services purchased from them on credit.

**Accounts receivable.** Amounts owed to a company by its customers or clients for goods or services sold to them on credit.

**Assets.** Economic resources owned or controlled by a business, which are expected to benefit future operations.

**Balance sheet.** A financial statement showing a company's assets, liabilities, and owner's equity on a given date. Also referred to as *Statement of Financial Position.*

**Business entity assumption.** The concept that a business is separate and distinct from its owner or owners and all other entities.

**Business transaction.** An economic event or activity that affects the financial position of a business entity and must be recorded.

**Capital.** Alternate term for *owner's equity.*

**Capital statement.** A financial statement that discloses the causes for the change in owner's equity that occurred during the period.

**Cost principle.** An accounting principle that requires resources and services to be recorded initially in company records at their acquisition cost.

**Creditor.** A person or company to whom a debt is owed. Creditors have a financial interest in (or claim to) the assets of the business.

**Expenses.** The cost of the goods and services surrendered or consumed in the process of generating revenue.

**Financial statements.** Periodic reports that communicate information, primarily financial in nature, and are designed to be useful in the decision-making process.

**Going concern assumption.** The assumption that a business will continue to operate indefinitely unless there is specific evidence to the contrary.

**Income statement.** A financial statement showing the revenues earned by the business, the expenses incurred in generating the revenues, and the resulting net income or net loss.

**Liabilities.** The obligations or debts that a business must pay in money or services at some time in the future.

**Net assets.** Total assets minus total liabilities.

**Net income.** The excess of revenues earned over expenses incurred for a given period of time.

**Net loss.** The excess of expenses incurred over revenues earned for a given period of time.

**Note payable.** A liability evidenced by a written promise to pay to another party a definite sum of money at some future determinable date.

**Objectivity principle.** The principle that accounting information must be free of bias and subject to verification by an independent party knowledgeable in accounting.

**Owner's equity.** A figure that represents the dollar value of ownership interest in (or ownership claims to) the assets of the business. Because owner's equity is always equal to total assets minus total liabilities, it is often referred to as *residual equity.*

**Owner's withdrawals.** The amounts of cash or other assets that have been taken from the company by its owner(s) for personal rather than for business use.

**Residual equity.** Alternate term for *owner's equity.*

**Revenues.** The inflow of cash or other resources received from customers or clients, which resulted from the sales of merchandise or the rendering of services, or from investments.

**Sole proprietorship.** A business owned by an individual.

**Statement of financial position.** Alternate title for *balance sheet.*

**Time period assumption.** The widely accepted notion that the life of a business can be divided into periods of time and that useful information concerning the activities of the business can be provided for those periods.

## REVIEW QUESTIONS

1. Describe the four basic accounting functions. [LO1a]
2. Describe the purpose or objective of each of the following financial statements:
   a. The income statement
   b. The balance sheet
   c. The capital statement [LO1b]
3. Name the three elements common to all income statements. [LO1b]
4. Name the three items that the heading of the income statement identifies. [LO1b]
5. Describe the two important accounting assumptions evident from the income statement. [LO1c]
6. Name the three sections of the body of the balance sheet. [LO1b]
7. What is meant by the cost principle? [LO1c]
8. Briefly discuss two reasons why accountants initially record assets at their historical cost. [LO1c]
9. Define *liabilities.* [LO1b]
10. Name the four circumstances that can change owner's equity. [LO1b]
11. Express the relationship among assets, liabilities, and owner's equity in equation form. [LO1d]
12. What is a business transaction? [LO2c]

## ANALYTICAL QUESTIONS

*Analytical Questions throughout the book will help you develop a deeper understanding of the chapter material.*

13. Why must the four basic functions of accounting be performed in the order in which they are listed? [LO1a]
14. State what accounting information would be missing if the set of principal financial statements excluded
    a. The income statement
    b. The balance sheet
    c. The capital statement [LO1b]
15. Assume that the assumptions of business entity and time period did not exist. In what way would accounting information supplied to us change? [LO1c]
16. How can we justify recording and maintaining assets at their cost when we know that the value of many assets changes over time? [LO1c]
17. Assume that the going concern assumption and objectivity principle did not exist. In what way would accounting information supplied to us change? [LO1c]
18. Why is owner's equity sometimes referred to as residual equity? [LO1b]
19. Why must total assets always be equal to total liabilities plus total owner's equity? [LO1d]
20. Without regard to the listings in the chapter, name five events that qualify as business transactions. Give reasons. [LO2c]

## IMPACT ANALYSIS QUESTIONS

*Impact Analysis Questions will appear at the end of each chapter throughout the book. They are designed to help you understand how a transaction, event, procedure, and/or accounting error affects key figures in financial statements or in other financial reports.*

*For each question that follows, indicate whether the accounting error would overstate [O], understate [U], or not affect [N] the specified key figures.* [LO2c]

21. Mr. Inept invested $4,000 cash in his business. The transaction was recorded as an increase in Cash and an increase in Accounts Payable.

    ______ Total Assets ______ Total Liabilities
    ______ Accounts Payable ______ Total Owner's Equity

22. Ms. Inept invested $3,000 cash in her business. The transaction was recorded as an increase in Office Equipment and an increase in her capital account.

    ______ Total Assets ______ Total Liabilities
    ______ Office Equipment ______ Total Owner's Equity

23. Mr. Unept purchased a car for $8,000. The transaction was recorded as an increase in Office Equipment and an increase in Accounts Payable, even though cash was paid for the car.

    ______ Total Assets ______ Total Liabilities
    ______ Office Equipment ______ Total Owner's Equity

24. Ms. Unept withdrew cash from her business. The transaction was recorded as a decrease in Office Equipment and a decrease in her capital account.

    ______ Total Assets ______ Cash
    ______ Office Equipment ______ Total Liabilities

25. Mr. Exept purchased office supplies and agreed to pay for them in thirty days. The transaction was recorded as an increase in Office Supplies and a decrease in Cash.

    ______ Total Assets ______ Cash
    ______ Office Supplies ______ Total Liabilities

## EXERCISES

*Exercises throughout the book will help you apply what you learned in the chapter to varied situations.*

EXERCISE 1–1 *(Transactions and the Accounting Equation)* Give examples of a transaction that would cause

a. One asset to increase and another to decrease without affecting liabilities or owner's equity
b. Total assets and total liabilities to decrease without affecting owner's equity
c. Total assets and total liabilities to increase without affecting owner's equity
d. Total assets and owner's equity to increase without affecting liabilities [LO1d,2c]

EXERCISE 1–2 *(Supply Missing Amount in Balance Sheet Data)* Determine

a. A company's total liabilities when its total assets are $120,000 and its total owner's equity is $72,000
b. The equity of the owner when the business has total assets of $30,000 and total liabilities of $35,000
c. A company's total assets when its total liabilities of $150,000 are equal to two-thirds of its total owner's equity [LO2b]

EXERCISE 1–3 *(Supply Missing Amount in Balance Sheet Data)* Using the following information, determine the company's total assets, total liabilities, and owner's equity. [LO2b]

| | | | |
|---|---|---|---|
| Accounts Payable | $12,000 | Cash | $ 8,000 |
| Accounts Receivable | 9,000 | Equipment | ? |
| Art Held, Capital | 30,000 | Land | 6,000 |
| Building | 40,000 | Mortgage Payable | 25,000 |

EXERCISE 1-4 *(Supply Appropriate Transaction)* Describe a transaction that will have the stated effect on the elements within the accounting equation:

a. Increase an asset and increase owner's equity
b. Increase one asset and decrease another asset
c. Increase an asset and increase a liability
d. Decrease an asset and decrease a liability
e. Decrease an asset and decrease owner's equity [LO1d,2c]

EXERCISE 1-5 *(Indicate Effect of Transaction on Assets, Liabilities, and Owner's Equity)* Seven transactions pertaining to a business entity are presented below.

a. The owner invested cash to start the business.
b. Purchased office equipment for cash.
c. Purchased a vehicle on credit.
d. Borrowed money from a bank.
e. Paid in cash some of the amount owed on the company vehicle.
f. Lent money to another company on a promise that it would soon be paid back.
g. Received cash representing the entire amount lent previously.

Using a tabular form, as shown below, identify each transaction by letter and then indicate its effect on the company's total assets, total liabilities, and owner's equity. The effects of the first transaction are indicated as an example. [LO2c]

| TOTAL ASSETS | TOTAL LIABILITIES | OWNER'S EQUITY |
|---|---|---|
| a. Increase | No effect | Increase |

## PROBLEMS

*Problems throughout the book will improve your skills in relating the chapter material to problem situations.*

PROBLEM 1-1 *(Prepare Income Statement from Randomly Listed Items)* From the following information, prepare an income statement for G. Ford's Political Consulting Company. The company began operating on October 1, 19X1, and the information below is taken from its records on October 31, 19X1. [LO2a]

| | | | |
|---|---|---|---|
| Salaries Expense | $3,500 | Interest Earned | $ 100 |
| Consulting Revenue | 9,300 | Advertising Expense | 600 |
| Rent Expense | 800 | Travel Expense | 1,700 |
| Telephone Expense | 200 | Utilities Expense | 300 |
| Maintenance Expense | 350 | Insurance Expense | 150 |

PROBLEM 1-2 *(Prepare Income Statement from Partial Data)* From the following information, prepare an income statement for the Leslie Karon Advertising Agency. The agency began operating on October 1, 19X1, and the information below is taken from its records on October 31, 19X1. The amount for Salaries Expense is missing, but it is known that the agency's net income for the month was $6,800. [LO2a]

| | | | |
|---|---:|---|---:|
| Advertising Expense | $ 3,700 | Travel Expense | $2,820 |
| Maintenance Expense | 230 | Rent Expense | 1,200 |
| Commission Revenue | 40,600 | Interest Expense | 180 |
| Insurance Expense | 240 | Utilities Expense | 570 |
| Salaries Expense | ? | Telephone Expense | 260 |

PROBLEM 1–3 *(Explain Transactions Listed in Tabular Form)* Six transactions of G. Bush Development Company, identified by the letters *a* through *f*, are summarized in the accompanying table. For each transaction, write a sentence explaining its probable nature. [LO2c]

| | | ASSETS | | | | | = LIABILITIES + | OWNER'S EQUITY |
|---|---|---:|---:|---:|---:|---:|---:|---:|
| | | CASH + | ACCOUNTS RECEIVABLE + | LAND + | BUILDING + | OFFICE EQUIPMENT = | ACCOUNTS PAYABLE + | G. BUSH, CAPITAL |
| | | -0- | -0- | -0- | -0- | -0- | -0- | -0- |
| | a. | +20,000 | | | | | | +20,000 |
| Bal. | | 20,000 | | | | | | 20,000 |
| | b. | −14,000 | | +4,000 | +10,000 | | | |
| Bal. | | 6,000 | | 4,000 | 10,000 | | | 20,000 |
| | c. | | | | | +3,000 | +3,000 | |
| Bal. | | 6,000 | | 4,000 | 10,000 | 3,000 | 3,000 | 20,000 |
| | d. | | +1,000 | | | −1,000 | | |
| Bal. | | 6,000 | 1,000 | 4,000 | 10,000 | 2,000 | 3,000 | 20,000 |
| | e. | − 2,000 | | | | | −2,000 | |
| Bal. | | 4,000 | 1,000 | 4,000 | 10,000 | 2,000 | 1,000 | 20,000 |
| | f. | + 500 | − 500 | | | | | |
| Bal. | | 4,500 | 500 | 4,000 | 10,000 | 2,000 | 1,000 | 20,000 |

PROBLEM 1–4 *(Prepare New Balance Sheet after Each Additional Transaction)* From the information shown below, prepare a balance sheet as of October 31, 19X1, for Mark Lane's Pizza Delivery Service. Also prepare a new balance sheet after the transaction on November 1 has been recorded and another new balance sheet after the transactions on November 3 have been recorded. [LO2b,2c]

| | | | |
|---|---:|---|---:|
| Accounts Receivable | $12,000 | Vehicles | $16,000 |
| Notes Payable | 2,700 | Accounts Payable | 9,900 |
| Cash | ? | M. Lane, Capital | 33,600 |
| Office Equipment | 10,300 | Supplies | 1,200 |

On November 1 the firm purchased another vehicle at a cost of $6,000 by paying 10% down and signing a note to pay the balance within six months. On November 3 a customer paid $3,100 to the company. This payment represents a collection of accounts receivable. Lane then made payment of $2,400 on its accounts payable.

PROBLEM 1–5 *(Prepare Balance Sheet from Randomly Listed Items)* From the following information, prepare a balance sheet for Rite Carter's Peanut Company as of October 31, 19X1. [LO2b]

| | | | |
|---|---:|---|---:|
| Accounts Payable | $ 3,400 | Land | $ 7,500 |
| Accounts Receivable | 1,900 | Office Equipment | 6,600 |
| Building | 46,000 | Mortgage Payable | 19,000 |
| Rite Carter, Capital | 39,300 | Notes Payable | 8,900 |
| Cash | 8,600 | | |

PROBLEM 1–6 *(Prepare Balance Sheet from Incomplete Data)* From the following information, prepare a balance sheet for H. Baker's Finance Company as of October 31, 19X1. [LO2b]

| | | | |
|---|---|---|---|
| Accounts Payable | $16,000 | D. Baker, Capital | ? |
| Cash | 9,300 | Accounts Receivable | 12,700 |
| Notes Payable | 4,400 | Supplies | 900 |
| Equipment | 19,300 | Prepaid Insurance | 600 |

PROBLEM 1–7 *(Prepare Balance Sheet from Partial Data)* Carole Burnit began operating her beauty parlor on October 2, 19X1. The information presented below was extracted from the company's records on October 31 of the same year.

| | | | |
|---|---|---|---|
| Vehicles | $9,500 | Mortgage Payable | $20,000 |
| Notes Receivable | 5,500 | Land | 9,800 |
| Accounts Payable | 6,300 | Accounts Receivable | 7,900 |
| Office Equipment | 5,200 | Building | 33,000 |
| | | Note Payable | 3,700 |

Two items and their amounts do not appear in the preceding list. One has been determined to be Cash, and its amount is equal to 10% of the company's total liabilities. You are asked to determine the other missing item and its amount and to prepare the company's balance sheet as of October 31, 19X1. [LO2b]

PROBLEM 1–8 *(Prepare Income Statement and Balance Sheet from Randomly Listed Items)* From the following information, prepare an income statement and a balance sheet for Court's Travel Service Company. Assume the information needed for the income statement covers the month of October and the information for the balance sheet is up to date as of October 31, 19X1, except for M. Court's capital amount. [LO2a,2b]

| | | | |
|---|---|---|---|
| Insurance Expense | $ 180 | Building | $27,800 |
| Equipment | 7,390 | Telephone Expense | 250 |
| Supplies Expense | 120 | Accounts Receivable | 8,210 |
| Commission Revenue | 23,200 | Note Payable | 6,400 |
| Maintenance Expense | 420 | Land | 2,000 |
| Cash | 9,480 | Rent Expense | 900 |
| Salaries Expense | 13,600 | M. Court, Capital (Oct. 1 balance) | 35,850 |
| Advertising Expense | 770 | Utilities Expense | 360 |
| Accounts Payable | 7,680 | Supplies | 410 |
| | | Travel Expense | 1,240 |

PROBLEM 1–9 *(Prepare Tabular Listing of Transactions)* Atlas Body Building Company had the following items and amounts among its assets, liabilities, and owner's equity on October 1, 19X1.

| | | | |
|---|---|---|---|
| Cash | $ 8,200 | Notes Payable | $ 7,900 |
| Accounts Receivable | 12,100 | Mortgage Payable | 11,500 |
| Land | 8,500 | Ed Rite, Capital | 45,900 |
| Building | 36,500 | | |

During the first few days of October the company engaged in the following transactions:

a. Collected $4,300 of Accounts Receivable.
b. Purchased a vehicle for $8,000 by paying 20% down and signing a written promise to pay the balance within sixty days.
c. Paid $2,000 on its Notes Payable liability.

d. The owner withdrew $1,000 in cash for his personal use.
e. Purchased office equipment that cost $1,600 on credit.
f. Sold for $200 cash two pieces of office equipment costing $200.

Using a tabular form, such as the one illustrated in Exhibit 1–4, show the effects of each of these transactions on the company's assets, liabilities, and owner's equity. [LO2c]

PROBLEM 1–10 *(Comprehensive Review Problem)* The following are randomly listed items as of October 20, 19X3 (except A, Capital) and represent transactions from October 1 to October 20.

| | | | |
|---|---|---|---|
| Salaries Expense | $15,000 | A, Capital (Oct. 1 balance) | $12,000 |
| Consulting Revenue | 50,000 | Maintenance Expense | 800 |
| Cash | 6,000 | Insurance Expense | 1,200 |
| Equipment | 10,000 | Utilities Expense | 900 |
| Accounts Receivable | 12,000 | Rent Expense | 5,100 |
| Travel Expense | 1,000 | Land | 5,000 |
| Advertising Expense | 12,000 | Supplies Expense | 1,000 |
| Accounts Payable | 11,000 | Miscellaneous Expense | 3,000 |

The following transactions occurred during the rest of October:
a. Collected $3,000 of Accounts Receivable.
b. Paid $2,000 of Accounts Payable.
c. Purchased additional land for $3,000 cash.
d. The owner withdrew $1,000.

Required:
1. Using a tabular form of the type illustrated in Exhibit 1–4, show the balances on October 20 for each asset, liability, and owner's equity item.
2. Using the same tabular form as in Requirement 1, show the effect of each of transactions *a* through *d* on the assets, liabilities, and owner's equity.
3. Prepare an income statement for the month of October 19X3.
4. Prepare a balance sheet as of October 31, 19X3. [LO2a,2b,2c]

## ALTERNATE PROBLEMS

*Alternate Problems throughout the book provide homework material similar in form to the regular problems, but with different figures that lead to different answers.*

PROBLEM 1–1A *(Prepare Income Statement from Partial Data)* (Alternate to Problem 1–2) From the information given below, prepare an income statement for the Brown Advertising Agency. The company began operating on November 1, 19X3, and the information is taken from its records on November 30, 19X3. The amount for Advertising Expense is missing, but it is known that the company's net income for the month was $17,000. [LO2a]

| | | | |
|---|---|---|---|
| Salaries Expense | $ 4,000 | Rent Expense | $1,000 |
| Advertising Expense | ? | Interest Expense | 200 |
| Commission Revenue | 40,000 | Utilities Expense | 600 |
| Maintenance Expense | 200 | Telephone Expense | 300 |
| Insurance Expense | 300 | | |

PROBLEM 1–2A *(Explain Transactions Listed in Tabular Form)* (Alternate to Problem 1–3) Five transactions of S. Watt's Wilderness Development Company identified by the letters *a* through *e* are summarized in the accompanying table. For each transaction, write a sentence describing its probable nature. [LO2c]

| | ASSETS | | | | = | LIABILITIES | | + | OWNER'S EQUITY |
|---|---|---|---|---|---|---|---|---|---|
| | CASH | + ACCOUNTS RECEIVABLE | + VEHICLES | + EQUIPMENT | = | ACCOUNTS PAYABLE | + NOTES PAYABLE | + | S. WATT, CAPITAL |
| Bal. | 10,700 | +3,900 | -0- | +2,000 | | =2,100 | -0- | | +14,500 |
| a. | + 2,100 | | | | | | | | 2,100 |
| Bal. | 12,800 | 3,900 | -0- | 2,000 | | 2,100 | -0- | | 16,600 |
| b. | − 2,000 | | +6,500 | | | | +4,500 | | |
| Bal. | 10,800 | 3,900 | 6,500 | 2,000 | | 2,100 | 4,500 | | 16,600 |
| c. | − 500 | | | | | | − 500 | | |
| Bal. | 10,300 | 3,900 | 6,500 | 2,000 | | 2,100 | 4,000 | | 16,600 |
| d. | − 800 | | | + 800 | | | | | |
| Bal. | 9,500 | 3,900 | 6,500 | 2,800 | | 2,100 | 4,000 | | 16,600 |
| e. | − 1,000 | | | +3,000 | | +2,000 | | | |
| Bal. | 8,500 | 3,900 | 6,500 | 5,800 | | 4,100 | 4,000 | | 16,600 |

PROBLEM 1–3A *(Prepare Balance Sheet from Partial Data)* (Alternate to Problem 1–7) Fillis Dillar began operating her beauty parlor on October 1, 19X3. The information presented below was extracted from the company's records on October 31 of the same year.

| | | | |
|---|---|---|---|
| Office Equipment | $ 5,000 | Mortgage Payable | $21,000 |
| Cars | 10,000 | Building | 30,000 |
| Notes Receivable | 5,000 | Land | 10,000 |
| Cash | 6,000 | Accounts Receivable | 8,000 |

Required:

Two items and their amount do not appear in the preceding list. One has been determined to be Accounts Payable, and its amount is equal to 20% of the company's total assets. You are asked to determine the other missing item and its amount and to prepare the company's balance sheet as of October 31, 19X3. [LO2b]

PROBLEM 1–4A *(Prepare Income Statement and Balance Sheet from Randomly Listed Items)* (Alternate to Problem 1–8) From the information given below, prepare an income statement and a balance sheet for the B. Rigg Sports Travel Company. Assume the information needed for the income statement covers the month of October and the information for the balance sheet is up to date as of October 31, 19X3, except for the B. Rigg capital amount. [LO2a,2b]

| | | | |
|---|---|---|---|
| Supplies Expense | $ 200 | Building | $28,000 |
| Cash | 10,000 | Rent Expense | 1,000 |
| Accounts Payable | 8,000 | B. Rigg, Capital (Oct. 1 balance) | 36,000 |
| Advertising Expense | 800 | Accounts Receivable | 8,000 |
| Commission Revenue | 24,000 | Utilities Expense | 300 |
| Insurance Expense | 200 | Travel Expense | 1,000 |
| Maintenance Expense | 400 | Land | 3,000 |
| Equipment | 8,000 | Notes Payable | 6,000 |
| Salaries Expense | 12,100 | Telephone Expense | 1,000 |

PROBLEM 1–5A *(Prepare Tabular Listing of Transactions)* (Alternate to Problem 1–9) W. Allen Body Building Company had the following items and amounts among its assets, liabilities, and owner's equity on September 30, 19X3.

| | | | |
|---|---|---|---|
| Cash | $ 9,000 | Notes Payable | $ 8,000 |
| Accounts Receivable | 12,000 | Mortgage Payable | 12,000 |
| Land | 8,000 | Allen, Capital | 45,000 |
| Building | 36,000 | | |

The following transactions occurred during October 19X3:

a. Collected $5,000 of Accounts Receivable.
b. Purchased a truck for $9,000 by paying 50% down and signing a note to pay the balance within ninety days.
c. The owner withdrew $2,000 in cash.
d. Paid $3,000 on the Notes Payable liability.
e. Purchased on credit office equipment for $2,000.
f. Returned some office equipment with a cost of $500 and received credit against the amount owed.

Required:

Using a tabular form such as the one illustrated in Exhibit 1 – 4, show the effects of each of these transactions on the company's assets, liabilities, and owner's equity. [LO2c]

# 2 Recording Business Transactions

### Learning Objectives

When you complete this chapter you will be able to

1. Answer the following questions:
   a. Why are documents used in recording business transactions?
   b. What kinds of items are included in Asset accounts? Liability accounts? Owner's equity accounts? Revenue accounts? Expense accounts?
   c. What are the rules of debit and credit?
   d. What is the purpose of a chart of accounts?
   e. How are journals used?
   f. What is the sequence of procedures in the accounting cycle?
2. Perform the following accounting functions:
   a. Enter transaction amounts directly into T accounts, applying the rules of debit and credit.
   b. Prepare a trial balance.
   c. Record transactions in a general journal and post the amounts in the appropriate ledger accounts.

The basic event with which accounting is concerned, as we have seen, is the business transaction. Every financial statement is simply a report of business transactions and their effects. The balance sheet is a report showing the cumulative effect that the business transactions engaged in by the entity since its beginning have had on its assets, liabilities, and owner's equity, stated in terms of the accounting equation:

Assets = Liabilities + Owner's Equity

In Chapter 1 you learned how to analyze the effects of a business transaction on the items in the accounting equation (that is, which items were increased and which were decreased) and how to prepare a new balance sheet after each transaction. That procedure is a good teaching example but is not used in the business world, where companies engage in numerous transactions daily. What we need is a system for recording and storing the data from these transactions so that we can prepare a set of financial statements at the end of the month or other accounting period.

In this chapter you will learn how business transactions are *identified, recorded, classified, summarized,* and *stored* for use in preparing financial statements and other financial reports. You will also learn how to use accounts to store transaction data and how to use the rules of debit and credit to record transactions in journals. Debit and credit rules for revenue and expense accounts are also included.

## BUSINESS DOCUMENTS—THE IDENTIFIERS OF TRANSACTIONS

***1a. Business documents provide evidence that transactions have occurred***

***1a. Business documents serve as the basis for accounting entries***

**Business documents** provide written or printed evidence that transactions have occurred and serve as the basis for entering transaction data in the accounting records. For example, when a business sells goods or services on credit, a sales invoice or sales ticket may be prepared. As another example, when a company buys goods or services on credit, it may receive a bill or invoice, which becomes the basis for supporting an entry to record the purchase and the accounts payable. Checks both issued and received, cash register tapes, invoices, bills, and statements are other examples of business documents that provide evidence that transactions have occurred.

Transaction data need to be recorded, classified, summarized, and stored. This chapter illustrates a system that satisfies these needs.

## THE ACCOUNT

An **account** is a form used to provide a record of the effect of transactions on each item that appears in a company's financial statements. The manner in which accounts are used is discussed and illustrated later in the chapter. The classification of accounts is covered now.

## CLASSIFYING ACCOUNTS

Accounts are classified into groups representing the elements of financial statements. The major classifications that we use follow the order in which they would appear in the balance sheet and income statement: Assets, Liabilities, Owner's Equity, Revenues, and Expenses.

*1b. Assets and liabilities are classified as current and noncurrent*

When assets and liabilities are reported in the balance sheet, they are often further subdivided to separate those that are current from those that are noncurrent. This separation provides information that is useful to the reader of the balance sheet.

## Asset Accounts

*1b. Current assets are cash or will become cash or be sold or used up during the firm's operating cycle or one year, whichever is longer*

**1. Current assets** are cash and other assets that are reasonably expected to be converted into cash, sold, or used up during the firm's normal operating cycle or within one year, whichever is longer.

An **operating cycle** is the average time period needed to complete a round of conversions that begin with cash outflow and end with cash inflow. The length of the operating cycle for a firm that performs a service, such as Tutorial Associates, should be much less than one year. A company that buys merchandise and sells that merchandise to customers probably has an operating cycle that is longer than a service company's cycle but nevertheless probably completes a number of cycles within a one-year period.

For companies that sell merchandise to customers on credit, the operating cycle may be diagramed as in Exhibit 2–1.

Current assets are usually listed on the balance sheet in the order of their presumed liquidity—that is, how long it will probably take to convert the assets into cash. The types of current assets commonly held by most businesses are listed and briefly explained below. You are probably familiar with most if not all

EXHIBIT 2–1

Operating Cycle for a Firm That Sells Merchandise on Credit

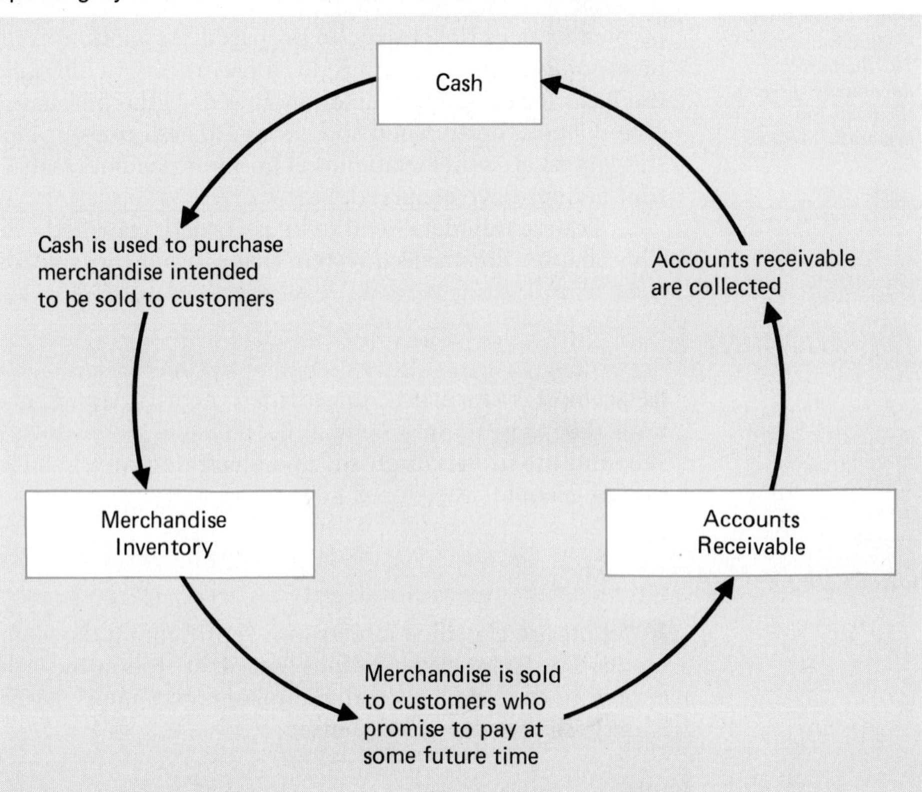

of them from your personal experience and from your recollection of the assets owned by Tutorial Associates.

*1b. Current assets include cash, marketable securities, notes receivable, accounts receivable, merchandise inventory, and prepaid expenses*

*Cash* consists of any medium of exchange that a bank will accept at face value for deposit, including currency, checks, bank deposits, and money orders.

*Marketable securities* are investments made in securities such as government bonds, corporate bonds, and corporate stock that are intended to be sold and converted into cash within a relatively short period of time.

*Notes receivable* are dollar claims that a company has against individuals or other businesses as evidenced by their written promise to pay a certain sum in money at a definite future date.

*Accounts receivable* are also dollar claims that a company has against its customers resulting from goods sold and/or services rendered to them on credit terms.

*Merchandise inventory* consists of goods owned by a company that it holds for purpose of sale to customers.

*Prepaid expenses* are amounts representing advance payments for items such as insurance, rent, and supplies. Unlike marketable securities, receivables, and inventories, prepaid expenses will not be converted into cash but will be consumed within one year or the operating cycle, whichever is longer.

**2. Noncurrent assets** are assets that are not expected to be converted into cash, sold or used up during the firm's normal operating cycle or within one year if the firm's operating cycle is shorter than one year. Such assets include the following:

*1b. Noncurrent assets include long-term investments; property, plant, and equipment; and intangible assets*

*Long-term investments* are assets that are not used in the normal operation of the business and that the company intends to hold for a period longer than a year or its operating cycle. Items in this category include securities and land being held for future use.

*Property, plant,* and *equipment* are assets that have relatively long lives, are used in the operation of the business, and are not intended for sale. Items in this category include land, buildings, machinery, and equipment.

*Intangible assets* are assets of a long-term nature that lack physical substance but are capable of providing future economic benefits because of the rights or privileges they confer. Items in this category include patents, copyrights, and trademarks.

## Liability Accounts

*1b. Current liabilities are debts or obligations due within the firm's operating cycle or one year, whichever is longer*

*1b. Current liabilities include notes payable, accounts payable, taxes payable, and salaries payable*

**3. Current liabilities** are the debts or obligations that will be due within the normal operating cycle of the company or within one year, whichever is longer. Most current liabilities are satisfied by making payment in cash. Examples of current liabilities are listed below.

*Notes payable* consist of amounts that a company owes to its creditors and are evidenced by a written promise to pay a definite sum of money at a definite future date.

*Accounts payable* are amounts that a company owes to its creditors and are incurred when a company buys goods and/or receives services on the basis of an oral or implied promise to pay in the future.

*Taxes payable* are amounts that a company owes to one or more governmental agencies and is required to pay within a specified period of time.

*Salaries payable* are amounts owed to a company's employees for services they have already rendered.

**4. Noncurrent liabilities,** often called *long-term liabilities*, are the debts or obligations that do not need to be paid within the next year or within the normal operating cycle, whichever is longer. Examples of noncurrent liabilities are listed below.

*1b. Noncurrent liabilities include long-term notes payable, mortgages payable, and bonds payable*

*Long-term notes payable* are debt that is evidenced by a written promise and will not be due in the near future.

*Mortgages payable* are debt that is evidenced by a written promise and for which the company has pledged a specific asset or assets as security.

*Bonds payable* are debt that has a due date more than a year away. This debt is usually evidenced by a formal document known as a *bond certificate.*

## Owner's Equity Accounts

Owner's equity, as we saw in Chapter 1, represents the dollar value of the owner's claim to the firm's assets. The owner's equity is equal to the net assets of the business, which is the difference between total assets and total liabilities. Transactions that affect the owner's equity of a business organized as a sole proprietorship or partnership are recorded in the accounts discussed below. One of the accounts, capital, is the basic account of owner's equity and is used interchangeably with owner's equity. The other three accounts — drawings, revenue, and expense, are subdivisions or components of owner's equity. The accounts used to record transactions that affect the owner's equity of a business organized as a corporation will be discussed later in the text.

*1b. The capital account is the basic owner's equity account*

**CAPITAL ACCOUNT** (The Basic Owner's Equity Account) When assets are invested in a firm by its owner or owners, the amount of the investment is recorded in the **capital account** established in the name of the owner. An example is the Stuart Hill, Capital, account in Chapter 1. Any additional investment by Hill is an increase in owner's equity and would be recorded as an increase in that same capital account bearing his name.

**DRAWINGS ACCOUNT** (A Subdivision or Component of Owner's Equity or Capital) If the owner withdraws cash or any other asset from the business for personal use, the amount is recorded in a **drawings account,** which is a decrease in owner's equity. Thus an account called Stuart Hill, Drawings, would be used to record the amount of cash or other assets withdrawn by Stuart Hill from his tutoring business.

*1b. Revenue accounts record increases in owner's equity resulting from the performance of services or the sale of goods*

**REVENUE ACCOUNTS** (A Subdivision or Component of Owner's Equity or Capital) Revenues are increases in owner's equity resulting from the performance of services or the sale of goods. When revenues earned exceed expenses incurred, the difference is called net income. A company will establish a revenue account to identify each source of the revenue and the amount of the revenue earned from that particular source for periods of time up to one year. Revenue account titles frequently used in industry to describe the source of the revenue are Sales, Fees Earned, Commissions Earned, Rent Revenue, and Interest Revenue.

*1b. Expense accounts record decreases in owner's equity resulting from the costs of goods and services used up in generating revenues*

**EXPENSE ACCOUNTS** (A Subdivision or Component of Owner's Equity or Capital) Expenses are decreases in owner's equity resulting from the costs of the goods and services used up in the process of generating revenues. If expenses exceed revenues, the company is operating at a net loss. Once again account titles will be descriptive concerning the nature of the expense. The larger and more complex the business becomes, the greater the number of expense accounts it will need to describe the nature of its activities. Account titles widely used are Cost of Goods Sold (for merchandising and manufacturing companies), Salaries Expense, Depreciation Expense, Rent Expense, Advertising Expense, Travel Expense, Supplies Expense, Utilities Expense, Maintenance Expense, Insurance Expense, and Interest Expense.

## MAINTAINING ACCOUNTS

The account is a basic record maintained within the company's accounting system. The accounting system will include a separate account for each item that appears on the financial statements discussed earlier. In a manual accounting system (sometimes called a pen-and-ink system) items are entered into the account by hand, and each account is kept on a separate card or sheet of paper. All the accounts of a specific business taken together are usually kept in a book or binder called a **ledger.**

Companies that use computerized accounting systems keep their records on magnetic tapes, disks, or other applicable devices. Their accounting records look different from those used in a manual system. Nevertheless, the purpose of recording, classifying, summarizing, and reporting financial data is the same under any system. Furthermore, all accounting systems are based upon the same underlying concepts. Because the manual system is easier to understand and illustrate, we will use it as our model in this book.

### The T Account

In its simplest form, an account has three parts:

1. A title, which states the name of the account
2. A left side, which is called the **debit** side (abbreviated Dr.)
3. A right side, which is called the **credit** side (abbreviated Cr.)

*2a. Effects of transactions are recorded on the left (debit) and right (credit) side of an account*

This form of account, which is often used to illustrate how transactions can be recorded in the accounts, is called a **T account** because of its similarity to the letter T, as illustrated below:

| TITLE OF THE ACCOUNT | |
|---|---|
| Left or debit side | Right or credit side |

Logically, then, amounts entered on the left side of an account are called ***debits,*** entering them is called **debiting,** and the account is said to be ***debited.*** Likewise, amounts entered on the right side of an account are called ***credits,*** entering them is called **crediting,** and the account is said to be ***credited.*** (Do not think of debits as always being additions or gains, or credits as always being subtractions or losses. In accounting the words DEBIT and CREDIT mean only LEFT or RIGHT, not increase or decrease.)

The cash account shown below is used to illustrate how data from transactions are entered and stored in T accounts:

| | CASH | |
|---|---|---|
| | 10,000 | 8,900 |
| | 3,400 | 6,700 |
| | 1,800 | 1,400 |
| | 1,300 | 2,600 |
| | 2,200 | *19,600* |
| | 4,100 | |
| *3,200* | *22,800* | |

Cash receipts (increases in cash) are entered vertically on the debit side of the account. Cash payments (decreases in cash) are entered vertically on the credit side of the account.

The debit total on the left side of the account is $22,800. This figure, called a **footing,** should be entered in a way that distinguishes it from the figures entered as a result of transactions that involve cash receipts. In our illustration the debit total or debit footing is printed in smaller type to avoid its being mistaken for an amount representing a cash receipt.

The credits entered on the right side of the account are also totaled, showing in our illustration total cash payments of $19,600.

### The Balance of an Account

The difference in dollars between the total debits and the total credits in an account is called the ***balance of the account,*** or the **account balance.** If the balance is a debit (a **debit balance**), the amount is inserted in the debit side of the account. If the balance is a credit (a **credit balance**), the amount is inserted in the credit side of the account. Like the footings, the account balance should be written smaller, in a different color, or in some other way so it will not be considered an additional debit or credit entry.

The cash account shown above has a debit balance of $3,200 ($22,800 − $19,600). If a balance sheet were to be prepared at this time, the company's current asset Cash would be reported at that amount, $3,200.

## DEBIT AND CREDIT RULES

The terms *debit* and *credit* are used to describe

1. The balance of an account (the Cash account has a *debit* balance of $3,200).
2. The recording of a transaction (we *debit* the Cash account when we record cash receipts and *credit* the cash account when we record cash payments).
3. The type of entry we make in an account (*debits* are amounts or entries on the left side of any account and *credits* are amounts or entries on the right side).

The system of debits and credits is simply a set of rules for recording increases and decreases in asset, liability, owner's equity, revenue, and expense accounts. Since debits or credits by themselves do not indicate increases or decreases, we must refer to a specific account to determine if the debits or the credits represent increases or decreases. How debits and credits are used to increase or decrease the three categories of accounts found on the balance sheet is shown in T-account format below:

| ASSETS | | = | LIABILITIES | | + | CAPITAL | |
|---|---|---|---|---|---|---|---|
| Debit to increase | Credit to decrease | | Debit to decrease | Credit to increase | | Debit to decrease | Credit to increase |

*1c. Debit and credit rules are related to the accounting equation*

Take special note of the relationship that the debit and credit rules have to the accounting equation. Assets are on the left side of the equal sign in the equation and are increased with left- or debit-side entries. Liabilities and owner's equity are on the right side of the equal sign in the equation and are increased with right- or credit-side entries.

We can now expand the basic accounting equation to include revenue, expense, and drawings accounts as follows:

Assets = Liabilities + Owner's Equity (Capital) + Revenues − Expenses − Drawings

Note that revenues, expenses, and drawings are placed to the right side of the equal sign in the equation along with owner's equity. This is because, as we have previously stated, revenues increase owner's equity, and expenses and drawings decrease owner's equity. Using the T-account format once again, the debit and credit rules for revenue, expense, and drawings accounts are as follows:

| REVENUES | | EXPENSES | | DRAWINGS | |
|---|---|---|---|---|---|
| Debit to decrease | Credit to increase | Debit to increase | Credit to decrease | Debit to increase | Credit to decrease |

Since revenues increase owner's equity and expenses and drawings decrease owner's equity, their debit and credit rules may be diagramed as shown in Exhibit 2–2. (Note that the revenue, expense, and drawings accounts are shown as debit and credit subdivisions of the capital account, which is the same as owner's equity.)

*EXHIBIT 2–2*

Debit and Credit Rules for Drawings, Expense, and Revenue Accounts

| CAPITAL (OWNER'S EQUITY) | | | | | |
|---|---|---|---|---|---|
| | | | Debit to decrease | Credit to increase | |
| DRAWINGS | | EXPENSES | | REVENUES | |
| Debit to increase | Credit to decrease | Debit to increase | Credit to decrease | Debit to decrease | Credit to increase |

You will find it helpful to memorize the rules of debit and credit and the way that they apply to asset, liability, and owner's equity (capital) accounts and to the subdivisions of owner's equity accounts—drawings, revenue, and expense accounts.

*1c. Debit and credit rules are summarized in Exhibit 2–3*

The rules for recording increases and decreases in these accounts together with a column to indicate their expected or normal balance are shown in Exhibit 2–3.

*EXHIBIT 2–3*

Debit and Credit Rules

| ACCOUNT | TO INCREASE | TO DECREASE | NORMAL BALANCE |
|---|---|---|---|
| Assets | Debit | Credit | Debit |
| Liabilities | Credit | Debit | Credit |
| Owner's Equity (Capital) | Credit | Debit | Credit |
| Drawings | Debit | Credit | Debit |
| Revenues | Credit | Debit | Credit |
| Expenses | Debit | Credit | Debit |

The expected or *normal* balance of any account is the side on which increases to the account are recorded. Knowing the normal balance of each account in a company's ledger may be useful in finding and detecting the cause of errors. If an account has a credit balance when its normally expected balance is a debit or vice versa, an error has probably been made.

## ANALYSIS OF TRANSACTIONS USING THE DEBIT-CREDIT RECORDING MODEL

### The Double-Entry System

The system for recording transactions that you are learning here is a **double-entry system.** It requires two things:

1. Every transaction must be recorded in at least two accounts.
2. The sum of the debit amounts recorded for each transaction must always be equal to the sum of the credit amounts recorded for that same transaction.

These two requirements are derived from the way the accounts fit into the accounting equation.

We will demonstrate by recording transactions directly into T accounts. To learn how to do so, let us use the transactions of Health Insurance Advisors—a management consulting firm that earns its revenue by advising client firms on the merits of various health insurance programs they might subscribe to for their employees.

*2a. Nineteen transactions are analyzed here and recorded directly into T accounts*

The first nineteen transactions of Health Insurance Advisors are listed below. We will analyze each one and record it in the appropriate accounts. We will find that in each case, as the principles of double-entry bookkeeping require, every transaction will affect at least two accounts. If more than one account is debited or more than one is credited, the sum of the debits must equal the sum of the credits.

TRANSACTION (1) On October 1 Paul Star took $20,000 of his personal money and deposited it in a checking account for Health Insurance Advisors.

*Analysis and recording into T accounts:*

| The asset Cash is increased by $20,000 | The owner's equity, Paul Star, Capital, is increased by $20,000 |
|---|---|
| *Increases in assets are recorded by debits* | *Increases in owner's equity are recorded by credits* |
| ∴ Debit Cash $20,000* | ∴ Credit Paul Star, Capital, $20,000 |

| CASH | |
|---|---|
| (1) 20,000 | |

| PAUL STAR, CAPITAL | |
|---|---|
| | (1) 20,000 |

TRANSACTION (2) On October 1 the company rented an office by paying $300, the rent for the month of October.

* The symbol ∴ means "therefore."

*Analysis and recording into T accounts:* The cost of renting the office is an October operating expense because the occupancy right the company buys will have expired by month-end. Expense items are recorded in separate expense accounts. Here the expense account used is called Rent Expense.

| The asset Cash is decreased by $300 | The expense Rent Expense is increased by $300 |
|---|---|
| *Decreases in assets are recorded by credits* | *Increases in expenses are recorded by debits* |
| ∴ Credit Cash $300 | ∴ Debit Rent Expense $300 |

**CASH**

| | Debit | | Credit |
|---|---|---|---|
| (1) | 20,000 | (2) | 300 |

**RENT EXPENSE**

| | Debit | | Credit |
|---|---|---|---|
| (2) | 300 | | |

TRANSACTION (3) On October 3 the company purchased office equipment costing $3,000 on credit from Allied Supply.

*Analysis and recording into T accounts:*

| The asset Office Equipment is increased by $3,000 | The liability Accounts Payable is increased by $3,000 |
|---|---|
| *Increases in assets are recorded by debits* | *Increases in liabilities are recorded by credits* |
| ∴ Debit Office Equipment $3,000 | ∴ Credit Accounts Payable $3,000 |

**OFFICE EQUIPMENT**

| | Debit | | Credit |
|---|---|---|---|
| (3) | 3,000 | | |

**ACCOUNTS PAYABLE**

| | Debit | | Credit |
|---|---|---|---|
| | | (3) | 3,000 |

TRANSACTION (4) On October 5 the company completed a consulting assignment and billed Topp Alloys, Inc., the client, $1,200 for the services performed.

*Analysis and recording into T accounts:* Revenue was earned when the company completed its consulting assignment, even though no cash was received at this time. What was received was Topp's promise to pay cash at some future time. This money claim against Topp is an asset called an account receivable.

| The asset Accounts Receivable is increased by $1,200 | The revenue Consulting Fees Earned is increased by $1,200 |
|---|---|
| *Increases in assets are recorded by debits* | *Increases in revenues are recorded by credits* |
| ∴ Debit Accounts Receivable $1,200 | ∴ Credit Consulting Fees Earned $1,200 |

**ACCOUNTS RECEIVABLE**

| | Debit | | Credit |
|---|---|---|---|
| (4) | 1,200 | | |

**CONSULTING FEES EARNED**

| | Debit | | Credit |
|---|---|---|---|
| | | (4) | 1,200 |

**TRANSACTION (5)** On October 8 the company purchased office supplies costing $400 on credit from Allied Supply.

*Analysis and recording into T accounts:*

| The asset Office Supplies is increased by $400 | The liability Accounts Payable is increased by $400 |
|---|---|
| *Increases in assets are recorded by debits* | *Increases in liabilities are recorded by credits* |
| ∴ Debit Office Supplies $400 | ∴ Credit Accounts Payable $400 |

| OFFICE SUPPLIES | |
|---|---|
| (5) 400 | |

| ACCOUNTS PAYABLE | |
|---|---|
| | (3) 3,000 |
| | (5) 400 |

*Note:* When financial statements are needed, the office supplies will be counted to determine the amount on hand. The difference between that amount and the amount purchased today represents the amount used during the period. The asset account Office Supplies will be reduced accordingly, and the related expense for supplies used will be recorded. The procedure for recording this transfer is discussed in Chapter 3. For the moment assume that none of the supplies have been consumed, and the entire amount appears as an asset.

**TRANSACTION (6)** On October 9 the company paid $80 for a newspaper advertisement describing its services.

*Analysis and recording into T accounts:*

| The asset Cash is decreased by $80 | The expense Advertising Expense is increased by $80 |
|---|---|
| *Decreases in assets are recorded by credits* | *Increases in expenses are recorded by debits* |
| ∴ Credit Cash $80 | ∴ Debit Advertising Expense $80 |

| CASH | |
|---|---|
| (1) 20,000 | (2) 300 |
| | (6) 80 |

| ADVERTISING EXPENSE | |
|---|---|
| (6) 80 | |

**TRANSACTION (7)** On October 10 the company spent $3,000 to buy some income-producing securities of the federal government. The securities are considered a short-term investment of excess cash.

*Analysis and recording into T accounts:* The transaction involves the exchange of one asset (Cash) for another (Marketable Securities).

| The asset Cash is decreased by $3,000 | The asset Marketable Securities is increased by $3,000 |
|---|---|
| *Decreases in assets are recorded by credits* | *Increases in assets are recorded by debits* |
| ∴ Credit Cash $3,000 | ∴ Debit Marketable Securities $3,000 |

CASH

| | | | |
|---|---|---|---|
| (1) | 20,000 | (2) | 300 |
| | | (6) | 80 |
| | | (7) | 3,000 |

MARKETABLE SECURITIES

| | | | |
|---|---|---|---|
| (7) | 3,000 | | |

TRANSACTION (8) On October 11 a consulting assignment was completed and $960 in cash representing full payment was received.

*Analysis and recording into T accounts:* This transaction increases the asset Cash and increases a revenue account, Consulting Fees Earned.

| The asset Cash is increased by $960 | The revenue Consulting Fees Earned is increased by $960 |
|---|---|
| *Increases in assets are recorded by debits* | *Increases in revenues are recorded by credits* |
| ∴ Debit Cash $960 | ∴ Credit Consulting Fees Earned $960 |

CASH

| | | | |
|---|---|---|---|
| (1) | 20,000 | (2) | 300 |
| (8) | 960 | (6) | 80 |
| | | (7) | 3,000 |

CONSULTING FEES EARNED

| | | | |
|---|---|---|---|
| | | (4) | 1,200 |
| | | (8) | 960 |

TRANSACTION (9) On October 12 the firm made a partial payment of $900 on the amount owed to Allied Supply.

*Analysis and recording into T accounts:*

| The asset Cash is decreased by $900 | The liability Accounts Payable is decreased by $900 |
|---|---|
| *Decreases in assets are recorded by credits* | *Decreases in liabilities are recorded by debits* |
| ∴ Credit Cash $900 | ∴ Debit Accounts Payable $900 |

CASH

| | | | |
|---|---|---|---|
| (1) | 20,000 | (2) | 300 |
| (8) | 960 | (6) | 80 |
| | | (7) | 3,000 |
| | | (9) | 900 |

ACCOUNTS PAYABLE

| | | | |
|---|---|---|---|
| (9) | 900 | (3) | 3,000 |
| | | (5) | 400 |

TRANSACTION (10) On October 16 two business automobiles were purchased. The automobiles cost $7,500 each and were acquired by paying $5,000 in cash and signing a note for $10,000.

*Analysis and recording into T accounts:*

| The asset Cash is decreased by $5,000 | The asset Vehicles is increased by $15,000 | The liability Notes Payable is increased by $10,000 |
|---|---|---|
| *Decreases in assets are recorded by credits* | *Increases in assets are recorded by debits* | *Increases in liabilities are recorded by credits* |
| ∴ Credit Cash $5,000 | ∴ Debit Vehicles $15,000 | ∴ Credit Notes Payable $10,000 |

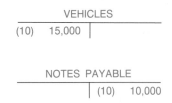

CASH

| | | | |
|---|---|---|---|
| (1) | 20,000 | (2) | 300 |
| (8) | 960 | (6) | 80 |
| | | (7) | 3,000 |
| | | (9) | 900 |
| | | (10) | 5,000 |

VEHICLES

| | | | |
|---|---|---|---|
| (10) | 15,000 | | |

NOTES PAYABLE

| | | | |
|---|---|---|---|
| | | (10) | 10,000 |

Although we debited only one account, we credited two accounts to record this transaction. For every transaction recorded, the sum of the debit amounts must equal the sum of the credit amounts. If more than two accounts are affected by a transaction, the sum of the amounts entered as debits must equal the sum of the amounts entered as credits.

TRANSACTION (11) On October 17 Health Insurance Advisors collected $700 of the amount owed by Topp Alloys, Inc.

*Analysis and recording into T accounts:*

| The asset Cash is increased by $700 | The asset Accounts Receivable is decreased by $700 |
|---|---|
| *Increases in assets are recorded by debits* | *Decreases in assets are recorded by credits* |
| ∴ Debit Cash $700 | ∴ Credit Accounts Receivable $700 |

CASH

| | | | |
|---|---|---|---|
| (1) | 20,000 | (2) | 300 |
| (8) | 960 | (6) | 80 |
| (11) | 700 | (7) | 3,000 |
| | | (9) | 900 |
| | | (10) | 5,000 |

ACCOUNTS RECEIVABLE

| | | | |
|---|---|---|---|
| (4) | 1,200 | (11) | 700 |

TRANSACTION (12) On October 18 travel expenses amounting to $150 were paid in cash.

*Analysis and recording into T accounts:*

| The asset Cash is decreased by $150 |
|---|
| *Decreases in assets are recorded by credits* |
| ∴ Credit Cash $150 |

| The expense Travel Expense is increased by $150 |
|---|
| *Increases in expenses are recorded by debits* |
| ∴ Debit Travel Expense $150 |

CASH

| | | | |
|---|---|---|---|
| (1) | 20,000 | (2) | 300 |
| (8) | 960 | (6) | 80 |
| (11) | 700 | (7) | 3,000 |
| | | (9) | 900 |
| | | (10) | 5,000 |
| | | (12) | 150 |

TRAVEL EXPENSE

| | | | |
|---|---|---|---|
| (12) | 150 | | |

TRANSACTION (13) On October 20 the company completed a consulting assignment and billed Wheatly Company, the client, $780 for services performed.

*Analysis and recording into T accounts:*

| The asset Accounts Receivable is increased by $780 |
|---|
| *Increases in assets are recorded by debits* |
| ∴ Debit Accounts Receivable $780 |

| The revenue Consulting Fees Earned is increased by $780 |
|---|
| *Increases in revenues are recorded by credits* |
| ∴ Credit Consulting Fees Earned $780 |

ACCOUNTS RECEIVABLE

| | | | |
|---|---|---|---|
| (4) | 1,200 | (11) | 700 |
| (13) | 780 | | |

CONSULTING FEES EARNED

| | | | |
|---|---|---|---|
| | | (4) | 1,200 |
| | | (8) | 960 |
| | | (13) | 780 |

TRANSACTION (14) On October 23 a check for $400 was drawn to pay for the office supplies previously purchased on credit.

*Analysis and recording into T accounts:*

| The asset Cash is decreased by $400 |
|---|
| *Decreases in assets are recorded by credits* |
| ∴ Credit Cash $400 |

| The liability Accounts Payable is decreased by $400 |
|---|
| *Decreases in liabilities are recorded by debits* |
| ∴ Debit Accounts Payable $400 |

| CASH | | | |
|---|---|---|---|
| (1) | 20,000 | (2) | 300 |
| (8) | 960 | (6) | 80 |
| (11) | 700 | (7) | 3,000 |
| | | (9) | 900 |
| | | (10) | 5,000 |
| | | (12) | 150 |
| | | (14) | 400 |

| ACCOUNTS PAYABLE | | | |
|---|---|---|---|
| (9) | 900 | (3) | 3,000 |
| (14) | 400 | (5) | 400 |

TRANSACTION (15) On October 27 Paul Star withdrew $1,200 from the business for his personal use.

*Analysis and recording into T accounts:* This transaction decreases the asset Cash and decreases Paul Star's equity in the assets of the business. In this situation a separate account called Drawings is used. Its purpose is to accumulate the figures that aggregately will show the amount of assets that the owner has withdrawn from his or her business during a period of time.

| The asset Cash is decreased by $1,200 | The Drawings account is increased by $1,200 |
|---|---|
| *Decreases in assets are recorded by credits* | *Increases in drawings are recorded by debits* |
| ∴ Credit Cash $1,200 | ∴ Debit Paul Star, Drawings, $1,200 |

| CASH | | | |
|---|---|---|---|
| (1) | 20,000 | (2) | 300 |
| (8) | 960 | (6) | 80 |
| (11) | 700 | (7) | 3,000 |
| | | (9) | 900 |
| | | (10) | 5,000 |
| | | (12) | 150 |
| | | (14) | 400 |
| | | (15) | 1,200 |

| PAUL STAR, DRAWINGS | | | |
|---|---|---|---|
| (15) | 1,200 | | |

TRANSACTION (16) On October 31 the firm paid salaries of $1,400 to recently hired company employees.

*Analysis and recording into T accounts:*

| The asset Cash is decreased by $1,400 | The expense Salary Expense is increased by $1,400 |
|---|---|
| *Decreases in assets are recorded by credits* | *Increases in expenses are recorded by debits* |
| ∴ Credit Cash $1,400 | ∴ Debit Salary Expense $1,400 |

CASH

| | | | |
|---|---|---|---|
| (1) | 20,000 | (2) | 300 |
| (8) | 960 | (6) | 80 |
| (11) | 700 | (7) | 3,000 |
| | | (9) | 900 |
| | | (10) | 5,000 |
| | | (12) | 150 |
| | | (14) | 400 |
| | | (15) | 1,200 |
| | | (16) | 1,400 |

SALARY EXPENSE

| | | | |
|---|---|---|---|
| (16) | 1,400 | | |

TRANSACTIONS (17), (18), (19) On October 31 the firm paid the following bills:

(17): Travel expenses of $110
(18): Telephone bill of $40
(19): Office equipment repairs of $70

*Analysis and recording into T accounts:* These transactions decrease the asset Cash and increase three separate expense accounts—Travel Expense, Telephone Expense, and Repairs Expense. We use three separate expense accounts so that we can identify the nature of each expense and use such data when reporting expenses on the income statement.

| | |
|---|---|
| The asset Cash is decreased by $110 | The expense Travel Expense is increased by $110 |
| *Decreases in assets are recorded by credits* | *Increases in expenses are recorded by debits* |
| ∴ Credit Cash $110 | ∴ Debit Travel Expense $110 |

| | |
|---|---|
| The asset Cash is decreased by $40 | The expense Telephone Expense is increased by $40 |
| *Decreases in assets are recorded by credits* | *Increases in expenses are recorded by debits* |
| ∴ Credit Cash $40 | ∴ Debit Telephone Expense $40 |

| | |
|---|---|
| The asset Cash is decreased by $70 | The expense Repairs Expense is increased by $70 |
| *Decreases in assets are recorded by credits* | *Increases in expenses are recorded by debits* |
| ∴ Credit Cash $70 | ∴ Debit Repairs Expense $70 |

CASH

| | | | |
|---|---|---|---|
| (1) | 20,000 | (2) | 300 |
| (8) | 960 | (6) | 80 |
| (11) | 700 | (7) | 3,000 |
| | | (9) | 900 |
| | | (10) | 5,000 |
| | | (12) | 150 |
| | | (14) | 400 |
| | | (15) | 1,200 |
| | | (16) | 1,400 |
| | | (17) | 110 |
| | | (18) | 40 |
| | | (19) | 70 |

TRAVEL EXPENSE

| | | |
|---|---|---|
| (12) | 150 | |
| (17) | 110 | |

TELEPHONE EXPENSE

| | | |
|---|---|---|
| (18) | 40 | |

REPAIRS EXPENSE

| | | |
|---|---|---|
| (19) | 70 | |

## SUMMARY OF TRANSACTIONS

The October activities of Health Insurance Advisors, represented by its nineteen completed transactions, have been analyzed and recorded in appropriate T accounts. In Exhibit 2–4 all the accounts are grouped together to show how the rules of debits and credits are followed and how the accounting equation is maintained. Note that, where appropriate, we have calculated the account balances by adding the debit and credit entries separately and then subtracting one set of totals from the other. For example, the balance in the Accounts Receivable account is calculated as follows:

ACCOUNTS RECEIVABLE

| Debit side of the account | Credit side of the account |
|---|---|
| 1,200 | 700 |
| 780 | |
| *1,980* | |

Thus the balance shown for this account is a debit balance of $1,280 ($1,980 – $700 = $1,280).

Remember that asset, expense, and drawings accounts normally have debit balances. Therefore, the total dollar amount posted to the debit side of these accounts should exceed the total dollar amount posted to the credit side. Remember also that liabilities, capital, and revenue accounts normally have credit balances. Therefore the total dollar amount posted to the credit side of these accounts should exceed the total dollar amount posted to the debit side.

## THE USE OF THREE-COLUMN LEDGER ACCOUNTS

Accounts in T form are convenient for purposes of analysis and illustration. In practice, however, a more elaborate account form will probably be used. A ledger account that has special rulings and three columns for entering dollar

*EXHIBIT 2–4*

Summary of Accounts for Health Insurance Advisors

ASSETS = LIABILITIES + OWNER'S EQUITY

## ASSETS

**CASH**

| | | | |
|---|---|---|---|
| (1) | 20,000 | (2) | 300 |
| (8) | 960 | (6) | 80 |
| (11) | 700 | (7) | 3,000 |
| | | (9) | 900 |
| | | (10) | 5,000 |
| | | (12) | 150 |
| | | (14) | 400 |
| | | (15) | 1,200 |
| | | (16) | 1,400 |
| | | (17) | 110 |
| | | (18) | 40 |
| | | (19) | 70 |
| Bal. | 9,010 | | |

**MARKETABLE SECURITIES**

| | | | |
|---|---|---|---|
| (7) | 3,000 | | |

**ACCOUNTS RECEIVABLE**

| | | | |
|---|---|---|---|
| (4) | 1,200 | (11) | 700 |
| (13) | 780 | | |
| Bal. | 1,280 | | |

**OFFICE SUPPLIES**

| | | | |
|---|---|---|---|
| (5) | 400 | | |

**OFFICE EQUIPMENT**

| | | | |
|---|---|---|---|
| (3) | 3,000 | | |

**VEHICLES**

| | | | |
|---|---|---|---|
| (10) | 15,000 | | |

## LIABILITIES

**ACCOUNTS PAYABLE**

| | | | |
|---|---|---|---|
| (9) | 900 | (3) | 3,000 |
| (14) | 400 | (5) | 400 |
| | | Bal. | 2,100 |

**NOTES PAYABLE**

| | | | |
|---|---|---|---|
| | | (10) | 10,000 |

## OWNER'S EQUITY

**PAUL STAR, CAPITAL**

| | | | |
|---|---|---|---|
| | | (1) | 20,000 |

**PAUL STAR, DRAWINGS**

| | | | |
|---|---|---|---|
| (15) | 1,200 | | |

**CONSULTING FEES EARNED**

| | | | |
|---|---|---|---|
| | | (4) | 1,200 |
| | | (8) | 960 |
| | | (13) | 780 |
| | | Bal. | 2,940 |

**SALARY EXPENSE**

| | | | |
|---|---|---|---|
| (16) | 1,400 | | |

**RENT EXPENSE**

| | | | |
|---|---|---|---|
| (2) | 300 | | |

**TRAVEL EXPENSE**

| | | | |
|---|---|---|---|
| (12) | 150 | | |
| (17) | 110 | | |
| Bal. | 260 | | |

**ADVERTISING EXPENSE**

| | | | |
|---|---|---|---|
| (6) | 80 | | |

**TELEPHONE EXPENSE**

| | | | |
|---|---|---|---|
| (18) | 40 | | |

**REPAIRS EXPENSE**

| | | | |
|---|---|---|---|
| (19) | 70 | | |

amounts is illustrated below by showing the postings of cash through transaction (14). Note that by having three money columns, we are able to enter not only debit and credit amounts but also a running balance to show a new balance for the account each time the account is debited or credited.

CASH — ACCOUNT NO. 1

| DATE | | EXPLANATION | POST. REF. | DEBIT | CREDIT | BALANCE |
|---|---|---|---|---|---|---|
| 19X1 Oct. | 1 | | | 20 000 | | 20 000 |
| | 1 | | | | 300 | 19 700 |
| | 9 | | | | 80 | 19 620 |
| | 10 | | | | 3 000 | 16 620 |
| | 11 | | | 960 | | 17 580 |
| | 12 | | | | 900 | 16 680 |
| | 16 | | | | 5 000 | 11 680 |
| | 17 | | | 700 | | 12 380 |
| | 18 | | | | 150 | 12 230 |
| | 23 | | | | 400 | 11 830 |

The account title and its number are shown at the top of the form. The *Date* of the transaction is shown in the first two columns. The *Explanation* column may be used for a variety of things, such as describing unusual items or making needed notations. The *Posting Reference (Post. Ref.)* column is used to list the page number of the journal where the journal entry for the transaction is recorded. (The use of a journal and the purpose of the reference column are explained later in this chapter.) The *Debit* and *Credit* columns are used to enter the dollar amounts resulting from transactions. In the *Balance* column the account's new balance is entered each time the account is debited or credited.

A major advantage of the three-column ledger account form is the balance column, which provides the account's balance at any date. For example, the company's cash balance of $11,830 on October 23 can easily be seen in the ledger account shown above.

## THE TRIAL BALANCE

*2b. A trial balance is prepared in three steps*

The equality of debit and credit balances in the accounts is tested periodically by preparing a **trial balance,** which is a two-column schedule listing the title and balance of every account, generally in the same order in which they appear in the ledger, at a specific date. The trial balance for Health Insurance Advisors is illustrated in Exhibit 2–5. It was prepared by taking the following steps:

1. The accounts appearing in the ledger were listed in the trial balance along with their current balances. The amounts for accounts having debit balances were entered in the left or debit column, and the amounts for accounts having credit balances were entered in the right or credit column on the trial balance.
2. Each money column was added.
3. The totals of each money column were compared to test the equality of debit and credit balances in the ledger.

EXHIBIT 2-5

HEALTH INSURANCE ADVISORS
Trial Balance
October 31, 19X1

| ACCOUNT TITLE | DEBITS | CREDITS |
|---|---|---|
| Cash | $ 9 010 | |
| Marketable Securities | 3 000 | |
| Accounts Receivable | 1 280 | |
| Office Supplies | 400 | |
| Office Equipment | 3 000 | |
| Vehicles | 15 000 | |
| Accounts Payable | | $ 2 100 |
| Notes Payable | | 10 000 |
| Paul Star, Capital | | 20 000 |
| Paul Star, Drawings | 1 200 | |
| Consulting Fees Earned | | 2 940 |
| Salary Expense | 1 400 | |
| Rent Expense | 300 | |
| Travel Expense | 260 | |
| Advertising Expense | 80 | |
| Telephone Expense | 40 | |
| Repairs Expense | 70 | |
| | $35 040 | $35 040 |

## PURPOSE AND LIMITATIONS OF A TRIAL BALANCE

A trial balance shows that

1. For every transaction, equal amounts of debits and credits were recorded
2. The balances for each account were computed accurately

However, a trial balance cannot prove that every transaction was correctly analyzed or that amounts were recorded in the proper accounts. In other words, a trial balance cannot guarantee that errors have not been made. For example, if the company received cash and erroneously entered the amount as a debit to Accounts Receivable, the balances of both the Cash account and the Accounts Receivable account would be incorrect. However, in the trial balance the sums of the debit and credit columns would still be equal. Furthermore, if a transaction that should have been recorded was omitted, two or more account balances would be incorrect. But a completed trial balance could not detect the error of omission because equal debit and credit amounts would have been omitted from the accounts and the trial balance debit and credit columns would still be equal.

The function of the trial balance is to prove that the ledger is in balance—that is, that equal amounts of debits and credits have been entered in the accounts for every transaction.

## THE CHART OF ACCOUNTS

One of the first steps in establishing an efficient accounting system is to determine the accounts that will be needed to accumulate and store accounting data and assign an identifying number to each account. The accounts used by a particular company will depend on several things, including the nature of its business activity, the size of the company, and the amount of detail needed in its financial reports. In general, a separate account should be established for each item expected to appear in the company's financial statements. The accounts should then be arranged in the ledger in financial statement order—that is:

Assets:
- Current assets
- Noncurrent assets

Liabilities:
- Current liabilities
- Noncurrent liabilities

Owner's Equity

Revenues

Expenses

*1d. A chart of accounts assigns an identifying number to each account a firm uses*

**A chart of accounts** is a listing of the account titles and the numbers that have been assigned to all accounts appearing in the general ledger. A simple chart of accounts suitable for Health Insurance Advisors is shown in Exhibit 2–6.

*EXHIBIT 2–6*

Chart of Accounts for Health Insurance Advisors

| No. | *Assets* | No. | *Revenues* |
|---|---|---|---|
| | Current assets: | 40 | Consulting Fees Earned |
| 1 | Cash | 41 | Interest Revenue |
| 2 | Marketable Securities | | *Expenses* |
| 5 | Notes Receivable | 60 | Salary Expense |
| 6 | Accounts Receivable | 61 | Rent Expense |
| 8 | Office Supplies | 64 | Travel Expense |
| | Noncurrent assets: | 68 | Advertising expense |
| 12 | Office Equipment | 71 | Telephone Expense |
| 14 | Vehicles | 74 | Repairs Expense |
| | *Liabilities* | | |
| | Current liabilities: | | |
| 20 | Accounts Payable | | |
| 21 | Notes Payable | | |
| | Noncurrent liabilities: | | |
| 26 | Loans Payable | | |
| | *Owner's Equity* | | |
| 30 | Paul Star, Capital | | |
| 31 | Paul Star, Drawings | | |

There are various reasons why numbers are used to identify an account; some of them are explained in this chapter. Note that within each category some numbers have been skipped. These numbers are being reserved for additional accounts that may be needed as the business expands. The numbering system used should be designed to accommodate the company's needs. For example, a small business may use a one-digit system and number its accounts consecutively, whereas a larger business may need two or even three-digit numbers to accommodate all its accounts.

Certain account titles, such as Accounts Receivable, Accounts Payable, and Inventory, have gained wide acceptance. For some accounts, however, more than one title is used. For example, the same account may be titled Vehicles by one company and Automobiles by another.

## THE USE OF JOURNALS

In this chapter we have illustrated the recording of business transactions by entering debits and credits directly in T accounts, which are a simple form of ledger account. For two reasons, however, this procedure is rarely used in practice. First, it would be difficult to follow an individual transaction, because its debit amount is entered in one or more accounts and its credit amount is entered in another account or accounts. Second, it would be difficult to find errors if transactions were entered directly in ledger accounts, especially for companies that have many transactions.

*1e. Journals list in the order of their occurrence every one of the firm's transactions, analyzed in terms of debits and credits*

To improve the system and to provide a link between the related debit and credit amounts entered in the accounts, we use a journal. **A journal** is a form of record that lists in the order of their occurrence every one of the firm's business transactions, analyzed in terms of debits and credits. Thus a transaction is analyzed and recorded in a journal before the amounts are entered in the appropriate individual accounts in the ledger. Because transactions are first recorded in the journal, it is sometimes called the **book of original entry.**

### The General Journal

A company may use more than one type of journal, depending on the nature of its business activity and its volume of transactions. In this text several types of journals will be discussed. The simplest and most flexible type is the **general journal.** It can be used to record any type of transaction.

The process of recording a transaction in a journal is called **journalizing.** The first four transactions of Health Insurance Advisors have been journalized in Exhibit 2 – 7 on page 54, together with the tenth transaction, so that you can see how a compound entry is recorded (an entry having more than one account debited and/or more than one account credited is called a **compound entry**). As you can see, a general journal provides columns for recording the following information about each transaction:

*1e,2c. Six items of information about each transaction are recorded in a general journal*

1. The date that the transaction occurred.
2. The titles of the accounts debited and credited.
3. The dollar amount to be debited, entered in the Debit amount column on the same line as the title of the account debited.
4. The dollar amount to be credited, entered in the Credit amount column on the same line as the title of the account credited.
5. A brief explanation of the transaction.
6. The numbers of the ledger accounts to which the debit and credit amounts were transferred. (This transfer, called *posting*, will be explained later in this chapter. The *Post. Ref.* [*Posting Reference*] column in the journal is not used until posting takes place.)

### Advantages of Using a Journal

*1e. The use of a journal in an accounting system offers four advantages*

By introducing a journal into the accounting system, we achieve the following advantages:

1. The journal shows in one place the debit and credit amounts resulting from each transaction.
2. The journal provides a chronological record of every transaction engaged in by a business. In effect, it serves as a company's diary. If it becomes necessary to review a transaction, its date can be used to locate the transaction in the journal.

3. The journal provides space for entering information about a transaction. For example, a brief written explanation can be given for each transaction. This explanation may be useful if there is a need to review complex transactions or develop transaction trends.
4. The journal reduces the possibility of error. If transactions are recorded directly in ledger accounts, we are less likely to detect the omission of a debit or credit. or the duplicate recording of a debit or credit.

EXHIBIT 2-7

GENERAL JOURNAL PAGE 1

| DATE | | ACCOUNT TITLES AND EXPLANATION | POST. REF. | DEBIT | CREDIT |
|---|---|---|---|---|---|
| 19X1 Oct. | 1 | Cash | | 20 000 | |
| | | Paul Star, Capital | | | 20 000 |
| | | Invested cash in the business | | | |
| | | | | | |
| | 1 | Rent Expense | | 300 | |
| | | Cash | | | 300 |
| | | Paid rent for the month of October | | | |
| | | | | | |
| | 3 | Office Equipment | | 3 000 | |
| | | Accounts Payable | | | 3 000 |
| | | Purchased office equipment on | | | |
| | | credit from Allied Supply | | | |
| | | | | | |
| | 5 | Accounts Receivable | | 1 200 | |
| | | Consulting Fees Earned | | | 1 200 |
| | | Completed assignment and billed | | | |
| | | Topp Alloys, Inc. for fees earned | | | |
| | | | | | |
| * | 16 | Vehicles | | 15 000 | |
| | | Cash | | | 5 000 |
| | | Notes Payable | | | 10 000 |
| | | Purchased two vehicles paying $5,000 | | | |
| | | down and signing a note for the | | | |
| | | balance of $10,000 | | | |

* Note that the entry on October 16 is out of sequence; it is shown in the journal at this time to illustrate the recording of a compound journal entry.

## THE TRANSFER OF AMOUNTS FROM THE JOURNAL TO LEDGERS—POSTING

### The Purpose of Posting

**Posting** is the process of transferring debit and credit amounts from the journal to the appropriate individual ledger accounts. As you will recall, the purpose of the journal is to show in one place the changes in specific ledger accounts caused by transactions. The purpose of posting is to show the effects that transactions have had on each individual ledger account, such as the effects of transactions on the asset account Cash.

The appropriate time to do the postings will depend on how many transactions a company has per day and on individual preference. Postings can be done after each transaction is recorded in the journal or at convenient time intervals such as the end of a day, week, or month.

### The Six-Step Posting Routine

The mechanics of posting are easy. It is a routine procedure that you can accomplish for each journal entry in six sequential steps:

*2c. Posting is accomplished in six steps*

1. Identify the first account title in the journal entry (the first account title will represent a debit to an account) and locate this account in the ledger.
2. Enter the date of the transaction as shown in the journal in the Date column of the ledger account.
3. Enter the amount of the debit as shown in the journal in the Debit column of the ledger account.
4. Enter in the Reference column of the ledger account the page number of the journal from which the entry is being posted.
5. Enter in the Posting Reference column of the journal the account number of the ledger account to which the debit amount was posted. This **cross-referencing** provides evidence that the debit amount in the journal has been posted.
6. Proceed to the next account named in the journal entry. If the next account named is a debit, repeat the preceding five steps. If the next account named in the entry is a credit, apply the preceding five steps for the credit part of the journal entry.

The posting process is illustrated in Exhibit 2 – 8 on page 56. The six steps in the process are applied to the first transaction of Health Insurance Advisors. (The steps are identified by circled numbers.)

## THE SEQUENCE OF PROCEDURES IN THE ACCOUNTING CYCLE

To record, classify, summarize, and report business transactions, the accountant must accomplish certain procedures in a given order. This sequence is known as the **accounting cycle.** The procedures that we have discussed thus far are applied in the following sequence:

*1f. The accounting cycle (as studied thus far) includes a sequence of seven procedures*

1. Prepare a chart of accounts.
2. Analyze each completed business transaction.
3. Journalize each completed business transaction.
4. Post amounts from the journal to their proper ledger accounts.
5. Obtain a balance for each ledger account.
6. Prepare a trial balance.
7. Prepare financial statements.

In Chapter 3 we will explain how adjusting entries are included in the accounting cycle and we will illustrate these entries for you. In Chapter 4 we will show you how the accounting cycle is completed.

*EXHIBIT 2–8*
The Six-Step Posting Process

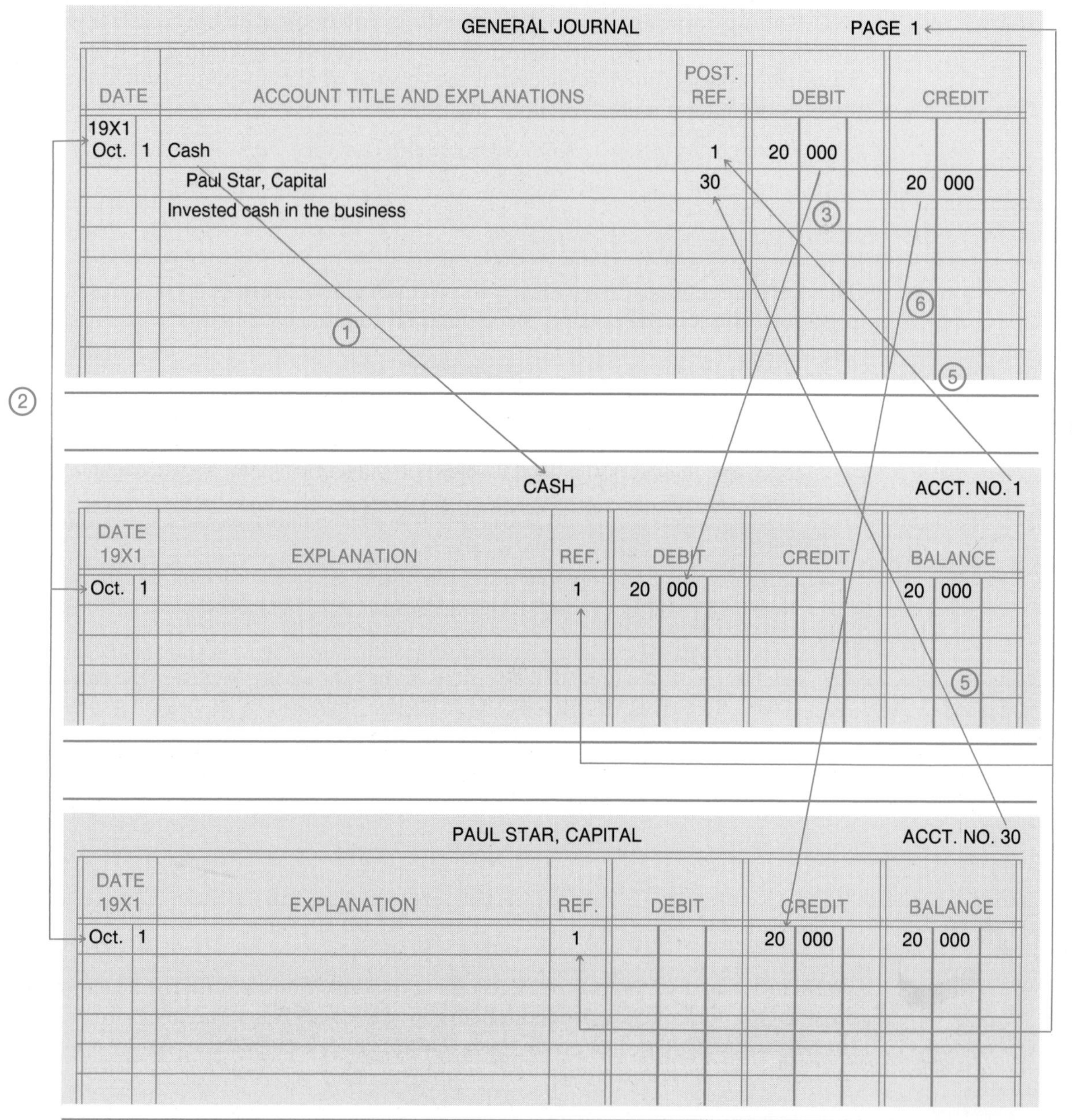

## HIGHLIGHT PROBLEM

Demonstrate your understanding of (1) journalizing, (2) posting, (3) cross-referencing, (4) obtaining account balances, and (5) preparing a trial balance by completing the requirements stated below.

1. Hart Interiors, newly organized by Judy Hart on October 1, had ten transactions during its first month of operations. These transactions must be recorded in a general journal. Shown on page 58 is the company's partially completed general journal. Complete it by entering the name of the account or accounts that should be debited and credited on each date. The company's chart of accounts is as follows:

| | | | |
|---|---|---|---|
| 1 | Cash | 31 | Judy Hart, Drawings |
| 3 | Accounts Receivable | 40 | Fees Earned |
| 10 | Office Equipment | 50 | Salaries Expense |
| 20 | Accounts Payable | 51 | Rent Expense |
| 30 | Judy Hart, Capital | 55 | Utilities Expense |

2. Make certain that all the debit and credit amounts recorded in the general journal were correctly posted to their appropriate ledger accounts. The names of the ledger accounts are shown above.

3. Check the general journal and each individual ledger account to make certain that all entries were properly cross-referenced.

4. Prepare an October 31, 19X1, trial balance.

GENERAL JOURNAL PAGE 1

| DATE | | ACCOUNT TITLE AND EXPLANATION | POST. REF. | DEBIT | CREDIT |
|---|---|---|---|---|---|
| 19X1 Oct. | 1 | | | 25 000 | |
| | | | | | 25 000 |
| | | Judy Hart invested cash in her business | | | |
| | | | | | |
| | 1 | | | 400 | |
| | | | | | 400 |
| | | Paid monthly rent | | | |
| | | | | | |
| | 4 | | | 6 000 | |
| | | | | | 2 000 |
| | | | | | 4 000 |
| | | Purchased office equipment. Paid one-third cash and promised to pay the balance | | | |
| | | | | | |
| | 9 | | | 800 | |
| | | | | | 800 |
| | | Earned and collected fee for completed work | | | |
| | | | | | |
| | 13 | | | 700 | |
| | | | | 700 | |
| | | | | | 1 400 |
| | | Completed work and received one-half payment and promise to receive the balance soon | | | |
| | | | | | |
| | 24 | | | 2 000 | |
| | | | | | 2 000 |
| | | Paid one-half of amount due for office equipment purchased on October 4 | | | |
| | | | | | |
| | 27 | | | 300 | |
| | | | | | 300 |
| | | Received partial payment for work completed and billed on the thirteenth | | | |
| | | | | | |
| | 30 | | | 700 | |
| | | | | | 700 |
| | | Paid part-time employees salary | | | |
| | | | | | |
| | 31 | | | 200 | |
| | | | | | 200 |
| | | Paid monthly utility bill | | | |
| | | | | | |
| | 31 | | | 500 | |
| | | | | | 500 |
| | | Judy withdrew cash for personal use | | | |

## GLOSSARY OF KEY TERMS

Account. A form used to provide a record of the effect of transactions on each item that appears in a company's financial statements.

Account balance. The difference in dollars between the total debits and the total credits in an account.

Accounting cycle. The sequence of accounting procedures that is performed during each accounting period in the life of a business enterprise.

Book of original entry. The book in which transactions are first recorded.

Business documents. Written or printed evidence that transactions have occurred.

Capital account. An account used to show the amount of assets invested in a firm by its owner or owners. The basic owner's equity account.

Chart of accounts. A listing showing the titles and account numbers that have been assigned to all accounts contained in the ledger.

Compound entry. A journal entry having more than one account debited and/or more than one account credited.

Credit. (1) The right-hand side of any account. (2) An entry on the right-hand side of any account.

Crediting. Entering dollar amounts on the right-hand side of an account.

Credit balance. The balance of an account when the sum of the credits entered in the account exceeds the sum of the debits entered in that account.

Cross-referencing. Entering in the journal the number of the ledger account to which an entry was posted, and entering in the ledger account the page number of the journal in which the entry and its amount can be found.

Current assets. Cash and other assets that are reasonably expected to be converted into cash, sold, or used up during the firm's normal operating cycle or within one year, whichever is longer.

Current liabilities. The debts or obligations that will be due within the normal operating cycle of the firm or within one year, whichever is longer. Current liabilities are generally satisfied by cash payments.

Debit. (1) The left-hand side of any account. (2) An entry on the left-hand side of any account.

Debiting. Entering dollar amounts on the left-hand side of an account.

Debit balance. The balance of an account when the sum of the debits entered in the account exceeds the sum of the credits entered in that account.

Double-entry system. A system for recording transactions such that the effect of every transaction is recorded in two or more accounts and transactions have equal amounts of debits and credits.

Drawings account. An account used to show the amount of cash or other assets the owner has taken from the business for his or her personal use. A subdivision or component of owner's equity.

Footing. Totaling a column of figures and showing the total in small or otherwise distinctly different figures under the last amount in the column.

General journal. A two-column record used to record a company's transactions in the order in which they occurred.

Journal. A form of record that lists in the order in which they occurred every one of the firm's transactions, analyzed in terms of debits and credits.

Journalizing. The process of recording transactions in the journal.

Ledger. A book or binder, or a computerized device, containing all of the accounts used by a particular firm.

Noncurrent assets. Assets that are not expected to be converted into cash, sold, or used during the firm's normal operating cycle or within one year if the operating cycle is shorter than one year.

Noncurrent liabilities (also called *long-term liabilities*). The debts or obligations that do not need to be paid within the next year or within the normal operating cycle, whichever is longer.

Operating cycle. The average time period needed by a company to complete its round of conversions that begin with cash outflow and end with cash inflow.

Posting. The process of transferring the debit amounts and the credit amounts from a journal to their appropriate ledger accounts.

T account. An account resembling the letter T which is often used to illustrate the debits and credits needed when recording the effects of a transaction involving individual assets, liabilities, or components of owner's equity.

Trial balance. A two-column schedule listing the title and balance of every account, generally in the same order in which they appear in the ledger, at a specific date. Accounts having debit balances will have their amounts listed in the left-hand money column, and accounts having credit balances will have their amounts listed in the right-hand money column. Totaling both columns tests the equality of debit and credit balances in the ledger.

## REVIEW QUESTIONS

1. Give five examples of business documents. [LO1a]
2. Name the five major classifications of accounts. [LO1b]
3. Name and describe two principal groups of assets. [LO1b]
4. What is meant by the term *operating cycle?* [LO1b]
5. Name and describe the two principal groups of liabilities. [LO1b]
6. Briefly define *owner's equity.* [LO1b]
7. Describe the three parts of a T account. [LO2a]
8. Name the three things described by the terms *debit* and *credit.* [LO1c]
9. Answer the following questions:
   a. Why are increases in revenues recorded by credits?
   b. Why are increases in expenses recorded by debits?
   c. Why are increases in drawings recorded by debits? [LO1c]
10. Describe the rules of debit and credit as they relate to
    a. Asset accounts
    b. Liability accounts
    c. The owner's capital account
    d. The drawings account
    e. Revenue accounts
    f. Expense accounts [LO1c]
11. What is meant by the *double-entry system?* [LO1c]
12. What is a trial balance? What two items of information are shown in a trial balance? [LO2b]
13. What is a chart of accounts? How are the accounts that are listed in a chart of accounts generally arranged? [LO1d]
14. What are the two reasons why debits and credits are rarely entered directly in ledger accounts in practice? [LO1e]
15. What is a journal? What use is made of a journal? [LO1e]
16. Why is a journal often called the book of original entry? [LO1e]
17. Name the six items of information contained in each transaction in a general journal. [LO1e]
18. What are the four advantages of using a journal? [LO1e]
19. What is the purpose of posting? [LO2c]
20. Describe the six-step posting routine. [LO2c]
21. Describe the sequence of procedures in the accounting cycle. [LO1f]

## ANALYTICAL QUESTIONS

22. Why is the information furnished by dividing assets into several categories on the balance sheet considered to be more useful to the statement readers than presenting only a composite asset figure? [LO1b]
23. "Today's assets are tomorrow's expenses." Explain this statement. Are any assets exceptions to this general statement? [LO1b]
24. "Owner's equity is sometimes referred to as a residual equity." Explain this statement. [LO1b]
25. If the rules of double-entry accounting were reversed (assets had credit balances, liabilities had debit balances, etc.), could financial statements be prepared in an acceptable and useful fashion? Why or why not? [LO1c]
26. Describe a transaction, other than those used as illustrations in the chapter, that would increase an asset account and increase a revenue account. [LO1c]

27. Describe a transaction, other than those used as illustrations in the chapter, that would increase one asset account and decrease another asset account. [LO1c]

28. Except for possible numerical errors, a trial balance must have an equality of debits and credits. Why is this true? [LO2b]

29. Compare and evaluate, from the point of view of analysis and the understanding of accounting, the process of journalizing and the process of posting. [LO2c]

## IMPACT ANALYSIS QUESTIONS

*For each error described, indicate whether it would overstate [O], understate [U], or not affect [N] the specified key figures.* [LO1c]

30. A vehicle was purchased on credit. The transaction was recorded by debiting the Vehicles account and crediting the Cash account.

    _______ Assets _______ Liabilities
    _______ Revenues _______ Owner's Equity

31. Cash was received for services performed. The transaction was recorded by debiting the Cash account and crediting the Accounts Receivable account.

    _______ Assets _______ Liabilities
    _______ Revenues _______ Expenses

32. Cash was paid to reduce the amount owed to a company for supplies previously purchased on credit. The transaction was recorded by debiting the Supplies account and crediting the Cash account.

    _______ Assets _______ Liabilities
    _______ Revenues _______ Owner's Equity

33. The company's owner withdrew cash for personal use. The transaction was recorded by debiting the Salary Expense account and crediting the Cash account.

    _______ Assets _______ Liabilities
    _______ Revenues _______ Expenses

## EXERCISES

EXERCISE 2-1 *(Describe Business Transactions)* Give an example of a business transaction that will result in

a. An increase in one asset and a decrease in another asset
b. An increase in an asset and an increase in a liability
c. An increase in an asset and an increase in owner's capital
d. A decrease in an asset and an increase in an expense
e. A decrease in an asset and a decrease in a liability
f. An increase in an asset and an increase in revenue
g. A decrease in an asset and an increase in owner's drawings [LO1c]

EXERCISE 2-2 *(Use the Debit and Credit Model)* For each item listed below, indicate how the item is increased and decreased by entering the words *debited* and *credited.* Also indicate the item's normal balance by entering the word *debit* or *credit* in the last column. [LO1c]

| ITEM | INCREASES | DECREASES | NORMAL BALANCE |
|---|---|---|---|
| Asset | | | |
| Liability | | | |
| Owner's Capital | | | |
| Owner's Drawings | | | |
| Revenue | | | |
| Expense | | | |

EXERCISE 2–3 *(Record Transactions Directly in T Accounts)* Use T accounts for recording increases and decreases in the following items: Cash, Accounts Receivable, Office Equipment, Accounts Payable, J. Silver—Capital, J. Silver—Drawings, Fees Earned, and Salaries Expense. The transactions are listed below; record them directly in T accounts, using the letters to identify the transactions.

a. J. Silver opened a service business by investing $8,000 in cash.
b. Purchased office equipment costing $1,500 on credit.
c. Received $600 in cash as a fee for services performed.
d. Billed a customer $900 as the fee for services performed.
e. Paid $500 of the amount owed for the purchase of office equipment, previously recorded in transaction *b*.
f. J. Silver withdrew $300 of business cash for personal use.
g. Received $200 of the amount owed by the customer from transaction *d*.
h. Paid salaries of $800 to part-time employees. [LO2a]

EXERCISE 2–4 *(Explain Transactions from T-Account Analysis)* Twelve transactions have been recorded directly in the T accounts shown below.

Required:

Explain the nature of each transaction that caused the debits and the credits. The letters in parentheses should be used to identify the transaction that has been entered. [LO2a]

CASH

| | | | |
|---|---|---|---|
| (a) | 40,000 | (b) | 300 |
| (d) | 900 | (c) | 5,000 |
| (h) | 100 | (e) | 3,000 |
| (i) | 2,000 | (g) | 500 |
| | | (k) | 2,000 |
| | | (l) | 4,500 |

NOTES PAYABLE

| | | | |
|---|---|---|---|
| (l) | 4,500 | (e) | 9,000 |
| | | (k) | 2,000 |

J. WARD, CAPITAL

| | | | |
|---|---|---|---|
| | | (a) | 40,000 |

ACCOUNTS RECEIVABLE

| | | | |
|---|---|---|---|
| (f) | 300 | (h) | 100 |
| (j) | 700 | | |

COMMISSIONS EARNED

| | | | |
|---|---|---|---|
| | | (d) | 900 |
| | | (f) | 300 |
| | | (j) | 700 |

EQUIPMENT

| | | | |
|---|---|---|---|
| (c) | 5,000 | (i) | 2,000 |
| (k) | 4,000 | | |

RENT EXPENSE

| | | | |
|---|---|---|---|
| (b) | 300 | | |

LAND

| | | | |
|---|---|---|---|
| (e) | 12,000 | | |

SALARIES EXPENSE

| | | | |
|---|---|---|---|
| (g) | 500 | | |

EXERCISE 2–5 *(Prepare a Trial Balance)* The accounts of Ordell Service Company as of October 31, 19X1, are listed below in alphabetical order. The Cash amount has purposely been omitted.

| | | | |
|---|---|---|---|
| Accounts Payable | $ 3,000 | Fees Earned | $40,900 |
| Accounts Receivable | 4,500 | Notes Payable | 8,000 |
| Cash | ? | Rent Expense | 3,600 |
| Equipment | 26,000 | Repairs Expense | 900 |
| F. Ordell, Capital | 25,000 | Salaries Expense | 26,600 |
| F. Ordell, Drawings | 7,200 | Utilities Expense | 1,800 |

Required:

Prepare a trial balance with the accounts listed in the preferred sequence. Determine the balance in the Cash account. [LO2b]

EXERCISE 2–6 *(Journalize Transactions)* Enter the following transactions in a two-column journal. Include, as part of each journal entry, a brief explanation of the transaction.

| | |
|---|---|
| Oct. 1 | Ed Gordon began a business by investing $12,000 in cash. |
| 3 | Paid monthly office rent of $500 in cash. |
| 5 | Received $1,200 from a client as commission for services performed. |
| 8 | Purchased a piece of office equipment. The terms of the purchase agreement called for 25% cash down and a written promise to pay the balance of $7,500 in ninety days. [LO2c] |

## PROBLEMS

PROBLEM 2–1 *(Analyze Transactions from T Accounts and Prepare a Trial Balance)* Sue Anton began a service business known as Anton's Dating Advisory Services on October 1. The company's transactions for October were entered directly in T accounts. On October 31, 19X1, these accounts appeared as shown below.

Anton's Dating Services Ledger Accounts, October 31, 19X1

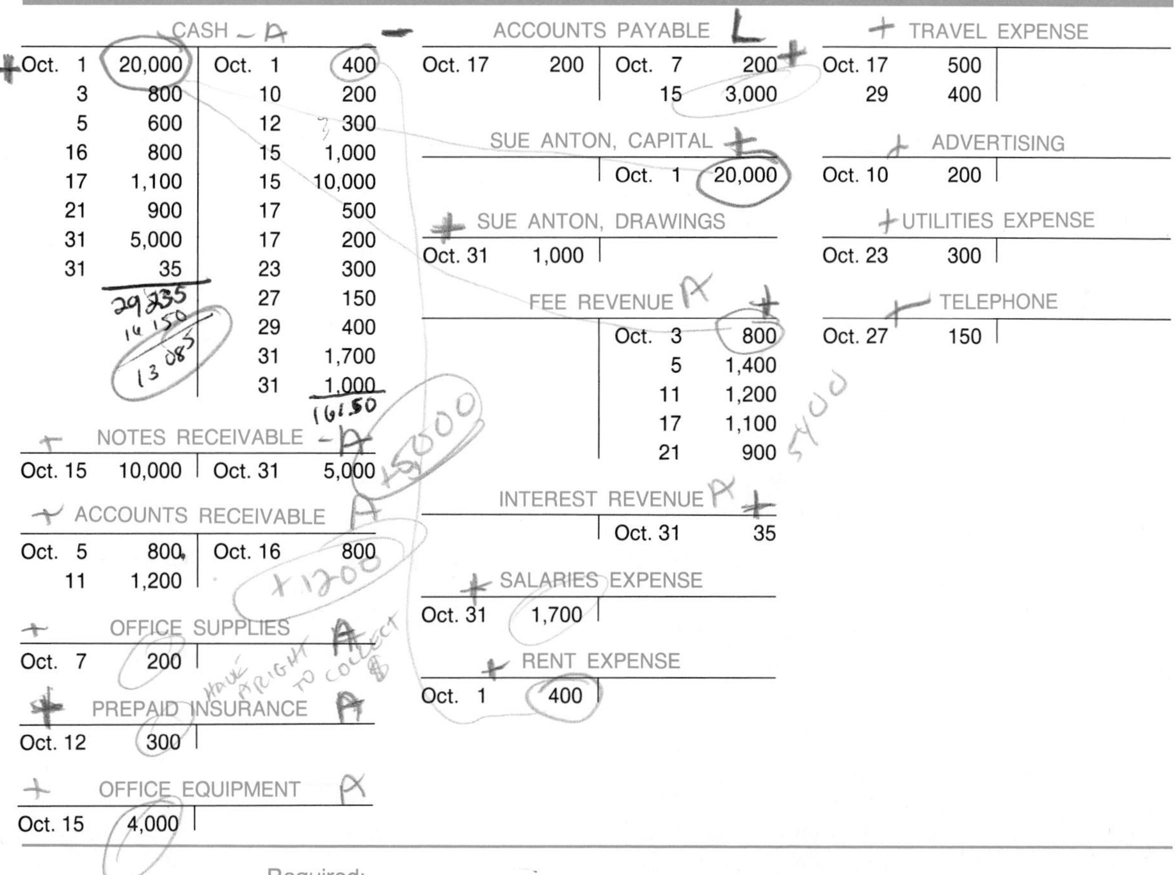

**CASH**

| Date | Debit | Date | Credit |
|---|---|---|---|
| Oct. 1 | 20,000 | Oct. 1 | 400 |
| 3 | 800 | 10 | 200 |
| 5 | 600 | 12 | 300 |
| 16 | 800 | 15 | 1,000 |
| 17 | 1,100 | 15 | 10,000 |
| 21 | 900 | 17 | 500 |
| 31 | 5,000 | 17 | 200 |
| 31 | 35 | 23 | 300 |
| | | 27 | 150 |
| | | 29 | 400 |
| | | 31 | 1,700 |
| | | 31 | 1,000 |

**NOTES RECEIVABLE**

| Date | Debit | Date | Credit |
|---|---|---|---|
| Oct. 15 | 10,000 | Oct. 31 | 5,000 |

**ACCOUNTS RECEIVABLE**

| Date | Debit | Date | Credit |
|---|---|---|---|
| Oct. 5 | 800 | Oct. 16 | 800 |
| 11 | 1,200 | | |

**OFFICE SUPPLIES**

| Date | Debit | Date | Credit |
|---|---|---|---|
| Oct. 7 | 200 | | |

**PREPAID INSURANCE**

| Date | Debit | Date | Credit |
|---|---|---|---|
| Oct. 12 | 300 | | |

**OFFICE EQUIPMENT**

| Date | Debit | Date | Credit |
|---|---|---|---|
| Oct. 15 | 4,000 | | |

**ACCOUNTS PAYABLE**

| Date | Debit | Date | Credit |
|---|---|---|---|
| Oct. 17 | 200 | Oct. 7 | 200 |
| | | 15 | 3,000 |

**SUE ANTON, CAPITAL**

| Date | Debit | Date | Credit |
|---|---|---|---|
| | | Oct. 1 | 20,000 |

**SUE ANTON, DRAWINGS**

| Date | Debit | Date | Credit |
|---|---|---|---|
| Oct. 31 | 1,000 | | |

**FEE REVENUE**

| Date | Debit | Date | Credit |
|---|---|---|---|
| | | Oct. 3 | 800 |
| | | 5 | 1,400 |
| | | 11 | 1,200 |
| | | 17 | 1,100 |
| | | 21 | 900 |

**INTEREST REVENUE**

| Date | Debit | Date | Credit |
|---|---|---|---|
| | | Oct. 31 | 35 |

**SALARIES EXPENSE**

| Date | Debit | Date | Credit |
|---|---|---|---|
| Oct. 31 | 1,700 | | |

**RENT EXPENSE**

| Date | Debit | Date | Credit |
|---|---|---|---|
| Oct. 1 | 400 | | |

**TRAVEL EXPENSE**

| Date | Debit | Date | Credit |
|---|---|---|---|
| Oct. 17 | 500 | | |
| 29 | 400 | | |

**ADVERTISING**

| Date | Debit | Date | Credit |
|---|---|---|---|
| Oct. 10 | 200 | | |

**UTILITIES EXPENSE**

| Date | Debit | Date | Credit |
|---|---|---|---|
| Oct. 23 | 300 | | |

**TELEPHONE**

| Date | Debit | Date | Credit |
|---|---|---|---|
| Oct. 27 | 150 | | |

Required:

1. Indicate the probable reason for the recorded debits and credits. Do this by describing the transactions that were recorded on the dates shown.
2. Determine the account balances and prepare a trial balance as of October 31, 19X1. [LO1c,2a,2b]

PROBLEM 2–2 *(Record Directly in T Accounts and Prepare a Trial Balance)* Art Harvey started a freeway limousine service company called Art's Limo and during a short period of operations completed the following transactions.

a. Began business by investing $9,000 in cash and a used limousine having a fair value of $8,000.
b. Paid office rent for the month, $200.
c. Paid $75 for an advertisement that will appear in the local newspaper.
d. Earned and collected $140 in fees earned by transporting clients during the first ten days of operating the business.
e. Paid a $600 premium for insurance. With this payment the policy is completely paid up for the year.
f. Purchased a typewriter costing $300 on credit from Hi-Way Supply Company.
g. Paid for the gas and oil used by the limousine, $80.
h. Earned and collected $210 in fees earned by transporting clients during the second ten days of operations.
i. Ran a special airport trip for the executives of City Company and billed the company $130.
j. Paid Hi-Way Supply Company $200 representing a partial payment for the typewriter acquired previously on credit.
k. Collected $260 in fees earned by transporting clients during the third ten days of operations.
l. Bought and paid for gas and oil used by the limousine, $110.
m. Collected in full the amount owed by City Company, $130.
n. Paid salary to a part-time driver, $90.
o. Art Harvey withdrew $150 in cash for personal use.

Required:

1. Use the following T accounts: Cash, Accounts Receivable, Prepaid Insurance, Office Equipment, Limousine, Accounts Payable, Art Harvey—Capital, Art Harvey—Drawings, Fee Revenue, Salaries Expense, Gas and Oil Expense, Rent Expense, and Advertising Expense. Record the transactions by entering the debits and credits directly in the T accounts. Use the transaction letters to identify each debit and credit amount.
2. Determine the account balances and prepare a trial balance using the date of October 31, 19X1. [LO2a,2b]

PROBLEM 2–3 *(Record Directly in T Accounts and Prepare a Trial Balance)* Stone Wall began a real estate agency called Wall Realty, and during a short period he completed the following transactions.

a. Began business by investing $12,000 in cash and an automobile having a fair value of $6,000.
b. Paid rent for one month on the office space, $400.
c. Purchased office equipment on credit, $2,500.
d. Received a cash commission for selling a house for a client, $600.
e. Paid for an advertisement to appear in a local newspaper, $100.
f. Completed a house sale and billed the client $800 as a commission on the sale.
g. Paid the premium on a two-year insurance policy, $400.
h. Paid $1,000 of the amount owed for the office equipment previously purchased on credit.
i. Received a cash commission for selling a house for a client, $500.
j. Received cash from the client billed in transaction *f*, $600.
k. Stone Wall withdrew $300 in cash for his personal use.
l. Paid salaries to the company's part-time employees, $700.

Required:

1. Use the following T accounts: Cash, Accounts Receivable, Prepaid Insurance, Office Equipment, Automobile, Accounts Payable, Stone Wall—Capital, Stone Wall—Drawings, Commission Revenue, Salaries Expense, Rent Expense, and Advertising Expense. Record the transactions by entering debits and credits directly in the T accounts. Use the transaction letters to identify each debit and credit amount.
2. Determine account balances and prepare a trial balance using the date of October 31, 19X3. [LO2a,2b]

PROBLEM 2–4 *(Prepare a Trial Balance)* The following accounts listed in alphabetical order are those of the Debbie Bune Voice Studio.

| | | | |
|---|---|---|---|
| Accounts Payable | $ 1,250 | Interest Expense | $ 130 |
| Accounts Receivable | 5,740 | Notes Payable | 3,200 |
| Advertising Expense | 960 | Prepaid Insurance | 360 |
| Building | 9,700 | Rent Expense | 1,800 |
| Cash | 2,630 | Repairs Expense | 430 |
| Commission Revenue | 15,880 | Salaries Expense | 5,620 |
| Debbie Bune, Capital | ? | Telephone Expense | 570 |
| Debbie Bune, Drawings | 1,540 | Travel Expense | 1,360 |
| Equipment | 6,300 | Utilities Expense | 1,190 |

Required:

Prepare a trial balance dated October 31, 19X1, with the accounts listed in a preferred sequence for preparing financial statements. Determine the balance in the Debbie Bune, Capital, account. [LO2b]

PROBLEM 2–5 *(Prepare Journal Entries, Post, and Prepare a Trial Balance)* A new writing clinic, Wolf Company, was started on October 1 by Tom Wolf. The company's transactions for its first month of operations are listed below.

| | | |
|---|---|---|
| Oct. | 1 | Began the business by investing cash of $32,000. |
| | 2 | Paid building rent for the month of October, $500. |
| | 5 | Purchased office equipment on credit from Rite Equipment Company, $3,200. |
| | 9 | Collected $900 in cash as a fee for services performed for a client. |
| | 11 | Paid $100 for an advertisement that will appear in a local newspaper announcing the opening of the business. |
| | 14 | Completed work for a client company and billed the company $1,300 for the services rendered. |
| | 14 | Purchased office supplies for $250 cash. |
| | 17 | Received $800 from a client as a fee for services rendered. |
| | 18 | Paid $1,600 of the amount owed to Rite Equipment Company. |
| | 20 | Received $400 representing a partial payment from the client billed on October 14. |
| | 23 | Paid the telephone bill, $75. |
| | 26 | Tom Wolf withdrew $900 in cash for personal use. |
| | 31 | Paid salaries to employees, $1,400. |

Required:

1. Prepare journal entries to record the transactions.
2. Post to three-column ledger accounts using the following account titles and numbers:

| | | | |
|---|---|---|---|
| 10 | Cash | 41 | Tom Wolf, Drawings |
| 12 | Accounts Receivable | 50 | Service Revenue |
| 16 | Office Supplies | 60 | Salaries Expense |
| 21 | Office Equipment | 61 | Rent Expense |
| 30 | Accounts Payable | 64 | Advertising Expense |
| 40 | Tom Wolf, Capital | 67 | Telephone Expense |

3. Prepare a trial balance as of October 31; 19X1. [LO2b,2c]

PROBLEM 2–6 *(Analyze T-Account Transactions, Record Journal Entries, and Prepare a Trial Balance)* Mark Hall started a service business known as Hallmark Advisory Company and completed a number of transactions during the month of October. The transactions were recorded by entering the debits and credits directly into T accounts and they appeared as shown below.

Required:

1. Record the transactions that appear in the T accounts in a general journal. Do this by using the dates to identify each transaction entered in the T accounts.
2. Determine the account balances and prepare a trial balance as of October 31, 19X1. [LO2b,2c]

Hallmark Advisory Company Ledger Accounts, October 31, 19X1

| CASH | | | |
|---|---|---|---|
| Oct. 2 | 25,000 | Oct. 2 | 300 |
| 5 | 700 | 6 | 800 |
| 17 | 1,300 | 15 | 200 |
| 22 | 1,200 | 15 | 900 |
| | | 18 | 300 |
| | | 24 | 400 |
| | | 25 | 700 |
| | | 29 | 500 |
| | | 31 | 1,000 |
| | | 31 | 600 |
| | | 31 | 1,300 |

| ACCOUNTS RECEIVABLE | | | |
|---|---|---|---|
| Oct. 12 | 1,200 | Oct. 22 | 1,200 |
| 21 | 1,600 | | |

| OFFICE SUPPLIES | | | |
|---|---|---|---|
| Oct. 9 | 300 | | |

| PREPAID INSURANCE | | | |
|---|---|---|---|
| Oct. 15 | 200 | | |

| OFFICE EQUIPMENT | | | |
|---|---|---|---|
| Oct. 6 | 4,400 | | |
| 18 | 700 | | |

| ACCOUNTS PAYABLE | | | |
|---|---|---|---|
| Oct. 18 | 300 | Oct. 9 | 300 |
| | | 18 | 700 |

| NOTES PAYABLE | | | |
|---|---|---|---|
| Oct. 31 | 1,300 | Oct. 6 | 3,600 |

| MARK HALL, CAPITAL | | | |
|---|---|---|---|
| | | Oct. 2 | 25,000 |

| MARK HALL, DRAWINGS | | | |
|---|---|---|---|
| Oct. 31 | 600 | | |

| FEE REVENUE | | | |
|---|---|---|---|
| | | Oct. 5 | 700 |
| | | 12 | 1,200 |
| | | 17 | 1,300 |
| | | 21 | 1,600 |

| SALARIES EXPENSE | | | |
|---|---|---|---|
| Oct. 15 | 900 | | |
| 31 | 1,000 | | |

| RENT EXPENSE | | | |
|---|---|---|---|
| Oct. 2 | 300 | | |

| TRAVEL EXPENSE | | | |
|---|---|---|---|
| Oct. 25 | 700 | | |

| ADVERTISING EXPENSE | | | |
|---|---|---|---|
| Oct. 24 | 400 | | |

| UTILITIES EXPENSE | | | |
|---|---|---|---|
| Oct. 29 | 500 | | |

PROBLEM 2–7 *(Prepare Journal Entries, Post, and Prepare a Trial Balance)* A new service business, Rite-Way Company, was started on October 1 by Tod Kenedy. The company's transactions for its first month of operations are listed below.

| | |
|---|---|
| Oct. 1 | Tod Kenedy began the business by opening a bank account in the firm's name using $20,000 of his personal savings. |
| 1 | Paid building rent for the month of October, $400. |

3 Purchased office equipment on credit from Jewel Supply Company, $2,800.
5 Paid $80 for an advertisement that will appear in the local newspaper.
9 Collected $750 in cash as a fee for services performed for a client.
11 Purchased office supplies on credit, $160.
15 Completed services for Atlas, a client company, and billed it $1,200.
17 Made a partial payment of $1,000 to Jewel Supply Company for the office equipment previously purchased.
19 Collected $620 in cash as a fee for services performed for a client.
22 Received partial payment of $400 from Atlas Company.
24 Paid travel expense of $120.
25 Paid the telephone bill, $45.
29 Tod Kenedy withdrew $700 in cash for personal use.
31 Paid part-time employees salaries of $1,100.

Required:

1. Prepare journal entries to record the above transactions.
2. Post the entries to three-column ledger accounts using the following account titles and numbers:

| | | | |
|---|---|---|---|
| 101 | Cash | 300 | Service Revenue |
| 103 | Accounts Receivable | 351 | Salaries Expense |
| 110 | Office Supplies | 352 | Rent Expense |
| 122 | Office Equipment | 355 | Travel Expense |
| 201 | Accounts Payable | 358 | Advertising Expense |
| 250 | Tod Kenedy, Capital | 362 | Telephone Expense |
| 251 | Tod Kenedy, Drawings | | |

3. Prepare a trial balance as of October 31, 19X1. [LO2b,2c]

PROBLEM 2–8 *(Prepare a Corrected Trial Balance)* Bates Company hired a new bookkeeper on October 1, 19X1. The bookkeeper had recently completed a basic accounting course at the local university. At the end of October the bookkeeper presented the following unbalanced trial balance.

BATES COMPANY
Trial Balance
October 31, 19X1

| | | |
|---|---|---|
| Cash | $ 4,270 | |
| Marketable Securities | 1,800 | |
| Accounts Receivable | 892 | |
| Notes Receivable | 180 | |
| Office Equipment | 1,650 | |
| Accounts Payable | | $ 2,587 |
| J. Bates, Capital | | 5,000 |
| J. Bates, Drawings | 500 | |
| Fee Revenue | | 16,405 |
| Interest Revenue | | 460 |
| Sales Salaries | 7,200 | |
| Office Salaries | 3,800 | |
| Rent Expense | 2,050 | |
| Office Expense | 740 | |
| Telephone Expense | 645 | |
| Travel Expense | 345 | |
| | $24,072 | $24,452 |

An examination of the ledger accounts showed that the trial balance did not balance because the following errors had been made:

a. A clerical error was made in adding the Telephone Expense account. It was totaled at $645 instead of $665.

b. Cash received from a customer on account was posted correctly to Accounts Receivable at $870, but numbers were transposed in posting to the Cash account, resulting in a posting of $780.

c. The purchase of file cabinets costing $290 on account was recorded as a debit to Office Expense and a credit to Accounts Payable.

d. Office Salaries of $900 was posted to Sales Salaries.

e. Interest revenue of $30 was received, and the Cash account was debited for $30 and the Interest Revenue account was credited for $300.

Required:

Prepare a corrected trial balance for Bates Company. [LO2b]

PROBLEM 2–9 *(Record Directly in T Accounts and Prepare a Trial Balance)* Carol Chaning owns a company that does manuscript typing and clerical work for a fee. On September 30, 19X1, the company's trial balance appeared as follows.

CHANING SERVICE AGENCY

Trial Balance

September 30, 19X1

| | | |
|---|---|---|
| Cash | $ 2,200 | |
| Office Supplies | 600 | |
| Office Equipment | 17,500 | |
| Vehicles | 8,500 | |
| Notes Payable | | $ 6,800 |
| C. Chaning, Capital | | 22,000 |
| | $28,800 | $28,800 |

The agency completed the following transactions during October:

a. Paid monthly rent, $200.

b. Purchased office supplies, $100, and office equipment, $300, on credit.

c. Paid for an advertisement that will appear in the local paper for two consecutive days, $50.

d. Paid for the supplies and office equipment purchased on credit in item *b*.

e. Completed clerical work for a client and collected a fee of $400.

f. Paid an employee for forty hours work at $5 an hour.

g. Completed clerical work and billed the client, $600.

h. Paid for gasoline and oil used in operating the vehicles, $30.

i. Received a check from the client billed in item g.

j. Paid telephone bill, $40.

k. Completed clerical work for a client and collected a fee of $300.

l. Made monthly payment of the note payable, $400.

m. Paid an employee for thirty hours work at $5 an hour.

n. Received a bill for gasoline and oil used in operating the vehicles, $50.

o. Carol Chaning withdrew $600 from the business for personal use.

p. Completed clerical work and billed the client $200.

Required:

1. Use the following T accounts: Cash, Accounts Receivable, Office Supplies, Office Equipment, Vehicles, Accounts Payable, Notes Payable, C. Chaning—Capital, C. Chaning—Drawings, Fees Earned, Salary Expense, Rent Expense, Vehicle Expense, Advertising Expense, and Telephone Expense.

2. Enter the amounts from the September 30 trial balance in the appropriate T accounts, identifying each amount by writing "Bal." (balance) before it.
3. Record the transactions by entering debits and credits directly in the T accounts. Use the transaction letters to identify each debit and credit amount.
4. Prepare a trial balance as of October 31, 19X1. [LO2a,2b]

PROBLEM 2–10 *(Comprehensive Review Problem)* A new service business, Exclusive Company, was started on October 1 by Jackie Law. The company's transactions for its first month of operations are listed below.

| | | |
|---|---|---|
| Oct. | 1 | The owner, Jackie Law, began the business by investing $14,000 in cash and a used automobile having a fair value of $7,000. |
| | 1 | Paid office rent for the month of October, $350. |
| | 2 | Paid $100 for an advertisement that will appear in the local newspaper. |
| | 2 | Purchased office equipment from A1-Brands Supply costing $3,500, paying 10% down and promising to pay the balance in the near future. |
| | 5 | Collected $420 from a client as a fee for services rendered. |
| | 8 | Paid for office supplies, $120. |
| | 8 | Collected $510 from a client as a fee for services rendered. |
| | 10 | Purchased office equipment from City Supply on credit, $1,400. |
| | 12 | Completed services for M&M Company, a client, and billed it $1,000. |
| | 16 | Paid travel expenses, $160. |
| | 19 | Paid the full amount owed to A1-Brands Supply. |
| | 19 | Collected $490 from a client as a fee for services rendered. |
| | 23 | Received partial payment of $500 from M&M Company. |
| | 24 | Completed services for Carlton Company, a client, and billed it $810. |
| | 26 | Paid utilities bill, $390. |
| | 29 | Paid travel expenses, $210. |
| | 30 | Jackie Law withdrew $1,000 in cash for personal use. |
| | 31 | Paid monthly salaries to part-time company employees, $1,300. |

Required:

1. Prepare journal entries to record the above transactions.
2. Post the entries to three-column ledger accounts. Use the ledger accounts you consider necessary.
3. Prepare a trial balance as of October 31, 19X1.
4. Indicate what effect (increase or decrease) each transaction had on
   a. Assets
   b. Liabilities
   c. Owner's Equity
   d. Revenues
   e. Expenses [LO1c,2b,2c]

## ALTERNATE PROBLEMS

PROBLEM 2–1A *(Record Directly in T Accounts and Prepare a Trial Balance)* (Alternate to Problem 2–2) M. Bagan began a real estate agency called Bagan Realty, and during a short period completed the following transactions.

a. Began business by investing $12,000 in cash and office equipment having a fair value of $6,000.
b. Paid rent for one month on the office space, $300.
c. Purchased an automobile on credit, $7,500.
d. Received a cash commission for selling a house for a client, $800.
e. Paid for an advertisement to appear in a local newspaper, $200.
f. Completed a house sale and billed the client $1,000 as a commission on the sale.
g. Paid the premium on a two-year insurance policy, $600.

h. Paid $1,200 of the amount owed for the automobile previously purchased on credit.
i. Received a cash commission for selling a house for a client, $800.
j. Received cash from the client billed in transaction *f*, $500.
k. M. Bagan withdrew $500 in cash for his personal use.
l. Paid salaries to the company's part-time employees, $900.

Required:

1. Use the following T accounts: Cash, Accounts Receivable, Prepaid Insurance, Office Equipment, Automobile, Accounts Payable, M. Bagan—Capital, M. Bagan—Drawings, Commission Revenue, Salaries Expense, Rent Expense, and Advertising Expense. Record the transactions by entering the debits and credits directly in the T accounts. Use the transaction letters to identify each debit and credit amount.
2. Determine the account balances and prepare a trial balance using the date of October 31, 19X3. [LO2a,2b]

PROBLEM 2–2A *(Prepare a Trial Balance)* (Alternate to Problem 2–4) The following accounts listed in alphabetical order are those of Bev Company.

| | | | |
|---|---|---|---|
| Accounts Payable | $ 2,000 | Interest Expense | $ 100 |
| Accounts Receivable | 4,000 | Notes Payable | 3,000 |
| Advertising Expense | 1,000 | Prepaid Insurance | 300 |
| Building | 10,000 | Rent Expense | 2,000 |
| Cash | 2,000 | Repairs Expense | 400 |
| Commission Revenue | 15,000 | Salaries Expense | 6,000 |
| Bev, Capital | ? | Telephone Expense | 600 |
| Bev, Drawings | 1,500 | Travel Expense | 1,300 |
| Equipment | 6,000 | Utilities Expense | 1,200 |

Required:

Prepare a trial balance dated October 31, 19X3, with the accounts listed in a preferred sequence for preparing financial statements. Determine the balance in the Bev, Capital, account. [LO2b]

PROBLEM 2–3A *(Prepare Journal Entries, Post, and Prepare a Trial Balance)* (Alternate to Problem 2–5) A new service business, Atone Company, was started on October 1 by Tom King. The company's transactions for its first month of operations are listed below.

| | |
|---|---|
| Oct. 1 | Began the business by investing cash of $32,000 and equipment worth $28,000. |
| 2 | Paid building rent for the month of October, $600. |
| 5 | Purchased an automobile on credit from Rite Equipment Company, $7,000. |
| 9 | Collected $1,000 in cash as a fee for services performed for a client. |
| 11 | Paid $300 for an advertisement that will appear in a local newspaper. |
| 14 | Completed work for a client company and billed the company $2,000. |
| 14 | Purchased office supplies for $300 cash. |
| 17 | Received $1,000 from a client as a fee for services rendered. |
| 18 | Paid $2,000 of the amount owed to Rite Equipment Company. |
| 20 | Received $500 representing a partial payment from the client billed on October 14. |
| 26 | Tom King withdrew $1,000 in cash for personal use. |
| 31 | Paid salaries to employees, $2,000. |

Required:

1. Prepare journal entries to record the transactions.
2. Post to three-column ledger accounts using the following account titles and numbers:

| | | | |
|---|---|---|---|
| 10 | Cash | 40 | Tom King, Capital |
| 12 | Accounts Receivable | 41 | Tom King, Drawings |
| 16 | Office Supplies | 50 | Service Revenue |
| 21 | Automobile | 60 | Salaries Expense |
| 25 | Equipment | 61 | Rent Expense |
| 30 | Accounts Payable | 64 | Advertising Expense |

3. Prepare a trial balance as of October 31, 19X3. [LO2b,2c]

PROBLEM 2–4A *(Analyze T-Account Transactions, Record Journal Entries, and Prepare a Trial Balance)* (Alternate to Problem 2–6) Ernie Troy opened a service business known as Troy Academic Advisory Company. He recorded the company's transactions by entering the debits and the credits directly into T accounts. The T accounts appear below.

Required:

1. Record the transactions that appear in the T accounts in a general journal. Do this by using the dates to identify each transaction entered in the T accounts.
2. Determine the account balances and prepare a trial balance as of October 31, 19X3. [LO2b,2c]

Troy Academic Advisory Company Ledger Accounts, October 31, 19X3

CASH

| | | | |
|---|---|---|---|
| Oct. 3 | 40,000 | Oct. 4 | 500 |
| 9 | 1,000 | 11 | 200 |
| 19 | 900 | 16 | 2,000 |
| 20 | 1,200 | 17 | 1,000 |
| | | 23 | 400 |
| | | 24 | 3,000 |
| | | 26 | 800 |
| | | 31 | 1,500 |

ACCOUNTS RECEIVABLE

| | | | |
|---|---|---|---|
| Oct. 14 | 1,600 | Oct. 19 | 900 |

OFFICE EQUIPMENT

| | | | |
|---|---|---|---|
| Oct. 7 | 2,000 | | |

VEHICLES

| | | | |
|---|---|---|---|
| Oct. 16 | 6,000 | | |

ACCOUNTS PAYABLE

| | | | |
|---|---|---|---|
| Oct. 17 | 1,000 | Oct. 7 | 2,000 |

NOTES PAYABLE

| | | | |
|---|---|---|---|
| Oct. 24 | 3,000 | Oct. 16 | 4,000 |

ERNIE TROY, CAPITAL

| | | | |
|---|---|---|---|
| | | Oct. 3 | 40,000 |

ERNIE TROY, DRAWINGS

| | | | |
|---|---|---|---|
| Oct. 26 | 800 | | |

FEE REVENUE

| | | | |
|---|---|---|---|
| | | Oct. 9 | 1,000 |
| | | 14 | 1,600 |
| | | 20 | 1,200 |

SALARIES EXPENSE

| | | | |
|---|---|---|---|
| Oct. 31 | 1,500 | | |

RENT EXPENSE

| | | | |
|---|---|---|---|
| Oct. 4 | 500 | | |

TRAVEL EXPENSE

| | | | |
|---|---|---|---|
| Oct. 23 | 400 | | |

ADVERTISING EXPENSE

| | | | |
|---|---|---|---|
| Oct. 11 | 200 | | |

PROBLEM 2–5A *(Prepare a Corrected Trial Balance)* (Alternate to Problem 2–8) Benson Company hired a new bookkeeper on October 1, 19X1. At the end of October the bookkeeper presented the following unbalanced trial balance.

BENSON COMPANY
Trial Balance
October 31, 19X1

| | | |
|---|---|---|
| Cash | $ 4,000 | |
| Marketable Securities | 2,000 | |
| Accounts Receivable | 1,000 | |
| Notes Receivable | 200 | |
| Office Equipment | 1,800 | |
| Accounts Payable | | $ 2,500 |
| B. Benson, Capital | | 5,000 |
| B. Benson, Drawings | 500 | |
| Fee Revenue | | 16,000 |
| Interest Revenue | | 500 |
| Sales Salaries | 8,000 | |
| Office Salaries | 3,500 | |
| Rent Expense | 2,000 | |
| Office Expense | 800 | |
| Telephone Expense | 600 | |
| Travel Expense | 600 | |
| | $25,000 | $24,000 |

An examination of the ledger accounts showed that the trial balance did not balance because the following errors had been made:

a. A clerical error was made in adding the Office Expense account. It was totaled at $800 instead of $1,000.

b. Cash received from a customer on account was posted correctly to the Accounts Receivable account at $1,000, but the posting to the Cash account was $1,200.

c. The purchase of file cabinets costing $300 on account was recorded as a debit to Office Salaries and a credit to Accounts Payable.

d. Sales Salaries of $1,000 was posted to Office Salaries.

e. Interest revenue of $500 was received, and the Cash account was debited for $1,500 and the Interest Revenue account was credited for $500.

Required:

Prepare a corrected trial balance for Benson Company. [LO2b]

# 3 *Adjusting the Accounts and Preparing Financial Statements*

### ***Learning Objectives***

When you complete this chapter you will be able to

1. Answer the following questions:
   a. What is the difference between the cash basis and the accrual basis of accounting?
   b. What are adjusting entries? What four principal situations require them?
   c. Why is the accrual basis of accounting more widely used than the cash basis?
2. Perform the following accounting functions:
   a. Prepare adjusting entries.
   b. Prepare financial statements from an adjusted trial balance.
   c. Prepare correcting entries.

To help people make decisions, accounting information must reach them as quickly and as often as they need it. The information must be current and must relate to the time period of interest to the decision maker.

Tax collectors, for example, and people who file tax returns need information relating to a specific year. Lenders and investors want updated financial information at least quarterly and annually. Owners and managers want reports on operational activity that cover specific periods of time. For their purposes, financial statements often are prepared monthly as well as quarterly and annually.

In Chapter 1 we noted that in order to provide financial statement users with timely information about a business, accountants divide its operating life into relatively short intervals of equal length called *accounting periods.* An **accounting period** is any time period for which an income statement is prepared. The income statement must show all revenues earned and all expenses incurred during a specified accounting period, and the balance sheet must show all assets owned, liabilities owed, and the owner's financial claim to the assets (expressed as owner's equity) at the end of the specified period. A problem encountered when preparing a company's financial statements for a given period is that some of its financial activities will affect its operating results and financial position for more than a single period.

To illustrate the problem, assume that on June 30 of the current year a company purchased a two-year insurance policy by paying a premium of $2,400. On that date the transaction would be recorded by debiting an asset account called Prepaid Insurance and crediting the asset account Cash. Because it is a two-year policy, its coverage extends beyond one accounting period. If financial statements were prepared three months later on September 30, the balance sheet should show an amount for Prepaid Insurance that recognizes that only twenty-one months of the original twenty-four months of insurance coverage remain. In addition, the income statement prepared for the three months ended September 30 should show that three months of insurance expense has been incurred during that period.

In this chapter we will learn the principles followed and procedures used to ensure that the financial effects of a company's activities are assigned to the appropriate accounting period. That is, the income statement will show the proper amounts for revenues earned and expenses incurred during the period, and the balance sheet will show the proper amounts for assets owned and liabilities owed at the end of that period.

## THE CASH BASIS AND THE ACCRUAL BASIS OF ACCOUNTING

### Cash Basis

There are two alternative methods of recording accounting transactions: the cash basis and the accrual basis. Some small businesses, many individuals, and certain professionals (such as physicians, lawyers, and accountants) maintain their accounting records on a **cash basis.** In cash basis accounting, revenues for goods sold or services rendered are not recorded until received in cash. Similarly, expenses incurred in the process of generating the revenues are not recorded until cash payments for those expenses are made. Thus, under the cash basis of accounting, net income for the period would be calculated as the difference between cash receipts from revenues and cash payments for expenses.

*1a. The cash basis: Revenues for goods sold or services rendered are not recorded until cash is received, and expenses incurred in generating the revenues are not recorded until cash is paid*

Focusing on the receipt and payment of cash does not adequately measure a company's operational performance for a given period of time. For example, it ignores the fact that revenues can be earned from the sale of goods and from the rendering of services either before or after the cash has been received. It also ignores the fact that expenses that helped to generate the revenues can be incurred in a period other than that in which they are paid for in cash.

### Accrual Basis

*1a. Accrual basis accounting is based on the revenue realization and matching principles*

The profession believes that a better measurement of a company's periodic net income can be achieved by using the **accrual basis** of accounting. Accrual-basis accounting is based on two accounting principles—**revenue realization principle** and **matching principle.**

**The Revenue Realization Principle**

Revenue should be recorded in the period in which it is earned.

Thus the time period in which the cash for the revenue is received is unimportant for the recognition of revenue.

**The Matching Principle**

Expenses incurred during a period should be matched against (deducted from) the revenues that these expenses helped to generate or earn during that same time period.

In accrual-basis accounting, therefore, revenue is recognized when it is earned, and expenses are recognized when they are incurred.

## ADJUSTING ENTRIES

To implement the accrual basis of accounting, we must be sure that when an income statement is prepared, it shows all the revenue and expenses applicable to the accounting period covered by the statement. We must be sure, too, that the balance sheet shows all the assets owned and liabilities incurred as of the last day of that period. The selection of an accounting period for which the financial statements will be prepared establishes a time period for reporting the effects of a company's activity (its transactions). Many transactions will affect amounts reported in the income statement and balance sheet only for the accounting period when these transactions occurred. Some transactions, however, will affect the amounts reported in the financial statements of two or more accounting periods. In addition, the company may have had activity that affects amounts reported for the current period but for which journal entries have not yet been recorded. As a result of these last two situations, we will need to adjust some of the accounts at the end of each accounting period to make certain that their balances reflect amounts that should be reported on the current financial statements.

*1b. Adjusting entries are needed to update account balances at the end of an accounting period*

The adjusting process is accomplished by recording and posting journal entries called **adjusting entries.** These are entries made at the end of an accounting period to update account balances before preparing financial statements.

To illustrate the need for adjustments, consider the end-of-the-period trial balance for Health Insurance Advisors prepared in Chapter 2 and reproduced in Exhibit 3–1 on page 76.

EXHIBIT 3-1

HEALTH INSURANCE ADVISORS
Unadjusted Trial Balance
October 31, 19X1

| | | |
|---|---|---|
| Cash | $ 9,010 | |
| Marketable Securities | 3,000 | |
| Accounts Receivable | 1,280 | |
| Office Supplies | 400 | |
| Office Equipment | 3,000 | |
| Vehicles | 15,000 | |
| Accounts Payable | | $ 2,100 |
| Notes Payable | | 10,000 |
| Paul Star, Capital | | 20,000 |
| Paul Star, Drawings | 1,200 | |
| Consulting Fees Earned | | 2,940 |
| Salaries Expense | 1,400 | |
| Rent Expense | 300 | |
| Travel Expense | 260 | |
| Advertising Expense | 80 | |
| Telephone Expense | 40 | |
| Repairs Expense | 70 | |
| | $35,040 | $35,040 |

The journal entry on October 2 that created the $400 balance in Office Supplies was

| | | |
|---|---|---|
| Office Supplies | 400 | |
| Accounts Payable | | 400 |
| To record the purchase of office supplies | | |

After shelving the office supplies in a supply closet, Paul Star and his employees began to use them. Some supplies are used each working day. The amount used represents a daily expense and a daily reduction of the asset Office Supplies. However, these daily reductions are not recorded in the accounts—for two reasons:

1. Information concerning the amount of office supplies used and the amount of office supplies remaining on hand is not needed on a daily basis.
2. Bookkeeping effort (and costs) can be saved by recording a single entry at the end of an accounting period to bring the account balance up to date (rather than entries each time supplies are used). This entry, known as an adjusting entry, shows the amount of office supplies used during the period. It also establishes an amount in the Office Supplies account that represents the cost of the office supplies remaining on hand at the end of the period.

If we assume that $100 of office supplies were used during the accounting period ending October 31, 19X1, the ledger accounts are adjusted on that date to show

A $300 balance in the Office Supplies account for purposes of the October 31 balance sheet

A $100 balance in the Office Supplies Expense account for purposes of the income statement covering that period

This adjustment is accomplished by an adjusting entry where the Office Supplies Expense account is debited for $100 and where the asset Office Supplies is credited for the same amount:

| | | |
|---|---|---|
| Office Supplies Expense . . . . . . . . . . . . . . . . . . . . . . . . . . . . . . . . . . . . . . . . | 100 | |
| Office Supplies . . . . . . . . . . . . . . . . . . . . . . . . . . . . . . . . . . . . . . . . | | 100 |
| To record office supplies used during the period | | |

Besides Office Supplies, several other accounts in the trial balance of Health Insurance Advisors do not reflect their proper balance. We will consider these in discussing the adjusting process in the next section.

## THE FOUR PRINCIPAL SITUATIONS THAT REQUIRE ADJUSTING ENTRIES

*1b. Four principal situations require adjusting entries*

Situations that call for end-of-the-period entries to adjust and update account balances can be classified into four groups as follows:

1. Recorded costs that must be apportioned between two or more accounting periods. (*Example:* The cost of equipment that will be used to generate revenues in both the current and future accounting periods.)
2. Recorded revenue that has been received in advance and must be apportioned between two or more accounting periods. (*Example:* Commissions collected in advance for services to be rendered in both the current and future accounting periods.)
3. Unrecorded expenses—that is, expenses that have been incurred in the current period but will be paid in a future period. (*Example:* Wages earned by employees in the current accounting period but not paid to them until a later accounting period.)
4. Unrecorded revenues—that is, revenues that have been earned in the current period but for which money will not be received until a future period. (*Example:* Commissions or fees earned in the current accounting period but not collected from or billed to the customers or clients until a later accounting period.)

## HOW ADJUSTING ENTRIES ARE MADE

To demonstrate the process of recording adjusting entries, let us consider a new firm, Windsor Time and Motion, which derives its revenue by performing consulting services. Exhibit 3–2 shows the trial balance prepared at the end of Windsor's first accounting period. A trial balance such as this, which lists all ledger accounts and their balances before they have been brought up to date by the adjusting process, is sometimes called an **unadjusted trial balance.**

### Situation 1—Apportioning Recorded Costs Between Two or More Accounting Periods

*1b. Sometimes recorded costs must be apportioned between accounting periods*

Companies often purchase assets that provide benefits during two or more accounting periods. Generally the transaction is initially recorded by debiting an asset account for the item's cost and crediting Cash or Accounts Payable. At the end of each accounting period that benefits from the asset, an appropriate portion of its cost is transferred from the asset account to an expense account by an adjusting entry. Two examples of apportioning the cost of an asset to the accounting periods benefited involve prepaid expenses and depreciation. Both are discussed and illustrated on the following pages.

*EXHIBIT 3–2*

WINDSOR TIME AND MOTION
Unadjusted Trial Balance
October 31, 19X1

| | | |
|---|---|---|
| Cash | $ 5,210 | |
| Accounts Receivable | 4,840 | |
| Notes Receivable | 6,000 | |
| Office Supplies | 390 | |
| Prepaid Insurance | 480 | |
| Office Equipment | 12,000 | |
| Vehicles | 10,800 | |
| Accounts Payable | | $ 2,830 |
| Unearned Rent Revenue | | 600 |
| Unearned Consulting Fees | | 1,200 |
| Notes Payable | | 4,000 |
| J. Lynn, Capital | | 25,000 |
| J. Lynn, Drawings | 1,500 | |
| Consulting Fees Earned | | 24,370 |
| Salaries Expense | 13,400 | |
| Rent Expense | 1,600 | |
| Travel Expense | 890 | |
| Advertising Expense | 540 | |
| Utilities Expense | 230 | |
| Repairs Expense | 120 | |
| | $58,000 | $58,000 |

## Prepaid Expenses

*1b,2a. Adjustments must be made for prepaid expenses*

Certain items such as insurance, rent, and supplies are often paid for before the benefits obtained from these payments have been received or used. These expenditures, called **prepaid expenses,** are usually recorded by debiting an asset account with a descriptive title such as Prepaid Insurance and crediting Cash. At the end of an accounting period, a portion or perhaps all of these goods or services paid for in advance will have been consumed or will have expired. The cost of the portion consumed or expired during the current accounting period is treated as an expense of that period. The cost of the portion not consumed or expired is treated as an asset that will benefit future operations. Of course the expense portion must be shown in the current income statement, and the asset in the balance sheet. We transfer an appropriate amount from the asset account to an expense account at the end of each accounting period by recording and posting adjusting entries. If, at the end of the period, adjusting entries to apportion the cost of prepaid expenses between an asset and an expense were not made, the financial statements would be incomplete and incorrect in two ways:

1. In the income statement, expenses would be understated and consequently net income would be overstated.
2. In the balance sheet, assets and owner's equity would both be overstated.

The adjustment process for prepaid expenses is illustrated by using two items that the Windsor Time and Motion Company pays for in advance of their use—insurance and office supplies.

**EXAMPLE 1: APPORTIONING THE COST OF AN INSURANCE POLICY** On October 1 the company purchased a one-year insurance policy, paying the full year's premium of $480 in advance. This transaction was recorded by debiting the asset account Prepaid Insurance and crediting Cash. The balance in the Prepaid Insurance account will remain at $480, as shown in Exhibit 3–2, until the end of an accounting period, when it will be adjusted.

The $480 expenditure provides insurance for one year and expires on a day-to-day basis. Thus, as each day in the month of October passed, a part of the protection benefits provided by the insurance expired and became an operating expense applicable to the month of October. By October 31, the end of the accounting period, one-twelfth of the $480 cost of the benefits has expired. Thus the adjusting entry needed on October 31 to record insurance expense of $40 ($\$480 \times \frac{1}{12} = \$40$) and to reduce the asset Prepaid Insurance is as follows:

| | | | |
|---|---|---|---|
| Oct. 31 | Insurance Expense | 40 | |
| | Prepaid Insurance | | 40 |
| | To record insurance expense for the month of October | | |

After the adjusting entry has been posted, the accounts affected will appear as follows:

| PREPAID INSURANCE | | | |
|---|---|---|---|
| Oct. 1 | 480 | Oct. 31 | 40 |

| INSURANCE EXPENSE | | | |
|---|---|---|---|
| Oct. 31 | 40 | | |

This adjusting entry does two things:

1. It reduces the balance in the Prepaid Insurance account to $440, the amount that reflects the cost of the unexpired insurance premium on October 31. This is the amount that will appear as an asset in the company's October 31 balance sheet.
2. It transfers $40 (the expired insurance cost) to the Insurance Expense account. This amount will appear as an operating expense in the company's current income statement.

**EXAMPLE 2: APPORTIONING THE COST OF OFFICE SUPPLIES** To conduct its business efficiently, Windsor Time and Motion needs office supplies such as business forms, stationery, and carbon paper. On October 3 the company purchased, on account, office supplies in sufficient quantity to last several months. The supplies cost $390. This transaction was recorded by debiting the asset account Office Supplies and crediting Accounts Payable. The balance in the Office Supplies account will remain at $390, as shown in Exhibit 3–2, until the end of an accounting period, when it will be adjusted. The reason is that no journal entries were made during the period to record the cost of the supplies that were used on a day-to-day basis. As mentioned earlier, it would be impractical and unnecessary to recognize the expense of consuming office supplies on a daily basis. Instead the cost of the supplies used is removed from the Office Supplies asset account at the end of the accounting period (before the financial statements have been prepared) by an adjusting entry. Generally the cost of the supplies used during the period is determined by first determining the cost of the supplies remaining at the end of the period. Then the difference between the amount shown as a balance in the Office Supplies Account and the amount determined for the supplies still on hand establishes the cost of supplies used during the period.

To illustrate, assume that a careful count taken by a Windsor employee on

October 31 reveals that office supplies having a cost of $250 are still on hand. The difference between the $390 balance shown in the Office Supplies account in Windsor's unadjusted trial balance and the $250 cost of the office supplies remaining on hand on that date is $140. This difference represents the cost of the office supplies used during the period. Therefore, an adjusting entry is needed on October 31 to recognize $140 of Office Supplies Expense and to reduce the asset Office Supplies by that same amount, as shown below.

| | | | |
|---|---|---|---|
| Oct. 31 | Office Supplies Expense . . . . . . . . . . . . . . . . . . . . . . . . . . . . . . . . | 140 | |
| | Office Supplies . . . . . . . . . . . . . . . . . . . . . . . . . . . . . . . . . . . | | 140 |
| | To record office supplies used during the month of October | | |

After the adjusting entry has been posted, the affected accounts will appear as follows:

| OFFICE SUPPLIES | | | |
|---|---|---|---|
| Oct. 3 | 390 | Oct. 31 | 140 |

| OFFICE SUPPLIES EXPENSE | | | |
|---|---|---|---|
| Oct. 31 | 140 | | |

The debit balance of $250 in the Office Supplies account will be shown as a current asset in the October 31 balance sheet. The $140 debit balance in the Office Supplies Expense account will be shown as an expense in the October income statement.

## Depreciation of Plant Assets

*1b,2a. Adjustments must be made for depreciation*

Plant assets, such as buildings, machinery, equipment, and vehicles, provide revenue-producing benefits for several years. To achieve proper matching, the expense of using the plant asset must be recorded in the same period as the revenues that the asset helped to produce. The amount of such expense, called *depreciation expense,* is determined by allocating (apportioning) the asset's acquisition cost over the number of periods expected to receive benefits from its use. Thus **depreciation** or ***depreciation expense*** refers to the *systematic allocation of a plant asset's cost (minus estimated residual value) to expense over the accounting periods expected to benefit from its use.*

To illustrate the process of preparing adjusting entries that will recognize depreciation expense for income statement reporting while reducing the carrying value of the plant asset for balance sheet reporting, we refer once again to Exhibit 3–2. Two plant assets, Office Equipment and Vehicles, are shown on Windsor's unadjusted trial balance.

**EXAMPLE 3: APPORTIONING THE COST OF OFFICE EQUIPMENT** The office equipment shown in the unadjusted trial balance in Exhibit 3–2 was purchased by the company on October 1 at a cost of $12,000 and is expected to provide revenue-producing benefits for eight years. At the end of eight years the residual or salvage value is expected to be zero. The amount of the asset's cost allocated to depreciation expense for the one-month period ending October 31, 19X1, is $125, calculated as follows: $12,000 ÷ 8 years = $1,500 per year; $1,500 ÷ 12 months = $125 per month. The adjusting entry to record the monthly depreciation expense for the office equipment is as follows:

| | | | |
|---|---|---|---|
| Oct. 31 | Depreciation Expense—Office Equipment. . . . . . . . . . . . . . . . . . . | 125 | |
| | Accumulated Depreciation—Office Equipment. . . . . . . . . . | | 125 |
| | To record depreciation for the month of October | | |

After the adjusting entry has been posted, the accounts affected will appear as follows:

| DEPRECIATION EXPENSE—OFFICE EQUIPMENT | |
|---|---|
| Oct. 31 125 | |

| ACCUMULATED DEPRECIATION—OFFICE EQUIPMENT | |
|---|---|
| | Oct. 31 125 |

The method used here to calculate depreciation of the office equipment is called the "straight-line" method because equal amounts of the asset's cost are allocated to equal time periods. Other acceptable depreciation methods will be discussed in a later chapter.

Note that in the depreciation entry a separate account called *Accumulated Depreciation—Office Equipment* was credited rather than the Office Equipment account. The **accumulated depreciation** account shows the amount of a depreciable plant asset's cost that has been allocated to depreciation expense since the asset was acquired. This procedure for recording depreciation allows the original acquisition cost to be retained in the plant asset account while providing information about the amount of depreciation expense that has been accumulated for the asset since the date of the purchase. The accumulated depreciation account is a *contra account.* **A contra account** is an account that is deducted from another related account when reported in the financial statements. A contra account has an opposite balance from the account to which it relates. Specifically, the Accumulated Depreciation—Office Equipment account is a **contra asset account**—an account having a credit balance that is shown in the balance sheet as a deduction from the asset to which it relates. It is deducted from the Office Equipment account when reported in the balance sheet, as illustrated below.

*1b,2a. Depreciation adjustments may be accumulated in a contra account, such as Accumulated Depreciation*

WINDSOR TIME AND MOTION
Partial Balance Sheet
October 31, 19X1

| | | |
|---|---|---|
| Plant and Equipment: | | |
| Office Equipment (at cost) | $12,000 | |
| Less: Accumulated Depreciation | 125 | $11,875 |

The Depreciation Expense—Office Equipment account will be reported as an operating expense in the company's income statement.

**EXAMPLE 4: APPORTIONING THE COST OF VEHICLES** The company owns a vehicle that was purchased on October 2 for $10,800 cash. At the time of purchase, the vehicle was given an estimated useful life of five years. Unlike the office equipment, which had an estimated *residual* or *scrap* value of zero at the end of its useful life, the vehicle is expected to have a residual value of $600 at the end of its estimated useful life. The monthly depreciation expense on the vehicle is $170, determined by dividing its cost minus its residual value by its estimated life in months: $10,800 cost − $600 of residual value = $10,200 of depreciable amount; $10,200 ÷ 60 months of estimated useful life = $170 of monthly depreciation expense. The procedure for determining the depreciation expense on any plant asset using the straight-line method would be essentially the same as that just outlined. Variations in the amount for the asset's acquisition cost, its estimated residual value, and its estimated useful life would cause the depreciation expense to be different with different assets. The journal entry to record the monthly depreciation expense for the vehicle is as follows:

| | | | |
|---|---|---|---|
| Oct. 31 | Depreciation Expense—Vehicles . . . . . . . . . . . . . . . . . . . . . . . . . . | 170 | |
| | Accumulated Depreciation—Vehicles . . . . . . . . . . . . . . . . . . | | 170 |
| | To record depreciation for the month of October | | |

After the adjusting entry has been posted, the accounts affected will appear as follows:

| DEPRECIATION EXPENSE—VEHICLES | | ACCUMULATED DEPRECIATION—VEHICLES | |
|---|---|---|---|
| Oct. 31 170 | | | Oct. 31 170 |

The Depreciation Expense—Vehicles account will be reported as an operating expense in the October income statement. The Accumulated Depreciation—Vehicles account will appear as a deduction from the Vehicles account in the October 31 balance sheet, as shown below.

WINDSOR TIME AND MOTION
Partial Balance Sheet
October 31, 19X1

| | | |
|---|---|---|
| Plant and Equipment: | | |
| Vehicles (at cost) | $10,800 | |
| Less: Accumulated Depreciation | 170 | $10,630 |

Office equipment and vehicles will then be reported on the balance sheet at their carrying values of $11,875 ($12,000 − $125) and $10,630 ($10,800 − $170), respectively. **Carrying value,** sometimes referred to as **book value,** is the net amount at which an asset is carried on the balance sheet. For depreciable assets, it is the difference between the balance in the plant asset account and the balance in its related accumulated depreciation account. Carrying value has no relationship to, and should not be interpreted as representing, the asset's market value, which is the amount for which the asset can be sold. Plant assets are reported on the balance sheet at their carrying value, not their market value.

### *Situation 2—Apportioning Revenue Received in Advance Between Two or More Accounting Periods*

*1b. Sometimes recorded revenues must be apportioned between accounting periods*

Companies sometimes receive cash or some other asset as payment for services they will render to their customers or clients during one or more future accounting periods. At the time that the cash or other asset is received, the amount is debited to an asset account, and an equal amount is credited to a liability account so that the accounting records will reflect the company's obligation to render future services. This type of liability, often referred to as *unearned revenue,* is discharged as the agreed-upon services are provided. Consequently, at the end of each accounting period during which the services are provided, an adjustment is needed to transfer an appropriate amount from the unearned revenue account (the liability account) to a revenue account.

For example, publishing companies usually receive money payments for magazine subscriptions in advance. These advance payments are recorded by debiting an asset account and crediting a liability account, as shown by the entry below where the advance payments totaled $600:

| | | | |
|---|---|---|---|
| Jan. 1 | Cash | 600 | |
| | Unearned Subscriptions Revenue | | 600 |
| | To record subscription money received in advance | | |

As the company delivers each issue of the magazine, it earns a portion of the advance payments. To transfer the earned portion of the advance payment from the Unearned Subscriptions Revenue account to the Subscriptions Revenue account, an adjusting entry such as the following is needed:

| | | | |
|---|---|---|---|
| Jan. 31 | Unearned Subscriptions Revenue | 50 | |
| | Subscriptions Revenue | | 50 |
| | To record subscription revenue earned during January | | |

We will further demonstrate the adjustment process for apportioning revenue received in advance by using two examples taken from the activity of Windsor Time and Motion Company.

**EXAMPLE 5: APPORTIONING RENT REVENUE RECEIVED IN ADVANCE** Having little use for the garage space obtained through its own rental agreement, Windsor Time and Motion decided to subrent the garage to make it revenue-producing. On October 16 Atlas Company agreed to rent the garage for $200 per month and paid three months' rent in advance by issuing a check for $600. Windsor recorded this transaction by debiting the $600 amount to the asset account Cash and crediting the amount to the Unearned Rent Revenue account (a liability account). Crediting a liability account was appropriate because no service had yet been provided to Atlas Company, the tenant, by Windsor Time and Motion, the landlord. However, an obligation to provide the agreed-upon space does exist, and consequently a liability for $600 appears in the Unearned Rent Revenue account in the company's unadjusted trial balance in Exhibit 3–2.

*1b,2a. Adjustments must be made for rent revenue received in advance*

It seems logical to assume that the rent revenue is earned proportionately over the three months. Therefore, by October 31, the end of the company's accounting period, half a month has passed since the cash payment was received and one-sixth of the $600 advance payment, or $100, has been earned by Windsor. That amount must be transferred from the Unearned Rent Revenue account to the Rent Revenue Earned account if the financial statements are to reflect appropriate amounts in both those accounts. The adjusting entry needed to reduce the liability account balance and record the rent revenue earned is as follows:

| | | | |
|---|---|---|---|
| Oct. 31 | Unearned Rent Revenue | 100 | |
| | Rent Revenue Earned | | 100 |
| | To record rent revenue earned during the month of October | | |

After the adjusting entry has been posted, the accounts affected will appear as follows:

| UNEARNED RENT REVENUE | | | |
|---|---|---|---|
| Oct. 31 | 100 | Oct. 16 | 600 |

| RENT REVENUE EARNED | | | |
|---|---|---|---|
| | | Oct. 31 | 100 |

The $500 credit balance in the Unearned Rent Revenue account is shown as a current liability in the October 31 balance sheet. The $100 credit balance in the Rent Revenue Earned account is shown as revenue in the October income statement. Unearned rent revenue differs from most other liabilities in that it can probably be satisfied by providing future services rather than requiring a future cash payment. Stated another way, Windsor Time and Motion has a current obligation to provide future services rather than to pay cash.

*1b,2a. Adjustments must be made for fees received in advance*

**EXAMPLE 6: APPORTIONING CONSULTING FEES RECEIVED IN ADVANCE** On certain consulting assignments, Windsor Time and Motion requests full payment from its clients before its employees begin to render services. On October 8 negotiations with a client firm culminated in an agreement that allowed Windsor to receive a $1,200 advance payment from a client. This payment was for services to be performed beginning on October 10 and continuing throughout the month of November.

The following entry would record the cash received:

| | | | |
|---|---|---|---|
| Oct. 10 | Cash | 1,200 | |
| | Unearned Consulting Fees | | 1,200 |
| | To record consulting fees received in advance | | |

The Unearned Consulting Fees account is a liability and appears in the company's trial balance prepared on October 31 and shown in Exhibit 3–2. As services are being performed, the fees are being earned. Assume that on October 31, the end of the accounting period, the company's client performance records show that 40% of this particular assignment has been completed, and therefore $480 ($1,200 × .40) of the consulting fees received in advance are earned. The following adjusting entry is needed to reduce the liability account balance and to record the revenue earned:

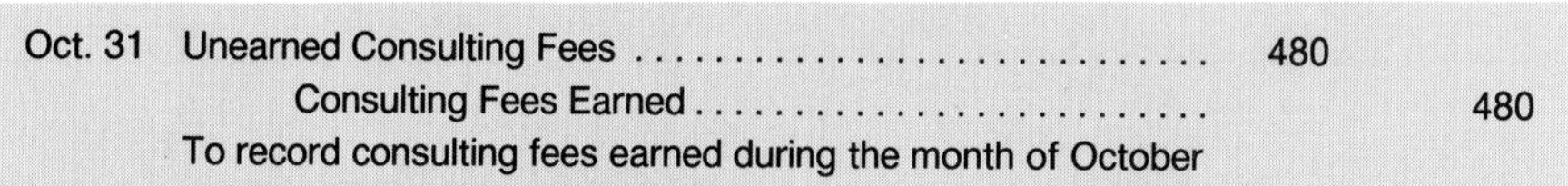

| | | | |
|---|---|---|---|
| Oct. 31 | Unearned Consulting Fees | 480 | |
| | Consulting Fees Earned | | 480 |
| | To record consulting fees earned during the month of October | | |

After the adjusting entry has been posted, the accounts affected will appear as follows:

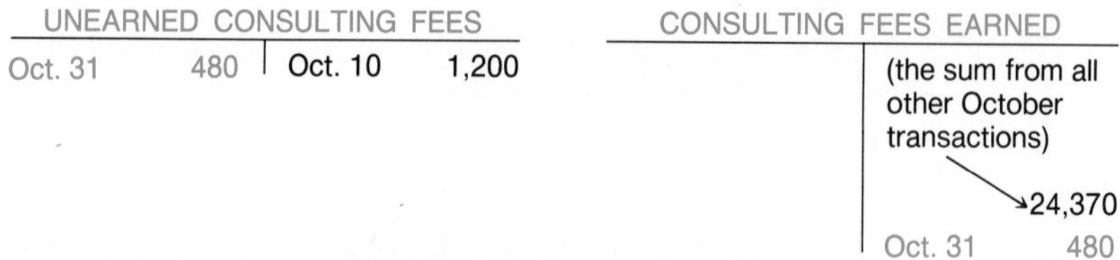

| UNEARNED CONSULTING FEES | | | |
|---|---|---|---|
| Oct. 31 | 480 | Oct. 10 | 1,200 |

CONSULTING FEES EARNED
(the sum from all other October transactions)
24,370
Oct. 31 480



The $720 credit balance remaining in the Unearned Consulting Fees account is shown as a current liability in the October 31 balance sheet. This liability will in the future be reduced, perhaps to zero, as additional services are provided during November. The aggregate, up-to-date balance of $24,850 ($24,370 + $480) in the Consulting Fees Earned account is shown as revenue in the October income statement.

## Situation 3 — Unrecorded Expenses

*1b. Sometimes expenses have been incurred but have not been recorded*

Most operating expenses are recorded when they are incurred. At the end of an accounting period, however, some expenses have usually been incurred but have not been recorded in the accounts.

These expenses are entered in the accounts by adjusting entries that debit an expense account to record the expense in the period in which it was incurred and credit a liability account to record the obligation to pay for the goods or services that have been received. Examples of expenses incurred but unrecorded at the end of an accounting period include portions of the salaries earned by the company's employees, interest on borrowed money, and taxes. All of these expenses accrue or accumulate day by day but are not paid or recorded on a daily basis.

Two examples taken from the activities and events of Windsor Time and Motion are used to illustrate the adjusting process for unrecorded expenses.

*1b,2a. Adjustments must be made to recognize accrued salaries expense*

EXAMPLE 7: ACCRUED SALARIES Windsor Time and Motion hired its employees during the first week of operations. Salaries total $3,350 per week for all employees. The company has a five-day work week beginning on Monday and ending on Friday, when the full week's salary is paid. Note that salaries expense and the corresponding liability accrue daily, although salaries are paid but once a week on Friday. Windsor's employees were last paid on Friday, October 28, and this payment covered the period of October 24 through October 28. However, the company operated on Monday, October 31, and salaries were earned on that day, although they remain unpaid as of October 31, the end of the accounting period. Because a payroll check will not be issued until Friday, November 4, the salary expense accrued on October 31 cannot be recorded in the proper accounting period without an adjusting entry. Assuming the five-day payroll of $3,350 is earned proportionately on each day of the week, the unrecorded salary expense and corresponding liability for salaries payable of $670 ($\frac{1}{5} \times \$3,350 = \$670$) is recorded by an adjusting entry as follows:

| | | | |
|---|---|---|---|
| Oct. 31 | Salaries Expense ........................................ | 670 | |
| | Salaries Payable .................................. | | 670 |
| | To record accrued salary expense for October | | |

After the adjusting entry has been posted, the affected accounts will appear as follows.

**SALARIES EXPENSE**

| | Debit | | Credit |
|---|---|---|---|
| | Oct. 7 | 3,350 | |
| | 14 | 3,350 | |
| | 21 | 3,350 | |
| | 28 | 3,350 | |
| 14,070 | 31 | 670 | |

**SALARIES PAYABLE**

| Debit | Credit | |
|---|---|---|
| | Oct. 31 | 670 |

The adjusted debit balance of $14,070 in the Salaries Expense account will appear as an expense in the company's October income statement. The credit balance of $670 in the Salaries Payable account will appear as a current liability in the company's October 31 balance sheet.

EXAMPLE 8: ACCRUED INTEREST Assume that the office equipment acquired on October 1, at a cost of $12,000, was purchased by paying $8,000 in cash and signing an interest-bearing note for the balance of $4,000. The note carries an interest rate of 15% per year, and the principal of the note plus the interest must be paid on December 31.

*1b,2a. Adjustments must be made to recognize accrued interest expense*

Although the interest does not have to be paid until December 31, like accrued salaries, interest accumulates or accrues daily. One month of interest expense, or \$50 ($\$4,000 \times .15 \times \frac{1}{12} = \$50$), accrued during October. The adjusting entry needed to record the interest expense incurred during October and the corresponding liability for interest payable is as follows:

| | | | |
|---|---|---|---|
| Oct. 31 | Interest Expense ...................................... | 50 | |
| | Interest Payable ...................................... | | 50 |
| | To record accrued interest expense for October | | |

After the adjusting entry has been posted, the affected accounts will appear as follows:

| INTEREST EXPENSE | | INTEREST PAYABLE | |
|---|---|---|---|
| Oct. 31 50 | | | Oct. 31 50 |

Interest expense is shown as an expense in the October income statement, and interest payable is reported as a current liability in the company's October 31 balance sheet.

## Situation 4—Unrecorded Revenue

Sometimes a company will provide goods or services to a customer or client near the end of an accounting period and the activity is not recorded at the end of the accounting period. In this situation, adjusting entries are needed to record the revenue earned and the related receivable. This type of revenue is often called *accrued revenue* and is entered in the records by an adjusting entry that debits an asset account and credits a revenue account.

*1b. Sometimes revenue has been earned but has not been recorded*

An example would be the interest on a note receivable which is earned daily but where the amount earned may not be received in cash until a future accounting period. At the end of an accounting period, before financial statements have been prepared, an adjusting entry is made that debits the Interest Receivable account and credits the Interest Revenue Earned account for the amount of interest accrued in the period.

Adjusting entries for unrecorded revenue are illustrated by the following two examples taken from the activity of Windsor Time and Motion.

**EXAMPLE 9: UNRECORDED RENT REVENUE** Having more than adequate parking facilities on its premises, Windsor on October 15 entered into an agreement to rent parking spaces to a neighboring firm for \$400 per month. The amount is payable on the fifteenth day of the following month (in this case on the fifteenth of November). Although Windsor did not receive a rent check in October, it has earned \$200 ($\frac{1}{2} \times \$400$) of the monthly rental revenue during October, which as of October 31 is not recorded in the accounts.

*1b,2a. Adjustments must be made to recognize accrued rental revenue*

The rent revenue that has been earned and the receivable that has been created are recorded by the following adjusting entry:

| | | | |
|---|---|---|---|
| Oct. 31 | Rent Receivable ...................................... | 200 | |
| | Rent Revenue Earned ............................... | | 200 |
| | To record rent revenue earned during October | | |

After the adjusting entry has been posted, the affected accounts will appear as follows:

| RENT RECEIVABLE | | | RENT REVENUE EARNED | |
|---|---|---|---|---|
| Oct. 31 | 200 | | Oct. 31 | 100 |
| | | | 31 | 200 |

The Rent Receivable account is shown as a current asset in the balance sheet, and the Rent Revenue Earned account is reported as revenue in the income statement.

*1b,2a. Adjustments must be made to recognize accrued interest revenue*

**EXAMPLE 10: UNRECORDED INTEREST REVENUE** Windsor Time and Motion accepted a \$6,000, 12%, interest-bearing note receivable from one of its clients on October 2. Both the principal amount of the note and the interest are due four months later on January 31. Although no cash was collected during October, interest for one month totaling \$60 ($\$6,000 \times .12 \times \frac{1}{12}$) was earned.

To record the interest earned during October and to recognize an asset for the interest receivable at the end of October, the following adjusting entry is needed at the end of the company's accounting period on October 31:

| | | | |
|---|---|---|---|
| Oct. 31 | Interest Receivable. . . . . . . . . . . . . . . . . . . . . . . . . . . . . . . . . . . . . . . . | 60 | |
| | Interest Revenue Earned . . . . . . . . . . . . . . . . . . . . . . . . . . . . . . . | | 60 |
| | To record interest earned during October | | |

After the adjusting entry has been posted, the affected accounts will appear as follows:

| INTEREST RECEIVABLE | | | INTEREST REVENUE EARNED | |
|---|---|---|---|---|
| Oct. 31 | 60 | | Oct. 31 | 60 |

The Interest Receivable account is shown as a current asset in the balance sheet, and the Interest Revenue Earned account is reported as revenue in the income statement.

## THE PLACE OF ADJUSTING ENTRIES IN THE ACCOUNTING CYCLE

As we have seen, the steps in the accounting cycle are performed in the following sequence:

1. Prepare a chart of accounts.
2. Analyze each completed business transaction.
3. Journalize each completed business transaction.
4. Post amounts from the journal to the appropriate ledger accounts.
5. Obtain balances for all ledger accounts.
6. Prepare a trial balance.
7. Prepare financial statements.

*2b. In the accounting cycle, adjusting entries are preliminary to preparation of financial statements*

In the Windsor Time and Motion illustration, we assumed that steps 1 through 6 of the cycle had been completed, and we focused on the need for adjustments that will bring the ledger account balances up to date before the financial statements are prepared. We see now that when adjusting entries are needed, step 7 (prepare financial statements) must be delayed until the account balances in the company's unadjusted trial balance are brought up to date.

*EXHIBIT 3–3*

| | WINDSOR TIME AND MOTION October 31, 19X1 | | | | | |
|---|---|---|---|---|---|---|
| | UNADJUSTED TRIAL BALANCE | | ADJUSTMENTS | | ADJUSTED TRIAL BALANCE | |
| ACCOUNTS | Debit | Credit | Debit | Credit | Debit | Credit |
| Cash | 5,210 | | | | 5,210 | |
| Accounts Receivable | 4,840 | | | | 4,840 | |
| Notes Receivable | 6,000 | | | | 6,000 | |
| Rent Receivable | | | (9) 200 | | 200 | |
| Interest Receivable | | | (10) 60 | | 60 | |
| Office Supplies | 390 | | | (2) 140 | 250 | |
| Prepaid Insurance | 480 | | | (1) 40 | 440 | |
| Office Equipment | 12,000 | | | | 12,000 | |
| Accumulated Depreciation—Office Equipment | | | | (3) 125 | | 125 |
| Vehicles | 10,800 | | | | 10,800 | |
| Accumulated Depreciation—Vehicles | | | | (4) 170 | | 170 |
| Accounts Payable | | 2,830 | | | | 2,830 |
| Salaries Payable | | | | (7) 670 | | 670 |
| Interest Payable | | | | (8) 50 | | 50 |
| Unearned Rent Revenue | | 600 | (5) 100 | | | 500 |
| Unearned Consulting Fees | | 1,200 | (6) 480 | | | 720 |
| Notes Payable | | 4,000 | | | | 4,000 |
| J. Lynn, Capital | | 25,000 | | | | 25,000 |
| J. Lynn, Drawings | 1,500 | | | | 1,500 | |
| Consulting Fees Earned | | 24,370 | | (6) 480 | | 24,850 |
| Rent Revenue Earned | | | | {(9) 200<br>(5) 100 | | 300 |
| Interest Revenue Earned | | | | (10) 60 | | 60 |
| Salaries Expense | 13,400 | | (7) 670 | | 14,070 | |
| Rent Expense | 1,600 | | | | 1,600 | |
| Travel Expense | 890 | | | | 890 | |
| Advertising Expense | 540 | | | | 540 | |
| Depreciation Expense—Office Equipment | | | (3) 125 | | 125 | |
| Depreciation Expense—Vehicles | | | (4) 170 | | 170 | |
| Office Supplies Expense | | | (2) 140 | | 140 | |
| Utilities Expense | 230 | | | | 230 | |
| Repairs Expense | 120 | | | | 120 | |
| Insurance Expense | | | (1) 40 | | 40 | |
| Interest Expense | | | (8) 50 | | 50 | |
| | 58,000 | 58,000 | 2,035 | 2,035 | 59,275 | 59,275 |

Therefore, after step 6 has been completed, the series of steps in the accounting cycle is revised to read as follows:

7. Prepare adjusting entries and post their amounts to the ledger accounts.
8. Prepare an adjusted trial balance.
9. Prepare financial statements.

Using the Windsor financial information, let us see how these three steps relate to the entire accounting process.

## PREPARING AN ADJUSTED TRIAL BALANCE

*2b. An adjusted trial balance is prepared after all adjusting entries have been made and posted*

We prepared ten needed adjusting entries for Windsor Time and Motion. After posting the dollar amounts from the adjusting entries to the ledger, we obtain new account balances and prepare another trial balance called an *adjusted trial balance.* An **adjusted trial balance** is a listing of all ledger accounts showing their balances after the adjusting entries have been posted. The adjusted trial balance provides two benefits:

1. Proof that the ledger is still in balance after all adjusting entries have been posted
2. A convenient form for the preparation of financial statements

Exhibit 3–3 shows the Windsor Time and Motion unadjusted trial balance, the account adjustments coming from the ten adjusting entries, and the resulting adjusted trial balance.

## PREPARING FINANCIAL STATEMENTS FROM THE ADJUSTED TRIAL BALANCE

We can now use the adjusted trial balance to prepare the financial statements. Note that the accounts are arranged in the trial balance in a convenient order as follows:

Assets
Liabilities
Owner's Equity
Revenues
Expenses

*2b. We use the adjusted trial balance to prepare the income statement*

The first financial statement to be prepared is the income statement because we need to know the amount of net income or net loss for purposes of calculating the change in owner's equity.

Windsor's income statement, showing all revenue and expense accounts with up-to-date balances (as they appear in the October 31 adjusted trial balance) is illustrated in Exhibit 3–4 on page 90.

*2b. Often a capital statement also is prepared*

A separate statement, called a **capital statement** or **statement of owner's equity,** is frequently prepared to show the causes for the change that took place in the capital account during the period. We looked briefly at the capital statement in Chapter 1. Owner's equity increases by the amount of reported net income (or decreases by the amount of reported net loss), and it decreases by the amount of withdrawals made by the owner.

During the month of October, J. Lynn's equity increased by $5,735, which is the excess of the reported net income over withdrawals for the period ($7,235 – $1,500). The capital statement is illustrated in Exhibit 3–5 on page 90.

EXHIBIT 3–4

| WINDSOR TIME AND MOTION<br>Income Statement<br>For the Month Ended October 31, 19X1 | | |
|---|---|---|
| Revenues: | | |
| Consulting Fees Earned | | $24,850 |
| Rent Revenue Earned | | 300 |
| Interest Revenue Earned | | 60 |
| Total Revenues | | $25,210 |
| Expenses: | | |
| Salaries | $14,070 | |
| Rent | 1,600 | |
| Travel | 890 | |
| Advertising | 540 | |
| Depreciation—Office Equipment | 125 | |
| Depreciation—Vehicles | 170 | |
| Office Supplies | 140 | |
| Utilities | 230 | |
| Repairs | 120 | |
| Insurance | 40 | |
| Interest | 50 | |
| Total Expenses | | 17,975 |
| Net Income | | $ 7,235 |

EXHIBIT 3–5

| WINDSOR TIME AND MOTION<br>Capital Statement<br>For the Month Ended October 31, 19X1 | |
|---|---|
| J. Lynn, Capital, Oct. 1, 19X1 | $25,000 |
| Add: Net income for October | 7,235 |
| Subtotal | 32,235 |
| Deduct: Withdrawals | 1,500 |
| J. Lynn, Capital, Oct. 31, 19X1 | $30,735 |

The updated owner's equity figure of $30,735 is reported in the Owner's Equity section of Windsor's balance sheet, as shown in Exhibit 3–6.

## WHY THE ACCRUAL BASIS OF ACCOUNTING IS USED

The previously illustrated financial statements were prepared on the *accrual basis* and in accordance with the *revenue realization* and *matching principles*. Although the accrual basis of accounting is widely used, some small businesses and certain professionals choose to maintain their records on the cash basis. Their choice will affect when—that is, at what point in time—financial information is entered in the accounting records. Consequently, it will also affect the information reported in the financial statements.

Under the cash basis of accounting, revenue is not recorded until received in cash and expenses are recorded in the period in which cash payment is made. Thus under cash-basis accounting, net income for the period is simply the difference between the *revenue received in cash* during that period and the *expenses paid in cash* during that same period.

EXHIBIT 3-6

WINDSOR TIME AND MOTION
Balance Sheet
October 31, 19X1

| ASSETS | | | |
|---|---|---|---|
| Current Assets: | | | |
| Cash | | $ 5,210 | |
| Accounts Receivable | | 4,840 | |
| Notes Receivable | | 6,000 | |
| Rent Receivable | | 200 | |
| Interest Receivable | | 60 | |
| Office Supplies | | 250 | |
| Prepaid Insurance | | 440 | |
| Total Current Assets | | | $17,000 |
| Plant Assets: | | | |
| Office Equipment | $12,000 | | |
| Less: Accumulated Depreciation | 125 | $11,875 | |
| Vehicles | $10,800 | | |
| Less: Accumulated Depreciation | 170 | 10,630 | |
| Total Plant Assets | | | 22,505 |
| Total Assets | | | $39,505 |
| LIABILITIES AND OWNER'S EQUITY | | | |
| Current Liabilities: | | | |
| Accounts Payable | | $ 2,830 | |
| Salaries Payable | | 670 | |
| Interest Payable | | 50 | |
| Unearned Rent Revenue | | 500 | |
| Unearned Consulting Fees | | 720 | |
| Notes Payable | | 4,000 | |
| Total Current Liabilities | | | $ 8,770 |
| Owner's Equity: | | | |
| J. Lynn, Capital | | | 30,735 |
| Total Liabilities and Owner's Equity | | | $39,505 |

In contrast, under the accrual basis of accounting, revenue is recorded when it is earned and expenses are recorded when incurred. Under accrual-basis accounting, net income is the difference between *all revenue earned* during a period and *all expenses incurred* to help produce that revenue.

The cash basis of accounting simplifies recordkeeping. It can be used with reasonably acceptable results by small businesses for which receivables, payables, and inventories are not important factors in determining net income. For most businesses, however, the accrual basis of accounting provides a measurement of net income that is more useful in analyzing and controlling business activities. Also, cash-basis financial statements are not considered to be in accordance with generally accepted accounting principles. Consequently, we use the accrual basis of accounting almost exclusively throughout this book.

*1c. The accrual basis provides a more useful net income figure. Also it is in accordance with GAAP*

## CORRECTING ENTRIES

Adjusting entries are needed to bring account balances up to date. On occasion we may also have to change an account balance to correct it for an error that was made in a journal entry but not discovered until after the amounts in the entry had been posted.

For example, assume that during October a company spent $300 to purchase a machine and recorded the transaction as follows:

| | | |
|---|---|---|
| Repairs Expense .............................................. | 300 | |
| Cash .............................................. | | 300 |
| To record the purchase of a machine | | |

Obviously, an error has been made, because the debit in this entry should be to an asset account titled Machinery instead of to an expense account. If the error is discovered in the journal before the amount has been posted, it can be corrected by drawing a line through the incorrect account title and writing the correct account title above it. A posting error where only the amount is wrong can be corrected in the same way.

*2c. Correcting entries are made in the journal to correct errors that have been recorded and posted to the wrong account*

However, when an amount is recorded in the wrong account and the error is not discovered until after posting has been completed (as you should assume happens in the example above), it is best to make a **correcting entry**—a journal entry to correct the error discovered. The following correcting entry is journalized and posted to correct the company's ledger accounts:

| | | |
|---|---|---|
| Machinery.............................................. | 300 | |
| Repairs Expense.............................................. | | 300 |
| To record the correction of a previous entry | | |

Note that the debit in this entry correctly records the fact that machinery has been purchased and when posted will correct the balance in the Machinery account. The credit to the Repairs Expense account will when posted remove the amount erroneously posted to that account from the previous entry.

## HIGHLIGHT PROBLEM

On November 1, 19X1, Kim Kranik organized a service company. The company has conducted business for one month, and on November 30, 19X1, prepared the accompanying unadjusted trial balance.

KRANIK CARETAKING COMPANY
Unadjusted Trial Balance
November 30, 19X1

| | | |
|---|---|---|
| Cash | $ 3,900 | |
| Accounts Receivable | 2,400 | |
| Office Supplies | 300 | |
| Prepaid Insurance | 1,200 | |
| Building | 24,000 | |
| Office Equipment | 6,000 | |
| Accounts Payable | | $ 4,300 |
| Unearned Commissions | | 900 |
| Mortgage Payable | | 15,000 |
| Kim Kranik, Capital | | 17,000 |
| Kim Kranik, Drawings | 1,500 | |
| Commissions Earned | | 18,200 |
| Salaries Expense | 12,000 | |
| Travel Expense | 2,900 | |
| Advertising Expense | 700 | |
| Utilities Expense | 500 | |
| | $55,400 | $55,400 |

Additional Information:

a. Office supplies remaining on hand on November 30 amount to $190.
b. The insurance policy was purchased on November 1. The $1,200 premium provides protection for one full year.
c. The building has an estimated useful business life of ten years and an estimated residual value of zero.
d. The office equipment has an estimated useful business life of five years and an estimated residual value of zero.
e. Of the commissions received in advance during November, $600 remains unearned on November 30.
f. The mortgage payable signed on November 1 has an interest rate of 12% per annum, payable on February 1 and every three months thereafter.
g. Salaries earned by company employees, but not yet paid, amount to $600.

Required:

On the basis of the information contained in the November 30 unadjusted trial balance and the additional information provided in items *a* through *g* above, prepare the adjusting entries that need to be recorded on November 30 if that date were to represent the end of an accounting period.

## GLOSSARY OF KEY TERMS

**Accounting period.** Any time period for which an income statement is prepared.

**Accrual basis.** An accounting basis whereby revenues are recorded in the accounting period in which they are earned regardless of whether or not received in cash, and expenses incurred in earning the revenues are recorded in the same accounting period regardless of whether or not paid in cash.

**Accumulated depreciation.** The amount of a depreciable plant asset's cost that has been allocated to depreciation expense since the asset was acquired. The accumulated depreciation account is a contra asset account that will be reported as a deduction from the related plant asset on the balance sheet.

**Adjusted trial balance.** A listing of all ledger accounts showing their balances after adjusting entries have been posted.

**Adjusting entries.** Journal entries made at the end of each accounting period to update account balances before preparing financial statements. The purpose is to report appropriate amounts for all accounts appearing in the end-of-the-period financial statements.

**Book value.** The net amount at which an asset is carried on the balance sheet. For assets subject to depreciation, book value is the difference between the balance in the plant asset account and the balance in its related accumulated depreciation account.

**Capital statement.** A statement that discloses the causes for the change in owner's equity that occurred during the period.

**Carrying value.** An alternate term for *book value.*

**Cash basis.** An accounting basis whereby revenues for goods sold or services rendered are recorded when the cash is received and expenses incurred in generating the revenues are recorded when the cash payments are made.

**Contra account.** An account that has an opposite balance from the account to which it relates and is deducted from the dollar amount of that related account when reported in the financial statements.

**Contra asset account.** An account having a credit balance that is shown in the balance sheet as a deduction from the asset to which it relates.

**Correcting entry.** A journal entry made to correct errors in the recording of a previous transaction that were discovered after the amounts had been posted.

**Depreciation.** A systematic process of allocating and charging to expense the cost (minus estimated residual value) of a plant asset over the accounting periods expected to receive benefits from its use.

**Matching principle.** A fundamental principle of the accrual basis of accounting which states that expenses incurred during a period should be matched against the revenues that these expenses helped to generate or earn during that same period.

**Prepaid expenses.** Assets that will expire over time or be consumed while operating the business. As the asset is expired or consumed, it becomes an expense.

**Revenue realization principle.** A principle that states that revenue should be recorded in the accounts in the period in which it is earned.

**Statement of owner's equity.** Alternate term for *capital statement*.

**Unadjusted trial balance.** Usually called a trial balance; it is a listing of all ledger accounts showing their balances before they have been brought up to date by the adjusting process.

# APPENDIX TO CHAPTER 3

## Adjusting Entries Needed When Original Entries Are Recorded in Revenue and Expense Accounts

In discussing adjusting entries so far, we have assumed that when expenses are prepaid, the transaction is recorded by debiting an asset account. In addition, we have assumed that when cash is received in advance for services that must be performed in the future, a liability account is credited for an amount equal to the advance payment. Thus the adjusting entries needed at the end of an accounting period take this form when illustrated in the main sections of the chapter:

*Debit* an Expense Account (such as Insurance Expense)
*Credit* the Prepaid Account (such as Prepaid Insurance)

*Debit* the Liability Account (such as Unearned Rent Revenue)
*Credit* a Revenue Account (such as Rent Revenue Earned)

This appendix will show the adjusting entries needed (1) when expense items paid for in advance of their use are originally debited to an expense account instead of to an asset account and (2) when revenues received in advance are originally credited to a revenue account instead of to a liability account.

When this happens, the adjusting entries needed at the end of the accounting period take the following form illustrated in this appendix:

*Debit* a Revenue Account (such as Rent Revenue Earned)
*Credit* the Liability Account (such as Unearned Rent Revenue)

*Debit* the Prepaid Account (such as Prepaid Insurance)
*Credit* an Expense Account (such as Insurance Expense)

This alternative approach does not represent a change in or from accrual-basis accounting. It is simply a different technique for arriving at the same end-of-the-period account balances needed for reporting in the financial statements. It is explained in this appendix because you will sometimes see it used in practice.

Let us take some of the Windsor company transactions and show the adjusting entries that would be needed if

1. Revenue received in advance is originally recorded by crediting a *revenue* account instead of a *liability* account
2. Expenses paid in advance are originally recorded by debiting an *expense* account instead of an *asset* account

## UNEARNED REVENUE ORIGINALLY CREDITED TO REVENUE ACCOUNTS

EXAMPLE 1 Recall that Windsor Time and Motion rented garage space to Atlas Company for $200 per month and on October 16 received a check for $600 representing three months' rent in advance. Using the alternative (revenue) approach for recording the transaction, the entire amount received in advance would be credited to the Rent Revenue Earned account as follows.

*Transaction entry* (orignal entry credited directly to a revenue account):

| | | | |
|---|---|---|---|
| Oct. 16 | Cash | 600 | |
| | Rent Revenue Earned | | 600 |

Of the $600 received on October 16, Windsor has earned $100 by October 31, and that is the amount that should appear as Rent Revenue Earned in its October income statement. The remaining amount of $500 is still unearned and should be shown in the balance sheet as a liability called Unearned Rent Revenue. The adjusting entry needed to have the accounts show their proper balances as of October 31 is as follows.

*Adjusting entry:*

| | | | |
|---|---|---|---|
| Oct. 31 | Rent Revenue Earned | 500 | |
| | Unearned Rent Revenue | | 500 |

EXAMPLE 2 On October 10 a client paid Windsor $1,200 in cash for services expected to be performed in the future. If this transaction was originally recorded by crediting a revenue account, the entry would be as follows.

*Transaction entry* (original entry credited directly to a revenue account):

| | | | |
|---|---|---|---|
| Oct. 10 | Cash | 1,200 | |
| | Consulting Fees Earned | | 1,200 |

Because the consulting assignment was 40% complete by October 31, consulting revenue earned during October is $480 ($1,200 × .40). The difference of $720 ($1,200 − $480) will be earned in one or more future accounting periods, and that amount should therefore be reported as a liability in the October 31 balance sheet. The entry needed to adjust the account balances on October 31 is as follows.

*Adjusting entry:*

| | | | |
|---|---|---|---|
| Oct. 31 | Consulting Fees Earned | 720 | |
| | Unearned Consulting Fees | | 720 |

## PREPAID EXPENSES ORIGINALLY DEBITED TO EXPENSE ACCOUNTS

EXAMPLE 3 A one-year insurance policy is purchased and the full year's premium of $480 is paid in advance. Using the alternative approach of recording the transaction by debiting an expense account instead of an asset account, the journal entry would be as follows.

*Transaction entry* (original entry debited directly to an expense account):

| | | | |
|---|---|---|---|
| Oct. 1 | Insurance Expense . . . . . . . . . . . . . . . . . . | 480 | |
| | Cash . . . . . . . . . . . . . . . . . . | | 480 |

On October 31 only one month of the twelve-month advance payment has expired. Therefore $40 ($480 ÷ 12 × 1) should appear as an expense in the October income statement. Eleven months of the premium remains unexpired and is assumed to benefit future periods. Therefore an amount ($440) representing the cost of the eleven-month prepayment should appear as an asset in the October 31 balance sheet. The entry needed to establish the asset account for $440 and to change the balance in the expense account to read $40 is as follows.

*Adjusting entry*:

| | | | |
|---|---|---|---|
| Oct. 31 | Prepaid Insurance . . . . . . . . . . . . . . . . . . | 440 | |
| | Insurance Expense . . . . . . . . . . . . . . . . . . | | 440 |

EXAMPLE 4 If prepaid expenses are originally debited to expense accounts instead of asset accounts, the purchase of office supplies costing $390 on October 3 would be recorded as follows.

*Transaction entry* (original entry debited directly to an expense account):

| | | | |
|---|---|---|---|
| Oct. 3 | Office Supplies Expense . . . . . . . . . . . . . . . . . . | 390 | |
| | Accounts Payable . . . . . . . . . . . . . . . . . . | | 390 |

Because $250 of office supplies remained on hand on October 31, that amount should appear as an asset in the October 31 balance sheet. The difference between the amount of office supplies purchased and the amount remaining on hand, $140 ($390 − $250 = $140), should appear as Office Supplies Expense in the October income statement. The adjusting entry needed to adjust the accounts so that they show proper balances as of October 31 is as follows.

*Adjusting entry*:

| | | | |
|---|---|---|---|
| Oct. 31 | Office Supplies . . . . . . . . . . . . . . . . . . | 250 | |
| | Office Supplies Expense . . . . . . . . . . . . . . . . . . | | 250 |

Regardless of which approach is used when the transactions described above are initially recorded, the objective of the adjusting entry recorded at the end of the accounting period is to establish the proper amount in the respective accounts. The adjustment process is carried out to ensure the proper matching of expenses incurred with revenues earned in the income statement and to report the correct balances for the accounts shown in the balance sheet.

## REVIEW QUESTIONS

1. Using the cash basis of accounting: (a) How is revenue recorded? (b) How are expenses recorded? [LO1a]
2. How does the matching principle relate to the recording of revenues and expenses? [LO1a]
3. How does the accrual basis of accounting apply the revenue realization principle and the matching principle to the recognition of revenue and expense? [LO1a]
4. Why are adjusting entries needed? [LO1b]
5. Describe the four principal situations that require adjusting entries. [LO1b]
6. What would be the effect on the income statement if adjustments for prepaid expenses that have expired or been consumed were not made? [LO2a]
7. What would be the effect on the balance sheet if adjustments for prepaid expenses that have expired or been consumed were not made? [LO2a]
8. What two things are accomplished when an adjusting entry that assigns part of the prepaid insurance to insurance expense is recorded and posted? [LO2a]
9. Define *depreciation*. [LO2a]
10. What are contra accounts? [LO2a]
11. Why is an unearned revenue account balance considered to be a liability? [LO2a]
12. Why are adjusting entries for unrecorded expenses needed? [LO2a]
13. Why are adjusting entries for unrecorded revenues needed? [LO2a]
14. What step in the accounting cycle must be delayed until adjusting entries are made? [LO2b]
15. What two benefits are provided by the adjusted trial balance? [LO2b]
16. What three financial statements are prepared from the data found in an adjusted trial balance? [LO2b]
17. Why is the accrual basis of accounting considered superior to the cash basis of accounting? [LO1c]
18. How is net income defined when the accrual basis of accounting is used? [LO1c]
19. What is the difference between adjusting and correcting entries? [LO2c]

## ANALYTICAL QUESTIONS

20. Why does the income statement show an approximation rather than an exact measurement of net income? [LO1a]
21. Why is the accrual basis of accounting a better measure of net income than the cash basis? "The change in cash during an accounting period is an important measure." Respond to this question and statement. [LO1a,1c]
22. What do we mean when we say that adjusting entries often reflect the effect of transactions and events that relate to more than a single accounting period? [LO1b]
23. Take each type of adjusting entry discussed in the chapter and indicate the effect of its omission on total assets, total liabilities, and total net income. That is, indicate whether the item would be overstated, understated, or unaffected by the omission. [LO1b,2a]
24. Why must financial statements be prepared from an adjusted trial balance rather than an unadjusted trial balance? [LO2b]
25. How can the use of the matching concept provide better information to help managers and owners decide whether to expand or contract business activity? [LO1c]

## IMPACT ANALYSIS QUESTIONS

*For each error described, indicate whether it would overstate [O], understate [U], or not affect [N] the specified key figures.* [LO1b,2a]

26. An adjusting entry was not made to record salaries earned by the employees but not yet paid by the company.

    _______ Assets _______ Liabilities
    _______ Expenses _______ Net Income

27. An adjusting entry was not made to recognize that some of the office supplies on hand at the beginning of the period had been used (consumed) during the period.

    _______ Assets _______ Revenues
    _______ Expenses _______ Net Income

28. An adjusting entry was not made at the end of the period to recognize the interest that was earned on the company's investments during the period.

    _______ Assets _______ Revenues
    _______ Expenses _______ Net Income

29. An adjusting entry was not made at the end of the period to recognize the rent revenue that was earned although not received during the period.

    _______ Assets _______ Revenues
    _______ Liabilities _______ Net Income

30. An adjusting entry was not made at the end of the period to recognize the amount of depreciation applicable to the period.

    _______ Assets _______ Liabilities
    _______ Expenses _______ Net Income

## EXERCISES

EXERCISE 3-1 *(Determine Effect of Errors on Reported Net Income)* For each of the following items, state whether the error increases or decreases net income for the period.

a. Fee revenue earned but not yet received was not recorded by an end-of-the-period adjusting entry.
b. Owing to a counting error, the office supplies remaining on hand was overstated. This overstated amount was used when the end-of-the-period adjusting entry was made.
c. Salaries earned but not yet paid at the end of the period were not recorded by an end-of-the-period adjusting entry.
d. Owing to a computation error, too much depreciation expense was recorded in the end-of-the-period adjusting entry.
e. Three months' rent was paid in advance on the first of the month, and the entire amount was debited to the Prepaid Rent account. No end-of-the-period adjusting entry was made to update this account balance.
f. Cash received from a customer in payment of an amount owed for services previously provided was recorded by debiting the Cash account and crediting the Fee Revenue account. No other entries relating to this event were made. [LO1b,2a]

EXERCISE 3-2 *(Prepare Adjusting Entries and Determine Their Financial Statement Classification)* The following information relates to Charter Company.

a. The company acquired a truck at a cost of $6,000. The useful life of the truck is estimated to be five years, with no residual value expected at the end of that five-year period.

Required:

Determine the amount of depreciation expense that occurs per month and per year. Prepare the adjusting entry needed to record the annual depreciation. Where would these accounts appear in the financial statements? What makes depreciation expense different from most other expenses found on the company's income statement?

b. The company, acting as the landlord, rents storage space for $300 per month with three months' rent expected in advance. On December 1 the company received a check for $900 from a newly acquired tenant. The company is now obligated to provide space to that tenant for three months beginning on December 1.

Required:

Prepare the entry that should be made on December 1 to record this transaction. Prepare the adjusting entry needed at the end of the period on December 31. Where would the accounts showing the effect of this renting activity appear in the financial statements prepared on December 31? What balances would they have? What makes the liability account created by these events different from most other liabilities found on the company's balance sheet? [LO2a,2b]

EXERCISE 3–3 *(Prepare Adjusting Entries)* Rite Company uses an annual accounting period and adjusts its accounts on December 31, the last day of that period.

Required:

On the basis of the following information, prepare the adjusting entries that would be needed on December 31.

a. The Office Supplies account had a balance of $360 on January 1. Although supplies were not purchased during the year, a physical count taken at the end of the year indicates that $90 of office supplies are still on hand.

b. The Prepaid Insurance account had a balance of $4,320 as the result of premiums paid on January 1. No additional premiums were paid during the year. The $4,320 of premiums paid on January 1 provide insurance coverage for a period of three full years.

c. Vehicle depreciation is calculated on a five-year estimated useful life with no expected salvage value. The balance in the Vehicles account on January 1 of the current year is $13,200, and no other amounts were posted to that account during the current year.

d. On December 10 an agreement was signed to provide twenty-five days of services to a client company. Rite Company charges the client $40 per day for these services, with the money payable at the end of the twenty-five-day period. There were fifteen chargeable days during the month of December.

e. A six-month bank loan in the amount of $20,000 was obtained on November 1 of the current year at an annual interest rate of 9%. No interest on this loan has been paid as of December 31, and no interest has been recorded. [LO2a]

EXERCISE 3–4 *(State the Effect of Adjustment Omission)* Assume that no adjustments for the facts contained in Exercise 3–3 were made. State the effect that each omission would have on reported net income, the owner's capital accounts balance, and the total assets and total liabilities as shown in the December 31 balance sheet. [LO2a,2b]

EXERCISE 3–5 *(Prepare Original and Adjusting Entries)* The Mall Playhouse sells tickets to its performances on a subscription basis.

Required:

For each transaction listed in items *a* through *e* below, prepare (1) the journal entry needed on the transaction date and (2) the adjusting entry needed to update account balances on December 31, the end of the accounting period.

a. On December 1 the Mall sold two thousand performance tickets for $24,000 cash. Holders of the tickets must use them on the date that the performances are given or forfeit the price of the ticket. The following schedule shows the number of tickets sold in advance of the performances for the $24,000: for the December performance, nine hundred tickets; for the January performance, seven hundred tickets; and for the February performance, four hundred tickets.

b. On December 1 the Mall borrowed $9,000 from State Bank. This amount, together with interest computed at 8% per year, is to be paid back on March 1 of next year.

c. On December 15 a two-year fire insurance policy was purchased by paying the premium of $2,640 in cash. (Insurance expense is calculated for each half month.)

d. On December 15 equipment costing $18,000 was purchased by paying $12,000 in cash and promising to pay the balance within thirty days. The equipment has an estimated useful life of five years with no residual value expected. (Depreciation is computed for each half month.)

e. On December 17 office supplies costing $290 were purchased on account. A count made on December 31 shows that $220 of the supplies are still on hand. [LO2a]

EXERCISE 3–6 *(Determine the Missing Amounts)* Determine the missing amounts indicated by the question marks for each of the four cases in the numbered columns shown below. Each numbered column should be treated independently. [LO2a]

| | 1 | 2 | 3 | 4 |
|---|---|---|---|---|
| Supplies on hand at the beginning of the period | 600 | 500 | 200 | ? |
| Supplies on hand at the end of the period | 400 | 350 | ? | 200 |
| Supplies purchased during the period | 500 | ? | 700 | 450 |
| Supplies used during the period | ? | 400 | 550 | 350 |

EXERCISE 3–7 *(State the Effects of Certain Adjusting Entries on the Elements in the Income Statement and the Balance Sheet)* Assume the following activities took place.

_____ 1. An adjusting entry to recognize the expired portion of an insurance policy premium was recorded and posted. The entry made when the premium was paid debited the Prepaid Insurance account and credited the Cash account for the cost of the premium.

_____ 2. An adjusting entry to recognize periodic depreciation was recorded and posted.

_____ 3. An adjusting entry to recognize the revenue earned for services performed during this period on monies received in a prior period was recorded and posted. When the cash was originally received, the transaction was recorded by debiting the Cash account and crediting the Unearned Revenue account.

_____ 4. An adjusting entry to recognize salaries earned but not yet paid was recorded and posted.

_____ 5. An adjusting entry to recognize interest earned but not yet received was recorded and posted.

_____ 6. An adjusting entry to recognize interest incurred on notes payable but not yet paid was recorded and posted.

Required:

A list of effects that an adjusting entry may have on the elements contained in the income statement and in the balance sheet can be described by one of the four choices that appear below. Place the appropriate letter in the blank shown next to items 1 through 6 above to indicate the effect of that item's adjusting entry.

a. Increase in assets, increase in revenues

b. Increase in revenues, decrease in liabilities

c. Increase in expenses, increase in liabilities

d. Increase in expenses, decrease in assets [LO2a]

## PROBLEMS

*Round all amounts to the nearest whole dollar.*

PROBLEM 3–1 *(Prepare Adjusting Entries)* The Valley Company operates with an accounting period of one full year ending on December 31. The following information is given. This information can be used as a basis for making all the necessary adjusting entries that are needed to bring the account balances up to date on December 31, 19X1.

a. The Office Supplies account had a $210 debit balance on January 1, and $360 of supplies were purchased during the year. A year-end physical count shows that office supplies costing $180 remain on hand.

b. A two-year fire insurance policy was purchased on January 1, at which time the entire insurance premium cost of $900 was debited to the Prepaid Insurance account.

c. Equipment purchased late last year for $14,000 was estimated to have a useful life of eight years and a residual value of $2,000. No entry for the current year's depreciation has yet been made.

d. On August 1 cash of $4,000 was received in advance for services to be rendered in the future. The transaction was recorded by debiting the Cash account and crediting the Unearned Service Revenue account. Once again on November 16, cash of $4,300 was received in advance for services, and again the Cash account was debited and the Unearned Service Revenue account was credited. On December 31 it was determined that 100% of the August 1 advance had been earned and 40% of the November 16 advance had been earned.

e. Salaries earned by company employees for the last two days of December have not been paid or recorded. Their earnings for those two days total $920.

f. A three-month bank loan for $8,000 was obtained on December 1. Annual interest on the loan is 10% per year. At December 31 no interest has been paid and none has been recorded.

g. On December 23 the company agreed to rent a piece of its equipment to another company. The agreement specified a rental period of no longer than twenty days and no shorter than four days at a cost of $60 per day, payable when the equipment is returned. On December 31 six workdays have passed since the equipment was rented.

Required:

Make the adjusting entries needed for each of the items *a* through g above. [LO2a]

PROBLEM 3–2 *(Prepare Original and Adjusting Entries)* The Universally Clean Company operates a clearinghouse to distribute magazines to student customers on a subscription basis. Listed below are seven transactions for the month of October.

Required:

For each of the following transactions, prepare (1) a journal entry as of the transaction date and (2) an adjusting entry, if one is needed, on October 31, the end of the company's accounting period.

a. On October 1 Universally Clean received a check representing three months' rent for space that will be provided to a client beginning on October 1 and ending on January 1 of the following year. The company charges $300 rent per month.

b. On October 10 Universally Clean purchased office supplies costing $370. A count made on October 31 shows that $280 of the supplies are still on hand.

c. On October 15 the company received cash from its magazine subscribers as follows:
$1,800 for one-year subscriptions
$5,400 for three-year subscriptions
$1,200 for five-year subscriptions
All subscriptions are for monthly publications, the first volume of which was in the mail by October 31.

d. On October 15 a two-year fire insurance policy was purchased by paying the premium of $864 in cash.

e. On October 15 equipment costing $12,000 was purchased by paying $9,000 in cash and promising to pay the balance within thirty days. The equipment has an estimated useful life of five years with no residual value expected. (Depreciation is computed for each half month.)

f. On October 20 Universally Clean obtained a $9,000 loan from City Bank. This amount, together with interest at 12% per year, is to be paid six months from now on April 20 of next year.

g. On October 21 the company rented a truck from Safe Drive Rental Service. The rental fee was established by a flat rate, payable upon entering the agreement. Universal paid $175 to obtain use of the truck for twenty-five consecutive days beginning on October 21. (There are eleven working days left in October.) [LO2a]

PROBLEM 3–3 *(Record Adjusting Entries)* Prepare the adjusting entries that will be needed at the end of the period on November 30, 19X1, for each of the following unrelated transactions and situations.

a. Salaries earned by employees as of November 30 but not yet recorded or paid amounted to $2,200.
b. A $12,000 note bearing interest at 15% per annum was received from a customer on November 1. The principal and interest are due in four months on March 1 of next year.
c. Rental revenue of $600 was collected in advance on November 1. The amount is applicable to November and December of this year and January of next year. On November 1 the entry was recorded by debiting the Cash account and crediting the Unearned Rental Revenue account for $600.
d. The Supplies account has a debit balance of $460 as of November 30. A physical count taken on that date indicates that supplies costing $170 are still on hand.
e. Equipment costing $10,000 was acquired on September 1 of the current year. The equipment has an estimated useful life of five years and an estimated residual value of $4,000. No entries for depreciation have been recorded in the past, but one is needed at this time.
f. The cost of all insurance premiums is recorded by debiting the Prepaid Insurance account and crediting the Cash account. On November 30 the expired insurance premiums amount to $820.
g. Storeroom space was rented on October 1 of the current year. Six months' rent, totaling $540, was paid in advance, at which time the Prepaid Rent account was debited and the Cash account was credited. No other amounts have been posted to the Prepaid Rent account as of November 30.
h. A building that cost $48,000 was estimated to depreciate at 5% annually. The building was acquired last year. No entries for depreciation have been recorded in the past, but one is needed at this time.
i. Interest expense incurred but not yet paid on a mortgage payable amounts to $125 as of November 30.
j. Interest earned on company investments remains stable at $540 per year. Payments are received quarterly on January 1, April 1, July 1, and October 1. No adjusting entries have been recorded since the last interest check was received on October 1, but one is needed at this time. [LO2a]

PROBLEM 3–4 *(Record Adjusting Entries and Determine Net Income)* Competitive Referral Service, owned by J. Weller, has the unadjusted trial balance on November 30, 19X1 as shown at the top of page 103.

The company started its activities on November 1, and it prepares adjusting entries monthly.

Additional Data:

a. The cost of office supplies remaining on hand is $160, as determined by a count taken on November 30.
b. The prepaid interest was established on November 1, by paying the interest in advance on the $3,000 note payable which is due in two months. The interest on the note is 10% per annum.
c. Office salaries earned but unpaid on November 30 amount to $310.
d. The rental of office facilities costs the company $300 per month. The $900 in the Prepaid Rent account represents three months' rent paid in advance on November 1.
e. The office equipment was purchased on November 1 and has an estimated useful life of ten years, with no salvage value expected after the ten years.

COMPETITIVE REFERRAL SERVICE
Unadjusted Trial Balance
November 30, 19X1

| | | |
|---|---|---|
| Cash | $ 6,200 | |
| Accounts Receivable | 2,240 | |
| Prepaid Interest | 50 | |
| Prepaid Rent | 900 | |
| Office Equipment | 6,600 | |
| Office Supplies | 265 | |
| Notes Payable | | $ 3,000 |
| Accounts Payable | | 1,800 |
| J. Weller, Capital | | 10,000 |
| Commission Revenue Earned | | 5,700 |
| Rental Revenue Earned | | 180 |
| Office Salaries Expense | 3,900 | |
| Maintenance Expense | 80 | |
| Advertising Expense | 395 | |
| Telephone Expense | 50 | |
| | $20,680 | $20,680 |

f. A total of $400 in commissions was received in cash before it was earned. The entry, recorded at the time the money was received, debited the Cash account and credited the Commission Revenue Earned account for the $400. On November 30, $300 of the payment received in advance remains unearned.

Required:

1. Prepare the adjusting entries needed to bring the account balances up to date on November 30.
2. Determine the amount of net income earned by the company during the month of November. [LO2a,2b]

PROBLEM 3-5 *(Prepare Adjusting Entries, Adjusted Trial Balance, and Income Statement)* The Academic Fortune Company has the following unadjusted trial balance on November 30, 19X1, the end of its first month of operations.

ACADEMIC FORTUNE COMPANY
Unadjusted Trial Balance
November 30, 19X1

| | | |
|---|---|---|
| Cash | $ 4,200 | |
| Accounts Receivable | 3,900 | |
| Government Bonds | 3,000 | |
| Office Supplies | 600 | |
| Prepaid Insurance | 900 | |
| Land | 18,500 | |
| Accounts Payable | | $ 1,570 |
| Unearned Commission Revenue | | 2,320 |
| Unearned Consulting Fees | | 9,460 |
| Mortgage Payable | | 10,000 |
| R. Lee, Capital | | 15,000 |
| Salaries Expense | 5,800 | |
| Office Expense | 400 | |
| Telephone Expense | 250 | |
| Travel Expense | 620 | |
| Utilities Expense | 180 | |
| | $38,350 | $38,350 |

Additional Data:

a. The $900 insurance premium was paid on November 1 and provides protection for three years.
b. Salaries are $1,450 for a five-day week. Payday is on Friday, and the last Friday in November was on the twenty-fifth, which of course is also the date on which the last salary entry was recorded.
c. The cost of office supplies remaining on hand on November 30 is $440, as determined by a count taken on that day.
d. $1,500 of the commission revenue received in advance was earned by November 30.
e. The investment in government bonds was made on November 1, at which time no interest was accrued. The bonds earn a 12% return annually, payable semiannually on April 30 and October 31.
f. Consulting fees earned as of November 30 amounted to $9,220.
g. Interest on the mortgage is paid quarterly beginning on January 31. The mortgage carries an annual interest rate of 15%, and although no interest has been paid, one month has accrued.

Required:

1. Prepare the adjusting entries needed on November 30.
2. Set up T accounts for each account shown in the unadjusted trial balance, and enter the amount representing its unadjusted balance as of November 30 in each account. Post the adjusting entries to the T accounts, and determine the updated account balances.
3. Prepare an adjusted trial balance.
4. Prepare an income statement for the month of November. [LO2a,2b]

PROBLEM 3–6 *(Prepare Adjusting Entries, Adjusted Trial Balance, and Financial Statements)* The Bates Company has the following unadjusted trial balance on November 30, 19X1, the end of its first month of operations.

BATES COMPANY

Unadjusted Trial Balance

November 30, 19X1

| | | |
|---|---|---|
| Cash | $ 4,600 | |
| Accounts Receivable | 3,800 | |
| Prepaid Insurance | 960 | |
| Office Supplies | 320 | |
| Office Equipment | 7,200 | |
| Accounts Payable | | $ 3,330 |
| Unearned Rental Revenue | | 800 |
| B. Bates, Capital | | 9,000 |
| B. Bates, Drawings | 1,400 | |
| Commission Revenue Earned | | 27,410 |
| Salaries Expense | 19,200 | |
| Rent Expense | 1,800 | |
| Travel Expense | 920 | |
| Utilities Expense | 340 | |
| | $40,540 | $40,540 |

Additional Data:

a. The insurance expense for November amounts to $160.
b. The cost of office supplies remaining on hand on November 30 is $140, as determined by a count taken on that day.
c. Salaries earned by company employees but not yet paid to them amounted to $300.
d. Parking space rented to a neighboring firm requires the tenant to pay two months' rent

in advance. The tenant's advance payment of $800 was received by Bates on November 1.

e. The office equipment has an estimated useful life of eight years with a residual value of zero.

Required:

1. Prepare the adjusting entries needed on November 30.
2. Set up T accounts for each account shown in the unadjusted trial balance, and enter the amount representing its unadjusted balance as of November 30 in each account. Post the adjusting entries to the T accounts, and determine the updated account balances.
3. Prepare an adjusted trial balance.
4. Prepare an income statement, a capital statement, and a balance sheet. [LO2a,2b]

PROBLEM 3–7 *(Prepare Adjusting Entries from Two Trial Balances)* Both the unadjusted and adjusted trial balances of Nix Company are shown in the accompanying exhibit.

NIX COMPANY
Trial Balances
November 30, 19X1

| | UNADJUSTED TRIAL BALANCE | | ADJUSTED TRIAL BALANCE | |
|---|---|---|---|---|
| Cash | $ 3,535 | | $ 3,535 | |
| Commissions Receivable | | | 175 | |
| Office Supplies | 1,490 | | 880 | |
| Prepaid Insurance | 1,270 | | 720 | |
| Prepaid Rent | 1,200 | | 900 | |
| Equipment | 8,800 | | 8,800 | |
| Accumulated Depreciation—Equipment | | $ 1,200 | | $ 1,480 |
| Vehicle | 3,700 | | 3,700 | |
| Accumulated Depreciation—Vehicle | | 800 | | 910 |
| Accounts Payable | | 1,010 | | 1,010 |
| Notes Payable | | 1,500 | | 1,500 |
| Salaries Payable | | | | 410 |
| Taxes Payable | | | | 40 |
| Interest Payable | | | | 25 |
| Unearned Commissions Revenue | | 320 | | 210 |
| D. Nix, Capital | | 10,000 | | 10,000 |
| D. Nix, Drawings | 3,700 | | 3,700 | |
| Commissions Revenue Earned | | 15,400 | | 15,685 |
| Salaries Expense | 6,200 | | 6,610 | |
| Rent Expense | | | 300 | |
| Office Supplies Expense | | | 610 | |
| Depreciation Expense—Equipment | | | 280 | |
| Depreciation Expense—Vehicle | | | 110 | |
| Insurance Expense | | | 550 | |
| Utilities Expense | 170 | | 170 | |
| Taxes Expense | 165 | | 205 | |
| Interest Expense | | | 25 | |
| | $30,230 | $30,230 | $31,270 | $31,270 |

Required:

Analyze the data contained in these trial balances and prepare the ten adjusting entries (already made by the company) that explain the changes in the account balances from the trial balance to the adjusted trial balance. [LO2a]

PROBLEM 3–8 *(Prepare Adjusting Entries from Income Statement and Trial Balance)* The October income statement for Chadley Company is shown below.

CHADLEY COMPANY
Income Statement
For the Month Ended October 31, 19X1

| | | |
|---|---|---|
| Revenue: | | |
| Consulting Fees Earned | | $18,700 |
| Rental Revenue Earned | | 600 |
| Interest Revenue Earned | | 100 |
| Total Revenue | | $19,400 |
| Expenses: | | |
| Salaries | $11,200 | |
| Rent | 1,900 | |
| Travel | 720 | |
| Advertising | 450 | |
| Depreciation | 120 | |
| Office Supplies | 110 | |
| Utilities | 230 | |
| Repairs | 60 | |
| Insurance | 90 | |
| Interest | 30 | |
| Total Expenses | | 14,910 |
| Net Income | | $ 4,490 |

The company's October 31 unadjusted trial balance, which was prepared before its income statement, is shown below.

CHADLEY COMPANY
Unadjusted Trial Balance
October 31, 19X1

| | | |
|---|---|---|
| Cash | $ 2,160 | |
| Accounts Receivable | 3,980 | |
| Notes Receivable | 12,000 | |
| Prepaid Insurance | 1,080 | |
| Office Supplies | 560 | |
| Equipment | 13,200 | |
| Accounts Payable | | $ 3,340 |
| Notes Payable | | 4,000 |
| Unearned Rental Revenue | | 1,800 |
| L. Chadley, Capital | | 20,500 |
| L. Chadley, Drawings | 1,400 | |
| Consulting Fees Earned | | 18,700 |
| Salaries Expense | 10,600 | |
| Rent Expense | 1,900 | |
| Travel Expense | 720 | |
| Advertising Expense | 450 | |
| Utilities Expense | 230 | |
| Repairs Expense | 60 | |
| | $48,340 | $48,340 |

Required:

1. Analyze the data contained in the unadjusted trial balance and the October income statement to determine (a) changes made in account balances by adjusting entries and (b) the new accounts established by the adjusting entries.
2. Prepare the seven adjusting entries that explain the changes in accounts and account balances from the unadjusted trial balance to the income statement. [LO2a,2b]

PROBLEM 3–9 *(Prepare Adjusting Entries)* On December 31, the company's year-end, the following information was available to help in making adjusting entries. No adjusting entries have been prepared at any time during the company's annual accounting period.

Required:

Prepare the adjusting entries needed for each item listed below.

a. Supplies costing $530 were purchased during the year and were debited to the Office Supplies account. At year-end the cost of supplies remaining on hand was determined to be $265. No supplies were on hand at the beginning of the year.

b. Salaries are established at $1,600 per five-day workweek. On December 31, 19X1, three days of salaries are earned but unpaid and unrecorded.

c. Two months' interest on investments of $9,000 made by the company has been earned as of year-end but has not yet been received. The investments earn 12% annually.

d. All equipment was acquired during the current year and is being depreciated over a five-year estimated useful life. Given below are the costs of three separate equipment purchases made this year together with their estimated residual values.

| | COST | RESIDUAL VALUE |
|---|---|---|
| January 1, 19X1 | $14,000 | $2,000 |
| April 30, 19X1 | 12,000 | 3,000 |
| September 1, 19X1 | 4,050 | -0- |

e. On February 1 the company purchased a three-year fire insurance policy, paying a premium of $972. The transaction was recorded by debiting the Prepaid Insurance account and crediting the Cash account.

f. All commission revenue is received in advance and is immediately recorded by crediting the Unearned Commission Revenue account. On January 1, 19X1, the balance in the Unearned Commission Revenue account was $7,900. Commissions received during the year totaled $98,000, and the amount of commissions received but still unearned at year-end amounted to $9,300. [LO2a]

PROBLEM 3–10 *(Prepare Correcting Entries, Adjusting Entries, Trial Balance, and Income Statement)* The Comclean Carpet Service Company began business three months ago. Joan Beyer, the owner, wanted to know whether she had made a profit during those first three months in which she operated the firm. Before an income statement could be prepared, Joan prepared a trial balance that provides the information needed to answer that question and found it did not balance. A copy of that trial balance is shown below.

COMCLEAN CARPET SERVICE COMPANY
Trial Balance
December 31, 19X1

| | | |
|---|---|---|
| Cash | $ 1,880 | |
| Accounts Receivable | 620 | |
| Supplies | 940 | |
| Equipment | 2,300 | |
| Vehicles | 16,800 | |
| Accounts Payable | | $ 790 |
| Unearned Service Revenue | | 260 |
| J. Beyer, Capital | | 18,000 |
| J. Beyer, Drawings | 4,700 | |
| Service Revenue | | 27,180 |
| Salaries Expense | 14,400 | |
| Rent Expense | 1,600 | |
| Vehicle Use Expense | 1,070 | |
| Utilities Expense | 910 | |
| Insurance Expense | 720 | |
| | $45,940 | $46,230 |

Frustrated by her experience, Joan then hired an accountant, who examined the records and found the following:

a. Supplies still on hand on December 31 totaled $360.
b. The balance in the Accounts Payable account was calculated incorrectly. The correct account balance is $590.
c. One-half of the service revenue received in advance has been earned.
d. A $100 cash payment made for equipment repair was incorrectly recorded. The amount was debited to the Equipment account and credited to the Cash account.
e. The equipment has an estimated useful life of five years and zero residual value.
f. The vehicles have an estimated useful life of four years and zero residual value.
g. Salaries earned but not yet paid or recorded amounted to $800 as of December 31.
h. The amount in the Insurance Expense account represents the cost of the premium on a two-year policy purchased three months ago on October 1, 19X1.
i. Cash of $230 was received from a customer immediately after services had been performed and the job completed. The transaction was recorded by debiting the Cash account for $230 and crediting the Service Revenue account for $320.

Required:

1. Set up T accounts for the accounts listed in the trial balance and these additional accounts: Prepaid Insurance, Accumulated Depreciation—Equipment, Accumulated Depreciation—Vehicles, Salaries Payable, Depreciation Expense—Equipment, Depreciation Expense—Vehicles, Supplies Expense, and Repairs Expense. Post the balances shown in the December 31, 19X1, trial balance as given.
2. Prepare the correcting and adjusting entries needed on December 31, 19X1, and post the amounts directly to the T accounts.
3. Determine the revised account balances.
4. Prepare an adjusted trial balance.
5. Prepare an income statement for the three months ended December 31, 19X1, to determine the net income earned by the company or the net loss incurred by the company during that period. [LO2a,2b,2c]

PROBLEM 3–11 *(Comprehensive Review Problem)* Statistics Enterprises was organized as a company on February 1, 19X1. The company's major revenue-producing activity is the processing of payroll and other data for client firms. On October 31, 19X1, nine months after the company had been organized, its owner, L. Sloan, wanted a set of financial statements prepared. The balance in the company's ledger accounts on that date is shown below.

STATISTICS ENTERPRISES
Unadjusted Trial Balance
October 31, 19X1

| | | |
|---|---|---|
| Cash | $ 6,500 | |
| Service Fees Receivable | 4,700 | |
| Prepaid Office Rent | 450 | |
| Prepaid Machine Rental | 1,200 | |
| Supplies on Hand | 610 | |
| Office Equipment | 4,400 | |
| Accounts Payable | | $ 2,200 |
| Notes Payable | | 2,400 |
| Unearned Service Fees | | 4,700 |
| L. Sloan, Capital | | 6,000 |
| Service Fees Earned | | 14,400 |
| Salaries Expense | 9,200 | |
| Maintenance Expense | 390 | |
| Advertising Expense | 450 | |
| Rent Expense | 1,800 | |
| | $29,700 | $29,700 |

Additional Data:

a. Interest accrued on the notes payable amounted to $40 as of October 31.

b. The asset account Prepaid Office Rent shows a two-month advance payment that was made on February 1. At that time it was agreed that this two-month advance payment would apply to October and November 19X1. Of course, no checks would need to be issued for the rent during those two months. The office rents for $225 per month.

c. Supplies remaining on hand cost $170, as determined by a count taken on October 31.

d. Salaries earned by company employees but not yet paid to them amount to $200 on October 31.

e. The new office equipment, purchased on February 3, has an estimated useful life of ten years with no expected residual value.

f. A machine used in the business was rented on February 1, 19X1, for a one-year period. The entire annual rental fee of $1,200 was paid in advance on that date.

g. Some clients willingly made advance payments to the company during its first nine months of operations. These transactions were recorded by debiting the Cash account and crediting the Unearned Service Fees account. The company, of course, understood its obligation to render services to these clients at some future time to earn the amounts paid to the company in advance. Services already rendered on these advance payments amounted to $3,600 as of October 31, 19X1.

h. Some clients pay only after services have been performed. On October 31 services amounting to $900 have been performed but have not yet been billed to the clients and therefore remain unrecorded at this time. (This amount is in addition to the amount that appears in the trial balance.)

Required:

1. Set up T accounts for the accounts listed in the trial balance and these additional accounts: Accumulated Depreciation—Office Equipment, Salaries Payable, Interest Payable, Machine Rental Expense, Depreciation Expense—Equipment, Supplies Expense, and Interest Expense. Post the balances shown in the trial balance to the T accounts.
2. Prepare the adjusting entries needed on October 31, 19X1, and post amounts directly to the T accounts.
3. Prepare an adjusted trial balance.
4. Prepare an income statement for the nine months ended October 31, 19X1.
5. Prepare a capital statement for the nine months ended October 31, 19X1.
6. Prepare a balance sheet as of October 31, 19X1. [LO1b,2a,2b]

## ALTERNATE PROBLEMS

*Round all amounts to the nearest whole dollar.*

PROBLEM 3–1A *(Prepare Adjusting Entries)* (Alternate to Problem 3–1) The Hilly Company operates with an accounting period of one full year ending on December 31. The following information is given as a basis for making adjusting entries on December 31, 19X1. Make the necessary adjusting entries.

a. The Office Supplies account had a $200 debit balance on January 1, and $300 of supplies were purchased during the year. A year-end physical count shows that office supplies costing $150 remain on hand.

b. A three-year fire insurance policy was purchased on January 1, at which time the entire insurance premium cost of $1,500 was debited to the Prepaid Insurance account.

c. Machinery purchased late last year for $21,000 was estimated to have a useful life of six years and a residual value of $3,000. No entry for the current year's depreciation has yet been made.

d. On September 1 cash of $6,000 was received in advance for services to be rendered in the future. The transaction was recorded by debiting the Cash account and crediting the Unearned Service Revenue account. Once again on October 16, cash of $4,300 was received in advance for services, and again the Cash account was debited and the Unearned Service Revenue account was credited. On December 31 it was determined that 90% of the September 1 advance had been earned and 30% of the October 16 advance had been earned.

e. Salaries earned by company employees for the last four days of December have not been paid or recorded. Their earnings for those four days total $1,200.

f. A six-month bank loan for $9,000 was obtained on December 1. Annual interest on the loan is 14% per year. At December 31 no interest has been paid and none has been recorded.

g. On December 21 the company agreed to rent a piece of its equipment to another company. The agreement specified a rental period of no longer than twenty days and no shorter than four days at a cost of $80 per day, payable when the equipment is returned. On December 31 eight workdays have passed since the equipment was rented.

Required:

Make the adjusting entries needed for each of the items *a* through g above. [LO2a]

PROBLEM 3–2A *(Prepare Original and Adjusting Entries)* (Alternate to Problem 3–2) The Universally Smug Company operates a clearinghouse to distribute magazines to customers on a subscription basis. Listed below are seven transactions for the month of October. For each transaction, prepare (1) a journal entry as of the transaction date and (2) an adjusting entry, if one is needed, on October 31, the end of the company's accounting period.

a. On October 1 Universally Smug received a check representing six months' rent for space that will be provided to a client beginning on October 1 and ending on April 1 of the following year. The company charges $300 rent per month.

b. On October 10 Universally Smug purchased office supplies costing $300. A count made on October 31 shows that $200 of supplies are still on hand.

c. On October 10 the company received cash from its magazine subscribers as follows:

  $2,400 for one-year subscriptions

  $5,400 for three-year subscriptions

  $3,000 for five-year subscriptions

  All subscriptions are for monthly publications, the first volume of which was in the mail by October 31.

d. On October 15 a three-year fire insurance policy was purchased by paying the premium of $900 in cash.

e. On October 15 equipment costing $12,000 was purchased by paying $10,000 in cash and promising to pay the balance within sixty days. The equipment has an estimated useful life of ten years with no residual value expected.

f. On October 10 Universally Smug obtained a $10,000 loan from City Bank. This amount, together with interest at 15% per year, is to be paid six months from now on April 10 of next year.

g. On October 21 the company rented a truck from Safe Drive Rental Service. The rental fee was established by a flat rate, payable upon entering the agreement. Universal paid $200 to obtain use of the truck for twenty consecutive days beginning on October 21. (Eleven working days have passed since the equipment was rented.) [LO2a]

PROBLEM 3–3A *(Prepare Adjusting Entries from Two Trial Balances)* (Alternate to Problem 3–7) Both the unadjusted and adjusted trial balances of Mix Company are shown below.

Required:

Analyze the data contained in these trial balances and prepare the nine adjusting entries (already made by the company) that explain the changes in the account balances from the trial balance to the adjusted trial balance. [LO2a]

MIX COMPANY
Trial Balances
November 30, 19X1

| | UNADJUSTED TRIAL BALANCE | | ADJUSTED TRIAL BALANCE | |
|---|---|---|---|---|
| Cash | $ 3,535 | | $ 3,535 | |
| Commissions Receivable | | | 375 | |
| Office Supplies | 1,490 | | 780 | |
| Prepaid Insurance | 1,270 | | 520 | |
| Prepaid Rent | 1,200 | | 900 | |
| Equipment | 8,800 | | 8,800 | |
| Accumulated Depreciation—Equipment | | $ 1,200 | | $ 1,680 |
| Vehicle | 3,700 | | 3,700 | |
| Accumulated Depreciation—Vehicle | | 800 | | 970 |
| Accounts Payable | | 1,010 | | 1,010 |
| Notes Payable | | 1,500 | | 1,500 |
| Salaries Payable | | | | 210 |
| Taxes Payable | | | | 140 |
| Unearned Commissions Revenue | | 320 | | 110 |
| D. Mix, Capital | | 10,000 | | 10,000 |
| D. Mix, Drawings | 3,700 | | 3,700 | |
| Commissions Revenue Earned | | 15,400 | | 15,985 |
| Salaries Expense | 6,200 | | 6,410 | |
| Rent Expense | | | 300 | |
| Office Supplies Expense | | | 710 | |
| Depreciation Expense—Equipment | | | 480 | |
| Depreciation Expense—Vehicle | | | 170 | |
| Insurance Expense | | | 750 | |
| Utilities Expense | 170 | | 170 | |
| Taxes Expense | 165 | | 305 | |
| | $30,230 | $30,230 | $31,605 | $31,605 |

PROBLEM 3-4A *(Prepare Adjusting Entries from Income Statement and Trial Balance)* (Alternate to Problem 3-8) The October income statement for Hadley Company is shown below.

HADLEY COMPANY
Income Statement
For the Month Ended October 31, 19X1

| | | |
|---|---|---|
| Revenue: | | |
| Consulting Fees Earned | | $19,300 |
| Interest Revenue Earned | | 100 |
| | | $19,400 |
| Expenses: | | |
| Salaries | $11,600 | |
| Rent | 1,500 | |
| Travel | 720 | |
| Advertising | 450 | |
| Depreciation | 120 | |
| Office Supplies | 110 | |
| Utilities | 230 | |
| Repairs | 60 | |
| Insurance | 70 | |
| Interest | 50 | |
| Total Expenses | | 14,910 |
| Net Income | | $ 4,490 |

The company's October 31 unadjusted trial balance, which was prepared before its income statement, is shown on page 112.

HADLEY COMPANY
Unadjusted Trial Balance
October 31, 19X1

| | | |
|---|---|---|
| Cash | $ 2,160 | |
| Accounts Receivable | 3,980 | |
| Notes Receivable | 12,000 | |
| Prepaid Insurance | 1,080 | |
| Office Supplies | 560 | |
| Equipment | 13,200 | |
| Accounts Payable | | $ 3,340 |
| Notes Payable | | 5,800 |
| L. Hadley, Capital | | 20,500 |
| L. Hadley, Drawings | 1,400 | |
| Consulting Fees Earned | | 18,700 |
| Salaries Expense | 10,600 | |
| Rent Expense | 1,900 | |
| Travel Expense | 720 | |
| Advertising Expense | 450 | |
| Utilities Expense | 230 | |
| Repairs Expense | 60 | |
| | $48,340 | $48,340 |

Required:

1. Analyze the data contained in the unadjusted trial balance and the October income statement to determine (a) changes made in account balances by adjusting entries and (b) the new accounts established by the adjusting entries.
2. Prepare the eight adjusting entries that explain the changes in accounts and account balances from the unadjusted trial balance to the income statement. [LO2a,2b]

PROBLEM 3–5A *(Prepare Adjusting Entries)* (Alternate to Problem 3–9) On December 31, the company's year-end, the following information was available to help in making adjusting entries. No adjusting entries have been prepared at any time during the company's annual accounting period.

a. When $500 of supplies were purchased during the year, the amount was debited to the Office Supplies account. At year-end the cost of supplies remaining on hand was determined to be $200. No supplies were on hand at the beginning of the year.
b. Salaries are established at $1,500 per five-day workweek. On December 31, 19X1, four days of salaries are earned but unpaid and unrecorded.
c. Two months' interest on investments of $11,000 made by the company has been earned as of year-end but has not yet been received. The investments earn 12% annually.
d. All equipment was acquired during the year and is being depreciated over a four-year estimated useful life. Given below are the costs of three separate equipment purchases made this year together with their estimated residual values.

| | COST | RESIDUAL VALUE |
|---|---|---|
| January 1, 19X1 | $15,000 | $3,000 |
| April 30, 19X1 | 9,000 | -0- |
| September 1, 19X1 | 4,580 | 500 |

Required:
Prepare the adjusting entries needed for each item listed above. [LO2a]

# 4 Completing the Accounting Cycle

## *Learning Objectives*

When you complete this chapter you will be able to

1. Answer the following questions:
   a. What is the purpose of the work sheet and what is its place in the sequence of the accounting cycle?
   b. What are the principal uses of a completed work sheet?
   c. What is the purpose of closing entries?
   d. What is the reason for reversing entries and when are they made?
2. Perform the following accounting functions:
   a. Prepare a ten-column work sheet.
   b. Prepare financial statements from a work sheet.
   c. Record adjusting entries using data from a work sheet.
   d. Journalize closing entries.
   e. Prepare an after-closing trial balance.
   f. Prepare reversing entries.

In the first three chapters we studied a sequence of accounting procedures. Some of these procedures are performed during each accounting period, and others are performed at its end. Taken together, these sequential procedures are known as the *accounting cycle.* In this chapter we will first summarize the complete accounting cycle and then learn how to carry out the procedures we have not yet studied.

## A SUMMARY OF THE ACCOUNTING CYCLE

The sequence of procedures in the accounting cycle was summarized in Chapter 3 as follows:

1. Prepare a chart of accounts.
2. Analyze each completed business transaction.
3. Journalize each completed business transaction.
4. Post amounts from the journal to the appropriate ledger accounts.
5. Obtain balances for all ledger accounts.
6. Prepare a trial balance.
7. Prepare adjusting entries and post their amounts to the ledger accounts.
8. Prepare an adjusted trial balance.
9. Prepare financial statements.

In this chapter we will add the following items to the accounting cycle:

***1a. A work sheet is used as a preliminary step in the preparation of financial statements***

The preparation of a work sheet, which makes it easier for accountants to complete steps 6 through 9 in the sequence

The process of closing out the accounts

To include these items, we expand steps 6 through 9 and add two new steps:

### THE EXPANSION OF STEPS 6–9

6. Prepare a trial balance in the first two columns of a work sheet.
7. Adjust the account balances by entering the adjustments within the work sheet.
8. Prepare an adjusted trial balance within the work sheet.
9. Prepare the following financial statements from the data contained within the work sheet:
   a. Income statement
   b. Capital statement (also called statement of owner's equity)
   c. Balance sheet
10. Record the adjusting entries in the general journal, using information available in the adjustments column of the work sheet, and post their amounts to the appropriate accounts in the ledger.

### ADDITIONAL STEPS

11. Record the closing entries and post their amounts to the appropriate accounts in the ledger.
12. Prepare an after-closing trial balance.

## PURPOSE OF THE WORK SHEET

If the reported financial information is to be timely and reliable, end-of-the-period procedures must be completed quickly and without error. To avoid errors in the permanent accounting records and to simplify the work at the end of an accounting period, a work sheet is sometimes prepared.

*1a. A work sheet is a multicolumn form that helps to organize the accounting information needed at the end of an accounting period*

**A work sheet** is a multicolumn form designed to gather and organize in one place information needed to prepare financial statements and to record the adjusting and closing entries. The work sheet is not a permanent accounting record, such as journals and ledgers. Nor does it ever become a public document, such as financial statements. It is merely a useful internal tool prepared by accountants. Although the completed work sheet contains the figures that will appear in the financial statements, you should not consider it a financial statement in itself. It is not a substitute for formal financial reporting.

If a manual system is used, a work sheet is usually prepared in pencil so that items and amounts can easily be erased and changed if necessary. Dollar signs, decimal points, and commas are not used when amounts are entered in the work sheet. If a word processor is used, erasing and revising data on the work sheet is relatively easy. Also, computer programming packages, such as LOTUS, facilitate the preparation of work sheets. In this chapter we will assume the use of a manual system.

*1a. A work sheet is prepared for four principal reasons*

In summary, the principal reasons for preparing a work sheet are to

*Minimize the possibility of making errors in the formal accounting records.* A completed work sheet contains all the accounting information needed to carry out the end-of-the-period accounting. If errors are made when the work sheet is prepared, they are easier to find and correct (by erasure) than would be possible if the errors were in the permanent accounting records such as journals and ledger accounts or in the financial statements themselves.

*Facilitate the recording of adjusting entries.* By having a pair of columns called Adjustments, the completed work sheet gathers in one place the amounts needed to record the adjusting entries in the journal. The design of the work sheet is such that it also lessens the possibility of overlooking an account that needs adjustment.

*Facilitate the recording of closing entries.* As we will see later in this chapter, the closing entries are needed at the end of each annual accounting period. The work sheet facilitates the recording of closing entries because it contains all the information needed to prepare them.

*Facilitate the preparation of financial statements.* The work sheet is a convenient "sorting device" for classifying the adjusted account balances according to the financial statements in which they will appear. Once the figures that belong in the financial statements appear in the work sheet columns designed for them, it is relatively simple to use them in preparing the formal financial statements.

## PREPARING THE WORK SHEET

Before preparing a work sheet, we need to understand its basic format. Although the work sheet is not a financial statement, it has a heading that shows

1. The name of the company
2. The title of the form (work sheet)
3. The period of time it covers

A typical work sheet has ten money columns. The columns are arranged in five pairs, each pair consisting of a debit and a credit column. An example is shown in Exhibit 4–1.

Five steps must be followed in preparing a work sheet. We will describe and illustrate each step sequentially using information from the Windsor Time and Motion company, with which we became acquainted in Chapter 3.

*EXHIBIT 4–1*

Work Sheet Format with No Accounts or Amounts Yet Entered

| ACCOUNT TITLES | TRIAL BALANCE | | ADJUSTMENTS | | ADJUSTED TRIAL BALANCE | | INCOME STATEMENT | | BALANCE SHEET | |
|---|---|---|---|---|---|---|---|---|---|---|
| | **Debit** | **Credit** | **Debit** | **Credit** | **Debit** | **Credit** | **Debit** | **Credit** | **Debit** | **Credit** |

*2a. We prepare a ten-column work sheet in five steps as illustrated in this section*

1. Enter the account titles and balances in the Account Titles and Trial Balance columns.

By introducing the work sheet into the accounting cycle, we have eliminated the need for a separate two-column trial balance. Instead we copy the titles and balances of the accounts as of October 31 directly from the ledger into the Account Titles and Trial Balance columns. After we have entered all account balances on the work sheet, we add the two columns to verify the equality of debit and credit amounts in the ledger, and we enter the trial balance totals. Keep in mind that this is an unadjusted trial balance taken before any adjusting entries have been posted to the accounts.

Exhibit 4–2 shows the work sheet with the company's October 31 trial balance entered in the first two of its ten money columns.

2. Enter the adjustments in the Adjustments columns.

The required adjustments for Windsor Time and Motion were explained in Chapter 3. We now enter these same adjustments in the Adjustments columns of the work sheet. Next we total the columns to make sure that the equality of debit and credit amounts is being maintained. Observe that each amount entered in the Adjustments columns is identified by a separate letter. This letter notation is used to link together the corresponding debit and credit parts of the entry. For example, the first adjustment that recognizes the expired portion of the insurance premium paid in advance is entered in the Adjustments column as a $40 debit (increase) to the Insurance Expense account and a $40 credit (decrease) to the Prepaid Insurance account. The corresponding debit and credit amounts of this entry are identified by the letter *a*.

If an adjustment should be made to an account that already appears in the trial balance, the amount of the adjustment is entered on the same line as the account title. If the adjustment is to an account that is not already in the trial balance, we write the title of the new account in the Account Title column of the work sheet on the first available line below the accounts listed for the trial balance. For example, the Insurance Expense account did not appear in the trial balance and was therefore added on the line below the trial balance totals.

Exhibit 4–3 shows the work sheet with all the account adjustments needed by Windsor Time and Motion entered in the third and fourth money columns called the Adjustments columns.

3. Enter the account balances as adjusted in the Adjusted Trial Balance columns.

To prepare the Adjusted Trial Balance, each account balance in the Trial Balance columns is added to or subtracted from the corresponding amounts, if any, in the Adjustments columns. The combined amounts for each account balance are extended on the same line and entered in the Adjusted Trial Balance columns. This process of combining the amounts entered on each line horizontally throughout the first four columns of the work sheet is called **cross-footing.**

For example, the Office Supplies account shows a debit balance of $390 in the Trial Balance debit column and a credit of $140 from adjustment *b* in the Adjustments credit column. The $390 debit amount and the $140 credit amount are combined to produce $250 (the amount of supplies remaining on hand) in the Adjusted Trial Balance debit column.

The work sheet as it would appear after amounts entered on each line have been combined and extended to the Adjusted Trial Balance columns is shown in Exhibit 4–4.

*EXHIBIT 4–2*

Account Balances are Entered in the Trial Balance Columns

| ACCOUNT TITLES | TRIAL BALANCE | | ADJUSTMENTS | | ADJUSTED TRIAL BALANCE | | INCOME STATEMENT | | BALANCE SHEET | |
|---|---|---|---|---|---|---|---|---|---|---|
| | Debit | Credit | Debit | Credit | Debit | Credit | Debit | Credit | Debit | Credit |
| Cash | 5 210 | | | | | | | | | |
| Accounts Receivable | 4 840 | | | | | | | | | |
| Notes Receivable | 6 000 | | | | | | | | | |
| Office Supplies | 390 | | | | | | | | | |
| Prepaid Insurance | 480 | | | | | | | | | |
| Office Equipment | 12 000 | | | | | | | | | |
| Vehicles | 10 800 | | | | | | | | | |
| Accounts Payable | | 2 830 | | | | | | | | |
| Unearned Rent Revenue | | 600 | | | | | | | | |
| Unearned Consulting Fees | | 1 200 | | | | | | | | |
| Notes Payable | | 4 000 | | | | | | | | |
| J. Lynn, Capital | | 25 000 | | | | | | | | |
| J. Lynn, Drawings | 1 500 | | | | | | | | | |
| Consulting Fees Earned | | 24 370 | | | | | | | | |
| Salaries Expense | 13 400 | | | | | | | | | |
| Rent Expense | 1 600 | | | | | | | | | |
| Travel Expense | 890 | | | | | | | | | |
| Advertising Expense | 540 | | | | | | | | | |
| Utilities Expense | 230 | | | | | | | | | |
| Repairs Expense | 120 | | | | | | | | | |
| Total | 58 000 | 58 000 | | | | | | | | |

*EXHIBIT 4–3*

Adjustments Keyed Together by Letter Notation and Entered in the Adjustments Columns

| ACCOUNT TITLES | TRIAL BALANCE | | ADJUSTMENTS | | ADJUSTED TRIAL BALANCE | | INCOME STATEMENT | | BALANCE SHEET | |
|---|---|---|---|---|---|---|---|---|---|---|
| | Debit | Credit | Debit | Credit | Debit | Credit | Debit | Credit | Debit | Credit |
| Cash | 5 210 | | | | | | | | | |
| Accounts Receivable | 4 840 | | | | | | | | | |
| Notes Receivable | 6 000 | | | | | | | | | |
| Office Supplies | 390 | | | (b) 140 | | | | | | |
| Prepaid Insurance | 480 | | | (a) 40 | | | | | | |
| Office Equipment | 12 000 | | | | | | | | | |
| Vehicles | 10 800 | | | | | | | | | |
| Accounts Payable | | 2 830 | | | | | | | | |
| Unearned Rent Revenue | | 600 | (e) 100 | | | | | | | |
| Unearned Consulting Fees | | 1 200 | (f) 480 | | | | | | | |
| Notes Payable | | 4 000 | | | | | | | | |
| J. Lynn, Capital | | 25 000 | | | | | | | | |
| J. Lynn, Drawings | 1 500 | | | | | | | | | |
| Consulting Fees Earned | | 24 370 | | (f) 480 | | | | | | |
| Salaries Expense | 13 400 | | (g) 670 | | | | | | | |
| Rent Expense | 1 600 | | | | | | | | | |
| Travel Expense | 890 | | | | | | | | | |
| Advertising Expense | 540 | | | | | | | | | |
| Utilities Expense | 230 | | | | | | | | | |
| Repairs Expense | 120 | | | | | | | | | |
| Total | 58 000 | 58 000 | | | | | | | | |
| Insurance Expense | | | (a) 40 | | | | | | | |
| Office Supplies Expense | | | (b) 140 | | | | | | | |
| Depreciation Expense–Office Equipment | | | (c) 125 | | | | | | | |
| Accumulated Depreciation–Office Equipment | | | | (c) 125 | | | | | | |
| Depreciation Expense–Vehicles | | | (d) 170 | | | | | | | |
| Accumulated Depreciation–Vehicles | | | | (d) 170 | | | | | | |
| Rent Revenue Earned | | | | (i) 200<br>(e) 100 | | | | | | |
| Salaries Payable | | | | (g) 670 | | | | | | |
| Interest Expense | | | (h) 50 | | | | | | | |
| Interest Payable | | | | (h) 50 | | | | | | |
| Rent Receivable | | | (i) 200 | | | | | | | |
| Interest Receivable | | | (j) 60 | | | | | | | |
| Interest Revenue Earned | | | | (j) 60 | | | | | | |
| Total | | | 2 035 | 2 035 | | | | | | |

*EXHIBIT 4–4*

Adjusted Account Balances Entered in the Adjusted Trial Balance Columns

| ACCOUNT TITLES | TRIAL BALANCE | | ADJUSTMENTS | | ADJUSTED TRIAL BALANCE | | INCOME STATEMENT | | BALANCE SHEET | |
|---|---|---|---|---|---|---|---|---|---|---|
| | Debit | Credit | Debit | Credit | Debit | Credit | Debit | Credit | Debit | Credit |
| Cash | 5 210 | | | | 5 210 | | | | | |
| Accounts Receivable | 4 840 | | | | 4 840 | | | | | |
| Notes Receivable | 6 000 | | | | 6 000 | | | | | |
| Office Supplies | 390 | | | (b) 140 | 250 | | | | | |
| Prepaid Insurance | 480 | | | (a) 40 | 440 | | | | | |
| Office Equipment | 12 000 | | | | 12 000 | | | | | |
| Vehicles | 10 800 | | | | 10 800 | | | | | |
| Accounts Payable | | 2 830 | | | | 2 830 | | | | |
| Unearned Rent Revenue | | 600 | (e) 100 | | | 500 | | | | |
| Unearned Consulting Fees | | 1 200 | (f) 480 | | | 720 | | | | |
| Notes Payable | | 4 000 | | | | 4 000 | | | | |
| J. Lynn, Capital | | 25 000 | | | | 25 000 | | | | |
| J. Lynn, Drawings | 1 500 | | | | 1 500 | | | | | |
| Consulting Fees Earned | | 24 370 | | (f) 480 | | 24 850 | | | | |
| Salaries Expense | 13 400 | | (g) 670 | | 14 070 | | | | | |
| Rent Expense | 1 600 | | | | 1 600 | | | | | |
| Travel Expense | 890 | | | | 890 | | | | | |
| Advertising Expense | 540 | | | | 540 | | | | | |
| Utilities Expense | 230 | | | | 230 | | | | | |
| Repairs Expense | 120 | | | | 120 | | | | | |
| Total | 58 000 | 58 000 | | | | | | | | |
| Insurance Expense | | | (a) 40 | | 40 | | | | | |
| Office Supplies Expense | | | (b) 140 | | 140 | | | | | |
| Depreciation Expense—Office Equipment | | | (c) 125 | | 125 | | | | | |
| Accumulated Depreciation—Office Equipment | | | | (c) 125 | | 125 | | | | |
| Depreciation Expense—Vehicles | | | (d) 170 | | 170 | | | | | |
| Accumulated Depreciation—Vehicles | | | | (d) 170 | | 170 | | | | |
| Rent Revenue Earned | | | | (i) 200<br>(e) 100 | | 300 | | | | |
| Salaries Payable | | | | (g) 670 | | 670 | | | | |
| Interest Expense | | | (h) 50 | | 50 | | | | | |
| Interest Payable | | | | (h) 50 | | 50 | | | | |
| Rent Receivable | | | (i) 200 | | 200 | | | | | |
| Interest Receivable | | | (j) 60 | | 60 | | | | | |
| Interest Revenue Earned | | | | (j) 60 | | 60 | | | | |
| Total | | | 2 035 | 2 035 | 59 275 | 59 275 | | | | |

4. Extend every account balance shown in the Adjusted Trial Balance columns to the Income Statement or the Balance Sheet columns.

Revenue and expense account balances are extended to the proper Income Statement debit or credit column. Asset and liability accounts and the two accounts—owner's capital and drawings—have their balances extended to the proper Balance Sheet debit or credit column. Extending of account balances should be done on a line-by-line basis, beginning with the first account listed, which is usually the Cash account. This procedure helps to reduce errors that can be made during the extension process, especially the common error of overlooking an amount that needs to be extended.

Exhibit 4–5 shows the work sheet with each amount taken from the adjusted trial balance extended to the proper financial statement column. Note that each amount in the Adjusted Trial Balance columns must be extended to only one of the four financial statement columns.

5. Total the Income Statement columns and the Balance Sheet columns. Enter the net income or net loss as a balancing figure in both the Income Statement and Balance Sheet columns and compute the four column totals again.

After all amounts have been extended to the last four columns, these columns are totaled by *footing* them. **Footing** is the addition or subtraction of items in a vertical column. Note that this has been done in Exhibit 4–6 and the totals appear as follows: Income Statement debit and credit columns, respectively, $17,975 and $25,210; Balance Sheet debit and credit columns, $41,300 and $34,065. The difference between the totals in the Income Statement columns is the net income or net loss for the period. In our illustration, revenues earned exceeded expenses incurred by $7,235 ($25,210 − $17,975), which is the Windsor Time and Motion company's net income for the month of October. The net income amount is entered in the Income Statement debit column to balance the two columns and also in the Balance Sheet credit column to balance those two columns (the owner's equity is increased by net income). A completed work sheet with all amounts extended and all columns totaled appears in Exhibit 4–6.

If the Balance Sheet columns do not have equal totals after the computed net income or net loss has been entered in the appropriate Balance Sheet column, one of the following types of errors may have occurred:

1. An account balance may not have been extended.
2. A balance may have been extended to the wrong column.
3. An error may have been made when adding one of the columns.

The fact that Balance Sheet columns have equal totals, however, does not ensure accuracy. For example, if an asset account balance is incorrectly extended to the debit column of the income statement or a revenue account balance is incorrectly extended to the credit column of the balance sheet, all work sheet columns will balance. But the net income and some other financial statement figures are wrong.

## USES OF THE COMPLETED WORK SHEET

The work sheet is useful because it summarizes in one place (on a ten-column form) information found in a number of other places (various financial records such as journals, ledgers, and statements). For example, by looking at a work

*EXHIBIT 4–5*

Account Balances Extended from the Adjusted Trial Balance Columns to the Income Statement and Balance Sheet Columns

| ACCOUNT TITLES | TRIAL BALANCE | | ADJUSTMENTS | | ADJUSTED TRIAL BALANCE | | INCOME STATEMENT | | BALANCE SHEET | |
|---|---|---|---|---|---|---|---|---|---|---|
| | Debit | Credit | Debit | Credit | Debit | Credit | Debit | Credit | Debit | Credit |
| Cash | 5 210 | | | | 5 210 | | | | 5 210 | |
| Accounts Receivable | 4 840 | | | | 4 840 | | | | 4 840 | |
| Notes Receivable | 6 000 | | | | 6 000 | | | | 6 000 | |
| Office Supplies | 390 | | | (b) 140 | 250 | | | | 250 | |
| Prepaid Insurance | 480 | | | (a) 40 | 440 | | | | 440 | |
| Office Equipment | 12 000 | | | | 12 000 | | | | 12 000 | |
| Vehicles | 10 800 | | | | 10 800 | | | | 10 800 | |
| Accounts Payable | | 2 830 | | | | 2 830 | | | | 2 830 |
| Unearned Rent Revenue | | 600 | (e) 100 | | | 500 | | | | 500 |
| Unearned Consulting Fees | | 1 200 | (f) 480 | | | 720 | | | | 720 |
| Notes Payable | | 4 000 | | | | 4 000 | | | | 4 000 |
| J. Lynn, Capital | | 25 000 | | | | 25 000 | | | | 25 000 |
| J. Lynn, Drawings | 1 500 | | | | 1 500 | | | | 1 500 | |
| Consulting Fees Earned | | 24 370 | | (f) 480 | | 24 850 | | 24 850 | | |
| Salaries Expense | 13 400 | | (g) 670 | | 14 070 | | 14 070 | | | |
| Rent Expense | 1 600 | | | | 1 600 | | 1 600 | | | |
| Travel Expense | 890 | | | | 890 | | 890 | | | |
| Advertising Expense | 540 | | | | 540 | | 540 | | | |
| Utilities Expense | 230 | | | | 230 | | 230 | | | |
| Repairs Expense | 120 | | | | 120 | | 120 | | | |
| Total | 58 000 | 58 000 | | | | | | | | |
| Insurance Expense | | | (a) 40 | | 40 | | 40 | | | |
| Office Supplies Expense | | | (b) 140 | | 140 | | 140 | | | |
| Depreciation Expense—Office Equipment | | | (c) 125 | | 125 | | 125 | | | |
| Accumulated Depreciation—Office Equipment | | | | (c) 125 | | 125 | | | | 125 |
| Depreciation Expense—Vehicles | | | (d) 170 | | 170 | | 170 | | | |
| Accumulated Depreciation—Vehicles | | | | (d) 170 | | 170 | | | | 170 |
| Rent Revenue Earned | | | | (i) 200<br>(e) 100 | | 300 | | 300 | | |
| Salaries Payable | | | | (g) 670 | | 670 | | | | 670 |
| Interest Expense | | | (h) 50 | | 50 | | 50 | | | |
| Interest Payable | | | | (h) 50 | | 50 | | | | 50 |
| Rent Receivable | | | (i) 200 | | 200 | | | | 200 | |
| Interest Receivable | | | (j) 60 | | 60 | | | | 60 | |
| Interest Revenue Earned | | | | (j) 60 | | 60 | | 60 | | |
| Total | | | 2 035 | 2 035 | 59 275 | 59 275 | | | | |

*EXHIBIT 4–6*

WINDSOR TIME AND MOTION

**Work Sheet**

**For the Month Ended October 31, 19X1**

| ACCOUNT TITLES | Trial Balance | | Adjustments | | Adjusted Trial Balance | | Income Statement | | Balance Sheet | |
|---|---|---|---|---|---|---|---|---|---|---|
| | Debit | Credit | Debit | Credit | Debit | Credit | Debit | Credit | Debit | Credit |
| Cash | 5 210 | | | | 5 210 | | | | 5 210 | |
| Accounts Receivable | 4 840 | | | | 4 840 | | | | 4 840 | |
| Notes Receivable | 6 000 | | | | 6 000 | | | | 6 000 | |
| Office Supplies | 390 | | | (b) 140 | 250 | | | | 250 | |
| Prepaid Insurance | 480 | | | (a) 40 | 440 | | | | 440 | |
| Office Equipment | 12 000 | | | | 12 000 | | | | 12 000 | |
| Vehicles | 10 800 | | | | 10 800 | | | | 10 800 | |
| Accounts Payable | | 2 830 | | | | 2 830 | | | | 2 830 |
| Unearned Rent Revenue | | 600 | (e) 100 | | | 500 | | | | 500 |
| Unearned Consulting Fees | | 1 200 | (f) 480 | | | 720 | | | | 720 |
| Notes Payable | | 4 000 | | | | 4 000 | | | | 4 000 |
| J. Lynn, Capital | | 25 000 | | | | 25 000 | | | | 25 000 |
| J. Lynn, Drawings | 1 500 | | | | 1 500 | | | | 1 500 | |
| Consulting Fees Earned | | 24 370 | | (f) 480 | | 24 850 | | 24 850 | | |
| Salaries Expense | 13 400 | | (g) 670 | | 14 070 | | 14 070 | | | |
| Rent Expense | 1 600 | | | | 1 600 | | 1 600 | | | |
| Travel Expense | 890 | | | | 890 | | 890 | | | |
| Advertising Expense | 540 | | | | 540 | | 540 | | | |
| Utilities Expense | 230 | | | | 230 | | 230 | | | |
| Repairs Expense | 120 | | | | 120 | | 120 | | | |
| Total | 58 000 | 58 000 | | | | | | | | |
| Insurance Expense | | | (a) 40 | | 40 | | 40 | | | |
| Office Supplies Expense | | | (b) 140 | | 140 | | 140 | | | |
| Depreciation Expense—Office Equipment | | | (c) 125 | | 125 | | 125 | | | |
| Accumulated Depreciation—Office Equipment | | | | (c) 125 | | 125 | | | | 125 |
| Depreciation Expense—Vehicles | | | (d) 170 | | 170 | | 170 | | | |
| Accumulated Depreciation—Vehicles | | | | (d) 170 | | 170 | | | | 170 |
| Rent Revenue Earned | | | | (i) 200<br>(e) 100 | | 300 | | 300 | | |
| Salaries Payable | | | | (g) 670 | | 670 | | | | 670 |
| Interest Expense | | | (h) 50 | | 50 | | 50 | | | |
| Interest Payable | | | | (h) 50 | | 50 | | | | 50 |
| Rent Receivable | | | (i) 200 | | 200 | | | | 200 | |
| Interest Receivable | | | (j) 60 | | 60 | | | | 60 | |
| Interest Revenue Earned | | | | (j) 60 | | 60 | | 60 | | |
| Total | | | 2 035 | 2 035 | 59 275 | 59 275 | 17 975 | 25 210 | 41 300 | 34 065 |
| Net Income | | | | | | | 7 235 | | | 7 235 |
| | | | | | | | 25 210 | 25 210 | 41 300 | 41 300 |

sheet we can see

The sources and the amount of revenues earned during the accounting period
The types and the amount of expenses incurred during the accounting period
The net income or net loss for the accounting period
The firm's cash position at the end of the accounting period
How much money is owed to the company at the end of the accounting period
How much money the company owes to others at the end of the accounting period

Generally, however, the work sheet is thought of as a tool used by the accountant to facilitate procedures required at the end of the accounting period. Once the work sheet is completed, it is used to

*1b. A completed work sheet has three principal uses*

1. Prepare the financial statements
2. Record the adjusting entries
3. Record the closing entries

We will now describe how the work sheet is used during each of these steps in the accounting cycle.

## Preparing the Financial Statements

*2b. Preparation of an income statement from a completed work sheet is shown in Exhibit 4–7*

After the work sheet has been completed, preparing the financial statements is relatively easy because all account balances have been sorted into Income Statement and Balance Sheet columns. The income statement shown in Exhibit 4–7 is prepared from the account balances listed in the Income Statement columns of the work sheet in Exhibit 4–6.

A second statement, referred to earlier as the capital statement, can also be prepared from the work sheet. The items needed for this statement are: the owner's capital account balance at the beginning of the period, the net income for the period, and the amount of drawings made by the owner during the period. All of these items are contained in the Balance Sheet columns of Exhibit 4–6.

EXHIBIT 4–7

WINDSOR TIME AND MOTION
Income Statement
For the Month Ended October 31, 19X1

| | | |
|---|---|---|
| Revenues: | | |
| Consulting Fees Earned | | $24,850 |
| Rent Revenue Earned | | 300 |
| Interest Revenue Earned | | 60 |
| Total Revenue | | $25,210 |
| Expenses: | | |
| Salaries | $14,070 | |
| Rent | 1,600 | |
| Travel | 890 | |
| Advertising | 540 | |
| Utilities | 230 | |
| Repairs | 120 | |
| Insurance | 40 | |
| Office Supplies | 140 | |
| Depreciation—Office Equipment | 125 | |
| Depreciation—Vehicles | 170 | |
| Interest | 50 | |
| Total Expenses | | 17,975 |
| Net Income | | $ 7,235 |

*2b. Preparation of a capital statement and balance sheet from the completed work sheet is shown in Exhibits 4–8 and 4–9*

The capital statement, and the balance sheet of Windsor Time and Motion, with figures taken from the Balance Sheet columns of the work sheet, are shown in Exhibits 4–8 and 4–9.

Note that the amounts shown for (1) total assets and (2) total liabilities and owner's equity in the formal balance sheet do not agree with the amounts shown as totals of the Balance Sheet columns in the work sheet. This is because of the contra accounts. The balances in the contra accounts (Accumulated Depreciation—Office Equipment and Accumulated Depreciation—Vehicles) are subtracted from the balances of their respective asset accounts in the balance sheet. The balance in the contra account (S. Lynn, Drawings) is subtracted in the capital statement to arrive at the October 31, 19X1 balance of S. Lynn, Capital.

*EXHIBIT 4–8*

WINDSOR TIME AND MOTION
Capital Statement
For the Month Ended October 31, 19X1

| | |
|---|---|
| J. Lynn, Capital, Oct. 1, 19X1 | $25,000 |
| Add: Net income for October | 7,235 |
| Subtotal | $32,235 |
| Deduct: Withdrawals during October | 1,500 |
| J. Lynn, Capital, Oct. 31, 19X1 | $30,735 |

*EXHIBIT 4–9*

WINDSOR TIME AND MOTION
Balance Sheet
October 31, 19X1

| | | | |
|---|---|---|---|
| **ASSETS** | | | |
| Current Assets: | | | |
| Cash | | | $ 5,210 |
| Accounts Receivable | | | 4,840 |
| Notes Receivable | | | 6,000 |
| Rent Receivable | | | 200 |
| Interest Receivable | | | 60 |
| Office Supplies | | | 250 |
| Prepaid Insurance | | | 440 |
| Total Current Assets | | | $17,000 |
| Plant and Equipment Assets: | | | |
| Office Equipment | $12,000 | | |
| Less: Accumulated Depreciation | 125 | $11,875 | |
| Vehicles | $10,800 | | |
| Less: Accumulated Depreciation | 170 | 10,630 | |
| Total Plant and Equipment Assets | | | 22,505 |
| Total Assets | | | $39,505 |
| **LIABILITIES AND OWNER'S EQUITY** | | | |
| Current Liabilities: | | | |
| Accounts Payable | | | $ 2,830 |
| Salaries Payable | | | 670 |
| Interest Payable | | | 50 |
| Unearned Rent Revenue | | | 500 |
| Unearned Consulting Fees | | | 720 |
| Notes Payable | | | 4,000 |
| Total Current Liabilities | | | $ 8,770 |
| Owner's Equity: | | | |
| J. Lynn, Capital | | | 30,735 |
| Total Liabilities and Owner's Equity | | | $39,505 |

## Recording the Adjusting Entries

*2c. Using the work sheet to record adjusting entries is illustrated here*

After the financial statements have been prepared, the adjusting entries are recorded in the journal and posted to the ledger. This step is needed so that the ledger account balances will agree with those shown in the work sheet and in the financial statements. The information needed for the adjusting entries, along with the amount and the title of the accounts to be debited and credited, appears in the completed work sheet.

The adjusting entries for Windsor Time and Motion are shown as they would appear after they had been recorded in the general journal on page 127.

## Recording the Closing Entries

The accounts for revenues, expenses, and drawings are used to record financial activities that cause owner's equity to change over a period of time. These accounts are called **temporary accounts** because after they have been used to accumulate data that cause owner's equity to change for a specified period (usually one year), we transfer their balances to a permanent type of account. This process is often referred to as the closing process. It allows us to start with a zero balance in each temporary account as we begin to accumulate revenue, expense, and drawings data for the next accounting period.

*1c. The purpose of closing entries is discussed here*

The journal entries made to transfer amounts from the temporary accounts (reduce the balances in those accounts to zero) are called **closing entries.** The purposes of closing entries are

1. To close the balance in all temporary accounts. By *close* we mean reduce the account balance to zero. By starting the new accounting period with zero balances in all temporary accounts, we separate the information accumulated in them during the last period from the information to be accumulated for the next period.
2. To produce an updated (end-of-the-period) balance in the owner's capital account. The balance in that account is then the same as the figure shown for owner's capital in the period-end balance sheet.

In carrying out the closing process, we establish a new temporary account called the **Income Summary account** (sometimes referred to as the ***Revenue and Expense Summary*** account or ***Profit and Loss Summary*** account). This account is used only in the end-of-the-period closing process. It summarizes all revenue and expense account balances and provides a single net income or net loss figure that must be transferred to the owner's capital account. As we shall see, the balance in the Income Summary account is also the net income or net loss for the period and must therefore be transferred to the owner's capital account.

Closing entries are generally prepared by following four sequential steps:

1. Close all revenue accounts by transferring the balance in each revenue account to the Income Summary account.
2. Close all expense accounts by transferring the balance in each expense account to the Income Summary account.
3. Close the Income Summary account by transferring its balance to the owner's capital account.
4. Close the Drawings account by transferring its balance to the owner's capital account.

## Closing Entries Illustrated

Many companies prepare monthly statements, but most of these companies close their accounts only once a year (any twelve-month period can constitute a year). For purposes of this illustration, however, we will record entries to close all the

GENERAL JOURNAL PAGE 5

| DATE | | ACCOUNT TITLES AND EXPLANATION | POST. REF. | DEBIT | CREDIT |
|---|---|---|---|---|---|
| 19X1 Oct. | 31 | Insurance Expense | | 40 | |
| | | Prepaid Insurance | | | 40 |
| | | To record insurance expense for October | | | |
| | | | | | |
| | 31 | Office Supplies Expense | | 140 | |
| | | Office Supplies | | | 140 |
| | | To record office supplies used in October | | | |
| | | | | | |
| | 31 | Depreciation Expense—Office Equipment | | 125 | |
| | | Accumulated Depreciation—Office Equipment | | | 125 |
| | | To record office equipment depreciation for October | | | |
| | | | | | |
| | 31 | Depreciation Expense—Vehicles | | 170 | |
| | | Accumulated Depreciation—Vehicles | | | 170 |
| | | To record depreciation of vehicles for October | | | |
| | | | | | |
| | 31 | Unearned Rent Revenue | | 100 | |
| | | Rent Revenue Earned | | | 100 |
| | | To record rent revenue earned during October | | | |
| | | | | | |
| | 31 | Unearned Consulting Fees | | 480 | |
| | | Consulting Fees Earned | | | 480 |
| | | To record fees earned during October | | | |
| | | | | | |
| | 31 | Salaries Expense | | 670 | |
| | | Salaries Payable | | | 670 |
| | | To record earned but unpaid October salaries | | | |
| | | | | | |
| | 31 | Interest Expense | | 50 | |
| | | Interest Payable | | | 50 |
| | | To record interest expense applicable to October | | | |
| | | | | | |
| | 31 | Rent Receivable | | 200 | |
| | | Rent Revenue Earned | | | 200 |
| | | To record rent revenue earned during October | | | |
| | | | | | |
| | 31 | Interest Receivable | | 60 | |
| | | Interest Revenue Earned | | | 60 |
| | | To record interest revenue earned during October | | | |

temporary accounts (revenue, expense, and owner's drawings) of Windsor Time and Motion on October 31, one month after the firm began operations.

*2d. We use amounts from the completed work sheet to record closing entries*

The information needed to prepare closing entries is available in the work sheet (Exhibit 4–6). The process is discussed and illustrated in four steps below.

**CLOSING THE REVENUE ACCOUNTS TO THE INCOME SUMMARY ACCOUNT** Revenue accounts have credit balances. Therefore, to reduce a revenue account balance to zero, it must be debited for an amount equal to its credit balance. The credit portion of the entry is made to the Income Summary account. The compound entry needed to close the three revenue accounts of Windsor Time and Motion is as follows:

| | | | |
|---|---|---|---|
| Oct. 31 | Consulting Fees Earned | 24,850 | |
| | Rent Revenue Earned | 300 | |
| | Interest Revenue Earned | 60 | |
| | Income Summary | | 25,210 |
| | To close the revenue accounts | | |

**CLOSING THE EXPENSE ACCOUNTS TO THE INCOME SUMMARY ACCOUNT** Expense accounts have debit balances. Each expense account is therefore credited for an amount equal to its balance, and the Income Summary account is debited for an amount equal to the total of the individual credits. The following entry is needed to close Windsor Time and Motion's expense accounts and transfer the sum of their balances to the Income Summary account:

| | | | |
|---|---|---|---|
| Oct. 31 | Income Summary | 17,975 | |
| | Salaries Expense | | 14,070 |
| | Rent Expense | | 1,600 |
| | Travel Expense | | 890 |
| | Advertising Expense | | 540 |
| | Utilities Expense | | 230 |
| | Repairs Expense | | 120 |
| | Insurance Expense | | 40 |
| | Office Supplies Expense | | 140 |
| | Depreciation Expense—Office Equipment | | 125 |
| | Depreciation Expense—Vehicles | | 170 |
| | Interest Expense | | 50 |
| | To close the expense accounts | | |

**CLOSING THE INCOME SUMMARY ACCOUNT TO THE CAPITAL ACCOUNT** After the entries to close the revenue and expense accounts have been posted, the balance in the Income Summary account is equal to the net income or net loss for the period.

> If the company had a *net income*, the Income Summary account has a *credit balance*, and the owner's capital account must be *increased* by that amount.
>
> Conversely, if the company had a *net loss*, the Income Summary account has a *debit balance*, and the owner's capital account must be *decreased* by that amount.

In any case, the balance in the Income Summary account must be transferred to the owner's capital account. Since Windsor Time and Motion had a net income of $7,235 for the one-month period ending on October 31, 19X1, the credit balance in its Income Summary account is transferred to the J. Lynn, Capital, account by the following entry:

| | | | |
|---|---|---|---|
| Oct. 31 | Income Summary | 7,235 | |
| | J. Lynn, Capital | | 7,235 |
| | To close the Income Summary account | | |

The effect of this entry is not only to close the temporary Income Summary account but also to transfer the balance in the account, representing net income, to J. Lynn's Capital account.

CLOSING THE DRAWINGS ACCOUNT TO THE CAPITAL ACCOUNT The owner's drawing account has a debit balance before the closing entries are posted. The amount in this account shows how much owner's equity was decreased during the period when the owner withdrew cash or other assets from the business for personal use. To establish the proper ending balance in the owner's capital account and to establish zero balances in the temporary accounts, we now close the drawings account by making the following entry:

| | | | |
|---|---|---|---|
| Oct. 31 | J. Lynn, Capital | 1,500 | |
| | J. Lynn, Drawings | | 1,500 |
| | To close the owner's drawings account | | |

## A SUMMARY OF THE CLOSING PROCESS

*2d. When we journalize closing entries, we use four procedures*

Let us summarize the procedures required in the closing process:

1. Close all revenue accounts by *debiting* each of them for the amount of their balances and *crediting* the *Income Summary* account for the sum of the individual debits.
2. Close all expense accounts by *crediting* each of them for the amount of their balances and *debiting* the *Income Summary* account for the sum of the individual credits.
3. Close the Income Summary account. A net income will be indicated when the account has a credit balance. In this case, *debit* the *account* for its balance and *credit* the *owner's capital account.* A net loss will be indicated when the account has a debit balance. In this case, *credit* the *account* for its balance and *debit* the *owner's capital account.*
4. Close the drawings account by *crediting* it for an amount equal to its balance and *debiting* the *owner's capital account* for the same amount.

After these steps have been completed, the revenue and expense accounts have zero balances and are ready for accumulation of the next period's revenues and expenses. The owner's drawing account and the Income Summary account also have zero balances. Furthermore, after all closing entries are recorded and posted, the balance in the owner's capital account is the same dollar figure that is shown for the owner's capital in the end of the period balance sheet.

Closing entries are necessary, not optional. For example, if Windsor's revenue accounts were not closed, they would continue to accumulate revenue data indefinitely. Thus they would have balances that represented the sum of many years of revenue-producing activities rather than having balances that represented the revenue-producing activities of the current year. Of course, the same would be true of expense accounts and the owner's drawing account if they were not closed.

Using the balances found in each of Windsor's temporary accounts, we can diagram the effects of the closing process, as shown in Exhibit 4–10.

*EXHIBIT 4–10*

Effects of the Closing Process

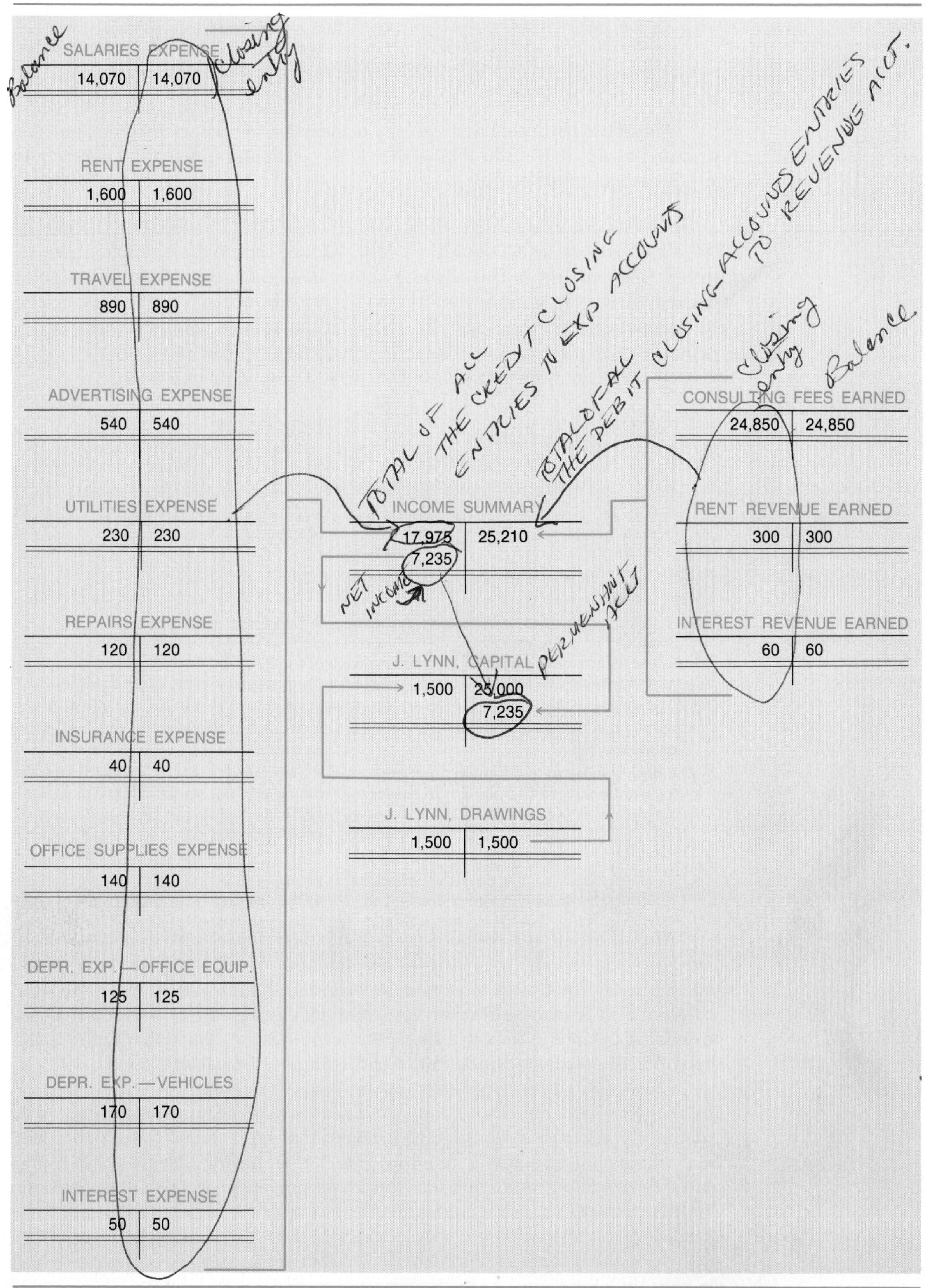

## THE AFTER-CLOSING TRIAL BALANCE

*2e. We prepare an after-closing trial balance after all temporary accounts have been closed*

To complete the accounting cycle after the revenue, expense, and owner's drawings accounts have been closed and the closing entries have been posted, we prepare an *after-closing trial balance.* The purpose of an **after-closing** (sometimes called **post-closing) trial balance** is to verify the equality of debit and credit amounts in the ledger accounts before we begin to accumulate information for the next accounting period. Because the closing process created zero balances in all temporary accounts, only the **permanent accounts** (all asset and liability accounts and the owner's capital account) will appear in the after-closing trial balance.

Windsor Time and Motion's after-closing trial balance is shown in Exhibit 4–11.

EXHIBIT 4–11

WINDSOR TIME AND MOTION
After-Closing Trial Balance
October 31, 19X1

| ACCOUNT TITLE | ACCOUNT BALANCE Debit | Credit |
|---|---|---|
| Cash | $ 5,210 | |
| Accounts Receivable | 4,840 | |
| Notes Receivable | 6,000 | |
| Rent Receivable | 200 | |
| Interest Receivable | 60 | |
| Office Supplies | 250 | |
| Prepaid Insurance | 440 | |
| Office Equipment | 12,000 | |
| Accumulated Depreciation—Office Equipment | | $ 125 |
| Vehicles | 10,800 | |
| Accumulated Depreciation—Vehicles | | 170 |
| Accounts Payable | | 2,830 |
| Salaries Payable | | 670 |
| Interest Payable | | 50 |
| Unearned Rent Revenue | | 500 |
| Unearned Consulting Fees | | 720 |
| Notes Payable | | 4,000 |
| J. Lynn, Capital | | 30,735 |
| | $39,800 | $39,800 |

## A COMMENT CONCERNING THE ACCOUNTING PERIOD

The maximum length of an accounting period is twelve consecutive months. Any twelve-month annual accounting period adopted by a company is referred to as the **fiscal year.** Fiscal years generally begin with the first day of a particular month selected by the company and end on the last day of the twelfth month from that point. Most companies choose to end their accounting period on December 31, although other twelve-month periods may be selected. Companies closing their accounting period on December 31 are said to have chosen a *calendar year-end.*

A fiscal year that ends when a firm's seasonal activities have reached the lowest point in its annual operating cycle is referred to as the **natural business year.** For example, the United Brands Company has a fiscal year ending on June 30; the fiscal year selected by the federal government begins on October 1 and ends twelve months later on September 30.

## REVERSING ENTRIES

### Why Reversing Entries Are Made

After the financial statements have been prepared and the closing entries have been recorded and posted, companies may choose to reverse some of their adjusting entries before entering transactions of the next accounting period. The entries made for this purpose are called **reversing entries** because the debits and credits are the reverse of those in the adjusting entries to which they relate. The reversing entry contains the same account titles and dollar amounts as the related adjusting entry, but the date is the first day of the next accounting period.

*1d. Reversing entries simplify the recording of a related entry in the next accounting period*

Reversing entries are optional, not required. The purpose of a reversing entry is to simplify the recording of a related entry in the next accounting period. Thus reversing entries may be beneficial when a company makes a lot of adjusting entries.

### Recording Reversing Entries

We will illustrate the reason for and the mechanics of reversing entries by referring to two adjusting entries taken from the Windsor Time and Motion examples shown earlier in the chapter.

Recall that the company's employees earned a salary on the last day of the accounting period (October 31, 19X1), which had not yet been paid or recorded. To record this one day of earned but unpaid salary, the following adjusting entry was made:

*2f. Two examples here show how reversing entries are prepared*

| | | | |
|---|---|---|---|
| Oct. 31 | Salaries Expense | 670 | |
| | Salaries Payable | | 670 |
| | To record earned but unpaid October salaries | | |

The next time salaries were paid (payday) was Friday, November 4, which is a date in the next accounting period. If the October 31 adjusting entry is not reversed, the following entry is made on November 4 to record payment of the payroll:

| | | | |
|---|---|---|---|
| Nov. 4 | Salaries Payable | 670 | |
| | Salaries Expense | 2,680 | |
| | Cash | | 3,350 |
| | To record payment of weekly salaries | | |

The entry on November 4 requires two debits—one to eliminate the liability account and the other to record the four days of salary expense applicable to November. Although this entry is not particularly difficult, bookkeeping could be simplified and errors avoided if every weekly salary payment (all fifty-two payments) were recorded in the same way. Thus on every payday the Salaries Expense account would be debited for a full week's pay, and the Cash account would be credited for an equal amount.

To accomplish this simplification, a reversing entry must be recorded on the first day of the next accounting period (November 1) to reverse the effects of the adjusting entry recorded on October 31. The accrued salaries adjusting entry of October 31 is reversed as follows:

| | | | |
|---|---|---|---|
| Nov. 1 | Salaries Payable .................................... | 670 | |
| | Salaries Expense ................................ | | 670 |
| | To reverse the accrued salaries adjusting entry | | |

Because the reversing entry was recorded and posted to the accounts, the Salaries Payable account now has a zero balance. The salary payment on November 4 can be recorded in the same way as each of the other fifty-one salary payments made throughout the year, as follows:

| | | | |
|---|---|---|---|
| Nov. 1 | Salaries Expense.................................... | 3,350 | |
| | Cash.......................................... | | 3,350 |
| | To record payment of weekly salaries | | |

After this entry has been posted, the Salaries Expense account, which was adjusted and closed on October 31, and reversed for $670 on November 1, would have a debit balance of $2,680 as shown in the T account below.

SALARIES EXPENSE

| | | | |
|---|---|---|---|
| Oct. 31 (Adjusting Entry) | 670 | Oct. 31 (Closing Entry) | 670 |
| Nov. 4 (Payment Entry) | 3,350 | Nov. 1 (Reversing Entry) | 670 |
| *Balance $2,680* | | | |

The $2,680 balance in the account represents the correct salaries expense for four workdays in November, calculated at $670 per day. The final balances in all affected accounts are the same whether reversing entries are used or not. However, by making a reversing entry on November 1, the recording of the payroll payment on November 4 is simplified.

For another example of an adjusting entry that can be reversed, refer to Windsor's agreement to rent parking spaces to a neighboring firm. In that situation, $200 of rent revenue was earned but not yet received on October 31, the end of the accounting period. As you will recall, to account for this situation we made the following adjusting entry:

| | | | |
|---|---|---|---|
| Oct. 31 | Rent Receivable.................................... | 200 | |
| | Rent Revenue Earned .......................... | | 200 |
| | To record rent revenue earned during October | | |

If the October 31 adjusting entry for rent receivable is not reversed, the entry to record receipt of the rent check on November 15 would be as follows (note that two credits are needed in the entry):

| | | | |
|---|---|---|---|
| Nov. 15 | Cash. | 400 | |
| | Rent Receivable | | 200 |
| | Rent Revenue Earned | | 200 |
| | To record collection of monthly rent | | |

If the company chooses to use reversing entries, the adjusting entry made on October 31 is reversed on November 1 as follows (note that reversing entries are exactly the opposite of adjusting entries):

| | | | |
|---|---|---|---|
| Nov. 1 | Rent Revenue Earned | 200 | |
| | Rent Receivable | | 200 |
| | To reverse the accrued rent receivable adjustng entry | | |

Because this reversing entry was recorded and posted to the accounts, the Rent Receivable account has a zero balance on November 1. Therefore the $400 of cash received on November 15 can be recorded as follows:

| | | | |
|---|---|---|---|
| Nov. 15 | Cash. | 400 | |
| | Rent Revenue Earned | | 400 |
| | To record collection of monthly rent | | |

Note that whether reversing entries are used or not, the adjusting and closing entries needed at the end of the accounting period are identical.

### Limitations of Reversing Entries

Reversing entries are designed to simplify the recordkeeping process. Because they reverse the effects of adjusting entries, they are frequently used when adjusting entries are made for accruals, as in the examples above. Adjusting entries for *depreciation* are not reversed. Furthermore, adjusting entries for prepaid expenses and revenues received in advance that were initially recorded in balance sheet accounts need not be reversed. A more-detailed discussion of adjusting entries is not needed here for an understanding of the sequence of procedures that constitute the accounting cycle.

## HIGHLIGHT PROBLEM

The first four columns of a ten-column work sheet prepared for Stewart Entertainments Company are shown on page 135.

Required:
Using the information provided, prepare the last six columns of a ten-column work sheet.

## GLOSSARY OF KEY TERMS

**After-closing trial balance.** A trial balance prepared after the revenue, expense, and owner's drawings accounts have been closed and the closing entries have been posted. It consists only of the permanent accounts. Its purpose is to verify the equality of debit and credit amounts in the general ledger accounts before we begin to accumulate information for the next accounting period.

| | Trial Balance | | Adjustments | |
|---|---|---|---|---|
| | Debit | Credit | Debit | Credit |
| Cash | 3 000 | | | |
| Notes Receivable | 4 000 | | | |
| Accounts Receivable | 2 000 | | | |
| Prepaid Insurance | 900 | | | (a) 100 |
| Vehicles | 16 300 | | | |
| Accounts Payable | | 4 000 | | |
| R. Stewart, Capital | | 20 000 | | |
| R. Stewart, Drawings | 2 000 | | | |
| Commission Revenue | | 21 500 | | |
| Salaries Expense | 12 000 | | (c) 400 | |
| Advertising Expense | 3 000 | | | |
| Rent Expense | 1 500 | | | |
| Utilities Expense | 800 | | | |
| | 45 500 | 45 500 | | |
| Insurance Expense | | | (a) 100 | |
| Depreciation Expense—Vehicles | | | (b) 200 | |
| Accumulated Depreciation—Vehicles | | | | (b) 200 |
| Salaries Payable | | | | (c) 400 |
| Interest Receivable | | | (d) 50 | |
| Interest Revenue | | | | (d) 50 |
| | | | 750 | 750 |

**Closing entries.** Journal entries made at the end of an accounting period to close the balances of revenue, expense, and owner's drawings accounts (the temporary accounts). This is accomplished by transferring their balances to the Income Summary account (for revenue and expense accounts) and to the owner's capital account (for the owner's drawings account). Closing entries are made to prepare the revenue, expense, and owner's drawings accounts for the accumulation of transactions data in the next accounting period and to update the balance in the owner's capital account.

**Cross-footing.** Combining amounts by adding or subtracting items on a line horizontally, in contrast to combining amounts by adding or subtracting items in a column vertically, which is often called *footing*.

**Fiscal year.** Any twelve-month annual accounting period adopted by a company.

**Footing.** Combining amounts by adding or subtracting items in a column vertically, in contrast to combining amounts by adding or subtracting items in a line horizontally, which is often called *cross-footing.*

**Income summary account.** An account used during the closing process to summarize the balances in the revenue and expense accounts and provide a single net income or net loss figure that must be transferred to the owner's capital account.

**Natural business year.** A fiscal year ending at a time when the firm's seasonal activities have reached the lowest point of activity in its annual operating cycle.

**Permanent accounts.** The accounts for assets, liabilities, and owner's capital. They accumulate information on a continuous basis.

**Post-closing trial balance.** An alternate title for *after-closing trial balance.*

**Reversing entries.** Entries made on the first day of a new accounting period to reverse the effects of certain adjusting entries made on the last day of the preceding accounting period.

**Temporary accounts.** The accounts for revenues, expenses, and owner's drawings. They are used during an accounting period to classify and accumulate changes affecting the owner's equity. They are closed at the end of each accounting period.

**Work sheet.** A multicolumn form designed to bring together and organize in one place the information needed to prepare financial statements and to record the adjusting and closing entries.

## REVIEW QUESTIONS

1. Explain how the work sheet modifies and expands the sequence of procedures in the accounting cycle. [LO1a]
2. State the four principal reasons for preparing a work sheet. [LO1a]
3. Name the three parts that constitute the heading of a work sheet. [LO1a,2a]
4. Name the five steps to be followed in preparing a work sheet. [LO2a]
5. What three types of errors may have occurred if the balance sheet columns in the work sheet do not have equal totals after the net income or net loss has been computed and entered in the appropriate balance sheet column? [LO2a]
6. What items of information can be found by examining a work sheet? [LO1b]
7. What are the three uses of a completed work sheet? [LO1b]
8. What three financial statements can be prepared from a completed work sheet? [LO2b]
9. Under what circumstances would the figure for total assets in the balance sheet be different from the figure shown as the total in the debit column of the balance sheet columns in the work sheet? [LO2b]
10. Why are adjusting entries recorded in the journal and posted to ledger accounts after the work sheet and financial statements have been prepared? [LO2c]
11. What are the two purposes of closing entries? [LO1c]
12. Explain the four sequential steps that are followed when preparing closing entries. [LO2d]
13. What types of accounts need to be closed? Why? [LO1c]
14. Explain the following: (a) Why is Income Summary credited when revenue accounts are closed? and (b) Why is Income Summary debited when expense accounts are closed? [LO2d]
15. Explain the two guidelines for closing the Income Summary account to the capital account. [LO2d]
16. What would happen to revenue and expense account balances if closing entries were not made? [LO1c,2d]
17. What is the purpose of an after-closing trial balance? [LO2e]
18. Why are there no temporary accounts in the after-closing trial balance? [LO2d,2e]
19. What is the purpose of reversing entries? [LO1d]
20. What type or types of adjusting entries are frequently reversed? [LO1d]

## ANALYTICAL QUESTIONS

21. Is the preparation of a work sheet a necessary part of the accounting cycle? Explain why or why not. [LO1a]
22. In preparing a work sheet, could we omit the adjusted trial balance columns? If we did omit them, what problems would this cause, if any, in completing the work sheet? [LO2a]
23. Explain why the preparation of financial statements is easier when a completed work sheet is available. [LO1b,2b]
24. Why are reversing entries optional rather than required? [LO1d]
25. Why is it beneficial to reverse adjusting entries for accruals? [LO1d]

## IMPACT ANALYSIS QUESTIONS

*For each error described, indicate whether it would overstate [O], understate [U], or not affect [N] the specified key figures.*

26. The amount shown for Unearned Rent Revenue in the credit column of the Adjusted Trial Balance columns in the work sheet was extended to the Income Statement credit column in the work sheet. [LO2a,2b]

    _______ Assets _______ Net Income
    _______ Liabilities _______ Owner's equity

27. The amount shown for Rent Receivable in the debit column of the Adjusted Trial balance columns in the work sheet was extended to the Income Statement debit column in the work sheet. [LO2a,2b]

    _______ Assets _______ Owner's Equity
    _______ Net Income _______ Revenue

28. The amount shown for Interest Revenue in the credit column of the Adjusted Trial Balance columns in the work sheet was extended to the Balance Sheet credit column in the work sheet. [LO2a,2b]

    _______ Assets _______ Net Income
    _______ Revenue _______ Owner's Equity

29. The amount shown for owner's drawings was not closed to owner's capital during the year-end closing process. [LO2d]

    _______ Assets _______ Net Income
    _______ Owner's Capital _______ Liabilities

## EXERCISES

EXERCISE 4–1 *(Extend Account Balances in a Work Sheet)* The accounts designated 1 through 12 below are alphabetically arranged. Each account balance would appear in one of the Adjusted Trial Balance columns in the work sheet on page 138.

Required:

Use a check mark to indicate in what column of the completed work sheet each account's dollar amount would be extended. Item X is shown as an example. [LO2a]

EXERCISE 4–2 *(Prepare Adjusting Entries from a Work Sheet)* Various accounts with their amounts taken from the Adjustments columns of a work sheet prepared on December 31, 19X1, are shown on page 138.

Required:

From this information, prepare the adjusting journal entries that are needed to update the ledger account balances. [LO2c]

*Work Sheet for Exercise 4–1*

| ACCOUNT | INCOME STATEMENT Debit | INCOME STATEMENT Credit | BALANCE SHEET Debit | BALANCE SHEET Credit |
|---|---|---|---|---|
| X. Cash | | | ✓ | |
| 1. Accounts Payable | | | | |
| 2. Accounts Receivable | | | | |
| 3. Accumulated Depreciation | | | | |
| 4. Cash | | | | |
| 5. Depreciation Expense | | | | |
| 6. Fee Revenue | | | | |
| 7. K. Hall, Capital | | | | |
| 8. K. Hall, Drawings | | | | |
| 9. Rent Revenue | | | | |
| 10. Salaries Expense | | | | |
| 11. Utilities Expense | | | | |
| 12. Vehicles | | | | |

*Work Sheet for Exercise 4–2*

| ACCOUNT | ADJUSTMENTS Debit | ADJUSTMENTS Credit |
|---|---|---|
| Prepaid Insurance | | (a) 240 |
| Office Supplies | | (b) 150 |
| Accumulated Depreciation, Equipment | | (c) 1,200 |
| Accumulated Depreciation, Vehicles | | (d) 2,500 |
| Salaries Expense | (e) 700 | |
| Insurance Expense | (a) 240 | |
| Office Supplies Expense | (b) 150 | |
| Depreciation Expense, Equipment | (c) 1,200 | |
| Depreciation Expense, Vehicles | (d) 2,500 | |
| Salaries Payable | | (e) 700 |
| | $4,790 | $4,790 |

EXERCISE 4–3 *(Prepare Closing Entries from T-Account Data)* Certain selected accounts of Ideal Company are shown below in T-account form.

| INTEREST RECEIVABLE | |
|---|---|
| 50 | |

| OFFICE SUPPLIES | |
|---|---|
| 200 | 80 |

| PREPAID INSURANCE | |
|---|---|
| 300 | 150 |
| 200 | |

| ACCUMULATED DEPRECIATION | |
|---|---|
| | 600 |
| | 125 |

| SALARIES PAYABLE | |
|---|---|
| | 320 |

| J. HALL, DRAWINGS | |
|---|---|
| 200 | |
| 1,900 | |

| FEE REVENUE | |
|---|---|
| | 6,000 |
| | 3,000 |
| | 8,000 |

| INTEREST REVENUE | |
|---|---|
| | 50 |

| SALARIES EXPENSE | |
|---|---|
| 10,800 | |
| 320 | |

| INSURANCE EXPENSE | |
|---|---|
| 150 | |

| DEPRECIATION EXPENSE | |
|---|---|
| 125 | |

| OFFICE SUPPLIES EXPENSE | |
|---|---|
| 80 | |

Required:
Indicate which accounts should be closed at the end of the accounting period, and journalize the entries needed to close those accounts. [LO2d]

EXERCISE 4–4 *(Determine Net Income and Prepare Closing Entries)* Various accounts with their amounts taken from the Income Statement columns of a work sheet prepared for Jeff Hall's company are shown below. The work sheet covers a three-month period ending on May 31, 19X1.

| ACCOUNT | INCOME STATEMENT Debit | Credit |
|---|---|---|
| Commission Revenue | | 23,500 |
| Rent Revenue | | 400 |
| Salaries Expense | 14,700 | |
| Advertising Expense | 2,100 | |
| Depreciation Expense | 800 | |
| Insurance Expense | 900 | |
| Supplies Expense | 200 | |

Required:
1. Determine the company's net income or net loss for the three-month period ending on May 31.
2. Although closing entries are generally made only at year-end, you are asked to prepare journal entries to close all temporary accounts. Jeff Hall (the company's owner) withdrew $2,400 cash for his personal use during the three months ended on May 31. [LO2b,2d]

EXERCISE 4–5 *(Correct Improperly Prepared Closing Entries)* The entries shown below were prepared to close a company's accounts at the end of its accounting period.

| | | |
|---|---|---|
| Commission Revenue | 88,000 | |
| Accumulated Depreciation | 7,200 | |
| Unearned Commission Revenue | 1,400 | |
| Income Summary | | 96,600 |
| To close the accounts | | |
| | | |
| Income Summary | 84,000 | |
| J. Hall, Drawings | | 9,300 |
| Salaries Expense | | 57,200 |
| Depreciation Expense | | 1,800 |
| Rent Expense | | 12,600 |
| Supplies Expense | | 3,100 |
| To close the accounts | | |
| | | |
| J. Hall, Capital | 12,600 | |
| Income Summary | | 12,600 |
| To close the account | | |

Required:
Although these entries are obviously incorrect, use the information given in them to prepare end-of-the-period closing entries that are correct. [LO2d]

EXERCISE 4–6 *(Determine Net Income and Prepare Closing Entries)* Various accounts with their amounts taken from the Income Statement columns of a work sheet prepared for Beverly Queen's company are shown below. The work sheet covers a three-month period ending on April 30, 19X1.

| ACCOUNT | INCOME STATEMENT | |
|---|---|---|
| | Debit | Credit |
| Consulting Fee Revenue | | 19,800 |
| Interest Revenue | | 400 |
| Salaries Expense | 12,200 | |
| Rent Expense | 3,600 | |
| Advertising Expense | 2,300 | |
| Travel Expense | 1,900 | |
| Insurance Expense | 800 | |
| Office Expense | 700 | |

Required:

1. Determine the company's net income or net loss for the three-month period ending on April 30.
2. Although closing entries are generally made only at year-end, you are asked to prepare journal entries to close all temporary accounts. Beverly Queen, the company's owner, withdrew $3,200 cash for her personal use during the three months ended on April 30. [LO2b,2d]

EXERCISE 4-7 *(Prepare Adjusting, Reversing, and Transaction Entries)* On December 31, 19X1, Melville Company had accrued salaries (salaries earned by company employees that had not yet been paid to them) of $590. A full week's salary payment totaling $2,460 was made to all employees on January 4, 19X2.

Required:

1. Prepare the adjusting entry needed on December 31, 19X1.
2. Prepare the reversing entry that could be made on January 1, 19X2.
3. a. Prepare the journal entry needed when the payroll was paid on January 4, 19X2, assuming the reversing entry was recorded and posted.
   b. Prepare the journal entry needed when the payroll was paid on January 4, 19X2, assuming no reversing entry was made on January 1. [LO2c,2f]

## PROBLEMS

PROBLEM 4-1 *(Prepare a Work Sheet)* The Spencer Company performs a service for which it receives a commission. On September 30, the end of the firm's accounting period, the following trial balance, shown at the top of page 141, was prepared.

Required:

Enter the trial balance in the Trial Balance columns of a ten-column work sheet and complete the work sheet using the following additional information:

a. Unexpired insurance at year-end, $260.
b. Office supplies remaining on hand amounted to $60 as determined by a physical count.
c. Estimated depreciation on office equipment, $1,660.
d. Of the commissions received in advance, $340 was earned by September 30.
e. Salaries earned but unpaid at year-end, $620. [LO2a]

PROBLEM 4-2 *(Complete a Work Sheet)* Shown on page 141 are four columns taken from a ten-column work sheet prepared by Everet Company. The Adjustments debit and credit columns have intentionally been omitted.

Required:

1. Prepare in general journal form the adjusting entries that change the amounts in the Trial Balance columns to the amounts in the Adjusted Trial Balance columns.

*Trial Balance for Problem 4-1*

SPENCER COMPANY
Trial Balance
September 30, 19X1

| | | |
|---|---|---|
| Cash | $ 9,350 | |
| Prepaid Insurance | 580 | |
| Office Supplies | 230 | |
| Office Equipment | 13,600 | |
| Accumulated Depreciation—Office Equipment | | $ 2,200 |
| Accounts Payable | | 1,740 |
| Unearned Commission Revenue | | 610 |
| J. Spencer, Capital | | 12,350 |
| J. Spencer, Drawings | 4,800 | |
| Commission Revenue | | 62,300 |
| Salaries Expense | 38,200 | |
| Rent Expense | 6,600 | |
| Advertising Expense | 4,800 | |
| Utilities Expense | 1,040 | |
| | $79,200 | $79,200 |

*Trial Balance for Problem 4-2*

| ACCOUNT | TRIAL BALANCE | | ADJUSTED TRIAL BALANCE | |
|---|---|---|---|---|
| | Debit | Credit | Debit | Credit |
| Cash | 4,200 | | 4,200 | |
| Commissions Receivable | 3,700 | | 4,500 | |
| Prepaid Insurance | 2,200 | | 1,500 | |
| Office Supplies | 1,300 | | 800 | |
| Equipment | 26,000 | | 26,000 | |
| Accumulated Depreciation—Equipment | | 5,200 | | 7,800 |
| Accounts Payable | | 6,100 | | 6,100 |
| Unearned Commission Revenue | | 900 | | 600 |
| Salaries Payable | | | | 1,300 |
| S. Everet, Capital | | 12,000 | | 12,000 |
| S. Everet, Drawings | 8,800 | | 8,800 | |
| Commission Revenue | | 92,400 | | 93,500 |
| Salaries Expense | 56,700 | | 58,000 | |
| Rent Expense | 4,800 | | 4,800 | |
| Travel Expense | 5,200 | | 5,200 | |
| Depreciation Expense | | | 2,600 | |
| Insurance Expense | | | 700 | |
| Utilities Expense | 3,700 | | 3,700 | |
| Office Supplies Expense | | | 500 | |
| | 116,600 | 116,600 | 121,300 | 121,300 |

2. Using all the information, prepare a ten-column work sheet for the three-month period ending March 31, 19X1. [LO2a,2c]

PROBLEM 4-3 *(Prepare a Work Sheet)* The following trial balance was taken from the ledger of the Crest Motivation Company, a management consulting firm, which has been operating for the past five years. The company's fiscal year-end is July 31.

Additional Information Available on July 31:

a. Interest earned but not yet received on the marketable securities, $130.
b. Insurance expired during the period, $680.
c. Supplies used during the period, $205.

CREST MOTIVATION COMPANY
Trial Balance
July 31, 19X1

| ACCOUNT | DEBIT | CREDIT |
|---|---|---|
| Cash | $ 8,540 | |
| Marketable Securities | 11,950 | |
| Consulting Fees Receivable | 5,400 | |
| Prepaid Insurance | 900 | |
| Supplies on Hand | 370 | |
| Data-Processing Equipment | 29,300 | |
| Accumulated Depreciation—Equipment | | $ 13,200 |
| Accounts Payable | | 2,910 |
| Notes Payable | | 3,200 |
| S. Crest, Capital | | 29,200 |
| S. Crest, Drawings | 3,500 | |
| Consulting Fee Revenue | | 102,720 |
| Interest Revenue | | 670 |
| Salaries Expense | 80,910 | |
| Rent Expense | 3,600 | |
| Travel Expense | 4,260 | |
| Utilities Expense | 1,980 | |
| Maintenance Expense | 570 | |
| Property Tax Expense | 620 | |
| | $151,900 | $151,900 |

d. Depreciation on equipment for the year, $2,800.
e. Interest accrued on the note payable since the note was taken out on September 30, $185.
f. Salaries earned but not yet paid, $410.
g. An unpaid property tax bill for $60 remained unrecorded at year-end.

Required:
Prepare a ten-column work sheet for the year ended July 31, 19X1. [LO2a]

PROBLEM 4-4 *(Prepare a Work Sheet from a Random List of Accounts)* Warner Space Brokers operates on a fiscal year ending July 31 and has just completed its fourth business year. The company's ledger accounts, with balances as they appeared before adjustments, are listed on page 143 in alphabetical order.

Required:
Using the information given on page 143:
1. Prepare a trial balance for Warner Space Brokers using the first two columns of a work sheet. Rearrange the accounts in financial statement order.
2. Complete the work sheet. The following additional information is available at the end of July:
   a. Salaries earned by company employees but not yet paid, $160.
   b. Office supplies costing $120 remained on hand as determined by a physical count taken on July 31.
   c. Accrued interest on the mortgage payable, $105.
   d. Insurance that remained unexpired, $660.
   e. One-half of the advances received by the company from its clients was earned by July 31.
   f. The equipment was estimated to have a useful life of eight years from the date of its purchase four years ago with no residual or salvage value expected.
   g. Accrued interest on the notes receivable, $80. [LO2a]

ACCOUNTS AND AMOUNTS
July 31, 19X1

| Account | Amount |
|---|---|
| Accounts Payable | $ 3,540 |
| Accounts Receivable | 5,920 |
| Accumulated Depreciation—Equipment | 13,200 |
| Advances from Clients | 760 |
| Advertising Expense | 1,010 |
| Cash | 6,140 |
| Equipment | 35,200 |
| Fee Revenue | 39,270 |
| Interest Expense | 420 |
| Mortgage Payable | 9,800 |
| Notes Receivable | 2,700 |
| Office Supplies | 550 |
| Prepaid Insurance | 990 |
| Rent Expense | 4,800 |
| Repairs Expense | 630 |
| Salaries Expense | 20,570 |
| Travel Expense | 1,220 |
| Utilities Expense | 820 |
| P. Warner, Capital | 19,000 |
| P. Warner, Drawings | 4,600 |

PROBLEM 4–5 *(Prepare a Work Sheet and Closing Entries)* A trial balance taken from the ledger of Richardson Forecasts at the end of its annual accounting period is shown below.

RICHARDSON FORECASTS
Trial Balance
December 31, 19X1

| ACCOUNT | DEBIT | CREDIT |
|---|---|---|
| Cash | $ 8,340 | |
| Accounts Receivable | 3,200 | |
| Notes Receivable | 7,000 | |
| Supplies | 1,260 | |
| Prepaid Insurance | 1,020 | |
| Equipment | 30,400 | |
| Accumulated Depreciation—Equipment | | $ 4,690 |
| Accounts Payable | | 3,950 |
| Taxes Payable | | 340 |
| T. Richardson, Capital | | 32,000 |
| T. Richardson, Drawings | 1,900 | |
| Service Revenue | | 60,480 |
| Interest Revenue | | 160 |
| Salaries Expense | 42,070 | |
| Rent Expense | 4,800 | |
| Utilities Expense | 1,290 | |
| Taxes Expense | 340 | |
| | $101,620 | $101,620 |

Additional Information Available at the End of December:

a. Interest earned on the notes but not yet received, $210.

b. Supplies used during the period, $940.

c. Unexpired insurance at year-end, $770.

d. Equipment depreciation, $3,300.
e. Salaries earned but unpaid and unrecorded at year-end, $720.

Required:
1. Prepare a ten-column work sheet for the year ended December 31, 19X1.
2. Prepare the closing entries. [LO2a,2d]

PROBLEM 4–6 *(Prepare an Adjusted Trial Balance, Closing Entries, and an After-Closing Trial Balance from a Random List of Accounts)* The following accounts, together with their adjusted balances, are those of Hemlock Relocation Company as of October 31, 19X1.

| | |
|---|---|
| Accounts Receivable | $13,265 |
| Depreciation Expense—Vehicles | 2,100 |
| Office Salaries Expense | 8,200 |
| Sales Salaries Expense | 21,450 |
| Vehicles | 10,700 |
| Legal Expense | 2,500 |
| Commission Revenue | 14,835 |
| Accumulated Depreciation—Vehicles | 3,200 |
| Rent Expense | 6,000 |
| A. Hemlock, Drawings | 9,000 |
| Supplies Expense | 1,270 |
| Advertising Expense | 3,770 |
| Accounts Payable | 12,275 |
| Utilities Expense | 840 |
| Travel Expense | 4,940 |
| Notes Receivable (due in 40 days) | 2,200 |
| Depreciation Expense—Equipment | 3,600 |
| A. Hemlock, Capital | 50,000 |
| Property Tax Expense | 1,030 |
| Telephone and Telegram Expense | 2,860 |
| Equipment | 36,400 |
| Service Revenue | 54,940 |
| Insurance Expense | 1,320 |
| Cash | 10,945 |
| Taxes Payable | 440 |
| Accumulated Depreciation—Equipment | 6,700 |

Required:
Using the information given above:
1. Prepare an adjusted trial balance. Do not prepare a complete ten-column work sheet. Rearrange the accounts in financial statement order.
2. Journalize the closing entries.
3. Prepare an after-closing trial balance. [LO2a,2d,2e]

PROBLEM 4–7 *(Prepare a Work Sheet, Closing Entries, and an After-Closing Trial Balance)* Scott Vacation Company operates with an annual accounting period that ends on December 31. On that date its trial balance appeared as shown on page 145.

To bring certain account balances up to date, the following additional information is provided at year end:
a. Salaries earned but not yet paid or recorded, $120.
b. One-third of the prepaid insurance has expired.
c. Supplies remaining on hand, $150.
d. Equipment has an estimated life of ten years (zero residual or salvage value).
e. Vehicles have an estimated life of five years ($500 of residual or salvage value estimated).
f. Accrued interest on the notes payable, $110.

Required:

1. Enter the trial balance in a ten-column work sheet and complete the work sheet.
2. From the data in the work sheet, prepare closing entries.
3. Prepare an after-closing trial balance. [LO2a,2d,2e]

SCOTT VACATION COMPANY
Trial Balance
December 31, 19X1

| ACCOUNT | DEBIT | CREDIT |
|---|---|---|
| Cash | $ 2,580 | |
| Supplies | 310 | |
| Prepaid Insurance | 630 | |
| Equipment | 12,160 | |
| Accumulated Depreciation—Equipment | | $ 2,980 |
| Vehicles | 7,000 | |
| Accumulated Depreciation—Vehicles | | 2,700 |
| Accounts Payable | | 880 |
| Notes Payable | | 7,200 |
| R. Scott, Capital | | 9,000 |
| R. Scott, Drawings | 1,500 | |
| Service Revenue | | 23,450 |
| Salaries Expense | 12,480 | |
| Rent Expense | 3,600 | |
| Travel Expense | 3,520 | |
| Commission Expense | 970 | |
| Advertising Expense | 840 | |
| Utilities Expense | 620 | |
| | $46,210 | $46,210 |

PROBLEM 4–8 *(Complete the Accounting Cycle from Trial Balance)* A trial balance for the Revere Alarm Associates taken at year-end October 31, 19X1, follows.

REVERE ALARM ASSOCIATES
Trial Balance
October 31, 19X1

| ACCOUNT | DEBIT | CREDIT |
|---|---|---|
| Cash | $ 4,000 | |
| Notes Receivable | 4,000 | |
| Accounts Receivable | 2,000 | |
| Prepaid Rent | 1,200 | |
| Prepaid Insurance | 660 | |
| Supplies | 420 | |
| Equipment | 12,200 | |
| Accounts Payable | | $ 3,800 |
| Notes Payable | | 2,500 |
| J. Revere, Capital | | 12,000 |
| J. Revere, Drawings | 1,180 | |
| Service Revenue | | 66,230 |
| Salaries Expense | 44,070 | |
| Rent Expense | 4,000 | |
| Advertising Expense | 9,200 | |
| Utilities Expense | 1,600 | |
| | $84,530 | $84,530 |

To bring certain account balances up to date, the following additional information is provided at year-end:

a. Supplies remaining on hand, $190.
b. Interest accrued on the notes receivable, $85.
c. Two-thirds of the prepaid rent has expired.
d. One-half of the prepaid insurance has expired.
e. Depreciation on the equipment, $990.
f. Interest accrued on the notes payable, $60.
g. Salaries earned but not paid, $270.

Required:

1. Enter the trial balance in a ten-column work sheet and complete the work sheet.
2. From the data in the work sheet, prepare an income statement, a capital statement, and a balance sheet.
3. From the data in the work sheet, prepare adjusting and closing entries.
4. Prepare an after-closing trial balance.
5. Prepare any reversing entries you think are necessary. [LO2a,2b,2c,2d,2e,2f]

PROBLEM 4–9 *(Prepare a Work Sheet and Record Adjusting Entries)* Eastern Advisors started operating on January 1, 19X1. To conserve the outflow of cash during its first year of operations, the company decided not to purchase transportation equipment or office equipment. Arrangements were made to rent transportation equipment on a daily use basis, and office equipment by paying an hourly rate. The company's accounts are brought up to date by adjusting entries at the end of each month. After six months of operations, the following trial balance was prepared.

EASTERN ADVISORS
Trial Balance
June 30, 19X1

| ACCOUNT | DEBIT | CREDIT |
|---|---|---|
| Cash | $11,500 | |
| Accounts Receivable | 3,550 | |
| Prepaid Insurance | 1,300 | |
| Prepaid Office Equipment Rental | 210 | |
| Supplies | 640 | |
| Accounts Payable | | $ 1,890 |
| Notes Payable | | 2,000 |
| Unearned Fee Revenue | | 1,120 |
| B. Rallo, Capital | | 15,000 |
| B. Rallo, Drawings | 10,000 | |
| Fee Revenue | | 54,200 |
| Salaries Expense | 43,600 | |
| Utilities Expense | 320 | |
| Office Equipment Rental Expense | 640 | |
| Insurance Expense | 400 | |
| Office Rent Expense | 900 | |
| Transportation Equipment Rental Expense | 770 | |
| Maintenance Expense | 380 | |
| | $74,210 | $74,210 |

The following information is available on June 30 and is to be used as a source for adjusting certain account balances:

a. Supplies remaining on hand, $480.
b. Unexpired insurance, $1,050.
c. A check for $210 was issued in advance on June 3 for the use of office equipment. Since

then the company has used the equipment for forty-five hours, and the equipment rental rate is $4 per hour.

d. Interest accrued on borrowed money (a note payable), $15.
e. Of the fees received in advance, only $320 remains unearned.
f. Salaries earned but not paid, $830.
g. Services to clients who did not pay in advance and who have not yet been billed, $710.
h. A bill for the rental of transportation equipment during the last two days of June (29 and 30) has not been received or recorded. The equipment rental charge is $25 per day.

Required:

1. Prepare a ten-column work sheet.
2. Journalize the adjusting entries. [LO2a,2c]

PROBLEM 4-10 *(Comprehensive Review)* The accounts for Hammond Graphic Concepts and their balances as they appeared at year-end before adjustments are shown below in alphabetical order.

HAMMOND GRAPHIC CONCEPTS
Accounts and Amounts
December 31, 19X1

| Account | Amount |
|---|---|
| Accounts Payable | $ 3,230 |
| Accounts Receivable | 4,720 |
| Accumulated Depreciation, Building | 4,000 |
| Accumulated Depreciation, Equipment | 8,400 |
| Advertising Expense | 810 |
| Building | 30,000 |
| Cash | 3,460 |
| D. Hammond, Capital | 65,000 |
| D. Hammond, Drawings | 4,700 |
| Equipment | 70,200 |
| Fee Revenue | 19,430 |
| Mortgage Payable | 24,000 |
| Notes Receivable | 2,100 |
| Prepaid Insurance | 980 |
| Rent Revenue | 550 |
| Repairs Expense | 530 |
| Salaries Expense | 4,600 |
| Supplies on Hand | 1,020 |
| Travel Expense | 810 |
| Utilities Expense | 680 |

Required:

Using the information given above:

1. Prepare a trial balance for Hammond Graphic Concepts using the first two columns of a work sheet. Rearrange the accounts in financial statement order.
2. Complete the work sheet. The following additional information is available at year-end.
   a. Depreciation on the equipment, $3,510.
   b. Unbilled fee revenue amounts to $410 and needs to be recorded.
   c. Accrued interest on the mortgage payable, $740.
   d. Accrued interest on notes receivable, $80.
   e. Amount of prepaid insurance, $630.
   f. Rent revenue is $50 per month; and although December's rent is earned and due, the tenant's check has not yet been received.

g. Salaries earned but not paid, $230.
h. Supplies remaining on hand, $240.
i. Depreciation on the building, $2,000.

3. From the data in the work sheet, prepare an income statement, a capital statement, and a balance sheet.
4. From the data in the work sheet, prepare adjusting and closing entries.
5. Prepare an after-closing trial balance.
6. Prepare any reversing entries you think are necessary. [LO2a,2b,2c,2d,2e,2f]

## ALTERNATE PROBLEMS

PROBLEM 4–1A *(Prepare a Work Sheet)* (Alternate to Problem 4–1) Aron Company performs a service for which it receives a commission. On September 30, the end of the firm's accounting period, the following trial balance was prepared.

ARON COMPANY
Trial Balance
September 30, 19X1

| | | |
|---|---|---|
| Cash | $ 9,350 | |
| Prepaid Insurance | 580 | |
| Office Supplies | 230 | |
| Office Equipment | 13,600 | |
| Accumulated Depreciation—Office Equipment | | $ 2,200 |
| Accounts Payable | | 1,740 |
| Unearned Commission Revenue | | 610 |
| J. Aron, Capital | | 12,350 |
| J. Aron, Drawings | 4,800 | |
| Commission Revenue | | 62,300 |
| Salaries Expense | 38,200 | |
| Rent Expense | 6,600 | |
| Advertising Expense | 4,800 | |
| Utilities Expense | 1,040 | |
| | $79,200 | $79,200 |

Required:
Enter the trial balance in the Trial Balance columns of a ten-column work sheet and complete the work sheet using the following additional information:

a. Unexpired insurance at year-end, $300.
b. Office supplies remaining on hand amounted to $100 as determined by a physical count.
c. Estimated depreciation on office equipment, $1,700.
d. Of the commissions received in advance, $500 was earned by September 30.
e. Salaries earned but unpaid at year-end, $700. [LO2a]

PROBLEM 4–2A *(Complete a Work Sheet)* (Alternate to Problem 4–2) Shown on page 149 are four columns taken from a ten-column work sheet prepared by Elwell Nutritionists.

Required:

1. Prepare the adjusting entries that change the amounts in the Trial Balance columns to the amounts in the Adjusted Trial Balance columns.
2. Using all the information, prepare a ten-column work sheet for the year ending May 31, 19X1. [LO2a,2c]

PROBLEM 4–3A *(Prepare a Work Sheet, Financial Statements, and Closing Entries)* (Alternate to Problem 4–5) A trial balance taken from the ledger of Richard Outplacements Outfit at the end of its annual accounting period is shown on page 149.

*Work Sheet for Problem 4-2a*

| ACCOUNT | TRIAL BALANCE Debit | TRIAL BALANCE Credit | ADJUSTED TRIAL BALANCE Debit | ADJUSTED TRIAL BALANCE Credit |
|---|---|---|---|---|
| Cash | 4,200 | | 4,200 | |
| Commissions Receivable | 3,700 | | 4,500 | |
| Prepaid Insurance | 2,200 | | 1,700 | |
| Office Supplies | 1,300 | | 700 | |
| Equipment | 26,000 | | 26,000 | |
| Accumulated Depreciation—Equipment | | 5,200 | | 6,200 |
| Accounts Payable | | 6,100 | | 6,100 |
| Unearned Commission Revenue | | 900 | | 300 |
| Salaries Payable | | | | 2,000 |
| S. Elwell, Capital | | 12,000 | | 12,000 |
| S. Elwell, Drawings | 8,800 | | 8,800 | |
| Commission Revenue | | 92,400 | | 93,800 |
| Salaries Expense | 56,700 | | 58,700 | |
| Rent Expense | 4,800 | | 4,800 | |
| Travel Expense | 5,200 | | 5,200 | |
| Depreciation Expense | | | 1,000 | |
| Insurance Expense | | | 500 | |
| Utilities Expense | 3,700 | | 3,700 | |
| Office Supplies Expense | | | 600 | |
| | 116,600 | 116,600 | 120,400 | 120,400 |

*Trial Balance for Problem 4-3a*

RICHARD OUTPLACEMENTS OUTFIT
Trial Balance
December 31, 19X1

| ACCOUNT | DEBIT | CREDIT |
|---|---|---|
| Cash | $ 8,340 | |
| Accounts Receivable | 3,200 | |
| Notes Receivable | 7,000 | |
| Supplies | 1,260 | |
| Prepaid Insurance | 1,020 | |
| Equipment | 30,400 | |
| Accumulated Depreciation—Equipment | | $ 4,690 |
| Accounts Payable | | 3,950 |
| Taxes Payable | | 340 |
| T. Richard, Capital | | 32,000 |
| T. Richard, Drawings | 1,900 | |
| Service Revenue | | 60,480 |
| Interest Revenue | | 160 |
| Salaries Expense | 42,070 | |
| Rent Expense | 4,800 | |
| Utilities Expense | 1,290 | |
| Taxes Expense | 340 | |
| | $101,620 | $101,620 |

Additional Information Available at the End of December:

a. Depreciation for the year, $3,000.

b. Salaries earned but not yet paid, $2,500.

c. Insurance expired during the period, $415.

d. Supplies remaining on hand at year-end, $900.
e. Interest earned but not yet received on the notes receivable, $110.

Required:
1. Prepare a ten-column work sheet for the year ended December 31, 19X1.
2. Prepare an income statement, a capital statement, and a balance sheet.
3. Prepare the closing entries. [LO2a,2b,2d]

PROBLEM 4–4A *(Prepare an Adjusted Trial Balance, Closing Entries, and an After-Closing Trial Balance from a Random List of Accounts)* (Alternate to Problem 4–6) The following accounts, together with their adjusted balances, are those of Himlock Home Security Experts as of October 31, 19X1.

| | |
|---|---|
| Accounts Receivable | $13,000 |
| Depreciation Expense—Vehicles | 1,100 |
| Office Salaries Expense | 8,200 |
| Sales Salaries Expense | 21,450 |
| Vehicles | 10,700 |
| Legal Expense | 2,500 |
| Commission Revenue | 14,570 |
| Accumulated Depreciation—Vehicles | 2,200 |
| Rent Expense | 5,000 |
| A. Himlock, Drawings | 8,000 |
| Supplies Expense | 1,000 |
| Advertising Expense | 3,500 |
| Accounts Payable | 12,275 |
| Utilities Expense | 3,380 |
| Travel Expense | 4,940 |
| Notes Receivable (due in 40 days) | 2,200 |
| Depreciation Expense—Equipment | 3,600 |
| A. Himlock, Capital | 50,000 |
| Property Tax Expense | 1,000 |
| Telephone and Telegram Expense | 2,890 |
| Equipment | 36,400 |
| Service Revenue | 54,940 |
| Insurance Expense | 1,320 |
| Cash | 10,945 |
| Taxes Payable | 440 |
| Accumulated Depreciation—Equipment | 6,700 |

Required:
Using the information given above:
1. Prepare an adjusted trial balance. Do not prepare a complete ten-column work sheet.
2. Journalize the closing entries.
3. Prepare an after-closing trial balance. [LO2a,2d,2e]

PROBLEM 4–5A *(Prepare a Work Sheet, Closing Entries, and an After-Closing Trial Balance)* (Alternate to Problem 4–7) Scoot Landscape Consultants Company operates with an annual accounting period that ends on December 31. On that date its trial balance appeared as on page 151. To bring certain account balances up to date, the following additional information is provided at year -end:
a. Salaries earned but not yet paid or recorded, $160.
b. One-fourth of the prepaid insurance has expired.
c. Supplies remaining on hand, $200.
d. Equipment has an estimated life of seven years (zero residual or salvage value).

SCOOT LANDSCAPE CONSULTANTS
Trial Balance
December 31, 19X1

| ACCOUNT | DEBIT | CREDIT |
|---|---|---|
| Cash | $ 3,000 | |
| Supplies | 390 | |
| Prepaid Insurance | 600 | |
| Equipment | 12,180 | |
| Accumulated Depreciation—Equipment | | $ 2,980 |
| Vehicles | 6,500 | |
| Accumulated Depreciation—Vehicles | | 2,700 |
| Accounts Payable | | 1,880 |
| Notes Payable | | 6,200 |
| R. Scoot, Capital | | 9,000 |
| R. Scoot, Drawings | 1,500 | |
| Service Revenue | | 23,450 |
| Salaries Expense | 12,490 | |
| Rent Expense | 3,600 | |
| Travel Expense | 3,520 | |
| Commission Expense | 970 | |
| Advertising Expense | 1,460 | |
| | $46,210 | $46,210 |

e. Vehicles have an estimated life of three years ($500 of residual or salvage value estimated).

f. Accrued interest on the notes payable, $140.

Required:

1. Enter the trial balance in a ten-column work sheet and complete the work sheet.
2. From the data in the work sheet, prepare closing entries.
3. Prepare an after-closing trial balance. [LO2a,2d,2e]

# 5 Accounting for a Merchandising Company

### *Learning Objectives*

When you complete this chapter you will be able to

1. Answer the following questions:
   a. How does accounting for merchandising companies resemble that for service companies? How does it differ?
   b. How does the perpetual inventory method differ from the periodic inventory method?
   c. What types of transactions constitute the sales revenue and cost of goods sold section of the income statement of a merchandising company?
   d. How do trade discounts differ from cash discounts?
2. Perform the following accounting functions:
   a. Journalize sales revenue transactions for a merchandising company.
   b. Journalize purchase transactions for a merchandising company that uses the gross invoice method.
   c. Journalize purchase transactions for a merchandising company that uses the net invoice method.
   d. Calculate the cost of goods sold of a merchandising company.
   e. Prepare the work sheet and financial statements for a merchandising company that uses the periodic inventory system.
   f. Prepare closing entries for a merchandising company that uses the periodic inventory system.

In the first four chapters we learned how to accumulate, summarize, and report accounting information for a business that renders personal services. As we have seen, a **service company** receives fees or commissions for providing services, and its periodic net income is determined by deducting from the fees and commissions earned the operating expenses incurred to generate the fees and commissions. In this chapter we focus on another important type of business, the **merchandising company,** whose primary business activity involves the purchase and sale of goods. Merchandising firms purchase goods with the intent to sell them to their customers at a price in excess of their cost. Thus net income for a merchandising firm is determined by subtracting from sales revenue (1) the cost of the goods sold and (2) their operating expenses.

*1a. Net income for service companies = fees or commission revenue earned minus operating expenses*

*1a. Net income for merchandising companies = revenue minus (1) cost of goods sold and (2) operating expenses*

The determination of net income for a merchandising firm can be shown in formula form as follows:

Sales − Cost of Goods Sold − Operating Expenses = Net Income

Merchandising firms may purchase and sell goods at the *retail level,* which includes department stores, sporting goods and specialty stores, and automobile dealerships. They may also purchase and sell goods at the *wholesale level,* which includes the electrical, plumbing, and lumber supply firms that sell their product to the retail shops or to commercial users.

*1a. Service and merchandising companies use the same basic accounting model and follow similar methods and practices*

All merchandising companies use the same basic accounting model discussed in the first four chapters. They also follow methods and practices similar to those used by service companies. Thus many of the concepts you will learn in this chapter expand on what you have already studied. We will introduce additional accounts and concepts to record transactions involving the purchase, handling, storage, and sale of merchandise.

Because merchandising firms purchase and sell goods, the valuation of their ending inventory and the determination of their cost of goods sold are given extensive treatment in the chapter. We will also develop a more-detailed income statement so that the results of a merchandising firm's profit-directed activities are fully disclosed.

The income statement for a merchandising firm consists of three sections: (1) the revenue section showing the net sales revenue earned from selling the company's products, (2) the cost of goods sold section showing the total cost of the products that were sold during the period, and (3) the operating expense section showing the expenses incurred in operating the company during the period. Most expenses incurred by a service firm are also incurred by a merchandising firm. The merchandising firm, however, will have additional expenses attributed to its buying and selling activities, such as delivery expenses.

We will begin our study of the accounting process for a merchandising firm by examining how the information in each section of the income statement is developed, beginning with sales in the revenue section.

## ACCOUNTING FOR SALES REVENUE

Revenues for a merchandising firm are generated from its sales of merchandise. To be financially successful, a merchandising firm must generate enough sales revenue to exceed both its cost of goods sold and its operating expenses and still provide a satisfactory remainder called net income. To provide information pertaining to a given period's sales revenue, it is necessary to account for (1) all sales (both cash and credit), (2) any related sales returns, and (3) any discounts on the selling price granted by the seller and taken by the buyer.

*1c,2a. To record a sale of merchandise, debit Cash or Accounts Receivable and credit Sales*

A sale of merchandise is recorded by debiting an asset account—Cash or Accounts Receivable—and crediting a **Sales Revenue,** or simply a **Sales account.**[1] The asset account debited depends on whether the sale was made for cash or on credit terms. The amount of the entry is determined by the selling price of the goods sold.

For example, a sale of merchandise for $600 cash is recorded as follows:

| | | |
|---|---|---|
| Cash | 600 | |
| Sales | | 600 |
| To record the sale of merchandise for cash | | |

The Sales account is used only for recording the sale of merchandise. If a merchandising company sold some of its equipment, the Equipment account would be credited, not the Sales account.

If a $600 sale of merchandise is made on credit, the entry to record the transaction would be as follows:

| | | |
|---|---|---|
| Accounts Receivable | 600 | |
| Sales | | 600 |
| To record the sale of merchandise on credit | | |

Note that revenue from the credit sale was considered earned even though the company will not receive cash from the customer until some later date. Under accrual accounting, revenue from the sale of merchandise is recorded when the merchandise is transferred from the company to the customer. As a result, the sales revenue earned in a given accounting period, as shown by the balance in the Sales account, may be substantially different from the amount of cash received from sales during that same period.

## Sales Returns and Allowances

To foster good customer relations, many merchandising companies have a "satisfaction guaranteed" policy. This allows customers to return unsatisfactory merchandise or accept a sales price adjustment. A customer may return merchandise—a sales return—because it was defective, was damaged in transit, or was for other reasons unsatisfactory. Generally, when a return occurs, the customer is given a cash refund or a credit that can be applied to his or her account. Sometimes the customer keeps the merchandise rather than return it and agrees to accept a price adjustment—a sales allowance—that can be applied against the original selling price of the merchandise.

These sales returns and sales allowances are really direct cancellations of sales. Consequently, they *could* be recorded by the following entry (assuming that the customer was given a credit of $120 for merchandise returned):

| | | |
|---|---|---|
| Sales | 120 | |
| Accounts Receivable | | 120 |
| To record a return of merchandise from a customer | | |

[1] If it isn't clear to you why these transactions are debited and credited as they are, review the explanation of the debit and credit rules in Chapter 2.

Most merchandising companies, however, debit a **Sales Returns and Allowances account,** which is a "contra" account to the Sales Revenue account.[2] Using a Sales Returns and Allowances account is recommended because the accounting records will then show total amounts for both sales revenue and sales returns and allowances. Sales returns and allowances result from customer dissatisfaction.

Maintaining a separate account for sales returns and allowances gives owners, managers, and others the opportunity to monitor the amount by looking for trends and to compare the amount with that of sales revenue. The relationship of these figures provides insight concerning the degree of customer dissatisfaction with the merchandise sold to them.

***1c,2a. To record a credit for return of unsatisfactory merchandise, debit Sales Returns and Allowances and credit Accounts Receivable***

Therefore the entry to record a sales return where the customer was given a $120 credit for the merchandise returned would be as follows:

| | | |
|---|---|---|
| Sales Returns and Allowances | 120 | |
| Accounts Receivable | | 120 |
| To record a return of merchandise from a customer | | |

The Sales Returns and Allowances account is always debited when merchandise is returned by a customer. The credit part of the entry depends on whether the customer is given a cash refund or a credit to his or her account. In our preceding illustration we assumed that the customer was given a credit, and we recorded the entry by debiting the Sales Returns and Allowances account and crediting Accounts Receivable.

If we now assume that the company was willing to give the customer a cash refund of $120, the entry to record the transaction would be as follows:

| | | |
|---|---|---|
| Sales Returns and Allowances | 120 | |
| Cash | | 120 |
| To record a return of merchandise from a customer | | |

## Sales Discounts

When merchandise is sold on credit, the terms for future payment must be clearly stated so that both parties understand the amount to be paid and the time of payment. Credit terms generally appear on the sales invoice and constitute part of the sales agreement. In some industries it is customary for invoices to become due within a relatively short period of time. In this case, the seller marks the sales invoice to indicate the terms, using symbols such as *n/10.* This means that the net or full invoice amount is due ten days after the invoice date. Net/30 would mean that the full invoice amount must be paid within thirty days of the invoice date. Another way of setting the terms for payment is, for example, *n/10, EOM.* This means that the net amount of the invoice is due ten days after the end of the month (**EOM**) in which the invoice is dated.

When the time period for which credit is given is long, it is common practice for the seller to offer a **cash discount.** The reason for giving a cash discount is to

[2] Recall that in Chapter 3 we discussed Accumulated Depreciation—Office Equipment as a contra asset account. Sales Returns and Allowances is a contra revenue account. Its rules of debit and credit are opposite to those for a revenue account: An increase in a contra revenue account is recorded by a debit, and a contra revenue account usually has a debit balance.

provide an incentive for the early payment of accounts.[3] Sales discounts, generally stated on the sales invoice, are expressed in various ways. For example, credit terms offering cash discounts may be stated as *2/10, n/30* or *2/EOM, n/60*. Terms of 2/10, n/30 mean that the customer (1) may deduct 2% from the gross invoice amount if payment is made within ten days after the invoice date, or alternatively (2) may wait and pay the full invoice amount at any time after the tenth day but not later than the thirtieth day after the invoice date. Terms of 2/EOM, n/60 mean that the customer (1) may deduct 2% from the gross invoice amount if payment is made by the end of the month, or alternatively (2) may wait and pay the full invoice amount at any time after the end of the month but before sixty days from the date of the invoice when full payment is due.

At the time of sale, the seller does not know if the customer will take advantage of the discount. Consequently, the general practice is to record the sale at its full invoice price. The recording of the discount (if taken) is delayed until the customer pays.

For example, assume that on October 10, Willow Company sold merchandise to a customer for $1,000 on credit terms of 2/10, n/30. The entry to record the sale (at full invoice price) is as follows:

| | | | |
|---|---|---|---|
| Oct. 10 | Accounts Receivable | 1,000 | |
| | Sales | | 1,000 |
| | To record the sale of merchandise on credit terms of 2/10, n/30 | | |

By the terms expressed in this sale, the customer is entitled to a cash discount if payment is made on or before October 20 or may pay Willow the full invoice price of $1,000 by November 9. If the customer pays on October 19 (within the discount period), Willow would record the collection of its receivable as follows:

| | | | |
|---|---|---|---|
| Oct. 19 | Cash | 980 | |
| | Sales Discount | 20 | |
| | Accounts Receivable | | 1,000 |
| | To record collection of accounts receivable, less a 2% discount | | |

If a customer returns some of the merchandise purchased on account, before paying for it, the terms of the discount apply only to the merchandise kept. For example, if the customer who purchased the $1,000 of merchandise on October 10 returns $200 of the merchandise on October 15, the discount terms apply only to $800, the gross invoice price of merchandise kept. Assuming that the customer makes payment on October 19, to take advantage of the discount, the check received would be for $784 ($800 − $16 discount = $784) and would be recorded as follows:

| | | | |
|---|---|---|---|
| Oct. 19 | Cash | 784 | |
| | Sales Discount | 16 | |
| | Accounts Receivable | | 800 |
| | To record collection of accounts receivable less a 2% discount | | |

[3] Because a cash discount is often viewed as another way of reducing (adjusting) the selling price of the merchandise sold, it is often referred to as a **sales discount**.

If a customer does not take advantage of the discount terms offered, the full invoice amount must be paid. Thus, if the customer chooses to pay the $1,000 amount on October 31 (twenty-one days after the invoice date and eleven days after the discount period expired), the entry for full invoice payment would be recorded as follows:

| | | | |
|---|---|---|---|
| Oct. 31 | Cash | 1,000 | |
| | Accounts Receivable | | 1,000 |
| | To record collection of accounts receivable | | |

As mentioned earlier, cash (sales) discounts are offered to encourage customers to pay their bills promptly. The seller benefits from this arrangement because

1. Cash will be available for use earlier, that is, before the end of the credit period
2. The dollar amount "tied up" in accounts receivable will be decreased
3. The risk of loss from uncollectible accounts receivable should be diminished

*1c,2a. The Sales Discounts account accumulates the amount of cash discounts taken by customers*

The **Sales Discounts account** accumulates the amount of cash discounts taken by customers during a period. Sales Discounts, like Sales Returns and Allowances, is a contra revenue account and as such has a debit balance. Both the Sales Returns and Allowances account and the Sales Discounts account are subtracted from **gross sales** to arrive at **net sales** in the income statement. The revenue section of Willow Company in Exhibit 5–1 illustrates the presentation.

EXHIBIT 5–1

WILLOW COMPANY
Partial Income Statement

| | | |
|---|---|---|
| Revenues: | | |
| Gross Sales | | $140,200 |
| Less: Sales Returns and Allowances | $1,300 | |
| Sales Discounts | 2,400 | 3,700 |
| Net Sales | | $136,500 |

## COST OF GOODS SOLD

We have said that merchandising firms buy finished products and sell them to their customers. Consistent with the matching principle, the net income for a merchandising firm (or for that matter any business entity) is determined by deducting from sales revenue the costs incurred to produce that revenue. For a merchandising firm, those costs consist of the cost of those products that were sold during the accounting period and any other operating expenses incurred during the period. By definition, then, the **cost of goods sold** for a merchandising firm is the cost (amount expended) for the products that have been sold. For a clothing store, the cost of goods sold would be the costs incurred in purchasing the suits, dresses, shirts, blouses, sweaters, and other merchandise that was sold during the period. The store's operating expenses would include expenses incurred in its selling and administrative activities, such as rent, salaries, advertising, and utilities.

To understand how the cost of goods sold for a given period is determined, we must discuss merchandise inventory and the net cost of purchases. This is done in the sections that follow.

## MERCHANDISE INVENTORY

The inventory of a merchandising firm is called **merchandise inventory,** or simply **inventory.** It consists of items held for sale in the normal course of the firm's business activities. We previously noted the kind of items that a clothing store would include in its inventory (suits, dresses, shirts, blouses, etc.). For a sporting goods store, inventory would consist of baseballs, footballs, basketballs, golf clubs, tennis racquets, skis, and other items of athletic equipment that a store of this type would be expected to sell.

The merchandise inventory on hand on the first day of the accounting period is called the **beginning inventory.** The merchandise inventory on hand on the last day of the accounting period is called the **ending inventory.** Of course, the ending inventory of one accounting period is always the beginning inventory of the next accounting period. The ending inventory is reported in the balance sheet as a current asset.

Determining the quantity and cost of the goods remaining on hand at the end of a period (ending inventory) and the cost of the goods sold during the period (cost of goods sold) is crucial in financial reporting. This is crucial because one establishes a valuation for the current asset inventory in the balance sheet and the other provides a significant figure for cost in the measurement of periodic net income.

The two alternative methods of accounting for merchandise inventory and the cost of goods sold are the *perpetual inventory method* and the *periodic inventory method.* These methods are described in the next two subsections.

### The Perpetual Inventory Method

*1b. The perpetual inventory method keeps continuous records of inventory sold and on hand*

Companies using the **perpetual inventory method** keep continuous records of the amount and cost of inventory on hand and of inventory sold. Under this system, an **inventory record card** (maintained by hand or processed electronically in a computer storage device) is kept for each inventory item to show the quantity, unit cost, and total cost for each purchase, each sale, and the inventory balance. When an inventory item purchased is received, the number of units received, the cost per unit, and the total cost are entered in this record. When an inventory item sold is shipped, the number of units shipped, the cost per unit, and the total cost of the units shipped is also entered in the same record. The balance columns show the inventory remaining on hand in number of units, cost per unit, and total cost.

Exhibit 5–2 contains an example of a perpetual inventory record card.

The perpetual inventory method involves keeping a current and continuous record of all inventory transactions on a separate inventory card for each type of inventory that the company holds. The system may be costly to maintain, especially when a company has to keep track of many different inventory items. To keep costs down, some companies will keep perpetual inventory records only for certain key inventory items.

*EXHIBIT 5-2*

Perpetual Inventory Record Card

SNOWGLIDE SKIS

| | | PURCHASED | | | SOLD | | | BALANCE | | |
|---|---|---|---|---|---|---|---|---|---|---|
| DATE | REFERENCE | Quantity | Unit Cost | Total Cost | Quantity | Unit Cost | Total Cost | Quantity | Unit Cost | Total Cost |
| Jan. 1 | Beginning Inventory | | | | | | | 20 | $90 | $1,800 |
| 5 | | | | | 3 | 90 | 270 | 17 | 90 | 1,530 |
| 8 | | | | | 2 | 90 | 180 | 15 | 90 | 1,350 |
| 10 | | 10 | 92 | 920 | | | | 15<br>10 | 90<br>92 | 2,270 |
| 13 | | | | | 5 | 90 | 450 | 10<br>10 | 90<br>92 | 1,820 |
| 15 | | | | | 4 | 90 | 360 | 6<br>10 | 90<br>92 | 1,460 |
| 18 | | 10 | 95 | 950 | | | | 6<br>10<br>10 | 90<br>92<br>95 | 2,410 |
| 20 | | | | | 6 | 90 | 540 | 10<br>10 | 92<br>95 | 1,870 |

The perpetual inventory method is widely used by companies that make the products they sell. (These manufacturing-type companies are discussed in later chapters.) It is also used extensively by merchandising companies that in a given accounting period sell a relatively few high-unit-value items, such as automobiles, appliances, fur coats, and furniture. (A full discussion and set of illustrations for the perpetual inventory method will be presented in Chapter 9.)

## The Periodic Inventory Method

Companies that sell low-value, high-volume items (such as the items generally sold in hardware stores, stationery stores, and drugstores) find that the costs of the perpetual inventory system are greater than the benefits received. Most of these companies, therefore, choose to use the alternative periodic inventory method in accounting for inventory and the cost of goods sold.

***1b. The periodic inventory method does not debit or credit inventory when merchandise is purchased or sold. Rather, a physical count determines the amount of the ending inventory***

Under the **periodic inventory method,** the Inventory account is not debited when merchandise is purchased and not credited when merchandise is sold. Instead the cost of inventory items purchased during the period is debited to a Purchases account, and only one entry—that which debits Cash or Accounts Receivable and credits Sales—is made to record a sale. The cost of the goods on hand (ending inventory) is determined by taking a physical inventory count.[4] Since under the periodic inventory method the cost of the goods sold is not recorded each time a sale is made, the ending inventory established by the physical count is needed to compute the cost of goods sold. The computation is made by deducting the ending inventory figure from the cost of the goods

[4] Basically, the procedure for taking a physical inventory count requires the following: (1) count each item of merchandise remaining on hand at the end of the accounting period, (2) multiply the quantity of each item of merchandise remaining on hand by its unit cost, and (3) add the resulting item costs to determine the cost of the ending inventory.

that were available for sale during the period. The items included in the calculation of cost of goods sold are

1. The cost of goods on hand at the beginning of the period (beginning inventory)
2. The cost of goods purchased during the period (net cost of purchases)
3. The cost of the unsold goods remaining on hand at the end of the period (ending inventory)

An example summarizing the cost of goods sold computation with assumed amounts is given below.

| | |
|---|---|
| Merchandise inventory at the beginning of the period | $12,000 |
| Add: Net cost of goods purchased during the period | 80,000 |
| Cost of goods available for sale | $92,000 |
| Less: Merchandise inventory at the end of the period | 14,000 |
| Cost of goods sold | $78,000 |

Note that the cost of the beginning inventory, $12,000 (determined by the physical count taken at the end of the last accounting period), plus the net cost of goods purchased during the year, determined the cost of the goods that were available for sale during the period ($12,000 + $80,000 = $92,000). Once those not sold are determined by physically counting the goods still on hand at the end of the period (in this case, $14,000), the cost of those that were sold is easily computed to be $78,000 ($92,000 − $14,000 = $78,000).

We will now discuss the procedures used to account for the net cost of goods purchased during a period, the $80,000 figure in our last example. We will assume the use of the periodic inventory method.

## NET COST OF GOODS PURCHASED

When the periodic inventory method is used, the net cost of goods purchased must also be computed. Figures for this computation are obtained from the ledger accounts, as we will see shortly. The **net cost of goods purchased** is made up of

The cost of the goods purchased (which can be obtained from the Purchases account balance)

Less adjustments for purchase returns and allowances (with amounts from these transactions recorded in a separate ledger account)

Less adjustments for purchase discounts (with amounts from these transactions recorded in a separate ledger account)

Plus adjustments for the cost of transporting the goods to the company (with amounts from these transactions recorded in a separate ledger account)

*2b. Under the gross invoice method, a merchandising firm records its purchases at the full invoice price*

These four items constituting the net cost of purchases are discussed and illustrated in the subsections that follow. In our illustrations, purchases are recorded at their full invoice price, commonly called the **gross invoice price.** The use of the gross invoice price in accounting for the cost of merchandise purchased is called the **gross invoice method,** or **gross purchases method.**

## Purchases

*1c,2b. When the periodic inventory method is used, merchandise purchased is recorded by debiting the Purchases account*

When the periodic inventory method is used, the cost of all merchandise purchased for resale is debited to a **Purchases account.** The Purchases account is a temporary account used to accumulate the cost of all the merchandise purchased during the period and will be closed at the end of each period.

If on January 3 a company using the periodic inventory method purchased $5,000 of merchandise on account, the transaction would be recorded as follows:

| | | | |
|---|---|---|---|
| Jan. 3 | Purchases. . . . . . . . . . . . . . . . . . . . . . . . . . . . . . . . . . . . . . . . . . . | 5,000 | |
| | Accounts Payable . . . . . . . . . . . . . . . . . . . . . . . . . . . . . . . | | 5,000 |
| | To record the purchase of merchandise on credit terms of 2/10, n/30 | | |

The Purchases account is used only to record merchandise purchased for resale. Items purchased for use in operating the business, such as vehicles, desks, and office supplies, are still recorded by debiting an asset account with an appropriate title.

## Purchase Returns and Allowances

*1c,2b. Adjustments for unsatisfactory merchandise returned to suppliers are debited to Accounts Payable and credited to Purchase Returns and Allowances*

As it was with sales, a purchase transaction may also involve ***purchase returns*** or ***purchase allowances.*** When merchandise purchased from a supplier is defective or otherwise unsatisfactory, the buyer generally returns it for credit or as an alternative accepts an allowance (that is, a price reduction) and keeps the merchandise. In any event, the cost of the merchandise returned or the amount of the allowance granted is credited to a **Purchase Returns and Allowances account.** For example, assume that $500 of the merchandise purchased on January 3 was returned to the supplier on January 9. The entry to record the purchase return would be as follows:

| | | | |
|---|---|---|---|
| Jan. 9 | Accounts Payable . . . . . . . . . . . . . . . . . . . . . . . . . . . . . . . . . . . . | 500 | |
| | Purchase Returns and Allowances . . . . . . . . . . . . . . . . . . | | 500 |
| | To record merchandise returned | | |

Purchase returns and allowances could be recorded by crediting the Purchases account. Instead we record them in a separate Purchase Returns and Allowances account where the amount for this type of business activity can be accumulated and provided to management and others.

The process of returning merchandise or negotiating allowances is both time-consuming and costly. An early step in controlling this cost is to develop a recordkeeping procedure that furnishes a dollar figure for purchase returns and allowances. Excessive returns may indicate that the company has poor purchasing practices or unreliable suppliers, in which case corrective action should be taken.

The Purchase Returns and Allowances account is a *contra* account to Purchases (that is, a contra expense account) whose balance is needed to help determine the net cost of purchases for a period.

## Purchase Discounts

When merchandise is purchased on account, the payment terms are stated on the invoice. Companies will frequently grant cash discounts to customers who pay promptly for goods purchased on credit. As explained earlier, when the seller gives a cash discount, it is called a *sales discount.* Conversely, when the buyer gets a *cash discount,* it is called a **purchase discount.**

Using data from previous transactions, we know that on January 3, the company purchased merchandise costing $5,000 on credit terms of 2/10, n/30. We also know that on January 9, merchandise costing $500 was returned. If the account balance ($4,500) is paid on January 11 (which is within ten days of the invoice date), the buyer would record the transaction as follows:

*1c,2b. The entry to record a purchase discount is shown here*

| | | | |
|---|---|---|---|
| Jan. 11 | Accounts Payable | 4,500 | |
| | Purchase Discounts | | 90 |
| | Cash | | 4,410 |
| | To record payment for merchandise purchased on January 3, less a 2% discount | | |

Note that the terms of the cash discount apply only to the amount still owed to the supplier after the amount of the purchase return has been deducted from the gross invoice amount. Generally speaking, when purchase discounts are offered, they should be taken even if the money has to be borrowed to make the payment within the specified time period. To illustrate this point, note that terms of 2/10, n/30 allow for a 2% discount if payment is made twenty days earlier than required. This is the equivalent of an annual interest rate of 36%, computed as follows:

A twenty-day period is approximately one-eighteenth of a year.
There are approximately eighteen twenty-day periods in a year.
Eighteen periods × 2% = 36% interest rate on an annual basis.

Although interest rates vary widely over time, it is reasonable to assume that a company can borrow at an annual interest rate considerably below 36%.

The balance in the **Purchase Discounts account** is the amount by which the cost of the goods purchased during a period was reduced as a result of making cash payments promptly (that is, within the specified discount period). The Purchase Discounts account is a *contra* account whose balance is used in determining the net cost of purchases for the period.

## Trade Discounts

*1d. A trade discount is a percentage reduction in published list prices*

Manufacturers and wholesalers often publish lists or catalogs showing the list price of their products. Certain customers, such as dealers, are frequently allowed deductions from the list prices quoted. These deductions are called **trade discounts.** It is important to distinguish between a cash discount, which is related to the prompt payment of an invoice, and a trade discount, which is a percentage reduction in published list prices. Trade discounts are used to determine the actual selling price of an item and are offered for the following reasons:

1. To avoid the cost of publishing catalogs simply to revise prices. Prices can be changed by changing the trade discounts available.

2. To reduce prices to customers who purchase large quantities.
3. To establish different prices to different types of customers. For example, price distinctions can be made between retailers, dealers, and wholesalers.

Trade discounts may be stated as a single rate or as a series of rates. When trade discounts are stated in a series, they are deducted in sequence and are often called **chain discounts,** or **series discounts.** To illustrate, first assume that merchandise having a list price of $1,000 is subject to a trade discount of 30%. The actual sales price is $700, computed as follows:

| | |
|---|---|
| List price | $1,000 |
| Less: Trade discount ($1,000 × 0.3) | 300 |
| Sales price | $ 700 |

Assume that if certain conditions are met, the merchandise is subject to discounts of 30% and 10%. Each discount applies to the net price after deducting any previous discounts. If the purchaser qualifies for both discounts, the actual sales price is $630, computed as follows:

| | |
|---|---|
| List price | $1,000 |
| Less: First trade discount ($1,000 × 0.3) | 300 |
| Remainder after first discount | 700 |
| Less: Second trade discount ($700 × 0.1) | 70 |
| Sales price | $ 630 |

Trade discounts *are not recorded* in the accounting records of either the buyer or the seller. They are used only to determine the actual selling price of the merchandise. In our second example, a selling price of $630 was established. Therefore both the seller and the buyer would use that amount when recording their sale and purchase, respectively. If a cash discount were available, it would apply to the actual sales price of $630.

## Transportation-In

When goods are purchased, costs will be incurred to transport them from the seller's premises to the buyer's premises. Sometimes the seller pays the transportation costs. Other times the buyer is responsible for paying the transportation costs. Transportation costs incurred by the buyer increase the cost of the merchandise acquired and could therefore be recorded by debiting the Purchases account directly. However, a more widely accepted procedure is to accumulate the cost of transportation on incoming merchandise in a **Transportation-In account** (sometimes called a **Freight-In account**). By establishing a separate account for transportation charges, we are able to provide information that management and others can monitor and attempt to control.

*1c,2b. The buyer records transportation charges on purchases by debiting Transportation-In*

To illustrate the journal entry to record transportation charges, assume that costs of $75 were incurred to ship merchandise from the supplier to the buyer. The sales agreement specifies that the buyer is responsible for these costs which the buyer paid on January 15.

| | | | |
|---|---|---|---|
| Jan. 15 | Transportation-In | 75 | |
| | Cash | | 75 |
| | To record the payment of transportation charges on merchandise purchased | | |

The Transportation-In account will be reported in the cost of goods sold section of the income statement as an addition to Purchases in establishing the net cost of purchases.

Two additional things should be noted: (1) the terms used in sales agreements to specify which party (the seller or the buyer) is responsible for paying transportation costs, and (2) the distinction in reporting between transportation costs incurred on merchandise purchased and transportation costs incurred on merchandise sold.

**SHIPPING TERMS** The terms used to specify which party is responsible for paying transportation costs are *FOB shipping point* and *FOB destination.* **FOB shipping point** is translated "free on board shipping point." It means that the buyer is responsible for paying any transportation costs incurred to ship the merchandise from the seller's location to the buyer's place of business. The term **FOB destination** is translated "free on board destination." It means that the seller is responsible for paying the transportation charges incurred to ship the merchandise to the buyer's location (destination).

When the buyer pays the transportation charges on merchandise shipped FOB shipping point, the amount paid is debited to the Transportation-In account and credited to the Cash account. Sometimes when goods are sold FOB shipping point, the seller will, as a matter of convenience, prepay the cost of transporting the items to the buyer's location. In this case, the buyer is obligated to pay to the seller an amount equal to the transportation costs plus the cost of the merchandise purchased. The obligation would be recorded by debiting both the Purchases account and the Transportation-In account for appropriate amounts. On other occasions, the buyer will pay the transportation costs on merchandise purchased FOB destination when the goods are received. Because the buyer is not responsible for paying transportation costs on merchandise purchased under these terms, the buyer will deduct that amount from the invoice amount when making payment.

Shipping terms also specify when title (ownership) to the merchandise passes (transfers) from seller to buyer.

When shipping terms are FOB shipping point, title to the merchandise passes to the buyer at the point of origin when the merchandise is placed on a carrier such as a truck, train, or plane. When merchandise is shipped FOB destination, title (ownership) does not transfer to the buyer until the merchandise reaches its destination.

To maintain information for determining amounts applicable to cost of goods sold, gross margin on sales, and operating expenses, we must distinguish between the transportation costs incurred on merchandise purchased and the transportation costs incurred on merchandise sold when entering these amounts in the accounting records. When the terms of the sale are FOB destination, the transportation costs incurred by the seller are recorded in a *Transportation-Out* or *Delivery Expense* account. Transportation-Out is an expense that should be reported in the operating expenses section of the income statement. Therefore it has no impact on the computation of cost of goods sold or gross margin on sales.

## ACCOUNTING FOR MERCHANDISE PURCHASED—THE NET INVOICE METHOD

In all the previous illustrations, purchase transactions were recorded at their gross invoice price, a procedure commonly referred to as the *gross invoice method* or the *gross purchases method*. You will recall that under this method, merchandise purchased is recorded at the gross, or full, invoice amount. Purchase discounts are recorded only if payment is made within the discount period specified by the seller.

*2c. Under the net invoice method, the buyer debits Purchases and credits Accounts Payable for the net invoice price*

Another method that may be used is the **net invoice method,** also called the **net purchases method.** Under this method, merchandise purchased is recorded at the net invoice amount, that is, full invoice amount less the cash discount allowed. To illustrate and contrast the methods, assume that on October 15 a company that uses the periodic inventory method purchased merchandise costing $8,000 on terms of 2/10, n/30. This transaction is recorded under the two methods as follows:

| GROSS INVOICE METHOD | | | | NET INVOICE METHOD | | | |
|---|---|---|---|---|---|---|---|
| Oct. 15 | Purchases | 8,000 | | Oct. 15 | Purchases | 7,840 | |
| | Accounts Payable | | 8,000 | | Accounts Payable | | 7,840 |
| | To record merchandise purchased on credit terms of 2/10, n/30 | | | | To record merchandise purchased on credit terms of 2/10, n/30 | | |

Note that under the net invoice method, the amount used in the entry to record the purchase is $7,840. Proponents of this method believe that purchase discounts reduce the cost of merchandise purchased and that its true cost is its net, not gross, cost. Discounts not taken are recorded as discounts lost (as we will illustrate below), and the amount of discounts lost should be viewed as an operating expense rather than an increase in the cost of purchases.

*2c. Under the net invoice method, payment within the discount period is recorded by debiting Accounts Payable and crediting Cash*

Returning to our example, if payment is made on October 23 (within the discount period), the discount may be taken. If the gross invoice method is used, the amount of the cash discount taken is recorded in a Purchase Discounts account. Under the net invoice method, cash discounts taken are not recorded. The entry to record the payment made on October 23 under each of the two methods is as follows:

| GROSS INVOICE METHOD | | | | NET INVOICE METHOD | | | |
|---|---|---|---|---|---|---|---|
| Oct. 23 | Accounts Payable | 8,000 | | Oct. 23 | Accounts Payable | 7,840 | |
| | Cash | | 7,840 | | Cash | | 7,840 |
| | Purchase Discounts | | 160 | | | | |
| | To record payment within the discount period | | | | To record payment within the discount period | | |

*2c. Under the net invoice method, discounts not taken are recorded in Purchase Discounts Lost*

If payment is not made by October 25, the discount is lost and $8,000 is owed and due to the supplier. Under the gross invoice method, the company has a liability on its books for the $8,000 amount. Under the net invoice method, the liability is on the books for $7,840, and therefore when payment is made after the discount period, the amount of the discount lost is recorded in a new account called **Purchase Discounts Lost.** For example, assume that payment is made on October 31. Since the discount period is over, the full invoice price of $8,000 must be paid and the entry under each of the two methods is as follows:

| GROSS INVOICE METHOD | | | | NET INVOICE METHOD | | | |
|---|---|---|---|---|---|---|---|
| Oct. 31 | Accounts Payable . . . . . . . . . . | 8,000 | | Oct. 31 | Accounts Payable. . . . . . . . . . | 7,840 | |
| | Cash . . . . . . . . . . . . . . . | | 8,000 | | Purchase Discounts Lost . . . . | 160 | |
| | | | | | Cash. . . . . . . . . . . . . . . | | 8,000 |
| | To record payment after the discount period | | | | To record payment after the discount period | | |

Companies lose discount privileges when they are unable to pay their invoices within the specified period of time. The cause may be inadequate cash balances or accounts payable personnel who are slow in processing invoices for payment. In any case, the net invoice method will provide a benefit in that it accumulates the amount of discounts lost in a separate account. This procedure places emphasis on the loss so that management can monitor the amount and create controls designed to minimize the amount. The gross invoice method does not provide a direct way to identify the amount of purchase discounts lost.

Although theoretically preferable, the net invoice method does not seem to be as widely used as the gross invoice method. Thus you should assume that the gross invoice method is used in all subsequent illustrations and end-of-the-chapter problems unless instructed differently.

## COST OF GOODS AVAILABLE FOR SALE

*1c,2d. Calculation of the cost of goods sold is illustrated in Exhibit 5–3*

The net cost of all merchandise purchased during a period, plus the cost of the merchandise on hand at the beginning of the period (the beginning inventory), is the total cost of the merchandise that could have been sold during the period. This amount is called the cost of goods available for sale. In the partial income statement shown in Exhibit 5–3, the cost of goods available for sale is shown as a line item for $207,300. It was computed by taking the balance in the Merchandise Inventory account at the beginning of the period ($20,000) and adding to it the net cost of purchases of $187,300 ($20,000 + $187,300 = $207,300).

## ENDING INVENTORY

At the end of the accounting period, a company using the periodic inventory method must take a physical count of the merchandise that is still on hand (unsold merchandise). Once the units counted have been associated with their appropriate costs, an amount representing the cost of the ending inventory can be determined. Assume, as shown in our illustration of a company's partial income statement, that the cost of the items remaining on hand at the end of the period (ending inventory) is $24,000. By subtracting the ending inventory amount of $24,000 from the cost of goods available for sale of $207,300, we determined that the cost of the goods sold during the period totaled $183,300.

## COST OF GOODS SOLD

The beginning inventory plus the net cost of purchases equals the cost of goods available for sale, and the cost of goods available for sale minus the ending inventory equals the cost of goods sold. These relationships, which are found in the income statement for companies using the periodic inventory method, can be summarized as follows:

Cost of Goods Available for Sale = Cost of the Beginning Inventory + Net Cost of Purchases

Cost of Goods Sold = Cost of Goods Available for Sale − Cost of the Ending Inventory

Gross Margin on Sales = Net Sales − Cost of Goods Sold

The accounts needed to accumulate merchandise costs under the periodic inventory method include the Purchases, Purchase Returns and Allowances, Purchase Discounts, and Transportation-In accounts. Exhibit 5–3 shows how all the components of the cost of goods sold are reported in that section of the income statement. The example is based on arbitrarily assumed amounts, includes two major sections of the income statement (the revenue section and the cost of goods sold section), and ends with an amount of $115,900 representing the gross margin on sales.

*EXHIBIT 5–3*

Partial Income Statement

| | | | | |
|---|---|---|---|---|
| Revenues: | | | | |
| Gross Sales | | | | $305,200 |
| Less: Sales Returns and Allowances | | | $1,700 | |
| Sales Discounts | | | 4,300 | 6,000 |
| Net Sales | | | | $299,200 |
| Cost of Goods Sold: | | | | |
| Merchandise Inventory, Jan. 1, 19X2 | | | $ 20,000 | |
| Purchases | | $190,000 | | |
| Less: Purchase Returns and Allowances | $1,500 | | | |
| Purchase Discounts | 3,800 | 5,300 | | |
| Net Purchases | | $184,700 | | |
| Add: Transportation-In | | 2,600 | | |
| Net Cost of Purchases | | | 187,300 | |
| Cost of Goods Available for Sale | | | $207,300 | |
| Less: Merchandise Inventory, Dec. 31, 19X2 | | | 24,000 | |
| Cost of Goods Sold | | | | 183,300 |
| Gross Margin on Sales | | | | $115,900 |

## MERCHANDISING ACCOUNTS SUMMARIZED

The activities of merchandising companies, especially those that use the periodic inventory method to account for ending inventory and the cost of goods sold, require a number of accounts not used by service companies. These additional accounts are summarized below.

*Sales account.* The Sales account is credited for the selling price of merchandise sold. Sales is classified as a revenue account. It appears in the revenue section of the income statement.

*Sales Returns and Allowances account.* The Sales Returns and Allowances account is debited for the selling price of the merchandise returned by customers and for amounts allowed as deductions from the original sales price for merchandise found defective by the buyer but not returned. Sales Returns and Allowances is classified as a contra revenue account. It appears in the income statement as a deduction from gross sales revenue.

*Sales Discounts account.* The Sales Discounts account is debited for the deductions that customers take from the gross sales price of merchandise they purchased when their payment is made within specified time limits. Sales Discounts is classified as a contra revenue account. It appears in the income statement as a deduction from gross sales revenue.

*Purchases account.* The Purchases account is debited for the purchase price of merchandise purchased. It appears as a component of the net cost of purchases in the cost of goods sold section of the income statement.

*Purchase Returns and Allowances account.* The Purchase Returns and Allowances account is credited for the cost of unsatisfactory merchandise returned to the supplier and for amounts allowed as deductions from the original purchase price for merchandise that, although retained, is found to be defective. Purchase Returns and Allowances is classified as a contra account to Purchases. It appears as a component of the net cost of purchases in the cost of goods sold section of the income statement.

*Purchase Discounts account.* The Purchase Discounts account is credited for the amounts that have been deducted from the original purchase price of merchandise when payment is made within the time period established by the seller. Purchase Discounts is classified as a contra account to Purchases. It appears as a component of the net cost of purchases in the cost of goods sold section of the income statement.

*Transportation-In account.* The Transportation-In account is debited for the cost of shipping merchandise from the seller's to the buyer's place of business. It appears as a component of the net cost of purchases in the cost of goods sold section of the income statement.

*Merchandise Inventory account.* The Merchandise Inventory account shows the cost of merchandise on hand and available for sale to customers. Merchandise Inventory is classified as a current asset and appears in the balance sheet. Under the periodic inventory method, the beginning inventory is added to the net cost of purchases to determine the cost of goods available for sale. The ending inventory is subtracted from the cost of goods available for sale to determine the cost of goods sold.

## END-OF-PERIOD PROCEDURES FOR A MERCHANDISING FIRM

The end-of-the-period procedures for a mechandising firm follow the same sequence of steps as those for a service firm. Thus at the end of the accounting period, after all the transaction entries have been recorded and posted to ledger accounts and the account balances have been determined, a work sheet can be prepared. This work sheet will help organize information needed for preparing financial statements and for journalizing the adjusting and closing entries.

Because many of the accounts used to record the effects of business transactions for a merchandising firm are the same as the ones used for a service firm, they are treated in the same way when reported and when preparing them for the next accounting period. New accounts associated with a merchandising firm or the ones associated specifically with merchandising firms that use the periodic inventory method should be observed carefully as we proceed through the end-of-the-period procedures to see how they are treated and reported.

Once the balances in all ledger accounts have been determined, we will continue the end-of-the-period process by illustrating

1. The preparation of a work sheet for a merchandising firm
2. The preparation of financial statements for a merchandising firm
3. The entries needed to close the temporary accounts at year-end

*2e. A work sheet for a merchandising company is illustrated in Exhibit 5–4*

**1. WORK SHEET FOR A MERCHANDISING FIRM** The format of a work sheet for a merchandising firm is similar to that for service firms except that some new accounts have been included. It serves the same purposes for the merchandising firm as it did when prepared for a service firm, namely, to help in preparing financial statements, adjusting entries, and closing entries. The completed work sheet of Cascade Lighting Outlet in Exhibit 5–4 will be used in the discussion that follows.

EXHIBIT 5–4

CASCADE LIGHTING OUTLET
Work Sheet
For the Year Ended December 31, 19X2

| | Trial Balance | | Adjustments | | Income Statement | | Balance Sheet | |
|---|---|---|---|---|---|---|---|---|
| | Debit | Credit | Debit | Credit | Debit | Credit | Debit | Credit |
| Cash | 4 200 | | | | | | 4 200 | |
| Accounts Receivable | 23 700 | | | | | | 23 700 | |
| Merchandise Inventory | 20 000 | | | | 20 000 | 23 000 | 23 000 | |
| Prepaid Insurance | 600 | | | (a) 200 | | | 400 | |
| Equipment | 18 000 | | | | | | 18 000 | |
| Accumulated Depreciation—Equipment | | 1 000 | | (b)1 800 | | | | 2 800 |
| Accounts Payable | | 11 000 | | | | | | 11 000 |
| S. Volta, Capital | | 50 000 | | | | | | 50 000 |
| S. Volta, Drawings | 15 000 | | | | | | 15 000 | |
| Sales | | 279 000 | | | | 279 000 | | |
| Sales Returns & Allowances | 3 000 | | | | 3 000 | | | |
| Sales Discounts | 4 500 | | | | 4 500 | | | |
| Purchases | 180 000 | | | | 180 000 | | | |
| Purchase Returns & Allowances | | 1 500 | | | | 1 500 | | |
| Purchase Discounts | | 3 500 | | | | 3 500 | | |
| Transportation | 2 000 | | | | 2 000 | | | |
| Salaries Expense | 45 000 | | (c)1 000 | | 46 000 | | | |
| Advertising Expense | 10 000 | | | | 10 000 | | | |
| Rent Expense | 12 000 | | | | 12 000 | | | |
| Utilities Expense | 8 000 | | | | 8 000 | | | |
| | 346 000 | 346 000 | | | | | | |
| Insurance Expense | | | (a) 200 | | 200 | | | |
| Depreciation Expense | | | (b)1 800 | | 1 800 | | | |
| Salaries Payable | | | | (c)1 000 | | | | 1 000 |
| | | | 3 000 | 3 000 | 287 500 | 307 000 | | |
| Net Income | | | | | 19 500 | | | 19 500 |
| | | | | | 307 000 | 307 000 | 84 300 | 84 300 |

As with all work sheets, the first two columns—the Trial Balance columns—show a listing of the account balances. These balances were taken from the ledger accounts on December 31, 19X2, the company's year-end.

Only three adjustments were needed to update the account balances as of December 31, 19X2. They are identified by amounts in the Adjustments columns and indicate the following:

a. Prepaid insurance was adjusted to reflect $200 of expired premium cost.
b. Annual depreciation expense on equipment was computed at $1,800.
c. Accrued salaries totaled $1,000 at year-end.

No other accounts needed to be adjusted, and so their amounts were extended directly from the Trial Balance columns to the Income Statement and Balance Sheet columns. In this work sheet the Adjusted Trial Balance columns were omitted. Accountants sometimes omit them, especially when only a few adjustments are entered in the Adjustments columns. Nevertheless, the combined figures from the Trial Balance and Adjustments columns are extended to the appropriate financial statement columns.

Pay close attention to the merchandising accounts (highlighted in Exhibit 5–4) and the way they are treated in the work sheet. They are the new accounts introduced in this chapter. Note especially that the balance of the Merchandise Inventory account ($20,000 in the Trial Balance debit column) is the cost of merchandise on hand at the beginning of the year. As you can see, this $20,000 amount is extended to the Income Statement debit column so that it can be added to the debit balance accounts that constitute the net cost of purchases. The Sales, Sales Returns and Allowances, and Sales Discounts account balances are extended to the appropriate Income Statement columns—Sales in the Income Statement credit column because it represents revenue, and Sales Returns and Allowances and Sales Discounts in the Income Statement debit column because they are contra accounts to Sales. The beginning Merchandise Inventory, Purchases, and Transportation-In balances are extended to the Income Statement debit column. Purchase Returns and Allowances and Purchase Discounts are extended to the Income Statement credit column. However, the treatment of the ending Merchandise Inventory in the work sheet needs special attention.

Recall that under the periodic inventory method, purchase and sales transactions are not entered in the Merchandise Inventory ledger account. Therefore the cost of the merchandise on hand at the end of the period cannot be obtained from that account. The $23,000 cost of the ending inventory for Cascade Lighting Outlet was determined by an inventory count. The procedure for entering the cost of the ending inventory in the work sheet is as follows:

> Enter the cost of the ending inventory ($23,000) in the Income Statement credit column and in the Balance Sheet debit column. The amount is entered in the Income Statement credit column because it must be subtracted from the cost of goods available for sale (whose amounts already appear in the work sheet Income Statement columns) to determine the cost of goods sold. The amount of the ending inventory is also extended to the Balance Sheet debit column to recognize that the ending inventory is an asset to be reported in the balance sheet.

The work sheet for a merchandising firm is completed in much the same way as that illustrated in Chapter 4 for a service firm. All the account balances are extended to either the Income Statement columns or the Balance Sheet columns. Then the net income ($19,500 for Cascade Lighting) is determined. The amount is titled net income and is entered in the Income Statement debit column and the Balance Sheet credit column. Finally, the last four columns are totaled to ensure that the equality of debits and credits has been maintained, and the work sheet is complete.

As part of the end-of-year process, adjusting entries are recorded from the information found in the Adjustments columns of the work sheet and are posted to the ledger accounts. The procedure for recording and posting these entries is the same for both merchandising and service firms.

**2. FINANCIAL STATEMENTS FOR A MERCHANDISING FIRM** After the work sheet has been completed, it should be used in preparing the financial statements. The three statements to be illustrated are the income statement, the capital statement, and the balance sheet.

*1c,2e. The income statement for a merchandising company is illustrated in Exhibit 5–5*

The *income statement* shown in Exhibit 5–5 was prepared from the information contained in the work sheet (Exhibit 5–4). Note the three major sections of the income statement for a merchandising company: revenue, cost of goods sold, and operating expenses. The company uses the periodic inventory method, and therefore many items are reported in the cost of goods sold section. The arrangement of these items should be examined carefully.

EXHIBIT 5–5

CASCADE LIGHTING OUTLET
Income Statement
For the Year Ended December 31, 19X2

| | | | | |
|---|---|---|---|---|
| Revenue: | | | | |
| Sales | | | | $279,000 |
| Less: Sales Returns and Allowances | | | $ 3,000 | |
| Sales Discounts | | | 4,500 | 7,500 |
| Net Sales | | | | $271,500 |
| Cost of Goods Sold: | | | | |
| Merchandise Inventory, Jan. 1, 19X2 | | | $ 20,000 | |
| Purchases | | $180,000 | | |
| Less: Purchase Returns and Allowances | $1,500 | | | |
| Purchase Discounts | 3,500 | 5,000 | | |
| Net Purchases | | $175,000 | | |
| Add: Transportation-In | | 2,000 | | |
| Net Cost of Purchases | | | 177,000 | |
| Cost of Goods Available for Sale | | | $197,000 | |
| Less: Merchandise Inventory, Dec. 31, 19X2 | | | 23,000 | |
| Cost of Goods Sold | | | | 174,000 |
| Gross Margin on Sales | | | | $ 97,500 |
| Operating Expenses: | | | | |
| Salaries | | | $ 46,000 | |
| Advertising | | | 10,000 | |
| Rent | | | 12,000 | |
| Utilities | | | 8,000 | |
| Insurance | | | 200 | |
| Depreciation | | | 1,800 | |
| Total Operating Expense | | | | 78,000 |
| Net Income | | | | $ 19,500 |

*2e. The capital statement for a merchandising company is illustrated in Exhibit 5–6*

The *capital statement* is prepared in the same way for a merchandising company as it is for a service company. Its purpose is to show the change that took place in owner's capital during the year. The owner's capital in Cascade Lighting Outlet was increased by net income and decreased by withdrawals. These changes in owner's capital are shown in the capital statement in Exhibit 5–6.

EXHIBIT 5-6

| CASCADE LIGHTING OUTLET | |
|---|---|
| Capital Statement | |
| For the Year Ended December 31, 19X2 | |
| S. Volta, Capital, Jan. 1, 19X2 ...... | $50,000 |
| Net Income for the Year ........... | 19,500 |
| Subtotal ...................... | $69,500 |
| Less: Drawings .................. | 15,000 |
| S. Volta, Capital, Dec. 31, 19X2 ..... | $54,500 |

*2e. The balance sheet for a mechandising company is illustrated in Exhibit 5-7*

The *balance sheet* for Cascade Lighting is shown in Exhibit 5-7. Note that the company's assets have been classified into current and long-term and that the ending inventory appears among the current assets. With one exception, the amounts were taken from the Balance Sheet columns of the work sheet. That exception applies to the owner's capital balance of $54,500, which was determined from information in the capital statement.

EXHIBIT 5-7

| CASCADE LIGHTING OUTLET | | |
|---|---|---|
| Balance Sheet | | |
| December 31, 19X2 | | |
| ASSETS | | |
| Current Assets: | | |
| Cash ........................... | $ 4,200 | |
| Accounts Receivable ............. | 23,700 | |
| Merchandise Inventory............ | 23,000 | |
| Prepaid Insurance................ | 400 | |
| Total Current Assets............ | | $51,300 |
| Long-Term Plant Assets: | | |
| Equipment...................... | $18,000 | |
| Less: Accumulated Depreciation ..... | 2,800 | |
| Total Long-Term Plant Assets ..... | | 15,200 |
| Total Assets ...................... | | $66,500 |
| LIABILITIES AND OWNER'S EQUITY | | |
| Current Liabilities: | | |
| Accounts Payable................ | $11,000 | |
| Salaries Payable ................. | 1,000 | |
| Total Current Liabilities.......... | | $12,000 |
| Owner's Equity: | | |
| S. Volta, Capital ................. | | 54,500 |
| Total Liabilities and Owner's Equity..... | | $66,500 |

**3. CLOSING ENTRIES FOR A MERCHANDISING FIRM** The purpose of closing entries is to clear out balances in (close) all revenue and expense accounts so that they will be ready to accumulate information in the next accounting period. The procedure here is the same as that described in Chapter 4 when the temporary accounts of a service firm were closed. However, when a merchandising firm uses the periodic inventory method, two items must be taken care of at year-end. This is done as a part of the closing entries process:

The beginning inventory balance is removed from the Merchandise Inventory account. This requires the posting of a credit to the account and therefore is usually done when all temporary accounts having debit balances are closed to the Income Summary account.

The ending inventory balance must be entered in the Merchandise Inventory account. This requires the posting of a debit to the account and therefore is usually done when all temporary accounts having credit balances are closed to the Income Summary account.

Crediting the beginning inventory and debiting the ending inventory as part of the closing entries merely expedites the journalizing process. Thus the closing entries in this chapter are really (1) *entries* to close out the temporary accounts and (2) *entries* to remove the beginning inventory balance and enter the ending inventory balance. The closing process can be summarized as follows:

1. *Close* all temporary accounts having *credit* balances by reducing their balances to *zero*, and *credit* the total to the *Income Summary account.* Use this entry to enter the ending inventory balance in the Merchandise Inventory account.
2. *Close* all temporary accounts having *debit* balances, except the drawings account, by reducing their balances to *zero*, and *debit* the total to the *Income Summary account.* Use this entry to remove the beginning inventory balance from the Merchandise Inventory account.
3. *Close* the balance in the Income Summary account by transferring it to the *owner's capital account.*
4. *Close* the balance in the owner's drawings account by transferring it to the *owner's capital account.*

The closing entries for Cascade Lighting Outlet are shown below.

*2f. Closing entries for a merchandising company that uses the periodic inventory system are illustrated here*

| | | | |
|---|---|---|---|
| Dec. 31 | Merchandise Inventory | 23,000 | |
| | Sales | 279,000 | |
| | Purchase Returns and Allowances | 1,500 | |
| | Purchase Discounts | 3,500 | |
| | Income Summary | | 307,000 |
| | To record the ending inventory and to close the temporary accounts having credit balances | | |

| | | | |
|---|---|---|---|
| Dec. 31 | Income Summary | 287,500 | |
| | Merchandise Inventory | | 20,000 |
| | Sales Returns and Allowances | | 3,000 |
| | Sales Discounts | | 4,500 |
| | Purchases | | 180,000 |
| | Transportation-In | | 2,000 |
| | Salaries Expense | | 46,000 |
| | Advertising Expense | | 10,000 |
| | Rent Expense | | 12,000 |
| | Utilities Expense | | 8,000 |
| | Insurance Expense | | 200 |
| | Depreciation Expense | | 1,800 |
| | To remove the beginning inventory and to close the temporary accounts having debit balances | | |

| | | | |
|---|---|---|---|
| Dec. 31 | Income Summary | 19,500 | |
| | S. Volta, Capital | | 19,500 |
| | To close the Income Summary account | | |

| | | | |
|---|---|---|---|
| Dec. 31 | S. Volta, Capital | 15,000 | |
| | S. Volta, Drawings | | 15,000 |
| | To close the Drawings account | | |

## HIGHLIGHT PROBLEM

The accompanying unadjusted trial balance is for Cheeper Audio & Video, a merchandising company.

CHEEPER AUDIO & VIDEO
Unadjusted Trial Balance
December 31, 19X1

| | | |
|---|---|---|
| Cash | $ 7,900 | |
| Accounts Receivable | 17,200 | |
| Merchandise Inventory, Jan. 1, 19X1 | 10,400 | |
| Prepaid Rent | 1,000 | |
| Equipment | 36,000 | |
| Accumulated Depreciation—Equipment | | $ 6,000 |
| Accounts Payable | | 7,500 |
| Taxes Payable | | 1,100 |
| M. Cheeper, Capital | | 50,000 |
| M. Cheeper, Drawings | 17,000 | |
| Sales | | 188,000 |
| Sales Returns and Allowances | 2,100 | |
| Sales Discounts | 3,500 | |
| Purchases | 107,600 | |
| Purchase Returns and Allowances | | 2,800 |
| Purchase Discounts | | 3,700 |
| Transportation-In | 2,000 | |
| Salaries Expense | 30,600 | |
| Rent Expense | 5,500 | |
| Advertising Expense | 13,800 | |
| Insurance Expense | 1,600 | |
| Utilities Expense | 2,900 | |
| | $259,100 | $259,100 |

Required:
Using the supplementary information given below, prepare
1. A work sheet for the year ended December 31, 19X1
2. An income statement for the year ended December 31, 19X1
3. The closing entries

Supplementary Information:

a. The company uses the periodic inventory method. An inventory taken on December 31, 19X1, established that the cost of the goods remaining on hand totaled $9,600.
b. The amount in the Prepaid Rent account is the result of a check issued on December 1, 19X1, for $1,000, at which time the Prepaid Rent account was debited and the Cash account was credited for that amount. Rent is $500 per month; the $1,000 check is for the rent applicable to December of this year and January of next year.
c. Depreciation expense is calculated to be $1,800 per year based on the equipment's estimated useful life of twenty years.
d. Salaries earned but unpaid at year-end amounted to $700.

## GLOSSARY OF KEY TERMS

**Beginning inventory.** Merchandise inventory on hand on the first day of an accounting period.

**Cash discount.** A deduction allowed from a gross invoice price when payment is made within a specified period of time. The price deduction is offered as an incentive to encourage prompt payment. A seller refers to the cash discount as a sales discount. A buyer refers to the cash discount as a purchase discount.

**Chain discounts.** A series of trade discounts expressed in percentages that can be deducted in sequence from a list price

**Cost of goods sold.** The amount expended for the products that have been sold. For a merchandising company, the cost of goods sold is equal to the beginning inventory plus the net purchases less the ending inventory.

**Ending inventory.** Merchandise inventory on hand on the last day of an accounting period.

**EOM.** A method to express the terms of a discount. EOM means end of month.

**FOB destination.** Terms for shipping goods under which the seller must bear the cost of shipping the goods to the buyer's location. Ownership of the goods passes to the buyer at the destination.

**FOB shipping point.** Terms for shipping goods under which the buyer must bear the cost of shipping the goods from the seller's location to the buyer's location. Ownership of the goods passes to the buyer at the shipping point.

**Freight-In account.** An alternate title for the *Transportation-In* account.

**Gross invoice method.** The use of the full invoice price in accounting for the cost of merchandise purchased. Also called *gross purchases method.*

**Gross margin on sales.** Net sales minus cost of goods sold.

**Gross purchases method.** Alternate term for *gross invoice method.*

**Gross sales.** The amount of a company's sales of merchandise for cash or on credit

**Inventory.** Alternate term for *merchandise inventory.*

**Inventory record card.** A continuous inventory record used to record quantities and cost of purchases and sales as they occur.

**Merchandise inventory.** Items held for sale in the normal course of the firm's business activities.

**Merchandising company.** A business entity that purchases goods with an intent to sell them at a price in excess of their cost.

**Net cost of goods purchased.** The cost of purchases less purchase returns and allowances and purchase discounts plus any transportation costs incurred by the buyer.

**Net invoice method.** The use of the net invoice price (full invoice price less anticipated cash discount) in accounting for the cost of merchandise purchases. Also called the *net purchases method.*

**Net purchases method.** Alternate term for *net invoice method.*

**Net sales.** Gross sales less sales returns and allowances and sales discounts.

**Periodic inventory method.** A method of accounting whereby the ending inventory is determined by counting and pricing the goods on hand, and the cost of goods sold is determined by adding the net cost of purchases to the beginning inventory and subtracting the ending inventory from that total.

**Perpetual inventory method.** A method of accounting for merchandise whereby continuous records of all purchase and sales transactions occurring during an accounting period are maintained. Thus the ending inventory and cost of goods sold can be determined from existing accounting records.

**Purchase discount.** Alternate term for *cash discount.*

**Purchase discounts account.** An account used under the periodic inventory method to record the reduction in the amount paid for merchandise purchased on account when payment is made within the discount period. A contra account to the Purchases account.

**Purchase discounts lost account.** An account used under the periodic inventory method to record the amount of discounts lost during the accounting period. This account is reported in the income statement as an operating expense.

**Purchase returns and allowances account.** An account used under the periodic inventory method to record the cost of merchandise returned to suppliers or the reduction granted by suppliers because the merchandise delivered was not fully satisfactory to the buyer. A contra account to the Purchases account.

**Purchases account.** An account used under the periodic inventory method to record the cost of merchandise purchased during the period.

**Sales account.** A revenue account used to record the

selling price of merchandise sold during the period.

Sales discount. Alternate term for *cash discount*.

Sales discounts account. An account used to accumulate the amount of cash discounts taken during a period by customers who have paid their open account balances within the discount period. A contra revenue account (contra to the Sales account).

Sales returns and allowances account. An account used to record the selling price of merchandise returned by customers or reductions from the selling price granted because the customer was not fully satisfied with the merchandise received. A contra revenue account (contra to the Sales account).

Sales revenue account. Alternate term for *Sales*.

Series discounts. An alternate term for *chain discounts*.

Service company. A business entity that receives fees or commissions for providing services.

Trade discounts. Percentage reductions from the list or catalog price of merchandise allowed to customers who qualify. Trade discounts establish an actual selling price and as such are not recorded in the accounts of the buyer or seller.

Transportation-In. An account used under the periodic inventory method to record transportation costs incurred by the buyer on merchandise purchased from a supplier.

## REVIEW QUESTIONS

1. How is net income determined in service companies? [LO1a]
2. How is net income determined in a merchandising company? [LO1a]
3. What three items must be accounted for to provide information pertaining to a given period's net sales? [LO2a]
4. Differentiate between the entries for the sale of merchandise for cash and those for the sale of merchandise on credit. What do these two entries have in common? [LO2a]
5. Why is the debit made to a contra revenue account for transactions involving sales returns and sales allowances? [LO2a]
6. Describe the journal entry made if a customer who buys merchandise on account pays for that merchandise within the discount time period allowed by the seller. [LO2a]
7. What types of companies generally use the perpetual inventory method? [LO1b]
8. What types of companies generally use the periodic inventory method? [LO1b]
9. What amount is recorded for purchases when the gross invoice method of accounting for the cost of merchandise purchased is used? [LO2b]
10. What is the Purchases account used for in the periodic inventory method? [LO2b]
11. Why is a contra expense account used to record transactions involving purchase returns and purchase allowances? [LO2b]
12. What information is contained in the contra expense account used to record transactions involving purchase discounts? [LO2b]
13. Give three reasons why trade discounts are used to determine the actual selling price of an item. [LO1d]
14. Why is a separate account used to accumulate all transportation charges on merchandise purchased? [LO2b]
15. Differentiate between FOB shipping point and FOB destination. [LO2b]
16. What amount is recorded for purchases when the net invoice method of accounting for the cost of merchandise purchased is used? [LO2c]
17. Under what conditions is a Purchase Discounts Lost account debited? [LO2c]
18. Describe how cost of goods sold is calculated when the periodic inventory method is used. [LO2d]
19. Name and describe the composition of eight accounts used by merchandising companies but not by service companies. [LO1c]
20. Describe the way that beginning and ending merchandise inventory accounts are handled in the work sheet of a merchandising company that uses the periodic inventory method. [LO2e]

21. Name and describe the components in the three major sections of the income statement for a merchandising company. [LO2e]
22. Describe the way that beginning and ending merchandise inventory accounts are handled in the closing entries process of a merchandising company. [LO2f]
23. Summarize the closing process in a merchandising company. [LO2f]

## ANALYTICAL QUESTIONS

24. "Accounting for service companies and merchandising companies is the same from a conceptual standpoint." Explain why this statement is true. [LO1a]
25. Why does a merchandising company have a cost of goods sold section in its income statement while a service company does not? [LO1a]
26. Name the special "contra" accounts used in the revenue and in the cost of goods sold sections of a merchandising company's income statement. Why are these "contra" accounts created? [LO1c,2a,2b,2c,2d]
27. Does the perpetual or the periodic inventory method provide better control over a company's inventory? Give the reasons for your answer. [LO1b]
28. Is it possible for the dollar amount representing the cost of goods sold for a period to be equal to the amount shown for the net cost of purchases for the same period? Explain why or why not. [LO2d]
29. When closing entries are made for a merchandising company, why is Merchandise Inventory debited in one entry and credited in another entry? [LO2f]

## IMPACT ANALYSIS QUESTIONS

*For each error described, indicate whether it would overstate [O], understate [U], or not affect [N] the indicated key figures. Assume that the periodic inventory method is used.*

30. A customer returned some merchandise purchased previously and was granted credit against her account. The transaction was recorded by debiting Accounts Receivable and crediting Sales Returns and Allowances. [LO2a]

    ______ Assets ______ Revenues
    ______ Expenses ______ Net Income

31. Received a freight bill for shipment of merchandise purchased on account. The transaction was recorded by debiting Delivery Expense and crediting Accounts Payable. [LO2b]

    ______ Assets ______ Cost of Goods Sold
    ______ Expenses ______ Net Income

32. Purchased equipment on credit and recorded the transaction by debiting Purchases and crediting Accounts Payable. [LO2b]

    ______ Assets ______ Cost of Goods Sold
    ______ Liabilities ______ Net Income

33. Returned damaged merchandise to a supplier and received a credit against the amount owed the supplier. The transaction was recorded by debiting Purchases Returns and Allowances and crediting Accounts Payable. [LO2b]

    ______ Assets ______ Cost of Goods Sold
    ______ Liabilities ______ Net Income

34. Sold office supplies at cost (no gain or loss on the sale). The transaction was recorded by debiting Cash and crediting Sales Revenue. [LO2a]

    ______ Assets ______ Cost of Goods Sold
    ______ Revenues ______ Net Income

## EXERCISES

*Assume the use of the periodic inventory method and that the gross invoice method is used for recording sales and purchases.*

EXERCISE 5–1 *(Record Sales Transactions)* On October 5, 19X1, Nigh Company sold $5,000 of merchandise on account to Western Company. Terms of the sale were 2/10, n/30.

On October 8, 19X1, Western Company returned merchandise found to be unsatisfactory and was granted an allowance of $600 to be applied against its unpaid account balance. On October 14, 19X1, Western paid the balance of its account in full.

Required:
Prepare the journal entries that Nigh Company would make to record these transactions. [LO2a]

EXERCISE 5–2 *(Determine Gross Purchases from Randomly Listed Accounts)* From the following data, determine an amount for gross purchases made during the period. [LO2b]

| | |
|---|---|
| Sales | $59,000 |
| Beginning Inventory | 18,000 |
| Purchase Discounts | 800 |
| Sales Returns | 1,500 |
| Ending Inventory | 16,000 |
| Cost of Goods Sold | 43,000 |
| Transportation-In | 2,000 |

EXERCISE 5–3 *(Make Computations from Randomly Listed Accounts)* Using the following accounts and their balances, compute (a) the net purchases, (b) the net cost of purchases, (c) the cost of goods available for sale, and (d) the cost of goods sold. [LO2d]

| | |
|---|---|
| Inventory, April 1, 19X1 (beginning) | $ 9,000 |
| Inventory, March 31, 19X2 (ending) | 10,500 |
| Purchases | 37,500 |
| Purchase Discounts | 700 |
| Transportation-In | 1,200 |
| Purchase Returns and Allowances | 1,800 |

EXERCISE 5–4 *(Determine Account Titles and Amounts for Purchases and Payments)* A company purchased merchandise having a list price of $8,000 and subject to trade discounts of 10% and 5%. The trade discounts were taken, and the merchandise was received with an invoice indicating terms of 5/10, n/30.

Required:
1. What account or accounts are debited and for how much to record the purchase?
2. What account or accounts are credited and for how much to record payment of the invoice within the discount period? [LO1d,2b]

EXERCISE 5–5 *(Perform Several Computations from Randomly Listed Data)* Using the following data, compute (a) the cost of goods sold, (b) the ending inventory, and (c) the net income. [LO2d,2e]

| | | | |
|---|---|---|---|
| Transportation-In | $ 1,400 | Operating Expenses | $25,000 |
| Sales Discounts | 700 | Sales | 62,300 |
| Beginning Inventory | 12,000 | Purchase Returns | 1,900 |
| Purchases | 32,500 | Gross Margin on Sales | 29,200 |

EXERCISES 5-6 *(Compute Amount of Inventory from Randomly Listed Data)* Using the following data, compute the amount of the beginning inventory. [LO2d]

| | |
|---|---|
| Transportation-In | $ 3,200 |
| Purchase Returns and Allowances | 1,700 |
| Cost of Goods Sold | 99,400 |
| Purchase Discounts | 2,500 |
| Ending Inventory | 38,400 |
| Purchases | 120,600 |

## PROBLEMS

*Unless otherwise indicated, assume the use of the periodic inventory method and that the gross invoice method is used for recording sales and purchases.*

PROBLEM 5-1 *(Prepare Journal Entries)* Stockdale Merchandise Mart had the following transactions during August 19X1.

| | | |
|---|---|---|
| Aug. | 1 | Purchased $1,600 of merchandise on account from Vail Video Company; terms 2/10, n/30. |
| | 2 | Sold $500 of merchandise to Tom Dunn, a customer, on account; terms 1/10, n/30. |
| | 4 | Sold $800 of merchandise to Lee O'Brien, a customer, on account; terms 2/10, n/30. |
| | 4 | Returned $200 of defective merchandise purchased on August 1 from Vail Video Company. A credit for that amount was allowed. |
| | 8 | Paid Vail Video Company the net amount owed for the merchandise purchased on August 1. |
| | 9 | Granted a $100 credit to Lee O'Brien for the return of some merchandise sold to O'Brien on August 4. |
| | 11 | Received payment in full from Tom Dunn for the merchandise sold to him on August 2. |
| | 12 | Purchased merchandise from United Firms on account. The merchandise has a list price of $6,000 subject to trade discounts of 20% and 10% and cash discount terms 5/10, n/30. Stockdale, the buyer, qualifies for the trade discount. |
| | 13 | Received payment in full from Lee O'Brien for the merchandise sold to him on August 4. |
| | 15 | Purchased $90 of office supplies on account from Americo Supply Company; terms 1/10, n/30. |
| | 16 | Paid transportation charges related to the merchandise purchased from United Firms, $60. The merchandise was shipped FOB shipping point. |
| | 18 | Sold $600 of merchandise to Lee Company, a customer, on account; terms 2/10, n/30. |
| | 20 | Merchandise having a sales price of $400 was sold for cash. |
| | 22 | Paid United Firms the net amount owed for the merchandise purchased on August 12. |

Required:
Prepare general journal entries to record the above transactions. [LO1d,2a,2b]

PROBLEM 5-2 *(Perform Income Statement Calculations)* See the table at the top of page 180.

Required:
Place the correct numbers where the blanks are shown. [LO2d,2e]

| | 19X3 | 19X4 | 19X5 |
|---|---|---|---|
| Sales | $110,000 | $ | $130,000 |
| Sales Returns and Allowances | | 3,000 | 2,000 |
| Sales Discounts | 2,000 | 4,000 | 3,000 |
| Net Sales | 100,000 | 120,000 | |
| Beginning Inventory | 8,000 | | 5,000 |
| Purchases | 75,000 | | 100,000 |
| Purchase Returns and Allowances | 3,000 | 2,000 | 1,000 |
| Purchase Discounts | | 2,000 | 3,000 |
| Net Purchases | 71,000 | 86,000 | |
| Cost of Goods Available for Sale | | | |
| Ending Inventory | | 5,000 | 6,000 |
| Cost of Goods Sold | 70,000 | | 95,000 |
| Gross Margin on Sales | | 30,000 | |
| Operating Expenses | | 17,000 | 16,000 |
| Net Income | 12,000 | | |

PROBLEM 5–3 *(Prepare an Income Statement from a Listing of Accounts)* The December 31, 19X3, adjusted trial balance and other documents of Country Garden Suppliers contained the following information.

| | |
|---|---|
| Transportation-In | $ 3,900 |
| Advertising Expense | 11,000 |
| Sales | 204,800 |
| Purchases | 115,600 |
| Purchase Returns | 2,100 |
| Salaries Expense | 47,000 |
| Notes Payable | 7,000 |
| Sales Discounts | 3,500 |
| Rent Expense | 12,000 |
| Utilities Expense | 10,000 |
| Sales Returns | 1,200 |
| Accounts Receivable | 22,400 |
| Purchase Discounts | 2,400 |

The company's merchandise inventory is determined on December 31 of each year by physically counting the merchandise remaining on hand. The figures below represent the result of those counts:

| | |
|---|---|
| Merchandise Inventory, January 1, 19X3 | $18,200 |
| Merchandise Inventory, December 31, 19X3 | 21,400 |

Required:

Prepare an income statement that shows detailed revenue, cost of goods sold, and operating expenses sections in good form. [LO2d,2e]

PROBLEM 5–4 *(Prepare a Work Sheet from a Trial Balance and Additional Information)* Georgetown Company, a retailing firm, ends its year on September 30. On that date in 19X2 the company prepared the unadjusted trial balance shown on page 181.

Additional Information:

a. Merchandise inventory on September 30, 19X2, $12,200.

GEORGETOWN COMPANY
Trial Balance
September 30, 19X2

| | | |
|---|---|---|
| Cash | $ 5,080 | |
| Accounts Receivable | 9,120 | |
| Merchandise Inventory, Oct. 1, 19X1 | 11,340 | |
| Store Supplies | 745 | |
| Prepaid Insurance | 860 | |
| Delivery Equipment | 16,200 | |
| Accumulated Depreciation—Delivery Equipment | | $ 2,630 |
| Accounts Payable | | 3,060 |
| Pat Lake, Capital | | 33,345 |
| Pat Lake, Drawings | 15,200 | |
| Sales | | 82,140 |
| Sales Returns and Allowances | 1,025 | |
| Sales Discounts | 1,245 | |
| Purchases | 49,330 | |
| Purchase Returns and Allowances | | 840 |
| Purchase Discounts | | 910 |
| Transportation-In | 740 | |
| Salaries Expense | 8,400 | |
| Rent Expense | 1,200 | |
| Advertising Expense | 1,390 | |
| Maintenance Expense | 240 | |
| Utilities Expense | 810 | |
| | $122,925 | $122,925 |

b. Expired insurance, $380.
c. Annual depreciation on the delivery equipment was computed and amounted to $3,600.
d. Store supplies remaining on hand, $270.
e. Unpaid and unrecorded salaries at year-end, $425.

Required:
Prepare a work sheet as of September 30, 19X2. [LO2e]

PROBLEM 5–5 *(Prepare a Work Sheet, an Income Statement, and Closing Entries from a Trial Balance and Additional Information)* Mayhill Engine Company ends its year on December 31. On December 31, 19X2, the company prepared the unadjusted trial balance as shown on page 182.

Additional Information:
a. End-of-the-year merchandise inventory determined by a physical count, $16,400.
b. Unexpired insurance at year-end, $860.
c. Supplies on hand, $230.
d. Building depreciation, 5% per year.
e. Office equipment depreciation, 10% per year.
f. Salaries earned but unpaid and unrecorded at year-end, $700.

Required:
1. Prepare a work sheet at December 31, 19X2.
2. Prepare an income statement.
3. Prepare the closing entries. [LO2d,2e,2f]

MAYHILL ENGINE COMPANY
Unadjusted Trial Balance
December 31, 19X2

| | | |
|---|---|---|
| Cash | $ 10,200 | |
| Accounts Receivable | 18,300 | |
| Merchandise Inventory, Jan. 1, 19X2 | 14,175 | |
| Prepaid Insurance | 1,660 | |
| Supplies | 665 | |
| Land | 18,000 | |
| Building | 62,000 | |
| Accumulated Depreciation—Building | | $ 16,000 |
| Office Equipment | 6,800 | |
| Accumulated Depreciation—Office Equipment | | 2,100 |
| Accounts Payable | | 12,800 |
| Mortgage Payable | | 11,000 |
| A. Hill, Capital | | 87,200 |
| A. Hill, Drawings | 18,000 | |
| Sales | | 183,200 |
| Sales Returns and Allowances | 600 | |
| Sales Discounts | 2,700 | |
| Purchases | 129,800 | |
| Purchase Returns and Allowances | | 1,400 |
| Purchase Discounts | | 2,600 |
| Transportation-In | 900 | |
| Salaries Expense | 23,000 | |
| Travel Expense | 5,200 | |
| Office Expense | 1,300 | |
| Utilities Expense | 2,200 | |
| Building Repair Expense | 800 | |
| | $316,300 | $316,300 |

PROBLEM 5-6 *(Prepare Journal Entries for Various Transactions)* Hatfield Department Store uses the periodic inventory method. A partial list of the company's transactions occurring during August is shown below.

| | | |
|---|---|---|
| Aug. | 3 | Purchased merchandise on account from Cory Company, $940; terms 2/10, n/30. |
| | 5 | Sold merchandise to Pic It Company for cash, $315. |
| | 6 | Sold merchandise on account to David Ales, $400; terms 2/10, n/30. |
| | 10 | Purchased merchandise on account from Johnson Products, $650; terms 2/10, n/30. |
| | 10 | Paid A & A Trucking $30 for transportation costs on the merchandise purchased from Johnson Products. Terms for the purchase were FOB shipping point. |
| | 12 | Merchandise having a sales price of $260 was sold for cash. |
| | 14 | Returned defective merchandise that cost $110 to Cory Company and received a credit. |
| | 16 | Received payment in full from David Ales for the sale made to him on August 6. |
| | 17 | Pic It Company returned $50 of merchandise it had purchased for cash on August 5 and was given a cash refund. |
| | 19 | Paid Johnson Products the net amount owed for the merchandise purchased on August 10. |
| | 21 | Sold merchandise on account to Garland Gourmet Garden, $840; terms 2/10, n/30. |
| | 24 | Paid Cory Company in full. |

Required:

1. Prepare general journal entries to record the above transactions, assuming the gross invoice method is used.

2. Prepare journal entries to record the transactions on August 3, 10, 19, and 24, assuming the net invoice method is used. [LO2a,2b,2c]

PROBLEM 5–7 *(Prepare an Income Statement from a Listing of Accounts)* The September 30, 19X1, adjusted trial balance and other documents of Gordon Trading Company contained the following information.

|  |  |
|---|---|
| Accumulated Depreciation—Delivery Equipment | $ 1,600 |
| Accumulated Depreciation—Machinery | 6,000 |
| Accounts Payable | 9,300 |
| Accounts Receivable | 12,100 |
| Advertising Expense | 6,820 |
| Cash | 6,880 |
| Delivery Equipment | 16,800 |
| Delivery Expense | 3,400 |
| Depreciation Expense—Delivery Equipment | 1,200 |
| Depreciation Expense—Machinery | 1,100 |
| Freight-In | 900 |
| Insurance Expense | 820 |
| Machinery | 28,300 |
| Maintenance Expense | 500 |
| Merchandise Inventory (beginning) | 6,200 |
| Office Supplies Expense | 400 |
| Purchases | 53,000 |
| Purchase Discounts | 800 |
| Purchase Returns and Allowances | 1,200 |
| Salaries Expense | 13,500 |
| Sales | 89,200 |
| Sales Discounts | 900 |
| Sales Returns | 1,100 |
| Taxes Expense | 1,700 |

The company's merchandise inventory is determined on September 30 of each year by physically counting the merchandise remaining on hand. The figures below show the result of those counts:

| | |
|---|---|
| Merchandise Inventory, September 30, 19X0 | $6,200 |
| Merchandise Inventory, September 30, 19X1 | 8,300 |

Required:
Prepare an income statement that shows detailed revenue, cost of goods sold, and operating expenses sections in good form. [LO2d,2e]

PROBLEM 5–8 *(Prepare a Work Sheet and Financial Statements from a List of Accounts and Other Information)* The list of accounts and their unadjusted balances on page 184 were taken from the ledger of Watts Office Machines Company on December 31, 19X1, the company's year-end.

Additional Information:
a. Merchandise inventory on December 31, 19X1, $23,300.
b. One-third of the prepaid insurance has expired.
c. Supplies remaining on hand, $170.
d. The cost of the equipment is being depreciated over a ten-year estimated life.
e. Unpaid and unrecorded salaries at year-end, $400.

| | |
|---|---|
| Cash | $ 3,995 |
| Accounts Receivable | 13,240 |
| Merchandise Inventory, Jan. 1, 19X1 | 22,800 |
| Prepaid Insurance | 360 |
| Supplies | 520 |
| Equipment | 15,000 |
| Accumulated Depreciation—Equipment | 4,500 |
| Accounts Payable | 11,990 |
| Taxes Payable | 390 |
| S. Palmer, Capital | 36,920 |
| S. Palmer, Drawings | 9,000 |
| Sales | 89,490 |
| Sales Returns and Allowances | 920 |
| Sales Discounts | 1,330 |
| Purchases | 56,320 |
| Purchase Returns and Allowances | 490 |
| Purchase Discounts | 1,125 |
| Transportation-In | 880 |
| Sales Salaries Expense | 11,800 |
| Rent Expense | 3,600 |
| Advertising Expense | 2,700 |
| Utilities Expense | 1,880 |
| Maintenance Expense | 560 |

Required:

1. Prepare a work sheet at December 31, 19X1.
2. Prepare an income statement, a capital statement, and a classified balance sheet. The income statement should show net revenue, cost of goods sold, operating expenses, and net income. [LO2d,2e]

PROBLEM 5-9 *(Prepare Journal Entries and a Partial Income Statement from Transactions and Other Information)* Bradley Recreation Supplies Company uses the periodic inventory method. A partial list of the company's transactions occurring during October is shown below.

Oct. 1 Purchased merchandise from Billard Company, $8,000; terms 2/10, n/30.

3 Sold merchandise on account to Johnson Supply, $3,000; terms 1/10, n/30.

4 Purchased merchandise from Franklin Company. The list price was $12,000 with a trade discount of 10% and terms of 2/10, n/30. Bradley Company qualifies for the trade discount.

6 Received payment made in full from Johnson Supply for the sale made on October 3.

8 Received a $200 allowance from Billard Company for merchandise damaged in transit.

9 Purchased merchandise from Krause Company, $2,000; terms 2/10, n/30.

11 Paid Billard Company the net amount owed for the merchandise purchased on October 1.

15 Sold merchandise on account to City Supply, $7,000; terms 1/10, n/30.

16 Paid Franklin Company the net amount owed for the merchandise purchased on October 4.

21 Sold merchandise on account to Guarantee Company, $5,500; terms 1/10, n/30.

24 Paid Krause Company the net amount owed for the merchandise purchased on October 9.

27 Purchased merchandise for cash, $4,000.
28 Paid transportation charges of $120 for the merchandise purchased on October 27. The merchandise was purchased FOB shipping point.
30 Returned $200 of defective merchandise purchased on October 27 and received a cash refund.

Required:
1. Prepare general journal entries to record the above transactions.
2. Prepare the cost of goods sold section of Bradley's income statement using the following amounts for the beginning and ending inventories:

| | |
|---|---|
| Beginning Merchandise Inventory | $7,700 |
| Ending Merchandise Inventory | 4,300 |

[LO2a,2b,2d,2e]

PROBLEM 5-10 *(Prepare an Income Statement and Closing Entries from Trial Balance Data)* Emerson Scales Company closes its accounts on December 31. After all accounts except inventory have been adjusted, its trial balance appears as follows.

EMERSON SCALES COMPANY
Trial Balance
December 31, 19X1

| | | |
|---|---|---|
| Cash | $ 17,700 | |
| Accounts Receivable | 39,600 | |
| Inventory, Jan. 1, 19X1 | 29,300 | |
| Prepaid Insurance | 2,200 | |
| Equipment | 24,000 | |
| Accumulated Depreciation—Equipment | | $ 9,000 |
| Accounts Payable | | 18,600 |
| Salaries Payable | | 2,200 |
| K. Emerson, Capital | | 76,400 |
| K. Emerson, Drawings | 20,000 | |
| Sales | | 320,000 |
| Sales Returns and Allowances | 7,200 | |
| Sales Discounts | 4,800 | |
| Purchases | 205,000 | |
| Purchase Returns and Allowances | | 4,500 |
| Purchase Discounts | | 5,200 |
| Transportation-In | 6,300 | |
| Salaries Expense | 52,700 | |
| Rent Expense | 12,000 | |
| Utilities Expense | 10,500 | |
| Depreciation Expense | 3,000 | |
| Insurance Expense | 1,600 | |
| | $435,900 | $435,900 |

The merchandise inventory on December 31, 19X1 (the end of the year), as determined by a count, amounted to $25,400.

Required:
1. Prepare an income statement showing net revenue, cost of goods sold, operating expenses, and net income.
2. Prepare closing entries. [LO2d,2e,2f]

PROBLEM 5-11 *(Prepare a Work Sheet, an Income Statement, and Closing Entries from a List of Accounts and Additional Information)* The following alphabetical list of accounts and their unadjusted balances was taken from the ledger of Tampa Paper Company at year-end December 31, 19X1.

|  |  |
|---|---|
| Accounts Payable | $ 9,500 |
| Accounts Receivable | 13,600 |
| Accumulated Depreciation—Equipment | 21,000 |
| Advertising Expense | 3,100 |
| Cash | 7,500 |
| Equipment | 60,000 |
| J. Tammy, Capital | 58,800 |
| J. Tammy, Drawings | 4,000 |
| Merchandise Inventory, Jan. 1, 19X1 | 11,500 |
| Prepaid Insurance | 1,700 |
| Purchase Discounts | 1,600 |
| Purchase Returns and Allowances | 2,100 |
| Purchases | 61,700 |
| Rent Expense | 8,000 |
| Salaries Expense | 11,600 |
| Sales | 96,900 |
| Sales Discounts | 3,400 |
| Sales Returns and Allowances | 2,300 |
| Utilities Expense | 1,500 |

Additional Information:

a. Merchandise inventory on December 31, 19X1, $17,200.

b. Unpaid and unrecorded salaries at year-end, $300.

c. All equipment was purchased at the same time and has an expected useful life of ten years (no salvage value).

d. An examination of policies showed $900 of unexpired insurance remaining at year-end.

Required:

1. Prepare a work sheet at December 31, 19X1. List all accounts in their expected order.
2. Prepare an income statement for the year ended December 31, 19X1, showing net revenue, cost of goods sold, operating expenses, and net income.
3. Prepare year-end closing entries. [LO2d,2e,2f]

PROBLEM 5–12 *(Comprehensive Review Problem)* The Advance Supplies Company prepared the trial balance shown on page 187.

Additional Information:

a. Ending merchandise inventory determined by physical count, $20,700.

b. Salaries earned but unpaid at year-end, $500.

c. Examination of policies showed $460 of unexpired insurance remaining at year-end.

d. Office supplies on hand at December 31, $100.

e. The buildings are being depreciated over a twenty-year useful life, and the equipment over a ten-year useful life (no expected salvage value).

f. All sales were on account.

g. Customers received credit on sales returns and allowances.

h. Cash collected on account (after sales discount deductions), $105,800.

i. All purchases were made on credit.

j. Cash payments made on account (after purchase discount deductions), $88,650.

Required:

1. Prepare journal entries to record the sales, sales returns and allowances, sales discounts, purchases, purchase discounts, and transportation-in (one summary entry for each of the six activities).
2. Prepare a work sheet at December 31, 19X2.

ADVANCE SUPPLIES COMPANY
Trial Balance
December 31, 19X2

| | | |
|---|---|---|
| Cash | $ 5,700 | |
| Notes Receivable | 2,000 | |
| Accounts Receivable | 8,200 | |
| Inventory (beginning) | 21,300 | |
| Prepaid Insurance | 860 | |
| Office Supplies | 240 | |
| Buildings | 27,000 | |
| Accumulated Depreciation—Buildings | | $ 6,200 |
| Equipment | 9,200 | |
| Accumulated Depreciation—Equipment | | 2,100 |
| Accounts Payable | | 7,850 |
| Mortgage Payable | | 9,000 |
| D. Royce, Capital | | 54,850 |
| Sales | | 120,000 |
| Sales Returns and Allowances | 3,800 | |
| Sales Discounts | 2,200 | |
| Purchases | 98,400 | |
| Purchase Discounts | | 1,900 |
| Transportation-In | 1,400 | |
| Salaries Expense | 16,700 | |
| Taxes Expense | 3,400 | |
| Maintenance Expense | 1,500 | |
| | $201,900 | $201,900 |

3. Prepare adjusting entries.
4. Prepare an income statement showing net revenue, cost of goods sold, operating expenses, and net income, and prepare a classified balance sheet.
5. Prepare closing entries. [LO2a,2b,2d,2e,2f]

## ALTERNATE PROBLEMS

*Assume the use of the periodic inventory method and that the gross invoice method is used for recording sales and purchases.*

PROBLEM 5–1A *(Prepare Journal Entries)* (Alternate to Problem 5–1) Broadside Merchandise Mart had the following transactions during November 19X8.

| | | |
|---|---|---|
| Nov. | 1 | Purchased $1,000 of merchandise on account from Bale Company; terms 1/10, n/30. |
| | 2 | Sold $1,500 of merchandise to Jim Jones, a customer, on account; terms 2/10, n/30. |
| | 4 | Sold $2,000 of merchandise to Bill Ponder, a customer, on account; terms 2/10, n/30. |
| | 4 | Returned $200 of defective merchandise purchased on November 1 from Bale Company. A credit for that amount was allowed. |
| | 8 | Paid Bale Company the net amount owed for the merchandise purchased on November 1. |
| | 9 | Granted a $100 credit to Jim Jones for the return of some merchandise sold to Jones on November 2. |
| | 11 | Received payment in full from Jim Jones for the merchandise sold to him on November 2. |
| | 12 | Purchased merchandise from Woolco on account. The merchandise |

has a list price of $5,000 subject to trade discounts of 30% and 20% and cash discounts terms 2/10, n/30. Broadside, the buyer, qualifies for the trade discount.

13 Received payment in full from Bill Ponder for the merchandise sold to him on November 4.

15 Purchased $90 of office supplies on account from Zubioko Supply Company; terms 5/10, n/30.

16 Paid transportation charges related to the merchandise purchased from Woolco, $60. The merchandise was shipped FOB shipping point.

18 Sold $1,600 of merchandise to Loan Company, a customer, on account; terms 1/10, n/30.

22 Paid Woolco the net amount owed for the merchandise purchased on November 12.

Required:
Prepare general journal entries to record the above transactions. [LO1d,2a,2b]

PROBLEM 5–2A *(Perform Income Statement Calculations)* (Alternate to Problem 5–2)

| | 19X1 | 19X2 | 19X3 |
|---|---|---|---|
| Sales | $ 90,000 | $____ | $____ |
| Sales Returns and Allowances | 8,000 | 31,000 | 20,000 |
| Sales Discounts | 2,000 | 4,000 | 3,000 |
| Net Sales | ____ | 120,000 | 125,000 |
| Beginning Inventory | 8,000 | ____ | 5,000 |
| Purchases | 85,000 | 90,000 | ____ |
| Purchase Returns and Allowances | 3,000 | 2,000 | 1,000 |
| Purchase Discounts | ____ | 2,000 | 3,000 |
| Net Purchases | 71,000 | ____ | 96,000 |
| Cost of Goods Available for Sale | ____ | ____ | ____ |
| Ending Inventory | ____ | 5,000 | 6,000 |
| Cost of Goods Sold | 70,000 | ____ | 95,000 |
| Gross Margin on Sales | ____ | 30,000 | ____ |
| Operating Expenses | ____ | 7,000 | 6,000 |
| Net Income | 2,000 | ____ | ____ |

Required:
Place the correct numbers where the blanks are shown. [LO2d,2e]

PROBLEM 5–3A *(Prepare an Income Statement from a Listing of Accounts)* (Alternate to Problem 5–3) The December 31, 19X3, adjusted trial balance and other documents of City Garden Company contained the following information.

| | |
|---|---|
| Advertising Expense | $ 11,000 |
| Transportation-In | 3,900 |
| Sales | 214,800 |
| Notes Payable | 7,000 |
| Purchases | 115,600 |
| Purchase Returns | 2,100 |
| Salaries Expense | 57,000 |
| Accounts Receivable | 22,400 |
| Sales Discounts | 3,500 |
| Rent Expense | 14,000 |
| Utilities Expense | 8,000 |
| Sales Returns | 1,200 |
| Purchase Discounts | 2,400 |

The company's merchandise inventory is determined on December 31 of each year by physically counting the merchandise remaining on hand. The figures below represent the result of those counts:

| | |
|---|---|
| Merchandise Inventory, January 1, 19X3 | $28,200 |
| Merchandise Inventory, December 31, 19X3 | 31,400 |

Required:
Prepare an income statement that shows detailed revenue, cost of goods sold, and operating expenses sections in good form. [LO2d,2e]

PROBLEM 5-4A *(Prepare a Work Sheet, an Income Statement, and Closing Entries from a Trial Balance and Additional Information)* (Alternate to Problem 5-5) Junehill Company ends its year on December 31. On December 31, 19X3, the company prepared the following unadjusted trial balance.

JUNEHILL COMPANY
Unadjusted Trial Balance
December 31, 19X3

| | | |
|---|---|---|
| Cash | $ 15,200 | |
| Accounts Receivable | 13,475 | |
| Merchandise Inventory, Jan. 1, 19X3 | 16,000 | |
| Prepaid Insurance | 1,660 | |
| Supplies | 665 | |
| Land | 16,000 | |
| Building | 64,000 | |
| Accumulated Depreciation—Building | | $ 6,000 |
| Office Equipment | 4,800 | |
| Accumulated Depreciation—Office Equipment | | 2,100 |
| Accounts Payable | | 22,800 |
| Mortgage Payable | | 11,000 |
| A. Hill, Capital | | 97,200 |
| A. Hill, Drawings | 18,000 | |
| Sales | | 173,200 |
| Sales Returns and Allowances | 600 | |
| Sales Discounts | 2,700 | |
| Purchases | 129,800 | |
| Purchase Returns and Allowances | | 1,400 |
| Purchase Discounts | | 2,600 |
| Transportation-In | 900 | |
| Salaries Expense | 23,000 | |
| Travel Expense | 5,200 | |
| Office Expense | 1,300 | |
| Utilities Expense | 2,200 | |
| Building Repair Expense | 800 | |
| | $316,300 | $316,300 |

Additional Information:

a. End-of-the-year merchandise inventory determined by a physical count, $15,400.
b. Unexpired insurance at year-end, $960.
c. Supplies on hand, $430.
d. Building depreciation, 4% per year.
e. Office equipment depreciation, 8% per year.
f. Salaries earned but unpaid and unrecorded at year-end, $900.

Required:

1. Prepare a work sheet at December 31, 19X3.
2. Prepare an income statement.
3. Prepare the closing entries. [LO2d,2e,2f]

PROBLEM 5–5A *(Prepare a Work Sheet and Financial Statements from a List of Accounts and Other Information)* (Alternate to Problem 5–8) The following list of accounts and their unadjusted balances were taken from the ledger of Hat's Company on December 31, 19X1, the company's year-end.

| | |
|---|---|
| Cash | $ 4,995 |
| Accounts Receivable | 12,240 |
| Merchandise Inventory, Jan. 1, 19X1 | 26,800 |
| Prepaid Insurance | 360 |
| Supplies | 520 |
| Equipment | 10,000 |
| Accumulated Depreciation—Equipment | 4,500 |
| Accounts Payable | 13,990 |
| Taxes Payable | 390 |
| S. Palms, Capital | 34,920 |
| S. Palms, Drawings | 9,000 |
| Sales | 86,490 |
| Sales Returns and Allowances | 920 |
| Sales Discounts | 1,330 |
| Purchases | 53,320 |
| Purchase Returns and Allowances | 490 |
| Purchase Discounts | 1,125 |
| Transportation-In | 880 |
| Sales Salaries Expense | 13,800 |
| Rent Expense | 2,600 |
| Advertising Expense | 2,700 |
| Utilities Expense | 1,880 |
| Maintenance Expense | 560 |

Additional Information:

a. Merchandise inventory on December 31, 19X1, $13,200.
b. One-fourth of the prepaid insurance has expired.
c. Supplies remaining on hand, $270.
d. The cost of the equipment is being depreciated over an eight-year estimated life.
e. Unpaid and unrecorded salaries at year-end, $600.

Required:

1. Prepare a work sheet at December 31, 19X1.
2. Prepare an income statement, a capital statement, and a classified balance sheet. The income statement should show net revenue, cost of goods sold, operating expenses, and net income. [LO2d,2e]

# 6 Accounting Systems — Manual and Automated

## Learning Objectives

When you complete this chapter you will be able to

1. Answer the following questions:
   a. What are the basic elements and procedures in an accounting system?
   b. What is the accounting process?
   c. What are the objectives and uses of special-purpose journals?
   d. What types of transactions are generally recorded in each special-purpose journal?
   e. What are the purposes of subsidiary ledgers and control accounts?
   f. What is the purpose of a general journal when special-purpose journals are used?
   g. What are the basic elements and procedures in a computerized accounting system? What are the special characteristics of microcomputer systems?
2. Perform the following accounting functions:
   a. Prepare entries in each special-purpose journal.
   b. Post amounts from special-purpose journals to subsidiary ledgers and control accounts.
   c. Record entries in a general journal when special-purpose journals are used, and post these entries to subsidiary ledger and control accounts.
   d. Prepare accounts receivable and accounts payable schedules and balance their totals with the related control accounts.

In earlier chapters we learned the accounting procedures and processes used to collect, record, classify, summarize, store, and report financial information both for companies that sell services and for those that sell merchandise. These procedures are carried out in a sequence called the *accounting cycle.*

***1a. An accounting system's elements are business documents, records, equipment, policies, and procedures. It (1) collects data, (2) organizes data, (3) stores data, and (4) provides reports***

We are now ready to move on to a new concept—that of an *accounting system.* An **accounting system** consists of the business documents, records, equipment, policies, and procedures used to record transactions and events that affect an entity's financial performance and its financial status. A good accounting system provides the means to (1) collect data, (2) organize data, (3) store data, and (4) provide reports that are useful to decision makers. Often, one of the first and most vital assignments performed by an accountant is to develop an accounting system that will meet the needs of the company for which it is designed.

## *STAGES IN DEVELOPING AN ACCOUNTING SYSTEM*

The development of an accounting system comprises four stages (the accountant should be involved in each one): (1) investigation, (2) design, (3) implementation, and (4) review for efficiency.

*Investigation.* Generally, the development process of an accounting system begins with a study of the nature of the business. It continues with an inquiry into probable types of transactions and events. Then it determines the information needs of management.

*Design.* Next the process proposes methods and procedures for collecting and organizing the data to meet management's needs.

*Implementation.* Once designed, the accounting system is installed and the implementation stage begins. This stage calls for careful planning and coordination by all the affected parties and requires the training of personnel responsible for operating the system.

*Review.* After implementation, the system is reviewed to test its efficiency. When functioning appropriately, the system should process and report information efficiently, accurately, and in a timely fashion.

## *A DIAGRAM OF THE ACCOUNTING PROCESS*

In developing an accounting system, a business must develop methods and procedures to collect, organize, store, and report the data shown in its financial reports. Exhibit 6–1 illustrates the sequence of these procedures, collectively referred to as the **accounting process.** The process is the same in both manual and computerized systems.

***1b. The accounting process is a sequence of procedures to collect, organize, store, and report the data shown in a firm's financial reports***

In a manual system we have the following sequence:

1. *Input.* Preparing or receiving business documents and recording transactions from these business documents in journals.
2. *Processing.* Posting transactions to ledgers.
3. *Output.* Preparing financial statements and other financial reports.

The accounting process for a computerized system uses the same input, processing, output sequence with different equipment and devices. Later in the chapter we will see how this is done.

## *ELEMENTS OF AN EFFICIENT MANUAL ACCOUNTING SYSTEM*

The main purpose of the accounting system is to process information for decision making that is relevant, reliable, and timely. Because most businesses have numerous transactions daily, a system must be developed that processes transac-

EXHIBIT 6-1

The Accounting Process

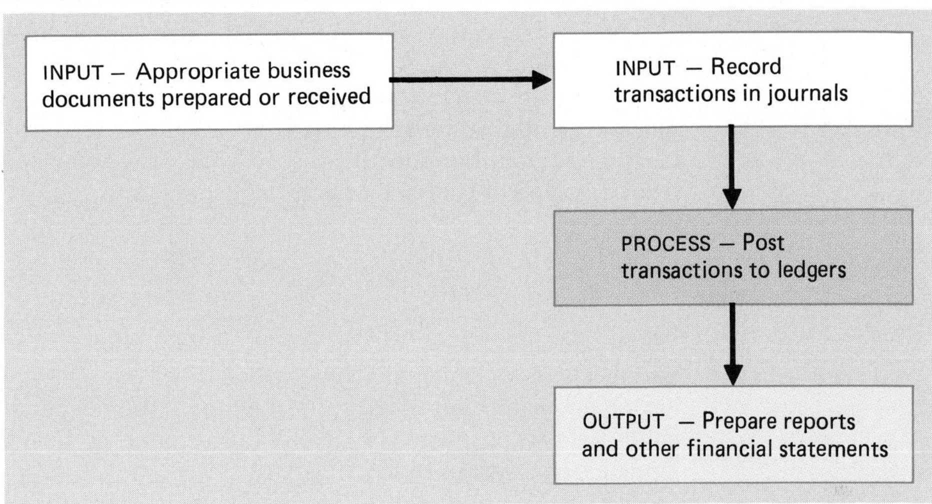


tions rapidly and efficiently. In a manual accounting system, as the name implies, personnel use human effort to prepare entries, post to ledger accounts, and prepare financial statements.

We now look at one of the elements of an efficient manual accounting system—one that can greatly reduce the time and effort needed to record and post business transactions.

## SPECIAL-PURPOSE JOURNALS

*1c. Special-purpose journals reduce labor and increase efficiency in the recording and posting of common recurring transactions*

As a first step in designing an efficient accounting system, companies often develop several types of *special-purpose journals.* Special-purpose journals greatly reduce the amount of work required to record and post transactions. They also allow for a **division of labor**—that is, they establish a means by which accounting information can be processed by several persons simultaneously.

Generally, **special-purpose journals** are introduced into the accounting system whenever a company has a large number of recurring transactions with common characteristics. Transactions of a merchandising firm that recur with frequency are of four types: (1) the sale of merchandise on credit, (2) the purchase of merchandise on credit, (3) the receipt of cash, and (4) the payment of cash.

*1d. Each special-purpose journal is used to record a specific type of transaction*

Four special journals are commonly used to record the four types of transactions likely to recur frequently.

| SPECIAL JOURNAL | TYPE OF TRANSACTION |
|---|---|
| **Sales Journal** | Sales of merchandise on credit |
| **Purchases Journal** | Purchases of merchandise on credit |
| **Cash Receipts Journal** | Receipts of cash |
| **Cash Payments Journal** | Payments of cash |

The general journal continues to be a part of the system and is used to record transactions other than those in the four types cited above. For example, the purchase of office supplies or any asset other than merchandise on credit would be recorded in the general journal. Also, adjusting, closing, correcting, and reversing entries would continue to be recorded in the general journal.

A combination of the four special journals and the general journal constitutes a manual accounting system that for many firms is capable of efficiently processing their transaction data. If necessary, other special-purpose journals may be introduced into the system. For example, a payroll journal (discussed in Chapter 12) may be added if its use will make the entering and posting of the data from this type of transaction more efficient.

## The Sales Journal

When merchandise is sold on credit, several copies of a sales invoice are prepared. The sales invoice includes the date of the sale, the invoice number, the customer's name and address, the amount of the sale, and the credit terms. One copy of the sales invoice is used by the accounting department as a basis for an entry in the sales journal.

*2a. Sales journal entries are prepared as in Exhibit 6–2*

A *sales journal* such as the one shown in Exhibit 6–2 is the special journal used to record sales of merchandise on credit. Entered in this sales journal are all the credit sales transactions that Able Company had during June 19X3.

*EXHIBIT 6–2*

SALES JOURNAL PAGE 16

| DATE | | ACCOUNT | INVOICE NUMBER | POST. REF. | AMOUNT |
|---|---|---|---|---|---|
| 19X3 | | | | | |
| June | 2 | Paul Carter | 100 | ✓ | 640 |
| | 5 | Henry Chambers | 101 | ✓ | 820 |
| | 8 | Steve Martin | 102 | ✓ | 380 |
| | 11 | Robert Morgan | 103 | ✓ | 1,260 |
| | 14 | Dave Christman | 104 | ✓ | 540 |
| | 17 | James Gray | 105 | ✓ | 280 |
| | 19 | Edward Campbell | 106 | ✓ | 760 |
| | 22 | Daniel Anderson | 107 | ✓ | 480 |
| | 25 | Alfred Greene | 108 | ✓ | 1,040 |
| | 29 | Herbert Ford | 109 | ✓ | 720 |
| | | | | | 6,920 |
| | 30 | Accounts Receivable debit—Sales credit | | | (4) (50) |

Several characteristics of the sales journal should be noted:

1. When a sales journal is used, each credit sale is entered on a single line.
2. The only transactions recorded in a sales journal are sales of merchandise on credit. Therefore the entries in the sales journal are self-explanatory, and no written explanation of the entry in this journal is required.
3. At the end of the accounting period, the total amount shown in the single money column ($6,920 in Exhibit 6–2) is posted twice: once as a debit to the Accounts Receivable account and once as a credit to the Sales account. This procedure eliminates posting separate debits and credits for each credit sale made during the period. Note that ledger account numbers (4) and (50) were placed below the money

column total to show that the dollar amounts have been posted to both the Accounts Receivable account and the Sales account. Note also that a check mark (✓) has been placed in the posting reference column of the sales journal opposite each amount to indicate that the amount has been posted to the customer's subsidiary account. Subsidiary accounts and the benefits of maintaining subsidiary ledgers are explained later in this chapter.

When a company has many credit sales transactions, the use of a sales journal enables it to process data more rapidly and at a reduced clerical cost. By using a sales journal, a company can

1. Eliminate the need to write the name of the accounts debited and credited for each entry, as is done when the general journal is the only book of entry used.
2. Eliminate the need to enter the amount of each credit sale in two different money columns, as must be done when the general journal is the only book of entry used.
3. Eliminate the need to write an explanation for each entry. Only when merchandise is sold on credit is the transaction recorded in the sales journal. Therefore all transactions entered in the sales journal are the same and, consequently, self-explanatory.
4. Save considerable time when posting amounts from the general journal to the ledger accounts. Posting for the sales journal is done periodically—perhaps at the end of a day, week, or month. To illustrate the efficiency in posting that can be achieved, assume that a company had five hundred transactions involving the sale of merchandise on credit during a particular month. If these five hundred transactions were recorded in a general journal, one thousand postings would be needed to transfer the amounts from the general journal to their proper accounts in the ledger. By using a sales journal and waiting to post until the end of the month, the company can reduce the number of postings to the general ledger from one thousand to two.

## The Purchases Journal

The *purchases journal* may be a single-column or multicolumn journal. Only purchases of merchandise on credit may be recorded in the single-column purchases journal shown in Exhibit 6–3. When we say single column, we mean single money column. However, as shown in Exhibit 6–3, the purchases journal also has columns for recording the date, supplier's name, terms of the purchase, and posting reference. The Terms column identifies and provides control over the cash discount terms, if any, that were offered by the supplier. The purchases journal uses the same transaction format as the sales journal. Each purchase of

*EXHIBIT 6–3*

PURCHASES JOURNAL — PAGE 8

| DATE | | ACCOUNT | TERMS | POST. REF. | AMOUNT |
|---|---|---|---|---|---|
| 19X3 | | | | | |
| June | 3 | Lowell and Company | 2/10, n/30 | ✓ | 800 |
| | 9 | Vista Company | 3/10, n/30 | ✓ | 1,100 |
| | 14 | Acme Supply House | n/30 | ✓ | 280 |
| | 19 | C-View Incorporated | 2/10, n/30 | ✓ | 650 |
| | 22 | Stewart and Sons | 1/10, n/30 | ✓ | 550 |
| | 29 | Lowell and Company | 2/10, n/30 | ✓ | 860 |
| | | | | | 4,240 |
| | 30 | Purchases debit—Accounts Payable credit | | | (60) (31) |

merchandise on credit is recorded by listing the invoice date, supplier's name, terms, and amount.

*2a. Purchases journal entries are prepared as in Exhibit 6–3*

The purchases journal shown in Exhibit 6–3 contains entries for all purchases of merchandise made on credit by Able Company during the month of June 19X3.

Several characteristics of the purchases journal should be noted:

1. When a purchases journal is used, all purchases of merchandise on credit are entered on a single line.
2. No written explanation of an entry made in this journal is needed.
3. At the end of the accounting period, the total amount shown in the single money column ($4,240 in Exhibit 6–3) is posted twice: once as a debit to the Purchases account and once as a credit to the Accounts Payable account.
   a. Account numbers for Purchases (60) and for Accounts Payable (31), established by the company's chart of accounts, are written below the column total to show that the two postings have been made.
   b. The check marks (✓) placed opposite each amount in the posting reference column of the Purchases Journal indicate that the amounts have been posted to a supplier's subsidiary account, as discussed in the next section of this chapter.

The purchases journal shown in Exhibit 6–3 was intentionally limited to one money column, and therefore only credit purchases of merchandise held for resale may be entered in this journal. If items such as office supplies or equipment are purchased on credit, the transaction is entered in the general journal or in another type of journal, such as a multicolumn purchases journal. Also, if merchandise (or any other asset) is purchased for cash, the transaction is recorded in a cash payments journal.

The advantages obtained from using a purchases journal are the same as those described earlier for a sales journal. These include timesaving advantages leading to reduced cost and increased efficiency.

## Subsidiary Ledgers and Control Accounts

The general ledger contains all the accounts that will appear on the company's financial statements, including its Accounts Receivable account and its Accounts Payable account. In previous chapters the entries involving credit sales *to* customers and cash collections *from* customers have been posted only to the Accounts Receivable account. Similarly, the entries involving credit purchases *from* suppliers and cash payments *to* suppliers have been posted only to the Accounts Payable account. This procedure established balances in those accounts that represent the total amount owed to a company by all of its customers (Accounts Receivable) and the total amount owed by the company to all suppliers (Accounts Payable). However, (1) the balance in the Accounts Receivable account does not provide information concerning the amounts that individual customers owe or the dates and dollar amounts of each transaction with a customer, and (2) the balance in the Accounts Payable account does not provide information concerning the amounts owed to individual suppliers or the dates and dollar amounts of each transaction with a supplier. To obtain that information, a company will establish a separate Accounts Receivable account for each customer and a separate Accounts Payable account for each supplier. If separate accounts were established in the general ledger, it would make that ledger bulky and unwieldy. For example, assume that a company had three thousand credit customers and two thousand suppliers. Its general ledger would include three thousand individual Accounts Receivable accounts and two thousand individual Accounts Payable accounts in addition to accounts for other assets, other liabilities, owner's equity, revenues, and expenses. Consequently, most companies keep the customer's accounts and the individual supplier's accounts in a separate ledger called a *subsidiary ledger*. As a result, we now have three separate ledgers:

One for individual customers' accounts, called an **accounts receivable ledger**

One for individual suppliers' accounts, called an **accounts payable ledger**

The *general ledger*, which contains all the accounts that will appear on the company's financial statements

The accounts receivable ledger and the accounts payable ledger are called subsidiary ledgers. A **subsidiary ledger** is a group of individual accounts that provide the detail of a general ledger account. For example, the individual customers' accounts in the accounts receivable subsidiary ledger provide the detail of the general ledger account Accounts Receivable. The general ledger account that is supported by the detail in the subsidiary ledger accounts is called the **control account.** Thus the Accounts Receivable account and the Accounts Payable account contained in the general ledger are control accounts. A company may use a number of control accounts. Examples include Accounts Receivable, Accounts Payable, Merchandise Inventory, and Equipment, in which case a separate subsidiary ledger is established for each control account. The balance in each control account will reflect the aggregate balances of the accounts in its related subsidiary ledger.

*1e. A control account reflects the aggregate balance in its related subsidiary ledger*

Returning to our examples of the Accounts Receivable and Accounts Payable control accounts:

The debit balance in the Accounts Receivable control account should be equal to the sum of the individual customers' account balances contained within its accounts receivable subsidiary ledger.

The credit balance in the Accounts Payable control account should be equal to the sum of the individual suppliers' account balances contained within its accounts payable subsidiary ledger.

The accounts receivable ledger is a group of separate accounts for each customer of the company. The accounts payable ledger is a group of separate accounts for each supplier of the company. As mentioned earlier, it may be beneficial to set up individual accounts in a subsidiary ledger to support the balance in other general ledger accounts. For example, the Equipment account may be supported by a subsidiary ledger if specific information about each item of owned equipment is important to its management.

*1e. Subsidiary ledgers provide four benefits*

Subsidiary ledgers are established to (1) reduce the size of the general ledger, (2) allow for a division of labor when amounts are posted, (3) minimize the possibility of making errors, and (4) provide additional detailed information useful to management in planning and controlling company activities.

## Posting to Subsidiary Ledgers and to Control Accounts

*2b. Posting from a sales journal to a subsidiary ledger and a general ledger control account is illustrated in Exhibit 6–4*

To illustrate the posting to subsidiary ledgers and control accounts, we refer again to the sales journal shown in Exhibit 6–2 and reproduced in Exhibit 6–4. Examine the illustration and note that each credit sale is posted to the individual customer's account in the accounts receivable subsidiary ledger. The total amount of sales for the month is posted as a debit to the Accounts Receivable control account and as a credit to the Sales account in the general ledger.

*EXHIBIT 6–4*

Posting from the Sales Journal to the General Ledger and the Accounts Receivable Subsidiary Ledger

***2b. The subsidiary ledger is posted daily; the general ledger is posted monthly***

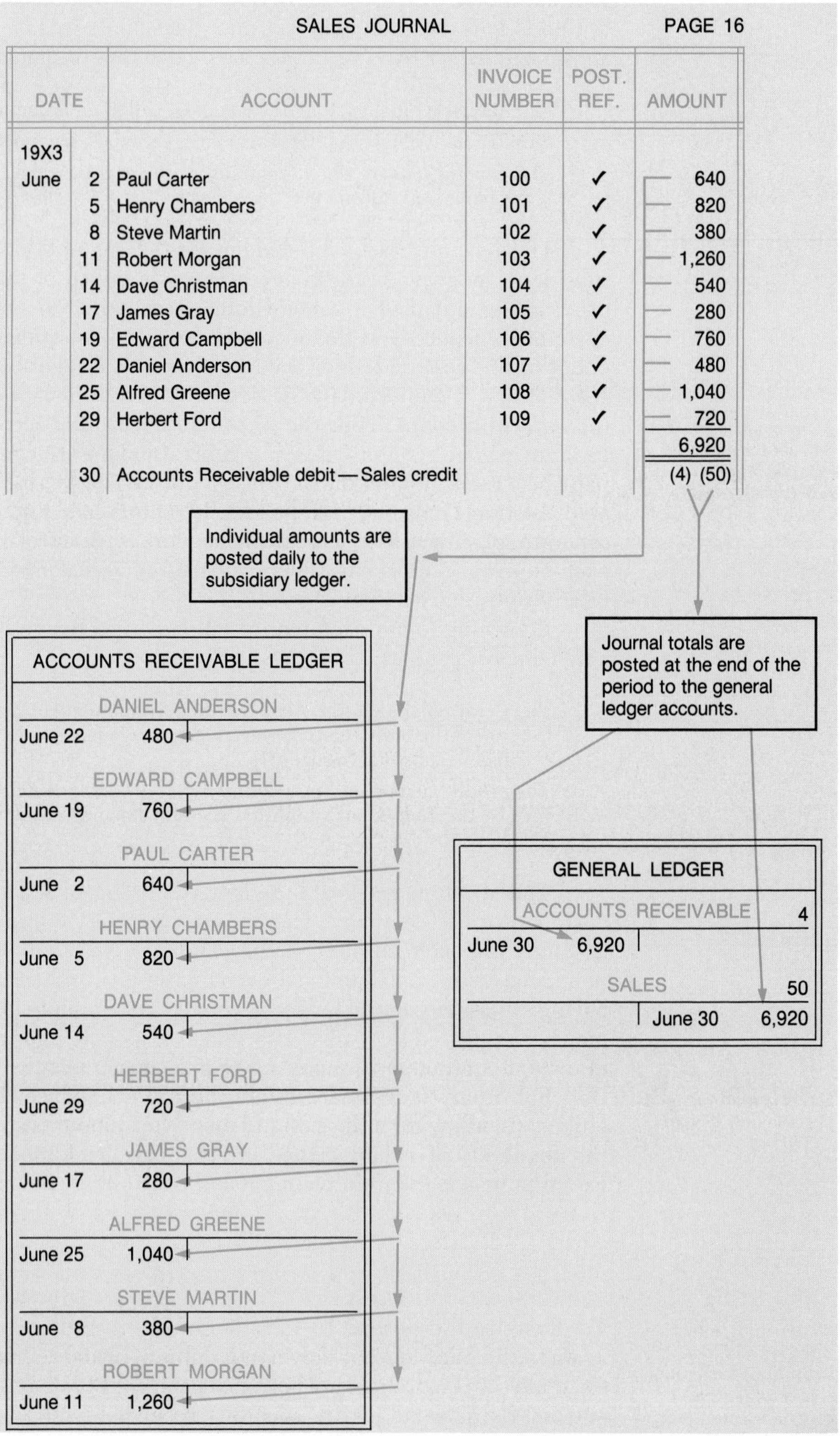


| DATE | | ACCOUNT | INVOICE NUMBER | POST. REF. | AMOUNT |
|---|---|---|---|---|---|
| 19X3 | | | | | |
| June | 2 | Paul Carter | 100 | ✓ | 640 |
| | 5 | Henry Chambers | 101 | ✓ | 820 |
| | 8 | Steve Martin | 102 | ✓ | 380 |
| | 11 | Robert Morgan | 103 | ✓ | 1,260 |
| | 14 | Dave Christman | 104 | ✓ | 540 |
| | 17 | James Gray | 105 | ✓ | 280 |
| | 19 | Edward Campbell | 106 | ✓ | 760 |
| | 22 | Daniel Anderson | 107 | ✓ | 480 |
| | 25 | Alfred Greene | 108 | ✓ | 1,040 |
| | 29 | Herbert Ford | 109 | ✓ | 720 |
| | | | | | 6,920 |
| | 30 | Accounts Receivable debit—Sales credit | | | (4) (50) |

Several things should be noted about the posting procedures illustrated in Exhibit 6–4:

1. Each credit sale is posted to the individual customer's subsidiary ledger account on the day the sale is made.
2. As each sale is being posted to the subsidiary ledger account, a check mark (✓) is placed in the Post. Ref. column to indicate that all information pertaining to the sale has been transferred to the appropriate subsidiary ledger account.
3. At the end of the month, the total amount of sales made on credit ($6,920) is posted to two general ledger accounts: as a debit to the Accounts Receivable control account and as a credit to the Sales account. After the postings have been completed, the debit balances in the individual customers' accounts, contained in the accounts receivable subsidiary ledger, are totaled to make certain that the total agrees with the debit balance in the Accounts Receivable control account.
4. The numbers assigned to the accounts debited and credited, (4) and (50) in this illustration, are placed beneath the total in the sales journal to indicate that posting to the general ledger has been completed.

*2b. Posting from a purchases journal is illustrated in Exhibit 6–5*

Exhibit 6–5 illustrates the procedure for posting from the purchases journal to the general ledger and to the accounts payable subsidiary ledger. (Note that the procedure is much the same as posting from the sales journal to the subsidiary and general ledgers.)

Several things should also be noted about the posting procedures illustrated in Exhibit 6–5 (see page 200):

1. Each entry in the purchases journal is posted to the individual supplier's subsidiary ledger account on the day the purchase is made.
2. As each purchase is being posted to the subsidiary ledger account, a check mark (✓) is placed in the Post. Ref. column to indicate that all the information pertinent to the purchase has been transferred to the appropriate subsidiary account.
3. At the end of the month, the total amount of purchases made on credit ($4,240) is posted to two general ledger accounts: as a debit to the Purchases account and as a credit to the Accounts Payable control account.
4. The numbers of the accounts debited and credited, (60) and (31), are placed beneath the total in the purchases journal to indicate that posting to the general ledger has been completed.

Periodically it is advisable to verify that the sum of the individual account balances in the accounts payable ledger is equal to the balance in the Accounts Payable control account.

## The Cash Receipts Journal

All the transactions involving the receipt of cash are recorded in the *cash receipts journal.* Common examples of transactions involving the receipt of cash are cash sales, the collection of accounts receivable from customers, and loans. To be effective for recording all sources of cash, the cash receipts journal must contain several columns. Therefore it is a multicolumn rather than single-column journal. Its design, including the number of dollar columns it should contain, depends on what sources of cash are available to the firm and how repetitive the transaction providing that source is. A goal for having special journals consists of reducing the time and effort needed to record and post transactions. This goal is best achieved by designating a money column for each account that will be debited or credited regularly.

*2a. Cash receipts journal entries are illustrated in Exhibit 6–6*

Exhibit 6–6 on page 201 shows a cash receipts journal in which the cash receipts transactions have been entered.

*EXHIBIT 6–5*

Posting from the Purchases Journal to the General Ledger and the Accounts Payable Subsidiary Ledger

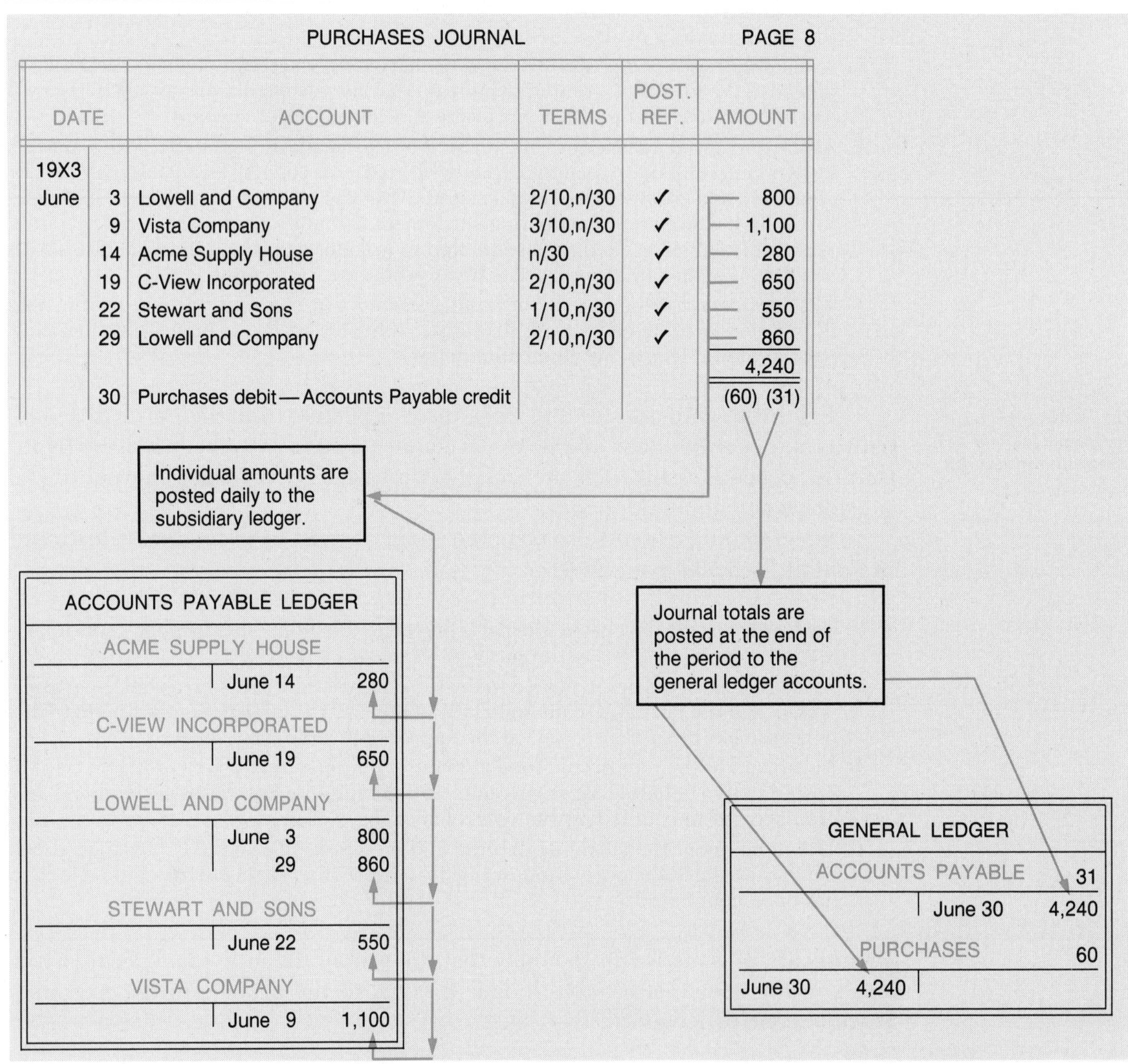


Several things should be noted about the format of the cash receipts journal shown in Exhibit 6–6:

1. Because all transactions involving cash receipts are recorded in this journal, the amount of every transaction entered will be placed in the first debit column.
2. Because cash receipts often come from cash sales, a Sales column is provided.
3. Cash receipts resulting from the collection of accounts receivable may involve a sales discount. In this case, the transaction is recorded in three different money columns headed Cash, Accounts Receivable, and Sales Discounts. Note that the customer's name is written in the Explanation column to identify the proper account to be credited in the accounts receivable ledger.
4. A column titled Other Sources is used to record cash received from sources other than cash sales or collections from accounts receivable. The name of the account is entered in the Other Sources column to identify the account to which the amount will be posted.

*EXHIBIT 6–6*
Cash Receipts Journal

CASH RECEIPTS JOURNAL — PAGE 6

| DATE | | EXPLANATION | DEBITS | | CREDITS | | | | | |
|---|---|---|---|---|---|---|---|---|---|---|
| | | | CASH | SALES DISCOUNTS | POST. REF. | ACCOUNTS RECEIVABLE | SALES | OTHER SOURCES | POST. REF. | AMOUNT |
| 19X3 June | 1 | Additional investment by owner | 2,000.00 | | | | | J. Owner, Capital | 40 | 2,000.00 |
| | 1 | Cash sales | 680.00 | | | | 680.00 | | | |
| | 3 | Cash sales | 710.00 | | | | 710.00 | | | |
| | 8 | Collection—Paul Carter | 627.20 | 12.80 | ✓ | 640.00 | | | | |
| | 11 | Proceeds of bank loan | 5,000.00 | | | | | Note Payable | 33 | 5,000.00 |
| | 13 | Cash sales | 440.00 | | | | 440.00 | | | |
| | 15 | Collection—Henry Chambers | 803.60 | 16.40 | ✓ | 820.00 | | | | |
| | 20 | Collection—Robert Morgan | 1,234.80 | 25.20 | ✓ | 1,260.00 | | | | |
| | 25 | Cash sales | 600.00 | | | | 600.00 | | | |
| | 27 | Collection—Dave Christman | 540.00 | | ✓ | 540.00 | | | | |
| | 30 | Cash sales | 360.00 | | | | 360.00 | | | |
| | | | 12,995.60 | 54.40 | | 3,260.00 | 2,790.00 | | | 7,000.00 |
| | | | (1) | (52) | | (4) | (50) | | | (✓) |

## Posting the Cash Receipts Journal to the General Ledger and the Accounts Receivable Subsidiary Ledger

As with the sales journal, entries in the cash receipts journal are posted to both the general ledger and the accounts receivable subsidiary ledger.

*2b. Posting from the cash receipts journal is illustrated in Exhibit 6–7*

The procedures for posting the entries in the cash receipts journal are illustrated in Exhibit 6–7 and summarized below.

As in the case of the sales journal and the purchases journal, several things should be noted about the posting procedures for the cash receipts journal:

1. Amounts entered in the Accounts Receivable credit column should be posted to the individual customers' accounts in the accounts receivable ledger immediately after they have been entered. Enter a check mark in the Post. Ref. column of the cash receipts journal to indicate that the amount has been posted. This immediate posting to the customer's account is necessary to make certain that each Accounts Receivable ledger account reflects the current status of that customer's account. This information is often used to determine a customer's credit rating and to monitor the company's collection policies.
2. Amounts entered in the Other Sources column should be posted to the general ledger account daily or at other convenient intervals throughout the month. Enter the number assigned to the account involved in the transaction in the Post. Ref. column to indicate that the amount has been posted. Most companies have only a few transactions that require an entry in the Other Sources column. Therefore posting immediately will not burden the recordkeeper and will eliminate some of the work required at the end of the month.
3. At the end of the month the cash receipts journal columns are totaled and ruled, as shown in Exhibit 6–7. The sum of the debit columns and the sum of the credit columns must be equal. This procedure, called *cross-footing*, obtained the following results in the illustrated cash receipts journal:

| DEBIT COLUMN TOTALS | | CREDIT COLUMN TOTALS | |
|---|---|---|---|
| Cash | $12,995.60 | Accounts Receivable | $ 3,260.00 |
| Sales Discounts | 54.40 | Sales | 2,790.00 |
| | | Other Sources | 7,000.00 |
| Total Debits | $13,050.00 | Total Credits | $13,050.00 |

4. After the totals of each column have been determined, the column totals are posted as follows:
   a. *Cash debit column.* Post as a debit to the Cash account. Enter the Cash account number (1) under the Cash column total to indicate that the amount has been posted.
   b. *Sales Discounts debit column.* Post as a debit to the Sales Discounts account. Enter the Sales Discounts account number (52) under the Sales Discounts column total to indicate that the amount has been posted.
   c. *Accounts Receivable credit column.* Post as a credit to the Accounts Receivable control account. Enter the Accounts Receivable account number (4) under the Accounts Receivable column total to indicate that the amount has been posted.
   d. *Sales credit column.* Post as a credit to the Sales account. Enter the Sales account number (50) under the Sales column total to indicate that the amount has been posted.
   e. *Other Sources column.* The Other Sources column amount is not posted in total because each entry in the column was posted individually during the month. The column is totaled only to verify that the debits and credits entered in the cash receipts journal are equal. Generally, a check mark is placed below the column total to indicate that the amount is not posted as a total.

EXHIBIT 6-7

**Posting from the Cash Receipts Journal to the General Ledger and the Accounts Receivable Subsidiary Ledger**

CASH RECEIPTS JOURNAL — PAGE 6

| DATE | | EXPLANATION | DEBITS: CASH | DEBITS: SALES DISCOUNTS | POST. REF. | CREDITS: ACCOUNTS RECEIVABLE | CREDITS: SALES | CREDITS: OTHER SOURCES | POST. REF. | AMOUNT |
|---|---|---|---|---|---|---|---|---|---|---|
| 19X3 | | | | | | | | | | |
| June | 1 | Additional investment by owner | 2,000.00 | | | | | J. Owner, Capital | 40 | 2,000.00 |
| | 1 | Cash sales | 680.00 | | | | 680.00 | | | |
| | 3 | Cash sales | 710.00 | | | | 710.00 | | | |
| | 8 | Collection—P. Carter | 627.20 | 12.80 | ✓ | 640.00 | | | | |
| | 11 | Proceeds of bank loan | 5,000.00 | | | | | Note Payable | 33 | 5,000.00 |
| | 13 | Cash sales | 440.00 | | | | 440.00 | | | |
| | 15 | Collection—H. Chambers | 803.60 | 16.40 | ✓ | 820.00 | | | | |
| | 20 | Collection—R. Morgan | 1,234.80 | 25.20 | ✓ | 1,260.00 | | | | |
| | 25 | Cash sales | 600.00 | | | | 600.00 | | | |
| | 27 | Collection—D. Christman | 540.00 | | ✓ | 540.00 | | | | |
| | 30 | Cash sales | 360.00 | | | | 360.00 | | | |
| | | | 12,995.60 | 54.40 | | 3,260.00 | 2,790.00 | | | 7,000.00 |
| | | | (1) | (52) | | (4) | (50) | | | (✓) |

Total is not posted

Individual amounts are posted daily to the subsidiary ledger.

Journal totals are posted at the end of the period to the general ledger account.

**ACCOUNTS RECEIVABLE LEDGER**

PAUL CARTER

| | | | |
|---|---|---|---|
| June 2 | 640 | June 8 | 640 |

HENRY CHAMBERS

| | | | |
|---|---|---|---|
| June 5 | 820 | June 15 | 820 |

DAVE CHRISTMAN

| | | | |
|---|---|---|---|
| June 14 | 540 | June 27 | 540 |

ROBERT MORGAN

| | | | |
|---|---|---|---|
| June 11 | 1,260 | June 20 | 1,260 |

**GENERAL LEDGER**

CASH — 1

| | | | |
|---|---|---|---|
| June 30 | 12,995.60 | | |

ACCOUNTS RECEIVABLE — 4

| | | | |
|---|---|---|---|
| June 30 | 6,920.00 | June 30 | 3,260.00 |

NOTE PAYABLE — 33

| | | | |
|---|---|---|---|
| | | June 11 | 5,000.00 |

J. OWNER, CAPITAL — 40

| | | | |
|---|---|---|---|
| | | June 1 | 2,000.00 |

SALES — 50

| | | | |
|---|---|---|---|
| | | June 30 | 6,920.00 |
| | | 30 | 2,790.00 |

SALES DISCOUNTS — 52

| | | | |
|---|---|---|---|
| June 30 | 54.40 | | |

The major reasons for using a cash receipts journal are (1) to reduce the time and effort required to record and post journal entries involving the receipt of cash and (2) to establish a division of labor.

In regard to the latter, to help ensure control over cash receipts, companies often separate the physical handling of cash from the recording of transactions that affect cash. Thus the entries in the cash receipts journal are usually prepared from a secondary source document, such as a cash register tape or a bank deposit slip. This approach minimizes the possibility of fraud or embezzlement because more than one person is responsible for preparing documents. These documents, when compared, must agree in all aspects, including dollar amount. Other aspects of internal control are examined in Chapter 7.

## The Cash Payments Journal

*2a. Cash payments journal entries are illustrated in Exhibit 6–8*

All the transactions involving payments of cash are recorded in the *cash payments journal,* sometimes called the **cash disbursements journal.**

The cash payments journal is multicolumn and quite similar in format to the cash receipts journal described earlier. Columns are designated for repetitive transactions, making it possible to obtain efficiency in the posting process, since posting can be done from column totals. Repetitive transactions recorded in this journal consist of payments to creditors for merchandise previously purchased on credit, payments for the cash purchase of merchandise, and payments for operating expenses. The cash payments journal in Exhibit 6–8 illustrates how the journal would look after the pertinent transactions had been entered.

Note that the cash payments journal has a column titled Check No. The number of the check used for each cash payment is listed in this column. An unbroken sequence of check numbers indicates that every check issued has been recorded in the cash payments journal. Numbering checks helps to maintain control over outgoing cash.

Note also that the illustrated cash payments journal has two credit columns and four debit columns. The two credit columns are

*Cash.* This column must be used for every transaction because only cash payment transactions are recorded in this journal.

*Purchase Discounts.* This column is used to enter purchase discounts that have been taken.

The four debit columns are

1. *Accounts Payable.* This column is used to enter payments made to vendors and suppliers who have extended credit to the company. The vendor's or supplier's name is written in the Explanation column to identify the payee. The name is needed so that the entry will be posted to the proper account in the accounts payable subsidiary ledger.
2. *Purchases.* This column is used to record all cash purchases of merchandise.
3. *Travel Expense.* This column is used to record all travel expense paid in cash. Because travel expense payments are repetitive for this company, a separate money column for recording this transaction has been provided in the cash payments journal.
4. *Other Payments.* This column is used to record all the cash payment transactions other than payments of accounts payable, cash purchases of merchandise, and cash payments for travel expense. The title of the account to be debited is written in the Other Payments column to identify the type of cash payment involved.

*EXHIBIT 6–8*

CASH PAYMENTS JOURNAL — PAGE 3

| DATE | | EXPLANATION | CHECK NO. | CREDITS | | DEBITS | | | | | | |
|---|---|---|---|---|---|---|---|---|---|---|---|---|
| | | | | CASH | PURCHASE DISCOUNTS | POST REF. | ACCOUNTS PAYABLE | PURCHASES | TRAVEL EXPENSE | OTHER PAYMENTS | POST. REF. | AMOUNT |
| 19X3 | | | | | | | | | | | | |
| June | 1 | June rent | 71 | 600 | | | | | | Rent expense | 65 | 600 |
| | 4 | Purchased merchandise | 72 | 200 | | | | 200 | | | | |
| | 6 | Travel expense | 73 | 30 | | | | | 30 | | | |
| | 9 | Paid Lowell and Company | 74 | 784 | 16 | ✓ | 800 | | | | | |
| | 11 | Travel expense | 75 | 35 | | | | | 35 | | | |
| | 14 | Paid Vista Company | 76 | 1,067 | 33 | ✓ | 1,100 | | | | | |
| | 16 | Purchased merchandise | 77 | 350 | | | | 350 | | | | |
| | 18 | Travel expense | 78 | 25 | | | | | 25 | | | |
| | 24 | Purchased merchandise | 79 | 400 | | | | 400 | | | | |
| | 26 | Paid C-View Incorporated | 80 | 637 | 13 | ✓ | 650 | | | | | |
| | 30 | Travel expense | 81 | 40 | | | | | 40 | | | |
| | 30 | Sales Salaries | 82 | 1,200 | | | | | | Salaries expense | 64 | 1,200 |
| | | | | 5,368 | 62 | | 2,550 | 950 | 130 | | | 1,800 |
| | | | | (1) | (61) | | (31) | (60) | (66) | | | (✓) |

*EXHIBIT 6–9*

**Posting from the Cash Payments Journal to the General Ledger and the Accounts Payable Subsidiary Ledger**

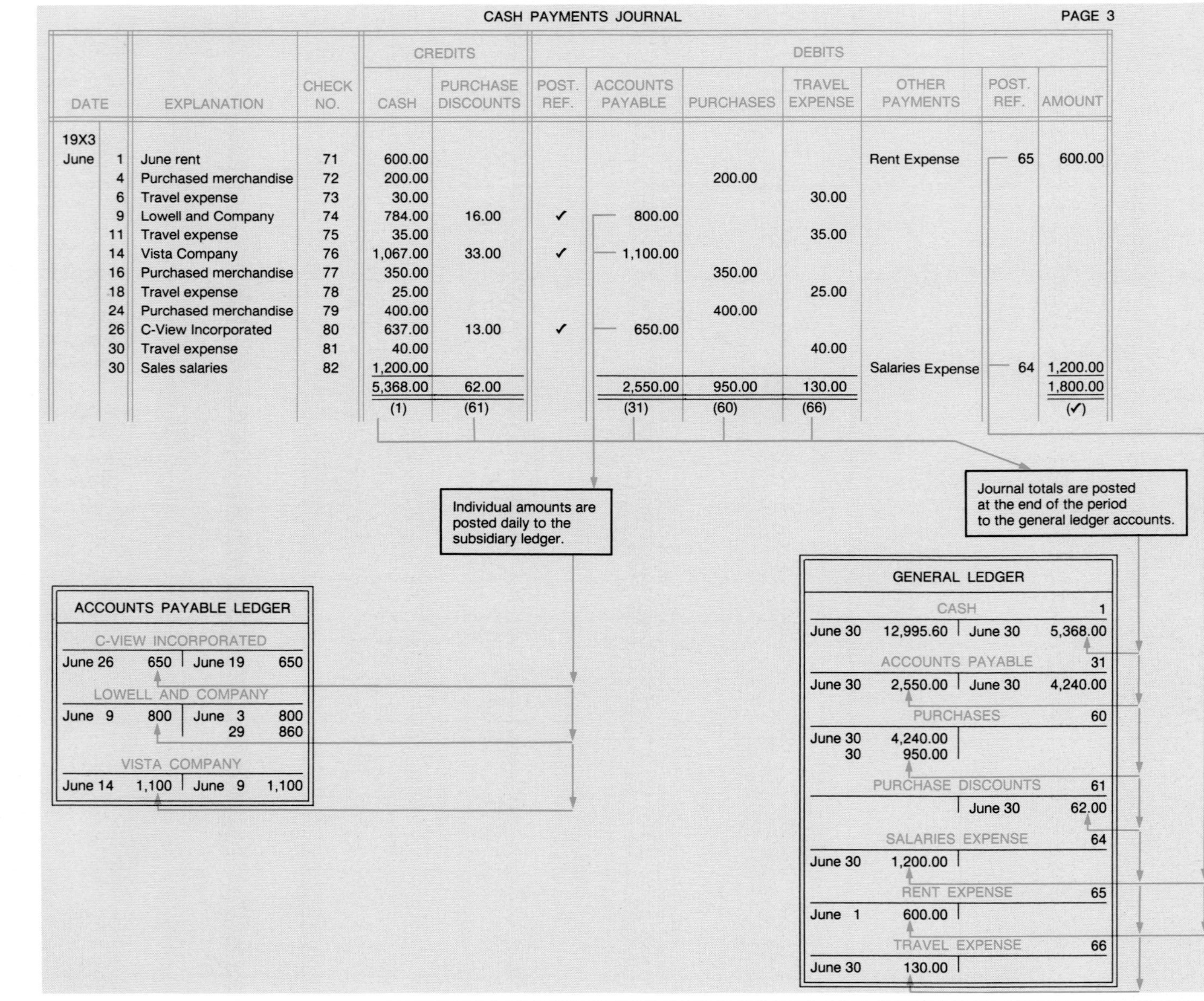

CASH PAYMENTS JOURNAL — PAGE 3

| | | | | CREDITS | | DEBITS | | | | | | |
|---|---|---|---|---|---|---|---|---|---|---|---|---|
| DATE | | EXPLANATION | CHECK NO. | CASH | PURCHASE DISCOUNTS | POST. REF. | ACCOUNTS PAYABLE | PURCHASES | TRAVEL EXPENSE | OTHER PAYMENTS | POST. REF. | AMOUNT |
| 19X3 | | | | | | | | | | | | |
| June | 1 | June rent | 71 | 600.00 | | | | | | Rent Expense | 65 | 600.00 |
| | 4 | Purchased merchandise | 72 | 200.00 | | | | 200.00 | | | | |
| | 6 | Travel expense | 73 | 30.00 | | | | | 30.00 | | | |
| | 9 | Lowell and Company | 74 | 784.00 | 16.00 | ✓ | 800.00 | | | | | |
| | 11 | Travel expense | 75 | 35.00 | | | | | 35.00 | | | |
| | 14 | Vista Company | 76 | 1,067.00 | 33.00 | ✓ | 1,100.00 | | | | | |
| | 16 | Purchased merchandise | 77 | 350.00 | | | | 350.00 | | | | |
| | 18 | Travel expense | 78 | 25.00 | | | | | 25.00 | | | |
| | 24 | Purchased merchandise | 79 | 400.00 | | | | 400.00 | | | | |
| | 26 | C-View Incorporated | 80 | 637.00 | 13.00 | ✓ | 650.00 | | | | | |
| | 30 | Travel expense | 81 | 40.00 | | | | | 40.00 | | | |
| | 30 | Sales salaries | 82 | 1,200.00 | | | | | | Salaries Expense | 64 | 1,200.00 |
| | | | | 5,368.00 | 62.00 | | 2,550.00 | 950.00 | 130.00 | | | 1,800.00 |
| | | | | (1) | (61) | | (31) | (60) | (66) | | | (✓) |

Individual amounts are posted daily to the subsidiary ledger.
Journal totals are posted at the end of the period to the general ledger accounts.

ACCOUNTS PAYABLE LEDGER

C-VIEW INCORPORATED

| | | | |
|---|---|---|---|
| June 26 | 650 | June 19 | 650 |

LOWELL AND COMPANY

| | | | |
|---|---|---|---|
| June 9 | 800 | June 3 | 800 |
| | | 29 | 860 |

VISTA COMPANY

| | | | |
|---|---|---|---|
| June 14 | 1,100 | June 9 | 1,100 |

GENERAL LEDGER

CASH — 1

| | | | |
|---|---|---|---|
| June 30 | 12,995.60 | June 30 | 5,368.00 |

ACCOUNTS PAYABLE — 31

| | | | |
|---|---|---|---|
| June 30 | 2,550.00 | June 30 | 4,240.00 |

PURCHASES — 60

| | | | |
|---|---|---|---|
| June 30 | 4,240.00 | | |
| 30 | 950.00 | | |

PURCHASE DISCOUNTS — 61

| | | | |
|---|---|---|---|
| | | June 30 | 62.00 |

SALARIES EXPENSE — 64

| | | | |
|---|---|---|---|
| June 30 | 1,200.00 | | |

RENT EXPENSE — 65

| | | | |
|---|---|---|---|
| June 1 | 600.00 | | |

TRAVEL EXPENSE — 66

| | | | |
|---|---|---|---|
| June 30 | 130.00 | | |

### Posting the Cash Payments Journal to the General Ledger and the Accounts Payable Subsidiary Ledger

Like those in the purchases journal, entries in the cash payments journal are posted to both the general ledger and the accounts payable subsidiary ledger.

*2b. Posting from a cash payments journal is illustrated in Exhibit 6–9*

The procedures for posting the entries in the cash payments journal are illustrated in Exhibit 6–9. Note the similarity between these procedures and the ones illustrated in Exhibit 6–7 for the posting of entries from the cash receipts journal.

As in the case of the sales, purchases, and cash receipts journals, several things should be noted about the posting procedures for the cash payments journal:

1. Amounts entered in the Accounts Payable debit column should be posted to the individual supplier's account in the accounts payable ledger immediately after they have been entered. Place a check mark in the Post. Ref. column of the cash payments journal to indicate that the amount has been posted.
2. Amounts entered in the Other Payments column should be posted to the general ledger account daily or at other convenient intervals throughout the month. Enter the number assigned to the account involved in the transaction in the Post. Ref. column to indicate that the amount has been posted.
3. At the end of the month, the cash payments journal columns are totaled and ruled, as shown in Exhibit 6–9. The sum of the debit columns and the sum of the credit columns must be the same. Verification that the debits and credits in our illustrated cash payments journal are equal is done as follows:

| CREDIT COLUMN TOTALS | | DEBIT COLUMN TOTALS | |
|---|---|---|---|
| Cash | $5,368 | Accounts Payable | $2,550 |
| Purchase Discounts | 62 | Purchases | 950 |
| | | Travel Expense | 130 |
| | | Other Payments | 1,800 |
| Total Credits | $5,430 | Total Debits | $5,430 |

4. The column totals for Cash and Purchase Discounts are posted at the end of the period as credits to their respective accounts in the general ledger. Account numbers (1) and (61) are entered below the respective column totals to indicate that the amounts have been posted. Post the column totals for Accounts Payable, Purchases, and Travel Expense as debits to their respective accounts in the general ledger. Enter account numbers (31), (60), and (66) below the respective column totals to indicate that the amounts have been posted. These postings are also made at the end of the period. The total in the Other Payments column is not posted because the individual amounts were posted when they were entered.

Note that only seven postings were needed to transfer all June amounts from the cash payments journal to the general ledger. If a general journal were used as the only book of entry, twenty-seven postings would be necessary. This example shows how the clerical work of recording and posting transactions can be reduced considerably by the use of special journals. It also shows how, as a result, the company can be more efficient in accumulating information and at a significantly lower clerical cost.

## ADDITIONAL COMMENTS ABOUT SPECIAL-PURPOSE JOURNALS

Special journals are identified in the Posting Reference column of the ledger accounts by abbreviations or initials. The journals with abbreviations that are frequently used follow.

| JOURNAL | ABBREVIATION |
|---|---|
| Sales Journal | S |
| Purchases Journal | P |
| Cash Receipts Journal | CR |
| Cash Payments Journal | CP |
| General Journal | GJ |

Note that the format of special journals is not standardized. We illustrated common versions throughout the chapter; however, the ones used by a particular company will depend on the nature of that company's activities and the repetitiveness of some of its transactions.

For example, a single-column purchases journal can easily be expanded to a multicolumn format. Exhibit 6–10 shows the format of a multicolumn purchases journal with transactions entered therein. It is shown for illustrative purposes only, but it does point out the versatility of special journals.

The multicolumn purchases journal provides a single credit column for accounts payable and several debit columns for the purchases of merchandise, transportation-in, store supplies, and office supplies. Other columns, if needed, could easily be added. The recording and posting procedures with a multicolumn purchases journal are similar to those already described. Amounts in the accounts payable column are posted daily to the individual suppliers' accounts in the accounts payable subsidiary ledger. Column totals are posted at the end of the month to their respective accounts in the general ledger.

*EXHIBIT 6–10*
Multicolumn Purchases Journal

PURCHASES JOURNAL

| DATE | | ACCOUNT CREDITED | TERMS | POST. REF. | CREDIT ACCOUNTS PAYABLE | DEBITS PURCHASES | TRANS-POR-TATION-IN | STORE SUPPLIES | OFFICE SUPPLIES |
|---|---|---|---|---|---|---|---|---|---|
| 19X3 | | | | | | | | | |
| June | 3 | Lowell and Company | 2/10, n/30 | ✓ | 800 | 800 | | | |
| | 5 | Wheatley Incorporated | n/30 | ✓ | 50 | | | 50 | |
| | 9 | Vista Company | 3/10, n/30 | ✓ | 1,100 | 1,100 | | | |
| | 14 | Acme Supply House | n/30 | ✓ | 280 | 280 | | | |
| | 15 | Systems Incorporated | n/30 | ✓ | 70 | | | | 70 |
| | 19 | C-View Incorporated | 2/10, n/30 | ✓ | 650 | 650 | | | |
| | 19 | Kline Transportation | n/30 | ✓ | 40 | | 40 | | |
| | 22 | Stewart and Sons | 1/10, n/30 | ✓ | 550 | 550 | | | |
| | 24 | Lowell and Company | 2/10, n/30 | ✓ | 860 | 860 | | | |
| | | | | | 4,400 | 4,240 | 40 | 50 | 70 |
| | | | | | (31) | (60) | (64) | (8) | (10) |

## GENERAL JOURNAL

*1f. When special-purpose journals are used, a general journal is used to record a few types of transactions and for correcting, adjusting, reversing, and closing entries*

When special journals are used, almost all the transactions can be recorded directly in one of them. Yet during a given accounting period, a company may have some transactions that cannot be efficiently handled in its special journals. These transactions are therefore recorded in the *general journal.* They do not occur frequently for the given company; otherwise it would consider starting another special journal to accommodate them. Examples of such transactions include

1. Sales returns and allowances
2. Purchase returns and allowances
3. The purchase and sale of assets (other than merchandise) on credit terms (when a single-column purchases journal and a single-column sales journal are being used)

*2c. General journal entries are recorded as illustrated here*

The general journal is also used for correcting entries, adjusting entries, reversing entries, and closing entries.

Described below are two typical transactions, both of which are posted to the subsidiary ledger accounts and to the general ledger accounts. However, neither can be recorded conveniently in any of the special journals discussed in this chapter.

On June 21 James Gray, a customer, returned $50 of merchandise that he had purchased on credit four days earlier. A credit for that amount was authorized and issued to him:

| | | | |
|---|---|---|---|
| June 21 | Sales Returns and Allowances | 50 | |
| | Accounts Receivable—Gray | | 50 |
| | To record merchandise returned by a customer for credit | | |

On June 30 merchandise costing $110 that had previously been purchased on credit from Lowell and Company was returned. Lowell accepted the return and issued a credit memo for the full amount:

| | | | |
|---|---|---|---|
| June 30 | Accounts Payable—Lowell | 110 | |
| | Purchase Returns and Allowances | | 110 |
| | To record merchandise returned to a supplier for credit | | |

These transactions are posted to the general ledger in the same manner as that described in earlier chapters. If the subsidiary ledgers discussed in this chapter are used, any debit or credit to accounts receivable or accounts payable must also be posted to the proper individual account in the subsidiary ledgers.

Thus the credit in the June 21 entry must be posted to both the Accounts Receivable control account and the subsidiary ledger account for James Gray. Also, the debit in the June 30 entry must be posted twice: once to the Accounts Payable control account and once to the subsidiary ledger account for Lowell and Company.

*2c. Posting from the general journal is illustrated in Exhibit 6–11*

The procedures for posting from the general journal to the general ledger and the subsidiary ledgers are illustrated in Exhibit 6–11.

EXHIBIT 6–11
Posting from the General Journal to the General Ledger and to the Accounts Receivable and Accounts Payable Subsidiary Ledgers

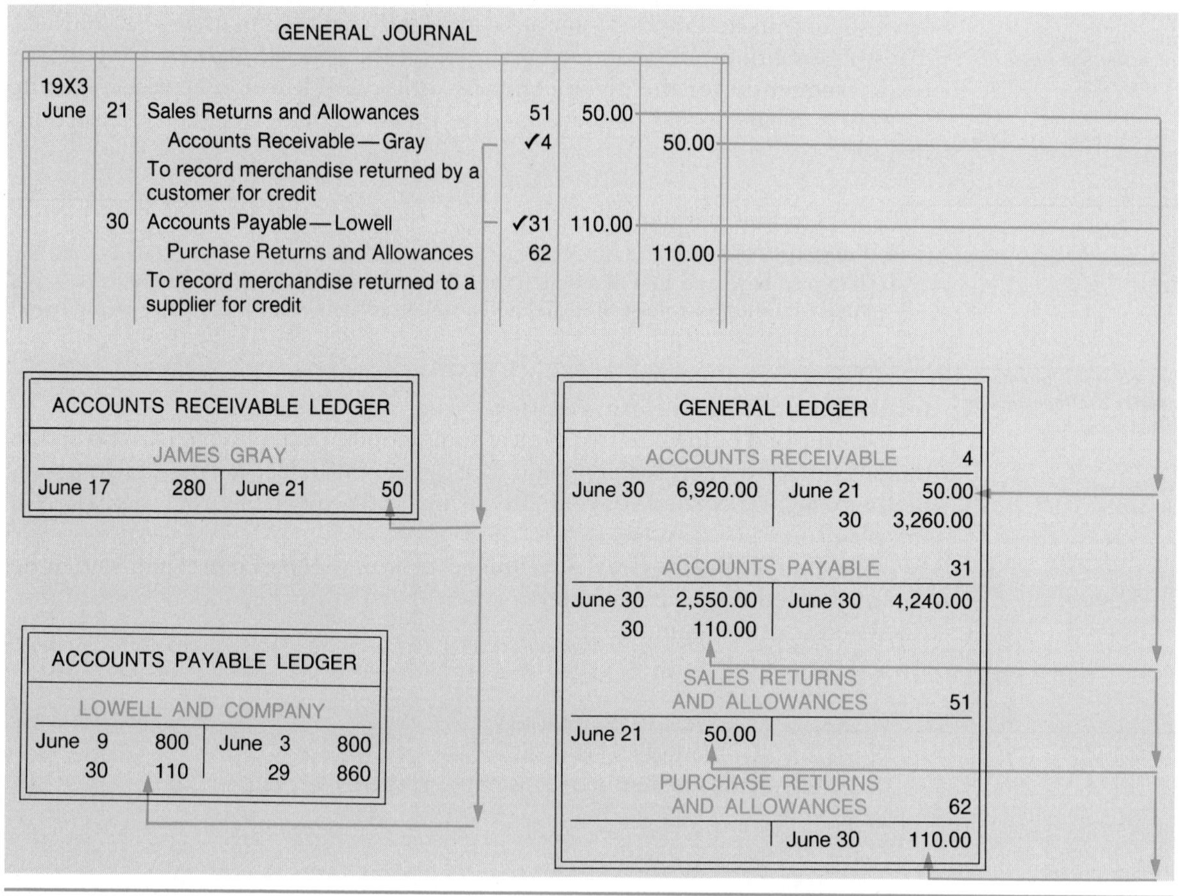

GENERAL JOURNAL

| Date | | Description | Ref. | Debit | Credit |
|---|---|---|---|---|---|
| 19X3 | | | | | |
| June | 21 | Sales Returns and Allowances | 51 | 50.00 | |
| | | Accounts Receivable—Gray | ✓4 | | 50.00 |
| | | To record merchandise returned by a customer for credit | | | |
| | 30 | Accounts Payable—Lowell | ✓31 | 110.00 | |
| | | Purchase Returns and Allowances | 62 | | 110.00 |
| | | To record merchandise returned to a supplier for credit | | | |

ACCOUNTS RECEIVABLE LEDGER

JAMES GRAY

| | | | |
|---|---|---|---|
| June 17 | 280 | June 21 | 50 |

ACCOUNTS PAYABLE LEDGER

LOWELL AND COMPANY

| | | | |
|---|---|---|---|
| June 9 | 800 | June 3 | 800 |
| 30 | 110 | 29 | 860 |

GENERAL LEDGER

ACCOUNTS RECEIVABLE 4

| | | | |
|---|---|---|---|
| June 30 | 6,920.00 | June 21 | 50.00 |
| | | 30 | 3,260.00 |

ACCOUNTS PAYABLE 31

| | | | |
|---|---|---|---|
| June 30 | 2,550.00 | June 30 | 4,240.00 |
| 30 | 110.00 | | |

SALES RETURNS AND ALLOWANCES 51

| | | | |
|---|---|---|---|
| June 21 | 50.00 | | |

PURCHASE RETURNS AND ALLOWANCES 62

| | | | |
|---|---|---|---|
| | | June 30 | 110.00 |

## SCHEDULES OF ACCOUNTS RECEIVABLE AND ACCOUNTS PAYABLE

*2d. Schedules of accounts receivable and accounts payable are prepared from balances in the subsidiary ledgers*

At the end of each accounting period, a trial balance is generally prepared to determine the equality of debits and credits in the general ledger. When subsidiary ledgers are used, schedules of accounts receivable and accounts payable are also prepared to verify that the sum of the balances in the subsidiary ledgers is equal to the balances in their respective control accounts.

The accounts receivable and accounts payable subsidiary ledgers are shown in Exhibit 6-12 as they would appear after all June postings.

Using the subsidiary ledger accounts, the schedules of Accounts Receivable and Accounts Payable at the bottom of page 211 were prepared.

*2d. The total of each schedule is checked against the balance in its control account*

The total of each schedule is checked to see that it agrees with the balance in its control account. The Accounts Receivable and Accounts Payable control accounts, as they would appear after all June postings, are shown below in T-account form.

ACCOUNTS RECEIVABLE 4

| | | | |
|---|---|---|---|
| June 30 | 6,920.00 | June 21 | 50.00 |
| | | 30 | 3,260.00 |

ACCOUNTS PAYABLE 31

| | | | |
|---|---|---|---|
| June 30 | 2,550.00 | June 30 | 4,240.00 |
| 30 | 110.00 | | |

EXHIBIT 6–12
Subsidiary Ledgers

**ACCOUNTS RECEIVABLE LEDGER**

DANIEL ANDERSON

| | | | |
|---|---|---|---|
| June 22 | 480 | | |

EDWARD CAMPBELL

| | | | |
|---|---|---|---|
| June 19 | 760 | | |

PAUL CARTER

| | | | |
|---|---|---|---|
| June 2 | 640 | June 8 | 640 |

HENRY CHAMBERS

| | | | |
|---|---|---|---|
| June 5 | 820 | June 15 | 820 |

DAVE CHRISTMAN

| | | | |
|---|---|---|---|
| June 14 | 540 | June 27 | 540 |

HERBERT FORD

| | | | |
|---|---|---|---|
| June 29 | 720 | | |

JAMES GRAY

| | | | |
|---|---|---|---|
| June 17 | 280 | June 21 | 50 |

ALFRED GREENE

| | | | |
|---|---|---|---|
| June 25 | 1,040 | | |

STEVE MARTIN

| | | | |
|---|---|---|---|
| June 8 | 380 | | |

ROBERT MORGAN

| | | | |
|---|---|---|---|
| June 11 | 1,260 | June 20 | 1,260 |

**ACCOUNTS PAYABLE LEDGER**

ACME SUPPLY HOUSE

| | | | |
|---|---|---|---|
| | | June 14 | 280 |

C-VIEW INCORPORATED

| | | | |
|---|---|---|---|
| June 26 | 650 | June 19 | 650 |

LOWELL AND COMPANY

| | | | |
|---|---|---|---|
| June 9 | 800 | June 3 | 800 |
| 30 | 110 | 29 | 860 |

STEWART AND SONS

| | | | |
|---|---|---|---|
| | | June 22 | 550 |

VISTA COMPANY

| | | | |
|---|---|---|---|
| June 14 | 1,100 | June 9 | 1,100 |

Schedule of Accounts Receivable
June 30, 19X3

| | |
|---|---|
| Daniel Anderson | $ 480 |
| Edward Campbell | 760 |
| Herbert Ford | 720 |
| James Gray | 230 |
| Alfred Greene | 1,040 |
| Steve Martin | 380 |
| Total (agrees with control account) | $3,610 |

Schedule of Accounts Payable
June 30, 19X3

| | |
|---|---|
| Acme Supply House | $ 280 |
| Lowell and Company | 750 |
| Stewart and Sons | 550 |
| Total (agrees with control account) | $1,580 |

Note that the total of each schedule agrees with the balance in its control account. Preparing a schedule of the account balances in each of the subsidiary ledgers serves the following purposes:

1. It verifies that the subsidiary ledgers are in agreement with the balance in their related control account.
2. For receivables, it establishes who owes the company money and how much each customer owes.
3. For payables, it establishes to whom the company owes money and how much is owed to each creditor.

## ADVANTAGES OF SPECIAL-PURPOSE JOURNALS — SUMMARIZED

We end this section of the chapter by summarizing the major advantages of special-purpose journals.

1. *Saving time in journalizing.* Only one line is needed to record each transaction, and a full explanation of the transaction is not necessary. The amount of writing is further reduced because account titles need not be repeated.
2. *Saving time in posting.* When a general journal is used, each entry must be posted separately to the general ledger. When special journals are used, only cumulative monthly figures are posted to the general ledger for most items appearing in the special journals.
3. *Providing for a division of labor.* Since several special journals are normally used, the recording process can be divided among several people, each of whom is responsible for a particular type of transaction.
4. *Streamlining the general ledger accounts by eliminating numerous postings and detail.* The number of postings to general ledger accounts is significantly reduced, and the number of accounts needed in the general ledger is limited to those reported in the financial statements.
5. *Facilitating analytical studies.* All common transactions are listed in chronological order in their respective journal.

## THE ACCOUNTING PROCESS IN A COMPUTERIZED SYSTEM

We remarked earlier that the input, processing, output sequence of the accounting process is the same in both manual and computerized systems. We will now look at some techniques and devices used in a computerized system and will compare one part of the computerized input, processing, output sequence with that of a manual system.

### Computer Input/Output Techniques and Devices

In a manual system pen-and-ink methods are used to record data in special journals. Financial statements and other output are printed or typed. In a computerized system a variety of devices are used.

*1g. A comparison between a batch processing system and an online processing system is shown in Exhibit 6–13*

As an example, look at Exhibit 6–13, which compares computerized with manual processing of credit sales data. The last two columns show how events in the accounting process are handled by two types of computerized systems. In a **batch processing system,** shown in column 3 of Exhibit 6–13, records of transactions are accumulated and are then periodically (for example, at the end of each day) entered into the computer system and processed at one time. In an **online processing system,** shown in column 4 of Exhibit 6–13, each transaction is entered into the computer system as it is initially recorded and is processed immediately.

An online processing system is *interactive*—it allows the computer program, by displaying questions or information on a video screen, to respond directly to input from the user. The user can also edit the data displayed on the screen.

Batch processing is characteristic of older systems in which all processing is often done by a large central computer called a *mainframe.*

*EXHIBIT 6–13*

Computerized vs. Manual Processing of Credit Sales Data

| (1) Event | (2) Manual System | (3) Computerized Batch Processing System | (4) Computerized Online System |
|---|---|---|---|
| 1. Prepare a sales invoice. | 1. Prepare the invoice by hand. | 1. Prepare the invoice by hand or keyboard entry. | 1. Prepare the invoice by hand or keyboard entry. |
| 2. Transfer the sales invoice data to the original record. | 2. Record the data by hand in the sales journal. | 2. Record the data on magnetic tape. | 2. Record the data into the CPU and to magnetic disk storage. |
| 3. Post the sales invoice data. | 3. Post the data by hand to the general ledger and the accounts receivable ledger. | 3. The computer reads the data into the CPU, where they are processed. | 3. The computer system processes the data. |
| 4. Prepare a list of accounts receivable balances. | 4. Prepare the list by hand from the accounts receivable ledger. | 4. The computer transfers the accounts receivable information to a printer or other output unit. | 4. The computer transfers the accounts receivable information back to the terminal printer and/or screen. |

Returning to Exhibit 6–13, Event 1 under both the batch and online systems consists of preparing the sales invoice, either by hand or by keyboard entry. The keyboard may be a computer input device that resembles a typewriter keyboard, or it may be the keyboard of an electronic cash register. When the sales invoice is prepared by hand, the information it contains must later be typed into the computer by way of the computer's keyboard. Keying the information directly into an electronic cash register, on the other hand, results in both the production of a printed sales receipt and the entry of the information into the computer. The device by which data are entered into (or delivered out of) a computer system is called a **terminal.**

Event 2 records the data on an electronic storage medium—**magnetic tape** or **magnetic disk,** which resembles the tapes and disks used in home stereos. Tapes can record (write) or play (read) data only in *sequential* order. To write to, or read from, any part of the tape, the unit must run the tape until the desired portion reaches the read/write head. Disks allow *random access*—the unit can write to, or read from, any desired portion of the disk almost instantly by moving the read/write head across the face of the disk to the proper track, much as we move the pickup arm of a phonograph. For batch processing, it is convenient to record transactions sequentially on a tape. For online processing, however, magnetic disks are used.

An early system for storage and retrieval of data by means of card punches, punched cards, card sorters, and card readers may still be seen in operation in some businesses. Punched-card systems have their limitations, and their use is declining.

In Event 2 of online processing, and Event 3 of batch processing, the data are fed into the computer's **central processing unit (CPU),** the part of the computer system that reads data and computer programs from the input units, executes the computer programs to process the data into information (Event 3), and writes the information on the output units.

Event 4 in both batch and online systems transfers information to an output device such as a screen or a printer. A **printer** is the part of the computer system that prints paper records that people can read without machine assistance.

Sometimes online and batch processing are combined. The terminal is used to check the customer's credit status and record the sale, and the sales invoices are used to update customers' accounts.

## MICROCOMPUTER SYSTEMS

A far-reaching change that has occurred in computerized systems in recent years is the creation of microcomputers. A *microcomputer* can be a "stand-alone computer" that need not be attached to a mainframe located in another area of the business establishment. (Mainframes are large computer installations connected to magnetic tape drives, remote terminals, and other devices.)

*1g. The configuration of a typical microcomputer system is illustrated here*

A microcomputer system can have several types of configurations. A typical configuration consists of

1. A processor
2. Some type of keyboard used for input
3. Some type of display screen used for verification and editing
4. Some type of printer used for output
5. Some type of storage medium

### The Processor

The processor (or central processing unit, as described earlier) executes the programs, controls the operations of the rest of the computer system, and contains the internal or working memory that stores program instructions and data. For microcomputers that are classified as personal computers, the hardware that houses the processor is a small rectangular metal box that can be placed on the corner of a desk.

The internal or working memory capacity differs with each type of processor. Typical capacities are 48,000, 64,000, 128,000, 256,000, or 512,000 characters (sometimes referred to as 48, 64, 128, 256, or 512 K). The greater the capacity, the more data the computer can store, and the more complex the programs can be. Random-access memory contains data that are erased when the computer is turned off. On the other hand, read-only memory contains characters that are part of the processor hardware and are not erased. Data in the random-access memory section of the processor must be transferred to some storage medium or they will be lost when the computer is shut down.

### The Keyboard

The keyboard is the device used to enter data and program instructions into the internal memory of the processor. A keyboard looks and operates much like a typewriter. Characters punched on a microcomputer keyboard are placed in the internal memory section of the processor and are displayed on a screen.

### The Display Screen

The display screen is contained in a separate metal or plastic box that could be permanently or temporarily attached to the processor. One fairly common method is to attach a cord from the display screen unit to the processor and place the screen unit on top of the processor. As users punch the character buttons on the keyboard, these characters appear on the display screen directly in front of them. The users can immediately edit the accuracy of the characters and, if necessary, change them.

### The Printer

Output appearing on a display screen is convenient for reviewing and editing. However, when the computer is turned off, the characters on the display screen, and in internal memory, disappear. To retain permanent printed output, a typical microcomputer system can also use some type of "hard-copy" printer. The data on the display screen, and in internal memory, can usually be printed by pushing a single common button on the keyboard.

A wide variety of printers are available that are compatible with many types of microcomputer systems. All that is usually needed is an interface cable to connect the processor to the printer.

### Storage Media

As an operator enters data into the internal memory section of the processor by typing characters on the keyboard, the same data can (and should) be recorded on some type of storage medium. In microcomputer systems, tape cassettes, hard disks, or diskettes (floppy disks) can be used. Diskettes are popular because of their small size, ease of handling, and reasonably large amount of storage capacity.

Many microcomputer processors contain slots or drives into which diskettes can be placed. By the use of a separate keyboard command, data previously typed into internal memory can be transferred to a diskette as a permanent record. Another keyboard command prints the data in internal memory. The advantage of transferring data from internal memory to a diskette is that these same data can be reprinted or fed back into the processor from the diskette as many times as desired. Data that are placed only in internal memory, however, are lost once the processor is turned off. To replace the same data in internal memory, if they have not been recorded on a diskette, the computer must be turned on and the keyboard input process repeated.

## HIGHLIGHT PROBLEM

The following problem is a practice problem designed to help you develop your ability to analyze a transaction and select the proper journal in which to record it when a number of special journals are being used. You are to analyze the transactions presented below and indicate which journal should be used to record each transaction, assuming the company uses the following set of journals:

| | |
|---|---|
| Sales Journal | single-column |
| Purchases Journal | single-column |
| Cash Receipts Journal | multicolumn |
| Cash Payments Journal | multicolumn |
| General Journal | two-column |

Transactions that occurred during the month of July:

| | | |
|---|---|---|
| July | 1 | Paid monthly rent, $600. |
| | 2 | Purchased $900 of merchandise on credit; terms 2/10, n/30. |
| | 2 | Purchased office supplies for $50 and paid cash. |
| | 3 | Sold $850 of merchandise on credit; terms 1/10, n/30. |
| | 4 | Sold merchandise for cash, $300. |
| | 8 | Purchased $600 of merchandise on credit; terms 2/10, n/30. |
| | 8 | Sold $940 of merchandise on credit; terms 1/10, n/30. |
| | 10 | Paid the amount due for the merchandise purchased on July 2. |
| | 12 | Returned $50 of defective merchandise purchased on July 8 and received a credit. |
| | 12 | Received payment for the sale made on July 3. |
| | 15 | Paid salaries, $620. |
| | 16 | Sold merchandise for cash, $470. |
| | 16 | Paid advertising expenses, $170 |
| | 18 | Granted a credit of $150 on merchandise returned from the sale made on July 8. |
| | 19 | Purchased an office typewriter on credit, $190. |
| | 22 | Sold $820 of merchandise on credit; terms 1/10, n/30. |
| | 24 | Received full payment for the credit sale made on July 8. |
| | 25 | Purchased $590 of merchandise on credit; terms 2/10, n/30. |
| | 29 | Purchased merchandise for cash, $175. |
| | 31 | Paid salaries, $580. |

## GLOSSARY OF KEY TERMS

**Accounting process.** The sequence of procedures used to collect, organize, store, and report the data shown in a firm's financial reports.

**Accounting system.** The business documents, records, equipment, policies, and procedures used to report transactions and events affecting an entity's financial performance and its financial status.

**Accounts payable ledger.** A ledger separate from the general ledger; it contains an account for each supplier or vendor. At the end of each accounting period, the total of the ledger accounts will equal the balance in the general ledger control account, Accounts Payable.

**Accounts receivable ledger.** A ledger separate from the general ledger; it contains an account for each credit customer. At the end of each accounting period, the total of the ledger accounts will equal the balance in the general ledger control account, Accounts Receivable.

**Batch processing system.** A computerized system in which, on a periodic basis, similar transactions are processed at one time.

**Cash disbursements journal.** Alternate title for *cash payments journal.*

**Cash payments journal.** A special journal used to record all the transactions involving payments of cash. Also called a *cash disbursements journal.*

**Cash receipts journal.** A special journal used to record all the transactions involving the receipt of cash.

**Central processing unit (CPU).** The part of the computer system that reads data and computer programs from the input units, executes the computer programs to process the data into information, and writes the information on the output units.

**Control account.** The general ledger account that is supported by the detail in the subsidiary ledger accounts.

**Division of labor.** Establishing a means by which accounting information can be processed by several persons simultaneously.

**Magnetic disk.** A data storage medium resembling a phonograph record, which rotates under a movable head and to or from which data can be read. A disk has random-access capabilities.

**Magnetic tape.** A data storage medium resembling home recording tape, to or from which data can be read. A tape has only sequential access capabilities.

**Online processing system.** A computerized system in which each transaction is entered into the computer system as it is initially recorded and is processed immediately.

**Printer.** The part of the computer system that prints

paper records that people can read without machine assistance.

**Purchases journal.** A special journal used to record all purchases of merchandise made on credit. If a single-column purchases journal is used, only purchases of merchandise held for resale are recorded in this special journal.

**Sales journal.** A special journal used to record all sales of merchandise made on credit.

**Special-purpose journals.** Any group of journals, each of which is designed to record a company's frequently recurring transactions.

**Subsidiary ledger.** A group of individual accounts that provide the detail of a general ledger account.

**Terminal.** An input/output device that allows people to communicate directly with the computer system.

## REVIEW QUESTIONS

1. What is an accounting system? [LO1a]
2. Describe the four stages involved in the development of an accounting system. [LO1a]
3. Describe the three-step sequence of the accounting process in a manual system. [LO1b]
4. Name the four types of transactions that recur with frequency in a merchandising company. [LO1c]
5. Name the four types of special-purpose journals used to record the transactions referred to in Question 4. [LO1d]
6. Describe four ways in which the use of a sales journal enables a merchandising company to process data more rapidly and at a reduced clerical cost. [LO1c,1d]
7. Why do almost all the companies that sell merchandise on credit keep individual accounts receivable records for each customer? [LO1e]
8. Why do almost all the companies that buy merchandise on credit keep individual accounts payable records for each supplier? [LO1e]
9. Describe the three separate ledgers kept by most companies when they have a significant number of accounts receivable and accounts payable. [LO1e]
10. Why are the Accounts Receivable and Accounts Payable general ledger accounts referred to as control accounts? [LO1e]
11. Describe four reasons why subsidiary ledgers are established. [LO1e]
12. Describe three transactions recorded in a general journal when the types of special journals described in this chapter are also used. [LO1f]
13. What three purposes are served by preparing a schedule of the account balances in each of the subsidiary ledgers? [LO1e]
14. Describe the five major advantages of special journals. [LO1c]
15. Differentiate between online processing and batch processing. [LO1g]
16. Differentiate between sequential order on magnetic tape and random access on magnetic disks. [LO1g]
17. What is the purpose of the central processing unit? [LO1g]
18. Name and describe the five parts of a typical configuration of a microcomputer system. [LO1g]

## ANALYTICAL QUESTIONS

19. "The accounting process is the same whether a manual or a computerized system is used." Explain the meaning of this statement. [LO1b]
20. Does the use of special journals change the rules of debit and credit when recording transaction entries? Explain why or why not. [LO1c]
21. During the month of October, the purchase of merchandise on credit was actually \$82,800. An error of \$1,000 was made when totaling the amount column of the purchases journal. How and when will this error be discovered? [LO1e,2a,2b]

22. Comment on the validity of the following statement: "By taking the customer accounts out of the Accounts Receivable general ledger account and placing them in a subsidiary ledger, the general ledger will no longer balance." [LO1e]
23. Explain why credit transactions should be posted to the subsidiary ledgers daily and need not be posted to the general ledger until the end of an accounting period. [LO1e,2b]
24. When a company uses special journals and records the return of merchandise previously purchased by a customer on credit in the general journal, the credit part of the entry must be posted twice. Does this cause the trial balance to be out of balance? Explain why or why not. [LO1f,2c]
25. Describe two types of errors that could cause the total of the accounts receivable schedule to be different from the total in the accounts receivable control account. [LO1e,2b]
26. In a computerized system, what are the advantages of using terminals to enter transactions rather than other input devices? [LO1g]
27. Why are certain microcomputer systems referred to as "stand-alone computers"? [LO1g]

## IMPACT ANALYSIS QUESTIONS

*For each error described, indicate whether it would overstate [O], understate [U], or not affect [N] the specified key figures.*

28. A check was received that fully paid a customer's account receivable. The transaction was recorded in the cash receipts journal by entering the amount of the check in the journal's Cash debit column and in its Sales credit column. [LO2a,2b]

    ______ Assets ______ Net Income
    ______ Revenue ______ Liabilities

29. A check sufficient to fully pay an amount owed to a supplier for merchandise previously purchased was mailed. A purchase discount was taken. The transaction was recorded in the cash payments journal by debiting accounts payable and crediting cash for equal amounts (the amount of the check). [LO2a,2b]

    ______ Assets ______ Net Income
    ______ Revenue ______ Liabilities

30. A purchase return was posted as a credit to the Sales Returns and Allowances account. [LO2c]

    ______ Assets ______ Net Income
    ______ Revenue ______ Liabilities

31. Equipment purchased on credit was recorded in the company's single-column purchases journal. [LO2a,2b,2c]

    ______ Assets ______ Net Income
    ______ Revenue ______ Liabilities

32. A sales return was posted as a debit to the Purchase Returns and Allowances account. [LO2c]

    ______ Assets ______ Net Income
    ______ Revenue ______ Liabilities

## EXERCISES

EXERCISE 6–1 *(Match Journals with Types of Transactions)* For each of the following transactions, name the journal to be used and the accounts that would be debited and credited. Assume that the company uses four special journals (with the purchases journal designed as a single-column journal) and a general journal.

a. Sale of merchandise on credit

b. Purchase of merchandise on credit
c. Payment of cash to a creditor
d. Adjusting entry to record accrued interest receivable
e. Sale of merchandise for cash
f. Purchase of equipment for cash
g. Payment of salaries
h. Purchase of merchandise for cash
i. Return of merchandise to a vendor for credit [LO1d,1f]

EXERCISE 6–2 *(Identify Appropriate Journals and Ledgers)* The Amroy Company uses a cash receipts journal, a cash payments journal, a sales journal, a single-column purchases journal, and a general journal.

a. At the end of the accounting period, the column total in the sales journal should be posted to what account or accounts? Is the posting a debit or a credit?
b. At the end of the accounting period, the column total in the purchases journal should be posted to what account or accounts? Is the posting a debit or a credit?
c. Identify the two subsidiary ledgers that would probably be used in conjunction with Amroy's journals.
d. In which of the journals would we expect to find the fewest transactions recorded?
e. In which of the journals would we expect to find the most transactions recorded?
f. In which of the journals are the adjusting and closing entries recorded?

[LO1d,1e,1f]

EXERCISE 6–3 *(Correct Transaction Errors)* In recording transactions and posting from various journals, the following errors were made. In each case, indicate how the error might be discovered or whether discovery is likely.

a. Correctly recorded a $95 sale of merchandise on credit in the sales journal but posted it to the customer's account in the subsidiary ledger as a $950 sale.
b. Correctly recorded a $450 purchase of merchandise on credit in the purchases journal but posted it to the supplier's account in the subsidiary ledger as a $45 purchase.
c. A $450 payment to a creditor was recorded in the cash payments journal as $540.
d. Underfooted (underadded) the Amount column in the sales journal by $300.
e. An addition error was made in determining the balance of a customer's account in the subsidiary ledger. [LO1d,1e]

EXERCISE 6–4 *(Identify Appropriate Journals)* A certain company uses the four special journals illustrated in this chapter (single-column for the purchases journal) and a general journal. Name the journal in which each of the following transactions would be recorded.

a. Owner's cash investment in the business
b. Sale of merchandise on credit
c. Purchase of merchandise for cash
d. Purchase of office supplies on account
e. Sale of merchandise for cash
f. Return of merchandise sold on credit
g. Collection from customers who previously bought merchandise on credit
h. Withdrawal of cash by the owner
i. Purchase of merchandise on credit
j. Return of merchandise purchased on credit [LO1d,1f]

EXERCISE 6–5 *(Match Transactions with Journal)* Identify the type of transaction(s) that would be recorded in

a. A sales journal (single-column)
b. A purchases journal (single-column)
c. A cash receipts journal
d. A cash payments journal

e. A general journal (identify at least three types of transactions, assuming the four special journals listed above were being used) [LO1d,1f]

EXERCISE 6–6 *(Enter Transactions in a Cash Receipts Journal)* The Ard Company had the following transactions during the first few days of October 19X3.

| | |
|---|---|
| Oct. 1 | Received payment from J. Winters, a customer, on account receivable of $750 less a 2% discount. |
| 2 | Sold merchandise for cash, $300. |
| 2 | Signed a note payable (interest due at maturity) for $5,000, and received a check in that amount. |
| 3 | Received payment from R. Summers, a customer, on account receivable of $500 less a 2% discount. |
| 3 | Received payment from L. Springs, a customer, on account receivable of $200. |

Required:
Prepare a cash receipts journal similar to the one shown in the text, and record each of the above transactions in that journal. [LO2a]

EXERCISE 6–7 *(Enter Transactions in a Cash Payments Journal)* The Sealy Company had the following transactions during the first few days of November 19X3.

| | |
|---|---|
| Nov. 1 | Purchased $400 of merchandise for cash from Artis Company; issued check no. 51. |
| 1 | Issued check no. 52 to Royal Realty for this month's rent of $600. |
| 2 | Issued check no. 53 to pay Shorter Company, a supplier, its invoice amount of $1,200 less a 2% discount. |
| 2 | Issued check no. 54 to pay Queen Company, a supplier, its invoice amount of $800. |
| 2 | Paid Delray Company, a supplier, its invoice amount of $1,850 less a 2% discount; issued check no. 55. |
| 3 | Used check no. 56 to withdraw $1,000 from the business for the owner's personal use. |

Required:
Prepare a cash payments journal similar to the one shown in the text, and record each of the above transactions in that journal. [LO2a]

EXERCISE 6–8 *(Post from Special Journals)* The Roundtree Company uses four special journals. On January 31, 19X8, the end of its first month of operations, the transactions recorded in the four special journals show the following:

| | |
|---|---|
| Sales Journal | Column total, $68,000 |
| Purchases Journal | Column total, $43,000 |
| Cash Receipts Journal | Accounts Receivable column total, $56,000 |
| Cash Payments Journal | Accounts Payable column total, $34,000 |

Required:
1. What postings would be made on January 31 from the column total in the sales journal?
2. What postings would be made on January 31 from the column total in the purchases journal? This is a single-column purchases journal.
3. What postings would be made on January 31 from the Accounts Receivable column total in the cash receipts journal?
4. What postings would be made on January 31 from the Accounts Payable column total in the cash payments journal?
5. What balances would appear in the Accounts Receivable control account and the Accounts Payable control account after all postings had been made? Assume that the

above transactions were the only ones affecting these accounts and that there were no beginning balances in either of the control accounts. [LO1e,2b,2d]

## PROBLEMS

PROBLEM 6–1 *(Record Transactions in Sales, Cash Receipts, and General Journals)* Selected transactions of Wayne Company for the month of October 19X2 are listed below.

| | | |
|---|---|---|
| Oct. | 1 | Sold merchandise to P. Moss, $400; terms 2/10, n/30; invoice no. 101. |
| | 3 | Borrowed $2,000 from the Lay-A-Way Finance Company, principal and interest to be repaid in ninety days. |
| | 8 | Received $250 from R. Toby representing the balance due from a sale made in August, discount not allowed. |
| | 11 | Sold merchandise to R. Blatt, $640; terms 2/10, n/30; invoice no. 102. |
| | 11 | Received payment from P. Moss pertaining to invoice no. 101 less the discount. |
| | 13 | Granted R. Blatt a credit of $40 for merchandise returned. |
| | 15 | Cash sales for the first fifteen days amounted to $810. |
| | 19 | Sold merchandise to J. Hein, $570; terms 2/10, n/30; invoice no. 103. |
| | 21 | Received payment from R. Blatt pertaining to invoice no. 102 less the discount. |
| | 25 | Sold land costing $55,000 for that amount. Terms of the sale were $20,000 cash and a note receivable for $35,000. |
| | 27 | Received $460 from L. Meyer representing the balance due from a sale made in September, discount not allowed. |
| | 31 | Cash sales for the last half of the month totaled $890. |

Required:

Record the above transactions using a cash receipts journal, a sales journal, and a general journal. Use the journal forms provided in the work papers, or prepare forms that follow the format of that illustrated in the chapter. [LO2a,2c]

PROBLEM 6–2 *(Record Transactions in Purchases, Cash Payments, and General Journals)* Selected transactions of the Erie Company for the month of April 19X2 are listed below.

| | | |
|---|---|---|
| April | 2 | Purchased merchandise for cash, $480; issued check no. 26. |
| | 4 | Purchased merchandise on credit from Willow Company, $900; terms 1/10, n/30. |
| | 5 | Purchased equipment for cash, $330; issued check no. 27. |
| | 7 | Issued check no. 28 for travel expense, $40. |
| | 7 | Issued check no. 29 for office supplies, $60. |
| | 9 | Purchased merchandise on credit from Varner Company, $740; terms n/30. |
| | 10 | Issued check no. 30 to Willow Company in payment of the $900 invoice less the discount. |
| | 10 | Received a $20 credit from Varner Company for defective merchandise that was returned. |
| | 13 | Purchased merchandise on credit from Falk Company, $660; terms 1/10, n/30. |
| | 15 | Issued check no. 31 to pay semimonthly wages of $375. |
| | 17 | Issued check no. 32 to fully pay the amount owed to Varner Company. |
| | 20 | Purchased merchandise for cash, $360; issued check no. 33. |
| | 21 | Issued check no. 34 for travel expense, $55. |
| | 24 | Issued check no. 35 to pay the $360 premium on a two-year fire insurance policy. |
| | 28 | Issued check no. 36 for travel expense, $30. |

30 Purchased merchandise on credit from Davis Company, $550; terms 2/10, n/30.

30 Issued check no. 37 to pay semimonthly wages of $390.

Required:

Record the above transactions using a single-column purchases journal, a cash payments journal, and a general journal. Use the journal forms provided in the work papers or prepare forms that follow the format of that illustrated in the chapter. [LO2a,2c]

PROBLEM 6–3 *(Record in General Journal and Identify Special Journals)* Presented below are selected transactions of the Baltic Company for the month of May 19X5.

May 1 P. Baltic, the owner made a cash investment of $15,000.

2 Paid three months' rent in advance. The rental charge is $100 per month.

3 Purchased merchandise on credit from Roland Company, $600; terms 2/10, n/30.

5 Paid weekly wages of $920 to company employees.

5 Sold merchandise for cash, $530.

8 Sold merchandise to J. Green, $840; terms 2/10, n/30.

8 Purchased merchandise for cash, $220.

9 Paid $300 to Bartley Company for merchandise purchased on account from it in March of this year. No discounts are permitted.

9 Sold merchandise for cash, $470.

12 Purchased merchandise on credit from Davis Company, $240; terms n/30.

14 Received payment of $400 from R. Wilkins, a customer, who is paying for merchandise sold to her in April of this year. The discount period had expired, and therefore no discount was taken.

18 Refunded $50 to a customer who returned defective merchandise previously purchased for cash.

23 Purchased merchandise on credit from Orange Company, $490; terms 1/10, n/30.

24 Purchased stationery for cash, $20.

27 Sold merchandise to K. Kullen, $960; terms 1/10, n/30.

30 Settled creditor's claim in full for merchandise previously purchased, $240, after taking a cash discount of $5.

30 Recorded monthly depreciation expense, $210.

Required:

1. Analyze the transactions and record them in a general journal.
2. State in which journal the transaction would be recorded if special journals were used. Assume single-column sales and purchases journals. [LO1d,2c]

PROBLEM 6–4 *(Record Transactions in Cash Receipts and Cash Payments Journals)* Hartley Company began business on September 1, 19X5. Its transactions involving the purchases and sales of merchandise on credit during September are recorded in the sales and purchases journals shown on page 223. All sales are made on terms of 2/10, n/30. The company's other September transactions were as follows:

Sept. 1 R. Hartley, the owner, invested $10,000 cash in the business.

1 Paid September rent of $600; issued check no. 100.

2 Purchased supplies for cash, $200; issued check no. 101.

5 Paid salaries of $1,200; issued check no. 102.

10 Received full payment from Holder Company, less the discount.

11 Paid Carrage Company in full, taking the discount; issued check no. 103.

12 Paid salaries of $800; issued check no. 104.

18 Received full payment from Yonkers & Sons, discount not allowed.

SALES JOURNAL PAGE 1

| DATE | | ACCOUNT DEBITED | INVOICE NUMBER | POSTED | AMOUNT |
|---|---|---|---|---|---|
| 19X5 | | | | | |
| Sept. | 3 | Holder Company | 100 | ✓ | 400 |
| | 5 | Yonkers & Sons | 101 | ✓ | 600 |
| | 9 | S. Bauer | 102 | ✓ | 300 |
| | 15 | L. Finch | 103 | ✓ | 800 |
| | 27 | R. Graves | 104 | ✓ | 1,500 |

PURCHASES JOURNAL PAGE 1

| DATE | | ACCOUNT CREDITED | TERMS | POSTED | AMOUNT |
|---|---|---|---|---|---|
| 19X5 | | | | | |
| Sept. | 2 | Carrage Company | 3/10, n/30 | ✓ | 1,500 |
| | 9 | Midas Company | 1/10, n/30 | ✓ | 400 |
| | 14 | Carrage Company | 2/10, n/30 | ✓ | 800 |
| | 27 | Loden Inc. | 1/15, n/30 | ✓ | 700 |

18 Received full payment from S. Bauer, less the discount.
18 Paid Midas Company in full, taking the discount; issued check no. 105.
19 Paid salaries of $900; issued check no. 106.
22 Received full payment from L. Finch, less the discount.
23 Paid Carrage Company in full, taking the discount; issued check no. 107.

Required:

1. Record the above September transactions in a cash receipts and cash payments journal. Use the forms provided in the work papers or prepare forms that follow the format of that illustrated in the chapter.
2. Foot and cross-foot both journals.
3. Explain the posting procedures to be followed when posting from the cash receipts and cash payments journals. [LO2a,2b]

PROBLEM 6–5 *(Identify Entries Posted to Subsidiary Accounts)* National Express Company uses a general journal and the four special journals illustrated in the text (single-column for the purchases journal). On October 31, 19X2, the accounts of J. Davis and D. Shore as they appeared in the accounts receivable and the accounts payable subsidiary ledgers, respectively, are as follows.

J. DAVIS

| DATE | | EXPLANATION | POST. REF. | DEBIT | CREDIT | BALANCE |
|---|---|---|---|---|---|---|
| Oct. | 2 | | S-5 | 675 | | 675 |
| | 5 | | GJ-4 | | 50 | 625 |
| | 12 | | CR-3 | | 625 | -0- |
| | 27 | | S-7 | 520 | | 520 |

D. SHORE

| DATE | | EXPLANATION | POST. REF. | DEBIT | CREDIT | BALANCE |
|---|---|---|---|---|---|---|
| Sept. | 28 | | P-3 | | 415 | 415 |
| Oct. | 3 | | GJ-4 | 20 | | 395 |
| | 7 | | CP-3 | 395 | | -0- |

Required:

1. Explain the nature of the entries posted to the J. Davis Accounts Receivable account, and indicate the journal from which the entry was posted.
2. Explain the nature of the entries posted to the D. Shore Accounts Payable account, and indicate the journal from which the entry was posted. [LO1d,1e,1f]

PROBLEM 6–6 *(Record Transactions Using All Four Special Journals and a General Journal)* The Pernell Company began business on October 1, 19X2, and adopted the following chart of accounts:

| | | | |
|---|---|---|---|
| 1 | Cash | 51 | Sales Discounts |
| 4 | Accounts Receivable | 52 | Sales Returns and Allowances |
| 6 | Prepaid Insurance | 60 | Purchases |
| 11 | Land | 61 | Purchase Discounts |
| 12 | Building | 62 | Purchase Returns and Allowances |
| 14 | Fixtures | 63 | Transportation-In |
| 25 | Accounts Payable | 70 | Salaries Expense |
| 26 | Notes Payable | 71 | Delivery Expense |
| 31 | Mortgage Payable | 72 | Maintenance Expense |
| 41 | R. Pernell, Capital | 73 | Utilities Expense |
| 42 | R. Pernell, Drawings | 74 | Insurance Expense |
| 50 | Sales | 75 | Depreciation Expense |

The transactions during October were as follows:

Oct. 1 R. Pernell invested $80,000 cash in the business.

3 Purchased land and a building. The cost of the building was $90,000; the cost of the land was $30,000. Payment of $15,000 was made by issuing check no. 1. A mortgage was obtained to cover the balance. (Use only one journal for the entire transaction.)

3 Purchased fixtures for the building from Store Equipment Company for cash. Check no. 2 was issued for $18,000 to pay for the fixtures in full.

7 Purchased merchandise on credit from Harmen Company, $16,500; terms 2/10, n/60.

8 Purchased merchandise on credit from Kalten Company, $21,900; terms 2/10, n/60.

9 Purchased a three-year insurance policy by paying a premium of $1,200. Check no. 3 was issued for that amount.

10 Purchased merchandise for cash, $9,000. Check no. 4 was issued for that amount.

10 Returned unsatisfactory merchandise in the amount of $3,600 to the Harmen Company and received credit.

12 Sold merchandise to W. Storms, $22,700; invoice no. 100; terms 1/10, n/30.

12 Sold merchandise to Kent Company, $18,600; invoice no. 101; terms 1/10, n/30.

13 Paid Harmen Company and Kalten Company the amounts due them,

less the applicable cash discount. Checks no. 5 and no. 6, respectively, were issued.

15 Cash sales for the first fifteen days totaled $3,600.

15 Paid semimonthly salaries of $5,100. Issued check no. 7 for that amount.

18 Sold merchandise to J. Fahey, $19,500; invoice no. 102; terms 1/10, n/30.

21 Sold merchandise to H. Benten, $17,100; invoice no. 103; terms 1/10, n/30.

21 Purchased merchandise on credit from B. Franklin, $10,800; terms 2/10, n/60.

21 Purchased $40 of maintenance supplies from the General Hardware Company, on credit; terms n/30.

21 H. Benten returned $3,000 of unsatisfactory merchandise. Credit was allowed for the entire amount.

22 W. Storms paid our invoice no. 100 in full, less the discount.

22 Received payment from Kent Company for the amount of invoice 101, less the discount.

25 Purchased merchandise on credit from Hawthorne Sales Company, $22,800; terms 2/10, n/30.

25 Paid transportation charges on merchandise received from Hawthorne Sales Company, $252; issued check no. 8. Terms of the sale were FOB shipping point.

26 Received payment from J. Fahey for the amount of invoice 102, less the discount.

28 Sold merchandise to W. Storms, $6,900; invoice no. 104; terms 1/10, n/60.

29 Paid utilities bill of $460; issued check no. 9.

29 Paid B. Franklin the invoice amount less the applicable discount; issued check no. 10.

29 H. Benten paid the amount due on invoice no. 103, less the discount.

31 Cash sales for the period October 15–31 totaled $4,650.

31 Paid semimonthly salaries of $5,400; issued check no. 11.

Required:

Using four special journals (single-column for the purchases journal) and a general journal, record all the October transactions. No columns are to be totaled. [LO2a,2c]

PROBLEM 6–7 *(Comprehensive Problem: Use Special Journals and the General Journal, Post, and Record Adjustments)* York Company engaged in the following transactions during the month of April 19X4.

April 1 The owner, E. York, invested $50,000 cash in the business.

1 Paid four months' rent in advance; issued check no. 101. Rent is $400 per month.

1 Purchased merchandise for cash, $2,000; issued check no. 102.

1 Purchased equipment on credit from Walden Company, $6,000.

2 Purchased merchandise on credit from R. Bailey, $2,000; terms 2/10, n/30.

2 Paid a $240 premium on a fire insurance policy effective for one year beginning today. Issued check no. 103 for that amount.

3 Purchased office supplies for cash, $175; issued check no. 104.

6 Purchased merchandise on credit from M. Allan, $1,600; terms 2/10, n/30.

7 Sold merchandise to Beth Thurman, $700; invoice no. 100; terms 3/10, n/30.

7 Sold merchandise for cash, $530.

7 Paid R. Bailey for the merchandise purchased on April 2, less the discount; issued check no. 105.

| | |
|---|---|
| 8 | Sold merchandise to Jan Todd, $300; invoice no. 101; terms n/30. |
| 9 | Sold merchandise to Hal Fein, $500; invoice no. 102; terms 1/10, n/30. |
| 9 | Paid for a local newspaper advertisement, $270; issued check no. 106. |
| 9 | Sold merchandise for cash, $680. |
| 10 | Purchased merchandise on credit from R. Bailey, $5,000; terms 2/10, n/30. |
| 13 | Purchased merchandise for cash, $1,200; issued check no. 107. |
| 13 | Received payment from Beth Thurman covering the amount of invoice no. 100, less the discount. |
| 14 | Invested $10,000 in marketable securities; issued check no. 108. |
| 14 | Made a partial payment of $1,000 to Walden Company for the equipment purchased on April 1; issued check no. 109. |
| 14 | Paid M. Allan for merchandise purchased on April 6, less the discount; issued check no. 110. |
| 16 | Received payment from Hal Fein covering the amount of invoice no. 102, less the discount. |
| 17 | Paid R. Bailey for merchandise purchased on April 10, less the discount; issued check no. 111. |
| 20 | Sold merchandise for cash, $660. |
| 21 | Received $50 cash from Jan Todd, representing a partial payment for goods purchased on invoice 101. |
| 23 | Purchased merchandise on credit from F. Dickson, $1,800; terms 2/10, n/30. |
| 24 | Sold merchandise to Art Benson, $700; invoice no. 103; terms 1/10, n/30. |
| 27 | Sold merchandise for cash, $890. |
| 28 | Paid April's maintenance bill, $160; issued check no. 112. |
| 29 | Paid April's utilities bill, $210; issued check no. 113. |
| 30 | Paid April's salaries, $1,500; issued check no. 114. |

Information for Adjustments:

| | |
|---|---|
| Prepaid rent as of April 30 | $ 1,200 |
| Prepaid insurance as of April 30 | 220 |
| Office supplies on hand as of April 30 | 125 |
| Depreciation expense (based on an estimated life of 5 years) | 100 |

Additional Information:

Assume that the company started business on April of this year. Assume further that the company records its transactions in four special journals (single-column for the sales and purchases journals) and a general journal and that all account balances are adjusted monthly.

Required:

1. Record the April transactions in the appropriate journals.
2. Total all columns in the special journals and rule off the columns.
3. Post all entries to the general ledger accounts. Assume that postings have been made to the subsidiary ledger accounts as required.
4. Prepare the adjusting entries needed at the end of the month and post them to the ledger accounts. [LO2a,2b,2c]

PROBLEM 6–8 *(Comprehensive Problem: Complete Part of the Accounting Cycle When Special Journals Are Used)* Shown below is the trial balance of Burnwell Company as it appeared on October 31, 19X5.

BURNWELL COMPANY
Trial Balance
October 31, 19X5

| | | |
|---|---|---|
| Cash | $ 74,720 | |
| Investments | 51,000 | |
| Accounts Receivable | 14,865 | |
| Notes Receivable | 25,000 | |
| Office Supplies | 620 | |
| Inventory | 56,780 | |
| Equipment | 127,400 | |
| Accumulated Depreciation—Equipment | | $ 2,700 |
| Accounts Payable | | 10,950 |
| Notes Payable | | 15,000 |
| S. Burnwell, Capital | | 158,830 |
| S. Burnwell, Drawings | 21,650 | |
| Sales | | 372,000 |
| Interest Revenue | | 230 |
| Sales Discounts | 5,630 | |
| Purchases | 187,350 | |
| Purchase Returns and Allowances | | 26,160 |
| Purchase Discounts | | 1,770 |
| Rent Expense | 3,500 | |
| Salaries Expense | 18,565 | |
| Interest Expense | 560 | |
| | $587,640 | $587,640 |

Shown below are the column totals and the details of certain columns resulting from the company's November transactions. These transactions have already been recorded in the various journals used by the company.

*Sales journal data for November:*

| | |
|---|---|
| Column total (from page 10 of sales journal) | $25,520 |

Details:

| | | |
|---|---|---|
| Nov. 4 | Terrance Co. | $4,620 |
| 10 | Lawrence Co. | 6,810 |
| 16 | James Milligan Co. | 2,250 |
| 21 | Lawrence Co. | 6,000 |
| 25 | James Milligan Co. | 465 |
| 29 | Hewlett Co. | 5,375 |

*Purchases journal data for November:*

| | |
|---|---|
| Column total (from page 6 of purchases journal) | $109,660 |

Details:

| | | |
|---|---|---|
| Nov. 1 | Karson Retailers | $26,830 |
| 11 | Altman Supply Co. | 45,525 |
| 14 | Karson Retailers | 17,760 |
| 21 | Perfection Ring Co. | 19,545 |

*Cash receipts journal data for November:*

| Column totals (from page 6 of cash receipts journal) | |
|---|---|
| Cash | $40,305 |
| Sales Discounts | 318 |
| Accounts Receivable | 18,456 |
| Sales | 5,085 |
| Other Sources | 17,082 |

Details of
Accounts Receivable column:

| | | |
|---|---|---|
| Nov. 1 | Hewlett Co. | $4,836 |
| 16 | Terrance Co. | 4,620 |
| 26 | Lawrence Co. | 3,000 |
| 28 | Lawrence Co. | 6,000 |

Other Sources column:

| | | |
|---|---|---|
| Nov. 4 | Notes Receivable | $15,000 |
| 9 | Interest Revenue | 82 |
| 18 | Investments | 2,000 |

*Cash payments journal data for November:*

| Column totals (from page 10 of cash payments journal) | |
|---|---|
| Cash | $97,357 |
| Purchase Discounts | 1,196 |
| Accounts Payable | 70,017 |
| Purchases | 1,986 |
| Other Payments | 26,550 |

Details of
Accounts Payable column:

| | | |
|---|---|---|
| Nov. 1 | Karson Retailing | $26,830 |
| 2 | Altman Supply Co. | 23,642 |
| 24 | Perfection Ring Co. | 19,545 |

Other Payments column:

| | | |
|---|---|---|
| Nov. 1 | Rent | $ 750 |
| 14 | Investments | 7,500 |
| 26 | Equipment | 1,500 |
| 29 | S. Burnwell, drawings | 1,800 |
| 29 | Notes Payable | 15,000 |

*General journal for November:*

| | | | PAGE 2 |
|---|---|---|---|
| 19X5 | | | |
| Nov. 4 | Notes Receivable | 10,029 | |
| | Accounts Receivable—Lawrence Co. | | 10,029 |
| | Received a 30-day note | | |
| 7 | Accounts Payable—Perfection Ring Co. | 10,950 | |
| | Notes Payable | | 10,950 |
| | Gave a 30-day note | | |
| 16 | Equipment | 7,500 | |
| | Accounts Payable—Merchants Machinery | | 7,500 |
| | Purchased equipment on account | | |
| 18 | Accounts Payable—Altman Supply Co. | 21,883 | |
| | Purchase Returns and Allowances | | 21,883 |
| | Returned some of merchandise purchased on November 11 | | |
| 25 | Office Supplies | 1,665 | |
| | Accounts Payable—Perfection Ring Co. | | 1,665 |
| | Purchased office supplies on account | | |

The Accounts Receivable balances as of October 31 consisted of two accounts:

| | |
|---|---|
| Hewlitt Co. | $ 4,836 |
| Lawrence Co. | 10,029 |
| | $14,865 |

The Accounts Payable as of October 31 consisted of one account:

| | |
|---|---|
| Perfection Ring Co. | $10,950 |

Required:

1. Post all totals and entries to the general ledger accounts and the subsidiary ledger accounts.
2. Prepare a trial balance.
3. Prepare schedules of accounts receivable and accounts payable, and see if their totals agree with the balances in the Accounts Receivable and Accounts Payable control accounts. [LO2b,2c,2d]

PROBLEM 6–9 *(Comprehensive Problem Using Special Journals)* B. Sedwick started a business on January 1, 19X3. During the first month the company had the following transactions.

| | |
|---|---|
| Jan. 1 | The owner started the company by investing $22,500 of personal cash in the business. |
| 1 | Paid three months' rent in advance by issuing check no. 1 for $900. |
| 2 | Purchased merchandise on credit from Hilton Company, $6,000; terms 1/10, n/30. |
| 3 | Sold merchandise to J. Pernell, $3,800; invoice no. 100; terms 1/10, n/30. |
| 5 | Sold merchandise to Staunton Corporation, $2,250; invoice no. 101; terms 1/10, n/30. |
| 9 | Purchased merchandise on credit from Hilton Company, $4,905; terms 1/10, n/30. |
| 9 | Sold merchandise on credit to J. Pernell, $1,250; invoice no. 102; terms n/30. |

| | |
|---|---|
| 9 | Paid for the rental of a delivery truck, \$42; issued check no. 2. (Record as delivery expense.) |
| 9 | The Staunton Corporation returned unwanted merchandise that cost \$450 and received a credit. |
| 11 | Purchased merchandise on credit from Melbrook & Company, \$4,710; terms 2/10, n/60. |
| 12 | Paid Hilton Company for the merchandise purchased on January 2, less the discount; issued check no. 3. |
| 12 | Sold merchandise for cash, \$3,500. |
| 12 | Paid salaries, \$1,320; issued check no. 4. |
| 12 | Returned defective merchandise purchased from Melbrook & Company and received a credit that amounted to \$860. |
| 12 | Purchased merchandise for cash, \$1,650; issued check no. 5. |
| 14 | Received payment from Staunton Corporation pertaining to invoice no. 101. The discount was taken. |
| 15 | J. Pernell paid one-half of the amount due on invoice no. 100. The discount was not allowed. |
| 15 | J. Pernell paid one-half of the amount due on invoice no. 102. |
| 15 | Sold merchandise to Blackthorn Company, \$1,650; invoice no. 103; terms 1/10, n/30. |
| 16 | Paid salaries, \$925; issued check no. 6. |
| 16 | Paid for the rental of a delivery truck, \$66; issued check no. 7. |
| 16 | Sold merchandise to J. Pernell, \$1,500; invoice no. 104; terms 1/10, n/30. |
| 17 | Paid Melbrook & Company for merchandise purchased on January 11, less the discount; issued check no. 8. |
| 20 | Purchased equipment for cash, \$5,500; issued check no. 9. |
| 20 | Sold merchandise to Blackthorn Company, \$2,100; invoice no. 105; terms 1/10, n/30. |
| 21 | Purchased merchandise for cash, \$780; issued check no. 10. |
| 22 | Purchased merchandise on credit from Wholesale Traders, \$5,700; terms 2/10, n/30. |
| 23 | Received payment from J. Pernell on invoice no. 104, less the discount. |
| 26 | Paid Wholesale Traders for the merchandise purchased on January 22, less the discount; issued check no. 11. |
| 28 | Discovered defects in the merchandise purchased from Wholesale Traders. It agreed to allow a credit of \$1,500 to be applied against the next purchase. |
| 29 | Received payment from Blackthorn Company on invoice no. 103. The discount period had expired. |
| 31 | Borrowed \$6,000 from the bank on a sixty-day note. |
| 31 | Paid salaries, \$990; issued check no. 12. |
| 31 | Sold merchandise for cash, \$1,500. |

Required:

Using the following chart of accounts:

| | | | |
|---|---|---|---|
| 1 | Cash | 20 | Sales |
| 3 | Accounts Receivable | 21 | Sales Returns and Allowances |
| 4 | Prepaid Rent | 22 | Sales Discounts |
| 5 | Prepaid Interest | 26 | Purchases |
| 8 | Equipment | 27 | Purchase Returns and Allowances |
| 10 | Accounts Payable | 28 | Purchase Discounts |
| 11 | Notes Payable | 30 | Salaries Expense |
| 17 | B. Sedwick, Drawings | 31 | Delivery Expense |
| 18 | B. Sedwick, Capital | | |

1. Record the transactions in the appropriate journals.
2. Indicate how the postings would be made from each of the journals. This requires entering posting references and indicating when specific posting should take place. [LO2a,2b,2c]

PROBLEM 6–10 *(Comprehensive Review Problem)* Presented below are selected transactions of the Atlantic Company for the month of April 19X2, the company's first month of operations.

| | | |
|---|---|---|
| April | 2 | A cash investment of $5,000 was made by J. Reynolds, the owner, who used personal funds to make the investment. |
| | 3 | Purchased merchandise on credit from Moe Company, $1,800; terms 2/10, n/30. |
| | 4 | Paid three months' rent in advance. The rental charge is $100 per month. Issued check no. 1. |
| | 5 | Sold merchandise on account to Landow Company, $940. |
| | 8 | Paid wages of $740 to company employees; issued check no. 2. |
| | 9 | Purchased merchandise on credit from Simko Company, $820; terms 1/10, n/30. |
| | 11 | Sold merchandise on account to Citron Company, $1,470. |
| | 12 | Received a partial payment on account from Landow Company, $440. |
| | 14 | Granted a $50 credit to Citron Company, which had been sold defective merchandise on April 11 on account. |
| | 16 | Purchased merchandise on credit from Moe Company, $490; terms 2/10, n/30. |
| | 18 | Purchased office supplies for cash, $20; issued check no. 3. |
| | 20 | Sold merchandise on account to Donaldson's, Inc., $950. |
| | 30 | Paid Moe Company $1,000 on account for the purchase made on April 3; issued check no. 4. |

Required:

1. The company uses four special journals: a sales journal, a single-column purchases journal, a cash receipts journal, and a cash payments journal, as well as a general journal. Record the transactions in the appropriate journal.
2. Post entries (where appropriate) to the accounts contained in (a) the accounts receivable subsidiary ledger and (b) the accounts payable subsidiary ledger.
3. Prepare a schedule of accounts receivable, and balance the total to the controlling account. (Separately determine the balance in the controlling account by reviewing the transactions that affect this account.)
4. Prepare a schedule of accounts payable, and balance the total to the controlling account. (Separately determine the balance in the controlling account by reviewing the transactions that affect this account.) [LO2a,2b,2c,2d]

## ALTERNATE PROBLEMS

PROBLEM 6–1A *(Record Transactions in Sales, Cash Receipts, and General Journals)* (Alternate to Problem 6–1) Selected transactions of Newton Company for the month of May 19X2 are listed below.

| | | |
|---|---|---|
| May | 2 | Sold merchandise to P. Jones, $600; terms 2/10, n/30; invoice no. 201. |
| | 4 | Borrowed $6,000 from Benefits Financial Company, principal and interest to be repaid in thirty days. |
| | 6 | Received $250 from R. Nexon representing the balance due from a sale made in April, discount not allowed. |
| | 11 | Sold merchandise to R. Klein, $960; terms 2/10, n/30; invoice no. 202. |
| | 14 | Received payment from P. Jones pertaining to invoice no. 201. |
| | 14 | Granted R. Klein a credit of $60 for merchandise returned. |
| | 15 | Cash sales for the first fifteen days amounted to $910. |

18 Sold merchandise to J. Gould, $970; terms 1/10, n/30; invoice no. 203.
19 Received payment from R. Klein pertaining to invoice no. 202, less the discount.
21 Sold land costing $55,000 for that amount. Terms of the sale were $10,000 cash and a note receivable for $45,000.
23 Received $460 from L. Mold representing the balance due from a sale made in September, discount not allowed.
31 Cash sales for the last half of the month totaled $790.

Required:

1. Record the above transactions using a cash receipts journal, a sales journal, and a general journal. Use the journal forms provided in the work papers, or prepare forms that follow the format of that illustrated in the chapter.
2. Give the reason why entries made in the general journal were not made in the special journals. [LO2a,2c]

PROBLEM 6–2A *(Record Transactions in Purchases, Cash Payments, and General Journals)* (Alternate to Problem 6–2) Selected transactions of the Edde Company for the month of June 19X2 are listed below.

June 2 Purchased merchandise for cash, $880; issued check no. 36.
4 Purchased merchandise on credit from W. Company, $800; terms 1/10, n/30.
5 Purchased equipment for cash, $230; issued check no. 37.
7 Issued check no. 38 for travel expense, $30.
7 Issued check no. 39 for office supplies, $20.
15 Issued check no. 40 to W. Company in payment of the $800 invoice.
15 Received a $40 credit from V. Company for defective merchandise that was returned.
15 Purchased merchandise on credit from Falkland Company, $660; terms 1/10, n/30.
15 Issued check no. 41 to pay semimonthly wages, $375.
23 Issued check no. 42 for travel expense, $95.
24 Issued check no. 43 to pay the $460 premium on a two-year fire insurance policy.
30 Purchased merchandise on account from D. Company, $650; terms 2/10, n/30.
30 Issued check no. 44 to pay semimonthly wages, $290.

Required:

Record the above transactions using a single-column purchases journal, a cash payments journal, and a general journal. Use the journal forms provided in the work papers or prepare forms that follow the format of that illustrated in the chapter. Explain the reasons why entries made in the general journal were not made in the special journals. [LO2a,2c]

PROBLEM 6–3A *(Identify Entries Posted to Subsidiary Accounts)* (Alternate to Problem 6–5) Nottingham Express Company uses a general journal and the four special journals illustrated in the text (single-column for the purchases journal). On January 31, 19X2, the accounts of B. Bass and D. Shane as they appeared in the accounts receivable and the accounts payable subsidiary ledgers, respectively, are as shown on page 233.

Required:

1. Explain the nature of the entries posted to the B. Bass Accounts Receivable account, and indicate the journal from which the entry was posted.
2. Explain the nature of the entries posted to the D. Shane Accounts Payable account, and indicate the journal from which the entry was posted. [LO1d,1e,1f]

B. BASS

| DATE | | EXPLANATION | POST. REF. | DEBIT | CREDIT | BALANCE |
|---|---|---|---|---|---|---|
| Jan. | 3 | | S-3 | 1 000 | | 1 000 |
| | 6 | | S-4 | 700 | | 1 700 |
| | 10 | | CR-4 | | 625 | 1 075 |
| | 15 | | S-6 | 600 | | 1 675 |
| | 20 | | S-8 | 480 | | 2 155 |
| | 22 | | GJ-5 | | 150 | 2 005 |

D. SHANE

| DATE | | EXPLANATION | POST. REF. | DEBIT | CREDIT | BALANCE |
|---|---|---|---|---|---|---|
| Jan. | 2 | | P-1 | | 100 | 100 |
| | 5 | | GJ-4 | 20 | | 80 |
| | 10 | | CP-3 | 80 | | 0 |
| | 12 | | P-2 | | 400 | 400 |

PROBLEM 6–4A *(Record Transactions Using All Four Special Journals and a General Journal)* (Alternate to Problem 6–6) The Powell Company began business on October 1, 19X2, and adopted the following chart of accounts:

| | | | |
|---|---|---|---|
| 1 | Cash | 60 | Purchases |
| 4 | Accounts Receivable | 61 | Purchase Discounts |
| 6 | Prepaid Insurance | 62 | Purchase Returns and Allowances |
| 14 | Equipment | 63 | Transportation-In |
| 25 | Accounts Payable | 70 | Salaries Expense |
| 26 | Notes Payable | 71 | Delivery Expense |
| 41 | E. Powell, Capital | 72 | Maintenance Expense |
| 42 | E. Powell, Drawings | 73 | Utilities Expense |
| 50 | Sales | 74 | Insurance Expense |
| 51 | Sales Discounts | 75 | Rent Expense |
| 52 | Sales Returns and Allowances | 76 | Depreciation Expense |

The transactions during October were as follows:

| | | |
|---|---|---|
| Oct. | 1 | E. Powell invested $75,000 cash in the business. |
| | 1 | Paid October's rent of $500; issued check no. 1. |
| | 1 | Purchased equipment for the store from Store Equipment Company for $8,000 cash; issued check no. 2. |
| | 5 | Purchased merchandise on credit from H. Company, $6,500; terms 1/10, n/60. |
| | 9 | Purchased merchandise on credit from K. Company, $15,000; terms 2/10, n/60. |
| | 10 | Purchased merchandise for cash, $8,000; issued check no. 3. |
| | 10 | Returned unsatisfactory merchandise in the amount of $2,000 to K. Company and received credit. |
| | 12 | Paid the H. Company and the K. Company the amounts due them, less discounts; issued checks no. 4 and 5, respectively. |

| | |
|---|---|
| 15 | Cash sales for the first fifteen days totaled $2,600. |
| 16 | Sold merchandise to J. Company on account, $14,500; invoice no. 100; terms 1/10, n/30. |
| 18 | Sold merchandise to I. Company on account, $8,000; invoice no. 101; terms 1/10, n/30. |
| 19 | Received payment from J. Company for the amount of invoice 100, less the discount. |
| 21 | I. Company returned merchandise in the amount of $1,000. Credit was allowed for the entire amount. |
| 24 | Sold merchandise to W. Company, $5,200; invoice no. 102; terms 1/10, n/60. |
| 29 | Paid utilities bill of $260; issued check no. 6. |
| 31 | Cash sales for the period October 15–31 totaled $4,650. |
| 31 | Paid salaries of $6,400; issued check no. 7. |

Required:

Using four special journals (single-column for the purchases journal) and a general journal, record all the October transactions. [LO2a,2c]

# 7 Internal Control and Control of Cash

## Learning Objectives

When you complete this chapter, you will be able to

1. Answer the following questions:
   a. What is internal control and what are some examples? Why are these controls needed?
   b. What is cash? How is cash presented on the balance sheet?
   c. What measures are taken to achieve adequate cash management?
   d. How is a petty cash fund established? How does it operate?
   e. What are the characteristics of checking accounts? Why is it necessary to prepare a bank reconciliation?
   f. How does the voucher system improve internal control over cash payments?
2. Perform the following accounting functions:
   a. Prepare the journal entries required to establish and replenish the petty cash fund.
   b. Prepare a bank reconciliation and adjust the accounting records based on the bank reconciliation.
   c. Record transactions in the voucher register and check register.

*1a. Internal controls are needed to avoid or detect improper transactions, to ensure the occurrence of transactions at the proper time, and to record transactions properly*

In earlier chapters we learned how to collect, record, classify, summarize, and report business transactions. We assumed that the business transactions we were concerned with were proper ones. However, the realities of business life are such that—unless effective controls exist—improper transactions may occur and not be detected, or transactions may not occur at the proper time. For example:

1. Badly needed purchase discounts could be lost if payments to creditors were not made within the discount period. Such laxness would be inefficient and might erase much of the company's net income for the accounting period.
2. In violation of the company's policy, sales on credit might be made to customers that are poor credit risks. The result could be credit sales with no cash collections coming from the resulting receivables.
3. Cash received from customers might be stolen. In an attempt to "cover up" the theft, records may be falsified.

Problems can arise also if transactions are not properly recorded. For example:

4. A company may incur some expenses on credit terms near the end of the accounting period. If the transaction is not recorded in the current accounting period, the financial statements prepared at the end of that period might be misleading because expenses would be understated and net income would be overstated.

## INTERNAL ADMINISTRATIVE CONTROL AND INTERNAL ACCOUNTING CONTROL

*1a. Internal control is divided into internal administrative control and internal accounting control*

To eliminate or minimize such undesirable occurrences, companies use **internal control.** This consists of a set of methods and procedures for (1) promoting operational efficiency and adherence to managerial policy (**internal administrative control**) and (2) safeguarding assets and ensuring the accuracy and reliability of account data (**internal accounting control**).

The cost and effort that go into establishing systems of internal control depend on the size of the company and other considerations. Almost all organizations use some internal control procedures. A procedure that is easily implemented, for example, is requiring two people to sign checks. Let us look briefly at examples of both aspects of internal control.

## EXAMPLES OF INTERNAL ADMINISTRATIVE CONTROL

### Avoiding Loss of Purchase Discounts

*1a. A system of processing invoices to ensure the taking of purchase discounts can help promote operational efficiency*

To minimize the chances of losing purchase discounts, a company must process its purchase invoices by the date necessary to earn the discount. For example, assume that a purchase invoice received from a creditor has a date of October 10 and a notation that the amount must be paid within ten days to earn a 2% discount. This invoice should be placed in the October 20 file. Likewise, an invoice dated October 11 with the same notation should be placed in the October 21 file. Each day the file should be examined to determine which invoices must be paid to earn the discount. Every effort should be made to pay these particular invoices on time.

### Avoiding Credit Extension to Poor Credit Risks

*1a. Approval of all credit sales in advance can help encourage adherence to managerial policies*

To minimize the chances of selling merchandise on credit to poor credit risks, a company could require that all credit sales be approved in advance by the credit manager or another appropriate official. This approval would not be made until the credit department had checked the customer's credit history. Such procedures would provide reasonable assurance that no credit sales were being made in violation of the company's credit policies.

## EXAMPLES OF INTERNAL ACCOUNTING CONTROL

### Avoiding Theft of Cash Receipts

*1a. Adequate separation of employee duties can help safeguard assets*

To reduce the chances of customers' cash receipts being stolen, a company could require that *different* employees handle different aspects of the transaction. For example, one employee could be responsible for depositing cash receipts in the bank and another for recording cash receipt transactions in the records. Thus collusion between these two people would have to occur before money could be taken and the theft covered up by manipulating the accounting records.

### Avoiding Failure to Record Unpaid Bills

*1a. Independent comparisons of records can help ensure reliability of financial records*

To reduce the chances of having an unpaid bill omitted from the records, a company could require that a designated employee compare, at the end of each accounting period, the total of the unpaid invoices with the credit balance in the Accounts Payable general ledger account. If the total of the unpaid invoices exceeds the balance in the Accounts Payable control account, there are unpaid invoices that need to be recorded. Later in this chapter we describe a voucher system that accomplishes some of the control objectives of ensuring reliable financial records.

## CHARACTERISTICS OF INTERNAL ACCOUNTING CONTROL

While a variety of factors contribute to a good system of internal accounting control, a good system should possess certain characteristics. In this section we discuss six:

1. Employee competence and integrity
2. Separation of incompatible functions
3. Proper authorization for transactions
4. Proper recording of transactions
5. Proper access to assets
6. Independent comparisons of assets with recorded accountability

### Employee Competence and Integrity

No system of internal accounting control can bridge the gap created by incompetent employees who are unable to handle their assigned tasks or dishonest employees who are determined to misappropriate company assets. If the person assigned to compare unpaid invoices with the balance in the Accounts Payable ledger account does not understand his or her responsibility, transactions could still go unrecorded. Separating the duties of the two employees by assigning one the responsibility for depositing cash receipts in the bank and the other the responsibility for recording cash receipt transactions in the records reduces the likelihood of fraud. However, if there is collusion between them to misappropriate the cash, the separation of their duties and responsibilities will not accomplish its intended purpose.

If employees are not competent or if they lack integrity, most other control measures designed to safeguard assets and produce accurate and reliable records will be rendered useless. It is for this reason that employee competence and integrity are listed as the first vital characteristic of internal accounting control.

### Separation of Incompatible Functions

Although the cost involved must be a consideration, different individuals, when possible, should handle different aspects of a given transaction. Separation of employee functions is also desirable. If possible from a cost point of view, different employees should be responsible for performing the following functions:

*Authorizing* a transaction

*Recording* a transaction in the accounting records

*Maintaining custody* of the asset or assets resulting from a transaction

*Comparing* physically the assets on hand with the related amounts recorded in the accounting records

As an example, this means that

Person *A* would authorize the purchase of an asset (assume merchandise inventory)

Person *B* would record the purchase in the accounting records when title to the merchandise passed to the buyer

Person *C* would take custody of the merchandise when it was received and would fill out a receiving report to verify receipt

Person *D* would periodically compare the amount of merchandise on hand determined by physical count with the amount shown for merchandise on hand in the accounting records

Some companies consider it too costly to employ four persons to perform these separate tasks. If they choose to be "economical" and assign only one or two persons to these four jobs, such companies must understand the possible consequences of that decision.

### Proper Authorization for Transactions

The separate person or persons *authorizing* transactions should act within the scope of their authority, and the transactions should conform to the terms of the authorizations. If this guidance is not followed, much of the benefit of separation of duties described in the previous section is lost.

For example, if the system requires that the credit manager or one of the credit department staff approve credit sales, it is improper for one of the salespeople to do so. Or if company policy prohibits an additional credit sale to customers having a bill from a previous purchase outstanding (unpaid) for ninety days or more, it is generally improper for the credit manager or one of the credit department staff to approve such a sale (without a good reason).

## Proper Recording of Transactions

The separate person or persons authorized to *record* transactions should record them at the amounts and in the period in which they were executed. The transactions must also be recorded in the proper ledger accounts. If this guideline is not followed, financial statements will be inaccurate and, therefore, misleading.

For example, an accounts payable clerk responsible for recording merchandise purchased on credit should

*Avoid* recording the purchase at its invoice cost minus an anticipated cash discount (unless the net purchases method is being used)

*Avoid* recording purchases in a given month if the terms of purchase indicate that title to the merchandise does not pass to the company until the following month

*Avoid* recording the purchase of merchandise by improperly debiting some other account, such as supplies expense

## Proper Access to Assets

Only *authorized* personnel should have *access* to assets. For example, only certain personnel should be permitted to receive purchased merchandise as it arrives at the company's location. When it arrives, an independent count of the items received should be made and recorded on a receiving report. This report should be sent to the accounts payable clerk (or an appropriate individual), who would then match the amounts on the receiving report with the amounts shown in the purchase invoice received from the supplier.

Access to assets by unauthorized personnel could result in the physical disappearance of merchandise, inaccurate accounting data, or other misappropriations of assets. To be effective, the company's internal accounting control system must ensure that only authorized personnel have physical access to or control over the company's assets.

## Independent Comparisons of Assets with Recorded Accountability

All the previously discussed characteristics of good internal accounting control should be accompanied by *independent comparisons* of assets on hand with assets reflected in the accounting records. These comparisons are so inherent a part of business-world operations that many of them are accepted as commonplace. For example:

Each day before the cashier deposits the day's cash receipts in the bank, a separate person *compares* the total of the deposit slip with the amount of cash receipts recorded in the accounting records.

Each month a separate person *reconciles* the cash balances on the company's books with the company's bank statement. (This procedure is discussed later in the chapter.)

Periodically (every three, six, or twelve months), separate personnel *compare* a count of merchandise on hand with the amount recorded on the books.

Without comparisons of this type, the company cannot be reasonably sure that assets have not been misappropriated and that the assets have not been recorded inaccurately.

## SUMMARY OF INTERNAL CONTROL

A good system of internal control begins with adequately trained, competent, and honest personnel and includes certain other attributes discussed above. The controls used are designed to assure management and others that the company's assets are being properly safeguarded, that accurate and reliable financial records are being maintained, that operational activities are being conducted efficiently, and that company policies and directives are being implemented.

In the following section we discuss cash, a universally desired asset that is therefore one of the assets most susceptible to theft and improper use. We will describe the application of internal control procedures to the receipt and disbursement of cash.

## CASH—WHAT IT IS

*1b. Cash is usually the first asset presented on the balance sheet. It includes the items listed here*

Cash is usually the first asset presented on a balance sheet because it is the most liquid asset a company holds. Included in **cash** are *coins, paper money, checks* (payable or endorsed to the company), *money orders*, and *money on deposit with banks*. However, postage stamps or postdated checks (checks that are dated in the future but cannot be deposited until that date) are excluded. These two items are classified as prepaid expenses and accounts receivable, respectively.

*1b. In general, any item a bank will accept as a deposit is cash*

When there is doubt about whether a particular item should be classified as cash, use this general rule: *Any item a bank will accept as a deposit should be included in cash.* For this reason, coins, paper money, checks, and money orders are classified as cash, whereas postage stamps, postdated checks, and promissory notes (which banks will not accept for deposit) are not a part of cash.

In the following sections we discuss the balance sheet presentation of cash, as well as methods and procedures used to verify and control cash.

## HOW CASH IS PRESENTED ON THE BALANCE SHEET

*1b. Cash is reported on the balance sheet as a single combined figure*

Companies frequently have more than one checking account. They also keep some cash on hand in the form of coin and paper money. Although companies maintain separate ledger accounts for cash held in each checking account and for cash on hand, they report one combined cash figure on the balance sheet. This combined amount is labeled *Cash on Hand and in Banks*, or simply *Cash*.

Management may, at some time, want to know the balances in each of its individual cash accounts. Other users of balance sheet information are generally not interested in specific cash account balances. They are more likely to be interested in the company's total cash and the way it compares with other balance sheet items, especially with its current debt. Combining cash amounts and presenting them as one aggregate amount keeps the balance sheet concise and understandable without sacrificing any needed disclosures.

*1b. Unlike unrestricted cash, cash that is restricted in its use is shown as a noncurrent asset*

Cash amounts may be unrestricted or restricted. Unrestricted amounts can be used at management's discretion in meeting the operating needs of the business. Unrestricted cash amounts are classified as a current asset and shown as the first item on a balance sheet. Restricted cash amounts are those that are set aside for a special purpose or are otherwise unavailable for operational needs. An example is a cash account that must be used to pay a noncurrent liability when it comes due at some future time. Restrictions are placed on cash as a result of a management decision, a contractual agreement, or some other legal requirement. Restricted cash amounts are classified as noncurrent assets. The financial report also includes a disclosure to indicate the nature of the restriction.

## CASH MANAGEMENT

Because cash is a high-risk asset susceptible to theft and/or misappropriation, it must be carefully safeguarded. Furthermore, since it is a high-volume asset (that is, many transactions result in cash receipts and cash payments), it is susceptible to errors and other irregularities. An important aspect of cash management consists of developing records, procedures, and systems that provide control over cash. Specifically, management must attempt to

1. Prevent the loss of cash due to theft or fraud
2. Provide an accurate accounting for cash receipts, cash payments, and cash balances
3. Maintain sufficient cash balances to cover operating needs and to satisfy maturing debt
4. Avoid holding excessive amounts of idle cash on hand or in checking accounts where they do not contribute to the company's earnings

From the moment cash is received until the moment it is deposited in a bank, it must be carefully safeguarded. The methods and procedures established to control cash depend on the size and nature of the company.

Some widely accepted methods and procedures for establishing control of cash are listed below. When examining them, recall that it is important for companies to determine whether the benefits obtained from these controls will exceed the cost of implementing them.

*1c. Adequate cash management entails a number of general measures; twelve are listed here*

1. The handling and custodianship of cash should be *separated* from the recordkeeping for cash.
2. The number of people who have *access* to cash should be limited.
3. The duties of receiving cash and disbursing cash should be *separated.*
4. A *record* should be made of all cash receipts at the time that money or checks are received.
5. *All* cash receipts should be deposited in bank accounts promptly, preferably on a daily basis.
6. *All* cash disbursements (except for small amounts paid out of petty cash) should be made by check.
7. Companies should use *consecutively prenumbered checks* and have a designated person responsible for their control and accountability.
8. Requests for check payments should be authorized by someone *other* than the person or persons who are authorized to sign the checks.
9. No checks should be signed unless they are supported by an *approved* invoice that justifies the payment.
10. After an authorized check has been drawn, the invoice supporting the check payment should be clearly marked "paid," showing the date of payment and check number. This procedure minimizes the risk of paying the amount due on a given invoice more than once.
11. Any check not actually used for payment should be clearly *marked "void."* Such checks should be maintained and filed so as to account for each prenumbered check.
12. Employees who have access to cash should be *bonded* by coverage with insurance to ensure against loss by fraudulent practices of the employee.

Use of the above procedures will help to protect and safeguard cash, making it less subject to theft or misuse.

## THE PETTY CASH FUND

In keeping with the basic principles of internal control, all large disbursements of cash should be made by check. Most businesses, however, find it convenient and practical to make small cash payments for such items as taxi fares, road tolls, parking fees, and postage stamps from a **petty cash fund.** Control over a petty cash fund is best achieved when petty cash is handled as an imprest fund of cash. An **imprest petty cash fund** is one that contains a specified amount of cash that is placed under the control of one person who uses it to make payments involving small dollar amounts. Under this system the fund, when it is close to being depleted, is replenished from the company's operating cash account up to the amount previously determined as being appropriate for the fund balance.

### Establishing the Petty Cash Fund

*1d,2a. A petty cash fund is established by entrusting funds to a petty cash fund cashier and making a journal entry*

The petty cash fund is established by estimating the amount of cash needed to handle those relatively small recurring payments that the company expects to have during a specified period, writing out a check to the petty cash fund cashier for the amount needed, and placing the proceeds from that check in a safe, a petty cash box, or a drawer. The amount should be large enough to handle the type of cash payments made from a fund over a relatively short time period, usually about a month.

To illustrate the accounting for the establishment of a petty cash fund, assume that on February 1, a check for $100 made payable to the petty cash fund cashier is cashed. The coin and currency proceeds are then placed in a petty cash box. The journal entry to record the establishment of the fund is as follows:

| | | | |
|---|---|---|---|
| Feb. 1 | Petty Cash ............................................. | 100 | |
| | Cash ............................................. | | 100 |
| | To establish a petty cash fund | | |

### Making Disbursements from the Petty Cash Fund

*1d. Petty cash vouchers are used in the operation of a petty cash fund*

Each time a payment is made from the fund, the petty cash fund cashier is required to fill out a **petty cash voucher.** This voucher is signed by the person who receives the money and initialed by the cashier, as illustrated below.

PETTY CASH VOUCHER

No. 34 DATE Feb. 3, 19X3

PAID TO Western Union
FOR Telegram
CHARGE TO Telegram Expense
AMOUNT $13.50

Fred Sist — Received by

BH — Approved by

Note that each petty cash voucher is sequentially numbered (number 34 in the illustration) and indicates the (1) date, (2) to whom the amount is paid, (3) the purpose of the expenditure, (4) the ledger account to be charged, and (5) the amount disbursed by the cashier.

If the person receiving payment can furnish documentation such as a receipt or an invoice, it should be attached to the petty cash voucher to support the disbursement of petty cash.

*1d. Surprise counts of the petty cash fund should be made periodically*

A petty cash voucher is prepared for every payment made from the fund and is placed in the petty cash box. Therefore the total of the cash in the cash box plus the total of the vouchers in the cash box should always equal the amount put in to establish the fund and the balance in the Petty Cash account. Surprise counts of the items in the fund should be made periodically to ensure that the fund money is being used properly and that no money has been misappropriated.

No journal entries are recorded when cash is disbursed from the fund. A summary journal entry is made when the fund is replenished, as illustrated in the next section.

## Replenishing the Petty Cash Fund

Note that no entries were made to record the cash payments made from the fund. These payments do, however, decrease the amount of cash available in the fund. At some point when the cash in the petty cash fund becomes low, the fund must be replenished—that is, restored to its original amount. This is accomplished by drawing a check in the amount of the sum of the vouchers in the fund. The journal entry to record the replenishment of the fund debits the expense accounts indicated on the petty cash vouchers and credits the cash account. For example, assume that on February 28, the cash in the fund is $8.10 and the petty cash vouchers summarized in numerical order are as follows.

| VOUCHER NO. | FOR | AMOUNT |
|---|---|---|
| 1 | Telegram | $13.50 |
| 2 | Postage Stamps | 9.00 |
| 3 | Road and Bridge Tolls | 5.70 |
| 4 | Telegram | 8.90 |
| 5 | Stationery | 7.80 |
| 6 | Road and Bridge Tolls | 4.30 |
| 7 | Postage Stamps | 6.00 |
| 8 | Freight Charges on Merchandise Purchased | 7.60 |
| 9 | Road and Bridge Tolls | 5.50 |
| 10 | Freight Charges on Merchandise Purchased | 14.00 |
| 11 | Stationery | 9.60 |

*1d,2a. The petty cash fund is replenished periodically. A single summary entry is made*

These vouchers represent monies paid out. However, petty cash expenditures are not recorded as they occur. Instead a single summary entry is made on February 28 when the petty cash fund is replenished. The entry to replenish the fund is as shown on page 244.

Recall that the Petty Cash account was debited when the fund was first established. Expense accounts are debited when the fund is replenished, and the Cash account (not the Petty Cash account) is credited. Thus the Petty Cash account in the general ledger is not affected by the replenishment entry, and it

| | | | |
|---|---|---|---|
| Feb. 28 | Telegram Expense | 22.40 | |
| | Postage Expense | 15.00 | |
| | Delivery Expense (road and bridge tolls) | 15.50 | |
| | Transportation-In (freight charges) | 21.60 | |
| | Stationery Expense | 17.40 | |
| | Cash | | 91.90 |
| | To replenish the petty cash fund | | |

remains at the fixed amount of $100. The amount will not change unless at some future time a decision is made to increase or decrease the amount of the fund.

The petty cash fund should be replenished when cash is needed or at the end of each accounting period even if the cash in the fund is sufficient. By doing so, all account balances will be brought up to date before the financial statements are prepared.

*1d. A petty cash book shows the amount of cash placed in the fund and the fund's payments*

Some companies use a **petty cash book** to enter each disbursement of cash made from the petty cash fund. The book's purpose is to show the amount of cash received and placed in the petty cash fund and the amount and purpose of each payment made from the petty cash fund. Although the petty cash book may take a variety of forms, the one illustrated in Exhibit 7–1 is typical.

The petty cash book is a supplementary record and is not an essential part of an imprest petty cash system.

EXHIBIT 7–1

Petty Cash Book

| DATE 19X5 | | VOUCHER OR CHECK NO. | RECEIPTS | PAYMENTS | DELIVERY EXPENSE | TRANSPORTATION-IN | POSTAGE EXPENSE | OTHER | |
|---|---|---|---|---|---|---|---|---|---|
| | | | | | | | | ACCOUNT | AMOUNT |
| Feb | 1 | Check 82 | 100.00 | | | | | | |
| | 3 | Voucher 1 | | 13.50 | | | | Telegram | 13.50 |
| | 5 | 2 | | 9.00 | | | 9.00 | | |
| | 5 | 3 | | 5.70 | 5.70 | | | | |
| | 8 | 4 | | 8.90 | | | | Telegram | 8.90 |
| | 11 | 5 | | 7.80 | | | | Stationery | 7.80 |
| | 13 | 6 | | 4.30 | 4.30 | | | | |
| | 17 | 7 | | 6.00 | | | 6.00 | | |
| | 20 | 8 | | 7.60 | | 7.60 | | | |
| | 22 | 9 | | 5.50 | 5.50 | | | | |
| | 25 | 10 | | 14.00 | | 14.00 | | | |
| | 27 | 11 | | 9.60 | | | | Stationery | 9.60 |
| | | Total | 100.00 | 91.90 | 15.50 | 21.60 | 15.00 | | 39.80 |
| | 28 | Check 301 | 91.90 | | | | | | |

## The Cash Over or Short Account

*1d. Errors in the petty cash fund are recorded in a Cash Over or Short account*

Regardless of the care exercised in handling the petty cash fund, some errors will inevitably be made. For example, the cashier may inadvertently give too little or too much change when paying a bill or reimbursing an employee. These errors become known when the remaining cash in the fund plus the sum of the vouchers differs from the amount originally placed in the petty cash fund. Of course, all errors should be investigated to determine their cause and eliminate their recurrence. Errors that cause shortages are recorded by debiting a **Cash Over or Short account,** and errors that cause overages are credited to that account.

To illustrate, assume that in our previous example the cash in the petty cash fund on February 28 was $6.60 (instead of the $8.10 that should have been there), with petty cash vouchers showing support for $91.90 of cash payments. The cash shortage of $1.50 would be recorded by debiting the Cash Over or Short account in the following replenishing entry:

| | | | |
|---|---|---|---|
| Feb. 28 | Telegram Expense | 22.40 | |
| | Postage Expense | 15.00 | |
| | Delivery Expense | 15.50 | |
| | Transportation-In | 21.60 | |
| | Stationery Expense | 17.40 | |
| | Cash Over or Short | 1.50 | |
| | Cash | | 93.40 |
| | To replenish the petty cash fund | | |

The ***Cash Over or Short account*** is used not only to record shortages or overages in the petty cash fund but also to record differences between the actual cash in a cash register and the amount "rung up" and recorded on the cash register. For example, assume that actual cash in the cash register is counted at $735, but the cash register tape shows cash sales of $733. The entry to record the cash, the cash sales, and the $2 overage is as follows:

| | | |
|---|---|---|
| Cash | 735 | |
| Cash Over or Short | | 2 |
| Sales | | 733 |
| To record cash sales | | |

If cash shortages during a period exceed cash overages, the Cash Over or Short account would have a *debit* balance and would be reported as an expense in the income statement.

Should cash overages exceed cash shortages, the Cash Over and Short account would have a *credit* balance and would be treated as revenue in the income statement.

Normally, few serious accounting problems arise from the use of an imprest petty cash system. The entire recordkeeping procedure can be summarized as follows.

| | |
|---|---|
| 1. The fund is established | A check is drawn for a specified amount and cashed. The Petty Cash account is debited and the Cash account is credited. |
| 2. Cash payments are made from the fund | No journal entries need be recorded. |
| 3. The fund is replenished | The amount of replenishment is equal to the total amount of cash disbursed from the fund plus or minus any shortage or overage. A journal entry debiting various expense accounts for the disbursements made from the fund and crediting cash is recorded. The replenishment entry does not involve the Petty Cash account. |

## BANK CHECKING ACCOUNTS

As stated earlier, an important aspect of internal control over cash is that all cash receipts should be deposited promptly in a bank checking account and all cash payments (except those authorized to be paid out of petty cash) should be made by prenumbered checks. Companies generally keep one or more checking accounts with one or more banks. By using a bank checking account, two records of cash are established. One record of cash is kept by the company and the other by the bank, which must periodically send bank statements to those who hold accounts (depositors).

*1e. A bank checking account entails the use of four business forms*

The business forms used in connection with a bank checking account are (1) a signature card, (2) a deposit ticket, (3) a check, and (4) a checking account bank statement.

### The Signature Card

When a checking account is opened, the bank requires that a **signature card** be signed by the depositor showing the signature of the person or persons authorized to sign checks drawn on the account. The card is retained at the bank and can be used by bank personnel to determine the authenticity of the signature or signatures on checks presented to them for payment.

### The Deposit Ticket

When making a deposit, the depositor fills out a **deposit ticket,** sometimes called a *deposit slip,* showing the amount of checks and/or currency deposited in the account. Deposit tickets come in various forms. They do, however, generally include space for writing in the account title or company name, the checking account number, the amount of cash deposited, and a listing of each check and the amount of each check to be deposited. The depositor is given a written or machine-imprinted receipt of the deposit, which can be used to determine whether all cash received was deposited.

Exhibit 7 – 2 contains a sample of a deposit ticket used by Last United Bank.

EXHIBIT 7 – 2

Deposit Ticket

Checking Deposit

Deposit Checking

LU Last United

Deposited in The Last United Bank, N.A. and accepted subject to the conditions of the Uniform Commercial Code.

Account Title (Name)

Date

Checking Account Number

| Cash | Dollars | Cents |
|---|---|---|
| Checks (List separately) | | |
| 1 | | |
| 2 | | |
| 3 | | |
| 4 | | |
| 5 | | |
| 6 | | |
| 7 | | |
| Total Deposit | | |

Below for Last United H.O. Use Only

Number of Items

| 0 | | |
|---|---|---|
| 2 | | |
| 4 | | |
| 5 | | |
| 6 | | |

| Type | Enc. |
|---|---|
| Del. | Chkd. |

Checking Deposit

DAC 1A Rev. 3-80 PTG 6-82

EXHIBIT 7–3
Bank Check

DAVID K. SAMUEL
100 SIXTH AVENUE
ANYWHERE, U.S.A. 01234

NO. ______

PAY
TO THE
ORDER OF ______________________________ $ ________ ______________ 19 ___ 1-108/280

______________________________ DOLLARS

LU MAIN OFFICE
LAST UNITED, N.A.
SOMEWHERE, USA 12603

ACCT. # ______________

FOR ______________ ______________

⑆2685680052⑆ 268⑉56805⑉5⑈.

## The Bank Check

A **check** is a written document signed by the depositor, instructing the bank to pay a specified sum of money to a designated payee. There are three parties to a check: (1) the *maker* (or drawer) who signs the check, (2) the *bank* on which the check is drawn, and (3) the *payee*, the person or organization to whose order the check is drawn.

Checks vary somewhat in form. Generally, they are serially prenumbered and include the name and address of the depositor.

Most banks use check forms on which the bank's identification number and the depositor's account number are printed in magnetic ink. High-speed electronic equipment, capable of "reading" the magnetic-ink numbers, sorts and posts the checks as charges to the depositor's account quickly and automatically.

Exhibit 7–3 shows a sample bank check.

## The Bank Statement

Once each month, usually at the beginning of the month, the bank sends the depositor a **bank statement** summarizing the activity that occurred in that account during the preceding month. The statement shows the balance in the account at the beginning of the month, each deposit and other amounts received by the bank during the period, each check and other amounts paid by the bank during the period, a new account balance every time it is changed by a receipt or payment, and the balance in the account at the end of the month.

Bank statements are generally mailed directly to the depositor. Included in the mailing of the statement are the checks paid by the bank (canceled checks) and notices of any bank charges or credits (debit or credit memoranda).

Debit memoranda (or memos) are bank notices that some amount, other than that represented by checks, has been charged to the depositor's account by the bank. Credit memoranda (or memos) are bank notices that some amount, other than that represented by deposits, has been added to the depositor's account by the bank.

Exhibit 7–4 contains an example of a monthly bank statement.

*EXHIBIT 7–4*

Bank Statement

**LAST UNITED STATEMENT**

David K. Samuel
100 Sixth Avenue
Anywhere, USA 01234

**LAST UNITED**
SOMEWHERE, USA

| PREVIOUS BALANCE | | CHECK AND DEBITS | | DEPOSITS AND CREDITS | | SERVICE CHARGE | | BALANCE ON STATEMENT DATE |
|---|---|---|---|---|---|---|---|---|
| 6,300.20 | − | 4,967.85 | + | 4,015.00 | − | 6.20 | = | 5,341.15 |

| Checks | | Deposits | Date | Balances |
|---|---|---|---|---|
| | | | 5-31-19X5 | 6,300.20 |
| 150.00<br>86.00 | 230.00 | | 6-1-19X5 | 5,834.20 |
| 325.80<br>75.40 | | 868.00 | 6-4-19X5 | 6,301.00 |
| 418.20 | 16.60 | | 6-6-19X5 | 5,866.20 |
| 512.50 | 103.80 | 474.00 | 6-8-19X5 | 5,723.90 |
| 118.00 | 316.40 | | 6-11-19X5 | 5,289.50 |
| 33.90 | 219.60 | | 6-15-19X5 | 5,036.00 |
| 44.70<br>112.40 | 109.70 | 320.00 | 6-18-19X5 | 5,089.20 |
| 217.60 | 18.50 | | 6-20-19X5 | 4,853.10 |
| 320.25 | | 500.00 | 6-24-19X5 | 5,032.85 |
| 78.20 | 330.20 | | 6-25-19X5 | 4,624.45 |
| 138.60 | 272.10 | 725.00 | 6-27-19X5 | 4,938.75 |
| 74.00<br>416.00 | 87.00 NSF | 212.00 | 6-28-19X5 | 4,573.75 |
| 142.40 | 6.20 SC | 916.00 | 6-30-19X5 | 5,341.15 |
| | | | | |
| | | | | |

Explanation of Symbols:
CM = Credit Memo
DM = Debit Memo
SC = Service Charge
EC = Error Correction
NSF = Non-sufficient Funds

## BANK RECONCILIATION

*1e. Ending cash balances in the bank statement and the company's records differ because of (1) timing differences and (2) errors*

The ending cash balance shown on the bank statement will seldom agree with the balance shown in the depositor's Cash account in its general ledger. The difference is caused by either or both of the following:

*Timing differences* in recording transactions. Certain transactions recorded in the company's accounts have not yet been recorded by the bank, and certain transactions recorded by the bank have not yet been recorded in the company's accounts.

*Errors* made by either the bank or the depositor when recording transactions.

The procedure for reconciling the difference between the amounts shown for the ending cash balance in the bank's records and in the depositor's records is called a **bank reconciliation.** It consists of a schedule listing the items and amounts that have caused the difference. Its purpose is to determine the reasons for the difference in cash balances, to establish the depositor's correct cash balance as of a given date, and to provide information that can be used to adjust the depositor's accounts if they need to be adjusted. A bank reconciliation can be viewed as an internal control device that establishes the company's correct cash balance on a specific date.

*1e. Timing differences may involve outstanding checks and deposits in transit*

Listed below are two common examples of one type of timing difference—transactions recorded in the company's accounts but not yet recorded by the bank at the time the bank statement was prepared.

1. **Outstanding checks.** These are checks issued and recorded by the depositor but not yet presented to the bank for payment. The result of outstanding checks is that there will be amounts deducted from the depositor's cash balance that have not yet been deducted from their bank account balance by the bank.
2. **Deposits in transit.** These are cash deposits made and entered on the depositor's cash records but not recorded by the bank in time to appear on the bank statement. For example, deposits made late in the day on the last day of the month may not be recorded by the bank until the next business day, which is in the following month. Deposits mailed to the bank on the last day of the month would not be recorded by the bank before the end-of-the-month bank statement was prepared. The result of deposits in transit is that amounts have been added to the depositor's cash balance that have not yet been added to their bank account balance by the bank.

*1e. Timing differences may involve bank service charges, NSF checks, credits for bank collections, and charges for bank payments*

Here are some common examples of another type of timing difference—transactions appearing on the current bank statement that have not yet been recorded in the company's accounts.

1. **Bank service charges.** These are amounts deducted by a bank from a depositor's account as payment for services rendered. Banks often charge a fee to cover the costs of handling a depositor's checking account. The amount of the fee charged is based on such factors as the average dollar balance maintained in the account and the number of checks and deposits processed during the period. Other checking account charges could include the cost of printing checks, a fee for certifying a check, and a fee for collecting on a note receivable. Generally, the company is not informed of the amount of the charge until the bank statement (together with a document stating the reason for and the amount of the charge) is received. As a result of bank service charges, there will be amounts deducted from the depositor's bank account balance that have not yet been deducted from the company's cash balance in its general ledger.
2. **Nonsufficient funds (NSF) checks.** An NSF check is a customer's check that has been deposited in the company's bank account but cannot be paid by the customer's bank because the customer's bank balance is less than the amount of the check. The company's bank deducts the amount from the company's cash balance, informs the company of its action, and returns the check to the company. The company then attempts to collect the amount from its customer. When a company receives notice

of an NSF check, it should deduct the amount from its cash balance immediately. Sometimes notice of an NSF check reaches the depositor in a period after the one in which the bank deducted the amount from the depositor's cash balance. Thus a timing difference occurs between the date on which the amount was deducted from the depositor's bank account balance and the date on which it will be recorded as a deduction in the depositor's accounting records.

3. **Credits for collections made directly by the bank.** A bank will often serve as an agent in collecting items such as promissory notes (notes receivable) for a depositor. When this service occurs, the bank increases the depositor's account and notifies the depositor of this action. Upon notification, the company records the collection in its accounting records. There may be a timing difference between the date on which the amount is collected by the bank and the date on which the company is notified of this collection. If so, there will be an amount added to the depositor's bank account balance that has not yet been recorded as an addition to the cash account in the company's general ledger.
4. **Charges for payments made directly by the bank.** A bank, when authorized, will serve as an agent in paying items such as promissory notes (notes payable) for a depositor. When payment is made, the bank deducts the amount from the depositor's account and immediately sends a debit memorandum informing the depositor of the transaction. Upon receiving notification of payment, the company records the transaction in its accounting records. Once again if a timing difference occurs, an amount is deducted from the depositor's bank account balance that has not yet been recorded as a deduction from the cash account in the company's general ledger.

On occasion, errors may be made by either the bank or the company. The most common errors include the transposition of numbers,[1] the misplacement of a decimal point, and adding or dropping zeros to or from a number. Errors not discovered by some other means will become apparent when reconciling the company's bank account. Any errors made by either the bank or the company should be corrected immediately.

## Procedures in Reconciling a Checking Account

*2b. A bank reconciliation is prepared in six steps*

The following procedures are used in finding the reconciling items and determining the adjusted (correct) cash balance:

1. *Compare the individual deposits listed on the bank statement with amounts of the individual deposits recorded in the company's accounting records.* This procedure will identify deposits recorded by the company that have not yet been recorded by the bank (deposits in transit). Any deposits not recorded by the bank are added to the balance per bank statement when reconciling. Also at this time, make certain that any deposits in transit of a prior period, which would have been included in last month's reconciliation, are shown among the deposits in the current month's bank statement.
2. *Compare the paid checks returned with those recorded in the company's accounting records.* To determine whether any written checks are still outstanding, arrange the paid checks returned in numerical order. Then compare these checks with those listed as outstanding on the preceding reconciliation and with those recorded in the cash payments journal during the current period. Checks issued that have not been paid by the bank are outstanding and are deducted from the balance per bank statement when reconciling. During the comparison process, make certain that all returned checks have actually been issued by the company, that amounts deducted from the company's cash balance by the bank agree with the amounts on the checks, and that the checks were properly endorsed.
3. *Note any payments made directly by the bank (these are usually supported by bank debit memoranda).* Gather all debit memoranda included with the bank statement

[1] For example, it is possible to transpose two numbers so that the correct amount of $397 is recorded as $379.

when it was mailed to identify any other items recorded by the bank but not yet recorded in the company's records. These include such items as bank service charges, NSF checks, and payments of promissory notes. If these items were not recorded in the cash payments journal, they must be deducted from the cash balance shown in the company's accounting records when reconciling.

4. *Note any collections made directly by the bank (which are generally supported by bank credit memoranda).* Gather the credit memos included with the bank statement to identify any items that were added to the bank statement balance by the bank but not yet recorded in the company's records. Credit items so identified are added to the cash balance shown in the company's accounting records when reconciling.
5. *Account for numerical errors.* If any numerical errors were made, they should have been discovered during the process of making the comparisons cited in the preceding steps. Of course, the bank must be notified of errors found in its records. The nature of the error will determine how it is treated when reconciling. The company's errors always affect the balance in the Cash account. Some errors require additions to while others require deductions from the company's Cash account balance. Errors made by the bank are either added to or deducted from the cash balance shown in the bank statement.
6. *Prepare the reconciliation statement.* Starting with both the cash balance per books and the cash balance per bank statement, reconcile these differing amounts to a corrected (or adjusted) cash balance. A bank reconciliation for Coleman Company as of November 30 is shown in Exhibit 7–5 and is supplemented by the explanation below.

EXHIBIT 7–5

COLEMAN COMPANY
Bank Reconciliation
November 30, 19X5

| | | |
|---|---|---|
| Balance per books | | $4,580 |
| Add: Proceeds of a note collected | | 600 |
| | | $5,180 |
| Deduct: NSF check of Frank Harley | $ 800 | |
| Bank service charge | 5 | 805 |
| Adjusted cash balance | | $4,375 |
| Balance per bank statement | | $7,360 |
| Add: Deposit in transit as of November 30 | | 1,140 |
| | | $8,500 |
| Deduct: Outstanding checks: | | |
| No. 321 | $ 730 | |
| No. 347 | 1,360 | |
| No. 363 | 835 | |
| No. 378 | 1,200 | 4,125 |
| Adjusted cash balance | | $4,375 |

## *Illustration of a Bank Reconciliation*

Coleman Company is preparing its bank reconciliation as of November 30, 19X5. The company's accounting records show that the balance in its Cash account is $4,580 on November 30, while the bank statement shows a cash balance of $7,360 on that same date. The purpose of the bank reconciliation is to identify the items that cause the difference in the cash balances and to determine the correct cash balance.

The illustration in Exhibit 7–5 shows that the format for a bank reconciliation is as follows.

All *appropriate* items are *added to* or *deducted from* the balance per books on November 30 to obtain the company's adjusted cash balance.

All *appropriate* items are then *added to* or *deducted from* the balance per bank statement on that same date to obtain the company's adjusted cash balance.

When the bank reconciliation has been completed, the two adjusted cash balances must, of course, be the same.

We will now identify each reconciling item used in the Coleman Company illustration and describe how it was treated in the bank reconciliation.

| RECONCILING ITEM | HOW THE ITEM IS TREATED IN THE BANK RECONCILIATION |
|---|---|
| 1. A credit memorandum included with the November bank statement showed that the bank had collected a promissory note for Coleman in the amount of $600 on November 30. | 1. The amount of this item is *added to the balance per books* because the transaction was recorded by the bank but has not yet been recorded in the company's accounting records. |
| 2. An NSF check from a customer (Frank Harley) for $800 was returned on November 29 and was included with the November bank statement. The bank deducted the amount from Coleman's bank account balance on that day. | 2. The amount of this item is *deducted from the balance per books* because the transaction was recorded by the bank but has not yet been recorded in the company's accounting records. |
| 3. A debit memorandum issued by the bank on November 30 for a $5 bank service charge was enclosed with the November bank statement. The bank deducted the amount from Coleman's bank account balance on that day. | 3. The amount of this item is *deducted from the balance per books* because the transaction was recorded by the bank but has not yet been recorded in the company's accounting records. |
| 4. A deposit of $1,140 was in transit on November 30. | 4. The amount of this item is *added to the balance per bank statement* because the transaction was recorded in the company's accounting records but has not yet been recorded by the bank. |
| 5. All checks issued in prior months have been returned with the bank statement. However, four checks issued in the current month (November) have not been returned. These outstanding checks are as follows: | 5. The aggregate amount of this item is *deducted from the balance per bank statement* because the transactions were recorded in the company's accounting records but have not yet been recorded by the bank. |

| DATE | CHECK NO. | AMOUNT |
|---|---|---|
| Nov. 24 | 321 | $ 730 |
| 27 | 347 | 1,360 |
| 29 | 363 | 835 |
| 30 | 378 | 1,200 |

Note that a bank reconciliation (as shown in Exhibit 7 – 5) is divided into two sections. One section begins with the balance according to the company's books and ends with the adjusted cash balance. The other section begins with the balance according to the bank statement and also ends with the adjusted cash balance.

### Entries Based on the Bank Reconciliation

In order to adjust Coleman Company's cash account balances to the correct amount, adjusting entries must be made for the reconciling items that affected the balance per books (as shown in the first section of Exhibit 7–5).

On the other hand, adjusting entries *are not* made for the reconciling items that affected the balance per bank (as shown in the second section of Exhibit 7–5). These items have already been recorded on Coleman Company's books.

*2b. Adjusting entries made from the bank reconciliation are shown here*

The adjusting entries needed for Coleman Company, based on its November 30 bank reconciliation, are as follows.

| | | | |
|---|---|---|---|
| Nov. 30 | Cash | 600 | |
| | Note Receivable | | 600 |
| | To record the collection of a note receivable by the bank | | |
| Nov. 30 | Accounts Receivable, F. Harley | 800 | |
| | Cash | | 800 |
| | To record a receivable from F. Harley in the amount of the NSF check returned by the bank | | |
| Nov. 30 | Bank Service Charge | 5 | |
| | Cash | | 5 |
| | To record the bank service charge | | |

After the adjusting entries have been posted, the company's records will be updated and the Cash account will have a balance of $4,375. This is the amount shown as the adjusted cash balance in the bank reconciliation and the amount that should be included on a November 30 balance sheet.

## THE VOUCHER SYSTEM

*1f. A voucher system verifies purchases, authorizes payment, and ensures proper recording of the transactions*

A **voucher system** is a formalized system for providing control over cash payments. The voucher system described in these sections covers all the transactions that require the payment of cash (except for payments made from petty cash). It consists of the records and procedures used to

*Verify* the purchase of goods and services charged to the buyer

*Authorize* paying for them

*Ensure* that the transactions were properly recorded

A properly functioning voucher system will ensure that every transaction involving a cash payment will be verified and recorded before a check is issued. The system uses the following documents and records: (1) vouchers, (2) a voucher register, (3) a check register, (4) a file for unpaid vouchers, and (5) a file for paid vouchers.

### What a Voucher Is

A **voucher** is a consecutively prenumbered document that provides written authorization to make a cash payment. A typical voucher has a front and a back side, as shown in Exhibit 7–6. One side summarizes the details of the invoice. The other side provides payment information and serves as a basis for recording the

*EXHIBIT 7–6*
Voucher

FRONT SIDE OF VOUCHER

ATLAS COMPANY

Pay to Lennar Company
220 South Drive
Columbus, OH

Voucher No. 89
Date Due 12/15
Date Paid 12/12
Check No. 367

| Date of Invoice | Invoice Number | Description | Amount |
|---|---|---|---|
| December 2 | 733 | 20 units - item cejell | $ 250.00 |

| Verification | Initials |
|---|---|
| Extension and footings | NL |
| Price per purchase order | BC |
| Quantities per receiving report | EK |
| Credit terms | CR |
| Distribution to accounts | BR |
| Approval for payments | J. Steele |

BACK SIDE OF VOUCHER

ACCOUNTING DISTRIBUTION

| Account Debited | Account Number | Amount |
|---|---|---|
| Purchases | 601 | $250.00 |
| Transportation-In | | |
| Advertising Expense | | |
| Delivery Expense | | |
| Utilities Expense | | |
| Salary Expense | | |
| Total | | $250.00 |

Voucher No. 89

Payee Lennar Company
220 South Drive
Columbus, Ohio

Payment Summary:

| | |
|---|---|
| Invoice cost | $250.00 |
| Cash discount | 5.00 |
| Net payment | $245.00 |

Check number 367

transaction. A major characteristic of the voucher system is that a voucher must be prepared authorizing an expenditure before a check can be issued.

Before an authorized individual approves the voucher for payment, several employees verify various aspects of the purchase and ascertain that the basis for recording the transaction has been established. The voucher preparation process includes the following:

The purchase order and invoice are *compared* to see if they agree in regard to type of goods, quantity, price, and credit terms.

The invoice and receiving report are *compared* to verify receipt of the goods ordered.

The invoice is *examined* to verify arithmetical accuracy.

The appropriate account to be debited is *determined* and inserted in the voucher.

After all the data except the details of payment have been inserted in the voucher, copies of the supporting documents, such as the purchase order, invoice, and receiving report, are usually attached to the voucher. Once the voucher has been approved for payment, it serves as a basis for an entry in a book called the *voucher register.*

## The Voucher Register

*2c. Recording of transactions in the voucher register is illustrated in Exhibit 7-7*

The **voucher register** is a multicolumn journal used as a book of original entry for all the transactions that require a cash payment. The voucher register takes the place of the purchases journal discussed in the preceding chapter. However, the voucher register is used to record all types of transactions requiring cash payments. The form of a voucher register varies depending on the size and nature of the business. A typical form of a voucher register is illustrated in Exhibit 7–7 on page 256.

Note that the vouchers are prenumbered and are entered in the voucher register in sequential order. All entries are recorded as a credit to Vouchers Payable and as a debit to the account or accounts to be charged for the expenditure. The new account title, **Vouchers Payable,** is frequently used as a substitute for Accounts Payable when the voucher system is used.

When a voucher is paid, the date of the payment and the number of the check are entered in the appropriate columns in the voucher register. With these items entered, it is easy to determine the amount of an individual unpaid voucher or the total amount for all unpaid vouchers.

Posting from the voucher register is similar to posting from the cash payments journal. Columns are totaled and cross-footed at the end of each month. Columns with account titles are posted as a debit or a credit to the appropriate accounts in the general ledger. Evidence that the posting has taken place is provided by placing the account number in parentheses just below the column total. Entries in the Other Accounts column are posted individually to the account named, and evidence of the posting is provided by entering the account number in the posting reference column.

## The Check Register

*2c. Recording of transactions in a check register is illustrated in Exhibit 7-8*

The payment of a voucher is recorded in a check register. A **check register** is a multicolumn journal that contains a record of all checks issued. In a voucher system the check register replaces the cash payments journal. Because each check issued is to pay a voucher that has previously been recorded as a voucher

*EXHIBIT 7–7*

Voucher Register

| Date | | Vou. No. | Payee | PAYMENT Date Paid | PAYMENT Check No. | VOUCHERS Payable Credit | Purchases Debit | Transport. In Debit | Adver. Debit | Delivery Debit | Utilities Debit | Salary Debit | Other Accounts Account | Other Accounts Post Ref. | Other Accounts Amount |
|---|---|---|---|---|---|---|---|---|---|---|---|---|---|---|---|
| Dec. | 1 | 87 | Style Company | 12/1 | 358 | 80 | | 80 | | | | | | | |
| | 1 | 88 | Cole Company | 12/5 | 361 | 210 | | | 210 | | | | | | |
| | 2 | 89 | Lennar Company | 12/12 | 367 | 250 | 250 | | | | | | | | |
| | 2 | 90 | Payroll | 12/2 | 359 | 1 200 | | | | | | 1 200 | | | |
| | 2 | 91 | First Equipment | | | 600 | | | | | | | Office Equipment | 203 | 600 |
| | 29 | 163 | Erie Delivery | 12/29 | 402 | 72 | | | | 72 | | | | | |
| | 29 | 164 | Lennar Company | | | 410 | 410 | | | | | | | | |
| | 30 | 165 | Common Utility | 12/31 | 403 | 68 | | | | | 68 | | | | |
| | 30 | 166 | Regional Telephone | 12/31 | 404 | 55 | | | | | 55 | | | | |
| | 30 | 167 | Payroll | 12/31 | 405 | 1 300 | | | | | | 1 300 | | | |
| | 31 | 168 | Merrill Company | | | 520 | 520 | | | | | | | | |
| | 31 | 169 | Atomic Freight | 12/31 | 406 | 60 | | 60 | | | | | | | |
| | 31 | 170 | Long Company | | | 370 | 370 | | | | | | | | |
| | | | | | | 23 600 | 15 960 | 210 | 320 | 145 | 165 | 6 200 | | | 600 |
| | | | | | | (300) | (600) | (602) | (603) | (604) | (605) | (606) | | | |

payable in the voucher register, only a few columns are needed in the check register. Exhibit 7–8 shows the typical form of a check register. The first column shows the date of the check. The second column shows the number of the check used. The third column identifies whom the check was made out to (the payee), and this is followed by a column indicating the number for the voucher being paid. In many cases, an entry in the check register results in a debit to Vouchers Payable, a credit to Purchases Discounts, and a credit to Cash. Therefore money columns are provided to enter amounts to be posted to those three accounts. The money columns in the check register are totaled and cross-footed at the end of each month, and the column totals are posted to the appropriate accounts in the general ledger. To provide evidence that the amounts have been posted, the ledger account numbers are written in parentheses under each column total.

*EXHIBIT 7–8*

Check Register

CHECK REGISTER

| Date | | Check Number | Payee | Voucher Number | Debit Vouchers Payable | Credit Purchase Discounts | Credit Cash |
|---|---|---|---|---|---|---|---|
| Dec. | 1 | 358 | Style Company | 87 | 80 | | 80 |
| | 2 | 359 | Payroll | 90 | 1,200 | | 1,200 |
| | 3 | 360 | T. M. Company | 76 | 650 | 13 | 637 |
| | 5 | 361 | Cole Company | 88 | 210 | | 210 |
| | 5 | 362 | Young Company | 73 | 500 | 15 | 485 |
| | . | . | . | . | . | . | . |
| | . | . | . | . | . | . | . |
| | . | . | . | . | . | . | . |
| | 29 | 402 | Erie Delivery | 163 | 72 | | 72 |
| | 31 | 403 | Common Utility | 165 | 68 | | 68 |
| | 31 | 404 | Regional Telephone | 166 | 55 | | 55 |
| | 31 | 405 | Payroll | 167 | 1,300 | | 1,300 |
| | 31 | 406 | Atomic Freight | 169 | 60 | | 60 |
| | | | | | 19,400 | 218 | 19,182 |
| | | | | | (300) | (601) | (100) |

## *Unpaid and Paid Vouchers Files*

When a voucher system is used, two files are needed—one for unpaid vouchers and the other for paid vouchers.

The unpaid voucher file contains vouchers that have been approved for payment and recorded in the voucher register but have not as yet been paid. Unpaid vouchers, which remain in that file until paid, should be filed by their due date. This filing procedure ensures that (1) discounts if allowed will not be missed simply because the time period granted has expired, and (2) accounts will be paid when due (assuming the company has adequate cash) to protect the company's credit rating. The amount due on each unpaid voucher represents the credit balance of an account (voucher) payable, making the unpaid voucher itself similar to an individual account payable in the accounts payable subsidiary ledger. Thus the unpaid voucher file substitutes for the accounts payable subsidiary ledger described in Chapter 6.

The paid voucher file contains all paid vouchers, arranged in numerical order. This file is useful for checking the details of previous cash payments, answering questions concerning specific payments, and providing information about specific expenditures.

When a voucher system is used, an accounts payable subsidiary ledger is not needed. However, the voucher system does not show in one place the aggregate amount owed to a particular supplier who may have two or more unpaid invoices outstanding. But if paid vouchers are filed in alphabetical order, a voucher system readily provides information pertaining to the amount of goods or services purchased from a given supplier over a period of time. Also, a voucher system provides good internal control over the acquisition of and payment for goods and services received.

## HIGHLIGHT PROBLEM

According to its accounting records, the Regal Company has a cash balance of *$4,230* on September 30, 19X7. The company's bank statement on the same date shows a cash balance of *$5,260.* To reconcile the bank account, the company determined the following.

A $180 deposit, placed in the bank's night depository on the evening of September 30, was not listed as a deposit on its September bank statement. Two checks issued in September were not included among the paid checks returned by the bank. They were: no. 57 for $370 and no. 60 for $910. Included among the returned checks was a credit memorandum showing that on September 29 the bank had collected on behalf of the company a non-interest-bearing $200 note receivable from J. Harris: Although Regal Company's bank balance increased by that amount on September 29, no entry pertaining to that transaction has as yet been made in the company's accounting records. Also included among the returned checks was a debit memorandum issued by the bank on September 30 showing that $10 was deducted from Regal's account as a charge for services rendered by the bank during the month of September. This transaction has not been recorded in the company's accounting records. The bank also returned with its statement an NSF check for $260. The check received by Regal from Ronald Evans, one of its customers, on September 26 had been included in that day's bank deposit. No entry has been made in the company's records to show the action taken by the bank on September 30, at which time the bank deducted the amount of the NSF check from Regal's bank balance.

Required:

1. Prepare a bank reconciliation for Regal Company as of September 30.
2. Prepare general journal entries to adjust the accounts.

## GLOSSARY OF KEY TERMS

**Bank reconciliation.** A procedure for reconciling the difference between the ending cash balance shown in the company's records and the ending cash balance shown in the bank statement. It consists of a schedule listing the items and amounts that have caused the difference.

**Bank service charges.** Amounts deducted by a bank from a depositor's account as payment for services rendered.

**Bank statement.** A statement of the balance in an account sent by a bank to its depositor along with paid checks and notices of any bank charges and bank credits (debit or credit memoranda).

**Cash.** An asset that includes coins, paper money, checks, money orders, and money on deposit with banks.

**Cash Over or Short account.** An account used to record shortages or overages in the petty cash fund. Also used to record amounts by which the actual cash receipts differ from amounts rung up on cash registers.

**Check.** A written document signed by the depositor, instructing the bank to pay a specified sum of money to a designated payee.

**Check register.** A multicolumn journal that contains a record of all checks issued.

**Deposit ticket.** A form filled out by the depositor showing the checks and/or currency deposited in the account.

**Deposits in transit.** Cash deposited and entered in the depositor's cash records but not received by the bank in time to appear on the bank statement.

**Imprest petty cash fund.** A petty cash system in which the balance of the petty cash account is established at a predetermined amount and remains at that amount unless the fund itself is either increased or decreased. All payments from the fund are documented by receipts or invoices.

**Internal accounting control.** See *internal control.*

**Internal administrative control.** See *internal control.*

**Internal control.** An organization's methods and procedures for (1) promoting operational efficiency and adherence to managerial policy *(internal administrative control)* and (2) safeguarding assets and ensuring the accuracy and reliability of accounting data *(internal accounting control)*.

**Nonsufficient funds (NSF) check.** A customer's check that has been deposited in the company's bank account but cannot be paid by the customer's bank because the customer's bank balance is less than the amount of the check.

**Outstanding checks.** Checks issued and recorded by a depositor but not yet presented to the depositor's bank for payment.

**Petty cash book.** A book that shows the amount of cash received and placed in the petty cash fund and the amount and purpose of each payment made from the petty cash fund.

**Petty cash fund.** A separate cash fund used for making relatively minor cash payments. This fund is generally used when writing a check is inefficient and impractical.

**Petty cash voucher.** A document issued and initialed by the petty cash custodian and signed by the person who receives money from the petty cash fund.

**Signature card.** A card signed by a depositor showing the signature of the person or persons authorized to sign checks drawn on the account.

**Voucher.** A consecutively prenumbered document providing written authorization for cash payments.

**Vouchers Payable.** An account title frequently used as a substitute for Accounts Payable when the voucher system is used.

**Voucher register.** A multicolumn journal used as a book of original entry for all transactions that require a cash payment.

**Voucher system.** A formalized system for providing control over cash payments. It consists of records and procedures to (1) verify the purchase of goods and services, (2) authorize paying for them, and (3) ensure that the transactions were properly recorded.

## REVIEW QUESTIONS

1. Differentiate between internal administrative control and internal accounting control. [LO1a]
2. Describe the six common characteristics of good internal accounting control. [LO1a]
3. What four functions should be separated in a good system of internal accounting control? [LO1a]
4. What general rule can be used when deciding whether a particular item should be classified as cash? [LO1b]
5. How are unrestricted cash amounts classified in the balance sheet? [LO1b]
6. Describe twelve widely accepted methods and procedures for establishing control of cash. [LO1c]
7. Why do most companies find it convenient to pay for some expenditures from a petty cash fund? [LO1d]
8. Explain how a petty cash fund is established. [LO1d]
9. Describe the purpose of and the contents of a petty cash voucher. [LO1d]
10. Describe what journal entries are made and when they are made when an imprest petty cash system is used. [LO2a]
11. Explain the purpose of a petty cash book. [LO1d]
12. Explain the purpose of a Cash Over or Short account when a petty cash fund is used. [LO1d]

13. Name and describe the business forms used in connection with a bank checking account. [LO1e]
14. What are the two reasons why the cash balance shown on the bank statement will seldom agree with the balance shown in the depositor's Cash account in its general ledger? [LO1e]
15. Describe six timing differences that necessitate the preparation of bank reconciliations. [LO1e,2b]
16. Describe the six procedures to be followed in reconciling a checking account. [LO2b]
17. Which section of the bank reconciliation shows data for the entries needed to adjust a company's accounts? [LO2b]
18. Name and describe the five documents and records used in a voucher system. [LO1f]
19. Describe the four-step process involved in voucher preparation. [LO1f]
20. Differentiate between a voucher register and a purchases journal. [LO2c]
21. When a voucher system is used, what journal is replaced by the check register? [LO2c]

## ANALYTICAL QUESTIONS

22. "Internal control over the asset cash is more "critical" than internal control over plant assets." Comment on this statement. [LO1a,1c]
23. Why are postdated checks classified as accounts receivable rather than cash on the balance sheet? [LO1b]
24. Why is segregation of duties important in a system of internal control over cash? [LO1a,1c]
25. What is an imprest petty cash fund? Explain how the fund is established and replenished, and describe the accounting entries that are needed. [LO1d,2a]
26. Give three reasons why there might be a shortage or an overage in the petty cash fund when it is replenished. [LO1d]
27. What conditions would have to exist for the ending cash balance in the company's records to be the same as the ending cash balance on the company's bank statement? [LO1e]
28. Why are some amounts on a bank reconciliation used to prepare adjusting entries and other amounts on a bank reconciliation not used to prepare adjusting entries? [LO2b]
29. Why would a company wish to use a voucher system when it has a purchases journal and a cash payments journal? [LO1f]
30. Why are a voucher register and a check register used in a voucher system? [LO2c]

## IMPACT ANALYSIS QUESTIONS

*For each error described, indicate whether it would overstate [O], understate [U], or not affect [N] the specified key figures.*

31. A $20 petty cash voucher was used to purchase postage stamps (none of which have been used). The voucher was lost. When replenishing the petty cash fund, the Cash Over or Short account was debited for $20. [LO2a]

    _______ Assets _______ Expenses
    _______ Revenues _______ Net Income

32. When preparing a bank reconciliation, a $400 customer's check returned NSF was incorrectly classified as a bank service charge. When preparing adjusting journal entries, the amount was debited to Bank Charges Expense. [LO2b]

    _______ Cash _______ Revenues
    _______ Total Assets _______ Expenses

33. The bank collected $8,200 on behalf of a depositor. The face value of the note was $8,000. The entire amount ($8,200) was added to the cash balance per the depositor's accounting records when the bank reconciliation was prepared, but the entire amount was credited to Notes Receivable when the adjusting entries were prepared. [LO2b]

| | |
|---|---|
| _______ Cash | _______ Revenues |
| _______ Total Assets | _______ Net Income |

34. On behalf of its depositor, the bank paid a $5,000 interest-bearing note to Mall Company. In preparing the bank reconciliation, $5,200 (the amount of the note plus interest) was deducted from the cash balance per the depositor's accounting records, but the entire amount was debited to Notes Receivable when adjusting entries were prepared. [LO2b]

| | |
|---|---|
| _______ Cash | _______ Expenses |
| _______ Liabilities | _______ Net Income |

35. When preparing the June 30, 19X5, bank reconciliation, Morris Vending Company discovered that a check written for the June rent had been recorded in the accounting records as $540, although issued and made out for the correct amount of $450. When preparing the bank reconciliation, the $90 difference was added to Cash shown in the company's accounting records but was credited to Miscellaneous Expense when the adjusting entry was prepared. [LO2b]

| | |
|---|---|
| _______ Cash | _______ Expenses |
| _______ Revenues | _______ Net Income |

## EXERCISES

EXERCISE 7–1 *(Analyze Control of Cash)* At Brent Company an employee had the following duties:

a. Handle and verify all cash receipts. This includes the cash contained in the cash registers at the end of each day and all checks received in the mail. The employee is also responsible for opening all incoming mail daily.
b. Deposit all cash and checks received in the bank.
c. Prepare all journal entries to record the receipt of cash.
d. Record reductions of receivables when customers make payments on account.
e. Prepare monthly statements of amounts owed to the company by each individual customer, and mail those statements to each customer.
f. Prepare the monthly bank reconciliation.

Required:

Comment on the weaknesses in the internal control over cash. Make recommendations that would improve control over cash. [LO1a,1c]

EXERCISE 7–2 *(Establish Definition of Cash)*

1. Identify by letter the items listed below that should be included in the company's cash balance.
   a. Postage stamps
   b. Petty cash on hand
   c. Checks payable to the company
   d. Postdated checks
   e. Deposits of coin and currency in transit
   f. Checks from customers returned by the bank and designated NSF
   g. Money orders on hand made payable to the company
   h. Money on deposit in checking accounts
   i. Money on deposit in savings accounts
   j. Money advanced to company employees
2. Indicate how each, if any, of the noncash items should be treated in the company's accounting records. [LO1b]

EXERCISE 7–3 *(Prepare a Journal Entry for a Petty Cash Fund)* The Rockfall Company maintains an impress petty cash fund of $250. On February 28 the fund contained cash of $39.55 and petty cash expense vouchers summarized as follows:

| | |
|---|---|
| Office supplies | $39.60 |
| Snow removal | 55.00 |
| Delivery expense | 43.90 |
| Postage | 21.00 |
| Transportation-In | 49.45 |

Required:

1. Prepare in general journal form an entry to replenish the petty cash fund.
2. If the company's fiscal year ended on January 31 when the fund had a cash balance of $210, should the fund have been replenished? Why or why not? [LO2a]

EXERCISE 7–4 *(Determine the Missing Amount in Reconciling a Bank Account)* Determine the correct amount and place it in the blank for situations *a* through *e* shown in the table below. [LO2b]

| | BALANCE PER COMPANY'S BOOKS | BALANCE PER BANK STATEMENT | BANK SERVICE CHARGES | OUTSTANDING CHECKS | DEPOSITS IN TRANSIT | ADJUSTED CASH BALANCE |
|---|---|---|---|---|---|---|
| (a) | $482.37 | $461.15 | $0.72 | $ 5.00 | $25.50 | $_____ |
| (b) | 753.88 | 703.29 | 0.74 | 50.15 | _____ | 753.14 |
| (c) | 442.85 | 487.53 | 0.47 | 64.40 | 19.25 | _____ |
| (d) | _____ | 119.28 | 0.77 | 29.62 | None | 89.66 |
| (e) | 597.50 | _____ | 0.35 | 26.75 | 50.00 | 597.15 |

EXERCISE 7–5 *(Prepare a Bank Reconciliation)* The October 19X5 bank statement for Easy Company shows an ending cash balance of $9,732. The cash balance in Easy Company's accounting records is $8,488 on that same date. The following items are the cause of the difference in the two amounts.

a. A deposit of $2,200 was in transit on October 31.
b. A check from Shortway Company, a customer, for $416 was returned NSF.
c. Outstanding checks amounted to $673.
d. Bank service charges for the month were $13.
e. A note collected by the bank on October 31 for $3,200 (including interest of $200) had not yet been recorded in the company's accounting records.

Required:

1. Prepare a bank reconciliation as of October 31, 19X5.
2. Prepare journal entries to adjust the accounts. [LO2b]

EXERCISE 7–6 *(Record Transactions Using a Voucher Register)* During the month of June, vouchers were prepared for the following transactions.

1. Voucher no. 131 was prepared payable to Mars Company for the purchase of merchandise, $1,000.
2. Voucher no. 132 was prepared payable to Sid's Supply for office equipment purchased, $5,000.
3. Voucher no. 133 was prepared payable to the Handy Shop for repairs made to old equipment, $50.
4. Voucher no. 134 was prepared payable to A. Kaufman for the payment of a non-interest-bearing note payable, $2,000.

During the month of June, checks numbered 206, 209, and 214 were issued to pay vouchers numbered 131, 132, and 134, respectively.

Required:
Use the voucher register provided in the work papers, or prepare a voucher register similar to the one illustrated in this chapter and record the transactions in the register. Use arbitrary June dates, or just indicate *June* in the date column. [LO2c]

## PROBLEMS

PROBLEM 7-1 *(State the Purpose of Internal Control Procedures)* Some widely accepted methods and procedures for establishing control over cash are as follows.

1. The functions involving the receipt of cash and the payment of cash should be handled by different persons.
2. All cash receipts are deposited in bank accounts promptly; preferably on a daily basis.
3. All cash payments must be approved and must be made by check (with an exception for certain disbursements from petty cash).
4. Checks are consecutively prenumbered, and a designated person is responsible for controlling them.
5. The person handling cash receipts does not have access to the accounts receivable records.
6. The petty cash fund is kept on an imprest basis.
7. Bank reconciliations are prepared on a monthly basis.

Required:
State the purpose of each of these procedures. [LO1a,1c]

PROBLEM 7-2 *(Distribute Internal Control Job Responsibilities)* Careful Company has three employees who must perform the following functions.

1. Handle all cash receipts (from cash registers and from checks received in the mail)
2. Open all incoming mail
3. Prepare bank deposit tickets
4. Make deposits in the bank
5. Maintain the check register
6. Prepare checks for signature
7. Maintain the voucher register
8. Maintain control over accounts receivable
9. Maintain control over accounts payable
10. Prepare monthly bank reconciliations

Required:
Distribute the functions among the three employees that would establish the best system of internal control possible under the conditions cited. [LO1a,1c]

PROBLEM 7-3 *(Record and Comment on Petty Cash Transactions)* On March 1, 1985, Rite Company established an imprest petty cash fund of $300. On March 31, 19X5, the fund consisted of cash and receipted vouchers to verify all expenditures made from the fund. These items are summarized below.

| | |
|---|---|
| Currency and coins | $ 8.30 |
| Petty cash vouchers for: | |
| Transportation-in | 62.30 |
| Office supplies | 43.90 |
| Telephone and telegrams | 16.70 |
| Delivery expense | 27.20 |
| Maintenance and repairs | 31.60 |
| Postage stamps | 23.00 |
| Loan to employee | 85.00 |

Required:

1. Prepare entries in general journal form to
   a. Establish the petty cash fund.
   b. Replenish the fund on March 31, 19X5, and increase it by $100 to a fund of $400.
2. Comment on whether the petty cash fund was handled satisfactorily. Include your views on the appropriateness of the type of disbursements made from the fund.

[LO2a]

PROBLEM 7–4 *(Use a Petty Cash Book and Prepare Journal Entries)* On January 1, 19X5, Kare Company decided to use a petty cash fund for making small cash expenditures. During the month of January, the following transactions took place.

| | |
|---|---|
| Jan. 1 | Drew check no. 105 payable to the company for $100, and cashed it to establish the fund. Appointed K. Sullivan, an employee, as the petty cashier with responsibility for control over the money in the fund and all recordkeeping pertaining to the fund. |
| 3 | Issued petty cash voucher 01 for $15.30 for office supplies purchased on that day. |
| 5 | Issued petty cash voucher 02 for $8.70 for repairs made to an office machine. |
| 8 | Issued petty cash voucher 03 for $10.20 for transportation charges on merchandise purchased for resale. |
| 9 | Issued petty cash voucher 04 for $7.50 for postage stamps. |
| 12 | Issued petty cash voucher 05 for $5.30 to reimburse an employee for travel expenses incurred in visiting a customer. |
| 16 | Issued petty cash voucher 06 for $8.10 for transportation charges on merchandise purchased for resale. |
| 18 | Issued petty cash voucher 07 for $16.40 for office supplies purchased. |
| 22 | Issued petty cash voucher 08 for $9.90 for transportation charges on merchandise purchased for resale. |
| 25 | Issued petty cash voucher 09 for a telegram costing $2.75. |
| 31 | Drew check no. 163 to replenish the petty cash fund. A cash count revealed that there was $14.35 remaining in the fund. |

Required:

1. Record the transactions in a petty cash book similar to the one illustrated in this chapter. Use appropriate column headings.
2. Prepare the journal entries to establish the petty cash fund on January 1 and to replenish the fund on January 31. [LO2a]

PROBLEM 7–5 *(Prepare a Bank Reconciliation)* Use the following information to prepare a bank reconciliation for Malta Company as of October 31, 19X5.

a. The company's cash account shows a balance of $16,469.14 on October 31.
b. The cash balance on the bank statement for the same date is $18,642.28.
c. A deposit of $2,612.45, representing the cash receipts of October 31, was not recorded by the bank until November 2.
d. A bank service charge for October of $11.40 has not yet been recorded by Malta Company.
e. A check received from Don Hill, a customer, for $319.00 and deposited by Malta Company was returned by the bank marked NSF.
f. Checks issued and mailed in October that have not cleared (been paid by) the bank as of October 31 are:

| | |
|---|---|
| No. 513 | $320.18 |
| No. 567 | 617.24 |
| No. 569 | 455.00 |
| No. 570 | 964.57 |

g. Check no. 553 correctly issued for $178.00 cleared the bank for that amount but was recorded in the check register as $187.00. The check was used to pay for repairs made to the company's office equipment.

h. The bank collected for Malta Company $3,100.00 on a note left with the bank for collection. The amount represents the face value of the note plus $100.00 in interest earned on the note. This transaction has not yet been recorded in Malta's accounting records.

i. The bank mistakenly charged Malta Company for a $350.00 check issued by Matta Company.

Required:

1. Prepare a bank reconciliation as of October 31, 19X5.
2. Indicate the amount of cash that should appear among the current assets on Malta's October 31, 19X5, balance sheet.
3. Prepare journal entries to adjust the accounts. [LO2b]

PROBLEM 7–6 *(Prepare a Bank Reconciliation)* Use the following information to prepare a bank reconciliation for Mataoe Company as of December 31, 19X3.

1. The company's bank reconciliation prepared as of November 30, 19X3, is shown below.

| | | |
|---|---|---|
| Balance per books, November 30 | | $5,230 |
| Deduct: Bank service charge | | 5 |
| Adjusted cash balance | | $5,225 |
| Balance per bank statement, November 30 | | $5,815 |
| Add: Deposit in transit | | 315 |
| | | $6,130 |
| Deduct: Outstanding checks: | | |
| No. 1156 | $500 | |
| No. 1158 | 250 | |
| No. 1159 | 155 | 905 |
| Adjusted cash balance | | $5,225 |

2. The bank statement issued on December 31, 19X3, shows a cash balance of $4,700. It also shows that three deposits and thirty sequentially numbered checks were processed during December and that a monthly service fee was charged. The activity is summarized below.

| | | |
|---|---|---|
| Dec. 1 | | $ 315 |
| 15 | | 530 |
| 21 | | 600 |
| | Total | $1,445 |

December charges against the account:

| | |
|---|---|
| Checks numbered 1158 through 1188 totaling | $2,555 |
| Bank service charge | 5 |

3. The company's accounting records show the following:
Cash receipts deposited during December:

| | |
|---|---|
| Dec. 16 | $ 530 |
| 22 | 600 |
| 31 | 1,100 |
| Total | $2,230 |

Checks disbursed during December:

| | |
|---|---|
| Checks numbered 1160 through 1188 totaling | $2,150 |
| Check numbered 1189 for | 100 |
| | $2,250 |

(*Hint:* To work this problem, you should compare amounts from the November 30, 19X3, bank reconciliation, the information about the bank's activity in December, and the information about the cash transactions entered in the company's accounting records for December. Pay close attention to the deposit in transit and to the outstanding checks listed in the November 30 bank reconciliation.) [LO2b]

PROBLEM 7–7 *(Correct a Bank Reconciliation)* On December 31, 19X2, Kimberly Company prepared the following bank reconciliation.

| | | |
|---|---|---|
| Balance per books, December 31 | | $5,200 |
| Add: Note receivable collected by bank | $500 | |
| Deposit in transit | 150 | 650 |
| | | $5,850 |
| Deduct: NSF check of J. Troy | | 80 |
| Adjusted cash balance | | $5,770 |
| Balance per bank statement, December 31 | | $5,850 |
| Deduct: Bank service charge | $ 5 | |
| Outstanding checks No. 162 | 185 | |
| No. 165 | 200 | 390 |
| | | $5,460 |
| Unlocated difference | | 310 |
| Adjusted cash balance | | $5,770 |

Required:

1. Identify the error or errors that caused the unlocated difference of $310.
2. Prepare a correct bank reconciliation as of December 31, 19X2.
3. Prepare any journal entries needed to adjust the company's accounts. [LO2b]

PROBLEM 7–8 *(Record Entries in a Voucher Register and a Check Register)* The Williams Company uses a voucher system and had the following transactions during the first half of April 19X5.

| | |
|---|---|
| April 1 | Prepared voucher no. 216 payable to R. Joyce for merchandise purchased, $800; terms 2/10, n/30. |
| 1 | Prepared voucher no. 217 payable to Len Rental Agency for April's rent, $420. |
| 2 | Prepared voucher no. 218 payable to Sue Supply for merchandise purchased, $650; terms 2/10, n/30. |
| 3 | Issued check no. 562 in payment of voucher no. 217. |
| 3 | Prepared voucher no. 219 payable to the Daily Record for advertising, $75. |
| 4 | Prepared voucher no. 220 payable to Loft Company for merchandise purchased, $550; terms 2/10, n/30. |
| 7 | Prepared voucher no. 221 payable to Fast Freight for transportation costs of $60 on merchandise purchased FOB shipping point. |

| | |
|---|---|
| 9 | Issued check no. 563 in payment of voucher no. 216. |
| 9 | Prepared voucher no. 222 payable to General Power for the monthly utility bill of $145. |
| 11 | Issued check no. 564 in payment of voucher no. 218. |
| 12 | Issued check no. 565 in payment of voucher no. 222. |
| 12 | Prepared voucher no. 223 payable to R. Joyce for merchandise purchased, $680; terms 2/10, n/30. |
| 14 | Issued check no. 566 in payment of voucher no. 220. |
| 15 | Prepared voucher no. 224 payable to payroll for semimonthly salaries of $2,800. |
| 15 | Prepared voucher no. 225 payable to Associated Company for merchandise purchased, $720; terms 2/10, n/30. |
| 15 | Issued check no. 567 in payment of voucher no. 224. |

Required:

1. Use the voucher register and the check register forms provided in the work papers, or prepare a voucher register and a check register similar to those illustrated in this chapter. Record the transactions in the voucher and check registers.
2. List the vouchers that would be in the unpaid vouchers file, and indicate the total amount of vouchers (accounts) payable as of April 15. Assume that there were no unpaid vouchers as of April 1. [LO2c]

PROBLEM 7–9 *(Use a Check Register to Record Transactions in a Voucher Register)*

| CHECK NO. | DATE | PAYEE | VOUCHER NO. | VOUCHERS PAYABLE DEBIT | PURCHASE DISCOUNTS CREDIT | CASH CREDIT |
|---|---|---|---|---|---|---|
| 913 | May 2 | Payroll | 262 | $2,500 | | $2,500 |
| 914 | 4 | Caldwell Merchandising Co. | 240 | 500 | $10 | 490 |
| 915 | 7 | Lowell Merchandising Co. | 245 | 600 | 12 | 588 |
| 916 | 9 | State Bank (including interest of $600) | 263 | 5,600 | | 5,600 |
| 917 | 15 | Eric Repair Shop | 265 | 90 | | 90 |
| 918 | 20 | Benson Repair Shop | 266 | 110 | | 110 |
| 919 | 23 | Wheel Transportation Co. | 268 | 155 | | 155 |
| 920 | 26 | Lowell Merchandising Co. | 248 | 700 | 14 | 686 |

Required:

Set up a voucher register using the format illustrated in the chapter. Enter the above transactions in the voucher register, assuming that they were entered in the voucher register prior to being entered in the check register. (*Hint:* Examine the payee in the check register to determine titles of the accounts that you think should be debited when making entries in the voucher register. Enter the vouchers in correct order.) [LO2c]

PROBLEM 7–10 *(Prepare a Bank Reconciliation)* Use the following information to prepare a bank reconciliation for the King Posters Company as of April 30, 19X5.

a. The company's Cash account shows a balance of $1,974.40 on April 30.

b. The cash balance on the bank statement for the same date is $2,184.20.

c. Checks that were written out during the month but have not yet cleared the bank (outstanding checks) are no. 357 for $15.30, no. 364 for $192.80, and no. 369 for $451.60.

d. A deposit of $510.00 representing the cash receipts of April 30 was not recorded by the bank until May 1.

e. A bank service charge for April of $11.20 has not yet been recorded by King Posters Company.

f. The company bookkeeper recorded $813.20 in the accounting records for a check issued to Alps Company, a supplier. The actual amount of the check (which is the correct amount) is $831.20.

g. On April 29 a customer stopped payment on a check given to King Posters Company on April 28. The check for $77.70 was deposited and recorded on the twenty-eighth (*Hint:* treated like an NSF check).

h. The bank collected for King Posters Company $175.00 on a non-interest-bearing note left with the bank for collection. This transaction has not yet been recorded in the company's accounting records.

i. The bank statement shows that $88.80 has been deducted from the company's cash balance for check no. 360, which was written out for $80.80. The check has been returned with the bank statement.

j. Included among the returned checks is a certified check for $187.50 made payable to the Hometown Municipality.

Required:

1. Prepare a bank reconciliation as of April 30, 19X5.
2. Prepare any journal entries needed to adjust the company's accounts. [LO2b]

## ALTERNATE PROBLEMS

PROBLEM 7–1A *(Prepare Journal Entries for a Petty Cash Fund)* (Alternate to Problem 7–3) Prepare journal entries for the following transactions involving an imprest petty cash fund.

1. Established a petty cash fund on March 1, $100.
2. Replenished the petty cash fund on March 27. The composition of the fund was as follows:
   a. Summarized vouchers were present for the following:

| | |
|---|---|
| Postage stamps | $15.50 |
| Freight charges on merchandise purchased | 20.30 |
| Delivery expenses on merchandise sold | 31.40 |
| Office supplies | 11.10 |
| Telegrams | 5.00 |

   b. Currency and coin in the fund on March 27 were counted and totaled $15.20. [LO2a]

PROBLEM 7–2A *(Prepare a Bank Reconciliation)* (Alternate to Problem 7–5) Use the following information to prepare a bank reconciliation for Artley Company as of January 31, 19X6.

1. The bank statement shows a cash balance of $4,520 as of January 31, 19X6.
2. The company's Cash account shows a balance of $3,320 for the same date.
3. Checks issued in January that have not yet cleared (been paid by) the bank are:

| | |
|---|---|
| No. 351 | $120 |
| No. 355 | 300 |
| No. 359 | 260 |

4. A deposit of $830 representing the cash receipts of January 31 did not appear on the January bank statement.
5. A bank service charge for $8 appeared on the January bank statement. The amount has not yet been recorded in the company's accounting records.
6. A check received from F. Walker, a customer, for $196 was deposited by Artley Company and returned by the bank marked NSF.
7. The January bank statement contained a credit memorandum for $1,558 representing the proceeds of a note left for collection. The note had a face value of $1,500, and the

$58 represents the amount of interest earned. The statement also contained a debit memorandum explaining that the bank had charged the company a $4 fee for the collection of the note. None of these items have been recorded in the company's accounting records.

Required:

1. Prepare a bank reconciliation as of January 1, 19X6.
2. Indicate the amount of cash that should appear among the current assets on Artley's January 31, 19X6, balance sheet.
3. Prepare journal entries to adjust the accounts. [LO2b]

PROBLEM 7–3A *(Correct a Bank Reconciliation)* (Alternate to Problem 7–7) On December 31, 19X2, Miller Company prepared the following bank reconciliation.

| | | |
|---|---|---|
| Balance per books, December 31 | | $5,200 |
| Add: Note receivable collected by bank | | 500 |
| | | $5,700 |
| Deduct: NSF check of J. Hill | $ 80 | |
| Outstanding checks | 390 | 470 |
| Adjusted cash balance | | $5,230 |
| Balance per bank statement, December 31 | | $5,855 |
| Add: Deposit in transit | | 150 |
| | | $6,005 |
| Deduct: Bank service charge | | 5 |
| | | $6,000 |
| Unlocated difference | | (770) |
| Adjusted cash balance | | $5,230 |

Required:

1. Identify the error or errors that caused the unlocated difference of $770.
2. Prepare a correct bank reconciliation as of December 31, 19X2.
3. Prepare any journal entries needed to adjust the company's accounts. [LO2b]

PROBLEM 7–4A *(Record Entries in a Voucher Register and Check Register)* (Alternate to Problem 7–8) Roman Company uses a voucher system and had the following transactions during the month of January 19X5.

| | |
|---|---|
| Jan. 2 | Purchased merchandise from Longly Company, $350; terms 2/10, n/30. Prepared voucher no. 1014. |
| 4 | Purchased merchandise from Holly Company, $550; terms 2/10, n/30. Prepared voucher no. 1015. |
| 5 | Received a bill from Jensen Company for a machine repair, $60. Prepared voucher no. 1016. |
| 6 | Received a bill from Roadway Company for transportation costs on merchandise purchased FOB shipping point, $45. Prepared voucher no. 1017. |
| 8 | Issued check no. 715 in payment of voucher no. 1017. |
| 10 | Issued check no. 716 in payment of voucher no. 1014. |
| 12 | Purchased merchandise from Indus Company, $600; terms 2/10, n/30. Prepared voucher no. 1018. |
| 14 | Issued check no. 717 in payment of voucher no. 1015. |
| 15 | Prepared voucher no. 1019 payable to payroll for semimonthly salaries of $2,600. |
| 15 | Issued check no. 718 in payment of voucher no. 1019. |
| 17 | Purchased merchandise from Guy Company, $1,200; terms 2/10, n/30. Prepared voucher no. 1020. |
| 20 | Issued check no. 719 in payment of voucher no. 1018. |

| | |
|---|---|
| 21 | Received a bill from Cole & Cole for legal fees incurred, $500. Prepared voucher no. 1021. |
| 22 | Issued check no. 720 in payment of voucher no. 1016. |
| 23 | Prepared voucher no. 1022 payable to General Power for the monthly utility bill of $210. |
| 24 | Issued check no. 721 in payment of voucher no. 1022. |
| 25 | Received a bill from Roadway Company for transportation costs on merchandise purchased FOB shipping point, $65. Prepared voucher no. 1023. |
| 28 | Purchased merchandise from Holly Company, $720; terms 2/10, n/30. Prepared voucher no. 1024. |
| 28 | Issued check no. 722 in payment of voucher 1020. |
| 31 | Prepared voucher no. 1025 payable to payroll for semimonthly salaries of $2,600. |
| 31 | Issued check no. 723 in payment of voucher 1025. |

Required:

1. Prepare a voucher register and a check register similar to those illustrated in this chapter. Record the transactions in the voucher and check registers.
2. List the vouchers that would be in the unpaid vouchers file, and indicate the total amount of vouchers (accounts) payable as of January 31. Assume that there were no unpaid vouchers as of January 1. [LO2c]

# 8 Notes and Accounts Receivable

### Learning Objectives

When you complete this chapter you will be able to

1. Answer the following questions:
   a. What are notes receivable? What kinds of transactions often result in their issuance?
   b. How do estimated losses from uncollectible accounts receivable arise when goods and services are sold on credit?
   c. How do credit card sales differ from other sales?
2. Perform the following accounting functions:
   a. Calculate the interest and maturity date on a promissory note.
   b. Prepare journal entries to record the transactions relating to notes receivable.
   c. Account for losses from uncollectible accounts, using both the direct write-off and the allowance methods.
   d. Determine the uncollectible accounts expense by using both the income statement and balance sheet approaches.
   e. Prepare the journal entry for writing off an uncollectible account when the allowance method is used.
   f. Prepare the journal entries to account for the recovery of an account receivable previously written off.
   g. Account for credit balances in accounts receivable.
   h. Prepare the journal entries that record bank and other credit card sales.

In earlier chapters we noted that a transaction involving a sale of goods or services is not always accompanied by an immediate payment in cash. Often the sale is made on credit, with the buyer agreeing to make payment within some specified period, such as thirty or sixty days. We will now look more closely at the accounting for credit transactions under a more general heading called *receivables*.

## WHAT RECEIVABLES ARE

*1a. Receivables commonly arise from sales on credit and the lending of money*

The term **receivables** refers to all money claims that a business has against individuals or organizations. Receivables can arise from various types of transactions. The three most common are the *sale* of goods or services on credit, which generally creates an *account receivable;* the *sale* of items involving relatively large dollar amounts with relatively long credit periods (usually more than sixty days), which generally creates a *note receivable;* and *lending* money, which generally creates a *note receivable.*

This chapter discusses the accounting for both notes and accounts receivable.

## NOTES RECEIVABLE: THE PROMISSORY NOTE

Many firms have **notes receivable,** which they report as assets on their balance sheet. A note receivable, or a **promissory note,** is an unconditional written promise to pay a definite sum of money on demand or at a fixed and determinable future time. A promissory note is generally received when a company engages in one or more of the following transactions:

*1a. Notes are generally received in four types of transactions*

1. *Sells* merchandise on credit terms longer than the customary thirty to sixty days
2. *Sells* a relatively high cost asset other than merchandise (such as equipment) on credit, with the credit period being comparatively long
3. *Lends* money to another company or individual
4. *Accepts* a note receivable in settlement of a customer's past-due accounts receivable

EXHIBIT 8–1
Promissory Note

*1a. Exhibit 8–1 illustrates the information in a promissory note*

$5,000 Denver, Colorado June 2, 19X5

sixty days AFTER DATE I PROMISE TO PAY

TO THE ORDER OF Hudson Company

Five thousand and 00/100 DOLLARS

PAYABLE AT Last State Bank

FOR VALUE RECEIVED WITH INTEREST AT 10%

Frank Cotton

Companies ask for promissory notes in situations such as those described above because the note often provides for the payment of interest by the debtor. A note is also advantageous to the creditor (holder) because it can usually be converted into cash by selling (discounting) it to a bank before it becomes due. Finally, a note is preferred because if legal action is necessary to collect it, a note shows in writing that the debtor acknowledged the debt, amount, and terms of payment.

The length of time between the end of the accounting period and the due date of the promissory note determines how the note is classified in the balance sheet. Notes due in less than a year are classified as current assets. Others are shown as long-term assets.

The person or entity who signs the note and promises to pay it at maturity is called the **maker.** The person or entity to whom payment is to be made is called the **payee.** In the note illustrated in Exhibit 8 – 1, Frank Cotton is the maker and Hudson Company is the payee.

*2b. Journal entries to record a promissory note are illustrated here*

ILLUSTRATIVE ENTRIES OF NOTES RECEIVABLE Hudson Company, the payee of the note, records it by making the following entry (it is the Hudson Company that lends Frank Cotton the $5,000):

| | | | |
|---|---|---|---|
| June 2 | Notes Receivable . . . . . . . . . . . . . . . . . . . . . . . . . . . . . . . . . . . | 5,000 | |
| | Cash. . . . . . . . . . . . . . . . . . . . . . . . . . . . . . . . . . . . . . . | | 5,000 |
| | To record money lent to Frank Cotton and a note received | | |

Frank Cotton, the maker of the note, records it by making the following entry (this is the debtor's entry creating a note payable):[1]

| | | | |
|---|---|---|---|
| June 2 | Cash . . . . . . . . . . . . . . . . . . . . . . . . . . . . . . . . . . . . . . . . . . . . | 5,000 | |
| | Notes Payable . . . . . . . . . . . . . . . . . . . . . . . . . . . . . . . . | | 5,000 |
| | To record money borrowed from Hudson Company and a note given | | |

A note may provide for the payment of interest for the use of the money during the time that the note is outstanding. These notes are called *interest-bearing notes.* Notes that do not provide for interest are called *non-interest-bearing.* On an interest-bearing note, the interest incurred by the maker of the note is an expense and is debited to an Interest Expense account in the accounting records of the maker. The interest earned by the payee on the note is revenue and is credited to an Interest Revenue account in the accounting records of the payee.

The face amount of the promissory note ($5,000 in our example) is called the **principal.** On a non-interest-bearing note, the amount due on the note's maturity date is its face amount. **Maturity date** refers to the date on which a note becomes due. On an interest-bearing note, the amount due on the maturity date is the **maturity value:** the note's principal (face amount) plus the interest.

## Determining the Maturity Date of a Promissory Note

*2a. Maturity date of a promissory note may be determined in four ways*

The maturity date of a promissory note may be determined by using one of the following methods:

[1] Accounting for notes payable and other current liabilities is discussed in Chapter 12.

1. The maturity date of the note may be *specified by a specific date*—for example, August 15, 19X5. When a note is written in this manner, there is no problem in determining the maturity date.
2. The maturity date of the note may be expressed as a *specified number of years* after its issuance date, such as "two years after date." The note's maturity date is determined by counting the number of years from its issuance date. For example, a note dated July 31, 19X5, due in two years would have a maturity date of July 31, 19X7.
3. The maturity date of the note may be expressed as a *specified number of months* after its issuance date, such as "three months after date." The note's maturity date is determined by counting the number of months from its issuance date. For example, a note dated July 15 due in three months would have a maturity date of October 15. In computing interest, each month is considered to be one-twelfth of a year. Thus interest on the three-month note would be computed by taking three-twelfths of the annual interest amount. (This is further illustrated in the following section.)
4. The maturity date of the note may be expressed as a *specified number of days* after its issuance date, such as "ninety days after date." When expressed in days, the maturity date is determined by counting the exact number of days that must pass after the note has been issued. When making the computation, exclude the date of the note and include its maturity date. For example, a note dated August 15 and due in ninety days would have a maturity date of November 13, determined as follows:

| | |
|---|---|
| Days remaining in August (31 minus 15) | 16 |
| Days in September | 30 |
| Days in October | 31 |
| Days in November (number of days needed to total 90) | 13 |
| | 90 |

## Determining Interest on a Promissory Note

**Interest** is a charge made for the use of money over time. To the borrower, interest is an *expense*. To the lender, interest is *revenue*. The formula for computing interest is as follows:

*2a. Interest on a promissory note = principal × rate of interest × time*

Principal × Rate of Interest × Time = Interest

Interest rates are usually stated in terms of a period of one year. Thus unless otherwise stated, the rate of interest on a note is assumed to be a yearly rate. For example, the interest on a $1,000, 9%, one-year note is $90, computed as follows:

$$\$1{,}000 \times \frac{9}{100} \times 1 = \$90$$

If the terms of the note were four months instead of a year, the interest charge would be $30, computed as follows:

$$\$1{,}000 \times \frac{9}{100} \times \frac{4}{12} = \$30$$

*2a. For convenience, a business year may be considered to be 360 days*

If the terms of the note are expressed in days, the exact number of days must be used in computing the interest. Some organizations, such as federal government agencies, would use the actual number of days in the year as the denominator. For example, 60 days would be considered to be 60/365 of a year. However, 360 days is often used as the denominator. As a matter of convenience in making calculations and to maintain consistency in illustrations, we will use a 360-day year when computing interest on notes that involve a period of less than a full year. Therefore the interest on a 60-day, 9% note for $1,000 would be $15, computed as follows:

$$\$1{,}000 \times \frac{9}{100} \times \frac{60}{360} = \$15$$

## ACCOUNTING FOR NOTES RECEIVABLE

Notes receivable are usually recorded in a single Notes Receivable ledger account. The Notes Receivable account is a control account, with the notes themselves providing the information needed to support the control account. Information such as the name of the maker, the principal amount, the rate of interest, and the maturity date can be determined by simply examining the individual notes on hand.

Accounting for notes receivable involves illustrating entries for the receipt of the note, the collection of the note, the end-of-the-period adjustment for interest revenue, a dishonored note, and a discounted note. Each of these entries is illustrated in the subsections that follow.

### Receipt of a Note

*2b. The entry to record receipt of a note is illustrated here*

Assume that Willow Company makes a $5,000 sale of merchandise on credit and receives a 90-day, 10% note receivable from its customer, J. Giles. The entry to record the receipt of the note and the related sales revenue is as follows:

| | | | |
|---|---|---|---|
| Oct. 1 | Notes Receivable . . . . . . . . . . | 5,000 | |
| | Sales . . . . . . . . . . | | 5,000 |
| | To record the sale of merchandise to J. Giles accepting a 90-day, 10% note | | |

### Collection of a Note

*2b. The entry to record collection of a note is illustrated here*

Ninety days later when this interest-bearing note is collected, the Cash account is debited for the amount received. The Notes Receivable account is credited for the note's principal amount (face value), and the Interest Revenue account is credited for the interest earned during the period of time that the note was held. The journal entry made ninety days later on December 30 to record the collection of the J. Giles note would be:

| | | | |
|---|---|---|---|
| Dec. 30 | Cash . . . . . . . . . . | 5,125 | |
| | Notes Receivable . . . . . . . . . . | | 5,000 |
| | Interest Revenue . . . . . . . . . . | | 125 |
| | Collected 90-day, 10% note from J. Giles including interest [$5,000 × (10/100) × (90/360) = $125] | | |

### Adjustments for Interest Earned at the End of the Accounting Period

A note received in one accounting period may not come due (mature) until the next accounting period. Because interest is a function of time, interest on the note is earned each day throughout the life of the note. In accordance with the *matching principle*, the amount of the interest earned must be apportioned between the two accounting periods. The basis for this apportionment is the number of days the note was held in each period.

*2b. An adjusting entry shows interest on the note earned during an accounting period*

For example, assume that on August 11, a 90-day, 10%, $7,200 note was received. The company prepares financial statements quarterly on March 31, June 30, September 30, and December 31. The following adjusting entry is needed on September 30 to show the interest earned for the fifty days the note was held during the accounting period ended September 30 and to establish an asset for the amount of the interest receivable at the end of that period:

| | | | |
|---|---|---|---|
| Sept. 30 | Interest Receivable.................................. | 100 | |
| | Interest Revenue.............................. | | 100 |
| | To record the interest earned while holding a 90-day, 10%, $7,200 note for 50 days [$7,200 × (10/100) × (50/360) = $100] | | |

*2b. An entry is made to record collection of a note in a subsequent period*

Assume that forty days later on November 9 (the note's maturity date), the note plus interest is collected. The entry to record the collection (assuming no reversing entry was made on October 1) is as follows:

| | | | |
|---|---|---|---|
| Nov. 9 | Cash............................................... | 7,380 | |
| | Notes Receivable.............................. | | 7,200 |
| | Interest Receivable............................. | | 100 |
| | Interest Revenue.............................. | | 80 |
| | Collected 90-day, 10% customer's note | | |

The interest earned was properly apportioned to each accounting period. The note was held for *fifty days* (August 11 to September 30) in the *first accounting period*, and the $100 of interest earned during that period was properly recognized in that period. The note was held for *forty days* (October 1 to November 9) in the *second accounting period*. The $80 of interest earned during that period [$7,200 × (10/100) × (40/360) = $80] was properly recognized, as shown by the $80 credit to the Interest Revenue account in the entry above.

## Recording a Dishonored Note

*2b. An entry is made to record a dishonored note*

If the maker of a note **defaults**—that is, fails to pay the obligation on its maturity date—the note is said to be **dishonored.** If this happens, the holder should make an entry to transfer the amount due from the Notes Receivable to the Accounts Receivable account. This shows that the maker of the note is still obligated to pay it and that the payee on the note intends to seek collection. To illustrate the recording of a dishonored note, assume that a ninety-day, 8% note receivable for $5,000 is dishonored at maturity by its maker, L. Newmark. The following entry would be made:

| | | | |
|---|---|---|---|
| Nov. 15 | Accounts Receivable, L. Newmark...................... | 5,100 | |
| | Notes Receivable............................. | | 5,000 |
| | Interest Revenue............................. | | 100 |
| | To record dishonored note of L. Newmark with interest at 8% for 90 days | | |

The entry removes the note from the Notes Receivable account and establishes L. Newmark as an account receivable. Note that the interest on the note is included in the account receivable and is recognized as earned in the current period even though it was not collected. This is because L. Newmark, the maker of the note, is legally obligated to pay the amount due on the note at its maturity date, which consists of its maturity value (principal plus interest).

Transferring dishonored notes receivable from the Notes Receivable account to the Accounts Receivable account serves two purposes:

1. The Notes Receivable account includes only those notes not yet matured and assumed to be collectible.
2. The creditor's (L. Newmark's) subsidiary account supporting the Accounts Receivable control account will show that it was created as a result of a dishonored note receivable. This information is useful in deciding on whether to grant future credit to this individual or organization.

## Discounting Notes Receivable

The holder of a note receivable can, by endorsing it and transferring it to a bank, convert the note into cash before its maturity date. This is referred to as **discounting** because the bank deducts its interest charge from the maturity value of the note and gives the endorser the proceeds. The amount of the proceeds paid to the endorser is the excess of the note's maturity value over the discount. The bank holds the note to maturity and then collects from the maker. If the maker defaults, the endorser is liable to the bank for payment. The endorser of a note is therefore *contingently liable* for the payment of the note. A **contingent liability** is a potential liability that will either be eliminated entirely or become an actual liability, depending on the occurrence of a future event or events. The future events in this situation are either payment by the maker, in which case no liability is assumed by the endorser, or default by the maker, in which case the contingent liability becomes an actual liability of the endorser. The endorser must then pay to the holder of the dishonored note (the bank) both the principal and the interest on the note.

Before proceeding with the accounting for discounted notes receivable, we need to understand certain terms:

1. The **discount** is the difference between the amount that the endorser receives from the bank when the note is transferred and its maturity value.
2. The **discount rate** is the interest rate charged by the bank when discounting a note receivable.
3. The **discount period** is the time period between the date on which the note is discounted with the bank and the note's maturity date.
4. **Proceeds** is the amount of cash received from the bank on the day the note receivable is transferred to the bank.

To illustrate the entries involved in discounting a note receivable, assume that on March 15 Metro Company received a $16,000, 75-day, 12% note from B. King, a customer. The entry to record the receipt of the note is as follows:

| | | | |
|---|---|---|---|
| March 15 | Notes Receivable | 16,000 | |
| | Sales | | 16,000 |
| | To record receipt of a note from B. King | | |

The note's maturity date is May 29, calculated as follows:

| | |
|---|---|
| Days remaining in March (31 minus 15) | 16 |
| Days in April | 30 |
| Days in May (number of days needed to total 75) | 29 |
| | 75 |

After holding the note for fifteen days, Metro discounted the note with its bank. The bank charges a discount rate of 15%. The amount of the discount is determined by taking the stipulated discount rate of 15% and applying it to the note's maturity value for the number of days from March 30, the discount date, to May 29, the note's maturity date. The amount of cash proceeds received by Metro is equal to the note's maturity value less the discount charged by the bank. The cash proceeds are determined as follows.

1. Determine the *maturity value* of the note. Interest is

$$\$16{,}000 \times .12 \times 75/360 = \$400$$

   Interest of \$400 plus principal of \$16,000 = maturity value of *\$16,400.*
2. Determine the *discount period* (the time period between the date the note is transferred to the bank [March 30] and the note's maturity date [May 29], or *sixty days*).
3. Compute the *discount* (the discount rate times the maturity value of the note for the discount period):

$$\$16{,}400 \times .15 \times 60/360 = \$410$$

4. Determine the *cash proceeds* (deduct the amount of the discount from the maturity value of the note):

$$\$16{,}400 - \$410 = \$15{,}990$$

*2b. An entry is made to record the discounting of a note receivable*

Metro's entry to record the discounting of the B. King note on March 30 would be as follows:

| | | | |
|---|---|---|---|
| March 30 | Cash | 15,990 | |
| | Interest Expense | 10 | |
| | Notes Receivable | | 16,000 |
| | To record discounting B. King's 12%, 75-day note with 60 days left at 15% | | |

In this example, the cash proceeds that were received when the note was discounted were less than the face amount of the note. The difference was debited to the Interest Expense account. The cash proceeds could be more than the face amount of the note, depending on the interest rates charged by the bank and the period of time between discounting and maturity date. For example, assume that Metro received cash proceeds of \$16,010 instead of \$15,990. The entry to record discounting of the B. King note would have been as follows:

| | | | |
|---|---|---|---|
| March 30 | Cash | 16,010 | |
| | Interest Revenue | | 10 |
| | Notes Receivable | | 16,000 |
| | To record discounting B. King's note | | |

*2b. The entry for discounted notes receivable contains either interest expense or interest revenue*

Thus the difference between the face amount of a discounted note and the proceeds from a discounted note is either interest expense or interest revenue as follows:

> If the cash proceeds are *less* than the face amount of the note, the difference is *interest expense.*
>
> If the cash proceeds are *greater* than the face amount of the note, the difference is *interest revenue.*

When a discounted note receivable matures, it is either paid by the maker or dishonored. If the maker pays the bank as agreed, no entries are required by the endorser. The payment relieves the endorser of his or her contingent liability. If the maker does not pay the note, the bank will notify the endorser that the note has been dishonored and will hold the endorser responsible for payment.

If B. King dishonored the note used in our previous example, the bank would require Metro Company to pay the note's maturity value plus a protest fee. **A protest fee** is a charge made by a bank for the effort and cost of notifying the endorser about the maker's default. This fee is generally added to the amount owed by the maker to the endorser as an account receivable when the endorser records the payment of the dishonored note.

*2b. An entry is made to record payment of a dishonored discounted note receivable plus protest fee*

For example, if the B. King note was dishonored and the bank charged a protest fee of $15, Metro Company would make the following entry on May 29 when it paid the bank the note's maturity value plus the protest fee:

| | | |
|---|---|---|
| Accounts Receivable, B. King | 16,415 | |
| Cash | | 16,415 |
| To record payment of the maturity value of discounted note dishonored by the maker, B. King, plus a protest fee of $15 | | |

The entry shows that B. King has an obligation to Metro Company for the maturity value of the note and for reimbursement of the protest fees paid. Metro Company classifies the receivable account as it would any other accounts receivable and makes every effort to collect the full amount from B. King.

## Disclosure of Discounted Notes Receivable

As stated previously, the endorser is contingently liable for all notes receivable discounted. On the balance sheet date, contingent liabilities are potential rather than actual liabilities. For this reason, they are not included in the liability section of the balance sheet. However, the following **full-disclosure principle** is applicable.

**Full-Disclosure Principle**

Financial statements and their accompanying notes must reveal (disclose) fully and completely all relevant data of a material nature pertaining to the financial position and operating results of the company for which the statements were prepared.

For example, a company could be contingently liable for pending lawsuits or additional tax assessments. Contingent liabilities may adversely affect the financial position of the company if future events cause them to become actual liabilities. Therefore they need to be disclosed. Disclosure is normally made in notes that accompany financial statements. The contingent liability caused by discounting notes receivable could be disclosed in a note that reads as follows:

Note 5: Contingencies:
At year-end the company was contingently liable for notes receivable discounted having an aggregate maturity value of $88,000.

## ACCOUNTS RECEIVABLE

Buying and selling on credit terms has become a standard business practice. Consequently, most sales of goods and services are now made on ten- to sixty-day terms. The asset that arises from a credit sale transaction is called an *account receivable*. As we saw in Chapter 5, the following entry would record the sale of merchandise on credit:

| | | |
|---|---|---|
| Accounts Receivable—J. Lott | 2,000 | |
| Sales | | 2,000 |
| To record a sale of merchandise on credit | | |

When the customer pays the amount due (assuming no sales discount), the transaction is recorded as follows:

| | | |
|---|---|---|
| Cash | 2,000 | |
| Accounts Receivable—J. Lott | | 2,000 |
| To record collection of an account receivable | | |

If special journals were used, these entries would be recorded in the sales journal and cash receipts journal, respectively.

*1b. Companies encourage credit sales to enhance net income*

Companies encourage credit sales because they are convenient and because companies believe that credit extension increases both sales and net income. Of course, no company would knowingly sell merchandise on credit to customers who at a later date would be unable or unwilling to pay. Historically, however, these sales sometimes take place. In an attempt to minimize the number and the dollar amount of credit sales that later prove to be uncollectible, many companies have established credit departments. These departments have the responsibility for determining the debt-paying ability of prospective customers.

Investigation of the credit worthiness of a prospective customer is a primary control procedure for minimizing credit losses. These investigations generally include an examination and analysis of the prospective customer's financial status. As part of the investigation, credit reports may be obtained from local or national credit bureaus. Dun & Bradstreet is one of the better-known credit-rating agencies. It, like others, accumulates, publishes, and sells credit information about businesses and individuals. On the basis of the information obtained, the credit department decides whether to approve or disapprove a credit sale to a particular customer.

*1b. Despite the care taken in extending credit, some accounts will be uncollectible, resulting in losses*

Regardless of the care taken to minimize the risk of extending credit, the company can still expect that some credit sales will be made to customers who will not pay. Inevitably, companies that sell on credit must be prepared to absorb the losses that arise from their uncollectible accounts. A company is said to have an effective credit-granting policy when it achieves an acceptable relationship between the losses on its uncollectible accounts and the potential income that can be derived from the revenue of credit sales.

## ACCOUNTING FOR UNCOLLECTIBLE ACCOUNTS

When it has been determined that a particular customer's account is uncollectible, the company incurs a loss. Losses from the failure to collect receivables are recognized as operating expenses and are given descriptive titles such as **uncollectible accounts expense, loss from uncollectible accounts,** or **bad debts expense.** Since there is no general rule used to determine when a particular account becomes uncollectible, two methods of accounting for uncollectible accounts have emerged: the *direct write-off method* and the *allowance method.*

### The Direct Write-Off Method

*2c. Under the direct write-off method, loss on an uncollectible account is recorded as an expense in the period when uncollectibility is recognized*

Under the **direct write-off method,** the loss from an uncollectible account is recorded as an expense during the period in which it is deemed to be uncollectible. For example, assume that a company with a calendar year-end had a $250 sale of merchandise on credit to Knox Co. and billed it on December 5. Assume further that several unsuccessful attempts are made to collect the amount due. By May 15 the company decides to write off the account as a loss. The journal entry to record the loss under the direct write-off method would be:

| | | | |
|---|---|---|---|
| May 15 | Uncollectible Accounts Expense . . . . . . . . . . . . . . . . . . . . . . . . . . | 250 | |
| | Acounts Receivable—Knox Co. . . . . . . . . . . . . . . . . . . . . . . | | 250 |
| | To write off the uncollectible account of Knox Co. | | |

This entry charges the loss from the uncollectible account as an expense of the current year, thereby reducing the current year's net income. The entry also reduces by $250 the accounts receivable appearing as an asset in the current year's balance sheet and eliminates the balance in the Knox Co. subsidiary ledger account.

Accounting for uncollectible account losses is simple under the direct write-off method. But the method violates the *matching principle* because uncollectible account losses are not *matched* with related sales.

You will recall from an earlier discussion that under the matching principle, net income is determined by matching expenses incurred in generating revenue with the revenue earned.

In the example used above, the revenue from the sale to Knox Co. is reported in last year's income statement, but the uncollectible account loss is reported in the current year's income statement. Thus expenses for last year were *understated,* causing last year's income to be *overstated.* Conversely, the expenses of the current year are *overstated,* causing the current year's net income to be *understated.*

Because the direct write-off method mismatches revenues and expenses, it is not the preferred way to account for losses from uncollectible accounts. In fact, its use can only be justified for companies that sell most of their goods or services on a cash basis but little on a credit basis. Therefore uncollectible account losses have no significant effect on their reported net income.

### The Allowance Method

The allowance method of accounting for uncollectible accounts does adhere to the matching principle. When the **allowance method** is used, the estimated losses arising from uncollectible accounts are recorded as expenses in the period in which the sales occurred.

*2c. Under the allowance method, estimated loss on uncollectible accounts is recorded by an adjusting entry*

Under the allowance method, losses from uncollectible accounts must be *estimated* at the end of each accounting period. The amount of the estimate becomes the *uncollectible accounts expense* for the period and is recorded by an adjusting entry.

To illustrate, assume that at the end of its first year of operations, a company with many credit customers has accounts receivable totaling $100,000. After a careful review of its receivables, management estimates that approximately $3,000 of its receivables will eventually prove to be uncollectible. Therefore the company's uncollectible accounts expense for the first year of operations is established at $3,000. The adjusting entry made on December 31, the end of the company's fiscal year, is as follows:

| | | | |
|---|---|---|---|
| Dec. 31 | Uncollectible Accounts Expense. . . . . . . . . . . . . . . . . . . . . . . . | 3,000 | |
| | Allowance for Uncollectible Accounts . . . . . . . . . . . . . . | | 3,000 |
| | To record the estimated uncollectible accounts expense | | |

Two things should be noted about the year-end adjusting entry. First, by debiting the Uncollectible Accounts Expense for $3,000, that amount will appear on the company's income statement and be deducted from the sales of that year. As a result, the estimated losses of selling on credit are *matched* with the sales revenue that selling on credit helped to generate.

Second, the estimated losses are credited to a new account called the *Allowance for Uncollectible Accounts* rather than being credited directly to the Accounts Receivable control account. An allowance account is credited because at the time the adjusting entry is made, it is not possible to identify which specific customers' accounts will prove to be uncollectible. Therefore none can be removed from the accounts receivable subsidiary ledger which supports the balance in the Accounts Receivable control account. If the Accounts Receivable account was credited in the adjusting entry but no customers' accounts were removed from the subsidiary ledger, there would be an imbalance between the Accounts Receivable control account and the accounts receivable subsidiary ledger.

The **Allowance for Uncollectible Accounts** is a contra account that is subtracted from Accounts Receivable in the current asset section of the balance sheet, as shown in Exhibit 8 – 2.

EXHIBIT 8 – 2

Partial Balance Sheet Showing Presentation of the Allowance for Uncollectible Accounts Account

| | | |
|---|---|---|
| Current Assets: | | |
| Cash | | $ 15,000 |
| Accounts Receivable | $100,000 | |
| Less: Allowance for Uncollectible Accounts | 3,000 | 97,000 |
| Merchandise Inventory | | 88,000 |
| Prepaid Expenses | | 5,000 |
| Total Current Assets | | $205,000 |

Uncollectible account losses result from making credit sales to customers who do not pay. Thus it can be argued that a loss from an uncollectible account is incurred at the moment such a sale is made. However, a company will not know until some time after the sale whether the customer's account is uncollectible. Therefore the amount of such losses must be estimated in advance.

Under the allowance method, the uncollectible accounts expense is estimated and matched against the sales revenue of the same period. The allowance method is considered the preferable way to account for losses from uncollectible accounts because it offers two major advantages:

1. In the income statement the estimated loss from uncollectible receivables is charged to the *same* period in which the revenue from credit sales was recorded.
2. The balance sheet shows the amount expected to be *realized* from the collection of the accounts receivable.

In the following sections we look at some methods commonly used to estimate the uncollectible account losses arising from credit sales.

## ESTIMATING UNCOLLECTIBLE ACCOUNTS EXPENSE

The estimate of uncollectible accounts expense is generally based on a company's past experience modified by forecasts concerning its future credit sales activity, anticipated changes in its credit-granting policies, and general economic conditions.

Assume, for example, that during the past several years a company has experienced uncollectible account losses equal to 2% of its sales. This percentage may have to be changed if the company develops some new internal credit strategy or if external forces, such as economic conditions, have changed. During periods of economic expansion and near full employment, the risk of loss for uncollectible accounts will probably be reduced. Therefore the percentage used to estimate the loss can be lowered. Conversely, in periods of widespread unemployment and economic contraction, granting credit is more risky and the percentage used in the past to estimate the loss may have to be raised.

Estimates can vary. If a low estimate of loss is made, the uncollectible accounts expense may be *understated*, causing reported net income to be *overstated*. Low loss estimates will also cause the net amount shown for accounts receivable in the balance sheet to be *overstated*. If the loss estimate is high, the uncollectible accounts expense may be *overstated*, causing net income and net accounts receivable to be *understated*.

Because in anticipating losses we are dealing with estimates, not certainty, problems can result. Nevertheless, to implement the matching concept, these estimates must be made. Accountants have found ways to make their estimates reliable and realistic.

Two methods are widely used to estimate the uncollectible accounts expense. One estimate is based on a percentage of sales or preferably net credit sales. The other estimate is based on a percentage of the accounts receivable. Both are described in the following sections.

### Estimate Based on Net Credit Sales

***1b,2d. Estimates of uncollectible accounts expenses can be based on net credit sales (the income statement approach)***

Drawing upon past experience, it is usually possible to establish a historical relationship between the amount of credit sales and the amount of uncollectible accounts incurred. Credit sales should be used because uncollectible accounts expenses do not result from cash sales. Likewise, using net credit sales (credit sales after deducting sales returns and allowances and sales discounts) is preferable to using gross credit sales. Once a relationship between net credit sales and uncollectible accounts has been established, it is used to calculate the amount for uncollectible accounts expense in the year-end adjusting entry.

To illustrate, assume that a company had net credit sales of $500,000 for the year 19X5. Its past experience indicates that generally 1% of its net credit sales prove uncollectible. The estimated uncollectible accounts expense for the year 19X5 would be $5,000 calculated as follows:

$$1\% \times \$500,000 = \$5,000$$

The adjusting entry to record the uncollectible accounts expense would be:

| | | | |
|---|---|---|---|
| Dec. 31 | Uncollectible Accounts Expense. . . . . . . . . . . . . . . . . . . . . . . . | 5,000 | |
| | Allowance for Uncollectible Accounts . . . . . . . . . . . . . . . | | 5,000 |
| | To record uncollectible accounts expense | | |

This method of estimating uncollectible accounts expense is often referred to as the **income statement approach** (or ***net credit sales method***) because by using net credit sales as a base, it emphasizes matching current revenues with the expenses incurred in generating those revenues. This approach establishes an amount that represents how much of this year's net credit sales *will not* be collected. That amount is debited to Uncollectible Accounts Expense at year-end.

The estimated loss from uncollectible accounts will then appear in the income statement for the year in which the sales were made. As a result, the estimated uncollectible accounts expense of $5,000 for the period used in our example is matched against the $500,000 of sales revenue earned during that period. As mentioned earlier, the percentage can be based on either a percentage of sales or a percentage of net credit sales. The important thing is to remain relatively consistent over time when attempting to establish a relationship between sales and uncollectible accounts.

The net credit sales method is widely used because it is simple and because it allows the uncollectible accounts expense to be matched against the sales revenue of the same period. When this method is used, however, the amount shown for accounts receivable in the balance sheet may not reflect the amount expected to be realized from their collection. Since estimates based on net credit sales emphasize the debit amount in the adjusting entry, the credit portion of the entry, posted to a permanent account which is not closed at the end of each year, could over time produce an unreasonable balance in the allowance account. Thus, when the income statement approach for estimating uncollectible accounts is used, the balance in the allowance account must be monitored for reasonableness. If it becomes too large or too small, it may be appropriate to revise the percentage figure applied to net sales.

### Estimate Based on Accounts Receivable

*1b,2d. Estimates of uncollectible accounts expenses can be based on a percentage of accounts receivable (the balance sheet approach)*

When the uncollectible accounts expense is estimated on the basis of accounts receivable, we are emphasizing a proper valuation in the balance sheet. The procedure involves determining a historical rate which when applied against the outstanding accounts receivable will provide the balance needed in Allowance for Uncollectible Accounts. Thus the approach focuses on reporting accounts receivable at net realizable value—the amount expected to be realized from their collection. It estimates how much of the year-end balance in the accounts receivable will not be collected. This amount represents the desired balance for the Allowance for Uncollectible Accounts account at year-end. The difference between this amount and the actual balance of the allowance account is the uncollectible accounts expense for the year.

To illustrate, assume that a company has determined that its uncollectible accounts normally amount to 3% of the year-end accounts receivable balance. At the end of the year, the company has accounts receivable of $70,000. Thus the company expects that $2,100 ($70,000 × 3%) of its accounts receivable will not be collected. The $2,100 also represents the desired balance in the Allowance for Uncollectible Accounts account. However, before the amount of the year-end adjusting entry can be determined, any existing balance in the allowance account must be considered. For example, if the Allowance for Uncollectible Accounts account currently shows a credit balance of $300 (balance before the adjustment), the amount by which it must be increased is $1,800. This is also the amount of the uncollectible account expense, as shown in the calculation below.

| | |
|---|---|
| Credit balance needed in the allowance account | $2,100 |
| Less: Existing credit balance in the allowance account | 300 |
| Amount by which the allowance account must be increased and the estimated uncollectible accounts expense | $1,800 |

The adjusting entry that increases the allowance account balance and recognizes the uncollectible accounts expense follows:

| | | | |
|---|---|---|---|
| Dec. 31 | Uncollectible Accounts Expense | 1,800 | |
| | Allowance for Uncollectible Accounts | | 1,800 |
| | To record the uncollectible accounts expense | | |

This method of estimating the uncollectible accounts expense is often referred to as the **balance sheet approach.** This approach establishes the balance needed in the allowance account in order to report accounts receivable at net realizable value (the amount expected to be realized from collection). The amount needed to create that balance in the allowance account is debited to the Uncollectible Accounts Expense account at year-end.

*1b,2d. The amount needed in the allowance account can be determined by the aging of accounts receivable*

AGING THE ACCOUNTS RECEIVABLE TO ESTABLISH THE BALANCE IN THE ALLOWANCE FOR UNCOLLECTIBLE ACCOUNTS Instead of establishing a percentage appropriate for the aggregate accounts receivable, some companies determine the amount needed in the allowance account by a procedure of **aging accounts receivable.** Aging accounts receivable involves reviewing each receivable balance and categorizing it according to the number of days it has been outstanding. The age categories may vary, but they often adhere to a pattern similar to the following:

*Current*
*1–30 days* past due
*31–60 days* past due
*61–90 days* past due
*91–120 days* past due
*Over 120 days* past due

After the amount of the receivables in each age category has been totaled, the totals are multiplied by an appropriate uncollectible accounts percentage developed from past experience. Different percentages are applied to different age category totals. The category totals are then summed to determine the balance needed in the Allowance for Uncollectible Accounts account.

Exhibit 8 – 3 illustrates the application of the aging procedure. Assume that the schedule was prepared for a company that sells merchandise on credit terms of net 30, and that the year-end balance in its Accounts Receivable account is $70,000.

*EXHIBIT 8–3*

Schedule of Customers' Accounts Receivable by Age

CUSTOMERS' ACCOUNTS RECEIVABLE

December 31, 19X5

| | | | NUMBER OF DAYS PAST DUE | | | | |
|---|---|---|---|---|---|---|---|
| CUSTOMER | ACCOUNT BALANCE | CURRENT | 1–30 | 31–60 | 61–90 | 91–120 | Over 120 |
| Abbate, J. | $ 600 | $ 600 | | | | | |
| Andersen, A. | 520 | | $ 520 | | | | |
| Benson, R. | 280 | | | $ 280 | | | |
| Brady, C. | 510 | 510 | | | | | |
| Buxton, A. | 330 | | | | | $ 330 | |
| Carroll, L. | 820 | 820 | | | | | |
| Clark, G. | 410 | | | | $ 410 | | |
| Crawford, M. | 870 | | 870 | | | | |
| Others listed alphabetically | 65,270 | 40,680 | 18,610 | 3,720 | 590 | 1,070 | $600 |
| Zega, B. | 390 | 390 | | | | | |
| Totals | $70,000 | $43,000 | $20,000 | $4,000 | $1,000 | $1,400 | $600 |

Note that the accounts are listed alphabetically. J. Abbate, the first account listed, shows a balance of $600. The amount is extended to the Current column, signifying that the customer has been billed within the last thirty days. A. Andersen's account of $520 is extended to the 1 – 30 Days Past Due column, signifying that the account is from thirty-one to sixty days old. R. Benson's account of $280 is extended to the 31 – 60 Days Past Due column, signifying that the account is from sixty-one to ninety days old, and so on.

The aging of accounts receivable is useful to management in evaluating its credit-granting policies and in monitoring collections. Aging identifies those customers whose accounts are delinquent and provides one of the better ways to estimate the company's credit losses. Generally, the older the uncollected account, the more difficult the collection.

The schedule in Exhibit 8 – 4 is used to determine the credit balance needed in the Allowance for Uncollectible Accounts. To make this determination, appropriate uncollectible rates based on past experience must be developed and applied to the six age categories. These totals are then added to determine the balance needed in the allowance account. In examining the schedule in Exhibit 8-4, note that

1. Only *1%* of the current accounts and *3%* of the accounts 1 – 30 days past due are estimated to be uncollectible
2. For the accounts 31 – 60 days, 61 – 90 days, 91 – 120 days, and over 120 days past due, *5%, 20%, 30%,* and *50%* are used, respectively

By applying those percentages to the appropriate column totals, we determine that the Allowance for Uncollectible Accounts account should have a credit balance of $2,150, calculated as shown in Exhibit 8–4.

EXHIBIT 8–4
Calculation to Estimate Losses from Uncollectible Accounts

| AGE CATEGORY | AMOUNT | PERCENTAGE ESTIMATED TO BE UNCOLLECTIBLE | REQUIRED BALANCE IN THE ALLOWANCE ACCOUNT |
|---|---|---|---|
| Current | $43,000 | 1% | $ 430 |
| 1–30 days past due | 20,000 | 3 | 600 |
| 31–60 days past due | 4,000 | 5 | 200 |
| 61–90 days past due | 1,000 | 20 | 200 |
| 91–120 days past due | 1,400 | 30 | 420 |
| Over 120 days past due | 600 | 50 | 300 |
| | $70,000 | | $2,150 |

Before the adjusting entry is made, it is necessary to consider the existing balance, if any, in the allowance account. Assume that the current credit balance in the allowance account is $300. The adjustment will be for $1,850, the amount needed to bring the account up to its required balance of $2,150.

The adjusting entry would be as follows:

| | | | |
|---|---|---|---|
| Dec. 31 | Uncollectible Accounts Expense | 1,850 | |
| | Allowance for Uncollectible Accounts | | 1,850 |
| | To record uncollectible accounts expense | | |

If, on the other hand, the allowance account had a debit balance of $200 prior to adjustment, the adjusting entry would be for *$2,350* ($200 + $2,150). As you can see, when the existing balance in the allowance account is a debit, that amount is added to the amount needed in the allowance account to derive the uncollectible accounts expense (which in this case was $2,350).

## WRITING OFF AN UNCOLLECTIBLE ACCOUNT

*2e. An entry is made to write off an uncollectible account to the Allowance for Uncollectible Accounts*

When a specific customer's account is deemed to be uncollectible, it should be written off against Allowance for Uncollectible Accounts by debiting the allowance account and crediting Accounts Receivable. For example, assume that an account receivable from R. Winslow in the amount of $290 has been deemed to be uncollectible. The entry to write off this account is as follows:

| | | | |
|---|---|---|---|
| Jan. 3 | Allowance for Uncollectible Accounts | 290 | |
| | Accounts Receivable, R. Winslow | | 290 |
| | To write off an uncollectible account | | |

The credit in the above entry is posted to both the Accounts Receivable control account in the general ledger and the R. Winslow account in the accounts receivable subsidiary ledger. Thus arithmetical agreement between the two ledgers is maintained.

Because the write-off entry affects two balance sheet accounts, it has no effect on net income. The appropriate expense effect on the net income was recognized in the preceding period by an adjusting entry. Thus the expense was recognized on an estimated basis at the end of the period in which the sale was recorded. Furthermore, the net amount of accounts receivable reported in the balance sheet is unchanged because individual accounts are written off against Allowance for Uncollectible Accounts, which is a contra account to Accounts Receivable.

To illustrate, assume that the Winslow account was written off on January 3 of the current year. The write-off entry would be posted to two balance sheet accounts as follows:

ACCOUNTS RECEIVABLE (CONTROL ACCOUNT)

| | | | DEBIT | CREDIT | BALANCE |
|---|---|---|---|---|---|
| Jan. | 1 | Balance | | | 70 000 |
| | 3 | | | 290 | 69 710 |

ALLOWANCE FOR UNCOLLECTIBLE ACCOUNTS

| | | | DEBIT | CREDIT | BALANCE |
|---|---|---|---|---|---|
| Jan. | 1 | Balance | | | 2 150 |
| | 3 | | 290 | | 1 860 |

The net amount expected to be collected from accounts receivable remains $67,850 both before and after the write-off entry, as calculated below:

| | BEFORE WRITE-OFF ENTRY | AFTER WRITE-OFF ENTRY |
|---|---|---|
| Accounts Receivable | $70,000 | $69,710 |
| Less: Allowance for Uncollectible Accounts | 2,150 | 1,860 |
| Net Amount Expected to Be Realized from Collection of Accounts Receivable | $67,850 | $67,850 |

## DIFFERENCES BETWEEN ESTIMATES AND ACTUAL WRITE-OFFS

The total amounts written off against the allowance account during the period will seldom if ever be equal to the balance that exists in the allowance account at the beginning of that period. If the total amount of the accounts written off during the period is *less* than the beginning balance in the allowance account, the account will have a *credit* balance at the end of the period before adjustment. Conversely, if the total amount of the accounts written off during the period *exceeds* the beginning balance in the allowance account, the account will have a *debit* balance at the end of the period before adjustment.

As long as the allowance for uncollectible accounts, before adjustment, has a relatively small debit or credit balance, no problem exists. However, if the before-adjustment debit or credit balances are large, previous estimates of uncollectible accounts were either insufficient or excessive. Prior years' financial statements may have been significantly misstated, and the company may need to change its estimates. Detailed illustrations of how to change these estimates are left to an advanced course.

## RECOVERY OF ACCOUNTS WRITTEN OFF

Sometimes after a company writes off one of its accounts receivable, the customer unexpectedly pays the amount in full or in part. When this recovery occurs, two entries should be made:

1. The *first* entry reverses the effect of the original entry that wrote off the account. Its purpose is to reinstate the customer's account so that it can be treated as a valid receivable.
2. The *second* entry records the cash collection from the customer.

*2f. Two entries are made to record recovery of an account previously written off*

For example, assume that a company collected $500 cash from D. Canon, a customer whose account was previously written off as uncollectible. The journal entries to reinstate the account and to record the cash collections are as follows (assuming that the allowance method of accounting for uncollectibles was used):

| | | | |
|---|---|---|---|
| March 1 | Accounts Receivable, D. Canon | 500 | |
| | Allowance for Uncollectible Accounts | | 500 |
| | To record reinstatement of D. Canon's account | | |
| March 1 | Cash | 500 | |
| | Accounts Receivable, D. Canon | | 500 |
| | To record collection of an account receivable | | |

By using two entries, the customer's account in the accounts receivable subsidiary ledger shows that after being written off, the account was subsequently collected. This information is important both to the company in determining whether to offer credit to this customer in the future, and to the customer whose credit standing may otherwise be impaired.

If the company had initially used the *direct write-off* method rather than the allowance method to write off the D. Canon account, the subsequent recovery would have been recorded as follows:

| | | | |
|---|---|---|---|
| March 1 | Accounts Receivable, D. Canon | 500 | |
| | Uncollectible Accounts Expense | | 500 |
| | To record reinstatement of D. Canon's account | | |
| March 1 | Cash | 500 | |
| | Accounts Receivable, D. Canon | | 500 |
| | To record collection of an account receivable | | |

## CREDIT BALANCES IN ACCOUNTS RECEIVABLE

Sometimes a customer's account in the accounts receivable subsidiary ledger has a credit balance. This occurs because customers sometimes overpay their accounts or return for credit merchandise previously paid for. When one or more customers' accounts have credit balances, the appropriate amount to show for accounts receivable is *the total of the customers' accounts with debit balances.* The total of the customers' accounts with credit balances should be shown as *a current liability*.

*2g. The total of credit balances in accounts receivable is shown as a current liability*

For example, assume that the balances in the Accounts Receivable control account are as follows:

| | |
|---|---|
| 120 accounts with debit balances totaling | $150,000 |
| 2 accounts with credit balances totaling | 2,600 |
| Net debit balance of the accounts receivable subsidiary ledger | $147,400 |

The customers' accounts with credit balances represent current liabilities. The balance sheet presentation should be as follows:

| | | | |
|---|---|---|---|
| Current Assets: | | Current Liabilities: | |
| Accounts Receivable | $150,000 | Credit Balances in Customers' Accounts | $2,600 |
| Less: Allowance for Uncollectible Accounts | X | | |

This procedure is in accordance with generally accepted accounting principles. Financial statement assets and liabilities should be shown at their gross amounts rather than being netted against each other.

## CREDIT CARD SALES

Cards issued by banks and companies which the holder can use to purchase goods and services on credit are called **credit cards.** Many retail businesses sell merchandise and services to customers who use credit cards to pay for their purchases. Some of the more widely used credit cards are American Express, Diners Club, MasterCard, and Visa.

When a credit card sale is made, the seller requires the purchaser to sign a form (invoice) showing the details of the sale, including the amount. The customer using the credit card is responsible for paying the company or bank that issued the card the full amount of the purchase. The seller then uses the signed form as a basis for receiving cash from the company or bank that issued the card. By allowing credit card sales, the seller obtains certain advantages that it would not achieve by limiting itself to cash sales and/or sales where it establishes the credit policies. For example, the company

*1c. Sellers gain several advantages from credit card sales*

1. Avoids *losses* resulting from uncollectible accounts
2. Collects cash (from the bank or credit card company) more *quickly* than it would from the customer using thirty-day credit
3. Avoids the *effort* and *expense* involved in credit investigation
4. Does not have to maintain an accounts receivable *ledger*
5. Eliminates the *costs* and *problems* involved in collecting from customers

The disadvantage is that banks and credit card companies charge a fee for their services. Because of this fee, the bank or credit card company does not pay

*1c. On their credit card sales, sellers pay a charge known as a discount*

the seller 100% of the credit card sale. The charge, known as a discount, is generally between 2% and 7% of the sale and is deducted directly from the credit card invoices when making payment.

To illustrate the journal entries needed when recording credit card sales, we must differentiate between bank credit card sales and other types of credit card sales.

## Bank Credit Card Sales

If a customer pays for a purchase by using a bank credit card, such as MasterCard or Visa, the seller may deposit the signed credit card form directly in its bank. The form is treated like the checks and cash received from others. The company making credit card sales can immediately record those sales as cash sales.

For example, assume that on a given day Martin Company made sales of $5,000 to customers who used one of the popular bank credit cards. Assume also that the signed credit card forms may be deposited in Martin's bank account in the same way as checks and currency. The journal entry to record the credit card sales, assuming the bank has a 5% discount charge, would be as follows:

*2h. An entry is made to record bank credit card sales*

| | | |
|---|---|---|
| Cash | 4,750 | |
| Credit Card Discount Expense | 250 | |
| Sales | | 5,000 |
| To record sales to customers who used bank credit cards | | |

## Other Credit Card Sales

Assume that a customer pays for a purchase using a company-issued credit card such as American Express or Diners Club. The form signed by the credit card holder does not represent a cash equivalent and therefore cannot be deposited directly in a bank. The signed form represents an accounts receivable from the credit card company and must be accounted for accordingly. For example, assume that at the end of a given day, Martin Company had sales of $5,000 to customers who paid with the American Express credit card. The journal entry to record these sales would be as follows:

*2h. An entry is made to record a company-issued credit card sale*

| | | |
|---|---|---|
| Accounts Receivable, American Express | 5,000 | |
| Sales | | 5,000 |
| To record sales to customers who used the American Express credit card | | |

Martin Company would mail the signed credit card forms to American Express, which pays them, less a discount (assumed to be 5%). When the cash, representing 95% of the face amount of the signed credit card forms, is received, Martin Company makes the following journal entry:

*2h. Another entry is made to record collection of cash from the credit card company*

| | | |
|---|---|---|
| Cash | 4,750 | |
| Credit Card Discount Expense | 250 | |
| Accounts Receivable, American Express | | 5,000 |
| To record the collection of accounts receivable from American Express less a 5% discount | | |

## HIGHLIGHT PROBLEM

PART I The following transactions are those of Winslow Landscaping Company.

**a.** On March 15 Winslow Landscaping received from F. Bates an $8,000, 90-day, 12% note dated today in settlement of an existing account receivable.

**b.** On April 14 Winslow Landscaping discounted the Bates note with its bank, which charges a discount rate of 15%.

**c.** Bates did not pay the note at maturity. The bank took action against Winslow Landscaping, which paid the amount in full plus a protest fee of $10. The management of Winslow Landscaping is convinced that the amount can be collected from Bates.

Required:

Prepare journal entries to record the above transactions.

PART II Armstrong Advertising Company has aged its accounts receivable and estimates its losses from uncollectible accounts at $3,700. The estimate was made on December 31, 19X5, at which time the company's Allowance for Uncollectible Accounts had a credit balance of $300.

During 19X6 the following transactions occurred:

**a.** On February 2 the company wrote off the account of D. Letters in the amount of $400.

**b.** On March 9 the company wrote off the account of L. Helms in the amount of $200.

**c.** On March 16 the company unexpectedly received a check for $400 from D. Letters.

Required:

1. Prepare the adjusting entry needed at year-end to record the uncollectible accounts expense for 19X5.
2. Prepare journal entries to record the 19X6 transactions shown as *a*, *b*, and *c* above.

## GLOSSARY OF KEY TERMS

**Aging accounts receivable.** Reviewing each accounts receivable balance and categorizing it according to the number of days it has been outstanding.

**Allowance for uncollectible accounts.** A contra account that is subtracted from Accounts Receivable in the current asset section of the balance sheet.

**Allowance method.** An accounting procedure whereby the losses from uncollectible accounts are estimated in advance and recorded as an expense in the period in which the sales occurred.

**Bad debts expense.** An alternate title for *Uncollectible accounts expense.*

**Balance sheet approach.** A method for determining the uncollectible accounts expense by establishing the balance needed in the allowance account.

**Contingent liability.** A potential liability that either will be eliminated entirely or will become an actual liability, depending on the occurrence of a future event or events.

**Credit cards.** Cards issued by banks and companies which the holder can use to purchase goods and services on credit.

**Default.** To fail to pay a note at its maturity date. The word *default* can also be a noun.

**Direct write-off method.** An accounting procedure whereby the losses from uncollectible accounts are recorded as an expense in the period in which the accounts receivable were determined to be uncollectible.

**Discount.** The difference between the amount that the endorser receives from the bank when the note is transferred and its maturity value.

**Discount period (of a note).** The period of time between the date a note is discounted with a bank or other financial institution and its maturity date.

**Discount rate (of a note).** The interest rate charged by a bank or financial institution when discounting a note receivable.

**Discounting (a note receivable).** Converting a note into cash before its maturity date by endorsing it and transferring it to a bank.

**Dishonored (note).** A note that the maker has failed to pay at its maturity date.

**Full-disclosure principle.** An accounting principle requiring that the financial statements and their accompanying notes reveal (disclose) fully and completely all relevant data of a material nature pertaining to the financial position and operating results of the company for which the statements were prepared.

**Income statement approach.** A method for determining the uncollectible accounts expense by establishing the balance needed in the expense account.

**Interest.** A charge made for the use of money over time.

**Loss from uncollectible accounts.** An alternate title for *Uncollectible accounts expense.*

**Maker (of a note).** The person or entity who signs a note and promises to pay it at maturity.

**Maturity date (of a note).** The date on which the principal amount of a note together with any interest is due and payable.

**Maturity value (of a note).** The amount due on the maturity date; the note's principal plus any interest.

**Note receivable.** An unconditional written promise to pay a definite sum of money on demand or at a fixed and determinable future time.

**Payee (of a note).** The person or entity to whom payment on a note is to be made.

**Principal (of a note).** The face amount of a promissory note.

**Proceeds (of a discounted note).** The amount of cash received from a bank or other financial institution when a note receivable is discounted: the maturity value of the note minus the interest charged for discounting the note before its maturity date.

**Promissory note.** An unconditional written promise to pay a certain sum of money on demand or at a fixed and determinable future time.

**Protest fee.** A fee charged by a bank or financial institution for the effort and cost of notifying the endorser of a note that the maker has dishonored (defaulted) the note.

**Receivables.** All money claims that a business has against individuals or organizations.

**Uncollectible accounts expense.** An account showing the loss a company incurs when an account receivable becomes uncollectible. This loss is recognized as an operating expense of the business.

## REVIEW QUESTIONS

1. Name the three most common types of transactions from which receivables can arise. [LO1a]
2. Describe the four types of transactions for which notes are generally received. [LO1a]
3. Name the items of information contained in a promissory note. [LO1a]
4. Describe three ways of determining the maturity date of a promissory note. [LO2a]
5. Define *interest.* How is interest classified on the financial statements of the borrower? On the financial statements of the lender? [LO2a]
6. Give the formula for computing interest. [LO2a]
7. What types of account are debited and credited when
   a. An interest-bearing note is received for merchandise received on credit?
   b. An interest-bearing note is collected?
   c. An adjustment is made for interest on a note at the end of an accountng period? [LO2b]
8. What two purposes are served by transferring dishonored notes receivable into the Accounts Receivable account? [LO2b]
9. What happens to a contingent liability on a discounted notes receivable if the maker pays the note? If the maker defaults on the note? [LO2b]
10. Describe the four-step process of calculating the cash proceeds of a discounted note. [LO2b]
11. When the cash proceeds are less than the face amount of a discounted note, how is the difference classified in the financial statements? When the proceeds are greater? [LO2b]
12. How is a contingent liability on a discounted note receivable disclosed in the financial statements? [LO2b]
13. Why do companies generally encourage credit sales? [LO1b]

14. How are losses from uncollectible accounts classified in the financial statements? [LO1b]
15. Differentiate between the direct write-off method and the allowance method of accounting for losses from uncollectible accounts. [LO2c]
16. What type of account is Allowance for Uncollectible Accounts? [LO2c]
17. Differentiate between the income statement approach and the balance sheet approach to estimating uncollectible accounts expense. [LO2d]
18. What is meant by the term *aging the accounts receivable?* [LO2d]
19. What journal entry is made to write off an uncollectible account when the allowance method is used? [LO2e]
20. Under what conditions will the allowance account have a credit balance at the end of the period before adjustment? A debit balance? [LO2c,2e]
21. What journal entries are made to show recovery of an account written off when the allowance method is used? When the direct write-off method is used? [LO2f]
22. How are credit balances in Accounts Receivable classified in the financial statements? [LO2g]
23. What advantages does a company obtain by allowing credit card sales? [LO1c]
24. Describe the difference between accounting for bank credit card sales and accounting for other credit card sales. [LO2h]

## ANALYTICAL QUESTIONS

25. "Since Accounts Receivable and Notes Receivable both represent monetary claims against others, why separate the amounts into two accounts?" Comment on this question. [LO1a]
26. A six-month note is received on October 31, and the interest cannot be legally collected until April 30 of next year. What is the rationale for preparing an adjusting entry on December 31 (year-end) to recognize the interest earned for two months? [LO2a,2b]
27. "The direct write-off method of accounting for uncollectible accounts is superior to the allowance method because the direct write-off method uses actual rather than estimated figures." Comment on this statement. [LO2c]
28. "If a company's dollar amount of accounts receivable is small, it does not matter whether the company uses the allowance method or the direct write-off method of accounting for uncollectible accounts expense." Explain why this statement is valid or not. [LO2c]
29. Under what circumstances would the balance in Allowance for Uncollectible Accounts be zero immediately before the adjusting entry for the estimated uncollectible accounts is prepared? [LO2c,2d]
30. Under what circumstances would the Allowance for Uncollectible Accounts have a debit balance immediately before the adjusting entry for the estimated uncollectible accounts is prepared? [LO2c,2d]
31. Explain the following:
    a. Why is the balance in Allowance for Uncollectible Accounts subtracted from Accounts Receivable in the balance sheet?
    b. Why doesn't the writing off of an uncollectible account against the allowance account reduce the estimated net realizable value of the company's accounts receivable? [LO2c,2e]
32. Data contained in an aging schedule may prove useful to management for purposes other than estimating the size of the balance required in the allowance account. Explain other uses of these data. [LO2d]
33. What would cause a customer's account receivable to have a credit balance? How would the credit balance be reported in the balance sheet? [LO2g]

## IMPACT ANALYSIS QUESTIONS

*For each error described, indicate whether it would overstate [O], understate [U], or not affect [N] the specified key figures.*

34. Doit Company discounts a $7,000 note receivable having a maturity value of $7,200 at its bank and receives proceeds of $7,060. When recording the entry, the company improperly credits $7,000 to the Sales account instead of to the Notes Receivable account. [LO2b]

_______ Assets _______ Revenues
_______ Net Income _______ Owner's Equity

35. Ral Company fails to collect its 60-day, 10%, $6,000 note receivable from a customer who has declared bankruptcy. Court papers indicate that creditors can expect fifty cents on the dollar, with payment scheduled within the next four months. Ral recorded the entry by debiting Uncollectible Accounts Expense and crediting Notes Receivable for the entire amount. [LO2b]

_______ Assets _______ Revenues
_______ Net Income _______ Expenses

36. Strom Company (with a calendar year-end of December 31) has on hand an interest-bearing note receivable from one of its customers. The note is dated November 1 and matures on April 30 of the following year. Strom failed to make a year-end adjusting entry to account for two months of accrued interest. [LO2a,2b]

_______ Assets _______ Revenues
_______ Net Income _______ Expenses

37. A company that uses the direct write-off method to account for its losses from uncollectible accounts determined that one of its customer's accounts receivable was uncollectible. The company's newly hired bookkeeper was informed of the uncollectible account and made the following entry: Debited Uncollectible Accounts Expense and credited Allowance for Uncollectible Accounts. [LO2c]

_______ Assets _______ Net Income
_______ Expenses _______ Owner's equity

38. A company that had previously estimated its uncollectible account losses at 3% of its net credit sales has inappropriately increased the percentage to 3.5% when making its year-end adjusting entry. [LO2d]

_______ Assets _______ Expenses
_______ Net Income _______ Owner's Equity

39. The sum of a company's Accounts Receivable amounts owed to them is $183,000. However, its accounts receivable subsidiary ledger shows a balance of $179,600. The difference is due to three customers' accounts that currently show credit balances. When preparing financial statements, the asset Accounts Receivable was incorrectly reported in the balance sheet at an amount net of its credit balances. [LO2g]

_______ Assets _______ Owner's Equity
_______ Liabilities _______ Net Income

## EXERCISES

EXERCISE 8–1 *(Calculate Interest)* Determine the interest on the notes listed below (use a 360-day year). [LO2a]

| | FACE AMOUNT | NUMBER OF DAYS | INTEREST RATE |
|---|---|---|---|
| (a) | $1,000 | 60 | 9% |
| (b) | 3,000 | 90 | 8 |
| (c) | 500 | 75 | 10 |
| (d) | 5,400 | 60 | 6 |
| (e) | 8,240 | 40 | 7 |

EXERCISE 8-2 *(Prepare Journal Entries for Receivable Transactions)* Safeway Company had the following transactions:

| | |
|---|---|
| Jan. 7 | Sold merchandise on credit to R. Gomez, $9,000; terms n/30. |
| March 3 | Received a $9,000, 90-day, 9% note from R. Gomez, who requested an extension of time to pay for the purchase. |
| April 2 | Safeway discounted the Gomez note at its bank at 10%. |
| June 1 | Received notice that Gomez dishonored the note. Safeway paid the bank the maturity value of the note plus a protest fee of $10. |
| June 15 | Received payment in full from Gomez. |

Required:
Prepare journal entries to record the above transactions. [LO2b]

EXERCISE 8-3 *(Prepare Journal Entries for Notes Receivable and Interest)* Carter Company had a balance of $100,000 in its Accounts Receivable on October 1, 19X2. The company's fiscal year ends on December 31. During the six-month period from October 1, 19X2, to March 31, 19X3, the following transactions relating to Notes Receivable occurred:

1. On October 1, 19X2, Carter accepted a six-month, 12% note from R. Hecker in settlement of Hecker's $20,000 account receivable. Interest on the note is due on its maturity date, April 1, 19X3.
2. On December 31, 19X2, Carter made a year-end adjusting entry for the interest earned on the Hecker note.
3. On April 1, 19X3, received payment in full for the note and interest.

Required:

1. Prepare journal entries to record the above transactions.
2. Assume that the October 1, 19X2, and December 31, 19X2, transactions occurred as listed above. However, assume also that on April 1, 19X3, R. Hecker dishonored the note. Prepare the journal entry required on April 1, 19X3. [LO2b]

EXERCISE 8-4 *(Use the Direct Write-Off Method and the Allowance Method to Account for Uncollectible Accounts)* Wilson Company had the following transactions during its first year of operations:

1. Made credit sales of $100,000 during the year.
2. Collected customers' accounts totaling $95,000.
3. Wrote off customer A's account in the amount of $400.
4. Wrote off customer B's account in the amount of $700.
5. Customer A unexpectedly paid $300 on the account previously written off in item 3 above. No additional payment is expected.

Required:

1. Prepare journal entries to record the summarized transactions cited above. Assume that Wilson uses the direct write-off method of accounting for uncollectible accounts.
2. Assume that Wilson uses the allowance method instead of the direct write-off method. Also assume that Wilson estimates that 1% of its sales will prove to be uncollectible. Calculate the difference between the amount reported for Uncollectible Accounts Expense in the first year if the allowance method is used and if the direct write-off method is used. [LO2c]

EXERCISE 8-5 *(Prepare Journal Entries Using the Allowance Method of Accounting for Uncollectible Accounts)* At December 31, 19X2, the end of its second year of operations, Shortway Company provided the information (see top of page 297) pertaining to accounts and amounts:

Required:

1. Prepare a journal entry to record the estimated loss on uncollectible accounts, assuming Shortway estimates that 1% of its net sales will prove to be uncollectible.

| | |
|---|---|
| Accounts Receivable | $100,000 |
| Net Sales | 500,000 |
| Allowance for Uncollectible Accounts (credit balance) | 350 |

2. Prepare a journal entry to record the estimated loss on uncollectible accounts, assuming the company estimates that 5% of outstanding accounts receivable rather than 1% of its net sales will prove to be uncollectible. [LO2c,2d]

EXERCISE 8-6 *(Estimate the Uncollectible Accounts from an Aging Schedule)* At the end of the year, the accounts receivable of Bluff Company totaling $50,000 were aged and categorized as follows:

| AGE CATEGORY | AMOUNT | PERCENTAGE ESTIMATED TO BE UNCOLLECTIBLE |
|---|---|---|
| Current | $28,000 | 1% |
| 1-30 days past due | 7,500 | 2 |
| 31-60 days past due | 5,500 | 3 |
| 61-90 days past due | 6,500 | 5 |
| Over 90 days past due | 2,500 | 10 |
| | $50,000 | |

Before the entry to record the estimated uncollectible accounts expense was prepared, the Allowance for Uncollectible Accounts account had a credit balance of $200.

Required:

1. Calculate the amount of accounts receivable estimated to be uncollectible.
2. Prepare the journal entry to record the estimated uncollectible accounts expense for the year.
3. Determine the amount that should be shown as the net realizable value of the accounts receivable on the year-end balance sheet. [LO2c,2d]

EXERCISE 8-7 *(Prepare Journal Entries Using the Allowance Method of Accounting for Uncollectible Accounts)* At the end of its fiscal year, selected accounts in the ledger of the Hartwell Corporation reveal the following information:

| | |
|---|---|
| Accounts receivable are | $ 80,000 |
| Net credit sales were | 960,000 |

Required:

Determine the expense expected to arise from uncollectible accounts under the assumptions indicated below, and prepare the journal entry to record the uncollectible accounts expense under each assumption.

1. The uncollectible accounts expense is estimated at 1% of the company's net credit sales, and
   a. The allowance account before adjustment has a credit balance of $400
   b. The allowance account before adjustment has a debit balance of $300
2. An aging and an analysis of each account in the accounts receivable subsidiary ledger indicates that the allowance account should have a balance of $6,900 after the year-end adjusting entry has been posted, and
   a. The allowance account before adjustment has a credit balance of $350
   b. The allowance account before adjustment has a debit balance of $150 [LO2d]

EXERCISE 8-8 *(Prepare Journal Entries for Credit Card Sales)* Selected transactions of Asiatic Company appear below.

Nov. 10 The company made sales of $800 to customers who used bank credit cards. The service charge on bank cards is 5%, and the company deposits the signed credit card invoices directly in its bank.

Nov. 10 The company made sales of $1,200 to customers who used the American Express credit card. American Express has a service charge of 4%, and the signed credit card invoices must be sent to the card company to obtain the cash.

Nov. 25 Received payment from American Express at 96% of the face value of all credit card invoices mailed on November 10.

Required:

Prepare journal entries to record the above transactions. [LO2h]

## PROBLEMS

PROBLEM 8–1 *(Prepare Journal Entries for Receivable Transactions)* Selected transactions completed by McInrow Company during the current year were as follows.

April 1 Sold merchandise on credit to Birdsong Company, $7,000; terms n/30.

15 Sold merchandise on credit to Westfield Company, $9,000, and accepted a 90-day, 9% note.

May 11 Accepted a $7,000, 60-day, 10% note from Birdsong Company in payment of its past due account receivable.

June 15 Sold merchandise on credit to Ellis Company, $4,000, and accepted a 45-day, 8% note.

20 Discounted the Birdsong Company note at the bank at 9%.

July 1 Sold merchandise on credit to Lendley Company, $10,000, and accepted a 120-day, 12% note.

10 Received notice that Birdsong Company dishonored its note. Paid the bank the maturity value of the note plus a protest fee of $10. McInrow believes the full amount can be collected from Birdsong.

14 Received from Westfield Company the amount due on the note dated April 15.

21 Discounted the Lendley Company note at the bank at 10%.

30 Ellis Company dishonored its note.

Required:

1. Prepare journal entries to record the above transactions. Assume that Lendley Company paid its note obligation in full on its due date.
2. Calculate the maturity date of the Lendley Company note. [LO2a,2b]

PROBLEM 8–2 *(Make Calculations and Prepare Journal Entries Involving Notes Receivable)* Information concerning five notes received by Brodie Company are detailed below.

| | DATE NOTE RECEIVED | FACE AMOUNT | TERM | INTEREST RATE | DATE DISCOUNTED | DISCOUNT RATE |
|---|---|---|---|---|---|---|
| (a) | July 15 | $10,000 | 6 months | 10% | Sept. 15 | 9% |
| (b) | Aug. 1 | 6,000 | 60 days | 8 | — | — |
| (c) | Sept. 6 | 5,000 | 90 days | 8 | Oct. 16 | 9 |
| (d) | Nov. 9 | 8,000 | 60 days | 9 | Dec. 19 | 10 |
| (e) | Dec. 21 | 3,000 | 30 days | 6 | — | — |

Required:

1. For each note, determine (1) its due date, (2) the amount of interest due at maturity, and (3) its maturity value.
2. Prepare journal entries to record the discounting of notes *a*, *c*, and *d*.

3. Prepare journal entries for notes *b* and *c*, both of which were dishonored by their maker (no protest fees were involved).
4. Prepare the adjusting entry to record the amount of interest earned on note *e* in the current year. [LO2a,2b]

PROBLEM 8–3 *(Prepare Journal Entries and Make Calculations for Receivable Transactions)* Selected transactions completed by Winters Company during the current year were as follows:

| | | |
|---|---|---|
| Jan. | 6 | Sold merchandise on credit to Post Company, $3,000; terms n/20. |
| | 30 | Accepted a $3,000, 60-day, 9% note from Post when it applied for an extension of time on its past due account receivable. |
| Feb. | 5 | Sold merchandise on credit to R. Quicks, $9,000, and accepted a 6-month, 10% note. |
| March | 1 | Discounted the Post Company note at the bank at 9%. |
| | 9 | Accepted a 90-day, 8% note from Leslie Company in payment of a past due account for $5,000. |
| | 31 | Received notice that Post Company dishonored its note. Paid the bank the maturity value of the note plus a protest fee of $8. Winters believes the full amount can be collected from Post. |
| April | 5 | Discounted the R. Quicks note at the bank at 9%. |
| | 18 | Discounted the Leslie Company note at the bank at 10%. |
| June | 7 | Sold merchandise on credit to Jetty Company, $6,000, and accepted a 60-day, 9% note. |
| | 17 | Discounted the Jetty Company note at the bank at 10%. |
| July | 9 | Received from Post Company the full amount shown in its account in the accounts receivable subsidiary ledger. |
| Aug. | 5 | Received notice that the R. Quicks note had been dishonored. Paid the bank the maturity value of the note plus a protest fee of $10. Winters believes the full amount can be collected from Quicks. |
| Oct. | 1 | Sold merchandise on credit to E. Ingle, $12,000, and accepted a 6-month, 10% note. |
| | 16 | Sold merchandise on credit to L. Starr, $4,000, and accepted a 60-day, 8% note. |
| Dec. | 15 | Received a check from L. Starr for the amount due on the note dated October 16. |
| | 31 | Wrote off as uncollectible the balance in the R. Quicks account receivable. Winters uses the direct write-off method to account for uncollectibles. |

Required:

1. Prepare journal entries to record the above transactions, including any interest accrued as of December 31 on the notes being held by Winters Company.
2. Determine the total amount of interest revenue earned and the total amount of interest expense incurred during the current year on all notes cited above. [LO2a,2b]

PROBLEM 8–4 *(Estimate Uncollectible Accounts Expense Using the Allowance Method)* Presented below are selected accounts of Alden Cuban Imports as of December 31, 19X5.

| | |
|---|---|
| Accounts Receivable | $40,000 |
| Allowance for Uncollectible Accounts (debit balance) | 200 |
| Sales | 260,000 |
| Sales Returns and Allowances | 10,000 |

Required:

1. Prepare the adjusting entry needed to record the uncollectible accounts expense for the year 19X5, assuming the company estimates that 1% of its net credit sales will prove to be uncollectible.

2. Prepare the adjusting entry needed to record the uncollectible accounts expense for the year 19X5, assuming the company estimates that 3% of its outstanding accounts receivable will prove to be uncollectible.
3. Prepare a journal entry to write off the account of Artis Company as uncollectible on March 20, 19X6 (the following year). The balance for Artis Company in the accounts receivable subsidiary ledger is $250. [LO2c,2d,2e]

PROBLEM 8–5 *(Estimate Uncollectible Accounts Expense Based on Aging the Accounts Receivable)* The Centaur Company has consistently provided for its uncollectible accounts expense at a rate of 1% of its net credit sales. Past experience with uncollectibles has revealed that the percentage has not remained stable. In fact, in the last five years the percentage relationship of uncollectibles to net credit sales has varied from 0.75% to as much as 2%. As a result, the Allowance for Uncollectible Accounts account has developed a debit balance. As of December 31, the company's year-end, the debit balance stands at $517.

After an executive meeting called to discuss the situation cited above, management decided to change its approach for estimating uncollectible account losses. Beginning with the current year-end, the company will age and analyze its customers' accounts in an attempt to establish their collectibility. After completing the aging schedule, an estimated loss percentage will be applied to each age category. Information concerning the amount of the receivables, their age (measured as current and in number of days past due), and the appropriate estimated loss percentage for each age category is shown below.

| AGE CATEGORY | AMOUNT | PERCENTAGE ESTIMATED TO BE UNCOLLECTIBLE |
|---|---|---|
| Current | $72,000 | 0.5% |
| 1–30 days past due | 19,500 | 1 |
| 31–60 days past due | 21,800 | 3 |
| 61–90 days past due | 6,000 | 10 |
| 91–120 days past due | 4,200 | 25 |
| Over 120 days past due | 1,400 | 50 |

Required:

1. Determine the amount of receivables estimated to be uncollectible.
2. Prepare the adjusting entry to recognize uncollectible accounts expense, and establish the appropriate balance in the allowance account. [LO2c,2d]

PROBLEM 8–6 *(Prepare Journal Entries Assuming Uncollectible Accounts Are Estimated as a Percentage of Accounts Receivable)* Presented below are selected accounts of Trans Company as of January 1, 19X5.

| | |
|---|---|
| Accounts Receivable | $70,000 |
| Allowance for Uncollectible Accounts (credit balance) | 3,000 |

During the year, credit sales were $300,000, and collections on these credit sales totaled $280,000. The following transactions pertaining to accounts receivable also occurred during 19X5.

| | |
|---|---|
| March 15 | Wrote off as uncollectible the account of T. Radics, $800. |
| May 22 | Wrote off as uncollectible the account of C. Blackburn, $1,500. |
| Aug. 3 | Unexpectedly received a $1,000 check from C. Blackburn pertaining to the account written off on May 22. Included with the check was a notice identifying the $1,000 amount as final settlement in a bankruptcy procedure. (This amount is not included in the $280,000 of credit sale collections cited above.) |
| Oct. 14 | Wrote off as uncollectible the account of W. Lister, $900. |

Dec. 31 Prepared the journal entry to record the estimated uncollectible accounts expense for the year. The company estimates that 3% of its outstanding accounts receivable will prove to be uncollectible.

Required:

1. Prepare journal entries to record (a) credit sales made in the current year and collections made on current sales during the current year, (b) the selected transactions dated March 15 through October 14, and (c) the year-end adjusting entry to record the uncollectible accounts expense.
2. Show how the Accounts Receivable account and the Allowance for Uncollectible Accounts account might appear in the balance sheet as of December 31, 19X5.

[LO2c,2d,2e,2f]

PROBLEM 8-7 *(Take Three Approaches in Using the Allowance Method of Accounting for Uncollectible Accounts Expense)* On the dates shown below, Zenith Company had the following accounts (all with normal balances, and the balance in the Allowance for Uncollectible Accounts account on December 31, 19X4, is after adjustment, and the balance in the Allowance for Uncollectible Accounts account on December 31, 19X5, is before adjustment):

| | DECEMBER 31, 19X4 | DECEMBER 31, 19X5 |
|---|---|---|
| Accounts Receivable | $100,000 | $120,000 |
| Allowance for Uncollectible Accounts | 5,500 | 250 |

During 19X5 the company had credit sales of $500,000, with sales returns and allowances on those credit sales of $30,000. The accounts receivable at the end of 19X5 were aged and categorized as follows:

| AGE CATEGORY | AMOUNT | PERCENTAGE ESTIMATED TO BE UNCOLLECTIBLE |
|---|---|---|
| Current | $100,000 | 1% |
| 1-30 days past due | 10,000 | 2 |
| 31-60 days past due | 3,000 | 3 |
| 61-90 days past due | 2,500 | 10 |
| Over 90 days past due | 4,500 | 30 |
| Total | $120,000 | |

Required:

Determine the amount of the accounts receivable estimated to be uncollectible, and prepare the appropriate adjusting entry under each of the following independent assumptions:

1. Uncollectible account losses are estimated on the basis of net credit sales at a rate of 1%.
2. Uncollectible account losses are estimated on the basis of the year-end balance in accounts receivable at a rate of 4%.
3. Uncollectible account losses are estimated on the basis of an account receivable aging schedule.

[LO2c,2d]

PROBLEM 8-8 *(Take Three Approaches in Using the Allowance Method of Accounting for Uncollectible Accounts Expense)* Famous Company had the following account balances before adjusting entries on December 31, 19X5:

| | |
|---|---|
| Accounts Receivable | $180,000 |
| Sales (all made on credit) | 840,000 |
| Allowance for Uncollectible Accounts (credit balance) | 350 |
| Sales Returns and Allowances | 40,000 |

The company also aged its accounts receivable and categorized them as follows:

| AGE CATEGORY | AMOUNT | PERCENTAGE ESTIMATED TO BE UNCOLLECTIBLE |
|---|---|---|
| Current | $ 76,000 | 0.5% |
| 1–30 days past due | 62,000 | 2 |
| 31–60 days past due | 22,000 | 5 |
| 61–90 days past due | 8,000 | 8 |
| Over 90 days past due | 12,000 | 40 |
| Total | $180,000 | |

Required:

1. Prepare the adjusting entry on December 31, 19X5, if uncollectible account losses are estimated on the basis of net credit sales at a rate of 1%.
2. Prepare the adjusting entry on December 31, 19X5, if uncollectible account losses are estimated on the basis of the year-end balance in accounts receivable at a rate of 4.5%.
3. Prepare the adjusting journal entry on December 31, 19X5, if uncollectible account losses are estimated on the basis of an accounts receivable aging schedule.

[LO2c,2d]

PROBLEM 8–9 *(Compare the Direct Write-Off Method and the Allowance Method)* Hillside Company has been in business for three years. Certain information pertaining to the company's activities is summarized below.

| | YEAR 1 | YEAR 2 | YEAR 3 |
|---|---|---|---|
| Sales* | $250,000 | $300,000 | $360,000 |
| Collections on credit sales | 142,000 | 234,000 | 254,000 |
| Accounts written off | 1,200 | 2,400 | 2,800 |

* Net credit sales were as follows: 60% of year 1 sales, 80% of year 2 sales, and 75% of year 3 sales.

Required:

1. Assume that Hillside used the direct write-off method of accounting for uncollectible account losses.
   a. Prepare the journal entry to show how the accounts written off in year 1 would have been recorded.
   b. Show the amount for and the presentation of accounts receivable in the balance sheet at the end of year 3.
   c. Calculate the total amount of uncollectible accounts expense that would have appeared in the company's income statement during the three-year period.
2. Assume that Hillside used the allowance method of accounting for uncollectible account losses. They are estimated on the basis of net credit sales at a rate of 1%.
   a. Prepare the adjusting entry needed at the end of years 1, 2, and 3, respectively.
   b. Show the amount for and the presentation of accounts receivable in the balance sheet at the end of year 3.
   c. Determine the total amount of uncollectible accounts expense that would have appeared in the company's income statement during the three-year period.
3. Of the two methods of accounting for uncollectible accounts expense, the direct write-off method and the allowance method, which method is preferred and why?

[LO2c,2d]

PROBLEM 8–10 *(Compare the Direct Write-Off Method with the Allowance Method)* Nutley Company has been in business for a number of years. Certain information pertaining to the company's activities during 19X5 is summarized below.

| | |
|---|---:|
| Sales (80% were credit sales) | $475,000 |
| Sales returns and allowances (All related to credit sales) | 5,000 |
| Collections made on accounts receivable | 350,000 |
| Accounts written off as uncollectible | 3,670 |
| Recovery of accounts previously written off | 320 |

Required:
Prepare journal entries for each situation as described in items *a* through *f* below, using first the direct write-off method and then the allowance method of accounting for uncollectible account losses.

a. Record the sales made on credit during the year.
b. Record the sales returns and allowances that were granted during the year.
c. Record the collections made on accounts receivable during the year.
d. Record the accounts written off during the year.
e. Record the recovery of accounts previously written off during the year.
f. Prepare the year-end adjusting entry, assuming the allowance method of accounting for uncollectible accounts is used. The estimate of uncollectible accounts expense is made on the basis of net credit sales using a rate of 1 percent.

Questions:
1. For the allowance method, assume that the Allowance for Uncollectible Accounts account had a credit balance of $3,500 on January 1, 19X5. Does the information affect the year-end adjusting entry? Why?
2. What method of accounting for uncollectible accounts, the direct write-off method or the allowance method, is preferred? Why? [LO2c,2d,2e,2f]

PROBLEM 8–11 *(Comprehensive Review)* Certain information and selected transactions of Dixie Company appear below.

| | |
|---|---:|
| Accounts Receivable balance, Jan. 1, 19X5 | $79,200 |
| Allowance for Uncollectible Accounts, Jan. 1, 19X5 (credit balance) | 2,640 |

Transactions for 19X5 and other information:

| | |
|---|---|
| Jan. 22 | Wrote off as uncollectible the account of R. Sweet, $315. |
| Feb. 17 | Unexpectedly received a check for $240 from Heller Company. The amount of the check is equal to the company's receivable that was written off as uncollectible last year. |
| 28 | Wrote off as uncollectible the account of Gerald Company, $555. |
| April 2 | Sold merchandise on credit to Allen Company, $2,000, and accepted a 90-day, 9% note. |
| 5 | Wrote off as uncollectible the account of K. Leeds, $730. |
| May 17 | Discounted Allen Company's note at the bank at 10%. |
| 19 | Received a check for $160 from Gerald Company, whose account had been written off on February 28 of this year. Dixie Company's management has determined that no additional monies can be expected from Gerald. |
| Aug. 9 | Received 20% of the $1,200 balance in the customer's account of Salem Company. The account receivable resulted from a credit sale made to Salem in October of last year. |
| 10 | Learned of Salem Company's bankruptcy and wrote off the remaining balance in that account as uncollectible. |
| Sept. 1 | Sold merchandise on credit to Downby Company, $8,000, and accepted a 6-month, 10% note. |
| 13 | Wrote off as uncollectible the account of J. Edwins, $625. |

Required:

1. Prepare journal entries to record the above transactions.
2. Prepare an adjusting entry to record the interest earned on the Downby note as of December 31, 19X5, Dixie Company's year-end.
3. Prepare the adjusting entry to record the uncollectible accounts expense for the year 19X5, using the following information. By aging and analyzing its accounts receivable, Dixie Company was able to estimate their realizable value. To report this value in its December 31 balance sheet, the balance in the Allowance for Uncollectible Accounts account must be $2,785 at year-end. [LO2a,2b,2c,2d,2e,2f]

## ALTERNATE PROBLEMS

PROBLEM 8–1A *(Make Calculations and Prepare Journal Entries Involving Notes Receivable)* (Alternate to Problem 8–2) Information concerning the notes received by Bribie Company are detailed below.

| | DATE NOTE RECEIVED | FACE AMOUNT | TERM | INTEREST RATE | DATE DISCOUNTED | DISCOUNT RATE |
|---|---|---|---|---|---|---|
| (a) | July 15 | $ 5,000 | 3 months | 10% | Sept. 15 | 9% |
| (b) | Aug. 1 | 16,000 | 30 days | 12 | — | — |
| (c) | Sept. 6 | 15,000 | 60 days | 12 | Oct. 16 | 9 |
| (d) | Nov. 9 | 18,000 | 60 days | 9 | Dec. 19 | 10 |
| (e) | Dec. 21 | 4,000 | 30 days | 6 | — | — |

Required:

1. For each note, determine (1) its due date, (2) the amount of interest due at maturity, and (3) its maturity value.
2. Prepare journal entries to record the discounting of notes *a*, *c*, and *d*.
3. Prepare journal entries for notes *b* and *c*, both of which were dishonored by the maker.
4. Prepare the adjusting entry to record the amount of interest earned on note *e* in the current year. [LO2a,2b]

PROBLEM 8–2A *(Prepare Journal Entries and Make Calculations for Receivable Transactions)* (Alternate to Problem 8–3) Selected transactions completed by Summer Company during the current year were as follows:

| | | |
|---|---|---|
| Jan. | 5 | Sold merchandise on credit to Post Company, $4,000; terms n/30. |
| | 30 | Accepted a $4,000, 90-day, 9% note from Post when it applied for an extension of time on its past due account receivable. |
| Feb. | 5 | Sold merchandise on credit to R. Quicks, $18,000, and accepted a 6-month, 10% note. |
| March | 1 | Discounted the Post Company note at the bank at 10%. |
| | 9 | Accepted a 60-day, 8% note from Leslie Company in payment of a past due account for $5,000. |
| | 31 | Received notice that Post Company dishonored its note. Paid the bank the maturity value of the note plus a protest fee of $8. Summer Company believes the full amount can be collected from Post. |
| April | 5 | Discounted the R. Quicks note at the bank at 10%. |
| | 18 | Discounted the Leslie Company note at the bank at 12%. |
| June | 7 | Sold merchandise on credit to Jetty Company, $6,000, and accepted a 90-day, 10% note. |
| | 17 | Discounted the Jetty Company note at the bank at 10%. |

| | | |
|---|---|---|
| July | 9 | Received from Post Company the full amount shown in its account in the accounts receivable subsidiary ledger. |
| Aug. | 5 | Received notice that the R. Quicks note had been dishonored. Paid the bank the maturity value of the note plus a protest fee of $10. Summer believes the full amount can be collected from Quicks. |
| Oct. | 1 | Sold merchandise on credit to E. Ingle, $22,000, and accepted a 6-month, 12% note. |
| | 16 | Sold merchandise on credit to L. Starr, $12,000, and accepted a 60-day, 10% note. |
| Dec. | 15 | Received a check from L. Starr for the amount due on the note dated October 16. |
| | 31 | Wrote off as uncollectible the balance in the R. Quicks account receivable. Summer uses the direct write-off method to account for uncollectibles. |

Required:

1. Prepare journal entries to record the above transactions, including any interest accrued as of December 31 on the notes being held by Summer Company.
2. Determine the total amount of interest revenue earned and the total amount of interest expense incurred on all notes cited above. [LO2a,2b]

PROBLEM 8–3A *(Estimate Uncollectible Accounts Expense Using the Allowance Method)* (Alternate to Problem 8–4) Presented below are selected accounts of Alfie Imports as of December 31, 19X5.

| | |
|---|---|
| Accounts Receivable | $ 50,000 |
| Allowance for Uncollectible Accounts (debit balance) | 300 |
| Sales | 360,000 |
| Sales Returns and Allowances | 20,000 |

Required:

1. Prepare the adjusting entry needed to record the uncollectible accounts expense for the year 19X5, assuming the company estimates that 2% of its net credit sales will prove to be uncollectible.
2. Prepare the adjusting entry needed to record the uncollectible accounts expense for the year 19X5, assuming the company estimates that 4% of its outstanding accounts receivable will prove to be uncollectible.
3. Prepare a journal entry to write off the account of Barts Company as uncollectible on April 30, 19X6 (the following year). The balance for Barts Company in the accounts receivable subsidiary ledger is $360. [LO2c,2d,2e]

PROBLEM 8–4A *(Estimate Uncollectible Accounts Expense Based on Aging the Accounts Receivable)* (Alternate to Problem 8–5) The Centurian Company has consistently provided for its uncollectible accounts expense at a rate of 2% of its net credit sales. Past experience with uncollectibles has revealed that the percentage has not remained stable. In fact, in the last five years the percentage relationship of uncollectibles to net credit sales has varied from 1.5% to as much as 3%. As a result, the Allowance for Uncollectible Accounts account has developed a debit balance. As of December 31, the company's year-end, the debit balance stands at $817.

After an executive meeting called to discuss the situation cited above, management decided to change its approach for estimating uncollectible account losses. Beginning with the current year-end, the company will age and analyze its customers' accounts in an attempt to establish their collectibility. After completing the aging schedule, an estimated loss percentage will be applied to each age category. Information concerning the amount of the receivables, their age (measured as current and in number of days past due), and the appropriate estimated loss percentage for each age category is shown below.

| AGE CATEGORY | AMOUNT | PERCENTAGE ESTIMATED TO BE UNCOLLECTIBLE |
|---|---|---|
| Current | $82,000 | 0.5% |
| 1–30 days past due | 29,500 | 1 |
| 31–60 days past due | 11,800 | 4 |
| 61–90 days past due | 16,000 | 12 |
| 91–120 days past due | 14,200 | 30 |
| Over 120 days past due | 11,400 | 60 |

Required:

1. Determine the amount of receivables estimated to be uncollectible.
2. Prepare the adjusting entry to recognize uncollectible account expense, and establish the appropriate balance in the allowance account. [LO2c,2d]

PROBLEM 8–5A *(Prepare Journal Entries Assuming Uncollectible Accounts Are Estimated as a Percentage of Accounts Receivable)* (Alternate to Problem 8–6) Presented below are selected accounts of Trite Company as of January 1, 19X5.

| | |
|---|---|
| Accounts Receivable | $70,000 |
| Allowance for Uncollectible Accounts (credit balance) | 3,000 |

During the year, credit sales were $400,000 and collections on these credit sales totaled $360,000. The following transactions pertaining to accounts receivable also occurred during 19X5.

| | |
|---|---|
| March 15 | Wrote off as uncollectible the account of T. Raid, $900. |
| May 22 | Wrote off as uncollectible the account of C. Black, $2,500. |
| Aug. 3 | Unexpectedly received a $2,000 check from C. Black pertaining to the account written off on May 22. Included with the check was a notice identifying the $2,000 amount as final settlement in a bankruptcy procedure. (This amount is not included in the $360,000 of credit sale collections cited above.) |
| Oct. 14 | Wrote off as uncollectible the account of H. Ladd, $750. |
| Dec. 31 | Prepared the journal entry to record the estimated uncollectible accounts expense for the year. The company estimates that 2.5% of its outstanding accounts receivable will prove to be uncollectible. |

Required:

1. Prepare journal entries to record (a) credit sales made in the current year and collections made on current sales during the current year, (b) the selected transactions dated March 15 through October 14, and (c) the year-end adjusting entry to record the uncollectible accounts expense.
2. Show how the Accounts Receivable account and the Allowance for Uncollectible Accounts account might appear in the balance sheet as of December 31, 19X5. [LO2c,2d,2e,2f]

# 9 *Inventories and Cost of Goods Sold*

### *Learning Objectives*

When you complete this chapter you will be able to

1. Answer the following questions:
   a. What is inventory? Why is inventory information important?
   b. What is the difference between the periodic inventory system and the perpetual inventory system?
   c. Why is a physical inventory count important? What problems are associated with making the count?
   d. What items constitute the cost of inventory?
   e. How are income determination and asset valuation during periods of changing prices affected by each of the following inventory cost-flow assumptions: (1) specific identification, (2) first-in, first-out (FIFO), (3) last-in, first-out (LIFO), and (4) average cost?
2. Perform the following accounting functions:
   a. Record journal entries using both the periodic and perpetual inventory systems.
   b. Calculate the effect of an inventory error on key balance sheet and income statement accounts for the current and subsequent years.
   c. Calculate the dollar amount of ending inventory and cost of goods sold using both the periodic inventory system and the perpetual inventory system under the four cost-flow assumptions listed in LO1e.
   d. Calculate the ending inventory using the three methods of applying the lower of cost or market rule.
   e. Calculate the ending inventory using the gross margin method of estimating inventory amounts and the retail method of estimating inventory amounts.

*1a. The definition of inventory is given here*

For many businesses, inventory represents the largest asset on their balance sheet, and cost of goods sold represents a significant item in determining their net income in their income statement. For merchandising businesses that purchase goods for resale, inventory consists of all goods owned by the firm and held for sale to customers in the regular course of business. For manufacturing businesses that make the goods they sell to customers, there are three types of inventory: raw materials (items to be processed into finished goods), work in process (items started but not yet completed), and finished goods (items completed and available for sale). Thus the term **inventory** can refer to (1) materials held for use in the later process of production, (2) materials in the process of production for such sale, or (3) finished merchandise held for sale in the regular course of business.

In this chapter we will be concerned only with inventories for a merchandising business. Inventories for a manufacturing business will be considered in a later chapter.

## DETERMINATION OF COST OF GOODS SOLD

You will recall that in Chapter 5 we determined the cost of goods available for sale during a period by adding to the beginning inventory the cost of the merchandise acquired during the period. This was expressed in equation form as follows:

Beginning Inventory + Cost of Goods Acquired (Net Cost of Purchases)
= Cost of Goods Available for Sale

At the end of each period, the cost of goods available for sale is separated into two elements: (1) the cost of the goods sold and (2) the cost of the ending inventory. This was also expressed in equation form as follows:

Cost of Goods Available for Sale − Ending Inventory = Cost of Goods Sold

Determining the amount of the ending inventory is important in income determination because it affects the amount that will be reported for the cost of goods sold. It is also important in assessing financial status because the ending inventory is reported as a current asset on the balance sheet.

## PERIODIC AND PERPETUAL INVENTORY SYSTEMS

The determination of ending inventory and cost of goods sold depends on the inventory system used. There are two principal inventory systems—the periodic and the perpetual. With the periodic inventory system, purchased merchandise is recorded by debiting the Purchases account. When merchandise is sold, revenue from the sale is recorded by crediting the Sales account. No other entry is made at the time of the sale to record the cost of the merchandise that was sold. As a result, the accounting records do not provide information about the cost of the merchandise sold or about the ending inventory. When the periodic inventory system is used, the cost of the ending inventory is determined by a physical count at the end of an accounting period. The cost of the goods sold is determined by calculation.

With the perpetual inventory system, accounting records provide continuous information pertaining to the cost of the merchandise on hand (inventory) and the cost of the goods sold. A perpetual inventory card such as that shown in Exhibit 9–1 is an important part of this system. A separate card is kept for each type of inventory item on hand. Each time the item is purchased or sold, data

*EXHIBIT 9–1*
Perpetual Inventory Card

ITEM SB-84 MAXIMUM 200
LOCATION Shelf 17 MINIMUM 20

| DATE | PURCHASED Units | Unit Cost | Total Cost | SOLD Units | Unit Cost | Total Cost | BALANCE Units | Unit Cost | Balance |
|---|---|---|---|---|---|---|---|---|---|
| Jan. 1 | | | | | | | 110 | 60 | $6,600 |
| 6 | | | | 20 | $60 | $1,200 | 90 | 60 | 5,400 |
| 7 | 40 | $65 | $2,600 | | | | {90<br>40 | {60<br>65 | <br>8,000 |
| 10 | | | | 70 | 60 | 4,200 | {20<br>40 | {60<br>65 | <br>3,800 |
| 12 | | | | 20 | 60 | 1,200 | 40 | 65 | 2,600 |
| 14 | | | | 10 | 65 | 650 | 30 | 65 | 1,950 |

For each purchase or sale, the inventory cards show the date of the transaction, the number of units bought or sold, the cost of the items per unit, and the total cost of the units bought or sold. The cards also show a "running" balance of the number of units on hand, their per unit cost, and the dollar balance of the inventory of the items on hand (also called the book inventory).

This inventory card shows that the first units sold are *assigned* the cost of the first (or earliest) units acquired. This is an example of one cost-flow assumption that can be used to assign costs to the units sold. This and other acceptable cost-flow assumptions are examined later in this chapter.

pertaining to the transaction are entered in the card. Collectively the cards represent a subsidiary ledger whose aggregate balances will be equal to the balance in the Inventory account.

When the perpetual inventory system is used, the costs of the items purchased are debited to the Inventory account (and entered in the specific inventory card). When an item or items are sold, two entries are recorded: (1) the cost of the item or items sold is debited to the Cost of Goods Sold account and credited to the Inventory account (with a corresponding entry in the appropriate inventory card or cards), and (2) the sales price is debited to the Cash or Accounts Receivable account and credited to the Sales account. Thus the Inventory account balance will show the cost of the merchandise on hand on a continuous basis, and the Cost of Goods Sold account balance will show the cost of the merchandise sold to date during the period. A physical inventory of each type of inventory item is usually taken only once a year at year-end to test the accuracy of the perpetual inventory records being maintained.

## RECORDING OF TRANSACTIONS — COMPARATIVE ILLUSTRATION

In this section we will demonstrate how six selected transactions of Marci Company, a merchandising firm, would be recorded under both the periodic and perpetual inventory systems. By presenting the entries to record the transactions side by side, we can readily see how the two systems differ.

*2a. Journal entries under both the periodic and perpetual inventory systems are illustrated on page 310*

TRANSACTION 1 Purchased on credit from Hurley Supply 500 items of product ZH having a total cost of $15,000 and terms of 2/10, n/30. Marci records purchases at the gross invoice amount.

| PERIODIC INVENTORY SYSTEM | | | PERPETUAL INVENTORY SYSTEM | | |
|---|---|---|---|---|---|
| Purchases | 15,000 | | Inventory | 15,000 | |
| Accounts Payable—Hurley | | 15,000 | Accounts Payable—Hurley | | 15,000 |
| To record merchandise purchased on credit | | | To record merchandise purchased on credit | | |

TRANSACTION 2 Marci returned 15 units of product ZH that were damaged or otherwise defective. Hurley granted a credit of $450, an amount equal to the cost of the defective units.

| PERIODIC INVENTORY SYSTEM | | | PERPETUAL INVENTORY SYSTEM | | |
|---|---|---|---|---|---|
| Accounts Payable—Hurley | 450 | | Accounts Payable—Hurley | 450 | |
| Purchase Returns and Allowances | | 450 | Inventory | | 450 |
| To record merchandise returned | | | To record merchandise returned | | |

TRANSACTION 3 Sold 100 units of ZH on credit to E. Best for $5,000, with terms of n/30. (The cost of the 100 units was $3,000.)

| PERIODIC INVENTORY SYSTEM | | | PERPETUAL INVENTORY SYSTEM | | |
|---|---|---|---|---|---|
| Accounts Receivable—Best | 5,000 | | Accounts Receivable—Best | 5,000 | |
| Sales | | 5,000 | Sales | | 5,000 |
| To record merchandise sold on credit | | | To record merchandise sold on credit | | |
| No entry to record the cost of the units sold | | | Cost of Goods Sold | 3,000 | |
| | | | Inventory | | 3,000 |
| | | | To record the cost of merchandise sold on credit | | |

*1b. A company that sells a variety of items having relatively low unit costs might use the periodic inventory system*

Note that under the periodic inventory system, no entry is made at the time of the sale to record either the cost of the items sold or a reduction in inventory. This is not an example of "sloppy recordkeeping." The firm using the periodic system often finds that it is impossible or impractical to determine the cost of units sold at the time that they are sold. For example, firms that sell a large variety of low-unit-cost items, such as hardware and drug stores, may find it is easier, less time-consuming, and less expensive to use a periodic rather than a perpetual inventory system.

When the periodic system is used, the balance in the Inventory account must be adjusted at the end of each accounting period to reflect the amount of inventory remaining on hand before financial statements can be prepared.

TRANSACTION 4 Transportation costs amounting to $200 that were incurred to obtain the 500 items of product ZH were paid.

| PERIODIC INVENTORY SYSTEM | | | PERPETUAL INVENTORY SYSTEM | | |
|---|---|---|---|---|---|
| Transportation-In | 200 | | Inventory | 200 | |
| Cash | | 200 | Cash | | 200 |
| To record payment of transportation charges on merchandise purchased | | | To record payment of transportation charges on merchandise purchased | | |

TRANSACTION 5 Marci paid Hurley's accounts payable in full after taking the 2% discount earned by paying within the specified time period.

| PERIODIC INVENTORY SYSTEM | | | PERPETUAL INVENTORY SYSTEM | | |
|---|---|---|---|---|---|
| Accounts Payable—Hurley . . . . . . . . | 14,550 | | Accounts Payable—Hurley . . . . . . . . | 14,550 | |
| Cash. . . . . . . . . . . . . . . . . . . . . | | 14,259 | Cash. . . . . . . . . . . . . . . . . . . . . | | 14,259 |
| Purchase Discount . . . . . . . . . | | 291 | Inventory . . . . . . . . . . . . . . . . | | 291 |
| To record payment to Hurley [($15,000 − $450) × 2% = $291] | | | To record payment to Hurley | | |

TRANSACTION 6 E. Best, a customer, returned for credit 5 of the units that were sold to her in transaction 3. Marci granted Best a credit of $250 (an amount equal to the selling price of the 5 units), which can be applied against the amount still owed on her account.

| PERIODIC INVENTORY SYSTEM | | | PERPETUAL INVENTORY SYSTEM | | |
|---|---|---|---|---|---|
| Sales Returns and Allowances. . . . . . | 250 | | Sales Returns and Allowances. . . . . . | 250 | |
| Accounts Receivable—Best . . . . . . . . . . . . . . . . . . . . . | | 250 | Accounts Receivable—Best . . . . . . . . . . . . . . . . . . . . . | | 250 |
| To record merchandise returned by a customer | | | To record merchandise returned by a customer | | |
| No entry to record the cost of units returned to inventory that were sold previously | | | Inventory. . . . . . . . . . . . . . . . . . . . . . | 150 | |
| | | | Cost of Goods Sold. . . . . . . . . | | 150 |
| | | | To record the return (at cost) of merchandise previously purchased to inventory (5 units × $30 a unit) | | |

Under the periodic inventory system (1) the Inventory account balance is not affected by sales returns and allowances transactions, and (2) no Cost of Goods Sold account is used when sales are made or when returned goods are accepted. Consequently, the cost of goods sold must be computed by using the amount determined by a physical count for the ending inventory.

In contrast, under the perpetual inventory system both the Inventory and the Cost of Goods Sold accounts are used when sales are made and when returned goods are accepted. The balance in the Cost of Goods Sold account represents the cumulative cost of all goods sold during a period.

Let us see how the Inventory account maintained under the perpetual inventory system would look after the six illustrated transactions that affected the account had been posted.

INVENTORY

| DATE | | EXPLANATION | POST. REF. | DEBIT | CREDIT | BALANCE |
|---|---|---|---|---|---|---|
| Jan. | 1 | Beginning balance | | | | 20 000 |
| | | Transaction 1—Purchases | | 15 000 | | 35 000 |
| | | Transaction 2—Purchase Return | | | 450 | 34 550 |
| | | Transaction 3—Sales | | | 3 000 | 31 550 |
| | | Transaction 4—Transportation Costs | | 200 | | 31 750 |
| | | Transaction 5—Purchase Discount | | | 291 | 31 459 |
| | | Transaction 6—Sales Return | | 150 | | 31 609 |

*1b. Companies that sell high-unit-cost items commonly use the perpetual inventory system*

Companies that sell high-unit-cost items, such as automobiles, home appliances, or fur coats, commonly use the perpetual inventory system. This system is expensive to maintain, but it produces current and continuous balances for inventory and cost of goods sold. Therefore financial statements can be prepared for any short period, including monthly, without taking a physical inventory each month. Another advantage attributed to the perpetual inventory system is that it provides information that can be used for planning and controlling the level of inventory.

## TAKING A PHYSICAL INVENTORY

### Purpose and General Techniques

*1c. A physical inventory count verifies records and determines losses under perpetual systems. Under periodic systems it must be taken in order to determine the cost of the inventory at the end of an accounting period*

As we stated earlier, the physical inventory on hand is counted at least once a year. The purpose of the inventory count depends somewhat on the inventory system being used. When a perpetual system is used, a physical count is taken to check on the accuracy of the inventory figure shown in the accounting records and to determine if any inventory losses from breakage, obsolescence, theft, or other causes have occurred. When a periodic system is used, a physical count is needed to determine the cost of the ending inventory, which in turn is needed to calculate the cost of goods sold.

Annual inventory counts are usually made near or at the end of the company's fiscal year. The advantage of counting at this time is that generally there are fewer items and less dollar value in the inventory at the end of the fiscal year. This is one reason why department stores often end their fiscal year on January 31.

Some companies hand-count inventory more than once a year. The frequency of inventory counts depends on their cost measured against the benefits expected to be obtained from taking the count.

A physical inventory involves counting or otherwise measuring the number of physical units of merchandise owned by the firm and available for sale—seemingly a simple process. But inventory counts can be time-consuming, costly, and complex. Items may be missed or double-counted; items that belong to other companies may be incorrectly included in the count. Therefore inventory counts must be carefully planned and supervised or the ending inventory figure may be erroneously overstated or understated.

The techniques for taking a physical inventory consist of (1) *counting* the items of unsold merchandise remaining on hand, (2) *multiplying* the count for each item type by its cost to determine the items' total cost, and (3) *adding* the item total costs to determine the cost of all units on hand (ending inventory).

Exhibit 9–2 illustrates this three-step procedure that resulted in an ending inventory of $205.

*EXHIBIT 9–2*
Steps in Taking a Physical Inventory

| ITEM | NUMBER OF UNITS COUNTED | COST | TOTAL COST |
|---|---|---|---|
| Hammers | 20 units | $4 per unit | $ 80 |
| Saws | 15 units | $7 per unit | 105 |
| Nails | 10 lbs. | $2 per lb. | 20 |
| Cost of Ending Inventory | | | $205 |

Some inventory items need to be weighed or measured. For example, scrap metal is weighed to determine its quantity; oil and gas are measured.

### Items Included in the Physical Count

Since only merchandise owned by a business at the close of the accounting period should be included in the inventory, care must be taken to ensure that all merchandise *owned*, regardless of where located, is included in the count. Care must also be taken to ensure that all merchandise *not owned* but held by the business is excluded from the count.

Here are examples of situations that should be carefully considered and understood by those responsible for the physical inventory count.

***1c. Merchandise in transit may belong to the buyer or to the seller, depending on its shipping terms***

1. At the close of the accounting period (the balance sheet date), *purchased* merchandise may be "in transit" from the supplier to the company. If such merchandise is designated *FOB shipping point,* title to the merchandise passes to the buyer on the day the goods are shipped. Therefore the merchandise *belongs* to the company and should be *included* in its ending inventory.
2. At the close of the accounting period (the balance sheet date), *sold* merchandise may be "in transit" from the company to one of its customers. If such merchandise is designated *FOB destination,* title to the merchandise does not pass to the customer until it arrives at the customer's place of business. Therefore this merchandise also *belongs* to the company and should be *included* in its ending inventory.
3. At the close of the accounting period (the balance sheet date), *purchased* merchandise may be "in transit" from the supplier to the company. If such merchandise is designated *FOB destination,* title to the merchandise does not pass to the company until it arrives at the company's location. Therefore the merchandise *does not belong* to the company and should be *excluded* from its ending inventory.
4. At the close of the accounting period (the balance sheet date), *sold* merchandise may be "in transit" from the company to the customer. If such merchandise is designated *FOB shipping point,* title to the merchandise passes to the customer on the day the goods are shipped. Therefore this merchandise *does not belong* to the company and should be *excluded* from its ending inventory.

***1c. Consigned merchandise is inventory of the consignor***

Another situation where physical location does not mean ownership involves merchandise held on **consignment.** The owner of the consigned merchandise is called the **consignor.** The person or company holding the consigned merchandise is called the **consignee.** In this arrangement the consignee has items of merchandise and has agreed to act on behalf of the consignor in selling the items for a commission. The consignor owns the merchandise regardless of where it is physically located and therefore includes the cost of consigned goods in its ending inventory. The consignee, an agent that physically possesses the items of merchandise, does not own them and excludes these goods when taking an ending inventory count.

## THE EFFECTS OF INVENTORY ERRORS

An error in the determination of the inventory at the end of the period will lead to the reporting of incorrect amounts for the cost of goods sold, gross margin on sales, and net income in the income statement. The error will also cause amounts reported for inventory, current assets, total assets, and owner's equity in the balance sheet to be incorrect. To demonstrate how an overstated or understated ending inventory affects several key figures reported in the financial statements, three illustrations using condensed financial statements will be given:

*2b. The effects of inventory errors are illustrated here*

In Illustration 1 the ending inventory is stated correctly at $40,000.
In Illustration 2 the ending inventory is overstated by $8,000.
In Illustration 3 the ending inventory is understated by $6,000.

*ILLUSTRATION 1*

Ending Inventory Correctly Stated at $40,000

| INCOME STATEMENT FOR THE YEAR | | |
|---|---|---|
| Net Sales | | $110,000 |
| Cost of Goods Sold: | | |
| Beginning Inventory | $ 39,000 | |
| Net Cost of Purchases | 75,000 | |
| Cost of Goods Available for Sale | $114,000 | |
| Less: Ending Inventory | 40,000 | |
| Cost of Goods Sold | | 74,000 |
| Gross Margin on Sales* | | $ 36,000 |
| Less: Operating Expenses | | 26,000 |
| Net Income | | $ 10,000 |

| BALANCE SHEET AT END OF YEAR | |
|---|---|
| Inventory | $ 40,000 |
| Other Assets | 100,000 |
| Total Assets | $140,000 |
| Liabilities | $ 60,000 |
| Owner's Equity | 80,000 |
| Total Liabilities and Owner's Equity | $140,000 |

* Same as gross profit on sales.

*ILLUSTRATION 2*

Ending Inventory Incorrectly Stated at $48,000 (Overstated by $8,000)

| INCOME STATEMENT FOR THE YEAR | | |
|---|---|---|
| Net Sales | | $110,000 |
| Cost of Goods Sold: | | |
| Beginning Inventory | $ 39,000 | |
| Net Cost of Purchases | 75,000 | |
| Cost of Goods Available for Sale | $114,000 | |
| Less: Ending Inventory | 48,000 | |
| Cost of Goods Sold | | 66,000 |
| Gross Margin on Sales | | $ 44,000 |
| Less: Operating Expenses | | 26,000 |
| Net Income | | $ 18,000 |

| BALANCE SHEET AT END OF YEAR | |
|---|---|
| Inventory | $ 48,000 |
| Other Assets | 100,000 |
| Total Assets | $148,000 |
| Liabilities | $ 60,000 |
| Owner's Equity | 88,000 |
| Total Liabilities and Owner's Equity | $148,000 |

*ILLUSTRATION 3*

Ending Inventory Incorrectly Stated at $34,000 (Understated by $6,000)

| INCOME STATEMENT FOR THE YEAR | | |
|---|---|---|
| Net Sales | | $110,000 |
| Cost of Goods Sold: | | |
| Beginning Inventory | $ 39,000 | |
| Net Cost of Purchases | 75,000 | |
| Cost of Goods Available for Sale | $114,000 | |
| Less: Ending Inventory | 34,000 | |
| Cost of Goods Sold | | 80,000 |
| Gross Margin on Sales | | $ 30,000 |
| Less: Operating Expenses | | 26,000 |
| Net Income | | $ 4,000 |

| BALANCE SHEET AT END OF YEAR | |
|---|---|
| Inventory | $ 34,000 |
| Other Assets | 100,000 |
| Total Assets | $134,000 |
| Liabilities | $ 60,000 |
| Owner's Equity | 74,000 |
| Total Liabilities and Owner's Equity | $134,000 |

Observe that in each illustration the cost of goods available for sale was constant and correctly reported at $114,000. It was the ending inventory and the cost of goods sold that varied. The variation was caused by errors in determining the amount that should be assigned to the ending inventory. Examining comparable amounts in the three sets of financial statements illustrated will reveal different amounts being reported for key financial statement items, as summarized below.

| | INCOME STATEMENT FIGURES FOR | | | BALANCE SHEET FIGURES FOR | | |
|---|---|---|---|---|---|---|
| | Cost of Goods Sold | Gross Margin on Sales | Net Income | Ending Inventory | Total Assets | Owner's Equity |
| Illustration 1: Inventory Correctly Stated | $74,000 | $36,000 | $10,000 | $40,000 | $140,000 | $80,000 |
| Illustration 2: Inventory Overstated by $8,000 | 66,000 | 44,000 | 18,000 | 48,000 | 148,000 | 88,000 |
| Illustration 3: Inventory Understated by $6,000 | 80,000 | 30,000 | 4,000 | 34,000 | 134,000 | 74,000 |

Because the ending inventory of one year becomes the beginning inventory of the next year, inventory errors have a "carryover effect."

Thus if the inventory is incorrectly stated at the end of a period, the net income for that period will be misstated and so will the net income for the next period. For example, if the inventory is incorrectly overstated at the end of 19X6, the net income for 19X6 will be overstated.

Furthermore, because the ending inventory for 19X6 becomes the beginning inventory for 19X7, it has a "carryover effect" and causes net income for that period to be understated by an amount equal to last year's overstatement. The amounts, although equal, have the opposite effect on reported net income. Inventory errors not corrected can affect amounts reported in the income statement for two consecutive years only. Although the net income reported for each year is incorrect, the amounts shown on the balance sheet at the end of the second year for assets and owner's equity will be correct.

The effects of inventory errors on various financial statement items can be summarized and diagramed as shown in Exhibit 9–3.

*EXHIBIT 9–3*

Effects of Inventory Errors

| | | INCOME STATEMENT ITEMS | | | BALANCE SHEET ITEMS | |
|---|---|---|---|---|---|---|
| | | Cost of Goods Sold | Gross Margin | Net Income | Inventory Balance | Owner's Equity |
| 19X6—Ending inventory is understated | Overstated | * | | | | |
| | Correct | | | | | |
| | Understated | | * | * | * | * |
| 19X7—Beginning inventory is understated | Overstated | | * | * | | |
| | Correct | | | | * | * |
| | Understated | * | | | | |
| 19X6—Ending inventory is overstated | Overstated | | * | * | * | * |
| | Correct | | | | | |
| | Understated | * | | | | |
| 19X7—Beginning inventory is overstated | Overstated | * | | | | |
| | Correct | | | | * | * |
| | Understated | | * | * | | |

## DETERMINING THE COST OF INVENTORY

The primary basis of accounting for inventory is **cost**, which is generally defined by the accounting profession as *the total of the applicable expenditures and charges directly or indirectly incurred in bringing an article or item to its present condition and location.* As applied to merchandise inventory, cost generally includes the following types of expenditures:

*1d. The items that generally constitute the cost of merchandise inventory are shown here*

1. The net *purchase* price
2. *Transportation* costs
3. *Insurance* on the merchandise while it is in transit
4. Special *handling* costs, *customs duties*, and other expenditures incurred in acquiring the merchandise

*1d. Two accounts are assigned a portion of the cost of goods available for sale*

Inventory costing is essentially a matter of assigning a portion of the cost of goods available for sale to inventory and to the cost of goods sold. To illustrate the assignment of costs with a simple example, assume the following:

1. The cost of each inventory item is $10 per unit.
2. The beginning inventory consists of 800 units.
3. During the period, 3,900 units were purchased.
4. At the end of the period, 500 units remained on hand.

The schedule below shows that the cost of goods available for sale was $47,000. It also shows that this amount was allocated (assigned) between the inventory and the cost of goods sold on the basis of number of units still on hand and number of units sold times the per unit cost of $10, respectively.

| | |
|---|---:|
| Beginning Inventory (800 units @ $10) | $ 8,000 |
| Add: Cost of Purchases (3,900 units @ $10) | 39,000 |
| Cost of Goods Available for Sale (4,700 units @ $10) | $47,000 |
| Less: Ending Inventory (500 units @ $10) | 5,000 |
| Cost of Goods Sold (4,200 units @ $10) | $42,000 |

Assigning the cost of goods available for sale to the ending inventory and to the cost of goods sold can also be diagramed as shown in Exhibit 9–4.

The example we have used is relatively simple because the unit cost of each inventory item is $10. In practice the situation is more complicated because purchase prices rarely remain constant during an accounting period. It is not uncommon to purchase identical inventory items at different unit cost prices during the period. The problem that now arises is determining which unit cost applies to the items in the ending inventory and which unit cost to the goods sold. The solution is to use a **cost-flow assumption** and assign costs of units of inventory acquired to the units in the ending inventory and to the units sold. A number of alternative methods for assigning costs to inventory and cost of goods sold exist. Four of the most widely used methods are

Specific identification
First-in, first-out (FIFO)
Last-in, first-out (LIFO)
Weighted average cost

EXHIBIT 9–4

Assigning the Cost of Goods Available for Sale to Ending Inventory and the Cost of Goods Sold

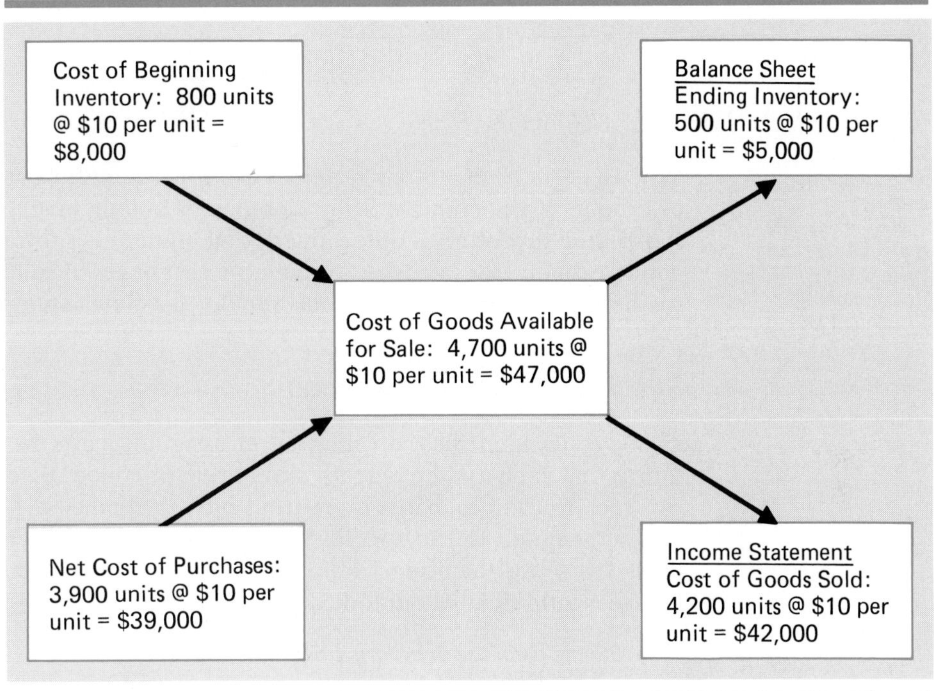


To explain and illustrate these methods, we will use the purchase and sales data relating to a single product of King Company as shown in the accompanying table.

Inventory Data: King Company, Product X

| | NUMBER OF UNITS | COST PER UNIT | TOTAL COST |
|---|---|---|---|
| Beginning Inventory | 10 | $100 | $ 1,000 |
| Purchases During the Month: | | | |
| Feb. 4 | 20 | 120 | 2,400 |
| Feb. 12 | 30 | 130 | 3,900 |
| Feb. 21 | 20 | 150 | 3,000 |
| Goods Available for Sale (in units and at cost) | 80 | | $10,300 |
| | **NUMBER OF UNITS** | **SELLING PRICE PER UNIT** | **TOTAL SALES** |
| Sales During the Month: | | | |
| Feb. 7 | 25 | $200 | $ 5,000 |
| Feb. 26 | 35 | 250 | 8,750 |
| Sales for the Month (in units and at selling price) | 60 | | $13,750 |
| Ending Inventory (units) | 20 | | |

In the illustrations that follow, we show four alternative methods for assigning the cost of goods available for sale (the $10,300) to ending inventory and cost of goods sold.

In the first set of illustrations we will assume that King Company uses a periodic inventory system whereby ending inventory is determined by a physical count. In the second set of illustrations we will assume that a perpetual inventory system is used whereby the balance in the Inventory account continuously represents the cost of goods on hand.

## COST ASSIGNMENTS USING A PERIODIC INVENTORY SYSTEM

*2c. Calculations of ending inventory and cost of goods sold under the periodic system using four cost-flow assumptions are illustrated here*

When a periodic inventory system is used, a cost must be assigned to the 20 units of Product X remaining in King Company's ending inventory. Once the cost of the ending inventory is determined, that amount is subtracted from the cost of goods available for sale to determine the cost of goods sold for the period. Let us see how this works with each acceptable cost-flow assumption.

### Specific Identification Method

The **specific identification** method of assigning costs to ending inventory requires that each unit be tagged, numbered, or coded. By doing so, the company can keep track of each inventory item and its actual cost. As a result, actual costs can be assigned to the specific items on hand when inventory is counted. To illustrate using the King Company data, assume that the 20 units of ending inventory physically counted can be identified and consist of

*5 units* from the *February 1* beginning inventory
*5 units* purchased on *February 12*
*10 units* purchased on *February 21*

The cost assigned to the ending inventory would be computed as follows.

Ending Inventory—Specific Identification Method

| | |
|---|---|
| 5 units @ $100 per unit (from beginning inventory) | $ 500 |
| 5 units @ $130 per unit (from February 12 purchase) | 650 |
| 10 units @ $150 per unit (from February 21 purchase) | 1,500 |
| 20 units—total ending inventory | $2,650 |

Cost of goods sold for the period could be determined by subtracting the cost assigned to the ending inventory from the cost of the goods available for sale, as shown below.

Cost of Goods Sold—Specific Identification Method

| | UNITS | COST |
|---|---|---|
| Cost of Goods Available for Sale | 80 | $10,300 |
| Less: Ending Inventory (shown above) | 20 | 2,650 |
| Cost of Goods Sold | 60 | $ 7,650 |

Specific identification has the advantage of pinpointing the cost of each item sold, and it might be used by companies with a relatively small number of dissimilar, high-priced items. However, this method would probably not be worthwhile for companies that sell a large number of identical items. The tagging or coding of individual units of merchandise and tracking the individual cost of each item sold would often be impractical, if not impossible.

Companies that sell cars, tractors, or boats might want to use the specific identification method. Most companies find that the recordkeeping costs exceed the benefits expected to be obtained from using this method and therefore choose another method of assigning costs to ending inventory and cost of goods sold.

### First-in, First-out (FIFO) Method

The **first-in, first-out (FIFO)** method is an inventory cost-flow assumption that assigns the cost of the *first* units purchased to the *first* units sold. Therefore:

> *Cost of goods sold* is assigned costs pertaining to the *earliest* purchases.
> *Ending inventory* is assigned costs pertaining to the *most recent* purchases.

Since under the periodic inventory system the ending inventory must be determined before the cost of goods can be calculated, the technique for assigning a cost to the ending inventory is to "work backward" on the layers of cost that constitute the cost of goods available for sale.

Referring again to the King Company data, we see that the 20 units purchased for $150 per unit on February 21 are the most recent purchase. The appropriate technique is to:

1. Assign the ending inventory a unit cost of $150 up to 20 units.

For example, if the ending inventory consists of 10 units, its cost is $1,500 ($150 × 10 units). If the ending inventory consists of 15 units, its cost is $2,250 ($150 × 15 units).

2. Assign any units above 20, and up to 50, a unit cost of $130 (the unit cost of the February 12 purchase).

For example, if the ending inventory consists of 30 units, its cost is $4,300, computed as follows.

$3,000 ($150 × 20 units)
+ $1,300 ($130 × 10 units) = $4,300

In our illustration King has 20 units in the ending inventory, and the costs are assigned to those units as follows.

Ending Inventory—FIFO Method

| | |
|---|---|
| 20 units from the February 21 purchase @ $150 | $3,000 |

The amount assigned to the cost of goods sold would be $7,300, computed as follows:

Cost of Goods Sold—FIFO Method

| | UNITS | COST |
|---|---|---|
| Cost of Goods Available for Sale | 80 | $10,300 |
| Less: Ending Inventory | 20 | 3,000 |
| Cost of Goods Sold | 60 | $ 7,300 |

Note that the cost of the ending inventory and consequently the cost of goods sold are different when we use the **FIFO** method than when we use the specific identification method. When items of inventory are acquired at different unit cost prices during a period, then each of the four cost-flow methods discussed in this chapter will produce different amounts for ending inventory and cost of goods sold.

The **FIFO** method is applied as if the first goods in (purchased) are the first ones sold. Thus the flow of *costs* tends to coincide with the actual flow of *goods* in many businesses (as just noted, the first merchandise purchased is often the first merchandise sold). Most companies try to sell the older goods first, especially if these goods are perishable or are subject to frequent style changes.

## *Last-in, First-out (LIFO) Method*

The **last-in, first-out (LIFO)** method is an inventory cost-flow assumption that assigns the cost of the *last* units purchased to the *first* units sold. Therefore:

> *Cost of goods sold* is assigned costs pertaining to the *most recent* purchases.
> *Ending inventory* is assigned costs from the *beginning inventory* and the *earliest* purchases.

The technique for calculating a **LIFO** ending inventory under the periodic inventory system is the opposite of that used when the **FIFO** ending inventory was calculated. Instead of "working backward" in the layers of costs, we "work forward."

Thus the **LIFO** cost of the 20 units in King Company's ending inventory would be $2,200, computed as follows:

Ending Inventory—LIFO Method

| | |
|---|---|
| 10 units from the beginning inventory @ $100 | $1,000 |
| 10 units from the purchase on February 4 @ $120 | 1,200 |
| 20 units—total ending inventory | $2,200 |

The amount assigned to cost of goods sold would then be $8,100, computed as follows:

Cost of Goods Sold—LIFO Method

| | UNITS | COST |
|---|---|---|
| Cost of Goods Available for Sale | 80 | $10,300 |
| Less: Ending Inventory | 20 | 2,200 |
| Cost of Goods Sold | 60 | $ 8,100 |

*1e. In periods of rising prices, the LIFO method will generally produce higher cost of goods sold than FIFO*

The LIFO method assigns the most recent costs to cost of goods sold. Note that in our example where costs were increasing, the LIFO method results in a cost of goods sold ($8,100) that is higher than the FIFO method ($7,300) and consequently results in a lower reported net income.

In a period of *rising* prices, the LIFO method will generally produce a *higher* cost of goods sold, a *lower* net income, and a *lower* ending inventory than would be obtained if the FIFO method were used.

The lower inventory amount obtained by the LIFO method does not relate meaningfully to the current cost of replacing the inventory. This is one of the disadvantages of using the LIFO method; sometimes some very old prices are assigned to the units remaining in the ending inventory. On the other hand, the income statement is more relevant under LIFO because the most recent inventory costs are charged against the current period's sales. Thus the LIFO method achieves a preferable matching on the income statement, where most current costs are matched with current selling prices.

## Weighted Average Cost Method

Under the **weighted average cost** method neither the first nor the last incurred costs are used to determine the ending inventory. Instead cost is allocated to inventory and to cost of goods sold on the basis of the weighted average cost of the items included in cost of goods available for sale.

1. The weighted average unit cost is computed by dividing the cost of goods available for sale by the number of units available for sale to determine an average unit cost.
2. This average cost is assigned to the units on hand to determine the ending inventory, and to the units sold to determine the cost of goods sold.

Using the weighted average cost method, the cost assigned to 20 units in King Company's ending inventory is $2,575, computed as follows:

Ending Inventory—Weighted Average Cost Method

| | |
|---|---|
| Cost of Goods Available for Sale | $10,300 |
| Number of Units Available for Sale | 80 |
| Average Cost per Unit ($10,300 ÷ 80) | $128.75 |
| Ending Inventory (20 units @ $128.75) | $ 2,575 |

The cost assigned to the cost of goods sold would be $7,725, computed as follows:

Cost of Goods Sold—Weighted Average Cost Method

| | |
|---|---|
| Cost of Goods Available for Sale | $10,300 |
| Less: Ending Inventory | 2,575 |
| Cost of Goods Sold | $ 7,725 |

Costs determined under the weighted average cost method are affected by the prices paid for the units in the beginning inventory as well as by the prices paid for all items purchased during the period. Thus the weighted average cost method tends to minimize the effects of changing prices. However, given a period of prolonged rising prices, the weighted average cost per unit will be less than the replacement cost per unit, and vice versa.

## COMPARISON OF COST ASSIGNMENT METHODS—PERIODIC INVENTORY SYSTEM

*2c. Cost assignment methods under the periodic system for all four cost-flow assumptions are compared in Exhibit 9–5*

The effects that the four alternative cost assignment methods have on ending inventory, cost of goods sold, gross margin on sales, and net income are summarized in Exhibit 9–5. The $3,200 of operating expenses was arbitrarily assumed for purposes of this illustration.

EXHIBIT 9–5

Comparison of Cost Assignment Methods—Periodic System

| | SPECIFIC IDENTIFICATION | FIFO | LIFO | WEIGHTED AVERAGE |
|---|---|---|---|---|
| Sales | $13,750 | $13,750 | $13,750 | $13,750 |
| Cost of Goods Sold: | | | | |
| Beginning Inventory | 1,000 | 1,000 | 1,000 | 1,000 |
| Purchases | 9,300 | 9,300 | 9,300 | 9,300 |
| Goods Available for Sale | 10,300 | 10,300 | 10,300 | 10,300 |
| Less: Ending Inventory | 2,650 | 3,000 | 2,200 | 2,575 |
| Cost of Goods Sold | 7,650 | 7,300 | 8,100 | 7,725 |
| Gross Margin on Sales | 6,100 | 6,450 | 5,650 | 6,025 |
| Operating Expenses | 3,200 | 3,200 | 3,200 | 3,200 |
| Net Income | $ 2,900 | $ 3,250 | $ 2,450 | $ 2,825 |

All four methods are recognized as acceptable alternatives. However, because the method selected affects ending inventory, cost of goods sold, gross margin on sales, and net income, full disclosure is required. *Full disclosure* means that a company indicates in its notes to the financial statements the method it uses for measuring the value of its ending inventory.

## COST ASSIGNMENTS USING A PERPETUAL INVENTORY SYSTEM

*2c. Calculations of ending inventory and cost of goods sold under the perpetual system using four cost-flow assumptions are illustrated here*

The same four cost-flow assignments are also appropriate when a company uses a perpetual inventory system. The difference is that

> Under the *periodic* inventory system, the ending inventory is determined by a physical count of the items on hand at the *end* of the period. The cost of goods sold is determined by adding the beginning inventory to the net cost of purchases and deducting the ending inventory.
>
> Under the *perpetual* inventory system, the balance in the Inventory account shows the amount of the ending inventory. The cost of goods sold is accumulated in the Cost of Goods Sold account *continuously throughout* the period.[1]

An inventory card or a record in a computer storage device is kept in both

[1] A physical count of the ending inventory is also made under the perpetual inventory system, but the dollar amount of the count is compared to the balance in the Inventory account.

quantities and dollars for each inventory item. A perpetual inventory card will be used in the illustrations that follow. As units are purchased or sold, the item's inventory card is adjusted to show the updated quantity on hand. The dollar figure accumulated for the cost of goods sold, and the dollar figure for the inventory at the end of the period, will depend on which cost-flow assignment has been adopted.

As we illustrate alternative ways to assign costs to the goods sold and to the goods remaining on hand, keep in mind that the actual physical flow of goods and the cost flow assumed are often quite different. There is no requirement that the cost-flow assumption adopted by a company be consistent with its physical movement of goods.

## Specific Identification Method

The specific identification method requires that the cost of each item sold be determined by identifying the specific purchase price of the unit sold.

The costs of the specific items sold are included in the cost of goods sold, and the costs of the specific items on hand are included in the inventory. The appeal of this method lies in the fact that actual costs are matched against actual revenue in income determination. It has limited application, however, because it is often impossible or impractical to segregate separate purchases and specifically identify the items sold. Using the King Company data once again, we would find that the ending inventory and the cost of goods sold would be $2,650 and $7,650, respectively, under both the periodic and perpetual inventory systems: When the specific identification method is used, the costs assigned to the 20 units remaining on hand were their specific costs, and the costs assigned to the 60 units sold were on the basis of the specific costs of those 60 items.

## First-in, First-out (FIFO) Method

An inventory record card for King Company's Product X prepared under the FIFO method of assigning costs is shown in Exhibit 9–6. It shows that the dollar

*EXHIBIT 9–6*

Inventory Record Card—Perpetual System—FIFO Method

| | PURCHASES | | | COST OF GOODS SOLD | | | BALANCE ON HAND | | |
|---|---|---|---|---|---|---|---|---|---|
| DATE | Number of Units | Unit Cost | Total Cost | Number of Units | Unit Cost | Total Cost | Number of Units | Unit Cost | Total Cost |
| Beginning Inventory | | | | | | | 10 | $100 | $1,000 |
| Feb. 4 | 20 | $120 | $2,400 | | | | 10 | 100 | |
| | | | | | | | 20 | 120 | 3,400 |
| 7 | | | | 10 | $100 | $1,000 | | | |
| | | | | 15 | 120 | 1,800 | 5 | 120 | 600 |
| 12 | 30 | 130 | 3,900 | | | | 5 | 120 | |
| | | | | | | | 30 | 130 | 4,500 |
| 21 | 20 | 150 | 3,000 | | | | 5 | 120 | |
| | | | | | | | 30 | 130 | |
| | | | | | | | 20 | 150 | 7,500 |
| 26 | | | | 5 | 120 | 600 | | | |
| | | | | 30 | 130 | 3,900 | 20 | 150 | 3,000 |
| Total | 70 | | $9,300 | 60 | | $7,300 | | | |

figure determined for the cost of goods sold (and the number of units removed from inventory) is based on the earliest-purchased units available for sale at the time of the sale. The units remaining on hand are therefore assigned the cost of the most recent purchases.

The card also shows that ending inventory and the cost of goods sold under a FIFO basis perpetual system are $3,000 and $7,300, respectively. As in all cases where FIFO is used, the inventory and cost of goods sold for King Company at the end of the period are the same whether a perpetual or a periodic inventory system is used.

### Last-in, First-out (LIFO) Method

An inventory record card for Product X prepared under the LIFO method of assigning costs is shown in Exhibit 9–7.

Under a LIFO basis perpetual inventory system, the cost of the last units acquired is assigned to cost of goods sold. Thus the cost of the last goods purchased is matched against revenue first in determining net income. To illustrate the procedure using King Company's data, note that on the inventory card the $2,900 cost of the sale made on February 7 was determined from two cost layers (two different acquisitions at two different unit costs):

> Of the 25 units sold, 20 are assigned the *$120 per unit* cost, a cost applicable to the last goods purchased on February 4.
>
> The other 5 units are assigned the *$100 per unit* cost, a cost applicable to units in the beginning inventory (the most recent cost layer available for assigning costs to the cost of goods sold).

Note that the ending inventory of $2,450 and the cost of goods sold of $7,850 determined on a LIFO basis using a perpetual inventory system are different from the ending inventory of $2,200 and the cost of goods sold of $8,100 determined on a LIFO basis using a periodic inventory system.

*EXHIBIT 9–7*

Inventory Record Card—Perpetual System—LIFO Method

| | PURCHASES | | | COST OF GOODS SOLD | | | BALANCE ON HAND | | |
|---|---|---|---|---|---|---|---|---|---|
| DATE | Number of Units | Unit Cost | Total Cost | Number of Units | Unit Cost | Total Cost | Number of Units | Unit Cost | Total Cost |
| Beginning Inventory | | | | | | | 10 | $100 | $1,000 |
| Feb. 4 | 20 | $120 | $2,400 | | | | 10<br>20 | 100<br>120 | 3,400 |
| 7 | | | | 20<br>5 | $120<br>100 | $2,400<br>500 | 5 | 100 | 500 |
| 12 | 30 | 130 | 3,900 | | | | 5<br>30 | 100<br>130 | 4,400 |
| 21 | 20 | 150 | 3,000 | | | | 5<br>30<br>20 | 100<br>130<br>150 | 7,400 |
| 26 | | | | 20<br>15 | 150<br>130 | $3,000<br>1,950 | 5<br>15 | 100<br>130 | 2,450 |
| Total | 70 | | $9,300 | 60 | | $7,850 | | | |

## Moving Average Method

*2c. The moving average method computes a new average unit cost after each purchase*

The weighted average method under the perpetual system is known as the **moving average** method because a new average unit cost is computed each time a purchase is made. Under the periodic system, you will recall, the average is taken only at the end of the period. When perpetual inventory records are used, an average unit cost is maintained.

The average unit cost is computed after each purchase by dividing the *total* cost of all units available for sale on a given date by the total number of units available for sale on that same date. This unit cost is then used in determining the cost of units sold until another purchase is made, when a new average unit cost is computed (hence the term *moving* or *changing* average cost).

Exhibit 9–8 demonstrates this concept of determining the cost of goods sold and ending inventory on a moving average unit cost basis under the perpetual inventory system.

*EXHIBIT 9–8*

Inventory Record Card—Perpetual System—Moving Average Method

| | PURCHASES | | | COST OF GOODS SOLD | | | BALANCE ON HAND | | |
|---|---|---|---|---|---|---|---|---|---|
| DATE | Number of Units | Unit Cost | Total Cost | Number of Units | Unit Cost | Total Cost | Number of Units | Unit Cost | Total Cost |
| Beginning Inventory | | | | | | | 10 | $100.00 | $1,000 |
| Feb. 4 | 20 | $120 | $2,400 | | | | 30 | 113.33 | 3,400 |
| 7 | | | | 25 | $113.33 | $2,833 | 5 | 113.33 | 567 |
| 12 | 30 | 130 | 3,900 | | | | 35 | 127.63 | 4,467 |
| 21 | 20 | 150 | 3,000 | | | | 55 | 135.76 | 7,467 |
| 26 | | | | 35 | 135.76 | 4,752 | 20 | 135.76 | 2,715 |
| Total | 70 | | $9,300 | 60 | | $7,585 | | | |

Examining Exhibit 9–8, we make two observations:

1. Each time a purchase is made, a new average unit cost is calculated.

For example, after the February 4 purchase of 20 units for $2,400, a new average unit cost of *$113.33* was computed as follows:

$3,400.00 ÷ 30 units = $113.33 (rounded)

2. Each time a sale is made, the previously calculated average unit cost is used to determine the cost of goods sold and consequently establishes the cost of the ending inventory at that time.

For example, on February 7 when 25 units were sold, a cost of goods sold of *$2,833.00* was determined as follows:

$113.33 average unit cost × 25 units sold = $2,833.00 (rounded)

After the February 7 sale of 25 units, the inventory is *$567.00*, computed as follows:

$3,400.00 − $2,833.00 = $567.00

or

$113.33 average unit cost × 5 units remaining on hand = $567.00 (rounded)

The same set of calculations is performed each time a purchase or sale is made. As a result, the figure accumulated for the cost of goods sold in the King Company illustration is $7,585 at year-end, and its ending inventory is $2,715.

## COMPARISON OF COST ASSIGNMENT METHODS—PERPETUAL INVENTORY SYSTEM

*2c. Cost assignment methods under the perpetual system for all four cost-flow assumptions are compared in Exhibit 9–9*

The effects that the four alternative cost assignment methods have on ending inventory, cost of goods sold, gross margin on sales, and net income are summarized in Exhibit 9–9. The figures for sales, beginning inventory, purchases, and operating expenses are the same as those used in Exhibit 9–5 when cost assignment methods using a periodic inventory system were compared.

*EXHIBIT 9–9*

Comparison of Cost Assignment Methods—Perpetual System

| | SPECIFIC IDENTIFICATION | FIFO | LIFO | MOVING AVERAGE |
|---|---|---|---|---|
| Sales | $13,750 | $13,750 | $13,750 | $13,750 |
| Cost of Goods Sold: | | | | |
| Beginning Inventory | 1,000 | 1,000 | 1,000 | 1,000 |
| Purchases | 9,300 | 9,300 | 9,300 | 9,300 |
| Goods Available for Sale | 10,300 | 10,300 | 10,300 | 10,300 |
| Less: Ending Inventory | 2,650 | 3,000 | 2,450 | 2,715 |
| Cost of Goods Sold | 7,650 | 7,300 | 7,850 | 7,585 |
| Gross Margin on Sales | 6,100 | 6,450 | 5,900 | 6,165 |
| Operating Expenses | 3,200 | 3,200 | 3,200 | 3,200 |
| Net Income | $ 2,900 | $ 3,250 | $ 2,700 | $ 2,965 |

## SUMMARY OF COST ASSIGNMENT METHODS

*1e,2c. Advantages and disadvantages of the four cost assignment methods are summarized here*

**SPECIFIC IDENTIFICATION** This method matches the cost flow with the physical flow of units through the company. Despite its theoretical merit, it cannot always be applied because the specific unit sold may not be clearly identifiable. This method works well for companies that sell relatively high priced items and keep only a few on hand.

**FIFO COST** This method requires that the cost of the first goods acquired be assigned to the first sold. Therefore, in a rising-price economy this method assigns lower costs to cost of goods sold, resulting in the reporting of a higher net income. Because the higher costs are assigned to the ending inventory, the balance sheet valuation of inventory more closely approximates its current replacement cost. The disadvantage of FIFO is that the method generally does a poor job of matching current costs with current revenue.

**LIFO COST** This method requires that the cost of the last goods acquired be assigned to the first sold, thereby matching most recent costs with current revenue. Advocates of LIFO emphasize its importance in income determination. However, when LIFO cost is used, the amount reported for inventory on the balance sheet will probably be below the current replacement cost of the items remaining on hand. During periods of rising prices, the LIFO method produces a lower net income, thus offering a tax advantage to the company that uses it.

AVERAGE COST This method matches against revenue a mathematically derived cost rather than any of the actual prices paid for the units sold. Average cost smoothes out the effect of price fluctuations on cost of goods sold and net income.

## FULL DISCLOSURE AND CONSISTENCY

Each of the four cost-flow assumptions is recognized as being an acceptable method for assigning costs to ending inventory and cost of goods sold. However, the full disclosure principle (introduced in Chapter 8) requires that the method selected be disclosed within the body of the company's financial statements or in their accompanying notes.

We have seen that a company can change its reported net income for an accounting period by changing its cost assignment method. If a different but acceptable method is a better reflection of the company's activity, a change should be made. Any change, however, no matter how desirable, should be tempered by the **consistency principle:**

**Consistency Principle**

An accounting method, once adopted among alternatives, should be used from period to period by the same business.

The consistency principle does not prohibit a company from changing from one inventory cost-flow assumption to another, but it does prohibit frequent or opportunistic changes. Its purpose is to make the financial statements of a particular company comparable from period to period.

Whenever a change in accounting method is made, the comparability of financial statements is preserved by an adequate disclosure of

The *nature* of the change
The *justification* for the change
The *effect* of the change on reported net income

This disclosure is usually made by parenthetical comments within the statements or by notes that accompany the statements.

## REPORTING INVENTORY AT AMOUNTS BELOW COST

The primary basis for valuing inventory is its historical cost as determined by an inventory-costing method such as **LIFO**. However, sometimes it may be appropriate to reduce the recorded value of inventory to a figure below its original cost. This situation is generally caused by inventory items that are damaged, physically deteriorated, or obsolete, which will significantly reduce the amount that can be obtained from the sale of the inventory. Another possibility is a decline in prices whereby replacement cost falls below original cost. We will now consider the proper accounting for such inventory.

VALUING INVENTORY AT NET REALIZABLE VALUE Inventory that can no longer be sold at a price above cost should be recorded at **net realizable value,** which is defined as estimated selling price of an inventory item less estimated selling and disposal costs.

Assume, for example, that a company has an electronic component with an original unit cost of $700. Style changes and other improvements in new models cause the unit's selling price to be reduced to $500, a reduction sufficient to ensure that the unit will be sold. Sales commissions and delivery costs estimated to be incurred on the sale of a unit amount to $30. The net realizable value of this electronic component is $470:

| | |
|---|---|
| Estimated Selling Price | $500 |
| Less: Estimated Selling and Disposal Costs | 30 |
| Net Realizable Value | $470 |

The unit is valued at $470 and should be reported in the company's balance sheet at that amount. The difference between its original cost of $700 and its net realizable value of $470, or $230, is reported as a loss in the current income statement. (This adheres to the matching principle, which requires that estimated losses be reported in the period in which they occurred.)

The journal entry to recognize the loss and to reduce the inventory to its net realizable value (assuming the perpetual system is used) is as follows:

| | | |
|---|---|---|
| Loss Due to Write-Down of Inventory | 230 | |
| Inventory | | 230 |
| To write down an inventory item to net realizable value | | |

**VALUING INVENTORY AT LOWER OF COST OR MARKET** A decline in the price level may cause the market value of the inventory to fall below its original cost. When this happens, the inventory is reduced to market value, and a loss is recognized. This approach to inventory valuation is guided by a rule known as the **lower of cost or market (LCM) rule.** The term **market,** as used in the phrase *lower of cost or market,* means the cost to replace the merchandise on the inventory date if purchased from the usual suppliers in the usual amounts. Thus *market* is not to be interpreted as price for which the inventory could be sold.

When the lower of cost or market rule is applied, inventory should be valued and reported either at its original cost or at the cost to replace it, whichever is lower. This approach, justified by the **conservatism principle,** often results in an inventory write-down.

**Conservatism Principle**

When choosing among alternative accounting methods, the one least likely to overstate assets or net income should be selected.

The inventory loss reflected by the write-down is reported currently even if the inventory items that lost value are still on hand. Accountants do not wait for the period in which the units are sold.

**METHODS OF APPLYING THE LOWER OF COST OR MARKET RULE** The lower of cost or market rule may be applied in one of three ways. It may be applied (1) directly to each item in the inventory, whereby the lower of cost or market for each item is selected for inventory valuation (the item-by-item method); (2) to each major category of inventory, in which case the lower of cost or market computed for each major category of inventory is used for inventory valuation (the category method); or (3) to the total inventory, in which case the lower of the total cost or total market computed for the entire inventory is used for inventory valuation (the total inventory method).

These three methods of applying the lower of cost or market rule are illustrated in Exhibit 9–10. In examining the exhibit, remember that the item's cost must first be determined by a cost-flow assumption such as specific identification, FIFO, LIFO, or average cost. *Market* refers to the item's current replacement cost.

Each application of the lower of cost or market rule represents an acceptable alternative for establishing the value of the ending inventory. Of course, the method chosen should be used consistently from period to period.

*EXHIBIT 9–10*

Application of Lower of Cost or Market Rule

| | | PER UNIT | | TOTALS | | LOWER OF COST OR MARKET | | |
|---|---|---|---|---|---|---|---|---|
| | QUANTITY | Cost | Market | Cost | Market | Individual Items | Major Categories | Total Inventory |
| *Garden Supplies:* | | | | | | | | |
| Lawn Mowers | 8 | $100 | $130 | $800 | $1,040 | $800 | | |
| Lawn Sprinklers | 6 | 15 | 20 | 90 | 120 | 90 | | |
| Rakes | 20 | 6 | 5 | 120 | 100 | 100 | | |
| Total | | | | 1,010 | 1,260 | | $1,010 | |
| *Paints:* | | | | | | | | |
| Style 117 | 12 | 5 | 5 | 60 | 60 | 60 | | |
| Style 146 | 15 | 4 | 6 | 60 | 90 | 60 | | |
| | | | | 120 | 150 | | 120 | |
| *Tools:* | | | | | | | | |
| Hammers | 9 | 7 | 6 | 63 | 54 | 54 | | |
| Saws | 20 | 15 | 12 | 300 | 240 | 240 | | |
| | | | | 363 | 294 | | 294 | |
| Total Inventory | | | | $1,493 | $1,704 | | | $1,493 |
| Inventory Valuation | | | | | | $1,404 | $1,424 | $1,493 |

**MODIFICATIONS OF THE LOWER OF COST OR MARKET RULE** The lower of cost or market practice originated a number of years ago when the principle of conservatism was considered to be important. In recent years this practice has been modified. Three guidelines are followed for modifying the general rule:

1. Inventory should be reported at *cost* (even though the replacement cost is lower) if there has not been, nor is there expected to be, any *reduction* in selling price.
2. Market value should not be *greater* than *net realizable value.*

Assume, for example, that a company has an inventory item that originally cost $30 but can be replaced for $24. If the selling price is $25 and estimated disposal costs are $5, the real loss in value is *$10* ($30 cost less $20 net realizable value). Therefore the item should be valued at *$20,* not at its higher replacement cost of *$24.*

3. Market value should not be *less* than *net realizable value, less a normal gross margin.*

Assume, for example, that a company has an item that originally cost $80 but can be replaced for $60. Also assume a selling price of $100, a gross margin of 20%, and disposal costs of $10.

The item's net realizable value less gross margin is:

| | | |
|---|---|---|
| Selling Price | | $100 |
| Less: Gross Margin of 20% | 20 | |
| Disposal Costs | 10 | 30 |
| | | $ 70 |

Because the net realizable value minus the gross margin is higher than the replacement cost of $60, the inventory is reported as $70.

In considering the three exceptions described above, remember this point: *The purpose of the lower of cost or market rule is to reduce the original acquisition cost to a more realistic updated value and to recognize the loss caused by the write-down of inventory in the accounting period in which the loss occurred.*

## ESTIMATING INVENTORY AMOUNTS

Regardless of the inventory system used, it is sometimes necessary or desirable to *estimate* the amount of ending inventory. There are four reasons for doing so:

1. *To verify an amount determined by a physical count.*
2. *To avoid the costly and time-consuming process of taking a physical count.* Recall that under the periodic inventory system, a physical count is needed to determine the ending inventory and to compute cost of goods sold. Physical counts are generally taken only once a year. Therefore companies that use the periodic inventory system must estimate their ending inventory monthly or quarterly if they have a need for interim financial statements. By estimating the amount of the ending inventory, an interim physical inventory count can be avoided.
3. *To test the reasonableness of the amount shown in the accounting records for ending inventory kept under the perpetual inventory system.*
4. *To establish the amount of inventory destroyed by a catastrophe such as a fire or flood.* An estimate of the amount of the inventory on hand prior to the catastrophe is needed to file an insurance claim.

Two approaches are commonly used to estimate an amount for the ending inventory: the *gross margin method* and the *retail method.*

### Gross Margin Method

*2e. The gross margin method estimates ending inventory by using an estimated rate of gross margin*

The **gross margin method,** sometimes called the *gross profit method,* of estimating the cost of ending inventory is based on the assumption that the rate of gross margin is approximately the same from period to period. For many businesses this assumption is realistic; but if it is not, the gross margin method will not produce valid results.

The rate itself is an estimate based upon the past and current experiences of the relationship between the two components of net sales: the gross margin on the sales and the cost of the goods sold. Once the gross margin rate is established, the ending inventory can be determined as follows:

1. *Multiply* the gross margin rate by the net sales to determine the estimated gross margin in dollars.
2. *Subtract* the estimated gross margin from the net sales to determine the estimated cost of goods sold.

3. *Subtract* the estimated cost of goods sold from the cost of goods available for sale to obtain the estimated ending inventory.

To illustrate the method, assume that the inventory on January 1 of the current quarterly period is $20,000, that the net purchases for the period January 1 through March 31 amounted to $75,000, and that net sales during that same period totaled $100,000. Finally, assume that the company estimates its gross margin rate to be $20% based on net sales. The estimated inventory on March 31 may be computed in three steps as follows.

1. Gross margin rate times net sales equals gross margin in dollars:

$$20\% \times \$100{,}000 = \textit{\$20,000}$$

2. Net sales minus gross margin equals cost of goods sold:

$$\$100{,}000 - \$20{,}000 = \textit{\$80,000}$$

3. Cost of goods available for sale minus cost of goods sold equals ending inventory:

$$\$95{,}000 - \$80{,}000 = \textit{\$15,000}$$

An alternative form for making the same determinations is to arrange the information in income statement format as shown below and proceed with the three-step calculation process described above.

| | | | |
|---|---|---|---|
| Net Sales | | $100,000 | (100%) |
| Beginning Inventory—Jan. 1 | $20,000 | | |
| Net Cost of Purchases | 75,000 | | |
| Cost of Goods Available for Sale | $95,000 | | |
| Less: Ending Inventory—March 31 | 15,000 | | |
| Cost of Goods Sold | | 80,000 | (80%) |
| Gross Margin on Sales | | $ 20,000 | (20%) |

## *Retail Method*

*2e. The retail method uses the cost-to-retail ratio to estimate ending inventory at cost*

The **retail method** of estimating the cost of an ending inventory is based on a percentage relationship between the cost of merchandise available for sale and the selling price of that same merchandise. As its name implies, the retail method is widely used by merchandising businesses, particularly department and discount stores. Businesses that choose to use the retail method must maintain supplementary records to accumulate the retail sales price of all merchandise acquired. The sales figure for the period is deducted from the retail sales price of the goods available for sale to determine the value of the ending inventory at retail sales prices. The inventory at retail is then converted to cost on the basis of the ratio of cost to retail sales price of the goods available for sale. This ratio is computed by dividing total goods available for sale at cost by the total goods available for sale at retail prices. For example, if the total goods available for sale at cost is $240,000 and the total goods available for sale at retail prices is $400,000, then the ratio of cost to retail is 60% ($240,000 ÷ $400,000 = 60%).

To illustrate the method, assume a company has accumulated the following data.

| | AT COST | AT RETAIL |
|---|---|---|
| Inventory (January 1) | $12,000 | $17,000 |
| Net Purchases* (January 1 – March 31) | 46,500 | 73,000 |
| Net Sales (January 1 – March 31) | — | 68,000 |

* Purchases minus purchases returns and purchases discounts.

The estimated inventory on March 31 may be computed in four steps as follows:

1. Determine the amount of goods available for sale at both cost and retail. The amount of goods available for sale consists of beginning inventory plus net purchases. In our example, this is $58,500 at cost ($12,000 + $46,500) and $90,000 at retail ($17,000 + $73,000).
2. Determine the relationship between the cost of the merchandise available for sale and the retail selling price of that same merchandise. The cost-to-retail ratio is 65% ($58,500 ÷ $90,000 = 65%).
3. Determine the estimated ending inventory at retail by deducting net sales for the period from the retail price of the goods available for sale during the period ($90,000 − $68,000 = an estimated ending inventory at retail of $22,000).
4. Determine the estimated ending inventory at cost by multiplying the ending inventory at retail by the cost-to-retail ratio ($22,000 × 65% = an estimated ending inventory at cost of $14,300).

A format for carrying out the four steps in estimating the ending inventory by using the retail method is shown below.

| | AT COST | AT RETAIL |
|---|---|---|
| Beginning Inventory—Jan. 1 | $12,000 | $17,000 |
| Net Cost of Purchases | 46,500 | 73,000 |
| Goods Available for Sale | $58,500 | $90,000 |
| Less: Net Sales | | 68,000 |
| Estimated Ending Inventory—March 31, at Retail | | 22,000 |
| Cost-to-Retail Ratio ($58,500 ÷ $90,000) | | 65% |
| Estimated Ending Inventory—March 31, at Cost ($22,000 × 65%) | $14,300 | |

Note that the cost of goods sold of $44,200, a figure needed for income determination, can be calculated from these data. This is done by subtracting the cost of the ending inventory from the goods available for sale at cost ($58,500 − $14,300 = *$44,200*).

The cost-to-retail ratio can also be used when retailers take a physical inventory. Department and discount stores normally mark the retail selling price on the items being held for sale. As the items are being counted, they can be listed and valued at their marked retail price. The total retail value of the goods on hand can easily be converted to cost by applying the cost-to-retail ratio.

For example, assume that the items on hand as determined by physical count were valued at their retail prices and the total of such prices was $140,000. If the cost-to-retail ratio is *80%*, then the ending inventory at cost is *$112,000* ($140,000 × 80% = $112,000).

## COMPARISON OF METHODS FOR ESTIMATING ENDING INVENTORY

The major difference between the gross margin method and the retail method of estimating ending inventory is as follows:

*2e. The gross margin method uses a gross margin rate based on past experience; the retail method, on a current cost to retail ratio*

1. The gross margin method uses a gross margin rate based on *experiences* from past periods.
2. The retail method uses a cost-to-retail ratio for goods available for sale, most of which were acquired during the *current* period.

*Both methods* are used when interim financial statements are needed by firms that do not want to incur the cost of frequent *physical inventory counts* or do not keep *perpetual inventory records.*

*Neither method* eliminates the need for a complete physical count of all merchandise on hand at least once a year. Physical counts verify the accuracy of the inventory records if such records are maintained and can help determine whether any inventory losses caused by damage, theft, or spoilage have occurred.

## HIGHLIGHT PROBLEM

The information below summarizes the purchases and sales of Niagra Company for the first quarter ending March 31. The company sells a single product and uses the periodic inventory system.

| PURCHASES | | | | SALES | | |
|---|---|---|---|---|---|---|
| Date | Units | Unit Cost | Total Cost | Date | Units | Selling Price |
| Jan. 8 | 50 | 90 | $4,500 | Jan. 12 | 100 | $120 |
| Feb. 2 | 100 | 92 | 9,200 | Feb. 9 | 80 | 125 |
| Feb. 19 | 60 | 94 | 5,640 | March 15 | 110 | 130 |
| March 3 | 80 | 95 | 7,600 | | | |
| March 12 | 40 | 98 | 3,920 | | | |
| March 27 | 80 | 100 | 8,000 | | | |

Inventory on January 1, the beginning of the period, consisted of 70 units costing $5,950.

Required:
Compute the ending inventory, cost of goods sold, and gross margin on sales using the

1. FIFO cost-flow assumption
2. LIFO cost-flow assumption
3. Weighted average cost-flow assumption

(*Hint:* It is helpful to determine both total sales in units and dollars and the cost of goods available for sale in units and dollars before doing the requirements.)

## GLOSSARY OF KEY TERMS

**Conservatism principle.** An accounting concept specifying that when choosing among alternative accounting methods, the one least likely to overstate assets or net income should be selected.

**Consignee.** A company or individual who receives and holds goods to sell on consignment. The consignee is not the owner of the goods being held.

**Consignment.** The transfer of possession but not ownership of goods to a sales agent.

**Consignor.** A company or individual who transfers goods to a consignee. The consignor retains ownership of the goods until sold by the consignee.

**Consistency principle.** An accounting principle that specifies that an accounting method, once adopted among alternatives, should be used from period to period by the same business. The purpose is to make the financial statements of a particular company comparable from period to period.

**Cost.** As it refers to merchandise inventory, the total of the applicable expenditures and charges directly or indirectly incurred in bringing an article or item of inventory to its existing condition and location.

**Cost-flow assumption.** A method of assigning the costs of units of inventory acquired to the units sold and to the units remaining on hand.

**First-In, First-Out (FIFO).** An inventory cost-flow assumption that assigns the costs of the first units acquired to the first units sold. The ending inventory is assigned the costs of the most recently acquired units.

**Gross margin method.** A method of estimating the cost of the ending inventory. It applies a gross margin rate developed from past experience to the current period's net sales to determine the estimated amount for gross margin on sales. The estimated gross margin on sales is subtracted from net sales to determine the estimated cost of goods sold, which in turn is subtracted from the cost of goods available for sale to obtain the estimated ending inventory.

**Inventory.** (1) Materials held for use in the later process of production, (2) materials in the process of production, or (3) finished merchandise held for sale in the regular course of business.

**Last-In, First-Out (LIFO).** An inventory cost-flow assumption that assigns the costs of the last units acquired to the first units sold. The ending inventory is assigned costs from the beginning inventory and the earliest purchases.

**Lower of cost or market (LCM) rule.** A method of inventory valuation under which the inventory is valued at cost or market, whichever is lower.

**Market.** The cost to replace merchandise on the inventory date if purchased from the usual suppliers in usual amounts.

**Moving average.** Term used for the weighted average method under the perpetual inventory system.

**Net realizable value.** The estimated selling price of an inventory item less its estimated selling and disposal costs.

**Retail method.** A method of estimating the cost of the ending inventory based on a percentage relationship between the cost of merchandise available for sale and the selling price of that same merchandise.

**Specific identification.** A method of assigning costs to the ending inventory by tagging, numbering, or coding each unit.

**Weighted average cost.** An inventory cost-flow assumption in which cost is allocated to inventory and to cost of goods sold on the basis of the weighted average cost of the items included in cost of goods available for sale.

## REVIEW QUESTIONS

1. What does inventory include? [LO1a]
2. The term *inventory* can refer to three things. Name these three things. [LO1a]
3. Describe the formula for determining cost of goods sold. [LO1a]
4. Differentiate between the entry for the purchase of merchandise when the periodic inventory system is used and the entry for the same transaction when the perpetual inventory system is used. [LO2a]
5. When the periodic inventory system is used, what entry, if any, is made to record the cost of goods sold at the time that a sale is made? [LO1b,2a]
6. When the perpetual inventory system is used, what two entries are recorded when items are sold? [LO1b,2a]
7. What purpose does an inventory count serve when a perpetual inventory system is used? When a periodic inventory system is used? [LO1c]
8. Differentiate between the way "in transit" merchandise is classified when it is designated FOB shipping point and when it is designated FOB destination. [LO1c]
9. In the year in which an inventory valuation error is made, which accounts shown in the financial statements and which dollar figures are affected by the error? [LO2b]
10. What is meant by the "carryover effect" of misstated ending inventory? [LO2b]
11. Name four expenditures in which the amount would be included in the cost of merchandise inventory. [LO1d]
12. Into which two elements must the cost of goods available for sale be separated in inventory costing? [LO1d]

13. Differentiate between the specific identification, the first-in, first-out (FIFO), and the last-in, first-out (LIFO) inventory cost-flow assumptions. [LO2c]
14. Differentiate between the weighted average cost method used under the periodic inventory system and the moving average cost method used under the perpetual inventory system. [LO2c]
15. What major advantages are attributed to each of the following cost-flow assumptions?
    a. Specific identification
    b. FIFO cost
    c. LIFO cost
    d. Average cost [LO2c]
16. During periods of rising prices, does the FIFO or the LIFO cost flow method result in the higher value for ending inventory? Why? [LO1e]
17. What is the lower of cost or market rule as it applies to inventory valuation? [LO2d]
18. Describe the three methods of applying the lower of cost or market rule to ending inventory valuation. [LO2d]
19. Describe the three guidelines used for modifications of the lower of cost or market rule. [LO2d]
20. Describe the three-step process of estimating inventory when the gross margin method is used. [LO2e]
21. Describe the four-step process of estimating inventory when the retail inventory method is used. [LO2e]
22. Briefly describe what the gross margin and retail methods of estimating inventory have in common and how they differ. [LO2e]

## ANALYTICAL QUESTIONS

23. "It does not matter whether a periodic or a perpetual inventory system is used because the figures reported in the financial statements will be the same at year-end." Comment on this statement. [LO1b,2a]
24. How can a company have items of inventory in its possession at year-end and still not own the items for inventory purposes? [LO1c]
25. "An overstatement of ending inventory for one year is automatically corrected in the next year. The net income for the combined two years is not misstated. Therefore accountants need not be concerned about inventory misstatements." True or false? Comment. [LO2b]
26. "The LIFO method of assigning costs is not 'realistic' because it does not reflect the actual physical flow of goods for most businesses." Comment on this statement. [LO1e,2c]
27. Why is it important to know which inventory cost-flow assumption was used when the financial position and operating results of different companies are being compared? [LO1e,2c]
28. Explain why a company is said to achieve income tax benefits when it uses the LIFO cost-flow assumption during periods of rising prices. [LO1e]
29. If the amount shown for inventory in the accounting records may be lowered from original cost to replacement cost under certain conditions, why should it not at times be raised from original cost to replacement cost? [LO2d]
30. If a company keeps accurate perpetual inventory records and counts the physical inventory on a regular basis, why should it ever be necessary to estimate inventory amounts? [LO2e]

## IMPACT ANALYSIS QUESTIONS

*For each error described, indicate whether it would overstate [O], understate [U], or not affect [N] the specified key figures.*

31. When taking a physical inventory, the company mistakenly included goods held on consignment in determining the amount of its ending inventory. [LO1c]

_______ Total Assets _______ Cost of Goods Sold
_______ Total Liabilities _______ Net Income

32. When taking a physical inventory, the company inadvertently missed some items in one of its warehouses. How does this error affect amounts reported for the current year only? [LO1c,2b]

_______ Total Assets _______ Net Income
_______ Owner's Equity _______ Gross Margin

33. What effect would the error stated in Question 32 (if not detected) have on amounts reported in the following year? [LO1c,2b]

_______ Total Assets _______ Net Income
_______ Owner's Equity _______ Gross Margin

34. A company changed its inventory accounting from the FIFO cost-flow assumption to the LIFO cost-flow assumption in 19X6. The year 19X6 was one of rising inventory costs and one in which the company purchased more items than it sold. [LO2c,1e]

_______ Total Assets _______ Revenue
_______ Cost of Goods Sold _______ Net Income

35. A company inappropriately increased the value of certain items in its inventory from their original cost to their higher replacement cost. [LO2d]

_______ Total Assets _______ Cost of Goods Sold
_______ Owner's Equity _______ Net Income

36. In using the retail method to compute ending inventory, a company used a cost-to-retail percentage of 20%, which was incorrect. The correct percentage is 30%. [LO2e]

_______ Total Assets _______ Cost of Goods Sold
_______ Owner's Equity _______ Net Income

## EXERCISES

EXERCISE 9–1 *(Compute Cost of Goods Sold, Gross Margin on Sales, and Gross Margin Percentage)* The following information was taken from the records of Meteor Company:

| | |
|---|---|
| Beginning Inventory | $ 15,000 |
| Ending Inventory | 19,500 |
| Purchases | 100,000 |
| Purchase Discounts | 2,500 |
| Purchase Returns | 4,000 |
| Sales | 153,000 |
| Sales Returns | 3,000 |
| Transportation-In | 1,000 |

Required:

1. Compute the cost of goods sold.
2. Compute the gross margin on sales and the gross margin percentage. [LO1d]

EXERCISE 9–2 *(Determine the Effects of Inventory Errors and Methods of Valuation)* When answering the questions in items 1 through 4 below, treat each item independently.

1. When taking the physical inventory, merchandise costing $2,000 was inadvertently overlooked. How did this error of omission affect the net income for the current year? What balance sheet items were also affected?
2. As a result of an inventory counting error, the December 31, 19X5, ending inventory was overstated by $5,000. What effect, if any, does the error have on the 19X5 reported net income? What effect, if any, does the error have on the 19X6 reported net

income? What effect, if any, would this error have on total owner's equity after the books are closed on December 31, 19X6?

3. Assume that an item in inventory that cost $40 could be sold for $55 and has a current replacement cost of $38. According to the lower of cost or market rule for inventory valuation, at what amount should the item be reported in the inventory?
4. Determine which of the following statements are true and which are false:
   a. In periods of economic contraction and price decline, the LIFO inventory method will yield an ending inventory that is higher than that determined by the FIFO inventory method.
   b. The FIFO inventory method assigns the most recent costs to inventory.
   c. The LIFO inventory method assigns the earliest costs to inventory.
   d. The inventory method used by a company must be disclosed in its financial statements or in the accompanying notes.
   e. In an economy where the overall trend in prices is upward, the use of the average cost method for inventory valuation will result in an income figure that is lower than that which would be reported if the FIFO method were used and higher than that which would be reported if the LIFO method were used. [LO1c,2b,1e,2d]

EXERCISE 9–3 *(Compute the Amounts to Supply Missing Data)* In each of the four cases that follow, fill in the blanks to supply the missing amounts. [LO1d]

| | CASE 1 | CASE 2 | CASE 3 | CASE 4 |
|---|---|---|---|---|
| Beginning Inventory | $ 5,500 | $ ____ | $ 6,200 | $ 5,300 |
| Purchases | 28,500 | 32,000 | ____ | 27,700 |
| Cost of Goods Sold | ____ | 31,500 | 25,800 | 32,000 |
| Cost of Goods Available for Sale | ____ | ____ | 27,800 | ____ |
| Ending Inventory | 4,500 | 4,000 | ____ | ____ |

EXERCISE 9–4 *(Make Corrections and Determine Effects of Inventory Errors)* Adare Company's income statements for the past three years are shown below.

| | 19X3 | 19X4 | 19X5 |
|---|---|---|---|
| Net Sales | $150,000 | $180,000 | $160,000 |
| Beginning Inventory | 25,000 | 22,000 | 28,000 |
| Net Cost of Purchases | 87,000 | 116,000 | 102,000 |
| Cost of Goods Available for Sale | 112,000 | 138,000 | 130,000 |
| Ending Inventory | 22,000 | 28,000 | 35,000 |
| Cost of Goods Sold | 90,000 | 110,000 | 95,000 |
| Gross Margin on Sales | 60,000 | 70,000 | 65,000 |
| Operating Expenses | 45,000 | 51,000 | 49,000 |
| Net Income | $ 15,000 | $ 19,000 | $ 16,000 |

During a recent review of Adare's accounting records, it was discovered that errors caused the 19X3 ending inventory to be overstated by $1,000 and the 19X4 ending inventory to be understated by $3,000. The 19X5 ending inventory is correct.

Required:

1. Prepare corrected income statements for 19X3, 19X4, and 19X5.
2. What is the cumulative effect of the errors on the figure shown for owner's equity in the company's balance sheet at the end of 19X5? [LO2b]

EXERCISE 9–5 *(Prepare Journal Entries Using the Periodic and Perpetual Inventory Methods)* Selected transactions of Yuban Company are listed below.

a. Merchandise costing $3,000, subject to discount terms of 2/10, n/30, was purchased on credit.

b. Merchandise costing $1,200 was purchased for cash.

c. Merchandise costing $500 and acquired in transaction *a* above was returned to the supplier, who granted full credit.

d. Merchandise costing $1,200 was sold to a customer for $2,000 on credit terms of n/30.

e. The liability created by the purchase of merchandise in transaction *a* above is paid in full and the related discount taken.

Required:

1. Prepare journal entries to record the above transactions using (a) the periodic inventory system and (b) the perpetual inventory system.
2. Assume that the balance in the Inventory account at the beginning of the period was $2,000. Also assume that a physical inventory count taken at the end of the period established that the cost of goods on hand amounted to $4,450. Prepare the entry needed, if any, to adjust the Inventory account at the end of the period. [LO2a]

EXERCISE 9–6 *(Use Various Cost-Flow Assumptions—Periodic Inventory System)* Inven Electronics Company has the following data pertaining to its beginning inventory and its purchases and sales for the month of January.

| | |
|---|---|
| Inventory, January 1 | 100 units @ $15 per unit |
| Purchases during January: | |
| Jan. 5 | 50 units @ $14 per unit |
| Jan. 8 | 75 units @ $16 per unit |
| Jan. 15 | 75 units @ $20 per unit |
| Jan. 20 | 100 units @ $21 per unit |
| Sales during January | 250 units |
| Inventory, January 31 | 150 units |

Required:

Compute Inven's cost of goods sold for January and its inventory at the end of January, using the following cost-flow assumptions (assume the periodic inventory method):

1. Specific identification (assume that one-fourth of the units in the January 1 inventory, all of the units purchased on January 5, 8, and 15, and one-fourth of the units purchased on January 20 were identified as those sold).
2. First-in, first-out (FIFO).
3. Last-in, first-out (LIFO).
4. Weighted average cost. [LO2c]

EXERCISE 9–7 *(Use FIFO and LIFO Cost-Flow Assumptions—Periodic and Perpetual Inventory Systems)* The following data and transactions pertain to an inventory item designated as ROM-5.

| | |
|---|---|
| January 1—Beginning Inventory | 55 units @ $320 = $17,600 |
| January 8—Purchased | 25 units @ $325 = $ 8,125 |
| January 9—Sold | 60 units |
| January 13—Purchased | 40 units @ $328 = $13,120 |
| January 19—Sold | 30 units |
| January 23—Purchased | 50 units @ $330 = $16,500 |
| January 25—Sold | 10 units |

Required:

1. Using the periodic inventory system and the FIFO cost-flow assumption, determine the cost of the 70 items on hand on January 31 and the cost of the 100 items sold during January.
2. Using the perpetual inventory system and the FIFO cost-flow assumption, determine the cost of the ending inventory and the cost of goods sold.

3. Using the periodic inventory system and the LIFO cost-flow assumption, determine the cost of the ending inventory and the cost of goods sold.
4. Using the perpetual inventory system and the LIFO cost-flow assumption, determine the cost of the ending inventory and the cost of goods sold. [LO2c]

EXERCISE 9–8 *(Apply the Lower of Cost or Market Rule)* On January 31, 19X5, Value Company developed the following data pertaining to units in its ending inventory.

| ITEM | NUMBER OF UNITS ON HAND | PER UNIT COST | COST TO REPLACE |
|---|---|---|---|
| U | 200 | $12.00 | $10.50 |
| V | 60 | 50.00 | 54.00 |
| W | 340 | 8.00 | 9.00 |
| X | 80 | 32.00 | 30.00 |
| Y | 120 | 25.00 | 29.00 |
| Z | 150 | 19.00 | 18.00 |

Required:

1. Determine the value of the ending inventory by applying the lower of cost or market rule (a) to each item in the inventory and (b) to the total inventory.
2. How will net income be affected by applying the lower of cost or market rule? What accounting concept is illustrated by the lower of cost or market rule? [LO2d]

EXERCISE 9–9 *(Use the Gross Margin Method)* Score Company uses the gross margin method to estimate its ending inventory so that its interim financial statements can be prepared on a quarterly basis. The following information is available on March 31.

Data from the period January 1 through March 31:

| | |
|---|---|
| Purchases | $69,500 |
| Purchases Returns | 6,700 |
| Purchases Discounts | 1,200 |
| Transportation-In | 400 |
| Sales | 89,800 |
| Sales Discounts | 1,600 |
| Sales Returns | 2,900 |

Additional Data:

Inventory at the beginning of the period was $18,600. Based upon its experiences over the past four years, the company has established that its average gross margin rate on net sales is 20%.

Required:

Use the gross margin method to estimate the cost of the inventory at March 31 and the cost of goods sold for the three months ended March 31. [LO2e]

EXERCISE 9–10 *(Use the Retail Method)* Rett Department Store estimates its ending inventory using the retail method. The following data are available on June 30.

| | COST | RETAIL |
|---|---|---|
| Inventory, June 1 | $11,000 | $ 20,000 |
| Purchases during June | 86,000 | 129,000 |
| Purchases Returns during June | 6,000 | 9,000 |
| Sales during June | | 115,000 |

Required:
Compute (a) the estimated cost of the inventory on June 30, (b) the cost of goods sold for June, and (c) the gross margin on sales for June. [LO2e]

## PROBLEMS

PROBLEM 9–1 *(Compute Cost of Goods Sold, Gross Margin, and Net Income)* Selected data of Hartley Lumber Company for the year ended December 31, 19X5, are summarized in the table below.

| | |
|---|---|
| Purchases | $405,000 |
| Purchases Discounts | 7,000 |
| Purchases Returns | 15,000 |
| Sales | 625,000 |
| Sales Discounts | 10,000 |
| Sales Returns | 18,000 |
| Transportation-In | 4,000 |
| Operating Expenses | 140,000 |

Inventory data are as follows:

| | |
|---|---|
| Inventory, January 1 | $50,000 |
| Inventory, December 31 | 70,000 |

Required:
1. Compute the (a) cost of goods sold, (b) gross margin, and (c) net income.
2. Assume that by applying the lower of cost or market rule on an item-by-item basis, the ending inventory would have been $63,000 instead of the $70,000 that was determined by using the major category basis. What effect would this have on the net income determined in 1*c* above—that is, if net income changed, by how much and in what direction? [LO1d,2d]

PROBLEM 9–2 *(Determine Net Income Under Various Cost-Flow Assumptions)* Selected data for Zorn Company for the year 19X6, some of which are in summarized form, appear below.

| | |
|---|---|
| Inventory, January 1 | 100 units @ $40 per unit |
| Purchases during January | 300 units @ $42 per unit |
| Purchases during February | 500 units @ $44 per unit |
| Purchases during April | 900 units @ $45 per unit |
| Purchases during June | 1,200 units @ $42 per unit |
| Purchases during September | 700 units @ $46 per unit |
| Purchases during November | 400 units @ $49 per unit |
| Sales during the year | 3,600 units totaling $273,600 |

Total operating expenses for the year were $89,500.

Required:
1. Prepare an income statement for the year ended December 31, 19X6, under each assumption listed below. The company uses the periodic inventory system and the (a) **FIFO** cost-flow assumption, (b) **LIFO** cost-flow assumption, (c) weighted average cost-flow assumption.
2. Which cost-flow assumption provides for the best matching of current costs with

current revenues? Which cost-flow assumption provides the most realistic inventory figure for reporting in the balance sheet? Why? [LO2c,1e]

PROBLEM 9–3 *(Determine the Effects of Inventory Errors)* At the end of 19X3 Pine Company determined the following from its accounting records:

| | |
|---|---|
| Net sales for the year 19X3 | $920,000 |
| Net cost of purchases for the year 19X3 | 550,000 |
| Operating expenses for the year 19X3 | 230,000 |

However, at the end of 19X4 the company discovered that errors made in the physical counting of inventory items had resulted in misstated amounts for the ending inventory in both 19X2 and 19X3. The amounts reported and the corrected amounts are shown below.

| | AS REPORTED | CORRECT AMOUNT |
|---|---|---|
| Ending Inventory, 19X2 | $55,000 | $48,000 |
| Ending Inventory, 19X3 | 52,000 | 50,000 |

The inventory at the end of 19X4 was determined correctly.

Required:

By referring to the data above, determine the effect, if any, of the inventory errors on items *a* through *e* listed below. Fill in the blanks to indicate the effect of the errors by using the terms *understated, overstated,* or *not misstated*—whichever is appropriate. [LO2b]

| | 19X2 | 19X3 | 19X4 |
|---|---|---|---|
| a. The Beginning Inventory was | ____ | ____ | ____ |
| b. The Ending Inventory was | ____ | ____ | ____ |
| c. The Cost of Goods Sold was | ____ | ____ | ____ |
| d. The Gross Margin was | ____ | ____ | ____ |
| e. The Net Income was | ____ | ____ | ____ |

PROBLEM 9–4 *(Determine the Effects of Inventory Errors)* In reviewing the records of Allway Company, which uses the periodic inventory system, you discovered the following:

1. Consigned goods received from Barth Company were on hand and were included in Allway's inventory at a cost of $7,000.
2. Goods costing $3,000 were purchased FOB shipping point on December 26. The goods were in transit from December 27 until January 3 when they were delivered to Allway. The purchase was properly recorded on December 26, but because the goods were not on hand at year-end they were not included in the ending inventory.
3. Allway sold goods and shipped them on December 29. The goods, which cost $4,000, were sold on credit for $6,000, FOB destination. The sale was recorded on December 29 and the goods, which were in transit to the customer, were not included in Allway's ending inventory. The goods arrived at their destination on January 5.
4. Goods purchased in December and costing $5,000 were received and included in the ending inventory. The purchase was erroneously recorded in the accounting records as a $500 purchase.
5. During the physical inventory count, merchandise costing $1,200 was counted twice. Also because of a clerical error, 500 units of merchandise costing $35 per unit were included in the inventory at a cost of $53 per unit.

The company had prepared the following income statement for the year ended December 31.

| | | |
|---|---|---|
| Sales | | $500,000 |
| Cost of Goods Sold: | | |
| Beginning Inventory | $ 60,000 | |
| Net cost of purchases | 350,000 | |
| Cost of Goods Available for Sale | $410,000 | |
| Ending Inventory | 80,000 | |
| Cost of Goods Sold | | 330,000 |
| Gross Margin | | $170,000 |
| Operating Expenses | | 110,000 |
| Net Income | | $ 60,000 |

You are satisfied that the beginning inventory and the operating expenses have been reported correctly. However, sales, net cost of purchases, and ending inventory figures need to be changed to reflect your findings.

Required:

1. Determine the correct figures for sales, net cost of purchases, and ending inventory.
2. Prepare a revised income statement using the corrected figures. [LO2b,lc]

PROBLEM 9-5 *(Compare the Periodic and Perpetual Inventory Systems)* During the month of January, Martin Company had the following selected transactions. The company uses the LIFO cost-flow assumption.

a. January 5, purchased 50 units @ $25 per unit
b. January 11, purchased 55 units @ $29 per unit
c. January 13, sold 50 units @ $100 per unit
d. January 15, purchased 70 units @ $30 per unit
e. January 17, purchased 60 units @ $30 per unit
f. January 17, sold 55 units @ $100 per unit
g. January 20, purchased 50 units @ $31 per unit
h. January 22, purchased 65 units @ $31 per unit
i. January 25, sold 50 units @ $100 per unit
j. January 30, sold 40 units @ $100 per unit

Beginning inventory consisted of 90 units @ $25 per unit.

Required:

1. Compute the number of units remaining in the ending inventory and the cost of the ending inventory assuming the company uses (a) the periodic inventory system and (b) the perpetual inventory system. Does the number of units remaining in the ending inventory differ for each system? Why or why not? Does the cost of the ending inventory differ for each system? Why or why not?
2. Prepare journal entries for the January transactions using the periodic inventory system.
3. Prepare journal entries for the January transactions using the perpetual inventory system. [LO2a,2c]

PROBLEM 9-6 *(Use Various Cost-Flow Assumptions—Periodic Inventory System)* At the end of 19X5, the first year of its operations, Hendley Corporation had 1,200 units of merchandise on hand. During 19X5 the following purchases had been made:

| DATE | QUANTITY | UNIT COST |
|---|---|---|
| January 4 | 700 | $ 9.00 |
| March 11 | 400 | 10.00 |
| April 22 | 1,000 | 9.50 |
| May 30 | 600 | 10.20 |
| July 14 | 300 | 10.50 |
| September 3 | 800 | 11.00 |
| October 18 | 500 | 11.70 |
| December 20 | 500 | 12.00 |

Required:
Assuming that the periodic inventory system is used, compute the ending inventory using the (a) FIFO cost-flow assumption, (b) LIFO cost-flow assumption, (c) weighted average cost-flow assumption. [LO2c]

PROBLEM 9–7 *(Complete a Narrative Comparison for Inventory Cost-Flow Assumptions)* The following questions relate to FIFO, LIFO, and weighted average cost-flow assumptions. Fill in each blank with one of the following phrases:

a. "Higher than the other two cost-flow assumptions."
b. "Lower than the other two cost-flow assumptions."
c. "Neither higher nor lower than the other two cost-flow assumptions."

1. During periods of rising prices, the weighted average cost-flow assumption produces a cost of goods sold that is

   ______________________________.

2. During periods of falling prices, the weighted average cost-flow assumption produces an ending inventory that is

   ______________________________.

3. During periods of rising prices, the FIFO cost-flow assumption produces a cost of goods sold that is

   ______________________________.

4. During periods of falling prices, the FIFO cost-flow assumption produces an ending inventory that is

   ______________________________.

5. During periods of rising prices, the LIFO cost-flow assumption produces a cost of goods sold that is

   ______________________________.

6. During periods of falling prices, the LIFO cost-flow assumption produces an ending inventory that is

   ______________________________.

7. During periods of rising prices, the LIFO cost-flow assumption produces a federal income tax liability that is

   ______________________________. [LO1e]

PROBLEM 9–8 *(Apply the Lower of Cost or Market Rule)* The year-end inventory of Variety Home and Garden Company determined by a physical count is summarized in the table below.

| | | PER UNIT | |
|---|---|---|---|
| | QUANTITY | Cost | Market |
| *Garden Supplies:* | | | |
| Mowers | 7 | $120 | $118 |
| Rotors | 12 | 110 | 112 |
| Backhoes | 15 | 90 | 95 |
| *Paints:* | | | |
| Latex | 5 | 8 | 5 |
| Enamel | 11 | 12 | 15 |
| Oil | 12 | 15 | 13 |
| *Tools:* | | | |
| Trimmers | 20 | 270 | 265 |
| Sprayers | 10 | 200 | 150 |

Required:

1. Determine the value of the ending inventory at lower of cost or market using each of the following methods: (a) the item-by-item method, (b) the major category method, and (c) the total inventory method.
2. Comment on why the amount of the ending inventory varies for each method.

[LO2d]

PROBLEM 9–9 *(Apply the Lower of Cost or Market Rule with Modifying Guidelines)* For several years X Company has used replacement cost whenever replacement cost was lower than original cost in valuing items in its inventory. This year, however, the company's new controller indicated that replacement cost would be used only if certain modifying guidelines were applied. To explain these guidelines, the following data were presented.

| ITEM | UNIT COST | UNIT REPLACEMENT COST | NORMAL SELLING PRICE | CURRENT SELLING PRICE | ESTIMATED COST TO COMPLETE AND DISPOSE OF INVENTORY ITEM |
|---|---|---|---|---|---|
| No. 1 | $10 | $ 9 | $15 | $12 | $1 |
| No. 2 | 15 | 12 | 20 | 20 | 2 |
| No. 3 | 20 | 17 | 25 | 24 | 1 |
| No. 4 | 15 | 16 | 20 | 20 | 1 |
| No. 5 | 20 | 19 | 25 | 20 | 2 |

Required:

For each inventory item numbered 1 through 5, indicate what per unit amount would be used to determine the value of the ending inventory at lower of cost or market, with modifying guidelines. (*Hint:* The gross margin amounts must be computed.) [LO2d]

PROBLEM 9–10 *(Use the Gross Margin Method)* On April 1, 19X5, the entire inventory of Mayflower Company was destroyed by a fire. Fortunately, the company's accounting records had been kept in an office that was not affected by the fire. The information shown below was taken from those records on the date of the fire.

| | |
|---|---|
| Merchandise Inventory, January 1 | $ 43,200 |
| Purchases | 339,000 |
| Purchases Discounts | 6,500 |
| Purchases Returns | 3,100 |
| Sales | 487,000 |
| Sales Discounts | 5,300 |
| Sales Returns | 4,100 |
| Transportation-In | 2,400 |
| General Expenses | 28,900 |
| Selling Expenses | 55,700 |

The last physical inventory was taken at the close of the company's accounting period on December 31, 19X4. In order to file an insurance claim, the company must estimate its inventory loss.

Required:

Using the gross margin method, determine the cost of the inventory destroyed by the fire on April 1. The gross margin based on net sales has averaged 30% over the past four years.

[LO2e]

PROBLEM 9–11 *(Use the Retail Method)* Star Sporting Goods Company uses the retail method to estimate the cost of its ending inventory. Data from the company's accounting records for the first three months are shown below.

| | AT COST | AT RETAIL |
|---|---|---|
| January 1, Beginning Inventory | $ 49,200 | $ 85,100 |
| Sales | | 500,700 |
| Transportation-In | 8,900 | |
| Purchases | 256,125 | 444,300 |
| Sales Returns | | 6,900 |
| Purchases Returns | 2,300 | 4,400 |
| Purchases Discounts | 4,800 | |
| Operating Expenses | 149,700 | |

Required:

1. Determine the cost of the March 31 inventory.
2. Prepare an income statement for the first quarter of the year.
3. Assume now that a physical inventory was taken on March 31 and established the cost of the ending inventory at $17,600. What factors may have caused the difference between the amount of the estimated inventory computed in Requirement 1 and the amount determined by the physical count? [LO2e]

PROBLEM 9–12 *(Compare Inventory Cost-Flow Assumptions—Periodic Inventory System)* Rae Merchandising Company, which began its first year of operations on January 1, 19X5, uses the periodic inventory system. Data on the company's purchases and sales for the year are shown below.

| | |
|---|---|
| Sales: $840,000 | The selling price remained stable at $8 per unit throughout the year |
| Purchases: 1/2 | 28,000 units at $5.00 per unit |
| 3/7 | 16,000 units at 5.50 per unit |
| 5/15 | 12,000 units at 5.70 per unit |
| 7/2 | 18,000 units at 5.60 per unit |
| 9/21 | 20,000 units at 5.75 per unit |
| 10/18 | 14,000 units at 5.80 per unit |
| 12/23 | 8,000 units at 6.00 per unit |

Summarized data pertaining to the company's operating expenses for the year 19X5 are as follows:

| | |
|---|---|
| Salaries | $180,400 |
| Rent | 31,000 |
| Advertising | 17,500 |
| Utilities | 12,700 |
| Depreciation | 13,200 |

The company's executives are aware that there are acceptable alternative inventory cost-flow assumptions and that in an economy of fluctuating prices, their selection will affect the valuation of ending inventory, the cost of goods sold, and consequently the reported net income. Before they are willing to make a decision regarding which inventory cost-flow assumption to use, they have engaged you to perform the following.

Required:

1. Determine the ending inventory using (a) the **FIFO** cost-flow assumption, (b) the **LIFO** cost-flow assumption, and (c) the weighted average cost-flow assumption (average cost may be computed to the nearest cent).
2. Prepare income statements under each of the cost-flow assumptions. Present them side by side in a manner that will enhance their comparability. [LO2c]

PROBLEM 9–13 *(Comprehensive Problem—Determine Effects of Errors and Make Corrections)* Standard Meter Company prepared the following condensed income statement for the month of September 19X5.

| | SEPTEMBER |
|---|---|
| Net Sales | $89,000 |
| Cost of Goods Sold: | |
| Beginning Inventory | 27,500 |
| Net Cost of Purchases | 59,700 |
| Cost of Goods Available for Sale | 87,200 |
| Ending Inventory | 26,900 |
| Cost of Goods Sold | 60,300 |
| Gross Margin | 28,700 |
| Less: Operating Expenses | 17,100 |
| Net Income | $11,600 |

The management of Standard Meter was concerned about and disappointed by its reported operational performance for the month of September. The statement indicated a gross margin of approximately 32% and a net income of slightly over 13%, based on net sales. Management's projected goal at the beginning of the month was to achieve a gross margin of 35% and a net income of 17%. It was agreed that the company's records should be reviewed by an outside authority to establish the reliability of the income statement. At a meeting on October 5, the company's board of directors approved the suggestion to engage the services of an independent public accounting firm. Its investigation disclosed the following:

a. Merchandise costing $600 was overlooked when a physical inventory was taken on September 30.
b. Merchandise costing $800 was on hand but was not counted during the physical inventory because it had been marked "sold." Further investigation revealed that title to the goods did not pass to the buyer until October 2 when the goods were shipped. The sale transaction was recorded properly on October 2.
c. A telephone bill representing an operating expense and applicable to the month of September was not recorded in September because the bill was not received until October 3. The amount was $45.
d. A clerical addition error was made when calculating the inventory on September 30. The error resulted in understating the ending inventory by $900.
e. Merchandise remained in a railroad car at the company's siding on September 30. Since it was not in the warehouse, it was overlooked by the team of inventory takers during the physical count. An examination of documents revealed that title to the goods had passed to Standard Meter Company on September 29, and that an entry debiting Purchases and crediting Accounts Payable for $2,600 was made on September 30.
f. Merchandise held on consignment was counted and included in the ending inventory at a cost of $1,400.

Required:

1. Determine the correct ending inventory and operating expense figures at September 30.
2. Prepare a revised income statement for the month of September.
3. Determine the gross margin and net income percentages based on the figures in the revised income statement. [LO1c,2b,1d]

## ALTERNATE PROBLEMS

PROBLEM 9–1A *(Compare Inventory Cost-Flow Assumptions—Periodic Inventory System)* (Alternate to Problem 9–2) Curious Company wishes to analyze different inventory cost-flow assumptions under conditions of both rising and falling prices. Therefore the following hypothetical data were developed for one month.

| | NUMBER OF UNITS | COST PER UNIT (ALTERNATIVE A) | COST PER UNIT (ALTERNATIVE B) |
|---|---|---|---|
| Beginning Inventory | 100 | $10 | $20 |
| Purchases: | | | |
| 1/10 | 50 | 11 | 19 |
| 1/12 | 70 | 13 | 18 |
| 1/20 | 50 | 15 | 18 |
| 1/22 | 80 | 15 | 16 |
| 1/25 | 100 | 16 | 15 |
| 1/29 | 60 | 17 | 12 |
| Sales | (400) | | |

Required:

1. Using the costs per unit shown in Alternative A, compute the cost of the ending inventory and the cost of goods sold for January using (a) the weighted average cost-flow assumption (average cost may be computed to the nearest cent), (b) the FIFO cost-flow assumption, and (c) the LIFO cost-flow assumption.
2. Complete the same requirements as in 1 above, using the costs per unit shown in Alternative B.
3. Comment on the differences in results obtained in Requirements 1 and 2. [LO2c,1e]

PROBLEM 9–2A *(Determine the Effects of Inventory Errors)* (Alternate to Problem 9–4) After preparing the partial income statement shown below, Butler Company's management became aware of the following:

Because some inventory items were overlooked during the physical count taken last year, this year's beginning inventory is understated by $3,800.

Because of computational errors, this year's ending inventory is overstated by $2,600.

Presented below is the partial income statement that contains these errors.

| | | |
|---|---|---|
| Net Sales | | $82,000 |
| Cost of Goods Sold: | | |
| Beginning Inventory | $23,700 | |
| Net purchases | 72,400 | |
| Cost of Goods Available for Sale | 96,100 | |
| Less: Ending Inventory | 32,500 | 63,600 |
| Gross Margin | | $18,400 |

Required:

1. Determine the effect of the inventory errors on (a) the cost of goods sold and (b) the gross margin. Also indicate whether the amounts are understated or overstated in the incorrect income statement.
2. Prepare a revised partial income statement using the corrected inventory figures. [LO2b,1c]

PROBLEM 9–3A *(Use Various Cost-Flow Assumptions—Perpetual Inventory System)* (Alternate to Problem 9–6) Hostos Company sells a single relatively high priced product. Transactions involving the purchases and sales of the product during April are shown on page 348.

The April 1 inventory was $7,000 and consisted of five units. The eleven units sold during April were sold at a uniform price, generating sales revenue of $24,200. Operating expenses for the month totaled $4,800.

| | |
|---|---|
| April 3 | Purchased 2 units @ $1,450 per unit |
| 8 | Sold 4 units |
| 9 | Purchased 5 units @ $1,500 per unit |
| 12 | Sold 4 units |
| 25 | Purchased 5 units @ $1,560 per unit |
| 29 | Sold 3 units |

Required:
Determine the ending inventory and prepare an income statement for the month of April under each assumption listed below. The company uses the perpetual inventory system and the

a. FIFO cost-flow assumption
b. LIFO cost-flow assumption
c. Moving average cost-flow assumption [LO2c]

PROBLEM 9–4A *(Use the Gross Margin Method)* (Alternate to Problem 9–10) During the past three years, Parklane Bowling Supplies Company developed the following data showing its sales, cost of goods sold, and gross margin.

| | 19X3 | 19X4 | 19X5 |
|---|---|---|---|
| Sales | $30,000 | $35,000 | $40,000 |
| Cost of Goods Sold: | | | |
| Inventory, January 1 | $ 5,000 | $ 8,000 | $ 9,000 |
| Purchases for Year | 20,000 | 21,000 | 24,900 |
| Cost of Goods Available for Sale | $25,000 | $29,000 | $33,900 |
| Inventory, December 31 | 8,000 | 9,000 | 10,000 |
| Cost of Goods Sold | $17,000 | $20,000 | $23,900 |
| Gross Margin | $13,000 | $15,000 | $16,100 |

On March 16, 19X6, a fire in the warehouse destroyed the company's entire inventory. The company wants to file an insurance claim for the amount of the loss and has asked you for help.

The following summarized data taken from the company's accounting records are available.

| | |
|---|---|
| Net Sales—January 1, 19X6, to March 16 | $9,500 |
| Net Cost of Purchases—January 1, 19X6, to March 16 | $6,800 |

Required:
Using the gross margin method, determine the cost of the inventory destroyed by the fire on March 16. Develop an average gross margin percentage from the information presented for the three-year period 19X3 through 19X5. [LO2e]

PROBLEM 9–5A *(Use the Retail Method)* (Alternate to Problem 9–11) Using the retail method of estimating the cost of the ending inventory, determine the missing amounts in each of the four cases listed below. Carry percentages to two decimal places and round results to the nearest dollar. [LO2e]

| | CASE 1 | CASE 2 | CASE 3 | CASE 4 |
|---|---|---|---|---|
| Beginning Inventory at Cost | $ 30,000 | $ 40,000 | $ 10,000 | $ 5,000 |
| Beginning Inventory at Retail | 50,000 | ______ | 20,000 | ______ |
| Net Purchases at Cost | 100,000 | 200,000 | 80,000 | 25,000 |
| Net Purchases at Retail | 130,000 | 250,000 | 100,000 | 40,000 |
| Net Sales | (120,000) | (190,000) | (120,000) | (50,000) |
| Ending Inventory at Retail | ______ | 110,000 | ______ | 5,000 |
| Ending Inventory at Cost | ______ | ______ | ______ | ______ |

# 10 Plant and Equipment: Acquisition and Depreciation

## *Learning Objectives*

When you complete this chapter you will be able to

1. Answer the following questions:
   a. What are noncurrent assets and plant and equipment assets and what are some examples of each?
   b. What is the meaning of the term *depreciation* as used in accounting?
   c. What items of data are needed to determine the periodic depreciation expense?
   d. How does the accelerated cost recovery system (ACRS) defer income taxes?
   e. How do capital expenditures differ from revenue expenditures?
2. Perform the following accounting functions:
   a. Determine the acquisition cost of different plant assets acquired under different terms and for different purposes.
   b. Compute periodic depreciation expense using the (1) straight-line method, (2) units-of-production method, (3) sum-of-the-year's-digits method, and (4) declining-balance method.
   c. Determine depreciation (1) for partial years, (2) when estimated useful life is revised, (3) when the group or composite method is used, and (4) for plant assets having low unit costs.

Assets, as we have seen, can be classified as current and noncurrent. Current assets consist of cash and of assets that can reasonably be expected to be converted into cash or consumed within one year or one operating cycle, whichever is longer. In this chapter we discuss certain noncurrent assets, those expected to provide benefits for more than one year or one operating cycle. For balance sheet reporting, these noncurrent assets are often classified according to their various characteristics. The four general classifications frequently used are (1) *investments,* (2) *plant and equipment,* (3) *natural resources,* and (4) *intangibles.* In this chapter (and in part of Chapter 11) we study the accounting for noncurrent assets classified as plant and equipment.

*1a. Noncurrent assets are of four general classifications*

## PLANT AND EQUIPMENT ASSETS

**Plant and equipment** are tangible, long-lived assets used in the operating activities of a business. They are not intended for resale to customers. Common examples include land, buildings, machinery, vehicles, equipment, tools, and furniture and fixtures. In past years **fixed assets** was a common term applied to this type of asset. Today the more popular terms are **property, plant, and equipment; plant assets;** or, as we will call them in this chapter, ***plant and equipment.***

*1a. Plant and equipment assets have three essential characteristics*

To be classified as plant and equipment an asset must possess three characteristics.

1. The asset must be used in the operations of the business.

Idle buildings or land being held for a future site or for speculative reasons should not be included in the classification plant and equipment. These assets are not being used in conducting the company's operating activities and should therefore be classified as long-term investments. It is also possible for an item to be properly classified as plant and equipment by one company and as inventory by another. For example, an automobile in a car dealer's showroom is an inventory item to the dealer. The same automobile purchased by an insurance company and used by an employee to visit and solicit business from clients is part of the insurance company's plant and equipment assets.

2. The asset must be expected to provide benefits for more than one year.

There is no standard regarding the minimum productive life necessary for an asset to be classified as plant and equipment. However, the common guide is that the asset must be capable of repeated use for a period lasting more than one year. A productive life of longer than one year is a characteristic that distinguishes an item properly classified as plant and equipment from an item such as supplies properly classified as a current asset.

3. The asset must be tangible in nature.

**Tangible** means having physical substance. To be classified as plant and equipment, the asset must have physical characteristics that can be seen and touched. Noncurrent assets used in the operations of the business, but lacking physical substance, are classified as *intangible* assets. Examples include patents, copyrights, franchises, and goodwill, which will be discussed in the next chapter.

## QUESTIONS INVOLVED IN ACCOUNTING FOR PLANT AND EQUIPMENT ASSETS

Several issues are involved in accounting for plant and equipment assets. They can be summarized by the following series of questions:

1. How is the *cost* of plant and equipment assets *determined?*
2. How should the *cost* of plant and equipment assets be *allocated* to expense over the periods expected to receive benefits from their use?
3. How should *subsequent expenditures* made to maintain and/or improve plant and equipment assets be *treated?*
4. How should the *disposal* of plant and equipment assets be *recorded?*

In the following sections we discuss the first three issues. The fourth issue will be examined in Chapter 11.

## DETERMINING THE COST OF PLANT AND EQUIPMENT ASSETS

*2a. The cost of a plant and equipment asset includes all expenditures reasonable and necessary to acquire and prepare the asset for its intended use*

The **cost** of a plant and equipment asset includes all the expenditures reasonable and necessary to acquire the asset and to prepare it for its intended use. This general rule will be used to determine the acquisition cost of specific plant assets discussed below.

**COST OF MACHINERY** The cost of a machine includes its purchase price (invoice price less any cash discounts) plus any sales tax, shipping charges incurred by the buyer, insurance on the asset while in transit, installation costs, and initial testing costs. In short, the cost of a machine includes all the expenditures reasonable and necessary to obtain it and get it ready for its intended use. If other expenditures resulting from carelessness or other unusual occurrences are incurred they should be treated as an expense of the current period, not as part of the asset cost.

To illustrate the accounting treatment of expenditures pertaining to a plant asset, assume that Classic Company purchases a machine having an invoice price of $20,000 with terms of 2/10, n/30. A sales tax of 5% and a transportation charge of $600 must be paid by the buyer. In addition, insurance costing $120 and paid for by the buyer was carried on the machine while in transit. The cost to install the machine was $525. Repair costs for damage to the machine caused by carelessness when company employees unpacked it were $75.

The cost of the machine and the amount to be debited to the Machinery account is $21,825, computed as follows:

| | |
|---|---|
| Invoice price of machine | $20,000 |
| Less: Cash discount (2% × $20,000) | 400 |
| Net cash price | $19,600 |
| Sales tax (5% × $19,600) | 980 |
| Transportation | 600 |
| Insurance | 120 |
| Installation | 525 |
| Cost of machine | $21,825 |

Note that all the expenditures except the one incurred to repair the damage were included in the cost of the machine. Damage repair costs, although associated with the machine, were not considered to be a reasonable and necessary expenditure to get the machine in place and ready for use. Therefore they are charged to the period as an expense.

A journal entry summarizing all the transactions pertaining to the machine is shown on page 352.

| | | | |
|---|---|---|---|
| July 1 | Machinery | 21,825 | |
| | Repairs Expense | 75 | |
| | Cash | | 21,900 |

*2a. Land cost includes the purchase price plus all expenditures to acquire title and prepare the land for its intended use*

COST OF LAND Land is an asset considered to have an unlimited useful life. The cost of land includes its negotiated purchase price plus other expenditures necessary in obtaining title to the property and preparing it for its intended use. These expenditures often include commissions to real estate agents, legal fees, surveying fees, accrued property taxes paid by the purchaser, and fees paid for clearing, grading, draining, and landscaping the property.

If a building on the land site must be removed in order to prepare the land for its intended use, the cost of removing the unwanted building (less amounts received from the sale of materials salvaged from the building) is included in the cost of the land.

To illustrate how costs associated with land acquisition are treated in accounting, assume that Classic Company purchases land to be used as a site for its new warehouse. The purchase price of the land is $90,000. Additional costs incurred to acquire title and prepare the land for its intended use were: real estate commissions, $3,500; legal fees, $1,800; survey fees, $400; building removal costs, $4,200; and drainage and landscaping fees, $2,700. The proceeds from the sale of materials from the demolished building amounted to $600.

The cost of the land and the amount to be debited to the Land account is $102,000, computed as follows:

| | | |
|---|---|---|
| Purchase price of land site | | $ 90,000 |
| Real estate commissions | | 3,500 |
| Legal fees | | 1,800 |
| Survey fees | | 400 |
| Removal of old building | $4,200 | |
| Less: Proceeds from sale of salvaged materials | 600 | 3,600 |
| Drainage and landscaping fees | | 2,700 |
| Cost of land | | $102,000 |

COST OF LAND IMPROVEMENTS Land improvements include such things as driveways, paved parking lots, fences, shrubbery, and sprinkler systems. When these items have limited lives and are subject to depreciation, their cost should be entered in a separate account called Land Improvements rather than in the Land account.

*2a. Cost of a purchased building includes its purchase price plus all expenditures to prepare it for its intended use*

COST OF BUILDINGS The cost of a purchased building includes its purchase price plus expenditures incurred for renovation and repair work that were needed to get the building ready for its intended use. When a company constructs a building for its own use, cost includes all the expenditures related to the construction project. Included would be the cost of materials and labor used in construction; the architectural, legal, and engineering fees; the cost of building permits; and the cost of insurance carried during construction. Generally, interest incurred during the construction period as a result of money borrowed to finance the construction is also included as part of the cost of the building.[1]

[1] Financial Accounting Standards Board, "Capitalization of Interest Cost," *Statement No. 34* (Stamford, Conn., 1979), par. 6.

*2a. Cost of equipment is determined like cost of machinery*

COST OF EQUIPMENT Like the cost of machinery, the cost of equipment includes all the expenditures incurred to purchase the equipment and get it ready for its intended use. These expenditures include invoice price less cash discounts, sales tax, shipping charges incurred by the buyer, insurance while the equipment is in transit, and installation and testing costs.

COST OF LEASED ASSETS Many companies choose to lease their plant and equipment assets rather than buy or make them. The accounting treatment given to certain long-term leased assets is similar to that given to purchased or self-constructed plant assets.

At this point it is only necessary to recognize that accounting similarities exist and that certain leased assets are classified as plant and equipment assets. A more-detailed discussion of accounting for leased assets is presented later in this text.

## ANOTHER CONSIDERATION WHEN DETERMINING COST

*2a. The lump-sum cost of group purchases must be apportioned among the assets acquired*

GROUP PURCHASES Sometimes a group of several different plant and equipment assets are purchased for one price. In such cases, the specific cost of each asset acquired in the group purchase is not identified. Therefore the group's total purchase price must be apportioned in a systematic way among the various assets acquired. The type of asset purchase being described here is called a **group purchase** or a **lump-sum acquisition** to indicate that several assets (a group) are being acquired for one (lump-sum) price. The apportionment of the one lump-sum price among the several assets acquired is normally done on the basis of the relative values of those assets.

To illustrate, assume that land, a building, and machinery are acquired at a cost of $200,000. An independent appraisal was obtained to value the assets at the following amounts: land, $48,000; building, $120,000; and machinery, $72,000. The $200,000 total cost can be apportioned to each asset as follows. (Remember that the total amount recorded cannot exceed $200,000 even though the total of the appraised values is $240,000.)

| | APPRAISED VALUE | PERCENTAGE OF TOTAL APPRAISED VALUE | | TOTAL COST | COST APPORTIONED TO EACH ASSET |
|---|---|---|---|---|---|
| Land | $ 48,000 | $ 48,000/240,000 = | 20% | × $200,000 = | $ 40,000 |
| Building | 120,000 | 120,000/240,000 = | 50 | × 200,000 = | 100,000 |
| Machinery | 72,000 | 72,000/240,000 = | 30 | × 200,000 = | 60,000 |
| Total | $240,000 | | 100% | | $200,000 |

The amount of cost apportioned to each asset is used when the purchase is recorded in the accounting records. The following entry would record the acquisition of the assets:

| | | Debit | Credit |
|---|---|---|---|
| July 1 | Land | 40,000 | |
| | Building | 100,000 | |
| | Machinery | 60,000 | |
| | Cash | | 200,000 |
| | To record the purchase of plant and equipment assets | | |

## DEPRECIATION

As mentioned earlier, all plant and equipment assets are expected to provide benefits for more than one year. When a company purchases such an asset, it is buying a bundle of service benefits that can be used to help generate revenues throughout the asset's useful life. Since all plant and equipment assets except land have limited useful lives, their service benefits are being consumed during the periods that the asset is used. As these service benefits are consumed, a portion of the asset's cost should be allocated (transferred) to expense. The process used to systematically allocate the cost of plant and equipment assets to the accounting periods benefited by their use is called **depreciation.**

*1b. Depreciation is the systematic allocation of the cost of plant and equipment assets to the accounting periods benefited by their use*

Depreciation often has a different meaning outside of accounting. Here the term *depreciation* often refers to a decline in the market value of an asset that an owner may have experienced while holding the asset. Although the market value of plant and equipment assets also changes while they are being held, these changes are not recorded in the accounting records. Accountants would suggest that since plant and equipment assets are acquired for use, not for resale, they should be recorded at their costs and that their costs should be allocated as an expense over their estimated useful lives. Simply put, in accounting, depreciation is a process of cost allocation, not a process of market valuation.

## DETERMINING THE AMOUNT OF PERIODIC DEPRECIATION

*1c. Three items of data about a plant asset are needed to determine its periodic depreciation expense*

To determine the amount of periodic depreciation for a plant asset, we need three items of data about the asset. We then need to select a method from several methods, each of which is acceptable for computing depreciation. The three items of data about the asset are (1) its *cost,* (2) its estimated useful *life,* and (3) its estimated *residual value* (which is the amount expected to be received when the asset is disposed of at the end of its useful life). Item 1, the asset's cost, has already been discussed. Therefore let us look in turn at items 2 and 3, estimated useful life and estimated residual value.

### Estimated Useful Life

*1c. Service benefits to be obtained from an asset may be measured in units of time or in units of activity and output*

The **estimated useful life** of a plant asset is an estimate of the expected benefits to be obtained from the asset before disposal. Service benefits may in turn be measured in units of time, such as years, or in units of activity or output, such as hours of operation or number of units produced. For example, a machine's useful life may be best measured in the number of hours expected to be obtained from its use (units of activity) rather than in the number of years (units of time) it is expected to be useful. On the other hand, a building's useful life is probably best measured in the number of years it is expected to be useful.

A plant asset's useful life refers to its usefulness to the business—that is, how long the company expects to benefit from its use. It is not a measurement of the asset's potential life. In fact, firms often dispose of assets before their service potential is completely exhausted.

For example, an electric typewriter may be able to provide benefits for ten or more years. However, because improved models are available more frequently, a given company may choose to trade in its old typewriters on new ones every three years. In this case, the company would use an estimated useful life of three years in determining the amount of asset cost that should be allocated to depreciation in each of the three years that the typewriters will be used.

*1c. The estimate of a plant asset's useful life is based, in part, on physical deterioration, obsolescence, and inadequacy*

The estimate of a plant asset's useful life is often based on the company's past experience with similar assets, with consideration being given to three additional factors: *physical deterioration, obsolescence,* and *inadequacy.*

**Physical deterioration** refers to the wear and tear on the asset caused by frequent use and exposure to such climatic elements as wind, rain, snow, and sun. An adequate maintenance program may be helpful in offsetting the effects that use and exposure have on an asset's useful life, but every depreciable plant asset will eventually wear out. Physical deterioration is probably the most important factor influencing the estimated useful life of the heavy equipment used in such industries as agriculture and construction.

**Obsolescence** results when inventions and technological changes develop new assets capable of providing superior services or the same services more efficiently than the existing assets. Obsolete assets are out-of-date assets. This factor plays an important role when estimating the useful life of equipment produced by high-tech companies in the computer and aerospace fields.

**Inadequacy** refers to the inability of an existing plant asset to provide enough service benefits to meet the current needs of its user. Inadequacy, like obsolescence, is difficult to predict, but it must be considered when estimating a plant asset's useful life.

### Estimated Residual Value

**Residual value,** sometimes called **salvage value** or **scrap value,** is the amount of a plant asset's cost expected to be recovered on its estimated date of disposal.

If a company plans to use a plant asset to a point where its potential service benefits are virtually consumed, its estimated residual value will probably be minimal or could even be zero. Conversely, if the company plans to dispose of the asset long before its potential service benefits have been exhausted, its estimated residual value might be substantial.

For example, if a company plans to use a vehicle for only two years, its potential service benefits will probably not be fully consumed and the asset may be expected to have a large residual value. On the other hand, if the company plans to use the vehicle for ten years, its expected residual value should be minimal.

*1c. A plant asset's cost less its estimated residual value equals its depreciable cost*

The excess of a plant asset's cost over its estimated residual value (an amount sometimes called the asset's **depreciable cost**) is the amount that should be recorded as depreciation expense during the asset's useful life.

## METHODS OF COMPUTING DEPRECIATION

There are several acceptable methods of computing depreciation. Four of the more frequently used methods are the (1) *straight-line* method, (2) *units-of-production* method, (3) *sum-of-the-years'-digits* method, and (4) *declining-balance* method. Each results in a different pattern of depreciation. That is, the application of each method will result in the recording of different amounts for depreciation expense in a given year during the asset's useful life. Each method is acceptable, and its selection should be based on how management assumes that the service benefits contained in the plant asset will be consumed. Furthermore, a company need not use a single method for all of its depreciable plant assets. The results of a survey covering six hundred companies indicated that 94% used the straight-line method, approximately 9% used the units-of-production method, and about 28% used an accelerated depreciation method such as the sum-of-the-years'-digits method or the declining-balance method.[2] The total percentage figure exceeds one hundred because some companies reported the use of different methods for different types of plant assets.

In the following sections we will compute depreciation using each of the four different methods. In each case, we will base our calculations on the following data:

| | |
|---|---|
| Cost of the plant asset (machine) | $95,000 |
| Estimated residual value | $ 5,000 |
| Estimated useful life in years | 5 years |
| Estimated useful life in units of production (total units expected to be produced by the machine during its useful life) | 360,000 units |

## Straight-line Method

The **straight-line method** is the simplest and most widely used method of computing depreciation. Under the straight-line method an equal share of the asset's depreciable cost is allocated to each accounting period in its estimated useful life. This method is most appropriate for depreciating plant assets that make a fairly uniform contribution to a company's revenue-producing activities during each period of their useful lives.

*2b. The straight-line method divides depreciable cost by the number of periods in the asset's estimated useful life*

The amount of depreciation for each period is determined by dividing the cost of the asset, less its residual value, by the number of periods in the asset's estimated useful life. Applying the asset information provided above, the depreciation expense for each year using the straight-line method is $18,000, as determined by the following formula:

$$\frac{\text{Cost} - \text{Estimated Residual Value}}{\text{Estimated Useful Life in Years}} \quad \text{or} \quad \frac{\$95{,}000 - \$5{,}000}{5 \text{ years}} = \text{Annual Depreciation of } \$18{,}000$$

As we have seen in earlier chapters, the journal entry to record depreciation is

| | | | |
|---|---|---|---|
| Dec. 31 | Depreciation Expense . . . . . . . . . . . . . . . . . . . . . . . . . . . . . . | 18,000 | |
| | Accumulated Depreciation—Machinery . . . . . . . . . . | | 18,000 |
| | To record annual depreciation | | |

As its title implies, the Depreciation Expense account appears as an operating expense in the current year's income statement. The Accumulated Depreciation—Machinery account appears in the balance sheet as a contra amount to Machinery. At the end of the first year, the plant asset would be reported on the balance sheet as follows:

| | | |
|---|---|---|
| Plant Assets: | | |
| Machinery | $95,000 | |
| Less: Accumulated Depreciation | 18,000 | 77,000 |

[2] *Accounting Trends and Techniques*, 36th ed. (New York: American Institute of Certified Public Accountants, 1982).

The $77,000 figure represents the asset's **undepreciated cost** (acquisition cost minus accumulated depreciation) and is frequently referred to as its **carrying** or **book value.**

A depreciation schedule for this plant asset for its five-year useful life is shown in Exhibit 10–1.

EXHIBIT 10–1

Depreciation Schedule—Straight-Line Method

| | DEPRECIATION EXPENSE | ACCUMULATED DEPRECIATION | CARRYING VALUE |
|---|---|---|---|
| Date of Purchase | $ — | $ — | $95,000 |
| Year 1 | 18,000 | 18,000 | 77,000 |
| Year 2 | 18,000 | 36,000 | 59,000 |
| Year 3 | 18,000 | 54,000 | 41,000 |
| Year 4 | 18,000 | 72,000 | 23,000 |
| Year 5 | 18,000 | 90,000 | 5,000 |

In examining the schedule, note that

The amount of depreciation charged as expense remains the same each year

The balance in the Accumulated Depreciation account increases at a *constant* amount of $18,000 per year until it equals the asset's depreciable cost of $90,000 at the end of the asset's useful life

The carrying value of the asset decreases at a constant amount of $18,000 per year until at the end of the asset's useful life it shows an amount equal to the asset's estimated residual value

## Units-of-Production Method

*2b. Under the units-of-production method depreciation is related to the asset's use rather than to the passage of time*

The **units-of-production method** is frequently used when an asset's service life can be better estimated in terms of output rather than years. In other words, depreciation is related to the asset's use rather than to the passage of time and therefore results in a charge that can vary from period to period. The method is often used to compute depreciation on assets whose life can be estimated in terms of driving miles, units of output, or flying hours. These assets include vehicles, machines, and airplanes.

To apply this method, the asset's life must be expressed in terms of productive output using relevant units such as hours, miles, or numbers produced. Depreciation is computed by first establishing a depreciation rate for the appropriate unit of productive output. That unit depreciation rate is then multiplied by the units of output that occurred during the period. The formula for determining depreciation under this method is

$$\frac{\text{Cost} - \text{Estimated Residual Value}}{\text{Estimated Units of Productive Output}} = \text{Depreciation per Unit of Productive Output}$$

Returning to asset data given in our example on page 356, let us assume that the machine processed 50,000 units of product in the first year. The depreciation for one unit of output would be 25 cents, and the depreciation for the first year would be $12,500 computed as follows:

$$\frac{\text{Cost of \$95,000} - \text{Estimated Residual Value of \$5,000}}{\text{360,000 Estimated Units of Productive Output}} = \text{\$.25 of Depreciation per Unit of Output}$$

$$\text{Depreciation Expense in Year 1} = \text{50,000 Units} \times \text{\$.25 per Unit, or \$12,500}$$

Assuming the machine produced 76,000 units in year 2, depreciation expense of $19,000 would be recorded (76,000 units × $.25 = $19,000) in that year.

A depreciation schedule for the machine using the units-of-production method with assumed numbers for the units produced each year is shown in Exhibit 10–2.

EXHIBIT 10–2

Depreciation Schedule—Units-of-Production Method

| | PRODUCTION IN UNITS | | DEPRECIATION EXPENSE | ACCUMULATED DEPRECIATION | CARRYING VALUE |
|---|---|---|---|---|---|
| Date of Purchase | | | $ — | $ — | $95,000 |
| Year 1 | 50,000 × .25 | = | 12,500 | 12,500 | 82,500 |
| Year 2 | 76,000 × .25 | = | 19,000 | 31,500 | 63,500 |
| Year 3 | 90,000 × .25 | = | 22,500 | 54,000 | 41,000 |
| Year 4 | 80,000 × .25 | = | 20,000 | 74,000 | 21,000 |
| Year 5 | 64,000 × .25 | = | 16,000 | 90,000 | 5,000 |

Note that under this method, the amount of depreciation expense depends on the asset's productive output. Therefore the carrying value of the asset decreases each year in direct relation to productive output until the residual value is reached.

When a plant asset provides service benefits that vary significantly from one period to another, the units-of-production depreciation method achieves a more appropriate matching of expenses with revenues. However, the method should be used only when the total units of productive output to be generated by an asset over its entire useful life can be estimated with reasonable reliability.

## *Sum-of-the-Years'-Digits Method*

*2b. The sum-of-the-years'-digits method charges more depreciation expense to the early years of an asset's useful life than to its later years*

The **sum-of-the-years'-digits method** is an **accelerated depreciation** method. This means that more depreciation expense is charged to the early years of an asset's useful life and a proportionately decreasing amount to the later years. Accelerated depreciation is appropriate for plant assets that are more efficient when new and therefore are assumed to provide more and better service benefits in the early years of their useful life and fewer service benefits as they become older.

Under the *sum-of-the-years'-digits method,* depreciation expense for each period is determined by multiplying the asset's depreciable cost by successively smaller fractions. The denominator of the fractions, which remains the same each year, is the sum of the digits representing the years of the asset's useful life (year 1, year 2, and so on). The numerators of the fractions, which change every year, consist of a number that shows how many years remain in the asset's life at the beginning of the year.

In our example the machine asset has an estimated useful life of five years, so its denominator is the sum of the digits representing the years in that asset's life, or *15*, computed as follows: 1 + 2 + 3 + 4 + 5 = *15*.[3] The numerators of the

[3] The fraction's denominator can also be determined by applying the following formula: $\text{Sum} = N\left(\frac{N+1}{2}\right)$, where $N$ = number of years of estimated life. Thus for an asset having a twenty-year life, the denominator would be 210 computed as follows: $20\left(\frac{20+1}{2}\right) = 210$.

fraction are the same digits taken in inverse order. Thus the fractions to be applied to the asset's depreciable cost are $\frac{5}{15}$ for the first year, $\frac{4}{15}$ for the second year, and then $\frac{3}{15}$, $\frac{2}{15}$, and $\frac{1}{15}$ for the remaining three years.

The amount of depreciation expense to be recorded in the first and second years of the machine's life under the sum-of-the-years'-digits method is $30,000 and $24,000, respectively, as computed below:

First Year—$\frac{5}{15} \times \$90,000 = \$30,000$

Second Year—$\frac{4}{15} \times \$90,000 = \$24,000$

Figures showing the application of the sum-of-the-years'-digits method for determining depreciation and other amounts applicable to the machine are in the schedule presented in Exhibit 10–3.

*EXHIBIT 10–3*

Depreciation Schedule—Sum-of-the-Years'-Digits Method

| | FRACTION USED | | COST LESS RESIDUAL VALUE | | DEPRECIATION EXPENSE | ACCUMULATED DEPRECIATION | CARRYING VALUE |
|---|---|---|---|---|---|---|---|
| Date of Purchase | | | $90,000 | | $ — | $ — | $95,000 |
| Year 1 | $\frac{5}{15}$ | × | 90,000 | = | 30,000 | 30,000 | 65,000 |
| Year 2 | $\frac{4}{15}$ | × | 90,000 | = | 24,000 | 54,000 | 41,000 |
| Year 3 | $\frac{3}{15}$ | × | 90,000 | = | 18,000 | 72,000 | 23,000 |
| Year 4 | $\frac{2}{15}$ | × | 90,000 | = | 12,000 | 84,000 | 11,000 |
| Year 5 | $\frac{1}{15}$ | × | 90,000 | = | 6,000 | 90,000 | 5,000 |

In this example we can see that the sum-of-the-years'-digits depreciation method achieves *accelerated depreciation* by assigning the larger fractions to the earlier years of the asset's life. The highest depreciation expense is therefore produced in the first year, followed by a gradual and constant declining amount ($6,000) of depreciation expense in the remaining years.

## Declining-Balance Method

*2b. The declining-balance method also charges more depreciation expense to the early years of an asset's useful life than to its later years*

The **declining-balance method** is another way of achieving accelerated depreciation. Under this method, depreciation expense for each period is determined by multiplying a fixed depreciation rate times the asset's undepreciated cost (carrying value). The fixed rate used is some multiple of the straight-line rate. When it is twice the straight-line rate, the depreciation method is called the **double-declining-balance method.** The double-declining-balance method, which can be used for both federal income tax purposes and financial reporting purposes, is the method illustrated here.

If an asset has an estimated useful life of four years, its depreciation rate under the straight-line method would be 25% (100 ÷ 4). This percentage rate is then doubled to obtain the double-declining-balance rate of *50%* (25% × 2). If an asset has an estimated life of five years, its straight-line depreciation rate is *20%* (100 ÷ 5). By doubling that rate we obtain the double-declining-balance rate of *40%* (20% × 2), which when applied to the carrying value of the depreciable asset determines the amount of depreciation expense to be recorded.

Returning to our original example on page 356, let us see how this method works. The machine has an estimated useful life of five years and therefore a straight-line depreciation rate of 20%. To depreciate the machine by the double-declining-balance method, we double the straight-line rate of 20%. We then apply the doubled rate of 40% to the asset's cost to determine depreciation for the first year and to its declining carrying value to determine depreciation thereafter. Depreciation in the first year would then amount to $38,000 ($95,000 × 40% = $38,000). In the second year the depreciation expense would drop to $22,800 computed at 40% times the asset's carrying value at the beginning of the second year [$57,000 carrying value ($95,000 − $38,000) at the beginning of the second year times 40% = $22,800]. The schedule in Exhibit 10–4 shows the computation of each year's depreciation expense under the double-declining-balance method, along with other amounts applicable to the machine during each year of its estimated five-year life.

Note that the asset's estimated residual value of $5,000 was not considered *in the computation* of depreciation expense under the declining-balance method except to recognize that the asset should not be depreciated below its estimated residual value. When residual value is reached, no more depreciation is charged. Thus depreciation in the last year of a plant asset's life under this method is the amount needed to reduce its carrying value to its residual value.

*EXHIBIT 10–4*

Depreciation Schedule—Double-Declining-Balance Method

| | COMPUTATION USING A FIXED RATE (40% × CARRYING VALUE) | DEPRECIATION EXPENSE | ACCUMULATED DEPRECIATION | CARRYING VALUE |
|---|---|---|---|---|
| Date of Purchase | | $ — | $ — | $95,000 |
| Year 1 | 40% × $95,000 | 38,000 | 38,000 | 57,000 |
| Year 2 | 40% × 57,000 | 22,800 | 60,800 | 34,200 |
| Year 3 | 40% × 34,200 | 13,680 | 74,480 | 20,520 |
| Year 4 | 40% × 20,520 | 8,208 | 82,688 | 12,312 |
| Year 5 | | 7,312* | 90,000 | 5,000 |

* Depreciation expense in year 5 is the amount needed to reduce the asset's carrying value to the estimated residual value of $5,000. Under the double-declining-balance method, depreciation expense in the last year of the asset's useful life is not computed by applying the fixed rate.

The depreciation schedule shown in Exhibit 10–4 summarizes several important aspects associated with the declining-balance method:

The depreciation rate remains *fixed* throughout the asset's life.

This fixed rate is applied to the *declining carrying value* of the asset.

The amount of depreciation expense is *largest* in the first year and declines in each succeeding year.

## COMPARISON OF DEPRECIATION METHODS

The straight-line, sum-of-the-years'-digits, and double-declining-balance are cost allocation methods that produce depreciation expense amounts that follow a certain pattern. On the other hand, the units-of-production method can allocate cost on an accelerated, equal, decelerated, or erratic basis, depending on variations in the asset's productive output. Thus depreciation expense amounts are not predictable when this method is used.

Exhibit 10–5 compares annual depreciation charges using each of the four depreciation methods by placing the amounts side by side. Once again the amounts were based on the data on page 356.

*EXHIBIT 10–5*

Comparison of Depreciation Methods

| | ANNUAL DEPRECIATION TO BE RECORDED USING | | | |
|---|---|---|---|---|
| YEAR | Straight-Line Method | Units-of-Production Method | Sum-of-The-Years'-Digits Method | Double-Declining-Balance Method |
| 1 | $18,000 | $12,500 | $30,000 | $38,000 |
| 2 | 18,000 | 19,000 | 24,000 | 22,800 |
| 3 | 18,000 | 22,500 | 18,000 | 13,680 |
| 4 | 18,000 | 20,000 | 12,000 | 8,208 |
| 5 | 18,000 | 16,000 | 6,000 | 7,312 |
| | $90,000 | $90,000 | $90,000 | $90,000 |

Note that when the straight-line method is used, an equal amount of depreciation expense is assigned to equal periods of time. Both the sum-of-the-years'-digits method and the double-declining-balance method achieve accelerated depreciation by allocating the largest portion of the cost of the machine to the early years of its useful life. As we can see, the double-declining balance method accelerates the depreciation even more during the early years than the sum-of-the-years'-digits-method does. All three time-related methods do, however, produce depreciation expense amounts that follow predictable patterns. On the other hand, the units-of-production method, which may achieve the best matching of expense against related revenues, produces depreciation expense amounts that are varied. Finally, we can see by the summed annual depreciation expense charges that the same total amount is ultimately allocated to depreciation expense under all four methods. That amount, $90,000 in this example, is the asset's acquisition cost less its estimated residual value.

## DEPRECIATION FOR PARTIAL YEARS

A plant asset may be purchased at any time during the year. In fact, it is more likely to expect that the purchase will be made at some time other than at the beginning or end of the year. When this happens, depreciation must be computed for part of a year.

Using the data from our previous example, we can illustrate the procedure for computing depreciation for partial periods by assuming that the machine is purchased on April 1, 19X6, and that the company's annual accounting period ends on December 31. Nine months' depreciation on the machine must be recorded on December 31, 19X6, the year in which the asset was acquired, and twelve months' depreciation must be recorded in the following year when the machine was used for the entire year. Examples showing the calculations to determine the amount of depreciation expense to be recorded in 19X6, the first partial-year depreciation, and 19X7, the first full-year depreciation, using all three depreciation methods based on time are given below. It should be pointed out that depreciation need not be computed to the nearest day or week for assets acquired during the month. Although variations exist, one common approach for computing depreciation on plant assets acquired during the year is to round the calculations to the nearest whole month. Therefore for an asset purchased on April 10, depreciation would be computed for the nine months beginning April 1.

*2c. Calculation of depreciation expense for a partial year is illustrated here*

| METHOD | AMOUNT OF DEPRECIATION EXPENSE TO BE RECORDED |
|---|---|
| Straight-line: | |
| 19X6—Fractional period (9 months) | |
| $90,000 ÷ 5 years = $18,000 × $\frac{9}{12}$ = | $13,500 |
| 19X7—Full year (12 months) | |
| $90,000 ÷ 5 years = | 18,000 |
| Sum-of-the-years' digits: | |
| 19X6—Fractional period (9 months) | |
| $90,000 × $\frac{5}{15}$ = $30,000 × $\frac{9}{12}$ = | 22,500 |
| 19X7—Full year (12 months) | |
| $90,000 × $\frac{5}{15}$ = $30,000 × $\frac{3}{12}$ = $ 7,500 | |
| $90,000 × $\frac{4}{15}$ = $24,000 × $\frac{9}{12}$ = 18,000 | 25,500 |
| Double-declining-balance: | |
| 19X6—Fractional period (9 months) | |
| $95,000 × 40% = $38,000 × $\frac{9}{12}$ = | 28,500 |
| 19X7—Full year (12 months) | |
| $95,000 × 40% = $38,000 × $\frac{3}{12}$ = $ 9,500 | |
| $57,000 × 40% = $22,800 × $\frac{9}{12}$ = 17,100 | 26,600 |

Note that when depreciation is calculated to the nearest month, annual depreciation figures are prorated. Of course, the units-of-production method was not included in our example because the computation of depreciation expense is based on the asset's productive output, not on the length of time that the asset was used under that method.

## REVISION OF DEPRECIATION RATES

*2c. When estimates are revised, depreciation expense is reallocated for current and future periods only (not for past periods)*

Because estimates of useful life and residual value are made at the time a depreciable asset is put into service, subsequent events may occur that cause the original estimates to change. These events are often brought about by changing conditions or by the gathering of new information. In any case, if the original estimates are no longer correct, the amount of depreciation expense based on those estimates will be either overstated or understated. The acceptable procedure is to use revised estimates in determining how much of the asset's remaining undepreciated cost should be charged to depreciation expense in the years remaining in the asset's useful life. As a result, the correction will affect only the amount of depreciation expense to be recorded in the current and future periods.

We will illustrate the concepts discussed above by using the following data pertaining to a company's depreciable plant asset.

| ASSET DATA | |
|---|---|
| Cost when acquired on January 1, 19X1 | $25,000 |
| Original estimate of useful life | 10 years |
| Original estimate of residual value | $ 5,000 |
| Annual depreciation expense (based on original data) | $ 2,000 |
| Accumulated depreciation at end of the sixth year ($2,000 × 6 yrs. = $12,000) | $12,000 |
| Carrying value (undepreciated cost) of asset at end of the sixth year ($25,000 − $12,000 = $13,000) | $13,000 |

At the beginning of 19X7 (after six years of asset use), it is estimated that the remaining useful life of the asset is eight years (instead of four) and that its residual value will be $3,000 (instead of $5,000). Depreciation expense for each of the remaining eight years is *$1,250*, computed as follows.

| | |
|---|---|
| Carrying value of asset at end of sixth year | $13,000 |
| Less: Estimated residual value as revised | 3,000 |
| Asset's remaining depreciable cost | $10,000 |
| Revised annual depreciation expense (computed as follows: $10,000 ÷ 8 yrs. = $1,250) | $ 1,250 |

Note that depreciation expense recorded in prior periods is not changed to reflect the change in the estimates of useful life and residual value that were made six years after the original estimates. When an accounting estimate is changed, only the amounts recorded in the current and future perods are affected.

## GROUP AND COMPOSITE DEPRECIATION

*2c. The group and composite depreciation methods make use of an average depreciation rate*

Large companies that have thousands of depreciable assets find it clerically convenient to establish groups of assets and determine depreciation for each group by using an average (depreciation) rate. The **group depreciation method** is used when relatively similar assets with approximately the same useful lives are placed together for purposes of computing depreciation. The **composite depreciation method** is used when the assets are dissimilar and have different useful lives. Under either method, an average depreciation rate is developed by

Computing the annual depreciation for *each* asset (or asset category) within the group

Determining the total annual depreciation by *summing* the individual annual amounts

*Dividing* the total annual depreciation by the total cost of the assets

The following chart illustrates this procedure numerically.

| ASSET | COST | RESIDUAL VALUE | DEPRECIABLE COST | ESTIMATED LIFE (YEARS) | DEPRECIATION (USE S.L. METHOD) |
|---|---|---|---|---|---|
| Autos | $ 90,000 | $10,000 | $ 80,000 | 4 | $20,000 |
| Trucks | 140,000 | 20,000 | 120,000 | 5 | 24,000 |
| Buses | 70,000 | 6,000 | 64,000 | 4 | 16,000 |
| | $300,000 | $36,000 | $264,000 | | $60,000 |

The group's average depreciation rate is 20%, determined by dividing the group's annual depreciation of $60,000 by the group's aggregate asset cost of $300,000. The group's average useful life is 4.4 years, determined by dividing the group's depreciable cost of $264,000 by the group's annual depreciation of $60,000.

Depreciation expense will be $60,000 ($300,000 × .20) per year and will be recorded by debiting Depreciation Expense and crediting Accumulated Depreciation for $60,000. If the composition of the assets within the group changes significantly (a new type of asset is added), a new average depreciation rate must be computed.

## DEPRECIATION OF PLANT ASSETS WITH LOW UNIT COSTS

*2c. For plant assets having low unit costs, the inventory depreciation method is often used*

Some types of plant assets are composed of numerous individual items with low unit costs. Examples include hand tools, patterns, dies, molds, and spare parts. Assets such as these are subject to breakage and pilferage, have relatively short lives, and require constant replacement. It would be costly and perhaps impractical to keep detailed records of the individual items in this group and to use the methods shown in the previous section to determine depreciation on those items. For these reasons, the **inventory depreciation method** is often used. Under this method, as these low-unit-cost plant assets are purchased, their cost is debited to a Hand Tools account (or one similarly titled). The balance in the Hand Tools account at the end of an accounting period will consist of the cost of the items on hand at the beginning of the period plus the cost of the items purchased during the period. At the end of the period, a physical inventory of the low-unit-cost items remaining on hand is taken with the items priced at their original cost. This ending inventory amount is then subtracted from the balance in the Hand Tools account, with the difference representing the expense for the period. Thus the amount of the expense is based on the dollar cost of the items used during the period, not on an allocation of their acquisition costs.

## DEPRECIATION FOR INCOME TAX PURPOSES

Depreciation methods used for income tax purposes may differ from those used for financial reporting. Prior to 1981 the most frequent difference was that the sum-of-the-years'-digits method and double-declining-balance method were often used for tax purposes while the straight-line method was being used for financial reporting.

*1d. The Accelerated Cost Recovery System (ACRS) allows more rapid depreciation for income tax purposes*

In 1981 Congress passed the Economic Recovery Act, which established a new method for determining depreciation for tax purposes called the **Accelerated Cost Recovery System (ACRS).** Although the Tax Reform Act of 1986 revised the ACRS guidelines it still generally permits more rapid depreciation than was allowed under previous laws.[4]

The ACRS accelerates depreciation in two ways. First, the system establishes several classes of depreciable assets with each class having a specified predetermined life. These assigned lives (called recovery periods) vary depending on the type of asset being used. For example, the revised ACRS has eight classes. Within each class, asset costs (not reduced by salvage values) are depreciated. Because the lives assigned to the assets in any given class are usually much shorter than the lives expected to be obtained from their use, depreciation is accelerated.

Second, assets belonging to either the 3-5-7 or 10-year class may be depreciated by using a 200 percent declining balance method. Assets in the 15 or 20 year class may be depreciated by using 150 percent declining balance. Residential and nonresidential property belong in the 27.5 or 31.5 year class and must be depreciated using the straight-line method. The use of the declining balance (for most business assets) and the rates allowed provide for accelerated depreciation.

More information about asset classifications and applicable notes for ACRS depreciation can be obtained in a series of published tables developed by the federal government.

---

[4] Because ACRS has caused a major change in the way income tax depreciation is determined, a basic understanding of its methodology is needed. However, this discussion provides only an overview; the Internal Revenue Code should be consulted for a more-detailed discussion.

## EXPENDITURES AFTER ASSET ACQUISITION

The term **expenditure** refers to a payment or the acceptance of an obligation to make a future payment. Companies frequently incur expenditures related to plant assets after they have been acquired. Depending on the nature of these after-acquisition expenditures, they will be recorded either as additions to a plant asset account or as an expense.

The general guidelines for making this determination are as follows:

If the expenditure is expected to provide benefits for *more than one* accounting period, an *asset* account should be debited.

If the expenditure is expected to benefit only the *current* period, an *expense* account should be debited.

### Capital versus Revenue Expenditures

*1e. Asset expenditures that provide benefits over more than the current accounting period are capital expenditures; otherwise they are revenue expenditures*

Expenditures incurred in purchasing a plant asset and any subsequent expenditures that will provide benefits over several accounting periods are called **capital expenditures.** All the capital expenditures associated with a particular asset are added to the cost of that asset. Expenditures that benefit only the current period are charged to expense accounts and are referred to as **revenue expenditures.**

At the time of the expenditure, it is not always easy to determine whether the expenditure will provide benefits over several periods or whether it will benefit only the current period. Yet the distinction is important because the treatment will affect the amount reported for net income in the current period as well as amounts reported for certain items in the year-end balance sheet.

Most of the expenditures incurred after an asset has been acquired and placed in service (after-acquisition expenditures) can be considered as either ordinary or extraordinary repairs and maintenance. Expenditures for ordinary repairs are revenue expenditures, and expenditures for extraordinary repairs are capital expenditures. Other after-acquisition expenditures qualifying as capital expenditures are those resulting in asset additions and asset betterments.

### A Closer Look at Capital Expenditures

A company obtains service benefits that extend over several accounting periods from after-acquisition expenditures that

*Extend* the useful life of a plant asset, or

*Increase* the quantity of services expected to be provided by a plant asset, or

*Increase* the quality of services expected to be provided by a plant asset.

*1e. Capital expenditures are debited to an asset account, revenue expenditures to expense accounts*

If the expenditure achieves one or more of these results, its cost should be debited to the related asset account and in accordance with the matching principle allocated to the current and future periods as depreciation. Expenditures that do not achieve any of the results cited above should be debited to expense accounts when incurred.

Companies incur several types of after-acquisition expenditures that qualify as capital expenditures. One such type is called **additions,** which are either additions to or expansions of existing assets. For example, a new wing or several floors may be added to an existing building. This cost was incurred after the building had originally been acquired and put to use. Since it will provide benefits over several years, it should be added to the cost of the building. Another type involves expenditures that result in betterments. Generally, **betterments** (sometimes called **improvements**) refer to expenditures made to acquire new components that significantly improve the operating capabilities of an existing plant asset. For example, the cost of installing elevators or an air-conditioning system in an existing building would qualify as an after-acquisition expenditure whose cost should be debited (added) to the asset *building.* Another type would be expenditures for extraordinary repairs such as major overhauls or reconditioning. **Extraordinary repairs** are major repairs that extend the useful life of a plant asset beyond the number of years originally intended. An extraordinary repair should therefore be treated as a capital expenditure. In this case the cost of the repair should be debited to the asset's Accumulated Depreciation account.

### A Closer Look at Revenue Expenditures

Minor repairs made to keep a plant asset in good operating condition, thereby maintaining its originally estimated useful life, are called **ordinary repairs.** The costs of such repairs are treated as revenue expenditures and consist primarily of the costs of regular maintenance, cleaning, painting, lubrication, and inspection. For example, vehicles need tuneups, small parts, fan belts, and so forth, on an ongoing and regular basis. The costs of those items are expensed as incurred. Machines need to be lubricated and cleaned. Buildings must be painted and heated, and their windows and carpeting must be repaired or replaced. These too are examples of revenue expenditures whose costs are recorded in expense accounts.

As a concluding note, the importance of distinguishing between capital expenditures and revenue expenditures and determining how that distinction affects reported net income cannot be overemphasized. If in the current period a capital expenditure is erroneously treated as a revenue expenditure, current expenses will be overstated and therefore net income will be understated. In subsequent years when part of the capital expenditure should have been allocated to an expense but was not, expenses will be understated and net income overstated. If in the current period a revenue expenditure is erroneously charged to an asset, current expenses will be understated, thus overstating net income. In addition, amounts from the improperly recorded asset will be allocated to expense in future years, therefore overstating expenses and understating net income in those years.

## HIGHLIGHT PROBLEM

Hi-Key Company purchased new equipment on January 1, 19X4, at a cost of $165,000. The equipment has an estimated useful life of five years and an estimated residual value of $15,000.

Required:

Prepare schedules to show the annual depreciation expense, the end-of-year accumulated depreciation, and the year-end carrying value of the asset for each year in its estimated life using each of the following depreciation methods:

a. Straight-line
b. Sum-of-the-years'-digits
c. Double-declining-balance

d. Units-of-production where estimated units of productive output consist of 300,000 units and productive output in each year is as follows:
   First year—40,000 units
   Second year—30,000 units
   Third year—70,000 units
   Fourth year—60,000 units
   Fifth year—100,000 units

## GLOSSARY OF KEY TERMS

**Accelerated Cost Recovery System (ACRS).** An accelerated depreciation method for tax purposes that can be used on certain assets acquired after 1980.

**Accelerated depreciation.** Any depreciation method that charges more depreciation expense to the early years of an asset's useful life and a proportionately decreasing amount to the later years.

**Additions.** Expenditures that are additions or expansions of existing assets. These are capital expenditures.

**Betterments.** Expenditures for new components that significantly improve the operating capabilities of an existing plant asset. Betterment expenditures are capitalized.

**Book value.** Alternate title for *carrying value*.

**Capital expenditures.** Expenditures incurred to purchase a plant asset and any subsequent expenditures to the plant asset that provide benefits over several accounting periods.

**Carrying value.** A plant asset's undepreciated cost —its acquisition cost minus its accumulated depreciation.

**Composite depreciation method.** A depreciation method that applies an average depreciation rate to the cost of a group of dissimilar assets having different useful lives.

**Cost (of a plant and equipment asset).** The sum of all expenditures that are reasonable and necessary to acquire the asset and prepare it for its intended use.

**Declining-balance method.** An accelerated depreciation method that determines depreciation expense for each period by multiplying a fixed depreciation rate times the asset's undepreciated cost (carrying value of the asset). The fixed depreciation rate is some multiple of the straight-line rate.

**Depreciable cost.** The excess of a plant asset's cost over its estimated residual value.

**Depreciation.** The process of systematic cost allocation that assigns a plant asset's acquisition cost to the accounting periods that benefit from that asset's use.

**Double-declining-balance method.** A declining-balance depreciation method in which the fixed depreciation rate used is double the straight-line rate.

**Estimated useful life.** An estimate of the expected benefits to be obtained from the use of a plant asset, measured in either number of years or units of activity or output.

**Expenditure.** A payment or acceptance of an obligation to make a future payment.

**Extraordinary repairs.** Major repairs that extend the useful life of a plant asset beyond the number of years originally estimated.

**Fixed assets.** Alternate term for *plant and equipment*.

**Group depreciation method.** A depreciation method whereby an average depreciation rate is applied to the cost of a group of relatively similar assets having approximately the same useful lives.

**Group purchase.** The acquisition of several plant and equipment assets for a single purchase price.

**Improvements.** Alternate term for *betterments*.

**Inadequacy.** The inability of an existing plant asset to provide enough service benefits to meet the current needs of its user.

**Inventory depreciation method.** A method to determine periodic depreciation for low-unit-cost, relatively short lived items properly classified as plant assets.

**Lump-sum acquisition.** Alternate term for *group purchase*.

**Obsolescence.** A status of a plant asset that results when technological changes develop new assets that can provide superior services or provide similar services more efficiently than the existing assets.

**Ordinary repairs.** Minor repairs made to keep a plant asset in good operating condition, thereby maintaining its originally estimated useful life.

**Physical deterioration.** The wear and tear of plant assets caused by frequency of use and exposure to climatic elements.

**Plant and equipment.** Tangible, long-lived assets used in the operating activities of the business rather than assets being held for resale.

**Plant assets.** Alternate term for *plant and equipment.*

**Property, plant, and equipment.** Alternate term for *plant and equipment.*

**Residual value.** The amount of a plant asset's cost expected to be recovered on its estimated date of disposal.

**Revenue expenditures.** Expenditures that provide benefits only during the current accounting period.

**Salvage value.** Alternate term for *residual value.*

**Scrap value.** Alternate term for *residual value.*

**Straight-line method.** A depreciation method that allocates an equal share of a plant asset's depreciable cost to each accounting period in the asset's estimated useful life.

**Sum-of-the-years'-digits method.** An accelerated depreciation method where the depreciation expense for each period is determined by multiplying the asset's depreciable cost by successively smaller fractions. (See text for details on constructing the fraction for each accounting period.)

**Tangible.** Having physical substance; able to be seen and touched.

**Undepreciated cost.** An asset's acquisition cost minus its accumulated depreciation.

**Units-of-production method.** A depreciation method in which the depreciable cost of a plant asset is allocated to each accounting period on the basis of the number of units produced by the asset during that accounting period.

## REVIEW QUESTIONS

1. What are the four classifications of noncurrent assets? [LO1a]
2. Describe the characteristics an asset must possess to be classified as plant and equipment. [LO1a]
3. What four questions can be used to summarize the issues involved in accounting for plant and equipment assets? [LO1a]
4. What types of expenditures are included in the cost of machinery? [LO2a]
5. Name the items included in the cost of land. [LO2a]
6. What are some examples of land improvements? [LO2a]
7. What items are included in the cost of a purchased building? [LO2a]
8. Name the items included in the cost of equipment. [LO2a]
9. Describe how the total cost of a group purchase is apportioned to the various plant and equipment assets acquired. [LO2a]
10. Why are plant and equipment assets (with the exception of land) depreciated? [LO1b]
11. Describe depreciation. [LO1b]
12. Explain how the term *depreciation* is often used outside of accounting. [LO1b]
13. Identify the three items of information needed to determine the periodic depreciation expense. [LO1c]
14. Differentiate between physical deterioration, obsolescence, and inadequacy of plant and equipment assets. [LO1c]
15. Briefly describe the difference between the straight-line, units-of-production, sum-of-the-years'-digits, and declining-balance depreciation methods. [LO2b]
16. How is the account Accumulated Depreciation—Machinery classified in the financial statements? [LO2b]
17. Which depreciation method uses estimated production output rather than years as a basis for computing depreciation? [LO2b]
18. Which two depreciation methods automatically cause more depreciation expense to be recorded in the early years of the life of an asset than in the later years? [LO2b]
19. How is depreciation on an asset determined if the asset is purchased during the year rather than at the beginning of a year? [LO2c]

20. What is done with the undepreciated cost of a plant asset when it becomes necessary to change the estimate of its useful life? [LO2c]
21. Describe the three-step process for developing an average depreciation rate when the group or composite depreciation method is used. [LO2c]
22. Name and describe the method used to depreciate plant assets having low unit costs. [LO2c]
23. Explain the computation of depreciation using the Accelerated Cost Recovery System (ACRS). [LO1d]
24. What guidelines are used to determine whether after-acquisition expenditures associated with plant and equipment assets should be recorded as additions to the assets or as expenses? [LO1e]
25. Name three results that a plant asset expenditure might achieve, any one of which will qualify that expenditure as a capital expenditure. [LO1e]
26. Name the three types of after-acquisition expenditures that qualify as capital expenditures. [LO1e]

## ANALYTICAL QUESTIONS

27. To be classified as plant and equipment, why must an asset possess all three characteristics discussed in the chapter? [LO1a]
28. Comment on the following statement: "The acquisition cost of a plant and equipment asset can exceed its invoice price." [LO2a]
29. Comment on the following statement: "Users of financial statements should not be concerned about the depreciation method used by a company. All methods charge the same amount of depreciation over the useful life of the asset." [LO1b,2b]
30. Comment on the following statement: "Users of financial statements should not be concerned about the depreciation methods used by a company. The total amount of depreciation cannot exceed the cost of the asset." [LO1b,2b]
31. Comment on the following statement: "It is not necessary to record depreciation on our plant assets this year because our improved maintenance program has kept the assets in a good state of repair." [LO1b]
32. Comment on the following statement: "Company A must be manipulating its net income because it is depreciating its vehicle over a five-year life. Company B purchased a similar vehicle and is using a three-year life for depreciation purposes." [LO1b,2b]
33. Comment on the following statement: "Depreciation need not be recorded this year because the market value of the asset exceeds the carrying value of the asset and the market value is rising each year." [LO1b]
34. Comment on the following statement: "Raising $100,000 to replace the asset should not be a problem because the balance in the accumulated depreciation account exceeds that amount." [LO1b]
35. Comment on the following statement: "Management should always use the straight-line method for depreciating plant assets for financial statement purposes. This method is simple. On the other hand, a company should always use an accelerated depreciation method for tax purposes." [LO2b]
36. How do the cost principle and the matching principle relate to accounting for plant assets? [LO1e]
37. Under what conditions should after-acquisition expenditures for a plant asset be capitalized rather than expensed? [LO1e]

## IMPACT ANALYSIS QUESTIONS

*For each error described, indicate whether it would overstate [O], understate [U], or not affect [N] the specified key figures.*

38. An asset's full acquisition cost was used when computing depreciation under the straight-line basis even though the asset has a relatively large estimated residual value. [LO2b]

_______ Assets _______ Revenues
_______ Net Income _______ Owner's Equity

39. An asset costs $100,000; it has an estimated residual value of $10,000 and an estimated useful life of six years. The asset was bought at the beginning of year 1. By mistake, depreciation was computed using the sum-of-the-years'-digits method when the straight-line method should have been used. Determine the effect of the mistake on the following items in year 1. [LO2b]

_______ Assets _______ Revenues
_______ Net Income _______ Owner's Equity

40. Using the data in Question 39, indicate the effect of the error on the following items in year 5. [LO2b]

_______ Expenses _______ Revenues
_______ Net Income _______ Liabilities

41. An asset has an estimated useful life of six years. At the end of the third year, it is determined that the estimated remaining useful life from that point is another five years instead of three. The estimated residual value is the same. No revised depreciation rate was used in the fourth year of the asset's life. [LO2c]

_______ Assets _______ Revenues
_______ Net Income _______ Owner's Equity

42. The company incorrectly capitalized an operating expense by debiting the cost of an ordinary repair to a plant asset account. The asset has a ten-year estimated useful life. Determine the effect of this error on the following items in year 1. [LO1e]

_______ Assets _______ Revenues
_______ Net Income _______ Owner's Equity

## EXERCISES

EXERCISE 10–1 *(Determine Acquisition Cost)* Loyal Company purchased land by paying $80,000 cash. Additional expenditures incurred by the company were as follows.

a. Real estate commissions, $4,000
b. Title search on the property, $900
c. Demolition of an old unwanted building on the property, $6,000
d. Property clearing and grading, $2,000
e. Construction and paving of a parking lot adjacent to the land site, $5,600
f. Property taxes accrued on the land prior to the purchase date, $400

The company received $1,200 from the sale of materials salvaged from the demolished building.

Required:

Determine the cost of the land (the appropriate amount to be debited to the land account). [LO2a]

EXERCISE 10–2 *(Determine Costs for Group or Lump-Sum Purchase)* On February 3, Daring Company purchased land, a building, and equipment for $800,000 cash. The assets were appraised on the next day at the following amounts:

Land—$100,000
Building—$650,000
Equipment—$250,000

Required:

Determine the amount of cost that should be assigned to each asset. Prepare a journal entry to record the purchase. [LO2a]

EXERCISE 10–3 *(Determine Costs for Group or Lump-Sum Purchase)* Assume the same facts as in Exercise 10–2 except that the assets were appraised at the following amounts:

Land—$190,000

Building—$460,000

Equipment—$200,000

Required:

Determine the amount of cost that should be assigned to each asset. Prepare a journal entry to record the purchase. [LO2a]

EXERCISE 10–4 *(Determine Acquisition Cost and Depreciation)* On January 2, 19X4, Val Company purchased a machine with a list price of $24,000. The credit terms were 2/10, n/60. Payment was made within the discount period and included a sales tax of $1,060. Val Company also paid freight charges of $310 for delivery of the machine, which was sent FOB shipping point. While company employees were removing the machine from the arrival platform, it was dropped and slightly damaged. The estimated repair cost was $90. Costs to install the machine amounted to $1,610, and the machine has an estimated useful life of five years and an estimated residual value of $1,000.

Required:

1. Determine the cost of the machine.
2. Assume that the machine was placed into use on January 4, 19X4. For comparison purposes, compute depreciation expense for each of the five years using the (a) straight-line method and (b) sum-of-the-years'-digits method.
3. Prepare the journal entry to record depreciation for 19X5 under the sum-of-the-years'-digits method. [LO2a,2b]

EXERCISE 10–5 *(Use Various Depreciation Methods—Partial Period)* On October 1, 19X0, Arias Company purchased a new vehicle for $14,000. The vehicle has an estimated useful life of four years and 80,000 miles. Its estimated residual value is $2,000. The vehicle was driven 16,000 miles in 19X0, 20,000 miles in 19X1, and 21,000 miles in 19X2. The company's fiscal year ends on December 31.

Required:

1. Determine the amount of depreciation expense to be recorded for 19X0, 19X1, and 19X2, using the following depreciation methods: (a) straight-line, (b) sum-of-the-years'-digits, and (c) units-of-production.
2. Prepare the journal entry to record depreciation expense on December 31, 19X0, under the units-of-production method. [LO2b,2c]

EXERCISE 10–6 *(Prepare Journal Entries for a Purchase, Extraordinary Repairs, and Depreciation)* The data in items *a* through *d* pertain to Zametta Company. Assume that all transactions were for cash.

a. Purchased a machine on January 3, 19X0.

   Invoice price—$50,000

   Cash discount taken—$1,250

   Sales tax paid—$2,000

   Transportation costs (the machine was delivered FOB shipping point)—$310

   Installation costs—$440

Prepare a journal entry to record the purchase.

b. On January 3, 19X0, the date of purchase, the machine's estimated useful life was seven years and its estimated residual value was $2,500.

Prepare a journal entry to record depreciation for each of the first two years, 19X0 and 19X1, using the straight-line method.

c. On January 2, 19X4, the beginning of the asset's fifth year of use, the company spent $6,000 on extraordinary repairs to the machine. The nature of the repairs is expected to add two more years to the machine's life (making its revised estimated useful life nine years). Estimated residual value continues to be $2,500.

Prepare a journal entry to record the extraordinary repair expenditure made on January 2, 19X4.

d. Based on the machine's revised data, prepare a journal entry to record depreciation on the machine on December 31, 19X4. [LO2a,2b,1e]

EXERCISE 10-7 *(Determine Acquisition Cost)* J. Brod, the owner of J. B. Dry Cleaners, purchased a new machine in February of the current year. She has asked you to review the following data of costs that have been incurred.

| | |
|---|---|
| List price of the machine (subject to a cash discount of 2% which was taken) | $28,600 |
| Transportation cost to obtain the machine shipped FOB shipping point | 240 |
| Cost to remove and scrap an old machine in order to make a suitable site for the new machine | 415 |
| Cost to install the new machine | 370 |
| Cost to insure the new machine after it was installed and operating | 180 |

Required:

Prepare a schedule listing the items to be included in the cost of the machine and determine its acquisition cost. [LO2a]

## PROBLEMS

PROBLEM 10-1 *(Determine the Acquisition Cost of Various Plant Assets)* Growth Company acquired a number of plant assets during its first year of operations. The company's bookkeeper used one account called Plant Assets and recorded all the following expenditures in that account.

a. Purchased a land site that included an old unusable building, $180,000.
b. Paid real estate commissions relating to the purchase, $9,200.
c. Paid fee for title search on the property, $1,200.
d. Purchased a machine (invoice price less a cash discount which was taken), $28,100.
e. Paid attorney a fee for work done in connection with the land purchase, $2,100.
f. Paid architect fees for work in designing a new building, $2,600.
g. Paid for a building permit, $400.
h. Paid for the demolition of the old building to prepare the site for a new building, $12,000.
i. Paid for delinquent taxes on the property acquired, $800.
j. Paid a premium to insure the machine while it was in transit, $120.
k. Paid building contractor for erecting a new building on the land site, $155,000.
l. Paid transportation costs on the machine delivered FOB destination, $240.
m. Paid for construction of a parking lot, $11,700.
n. Paid costs incurred to build a concrete foundation for the new machine (foundation is not usable elsewhere), $470.
o. Paid for parking lot lights (including installation), $3,300.
p. Paid to have the new machine installed, $620.
q. Paid to erect a fence around the newly acquired property, $4,200.
r. Paid to have test runs made on the new machine, $330.
s. Paid for ordinary and minor machine repairs, $55.

In addition to the above, it was determined that when materials salvaged from the demolished building were sold for $2,000, the bookkeeper recorded the transaction by debiting that amount to the Cash account and crediting the same amount to an account called Supplementary Revenue.

Required:

1. Prepare a schedule with six column headings as follows: Description of Item, Land, Buildings, Machinery, Land Improvements, Other.

   List items *a* through *s* in the Description column of the schedule, and place the dollar amount of that item in one of the other columns depending on how the amount should be treated for accounting purposes.
2. Enter the amount received from the sale of salvaged materials in an appropriate column of the schedule (once again depending on how the transaction should be treated for accounting purposes).
3. Prepare a journal entry to eliminate the balance in the Plant Assets account and assign transaction amounts to their appropriate accounts.
4. Prepare a journal entry, if one is needed, to correct the bookkeeper's recording of the transaction pertaining to the sale of salvaged material.
5. Prepare a journal entry or entries to record nine months of depreciation on Growth Company's depreciable plant assets. Data needed to compute depreciation are provided below. [LO2a,2b,2c,1e]

| ASSET | USEFUL LIFE | RESIDUAL VALUE | DEPRECIATION METHOD |
|---|---|---|---|
| Buildings | 20 years | $30,000 | Straight-line |
| Machinery | 7 years | 5,000 | Sum-of-the-years'-digits |
| Land improvements | 12 years | 0 | Straight-line |

PROBLEM 10–2 *(Determine Acquisition Cost and Depreciation)* Progressive Company paid $86,000 for a machine. The machine had to be installed and tested at an additional cost of $3,000. Its estimated useful life is five years, and its estimated residual value is $5,000. The machine was placed into service during the first week of January 19X3. The company's year ends on December 31.

Required:

Compute the depreciation for each of the five years using the following depreciation methods: (a) straight-line, (b) sum-of-the-years'-digits, (c) double-declining-balance, and (d) units-of-production, assuming that productive output during the machine's life is expected to be as follows:

19X3—18,000 units
19X4—25,000 units
19X5—22,000 units
19X6—34,000 units
19X7—21,000 units [LO2a,2b]

PROBLEM 10–3 *(Compute Depreciation Using the Group Depreciation Method)* Weston Company has several hundred depreciable assets and therefore uses the group method to compute depreciation. The composition of the company's plant assets has not changed significantly during the current year. The following data are available.

| PLANT ASSETS | COST | RESIDUAL VALUE | USEFUL LIFE | METHOD |
|---|---|---|---|---|
| Autos | $ 960,000 | $ 80,000 | 4 years | Straight-line |
| Trucks | 1,200,000 | 100,000 | 5 years | Straight-line |
| Cranes | 640,000 | 50,000 | 5 years | Straight-line |
| Earth movers | 1,500,000 | 70,000 | 6 years | Straight-line |

Required:

1. Compute the average depreciation rate and the average useful life using the group depreciation method.

2. Prepare a journal entry to record the depreciation expense for the current year, using the group depreciation method.
3. What is the primary advantage of grouping similar plant assets and applying an average depreciation rate to the entire group? [LO2c]

PROBLEM 10–4 *(Record Extraordinary Repairs, Improvements, and Depreciation Expense)* On January 2, 19X3, Ward Company purchased a new machine at a cost of $85,000. The machine was immediately installed and made ready for use at a cost of $3,000. Its estimated useful life is eight years, and its estimated residual value is $8,000. Ward uses the straight-line depreciation method.

On January 2, 19X5, the company completely overhauled the machine at a cost of $8,400. The overhaul, considered an extraordinary repair, extended the machine's estimated useful life to twelve years (four more than the original estimate). Estimated residual value remained the same.

On January 2, 19X7, the company made an improvement to the machine that cost $3,800. This improvement increased the machine's productivity but not its useful life and increased estimated residual value to $9,000.

Required:

Prepare journal entries to record

1. The purchase of the machine and its installation cost on January 2, 19X3
2. Depreciation expense on the machine on December 31, 19X3
3. The overhaul of the machine on January 2, 19X5
4. Depreciation expense on December 31, 19X5
5. The improvement made to the machine on January 2, 19X7
6. Depreciation expense on December 31, 19X7 [LO2a,2b,1e]

PROBLEM 10–5 *(Use and Evaluate Depreciation Methods)* On January 4, 19X5, Anchor Company purchased a machine for $130,000. The machine is expected to have a useful life of five years and a residual value of $10,000. The company's management wants to make comparisons of various depreciation methods because they can significantly affect reported net income.

Required:

1. Prepare a schedule like the one shown below. Compute the annual depreciation and enter that amount and the end-of-the-year carrying value for each of the five years of the asset's useful life and for each of the three listed depreciation methods as shown in the column headings.

| | STRAIGHT-LINE | | SUM-OF-THE-YEARS'-DIGITS | | DOUBLE-DECLINING BALANCE | |
|---|---|---|---|---|---|---|
| YEAR | Depreciation Expense | Carrying Value | Depreciation Expense | Carrying Value | Depreciation Expense | Carrying Value |
| Date of Purchase | $ — | $130,000 | $ — | $130,000 | $ — | $130,000 |
| Year 1 | | | | | | |
| Year 2 | | | | | | |
| Year 3 | | | | | | |
| Year 4 | | | | | | |
| Year 5 | | | | | | |

2. Which depreciation method would
   a. Result in the highest reported net income taken aggregately for the first two years of the machine's estimated life?
   b. Result in the lowest reported net income taken aggregately for the first two years of the machine's estimated life? [LO2b]

PROBLEM 10–6 *(Classify and Record Capital and Revenue Expenditures)* Klein Company had the following cash transactions during 19X4.

a. Paid the fee charged for surveying a parcel of newly acquired land, $1,000.
b. Paid for normal tuneup service on a company vehicle, $120.
c. Paid for insurance on a machine while it was in transit from the seller, $75.
d. Paid architect for designing a new building, $3,600.
e. Paid the cost to install a newly acquired machine, $540.
f. Paid the cost of an extraordinary repair that is expected to extend the useful life of a vehicle by two years, $1,750.
g. Paid an attorney for work related to the newly acquired land, $1,300.
h. Paid the costs to paint a building acquired three years ago, $315.
i. Paid for a building permit, $350.
j. Paid for a fence that was erected around the newly acquired land, $6,200.
k. Paid to replace the tires on the company vehicle, $280.
l. Paid for window repairs on the building that was being painted, $80.
m. Paid for the construction of a parking lot to be used by company employees, $7,400.
n. Made partial payment to building contractor hired to erect a new building, $50,000.
o. Paid for test runs on a recently acquired machine (testing was necessary before using the machine), $500.

Required:

1. For each transaction described above, indicate whether the expenditure should be treated as a capital expenditure or as a revenue expenditure. Indicate the title of the account to be debited in each case. [LO1e,2a]

PROBLEM 10–7 *(Use Revised Depreciation Rates)* The Newmark Company, which uses the straight-line depreciation method, purchased three machines on January 10, 19X0. Data relating to each machine are shown below.

| | MACHINE A | MACHINE B | MACHINE C |
|---|---|---|---|
| Cost | $20,000 | $37,000 | $53,600 |
| Useful life | 5 years | 7 years | 8 years |
| Residual value | None | $ 2,000 | $ 4,000 |

During 19X0 and 19X1, Machine B was used much more than originally planned. Machine A was used as planned, and Machine C was used sparingly. This experience prompted management to reexamine both estimated useful lives and estimated residual values originally assigned to each of the machines. As a result, certain revisions were made and the data shown below were submitted.

| AS OF JANUARY 1, 19X2 | ESTIMATED REMAINING USEFUL LIFE | ESTIMATED RESIDUAL VALUE |
|---|---|---|
| Machine A | 3 years (no change) | None (no change) |
| Machine B | 3 years (reduced by 2) | $2,000 (no change) |
| Machine C | 6 years (no change) | $7,000 (increased by $3,000) |

Required:

1. Compute the amount of depreciation expense that should be recognized for each machine in 19X0 and 19X1. The company records depreciation expense to the nearest month.
2. Compute the amount of depreciation expense that should be recognized for each machine in 19X2.
3. Prepare the journal entry or entries to record depreciation expense for the year 19X2. (Use one journal entry for all three machines.) [LO2b,2c]

PROBLEM 10–8 *(Identify Acquisition Cost Errors and Their Effect on Reported Net Income)* On March 1, 19X5, a company purchased a used machine costing $14,400. The machine was delivered and installed the next day at a cost of $280. After spending an additional $920 to recondition the machine, it was placed in service on April 1. The straight-line method of depreciation is used, and the machine has an estimated useful life of ten years with no residual value expected. On December 31, 19X8, the asset was reported on the company's balance sheet as follows:

| | | |
|---|---|---|
| Machinery | $14,400 | |
| Less: Accumulated Depreciation | 5,520* | $8,880 |

* Depreciation taken in 19X5 was $1,200.

The company's income statement showed the following net incomes for each of the last four years:

| | |
|---|---|
| 19X5 | $19,400 |
| 19X6 | 21,380 |
| 19X7 | 22,760 |
| 19X8 | 23,100 |

Required:
Prepare a schedule that will show the errors, if any, that were made in determining the asset's acquisition cost and year-end depreciation expense. If necessary, correct the reported net income and show the amounts that should have been reported for each of the four years 19X5 through 19X8. [LO2a,2b,2c]

PROBLEM 10–9 *(Comprehensive Problem)* On February 12, 19X3, Yardley Company paid $28,000 to purchase a machine. Delivery charges and insurance covering the machine while in transit cost Yardley an additional $400 and were paid on February 14, 19X3. The machine was installed and tested before being used operationally. This cost the company $1,600, which was paid on February 26, 19X3. Based upon past experience with similar assets, the machine is expected to have a useful life of eight years and a residual value of $3,000. The machine was put into service on March 2, 19X3.

On April 1, 19X3, the company negotiated to purchase a group of several assets for a total cash price of $400,000. The assets consisted of land, a main building, and a secondary building that will be used as a warehouse. The assets were independently appraised on the date of their purchase at the following amounts:

Land—$110,000

Main Building—$275,000

Secondary Building—$55,000

Required:

1. Determine the cost of the machine and prepare journal entries to record its purchase.
2. Prepare a schedule to determine the amount of cost that should be assigned to each asset acquired in the group purchase. Prepare a journal entry to record the purchase.
3. Compute the amount of depreciation expense to be recorded for each plant asset for each of the first two years ending on December 31, 19X3 and 19X4. Use the following data:

   Machine—Estimated useful life of eight years, a $3,000 residual value, and the sum-of-the-years'-digits method is used.

   Building—Estimated useful life of twenty years, a $10,000 residual value, and the straight-line method is used.

Warehouse—Estimated useful life of eight years, no residual value, and the double-declining-balance method is used.

4. Prepare a journal entry or entries to record the depreciation expense for 19X3. [LO1e,2a,2b,2c]

## ALTERNATE PROBLEMS

PROBLEM 10–1A *(Determine Acquisition Cost and Depreciation)* (Alternate to Problem 10–2) Bevco Company, a maker of ceramic dolls, purchased a firing oven for use in the operations of its business. The following data relate to the oven.

Cash price paid to the seller, $10,600

Delivery charges (FOB shipping point), $140

Installation costs, $260

Estimated useful life:
In years, 6 years
In hours of operation, 50,000 hours

Estimated residual value, $1,000

Date oven was put into use, May 1, 19X0

During 19X0 the oven was used for 4,050 hours. During 19X1 and 19X2 the oven was used for 8,200 and 9,600 hours, respectively.

Required:

1. Determine the amount of depreciation expense that should be recognized in 19X0, 19X1, and 19X2, respectively, and the asset's carrying value at the end of each of those years. The company's year ends on December 31. Use the following depreciation methods: (a) straight-line, (b) sum-of-the-years'-digits, (c) double-declining-balance, and (d) units-of-production. Round amounts to nearest dollar.
2. Which method would result in the lowest reported net income for each of the years 19X0, 19X1, and 19X2? [LO2a,2b]

PROBLEM 10–2A *(Compute and Record Group Depreciation)* (Alternate to Problem 10–3) The following information was taken from the plant asset records of Hi-Adventure Company.

| ASSET | ACQUISITION COST | RESIDUAL VALUE | USEFUL LIFE IN YEARS | METHOD |
|---|---|---|---|---|
| A | $ 60,000 | 0 | 6 | Straight-line |
| B | 50,000 | $ 2,000 | 8 | Straight-line |
| C | 90,000 | 5,000 | 5 | Straight-line |
| D | 120,000 | 10,000 | 10 | Straight-line |
| E | 80,000 | 8,000 | 6 | Straight-line |

All assets were acquired more than one year ago; none is more than three years old.

Required:

1. Compute the average depreciation rate and the average useful life using the group depreciation method.
2. Prepare a journal entry to record the depreciation expense for the current year, using the group depreciation method.
3. What is the primary advantage of grouping similar plant assets and applying an average depreciation rate to the entire group? [LO2c]

PROBLEM 10–3A *(Compute Depreciation Methods)* (Alternate to Problem 10–5) On January 3, 19X3, Goodway Company purchased a new machine for $75,000. The machine has an estimated useful life of eight years and an estimated residual value of $3,000. Management wanted some comparative data on the amount of depreciation expense that would be recorded under various depreciation methods and has consulted you on this matter.

Required:

Prepare a schedule showing the amount of depreciation expense that would be recognized for each year in the asset's estimated useful life using the following depreciation methods: (a) straight-line, (b) sum-of-the-years'-digits, and (c) double-declining-balance. [LO2b]

PROBLEM 10–4A *(Use Revised Depreciation Rate)* (Alternate to Problem 10–7) On January 2, 19X3, Salter Company purchased a machine costing $45,000. The machine has an estimated useful life of six years and an estimated residual value of $3,000. The company calculates depreciation using the straight-line method. The machine was placed into service on January 6, 19X3. After three years of use, it was evident that the machine would last only two more years (or a total of five years) and would have an estimated residual value of only $2,000.

Required:

1. Determine the amount of depreciation expense to be recorded in the first three years of the asset's life.
2. Determine the amount of revised depreciation expense to be recorded in the fourth and fifth years of the asset's life. [LO2b,2c]

# 11 Plant and Equipment: Disposals, Natural Resources, and Intangibles

## Learning Objectives

When you complete this chapter, you will be able to

1. Answer the following questions:
   a. How do the financial accounting and the income tax rules differ on certain exchanges of plant assets?
   b. How are subsidiary ledgers used for plant assets?
   c. In what ways are plant assets reported in the financial statements, and what disclosures are required?
   d. What are the unique characteristics of intangible assets, and how are intangible assets written off?
2. Perform the accounting for the following:
   a. The discard, sale, or exchange of plant assets.
   b. Natural resources, including the computation of depletion and the journal entry to record depletion.
   c. Intangible assets, including the computation of amortization and the journal entry to record amortization.

In this chapter we continue the discussion of long-term assets we began in Chapter 10. We now examine the accounting for disposal of plant and equipment assets, for natural resources, and for intangible assets.

## PLANT ASSET DISPOSALS

A plant asset eventually wears out or becomes obsolete or inadequate. When this happens, the asset may be discarded, sold, or traded in on a new one. Some aspects of the accounting treatment depend on which of these three actions is taken. In all cases, however, we must

*Record* depreciation from the date it was last recorded to the date the asset was disposed of

*Remove* the carrying value of the asset from the accounts

We remove carrying value by

*Debiting* the related accumulated depreciation account for the total depreciation taken on the asset to the date of disposal

*Crediting* the asset account for its cost

We will look at a number of examples that illustrate the accounting practices to be followed when a plant asset is discarded, sold, or traded in on a new asset.

### Discarding a Plant Asset

*2a. No loss is recorded on discard of a fully depreciated plant asset*

When a plant asset is no longer useful to the business and has no market value, it is discarded or scrapped. If the asset has been fully depreciated, there is no loss on the disposal. If the asset is discarded before it has been fully depreciated, there would be a loss on its disposal. Both situations are illustrated below.

*Situation 1: Discarding a fully depreciated asset.* Assume that a machine acquired at a cost of $20,000 became fully depreciated as of December 31, 19X5, and was discarded as worthless on February 4, 19X6. The entry to record the discard is:

| | | | |
|---|---|---|---|
| Feb. 4 | Accumulated Depreciation—Machinery . . . . . . . . . . . . . . . . . | 20,000 | |
| | Machinery . . . . . . . . . . . . . . . . . . . . . . . . . . . . . . . . . . . . | | 20,000 |
| | To record the discard of a fully depreciated machine | | |

*2a. Undepreciated cost is recognized as a loss on the discard of a plant asset*

*Situation 2: Discarding a partially depreciated asset.* Assume now that a machine acquired at a cost of $15,000 is discarded as worthless on January 2, 19X6. In this case, the asset's undepreciated cost is recognized as a loss on disposal. For example, if this machine had an Accumulated Depreciation account balance of $11,000 on the day of its disposal, the entry to remove the plant asset accounts and record the loss would be as follows:

| | | | |
|---|---|---|---|
| Jan. 2 | Accumulated Depreciation—Machinery. . . . . . . . . . . . . . . . . . | 11,000 | |
| | Loss on Disposal of Plant Assets . . . . . . . . . . . . . . . . . . . . . . . | 4,000 | |
| | Machinery . . . . . . . . . . . . . . . . . . . . . . . . . . . . . . . . . . . . | | 15,000 |
| | To record the discard of a partially depreciated machine | | |

The entry removes the balances in the Machinery and Accumulated Depreciation accounts and recognizes the difference between the two amounts ($15,000 − $11,000 = $4,000) as a loss on disposal. Losses and gains on the disposal of plant assets are generally included with "Other Expenses" or "Other Income" on a classified income statement.

*2a. Cost of removal is added to loss on disposal of a plant assset*

*Situation 3: Expenditure incurred when discarding.* Sometimes it is necessary to pay to have a worthless plant asset removed. The amount of the payment increases the loss on the asset's disposal. For example, if the company paid $300 to have the machine removed, the entry (using the data from our last example) would be as follows:

| | | | |
|---|---|---|---|
| Jan. 2 | Accumulated Depreciation—Machinery | 11,000 | |
| | Loss on Disposal of Plant Assets | 4,300 | |
| | Machinery | | 15,000 |
| | Cash | | 300 |
| | To record the disposal of a partially depreciated machine with disposal costs of $300 | | |

If a company is still using an asset that is fully depreciated, its cost and accumulated depreciation should not be removed from the accounts. The accounts provide evidence of the continued use of such assets, which is a control function that accountants want to maintain.

## Selling a Plant Asset

Another way to dispose of a plant asset is to sell it. If the selling price is more than the carrying value of the asset, a gain will be recognized. If the selling price is less than the carrying value of the asset, a loss will be recognized. If the selling price is equal to the carrying value of the asset (less likely), no gain or loss will be recognized on the disposal.

To illustrate each of these possibilities, assume that a machine was purchased on January 2, 19X2, for $28,000 and was sold on October 1, 19X6. On the date of purchase, the machine was expected to have a useful life of seven years and residual value of $2,800. Depreciation entries have been recorded each December 31 by using the straight-line method. The Accumulated Depreciation account has a balance of $14,400 on December 31, 19X5, representing the depreciation recorded on the machine through that date.

*2a. Depreciation must be recorded for the partial year up to the date of disposal*

Before recording the sale, an entry must be made to record depreciation for the nine months in the current year (January 1 to October 1, 19X6) and bring the balance in the Accumulated Depreciation account up to-date as follows:

| | | | |
|---|---|---|---|
| Oct. 1 | Depreciation Expense—Machinery | 2,700 | |
| | Accumulated Depreciation—Machinery | | 2,700 |
| | To record nine months of depreciation on machinery sold ($28,000 − $2,800 = $25,200; $25,200 ÷ 7 = $3,600; $3,600 × $\frac{9}{12}$ = $2,700) | | |

After this entry has been posted, the Accumulated Depreciation account will have a balance of *$17,100* ($14,400 + $2,700), and the machine will have a carrying value of *$10,900* ($28,000 − $17,100).

The entries to record the sale of the machine using three independent assumptions about its selling price are illustrated below.

*Situation 1: Selling a plant asset for an amount that is equal to its carrying value.* If the machine is sold for $10,900, no gain or loss is recognized and the entry is as follows:

*2a. Entries are illustrated here for the sale of a plant asset at carrying value, at more than carrying value, and at less than carrying value*

| | | | |
|---|---|---|---|
| Oct. 1 | Cash | 10,900 | |
| | Accumulated Depreciation—Machinery | 17,100 | |
| | Machinery | | 28,000 |
| | To record the sale of a machine | | |

The entry records the cash received and removes the cost of the machine and its related accumulated depreciation from the accounts.

*Situation 2: Selling a plant asset for an amount that exceeds its carrying value.* If the machine is sold for $11,500, a gain of $600 representing the difference between the asset's selling price and its carrying value ($11,500 − $10,900 = $600) is recognized and the entry is as follows:

| | | | |
|---|---|---|---|
| Oct. 1 | Cash | 11,500 | |
| | Accumulated Depreciation—Machinery | 17,100 | |
| | Machinery | | 28,000 |
| | Gain on Disposal of Plant Assets | | 600 |
| | To record the sale of a machine | | |

*Situation 3: Selling a plant asset for an amount than is less that its carrying value.* If the machine is sold for $10,600, a loss of $300 representing the difference between the asset's selling price and its carrying value is recognized and the entry is as follows:

| | | | |
|---|---|---|---|
| Oct. 1 | Cash | 10,600 | |
| | Accumulated Depreciation—Machinery | 17,100 | |
| | Loss on Disposal of Plant Assets | 300 | |
| | Machinery | | 28,000 |
| | To record the sale of a machine | | |

## Exchanging Plant Assets

A third way to dispose of a plant asset is to trade it in for another one. In such transactions the trade-in allowance granted for the old asset is deducted from the price of the new asset, and the remaining balance is paid according to the credit terms. The accounting treatment given to a trade-in depends on whether the assets exchanged are similar or dissimilar.

EXCHANGING SIMILAR ASSETS **Similar plant assets** are those of the same general type that perform the same function in a business. If in the exchange of similar assets the trade-in allowance granted for the old plant asset is less than its carrying value, a loss results and that loss is recognized immediately. However, if in the exchange of similar assets the trade-in allowance granted for the old plant asset is greater than its carrying value, the gain that results is not recognized at the time of the exchange. Thus the gains and losses resulting from the exchange of similar assets are handled differently in the accounting records. Losses are recognized immediately, and gains are not recognized immediately.[1]

*Situation 1: Recognition of loss.* Here we illustrate the accounting when an asset is traded for a similar one and the loss indicated is recorded immediately. Assume that a machine that originally cost $28,000 and has an accumulated depreciation of $20,000 is traded for a new machine on March 2, 19X5. The list price of the new machine is $35,000. A trade-in allowance of $5,000 was received on the old machine, and the balance was paid in cash. The old machine has a carrying value of $8,000 on the trade-in date determined as follows:

| | |
|---|---|
| Cost of old machine | $28,000 |
| Less accumulated depreciation | 20,000 |
| Carrying value at date of exchange | $ 8,000 |

***2a. For exchanges of similar plant assets, the excess of an asset's carrying value over its trade-in allowance is recorded as a loss***

The amount of loss to be recognized on the exchange is the excess of the carrying value of the machine traded in over the trade-in allowance granted ($8,000 − $5,000), or $3,000. The entry to record the exchange transaction is as follows:

| | | | |
|---|---|---|---|
| March 2 | Machinery | 35,000 | |
| | Accumulated Depreciation—Machinery | 20,000 | |
| | Loss on Disposal of Plant Assets | 3,000 | |
| | Machinery | | 28,000 |
| | Cash | | 30,000 |
| | To record the exchange of an old machine for a new one having a similar use | | |

Note that the journal entry records the new machine at its cash price of $35,000 (the amount that would have been paid if the machine had been purchased outright with no trade-in). The entry also removes the cost of the old machine and its related accumulated depreciation from the accounts and recognizes the loss on the exchange.

***2a. For exchanges of similar plant assets, a gain on trade-in is not recognized in the accounts***

*Situation 2: Nonrecognition of gain.* Here we illustrate the accounting when an asset is traded for a similar one and the gain indicated is not immediately recognized. Assume now that in acquiring the $35,000 machine, a $9,000 rather than a $5,000 trade-in was received and the remaining balance of $26,000 was paid in cash. Because the trade-in allowance granted on the old asset exceeds its carrying value, the difference of $1,000 ($9,000 − $8,000 = $1,000) represents a book gain. However, this gain is not recognized in the accounts when the exchange transaction is recorded. The new machine is recorded at its cash price less the gain not recognized, or $34,000. Thus the cost basis of the new machine is computed as follows:

| | |
|---|---|
| Cash price of new machine | $35,000 |
| Less: Gain not recognized | 1,000 |
| Recorded amount of new machine | $34,000 |

[1] See Accounting Principles Board, "Accounting for Nonmonetary Transactions," *Opinion No.* 29 (New York: AICPA, 1973).

The cost of the new machine could also be determined by adding the cash paid to acquire it ($26,000) to the carrying value of the old machine ($8,000), or $34,000.

The following entry would record the exchange transaction:

| | | | |
|---|---|---|---|
| March 2 | Machinery | 34,000 | |
| | Accumulated Depreciation—Machinery | 20,000 | |
| | Machinery | | 28,000 |
| | Cash | | 26,000 |
| | To record the exchange of an old machine for a new one having a similar use | | |

The nonrecognition of the $1,000 gain at the time of the exchange is actually a *postponement* of that gain. For example, assume that at a later date the new machine having a cost basis of $34,000, not $35,000, is sold or discarded. Any gain on the transaction will be increased by $1,000, and any loss will be reduced by $1,000. Furthermore, if the machine is kept for its entire estimated useful life, the total amount of depreciation expense recorded over that life will be $1,000 less than the amount recorded had the depreciation been based on the machine's $35,000 cash price.

*2a. For exchanges of dissimilar plant assets, gains and losses are recognized immediately*

EXCHANGING DISSIMILAR ASSETS **Dissimilar plant assets** are assets that are not of the same general type and do not perform the same function in a business. When dissimilar assets are exchanged, the resulting gains or losses are recognized immediately.

*Situation 1: Recognition of loss.* It is not a common business practice to trade in an asset having one purpose for another asset having a dissimilar purpose or function. For purposes of this example, however, assume that on April 1 cash of $6,000 and a vehicle that cost $12,000 with an accumulated depreciation of $5,000 are traded for a computer having a cash price of $10,000. The following entry would record the exchange transaction:

| | | | |
|---|---|---|---|
| April 1 | Equipment | 10,000 | |
| | Accumulated Depreciation—Vehicle | 5,000 | |
| | Loss on Disposal of Plant Assets | 3,000 | |
| | Vehicle | | 12,000 |
| | Cash | | 6,000 |
| | To record a computer acquired in exchange for a vehicle and cash | | |

Note that the equipment received (computer) is recorded at its cash price or fair market value,[2] not at list price. The entry also removes the cost of the vehicle and its related accumulated depreciation from the accounts and recognizes a loss on the transaction. The loss is computed as follows:

| | |
|---|---|
| Carrying value of vehicle given in exchange | $ 7,000 |
| Cash paid in exchange | 6,000 |
| Value given in exchange | 13,000 |
| Less: Cash price (fair market value) of computer acquired in exchange | 10,000 |
| Loss on exchange | $ 3,000 |

[2] **Fair market value** refers to a value determined by informed buyers and sellers from aggregate data available.

*Situation 2: Recognition of gain.* Assume the same facts as in situation 1 except that the computer received has a cash price (fair market value) of $15,000. When recording the transaction, a gain of $2,000 on the exchange would be recognized and the entry would be as follows:

| | | | |
|---|---|---|---|
| April 1 | Equipment | 15,000 | |
| | Accumulated Depreciation—Vehicle | 5,000 | |
| | Vehicle | | 12,000 |
| | Cash | | 6,000 |
| | Gain on Disposal of Plant Assets | | 2,000 |
| | To record a computer acquired in exchange for a vehicle and cash | | |

The gain is determined by deducting values assigned to the assets given in exchange (carrying value of vehicle, $7,000, plus $6,000 cash, or $13,000) from the fair market value of the assets acquired in exchange (cash price of computer, $15,000).

### Federal Income Tax Rules for Exchanges of Plant Assets

For federal income tax purposes, *neither* gains nor losses are recognized when *similar* productive assets are exchanged and cash is *paid* (rather than received) by the taxpayer. Thus the treatment of a nonrecognized gain for tax purposes is consistent with the treatment prescribed for financial reporting purposes.

***1a. When an exchange of similar plant assets results in a loss, financial accounting and income tax rules differ***

When the exchange results in a loss, federal income tax laws and financial accounting practices differ:

For *financial accounting* purposes, the loss on the exchange of one plant asset for another is recognized immediately.

For *tax* purposes, the loss cannot be recognized.

To illustrate, assume that old equipment that cost $30,000 and has accumulated depreciation of $20,000 is traded in on new equipment with a cash price of $45,000. A trade-in allowance of $5,000 is received and $40,000 is paid in cash. For federal income tax purposes, the new equipment has a cost basis of *$50,000* (equal to the carrying value of the old asset plus the cash paid, $10,000 + $40,000 = $50,000). The indicated loss of $5,000 (representing the difference between the carrying value of the old asset of $10,000 less its trade-in allowance of $5,000) is not recognized immediately for tax purposes. Instead it is included in the cost basis of the new asset, making its cost basis *$5,000* higher than its cash price. Depreciation expense for tax purposes will be based upon the asset's cost basis of $50,000, not on its cash price of $45,000. As a result, the $5,000 loss not immediately recognized is recognized over the life of the new equipment through higher depreciation charges.

## CONTROL OF PLANT ASSETS—SUBSIDIARY LEDGERS

Management is responsible for establishing an internal control system for its plant assets. The system varies depending on the size and complexity of the business and the composition of its assets. All systems require formal records. For

*EXHIBIT 11–1*

Plant Asset Subsidiary Ledger Cards

*Subsidiary Plant Asset*

Item: Delivery Truck

Serial No: 3ST624963

Location: Garage 1

Estimated Life: 5 years

Depreciation Method: S.L.

General Ledger Account: Delivery Equipment

Purchased From: Lane Motors

Estimated Residual Value: $1,000

Depreciation per year: $3,200

| DATE | EXPLANATION | POST. REF. | ASSET DEBIT | ASSET CREDIT | ASSET BALANCE | DEPRECIATION DEBIT | DEPRECIATION CREDIT | DEPRECIATION BALANCE |
|---|---|---|---|---|---|---|---|---|
| 19X4 Jan. 1 | | CP 12 | 17 000 | | 17 000 | | | |
| Dec. 31 | | GJ 6 | | | | | 3 200 | 3 200 |
| 19X5 Dec. 31 | | GJ 11 | | | | | 3 200 | 6 400 |
| 19X6 Dec. 31 | | GJ 15 | | | | | 3 200 | 9 600 |

*Subsidiary Plant Asset*

Item: Van

Serial No: 8GR748639

Location: Garage 1

Estimated Life: 4 years

Depreciation Method: S.L.

General Ledger Account: Delivery Equipment

Purchased From: Lane Motors

Estimated Residual Value: $2,500

Depreciation per year: $4,000

| DATE | EXPLANATION | POST. REF. | ASSET DEBIT | ASSET CREDIT | ASSET BALANCE | DEPRECIATION DEBIT | DEPRECIATION CREDIT | DEPRECIATION BALANCE |
|---|---|---|---|---|---|---|---|---|
| 19X4 April 1 | | CP 86 | 18 500 | | 18 500 | | | |
| Dec. 31 | | GJ 6 | | | | | 3 000* | 3 000 |
| 19X5 Dec. 31 | | GJ 11 | | | | | 4 000 | 7 000 |
| 19X6 Dec. 31 | | GJ 15 | | | | | 4 000 | 11 000 |

* Depreciation from April 1, 19X4 to December 1, 19X4.

EXHIBIT 11–2

Plant Asset Control Accounts

DELIVERY EQUIPMENT — ACCOUNT NO. 44

| DATE | | EXPLANATION | POST. REF. | DEBIT | CREDIT | BALANCE |
|---|---|---|---|---|---|---|
| 19X4 Jan. | 1 | | CP 12 | 17 000 | | 17 000 |
| April | 1 | | CP 86 | 18 500 | | 35 500 |

ACCUMULATED DEPRECIATION—DELIVERY EQUIPMENT — ACCOUNT NO. 45

| DATE | | EXPLANATION | POST. REF. | DEBIT | CREDIT | BALANCE |
|---|---|---|---|---|---|---|
| 19X4 Dec. | 31 | | GJ 6 | | 6 200 | 6 200 |
| 19X5 Dec. | 31 | | GJ 11 | | 7 200 | 13 400 |
| 19X6 Dec. | 31 | | GJ 15 | | 7 200 | 20 600 |

small companies, the records may be handwritten; larger businesses will probably use computers. The records generally contain information that identifies the asset, its location, acquisition cost, estimated life, depreciation method used, residual value (if any), annual depreciation, accumulated depreciation to date, and any other data considered pertinent.

Many businesses divide their plant assets into functional groups and provide in their general ledger a separate plant asset account and a separate accumulated depreciation account for each functional group. For example, a retail appliance store might have separate asset and accumulated depreciation accounts for its delivery equipment, store equipment, and office equipment. Each plant asset account and related accumulated depreciation account is usually a control account that is supported by detailed subsidiary records. The subsidiary records generally consist of cards, with a separate card for each item included in the control account. Each card in the subsidiary ledger has an identification number, which should also be affixed to the asset itself. This number helps to identify items, which in turn helps to increase control over them. Although there are many variations in the form of subsidiary records for plant assets, they generally have spaces for recording the date the asset was acquired, its cost, useful life, residual value, depreciation method used, annual depreciation, accumulated depreciation, and any other useful data.

*1b. Subsidiary ledgers provide detailed information about plant assets*

Exhibit 11–1 contains an example of two subsidiary record cards—one for a truck and one for a van. They are the records that provide support for the control accounts in Exhibit 11–2, the $35,500 debit balance in Delivery Equipment control account (consisting of a $17,000 truck plus an $18,500 van) and the $20,600 credit balance in Accumulated Depreciation—Delivery Equipment control account (consisting of the depreciation taken on the truck [$9,600] and the depreciation taken on the van [$11,000]).

## REPORTING PLANT ASSETS IN THE FINANCIAL STATEMENTS

*1c. Financial Statements should disclose the balance of each major group of depreciable assets, together with accumulated depreciation*

The balance of each major class of depreciable assets, together with the related accumulated depreciation either by major class or in total, should be disclosed in the financial statements or in the notes thereto.[3] Some companies make a rather detailed presentation of plant assets right in the balance sheet, as shown in the following partial balance sheet.

| | COST | ACCUMULATED DEPRECIATION | CARRYING VALUE |
|---|---|---|---|
| Plant Assets: | | | |
| Land | $ 100,000 | $ — | $100,000 |
| Buildings | 500,000 | 200,000 | 300,000 |
| Equipment | 600,000 | 250,000 | 350,000 |
| Vehicles | 80,000 | 20,000 | 60,000 |
| Total Plant Assets | $1,280,000 | $470,000 | $810,000 |

Another frequently used presentation follows:

| | | |
|---|---|---|
| Plant Assets: | | |
| Land | $ 100,000 | |
| Buildings | 500,000 | |
| Equipment | 600,000 | |
| Vehicles | 80,000 | |
| | $1,280,000 | |
| Less: Accumulated Depreciation | 470,000 | $810,000 |

Sometimes the balances in plant asset accounts are combined with related accumulated depreciation accounts and are shown as single figures. For example, Exxon Corporation has reported plant assets in its balance sheet as follows:

| | |
|---|---|
| Property, plant and equipment, at cost, less accumulated depreciation and depletion of $17,519,872,000 . . . . . . . . . . . . . . . . | $35,285,519,000 |

Regardless of which approach is used, the following information pertaining to plant assets must be disclosed in the financial statements or in notes thereto:

*1c. Four items of information about plant assets must be disclosed in the financial statements*

1. Depreciation expense for the period
2. Balances of major classes of depreciable assets, by nature or function, at the balance sheet date
3. Accumulated depreciation, either by major classes of depreciable assets or in total, at the balance sheet date, and
4. A general description of the method or methods used in computing depreciation with respect to major classes of depreciable assets.[4]

---

[3] Accounting Principles Board, "Omnibus Opinion 1967," *Opinion No. 12* (New York: AICPA, 1967), par. 5.

[4] Ibid.

# NATURAL RESOURCES

## The Composition of Natural Resources

Natural resources, like plant assets, are also expected to provide benefits for more than one year. Examples include

Mineral deposits
Oil and gas reserves
Coal fields
Tracts of standing timber

**Natural resources** (sometimes called **wasting assets**) differ from plant assets in that they are physically consumed, through removal, in the production process. In their natural state they represent inventories that will be converted into a product by pumping, cutting, or mining.

For example, a tract of standing timber is an inventory of uncut lumber until changed into a finished product that can be sold to customers. Until converted, natural resources are shown on the balance sheet as long-term assets, bearing descriptive titles such as Mineral Deposits, Oil and Gas Reserves, and Timber Lands.

*2b. Natural resources are recorded at acquisition cost*

Natural resources are recorded at acquisition cost, which may include some costs for exploration and development. As the resource is being converted by a pumping, cutting, or mining process, the asset account must be proportionately reduced. For example, the carrying value of a coal mine is reduced as each ton of coal is extracted. As a result, a portion of the asset's original cost is gradually transferred and assigned to a depletion account.

## Depletion

*2b. Under the units-of-production method, depletion is computed in the same way as depreciation*

The term **depletion** is used to describe the process of cost allocation that assigns a portion of the cost of a natural resource to the units removed during a period. Under the units-of-production method, depletion is computed in the same way as depreciation: The *cost* of the natural resource, less its *estimated* residual value, is divided by an *estimate* of the number of units, such as barrels of oil or tons of coal, contained in the natural resource.

For example, assume that a coal mine containing an estimated 1,000,000 tons of uniform grade coal cost \$3,300,000. Assume further that the property is expected to have a residual value of \$300,000 after its contents have been extracted. The depletion charge per ton of coal is *\$3* computed as follows: [(\$3,300,000 − \$300,000 = \$3,000,000) ÷ (1,000,000 tons)]. If 200,000 tons of coal are mined during the year, the depletion amounting to *\$600,000* (200,000 tons × \$3 per ton) would be recorded as follows:

| | | | |
|---|---|---|---|
| Dec. 31 | Depletion—Coal Mine | 600,000 | |
| | Accumulated Depletion—Coal Mine | | 600,000 |
| | To record depletion for the year | | |

The Accumulated Depletion account is a contra asset account and is presented in the balance sheet as a deduction from the cost of the coal mine in a presentation similar to the following:

| | | |
|---|---|---|
| Coal Mine | $3,300,000 | |
| Less: Accumulated Depletion | 600,000 | $2,700,000 |

If the 200,000 tons of coal extracted are sold by the end of the year, the $600,000 of depletion will be charged to expense and will appear in the current year's income statement. However, if a portion of the mined coal remains unsold at year-end, the $600,000 of depletion must be allocated proportionately. The portion assigned to the unsold coal represents inventory and is reported as a current asset on the balance sheet. The portion assigned to the coal sold is reported as an expense on the income statement.

*2b. Only those extracted natural resources that are sold are reported as Depletion Expense*

For example, if 150,000 tons of the extracted coal were sold during the year, only *$450,000* (150,000 tons × $3) of the $600,000 of depletion would be charged to expense and reported on the income statement. The remaining *$150,000* of depletion would be reported as coal inventory on the balance sheet. The following entry would record the assignment of depletion to expense and to the asset:

| | | | |
|---|---|---|---|
| Dec. 31 | Depletion Expense . . . . . . . . . . | 450,000 | |
| | Coal Inventory . . . . . . . . . . | 150,000 | |
| | Depletion—Coal Mine . . . . . . . . | | 600,000 |
| | To record the allocation of depletion | | |

To extract a natural resource, it may be necessary to construct a building and install some equipment on the site. The cost of these plant assets should be depreciated over their estimated useful lives or over the life of the natural resource, whichever is shorter. Generally, depreciation is computed on the same basis as depletion by using the units-of-production method. For example, if mining equipment having a cost of $500,000 and no residual value were installed in the coal mine of our preceding illustration, the depreciation charge based on the life expectancy of the coal mine would be *$.50* per unit mined ($500,000 ÷ 1,000,000 tons). Depreciation was computed in the same way as depletion (by using the units-of-production method) because the equipment is assumed to have the life span of the mine, after which time it will no longer be useful to anyone. Depreciation expense for the mining equipment in the current year would be *$100,000* ($.50 × 200,000 tons).

Because the cost of a mine or any other natural resource generally involves large sums of money, accounting for these resources takes on added significance.

*2b. Estimates of number of recoverable units of a natural resource may need to be revised*

One of the more formidable problems is estimating the number of recoverable units held by the resource. If original estimates are ever revised, the depletion rate per unit must also be revised. The procedure for revising depletion rates is the same as that followed when depreciation rates are revised. Briefly stated, the *remaining* carrying value of the natural resource is spread over the *new* estimate of recoverable units.

## INTANGIBLE ASSETS AND AMORTIZATION

*1d. Intangible assets have no physical substance but convey certain rights and privileges*

Assets that are long-lived (expected to provide benefits for more than one year) but have no physical substance are called **intangible assets.** They contribute to a firm's earnings capability by virtue of certain rights and privileges associated with them. Examples of intangible assets are patents, copyrights, trademarks, franchises, and goodwill.

*1d, 2c. The accounting for intangible assets is similar to that for plant assets*

The accounting for intangible assets is similar to that described for plant assets in that

Intangible assets are initially recorded at their acquisition *cost*

Their costs are systemically allocated to expense over their estimated *useful* life or in some cases their legal life, whichever is shorter

Intangible assets are often shown in a separate section of the balance sheet following plant assets and natural resources. They are reported at cost or at the portion of their cost that has not yet been amortized. **Amortization** is the allocation of the cost of an intangible asset to the periods expected to benefit from its use.

*1d,2c. Allocation of the cost of an intangible asset to the periods expected to benefit from its use is called amortization*

Amortization is similar to depreciation of plant assets and depletion of natural resources. It is a cost allocation process that assigns the acquisition cost of an intangible asset to the periods benefiting from its use. Periodic amortization is recorded by

*Debiting* amortization expense and

*Crediting* the intangible asset account itself, rather than crediting a contra-asset account such as accumulated amortization.

Although this is common practice, it would nevertheless be acceptable to use an accumulated amortization account comparable to the accumulated depreciation account used for plant assets or the accumulated depletion account used for natural resources.

*1d,2c. Intangible assets are amortized over the shortest of their expected useful life, their legal life, or forty years*

Intangible assets should be amortized over the shorter of their expected useful life or their legal life. Current accounting practice requires that the cost of an intangible asset acquired after October 31, 1970, be amortized over a period of not more than forty years. Furthermore, the straight-line method of amortization must be used unless it can be demonstrated that another method is more appropriate.[5] Thus the patents we discuss in the following sections should be amortized using the straight-line method over (1) their expected useful life, (2) their legal life, or (3) forty years, whichever is shortest.

## Patents

A **patent** is an exclusive right, granted by the U.S. Patent Office, to use, manufacture, and sell a particular product or process. Patents are issued to encourage the invention of new machines and processes. Polaroid film is an example of a product manufactured under a patent. Patents are granted for seventeen years and cannot be renewed. However, if modifications or improvements are made, a new patent may be obtained for the improved version.

Patents may be obtained on new products and processes developed by a company's own research facilities, or they may be purchased from others. The costs of acquiring a patent on products or processes developed internally are usually minimal, consisting of nothing more than document filing and legal fees. For this reason, they are generally charged immediately to expense accounts. When a patent is purchased from the inventor or other holder, the purchase price should be debited to the Patents account. In addition, any legal costs incurred to defend the patent successfully should also be debited to the Patents account.

[5] Accounting Principles Board, "Intangible Assets," *Opinion No. 17* (New York: AICPA, 1970), par. 29.

*2c. Entries to record the purchase and amortization of a patent are illustrated here*

To illustrate the accounting for patents, assume that a patent granted to a developer four years earlier was purchased from that holder on January 2 for $100,000. The following entry would record the purchase:

| | | | |
|---|---|---|---|
| Jan. 2 | Patents | 100,000 | |
| | Cash | | 100,000 |
| | To record the purchase of a patent | | |

The patent's remaining legal life is thirteen years. But if its estimated useful life is ten years, its costs should be amortized over that period, since it is shorter. The entry to record patent amortization at the end of the year is as follows:

| | | | |
|---|---|---|---|
| Dec. 31 | Amortization Expense—Patents | 10,000 | |
| | Patents | | 10,000 |
| | To record patent amortization for the year | | |

All **research and development costs**—costs incurred in the search for new products or processes—must be expensed as incurred. This rule was established to achieve uniformity among companies in the treatment of research and development costs. Before 1975 some companies, such as Du Pont, charged research and development costs to expense when incurred. Other companies, such as Lockheed, capitalized sizable amounts of such costs. The requirement enhances comparability between companies. It also recognizes the high degree of uncertainty about future benefits to be obtained from research and development costs. (Not all R&D projects are successful.) As a result, all research and development costs not reimbursable from a governmental agency or other parties must be charged to expense when incurred.[6]

## Copyrights

**A copyright** is an exclusive right granted by the federal government to publish, sell, or control a literary or artistic work for the life of the creator plus fifty years. The cost of obtaining a copyright is nominal and is often charged to expense immediately. Copyrights can also be purchased, but generally at a high cost. In this case, the purchase price is debited to a Copyright account. Purchased copyrights are amortized over their useful life, not exceeding forty years. Because copyrights generally are capable of providing benefits for only a few years, the costs are usually amortized over relatively short periods. Periodic copyright amortization is recorded by *debiting* an account called Amortization Expense—Copyrights and *crediting* the asset account Copyrights.

## Trademarks and Trade Names

**Trademarks and trade names** are words, symbols, designs, or other devices that identify a particular product or group of products. A well-known example is the unique symbol for Coca-Cola and the use of the word *Coke.* A trademark may be registered with the U.S. Patent Office, which gives the owner the exclusive right

[6] Financial Accounting Standards Board, "Accounting for Research and Development Costs," *Statement No. 2* (Stamford, Conn., 1974), par. 12.

to use it for a period of twenty years. Registration is renewable for additional twenty-year periods as long as the trademark is used continuously. Although this feature could give a trademark an unlimited useful life, its revenue-producing benefit may be confined to only a few years.

Companies may develop trademarks internally or they may purchase them from others. In either case the cost, if material, should be *capitalized* as an asset and *amortized* over the benefit period, not to exceed forty years.

Costs of internally developed trademarks that should be capitalized and amortized include registration fees, attorneys' fees, design fees, and costs incurred in connection with defending trademark rights.

## Leaseholds

Companies frequently rent property for a specified period under a contract called a **lease.** The company or person acquiring the right to possess and use the property is the **lessee;** the owner of the property is the **lessor.** The rights of possession and use granted to the lessee are called a **leasehold.** Examples of assets commonly leased are buildings, vehicles, machinery, and office equipment.

Some leases require no advance payment from the lessee but do require regular monthly installments. In such cases, a leasehold account is not used and the monthly payments are *debited* to a *Rent Expense* account.

For leases that extend over long periods, the lease agreement frequently requires the lessee to make a lump-sum payment at the time the lease is signed. In this case, the lessee should *debit* the amount of the prepayment to a *Leasehold* account and charge the amount to *Rent Expense* over the periods covered by the advance payment.

To illustrate, assume that a company enters into an agreement to lease office space from the building's owner for five years beginning on January 1, 19X5. The lease contract requires a prepayment of $50,000 plus annual payments of $30,000 on December 31 of each year. The advance payment is recorded as follows:

*2c. An entry is made to a Leasehold account for advance payment on leased space*

| | | | |
|---|---|---|---|
| Jan. 1 | Leasehold. . . . . . . . . . . . . . . . . . . . . . . . . . . . . . . . . . . . . . . . . | 50,000 | |
| | Cash . . . . . . . . . . . . . . . . . . . . . . . . . . . . . . . . . . . . . . | | 50,000 |
| | To record advance payment on leased office space | | |

*2c. An adjusting entry is used to record the periodic amortization of the Leasehold account*

The Leasehold account is an intangible asset and appears in the lessee's balance sheet. On December 31 of each year, the annual payment of $30,000 and the $10,000 periodic amortization of the Leasehold account ($50,000 ÷ 5 years = $10,000) are recorded as follows:

| | | | |
|---|---|---|---|
| Dec. 31 | Rent Expense . . . . . . . . . . . . . . . . . . . . . . . . . . . . . . . . . . . . . | 40,000 | |
| | Leasehold. . . . . . . . . . . . . . . . . . . . . . . . . . . . . . . . . . | | 10,000 |
| | Cash . . . . . . . . . . . . . . . . . . . . . . . . . . . . . . . . . . . . . | | 30,000 |
| | To record the annual rent payment and the amortization of a leasehold | | |

Under certain leasing arrangements, the lessor transfers to the lessee substantially all of the rights and risks related to the ownership of the leased property. This is considered an installment purchase of the property and should be recorded as such. Chapter 16 discusses in greater detail the accounting for this type of lease.

## Leasehold Improvements

Alterations or improvements made to leased property by the lessee are called **leasehold improvements.** Examples include constructing partitions and installing an improved lighting system in a leased building. The alterations or improvements become a permanent part of the leased property and revert to the lessor at the end of the lease. The lessee debits the cost of the alterations and improvements to a *Leasehold Improvements* account and amortizes that cost over the life of the lease or the life of the improvements, whichever is shorter. The amortization entry usually debits a Rent Expense account and credits the Leasehold Improvements account.

To illustrate, assume that a lessee makes improvements to a building leased for five years. The improvements made at the beginning of the lease period cost $20,000 and have an expected useful life of eight years. The expenditure for the improvements is recorded as follows:

*2c. An entry is shown here to record an expenditure for leasehold improvements*

| | | | |
|---|---|---|---|
| Jan. 3 | Leasehold Improvements | 20,000 | |
| | Cash | | 20,000 |
| | To record improvements to a leased building | | |

*2c. An ajdusting entry is used to record the periodic amortization of the cost of leasehold improvements*

The Leasehold Improvements account is an intangible asset. Since the improvements cannot be removed by the lessee after the lease term expires, benefits can only be obtained by the lessee for the five-year period and the asset's cost should be amortized over that time. The following entry would record the amortization:

| | | | |
|---|---|---|---|
| Dec. 31 | Rent Expense | 4,000 | |
| | Leasehold Improvements | | 4,000 |
| | To record amortization of leasehold improvements | | |

## Franchises

**A franchise** is an exclusive right granted by a company or a governmental agency to conduct business at a specified location or in a particular geographic area. Familiar examples of franchises are the right to operate fast-food restaurants such as McDonald's or Burger King. Municipalities frequently grant franchises to companies, giving them the exclusive right to operate bus line routes or to provide services such as trash removal.

The cost of a franchise may be substantial, in which case the cost should be *recorded* as an intangible asset and *amortized* over the life of the franchise. If the franchise is indefinite in duration or is perpetual, its cost should be amortized over the estimated benefit period, but in no case should the period exceed forty years. When the cost of a franchise is small, it may be charged to expense when incurred. The periodic payments required under a franchise (such as fees based upon periodic income) should be charged to expense when incurred.

## Organization Costs

The costs associated with the formation of a company are called **organization costs.** These costs may be numerous and substantial, particularly for a corporation. They generally occur before the company begins operations or during its early stages of operations. Costs of this type are *debited* to an intangible asset account called *Organization Costs.*

Although it can be argued that organization costs provide benefits to the company over its entire life, they too must be amortized over a period not to exceed forty years. Since the benefit period cannot be determined with certainty, companies choose an arbitrary period, with five years commonly used as the period of time over which the costs are amortized. The selection is probably influenced by the IRS rule that established five years as the minimum amortization period allowed for federal income tax purposes. Annual amortization is recorded by *debiting* an Amortization Expense account and *crediting* the Organization Costs account.

## Goodwill

The term *goodwill* means many things. Generally, it refers to the favorable reputation that a company has developed among its customers. In accounting, goodwill has a special meaning: **Goodwill** is *the potential of a company to earn a rate of return on its net assets (total assets minus total liabilities) that is greater than the normal rate of return for companies operating in the same line of business.* Goodwill is created by many factors, including favorable customer relations, advantageous location, product superiority, superior management, operating efficiency, and reputation.

To demonstrate the concept of above-average earnings, assume the following data about Company A and Company B, which operate in the same industry.

| | COMPANY A | COMPANY B |
|---|---|---|
| Net assets (excluding goodwill) | $8,000,000 | $8,000,000 |
| Normal rate of return for the industry | 10% | 10% |
| Normal return on net assets | $ 800,000 | $ 800,000 |
| Actual net income (averaged for the past five years) | 960,000 | 800,000 |
| Earnings above average for the past five years | $ 160,000 | $ 0 |

Because Company A has an above-average earnings rate (12% compared with the industry average of 10% computed as follows: $960,000 ÷ $8,000,000 = 12%), goodwill is said to exist. That is, one or more of the intangible factors cited above that create goodwill were in existence and helped the company generate its excess earnings. Furthermore, if both companies were offered for sale and the above-average earnings rate of Company A was expected to continue, a potential buyer would probably have to pay more to acquire Company A than Company B, although both have the same amount of net assets.

If the buyer does pay more for the business than the **fair market value** of the net assets being acquired, there is evidence that goodwill has been purchased. In such cases, the buyer assigns the amount by which the purchase price exceeds the fair market value of the net assets acquired to a Goodwill account. Goodwill is recorded in the accounts only when it has been purchased.

*2c. Three methods for determining the cost of goodwill are discussed here*

There are several approaches for determining a cost value for goodwill when a business is purchased. Three common methods follow.

1. The buyer and the seller in negotiation may establish an arbitrary value for the goodwill of the business being sold. For example, assume that a buyer is willing to pay $8,500,000 to acquire Company A in its entirety and the seller is willing to accept that amount. If both agree that the fair value of the net assets of Company A is $8,000,000, they have arbitrarily valued goodwill at $500,000. In the purchase transaction, the amount by which the purchase price exceeds the fair value of the net assets acquired should be recorded in a Goodwill account.
2. Goodwill may be valued at some multiple by which expected earnings exceed average earnings. For example, if Company A's earnings are expected to exceed average earnings by $160,000 for at least the next four years, goodwill may be valued at four times the amount that earnings are expected to exceed average, or at $640,000 (4 × $160,000). The multiple applied to the above average earnings could of course vary, and in any case it establishes an arbitrary value for goodwill. In this example the purchase price for Company A would be $8,640,000, of which $640,000 represents purchased goodwill and would be recorded in the Goodwill account.
3. Goodwill may be valued by capitalizing expected earnings in excess of average earnings at the normal rate of return for the industry. Capitalizing earnings that are above average means dividing those earnings by the normal rate of return. For example, assume that Company A is expected to continue to have earnings each year that exceed the average for companies in its industry by $160,000 and that the normal rate of return in the industry is 10%. The excess earnings may be capitalized at 10% to establish a goodwill value of $1,600,000 ($160,000 ÷ 10% = $1,600,000). Note that when goodwill is valued under this approach, it shows the amount that would have to be invested at the normal rate of return to earn the extra $160,000 each year ($1,600,000 × 10% = $160,000).

In summary, the following points regarding goodwill should be kept in mind:

1. Internally developed goodwill is not recorded in the accounts.
2. Goodwill is recorded in the accounts only when it has been purchased.
3. Purchased goodwill, representing the part of the purchase price of a business that exceeds the fair market value of the net assets acquired, is debited to a Goodwill account.
4. Purchased goodwill is reported in the balance sheet as an intangible asset.
5. Because the benefits derived from purchased goodwill eventually disappear, its recorded cost should be amortized over the number of years of expected benefit, but in no case should that period exceed forty years.

## HIGHLIGHT PROBLEM

This problem consists of two independent sections, A and B.

A. The office equipment of Daultry Company consists of a computer and a copy machine. Data concerning these plant assets appear below.

| ASSETS | ACQUISITION DATE | COST | USEFUL LIFE | RESIDUAL VALUE | DEPRECIATION METHOD |
|---|---|---|---|---|---|
| Computer | 1/1/X3 | $25,000 | 5 years | $5,000 | S.L. |
| Copier | 1/1/X2 | 12,500 | 6 years | 500 | S.L. |

July 1, 19X6—The computer was traded in on a new one having a list price of $30,000. To complete the exchange, Daultry paid $22,000 in cash.

December 31, 19X6—The copier was traded in on a new one having a list price of $18,000. Daultry received a trade-in allowance of $3,000 for the old copier.

Required:

1. Prepare journal entries to record each exchange transaction, along with the entries to record depreciation up to the date of the disposals.
2. Prepare the journal entry made on December 31, 19X6, to record the partial year's depreciation on the new computer. The straight-line depreciation method is used, and the copier has an estimated life of four years with an estimated residual value of $6,000.

B. Foresight Company paid cash to acquire the following assets during 19X6.

April 1—A patent for $90,000. The patent has a remaining legal life of twelve and one-half years. However, the company expects to receive benefits from its use for only ten years.

August 31—A trademark for $120,000. The company believes the trademark will have a perpetual life.

The company also made substantial improvements to a building that it occupies under a ten-year lease agreement that began on January 1, 19X6. The improvements, which were completed on June 30, 19X6, cost $57,000.

Required:

1. Prepare journal entries to record the above transactions.
2. Prepare the journal entries to record amortization for the current year.

## GLOSSARY OF KEY TERMS

**Amortization.** The allocation of the cost of an intangible asset to the periods expected to benefit from its use.

**Copyright.** An exclusive right granted by the federal government to publish, sell, or control a literary or artistic work for the life of the creator plus fifty years.

**Depletion.** The process of cost allocation that assigns a portion of the cost of a natural resource to the units that are removed during a period.

**Dissimilar plant assets.** Plant assets that are not of the same general type and do not perform the same function in a business.

**Fair market value.** Value determined by informed buyers and sellers from aggregate data available.

**Franchise.** An exclusive right granted by a company or a governmental agency to conduct business at a specified location or in a particular geographic area.

**Goodwill.** The potential of a company to earn a rate of return on its net assets that is greater than the normal rate of return for companies operating in the same line of business.

**Intangible assets.** Long-lived assets that have no physical substance but contribute to the earnings capability of a firm by virtue of the rights and privileges associated with them.

**Lease.** A contract that grants the right to possess and use property.

**Leasehold.** The rights of possession and use of property granted to the lessee under a lease contract.

**Leasehold improvements.** Alterations or improvements to a leased property made by the lessee.

**Lessee.** A person or company given the right to possess and use property under the terms of a lease contract.

**Lessor.** A person or company that has given another the right to possess and use property under the terms of a lease contract—the property owner.

**Natural resources.** Assets such as mines, oil reserves, gas deposits, ore deposits, and timber tracts that will be physically consumed as units are removed and converted into inventory.

**Organization costs.** Costs associated with the formation of a company.

**Patent.** An exclusive right granted by the U.S. Patent Office to use, manufacture, and sell a particular product or process for a period of seventeen years.

**Research and development costs.** Costs incurred in the search for new products or processes. These costs must be expensed when incurred.

**Similar plant assets.** Plant assets of the same general type that perform the same function in a business.

**Trademarks and trade names.** Words, symbols, designs, or other devices that identify a particular product or group of products.

**Wasting assets.** Alternate term for *natural resources.*

## REVIEW QUESTIONS

1. In all cases, what two steps must be performed when an asset is discarded, sold, or traded in on a new one? [LO2a]
2. What happens to the undepreciated cost of a partially depreciated asset that is discarded? [LO2a]
3. When a company discards a plant asset, how is the cost of the removal of the asset treated in the journal entry that shows the disposal? [LO2a]
4. Describe the journal entry that is made if a plant asset is sold (a) for an amount equal to its carrying value, (b) for an amount that exceeds its carrying value, and (c) for an amount that is less than its carrying value. [LO2a]
5. Differentiate between similar plant assets and dissimilar plant assets. [LO2a]
6. How is a loss on the exchange of similar assets treated in accounting? How is a gain treated? [LO2a]
7. How is a loss on the exchange of dissimilar assets treated in accounting? How is a gain treated? [LO2a]
8. Explain the difference between federal income tax rules and financial accounting practices for exchanges of plant assets. [LO1a]
9. Describe the content of plant asset subsidiary ledger cards. [LO1b]
10. What two control accounts are maintained for plant assets? [LO1b]
11. Explain three different ways for reporting plant assets in the balance sheet. [LO1c]
12. Name the four items of information pertaining to plant assets that must be disclosed in the financial statements or in notes thereto. [LO1c]
13. Differentiate between natural resources and plant assets. [LO1d]
14. Describe how natural resource depletion is computed. [LO2b]
15. How is the depletion cost of the units removed from a natural resource that have not been sold at the end of the accounting period reported in the financial statements? [LO2b]
16. Give five examples of intangible assets. [LO1d]
17. On what basis is the cost of an intangible asset allocated to expense? [LO1d,2c]
18. In what section of the financial statements are intangible assets reported? At what amount are they reported? [LO1d]
19. Differentiate between a patent and a copyright. In what way is the accounting for both of these intangible assets similar? [LO2c]
20. How are research and development costs accounted for? [LO2c]
21. How are the costs of internally developed or purchased trademarks accounted for? [LO2c]
22. Differentiate between the accounting for leases that only require regular monthly payments and leases that require an advance lump-sum payment. [LO2c]
23. Over what period of time are the following intangible assets amortized: (1) leasehold improvements, (2) franchises, and (3) organization costs? [LO2c]
24. Describe three approaches for determining a cost value for goodwill when a business is purchased. [LO2c]

## ANALYTICAL QUESTIONS

25. Why are gains recognized on the exchanges of dissimilar assets and not recognized on the exchanges of similar assets? [LO2a]
26. Discuss the validity of the following statement. "If at the time a plant asset was acquired, its useful life and residual value were known with certainty, there would never be a gain or loss upon its disposal." [LO2a]
27. Discuss the difference between the financial accounting and income tax rules on certain exchanges of plant assets. [LO1a]

28. What are the similarities and the differences between depreciation, depletion, and amortization? [LO1d,2b,2c]
29. Discuss factors you consider important in reaching the conclusion that research and development costs should be expensed as incurred. [LO1d,2c]
30. Why is goodwill recorded only when purchased? [LO1d,2c]

## *IMPACT ANALYSIS QUESTIONS*

*For each error described, indicate whether it would overstate [O], understate [U], or not affect [N] the specified key figures.*

31. Annual depreciation expense was recorded on a fully depreciated plant asset because it remained in service throughout the current year. [LO2a]

_______ Assets _______ Revenue
_______ Owner's Equity _______ Net Income

32. A plant asset was exchanged for a new one of the same general type that will perform the same function in the business. A gain was recognized when the exchange transaction was recorded. [LO2a]

_______ Assets _______ Liabilities
_______ Owner's Equity _______ Net Income

33. A building that could normally be used for twenty-five years is constructed on the site of a copper mine. The copper content of the mine is expected to be entirely extracted over a period of ten years, after which it and the building will no longer be useful to the firm. In the first year one-tenth of the copper contained in the mine was extracted and depletion was recorded. In that same year the building was depreciated using the straight-line method with a twenty-five-year estimated life and a zero residual value. [LO2b]

_______ Assets _______ Liabilities
_______ Owner's Equity _______ Net Income

34. A company purchased a patent at the beginning of its current fiscal year. The patent has an estimated useful life of ten years. The cost of the patent is being amortized over its legal life of seventeen years. [LO1d,2c]

_______ Assets _______ Revenue
_______ Expenses _______ Net Income

35. A certain company recognizes that it has good customer relations, a favorable location, high-quality products to sell, suppliers that are eager to do business with the company, excellent relationships with employees, and an overall superior reputation. Therefore the company established an amount for goodwill and recorded it in the accounts at the beginning of the current year. The amount is also being amortized over forty years. [LO1d,2c]

_______ Assets _______ Liabilities
_______ Expenses _______ Revenue

## *EXERCISES*

EXERCISE 11-1 *(Prepare Journal Entries to Record the Sale and Discarding of Plant Assets)* The Glenpoint Company purchased a machine for $19,500 on January 3, 19X2. The machine is depreciated using the straight-line method with an estimated useful life of six years and a residual value of $1,500. Depreciation expense was last recorded on December 31, 19X5.

Required:

1. Prepare the journal entries to record the partial year's depreciation to the dates of disposal as given in Requirements 2a, 2b, 2c, and 2d below.
2. Prepare the journal entries to record the disposal of the machine assuming each of the following conditions independently:

a. The machine was scrapped on April 30, 19X6.
b. The machine was sold for $6,500 on June 30, 19X6.
c. The machine was sold for $5,000 on June 30, 19X6.
d. The machine was sold for $5,250 on October 1, 19X6. [LO2a]

EXERCISE 11–2 *(Prepare Journal Entries to Record the Exchange of Similar Plant Assets)* On January 2, 19X6, Braden Construction Company exchanged used equipment with a cost of $50,000 and accumulated depreciation of $40,000 for new similar equipment. The new equipment has a cash purchase price of $70,000.

Required:

1. Prepare the journal entry to record the exchange of the equipment for financial accounting purposes assuming a trade-in allowance of $8,000 was received for the old equipment and the balance was paid in cash.
2. Prepare the journal entry to record the exchange of the equipment for financial accounting purposes assuming a trade-in allowance of $12,000 was received for the old equipment and the balance was paid in cash. [LO2a]

EXERCISE 11–3 *(Prepare Journal Entries to Record the Exchange of Dissimilar Plant Assets)* Eller Company exchanged its used machine having a cost of $30,000 and accumulated depreciation of $20,000 for a vehicle. The vehicle's cash price is $15,000.

Required:

1. Prepare the journal entry to record the exchange of these dissimilar assets assuming a trade-in allowance of $12,000 was received for the used machine and the balance was paid in cash.
2. Prepare the journal entry to record the exchange of these dissimilar assets assuming a trade-in allowance of $5,000 was received for the used machine and the balance was paid in cash. [LO2a]

EXERCISE 11–4 *(Compute Depletion Charges for Natural Resources)* Lookout Company recently purchased for $6,800,000 a tract of land containing an estimated 700,000 tons of ore. Equipment needed to extract the ore was also acquired and installed on site at a cost of $840,000. The company expects to work the mine for ten years, after which it anticipates that the land could be sold for $500,000 and the equipment would be worthless and therefore abandoned.

Required:

1. a. Prepare the journal entry to record depletion of the mine for the first year assuming that 50,000 tons of ore were removed and sold.
   b. Prepare the journal entry to record depreciation of the mining equipment for the first year using the units-of-production method.

At the beginning of the second year, the estimate of the mine's ore content was revised. At this time it was determined that only 600,000 tons of ore remained in the mine.

2. a. Compute the revised depletion charge per ton and the depletion expense for the second year, during which 40,000 tons of ore were removed and sold.
   b. Compute the depreciation expense for the mining equipment in the second year. [LO2b]

EXERCISE 11–5 *(Prepare Journal Entries for Acquisition and Amortization of Intangible Assets)* Worldwide Company had the following transactions during 19X6, the first year of its operations.

1. A trademark was granted to the company giving it the exclusive right to use a globe as a symbol to identify the company and its products. The cost of obtaining the trademark, which is assumed to have an indefinite life, was $20,000.
2. Organization costs, which consist primarily of legal fees, were $7,000. These costs are assumed to benefit the company over its entire life.
3. A three-year-old patent was purchased for $79,800. The patent is expected to contribute to the earnings capability of the company for seven years.

4. A copyright was purchased for $44,000. Although the copyright legally protects its owner for a number of years, the company estimates that it will be useful for only five more years.

Required:
Assuming all the intangibles were acquired during the first week of January 19X6:
1. Prepare journal entries to record their acquisition.
2. Prepare separate journal entries to record amortization on each asset for the current year ending December 31, 19X6. The company always uses the maximum amortization period allowed. [LO1d,2c]

EXERCISE 11–6 *(Evaluate Goodwill)* The management of Frost Company has expressed an interest in buying Dewdrop Company, which it feels can help in merchandising its product. It has been determined that Dewdrop's net assets have a fair market value of $600,000 and that the company's annual net income in the past few years has averaged $75,000. In this industry 10% is considered a normal rate of return on net assets.

Required:
1. Determine the amount by which Dewdrop Company's average earnings exceed the industry's normal earnings.
2. Determine the total price that Frost Company would pay for Dewdrop Company under each of the following assumptions:
   a. Frost will pay an amount equal to three years' above-average earnings for Dewdrop Company's goodwill.
   b. The amount to be paid for Dewdrop's goodwill will be determined by capitalizing its above-average annual earnings at 25%.
3. Would goodwill increase or decrease with regard to the amount determined in Requirement 2b if above-average annual earnings were capitalized at 15% instead of 25%? By how much? [LO1d,2c]

## PROBLEMS

PROBLEM 11–1 *(Prepare Journal Entries for the Sale and Discarding of Plant Assets)* Data as of January 1, 19X6, for five plant assets owned by Halsted Company are shown below.

| ASSET | COST | USEFUL LIFE | RESIDUAL VALUE | ACCUMULATED DEPRECIATION | DEPRECIATION METHOD |
|---|---|---|---|---|---|
| Machine A | $14,000 | 5 years | $2,000 | $ 7,000 | S.L. |
| Machine B | 27,000 | 8 years | 3,000 | 16,500 | S.L. |
| Fixtures | 10,000 | 6 years | 1,000 | 7,500 | S.L. |
| Vehicle 1 | 16,200 | 4 years | 2,200 | 8,300 | Miles |
| Vehicle 2 | 18,500 | 5 years | 500 | 12,400 | S.L. |

During 19X6 the following transactions took place:

Machine A—was sold on April 1 for $3,000 cash.

Machine B—was sold on May 31 for $10,000 cash.

Fixtures—were dismantled and scrapped on June 30.

Vehicle 1—although it had not been driven for all of its expected 50,000 miles, it was sold on August 3 for $4,800. In 19X6 the vehicle was driven for 12,000 miles.

Vehicle 2—was sold on October 1 for $3,400.

Required:
For each of the five plant assets, prepare (a) the journal entry to record depreciation to the date of its disposal, and (b) the journal entry to record its disposal. [LO2a]

PROBLEM 11-2 *(Prepare Journal Entries for Sale and Exchange of Plant Assets)* Solbe Company had a machine with the following cost and accumulated depreciation recorded in the accounts as of July 1, the date of its disposal.

| | |
|---|---|
| Machinery | $60,000 |
| Accumulated Depreciation | 48,000 |
| Carrying Value | $12,000 |

Required:
Prepare the journal entry to record each of the following transactions independently of each other. For exchanges, use the financial accounting method instead of the income tax rule.

1. The machine was sold for $15,000 cash.
2. The machine was sold for $8,000 cash.
3. The machine was exchanged for a similar machine having a cash purchase price of $75,000. A trade-in allowance of $20,000 was received for the old machine, and the balance of $55,000 was paid in cash.
4. The machine was exchanged for a similar machine having a cash purchase price of $90,000. A trade-in allowance of $10,000 was received for the old machine, and the balance of $80,000 was paid in cash.
5. The machine was exchanged for a vehicle having a cash purchase price of $16,000. A trade-in allowance of $5,000 was received for the old machine, and the balance of $11,000 was paid in cash.
6. The machine was exchanged for a patent having a cash purchase price of $55,000. A trade-in allowance of $15,000 was received for the old machine, and the balance of $40,000 was paid in cash. [LO2a]

PROBLEM 11-3 *(Compute Depletion for Natural Resources)* Sawyer Company purchased a coal mine containing an estimated 1,000,000 tons of commercially useful coal for $9,200,000. The company estimates that the ore will be extracted over a period of eight years, after which it expects that the land can be sold for $200,000. During the first two years, the following number of tons of coal were mined and sold:

| | |
|---|---|
| 19X3 | 80,000 tons |
| 19X4 | 120,000 tons |

Required:

1. Compute depletion expense for 19X3 and 19X4.
2. Determine the mine's carrying value at the end of 19X4.
3. Assume that at the beginning of 19X5, a geologist determined that approximately 900,000 recoverable tons of coal remained in the mine. Compute the depletion charge per ton that should be used in 19X5. [LO2b]

PROBLEM 11-4 *(Prepare Journal Entries for Acquisition and Amortization of Intangible Assets)* Selected transactions and events for Exlight Company are presented below.

| | |
|---|---|
| Jan. 2 | Paid all fees incurred in organizing the company. The entire cost including legal fees totaled $8,000. |
| March 1 | Purchased a patent for $24,000. The patent had a remaining life of twelve years when purchased, but the company expects it to be useful for only five years. |
| May 31 | Purchased a franchise giving Exlight Company the exclusive right to distribute a new product within the state where the company is located. The franchise was granted for a ten-year period with no right of renewal and cost $72,000. |

| | | |
|---|---|---|
| July | 1 | Signed a contract to lease a sales office. The lease is for five years and requires an advance payment of $60,000, with future annual payments of $60,000 to be made on July 1 of each subsequent year. |
| Aug. | 31 | Paid $5,400 in legal fees for successfully defending the patent purchased on March 1 of this year. The company does not believe that the patent's expected useful life has been changed as a result of this action. |
| Nov. | 1 | Partitions costing $14,280 were installed in the sales office leased on July 1. The partitions designed to improve efficiency within this particular office have a use guarantee of eight years. The lease on the sales office is not renewable. |

Required:

1. Prepare journal entries to record the above transactions.
2. Prepare separate journal entries to record the amortization expense on each asset for the current year ending December 31. Show all computations in good form. The company always uses the maximum amortization period allowed. [LO1d,2c]

PROBLEM 11–5 *(Evaluate Goodwill)* Valarie Torres has for several months been looking for a business that she could purchase. She believes she finally found a good one in Oakridge Company, which has been earning an average of $18,000 per year for the last five years. Other companies in the industry would have averaged $15,000 per year based on the same amount of net assets over the same period of time. Oakridge Company's current balance sheet is shown below.

| | | |
|---|---|---|
| Current Assets: | | |
| Cash | $ 15,000 | |
| Inventory | 60,000 | |
| Office Supplies | 2,000 | |
| Total Current Assets | | $ 77,000 |
| Plant Assets: | | |
| Land | $ 10,000 | |
| Building | 150,000 | |
| Equipment | 90,000 | |
| | $250,000 | |
| Less: Accumulated Depreciation | 120,000 | 130,000 |
| Total Assets | | $207,000 |
| Current Liabilities: | | |
| Accounts Payable | | $ 12,000 |
| Long-Term Liabilities: | | |
| Notes Payable | | 80,000 |
| Total Liabilities | | $ 92,000 |
| A. Rivers, Capital | | 115,000 |
| Total Liabilities and Owner's Equity | | $207,000 |

Valarie and A. Rivers, the owner of Oakridge, agree that the amounts shown for all assets and liabilities except land are realistic and are essentially equal to their fair market values.

The land, which was purchased a few years ago, currently has a fair market value of $30,000. Valarie agrees with this assessment of the land value and is now preparing to make an offer to purchase the company. If the offer is accepted, Valarie will acquire all of the company's assets except cash and will assume all of its liabilities.

Required:

1. Determine the fair market value of Oakridge Company's net assets (exclusive of cash).
2. Determine the average rate of return Oakridge has earned on its net assets. (Exclude cash and use an adjusted value for land based on its market value.)
3. Determine the amount Valarie will pay for the company's goodwill under each assumption listed below.

a. Valarie is willing to pay an amount equal to eight times the company's above-average annual earnings for the past five years.

b. Valarie is willing to pay an amount equal to the value computed by capitalizng the annual above-average earnings at 12%. [LO1d,2c]

PROBLEM 11-6 *(Compute and Prepare Journal Entries for Depletion of Natural Resources and Depreciation of Closely Related Plant Assets)* On April 2, 19X5, United Oil Company purchased an oil field for $22,000,000. The field is estimated to contain 5,000,000 barrels of oil and to have a residual value of $2,000,000 after all the oil has been removed. On June 1 equipment costing $800,000 was installed on the site and the company began pumping oil. The equipment will have no usefulness after the oil field has been depleted and will be scrapped or abandoned at that time. During 19X5, 500,000 barrels of oil were removed from the field and sold. During 19X6, 770,000 barrels of oil were removed and 700,000 barrels were sold.

Required:

1. Compute the depletion charge per barrel. Prepare the journal entry to record depletion of the oil field for 19X6. Include the journal entry to record the assignment of depletion to expense and to the asset.
2. Prepare the journal entry to record depreciation of the equipment for 19X6 using the units-of-production method.
3. Prepare a partial balance sheet showing how the oil field and the equipment would be reported at the end of 19X6. [LO2b]

PROBLEM 11-7 *(Prepare Journal Entries and Describe Financial Statement Reporting for Several Noncurrent Asset Transactions)* On December 31, 19X6, the Neptune Company had, among others, the accounts listed below.

|  |  |
|---|---|
| Accumulated Depreciation—Building | $ 17,200 |
| Accumulated Depreciation—Equipment | 36,600 |
| Accumulated Depreciation—Furniture and Fixtures | 3,900 |
| Building | 64,000 |
| Equipment | 88,000 |
| Franchise | 57,000 |
| Furniture and Fixtures | 11,700 |
| Land | 40,000 |
| Mining Property (original cost $900,000) | 666,900 |
| Organization Costs | 6,800 |
| Patents | 7,700 |

Additional information relating to some of these accounts is given below.

*Mining Property.* Acquired in 19X3, at which time it was estimated that 200,000 tons of ore could be extracted from the mine. A total of 20,000 tons were extracted and sold in 19X6.

*Building.* Acquired in 19X0. Estimated useful life established at that time was twenty years with no residual value expected. The straight-line method of depreciation is being used.

*Equipment.* Acquired late in 19X1. Estimated useful life is ten years, with a residual value of $2,000 expected at the end of that period. The straight-line method of depreciation is being used.

*Furniture and Fixtures.* Acquired early in 19X1. Estimated useful life is fifteen years, with no residual value expected. The straight-line method of depreciation is being used.

*Patents.* Acquired in 19X3 at an original cost of $9,350. The patent is being amortized over its legal life.

*Franchise.* Acquired in January 19X4 at a cost of $60,000. The franchise has an indefinite life.

*Organization Costs.* Incurred during January 19X0. Total cost $8,000. Although assumed to have an indefinite life, the organization costs are being amortized.

Required:
1. Prepare separate journal entries to record depreciation, depletion, and amortization for the current year ending December 31, 19X6.
2. Describe how each item listed above would be reported on the December 31, 19X6, balance sheet. [LO1c,1d,2b,2c]

PROBLEM 11–8 *(Prepare Journal Entries for Disposal of Plant Assets)* On January 3, 19X3, Anchor Company purchased a machine for $27,000. The machine had an estimated useful life of six years and a residual value of $3,000. Depreciation is determined by the straight-line method.

Required:
Assuming the machine is disposed of on June 30, 19X6:
1. Prepare the journal entry to record the depreciation expense for the six months in 19X6.
2. Prepare journal entries to record the disposal of the machine under each of the following assumptions:
   a. The machine was sold for $15,000 cash.
   b. The machine was sold for $10,500 cash.
   c. The machine was exchanged for a new machine having a similar purpose and a cash price of $35,000. A trade-in allowance of $14,000 was received for the old machine, and the balance of $21,000 was paid in cash. (Use the financial accounting method.)
   d. The machine was exchanged for a new machine having a similar purpose and a cash price of $35,000. A trade-in allowance of $5,000 was received for the old machine, and the balance of $30,000 was paid in cash. (Use the financial accounting method.)
   e. Use the same data in *d* above and record the exchange transaction using the income tax rule. [LO1a,2a]

PROBLEM 11–9 *(Exchange of Plant Assets—Comprehensive Problem)* On January 3, 19X6, Purity Company exchanged an old machine for a new machine having a cash purchase price of $64,000. The old machine originally cost $48,000 and had a carrying value of $16,000 on the date of the exchange.

Four separate and independent situations relating to the exchange appear below.
1. The machine was exchanged for one of the same general type that performs the same function. A trade-in allowance of $10,000 was received for the old machine, and the balance was paid in cash.
2. The machine was exchanged for one of the same general type that performs the same function. A trade-in allowance of $18,000 was received for the old machine, and the balance was paid in cash.
3. The machine was exchanged for one of a different type that does not perform the same function. A trade-in allowance of $20,000 was received for the old machine, and the balance was paid in cash.
4. The machine was exchanged for one of a different type that does not perform the same function. A trade-in allowance of $14,000 was received for the old machine, and the balance was paid in cash.

Required:
1. For each of the four situations, prepare a journal entry to record the exchange of the machines in the way that conforms with financial accounting methods.
2. Using the data described in situation 1 (and the related exchange journal entry), compute depreciation expense for the first year of the new asset's life. Assume that the machine's estimated useful life is five years and estimated residual value is $10,000. The sum-of-the-years'-digits method is used to compute depreciation. [LO2a]

## ALTERNATE PROBLEMS

PROBLEM 11–1A *(Prepare Journal Entries for Sale and Discarding of Plant Assets)* (Alternate to Problem 11–1) On January 2, 19X3, Pro All Company paid $14,000 to purchase a machine. The machine has an estimated useful life of five years and an estimated residual value of $2,000. Depreciation was last recorded on December 31, 19X5, at which time the accumulated depreciation on the machine was $7,200.

Required:

1. Prepare the journal entries to record the partial year's depreciation to the dates of disposal as given in Requirements 2a, 2b, 2c, and 2d below.
2. Prepare the journal entry to record the disposal of the machine assuming each of the following conditions independently:
   a. The machine was scrapped on November 30, 19X6.
   b. The machine was sold for $5,000 on July 31, 19X6.
   c. The machine was sold for $5,700 on July 31, 19X6.
   d. The machine was sold for $5,000 on October 1, 19X6. [LO2a]

PROBLEM 11–2A *(Prepare Journal Entries for Sale and Exchange of Plant Assets)* (Alternate to Problem 11–2) The management of Bates Company had certain plant assets that it was anxious to sell or exchange. As of December 31, 19X5, data pertaining to these assets were as follows:

Office Equipment: Cost, $80,000; Accumulated Depreciation, $30,000
Building: Cost, $240,000; Accumulated Depreciation, $180,000
Machinery: Cost, $150,000; Accumulated Depreciation, $60,000

The company completed the following transactions on January 3, 19X6:

1. The old office equipment was exchanged for new office equipment having a cash purchase price of $125,000. A trade-in allowance of $35,000 was received for the old equipment, and the balance of $90,000 was paid in cash.
2. The machinery was exchanged for a small warehouse having a cash purchase price of $100,000. A trade-in allowance of $75,000 was received for the old machinery, and the balance of $25,000 was paid in cash.
3. The building was sold for $50,000.

Required:

Prepare journal entries to record the above transactions independently of each other. For exchanges, use the financial accounting method instead of the income tax rule. [LO2a]

PROBLEM 11–3A *(Prepare Journal Entries and Determine Carrying Values for Natural Resources and Intangibles)* (Alternate to Problem 11–4) Selected transactions and events of Westway Company at various times during the company's life are given below.

1. Organization costs consisting primarily of legal fees were incurred during the first week in January 19X4 and totaled $7,500. The company amortizes organization costs over five years.
2. A patent costing $42,000 was purchased from its inventor on March 2, 19X4. The patent had a remaining life of eleven years when purchased, but the company has been amortizing its cost over an estimated useful life of seven years.
3. In October 19X4 the company purchased the Dana Slope mine for $56,000,000. The mine is estimated to contain 1,000,000 tons of ore and has an estimated residual value of $500,000. Mining operations began in January 19X5. Production and sales records show the following: 19X5, 125,000 tons mined and sold; 19X6, 200,000 tons mined and 180,000 tons sold.
4. During the first week in January 19X5, mining equipment costing $610,000 was installed at the Dana Slope site. The equipment is being depreciated using the units-of-production method and is expected to have a residual value of $10,000 after the mine's ore has been completely extracted.

5. On July 2, 19X5, a franchise granting the company exclusive rights to distribute one of its products within a tri-state area was purchased for $58,000. The franchise right was granted for ten years and is being amortized over that period.
6. On July 1, 19X6, the company signed a five-year lease agreement giving it the right to possess and use a warehouse. The lease agreement requires that on July 1 of each year a full year's rent of $12,000 be paid in advance. The lease is noncancelable and can be renewed by Westway for two more five-year periods.
7. On September 1, 19X6, the company paid $6,720 to a contractor who had installed a new floor and a concrete loading platform in the leased facility. The improvements have an estimated life of twenty-five years with no residual value.

Required:

1. Prepare journal entries to record each of the two transactions that occurred during 19X6.
2. Prepare separate journal entries to record depreciation, depletion, and amortization for the current year ending December 31, 19X6.
3. Prepare a list identifying each asset that has been acquired and its carrying value as of December 31, 19X6. [LO1d,2b,2c]

PROBLEM 11-4A *(Evaluate Goodwill)* (Alternate to Problem 11–5) The owners of Stewart Company are interested in selling their business if they can get an acceptable price. They have asked you to help determine a "bench mark" selling price that can be used when negotiating with a potential buyer. Using information contained in the company's financial statements, you prepared the following summary.

| YEAR | NET ASSETS | REPORTED NET INCOME |
|---|---|---|
| 19X1 | $240,000 | $23,550 |
| 19X2 | 262,000 | 27,480 |
| 19X3 | 286,000 | 30,900 |
| 19X4 | 314,000 | 32,600 |
| 19X5 | 336,000 | 34,970 |

You believe that the balance sheet has consistently shown fair values for all assets and liabilities. Your approach in determining the company's return on its net assets is to relate the average net assets held for the past five years with the actual average annual earnings for the same period.

The normal rate of return on net assets for companies in the same industry is 9%.

Required:

1. Determine a "bench mark" selling price for the company assuming that implied goodwill can be measured by multiplying the above-average earnings by 5.
2. Determine a "bench mark" selling price for the company assuming that implied goodwill can be measured by capitalizing the above-average earnings at 18%.
3. Assume that the negotiations between buyer and seller result in the company's being sold on January 5, 19X6, for $358,000. Assume also that in the first year after the company was purchased, it earned a 10% return based on the net assets acquired on January 5 (excluding goodwill). Determine the reported net income for the first year assuming goodwill is amortized over a period of twenty years. [LO1d,2c]

PROBLEM 11-5A *(Describe Financial Statement Reporting and Determine Carrying Values for Noncurrent Assets)* (Alternate to Problem 11–7) The following selected accounts and amounts were taken from the December 31, 19X6, adjusted trial balance of Monterray Company.

| | |
|---|---|
| Cash | $ 20,000 |
| Equipment | 180,000 |
| Accumulated Depletion—Mineral Deposits | 330,000 |
| Equipment Repairs | 11,000 |
| Inventories | 83,000 |
| Accumulated Depreciation—Buildings | 60,000 |
| Land | 95,000 |
| Patents | 40,000 |
| Accumulated Depreciation—Equipment | 35,000 |
| Buildings | 240,000 |
| Trademarks | 52,000 |
| Vehicles | 74,000 |
| Mineral Deposits | 580,000 |
| Accumulated Depreciation—Vehicles | 14,000 |

Required:

1. Using the data above, describe how the company's noncurrent assets would be reported on the December 31, 19X6, balance sheet.
2. Determine the total carrying value of all of the company's noncurrent assets as of December 31, 19X6. [LO1c]

# 12 *Current Liabilities and Payroll Accounting*

### *Learning Objectives*

When you complete this chapter you will be able to

1. Answer the following questions:
   a. What are *liabilities* and how are they measured and reported?
   b. What are the principal objectives of accounting for liabilities?
   c. What are the characteristics of current liabilities?
   d. What are *contingent liabilities* and how should they be reported?
   e. What are the characteristics of payroll accounting and internal accounting control associated with payroll?
   f. What kinds of records and procedures are used in payroll accounting?
2. Perform the following accounting functions:
   a. Identify several current liabilities that have a definite maturity value and apply acceptable accounting measurement practices to compute, record, and report them.
   b. Identify several current liabilities that have an estimated maturity value and apply acceptable accounting measurement practices to compute, record, and report them.
   c. Determine an employee's gross earnings, identify and calculate the various earnings deductions, and compute an employee's net earnings.
   d. Prepare the journal entry to record payroll.
   e. Identify, calculate, and prepare the journal entry to record payroll taxes levied on the employer.

In the five preceding chapters we discussed the nature, measurement, and reporting of certain assets and their related income statement accounts. In this chapter we begin a similar discussion of liabilities.

First we give a brief and general discussion of liabilities. Then we focus on obligations properly classified as *current liabilities.* Since several current liabilities are associated with a company's payroll, our discussion includes payroll accounting. Long-term liabilities are covered in Chapter 16.

## THE NATURE OF LIABILITIES

**Liabilities** are obligations resulting from past transactions that require the future payment of assets or the future performance of services.

*1a. A liability has three characteristics*

Note that from the definition, a liability has three stated or implied characteristics:

There is a *present duty* or *responsibility.*

Liabilities are the result of *past transactions.*

The obligation will require a *future sacrifice* of *economic benefits.*

*1b. The principal objectives of accounting for liabilities are stated here*

The objectives of accounting for liabilities are to

Be certain that all liabilities have been recorded. At a minimum this involves a search for unpaid invoices, the recognition of accrued liabilities, and a review of all conditions pertaining to advance payments received from customers. Failure to record a liability is often accompanied by failure to record an expense, which results in an overstated net income.

Be certain that all liabilities are valued in accordance with generally accepted accounting principles. As we will learn, some liabilities are valued at the amount of money needed to settle the obligation or the fair market value of the goods and services to be provided. Others are valued based on concepts of the time value of money (discussed more fully in Chapter 16). The existence of a liability is usually known, yet the amount will sometimes need to be estimated. The importance of liability valuation is clear in that it impacts key elements reported in the financial statements and affects income determination.

Be certain that the liabilities are properly classified as to current and long-term when reported in the balance sheet. Separating current liabilities from long-term liabilities in the balance sheet provides information as to how much demand will be placed on current assets to meet current liabilities in the short run. This and other measures of a company's short-term debt-paying ability will be examined in Chapter 19.

### Current Liabilities

*1c. Current liabilities are expected to be paid within an operating cycle or a year, whichever is longer.*

**Current liabilities** are debts or other obligations that (1) are expected to be paid within an operating cycle or a year, whichever is longer, and (2) will require the use of an existing current asset, such as cash, or the creation of another current liability. Those that need not be paid within an operating cycle or a year are classified as long-term liabilities.

*1c. Some current liabilities have definite maturity values; others have estimated maturity values*

For purposes of presentation, we have divided current liabilities into two groups. The first group consists of those liabilities whose amount (maturity value) is definitely known on the balance sheet date. Included in this group are accounts and notes payable. The second group consists of those liabilities whose amount (maturity value) is not definitely known on the balance sheet date, such as a corporate liability for income taxes payable. Liabilities found in the first group will be discussed first.

## CURRENT LIABILITIES WITH DEFINITE MATURITY VALUES

Most current liabilities have definite maturity values. They generally arise from contractual relationships that exist between a company and its vendors, lending institutions, employees, and customers. These contractual relationships provide evidence that one party to the contract has incurred a liability for a specific or determinable dollar amount. In discussing the liabilities included in this group, we will review items discussed earlier in the text, cover others in more detail, and introduce new ones.

### Accounts Payable

*2a. Accounts Payable have a definite maturity value*

Accounts payable are amounts owed for goods, supplies, equipment, or services that are purchased on credit. When items are purchased on credit, there is an oral or implied promise to pay for them. This promise to pay is the account payable whose amount can be determined with certainty. Accounting for accounts payable was covered in previous chapters and is fairly routine.

### Notes Payable

*2a. Short-term notes have a definite maturity value*

A short-term **note payable** is a liability evidenced by the issuance of a written promise to pay a definite sum of money, usually with interest, on demand or at a definite date in the future.

The most common reasons for issuing notes payable are

To borrow money from a bank or other financial institution
To obtain an extension of time for payment on an account payable
To acquire goods, other assets, or services from a supplier

Each of these uses of notes payable is illustrated in the following sections.

BORROWING MONEY Many companies borrow money for short periods of time as a planned business practice.

*2a. A journal entry is made to record the issuance of a note*

To illustrate the accounting for a short-term loan, assume that on September 1 Gateway Company borrowed $10,000 from its bank for six months at an annual interest rate of 12%. The agreement provides for payment of the note's face amount, plus interest, on March 1. The following entry would record the transaction:

| | | | |
|---|---|---|---|
| Sept. 1 | Cash | 10,000 | |
| | Notes Payable | | 10,000 |
| | To record the borrowing of $10,000 for six months at 12% | | |

*2a. A year-end adjusting entry is made for interest incurred on a note*

Note that the cash obtained equaled the face value of the note. Interest on the borrowed money will be collected by the bank when the loan is repaid. However, since interest accrues each day over the life of the loan, Gateway—having a calendar year-end—would make the following entry on December 31 to recognize four months of accrued interest:

| | | | |
|---|---|---|---|
| Dec. 31 | Interest Expense | 400 | |
| | Interest Payable | | 400 |
| | To accrue interest for four months on a 12%, $10,000 note | | |

*2a. An entry is made when the note is paid*

Assuming that the company does not make reversing entries, the entry when the note and interest are paid on March 1 of the next year is as follows:

| | | | |
|---|---|---|---|
| March 1 | Notes Payable | 10,000 | |
| | Interest Payable | 400 | |
| | Interest Expense | 200 | |
| | Cash | | 10,600 |
| | To record payment of the interest-bearing note | | |

Another and perhaps more common way for banks to lend money is to deduct interest at the time the loan is made. This is called *discounting the note payable.* Interest is deducted in advance, and the borrower receives the difference between the face value of the note and the interest. If the bank discounts Gateway's note at 12% for six months, it will deduct from the face amount of the note 180 days' interest at 12%, or $600. Gateway receives the difference, or $9,400 (called *proceeds*).

*2a. An entry is made to record discounting of a note payable*

The following entry would record the transaction:

| | | | |
|---|---|---|---|
| Sept. 1 | Cash | 9,400 | |
| | Discount on Notes Payable | 600 | |
| | Notes Payable | | 10,000 |
| | To record borrowing on a six-month $10,000 note discounted at 12% [$10,000 × .12 × (180/360) = $600 interest] | | |

The $600 balance in the Discount on Notes Payable account represents the full amount of interest to be incurred over the life of the note. This amount must eventually be transferred from the discount account to the Interest Expense account. The process of transferring the amount in the Discount on Notes Payable account to the Interest Expense account is called *amortizing the discount.* The discount on a short-term note payable is generally amortized by using the straight-line method. The year-end adjusting entry that amortizes four months of the discount and recognizes interest expense is as follows:

*2a. A year-end adjusting entry is made to amortize discount on a note payable*

| | | | |
|---|---|---|---|
| Dec. 31 | Interest Expense | 400 | |
| | Discount on Notes Payable | | 400 |
| | To record amortization of discount on note | | |

To show the proper amount for the liability on the balance sheet, the remaining balance in Discount on Notes Payable is deducted from the Notes Payable as a contra-liability account as follows:

PARTIAL BALANCE SHEET

| | | |
|---|---|---|
| Current Liabilities: | | |
| Accounts Payable | | $37,800 |
| Notes Payable | $10,000 | |
| Less: Discount on Notes Payable | 200 | 9,800 |

*2a. An entry is made to record payment of a note*

On March 1 of the following year, the note is paid and the transaction recorded as follows:

| | | | |
|---|---|---|---|
| March 1 | Notes Payable | 10,000 | |
| | Interest Expense | 200 | |
| | Discount on Notes Payable | | 200 |
| | Cash | | 10,000 |
| | To record payment of the note and interest expense incurred since year-end | | |

There is a major difference between the effective annual interest rate on the two notes just described. Borrowing money by issuing a $10,000, 12% interest-bearing note results in an effective annual interest rate of 12%. However, borrowing money by discounting a $10,000 note at 12% results in a somewhat higher effective annual interest rate. Both notes require the same interest payment of $600. But in the first note, the borrower receives $10,000; in the second note, the borrower receives only $9,400. The differences in the effective annual interest rate can be compared as follows:

| | INTEREST CHARGED | AMOUNT RECEIVED | EFFECTIVE INTEREST RATE* |
|---|---|---|---|
| Note 1 | $600 | $10,000 | $600/($10,000 × $\frac{1}{2}$) = 12.00% |
| Note 2 | $600 | 9,400 | $600/($ 9,400 × $\frac{1}{2}$) = 12.77% |

* The amount received is multiplied by one-half to reflect the borrowing period of one-half a year.

**EXTENSION OF TIME** A company temporarily short of cash will be unable to pay an amount currently due on an account payable. Sometimes a note payable is given to obtain an extension of time for payment. The amount of the note payable is generally equal to the amount of the account payable. The note, however, includes interest that will be charged on that amount for the length of the extension period granted.

*2a. An entry is made to record issuance of a note to extend time to pay an account payable obligation*

To illustrate, assume that Gateway Company has an obligation to Woods Company on accounts payable in the amount of $3,000. On March 15, when the amount is due, Gateway is temporarily short of cash and cannot pay. Woods agrees to accept a sixty-day, 12%, $3,000 note in granting an extension on the due date of the account payable. Gateway records the issuance of the note as follows:

| | | | |
|---|---|---|---|
| March 15 | Accounts Payable—Woods Company | 3,000 | |
| | Notes Payable | | 3,000 |
| | To record issuance of a 60-day, 12% note | | |

It should be noted that Gateway has not paid the debt. It has merely replaced one obligation (Accounts Payable) with another obligation (Notes Payable), agreeing to pay the $3,000 amount plus interest in sixty days.

On May 14, the due date of the note, Gateway will pay Woods $3,060. This amount is equal to the face value of the note plus interest of $60 ($3,000 × 12% × $\frac{60}{360}$). The entry to record payment of the note and its interest is as follows:

| | | | |
|---|---|---|---|
| May 14 | Notes Payable | 3,000 | |
| | Interest Expense | 60 | |
| | Cash | | 3,060 |
| | To record payment of note issued to Woods Company | | |

**TO ACQUIRE ASSETS OR SERVICES** Companies may at times issue short-term notes to their suppliers in exchange for merchandise or other assets. The note is generally issued for the total amount due at maturity. When recording the transaction, we must determine what portion of the note's full amount should be assigned to the cost of the asset acquired, and what portion should be assigned to the cost of using borrowed money.

To illustrate, assume that a company purchases merchandise by issuing a note payable due in six months for $21,200. How should the $21,200 be assigned to its two components: (1) the cost of the items acquired and (2) the cost of using borrowed money? The assignment is generally made by determining how much the merchandise would cost on the date it was acquired if it were purchased for cash instead of by issuing a note. Let us say the amount would be $20,000. Then the amount assigned to the cost of the merchandise acquired would be $20,000, and the remainder of $1,200 would be assigned to the cost of borrowed money.

*2a. An entry is made to record purchase of an asset with a short-term note*

If we assume that this transaction occurred on February 1, the entry to record it using the perpetual inventory system would be as follows:

| | | | |
|---|---|---|---|
| Feb. 1 | Inventory | 20,000 | |
| | Discount on Notes Payable | 1,200 | |
| | Notes Payable | | 21,200 |
| | To record merchandise purchased with a six-month note payable | | |

Note that once again the Discount on Notes Payable, a contra-liability account, is used to record the amount of interest to be incurred over the life of the note.

When six months later—on August 1—the note is paid, the transaction is recorded as follows:

| | | | |
|---|---|---|---|
| Aug. 1 | Notes Payable | 21,200 | |
| | Interest Expense | 1,200 | |
| | Discount on Notes Payable | | 1,200 |
| | Cash | | 21,200 |
| | To record payment of the note plus interest | | |

## Dividends Payable

Cash dividends are distributions of a corporation's earnings to its shareholders. Because the timing and amounts of dividends are determined by the corporation's board of directors, they do not accrue like interest on debt. When the board officially declares a cash dividend, it becomes a liability of the corporation until paid. Dividends are usually paid within a few weeks after they have been declared. During this relatively short period, dividends payable represent a current liability of the corporation. More will be said about accounting for dividends in Chapter 15.

## Current Portions of Long-Term Debt

*1c. Current portions of long-term debt are current liabilities*

Long-term debt may be issued so that it matures in a series of installments covering several years. If a portion of long-term debt is due within one year or the operating cycle, whichever is longer, that portion is a current liability.

For example, assume that a firm obtains a $400,000 loan to be paid in installments of $50,000 per year for the next eight years. The $50,000 installment due within *one year* is reported as a *current liability.* The remaining $350,000 is reported as a long-term liability.

## Sales and Excise Taxes Payable

Most states levy a sales tax on various products and services sold in the state. Certain products and services are subject to both sales and federal excise taxes. The tax laws usually require the seller to collect the taxes from the customer and remit the amount collected periodically. The amount collected represents a current liability until it is remitted to the appropriate government agency.

To illustrate the accounting, assume that a product with a $500 selling price is subject to a 5% sales tax and a 10% excise tax and is sold for cash on May 1. The entry to record the sale is as follows:

| | | | |
|---|---|---|---|
| May 1 | Cash | 575 | |
| | Sales | | 500 |
| | Sales Tax Payable | | 25 |
| | Excise Tax Payable | | 50 |
| | To record a sale of merchandise and the collection of related taxes | | |

The sale is recorded at $500, and the taxes collected from the customer are recorded as liabilities. The liabilities will be eliminated when the amounts collected are remitted to the government.

Instead of recording the sales and excise tax liabilities at the time of sale, some companies find it more convenient to credit the Sales account for the entire amount collected (which would include these taxes), and make an adjustment at the end of each period to record both the sales and excise taxes payable. For example, assume a company using this method credited its Sales account for $672,000 during the period, and all sales are subject to a 5% sales tax and a 7% excise tax. The figure entered in the Sales account includes the sales price of the items sold plus the sales tax and the excise tax. The company's actual sales revenue figure for the period is $600,000, determined as follows: ($672,000 ÷ 1.12 = $600,000). The amount of sales tax payable is $30,000 ($600,000 of sales × .05 = $30,000) and the amount of excise tax payable is $42,000 ($600,000 × .07 = $42,000).

The entry to adjust the Sales account and record the liabilities for sales taxes and excise taxes would be:

| | | |
|---|---|---|
| Sales | 72,000 | |
| Sales Tax Payable | | 30,000 |
| Excise Tax Payable | | 42,000 |
| To remove sales and excise taxes from the Sales account and record the liabilities for these taxes. | | |

## Accrued Liabilities

**Accrued liabilities** are obligations for expenditures that have been incurred but have not yet been recorded or paid. At the end of an accounting period, the obligation for accrued expenses is recognized by adjusting entries. Examples of expenses for which accruals are made include salaries, interest, property tax, and income tax. The accrual of interest first discussed in Chapter 3 is reviewed here. Accruals for property taxes and income taxes are discussed in the section on liabilities whose amount is not definitely known, and accruals for salaries are discussed later in this chapter.

INTEREST Interest accrues daily on all interest-bearing notes. When a note is issued in one accounting period and is repaid in another, an adjusting entry is needed at year-end to record the interest expense incurred during the period and the liability for interest payable that exists at the end of that period. To illustrate, assume that on October 1 Gateway Company borrowed $20,000 by issuing to its bank a six-month, 10%, interest-bearing note for that amount. If the company's accounting period ends on December 31, by then three months', or $500, of interest ($\$20{,}000 \times 10\% \times \frac{3}{12} = \$500$) has accrued on the note. The adjusting entry to record the accrued interest expense and interest obligation up to this point in time is as follows:

| | | | |
|---|---|---|---|
| Dec. 31 | Interest Expense .................................... | 500 | |
| | Interest Payable ................................ | | 500 |
| | To record accrued interest on a note payable | | |

## Unearned Revenues

**Unearned revenues,** sometimes called **deferred revenues,** are noncash obligations resulting from amounts received before they have been earned. The obligation is created when a customer or a client pays for goods or services before receiving them. These advance payments are recorded as current liabilities and remain current liabilities until the goods are delivered or the services are rendered. Two common examples of transactions that create a liability for unearned revenue are given below.

ADVANCE PAYMENTS THAT CREATE AN OBLIGATION TO PROVIDE FUTURE SERVICES Assume that Gateway Company provides cleaning services for client companies. On September 1 Gateway received a $4,200 advance payment from a client for cleaning services to be performed over the next six months. The following entry would record the cash received in advance:

| | | | |
|---|---|---|---|
| Sept. 1 | Cash ............................................... | 4,200 | |
| | Unearned Service Revenue ...................... | | 4,200 |
| | To record fees received in advance | | |

When services are performed, the liability for unearned service revenue is reduced or completely eliminated, and service revenue earned is recognized. For example, the entry to record services that were completed in September is as follows:

| | | | |
|---|---|---|---|
| Sept. 30 | Unearned Service Revenue | 700 | |
| | Service Revenue | | 700 |
| | To record service revenue earned | | |

The liability for Unearned Service Revenue has been reduced to $3,500 and will be further reduced in the future as Gateway continues to perform services for the client.

**ADVANCE PAYMENTS THAT CREATE AN OBLIGATION TO PROVIDE FUTURE PRODUCT** Assume that Gateway is a magazine publishing company that requires subscribers to pay for subscriptions in advance. When Gateway receives cash for a subscription order, a liability representing the company's obligation to deliver magazines in the future is created. For example, if on October 1 Gateway received checks totaling $3,600 from customers who subscribed to twelve monthly issues of its magazine, the entry to record the cash received is as follows:

| | | | |
|---|---|---|---|
| Oct. 1 | Cash | 3,600 | |
| | Subscriptions Collected in Advance | | 3,600 |
| | To record subscription orders taken | | |

Subscriptions Collected in Advance should be reported as a current liability on the balance sheet. No revenue was recognized on October 1, the transaction date, because at that time no magazines had as yet been delivered. The amount of revenue recognized, and consequently the amount by which the liability is reduced, is dependent on the number of magazines delivered at a given point in time. For example, if by December 31, the company's year-end, three issues of the magazine had been delivered, $900 ($\$3{,}600 \times \frac{3}{12} = \$900$) of revenue should be recognized, and the liability for Subscriptions Collected in Advance should be reduced by that same amount. The adjusting entry to accomplish this is as follows:

| | | | |
|---|---|---|---|
| Dec. 31 | Subscriptions Collected in Advance | 900 | |
| | Subscriptions Revenue | | 900 |
| | To record subscription revenue earned | | |

The $2,700 balance that remains in the Subscriptions Collected in Advance account is reported on the balance sheet as a current liability and will be recognized as revenue in future periods when the remaining magazines are delivered.

## CURRENT LIABILITIES WITH ESTIMATED MATURITY VALUES

We know that current liabilities with estimated maturity values exist on the day the balance sheet is to be prepared, but we do not know the exact amount that is owed. Liabilities belonging to this group must of necessity show amounts that are based upon estimates. Their exact amounts cannot be determined until a later date. Examples include property taxes payable, income taxes payable, and product warranty obligations. In each of these cases, the problem is to estimate and record the amount of the liability so that it can be reported on the current balance sheet.

## Property Taxes Payable

*2b. Property taxes payable are current liabilities that have an estimated maturity value*

Property taxes levied on real property, such as land and buildings, are a major source of revenue for local government units. The tax is usually based on the assessed value (the value assigned by the tax assessor) of property owned by residents and local businesses.

Problems sometimes arise in estimating the amount of property taxes to be recorded for a given period. This is because property taxes are usually assessed annually based on the fiscal year of the taxing authority, but this date rarely corresponds to the actual date on which the property is assessed. Thus it is often necessary for companies to initially estimate the amount of property taxes applicable to each month of the year. Only when the tax bill is received will the company be able to compare the amount of the estimate with the actual amount of tax to be paid.

To illustrate, assume that Gateway is located in a city that has a fiscal year of July 1 to June 30. The city's assessment date is October 1 of the fiscal year beginning the previous July 1, and its tax payment date is November 15. On July 1 Gateway can only estimate its property taxes for the coming year, which it does at $30,000. This estimate is based on last year's tax bill plus any publicized information about expected tax rate changes. On July 31 the company should make the following adjusting entry to record $2,500 ($30,000 ÷ 12 months = $2,500) of accrued property taxes applicable to the month of July:

| | | | |
|---|---|---|---|
| July 31 | Property Tax Expense.............................. | 2,500 | |
| | Property Tax Payable.......................... | | 2,500 |
| | To record estimated property tax expense for the month | | |

The same entry would be repeated on August 31 and September 30. On October 1 when Gateway receives its property tax bill, its actual annual property tax would be known. Let us assume the bill was for $30,360; then Gateway's actual property tax per month can be determined at $2,530 ($30,360 ÷ 12 months = $2,530). The difference between the actual property tax expense for July, August, and September and the estimated property tax expense recorded for that same three-month period is $90 ($30 difference per month × 3 months = $90). Because the difference is small, the amount can be added to the property tax expense recorded for October, making that month's amount $2,620 (actual monthly tax expense of $2,530 plus $90 for the amount previously underestimated). The entry recorded on October 31 would be as follows:

| | | | |
|---|---|---|---|
| Oct. 31 | Property Tax Expense.............................. | 2,620 | |
| | Property Tax Payable.......................... | | 2,620 |
| | To record property tax expense for the month | | |

After the October entry has been posted, the Property Taxes Payable account has a balance of $10,120. The entry to record the property tax payment made on November 15 is as follows:

| | | | |
|---|---|---|---|
| Nov. 15 | Property Taxes Payable ............................ | 10,120 | |
| | Prepaid Property Taxes ............................ | 20,240 | |
| | Cash...................................... | | 30,360 |
| | To record payment of property taxes | | |

Beginning on November 30, and continuing for each month until June 30, the amount in the Prepaid Property Taxes account will be written off to expense at the rate of $2,530 per month. The adjusting entry made on November 30 illustrates the process:

| | | | |
|---|---|---|---|
| Nov. 30 | Property Tax Expense | 2,530 | |
| | Prepaid Property Taxes | | 2,530 |
| | To record property tax expense for the month | | |

This entry, together with seven identical ones recorded at the end of each month from December 31 to June 30, will reduce the Prepaid Property Taxes account until it has a zero balance. In July of the next fiscal year, the process begins again.

## Income Taxes Payable

*2b. Income taxes payable are current liabilities that have an estimated maturity value*

Corporations are legal entities whose income is taxed by the federal government, most state governments, and some municipal governments. Single proprietorships and partnerships are not considered taxable entities, and their net income is not subject to income taxes. However, the individual owners of these businesses must include their share of the firm's business income on their personal tax returns. The amount of a corporate entity's income tax liability depends on the results of its operations and therefore cannot be accurately determined until after the end of the year.

However, because income taxes are an expense of the year in which the income is earned, an estimate of the amount must be recorded in that period. If a company estimated its tax liability at $15,000, the following entry would be recorded:

| | | | |
|---|---|---|---|
| Dec. 31 | Income Tax Expense | 15,000 | |
| | Income Tax Payable | | 15,000 |
| | To record estimated income taxes | | |

The Income Tax Payable account is reported as a current liability on the balance sheet, and the Income Tax Expense account is reported as an expense on the income statement. The computation of income subject to tax and the corresponding tax liability is discussed more fully in Chapter 28.

## Product Warranty Obligations

*2b. Product warranty obligations are current liabilities that have an estimated maturity value*

Sometimes a seller places a guarantee or warranty on its product when that product is sold. For example, the warranty may state that the seller is willing to repair or replace goods that malfunction within a specified period of time after they have been sold.

**Warranty** obligations result from such statements. Since the warranty is a feature of the product being sold, the cost of providing the warranty should be recorded in the same period in which the product is sold. To accomplish this, the cost of the warranty must be estimated. The actual cost of providing warranty services will not be known until some time in the future. To illustrate how product warranty accounting works, assume that Gateway Company offers a twelve-month product warranty for services on its window air conditioners. The company estimates that 2% of the air conditioners sold will be returned for service under the warranty and that the average cost per claim will be $10. If five hundred air conditioners were sold during June, the estimated costs of fulfilling the terms of the warranty would be $100 ($500 \times .02 \times \$10 = \$100$). The estimated liability would be recorded by an adusting entry on June 30 as follows:

| | | | |
|---|---|---|---|
| June 30 | Product Warranty Expense. . . . . . . . . . . . . . . . . . . . . . . . . . . . . . . . | 100 | |
| | Product Warranty Liability . . . . . . . . . . . . . . . . . . . . . . . . . . | | 100 |
| | To record estimated product warranty costs on June sales | | |

When an air conditioner under the product warranty is returned for service, the cost of servicing it is charged against the Product Warranty Liability account. Assume, for example, that on August 12 a customer returned an air conditioner that malfunctioned. If Gateway incurs costs of $15 for replacement parts used to service the item, the transaction would be recorded as follows:

| | | | |
|---|---|---|---|
| Aug. 12 | Product Warranty Liability. . . . . . . . . . . . . . . . . . . . . . . . . . . . . . . . | 15 | |
| | Inventory of Parts. . . . . . . . . . . . . . . . . . . . . . . . . . . . . . . . . . | | 15 |
| | To record costs to service an item under product warranty | | |

Actual product warranty costs are seldom equal to the company's estimate. When the amount of overestimate or underestimate is small, the warranty expense recorded in the next period may be increased or decreased. While estimated liabilities cannot be measured with precision, the accountant must use all the available data to make reasonable estimates. Failure to record estimated liabilities *understates* a firm's expenses, *overstates* its net income and owner's equity, and *understates* its liabilities reported at the end of that period.

## Contingent Liabilities

*1d. Contingent liabilities are obligations that are indefinite as to existence and amount*

Certain current liabilities are indefinite as to existence and amount. These are referred to as contingent liabilities. A **contingent liability** is a potential liability that will become an actual liability only if certain future events occur or do not occur. Thus before we can be sure that a liability actually exists and the amount of that liability, some future event must take place or fail to take place. Contingencies arise from lawsuits, discounting of notes receivable, possible tax assessments, and other causes.

Accounting for a contingent liability depends on how one makes a judgment concerning the likelihood that a specific future event will or will not take place. To provide guidance in evaluating the likelihood of a specific future event's taking place, three categories have been established: *probable, reasonably possible*, and *remote.*

*1d. Accounting differs for different categories of likelihood that a future event will or will not take place*

Different accounting treatment is recommended for each category of likelihood. If the future event will *probably* occur and the amount of liability can be *reasonably estimated*, the liability and corresponding loss should be recorded in the accounting records. If the amount cannot be reasonably estimated, no entry can of course be made—in which case a footnote to the financial statements should be prepared describing the nature of the contingency and the fact that the amount cannot be reasonably estimated.

If the likelihood of the future event is deemed to be *reasonably possible,* the related contingency should be fully disclosed in a footnote. On the other hand, contingent liabilities that have only a remote chance of becoming actual liabilities need not be recorded or disclosed.

## PAYROLL ACCOUNTING

Salaries, wages, and related payroll taxes are significant expenses for most businesses. For example, Exxon Corporation reported salaries, wages, and employee benefits of $3.4 billion for a given year for its 130,000 employees. Companies in the service industry, such as banks, often have payroll costs representing 50% or more of their total operating costs.

Payroll accounting can be complicated because of various federal and state laws. Before discussing the mechanics of payroll accounting, we will briefly describe some essential features of a payroll system. The payroll system should be designed to accomplish the following:

1. Generate paychecks to pay each employee the correct amount at the time it was promised. Paychecks should be accompanied by detailed information indicating how the net amount received by the employee was calculated.
2. Accumulate payroll information on each employee and in aggregate as required by various governmental agencies, and provide appropriate reports and timely remittances of amounts due to those agencies.
3. Prevent errors or acts of fraud whereby checks are issued for incorrect amounts or are being received by nonauthorized persons. All of us have probably heard stories about companies whose payroll system has overpaid employees, generated duplicate paychecks, issued checks to employees who have been terminated, and issued checks to fictitious employees.

### Internal Accounting Control Over Payroll

Accounting for the acquisition and cost of personnel services requires strong internal accounting control to safeguard funds and to ensure the accurate and timely processing of payroll data. Sound internal accounting control is an integral part of an effective manual or computerized payroll system.

***1e. Internal accounting control over payroll involves separating certain payroll functions***

One key to achieving strong internal accounting control over payroll is to separate the duties of hiring employees from the duties of paying employees. In most businesses payroll duties (or functions) include the following:

*The hiring function.* All new employees should be required to prepare a personnel record showing, at a minimum, job description, salary or wage rate, fringe benefits, number of withholding allowances claimed, and employee-authorized payroll deductions. The personnel department is responsible for maintaining and updating the employee's personnel record.

*The timekeeping function.* Businesses generally use a document to record the amount of time for which an employee will be paid. Salaried personnel are generally paid on the basis of a contract. Employees paid on an hourly basis generally use a time clock to record the number of hours worked during a given pay period. This is then used as the basis for calculating the employee's pay.

*The recordkeeping function.* Data from timekeeping together with data from personnel are used to maintain payroll records and prepare individual paychecks.

*The distribution function.* The distribution of paychecks should be handled by a department or person separated from any of the functions discussed above. In large organizations the distribution of paychecks is generally the responsibility of a paymaster who is a member of the finance department.

This list of payroll-system functions is not all-inclusive. Its purpose is to emphasize that strong internal accounting control over payroll procedures requires the separation of duties. Of course, for a small, individually owned business, separation may not be needed. The owner may know all the employees and how much each employee should be paid for work performed during each pay period.

We are now ready to discuss accounting for payroll and related payroll taxes beginning with the computation of gross earnings.

## GROSS EARNINGS

*1f,2c. Computation of gross earnings is explained here*

**Gross earnings** consist of the total amount of an employee's salary or wages before any payroll deductions have been subtracted. The term *salaries* refers to the compensation paid to an employee on a weekly, semimonthly, or monthly basis without regard to the number of hours worked during the period. *Wages* refers to compensation paid to an employee on the basis of the number of hours worked or the number of units produced. Payroll periods for wage earners are generally weekly or biweekly. Employers may supplement salaries or wages by offering bonuses, commissions, profit sharing, and cost-of-living adjustments.

Salary and wage rates are determined either from a negotiated labor contract or by mutual agreement between the company and the employee. Most businesses are subject to the provisions of the **Fair Labor Standards Act** (also called the ***Wages and Hours Law***). The law sets minimum hourly wages and regulates overtime, requiring employers to pay at least one and one-half times the regular hourly rate for all hours worked in excess of forty hours per week. It also provides equal pay standards for workers in industries engaged in interstate commerce.

Certain executive, administrative, and supervisory employees are exempt from the one and one-half times requirement, and certain industries such as hotel and restaurant businesses are also exempt from the overtime requirement of the law.

To illustrate the computation of gross earnings, assume that Tracy Warren, an employee, earns a regular hourly wage of $6. In addition, Tracy is paid an overtime rate of one and one-half times the regular rate for all hours worked over eight in any weekday, and twice the regular rate for work on a weekend or a holiday. The schedule below shows the hours Tracy worked during the week ending January 20, 19X7.

| DAY | TOTAL HOURS WORKED | REGULAR HOURS | OVERTIME HOURS |
|---|---|---|---|
| Monday | 8 | 8 | 0 |
| Tuesday | 10 | 8 | 2 |
| Wednesday | 9 | 8 | 1 |
| Thursday | 8 | 8 | 0 |
| Friday | 10 | 8 | 2 |
| Saturday | 4 | 0 | 4 |
| Total | 49 | 40 | 9 |

Tracy's gross earnings for the week are $333, computed as follows:

| | | |
|---|---|---|
| Regular pay | 40 hours × $6 = | $240 |
| Overtime pay—weekdays | 5 hours × $6 × 1.5 = | 45 |
| Overtime pay—weekend | 4 hours × $6 × 2 = | 48 |
| Gross earnings | | $333 |

## DEDUCTIONS FROM GROSS EARNINGS

*1f,2c. Computations of deductions from gross earnings are explained here*

From our own work experiences we know that our net earnings *(take-home pay)* will be less than our gross earnings. This is because certain deductions are subtracted from gross earnings to arrive at net earnings. Many of these deductions are required by law; others we may have authorized. Deductions required by law are **FICA** taxes, federal income taxes, state and city income taxes (required by most states and some cities), and state unemployment compensation tax on employees (where applicable by state law). Deductions authorized by us vary widely but often include such items as premiums on medical, health, and life insurance; contribution to a retirement or pension plan; U.S. savings bonds; savings to be deposited with a credit union; contributions to charities; and union dues.

### FICA Taxes

The *Federal Insurance Contributions Act (FICA)*, commonly called the ***Social Security Act***, provides that qualified workers who retire after reaching a specified age receive monthly retirement payments and certain medical benefits. In addition, the act provides benefits to a worker who becomes disabled and survivor's benefits to the family of a worker in the case of death.

The Social Security programs are financed by taxes levied on salaries or wages paid to employees and on self-employment income. **FICA taxes** are levied on both employers and employees based on a schedule established by Congress. The schedule establishes the tax rate and the maximum amount of each employee's earnings subject to the tax. In recent years both the tax rate and the earnings subject to tax have increased significantly. This increase can be seen in the accompanying table. An attempt to project the amounts closer to the present date would not be useful because they are subject to change at any time (by congressional action), and publicized projections have frequently been revised. Since the limit and percent increase frequently, a rate of 7% and a maximum of $40,000 will be used in all problems in this text.

| YEAR | BASE (MAXIMUM EARNINGS SUBJECT TO FICA TAX) | TAX RATE ON EMPLOYEES | MAXIMUM FICA TAX TO BE WITHHELD FROM AN EMPLOYEE IN A CALENDAR YEAR (ROUNDED) |
|---|---|---|---|
| 1937 | $ 3,000 | 1.0% | $ 30 |
| 1951 | 3,600 | 1.5 | 54 |
| 1972 | 9,000 | 5.2 | 468 |
| 1979 | 22,900 | 6.13 | 1,404 |
| 1983 | 35,700 | 6.70 | 2,392 |
| 1985 | 39,600 | 7.05 | 2,792 |
| 1986 | 42,000 | 7.15 | 3,003 |

The employer is required to withhold as a **FICA** tax a portion of the earnings of each of its employees, subject to a maximum, on each payday. The amount of the FICA tax is calculated at the current rate until the annual maximum earnings subject to the tax is reached. For example, assume that Tracy Warren, who had gross earnings of $333 for the week ended January 20, 19X7, had not yet earned the annual maximum amount during 19X7. The amount of FICA tax to be withheld from her current paycheck is $23.31 ($333.00 × .07).

This amount is the employee's contribution to the Social Security programs. As we will explain later, the employer must also contribute to the programs based on the earnings of each of its employees. It must also remit the amounts to the Internal Revenue Service on a timely basis as prescribed by law.

### Federal Income Taxes

The federal government requires employers to act as tax-collecting agents and withhold income taxes from salaries or wages before they are paid. The amount to be withheld from each employee's gross earnings is determined by the amount of the earnings and by the number of the employee's exemptions. Each employee is entitled to one exemption for himself or herself and one for each dependent. Additional exemptions may be claimed if the employee or the employee's spouse is blind or over sixty-five years of age. Thus a married couple, neither of whom is over sixty-five years old or blind, with three dependent children, would claim five exemptions. All employees are required to file an **Employee's Withholding Allowance Certificate (Form W-4)** with their employer to indicate the number of exemptions claimed (see Exhibit 12–1).

*EXHIBIT 12–1*

Withholding Allowance Certificate—Form W-4

Form **W-4** (Rev. January 1986) | Department of the Treasury—Internal Revenue Service | **Employee's Withholding Allowance Certificate** | OMB No. 1545-0010 Expires: 11-30-87

1 Type or print your full name: TRACY WARREN
2 Your social security number: 542-14-5437

Home address (number and street or rural route): 22 ROCK ROAD
City or town, state, and ZIP code: SARASOTA, FLORIDA 33583

3 Marital Status: ☐ Single ☒ Married ☐ Married, but withhold at higher Single rate
**Note:** If married, but legally separated, or spouse is a nonresident alien, check the Single box.

4 Total number of allowances you are claiming (from line F of the worksheet on page 2) . . . . . 3
5 Additional amount, if any, you want deducted from each pay . . . . . $
6 I claim exemption from withholding because (see instructions and check boxes below that apply):
a ☐ Last year I did not owe any Federal income tax and had a right to a full refund of **ALL** income tax withheld, **AND**
b ☐ This year I do not expect to owe any Federal income tax and expect to have a right to a full refund of **ALL** income tax withheld. If both a and b apply, enter the year effective and "EXEMPT" here . . . ▶ Year 19
c If you entered "EXEMPT" on line 6b, are you a full-time student? . . . . . ☐Yes ☐No

Under penalties of perjury, I certify that I am entitled to the number of withholding allowances claimed on this certificate, or if claiming exemption from withholding, that I am entitled to claim the exempt status.
**Employee's signature ▶** Tracy Warren **Date ▶** January 4 19 84

7 Employer's name and address **(Employer: Complete 7, 8, and 9 only if sending to IRS)**: WINDSOR COMPANY, 260 SOUTH DRIVE SARASOTA, FLORIDA 33583
8 Office code
9 Employer identification number: 45-2177836

Detach along this line. Give the top part of this form to employer; keep the lower part for your records.

To determine the amount of federal income taxes to be withheld from an employee's gross earnings, most employers use a **Wage-Bracket Withholding**

Table like the one shown in Exhibit 12–2. These tables show the amounts to be withheld from employees' salaries or wages at various levels of gross earnings and for various numbers of withholding allowances (exemptions).

*EXHIBIT 12–2*

Wage-Bracket Withholding Table

MARRIED Persons—WEEKLY Payroll Period
(For Wages Paid After December 1984)

| And the wages are— | | And the number of withholding allowances claimed is— | | | | | | | | | | |
|---|---|---|---|---|---|---|---|---|---|---|---|---|
| | | 0 | 1 | 2 | 3 | 4 | 5 | 6 | 7 | 8 | 9 | 10 |
| At least | But less than | The amount of income tax to be withheld shall be— | | | | | | | | | | |
| $300 | $310 | $36 | $32 | $29 | $26 | $23 | $20 | $17 | $14 | $11 | $ 9 | $ 6 |
| 310 | 320 | 38 | 34 | 31 | 28 | 24 | 21 | 18 | 16 | 13 | 10 | 8 |
| 320 | 330 | 39 | 36 | 32 | 29 | 26 | 23 | 20 | 17 | 14 | 11 | 9 |
| 330 | 340 | 41 | 38 | 34 | 31 | 28 | 24 | 21 | 18 | 16 | 13 | 10 |
| 340 | 350 | 43 | 39 | 36 | 32 | 29 | 26 | 23 | 20 | 17 | 14 | 11 |
| 350 | 360 | 45 | 41 | 38 | 34 | 31 | 28 | 24 | 21 | 18 | 16 | 13 |
| 360 | 370 | 47 | 43 | 39 | 36 | 32 | 29 | 26 | 23 | 20 | 17 | 14 |
| 370 | 380 | 48 | 45 | 41 | 38 | 34 | 31 | 28 | 24 | 21 | 18 | 16 |
| 380 | 390 | 50 | 47 | 43 | 39 | 36 | 32 | 29 | 26 | 23 | 20 | 17 |
| 390 | 400 | 52 | 48 | 45 | 41 | 38 | 34 | 31 | 28 | 24 | 21 | 18 |
| 400 | 410 | 55 | 50 | 47 | 43 | 39 | 36 | 32 | 29 | 26 | 23 | 20 |
| 410 | 420 | 57 | 52 | 48 | 45 | 41 | 38 | 34 | 31 | 28 | 24 | 21 |
| 420 | 430 | 59 | 55 | 50 | 47 | 43 | 39 | 36 | 32 | 29 | 26 | 23 |
| 430 | 440 | 61 | 57 | 52 | 48 | 45 | 41 | 38 | 34 | 31 | 28 | 24 |
| 440 | 450 | 63 | 59 | 55 | 50 | 47 | 43 | 39 | 36 | 32 | 29 | 26 |
| 450 | 460 | 66 | 61 | 57 | 52 | 48 | 45 | 41 | 38 | 34 | 31 | 28 |
| 460 | 470 | 68 | 63 | 59 | 55 | 50 | 47 | 43 | 39 | 36 | 32 | 29 |
| 470 | 480 | 70 | 66 | 61 | 57 | 52 | 48 | 45 | 41 | 38 | 34 | 31 |
| 480 | 490 | 73 | 68 | 63 | 59 | 55 | 50 | 47 | 43 | 39 | 36 | 32 |
| 490 | 500 | 75 | 70 | 66 | 61 | 57 | 52 | 48 | 45 | 41 | 38 | 34 |
| 500 | 510 | 78 | 73 | 68 | 63 | 59 | 55 | 50 | 47 | 43 | 39 | 36 |
| 510 | 520 | 80 | 75 | 70 | 66 | 61 | 57 | 52 | 48 | 45 | 41 | 38 |
| 520 | 530 | 83 | 78 | 73 | 68 | 63 | 59 | 55 | 50 | 47 | 43 | 39 |
| 530 | 540 | 85 | 80 | 75 | 70 | 66 | 61 | 57 | 52 | 48 | 45 | 41 |
| 540 | 550 | 88 | 83 | 78 | 73 | 68 | 63 | 59 | 55 | 50 | 47 | 43 |
| 550 | 560 | 90 | 85 | 80 | 75 | 70 | 66 | 61 | 57 | 52 | 48 | 45 |
| 560 | 570 | 93 | 88 | 83 | 78 | 73 | 68 | 63 | 59 | 55 | 50 | 47 |
| 570 | 580 | 95 | 90 | 85 | 80 | 75 | 70 | 66 | 61 | 57 | 52 | 48 |
| 580 | 590 | 98 | 93 | 88 | 83 | 78 | 73 | 68 | 63 | 59 | 55 | 50 |

The illustrated table is for married employees and is applicable to a weekly payroll period. Different tables have been prepared for single employees and for payroll periods that are biweekly, semimonthly, and monthly.

Using the table, the amount of federal income tax to be withheld from an employee's gross earnings can easily be determined. First, locate the employee's wage bracket in the first two columns and then follow the line of the wage bracket to the column showing the number of withholding allowances claimed by the employee. For example, Tracy Warren's gross earnings were $333 for the week ending January 20, and she claims three withholding allowances. Her wage bracket is the fourth down from the top, reading "at least $330 but less than $340." The amount of federal income tax to be withheld from her pay is found four money columns over under "three withholding allowances claimed" and is $31.

## State and City Income Taxes

Most states and some cities levy income taxes on the gross earnings of employees. Like federal income taxes, these income taxes must be withheld by the employer. Procedures for determining the amounts of such withholdings follow patterns similar to those used for federal income taxes.

## Other Deductions

All the states have unemployment insurance programs. Most states finance the program by taxes levied only on the employer. In a few states the tax is also levied on the salaries and wages paid to employees up to a limit or ceiling amount of annual earnings. In those few states in which the tax is imposed on employees, the employer must withhold the tax from employee's earnings.

In addition to payroll deductions required by law, many employees authorize other deductions that are made for their benefit or convenience. Examples, you will recall, include deductions for the payment of insurance premiums, for contributions to pension or retirement plans, for savings, and for contributions to charities. In any case, deductions are amounts withheld from an employee's gross earnings, and these withholdings generally result in current liabilities for the employer. The liabilities are eliminated when the employer pays the amounts withheld to the appropriate agencies and organizations.

## Computation of Employee Net Earnings

Gross earnings less payroll deductions equals the amount to be paid to the employee called **net earnings** or ***net pay.*** The computation of Tracy Warren's net earnings of $254.39 for the week ending January 20, 19X7, is shown below.

| | | |
|---|---|---|
| Gross earnings for the week | | $333.00 |
| Deductions: | | |
| FICA tax | $23.31 | |
| Federal income taxes | 31.00 | |
| State income taxes | 8.20 | |
| Medical insurance | 9.10 | |
| U.S. savings bonds | 5.00 | |
| Union dues | 2.00 | |
| Total deductions | | 78.61 |
| Net earnings | | $254.39 |

You will recall that Tracy's gross earnings (including regular and overtime pay) for the week were $333. All of these earnings were subject to FICA tax, which computed at the rate of 7% totaled $23.31. Federal income taxes withheld determined by her employer were $31.00. Following similar procedures, state income tax withholding of $8.20 was also determined. The deduction for union dues may or may not be a voluntary deduction. Nevertheless, that deduction plus authorized deductions for medical insurance premiums and U.S. savings bonds were made, leaving Tracy with net earnings of $254.39.

### Employer's Liability for Amounts Withheld

The amounts withheld from an employee's earnings, whether mandated or voluntarily authorized, are liabilities of the employer. In withholding the amounts, the employer acts as a collection agent for the various governmental agencies, labor union, or designated organizations. The employer must maintain adequate records to

Support the reason and purpose of the withholdings
Provide data for filing reports concerning the withholdings
Make timely payments of the amounts withheld

In addition, the employer usually prepares a statement of earnings attached to the paycheck of each employee to identify each withholding and to explain how the net earnings were determined. When financial statements are prepared, the withheld amounts that have not yet been remitted to appropriate agencies are reported as current liabilities on the employer's balance sheet.

## PAYROLL RECORDS AND PROCEDURES

The records and procedures used in accounting for payroll will vary from company to company depending on the number of employees and the extent of automation. With the increasing use of in-house computers and the availability of time-sharing services, most companies have automated payroll accounting systems. However, some companies with few employees continue to process payroll data manually. Whether automated or manual, there are several records and procedures common to most payroll systems. In this section we describe and illustrate certain basic records and procedures common to most payroll systems. Because of its simplicity of illustration, we will use a nonautomated form.

### Payroll Register

A **Payroll Register** is a multicolumn form used by an employer to assemble and summarize the data needed to prepare the payroll. It contains a listing of each employee's gross earnings, deductions, and net earnings for a given payroll period. Although its design may vary somewhat depending on the number of employees, the payroll classifications, and the extent of automation, the one shown in Exhibit 12–3 (see page 428) provides the information needed.

The nature of the data appearing in the illustrative Payroll Register is self-evident from the column headings. The name of the employee, number of hours worked during the pay period, and gross earnings based on those hours are entered in the appropriate columns. A separate column is provided for each type of deduction from gross earnings. Each employee's net earnings—the amount each will be paid—is shown in a separate column followed by the number of the check used to make that payment. Take a moment to observe how Tracy Warren's payroll data applicable to the payroll period are entered on one line of the Payroll Register. The last two columns divide the payroll into categories indicating the expense accounts that should be debited when the payroll is recorded in the accounting records.

As shown in Exhibit 12–3, the columns of the Payroll Register are totaled at the end of each pay period. These totals are then used to record the payroll in the accounting records.

*EXHIBIT 12–3*

Payroll Register

| PAY PERIOD: WEEK ENDED JANUARY 20, 1987 | | | | | | | | | | | | | | | |
|---|---|---|---|---|---|---|---|---|---|---|---|---|---|---|---|
| | | EARNINGS | | | DEDUCTIONS | | | | | | PAYMENTS | | ACCOUNT DEBITED | |
| EMPLOYEE | HOURS | Regular | Overtime | Total | FICA Tax | Fed. Inc. Tax | State Inc. Tax | Medical Insurance | U.S. Savings Bonds | Union Dues | Net Earnings | Check No. | Sales Sal. Exp. | Office Sal. Exp. |
| Bill Darkus | 40 | 240 00 | – | 240 00 | 16 80 | 25 00 | 5 60 | 5 90 | – | 2 00 | 184 70 | 51 | 240 00 | |
| Bob Gable | 44 | 340 00 | 51 00 | 391 00 | 27 37 | 51 00 | 14 70 | 10 20 | 8 00 | 2 00 | 277 73 | 52 | 391 00 | |
| Ken Monday | 40 | 280 00 | – | 280 00 | 19 60 | 38 00 | 8 50 | 5 90 | 5 00 | 2 00 | 201 00 | 53 | 280 00 | |
| Beth Orr | 40 | 320 00 | – | 320 00 | 22 40 | 44 00 | 11 30 | 9 10 | 5 00 | – | 228 20 | 54 | | 320 00 |
| John Reyes | 46 | 240 00 | 54 00 | 294 00 | 20 58 | 35 00 | 7 40 | 5 90 | – | – | 225 12 | 55 | | 294 00 |
| Sheri Ross | 40 | 300 00 | – | 300 00 | 21 00 | 40 00 | 9 10 | 5 90 | 8 00 | 2 00 | 214 00 | 56 | 300 00 | |
| Tracy Warren | 49 | 240 00 | 93 00 | 333 00 | 23 31 | 31 00 | 8 20 | 9 10 | 5 00 | 2 00 | 254 39 | 57 | 333 00 | |
| Totals | | 1 960 00 | 198 00 | 2 158 00 | 151 06 | 264 00 | 64 80 | 52 00 | 31 00 | 10 00 | 1585 14 | | 1 544 00 | 614 00 |

### Recording the Payroll

*2d. An entry is made to record the payroll expense*

The payroll journal entry based on the Payroll Register shown in Exhibit 12–3 is as follows (the entry records the payroll expense and the employer's related liabilities):

| | | | |
|---|---|---|---|
| Jan. 20 | Sales Salaries Expense | 1,544.00 | |
| | Office Salaries Expense | 614.00 | |
| | FICA Taxes Payable | | 151.06 |
| | Employee's Federal Income Taxes Payable | | 264.00 |
| | Employee's State Income Taxes Payable | | 64.80 |
| | Medical Insurance Payable | | 52.00 |
| | U.S. Savings Bonds Payable | | 31.00 |
| | Union Dues Payable | | 10.00 |
| | Salaries Payable | | 1,585.14 |
| | To record the payroll for the week ended January 20 | | |

### Employee Earnings Record

Another payroll record that employers maintain is called an **Employee Earnings Record** (see Exhibit 12–4). It provides a summary of each employee's gross earnings, deductions, and net earnings for each payroll period and the cumulative gross earnings for the year to date. Information to update the Employee Earnings Record is taken at the end of each pay period from the related line in the Payroll Register. This updating procedure can be observed by noting the last entry in Tracy Warren's earnings record. It shows data from the line in the Payroll Register relating to Tracy's payroll for the week ended January 20.

The information contained in the Employee Earnings Record must be updated because (1) it is needed to prepare certain quarterly payroll reports, as we will discuss later in the chapter; (2) the amount shown for cumulative gross earnings is needed in computing taxes, such as FICA taxes, where tax rates are applied to an employee's gross earnings only until a maximum or ceiling amount of those earnings has been reached (also discussed in more detail later); and (3) it provides information needed to prepare a **Wage and Tax Statement (Form W-2)** at the end of the year. This statement (see Exhibit 12–5) prepared by the employer contains a considerable amount of information, including the employee's gross earnings for the calendar year (item 10), the earnings subject to FICA tax (item 13), the federal and state income taxes withheld (items 9 and 17), and the FICA taxes withheld (item 11).

The employer must give each employee several copies of this statement and must also send a copy to the Social Security Administration. The employee uses the information contained in the form to file his or her income tax returns, and a copy of the form must be attached to each return filed.

## PAYROLL TAXES OF THE EMPLOYER

Up to this point we have discussed only the taxes levied against employees and withheld by employers. Most employers are also subject to federal and state taxes. The three major **payroll taxes** that the employer must pay are the FICA tax, federal unemployment tax, and state unemployment tax. These taxes are an operating expense of the business. The salaries and wages subject to each tax must be determined on the basis of each employee's earnings record.

*EXHIBIT 12–4*

Employee Earnings Record

| | | | | | |
|---|---|---|---|---|---|
| EMPLOYEE'S NAME | Tracy Warren | DATE OF EMPLOYMENT | October 19, 19X0 | POSITION | Sales Rep. |
| ADDRESS | 22 Rock Road | DATE OF TERMINATION | | HOURLY RATE | $6.00 |
| | Sarasota, Florida 33583 | MARITAL STATUS | M | | |
| SOCIAL SECURITY NUMBER | 542-14-5437 | EXEMPTIONS | 3 | | |
| DATE OF BIRTH | November 3, 1950 | | | | |

| | | EARNINGS | | | DEDUCTIONS | | | | | | | |
|---|---|---|---|---|---|---|---|---|---|---|---|---|
| PERIOD ENDING | TOTAL HOURS | Regular | Overtime | Gross | FICA Tax | Fed. Inc. Tax | State Inc. Tax | Medical Insurance | U.S. Savings Bonds | Union Dues | NET EARNINGS | CUMULATIVE GROSS EARNINGS |
| Jan. 6 | 40 | 240.00 | — | 240.00 | 16.80 | 20.00 | 5.30 | 9.10 | 5.00 | 2.00 | 181.80 | 240.00 |
| 13 | 42 | 240.00 | 18.00 | 258.00 | 18.06 | 22.00 | 5.90 | 9.10 | 5.00 | 2.00 | 195.94 | 498.00 |
| 20 | 49 | 240.00 | 93.00 | 333.00 | 23.31 | 31.00 | 8.20 | 9.10 | 5.00 | 2.00 | 254.39 | 831.00 |

EXHIBIT 12–5

Wage and Tax Statement—Form W-2

| 1 Control number | | OMB No. 1545-0008 | |
|---|---|---|---|
| 2 Employer's name, address, and ZIP code<br>WINDSOR COMPANY<br>260 SOUTH DRIVE<br>SARASOTA, FLORIDA 33583 | | 3 Employer's identification number<br>45-2177836 | 4 Employer's State number |
| | | 5 Statutory employee ☐ Deceased ☐ Legal rep. ☐ 942 emp. ☐ Subtotal ☐ Void ☐ | |
| | | 6 Allocated tips | 7 Advance EIC payment |
| 8 Employee's social security number<br>542-14-5437 | 9 Federal income tax withheld<br>1,885.40 | 10 Wages, tips, other compensation<br>15,600.00 | 11 Social security tax withheld<br>1,092.00 |
| 12 Employee's name, address, and ZIP code<br>TRACY WARREN<br>22 ROCK ROAD<br>SARASOTA, FLORIDA<br>33583 | | 13 Social security wages<br>15,600.00 | 14 Social security tips |
| | | 16 | |

| 17 State income tax | 18 State wages, tips, etc. | 19 Name of State |
|---|---|---|
| 410.60 | | FLORIDA |
| 20 Local income tax | 21 Local wages, tips, etc. | 22 Name of locality |

Form W-2 Wage and Tax Statement **1985** Copy 1 For State, City, or Local Tax Department
Employee's and employer's copy compared ☐

## FICA Taxes

Employers are required to contribute to the Federal Insurance Contributions Act program for each employee. In 1986, the employer's tax rate was 7.15%. Thus the employer is required to match the amount of FICA tax withheld from each employee's pay. The employer is liable for the combined tax (which would be 14.3%) of the first $42,000 of each employee's earnings; 7.15% of which was paid by the employee, and 7.15% by the employer. The rate was applied to the first $42,000 of gross earnings for each employee.

For example, assume that a company had two employees. One had gross earnings of $400, and the other had gross earnings of $600. The company would have had to pay FICA taxes of $71.50 ($600 + $400 × .0715), assuming that neither employee had reached a cumulative gross earnings of $42,000, the maximum annual earnings subject to that tax. As with the employee portion, we will use a rate of 7% on the first $40,000 of each employee's earnings in the exercises and problems.

## Federal Unemployment Tax

The Federal Unemployment Tax Act (FUTA) is another part of the national Social Security program. It functions as a joint program between the federal government and the various states and is designed to provide temporary benefits in the form of compensation to persons who become unemployed as a result of economic forces beyond their control. **Federal unemployment taxes** levied on employers are not paid directly to the unemployed but are allocated among the states to pay a portion of the costs of their joint federal-state unemployment programs. Note that the act levies the tax on employers only, not on employees.

The rate and the maximum amount subject to the tax are frequently revised by Congress. For our purposes, we will assume a **FUTA** tax rate of 3.5% on the first $7,000 earned by each employee during a calendar year. The employer is, however, allowed to reduce the rate because of credits received for amounts paid to the state unemployment compensation plan. The maximum credit is 2.7%, and since most states have established a tax rate of 2.7% for their own programs, the employer is usually subject to a **FUTA** tax of 0.8% (3.5% − 2.7% = 0.8%) on each employee's gross earnings up to $7,000.

### State Unemployment Tax

The amounts paid as benefits to unemployed persons are financed by **state unemployment taxes** levied on the employer. Some states levy taxes on both employer and employee. Although the rates of tax and the tax base vary from state to state, the usual tax rate on employers is 2.7% and is based on the first $7,000 earned by each employee during the calendar year. Many states have instituted a merit-rating system to reduce the rates for employers who maintain a stable work force and provide workers with steady employment.

In our problems and illustrations we will assume a tax rate of 2.7% based on the first $7,000 of each employee's earnings. We will also assume that the tax is levied only on the employer.

### Recording Payroll Taxes

The entry to record the employer's payroll taxes is usually made at the same time that the payroll is recorded. To illustrate, we will again use the data from the Payroll Register in Exhibit 12–3. Because the payroll data relate to the week ending January 20, we assume that no employee has accumulated gross earnings in excess of $7,000 (the first maximum taxable salary level to be reached). The register shows gross earnings for the week of $2,158.00. Therefore the FICA tax is *$151.06* (.07 × $2,158); the federal unemployment tax is *$17.26* (.008 × $2,158); and the state unemployment tax is *$58.27* (.027 × $2,158). The journal entry to record the payroll tax expense for the week and the liabilities for the taxes accrued is as follows:

| | | | |
|---|---|---|---|
| Jan. 20 | Payroll Tax Expense | 226.59 | |
| | FICA Taxes Payable | | 151.06 |
| | Federal Unemployment Taxes Payable | | 17.26 |
| | State Unemployment Taxes Payable | | 58.27 |
| | To record payroll taxes for the week ended January 20 | | |

### Payment of Payroll and Payroll-Related Taxes

Payment of the payroll and each of the payroll-related taxes is recorded in the same way as the payment of other liabilities. That is, cash is credited and the appropriate liability is debited when the payment transaction is recorded.

Employers who deduct large amounts of taxes from their payroll are, however, required to remit those amounts in accordance with the law. They must also provide a considerable amount of detail to government agencies on required forms.

For example, the federal income tax and **FICA** tax withheld from employees are detailed and combined with the employer's **FICA** tax on a single return called the **Employer's Quarterly Federal Tax Return (Form 941).** The form covers a three-month calendar quarter and must be filed, together with a check for the amount due, by the last day of the month after the end of each calendar quarter. When the amount of the combined taxes is high even for short payroll periods, the federal government requires employers to make payments as often as weekly, semimonthly, or monthly. The payments are made by depositing the money to the credit of the Internal Revenue Service at an authorized commercial bank or a Federal Reserve Bank.

Federal unemployment tax returns and payments are made on an annual basis if the amount of the tax is less than a stipulated minimum. If not, quarterly payments are required and an annual return is filed. The return is called the *Employer's Annual Federal Unemployment Tax Return (Form 940)*, and it must be filed by January 31 for the previous calendar year. State laws vary, but most require employers to file a state unemployment tax return quarterly and to pay the tax at that time.

## PAYROLL TAXES—SUMMARIZED

Some of the payroll taxes discussed in the previous sections are levied against the employers, some against the employees, and some against both. Exhibit 12–6 summarizes the responsibility related to payroll taxes.

*EXHIBIT 12–6*
Summary of Taxes Related to Payroll

| TAX | LEVIED ON EMPLOYER | LEVIED ON EMPLOYEE |
|---|---|---|
| Federal Income Tax | | X |
| State Income Tax | | X |
| Social Security Tax (FICA) | X | X |
| Federal Unemployment Tax | X | |
| State Unemployment Tax | X | X (in certain states only) |

## HIGHLIGHT PROBLEM

Slater Company's year ends on December 31. Listed below are selected transactions that occurred during January 19X8.

**a.** On January 15 the company borrowed money from City Bank by issuing a six-month note having a face value of $12,000. The bank deducted interest at 10% and gave the company the proceeds of $11,400.

**b.** The company had sales of $150,000. All sales were made for cash. All items sold were subject to a 6% state sales tax. Sales taxes must be remitted to the state on April 1, 19X8.

**c.** The company offers a warranty on its products. It estimates that fifty of the items sold during January will require warranty work costing an average of $20 per claim. None of the items sold during January have as yet been returned for warranty work.

**d.** The company pays its employees once a month. Total salaries for January were $30,000, classified as follows:

| | |
|---|---|
| Sales | $24,000 |
| Office | 6,000 |

Additional data taken directly from the payroll register follow:

| | |
|---|---|
| Federal income taxes withheld | $4,800 |
| State income taxes withheld | 900 |
| FICA taxes withheld | 2,100 |
| Medical insurance premiums withheld | 560 |
| Union dues withheld | 230 |

Required:

1. Prepare the journal entry or entries to record the following:
   a. The note issued on January 15.
   b. The January sales including the liability for sales taxes. Assume that a summary entry is made on January 31.
   c. The estimated liability for product warranties on January 31 for the items sold during January.
   d. January's payroll. Assume that employees will be paid on February 1, 19X8.
   e. The payroll taxes related to the January payroll. Assume that 100% of the gross earnings is subject to 7% FICA tax because none of the employees have exceeded the annual maximum amount of earnings on which these taxes are levied. The state and federal unemployment insurance tax rates are 2.7% and 0.8% and are levied on the entire $30,000 of gross earnings because none of the employees has exceeded the set annual maximum.
   f. The recognition of accrued interest expense on January 31 for the bank note issued on January 15.
2. Determine the total payroll expense for the month of January.

## GLOSSARY OF KEY TERMS

**Accrued liabilities.** Obligations for expenses that have been incurred but have not yet been recorded or paid.

**Contingent liability.** A potential liability that will become an actual liability only if certain future events occur or do not occur.

**Current liabilities.** Debts and obligations that are expected to be paid within an operating cycle or a year, whichever is longer, and require the use of an existing current asset or the creation of another current liability.

**Employee Earnings Record.** A multicolumn record showing for each employee the hours worked, gross earnings, deductions, and net earnings for each payroll period and the cumulative gross earnings for the year to date.

**Employee's Withholding Allowance Certificate (Form W-4).** A form prepared by each employee stating his or her marital status and the number of withholding allowances (exemptions) claimed.

**Employer's Quarterly Federal Tax Return (Form 941).** A form prepared by the employer at the end of each calendar quarter showing the amount of federal income tax withheld from employees, the amount of gross salaries and wages paid to employees who were subject to FICA taxes, the amount of FICA taxes to be paid, the amount of deposits made during the period, and the amount due with the tax return.

**Fair Labor Standards Act.** A federal law that sets minimum hourly wages, regulates overtime, and provides equal pay standards for workers in industries engaged in interstate commerce.

**Federal unemployment taxes.** Taxes levied on employers by the federal government. The taxes collected are used to pay a portion of the costs of the joint federal-state unemployment programs that provide temporary benefits to persons who become unemployed as a result of economic forces beyond their control.

**FICA taxes.** Federal Insurance Contribution Act taxes paid by both employers and employees; otherwise known as Social Security taxes.

**Gross earnings.** The total amount of an employee's salary or wages before any payroll deductions have been subtracted.

**Liabilities.** Obligations resulting from past transactions that require the future payment of assets or the future performance of services.

**Net earnings.** Gross earnings less payroll deductions.

**Note payable.** A liability evidenced by the issuance of a written promise to pay a definite sum of money, usually with interest, on demand or at a definite date in the future.

**Payroll Register.** A multicolumn form used by an employer to assemble and summarize the data needed to prepare the payroll. It contains a listing of each employee's gross earnings, deductions, and net earnings for a given payroll period.

**Payroll taxes.** Taxes levied on employers based on the gross earnings (with established annual limits) of their employees.

**State unemployment taxes.** Taxes levied on employers and in a few states on the employee by state governments. The taxes collected are used to pay temporary benefits to persons who become unemployed as a result of economic forces beyond their control.

**Unearned revenues.** Noncash obligations resulting from amounts received before they have been earned. Sometimes called *deferred revenues.*

**Wage and Tax Statement (Form W-2).** A form prepared by the employer and given to every employee and the Social Security Administration. The form shows the employee's gross earnings for the calendar year, the earnings subject to FICA tax, the federal and state income taxes withheld, and the FICA taxes withheld.

**Wage-bracket withholding table.** A table that is provided by the government and is used to determine the amount of federal income tax to withhold from the gross earnings of employees.

**Warranty.** A promise made by a seller or manufacturer to remedy a malfunctioning or defective product within a specified period of time after acquisition.

## REVIEW QUESTIONS

1. Describe the three characteristics involved in the definition of a liability. [LO1a]
2. Describe the three stated or implied objectives of accounting for liabilities. [LO1b]
3. What are current liabilities? [LO1c]
4. Name seven current liabilities that have definite maturity values. [LO2a]
5. Give three reasons why notes payable are issued. [LO2a]
6. Explain why money borrowed when the interest is deducted in advance causes a higher effective annual interest rate on the borrowed money. [LO2a]
7. Under what circumstances would a portion of long-term debt be classified as a current liability? [LO2a]
8. Differentiate between accrued liabilities and other current liabilities. [LO2a]
9. Why are unearned revenues referred to as noncash obligations? [LO2a]
10. Why is Income Tax Payable an estimated liability? [LO2b]
11. How are the Income Tax Expense account and the Income Tax Payable account reported in the financial statements? [LO2b]
12. What causes warranty obligations to occur? [LO2b]
13. Explain how product warranty liability is calculated. [LO2b]
14. What is a contingent liability and what causes a contingent liability to arise? [LO1d,2b]
15. Name and describe the three categories of likelihood that pertain to a decision as to whether a specific future event will occur. [LO1d,2b]
16. Describe the accounting treatment recommended for each category of likelihood referred to in Question 15. [LO1d,2b]
17. Describe three things a payroll system should be designed to accomplish. [LO1e]
18. Compare and contrast the four duties or functions that should be separated to achieve strong internal accounting control in a payroll system. [LO1e]
19. Differentiate between salaries and wages. [LO1e]
20. What provisions of the Fair Labor Standards Act are important in the determination of gross earnings? [LO1e,2c]

21. Identify deductions from gross earnings that are required by law. [LO1e,2c]
22. Identify deductions from gross earnings often authorized by the employee. [LO1e,2c]
23. Define *Payroll Register* and describe its contents. [LO1f]
24. Describe the contents of an Employee Earnings Record. [LO1f]
25. Describe the contents of a Wage and Tax Statement. [LO1f]
26. Name three major payroll taxes that an employer must pay. [LO2e]
27. Describe the contents of an Employer's Quarterly Federal Tax Return and an Employer's Annual Federal Unemployment Tax Return. [LO2e]

## ANALYTICAL QUESTIONS

28. Why is it important to separate current and long-term liabilities on the balance sheet? [LO1c]
29. What is the rationale for classifying revenue received in advance as a liability? [LO2a]
30. Comment on the following statement: "When borrowing money on a note, it makes no difference to our company if the bank deducts the interest when the money is borrowed or if the interest must be paid at the time that the note matures." [LO2a]
31. Comment on the following statement: "When we offer a warranty on the product we sell, there is no need to recognize a liability because we don't know who or how many customers will use the warranty." [LO2b]
32. Businesses operate on many contingencies. How can you tell whether a contingency should be recorded in the accounts? [LO1d,2b]
33. Comment on the following statement: "How can I prevent a dishonest employee in the payroll department from putting a fictitious name or the name of a former employee in the Payroll Register, preparing a paycheck to the order of that name, and cashing it?" [LO1e]

## IMPACT ANALYSIS QUESTIONS

*For each error described, indicate whether it would overstate [O], understate [U], or not affect [N] the specified key figures.*

34. Beta Company incurred an expense on December 26, 19X6. No entry was made to record this transaction until January 2, 19X7. [LO2a]

    ______ Assets ______ Net Income
    ______ Liabilities ______ Owner's Equity

35. Zeta Company did not record a machine repair bill received on December 31, 19X6. The repairs were made in December and the bill should have been recorded. [LO2a]

    ______ Assets ______ Net Income
    ______ Liabilities ______ Owner's Equity

36. When estimating income tax expense for the year 19X6, the company multiplied its tax rate times $50,000 instead of times $40,000, the correct amount of its taxable income. [LO2b]

    ______ Assets ______ Expenses
    ______ Liabilities ______ Net Income

37. When making out the payroll for the current period, the employer calculated the net pay for one of its employees by incorrectly withholding federal income taxes based on four exemptions rather than three. The incorrect amount was used when the check was prepared; therefore the amount paid to the employee was incorrect. [LO2c]

    ______ Assets ______ Expenses
    ______ Liabilities ______ Net Income

38. When calculating payroll tax expenses for the year 19X7, the company omitted Federal Unemployment Tax Expense. [LO2e]

_______ Assets _______ Expenses
_______ Liabilities _______ Net Income

## EXERCISES

EXERCISE 12–1 *(Prepare Journal Entries for an Interest-Bearing Note Payable)* On June 1 Leeds Company borrowed $15,000 from its bank by signing a three-month, 10% note for $15,000.

Required:

1. Prepare journal entries to record the issuance of the note and the payment of the note on its maturity date. Leeds's year ends on December 31.
2. Assume that the note was issued on November 1 instead of June 1. Prepare journal entries to record the issuance of the note, the year-end interest accrual, and the payment of the note on its maturity date. [LO2a]

EXERCISE 12–2 *(Prepare Journal Entries for a Discounted Note Payable)* On November 1 Hamilton Company borrowed money by issuing a $15,000, three-month note payable to its bank. The bank deducted interest at 10% and gave Hamilton the proceeds on the same day.

Required:

1. Prepare journal entries to record the issuance of the note, the year-end interest accrual (the company's year ends on December 31), and the payment of the note on its maturity date.
2. Compute the effective interest rate paid on the borrowed money. [LO2a]

EXERCISE 12–3 *(Prepare Journal Entries for Notes Issued to Purchase Inventory)* On October 1 Jay Company signed a six-month note for $28,600 (which is also the amount due at maturity) and gave it to Zerron Company. The note, plus a cash down payment of $5,000, was used to acquire merchandise having a cash purchase price of $30,000.

Required:

1. Prepare the journal entries made by Jay Company on October 1 and December 31 of the current year. Jay Company's year ends on December 31.
2. Prepare the journal entry or entries made by Jay Company on April 1 of the following year, the day on which the note must be paid. (Assume the note was paid.) [LO2a]

EXERCISE 12–4 *(Compute and Prepare Journal Entry for Sales and Excise Taxes)* Clearview Company received $960,940 from cash sales made to customers during January. The amount includes a state sales tax of 6% and a federal excise tax of 9%.

Required:

1. Determine the amount of sales revenue to be reported on the sales described above.
2. Prepare a journal entry to record in aggregate the January sales. [LO2a]

EXERCISE 12–5 *(Estimate Product Warranty Liability)* Goodbe Company sells electric mixers. Each mixer carries an unconditional warranty providing for free replacement in case of product failure during the ninety days following the date of sale. Based on past experience and other factors, Goodbe estimates that 3% of the mixers sold during 19X7 will have to be replaced and that the average cost of replacement will be $20 per unit. During January 19X7 Goodbe sold 15,000 mixers, and 300 were later replaced under the terms of the warranty.

Required:

1. Prepare a journal entry dated January 31 to record the estimated liability for product warranties based on January's sales.
2. Prepare a journal entry dated March 31 to record the cost of the mixers replaced under the warranty up to this point in time. [LO2b]

EXERCISE 12–6 *(Determine Gross and Net Earnings)* Ann Wren, a receptionist, is paid at the rate of $8 per hour. Overtime pay is at one and one-half times her regular hourly rate. Ann worked forty-four hours this week. Her gross earnings prior to this week were $4,600. Ann is married and claims four withholding allowances on her Form W-4. Withholdings for FICA taxes and federal income taxes are the only amounts deducted when determining the amount of her paycheck.

Required:
Compute the following amounts for Ann's current weekly wages:

1. Regular earnings
2. Overtime earnings
3. Gross earnings
4. FICA taxes
5. Federal income tax withheld (use Wage-Bracket Withholding Table in Exhibit 12–2)
6. Net earnings [LO2c]

EXERCISE 12–7 *(Prepare Journal Entries for Payroll)* For the week ended May 15, Sutton Company's Payroll Register shows salaries and gross wages of $120,000. Of this amount, $8,000 is not subject to FICA taxes and $70,000 is not subject to federal and state unemployment taxes. The company withheld $17,500 of federal income taxes, $3,600 of state income taxes, $2,900 for medical insurance premiums, and $800 for union dues from the employees' payroll checks. The employees have a FICA tax rate of 7% and are not subject to state unemployment taxes. The company's applicable tax rates are: FICA tax, 7%; state unemployment tax, 2.7%; and federal unemployment tax, .8%.

Required:

1. Prepare a journal entry to record the payroll for the week ended May 15. Employees are paid on May 17.
2. Prepare a journal entry to record the employer's payroll tax expense. [LO1f,2c,2d,2e]

EXERCISE 12–8 *(Determine Payroll Amounts and Make the Payroll Journal Entry)* Wally Arthur, a steel worker, earns $10 per hour. In accordance with the union contract, *overtime* is defined as hours worked in excess of forty per week and is paid at one and one-half times the regular hourly rate. In addition, any work on Sundays or holidays is paid at twice the regular rate.

For the week just ended, Wally worked a total of fifty-two hours, including four on a holiday. His paycheck (net pay) was $455.60. Deductions from his gross earnings were as follows: federal income taxes; FICA tax (on the full amount), 7%; medical insurance premiums, $10.00; and union dues, $4.00.

Required:

1. Compute the following amounts for Wally's current weekly wages:
   a. Gross earnings
   b. FICA tax deduction
   c. Federal income tax deduction
2. Prepare a journal entry to record the payroll and payroll deduction assuming Wally's paycheck will be drawn two days after the pay period ends. [LO1f,2c,2d]

## PROBLEMS

PROBLEM 12–1 *(Prepare Journal Entries for Notes Issued in Exchange for a Machine)* On August 1, 19X6, Langley Company purchased a machine at a cost of $60,000. The company paid $20,000 in cash as a down payment and gave a 12%, six-month note payable for the balance. The company's year ends on December 31.

Required:

1. Prepare the journal entry to record the purchase of the machine on August 1, 19X6.
2. Prepare the journal entry to record the accrual of interest expense on December 31, 19X6.
3. Prepare the journal entry to record payment of the note on its maturity date, February 1, 19X7. [LO2a]

PROBLEM 12–2 *(Prepare Journal Entries and Balance Sheet Section for Notes Payable Transactions)* Tactic Company had the following transactions during the fiscal year ended December 31:

| | |
|---|---|
| May 1 | Borrowed money from Local Bank by issuing a $40,000, nine-month note payable. The bank deducted interest at 12% and gave the company the proceeds on the same day. |
| June 15 | Issued a $6,000 note to Richards Company in settlement of an overdue account payable with that firm for that amount. The note was for one month due on July 15 and carried an interest rate of 10%. |
| July 1 | Paid $10,000 cash and issued a $50,000 note to Georgia Supply for the purchase of equipment costing $60,000. The note was due in 120 days and carried an interest rate of 15%. |
| July 15 | The note to Richards Company was paid in full. |
| Sept. 1 | Issued a six-month note to Kingsley Company for $20,200, which is the amount due at the note's maturity date. The note plus a cash down payment of $6,000 was used to acquire equipment having a cash purchase price of $25,000. |
| Oct. 29 | The note to Georgia Supply was paid in full. |

Required:

1. Prepare journal entries to record the above transactions.
2. Prepare adjusting entries to record the accrual of interest expense on December 31.
3. Prepare the current liability section of Tactic Company's balance sheet as of December 31. Assume that the only other current liability that the company had on this date was accounts payable of $82,700. [LO2a]

PROBLEM 12–3 *(Calculate and Prepare Journal Entry for Sales and Excise Taxes)* During January 19X6 Singer Company recorded sales of $192,100. The procedure used by Singer when recording sales is to include in the sales figure all amounts related to sales taxes and excise taxes. By analyzing the Sales account for January, the following was determined:

a. One-half of sales was subject to both a 5% sales tax and an 8% excise tax.
b. The balance of sales was not subject to either sales tax or excise tax.

Required:

1. Calculate the amount of sales revenue to be reported for January 19X6, and determine the appropriate amount to be reported as liabilities for sales taxes and for excise taxes.
2. Prepare a journal entry to correct the balance in the Sales account. [LO2a]

PROBLEM 12–4 *(Make Computations and Prepare Journal Entries for Property Tax)* Gramacy Company prepares monthly financial statements and ends its fiscal year on October 31. The company owns an office complex in Southfield, a city where taxes are assessed on February 3 of each year with payment due by March 31. The city's fiscal year ends five months after the assessment date on June 30. For the city tax year ending June 30, 19X6, Gramacy paid $18,000 in property taxes.

Required:

1. Determine the amount of property tax expense that should be recorded for July 19X6. Property taxes for the coming year are expected to increase by 8%.
2. Assume that the tax bill received on February 15, 19X7, was for $19,800 and that the estimate made in July was used to record property tax entries through January 31 of the current year (seven consecutive months). Prepare a journal entry for property tax

expense on February 28, 19X7. The company treats small differences between estimated and actual property taxes as expenses in the month in which the difference is known.

3. Prepare the journal entry to record the property tax payment on March 31, 19X7. [LO2a]

PROBLEM 12–5 *(Prepare Journal Entries and Make Computations for Product Warranty Transactions)* E-Z Muffler Company, experiencing intense competition for its product, has decided to offer a one-year free repair or replacement warranty on all new mufflers sold. In the first three months after the warranty offer, the following data were compiled.

| | JANUARY | FEBRUARY | MARCH |
|---|---|---|---|
| Sales of mufflers in dollars | $9,000 | $8,600 | $12,000 |
| Estimated repair and replacement costs as a percentage of sales dollars | 5% | 5% | 5% |
| Actual cost of warranty claims | $410 | $440 | $575 |

Required:

1. Assuming financial statements were prepared at the end of each month, prepare journal entries to recognize the estimated product warranty expense for each of the first three months.
2. Prepare the journal entry to record the actual cost of repair and replacement services under the warranty for March. Assume that the costs incurred were: replacement mufflers and parts (taken from inventory), $340; labor (paid in cash), $235.
3. Determine the balance in the Product Warranty Liability account as of March 31. Why is there a balance in the account? [LO2b]

PROBLEM 12–6 *(Determine and Record Gross and Net Earnings)* Amy Stewart, a restaurant manager, earns $10 per hour. She is paid an overtime rate of one and one-half times her regular pay rate for hours worked in excess of forty from Monday through Friday, and twice her regular pay rate for hours worked on the weekend or holidays. Her time sheet for the week just ended shows that she worked forty-nine hours as follows:

| | |
|---|---|
| Monday through Friday | 44 hours (including 4 hours of overtime on Friday) |
| Saturday | 5 hours (6 P.M. until 11 P.M.) |

Her payroll deductions are as follows:

| | |
|---|---|
| Federal income tax | $66.50 |
| State income tax | 13.10 |
| FICA tax (all wages applicable at 7%) | |
| Medical insurance premiums | 8.20 |

Required:

1. Calculate Amy Stewart's gross and net earnings for the week just ended.
2. Prepare a journal entry to record the payroll and payroll deductions assuming Amy is not paid until Wednesday of the following week. [LO2c,2d]

PROBLEM 12–7 *(Prepare Payroll Journal Entries)* The payroll records of Grant Company for the first week of February showed total salaries earned by employees of $26,000. This total was divided into categories and classified as follows:

| | |
|---|---|
| Sales salaries | $16,000 |
| Administrative salaries | 8,000 |
| Office salaries | 2,000 |

The amounts withheld from the employees' pay consisted of FICA taxes, 7%; federal income taxes, $3,900; state income taxes, $780; and group medical insurance premiums, $310.

Required:

1. Prepare a journal entry to record the payroll. Assume that all salaries are subject to FICA taxes and that employees are paid on the day the payroll is recorded.
2. Prepare a journal entry to record the employer's payroll tax expense. Assume that the employer's tax rates are as follows: FICA tax, 7%; state unemployment tax, 2.7%; and federal unemployment tax, .8%. The entire payroll is subject to these taxes.
3. Determine the company's total payroll expense for the first week of February.

[LO1f,2c,2d,2e]

PROBLEM 12–8 *(Prepare a Payroll Register and Payroll Journal Entries)* Royal Company has five employees. Certain payroll data for the week ending October 15 are presented below.

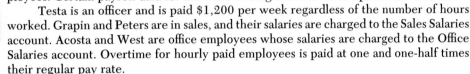

Testa is an officer and is paid $1,200 per week regardless of the number of hours worked. Grapin and Peters are in sales, and their salaries are charged to the Sales Salaries account. Acosta and West are office employees whose salaries are charged to the Office Salaries account. Overtime for hourly paid employees is paid at one and one-half times their regular pay rate.

| EMPLOYEE | HOURS WORKED Reg | OT | PAY RATE | FEDERAL INCOME TAXES | STATE INCOME TAXES | GROUP MEDICAL INSURANCE | CUMULATIVE EARNINGS TO END OF PRIOR WEEK |
|---|---|---|---|---|---|---|---|
| I. Acosta | 40 | 2 | $6.50 | $31.50 | $5.50 | $9.00 | $ 4,200 |
| B. Grapin | 40 | 4 | 8.00 | 49.00 | 7.00 | 9.00 | 12,400 |
| F. Peters | 40 | 0 | 9.00 | 41.70 | 6.00 | 8.00 | 6,900 |
| R. Testa | 40 | 0 | Salary | 85.20 | 10.00 | 9.00 | 39,600 |
| D. West | 40 | 5 | 7.00 | 43.80 | 6.50 | 8.00 | 9,300 |

The FICA tax rate is 7% for employees and 7% for employers on each employee's first $40,000 of gross earnings. The unemployment tax rates are 2.7% for the state and 0.8% for the federal, both levied on the employer only and both based on each employee's first $7,000 of gross earnings.

Required:

From the information given, prepare the following:

1. A payroll register for the week ending October 15.
2. A journal entry to record the payroll for this period.
3. A journal entry to record the employer's payroll tax expense for this period.

[LO1f,2c,2d,2e]

PROBLEM 12–9 *(Make Calculations and Prepare Payroll Journal Entries)* Information pertaining to the payroll of Farley Company for the week ending September 28 was compiled and is presented below.

| EMPLOYEE | GROSS EARNINGS | FEDERAL INCOME TAXES | STATE INCOME TAXES | MEDICAL INSURANCE DEDUCTION | UNION DUES DEDUCTED | CUMULATIVE EARNINGS TO END OF PRIOR WEEK |
|---|---|---|---|---|---|---|
| D. Barry | $300 | $ 36 | $ 9 | $ 8 | $4 | $11,900 |
| H. Geiss | 500 | 60 | 15 | 10 | 4 | 5,500 |
| M. Rahn | 550 | 112 | 28 | 10 | 5 | 22,300 |
| E. Suarez | 1,050 | 158 | 36 | 12 | 5 | 39,900 |
| P. Zanis | 400 | 59 | 14 | 8 | 4 | 4,660 |

The gross earnings for E. Suarez are charged to the Administrative Salaries account. Geiss and Zanis have their gross earnings charged to the Sales Salaries account, and Barry and Rahn have their gross earnings charged to the Office Salaries account.

The FICA tax rate is 7% for employees and 7% for employers based on the first $40,000 earned by each employee. The state unemployment tax rate is 2.7%, and the federal unemployment tax rate is 0.8%, each of which is applied to each employee's first $7,000 of gross earnings. Unemployment taxes are levied only on the employer.

Required:

1. Calculate the FICA tax withheld and determine the net pay for each employee.
2. Prepare a journal entry to record the payroll.
3. Prepare a journal entry to record the employer's payroll tax expense.

[LO1f,2c,2d,2e]

PROBLEM 12–10 *(Prepare Payroll Journal Entries and Balance Sheet Presentation of Payroll Liabilities)* Edison Company has monthly pay periods and draws checks to pay employees on the first day of the following month. During September of the current year, the company's employees earned salaries and wages totaling $136,000, classified as follows: sales personnel, 70% of the total; office personnel, 20% of the total; and officers, $13,600. FICA tax withheld from employees is at a 7% rate on each employee's first $40,000 of gross earnings. At the end of September all the employees have cumulative gross earnings below the $40,000 taxable limit except two officers. These officers reached the gross earnings limit during August and together earned $10,600 during September. Other deductions from the September payroll were as follows:

| | |
|---|---:|
| Federal income taxes | $20,400 |
| State income taxes | 3,200 |
| Group medical insurance | 1,660 |
| Credit Union savings | 4,100 |

Required:

1. Prepare a journal entry to record September's payroll.
2. Prepare a journal entry to record the employer's payroll tax expense. The employer's FICA tax rate is 7%. The state unemployment tax rate is 2.7%, and the federal unemployment tax rate is 0.8%, each of which is levied on the employer only and is based on each employee's first $7,000 of gross earnings. Twenty-five percent of September's gross earnings is subject to unemployment taxes.
3. Prepare the current liability section of Edison Company's balance sheet as of September 30. Assume that the only other current liability that the company had on this date was accounts payable of $82,700. [LO1f,2c,2d,2e]

## ALTERNATE PROBLEMS

PROBLEM 12–1A *(Prepare Journal Entries and Balance Sheet Section for Notes Payable Transactions)* (Alternate to Problem 12–2) Franklin Company had the following transactions during the fiscal year ended September 30:

| | |
|---|---|
| Jan. 15 | Purchased equipment costing $50,000 from Hartley Supply. Paid 20% down and gave a 12% note due May 15 for the balance. |
| Feb. 1 | Issued an $8,000 note to A. Singer in settlement of an overdue account payable for that same amount. The note is due in two months with interest at 9%. |
| March 15 | Borrowed $25,000 at 10% from City Bank. The note is due one year from today. The bank deducted the interest and gave Franklin the proceeds. |

| | | |
|---|---|---|
| April | 1 | The note to A. Singer was paid in full. |
| May | 1 | Issued a six-month note to Zeller Company for $15,000, which is the amount due at the note's maturity date. The note plus a cash down payment of $5,000 was used to acquire equipment having a cash purchase price of $19,250. |
| May | 15 | The note to Hartley Supply was paid in full. |

Required:

1. Prepare journal entries to record the above transactions.
2. Prepare adjusting entries to record the accrual of interest expense on September 30.
3. Prepare the current liability section of Franklin Company's balance sheet as of September 30. Assume that the only current liability that the company had on this date was accounts payable of $53,400. [LO2a]

PROBLEM 12–2A *(Calculate and Prepare Journal Entry for Sales and Excise Taxes)* (Alternate to Problem 12–3) During January 19X6 Sower Company recorded sales of $432,225. The procedure used by Sower when recording sales is to include in the sales figure all amounts related to sales taxes and excise taxes. By analyzing the Sales account for January, the following was determined:

a. One-third of sales was subject to both a 6% sales tax and a 7% excise tax.
b. The balance of sales was not subject to either sales tax or excise tax.

Required:

1. Calculate the amount of sales revenue to be reported for January 19X6, and determine the appropriate amount to be reported as liabilities for sales taxes and for excise taxes.
2. Prepare a journal entry to correct the balance in the Sales account. [LO2a]

PROBLEM 12–3A *(Make Computations and Prepare Journal Entries for Property Tax)* (Alternate to Problem 12–4) Garmony Company prepares monthly financial statements and ends its fiscal year on November 30. The company owns a building in Northfield, a city where taxes are assessed on February 3 of each year with payment due by March 31. The city's fiscal year ends five months after the assessment date on June 30. For the city tax year ending June 30, 19X6, Garmony paid $20,000 in property taxes.

Required:

(All amounts should be rounded to the nearest dollar.)

1. Determine the amount of property tax expense that should be recorded for July 19X6 if property taxes for the coming year are expected to increase by 10%.
2. Assume that the tax bill received on February 15, 19X7, was for $21,700 and that the estimate made in July was used to record property tax entries through January 31 of the current year (seven consecutive months). Prepare a journal entry for property tax expense on February 28, 19X7. The company treats small differences between estimated and actual property taxes as expenses in the month in which the difference is known.
3. Prepare the journal entry to record the property tax payment on March 31, 19X7. [LO2a]

PROBLEM 12–4A *(Prepare Journal Entries and Make Computations for Product Warranty Transactions)* (Alternate to Problem 12–5) A-G Battery Company, experiencing intense competition for its product, has decided to offer a one-year free repair or replacement warranty on all new batteries sold. In the first three months after the warranty offer, the following data were compiled.

| | JANUARY | FEBRUARY | MARCH |
|---|---|---|---|
| Sales of batteries in dollars | $12,000 | $9,800 | $15,000 |
| Estimated repair and replacement costs as a percentage of sales dollars | 6% | 6% | 6% |
| Actual cost of warranty claims | $520 | $630 | $775 |

Required:

1. Assuming financial statements were prepared at the end of each month, prepare journal entries to recognize the estimated product warranty expense for each of the first three months.
2. Prepare the journal entry to record the actual cost of repair and replacement services under the warranty for March. Assume that the costs incurred were: replacement batteries and parts (taken from inventory), $440; labor (paid in cash), $335.
3. Determine the balance in the Product Warranty Liability account as of March 31. Why is there a balance in the account? [LO2b]

PROBLEM 12–5A *(Prepare Payroll Journal Entries)* (Alternate to Problem 12–7) Payroll data for the week ended January 12, compiled for Multa Company, are shown below.

| ITEM | AMOUNT |
|---|---|
| Salaries | $120,000—50% Sales<br>—10% Office<br>—40% Executive |
| FICA taxes: | |
| Employer's contribution | 7.0% |
| Employees' contribution | 7.0% |
| Federal income taxes withheld | $24,600 |
| State income taxes withheld | $2,900 |
| Federal unemployment taxes | 0.8% |
| State unemployment taxes | 2.7% |

On this date no employee has yet exceeded the maximum earnings subject to the applicable taxes.

Required:

Prepare the journal entry to record (a) the weekly payroll, (b) the payroll tax expense, and (c) the payment of net earnings to the employees on January 12. [LO1f,2c,2d,2e]

PROBLEM 12–6A *(Prepare a Payroll Register and Payroll Journal Entries)* (Alternate to Problem 12–8) Ruskin Company has provided the following information pertaining to its weekly payroll, which ended on November 3.

Franco, Kalok, and Lopez are sales personnel. Alston and Kirk are office workers. All employees are paid one and one-half times their regular pay rate for overtime hours worked.

| EMPLOYEE | HOURS WORKED Reg | OT | PAY RATE | FEDERAL INCOME TAXES | STATE INCOME TAXES | GROUP MEDICAID INSURANCE | CUMULATIVE EARNINGS TO END OF PRIOR WEEK |
|---|---|---|---|---|---|---|---|
| G. Alston | 40 | 4 | $6.00 | $30.00 | $6.00 | $3.00 | $ 5,240 |
| M. Franco | 40 | 2 | 8.00 | 32.00 | 6.00 | 3.00 | 13,990 |
| R. Kalok | 40 | 0 | 9.00 | 51.00 | 8.50 | 3.00 | 15,770 |
| B. Kirk | 40 | 5 | 5.00 | 28.00 | 5.50 | 3.00 | 6,900 |
| E. Lopez | 40 | 6 | 7.00 | 36.00 | 7.00 | 3.00 | 12,680 |

The FICA taxes are levied on employees at a rate of 7% and on employers at a rate of 7% based on each employee's first $40,000 of gross earnings. The state unemployment tax rate is 2.7% (levied on employers only), and the federal unemployment tax rate is 0.8% based on each employee's first $7,000 of gross earnings.

Required:

From the information given, prepare the following:

1. A payroll register for the week ending November 3.
2. A journal entry to record the payroll for this period.
3. A journal entry to record the employer's payroll tax expense for this period.

[LO1f,2c,2d,2e]

# 13 Partnerships

## Learning Objectives

When you complete this chapter you will be able to

1. Answer the following questions:
   a. What are a partnership's purposes, major characteristics, and advantages and disadvantages?
   b. What are the unique aspects of accounting for partnerships?
2. Perform the following accounting functions:
   a. Prepare journal entries for the formation of a partnership.
   b. Prepare a schedule showing how partnership income is divided among the partners according to the provisions of the partnership agreement.
   c. Prepare a statement of partners' capital.
   d. Prepare journal entries for a person's admittance to a partnership.
   e. Prepare journal entries for a person's withdrawal from a partnership.
   f. Compute the distribution of assets to the partners and prepare journal entries required when a partnership is liquidated.

Partnership accounting, like all accounting, is designed to provide information needed by decision makers, particularly the partners themselves. For example, partners might ask such practical questions as the following:

> How do I get money out of this partnership?
>
> Are there any limitations on the amount of money I can take out?
>
> If we want to admit a new partner, how do we do it? How do the accounting data help us in determining how to admit a new partner—or release a current one?

In this chapter we will see how partnership accounting answers such questions.

The **Uniform Partnership Act,** which has been adopted by most states, defines **partnership** as "an association of two or more persons to carry on as co-owners of a business for profit."

*1a. People form partnerships to gain advantages from utilizing combined capital, skills, and experience*

People join together to form partnerships for a number of reasons. Generally they are formed to obtain the advantage of combining the capital resources, managerial skills, and experience of the partners in an effort to achieve a common business goal. Many businesses operating in the service industry are organized as partnerships. For example, physicians, dentists, attorneys, and accountants often practice their profession as partners in a partnership. Partnerships can vary in size from organizations with two partners to those (like large international accounting firms) with over one thousand partners.

Before discussing partnership accounting, we need to learn about the partnership form of business organization by first examining some of its major characteristics.

## CHARACTERISTICS OF A PARTNERSHIP

Partnerships have several distinctive characteristics that have important accounting implications. These characteristics are discussed below.

*1a. Distinctive characteristics of partnerships are listed here*

**EASE OF FORMATION** Like sole proprietorships, which we have been discussing up to this point in the text, partnerships are relatively easy to form. No legal permissions or approvals are required. All that is needed is an agreement between two or more persons to start a business with the object of earning a profit. The agreement, which constitutes a contract, should specify all the matters that if not clearly expressed could result in subsequent disputes. Although the agreement need not be in writing to be binding on the partner, it is usually preferable that it be written so as to have a document showing exactly what the partners have agreed to.

**VOLUNTARY ASSOCIATION** A partnership is a voluntary association of individuals into which another person cannot be forced. Each partner is legally responsible for the business acts of his or her partners when these acts are within the scope of the partnership. For this and other reasons it is important that an individual be able to select the people who will join together as partners in a partnership.

**NO SEPARATE LEGAL ENTITY** A partnership is not a legal entity in itself. The partners are themselves the entities. Each partner is personally liable for the debts of the partnership. Furthermore, a partnership is not taxed as a separate entity. Instead its net income or net loss is divided among the individual partners per agreement and is reported on their individual tax returns.

UNLIMITED LIABILITY The characteristic of a partnership called **unlimited liability** makes each partner personally liable to creditors for all debts incurred by the partnership. This means that if the creditors of the partnership cannot be paid from the partnership's assets, they may seek to have their claim satisfied from the personal assets of the individual partners. This is the unlimited liability characteristic of a partnership. That is, a partner's liability for partnership debts is not limited to the amount he or she has invested in the partnership.

LIMITED LIFE A partnership has a **limited life.** A partnership dissolves with any change in the personnel of its membership. For example, a partnership dissolves when (1) a partner withdraws, (2) a partner goes bankrupt, (3) a partner is incapacitated, (4) a partner dies. Furthermore, a partnership will be dissolved when the period specified in the agreement expires or when the objective specified in the agreement has been achieved. Similarly, the admission of a new partner dissolves the old partnership. In some of these cases, the partnership's business activity stops immediately and the partnership ceases to exist. In other cases, the continuing partners form a new partnership and continue to operate without any noticeable interruption of business activity.

MUTUAL AGENCY Normally, there is **mutual agency** in a partnership in that every partner is an agent for the partnership and for all the other partners. Thus when conducting business, a partner represents the other partners and can bind them to any contract when acting within the apparent scope of the business. For example, a partner in a merchandising firm can bind the partnership to contracts to buy and sell merchandise, lease a building, acquire equipment, or hire employees. These are activities well within the scope of business conducted by a merchandising firm. Activities outside the scope of the partnership require authorization by all partners. For example, a partner in a law firm, acting alone, could not bind his or her partners to a contract to sell land owned by the partnership.

CO-OWNERSHIP OF PARTNERSHIP PROPERTY AND INCOME In accordance with the Uniform Partnership Act, partners are co-owners of a business entity. When partners invest assets in a partnership, they do not retain any personal right to them. The assets invested become the property of all partners jointly. For example, if partner A invests in a partnership by contributing his or her personal automobile, the automobile becomes an asset of the partnership and is owned jointly by all the partners in the firm. Similarly, a partnership's net income or net loss belongs to all the partners and is distributed among them according to their agreement.

## PARTNERSHIP ADVANTAGES AND DISADVANTAGES

*1a. Partnerships offer certain advantages and disadvantages when compared with sole proprietorships and corporations*

A major advantage of a partnership (as contrasted with a sole proprietorship) is that it provides the opportunity to utilize the combined managerial skills and experience of the individual partners. A partnership is easier and less costly to organize than a corporation. Generally, it is not subject to as much government regulation as corporations, nor is it subject to the tax burden of a corporation. Furthermore, partners have more freedom to act because they do not have to report to stockholders or a corporate board of directors.

Limited life, unlimited liability, and mutual agency do cause certain problems, however. If the business needs a large amount of invested capital, the unlimited-liability aspect of a partnership could make it difficult to raise the necessary funds. Stockholders of a corporation have at risk only the amount that they invest, whereas the personal assets of a partner can be used to settle the claims of creditors. Transferring an ownership interest in a partnership is difficult, and the potential for incurring extensive personal liability resulting from the acts of other partners is always a threat.

## THE PARTNERSHIP CONTRACT

As mentioned earlier, a partnership can be formed by an oral agreement. It is, however, good business practice to have a written document that sets forth the terms under which the partners will conduct partnership business. The partners' written agreement is called the **partnership contract** or the **articles of partnership** and should include such important items as the following:

Partnership name and location of the business.

Nature and purpose of the business.

Names of the partners and the rights and duties of each partner.

Manner in which profits or losses will be shared.

Amount initially invested by each partner and the way in which noncash assets are to be valued. Provisions concerning future investment.

Amount or provision for limitations on the amount of assets that each partner is allowed to withdraw.

A statement detailing the conditions under which new partners are admitted to the partnership.

A statement detailing the conditions under which old partners are allowed to withdraw.

Authority of each partner in contract situations.

Procedures to be followed in the event of a dispute among the partners.

A statement detailing how the partnership and the partners are affected by the death of a partner.

Procedures to be followed when the partnership is dissolved.

A statement specifying who will maintain the company's financial records, where they will be kept, and when financial statements will be prepared and made available to the partners.

## UNIQUE ASPECTS OF ACCOUNTING FOR PARTNERSHIPS

*1b. The unique aspects of accounting for partnerships involve transactions that affect owner's equity*

Accounting for a partnership is essentially the same as accounting for a sole proprietorship. This involves using the same procedures, techniques, and principles discussed in preceding chapters. Journals and schedules are used for the same purposes and with little, if any, alteration. There is, however, a major difference in accounting for owner's equity. Ownership interests in a partnership belong to two or more partners. These interests are not always equal because both the amounts invested and the amounts withdrawn by each partner may vary. Furthermore, we will see that the profit or loss reported each period is divided among the partners in accordance with the partnership agreement, which may result in an unequal distribution among partners. Because the ownership interest of each partner can vary, a separate capital account and separate drawings account is maintained for each partner. A partner's *capital* account is credited when assets are *invested* in the partnership by that partner. A partner's *drawings* account is debited when assets are *withdrawn* from the partnership by that partner. At the end of the accounting period, the balance in each partner's drawings account is closed to his or her capital account. These are the same procedures followed in accounting for the capital transactions of a single proprietor—the only difference is that more than one capital account and more than one drawings account are needed. Most transactions for a partnership are handled the same as they are for a single proprietorship. The unique aspects of partnership accounting involve

The formation of a partnership
The manner in which partnership net income or loss is divided
Partnership financial statements
The admittance and withdrawal of a partner
The death of a partner
Partnership liquidation

These aspects of accounting for partnerships are discussed in the rest of this chapter.

## THE FORMATION OF A PARTNERSHIP

Accounting for partnerships begins when the partners (owners) invest their personal assets in the business. When this happens, a journal entry is made to record the investment of each partner in the partnership. The various assets contributed by a partner are *debited* to the proper asset accounts. If the partner's liabilities are assumed by the partnership, the appropriate liability accounts are *credited.* The journal entry is completed by *crediting* the partner's capital account for the net amount (the difference between the assets contributed and the liabilities assumed). When assets other than cash are invested, the partners must agree on their value. The value of noncash assets is usually their fair market value on the date they are transferred to the partnership.

To illustrate, assume that R. Blake and J. Max, sole owners of competing businesses, agree to combine their companies and form a partnership. The partners are to contribute all the assets of their previous business. They also agree that the partnership is to assume the liabilities of the separate businesses. The amounts of noncash assets represent their fair market value as agreed to by the partners. The journal entry to record the assets contributed and the liabilities transferred to the partnership by R. Blake is as follows:

| | | | |
|---|---|---|---|
| Oct. 1 | Cash | 8,200 | |
| | Accounts Receivable | 17,600 | |
| | Merchandise Inventory | 21,500 | |
| | Equipment | 35,000 | |
| | Allowance for Uncollectible Accounts | | 400 |
| | Accounts Payable | | 11,900 |
| | R. Blake, Capital | | 70,000 |
| | To record investment of R. Blake | | |

Note that receivables contributed to the partnership are recorded at their face amount, with a credit to a contra account for accounts whose future collectibility is uncertain. The agreed-upon amount for the equipment represents its fair market value and acquisition cost to the partnership. This amount may differ from the balances appearing in the accounts of Blake's single proprietorship on the day the partnership was formed. For example, the equipment may have cost

Blake $55,000, and depreciation of $18,000 may have been recorded up to date. However, because the fair market value of the equipment is $35,000 on the day the partnership is formed, that figure, not the asset's book value of $37,000, is used to record Blake's investment of equipment in the partnership.

To provide another illustration, assume that E. Lake and R. Grace agree to form a partnership on April 1, 19X8. Lake will contribute assets with the following agreed-upon values: accounts receivable, $6,000 (all deemed collectible); inventory, $24,000; supplies; $2,000; and equipment, $40,000. The partnership will also assume Lake's liability for accounts payable totaling $12,000. Grace will invest cash of $25,000 and a vehicle having an agreed-upon fair market value of $15,000.

*2a. An entry is made to record initial investments of partners*

The journal entries that record the initial investments of Lake and Grace are as follows:

| | | | |
|---|---|---|---|
| April 1 | Accounts Receivable | 6,000 | |
| | Inventory | 24,000 | |
| | Supplies | 2,000 | |
| | Equipment | 40,000 | |
| | Accounts Payable | | 12,000 |
| | E. Lake, Capital | | 60,000 |
| | To record investment of E. Lake | | |
| April 1 | Cash | 25,000 | |
| | Vehicle | 15,000 | |
| | R. Grace | | 40,000 |
| | To record investment of R. Grace | | |

## DIVISION OF PARTNERSHIP NET INCOME OR NET LOSS

Partnership net income can be divided in any way agreed upon by the partners. If all partners provide equal services and contribute equal amounts of capital, each one's share of net income (or loss) might be the same. In most partnerships, however, the value of services provided by the partners varies. Furthermore, partners sometimes have unequal capital investments in the partnership. Most partnership agreements contain provisions that recognize differences in the services performed by each partner and in the amounts of capital invested by each partner when sharing partnership net income or loss. If the services of one partner are much more valuable to the partnership than those of another, the differences can be recognized by providing allowances for salaries. Partnership salaries are simply a means to divide partnership income in an equitable manner; they are not salaries in a legal sense. Partners are the owners of the partnership, not its employees. Differences in capital invested can also be recognized by allowing interest on capital account balances. Partners invest in the partnership to earn a return in the form of income, not for interest. Thus when interest is said to be allowed on capital invested, it is simply another way to achieve an equitable division of partnership income and is not the same as interest paid on borrowed money.

There are several ways for partners to share partnership income (or losses). Some of the more common ways are

Based on an agreed-upon ratio
Based on the ratio of capital account balances

Based on salary allowances to partners, with remaining net income or loss divided by an agreed-upon ratio

Based on interest allowances to partners, with remaining net income or loss divided by an agreed-upon ratio

Based on both salary and interest allowances to partners, with remaining net income or loss divided by an agreed-upon ratio

Let us now look at how each of these methods works.

## An Agreed-Upon Ratio

If the partnership agreement is silent on the matter of how net income (or losses) should be divided among the partners, the law provides that income and losses are to be shared equally. Any ratio other than equal must be stated in the agreement. Ratios are established in order to recognize and reward differences in services performed and in capital contributed. For example, it may be appropriate to establish (by agreement) income-sharing ratios of 50%, 30%, and 20% for a three-person partnership. In any case, it is crucial that partnership net income be divided among the partners in exact accordance with their partnership agreement.

*2b. Partnership income may be divided according to an agreed-upon ratio*

To illustrate the division of partnership net income based on an agreed-upon ratio, assume that the TW Partnership has a net income of $70,000 at the end of its first year of operations. Assume also that 70% of the net income goes to Bill Tucker and 30% to Kim Ward, both of whom are partners in the firm.

The computation of each partner's share of the net income and the journal entry to record the division of the net income are as follows:

| DIVISION OF NET INCOME | |
|---|---|
| Bill Tucker ($70,000 × .70) | $49,000 |
| Kim Ward ($70,000 × .30) | 21,000 |
| Net Income | $70,000 |

| | | | |
|---|---|---|---|
| Dec. 31 | Income Summary | 70,000 | |
| | Tucker, Capital | | 49,000 |
| | Ward, Capital | | 21,000 |
| | To close the income summary account and divide partnership net income according to the agreement | | |

Partnership losses are also divided in the same 70 : 30 ratio unless there is a separate loss provision contained within the partnership agreement.

## Based on the Ratio of Capital Account Balances

For some businesses, net income is closely related to the amount of money invested in the business. When this is the case, a division of that net income based on the ratio of the partners' capital account balances may provide the fairest method of sharing the income. To illustrate using the TW Partnership data, the net income might be divided based on either the partners' beginning of the year or the average capital account balances.

The partners' capital and drawings accounts as they appeared at the end of the first year, before the $70,000 of partnership net income had been divided, are shown below.

| BILL TUCKER, CAPITAL | | | |
|---|---|---|---|
| | | Jan. 1 | 120,000 |
| | | April 1 | 30,000 |

| KIM WARD, CAPITAL | | | |
|---|---|---|---|
| | | Jan. 1 | 80,000 |

| BILL TUCKER, DRAWINGS | | | |
|---|---|---|---|
| July 1 | 20,000 | | |

| KIM WARD, DRAWINGS | | | |
|---|---|---|---|
| April 1 | 10,000 | | |

INCOME SHARED ON BASIS OF BEGINNING CAPITAL ACCOUNT BALANCES The capital balances at the beginning of the year are $200,000 as follows:

| | |
|---|---|
| Bill Tucker, Capital | $120,000 |
| Kim Ward, Capital | 80,000 |
| Total capital invested | $200,000 |

The capital ratios are 60 : 40 respectively, calculated as follows:

$$\text{Bill Tucker: } \frac{\$120,000}{\$200,000} = \frac{3}{5}, \text{ or } 60\%$$

$$\text{Kim Ward: } \frac{\$\ 80,000}{\$200,000} = \frac{2}{5}, \text{ or } 40\%$$

The computation of each partner's share of net income and the journal entry to record the division of the net income are as follows:

*2b. Partnership income may be divided based upon the ratio of partners' beginning capital account balances*

| DIVISION OF NET INCOME | |
|---|---|
| Bill Tucker ($70,000 × .60) | $42,000 |
| Kim Ward ($70,000 × .40) | 28,000 |
| Net Income | $70,000 |

| | | | |
|---|---|---|---|
| Dec. 31 | Income Summary | 70,000 | |
| | Tucker, Capital | | 42,000 |
| | Ward, Capital | | 28,000 |
| | To close the income summary account and divide partnership net income according to the agreement | | |

Note that in this instance, the division of income is different from that calculated for the agreed-upon ratio.

*2b. Partnership income may be divided according to the ratio of the average capital account balances*

INCOME SHARED ON BASIS OF THE RATIO OF AVERAGE CAPITAL ACCOUNT BALANCES Using beginning capital account balances to divide net income may not be fair because it does not recognize changes in the partners' investments during the period. A more equitable method may be to use average capital account balances. The procedure requires that each partner's capital investment be weighted by multiplying the amount invested by the portion of the year these invested resources were committed to the firm. Using the data from the TW Partnership, the calculations for the average capital account balances and the division of net income are as follows:

AVERAGE CAPITAL INVESTMENT BALANCES

| | Capital Account Balance | × | Months That Investment Amount Remained Unchanged | | Total | Average Capital Account Balances |
|---|---|---|---|---|---|---|
| Bill Tucker | $120,000 | × | 3 months | = | $ 360,000 | |
| | 150,000 | × | 3 months | = | 450,000 | |
| | 130,000 | × | 6 months | = | 780,000 | |
| | | | | | $1,590,000 ÷ 12 = | $132,500 |
| Kim Ward | $ 80,000 | × | 3 months | = | $ 240,000 | |
| | 70,000 | × | 9 months | = | 630,000 | |
| | | | | | $ 870,000 ÷ 12 = | $ 72,500 |
| Total Average Capital Account Balance | | | | | | $205,000 |

Note that the capital account balance is changed by investments and by withdrawals. Tucker had $120,000 invested from January 1 to April 1. He then invested an additional $30,000, bringing his invested capital up to $150,000. On July 1 he withdrew $20,000, reducing his invested capital to $130,000. The average capital ratios are 64.6% and 35.4%, respectively, calculated as follows:

$$\text{Bill Tucker: } \frac{\$132{,}500}{\$205{,}000} = 64.6\% \text{ (rounded)}$$

$$\text{Kim Ward: } \frac{\$\ 72{,}500}{\$205{,}000} = 35.4\% \text{ (rounded)}$$

The computation of each partner's share of the $70,000 of net income and the journal entry to record the division of net income are as follows:

DIVISION OF NET INCOME

| | | |
|---|---|---|
| Bill Tucker | ($70,000 × .646) | $45,220 |
| Kim Ward | ($70,000 × .354) | 24,780 |
| | | $70,000 |

| | | | |
|---|---|---|---|
| Dec. 31 | Income Summary | 70,000 | |
| | Tucker, Capital | | 45,220 |
| | Ward, Capital | | 24,780 |
| | To close the income summary account and divide partnership net income according to the agreement | | |

## *Allowances for Salaries*

*2b. Partnership agreements may provide for salary allowances to partners*

Partners may agree that the most equitable plan of income sharing is to provide allowances for salaries that will recognize that the services provided by one partner may be more valuable than the services provided by another. Salary allowances recognize differences in each partner's managerial skills, ability to conduct the affairs of the business, time devoted to the business, and seniority.

These are not salaries in the legal sense. They represent a way of dividing income among the partners in an equitable manner. Any remaining net income after salary allowances have been accounted for is shared in an agreed-upon ratio.

To illustrate, assume that Tucker and Ward's partnership agreement provides that salary allowances are to be *$18,000* and *$12,000*, respectively, and that any remaining net income is to be divided *equally*. Under this agreement, the $70,000 of net income would be shared by each partner as shown in the schedule below.

DIVISION OF NET INCOME

| | Tucker | Ward | Total |
|---|---|---|---|
| Salary allowances to partners | $18,000 | $12,000 | $30,000 |
| Remaining income to be divided equally* | 20,000 | 20,000 | 40,000 |
| Total | $38,000 | $32,000 | $70,000 |

* The remainder is $40,000, representing the difference between the net income of $70,000 and the salary allowances of $30,000.

The entry to record the division of net income is as follows:

| | | | |
|---|---|---|---|
| Dec. 31 | Income Summary | 70,000 | |
| | Tucker, Capital | | 38,000 |
| | Ward, Capital | | 32,000 |
| | To close the income summary account and divide partnership net income according to the agreement | | |

### Allowances for Interest

*2b. Partnership agreements may provide for interest allowances to partners*

Partners seldom make equal contributions to the firm. The partners may agree that when the capital investment maintained by each partner is unequal, a system of reward based on capital investments should be established. Generally this is done by allowing interest. This too is a way of dividing income among the partners in an equitable manner. In this case, a portion of the net income is allocated to each partner in the form of interest, with the amount based on the partner's capital account balance.

The interest allowance can be computed on the beginning or average capital account balance. To illustrate the division of the $70,000 of partnership net income to Tucker and Ward when interest allowances are provided, assume the following: Interest of 12% is allowed to both partners based on their average capital balances, and any remaining net income is to be divided equally. Average capital balances for Tucker and Ward as previously computed are $132,500 and $72,500, respectively. Under this agreement, the $70,000 of net income would be shared by each partner as shown in the schedule at the top of page 456.

The entry to record the division of net income is as follows:

| | | | |
|---|---|---|---|
| Dec. 31 | Income Summary | 70,000 | |
| | Tucker, Capital | | 38,600 |
| | Ward, Capital | | 31,400 |
| | To close the income summary account and divide partnership net income according to the agreement | | |

DIVISION OF NET INCOME

| | Tucker | Ward | Total |
|---|---|---|---|
| Interest allowance on average capital invested | | | |
| $132,500 × 12% | $15,900 | | $15,900 |
| $ 72,500 × 12% | | $ 8,700 | $ 8,700 |
| Remaining income to be divided equally | | | |
| ($70,000 − $24,600 = $45,400) | 22,700 | 22,700 | 45,400 |
| Total | $38,600 | $31,400 | $70,000 |

## Allowances for Salaries and Interest

*2b. Partnership agreements may provide for salaries and interest allowances, and a sharing of remaining income*

Partnership agreements are sometimes written to include both salary allowances and interest allowances. To illustrate, assume that the partners agree that (1) interest of *10%* is to be allowed on their average capital balances, and (2) Tucker should have an annual salary allowance of *$15,000* and Ward should have one of *$10,000*. Any remaining income is to be shared equally. The calculations and journal entry to show how the partnership income of $70,000 is to be divided among the partners are as follows.

DIVISION OF NET INCOME

| | Tucker | Ward | Total |
|---|---|---|---|
| Salary allowances to partners | $15,000 | $10,000 | $25,000 |
| Interest allowance on average capital invested | | | |
| $132,500 × 10% | 13,250 | | 13,250 |
| $ 72,500 × 10% | | 7,250 | 7,250 |
| Total salary and interest allowances | $28,250 | $17,250 | $45,500 |
| Remaining income to be divided equally | | | |
| ($70,000 − $45,500 = $24,500) | 12,250 | 12,250 | 24,500 |
| Total | $40,500 | $29,500 | $70,000 |

| | | Debit | Credit |
|---|---|---|---|
| Dec. 31 | Income Summary | 70,000 | |
| | Tucker, Capital | | 40,500 |
| | Ward, Capital | | 29,500 |
| | To close the income summary account and divide partnership net income according to the agreement | | |

In previous illustrations the partnership's net income has exceeded the sum of the salary and interest allowances. What if the opposite should happen? That is, what happens when the sum of the salary and interest allowances exceeds net income? The same method is used to share the income. Because the allowances exceed the net income, the remaining balance is a negative figure and is divided equally between the partners. To illustrate, assume that Tucker and Ward have the same salary and interest allowances as in the preceding illustration, but the partnership net income is only $30,000 this time. The schedule at the top of page 457 shows how the $30,000 is divided between the partners.

Note that the sum of all agreed-upon allowances, $45,500, exceeds net income by $15,500. Thus $7,750 ($\frac{1}{2}$ of $15,500), the negative amount to be

DIVISION OF NET INCOME

| | Tucker | Ward | Total |
|---|---|---|---|
| Salary allowances | $15,000 | $10,000 | $25,000 |
| Interest allowances | 13,250 | 7,250 | 20,500 |
| Total | $28,250 | $17,250 | $45,500 |
| Excess of allowances over net income (a negative amount) to be divided equally ($45,500 − 30,000 = $15,500) | ( 7,750) | ( 7,750) | (15,500) |
| Total | $20,500 | $ 9,500 | $30,000 |

divided equally, was deducted from each partner's total allowances to determine the partner's share of net income.

The entry to record the division of net income is as follows:

| | | | |
|---|---|---|---|
| Dec. 31 | Income Summary . . . . . . . . . . . . . . . . . . . . . . . . . . . . . . . . . | 30,000 | |
| | Tucker, Capital. . . . . . . . . . . . . . . . . . . . . . . . . . . . . . | | 20,500 |
| | Ward, Capital . . . . . . . . . . . . . . . . . . . . . . . . . . . . . . | | 9,500 |
| | To close the income summary account and divide the partnership net income according to the agreement | | |

The partners would share a net loss in the same manner. In this case, the procedure would begin with a negative number (the amount of the loss), and the amount to be divided after provisions for salary and interest allowances had been made would be a larger negative number.

To illustrate assume that Tucker and Ward have the same salary and interest allowances as in the preceding illustration, but that the TW Partnership had a net loss of $50,000 for its first year of operations. The schedule below shows the manner in which the net loss would be shared by the partners.

DIVISION OF NET INCOME

| | Tucker | Ward | Total |
|---|---|---|---|
| Salary allowances | $15,000 | $10,000 | $25,000 |
| Interest allowances | 13,250 | 7,250 | 20,500 |
| Total | $28,250 | $17,250 | $45,500 |
| Allowances plus the net loss is the negative amount to be divided equally ($45,500 + $50,000 = $95,500) | ( 47,750) | ( 47,750) | ( 95,500) |
| Total | ($19,500) | ($30,500) | ($50,000) |

The entry to record the division of the net loss is as follows:

| | | | |
|---|---|---|---|
| Dec. 31 | Tucker, Capital . . . . . . . . . . . . . . . . . . . . . . . . . . . . . . . . . | 19,500 | |
| | Ward, Capital. . . . . . . . . . . . . . . . . . . . . . . . . . . . . . . . . . | 30,500 | |
| | Income Summary. . . . . . . . . . . . . . . . . . . . . . . . . . . | | 50,000 |
| | To close the income summary account and divide partnership net loss according to the agreement | | |

## PARTNERSHIP FINANCIAL STATEMENTS

*1b,2c. A unique aspect of accounting for partnerships is the statement of partners' capital*

In most respects, the financial statements of a partnership are like those of a sole proprietorship. However, certain differences arise because a partnership has two or more co-owners. These differences are as follows: (1) Each partner's capital account is shown in the equity section of the balance sheet or in a supporting schedule. (2) Details concerning the division of net income should be disclosed. This can be done by adding a section to the income statement (as shown in Exhibit 13–1) or by presenting the data in a supporting schedule. (3) **A statement of partners' capital** is prepared to show the changes in partners' equity interest that took place during the period. This statement is prepared in a number of ways, one of which is illustrated in Exhibit 13–2.

EXHIBIT 13–1

TW PARTNERSHIP
Income Statement
For the Year Ended December 31, 19X7

| | | |
|---|---|---|
| Sales | | $810,000 |
| Cost of Goods Sold | | 530,000 |
| Gross Profit Margin | | $280,000 |
| Operating Expenses: | | |
| Selling Expenses | $120,000 | |
| General Expenses | 60,000 | |
| Financial Expenses* | 30,000 | 210,000 |
| Net Income | | $ 70,000 |

DIVISION OF NET INCOME TO PARTNERS

| | Tucker | Ward | Total |
|---|---|---|---|
| Salary | $15,000 | $ 10,000 | $ 25,000 |
| Interest | 13,250 | 7,250 | 20,500 |
| Remainder | 12,250 | 12,250 | 24,500 |
| Total | $40,500 | $ 29,500 | $ 70,000 |

* Interest is an example.

EXHIBIT 13–2

TW PARTNERSHIP
Statement of Partners' Capital
For the Year Ended December 31, 19X7

| | Tucker | Ward | Total |
|---|---|---|---|
| Capital Balances, January 1, 19X7 | $120,000 | $ 80,000 | $200,000 |
| Add: Additional Investment | 30,000 | -0- | 30,000 |
| Net Income | 40,500 | 29,500 | 70,000 |
| Total | $190,500 | $109,500 | $300,000 |
| Less: Withdrawals | 20,000 | 10,000 | 30,000 |
| Capital Balances, December 31, 19X7 | $170,500 | $ 99,500 | $270,000 |

## ADMITTANCE OF A PARTNER

A new partner may gain admittance to a partnership in one of two ways. The new partner could purchase an interest from one or more of the current partners, or the new partner could invest in the partnership. In either case, the additional person cannot gain admittance to the partnership without the consent of all the current partners.

## Purchase of an Interest

*2d. An entry is prepared when a new partner buys an interest from a current partner*

Sometimes an additional person is admitted to an existing partnership by purchasing an interest from one or more of the current partners. The transaction is between the new partner and the partner or partners selling part or all of their interests in the partnership. Payment for the interest is made directly to the partner or partners selling the interest. Thus the only entry needed is one that transfers the proper amount from the capital account or accounts of the selling partner or partners to a capital account established for the buying (incoming) partner.

For example, assume that Bill Arnold, a partner in the ABC Partnership, has a $60,000 balance in his capital account. Assume further that on March 8 he arranges to sell his interest in the partnership to Liz Dalton for $85,000. The firm's other partners have been consulted and have consented to the sale.

The following entry would record the admission of Dalton by a purchase of an interest:

| | | | |
|---|---|---|---|
| March 8 | Arnold, Capital | 60,000 | |
| | Dalton, Capital | | 60,000 |
| | To record transfer of B. Arnold's capital interest to L. Dalton | | |

Note that the entry is for $60,000, the book value of the capital interest purchased, not for $85,000, the amount paid for that interest. The $85,000 that Dalton paid Arnold is a personal transaction between those two persons and is not recorded in the accounts of the partnership. If Dalton had paid Arnold $10,000 or $100,000 for his $60,000 interest, the same entry shown above would have been the only entry recorded in the accounts of the partnership.

To show the accounting for a related example, assume this time that Liz Dalton is admitted to the partnership by purchasing one-half of Bill Arnold's $60,000 and one-half of Laura Baugh's $80,000 capital interest in the partnership. The negotiated price for acquiring this interest is $90,000.

The only entry needed on the partnership books is the one to transfer capital interests:

| | | | |
|---|---|---|---|
| March 8 | Arnold, Capital | 30,000 | |
| | Baugh, Capital | 40,000 | |
| | Dalton, Capital | | 70,000 |
| | To record the transfer of one-half of B. Arnold's and L. Baugh's capital interest to L. Dalton | | |

## Investment in the Partnership

Instead of purchasing an interest from a current partner, a person may gain admittance to an existing partnership by investing cash or other assets in the business. Because the invested assets become the property of the partnership, both the total assets and the total equities of the firm increase. For example, assume that the ABC Partnership had assets and equities before the investment by a new partner as follows:

| ASSETS | | EQUITIES | |
|---|---|---|---|
| Cash | $ 30,000 | Arnold, Capital | $ 60,000 |
| Other Assets | 110,000 | Baugh, Capital | 80,000 |
| Total Assets | $140,000 | Total Equities | $140,000 |

On March 8 the partners agree to admit Dalton to a one-third interest in the partnership for a cash investment of $70,000. After the investment the firm's cash will be $100,000, and total assets and total equities will be $210,000. Since Dalton's $70,000 investment secures a one-third interest in the firm, her capital account is established for that amount ($\$70,000 \div \$210,000 = \frac{1}{3}$). The entry to record Dalton's investment is as follows:

*2d. An entry is required when a new partner gains admittance by investing assets*

| | | | |
|---|---|---|---|
| March 8 | Cash | 70,000 | |
| | Dalton, Capital | | 70,000 |
| | To record the admittance of L. Dalton to a one-third interest in the firm | | |

If Dalton had invested assets other than cash, their value would have had to be established and agreed to by all partners. Although Dalton has obtained a one-third equity interest in the net assets of the new partnership, she is not necessarily entitled to one-third of its income. The sharing of income (and losses) is a separate matter on which the partners must agree. Once Dalton is admitted to the partnership, a new income-sharing provision should be established and stated in the partnership agreement.

### *Investment with Bonus to Original Partners*

Sometimes an incoming partner is willing to invest an amount in excess of the amount of partnership interest to be obtained. This often happens when investing in a partnership that has had or anticipates that it will have exceptional performance, such as above-average earnings.

For example, an incoming partner may be willing to pay $90,000 for a $70,000 equity interest in a successful partnership just to have the opportunity to share in its net income. The $20,000 difference between the $90,000 invested by the new partner and the $70,000 of equity interest obtained in the partnership by the new partner is called a *bonus*. The bonus is shared by the original partners (credited to their capital accounts) in accordance with the income- and loss-sharing ratio that existed before the new partner was admitted.

To illustrate the accounting when a bonus is shared by the original partners, we change our previous example slightly. This time assume that Arnold and Baugh have been partners in the ABC Partnership for several years. Their capital account has increased consistently and currently shows balances of $140,000 for Arnold and $160,000 for Baugh. On March 8 Liz Dalton joins the firm by investing $100,000 cash for a one-fifth interest. The amount of Dalton's interest (capital account credit) can be determined as follows:

| | |
|---|---|
| Net assets (equities of the partners in the original partnership [$140,000 + $160,000]) | $300,000 |
| Investment made by new partner (Dalton) | 100,000 |
| Net assets (total equities of the partners in the new partnership) | $400,000 |
| Equity interest of new partner (Dalton) equal to $\frac{1}{5}$ of $400,000, or $80,000 | $ 80,000 |

The $20,000 difference between Dalton's investment of $100,000 and the $80,000 of equity interest obtained is a bonus to be shared by Arnold and Baugh. Sharing the bonus in accordance with their income- and loss-sharing ratio compensates the original partners for making the partnership successful. In this case, Arnold's capital account would be credited for $12,000 (60% of the $20,000 bonus), and Baugh's capital account would be credited for $8,000 (40% of the $20,000 bonus).

*2d. An entry is prepared to record a bonus allocation to the original partners*

The following entry would record Dalton's admittance to the partnership:

| | | | |
|---|---|---|---|
| March 8 | Cash | 100,000 | |
| | Arnold, Capital | | 12,000 |
| | Baugh, Capital | | 8,000 |
| | Dalton, Capital | | 80,000 |
| | To record the admittance of L. Dalton and the bonus allocation to B. Arnold and L. Baugh | | |

## *Investment with Bonus to New Partner*

There are several reasons why the members of an existing partnership may want to bring in a new partner. The new partner's investment of cash or noncash assets may be something badly needed by the firm. On the other hand, a new partner may be attractive because the individual has unique skills, technical abilities, managerial talents, or business contacts that can benefit the firm. For these reasons, the original partners may be willing to give the incoming partner a bonus in the form of an equity interest in the firm that is larger than the amount that he or she invests.

To illustrate, assume the same facts as those stated in the preceding example except that this time Dalton is offered the one-fifth equity interest in the partnership for a cash investment of $60,000, not $100,000. If she accepts, her equity interest (capital account credit) is $72,000, determined as follows:

| | |
|---|---|
| Net assets (equities of the partners in the original partnership [$140,000 + $160,000]) | $300,000 |
| Investment made by new partner (Dalton) | 60,000 |
| Net assets (total equities of the partners in the new partnership) | $360,000 |
| Equity interest of new partner (Dalton) equal to $\frac{1}{5}$ of $360,000, or $72,000 | $ 72,000 |

The $12,000 difference between the $72,000 equity interest and the $60,000 invested by Dalton is a bonus given to her by the original partners as an incentive to join the firm. The amount of the bonus is debited to the capital accounts of Arnold and Baugh in proportion to their original income- and loss-sharing ratio, which is 60% for Arnold and 40% for Baugh.

*2d. An entry is prepared to record a bonus allocation to a new partner*

The entry to record Dalton's admittance to the partnership is as follows:

| | | | |
|---|---|---|---|
| March 8 | Cash | 60,000 | |
| | Arnold, Capital | 7,200 | |
| | Baugh, Capital | 4,800 | |
| | Dalton, Capital | | 72,000 |
| | To record the admittance of L. Dalton, including the bonus | | |

### Recognition of Goodwill

Instead of allowing bonuses to the partners, an alternative method sometimes used is to recognize goodwill attributable to either the old partners or to the incoming partner. If goodwill is attributed to the old partnership then the amount recorded should be allocated to the capital accounts of the old partners according to their income-sharing ratio. If the goodwill is attributable to the incoming partner his or her capital account is credited for an amount equal to the total of his or her investment plus the amount recorded as goodwill.

Although the recording of goodwill is justifiable, the bonus method appears to be the method more frequently used.

## WITHDRAWAL OF A PARTNER

A partner may withdraw from a partnership in three ways:

By *selling* his or her equity interest to an *outside party* (which requires the consent of the remaining partners)

By *selling* his or her equity interest to one or more of the *remaining partners* (which requires the consent of all partners)

By *withdrawing* partnership assets in settlement of his or her equity interest

### Sale of Equity Interest to Outside Party

*2e. An entry is made to record a partner's withdrawal by sale of equity interest to an outside party*

The sale of an equity interest to an outside party is a personal transaction between the incoming and withdrawing partners. The total assets and total capital of the partnership do not change. The only entry recorded on the partnership books is one that transfers the amount in the capital account of the withdrawing partner to the capital account of the incoming partner.

For example, assume that Bill Arnold, after receiving the consent of the other partners, withdraws from the ABC Partnership by selling his $60,000 equity interest to Eric Cole. Cole's payment, which could be equal to, greater than, or less than $60,000, goes directly to Arnold, not to the partnership. The only entry recorded on the partnership books is the one shown below:

| | | | |
|---|---|---|---|
| March 8 | Arnold, Capital | 60,000 | |
| | Cole, Capital | | 60,000 |
| | To record Arnold's withdrawal from and Cole's admittance to the partnership | | |

### Sale of Equity Interest to Remaining Partners

In the sale of an equity interest to one or more of the partners remaining in the firm, the remaining partner(s) use their personal funds to buy out the withdrawing partner. Since payment goes directly to the withdrawing partner, this is a personal transaction between the remaining partner(s) and the withdrawing partner and as such is not recorded on the partnership books. Only the resulting changes in the partners' capital accounts need to be recorded.

*2e. An entry is made to record a partner's withdrawal by sale of equity interest to remaining partners*

For example, assume that Bill Arnold, who has a capital account balance of $60,000, is willing to sell his interest in the partnership to Baugh and Dalton. They agree to buy him out. Each pays Arnold $40,000 and will share his equity interest equally. The only entry needed on the partnership books is the one shown below:

| | | | |
|---|---|---|---|
| March 8 | Arnold, Capital | 60,000 | |
| | Baugh, Capital | | 30,000 |
| | Dalton, Capital | | 30,000 |
| | To record transfer of Arnold's partnership interest to Baugh and Dalton | | |

## *Withdrawing Assets from the Partnership*

The partnership agreement should clearly state the procedures to be followed when a partner withdraws from the firm. Agreements often provide for an audit of the accounting records and a revaluation of partnership assets. The revaluation places the assets on the books at their fair market value. Any increase or decrease in asset values resulting from revaluation is generally divided among the partners using the income- and loss-sharing ratio. This procedure adjusts the partners' capital account balances to reflect the current value of each partner's equity interest. This is important because the agreement may permit the retiring partner to withdraw assets equal to the amount of his or her restated capital account balance.

For example, assume that Arnold is retiring from the ABC Partnership, whose partners Arnold, Baugh, and Dalton share income 50:25:25, respectively. The partnership agreement provides for asset revaluation upon the retirement of a partner. Just prior to revaluation, the ABC Partnership balance sheet appeared as follows:

| ASSETS | | | LIABILITIES AND OWNER'S EQUITY | |
|---|---|---|---|---|
| Cash | | $30,000 | Accounts Payable | $15,000 |
| Accounts Receivable (net) | | 40,000 | Other Liabilities | 25,000 |
| Inventory | | 60,000 | Arnold, Capital | 60,000 |
| Plant Assets | $160,000 | | Baugh, Capital | 80,000 |
| Less: Accum. Depr. | 40,000 | 120,000 | Dalton, Capital | 70,000 |
| Total | | $250,000 | Total | $250,000 |

Appraisals indicate that the inventory should be valued at $66,000, the plant assets should be valued at $200,000, with accumulated depreciation of $50,000.

The entry to record the revaluations and restate equity interests is as shown at the top of page 464.

Note that gains or losses resulting from revaluation are shared by the partners in accordance with their income- and loss-sharing ratio, and their capital accounts were credited accordingly. After the revaluation entry has been re-

| | | | |
|---|---|---|---|
| March 8 | Inventory | 6,000 | |
| | Plant Assets | 40,000 | |
| | Accumulated Depreciation | | 10,000 |
| | Arnold, Capital | | 18,000 |
| | Baugh, Capital | | 9,000 |
| | Dalton, Capital | | 9,000 |
| | To record the revaluation of certain assets and liabilities | | |

corded and posted, the balance sheet would show revised amounts for assets and partners' capital accounts as follows.

| ASSETS | | | LIABILITIES AND OWNER'S EQUITY | |
|---|---|---|---|---|
| Cash | | $ 30,000 | Accounts Payable | $ 15,000 |
| Accounts Receivable (net) | | 40,000 | Other Liabilities | 25,000 |
| Inventory | | 66,000 | Arnold, Capital | 78,000 |
| Plant Assets | $200,000 | | Baugh, Capital | 89,000 |
| Less: Accum. Depr. | 50,000 | 150,000 | Dalton, Capital | 79,000 |
| Total | | $286,000 | Total | $286,000 |

*2e. The entry shows the withdrawal of a partner taking partnership assets*

Assume that the partnership agreement allows the retiring partner to take from the firm cash equal to his or her restated capital account balance. Furthermore, if the cash balance is not sufficient to settle the equity interest, he or she will receive an interest-bearing promissory note for the balance. The entry to record Arnold's withdrawal is as follows:

| | | | |
|---|---|---|---|
| March 8 | Arnold, Capital | 78,000 | |
| | Cash | | 30,000 |
| | Note Payable | | 48,000 |
| | To record Arnold's withdrawal from the firm | | |

*2e. Remaining partners share a withdrawing partner's unwithdrawn book equity*

Sometimes a partner is willing to take less than the restated value of his or her equity interest when withdrawing from the partnership. In such cases, the remaining partners share the amount of the equity not withdrawn in accordance with their income- and loss-sharing ratio.

For example, assume that Arnold is anxious to withdraw from the ABC Partnership and agrees to accept $20,000 in cash and a $50,000 promissory note for his equity interest of $78,000. Because the settlement is for $8,000 less than the balance in Arnold's capital account, that amount will be divided between the remaining partners, Baugh and Dalton, in accordance with their income- and loss-sharing ratio. The income- and loss-sharing ratio was Arnold, 50; Baugh, 25; and Dalton, 25. Since Baugh and Dalton share income equally, they will divide the $8,000 equally and increase their capital accounts by $4,000 each. Thus the entry to record Arnold's withdrawal is as follows:

| | | | |
|---|---|---|---|
| March 8 | Arnold, Capital | 78,000 | |
| | Cash | | 20,000 |
| | Notes Payable | | 50,000 |
| | Baugh, Capital | | 4,000 |
| | Dalton, Capital | | 4,000 |
| | To record Arnold's withdrawal from the firm | | |

Sometimes a partner is offered more than the restated value of his or her equity interest to withdraw from the partnership. This occurs when the partners continuing in the business are anxious to do business without a certain partner.

To illustrate the accounting, assume that Arnold is withdrawing from the ABC Partnership and is to receive $25,000 in cash and a promissory note for $60,000 for his $78,000 equity interest. The entry to record Arnold's withdrawal is as follows:

| | | | |
|---|---|---|---|
| March 8 | Arnold, Capital | 78,000 | |
| | Baugh, Capital | 3,500 | |
| | Dalton, Capital | 3,500 | |
| | Cash | | 25,000 |
| | Notes Payable | | 60,000 |
| | To record Arnold's withdrawal from the firm | | |

***2e. Remaining partners may share a charge for payment in excess of capital to a withdrawing partner***

Note that in this case the excess payment of $7,000 is charged against the capital accounts of the remaining partners in their income- and loss-sharing ratio.

## DEATH OF A PARTNER

The death of a partner dissolves the partnership because the original association has been changed. The partnership agreement should state the procedures to be followed for determining the deceased partner's equity interest at the time of death and the manner in which settlement will be made with the deceased partner's estate.

These procedures conform to those used when a partner withdraws. The surviving partners may purchase the deceased partner's equity in the firm, it may be sold to outsiders, or certain partnership assets may be withdrawn and delivered to the estate. The accounting for these procedures has already been discussed.

## PARTNERSHIP LIQUIDATION

The process of terminating a business and discontinuing its operations is called **liquidation.** Liquidation involves

*Selling* the firm's noncash assets

*Paying* its creditors

*Distributing* the remaining cash or other assets to the partners according to their equity interest

Liquidations can be complex, and the complexities are covered in advanced accounting texts. We will look here at the fundamentals.

To illustrate the accounting for a partnership liquidation, assume that on March 8, 19X5, Arons, Beck, and Carter, the partners in ABC Company, decided to suspend operations and terminate their business. The partners have been sharing income and losses as follows: Arons, 50%; Beck, 30%; Carter 20%. After ceasing their normal business activities and closing the temporary accounts, the partnership's condensed balance sheet was prepared:

| ASSETS | | LIABILITIES AND OWNER'S EQUITY | |
|---|---|---|---|
| Cash | $ 20,000 | Accounts Payable | $ 70,000 |
| Accounts Receivable | 50,000 | Arons, Capital | 80,000 |
| Inventory | 60,000 | Beck, Capital | 60,000 |
| Plant Assets (net of accumulated depreciation) | 130,000 | Carter, Capital | 50,000 |
| Total | $260,000 | Total | $260,000 |

These data will be used to show three examples of circumstances that can occur in liquidations: (1) *gain* on sale of partnership assets, (2) *loss* on sale of partnership assets where capital account balances are sufficient to absorb the loss, and (3) *loss* on sale of partnership assets where one or more capital account balances are not sufficient to absorb the loss.

## Gain on Sale of Partnership Assets

The first step in liquidating the partnership is to sell its noncash assets. In this example we will illustrate the accounting when there is a gain on the sale of partnership assets. Therefore assume the following:

Inventory of $60,000 was sold for $75,000 cash, resulting in a gain of $15,000

Plant assets of $130,000 (net of accumulated depreciation) were sold for $150,000 cash, resulting in a gain of $20,000

Accounts receivable of $50,000 were sold for $45,000 cash, resulting in a loss of $5,000

Aggregate gain on the sale of noncash assets, often called gain or loss from realization of assets, amounted to $30,000 ($15,000 + $20,000 − $5,000 = $30,000)

The entry to record the sale of noncash assets is as follows:

| | Debit | Credit |
|---|---|---|
| Cash | 270,000 | |
| Accounts Receivable | | 50,000 |
| Inventory | | 60,000 |
| Plant Assets | | 130,000 |
| Gain or Loss from Realization of Assets | | 30,000 |
| To record sale of assets | | |

The gain is then divided among the partners, and the amounts are credited to their respective capital accounts in accordance with their income-sharing ratios. The entry to allocate the net gain to the partners' capital accounts is as follows:

| | Debit | Credit |
|---|---|---|
| Gain or Loss from Realization of Assets | 30,000 | |
| Arons, Capital | | 15,000 |
| Beck, Capital | | 9,000 |
| Carter, Capital | | 6,000 |
| To divide the net gain on the sale of assets according to the income-sharing ratio | | |

The partnership's condensed balance sheet would now be as follows:

| ASSETS | | LIABILITIES AND OWNER'S EQUITY | |
|---|---|---|---|
| Cash | $290,000 | Accounts Payable | $ 70,000 |
| | | Arons, Capital | 95,000 |
| | | Beck, Capital | 69,000 |
| | | Carter, Capital | 56,000 |
| Total | $290,000 | Total | $290,000 |

The next step would be to pay the creditors the $70,000 owed to them and record the payment as follows:

| | | |
|---|---|---|
| Accounts Payable | 70,000 | |
| Cash | | 70,000 |
| To record payment of liabilities | | |

The final distribution of cash is made in accordance with the balances in the partners' respective capital accounts. The entry to record distribution of the remaining partnership cash to the partners is as follows:

| | | |
|---|---|---|
| Arons, Capital | 95,000 | |
| Beck, Capital | 69,000 | |
| Carter, Capital | 56,000 | |
| Cash | | 220,000 |
| To record distribution of remaining cash to partners | | |

Note that the cash distributed to the partners (after all creditors have been paid) is determined by the balance in their respective capital accounts. Cash distributions are *not* made in accordance with the partners' income-sharing ratio.

A partnership liquidation schedule that summarizes the liquidation process is shown in Exhibit 13–3. This schedule functions as a worksheet and aids in organizing and determining the entries needed to record a liquidation.

### *Loss on Sale of Partnership Assets: Capital Account Balances Sufficient*

*2f. A liquidation schedule when there is an absorbable loss on sale of partnership assets is illustrated in Exhibit 13–4*

Sometimes noncash assets are sold at a loss. If all partners have credit balances in their capital accounts that are large enough to absorb their share of the loss, we follow procedures similar to those used in the preceding example. To illustrate, assume that the partnership's noncash assets were sold for $200,000 instead of $270,000. We would recognize a loss of $40,000 (Accounts Receivable $50,000 + Inventory $60,000 + Plant Assets $130,000 = $240,000 − $200,000 cash received = $40,000 loss). We would then divide it among the partners, and the amounts would be debited to their respective capital accounts in accordance with their income-sharing ratio. The $70,000 of Accounts Payable would be paid, and the remaining *$150,000* in cash would be distributed to the partners in accordance with the balance in their respective capital accounts.

The partnership liquidation schedule shown in Exhibit 13–4 summarizes these transactions and events.

*EXHIBIT 13–3*

ARONS, BECK, AND CARTER

Partnership Liquidation Schedule
March 8, 19X5

| EXPLANATION | CASH | + | NONCASH ASSETS | = | ACCOUNTS PAYABLE | + | ARONS, CAPITAL | + | BECK, CAPITAL | + | CARTER, CAPITAL | + OR − | GAIN (LOSS) FROM REALIZATION |
|---|---|---|---|---|---|---|---|---|---|---|---|---|---|
| Beginning Balances | $ 20,000 | | $240,000 | | $70,000 | | $80,000 | | $60,000 | | $50,000 | | — |
| Sale of Receivables | 45,000 | | (50,000) | | — | | — | | — | | — | | $ (5,000) |
| Sale of Inventory | 75,000 | | (60,000) | | — | | — | | — | | — | | 15,000 |
| Sale of Plant Assets | 150,000 | | (130,000) | | — | | — | | — | | — | | 20,000 |
| | $290,000 | | $ 0 | | $70,000 | | $80,000 | | $60,000 | | $50,000 | | $30,000 |
| Division of Gain on Sale of Noncash Assets (5 : 3 : 2) | — | | — | | — | | 15,000 | | 9,000 | | 6,000 | | (30,000) |
| | $290,000 | | $ 0 | | $70,000 | | $95,000 | | $69,000 | | $56,000 | | $ 0 |
| Payment of Liabilities | 70,000 | | — | | 70,000 | | — | | — | | — | | — |
| | $220,000 | | $ 0 | | $ 0 | | $95,000 | | $69,000 | | $56,000 | | $ 0 |
| Cash Distribution to Partners (according to the balances in their capital accounts) | (220,000) | | — | | — | | (95,000) | | (69,000) | | (56,000) | | — |
| | $ 0 | | $ 0 | | $ 0 | | $ 0 | | $ 0 | | $ 0 | | $ 0 |

*EXHIBIT 13–4*

ARONS, BECK, AND CARTER

Partnership Liquidation Schedule

March 8, 19X5

| EXPLANATION | CASH | + | NONCASH ASSETS | = | ACCOUNTS PAYABLE | + | ARONS, CAPITAL | + | BECK CAPITAL | + | CARTER, CAPITAL | + OR – | GAIN (LOSS) FROM REALIZATION |
|---|---|---|---|---|---|---|---|---|---|---|---|---|---|
| Beginning Balances | $ 20,000 | | $240,000 | | $70,000 | | $80,000 | | $60,000 | | $50,000 | | — |
| Sale of Noncash Assets | 200,000 | | (240,000) | | — | | — | | — | | — | | ($40,000) |
| | $220,000 | | $ 0 | | $70,000 | | $80,000 | | $60,000 | | $50,000 | | ($40,000) |
| Division of Loss on Sale of Noncash Assets (5:3:2) | — | | — | | — | | (20,000) | | (12,000) | | (8,000) | | 40,000 |
| | $220,000 | | $ 0 | | $70,000 | | $60,000 | | $48,000 | | $42,000 | | $ 0 |
| Payment of Liabilities | 70,000 | | — | | 70,000 | | — | | — | | — | | — |
| | $150,000 | | $ 0 | | $ 0 | | $60,000 | | $48,000 | | $42,000 | | $ 0 |
| Cash Distribution to Partners (according to the balances in their capital accounts) | (150,000) | | — | | — | | (60,000) | | (48,000) | | (42,000) | | — |
| | $ 0 | | $ 0 | | $ 0 | | $ 0 | | $ 0 | | $ 0 | | $ 0 |

*2f. Entries to record a liquidation when there is an absorbable loss on sale of partnership assets are illustrated here*

The general journal entries to record the liquidation of the partnership under these circumstances are as follows:

*Sale of assets:*

| | | |
|---|---|---|
| Cash | 200,000 | |
| Gain or Loss from Realization of Assets | 40,000 | |
| Accounts Receivable | | 50,000 |
| Inventory | | 60,000 |
| Plant Assets | | 130,000 |

*Division of loss:*

| | | |
|---|---|---|
| Arons, Capital | 20,000 | |
| Beck, Capital | 12,000 | |
| Carter, Capital | 8,000 | |
| Gain or Loss from Realization of Assets | | 40,000 |

*Payment of liabilities:*

| | | |
|---|---|---|
| Accounts Payable | 70,000 | |
| Cash | | 70,000 |

*Cash distribution to partners:*

| | | |
|---|---|---|
| Arons, Capital | 60,000 | |
| Beck, Capital | 48,000 | |
| Carter, Capital | 42,000 | |
| Cash | | 150,000 |

## Loss on Sale of Partnership Assets: Capital Account Balances Not Sufficient

Sometimes when partnership assets are sold at a loss, the size of the loss is so large that it causes one or more partners to have a debit balance in their capital account after the loss has been divided. A partner with a debit balance in his or her capital account must, if able, contribute cash or other personal assets to the partnership to eliminate the debit balance. If this is done, the partnership will have enough assets to pay the other partners amounts equal to their capital balances, thus completing the liquidation.

To illustrate this situation, assume that the partnership's noncash assets are sold for $60,000. The entries to record the sale and the division of the $180,000 loss (carrying value of noncash assets $240,000 − $60,000 sales price of those assets = $180,000 loss from their realization) are as follows:

*Sale of assets:*

| | | |
|---|---|---|
| Cash | 60,000 | |
| Gain or Loss from Realization of Assets | 180,000 | |
| Accounts Receivable | | 50,000 |
| Inventory | | 60,000 |
| Plant Assets | | 130,000 |

*Division of loss:*

| | | |
|---|---|---|
| Arons, Capital | 90,000 | |
| Beck, Capital | 54,000 | |
| Carter, Capital | 36,000 | |
| Gain or Loss from Realization of Assets | | 180,000 |

After the realization loss has been posted to the accounts, the capital account of Arons will have a $10,000 debit balance while the capital accounts of Beck and Carter will have credit balances of $6,000 and $14,000, respectively. The schedule below shows how these amounts were determined.

| | ARONS, CAPITAL | BECK, CAPITAL | CARTER, CAPITAL | TOTAL CAPITAL |
|---|---|---|---|---|
| Capital balances before sale of noncash assets | $80,000 | $60,000 | $50,000 | $190,000 |
| Division of loss on sale of noncash assets (5:3:2) | (90,000) | (54,000) | (36,000) | (180,000) |
| Capital balances after realization loss is posted | ($10,000) | $ 6,000 | $14,000 | $ 10,000 |

After the creditors have been paid $70,000, there is only $10,000 of cash left in the partnership ($20,000 + $60,000 on the sale − $70,000 paid to creditors). This is not enough to cover the capital balances of Beck and Carter. However, if Arons pays $10,000 into the partnership, his capital account deficit would be covered and the partnership would have $20,000 in cash. To complete the liquidation, the money must be distributed to Beck and Carter based on their capital account balances.

The entries to record payment of liabilities, the receipt of Arons's $10,000 to cover his capital account deficit, and the distribution of remaining cash are as follows:

*Payment of liabilities:*

| | | |
|---|---|---|
| Accounts Payable | 70,000 | |
| Cash | | 70,000 |

*Receipt of cash to cover Arons's capital account deficit:*

| | | |
|---|---|---|
| Cash | 10,000 | |
| Arons, Capital | | 10,000 |

*Distribution of remaining cash:*

| | | |
|---|---|---|
| Beck, Capital | 6,000 | |
| Carter, Capital | 14,000 | |
| Cash | | 20,000 |

EXHIBIT 13-5

ARONS, BECK, AND CARTER
Partnership Liquidation Schedule
March 8, 19X5

| EXPLANATION | CASH | + | NONCASH ASSETS | = | ACCOUNTS PAYABLE | + | ARONS, CAPITAL | + | BECK, CAPITAL | + | CARTER, CAPITAL | + OR − | GAIN (LOSS) FROM REALIZATION |
|---|---|---|---|---|---|---|---|---|---|---|---|---|---|
| Beginning Balances | $20,000 | | $240,000 | | $70,000 | | $ 80,000 | | $60,000 | | $50,000 | | — |
| Sale of Noncash Assets | 60,000 | | (240,000) | | — | | — | | — | | — | | ($180,000) |
| | $80,000 | | $ 0 | | $70,000 | | $ 80,000 | | $60,000 | | $50,000 | | ($180,000) |
| Division of Loss on Sale of Noncash Assets (5:3:2) | — | | — | | — | | (90,000) | | (54,000) | | (36,000) | | 180,000 |
| | $80,000 | | $ 0 | | $70,000 | | $(10,000) | | $ 6,000 | | $14,000 | | $ 0 |
| Payment of Liabilities | 70,000 | | — | | 70,000 | | — | | — | | — | | — |
| | $10,000 | | $ 0 | | $ 0 | | $(10,000) | | $ 6,000 | | $14,000 | | $ 0 |
| Receipt of Cash from Arons | 10,000 | | — | | — | | 10,000 | | — | | — | | — |
| | $20,000 | | $ 0 | | $ 0 | | $ 0 | | $ 6,000 | | $14,000 | | $ 0 |
| Cash Distribution to Partners (according to the balances in their capital accounts) | (20,000) | | — | | — | | — | | (6,000) | | (14,000) | | — |
| | $ 0 | | $ 0 | | $ 0 | | $ 0 | | $ 0 | | $ 0 | | $ 0 |

All of these transactions and events are summarized in the partnership liquidation schedule shown in Exhibit 13–5.

Let us assume that instead of contributing $10,000 to the partnership, Arons is unwilling or unable to provide the cash needed to cover the debit balance in his capital account. In this situation, the remaining partners must share the amount of the deficit in their remaining income- and loss-sharing ratio, which is 3 : 2. Beck will have three-fifths of the deficit, or $6,000 debited to his capital account. Carter will have two-fifths of the deficit, or $4,000 debited to his capital account. The entry to record the absorption of the deficit in Arons's capital account by Beck and Carter is as follows:

| | | |
|---|---|---|
| Beck, Capital | 6,000 | |
| Carter, Capital | 4,000 | |
| Arons, Capital | | 10,000 |

After the entry has been posted, Beck's capital account will have a zero balance and Carter's capital account will have a $10,000 credit balance (an amount equal to the cash remaining in the partnership). To complete the liquidation, the cash is distributed to Carter and the following entry is prepared:

| | | |
|---|---|---|
| Carter, Capital | 10,000 | |
| Cash | | 10,000 |

Sometimes the partner with a debit capital account balance, Arons in this example, can pay only a part of his or her deficiency. This does not change the entry; only the amount is different. When the amount paid into the partnership does not fully cover the deficiency, the remaining partners must absorb whatever deficiency is left in their income- and loss-sharing ratio.

## HIGHLIGHT PROBLEM

D. Alexis, J. Bramble, and K. Costa have been partners in the ABC Partnership for several years. Their partnership agreement provides salary allowances to Alexis, Bramble, and Costa of $15,000, $12,000, and $10,000, respectively. Income after salary allowances is to be shared by the partners in a 4 : 2 : 4 ratio.

During the year 19X5 the partners withdrew partnership assets as follows: Alexis, $24,200; Bramble, $15,600; and Costa, $27,200. Partnership net income for 19X5 was $75,000.

Required:

1. Prepare a schedule showing how the net income of $75,000 is shared by the partners.
2. Prepare a Statement of Partners' Capital for the year ended December 31, 19X5. On January 1, 19X5, the partners had capital account balances as follows: Alexis, $92,000; Bramble, $85,000; and Costa, $76,000.
3. Prepare journal entries to record the liquidation of the partnership, which took place on January 1, 19X6. On that date the partnership had assets consisting of cash of $40,000 and noncash assets of $315,000. Liabilities on that date totaled $94,000. In liquidation the noncash assets were sold for $275,000, the creditors were paid, and the remaining cash was distributed to the partners.

## GLOSSARY OF KEY TERMS

**Articles of partnership.** Alternate term for *partnership contract* or *partnership agreement.*

**Limited life.** A partnership characteristic that dissolves the partnership with any change in the personnel of its membership. This includes the admittance of a new partner and the withdrawal, bankruptcy, incapacitation, or death of a partner.

**Liquidation.** The process of terminating a business and discontinuing its operations. It involves selling its noncash assets, paying the creditors, and distributing the remaining cash to the owners.

**Mutual agency.** A partnership characteristic whereby each partner is an agent for the partnership and for all other partners and has the authority to legally bind the partnership to contracts.

**Partnership.** An association of two or more persons to carry on as co-owners of a business for profit.

**Partnership contract.** The contract or agreement made among the partners in the partnership that sets forth the terms under which they will conduct the partnership business.

**Statement of partners' capital.** A financial statement that shows the changes in partners' equity interest that took place during the period.

**Uniform Partnership Act.** Uniform legislation enacted by most states to govern the formation, operation, and liquidation of partnerships.

**Unlimited liability.** A partnership characteristic making each partner personally liable to creditors for all debts incurred by the partnership.

## REVIEW QUESTIONS

1. Why do people join together to form partnerships? [LO1a]
2. Name seven distinctive characteristics of partnerships. [LO1a]
3. Describe the advantages and disadvantages of a partnership as contrasted with other forms of business organization. [LO1a]
4. What important items should be included in a partnership contract? [LO1a]
5. What part of the financial statements must be accounted for differently when a partnership is used rather than a sole proprietorship? [LO1b]
6. Name the five unique aspects relating to partnership accounting. [LO1b]
7. Describe the type of journal entry made when partners invest their personal assets to form a partnership. [LO2a]
8. Name five common ways in which partnership net income may be divided among the partners. [LO2b]
9. Describe how an income statement prepared for a partnership might differ from one prepared for a sole proprietorship. [LO2c]
10. Describe the purpose and content of a statement of partners' capital. [LO2c]
11. In what two ways can a new partner gain admittance to an existing partnership? [LO2d]
12. Why would an incoming partner be willing to invest an amount in excess of the amount of partnership interest obtained? How is that transaction accounted for? [LO2d]
13. Why would the original partners in a firm be willing to give an incoming partner a bonus in the form of an equity interest in the firm that is larger than the amount that he or she invests? How is the transaction accounted for? [LO2d]
14. In what three ways may a partner withdraw from a partnership? [LO2e]
15. How is the difference accounted for when a withdrawing partner is willing to take less than the restated value of his or her equity interest when withdrawing from the partnership? [LO2e]
16. What happens to the partnership when one of the partners dies? [LO2e]
17. Describe the three steps involved in liquidating a partnership. [LO2f]
18. When a partnership is liquidated, how is a gain on the sale of partnership assets accounted for? [LO2f]
19. When a partnership is liquidated, how is a loss on the sale of partnership assets accounted for when the capital account balance for each partner is sufficient to absorb his or her share of the loss? [LO2f]

20. When a partnership is liquidated, how is a loss on the sale of partnership assets accounted for when the capital account balances for one or more partners are not sufficient to absorb his or her share of the loss? [LO2f]

## ANALYTICAL QUESTIONS

21. Partners are not paid salaries in the legal sense but are given salary allowances. What is the difference between a salary allowance and a salary expense? How are salary allowances reported in the financial statements? [LO2b]
22. How is it possible to provide for an equitable sharing of net income among partners when each partner has a different amount of capital invested in the partnership? [LO2b]
23. Comment on the validity of the following statement: "The partner who works the most hours deserves the largest share of the partnership net income." [LO2b]
24. Manny Reeves wishes to join an existing partnership. He is told by the existing partners that a cash investment of $50,000 is required to receive a capital balance of $42,000. Why might Reeves agree to this arrangement? [LO2d]
25. Partnership liquidation gains and losses are shared according to the partners' income- and loss-sharing ratio. However, the final cash settlement is made in accordance with the balances in the partners' capital accounts. Explain why the settlement is made in this way. [LO2f]

## IMPACT ANALYSIS QUESTIONS

*For each error described, indicate whether it would overstate [O], understate [U] or not affect [N] the specified key figures.*

26. Parson and Larson had capital balances of $30,000 and $40,000, respectively, before deciding to admit Carson to the partnership with an investment of $30,000. Carson was to receive a one-third interest in the partnership. An entry was made debiting cash and crediting Carson's capital account for $30,000. [LO2d]

    _______ Parson, Capital _______ Larson, Capital
    _______ Carson, Capital

27. Assume the same situation as in Question 26 except that Carson was to receive a one-fourth interest in the partnership. [LO2d]

    _______ Parson, Capital _______ Larson, Capital
    _______ Carson, Capital

28. Jensen, Bensen, and Wensen had an income-sharing agreement that called for them to share income and losses in a 40%, 40%, and 20% ratio, respectively. However, the bookkeeper assigned one-third of the net income to each partner. [LO2b]

    _______ Jensen, Capital _______ Bensen, Capital
    _______ Wensen, Capital

29. Assume the same situation as in Question 28 except that the bookkeeper credited 50%, 40%, and 10% of the net income to Jensen, Bensen, and Wensen, respectively. [LO2b]

    _______ Jensen, Capital _______ Bensen, Capital
    _______ Wensen, Capital

30. Halley, Calley, and Malley had an income-sharing agreement that called for each partner to receive one-third of income and losses. When the partnership was liquidated, the net assets were sold at a loss. The bookkeeper incorrectly debited 40%, 30%, and 30% of the loss to the Halley, Calley, and Malley capital accounts, respectively. [LO2b,2f]

    _______ Halley, Capital _______ Calley, Capital
    _______ Malley, Capital

## EXERCISES

EXERCISE 13–1 *(Prepare Journal Entries for Forming a Partnership)* Cross and Decker agree to form a partnership on September 1. Cross contributed the following assets, all of which are stated at their fair market value: supplies, $300; equipment, $16,000; vehicle, $4,000. There is also a $5,000 note payable on the equipment that will be assumed by the partnership. Decker contributed $18,000 in cash.

Required:
Prepare separate journal entries to record each partner's initial investment. [LO2a]

EXERCISE 13–2 *(Prepare Schedules to Show Division of Net Income and Net Loss)* Kriss, Long, and Manden formed a partnership by investing cash of $30,000, $10,000, and $50,000, respectively. The partnership agreement contained the following provisions related to income sharing: Each partner is allowed 10% interest on his or her original investment. Kriss and Long have salary allowances of $12,000 each. Manden's salary allowance is $20,000. Remaining net income is to be shared equally.

Required:
Prepare schedules to show each partner's share of net income or loss under the following independent situations:

1. Net income was $80,000.
2. Net income was $38,000.
3. Net loss was $16,000. [LO2b]

EXERCISE 13–3 *(Prepare Journal Entries to Record Division of Net Income)* Archer, Stokes, and Warren formed a partnership by investing $20,000, $30,000, and $60,000 in cash, respectively. The partnership's net income for the first year was $42,000.

Required:

1. Prepare the journal entry to record the division of net income under each of the following assumptions:
   a. Income is shared by Archer, Stokes, and Warren in the agreed-upon ratio of 5 : 3 : 2.
   b. The partners agreed to share income in the ratio of their original capital investments.
   c. The partners agreed to the following: interest allowances of 8% to each partner based upon the amount of his or her initial investment; salary allowances of $4,000, $12,000, and $10,000 to Archer, Stokes, and Warren, respectively; and any remaining net income is to be shared equally.
2. Repeat Requirement 1 for each assumption described in items *a* through *c*, assuming this time that the partnership's net income for the first year was $18,000. [LO2b]

EXERCISE 13–4 *(Prepare Journal Entries to Record Admittance of a New Partner)* Stern and Powers are partners having capital account balances of $50,000 and $30,000, respectively. They share income and losses in a ratio of 6 : 4. The partners have agreed to admit Marion to the partnership for a cash investment of $40,000.

Required:
Prepare the journal entry to record Marion's admittance to the partnership under each of the following conditions:

1. Marion receives a one-third equity interest.
2. Marion receives a one-fourth equity interest.
3. Marion receives a two-fifths equity interest. [LO2d]

EXERCISE 13–5 *(Prepare Journal Entries to Record Withdrawal of a Partner)* Shorter, Jennings, and Carson are partners who share income and losses in a 5 : 3 : 2 ratio. They have respective capital balances of $30,000, $50,000, and $20,000 at the time of Carson's withdrawal from the partnership.

Required:

Prepare the journal entry to record Carson's withdrawal under each of the following assumptions:

1. Carson receives cash of $20,000 from the partnership.
2. Carson receives cash of $28,000 from the partnership.
3. Carson receives cash of $16,000 from the partnership. [LO2e]

EXERCISE 13–6 *(Prepare Journal Entries to Record Partnership Liquidation)* Hall, Gomez, and Smoke are partners who share income in the ratio of 4:3:3. On November 3 when the partners agreed to liquidate their business, the company's accounts were as follows:

| | |
|---|---|
| Cash | $10,000 |
| Noncash Assets | 65,000 |
| Liabilities | 15,000 |
| Hall, Capital | 5,000 |
| Gomez, Capital | 30,000 |
| Smoke, Capital | 25,000 |

The noncash assets were sold for cash of $40,000.

Required:

Prepare journal entries to record the following:

1. Sale of the noncash assets.
2. Division of the gain or loss realized on the sale of the noncash assets.
3. Payment to creditors.
4. a. (Assume that Hall pays cash to the partnership in an amount sufficient to cover his capital account debit balance.) Payment by Hall and the distribution of cash to the partners.
   b. (Assume that Hall does not pay anything to cover his capital account debit balance.) Assignment of Hall's capital account debit balance and the distribution of cash to the partners. [LO2f]

EXERCISE 13–7 *(Prepare Journal Entries to Record Partnership Liquidation)* Mayo, Sloan, and Lane are partners with capital accounts of $44,000, $56,000, and $38,000, respectively. They share income and losses in the ratio of 3:5:2. When the partners agreed to liquidate, the business had cash of $35,000, noncash assets totaling $165,000, and liabilities of $62,000. On May 23 all noncash assets were sold for $180,000, the creditors were paid, and the final distribution of cash was made.

Required:

Prepare the journal entries to record the following:

1. Sale of the noncash assets.
2. Division of the gain or loss realized on the sale of the noncash assets.
3. Payment to creditors.
4. Distribution of cash to the partners. [LO2f]

## PROBLEMS

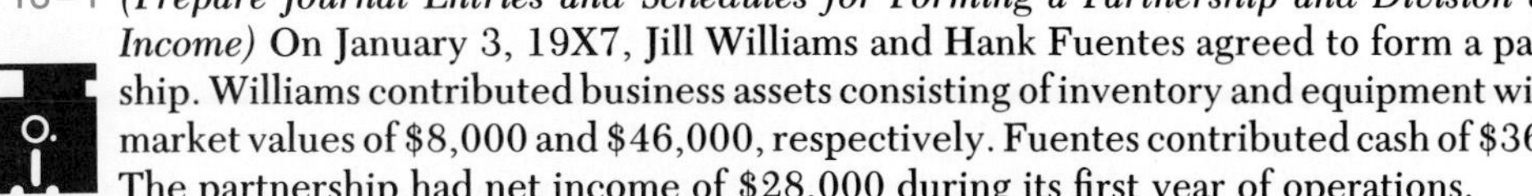

PROBLEM 13–1 *(Prepare Journal Entries and Schedules for Forming a Partnership and Division of Net Income)* On January 3, 19X7, Jill Williams and Hank Fuentes agreed to form a partnership. Williams contributed business assets consisting of inventory and equipment with fair market values of $8,000 and $46,000, respectively. Fuentes contributed cash of $36,000. The partnership had net income of $28,000 during its first year of operations.

Required:
1. Prepare separate journal entries to record each partner's initial investment.
2. Prepare schedules to show each partner's share of net income under each of the following plans:
   a. Income is shared in a ratio of 4 : 6.
   b. Income is shared in a ratio based upon the partners' initial capital investments.
   c. Income is shared by providing interest allowances at 10% to each partner based upon the amount of his or her initial investment, with any remainder divided equally.
   d. Income is shared by providing salary allowances of $8,000 for Williams and $12,000 for Fuentes, with any remainder divided 7 : 3, respectively. [LO2a,2b]

PROBLEM 13–2 *(Prepare Journal Entries to Record Division of Net Income and Net Loss)* Glenn and Beamer formed a partnership. Glenn invested $30,000, and Beamer invested $10,000.

Required:
1. Prepare journal entries to divide the $24,000 of net income earned during the company's first year of operations under each of the following assumptions:
   a. The partnership agreement is silent on how income is to be shared.
   b. The partners share income in the ratio of their beginning-of-the-period capital account balances.
   c. The partners share income by providing interest allowances at 8% to each partner based on their beginning-of-the-period capital account balances, with any remainder divided equally.
   d. The partners share income by providing salary allowances of $5,000 for Glenn and $8,000 for Beamer, with any remainder divided 4 : 6, respectively.
2. Assume that during its first year of operations, the partnership earned net income of $10,000 instead of $24,000. Prepare journal entries to divide that amount of net income under each of the assumptions labeled *a* through *d* above.
3. Assume now that the partnership incurred a $4,000 net loss during its first year of operations. Prepare journal entries to divide the loss under each of the assumptions labeled *a* through *d* above. [LO2b]

PROBLEM 13–3 *(Prepare Schedules to Show Division of Net Income and Prepare Statement of Partners' Capital)* Todd, Ward, and Best are partners in a distributing business. Data pertaining to the partners' capital accounts for 19X5 are as follows.

| | BEGINNING CAPITAL ACCOUNT BALANCES | INVESTMENTS DURING THE YEAR | AVERAGE CAPITAL ACCOUNT BALANCES |
|---|---|---|---|
| Todd | $15,000 | $10,000 | $20,000 |
| Ward | 20,000 | 20,000 | 30,000 |
| Best | 50,000 | — | 50,000 |

Net income for the year ended December 31, 19X5, was $18,000.

Required:
1. Prepare schedules to show each partner's share of net income under each assumption made below:
   a. Income is shared in a ratio based upon each partner's average capital account balance for the period.
   b. Income is shared by providing interest allowances at 12% to each partner based upon his or her average capital account balance, with any remainder divided equally.
   c. Income is shared by providing interest allowances at 6% to each partner based upon his or her average capital account balance, salary allowances of $8,000, $5,000, and $3,000 for Todd, Ward, and Best, respectively, with any remainder divided 4 : 3 : 3.

2. Prepare a statement of partners' capital. Additional data follow:
   a. When partnership assets were withdrawn from the firm by the partners, the transactions were recorded by debiting their individual drawings accounts. The balances in those drawings accounts at year-end were as follows: Todd, $10,200; Ward, $7,500; and Best, $3,800.
   b. The partnership net income is divided as provided for in Requirement 1*b*, above. [LO2b,2c]

PROBLEM 13–4 *(Prepare Journal Entries to Record Admittance of a New Partner)* Blake and Kean were partners in a profitable business that needed certain managerial skills in order to expand. On February 15 the partners met Tabor, who they felt had the skills they were seeking. On that same day when Blake and Kean had capital account balances of $50,000 and $30,000, respectively, they agreed to admit Tabor to the partnership. The original partners have been sharing net income in a 3:2 ratio.

Required:
Prepare the journal entry to record Tabor's admittance to the partnership for each of the following situations:
1. Tabor pays Blake $35,000 for 50% of his equity interest.
2. Tabor pays Blake $20,000 for 25% of his equity interest and pays Kean $12,500 for 25% of her equity interest.
3. Tabor invests $20,000 cash in the partnership for a 20% equity interest.
4. Tabor invests $40,000 cash in the partnership for a 25% equity interest.
5. Tabor invests $70,000 cash in the partnership for a 50% equity interest. [LO2d]

PROBLEM 13–5 *(Prepare Journal Entries to Record Withdrawal of a Partner)* Mason, Danza, and Clark are partners in Action Company, which started operations three years ago. They share income and losses in a 3:3:4 ratio. On October 15 of the current year, Clark withdraws from the partnership. The company's after-closing trial balance on that date is presented below.

ACTION COMPANY
After-Closing Trial Balance
October 15, 19X5

| | | |
|---|---|---|
| Cash | $ 20,000 | |
| Accounts Receivable | 50,000 | |
| Inventory | 30,000 | |
| Equipment | 125,000 | |
| Accumulated Depreciation | | $ 25,000 |
| Accounts Payable | | 30,000 |
| Mason, Capital | | 80,000 |
| Danza, Capital | | 50,000 |
| Clark, Capital | | 40,000 |
| | $225,000 | $225,000 |

Required:
Prepare the journal entry or entries to record the withdrawal of Clark for each of the following situations:
1. Clark sells his interest to Danza for $50,000.
2. Clark sells one-half of his interest to Mason and one-half of his interest to Danza for $27,000 each.
3. Clark receives cash of $30,000 and a note for $25,000 from the partnership for his interest.
4. Clark receives cash of $34,000 for his interest.
5. Clark is paid cash equal to the balance in his capital account after the accounts have been adjusted to recognize fair market value as follows: Accounts Receivable are re-

valued at $46,000; Inventory was increased by $10,000; Equipment is restated at $150,000; and the Accumulated Depreciation is increased by $5,000. [LO2e]

PROBLEM 13–6 *(Prepare Journal Entries to Record Partner Admittance and Withdrawal, and Compute Division of Net Income)* On January 5, 19X6, Carson and Taylor formed a partnership and invested $25,000 and $30,000, respectively. The partnership agreement provides an annual salary allowance of $10,000 for Carson, with any remaining income divided equally. Net income for the first year was a disappointing $7,000. During 19X6 Carson's withdrawals totaled $9,500 and Taylor's totaled $4,500.

In an effort to increase sales, Jordon, who is known to have excellent business contacts, was admitted to the firm. This occurred on January 9, 19X7, when Jordon purchased one-third of Carson's equity interest for $10,000. Payment went directly to Carson. At this time the income-sharing agreement was rewritten to provide for annual salary allowances of $7,000 and $5,000 for Carson and Jordon, respectively, with any remaining income divided equally. Net income for 19X7 almost quadrupled to $27,000. The partners, who had agreed to limit their withdrawals during the year, had year-end drawing account balances as follows: Carson, $7,000; Taylor, $3,000; and Jordon, $10,000.

On January 1, 19X8, Carson announced his retirement from the partnership. The firm purchased his equity interest on that date for $25,000.

Required:

1. Prepare a schedule to show Carson's and Taylor's shares of the 19X6 net income.
2. Determine the balances in Carson's and Taylor's capital accounts as of December 31, 19X6.
3. Prepare the journal entry to record Jordon's admittance to the partnership.
4. Prepare a schedule to show each partner's share of the 19X7 net income.
5. Determine the balances in each partner's capital account as of December 31, 19X7.
6. Prepare the journal entry to record Carson's withdrawal from the partnership.
7. Without changing your solution to Requirement 3, prepare the journal entry on January 9, 19X7, assuming Jordon was admitted to the partnership by investing $18,000 in the firm rather than buying a third of Carson's equity interest. Assume further that Jordon received a one-third equity interest in the firm. [LO2b,2d,2e]

PROBLEM 13–7 *(Prepare Journal Entries to Record Partnership Liquidation)* Moore, Dean, and Lee are partners who share net income and losses in a 5:3:2 ratio, respectively. On October 7, 19X6, they decide to liquidate the business. An after-closing trial balance prepared on that date is shown below.

After-Closing Trial Balance
October 7, 19X6

| | | |
|---|---|---|
| Cash | $ 18,000 | |
| Marketable Securities | 26,000 | |
| Accounts Receivable | 44,000 | |
| Allowance for Uncollectible Accounts | | $ 1,000 |
| Inventory | 35,000 | |
| Equipment | 90,000 | |
| Accumulated Depreciation | | 30,000 |
| Accounts Payable | | 23,000 |
| Notes Payable | | 36,000 |
| Moore, Capital | | 6,000 |
| Dean, Capital | | 73,000 |
| Lee, Capital | | 44,000 |
| | $213,000 | $213,000 |

Required:

Prepare journal entries to record the following:

1. Sold all noncash items on the dates and for the amounts shown below.

| | | |
|---|---|---|
| October | 8 | Sold the marketable securities for $33,000. |
| | 9 | Sold the accounts receivable to a finance company for $36,000. |
| | 11 | Sold the inventory for $48,000. |
| | 15 | Sold the equipment to a used-equipment company for $25,000. |

2. On October 15 after all noncash assets had been sold, the gain or loss realized on their sale was divided and assigned to the partners' capital accounts.
3. All partnership liabilities were paid on October 17.
4. a. (Assume that any partner with an equity deficiency is able to pay that amount to the partnership). On October 20 the receipt of cash from the deficient partner, and on the following day the distribution of partnership cash to the partners.
   b. (Assume that any partner with an equity deficiency is unable to pay that amount to the partnership.) On October 20 the assignment of any deficit capital accounts balances to partners having credit balance capital accounts, and on the following day the distribution of the partnership's remaining cash. [LO2f]

PROBLEM 13–8 *(Prepare Schedules and Journal Entries for Partnership Liquidation)* Ames, Hall, and Kent are partners who share net income and losses in a 4 : 4 : 2 ratio, respectively. On November 3, 19X6, they decide to liquidate the business. Company accounts and their balances after adjustments and in summary form are shown below.

| | |
|---|---|
| Cash | $ 30,000 |
| Noncash Assets | 180,000 |
| Liabilities | 50,000 |
| Ames, Capital | 70,000 |
| Hall, Capital | 10,000 |
| Kent, Capital | 80,000 |

Required:

1. Prepare two separate partnership liquidation schedules for the independent cases represented by the information in *a* and *b* below.
   a. The noncash assets were sold for $100,000. None of the partners have personal assets that can be contributed (invested) in the partnership. The liabilities were paid, and the cash remaining in the partnership was distributed to the partners.
   b. The noncash assets were sold for $200,000. All the partners have personal assets in excess of $100,000. The partnership liabilities were paid, and any remaining cash was distributed to the partners.
2. Prepare journal entries to record the activity presented in Requirement 1*a* above. Assume that everything occurred on November 3, 19X6. [LO2f]

PROBLEM 13–9 *(Comprehensive Problem)* Harris and Sheldon formed a partnership to operate a real estate agency. Certain transactions and events pertaining to the partnership are listed below.

*19X6*

| | |
|---|---|
| Jan. 24 | The partnership was formed. Harris contributed the following assets: cash, $15,000; supplies, $1,000; and used equipment having a fair market value of $14,000. Assets contributed by Sheldon consisted of cash, $30,000, and a vehicle that cost Sheldon $11,200 and currently has a fair market value of $10,000. |
| Dec. 31 | The partnership had net income of $18,000 in this its first year of operations. The partnership agreement specifies that income and losses are divided by allowing 10% interest on each partner's initial investment; salary allowances of $10,000 and $15,000 for Harris and Sheldon, respectively, with any remaining net income divided equally. As per their agreement, the partners did not withdraw any partnership assets for their personal use during this first year of business activity. |

| | |
|---|---|
| *19X7* | |
| Jan. 3 | The partners agreed to admit Jamie Brill, an experienced broker with a following in the commercial sector of the business, into their partnership. Brill invested $32,000 for a one-third equity interest in the business. The bonus was transferred in equal amounts from the capital accounts of the original partners to Brill's capital account. |
| Dec. 31 | The net income earned by the partnership in 19X7 amounted to $42,000. The new partnership agreement specifies that income and losses will be divided by allowing 12% interest on each partner's beginning-of-the-year capital balance (for this year that includes Jamie Brill's capital balance as of January 3, the day he was admitted to the partnership), and salary allowances of $8,000 and $12,000 for Harris and Sheldon, respectively, with any remainder in a 2:2:6 ratio. This year the partners made personal withdrawals of partnership assets totaling $15,360 for Harris, $27,280 for Sheldon, and $19,360 for Brill. |
| *19X8* | |
| Jan. 5 | Because of many disagreements among the partners (especially related to what some believed to be excessive withdrawal of partnership assets), the partners decided to liquidate the business. A summary of the partnership's assets and liabilities at this time revealed the following: cash, $16,000; noncash assets, $162,000; liabilities, $78,000. In liquidation, the noncash assets were sold for $120,000 and, per a new written agreement dated January 3, 19X8, gains or losses on the sales of assets were divided equally. To complete the partnership liquidation, all liabilities were paid and the remaining cash was distributed to the partners. |

Required:

1. Prepare separate journal entries to record the investment of the original partners on January 24, 19X6.
2. Prepare a journal entry to record the division of the first year's net income. Support amounts with computation schedules.
3. Prepare the journal entry or entries to record the admittance of Brill to the partnership on January 3, 19X7.
4. Prepare a journal entry to record the division of the second year's net income. Support amounts with computation schedules.
5. Prepare a statement of partners' capital as of December 31, 19X7.
6. Prepare a partnership liquidation schedule and the journal entries to record the liquidation of the partnership on January 5, 19X8. [LO2a,2b,2c,2d,2f]

## ALTERNATE PROBLEMS

PROBLEM 13–1A *(Prepare Journal Entries and Schedules for Forming a Partnership and Division of Net Income)* (Alternate to Problem 13–1) On January 3, 19X7, M. Cole and T. David agreed to form a partnership. Cole contributed business assets consisting of inventory and equipment with fair market values of $12,000 and $55,000, respectively. David contributed cash of $33,000. The partnership had net income of $36,000 during its first year of operations.

Required:

1. Prepare separate journal entries to record each partner's initial investment.
2. Prepare schedules to show each partner's share of net income under each of the following plans:

a. The partners share income in a ratio of 3:7.
b. The partners share income in a ratio based upon their initial capital investments.
c. The partners share income by providing interest allowances at 8% to each partner based upon the amount of their initial investment, with any remainder divided equally.
d. The partners share income by providing salary allowances of $6,000 for Cole and $14,000 for David, with any remainder divided 6:4, respectively. [LO2a,2b]

PROBLEM 13–2A *(Prepare Journal Entries to Record Division of Net Income and Net Loss)* (Alternate to Problem 13–2) Acker and Boomer formed a partnership. Acker invested $40,000, and Boomer invested $20,000.

Required:

1. Prepare journal entries to divide the $26,000 of net income earned during the company's first year of operations under each of the following assumptions:
   a. The partnership agreement is silent on how income is to be shared.
   b. The partners share income in the ratio of their beginning-of-the-period capital account balances.
   c. The partners share income by providing interest allowances at 10% to each partner based on their beginning-of-the-period capital account balances, with any remainder divided equally.
   d. The partners share income by providing salary allowances of $8,000 for Acker and $12,000 for Boomer, with any remainder divided 7:3, respectively.
2. Assume that during its first year of operations, the partnership earned net income of $12,000 instead of $26,000. Prepare journal entries to divide that amount of net income under each of the assumptions labeled *a* through *d* above.
3. Assume now that the partnership incurred a net loss of $6,000 during its first year of operations. Prepare journal entries to divide the loss under each of the assumptions labeled *a* through *d* above. [LO2b]

PROBLEM 13–3A *(Prepare Journal Entries to Record Admittance of a New Partner)* (Alternate to Problem 13–4) Tucker and Wall were partners in a successful business that needed a person with certain managerial talent in order to expand. On February 15 the partners met Dawson, who they felt had the talent they were seeking. On that same day when Tucker and Wall had capital account balances of $40,000 and $20,000, respectively, they agreed to admit Dawson to the partnership. The original partners have been sharing net income in a 6:4 ratio.

Required:

Prepare the journal entry to record Dawson's admittance to the partnership for each of the following situations:

1. Dawson pays Tucker $25,000 for 50% of her equity interest.
2. Dawson pays Tucker $8,000 for 25% of her equity interest.
3. Dawson invests $20,000 cash in the partnership for a 20% equity interest.
4. Dawson invests $40,000 cash in the partnership for a 30% equity interest.
5. Dawson invests $40,000 cash in the partnership for a 50% equity interest. [LO2d]

PROBLEM 13–4A *(Prepare Journal Entries to Record Withdrawal of a Partner)* (Alternate to Problem 13–5) Davis, Eden, and Franco are partners in Excite Company, which started operations two years ago. Per agreement they share income and losses in a 4:4:2 ratio. On August 12 of the current year, Franco withdraws from the partnership. The company's after-closing trial balance on that date is presented on page 484.

EXCITE COMPANY

After-Closing Trial Balance
August, 12, 19X5

| | | |
|---|---|---|
| Cash | $ 25,000 | |
| Accounts Receivable | 65,000 | |
| Inventory | 40,000 | |
| Equipment | 100,000 | |
| Accumulated Depreciation | | $ 20,000 |
| Accounts Payable | | 50,000 |
| Davis, Capital | | 60,000 |
| Eden, Capital | | 70,000 |
| Franco, Capital | | 30,000 |
| | $230,000 | $230,000 |

Required:

Prepare the journal entry or entries to record the withdrawal of Franco for each of the following independent situations:

1. Franco sells his interest to Davis for $40,000.
2. Franco sells one-third of his interest to Davis for $12,000 and two-thirds of his interest to Eden for $24,000.
3. Franco receives cash of $20,000 and a note for $22,000 from the partnership for his interest.
4. Franco receives cash of $26,000 for his interest.
5. Franco is paid cash equal to the balance in his capital account after the accounts have been adjusted to recognize fair market value as follows: An Allowance for Uncollectible Accounts of $2,000 is established for the Accounts Receivable; the Inventory is increased to $47,000; Equipment is restated at $170,000; the Accumulated Depreciation is increased to $40,000. [LO2e]

PROBLEM 13–5A *(Prepare Journal Entries to Record Partnership Liquidation)* (Alternate to Problem 13–7) Dudley, Elliott, and Frey are partners who share net income and losses in a 4:4:2 ratio, respectively. On May 26, 19X7, they decide to liquidate the business. An after-closing trial balance prepared on that date is shown below.

After-Closing Trial Balance
May 26, 19X7

| | | |
|---|---|---|
| Cash | $ 12,000 | |
| Marketable Securities | 15,000 | |
| Accounts Receivable | 28,000 | |
| Allowance for Uncollectible Accounts | | $ 600 |
| Inventory | 31,000 | |
| Equipment | 70,000 | |
| Accumulated Depreciation | | 20,400 |
| Accounts Payable | | 26,000 |
| Notes Payable | | 18,000 |
| Dudley, Capital | | 32,000 |
| Elliott, Capital | | 9,000 |
| Frey, Capital | | 50,000 |
| | $156,000 | $156,000 |

Required:

Prepare journal entries to record the following:

1. Sold all noncash items on the dates and for the amounts shown below.

| | |
|---|---|
| May 27 | Sold the marketable securities for $21,000. |
| 27 | Sold the accounts receivable to a finance company for $18,500. |
| 28 | Sold the inventory for $35,300. |
| 31 | Sold the equipment to a used-equipment company for $18,200. |

2. On May 31 after all noncash assets had been sold, the gain or loss realized on their sale was divided and assigned to the partners' capital accounts.
3. All partnership liabilities were paid on June 2, 19X7.
4. a. (Assume that any partner with an equity deficiency is able to pay that amount to the partnership.) On June 5 the receipt of cash from the deficient partner, and on the following day the distribution of partnership cash to the partners.
   b. (Assume that any partner with an equity deficiency is unable to pay that amount to the partnership.) On June 5 the assignment of any deficit capital account balances to partners having credit balance capital accounts, and on the following day the distribution of the partnership's remaining cash. [LO2f]

# 14 Corporations: Organization and Contributed Equity

### *Learning Objectives*

When you complete this chapter you will be able to

1. Answer the following questions:
   a. What is a corporation, and what are the distinctive characteristics and the advantages and disadvantages of the corporate form of business organization?
   b. How is a corporation formed and managed? What are the rights of stockholders and the roles of the corporate board of directors and corporate officers?
   c. What are the distinctive features of the stockholders' equity section of a corporation's balance sheet?
   d. What are the differences between authorized, issued, and unissued capital stock, and between par value, stated value, and no-par capital stock?
   e. What are the differences between common and preferred stock, and what special privileges are normally granted to each?
2. Perform the following accounting functions:
   a. Compute preferred stock and common stock dividends.
   b. Perform the accounting for the issuance of capital stock, including noncash issuances and donated capital.
   c. Perform the accounting for subscriptions to capital stock.
   d. Demonstrate how to compute book value per common share.

Although there are fewer corporations than proprietorships or partnerships, the corporate form of business organization dominates the U.S. economy. Corporations generate more dollars of revenue and net income, own more assets, employ more people, and produce more output of goods and services. In terms of economic significance, corporations are clearly the most important form of business organization. Most of the largest U.S. companies, such as Exxon and General Motors as well as many smaller ones, are organized as corporations. At some time you are likely to be associated with a corporation, either as an employee or as an owner of its shares. For these reasons, it is important that you become familiar with corporate structure and understand the accounting for corporate ownership.

## WHAT A CORPORATION IS

***1a. A corporation is a separate legal entity apart from its owners***

Unlike a proprietorship and a partnership, a **corporation** is a legal entity separate and apart from its owners. In a widely quoted definition, Chief Justice John Marshall in 1819 described a corporation as "an artificial being, invisible, intangible, and existing only in the contemplation of the law."

As a legal entity, a corporation may buy, own, and sell property in its own name. In addition, a corporation can enter into contracts with others and can sue or be sued in court. It also pays income tax and in general conducts business in the same way as a person. Ownership in a corporation is represented by transferable shares of stock, and the owners, called **stockholders,** are not personally liable for the corporation's debts.

## ADVANTAGES OF THE CORPORATE FORM OF ORGANIZATION

***1a. The nature of a corporation gives it certain distinctive advantages***

The corporate form of business organization has a number of advantages over the sole proprietorship and partnership forms. Among them are the following.

### Existence as a Separate Legal Entity

A corporation has a separate legal existence. It can, through its agents, conduct business with the same rights, duties, and responsibilities as a person.

### Limited Liability for Stockholders

As a separate legal entity, a corporation is responsible for the liabilities incurred in its corporate name. Thus the creditors of a corporation have a claim against the assets of the corporation, not against the personal assets of the stockholders. Because the stockholders, who are the owners of the corporation, have no personal liability for corporate debt, the amount they have at risk is the amount they invested in the corporation. Stated another way, the liability that each stockholder has for corporate debt is limited to the amount paid for his or her shares of stock. Contrast this with partnerships where one or more partners may be held personally liable for the debts of the partnership, thus risking personal as well as company assets. For an investor, **limited liability** is one of the major advantages of the corporate form of organization.

### Ease of Transferring Ownership Rights

Ownership rights in a corporation are represented by shares of stock. These shares can be transferred to other individuals or entities either directly or indirectly through private sales, brokerage firms, or established stock exchanges. Furthermore, the transfer of shares among shareholders does not require approval of the corporation itself and does not affect its accounts or its operations.

### Continuous Existence

Continuous existence refers to the fact that a successful corporation may continue to operate indefinitely. As a separate legal entity, a corporation continues to exist despite changes in its ownership. In contrast, a change in ownership caused by the withdrawal, incapacity, or death of an owner terminates a sole proprietorship or a partnership. The transfer of ownership shares has no effect on the corporation's ability to conduct its normal activity. Therefore corporations have continuous existence, often referred to as *unlimited lives.*

### Potential for Raising Larger Amounts of Capital

Limited liability for stockholders and easily transferable shares make stock ownership an attractive investment. These in turn enable a corporation to raise large amounts of capital by combining the investment capital of many stockholders. The right to sell shares of ownership in itself generally enables corporations to raise larger amounts of capital than partnerships can. The latter's capital-raising ability is limited by the number of partners and their individual wealth. The market of individuals and institutions that invest in corporations by buying their stock is considerable. Some corporations have thousands of stockholders; others have more than a million. These are generally referred to as *publicly held* corporations. Corporations owned by relatively few stockholders are referred to as *closely held.*

### No Mutual Agency

A stockholder, although legally a part owner of the corporation, does not have the power to bind the corporation to contracts. In contrast, a partnership can be bound by the actions of its partners.

### Professional Management

Stockholders own the corporation but do not manage its daily activities. Stockholders elect the board of directors, which has the broad responsibility for administering the corporation's affairs. The directors, in turn, hire a president and other corporate officers to manage the details of the business. This arrangement, which separates corporate management from corporate ownership, allows the corporation to seek out and hire the best managerial talent available for conducting the activities of the business.

## DISADVANTAGES OF THE CORPORATE FORM OF ORGANIZATION

*1a. The corporate form also has several disadvantages*

The corporate form of organization also has some disadvantages when compared with sole proprietorships and partnerships. Among the major disadvantages are the following.

### Greater Government Regulation

A corporation is created by fulfilling the requirements of state laws. These same laws can subject the corporation to a significant amount of regulation and control that is not imposed on proprietorships or partnerships. Corporations are responsible for filing reports with the state where their charter was granted. In addition, many corporations are subject to federal regulations. For example, federal laws administered by the Securities and Exchange Commission (SEC) regulate the securities markets in which shares of publicly held corporations are bought and sold. Publicly held corporations must also file extensive periodic reports with the SEC, which become public documents.

### Greater Tax Burden

Corporations as separate business entities are subject to various taxes not levied on sole proprietorships or partnerships. For example, corporations are subject to federal and state income taxes, the combination of which often exceeds 40% of the corporation's before-tax income. Stockholders often receive a share of the corporation's after-tax income, which is usually in cash paid out as dividends. The dividend received is taxable income to the stockholder. Thus a corporation's income is actually taxed twice—first as corporate income and again as personal income when distributed to the stockholders as dividends.

### Separation of Owners and Managers

Sometimes the hiring of professional managers who are separate from the owners is an advantage; at other times it can be a disadvantage. Sometimes managers make decisions that are beneficial to themselves but not to the company as a whole or to its shareholders. Corporate stockholders may not be in a position to determine whether management has made appropriate decisions and may often find it difficult to exercise any control over the management's actions.

## FORMING A CORPORATION

*1b. A corporation is formed by obtaining a state charter*

A corporation is created by obtaining a **corporate charter** from one of the fifty states. Although state laws differ, generally a charter application must be signed by three or more individuals called *incorporators,* each of whom will become an owner of the prospective corporation's stock. The incorporators' names are filed with the appropriate state official. Charter applications typically require the following information:

- The name of the proposed corporation
- The legal address of its principal office within the state
- The date of incorporation
- The nature and purpose of the business to be conducted
- A description of each type (class) of stock that the corporation will be authorized to issue
- The number of shares of each class of stock authorized
- A description of the rights and preferences assigned to each class of stock
- The names and addresses of the incorporators

After the application has been approved and all fees have been paid, the charter is issued. This brings the corporation into existence with authority to conduct business as a separate legal entity.

Then the stockholders hold a meeting during which the members of the board of directors are elected, and corporate bylaws are adopted. The bylaws indicate how the corporation will be governed and include policy statements as to how company affairs will be conducted. Then the board of directors holds a meeting to appoint a president and other officers who will operate the company. Once this is accomplished and the initial capital is raised by selling shares of the corporation's stock, the corporation is ready to begin operating.

## ORGANIZATION COSTS

The costs of forming a corporation, called **organization costs,** include such items as the incorporation fee paid to the state; the legal, accounting, and promotional fees; the cost of printing stock certificates; and the various other expenditures necessary to form the corporation. As these costs are being incurred, the amounts are debited to an intangible asset account called Organization Costs. Organization costs are incurred to create the corporation and should be of benefit to the corporation throughout its entire life.

However, since the life of a corporation is indeterminable, the years of benefit cannot be pinpointed. Thus organization costs, like all other intangible assets, are amortized over *an estimated benefit period, which in no case should exceed forty years.* Because current income tax regulations allow organization costs to be amortized over a period of not less than five years, many companies amortize these costs over *five years for both federal income tax and financial accounting purposes.*

## CORPORATE OWNERSHIP AND MANAGEMENT

Although the control of a corporation rests ultimately with its stockholders (owners), this control is exercised indirectly through the election of a board of directors. The board, elected by the stockholders, is responsible for setting overall corporate policies. The board, in turn, selects and elects the corporate officers, who typically include a president, one or more vice-presidents, a treasurer, a controller, and a secretary. These individuals manage the day-to-day activities of the business and carry out the policies set by the board.

*1b. Typical corporate organization structure is illustrated in Exhibit 14–1*

Exhibit 14–1 shows a typical corporate organization structure. Note that the lines of authority extend from the stockholders to the board of directors, to the president, and to other officers. Note also that each vice-president is in charge of a major function of the business. The controller is the chief accounting officer, the treasurer is the chief financial officer, and the secretary is an administrative officer.

### Stockholders

*1b. Owners of corporate stock have certain rights and privileges*

Stockholders do not normally participate in the day-to-day management of the company. Their involvement in corporate affairs is generally limited to electing the board of directors and voting on certain issues during meetings of the stockholders. An individual stockholder can, however, become directly involved in the daily management of the company by being elected to the board of directors or by being appointed an officer of the company. Stockholders do have certain rights and privileges. These, unless otherwise stated, usually include the following:

EXHIBIT 14–1

Corporate Organization Structure

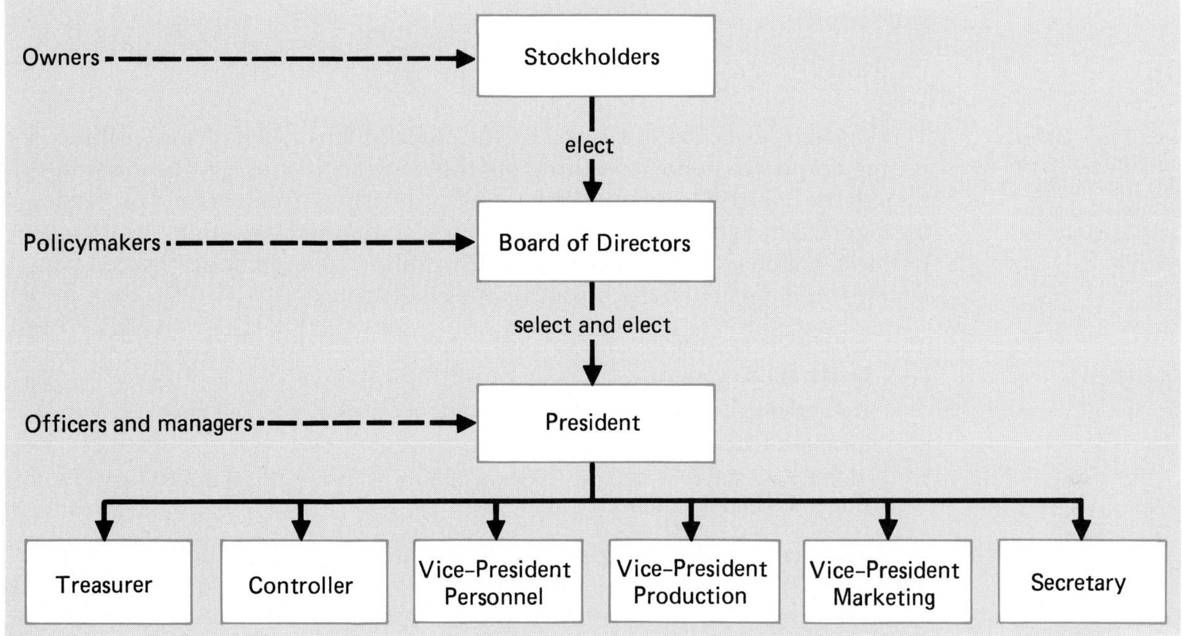


The right to dispose of their shares. Stockholders generally dispose of their shares through sale or gift. In either case, corporate ownership has been transferred.

The right to indirectly participate in the management of the company by voting for directors and on other matters that may be brought before them at stockholders' meetings.

The right to share in corporate earnings by receiving dividends when declared by the board of directors. Dividends are a distribution of corporate assets, usually cash, to the company's stockholders.

The right to purchase a portion of any new shares issued by the corporation. This **preemptive right** allows each stockholder to purchase new shares in proportion to his or her current holdings. This assures each stockholder that he or she can maintain the same percentage of ownership in the corporation after a new issuance of stock as before. For example, assume that J. Toney owns 10% of the stock of a corporation by virtue of owning 10,000 of the company's 100,000 outstanding shares. If the company plans to issue 50,000 new shares, Toney has the right to purchase 10 percent of that amount, or 5,000 shares, and thereby maintain his percentage of ownership in the corporation. In large corporations stockholders often waive their preemptive right in order to give management more flexibility when issuing new shares.

The right to share in the distribution of corporate assets if the corporation is liquidated. When a corporation is being liquidated, all the creditors are paid in full. Any remaining assets are then distributed to the stockholders in proportion to the number of shares they own.

Stockholders generally meet once a year to elect directors and conduct other business as provided by the corporate bylaws. Other business may include a discussion and a vote on such matters as proposed changes in the charter, the issuance of additional stock, the selection of outside auditors, and the revision of pension and stock option plans. Each stockholder is entitled to one vote for each share of voting stock held. Stockholders who do not personally attend the annual meeting may vote by proxy. A **proxy** is a legal document, signed by a stockholder, giving another person the authority to vote the stockholder's shares. Stockholders frequently give the voting authority to current management, which allows management to vote on corporate issues on behalf of the corporation's stockholders.

### Board of Directors

***1b. The board of directors is elected by the stockholders and is responsible for setting corporate policy***

The **board of directors** is elected by the stockholders and has responsibility for setting corporate policy and directing the management of the corporation. Although the board delegates most day-to-day decisions to officers and professional managers, it does maintain its authority for planning and implementing the major business policies of the corporation. In addition to appointing the company's administrative officers, the board's duties include

Authorizing contracts

Declaring dividends

Authorizing long-term borrowing, additional stock issues, and major projects

Establishing executive salaries

Monitoring and reviewing the system of internal controls and the work of the outside independent auditors

The board of directors is normally composed of several corporate officers (often referred to as insiders) and several persons not employed by the company (often referred to as outsiders). The purpose of having several outsiders serve as board members is to obtain more objectivity in the evaluation of management's performance.

The actions of the board are recorded in the minutes of each meeting. The *minutes book,* which includes the details of the board's decisions, is an important document to the accountant. It provides the authorization for certain transactions that need to be recorded in the accounting records.

### Corporate Officers

***1b. Corporate officers usually include a president, vice-presidents, treasurer, secretary, and controller***

The *president* and various other administrative officers are responsible for carrying out the policies set by the board and for managing the day-to-day activities of the business. The president is the chief executive officer and is directly responsible to the board for the operations of the company. Other administrative officers generally consist of the vice-presidents, treasurer, secretary, and controller.

The *vice-presidents* report to the president and are generally responsible for specific functional operations, such as marketing, production, personnel, and finance.

The *treasurer* is the custodian of company funds and is responsible for the planning and control of the company's cash.

The *secretary* keeps minutes of the directors' and stockholders' meetings, represents the company in most legal and contractual matters, and is in charge of many company records.

The *controller* is the chief accountant responsible for maintaining the accounting records, keeping an adequate system of internal control, preparing financial statements and tax returns, preparing reports required by other agencies, and developing a budget.

## STOCKHOLDERS' EQUITY

The major difference in accounting for a corporation and accounting for a sole proprietorship or a partnership involves the owners' equity. The treatment of the assets and liabilities of a corporation is similar to that of all other forms of business

*1c. Stockholders' equity generally is divided into contributed capital and retained earnings*

organization. In a corporation's balance sheet the term **stockholders' equity** is used to express the owners' claims to business assets instead of the term *owners' equity*. Furthermore, state incorporation laws generally require that the stockholders' equity section of a corporate balance sheet be divided into two broad categories—*contributed capital* and *retained earnings.* The main objective of this division is to clearly indicate the two main sources of stockholders' equity.

**Contributed capital** shows the amount of resources contributed (invested) in the corporation by the stockholders. **Retained earnings** shows the amount of income (resources) earned by the corporation and retained in the business.

The stockholders' equity section of a corporation's balance sheet can be divided into subsections to show the sources of its stockholders' equity, as illustrated below.

STOCKHOLDERS' EQUITY

| | |
|---|---|
| Contributed Capital: | |
| Preferred Stock, $10 par value, 25,000 shares authorized, 10,000 shares issued and outstanding | $100,000 |
| Common Stock, $5 par value, 300,000 shares authorized, 100,000 shares issued and outstanding | 500,000 |
| Paid-in Capital in Excess of Par Value—Preferred | 20,000 |
| Paid-in Capital in Excess of Par Value—Common | 80,000 |
| Total Contributed Capital | $700,000 |
| Retained Earnings | 250,000 |
| Total Stockholders' Equity | $950,000 |

*1c. The contributed capital subsection provides detailed information about the corporation's stock*

Note that the contributed capital subsection of the stockholders' equity provides a considerable amount of detailed information about the corporation's stock, including the following:

The types of stock issued, preferred and common

Their par value, $10 for the preferred and $5 for the common

The number of shares authorized by the corporate charter, 25,000 of the preferred and 300,000 of the common

The number of shares issued by the corporation, 10,000 of the preferred and 100,000 of the common

The number of shares of **outstanding stock,** that is, the number of shares held by the stockholders

The amount that stockholders paid for the shares issued in excess of their par value, $20,000 in excess of their par value for the preferred shares and $80,000 in excess of their par value for the common shares

The remainder of this chapter discusses the issues and examines the accounting for the items reported in the contributed capital section of stockholders' equity. Retained earnings is discussed in the next chapter.

## CAPITAL STOCK

*1d. Capital stock includes authorized, issued, and unissued shares*

The general term used to describe shares of ownership in a corporation is **capital stock.** Each owner receives from the corporation a legal document called a **stock certificate.** This certificate indicates the number of shares of the corporation's stock owned, the class of stock, its par or stated value if any, and the preferential rights or restrictions applicable to the shares.

The corporation's charter indicates the number of shares of each class of capital stock that the corporation is authorized to issue and the par or stated value, if any, assigned to those shares.

> **Authorized shares** represent the maximum number of shares of each class of capital stock the corporation is permitted to issue.
>
> **Issued shares** is the term used to describe the authorized shares of stock that have been issued (distributed) to the stockholders.

It is normal to expect a corporation to obtain authorization to issue more shares than it plans to sell or otherwise distribute immediately. This allows the corporation to issue additional shares at some future time without asking the state for an amendment to the charter that would increase the number of authorized shares. Shares that are authorized but not yet issued are referred to as **unissued shares,** and they represent a means for raising additional monies in the future.

To illustrate, assume that a corporation is authorized to issue 500,000 shares of capital stock and that 300,000 shares have been issued. The corporation would at this point have 200,000 unissued shares, which may at some future time be sold or otherwise distributed.

### Par Value

***1d. In some states, stock must be assigned a par value***

In some states the incorporation laws require that stock be given a par value. **Par value** is a per share amount determined arbitrarily and assigned to the stock by the company's incorporators at the time they apply for the corporate charter. The par amount is printed on each stock certificate and is recorded in the capital stock accounts. In some states par value establishes a minimum amount of **legal capital** that must be retained in the business. The amount established as the corporation's legal capital cannot be distributed to stockholders unless the corporation is being liquidated and some assets remain after all the creditors have been paid. Legal capital specifies the minimum amount of resources invested in the corporation by the stockholders that must be retained in the corporation for the protection of its creditors.

The par value of a company's stock is no indication of its worth or market value. At any one point in time, the market value per share may be considerably above its par value. For example, both Polaroid and Revlon have had common stock with a par value of one dollar per share, and Sears has common stock with a par value of seventy-five cents per share. In each case, the company's market value per share is considerably above those amounts.

### No-Par Stock

***1d. No-par stock is stock without an assigned par value***

**No-par stock** does not have a par value per share. It wasn't until 1912 that New York State passed the first law permitting the issuance of this type of stock. One intent of this law was to eliminate some of the misunderstandings that had developed about the significance of par value. Today all the states permit the issuance of no-par stock. Since no arbitrary value is assigned to these shares, some states require that the entire amount received from the sale of no-par stock be considered legal capital.

### No-Par Stock with a Stated Value

*1d. In many states the board of directors may assign a stated value to no-par stock*

In many states the board of directors may assign a stated value to no-par stock. When a stated value is assigned to the shares, the shares are said to be **stated value stock,** or simply *no-par stock.* A stated value serves the same purpose as par value in that it is used to determine a corporation's legal capital.

## CLASSES OF STOCK

To appeal to the diverse interests of as many investors as possible, many corporations issue two types of capital stock—common and preferred.

### Common Stock

When only one class of stock is issued, it is called **common stock.** It is the most basic class of stock and is issued by every corporation. Unless otherwise stated, common stockholders have the previously mentioned basic rights that accompany the ownership of shares.

*1e. Common stock represents a corporation's residual equity*

Common stock represents the *residual equity* of a corporation. This means that claims to corporate assets by creditors and preferred stockholders rank ahead of claims by common stockholders. If the corporation liquidates, common stockholders receive assets only after all the obligations to creditors and preferred stockholders have been satisfied.

### Preferred Stock

*1e. Preferred stock offers special features to meet investors' objectives*

In addition to common stock, many corporations issue one or more types of **preferred stock.** Each type of preferred stock will have its own special preferences or restrictions that distinguish it from common stock or other types of preferred. By having various and distinctive features, the preferred stock may be more capable of meeting the objectives of certain potential investors.

For example, preferred stock often appeals to investors who want less risk and market volatility than that assumed in common stock ownership and yet maintain a stable and steady dividend. Preferred stock attempts to meet a variety of investment objectives by providing various preferential rights not available to common stockholders. These preferential rights of preferred stock generally include one or more of the following:

Preference as to **dividends** (distributions of earnings in the form of cash, other assets, or shares of the corporation's own stock to its stockholders)

Preference as to assets if the corporation is liquidated

Convertible at the option of the holder

Callable at the option of the corporation

Preferred stockholders often have limited or no voting rights in corporate affairs, rights normally granted to common stockholders.

### Preference as to Dividends

*1e. Preferred stock usually has preference as to dividends*

Preferred stock usually has preference as to dividends. Thus the preferred stockholders are entitled to receive a dividend before any dividend can be paid to the common stockholders. The preference dividend is usually expressed as either

A *dollar* amount per share or
A *percentage* of the stock's par value.

The shares may be issued, for example, as either

"$5 preferred," meaning a yearly dividend of $5 per share, or
"$100 par value, 5% preferred," which also means a yearly dividend of $5 per share (5% of the $100 par value equals $5).

There is of course no assurance that the stipulated preference dividend will always be paid. As with dividends on common stock, the obligation to pay dividends on preferred stock occurs only if they are declared by the board of directors.

The dividend preference on most preferred stock is *cumulative*. When dividends are not declared on **cumulative preferred stock,** the amount of the undeclared dividends accumulates. This accumulated amount, representing the dividends not paid in past years, plus the current year's regular preference dividend, must be declared and paid before dividends can be paid to common stockholders. Dividends not declared or paid on cumulative preferred stock are called **dividends in arrears.** They represent dividends not paid in past years whose future payment depends on a dividend declaration by the board of directors. Dividends in arrears are not liabilities of the corporation and are not recorded in the accounting records. However, the amount of the dividends in arrears should be reported and disclosed in the notes that accompany the financial statements.

To illustrate the distribution of dividends for cumulative preferred stock, assume that a corporation has the following:

*1e,2a. Distribution of dividends for cumulative preferred stock is illustrated here*

2,000 shares of $100 par value, 6% cumulative preferred stock outstanding
40,000 shares of $10 par value common stock outstanding

No dividends have been paid during the past two years, but the board of directors has declared a $90,000 dividend in the current year. The $90,000 dividend distribution would be allocated to the preferred and common stockholders as shown in the schedule below.

| | PREFERRED DIVIDEND | COMMON DIVIDEND | TOTAL DIVIDEND |
|---|---|---|---|
| Dividends in Arrears—Two Years ($6 × 2,000 shares × 2 yrs.) | $24,000 | — | $24,000 |
| Current-Year Preference Dividend ($6 × 2,000 shares) | 12,000 | — | 12,000 |
| Amount Remaining ($90,000 − $36,000 = $54,000) to Common | — | $54,000 | 54,000 |
| Total Amount Distributed | $36,000 | $54,000 | $90,000 |
| Dividends per Share: | | | |
| $36,000/2,000 shares | $18.00 | | |
| $54,000/40,000 shares | | $ 1.35 | |

If in our preceding example the board had declared a $30,000 dividend, preferred stockholders would have received the entire amount, no dividend would have been available for common stockholders, and there would still have been $6,000 of dividends in arrears to preferred stockholders.

If the stock is **noncumulative preferred stock,** any undeclared dividends are lost and will never be paid. For this reason, investors have been reluctant to buy preferred stock that is noncumulative; therefore few companies have issued such shares.

Most preferred stock is nonparticipating. This means that the preferred stockholders are limited to receiving the amount of their specified dividend and no more. Sometimes the preferred stock is participating. **Participating preferred stock** has a feature that makes the preferred stockholder eligible to receive a larger dividend than the specified dividend amount. The extent of participation varies widely, leading to the descriptive titles of *partially* and *fully participating* preferred stock.

*1e,2a. Distribution of dividends for participating preferred stock is illustrated here*

To illustrate a dividend distribution, assume that the preferred stock of the corporation in the preceding illustration has a participating feature. The feature provides that if the dividend to be distributed exceeds the preferred's specified dividend, a comparable rate should be used to allocate dividends to the common. The amount remaining is to be apportioned so that both classes of stock receive the same rate of distribution. According to these terms, the $90,000 dividend distribution would be allocated to the preferred and common stockholders as shown in the schedule below.

| | PREFERRED DIVIDEND | COMMON DIVIDEND | TOTAL DIVIDEND |
|---|---|---|---|
| Total Par Value of Stock Outstanding | $200,000 | $400,000 | $600,000 |
| Preferred Dividends in Arrears ($6 × 2,000 shares × 2 yrs.) | $ 24,000 | — | $ 24,000 |
| Current Specified Dividend to Preferred ($6 × 2,000 shares) | 12,000 | — | 12,000 |
| Matching Rate to Common Shareholders (6% × $400,000 par value) | — | $ 24,000 | 24,000 |
| Remaining Dividend Amount of $30,000 allocated to give each class the same rate [$30,000 ÷ $600,000 (the total par value of both classes of stock) = 5%] | | | |
| 5% × $200,000 | 10,000 | — | 10,000 |
| 5% × $400,000 | — | 20,000 | 20,000 |
| Total Amount Distributed | $ 46,000 | $ 44,000 | $ 90,000 |
| Dividends per Share | $ 23.00 | $ 1.10 | |

Note that the procedure for allocating the dividends is as follows:

Arrearage dividends, if any, must be allocated first.

The specified preference dividend (in this case $6 per share or, in total, 6% times the stock's par value of $200,000) is allocated next.

An amount based on a matching rate is then allocated to the common stockholders. The amount is determined by multiplying the same rate that the preferred received times the par value of the common (6% matching rate times $400,000 par value).

The remaining amount is then allocated to the common and preferred so that both receive the same rate of distribution. This rate is determined by dividing the number of dollars remaining to be distributed by the total par value of both classes of stock.

The extent of participation may vary. For example, the preferred shares may be entitled to participate to 9%, in which case they would be called partially participating. Using the data from our previous illustration, the partially participating preferred stock would be entitled only to an additional 3% over their regular dividend of 6%, with the remaining amount being distributed to the common stockholders.

Because most preferred stock is nonparticipating, we will go no further with our discussion of participating preferred stock. For nonparticipating preferred stock, dividends are allocated first for arrearage amounts, if any, next for the stock's preference dividend, and then any remaining amount is entirely allocated to the common stockholders.

### Preference as to Assets

*1e. Preferred stock may have preference as to assets*

Preferred stock generally has a preference in its claim to assets if the corporation is liquidated. When a corporation is terminated, creditors' claims must be paid first. If the firm is being liquidated and assets remain after the creditors have been paid, the preferred stockholders are entitled to receive payment equal to the par value of their stock (or a higher liquidation value if one is stated) before any payment is made to common stockholders. This preference also includes payment for any dividends in arrears on cumulative preferred stock.

### The Convertible Feature

*1e. The convertible feature of some preferred stocks makes the shares more appealing to investors*

Some preferred stocks carry a *convertible* feature. This means that the holders of **convertible preferred stock** can exchange their preferred shares for common shares in a specified exchange ratio. For example, one share of preferred stock may be convertible, at the option of the holder, to three shares of common stock.

The convertible feature makes the shares more appealing to investors. If the market price of the common stock rises, the conversion feature will allow the preferred stockholders to benefit from the increase. This is because the market price of the convertible preferred stock will tend to approximate the market price of the common stock into which it can be converted after adjusting for the exchange ratio. Using the exchange ratio of our preceding example, if the market price of common went from $25 per share to $30, then given the exchange ratio of 3 to 1 the market price of preferred would have gone up $15 during the same period.

### The Call Provision

*1e. Most preferred stocks include a call provision*

Most preferred stocks include a **call provision,** which gives the corporation the right to redeem the stock on demand or in accordance with specified terms at a stipulated **call price.** The call price, sometimes called the *redemption price,* is usually set above the stock's original issuance price. For example, preferred stock issued on March 1, 1985, at $20 per share may be callable at any time after February 28, 1990, at $25 per share. The call is at the option of the corporation, not the shareholder. Having a call provision gives the corporation some flexibility in deciding on the type of securities represented in stockholders' equity.

### Stock Features — Summarized

We have seen that all corporations issue common stock, and common stockholders have voting privileges. Many corporations also issue preferred stock, and some corporations issue two or more types of preferred stock. Although preferred stockholders usually have limited voting rights or no voting rights, their shares have features that give them certain advantages not available to common stockholders. These features provide specific rights or restrictions and usually relate to dividends, priorities on claims to assets, convertibility, and callability.

## ACCOUNTING FOR THE ISSUANCE OF PAR VALUE STOCK

When par value stock is issued for cash, the transaction is recorded as follows: (1) the Cash account is debited for the amount received, (2) the Common Stock (or Preferred Stock) account is credited for the par value of the shares issued, and (3) a separate account called Paid-in Capital in Excess of Par Value is credited for the amount by which the selling price of the shares exceeded their par value.

First we will illustrate the accounting when par value stock is issued for cash at an amount equal to its par value. Thus in this first example we will not need the Paid-in Capital in Excess of Par Value account. Assume that Gentry Corporation is authorized to issue *20,000* shares of $100 par value preferred stock and *100,000* shares of $5 par value common stock. Assume further that *5,000* preferred shares and *40,000* common shares were issued for cash at amounts equal to their respective par values. The entry to record the transaction is as follows:

***2b. An entry is made to record the receipt of cash and the issuance of stock***

| | | |
|---|---|---|
| Cash | 700,000 | |
| Preferred Stock | | 500,000 |
| Common Stock | | 200,000 |
| Issued 5,000 shares of $100 par value preferred stock and 40,000 shares of $5 par value common stock at par for cash | | |

The Preferred and Common Stock accounts are controlling accounts. It is important to maintain records showing at a minimum each stockholder's name, address, and number of shares owned. This information is needed for the issuance of dividend checks, financial reports, and voting forms. These individual stockholder accounts are kept in a subsidiary ledger called the **stockholders' ledger.**

Now we will assume that the par value stock is issued for an amount in excess of its par value. This requires crediting the **Paid-in Capital in Excess of Par Value** account for the amount by which the proceeds received exceed the par value of the shares issued.

***2b. Paid-in Capital in Excess of Par Value is credited for the excess of proceeds over par value***

For example, assume that Gentry Corporation issues 40,000 of its common shares for cash at $8 per share. The entry to record the receipt of cash and the issuance of the stock is as follows:

| | | |
|---|---|---|
| Cash | 320,000 | |
| Common Stock | | 200,000 |
| Paid-in Capital in Excess of Par Value—Common | | 120,000 |
| Issued 40,000 shares of $5 par value common stock for $8 per share | | |

Note that

Cash is *debited* for *$320,000,* the amount received

Common Stock is *credited* for *$200,000,* the par value of the shares issued

The amount received in excess of the stock's par value, *$120,000,* is *credited* to the Paid-in Capital in Excess of Par Value—Common account.

Thus our illustration shows that when we are accounting for the issuance of stock:

Cash (or on occasion some other asset) is debited when the stock is issued.

The stockholders' equity accounts will identify the class of stock issued (either common or preferred).

The proceeds from the sale of the stock are divided into that portion attributable to the stock's par value and that portion in excess of the par value.

The amount paid in excess of par value is sometimes called a premium, in which case the account title Premium on Common Stock may be used instead of Paid-in Capital in Excess of Par Value—Common. Regardless of which account title is used, the amount paid in excess of par value is part of the corporation's total contributed capital and is shown in the stockholders' equity section of the balance sheet, as illustrated below.

STOCKHOLDERS' EQUITY

| | |
|---|---|
| Contributed Capital: | |
| Common Stock, $5 par value, 100,000 shares authorized, 40,000 shares issued and outstanding | $200,000 |
| Paid-in Capital in Excess of Par Value | 120,000 |
| Total Contributed Capital | $320,000 |
| Retained Earnings* | 100,000 |
| Total Stockholders' Equity | $420,000 |

* Amount arbitrarily assumed.

If we assume that 5,000 of Gentry Corporation's $100 par value preferred shares are now issued at $120 per share instead of $100 per share, the entry would be as follows:

| | | |
|---|---|---|
| Cash | 600,000 | |
| Preferred Stock | | 500,000 |
| Paid-in Capital in Excess of Par Value—Preferred | | 100,000 |
| Issued 5,000 shares of $100 par value preferred stock for $120 per share | | |

If a corporation issues stock for less than its par value, it is said to be issued at a **discount.** Only a few states permit this practice because stockholders are then investing less than the minimum legal capital. In some of these states the stockholders are contingently liable to the corporation's creditors for the amount of the discount. If the corporation has been liquidated and there are not enough assets to pay the creditors in full, the stockholders can be assessed for additional monies up to the amount of the discount on their shares.

*2b. Discount on Common Stock is debited when stock is issued at less than par*

To illustrate, assume that Gentry Corporation issues 40,000 of its $5 par value common shares for cash at $3 per share. This is $2 per share below par value, and the total discount of $80,000 ($2 × 40,000 shares) will be debited to the Discount on Common Stock account.

The entry to record the transaction is as follows:

| | | |
|---|---|---|
| Cash | 120,000 | |
| Discount on Common Stock | 80,000 | |
| Common Stock | | 200,000 |
| Issued 40,000 shares of $5 par value common stock for $3 per share | | |

The amount of the discount is debited to the Discount on Common Stock account. This is a contra account, shown in the stockholders' equity section of the balance sheet as a deduction from the Common Stock account. This presentation is used so that the amount actually invested in the corporation by the preferred and common stockholders can be determined.

## ACCOUNTING FOR THE ISSUANCE OF NO-PAR STOCK

*2b. In some states, all the proceeds from sale of no-par stock must be credited to a capital stock account*

In some states, when a corporation issues no-par stock, the entire proceeds from the sale become minimum legal capital and must be credited to a capital stock account. For example, assume that Gentry Corporation's capital stock is no-par common and that 40,000 shares are issued at $7 per share. The entire proceeds of $280,000 are credited to the no-par common stock account as follows:

| | | |
|---|---|---|
| Cash | 280,000 | |
| Common Stock, No-par | | 280,000 |
| Issued 40,000 shares of no-par common stock for $7 per share | | |

In other states, the board of directors may assign a stated value per share to the firm's no-par stock. The stated value then becomes minimum legal capital and is credited to a capital stock account. If the stock is issued at an amount in excess of the stated value, the excess is credited to a contributed capital account, such as Paid-in Capital in Excess of Stated Value—Common.

To illustrate the entry when no-par stock having a stated value is issued, assume that Gentry's directors assigned a stated value of $5 to the firm's no-par common stock. The entry to record the issuance of 40,000 shares of the no-par common stock for $7 per share is as follows:

| | | |
|---|---|---|
| Cash | 280,000 | |
| Common Stock, No-par | | 200,000 |
| Paid-in Capital in Excess of Stated Value—Common | | 80,000 |
| Issued 40,000 shares of no-par common stock with a $5 stated value for $7 per share | | |

The Paid-in Capital in Excess of Stated Value account is treated in the same way as the Paid-in Capital in Excess of Par Value account. Both represent a part of total contributed capital. Because they are seldom part of legal capital, they are reported as separate components of contributed capital in the stockholders' equity section of the balance sheet as follows:

| STOCKHOLDERS' EQUITY | |
|---|---|
| Contributed Capital | |
| Common Stock, $5 stated value, 100,000 shares authorized, 40,000 shares issued and outstanding | $200,000 |
| Paid-in Capital in Excess of Stated Value | 80,000 |
| Total Contributed Capital | $280,000 |
| Retained Earnings | 100,000 |
| Total Stockholders' Equity | $380,000 |

## ACCOUNTING FOR STOCK ISSUANCE IN EXCHANGE FOR SERVICES OR NONCASH ASSETS

As shown in all our previous examples, corporations normally issue their stock for cash. The cash is then used for various corporate purposes, such as the purchase of assets and the payment of expenses. Sometimes, however, a corporation may issue stock in a direct exchange for noncash assets, such as land, buildings, or patents. Stock may also be issued to attorneys, corporate promoters, and other professionals in payment for the services they provided, particularly at the time the corportion was formed.

When shares are issued for noncash assets, a question arises as to what amount should be used to record the exchange. For example, when assets are acquired by purchase, they are recorded in the accounts at their cost. Purchased services are also recorded at cost—but how is cost determined when stock rather than cash is given in exchange for the assets or for the services acquired? The general rule is that *the assets or services acquired are recorded at their fair market value or at the fair market value of the stock issued, whichever is more clearly and objectively determinable.*

If the corporation's stock is actively traded on one of the stock exchanges, its market value is not only easy to obtain but perhaps the best way to measure value. When the stock is not actively traded, the values to be assigned to the assets or services acquired must be determined carefully, and this may become the responsibility of the board of directors.

To illustrate the accounting, assume that Gentry's attorney agreed to accept 300 shares of the company's $5 par value common stock for services performed when the corporation was formed. At the times the shares were issued, their market value was not determinable. However, for the legal and promoting work performed, the attorney would have billed the company $2,000. The journal entry to record the transaction follows:

***2b. An entry is made to record the issuance of stock in return for services***

| | | |
|---|---|---|
| Organization Costs . . . . . . . . . . | 2,000 | |
| Common Stock. . . . . . . . . . | | 1,500 |
| Paid-in Capital in Excess of Par Value—Common. . . . . . . . | | 500 |
| Issued 300 shares of $5 par value common stock for attorney's services | | |

Because the company's stock was not actively traded, its market value could not be determined at the time the shares were issued.

The Organization Costs account was *debited* for *$2,000,* the value of the services rendered by the attorney, an amount more clearly and objectively determinable at the time the shares were issued.

The Common Stock account was *credited* for the *par value* of the shares issued.

The *difference* between the fair value of the asset acquired and the par value of the shares issued was *credited* to Paid-in Capital in Excess of Par Value—Common.

For another example, assume that six months later, when the company's stock was actively trading at $8 per share, 2,000 shares were given to another company in exchange for a recently developed patent. The fair market value of the patent is not clearly determinable to either party to the transaction. Therefore the entry to record the exchange (based on the market value of shares) is as follows:

***2b. An entry is made to record the issuance of stock in exchange for a patent***

| | | |
|---|---|---|
| Patents. . . . . . . . . . . . . . . . . . . . . . . . . . . . . . . . . . . . . . . . . . . . . . | 16,000 | |
| Common Stock. . . . . . . . . . . . . . . . . . . . . . . . . . . . . . . . . . . . . . . | | 10,000 |
| Paid-in Capital in Excess of Par Value—Common. . . . . . . . . | | 6,000 |
| Issued 2,000 shares of $5 par value common stock in exchange for a patent | | |

## ACCOUNTING FOR DONATED CAPITAL

*2b. Donated assets are credited to Donated Capital*

Although it rarely occurs, a corporation may occasionally receive a donation of assets from a shareholder, municipality, or other party. For example, some cities give land to a corporation that promises to construct facilities on that land. The city benefits directly by increasing its tax base and indirectly by increasing local employment. The corporation receiving the land (or any other asset) records the donation by debiting the asset account for its fair market value and crediting a separate contributed equity account called Donated Capital.

To illustrate, assume that Gentry receives a donation of land having a fair market value of $150,000. The following entry would be recorded:

| | | |
|---|---|---|
| Land. . . . . . . . . . . . . . . . . . . . . . . . . . . . . . . . . . . . . . . . . . . . . . . . . | 150,000 | |
| Donated Capital . . . . . . . . . . . . . . . . . . . . . . . . . . . . . . . . . . . . | | 150,000 |
| To record donated land at its fair market value | | |

The Donated Capital account is part of the corporation's contributed capital and is shown in the stockholders' equity section of its balance sheet.

## ACCOUNTING FOR STOCK SUBSCRIPTIONS

Corporations sometimes issue stock on a **stock subscription** basis. In such cases, the purchaser (investor) agrees to purchase a specified number of shares at an agreed-upon price per share. The terms may provide for payment in full at some future date or for installment payments over a period of time. When the stock is subscribed, a contract exists, and the corporation acquires a receivable from the subscriber. If the stock is subscribed for at par, the subscription price is debited to the asset account Subscriptions Receivable and credited to a separate account called Common (or Preferred) Stock Subscribed.

The Subscriptions Receivable account is an asset account showing the amount owed to the corporation by its subscribers. The Stock Subscribed account represents part of the corporation's minimum legal capital. The presence of this account shows that stock subscribed for has not been fully paid for and, therefore, the shares have not been issued. Thus in a sense the Stock Subscribed account represents a temporary stockholders' equity account. The account will remain open only until the shares are paid for in full and certificates are issued.

When stock is subscribed for at a price above par or stated value, the Subscriptions Receivable account is debited for the subscription price. The Stock Subscribed account is credited for the stock's par or stated value, and the difference between the subscription price and the par or stated value is credited to the Paid-in Capital in Excess of Par (or Stated) Value account. In those rare cases where the subscription price is less than the stock's par or stated value, the difference is debited to a Discount on Common (or Preferred) Stock account.

To illustrate the entries for subscriptions and stock issuance, assume that on March 1 Gentry Corporation receives a subscription to 10,000 shares of its $5 par value common stock at $9 per share. The agreement requires the investor to make a down payment of one-third of the purchase price. The remaining amount is due in two equal installments on May 1 and July 1. The entries to record the subscription and the down payment are as follows.

*2c. Entries are made to record subscriptions to capital stock*

| | | | |
|---|---|---|---|
| March 1 | Subscriptions Receivable—Common | 90,000 | |
| | Common Stock Subscribed | | 50,000 |
| | Paid-in Capital in Excess of Par Value—Common | | 40,000 |
| | Received subscriptions for 10,000 shares of $5 par value common stock at $9 per share | | |
| March 1 | Cash | 30,000 | |
| | Subscriptions Receivable—Common | | 30,000 |
| | Collected one-third payment for subscriptions to 10,000 common shares | | |

When the installment payments of May 1 and July 1 are received, Cash is debited and Subscriptions Receivable—Common is credited, just as in the down payment entry recorded above. After all agreed-to payments have been received, the corporation will issue the stock certificate to the investor. In our example this will happen on July 1. The entries to record collection of the agreed-upon amounts and issuance of the fully paid-for shares are as follows.

| | | | |
|---|---|---|---|
| May 1 | Cash | 30,000 | |
| | Subscriptions Receivable—Common | | 30,000 |
| | Collected one-third payment for subscriptions to 10,000 common shares | | |
| July 1 | Cash | 30,000 | |
| | Subscriptions Receivable—Common | | 30,000 |
| | Collected one-third payment for subscriptions to 10,000 common shares | | |
| July 1 | Common Stock Subscribed | 50,000 | |
| | Common Stock | | 50,000 |
| | Issued a stock certificate for 10,000 shares of $5 par value common stock | | |

If financial statements were prepared on May 31, 19XX, before the final payment on the subscription was received, the Subscriptions Receivable account with its $30,000 debit balance would be reported as a current asset on the balance sheet.

The Common Stock Subscribed account having a balance of $50,000 on that date is reported as a component of contributed capital in the stockholders' equity section of the balance sheet.

## STOCK VALUES

In addition to par value, stated value, and redemption value, which we have already discussed, the terms *market value* and *book value* are often encountered and associated with a corporation's stock.

## Book Value

*2d. Book value per share measures the claim that an owner of one share of stock has in the corporation's net assets*

The **book value per share** of common stock measures the portion of stockholders' equity represented by one share of stock. Or put another way, it provides a measurement of the amount of claim that each share of stock has against the net assets of the corporation. If a corporation has issued only one type of stock, book value per share is determined by dividing total stockholders' equity by the number of shares outstanding plus shares subscribed but not issued.

For example, assume that Gentry's balance sheet has the following stockholders' equity section:

| | |
|---|---|
| Contributed Capital: | |
| Common Stock, $5 par value, 100,000 shares authorized, 40,000 shares issued and outstanding | $200,000 |
| Paid-in Capital in Excess of Par Value | 120,000 |
| Total Contributed Capital | $320,000 |
| Retained Earnings | 180,000 |
| Total Stockholders' Equity | $500,000 |

Book value per share is $12.50, computed as follows:

$$\frac{\text{Total Stockholders' Equity}}{\text{Number of Shares Outstanding plus Shares Subscribed}} = \frac{\$500{,}000}{40{,}000} = \$12.50 \text{ per share}$$

Book value per share is another corporate financial measure that when monitored over time may provide some useful information. It should not, however, be confused with market value per share, which is determined by the supply and demand for the corporation's shares. Book values do change when earnings are retained in the business rather than distributed as a dividend, which in turn contributes to corporate growth. When earnings are retained, stockholders' equity increases. If the number of shares outstanding remains relatively stable while stockholders' equity increases, book value per share will increase.

When a corporation has both preferred and common stock outstanding, total stockholders' equity must be allocated between the two classes of stock. The general rule is to subtract from total stockholders' equity the amount that would be distributed to preferred stockholders (before any distribution would be made to common stockholders) should the corporation be terminated. This means that the portion of stockholders' equity allocated to preferred stock is its call price plus any dividends in arrears. The sum of these two items is subtracted from total stockholders' equity to determine the amount of stockholders' equity that can be attributed to common stock. The book values per share for each class of stock can then be determined by dividing the portion of stockholders' equity assigned to each class by their respective number of shares outstanding.

For example, assume that the stockholders' equity section of Gentry's balance sheet is as follows:

| | |
|---|---|
| Contributed Capital: | |
| Preferred Stock, $100 par value, 8% cumulative and nonparticipating, 20,000 shares authorized, 5,000 shares issued and outstanding, callable at $110 | $ 500,000 |
| Common Stock, $5 par value, 100,000 shares authorized, 40,000 shares issued and outstanding | 200,000 |
| Paid-in Capital in Excess of Par Value—Common | 120,000 |
| Total Contributed Capital | $ 820,000 |
| Retained Earnings | 180,000 |
| Total Stockholders' Equity | $1,000,000 |

Assume that dividends on the preferred stock are $80,000 in arrears. The allocation of Gentry's total stockholders' equity shows that the portion assigned to preferred shares is $630,000 and the portion assigned to common shares is $370,000 as follows:

| | | |
|---|---|---|
| Total Stockholders' Equity | | $1,000,000 |
| Allocated to Preferred Stock: | | |
| Call price (5,000 shares × $110) | $550,000 | |
| Preferred dividends in arrears | 80,000 | |
| Stockholders' equity assigned to preferred stock | | $ 630,000 |
| Stockholders' equity assigned to common stock | | $ 370,000 |

Book value per share for each class of stock is computed as follows:

Preferred stock: $630,000 ÷ 5,000 shares = $126.00 per share
Common stock: $370,000 ÷ 40,000 shares = $ 9.25 per share

Book value is not the same as liquidation value. If a corporation is liquidated, its assets will probably sell at prices quite different from the amounts at which they are carried on the books. Book value is based on historical cost, not on amounts realized when assets are sold.

### Market Value

The **market value** of a share of stock is the price at which a share can be bought or sold. Although many things influence the market price of a company's stock, expectations play a significant role. The investment community forms opinions of a particular company's future earnings capacity, its dividends per share, and its position in the industry. Opinions on the general state of the economy, both current and future, also affect the market value of a company's stock.

## HIGHLIGHT PROBLEM

The stockholders' equity section of Warwick Corporation's balance sheet on December 31, 19X5, is presented below.

| STOCKHOLDERS' EQUITY | |
|---|---|
| Contributed Capital: | |
| Preferred Stock, $100 par value, 9% cumulative and nonparticipating, 50,000 shares authorized, 10,000 shares issued and outstanding, callable at $120 | $1,000,000 |
| Common Stock, $5 stated value, 200,000 shares authorized, 100,000 shares issued and outstanding | 500,000 |
| Paid-in Capital in Excess of Par Value—Preferred | 80,000 |
| Paid-in Capital in Excess of Stated Value—Common | 300,000 |
| Total Contributed Capital | $1,880,000 |
| Retained Earnings | 740,000 |
| Total Stockholders' Equity | $2,620,000 |

Selected transactions affecting stockholders' equity were completed during the first three months of 19X6 as follows:

| | |
|---|---|
| Jan. 5 | Issued 2,000 shares of preferred stock at $120 per share. |
| Jan. 15 | Issued 3,000 shares of common stock in exchange for land having a fair market value of $18,000. |
| Feb. 1 | Received subscriptions to 10,000 shares of common stock at $8 per share, along with a down payment equal to one-half of the subscription price. The remainder of the subscription price is payable in two equal installments due on March 1 and May 1. |
| March 1 | Collected the first installment on the subscription contract. |

Required:

1. Prepare journal entries to record the above transactions.
2. Prepare the stockholders' equity section of the balance sheet on March 31, 19X6. The retained earnings on that date has been increased by the amount of net income reported for the first quarter of 19X6 and decreased by the quarterly dividends declared on both the preferred and the common stock. The correct retained earnings on March 31, 19X6, is $860,500.
3. Compute the book value per share of preferred stock and of common stock. The preferred stock has a call price of $120. No dividends are in arrears on the preferred stock.
4. Answer the following questions:
   a. What is the dividend per share on the preferred stock?
   b. How much of a dividend must be declared annually to satisfy the preferred dividend preference?
   c. How many shares of preferred stock are unissued on March 31, 19X6?

## GLOSSARY OF KEY TERMS

**Authorized shares.** The maximum number of shares of each class of capital stock that may be issued by a corporation as specified in its charter.

**Board of directors.** Persons elected by common stockholders to set corporate policy and direct the management of a corporation.

**Book value per share.** A measurement of the amount of claim that each share of stock has against the net assets of the corporation.

**Call price.** The price that the corporation must pay for each share of callable preferred stock if the corporation decides to redeem (call) the preferred shares.

**Call provision.** Provision in preferred stock that gives the corporation the right to redeem the stock on demand or in accordance with specified terms at a stipulated call price.

**Capital stock.** Shares of ownership in a corporation. The term may be used when referring to either common or preferred stock.

**Common stock.** The most basic class of stock, which usually has all stockholders' rights, including the right to dispose of their shares, the preemptive right, the right to vote, the right to share in net income, and the right to share in assets upon liquidation.

**Contributed capital.** A component of stockholders' equity. The amount of resources contributed (invested) in the corporation by the stockholders.

**Convertible preferred stock.** Preferred stock that gives the owner the option to exchange his or her preferred shares for the company's common shares in a specified ratio.

**Corporate charter.** A document issued by a state to the incorporators that gives legal status to a corporation.

**Corporation.** A business entity that is chartered by the state and has a continuous life and is treated legally as independent and separate from its owners. An entity where ownership is represented by transferable shares of stock and where owners are not personally liable for the corporation's debts.

**Cumulative preferred stock.** Preferred stock with the feature that if dividends are omitted or reduced in any year, the amount accumulates and must be paid before any dividends can be paid on the common stock.

**Discount (on capital stock).** The difference between the par value or stated value of stock and the amount below the par or stated value received from the investor (stockholder) at the time the stock was issued.

**Dividends.** A distribution of earnings in the form of

cash, other assets, or shares of the corporation's own stock to its stockholders.

**Dividends in arrears.** Undeclared prior period dividends on cumulative preferred stock. These dividends must be paid to preferred shareholders before any dividends can be paid to the common shareholders.

**Issued shares.** Authorized shares of stock that have been issued (distributed) to the stockholders.

**Legal capital.** A specified minimum amount that must be retained in the corporation. The minimum legal capital is usually equal to the aggregate par or stated value of the capital stock issued by the corporation.

**Limited liability.** A characteristic of the corporate form of business organization whereby its owners (stockholders) are liable for the debts and obligations of a corporation only to the extent of the amount invested to acquire the corporate shares.

**Market value (of a share of stock).** The price at which a share of stock can be bought or sold. Once the stock is issued, its market price continually changes.

**Noncumulative preferred stock.** Preferred stock on which the right to receive dividends is lost in any year in which dividends are not declared.

**No-par stock.** Stock that does not have a par value per share.

**Organization costs.** Costs of forming a corporation, such as fees paid to the state, attorneys, promoters, and other professionals.

**Outstanding stock.** Authorized stock that has been issued and is still being held by investors.

**Paid-in capital in excess of par (or stated) value.** The excess of the stock's issuance price over its par (or stated) value.

**Participating preferred stock.** Preferred stock that has the right to share in dividends above its specified preference amount.

**Par value.** An arbitrary amount assigned to a share of stock by the corporation's incorporators.

**Preemptive right.** The right of a stockholder to purchase additional shares of stock in proportion to his or her current holdings in the event that more stock of the same class is issued by the corporation.

**Preferred stock.** A class of stock given certain preferences over common stock when it comes to the exercise of stockholders' rights.

**Proxy.** A legal document, signed by a stockholder, giving another person the right to vote the stockholder's shares.

**Retained earnings.** A component of stockholders' equity. The amount of income (resources) earned by the corporation and retained in the business.

**Stated value stock.** No-par stock that has a stated value assigned to it by the corporation's board of directors.

**Stock certificate.** A legal document that is issued by a corporation and indicates the number of shares owned by the stockholder, the par value per share, and other relevant data.

**Stock subscription.** A contractual agreement to purchase shares of stock from a corporation at an agreed-upon price per share with payment made at some future date or in a series of installments.

**Stockholders.** The owners of a corporation; the persons who own shares of the corporation's stock.

**Stockholders' equity.** Term used in a corporation's balance sheet instead of owners' equity.

**Stockholders' ledger.** A subsidiary record showing at a minimum the name, address, and number of shares owned by each stockholder.

**Unissued shares.** Authorized shares of stock that have not yet been issued.

## REVIEW QUESTIONS

1. Name and briefly discuss seven advantages of the corporate form of business organization. [LO1a]
2. Name and briefly discuss three disadvantages of the corporate form of business organization. [LO1a]
3. Name eight items of information that generally must be included in a corporate charter application. [LO1b]
4. How are organization costs reported in the financial statements? How are these costs written off? [LO1b]
5. Describe five rights and privileges normally given to corporate stockholders. [LO1b]
6. What principal areas of corporate affairs are the responsibility of the board of directors? [LO1b]
7. Name five duties of a corporate board of directors. [LO1b]

8. Describe the responsibilities usually assigned to the following corporate officers: (a) president, (b) vice-presidents, (c) treasurer, (d) secretary, and (e) controller. [LO1b]
9. Differentiate between contributed capital and retained earnings. [LO1c]
10. Name six items of information normally reported under the caption "Contributed Capital" in the stockholders' equity section of the balance sheet. [LO1c]
11. Differentiate between (a) authorized shares, (b) unissued shares, and (c) issued shares. [LO1d]
12. Differentiate between (a) par value capital stock, (b) no-par capital stock with a stated value, and (c) no-par capital stock. [LO1d]
13. Differentiate between common stock and preferred stock. [LO1e]
14. What is meant by the statement that common stock represents the residual equity of a corporation? [LO1e]
15. Name the four preferential rights features of preferred stock. [LO1e]
16. In what two ways can preferred dividends be expressed or labeled? [LO1e]
17. Define *cumulative preferred stock.* [LO1e,2a]
18. What is meant by the phrase *dividends in arrears*? [LO1e,2a]
19. Define *participating preferred stock.* [LO1e,2a]
20. When a corporation is terminated, which claims must be paid first? [LO1e]
21. What is a convertible feature on preferred stock? [LO1e]
22. What is a call provision on preferred stock? [LO1e]
23. What accounts need to be debited and credited when common stock is issued for cash at its par value? [LO2b]
24. What accounts need to be debited and credited when common stock is issued for cash at a price above its par value? [LO2b]
25. What accounts need to be debited and credited when common stock is issued for cash at a price below its par value? [LO2b]
26. What accounts need to be debited and credited when no-par common stock is issued for cash? [LO2b]
27. At what amounts are noncash assets recorded when they are received in exchange for the corporation's stock? [LO2b]
28. What accounts need to be debited and credited when land is donated to a corporation? [LO2b]
29. Differentiate between stock sold on a subscription basis and stock sold for cash? [LO2c]
30. How is the Common Stock Subscribed account reported in the financial statements? [LO2c]
31. Differentiate between book value per share and market value per share. [LO2d]
32. How is book value per share calculated when a corporation issues only one type of stock? [LO2d]

## ANALYTICAL QUESTIONS

33. Why are corporations subject to laws that place limits on the amount of dividends that can be declared, but no similar laws exist to limit the amount of partnership or sole proprietorship withdrawals? [LO1a]
34. Differentiate between the role of a corporate board of directors and that of the owners of a partnership. [LO1b]
35. What distinctive features will readers find in the stockholders' equity section of a corporation's balance sheet that will not be found in the owners' equity section of a partnership balance sheet? [LO1c]
36. Why would a company issue no-par capital stock in place of par value capital stock? [LO1d]

37. If preferred stockholders have so many rights and privileges, why would investors want to purchase common stock? [LO1e,2a]
38. A manager of a local corporation said that the corporation could add to its reported net income by selling its stock at a premium. When questioned further, the manager said that the corporation would earn a profit on every share sold above the stock's stated value of $5 and that the timing was right because the stock sold yesterday at $8 per share. Comment on the manager's statements. [LO2b]
39. A corporation issues common stock that has no established market value in exchange for land that has had a number of different appraisals. How would you determine the dollar amount of this transaction? [LO2b]
40. "In the long run there really is no difference between common stock issued for cash and common stock issued on a subscription basis." Comment on this statement. [LO2c]
41. "The common stock of Corporation X has a book value of $1 per share. The common stock of Corporation Z has a book value of $5 per share. This is evidence that the value of Corporation Z's common stock is five times as much as the value of Corporation X's common stock." Comment on this assertion. [LO2d]
42. A friend made the following statement: "I'm not worried about the market price of my shares in Corporation A. I paid $20 a share and the latest report said they have a book value of $24 a share. How can I lose? Even if the corporation terminates, I would receive $4 over my cost per share in liquidation." Comment on this statement. [LO2d]

## IMPACT ANALYSIS QUESTIONS

*For each error described, indicate whether it would overstate [O], understate [U], or not affect [N] the key figures.*

43. When capital stock with a par value of $10 was issued at $12 per share, the $2 difference between the par value and the issuance price was credited to a revenue account. [LO2b]

_______ Total Stockholders' Equity _______ Retained Earnings
_______ Total Assets _______ Net Income

44. When capital stock with a par value of $10 was issued at $8 per share, the $2 difference between the par value and the issuance price was debited to an expense account. [LO2b]

_______ Total Stockholders' Equity _______ Retained Earnings
_______ Total Assets _______ Net Income

45. When common stock was issued for land, the land was incorrectly recorded at $10,000 rather than $12,000 when the entry was made. [LO2b]

_______ Total Stockholders' Equity _______ Retained Earnings
_______ Total Assets _______ Net Income

46. When capital stock was subscribed for, an incorrect entry was made debiting a receivable account and crediting a liability account. [LO2c]

_______ Total Stockholders' Equity _______ Retained Earnings
_______ Total Liabilities _______ Net Income

47. When cash was collected for stock previously subscribed to, an incorrect entry was made debiting cash and crediting common stock subscribed. [LO2c]

_______ Total Stockholders' Equity _______ Retained Earnings
_______ Total Assets _______ Net Income

## EXERCISES

EXERCISE 14–1 *(Record the Issuance of Stock)* Reardon Corporation is authorized to issue 200,000 shares of common stock.

Required:

Prepare a journal entry to record the issuance of 50,000 shares at $20 per share assuming that

1. The stock has a par value of $5 per share.
2. The stock is no-par stock.
3. The stock is no-par having a stated value of $8 per share. [LO2b]

EXERCISE 14–2 *(Record the Issuance of Stock)* Springfield Corporation is authorized to issue 100,000 shares of $5 par value common stock. The following transactions occurred during the company's first year of operations:

1. Issued 20,000 shares at $20 per share.
2. Issued 300 shares in exchange for organizational services. The services have a fair market value of $6,000.
3. Accepted land with a fair market value of $40,000 as a donation from the city where the corporation has agreed to build an outlet store.
4. Issued 3,000 shares in exchange for land and a building appraised at $10,000 and $60,000, respectively.

Required:

Prepare journal entries to record the above transactions. [LO2b]

EXERCISE 14–3 *(Prepare the Stockholders' Equity Section of a Balance Sheet)* The following accounts and balances were taken from the records of Galaxy Corporation.

| | |
|---|---|
| Subscriptions Receivable—Common | 80,000 debit |
| Common Stock—$10 par value, 100,000 shares authorized, 40,000 shares issued | 400,000 credit |
| Discount on Common Stock | 120,000 debit |
| Common Stock Subscribed | 100,000 credit |
| Preferred Stock—$50 par value, 8% cumulative, 20,000 shares authorized, 10,000 shares issued | 500,000 credit |
| Paid-in Capital in Excess of Par Value—Preferred Stock | 150,000 credit |
| Retained Earnings | 210,000 credit |

Required:

Prepare the stockholders' equity section of the balance sheet. [LO1c]

EXERCISE 14–4 *(Calculate Dividend Distributions)* Paragon Corporation has 10,000 shares of $100 par value, 9% cumulative preferred stock outstanding and 30,000 shares of $5 stated value common stock outstanding. The company issued all the shares on January 3, 19X1, the day it began operations. The company's board of directors declared cash dividends in three of the first four years as follows:

| | |
|---|---|
| 19X1 | $120,000 |
| 19X2 | NONE |
| 19X3 | $150,000 |
| 19X4 | $180,000 |

Required:

Determine the total cash dividends and dividends per share distributed to the preferred and common stockholders during each of the four years. Disclose the amount, if any, of dividends in arrears at the end of each year. [LO2a]

EXERCISE 14–5 *(Record Stock Subscriptions)* On March 31 Peppy Corporation sold 10,000 shares of $5 par value common stock on a subscription basis for $20 per share. The subscription contract required a down payment of 20% of the purchase price, with the remainder due in two equal installments on April 30 and May 31.

Required:

Prepare journal entries to record

1. The stock subscription
2. The cash received as the down payment
3. The receipt of the remaining amounts due on the subscriptions
4. The issuance of the stock certificates [LO2c]

EXERCISE 14–6 *(Analyze Stockholders' Equity Accounts)* The following accounts and balances appeared in the records of Sky-Hi Corporation at the end of its first two years of existence.

| | 19X6 | 19X5 |
|---|---|---|
| Preferred Stock, $10 par value, 8% cumulative | $150,000 | $100,000 |
| Common Stock, $1 stated value | 70,000 | 50,000 |
| Paid-in Capital in Excess of Par Value, Preferred Stock | 130,000 | 80,000 |
| Paid-in Capital in Excess of Stated Value, Common Stock | 300,000 | 200,000 |
| Retained Earnings | 120,000 | 80,000 |

Required:

Determine the following:

1. How many shares of preferred stock were issued during 19X5 and what was the average price paid per share?
2. How many shares of common stock were issued during 19X5 and what was the average price paid per share?
3. How many shares of preferred stock were issued during 19X6 and what was the average price paid per share?
4. How many shares of common stock were issued during 19X6 and what was the average price paid per share?
5. What was the company's total contributed capital at the end of 19X5 and 19X6, respectively? [LO2b]

EXERCISE 14–7 *(Record the Issuance of Preferred and Common Stock)* Royal Corporation's charter authorizes the company to issue 50,000 shares of $100 par value, 10% cumulative preferred stock and 100,000 shares of $5 par value common stock. The following transactions affecting stockholders' equity were completed during the first year of operations.

| | | |
|---|---|---|
| Jan. | 5 | Sold 10,000 preferred shares at $105 per share. |
| | 8 | Sold 30,000 common shares at $8 per share. |
| | 9 | Issued 1,000 common shares to professionals for services rendered in organizing the company. The shares given to these professionals paid for their services in full, which had been billed to Royal at $8,000. |
| Feb. | 2 | Issued 500 preferred shares in exchange for land appraised at $60,000. |
| | 5 | Issued 10,000 common shares in exchange for a building. On this date the common shares were trading actively at $9 per share. |
| | 20 | Accepted subscriptions to 5,000 common shares at $10 per share. The subscription contract required a down payment of 30% of the purchase price, with the remainder due in two equal installments on March 15 and April 15. |
| March | 15 | Collected cash representing the first installment on the subscription contract. |

Required:

Prepare journal entries to record the above transactions. [LO2b,2c]

EXERCISE 14–8 *(Determine Book Values per Share)* The stockholders' equity section of Hi-Fly Corporation's balance sheet on December 31, 19X6 is shown below.

| | |
|---|---|
| Contributed Capital: | |
| Preferred Stock, $50 par value, 10% cumulative, 50,000 shares authorized, issued, and outstanding | $2,500,000 |
| Common Stock, $10 par value, 200,000 shares authorized, 100,000 shares issued and outstanding | 1,000,000 |
| Paid-in Capital in Excess of Par Value, Common | 200,000 |
| Total Contributed Capital | $3,700,000 |
| Retained Earnings | 1,200,000 |
| Total Stockholders' Equity | $4,900,000 |

There is $100,000 of dividends in arrears on the preferred stock, which is callable at $55 per share.

Required:

Determine the book value per share for each class of stock (preferred and common). [LO2d]

## PROBLEMS

PROBLEM 14–1 *(Record Stock Issuance and Prepare Stockholders' Equity Section)* Carter Corporation was organized on January 5. The company's charter authorizes the issuance of 10,000 shares of $100 par value, 9% cumulative preferred stock and 100,000 shares of no-par common stock. The board of directors has established a $5 stated value on the common stock. The following transactions affecting stockholders' equity were completed during the year.

| | |
|---|---|
| Jan. 5 | Issued 500 common shares to Carter's attorneys and accountants in exchange for payment of a $12,000 bill for professional services rendered in organizing the company. |
| Jan. 7 | Issued 2,000 preferred shares at par and 10,000 common shares at $20 per share. |
| March 12 | Exchanged 9,000 shares of common stock for land having an appraised value of $80,000 and a building having an appraised value of $120,000. |
| Sept. 1 | Accepted subscriptions to 20,000 shares of common stock at $25 per share. Cash totaling 30% of the subscription price was received as a down payment. |
| Sept. 15 | Collected one-half of the amount due on the common stock subscription contract. |
| Oct. 3 | Accepted subscriptions to 1,000 shares of preferred stock at $120 per share, along with cash representing one-third of the subscription price. The remainder of the subscription price is payable in two equal installments due on November 15 and January 15. |
| Oct. 15 | Collected the last installment on the subscribed stock of September 1 and issued the stock certificates. |
| Nov. 15 | Collected the first installment on the subscribed stock of October 15. |

Required:

1. Prepare journal entries to record the above transactions.
2. Prepare the stockholders' equity section of the balance sheet as of December 31. Assume that the Retained Earnings account has a balance of $38,500. [LO1c,2b,2c]

PROBLEM 14–2 *(Prepare the Stockholders' Equity Section of a Balance Sheet)* A partial list of accounts and balances taken from the after-closing trial balance of Friendly Corporation on December 31, 19X6, is shown on page 514.

The preferred stock has a $100 par value; 5,000 shares are authorized, and 1,000 shares have been issued and are outstanding. The common stock has a $2 stated value; 400,000 shares are authorized, and 100,000 shares have been issued and are outstanding.

| | DEBIT | CREDIT |
|---|---|---|
| Common Stock | | $200,000 |
| Retained Earnings | | 112,000 |
| Subscriptions Receivable—Common | $180,000 | |
| Preferred Stock | | 100,000 |
| Paid-in Capital in Excess of Stated Value, Common | | 420,000 |
| Common Stock Subscribed | | 50,000 |
| Paid-in Capital in Excess of Par Value, Preferred | | 80,000 |
| Donated Capital | | 35,000 |

Required:

Prepare the stockholders' equity section of the balance sheet. [LO1c]

PROBLEM 14–3 *(Determine Dividend Distributions)* Venice Corporation had 6,000 shares of its $100 par value, 8% cumulative preferred stock and 40,000 shares of its $10 stated value common stock outstanding for the years 19X3 through 19X6. The company declared cash dividends of $108,000, $36,000, $50,000, and $148,000 for those years.

Required:

1. Determine the total cash dividends and dividends per share distributed to the preferred and common stockholders during each of the four years. Disclose the amount, if any, of dividends in arrears at the end of each year.
2. Using the same data, make the computations assuming this time that the preferred stock is noncumulative instead of cumulative. [LO2a]

PROBLEM 14–4 *(Record Stock Subscriptions)* Lively Corporation is authorized to issue 300,000 shares of $5 par value common stock. The following transactions affecting stockholders' equity accounts occurred during the first six months of 19X6.

| | |
|---|---|
| Jan. 3 | Received subscriptions for 50,000 shares of stock at $12 per share. The subscription contract required a down payment of one-third of the subscription price, with the remainder due in two equal installments on February 1 and April 1. |
| Jan. 28 | Issued 10,000 shares in exchange for land and a building appraised at $52,000 and $92,000, respectively. |
| Feb. 1 | The first installment on the subscription contract was received in cash. |
| April 1 | The final installment on the subscription contract was received in cash, and the stock certificates were issued. |
| June 20 | Accepted land having a fair market value of $38,000 as a donation from the city. |

Required:

Prepare journal entries to record the above transactions. [LO2c]

PROBLEM 14–5 *(Analyze Stockholders' Equity Accounts)* At the close of the current year, the stockholders' equity section of Jesse Corporation's balance sheet appeared as follows.

| | |
|---|---|
| Contributed Capital: | |
| Preferred Stock, $40 par value, 10% cumulative, 100,000 shares authorized | $1,600,000 |
| Common Stock, $2 stated value, 300,000 shares authorized | 400,000 |
| Common Stock Subscribed | 60,000 |
| Paid-in Capital in Excess of Par Value, Preferred | 320,000 |
| Paid-in Capital in Excess of Stated Value, Common | 2,800,000 |
| Total Contributed Capital | $5,180,000 |
| Retained Earnings | 1,720,000 |
| Total Stockholders' Equity | $6,900,000 |

Required:

On the basis of the data given in the stockholders' equity section above, answer each of the following questions. Show calculations where appropriate.

1. How many shares of preferred stock have been issued?
2. What is the annual preference dividend in total, and what is the annual preference dividend per share on preferred stock?
3. How many shares of common stock have been issued?
4. How many shares of common stock are subscribed?
5. What is the average price per share received by the corporation for its preferred shares?
6. What is the average price per share received by the corporation for its common shares (including the subscribed stock)?
7. Could the amount in the asset account Subscriptions Receivable—Common exceed, be less than, or be equal to the amount in the Common Stock Subscribed account? Explain.
8. What amount represents the corporation's minimum legal capital? [LO2a,2b,2c]

PROBLEM 14–6 *(Compute Book Values per Share)* Revival Corporation's stockholders' equity on December 31, 19X6, is presented below.

| | |
|---|---|
| Contributed Capital: | |
| Preferred Stock, $100 par value, 8% cumulative, 50,000 shares authorized, 30,000 shares issued and outstanding | $3,000,000 |
| Paid-in Capital in Excess of Par Value, Preferred | 240,000 |
| Common Stock, $5 par value, 500,000 shares authorized, 200,000 shares issued and outstanding | 1,000,000 |
| Paid-in Capital in Excess of Par Value, Common | 1,400,000 |
| Total Contributed Capital | $5,640,000 |
| Retained Earnings | 720,000 |
| Total Stockholders' Equity | $6,360,000 |

Required:

For each of the following independent cases, compute the book value per share for the preferred stock and the common stock.

1. The preferred stock is callable at $110, and no dividends are in arrears.
2. The preferred stock is callable at par, and preferred dividends are $180,000 in arrears.
3. The preferred stock is callable at $105, and preferred dividends are two years in arrears. [LO2d]

PROBLEM 14–7 *(Determine Dividend Distributions)* Sensation Corporation has outstanding 10,000 shares of $50 par value, 10% cumulative preferred stock and 60,000 shares of $5 par value common stock. The company has declared cash dividends of $176,000 during the current year.

Required:

1. Determine the total cash dividends and dividends per share distributed to each class of stock, assuming that there are no dividends in arrears.
2. Determine the total cash dividends and dividends per share distributed to each class of stock, assuming that one year's dividends are in arrears on the preferred stock.
3. Determine the total cash dividends and dividends per share distributed to each class of stock, assuming that the 10% preferred stock is partially participating (up to 12%) and there are no dividends in arrears.
4. Determine the total cash dividends and dividends per share distributed to each class of stock, assuming that the 10% preferred stock is fully participating and there are no dividends in arrears. [LO2a]

PROBLEM 14–8 *(Record Stock Issuance, Prepare Stockholders' Equity Section, and Compute Book Value per Share)* The Hi-Lite Corporation was organized on January 8 of the current year with authorization to issue 20,000 shares of $50 par value, 12% cumulative preferred stock and 100,000 shares of $10 par value common stock. The following transactions affecting stockholders' equity were completed during the year.

| | |
|---|---|
| Jan. 12 | Issued 20,000 shares of common stock for $300,000. |
| Jan. 15 | Issued 500 shares of common stock to attorneys in exchange for their services in organizing the corporation. The services were valued based on their billing of $8,000. |
| March 10 | Issued 1,000 shares of preferred stock in exchange for equipment having a fair market value of $52,000. |
| April 1 | Accepted land having a fair market value of $60,000 as a donation from the city. |
| April 4 | Issued 5,000 shares of preferred stock for $58 per share. |
| June 1 | Accepted subscriptions to 26,500 shares of common stock at $20 per share. A down payment equal to 40% of the subscription price accompanied the subscription. |
| July 15 | Collected the balance on the subscribed stock of June 1 and issued the stock certificates. |
| Nov. 10 | Accepted subscriptions to 2,000 shares of preferred stock at $55 per share. A down payment equal to 50% of the subscription price accompanied the subscription. The balance is due on January 15. |

Required:

1. Prepare journal entries to record the above transactions.
2. Prepare the stockholders' equity section of the balance sheet as of December 31. Assume that the Retained Earnings account has a balance of $47,200.
3. Compute the book value per share of the preferred stock and common stock as of December 31. Assume that no dividends are in arrears on the preferred shares and that the call price on the preferred stock is $60 per share. [LO1c,2b,2c,2d]

PROBLEM 14–9 *(Comprehensive Problem)* The stockholders' equity section of Futura Corporation's balance sheet on January 1, 19X6, is presented below.

| | |
|---|---|
| Contributed Capital | |
| Preferred Stock, $50 par value, 10% cumulative, 100,000 shares authorized, 20,000 shares issued and outstanding | $1,000,000 |
| Paid-in Capital in Excess of Par Value, Preferred | 140,000 |
| Common Stock, $10 stated value, 200,000 shares authorized, 40,000 shares issued and outstanding | 400,000 |
| Paid-in Capital in Excess of Stated Value, Common | 320,000 |
| Total Contributed Capital | $1,860,000 |
| Retained Earnings | 710,000 |
| Total Stockholders' Equity | $2,570,000 |

The following transactions occurred during the year.

| | |
|---|---|
| Jan. 19 | Sold 10,000 shares of common stock for $180,000. |
| Feb. 15 | Accepted subscriptions to 30,000 shares of common stock at $19 per share. Received cash for one-third of the subscription price at this time. The remainder of the subscription price is payable in two equal installments due on April 15 and June 15. |
| April 4 | Issued 5,000 shares of preferred stock in exchange for land and a building having fair market values of $70,000 and $200,000, respectively. |
| April 15 | Collected the first installment on the subscription contract of February 15. |
| May 7 | Sold 3,000 shares of common stock for $22 per share. |

| | |
|---|---|
| June 15 | Collected the final installment on the subscription contract of February 15 and issued the stock certificates. |
| Aug. 10 | Sold 5,000 shares of preferred stock for $55 per share. |
| Sept. 7 | Accepted land having a fair market value of $48,000 as a donation. |

Required:

1. Prepare journal entries to record the above transactions.
2. Prepare the stockholders' equity section of the balance sheet as of December 31, 19X6. Assume that dividends were paid to both preferred and common stockholders and that the Retained Earnings account balance on December 31, 19X6, is $930,000.
3. Compute the book value per share of the preferred stock and common stock as of December 31, 19X6. The preferred stock is callable at $55 per share.
4. Compute the book value per share of the preferred stock and common stock as of December 31, 19X6. Assume this time that the preferred stock is callable at $60 per share, and one year's preferred dividends are in arrears. [LO1c,2a,2b,2c,2d]

## ALTERNATE PROBLEMS

PROBLEM 14–1A *(Record Stock Issuance and Prepare Stockholders' Equity Section)* (Alternate to Problem 14–1) Sensation Corporation was organized on January 4. The company's charter authorizes the issuance of 20,000 shares of $50 par value, 12% cumulative preferred stock and 75,000 shares of no-par common stock. The board of directors has established a $2 stated value on the common stock. The following transactions affecting stockholders' equity were completed during the year.

| | |
|---|---|
| Jan. 4 | Issued 600 common shares to the company's attorneys and accountants in exchange for payment of a $2,500 bill for professional services rendered in organizing the company. |
| Jan. 9 | Issued 4,000 preferred shares at par and 15,000 common shares at $4 per share. |
| March 15 | Exchanged 8,400 shares of common stock for equipment having an appraised value of $40,000. |
| Sept. 3 | Accepted subscriptions to 30,000 shares of common stock at $6 per share. Cash totaling 30% of the subscription price was received as a down payment. |
| Oct. 1 | Collected one-half of the amount due on the common stock subscription contract. |
| Oct. 12 | Accepted subscriptions to 3,000 shares of preferred stock at $60 per share, along with cash representing one-third of the subscription price. The remainder of the subscription price is payable in two equal installments on November 16 and January 31. |
| Nov. 1 | Collected the last installment on the subscribed stock of September 3 and issued the stock certificates. |
| Nov. 16 | Collected the first installment on the subscribed stock of October 12. |

Required:

1. Prepare journal entries to record the above transactions.
2. Prepare the stockholders' equity section of the balance sheet as of December 31. Assume that the Retained Earnings account has a balance of $23,700. [LO1c,2b,2c]

PROBLEM 14–2A *(Determine Dividend Distributions)* (Alternate to Problem 14–3) Baldwin Corporation had the following stocks issued and outstanding when the board of directors declared a $290,000 dividend:

Preferred stock: 10,000 shares, 10%, $50 par value

Common stock: 60,000 shares, $8 par value

Required:
Determine the total cash dividend and the dividends per share to be distributed to the preferred and common stockholders under each of the following independent conditions.
1. The preferred stock is noncumulative and nonparticipating.
2. The preferred stock is cumulative and nonparticipating, and dividends are two years in arrears.
3. The preferred stock is cumulative and participating to 12%. Dividends are one year in arrears.
4. The preferred stock is cumulative and fully participating. There are no dividends in arrears. [LO2a]

PROBLEM 14–3A *(Record Stock Subscriptions)* (Alternate to Problem 14–4) Opto Corporation is authorized to issue 500,000 shares of no-par common stock having a stated value of $2 per share. The following transactions affecting stockholders' equity accounts occurred during the first six months of 19X5.

| | |
|---|---|
| Jan. 2 | Received subscriptions for 80,000 shares of stock at $8 per share. The subscription contract required a down payment of one-half of the subscription price, with the remainder due in two equal installments on February 15 and April 1. |
| Jan. 26 | Issued 20,000 shares in exchange for land and a building appraised at $60,000 and $110,000, respectively. |
| Feb. 15 | The first installment on the subscription contract was received in cash. |
| April 1 | The final installment on the subscription contract was received in cash, and the stock certificates were issued. |
| June 27 | Accepted land having a fair market value of $25,000 as a donation from the city. |

Required:
Prepare journal entries to record the above transactions. [LO2c]

PROBLEM 14–4A *(Analyze Stockholders' Equity Accounts)* (Alternate to Problem 14–5) Shown below is the stockholders' equity section of the balance sheet of Faulty Corporation as prepared by one of its employees.

| | |
|---|---:|
| Preferred Stock, $50 par value, 10% cumulative | $250,000 |
| Paid-in Capital in Excess of Par Value, Preferred | 40,000 |
| Common Stock, $10 par | 100,000 |
| Common Stock Subscribed | 30,000 |
| Paid-in Capital in Excess of Par Value, Common | 156,000 |
| Retained Earnings | 83,000 |
| Total Stockholders' Equity | $659,000 |

Required:
This stockholders' equity section omitted several important facts which you have been asked to determine. To do this, answer each of the following questions using the data given above. Show supporting computations where appropriate.
1. How many shares of preferred stock have been issued?
2. How many shares of common stock have been issued?
3. How many shares of common stock have been subscribed but not yet issued?
4. What was the average price per share received by the corporation for its preferred shares?
5. What was the average price per share received by the corporation for its common shares, including common stock subscribed?
6. What is the total contributed capital of the corporation?
7. What is the annual preference dividend in total and per share on the preferred stock?

8. Could the amount in the asset account Subscriptions Receivable—Common exceed, be less than, or be equal to the amount in the Common Stock Subscribed account? Explain.
9. What amount represents the corporation's minimum legal capital? [LO2a,2b,2c]

PROBLEM 14–5A *(Compute Book Values per Share)* (Alternate to Problem 14–6) Foremost Corporation's stockholders' equity on December 31, 19X5, is presented below.

| | |
|---|---|
| Contributed Capital: | |
| Preferred Stock, $100 par value, 10% cumulative, 80,000 shares authorized, 20,000 shares issued and outstanding | $2,000,000 |
| Paid-in Capital in Excess of Par Value, Preferred | 430,000 |
| Common Stock, no-par with a stated value of $5; 750,000 shares authorized, 300,000 shares issued and outstanding | 1,500,000 |
| Paid-in Capital in Excess of Stated Value, Common | 2,600,000 |
| Total Contributed Capital | $6,530,000 |
| Retained Earnings | 470,000 |
| Total Stockholders' Equity | $7,000,000 |

Required:

For each of the following independent cases, compute the book value per share for the preferred stock and for the common stock.

1. The preferred stock is callable at $108, and no dividends are in arrears.
2. The preferred stock is callable at par, and preferred dividends are two years in arrears.
3. The preferred stock is callable at $112, and preferred dividends are three years in arrears. [LO2d]

# 15 Corporations: Retained Earnings, Dividends, Treasury Stock, and Income Reporting

## *Learning Objectives*

When you complete this chapter you will be able to

1. Answer the following questions:
   a. What is retained earnings and what is the composition of that account?
   b. How do cash dividends, stock dividends, and stock splits differ, and how are they accounted for?
   c. What is the nature of prior period adjustments, and how are they reported in financial statements?
   d. What is treasury stock?
   e. What are appropriations or restrictions of retained earnings, and how are they disclosed in the financial statements?
   f. How are discontinued operations, extraordinary items, and accounting changes disclosed and reported in the income statement?
2. Perform the following accounting functions:
   a. Prepare journal entries to record the acquisition and reissuance of treasury shares.
   b. Prepare a statement of retained earnings.
   c. Prepare a comprehensive stockholders' equity section of a balance sheet.
   d. Prepare a comprehensive income statement.
   e. Compute primary and fully diluted earnings per share.

In Chapter 14 we noted that corporate stockholders' equity, when presented in a balance sheet, is divided into two components: contributed capital and retained earnings. This division clearly indicates the sources of stockholders' equity. *Contributed capital* represents investment in the corporation, while *retained earnings* represents income earned and retained in the business. We will now look at the retained earnings component.

## THE NATURE OF RETAINED EARNINGS

*1a. Retained earnings represents the portion of the corporation's accumulated net income that has not been distributed to its shareholders as a dividend*

Net income represents the excess of revenues over expenses and increases stockholders' equity, with the latter change shown in the corporation's balance sheet as an increase in retained earnings. Retained earnings represents the portion of a corporation's accumulated net income that has not been distributed to its stockholders as a dividend. A company's board of directors may choose to retain some of the assets generated from the company's profitable operations for a variety of reasons, including current business needs and future growth.

Note, however, that when a company has retained earnings, it does not mean that the company has cash or any other specific assets equal to the amount of its retained earnings. A credit balance in the Retained Earnings account does, however, indicate that net income has been retained, which in turn means that net assets (total assets minus total liabilities) have increased.

The Retained Earnings account will have a debit balance if a company's accumulated net losses and distributions to stockholders have exceeded its accumulated net income. This debit balance in Retained Earnings is called a **deficit** and is shown as a deduction from contributed capital in the stockholders' equity section of the balance sheet.

*1a. A number of factors affect the Retained Earnings account*

Actually, a number of factors affect the Retained Earnings account. The primary ones are

- Periodic net income or net loss
- Dividends
- Prior period adjustments
- Reissuance of treasury stock under certain conditions
- Appropriation of retained earnings

Each factor is discussed in the following sections.

## NET INCOME OR NET LOSS

Net income increases retained earnings, while net loss decreases it.

Recall that during the year-end closing process, the net income or net loss of a sole proprietorship or a partnership was transferred from the Income Summary account to the owners' individual capital accounts. The closing process for a corporation is similar except that income or loss is transferred to the Retained Earnings account instead of the individual capital accounts. For example, if a company's net income for the year is $300,000, the entry to transfer that amount to Retained Earnings is as follows:

| | | | |
|---|---|---|---|
| Dec. 31 | Income Summary | 300,000 | |
| | Retained Earnings | | 300,000 |
| | To close the Income Summary account | | |

The entry increases Retained Earnings and total stockholders' equity by $300,000. If a company has a net loss of $150,000, the following journal entry would transfer the loss to Retained Earnings:

| | | | |
|---|---|---|---|
| Dec. 31 | Retained Earnings. . . . . . . . . . . . . . . . . . . . . . . . . . . . . . . | 150,000 | |
| | Income Summary. . . . . . . . . . . . . . . . . . . . . . . . . . . | | 150,000 |
| | To close the Income Summary account | | |

The entry decreases Retained Earnings and total stockholders' equity by $150,000.

## DIVIDENDS

*Dividends*, as we saw in Chapter 14, are distributions of cash, assets other than cash, or shares of the corporation's own stock to its stockholders. Although cash dividends are the most common, all dividends, whatever their form, result in a decrease in retained earnings.

The authority to declare dividends belongs solely to the board of directors. Many corporations, especially those whose shares are widely held, try to maintain a stable dividend record. These companies are attractive to investors who count on receiving dividend payments at regular intervals of time, such as annually, semiannually, or quarterly.

Three dates are important to the discussion of dividends. In the order in which they occur, these are (1) the declaration date, (2) the record date, and (3) the payment date.

The **declaration date** is the date on which the board of directors takes formal action in declaring the dividend. The type of dividend (cash, other assets, or shares of stock), the amount of the dividend, and the record and payment dates are specified at this time. Because the dividend declaration legally commits the corporation to pay the dividend, a journal entry to recognize the dividend liability must be recorded on this date.

The **record date** is the date (selected by the board of directors) on which ownership of the stock of a company is determined for the purpose of establishing who has a right to receive the dividend. Stock ownership may change daily (by the buying and selling of shares), so it is important that a list consisting of the names and addresses of stockholders be compiled on the date of record. Those who own the stock on that date are entitled to receive the dividend even if they dispose of their shares before the payment date. Thus shares sold between the record date and the payment date are sold **ex-dividend,** meaning that the purchaser of the stock has no right to the current dividend. The record date is usually a few weeks after the declaration date and a few weeks before the payment date, which allows time for the processing of shareholders' data. No journal entry is needed on the date of record.

The **payment date** is the date (selected by the board of directors) on which the dividend will be distributed to the stockholders of record. A journal entry is needed on this date to record the distribution of cash or the distribution of noncash assets or shares of stock.

The following example of a typical dividend announcement shows the sequencing of these three important dates:

> On March 20 (the declaration date) the board of directors of Polo Corporation declared a dividend of $180,000 or $2 per common share to the stockholders of record on April 10 (the record date), payable on April 30 (the payment date).

## Cash Dividends

*1b. Most dividends are paid in cash*

Most dividends are paid in cash. Three conditions must exist before a cash dividend can be distributed:

1. Formal action by the board of directors
2. An adequate balance in Retained Earnings
3. Sufficient cash to pay the dividend

The legality of the dividend is normally related to the balance in the corporation's Retained Earnings account. The incorporation laws of most states prohibit the declaration of a dividend that exceeds the total undistributed net income of the company, as shown by the credit balance in its Retained Earnings account. Thus to be legally able to declare a dividend, a corporation must have sufficient retained earnings.[1]

We know that the amount of retained earnings is not directly related to cash. Therefore having a large amount of retained earnings does not necessarily mean that the corporation has sufficient cash to pay the dividend. The cash provided by earnings may have been used to purchase other assets such as inventory or equipment or may have been used for other purposes such as the reduction of liabilities.

Cash dividends on common stock are usually stated in terms of dollars and cents rather than as a percentage of par. Cash dividends on preferred stock may be stated either in dollars and cents or as a percentage of par. For example, a corporation may declare a dividend of $2 per share on the 30,000 common shares outstanding and distribute cash of $60,000 (30,000 shares × $2 per share) to its common stockholders. It may also declare a $5 per share dividend on the 10,000 shares of $50 par, 10% preferred stock outstanding and distribute cash of $50,000 (10,000 shares × $5 per share) to its preferred stockholders.

*1b. The complete sequence of accounting for cash dividends is illustrated here*

The following illustration demonstrates the complete sequence of accounting for cash dividends. On November 10 the board of directors of Supra Corporation declared a cash dividend of $2 per share on its 30,000 outstanding shares of common stock. The dividend is to be paid on December 20 to stockholders of record on December 1. Two entries are needed, one to record the dividend declaration (on the declaration date) and the other to record payment of the dividend (on the payment date) as follows:

| | | | |
|---|---|---|---|
| Nov. 10 | Retained Earnings. . . . . . . . . . . . . . . . . . . . . . . . . . . . . . . . . | 60,000 | |
| | Cash Dividends Payable . . . . . . . . . . . . . . . . . . . . . . . | | 60,000 |
| | To record a cash dividend of $2 per share on 30,000 common shares outstanding | | |
| Dec. 20 | Cash Dividends Payable . . . . . . . . . . . . . . . . . . . . . . . . . . . | 60,000 | |
| | Cash. . . . . . . . . . . . . . . . . . . . . . . . . . . . . . . . . . . . . . | | 60,000 |
| | To record payment of the dividend declared on November 10 | | |

An entry is required on November 10, the declaration date, because the company becomes legally obligated to pay the dividend. No entry is required on

[1] Some state laws do allow dividends to be paid to the extent that they do not reduce total stockholders' equity below the corporation's minimum legal capital. Such dividends are called **liquidating dividends** because the shareholders are receiving all or part of their paid-in capital investment. This means that the stockholders are receiving a return *of* their investment, not a return *on* their investment. Liquidating dividends are generally paid only by corporations that are terminating, or permanently reducing the size of, their operations.

December 1, the date of record, since that date is used only to identify those stockholders entitled to receive the dividend. The entry on the payment date eliminates the dividend liability from the accounts.

Some companies prefer to debit a temporary account called Dividends rather than debiting Retained Earnings on the date the dividend is declared. The Dividends account is then closed to Retained Earnings at the end of the accounting period. Using the Dividends account is simply an alternative recording practice. In either case, the dividend declaration reduces Retained Earnings.

## Stock Dividends

***1b. A stock dividend is a pro rata distribution of additional shares of a corporation's own stock to its shareholders***

Sometimes corporations declare a stock dividend rather than a cash dividend. A **stock dividend** is a pro rata distribution of additional shares of a corporation's own stock to its shareholders. The additional shares are issued in proportion to each stockholder's present ownership in the company.

For example, if a corporation issues a 10% stock dividend, each shareholder receives one additional share for every ten shares owned. Most stock dividends consist of the distribution of additional shares of common stock to common stockholders. Distribution of common stock to preferred stockholders, or vice versa, is unusual. Consequently, our discussion will be limited to the usual form of stock dividends, additional common shares distributed to common shareholders.

In a stock dividend, no cash (or other corporate asset) is distributed to the stockholders. A stock dividend, unlike a cash dividend (which reduces corporate assets and stockholders' equity by the same amount), *has no effect on corporate assets or on the* total *amount of stockholders' equity.* A stock dividend does affect the capital structure of the issuing corporation because when a stock dividend is declared, an amount is transferred from retained earnings to contributed capital. The amount transferred is determined either on the basis of the market value of the additional shares issued as a dividend or on the basis of the par or stated value of those shares, as discussed in the following sections.

**REASONS FOR ISSUING A STOCK DIVIDEND** There are several reasons why a corporate board of directors may declare a stock dividend. Two frequently cited ones are listed below.

> *To conserve cash.* Many profitable companies issue stock dividends to conserve cash for other purposes. This might include the financing of planned plant expansion or the desire to conduct research in new areas. A stock dividend allows the corporation to make a distribution to its shareholders showing them some evidence of corporate well-being, without using cash or any other corporate asset.
>
> *To reduce the market price of the shares.* This is usually accomplished by large stock dividends or stock splits, which reduce the market price of the shares by significantly increasing the number of shares outstanding.

Corporate directors may feel that by lowering the market price per share, they will attract a broader group of investors. (The lower market price makes the stock more affordable to individuals with small amounts to invest and thereby expands the corporation's potential ownership base.)

**SMALL STOCK DIVIDENDS** The laws of most states require that a minimum amount (equal to the par or stated value of the additional shares issued in the stock dividend) be transferred from Retained Earnings to Common Stock. However, in accounting for stock dividends the profession has made a distinction between small and large stock dividends.

For small stock dividends (defined as less than 20% to 25% of the number of shares previously outstanding), the profession recommends that Retained Earnings be reduced and contributed capital increased by an amount equal to the fair value of the additional shares issued.[2]

This view assumes that a small distribution of additional shares does not immediately or significantly affect the market price of the shares. As a result, "many recipients of stock dividends look upon them as distributions of corporate earnings and usually in an amount equivalent to the fair value of the additional shares issued."[3] For this reason, the fair value, usually the market price per share, is considered the proper amount to use to account for a small stock dividend.

***1b. The accounting for small stock dividends is illustrated here***

To illustrate the accounting for a small stock dividend, assume that Supra Corporation has the following stockholders' equity.

| | |
|---|---|
| Contributed Capital: | |
| Common Stock, $5 par value, 100,000 shares authorized, 30,000 shares issued and outstanding | $150,000 |
| Paid-in Capital in Excess of Par Value | 100,000 |
| Total Contributed Capital | $250,000 |
| Retained Earnings | 300,000 |
| Total Stockholders' Equity | $550,000 |

Assume further that the board of directors declares a 10% stock dividend on December 10, distributable on January 15, to the stockholders of record on December 31. The market price of the stock on December 10 was $20 per share. The entry to record the declaration of the stock dividend is as follows:

| | | | |
|---|---|---|---|
| Dec. 10 | Retained Earnings | 60,000 | |
| | Stock Dividend Distributable | | 15,000 |
| | Paid-in Capital in Excess of Par Value | | 45,000 |
| | To record the declaration of a 10% stock dividend on 30,000 shares of common stock | | |

Note that the effect of the stock dividend is to transfer $60,000 from Retained Earnings to contributed capital accounts and to increase by 3,000 the number of shares outstanding. The specific accounts affected and the computation of the amounts are outlined below.

The *Retained Earnings* account is debited for the market value of the shares to be issued. The amount is computed as follows: 30,000 shares × .10 = 3,000 shares to be issued × $20 (the current market price per share) = $60,000.

The *Stock Dividend Distributable* account is credited for the par value of the shares to be issued (3,000 shares × $5 = $15,000). The Stock Dividend Distributable account is not a liability because the company has no obligation to distribute cash or any other corporate asset. The obligation is to distribute additional shares of stock. If a balance sheet is prepared between the date of declaration and the date of issuance, the Stock Dividend Distributable account is reported as a separate item of contributed capital. The equity section of Supra Corporation's balance sheet shown on page 526 demonstrates the reporting of a stock dividend distributable.

[2] *Accounting Research and Terminology Bulletins—Final Edition,* No. 43 (New York: American Institute of Certified Public Accountants, 1961), Chap. 7, Sec. B, par. 10.
[3] Ibid.

*Paid-in Capital in Excess of Par Value* is credited for the amount that total market value of the shares to be issued exceeds their total par value. In this example, total market value ($60,000) exceeds total par value ($15,000) by $45,000.

After the dividend declaration entry has been posted, the stockholders' equity section of Supra Corporation's balance sheet would appear as follows:

| | |
|---|---|
| Contributed Capital: | |
| Common Stock, $5 par value, 100,000 shares authorized, 30,000 shares issued and outstanding | $150,000 |
| Common Stock Dividend Distributable | 15,000 |
| Paid-in Capital in Excess of Par Value | 145,000 |
| Total Contributed Capital | $310,000 |
| Retained Earnings | 240,000 |
| Total Stockholders' Equity | $550,000 |

The entry to be made on January 15, when the shares are issued, is as follows:

| | | | |
|---|---|---|---|
| Jan. 15 | Stock Dividend Distributable | 15,000 | |
| | Common Stock | | 15,000 |
| | To record the issuance of a stock dividend of 3,000 shares | | |

Note that the entries cause retained earnings to decrease and *total* contributed capital to increase by equal amounts. Thus Supra's total stockholders' equity is unchanged by the stock dividend, as the schedule shown below demonstrates.

| STOCKHOLDERS' EQUITY ACCOUNTS | BEFORE STOCK DIVIDEND | AFTER STOCK DIVIDEND |
|---|---|---|
| Common Stock, $5 par value | $150,000 | $165,000 |
| Paid-in Capital in Excess of Par Value | 100,000 | 145,000 |
| Total Contributed Capital | $250,000 | $310,000 |
| Retained Earnings | 300,000 | 240,000 |
| Total Stockholders' Equity | $550,000 | $550,000 |

The process of rearranging stockholders' equity is often referred to as the **capitalization of retained earnings.** Note three important points:

Sixty thousand dollars of retained earnings is capitalized and is transferred to contributed capital accounts.

There are 3,000 additional shares of common stock outstanding.

The proportionate ownership in the corporation of each stockholder remains unchanged.

To illustrate the last point, assume that an individual owned 1,500 shares of Supra Corporation's stock before, and 1,650 shares after, the stock dividend. The proportionate share of ownership remains unchanged, as shown below.

| | BEFORE STOCK DIVIDEND | AFTER STOCK DIVIDEND |
|---|---|---|
| Total stockholders' equity | $550,000 | $550,000 |
| Number of shares outstanding | 30,000 | 33,000 |
| Shares owned by individual | 1,500 | 1,650 |
| Percentage owned by individual (line 3 ÷ line 2) | 5% | 5% |
| Individual's share of total stockholders' equity (5% × $550,000) | $ 27,500 | $ 27,500 |

LARGE STOCK DIVIDENDS When new shares amounting to more than 20% to 25% of the number of shares previously outstanding are issued, an immediate and significant drop in the price per share can be expected. In accounting for large stock dividends, the amount transferred from retained earnings to contributed capital is based on the par or stated value (not the market value) of the shares issued.

*1b. The accounting for large stock dividends is illustrated here*

To illustrate, return to Supra Corporation's stockholders' equity accounts as they first appeared on page 525 and assume the following. On December 10, when the corporation's shares were selling for $20 per share, the board declared a 30% stock dividend. In this case, 9,000 additional shares will be issued (30,000 shares × .30). Their aggregate par value (not market value) is $45,000 (9,000 shares to be issued × $5 par value per share), and that amount is used to record the transfer from retained earnings. The entries to record the large stock dividend declaration and the issuance of the shares are as follows:

| | | | |
|---|---|---|---|
| Dec. 10 | Retained Earnings | 45,000 | |
| | Stock Dividend Distributable | | 45,000 |
| | To record the declaration of a 30% stock dividend on 30,000 shares of common stock | | |
| Jan. 15 | Stock Dividend Distributable | 45,000 | |
| | Common Stock | | 45,000 |
| | To record the issuance of a stock dividend of 9,000 shares | | |

After the distribution of the shares, the stockholders' equity section of Supra Corporation's balance sheet would be as follows.

| | |
|---|---|
| Contributed Capital: | |
| Common Stock, $5 par value, 100,000 shares authorized, 39,000 shares issued and outstanding | $195,000 |
| Paid-in Capital in Excess of Par Value | 100,000 |
| Total Contributed Capital | $295,000 |
| Retained Earnings | 255,000 |
| Total Stockholders' Equity | $550,000 |

## Stock Splits

As mentioned earlier, a corporation may wish to reduce the per share market price of its stock to make it more attractive to a wider range of investors. This can be accomplished by declaring a large stock dividend or by declaring a stock split.

*1b. A stock split increases the number of shares outstanding and reduces the stock's par or stated value proportionately*

A **stock split** increases the number of shares authorized, issued, and outstanding and reduces the stock's par or stated value proportionately.

For example, assume that a corporation has 100,000 shares of $10 par value common stock outstanding. The stock has a current market price of $100 per share. To reduce the market price of the shares for wider trading, the board of directors approves a 4-for-1 stock split. The split reduces the par value of each share from $10.00 to $2.50 ($10 ÷ 4) and will increase the number of shares outstanding from 100,000 to 400,000 (100,000 × 4). The shares outstanding before the split are recalled, and new stock certificates are issued—four new shares issued for each share recalled. A stockholder who owned 100 shares of the $10 par value stock before the split now owns 400 shares of the $2.50 par value stock. A stock split does not change the balances in any of the stockholders' equity accounts. The only amounts that change on the balance sheet are the number of shares authorized, issued, and outstanding and the par or stated value per share.

Because the stock split does not change the dollar balances in any of the stockholders' equity accounts, no journal entry need be recorded. However, a memorandum notation is usually placed in the journal and in the Common Stock account to indicate that the par value has been reduced and the number of shares increased.

To summarize, both stock dividends and stock splits increase the number of shares outstanding without changing either total stockholders' equity or the proportionate share of ownership that each stockholder has in the corporation. But they are accounted for differently. A stock dividend requires an entry to transfer an amount from the Retained Earnings account to a contributed capital account or accounts. A stock split requires only a memorandum-type entry to indicate the change in the par or stated value per share.

## PRIOR PERIOD ADJUSTMENTS

*1c. A prior period adjustment adjusts the beginning balance of retained earnings to correct an error in the net income of a prior period*

Another factor that affects retained earnings directly is a **prior period adjustment.** This adjustment is made to the beginning balance of retained earnings and corrects an error made in the determination of net income in a prior period.

Errors discovered in the same period in which they occurred should be corrected in that period's financial statements. However, errors discovered in an accounting period subsequent to the period in which the errors were made are treated as prior period adjustments. In accounting for prior period adjustments, retained earnings is increased or decreased directly because the net income of the year or years affected by the error has already been closed to the Retained Earnings account.

To illustrate, assume that Supra Corporation discovered in December 19X6 that a mathematical error had been made in 19X5 when computing depreciation on its machinery. As a result, depreciation expense for 19X5 was understated by $55,000. The journal entry to record the prior period adjustment, assuming no tax effect (a topic to be discussed shortly), is as follows:

| | | | |
|---|---|---|---|
| Dec. 31 | Retained Earnings | 55,000 | |
| | Accumulated Depreciation—Machinery | | 55,000 |
| | To correct the error in recording depreciation in 19X5 | | |

In the 19X5 closing entries, the net income credited to retained earnings was overstated by $55,000. The debit to the Retained Earnings account in the above entry corrects the balance in that account. In addition, the error also caused the Accumulated Depreciation—Machinery account to be understated by $55,000 on the 19X5 balance sheet. The credit to Accumulated Depreciation—Machinery corrects the balance in that account.

Prior period adjustments either increase or decrease Retained Earnings, depending on how the error affected net income in the year it was made. They are, however, rather uncommon in practice. Sophisticated internal control systems and annual audits by Certified Public Accountants have significantly reduced material errors that require correction by a prior period adjustment.

## TREASURY STOCK

*1d. Stock previously issued that has been reacquired by the corporation but not retired or reissued is called treasury stock*

Corporations frequently purchase shares of their own outstanding stock from the stockholders. The reacquired stock is called **treasury stock.** By definition, treasury stock is a corporation's own stock, either common or preferred, that has been issued and reacquired by the corporation but has not been retired or reissued. Although treasury stock is usually acquired by purchase, stock donated to the corporation by its stockholders also meets the criteria established by the definition.

Some of the reasons why a corporation purchases its own stock are

To have shares available for distribution to employees under stock purchase, stock option, or stock bonus plans

To support the market price of the shares by stimulating trading in the stock

To buy out the ownership interest of a particular stockholder or group of stockholders

To have shares available for use in such activities as the future acquisition of another company or companies

To achieve the benefits anticipated from purchasing the shares when they appear to be selling at an unusually low price and later selling those shares at a higher price

To increase reported earnings per share by decreasing the number of outstanding shares

For these and other reasons many corporations, especially large ones, are actively involved in the purchase of their own shares.

A corporation may hold treasury shares for an indefinite period of time, reissue them at any time, or retire them. While held, treasury shares are similar to unissued shares in that they have no rights until the shares are reissued. Thus treasury shares do not have voting rights and are not entitled to receive cash dividends, execute the preemptive right, or share in assets if the corporation is liquidated. There is, however, a major difference between treasury stock and unissued stock. If the stock was originally issued at or in excess of its par value, and then reacquired as treasury stock, it can be reissued at less than its par value without the purchaser's incurring a discount liability.

### Purchases of Treasury Stock

There are several methods of accounting for the purchase of treasury stock. The most commonly used one (and the one illustrated here) is the cost basis. When the stock is purchased by the corporation, the Treasury Stock account is debited and the Cash account is credited for the cost of the shares acquired. The par or stated value of the shares and the price at which the stock was originally issued are ignored. For example, assume that on August 12 Supra Corporation purchased

*2a. An entry is made to record the purchase of treasury shares at cost*

1,000 shares of its own stock at $30 per share. The entry to record the purchase is as follows:

| | | | |
|---|---|---|---|
| Aug. 12 | Treasury Stock | 30,000 | |
| | Cash | | 30,000 |
| | Purchased 1,000 shares of treasury stock at $30 per share | | |

Because a corporation cannot own part of itself, the Treasury Stock account is not reported as an asset. Instead it is treated as a contra-stockholders' equity account and reported in the balance sheet as a deduction from the total of contributed capital and retained earnings.

The journal entry that records the purchase of treasury stock shows that the corporation reduces both its assets and its stockholders' equity in equal amounts. After the transaction has been completed and recorded, the stockholders' equity section of Supra Corporation's balance sheet will appear as follows.

STOCKHOLDERS' EQUITY

| | |
|---|---|
| Contributed Capital: | |
| Common Stock, $5 par value, 100,000 shares authorized, 39,000 shares issued, 38,000 shares outstanding | $195,000 |
| Paid-in Capital in Excess of Par Value | 100,000 |
| Total Contributed Capital | $295,000 |
| Retained Earnings | 255,000 |
| Total Contributed Capital and Retained Earnings | $550,000 |
| Less: Treasury Stock, 1,000 shares, at cost | 30,000 |
| Total Stockholders' Equity | $520,000 |

## Reissuance of Treasury Stock

The treasury shares may be reissued at a price above, below, or equal to their cost. When the treasury shares are reissued at cost, the transaction is recorded by reversing the entry used to record their purchase. If Supra Corporation sells the 1,000 treasury shares for $30 per share, Cash is debited and Treasury Stock is credited for $30,000. The sale eliminates all the treasury shares, and the credit to the Treasury Stock account eliminates the balance in that account.

When the treasury shares are reissued at a price above their cost, Cash is debited for the amount received, Treasury Stock is credited for the cost of the shares reissued, and the difference is credited to an account called Paid-in Capital from Treasury Stock Transactions. For example, assume that on October 10, 300 of the 1,000 treasury shares acquired on August 12 are reissued at $40 per share. The entry to record the reissuance is as follows:

*2a. An entry is made to record the reissuance of treasury shares*

| | | | |
|---|---|---|---|
| Oct. 10 | Cash | 12,000 | |
| | Treasury Stock | | 9,000 |
| | Paid-in Capital from Treasury Stock Transactions | | 3,000 |
| | Sold 300 shares of treasury stock that cost $30 per share for $40 per share | | |

If the treasury shares are reissued at a price below their cost, Paid-in Capital from Treasury Stock Transactions is debited for the difference between the cost and the reissue price. Continuing with our example, assume that on November 20, 500 of the remaining 700 treasury shares were reissued at $25 per share. The entry to record the reissuance is as follows:

| | | | |
|---|---|---|---|
| Nov. 20 | Cash | 12,500 | |
| | Paid-in Capital from Treasury Stock Transactions | 2,500 | |
| | Treasury Stock | | 15,000 |
| | Sold 500 shares of treasury stock that cost $30 per share for $25 per share | | |

If there is no Paid-in Capital from Treasury Stock Transactions account or the balance in that account is insufficient to cover the excess of cost over the reissue price, the Retained Earnings account is debited. For example, assume that on December 12 the 200 remaining shares of treasury stock were reissued at $20 per share. The entry to record the transaction is as follows:

| | | | |
|---|---|---|---|
| Dec. 12 | Cash | 4,000 | |
| | Paid-in Capital from Treasury Stock Transactions | 500* | |
| | Retained Earnings | 1,500 | |
| | Treasury Stock | | 6,000 |
| | Sold 200 shares of treasury stock that cost $30 per share for $20 per share | | |

Our examples have been kept simple. We eliminated some arithmetic complexities by avoiding the acquisition of treasury shares at different dates with different costs. Companies that have many treasury stock transactions keep records to ensure that cost data are available when the stock is reissued.

Note that no gains or losses are ever recorded when treasury stock is sold. That is because treasury stock is not an asset. Corporate net income or net loss should be determined by measuring the results of the corporation's business activities, not from activities involving the purchase and reissuance of its own shares of stock.

## APPROPRIATION OF RETAINED EARNINGS

*1e. An appropriation of retained earnings is a journal entry or disclosure that indicates the earmarking of corporate assets*

Corporations often place restrictions on part of retained earnings. The restriction, called **appropriation of retained earnings,** indicates that some corporate assets generated through earnings are earmarked for purposes other than payments of dividends. Some restrictions are made voluntarily by the board of directors; others are contractual or legal. Examples of restrictions on a part of retained earnings include the following:

Voluntary—to decrease dividend payments and thus accumulate assets for a special purpose (such as plant expansion)

Contractual—to meet a requirement in a debt contract that stipulates that a certain amount of earned corporate assets be retained in the business to protect the claims of individual creditors (such as bondholders)

Legal—to meet a state law requirement that often stipulates that retained earnings be restricted in an amount equal to the cost of treasury stock held by the corporation

* The $3,000 credited on October 10 minus the $2,500 debited on November 20 leaves a $500 balance in the Paid-in Capital from Treasury Stock Transactions account.

Restrictions on retained earnings may be achieved and communicated in either of two ways: by making a journal entry that appropriates retained earnings or by adding a note to the financial statements that discloses the nature of the restrictions.

When a journal entry is used to appropriate retained earnings, it transfers a dollar amount from the unrestricted Retained Earnings account to another stockholders' equity account called Retained Earnings Appropriated. For example, assume that the board of directors of Supra Corporation plans to expand its plant capacity over the next few years. Its plans call for financing much of this expansion by retaining assets generated by earnings. On June 1, 19X6, the board takes action by passing a resolution to appropriate $100,000 of retained earnings. The entry to record the appropriation is as follows:

*1e. An entry is made to record an appropriation of retained earnings*

| | | | |
|---|---|---|---|
| June 1 | Retained Earnings . . . . . . . . . . . . . . . . . . . . . . . . . . . . . . . | 100,000 | |
| | Retained Earnings Appropriated for Plant Expansion. . . . . . . . . . . . . . . . . . . . . . . . . . . . . . . . . . | | 100,000 |
| | To record the appropriation of retained earnings for plant expansion | | |

An appropriation of retained earnings has no effect on the company's assets, total retained earnings, or total stockholders' equity. The entry involves two separate Retained Earnings accounts. Thus the sum of the two accounts is equal to the balance that appeared in the Retained Earnings account before the appropriation entry was recorded.

By appropriating retained earnings, we are able to communicate that assets in that amount will be retained for the purpose designated and nothing more. The appropriation of retained earnings does not indicate that cash or any other asset has been set aside to achieve the designated purpose.

*1e. The appropriation of retained earnings is shown in the stockholders' equity section of the balance sheet*

The stockholders' equity section of Supra Corporation's balance sheet below shows how the appropriation of retained earnings may be reported.

STOCKHOLDERS' EQUITY

| | | |
|---|---|---|
| Contributed Capital: | | |
| Common Stock, $5 par value, 100,000 shares authorized, 39,000 shares outstanding. . . . . . . . . . . . . . . . . . . . . . . . . . . . . . . . . . . . . . . . . . . . . . . . . | | $195,000 |
| Paid-in Capital in Excess of Par Value . . . . . . . . . . . . . . . . . . . . . . . . . . | | 100,000 |
| Total Contributed Capital . . . . . . . . . . . . . . . . . . . . . . . . . . . . . . . . . . . | | $295,000 |
| Retained Earnings: | | |
| Retained Earnings Unappropriated . . . . . . . . . . . . . . . . . . . . . . . . . . . . . . | $155,000 | |
| Retained Earnings Appropriated for Plant Expansion. . . . . . . . . . . . . . . . . | 100,000 | |
| Total Retained Earnings . . . . . . . . . . . . . . . . . . . . . . . . . . . . . . . . . . . . | | 255,000 |
| Total Stockholders' Equity . . . . . . . . . . . . . . . . . . . . . . . . . . . . . . . . . . . | | $550,000 |

When the appropriation of retained earnings is no longer needed, the appropriation is removed by transferring the amount back to the Retained Earnings account. Thus when the plant expansion is completed (or the plans canceled), the appropriation would be removed by the following entry:

*1e. An entry is made to remove an appropriation of retained earnings*

| | | | |
|---|---|---|---|
| March 31 | Retained Earnings Appropriated for Plant Expansion. . . . . . . . . . . . . . . . . . . . . . . . . . . . . . . . . . . . . . . | 100,000 | |
| | Retained Earnings. . . . . . . . . . . . . . . . . . . . . . . . . . | | 100,000 |
| | To remove the appropriation of retained earnings | | |

*1e. An appropriation of retained earnings may be disclosed in a note that accompanies a balance sheet*

Information concerning the appropriation of retained earnings can also be disclosed in a note that accompanies the financial statements. This method seems to be the choice of an increasing number of companies. The note must clearly describe all legal, contractual, or discretionary provisions and show the nature and amount of the appropriation.

For example, the appropriation data appearing in the foregoing illustration could be disclosed in a note that accompanies the balance sheet and might appear as follows:

| | |
|---|---|
| Contributed Capital: | |
| Common Stock, $5 par value, 100,000 shares authorized, 39,000 shares outstanding | $195,000 |
| Paid-in Capital in Excess of Par Value | 100,000 |
| Total Contributed Capital | $295,000 |
| Retained Earnings (see note 5) | 255,000 |
| Total Stockholders' Equity | $550,000 |

Note 5—Retained earnings in the amount of $100,000 is appropriated for plant expansion; the remaining $155,000 is unrestricted.

## STATEMENT OF RETAINED EARNINGS

We have now completed our discussion of the primary factors that cause changes in the Retained Earnings account. These changes are often disclosed in the statement of retained earnings, one of the financial statements published by a corporation in its annual report to stockholders. The statement of retained earnings shows what caused the balance in the Retained Earnings account to change during the period covered by the statement. Exhibit 15–1 shows the statement of retained earnings for Supra Corporation. Although the amount of detail presented in the statement varies, this one is fairly comprehensive. It shows how prior period adjustments as well as net income and dividends are reported.

*2b. A statement of retained earnings is illustrated in Exhibit 15–1*

EXHIBIT 15–1

SUPRA CORPORATION
Statement of Retained Earnings
For the Year Ended December 31, 19X6

| | | |
|---|---|---|
| Retained Earnings, December 31, 19X5 | | $255,000 |
| Deduct: Prior Period Adjustment for the correction of an error in computed depreciation (net of taxes) | | 55,000 |
| Retained Earnings as adjusted, December 31, 19X5 | | $200,000 |
| Add: Net Income for 19X6 | | 260,000 |
| Total | | $460,000 |
| Deduct: Dividends Declared in 19X6: | | |
| Cash Dividends | $60,000 | |
| Stock Dividends | 60,000 | 120,000 |
| Retained Earnings, December 31, 19X6 | | $340,000 |

## A COMPREHENSIVE STOCKHOLDERS' EQUITY SECTION OF A BALANCE SHEET

*2c. A comprehensive stockholders' equity section of a balance sheet is illustrated in Exhibit 15–2*

We have discussed various accounts that may appear in the stockholders' equity section of the balance sheet. Exhibit 15–2 is a comprehensive illustration showing how stockholders' equity accounts may be reported in the balance sheet. It includes such descriptive information as shares authorized, issued, outstanding, preferences, and par values. These data, which are needed for full and fair disclosure, may as an alternative be shown in notes accompanying the financial statements. Although the terminology used and the amount of detail provided may vary somewhat in practice, the illustration should be examined carefully for form and content.

EXHIBIT 15–2

Stockholders' Equity

| | | |
|---|---|---|
| Contributed Capital: | | |
| Preferred Stock, $100 par value, $9 cumulative and nonparticipating, 75,000 shares authorized, 30,000 shares issued and outstanding | | $3,000,000 |
| Common Stock, $5 par value, 200,000 shares authorized, 80,000 shares issued, 75,000 shares outstanding | | 400,000 |
| Common Stock Subscribed, 20,000 shares | | 100,000 |
| Common Stock Dividend Distributable, 8,000 shares | | 40,000 |
| Paid-in Capital in Excess of Par Value—Preferred | | 250,000 |
| Paid-in Capital in Excess of Par Value—Common | | 920,000 |
| Paid-in Capital from Treasury Stock Transactions | | 80,000 |
| Donated Capital | | 110,000 |
| Total Contributed Capital | | $4,900,000 |
| Retained Earnings: | | |
| Retained Earnings—Unappropriated | $1,050,000 | |
| Retained Earnings—Appropriated for Plant Expansion | 550,000 | |
| Total Retained Earnings | | 1,600,000 |
| Total Contributed Capital and Retained Earnings | | $6,500,000 |
| Less: Treasury Stock, 5,000 common shares, at cost | | 110,000 |
| Total Stockholders' Equity | | $6,390,000 |

## CORPORATE INCOME REPORTING

The determination of periodic net income is one of the primary functions of accounting. Corporations that cannot consistently generate net income generally do not stay in business very long, and those who invested their resources in these businesses generally lose some or all of the amounts invested. On the other hand, corporations that consistently earn sizable amounts of net income are usually able to give investors the benefits they seek. The income earned for a period usually affects how much will be paid out in dividends and frequently influences the market price of the shares. Generally, the higher the net income, the higher the dividend payout and the higher the market price of the shares, and vice versa.

In the following sections we will show how a corporate income statement is prepared to disclose its earning activities in a way that is informative and useful in evaluating current earnings and in predicting future earnings.

## INCOME STATEMENT SECTIONS

*2d. A comprehensive income statement is illustrated in Exhibit 15–3*

Income or loss from normal and recurring operating activities is identified on the income statement as **income from continuing operations** (see Exhibit 15–3). It is determined from revenue and expense items considered normal and recurring to the operations of the particular business. Since income from continuing operations relates to revenue and expense activities that are expected to continue in the future, it is considered a useful figure in predicting future income. Items resulting from transactions or events that are unusual and nonrecurring could significantly affect the net income reported for the current period, although they are not indicative of what is expected in the future.

For this reason we reported items resulting from unusual and nonrecurring transactions and events separately in the income statement *after* income or loss from continuing operations. These items can be divided into three categories and identified as (1) discontinued operations, (2) extraordinary items, and (3) changes in accounting principles.

EXHIBIT 15–3

Comprehensive Income Statement

RIVAL CORPORATION
Income Statement
For the Year Ended December 31, 19X6

| | | |
|---|---|---|
| Revenues: | | |
| Net sales | | $4,900,000 |
| Other revenue | | 250,000 |
| Total revenue | | $5,150,000 |
| Operating Expenses: | | |
| Cost of goods sold | $2,900,000 | |
| Selling expenses | 950,000 | |
| Administrative expenses | 500,000 | |
| General expense | 100,000 | 4,450,000 |
| Income from Continuing Operations before Taxes | | $ 700,000 |
| Income Tax Expense | | 280,000 |
| Income from Continuing Operations | | $ 420,000 |
| Discontinued Operations: | | |
| Operating income of discontinued segment (net of taxes, $40,000) | $ 60,000 | |
| Loss on disposal of segment (net of tax savings, $48,000) | (72,000) | (12,000) |
| Income before Extraordinary Items | | $ 408,000 |
| Extraordinary Item: Loss from earthquake damage (net of tax savings, $36,000) | | (54,000) |
| Income before Cumulative Effect of an Accounting Change | | $ 354,000 |
| Cumulative effect of change in depreciation method (net of taxes, $32,000) | | 48,000 |
| Net Income | | $ 402,000 |
| Earnings per Common Share: | | |
| Income from continuing operations | | $2.10 |
| Discontinued operations | | (.06) |
| Income before extraordinary item and cumulative effect of accounting change | | $2.04 |
| Extraordinary loss | | (.27) |
| Cumulative effect of accounting change | | .24 |
| Net income | | $2.01 |

The data on earnings per common share are based on 200,000 weighted average number of common shares outstanding. There are no potentially dilutive securities.

## Discontinued Operations

A large corporation may have one or more segments of business. For example, Allied-Signal Inc., a large industrial corporation, lists aerospace and automotive among its business segments. A **business segment** refers to "a component of an entity whose activities represent a separate major line of business or a certain class of customers."[4] Sometimes a company will sell, abandon, or otherwise dispose of an entire segment of its business.

Because the disposal of a business segment is an important event qualifying as unusual and nonrecurring, the gain or loss resulting from the disposal is reported as a separate item in the income statement. Reporting requirements for discontinued operations are quite complex, and therefore only the major provisions are covered here. Exhibit 15–3 shows how gains and losses from discontinued operations are reported in an income statement. Note that a separate income statement category called **Discontinued Operations** is provided. It appears immediately after Income from Continuing Operations and shows two items of information concerning discontinued operations:

*1f. Information about a discontinued operation is reported separately in the income statement*

> The income (or loss) of the current year that resulted from operating the business segment that has been disposed of
>
> The gain or loss from the disposal of the business segment

Both figures are shown **net of income taxes.** This is known as **intraperiod tax allocation,** which is the process of apportioning the total income tax expense (or income tax savings) for the year to each of the items shown in the designated categories in the income statement. For example, Exhibit 15–3 shows that \$280,000 of income tax expense relates to the income from continuing operations and that \$40,000 of income tax expense, shown parenthetically, relates to the income from operating the business segment that was disposed of during the current period. Note that when losses occur such as the loss on the disposal of the business segment, an income tax savings results and is so identified. Based on Rival Corporation's assumed tax rate of 40%, the loss incurred on the disposal of the business segment must have been \$120,000 before taxes. Because the \$120,000 loss will reduce taxable income by that amount, it will also reduce the amount of tax paid by \$48,000 (\$120,000 × 40% = \$48,000). This amount is shown parenthetically as a tax savings. Therefore the net of tax loss to be used in the determination of the current year's net income is \$72,000 (a \$120,000 loss on disposal − a \$48,000 tax savings = \$72,000 of reported loss).

Other unusual and nonrecurring transactions and events such as extraordinary items and changes in accounting principles are also reported as separate categories in the income statement by using a net-of-tax-effect approach.

## Extraordinary Items

**Extraordinary items** are events and transactions that are unusual in nature, infrequent in occurrence, and significant in amount. The Accounting Principles Board describes an unusual and infrequent event or transaction in the following terms:

> *Unusual Nature*—the underlying event or transaction should possess a high degree of abnormality and be a type clearly unrelated to, or only incidentally related to, the

[4] *Opinions of the Accounting Principles Board, No. 30,* "Reporting the Results of Operations" (New York: American Institute of Certified Public Accountants, 1973), par. 13.

ordinary and typical activities of the entity, taking into account the environment in which the entity operates.

*Infrequency of Occurrence*—the underlying event or transaction should be a type that would not reasonably be expected to recur in the foreseeable future, taking into account the environment in which the entity operates.[5]

Transactions and events that meet both of the above criteria are rare. Some that qualify for reporting as extraordinary items are gains or losses resulting from (1) major casualties such as floods, earthquakes, and tornadoes, (2) the expropriation of property by foreign governments, and (3) the enactment of a new law. In addition, the Financial Accounting Standards Board has ruled that a few other specifically identified gains or losses must be reported as extraordinary items, including any material gain or loss resulting from the early extinguishment of debt.

*1f. Extraordinary items are reported separately on the income statement*

Extraordinary items shown net of their tax effects are reported separately in the income statement following income from continuing operations but after gains or losses from discontinued operations if any were reported. The presentation of a loss resulting from an extraordinary item (earthquake damage) is shown in Exhibit 15–3.

Transactions and events that are *either* unusual in nature or infrequent in occurrence but not *both,* such as gains or losses on the disposal of plant assets, do not qualify as extraordinary items. They should be reported among the items that determine income from continuing operations.

Gains and losses that do result from extraordinary items, like those that result from discontinued operations, are reported separately to show readers of the income statement that transactions and events causing these types of gains or losses are significantly different from the firm's regular and ongoing business activities.

## Changes in Accounting Principles

To respond to changing circumstances, a company may occasionally find it appropriate to change from one generally accepted accounting principle to another. The accounting profession has stated that a **change in accounting principle** "results from the adoption of a generally accepted accounting principle different from the one used previously for reporting purposes."[6] For example, a company should change its method of depreciation from the sum-of-the-years'-digits method to the straight-line method if the benefits derived from the assets' use are no longer being consumed in an accelerated fashion.

As you would expect, a change from one generally accepted accounting principle to another may have a significant effect on key financial statement amounts. To help the reader of the financial statements understand the effect of an accounting change, considerable disclosure is required. This includes information concerning the nature of the change, its justification, and its effect on the current period's net income.

*1f. Information concerning an accounting change must be disclosed in the notes to the financial statements*

In addition, the cumulative effect of the change is generally reported separately in the income statement immediately after extraordinary items, if any. The **cumulative effect of a change in accounting principle** is the effect that the new accounting principle would have had on the net income of all prior years if it,

[5] Ibid., par. 20.

[6] *Opinions of the Accounting Principles Board, No. 20,* "Accounting Changes" (New York: American Institute of Certified Public Accountants, 1971), par. 7.

instead of the old accounting principle, had been used in those past years. Since it is assumed that a change in principle is made at the beginning of the year, the cumulative effect is measured as the difference between the balance in the Retained Earnings account at the beginning of the year and the balance that would have been in that account at the beginning of the year had the new accounting principle always been used.

For example, assume that Rival Corporation has for a number of years used the sum-of-the-years'-digits method to depreciate its equipment. In 19X6 management decides to change to the straight-line method because it believes that this method will better reflect how the service benefits of the equipment are being used. The cumulative effect of the change to the beginning of 19X6 is computed in the schedule below.

Cumulative Effect of Change in Depreciation

| | |
|---|---|
| Depreciation taken by using the sum-of-the-years'-digits method for all years prior to 19X6 | $290,000 |
| Less: Depreciation that would have been taken by using the straight-line method during those years | 210,000 |
| Cumulative effect of accounting change | $ 80,000 |

The cumulative effect of the accounting change, assuming an income tax rate of 40%, will increase net income by $48,000 and be reported as shown in Exhibit 15–3.

In our discussion of how certain special items should be reported in the income statement, we have purposely used assumed amounts and simple computations. More-complex income reporting procedures are covered in advanced accounting courses. Our purpose here was to briefly describe some of the features of the corporate income statement and emphasize its usefulness.

## EARNINGS PER SHARE

One of the most widely quoted accounting statistics is *earnings per share* of common stock. Data relating to earnings per share (EPS) are often reported in the financial pages of daily newspapers, financial magazines, and various statistical services. The data are of primary interest not only to present and potential investors but to security analysts, who use it to

Evaluate the past performance of a business
Compare performance with that of other companies
Assess prospects for future earnings and dividend distributions

The Accounting Principles Board recognized the significance of this figure when it concluded that earnings per share of common stock should be shown on the face of the income statement.[7]

[7] *Opinions of the Accounting Principles Board, No. 15,* "Earnings per Share" (New York: American Institute of Certified Public Accountants, 1969), par. 12.

## Simple Capital Structure

*2e. If only common stock is outstanding, earnings per share = net income ÷ average number of shares outstanding*

If a corporation has only common stock outstanding, **earnings per share** is determined by dividing net income by the average number of shares outstanding. If the corporation also has nonconvertible preferred stock outstanding, the preferred dividend requirement for the year must be subtracted from the net income, and only the remaining amount is divided by the average number of common shares outstanding to determine earnings per share. Also if the number of common shares outstanding changes during the year, it will be necessary to compute a weighted average number of common shares outstanding for the year for use in determining earnings per share. For example, if a company had 200,000 shares of common stock outstanding at the beginning of the year and issued 80,000 additional shares on October 1, the weighted average number of common shares outstanding (based on the number of months that the shares were outstanding during the year) is 220,000 shares computed as follows:

| | |
|---|---|
| 200,000 shares × $\frac{9}{12}$ of a year | 150,000 |
| 280,000 shares × $\frac{3}{12}$ of a year | 70,000 |
| Weighted average number of shares outstanding | 220,000 |

Thus the basic earnings-per-share amount is computed by dividing the net income applicable to common stock by the weighted average number of common shares outstanding. This can be expressed in formula form as follows:

$$\text{EPS} = \frac{\text{Net Income} - \text{Preferred Dividends}}{\text{Weighted Average Number of Common Shares Outstanding}}$$

To illustrate, assume that the corporation having 220,000 weighted average common shares outstanding also had 10,000 shares of \$8 preferred stock outstanding during the entire year. Assume further that its reported net income for that year was \$432,000. Then its earnings per share of common stock would be \$1.60, computed as follows:

$$\frac{\$432{,}000 - \$80{,}000}{220{,}000} = \$1.60$$

The earnings-per-share calculations shown above are for corporations having a simple capital structure. Corporations are said to have a **simple capital structure** when they have no outstanding convertible securities (such as bonds or preferred stock) or outstanding stock purchase rights or options that could be converted into common stock. Corporations having a simple capital structure report one earnings-per-share figure calculated by using the basic formula shown above.

## Complex Capital Structure

Many corporations have a **complex capital structure.** This means that they have convertible securities, stock purchase rights, or options that can be converted into common stock. These items have the potential for diluting (reducing) earnings per common share because certain actions taken by those who own them would cause the company to issue additional shares of stock. For example, the owners of convertible preferred stock may at any time exchange them for a specified number of common shares.

Corporations with complex capital structures report two earnings-per-share amounts — primary earnings per share and fully diluted earnings per share. When calculating these amounts, we make certain assumptions about the corporation's potentially dilutive securities. In calculating **primary earnings per share,** we assume that only certain securities were converted, causing new stock to be issued. These securities are the ones most likely to be converted into common stock and are called **common stock equivalents.** The accounting profession has established criteria for determining whether a potentially dilutive security is a common stock equivalent. For our purposes, recognize that securities qualifying as common stock equivalents are treated as the equivalent of common stock in the computation of earnings per share. In calculating **fully diluted earnings per share,** we assume that all potentially dilutive securities were converted, causing new stock to be issued regardless of how unlikely it may be that conversion will actually occur.

The determination of whether a potentially dilutive security is a common stock equivalent is made once — when the security is issued. If it qualifies at that time, it remains a common stock equivalent for purposes of computing earnings per share for as long as it remains outstanding.

The rules for determining whether a potentially dilutive security should be included in the calculation of primary earnings per share or fully diluted earnings per share or both are complex, and detailed coverage will not be attempted here.

To illustrate the computation of primary and fully diluted earnings per share, assume that Compete Corporation had the following capital structure and reported the following net income:

*2e. Computations of primary and fully diluted earnings per share are illustrated here*

*Preferred stock* — 5,000 shares of cumulative, convertible preferred stock outstanding for the entire year. The preferred dividend is \$8 per share, and each share is convertible into four shares of common stock. The stock is a potentially dilutive security but did not meet the APB criteria for a common stock equivalent at the date of issuance.

*Common stock* — 100,000 shares, which were outstanding for the entire year.

*Net income for the year* — \$540,000.

Computations for the per share amounts are shown below.

$$\text{Primary EPS} = \frac{\text{Net Income} - \text{Preferred Dividends}}{\text{Weighted Average Number of Common Shares Outstanding}}$$

$$= \frac{\$540{,}000 - \$40{,}000}{100{,}000} = \$5.00$$

$$\text{Fully Diluted EPS} = \frac{\text{Net Income Applicable to Common Stock}}{\text{Weighted Average Number of Common Shares Outstanding plus the Potentially Dilutive Security (Preferred Stock)}}$$

$$= \frac{\$540{,}000}{100{,}000 + 20{,}000} = \$4.50$$

Note that both the numerator and the denominator changed in the calculation of fully diluted earnings per share. Conversions of convertible securities are assumed to take place as of the beginning of the year (if the security was outstanding for the entire year). The assumed conversion of the preferred stock means that none would be outstanding, and consequently no dividends would be paid.

This makes the entire net income ($540,000) applicable to common shares, which increased to 120,000 shares as a result of the assumed conversion.

As we have seen, earnings-per-share figures are hypothetical and are based on "as if" assumptions concerning the conversion of certain securities into common stock. In the preceding example, we made the conversion assumption when computing fully diluted earnings per share, even though the preferred stock was not actually converted into common stock.

## PRESENTATION OF EARNINGS-PER-SHARE DATA

Earnings per share is reported in the income statement. If there are nonrecurring items in the statement, per share amounts must be shown for:

Income from continuing operations
Income before extraordinary items and cumulative effect of accounting changes
Cumulative effect of an accounting change
Net Income

Per share amounts for gains or losses on discontinued operations and for gains or losses on extraordinary items may also be presented.

We have now concluded our study of corporate income reporting. Exhibit 15–3 showed the presentation of a comprehensive income statement, the purpose being to illustrate the various items discussed above. It should be recognized, however, that rarely would a company have all of these nonrecurring items in one year.

## HIGHLIGHT PROBLEM

Information pertaining to the income statement accounts of Golden Corporation as of December 31, 19X6, is presented below.

| | |
|---|---:|
| Cost of goods sold | $105,000 |
| Loss from property expropriated in South Transylvania (before tax) | 40,000 |
| Selling expenses | 29,000 |
| Loss from labor strike (considered unusual but recurring) (before tax) | 12,000 |
| Gain on disposal of business segment (before tax) | 10,000 |
| Sales Revenue | 270,000 |
| Administrative expenses | 18,000 |
| Loss from the operations of the discontinued segment (before tax) | 15,000 |
| Interest expense | 4,000 |

Assume that the company is taxed at a rate of 40% on all applicable items. There are 5,000 shares of cumulative convertible preferred stock which were outstanding during the entire year and on which the annual cash dividend is $2 per share. Each preferred share is convertible into two shares of common stock. At issuance, the preferred stock did not qualify as a common stock equivalent. The weighted average number of common shares outstanding for purposes of computing primary earnings per share has been established as 20,000.

Required:
Prepare an income statement for the company and include earnings-per-share data on the face of the statement.

## GLOSSARY OF KEY TERMS

**Appropriation of retained earnings.** A journal entry or disclosure that informs stockholders and others that some corporate assets generated from earnings are earmarked for purposes other than the payment of dividends.

**Business segment.** A component of a business whose activities represent a separate major line of business or class of customer.

**Capitalization (of retained earnings).** A rearrangement of stockholders' equity that decreases Retained Earnings and increases Contributed Capital in equal amounts.

**Change in accounting principle.** A change from one generally accepted accounting principle or method to another generally accepted principle or method.

**Common stock equivalents.** Securities that are likely to be converted into common stock.

**Complex capital structures.** A corporate capital structure that has outstanding securities, or outstanding stock purchase rights, or options that could be converted into common stock.

**Cumulative effect of a change in accounting principle.** The total effect that the new accounting principle would have had on the net income of all prior years if the new, instead of the old, accounting principle had been used in those years.

**Declaration date.** The date on which a dividend is formally declared by the corporation's board of directors.

**Deficit.** Term used to indicate a debit balance in the Retained Earnings account.

**Discontinued operation.** A segment of a business that is no longer a part of the ongoing operations of the company.

**Earnings per share.** Net income available to the common stock divided by the weighted average number of common shares outstanding during the period.

**Ex-dividend.** Term describing shares of stock purchased between the record date and the payment date. The buyer of the stock does not acquire the right to the current dividend.

**Extraordinary items.** Events and transactions that are unusual in nature, occur infrequently, and are significant in amount.

**Fully diluted earnings per share.** An earnings-per-share figure computed under the assumption that all potentially dilutive securities were converted into common stock.

**Income from continuing operations.** A component of the income statement showing the income or loss generated by normal and recurring activities of the company.

**Intraperiod tax allocation.** The process of apportioning the corporation's income tax expense (or income tax savings) among the following reported items: income from continuing operations, discontinued operations, extraordinary items, changes in accounting principle, and prior period adjustments.

**Liquidating dividends.** Distributions of assets by a corporation to its shareholders which constitute a return of their contributed capital, not a distribution of assets attributable to corporate earnings.

**Net of income taxes.** A phrase used in connection with discontinued operations, extraordinary items, changes in accounting principles, and prior period adjustments. These items are shown in the financial statements at the dollar amounts remaining after deducting the effect of applicable taxes.

**Payment date.** The date (selected by the board of directors) on which a dividend will be distributed to stockholders of record.

**Primary earnings per share.** An earnings-per-share figure computed under the assumption that only certain securities were converted into common stock.

**Prior period adjustment.** An adjustment made to the beginning balance of retained earnings that corrects an error made in the determination of net income in a prior period.

**Record date.** The date (selected by the board of directors) on which ownership of shares is determined for purposes of establishing who has the right to receive the dividend.

**Simple capital structure.** A corporate capital structure that contains no outstanding securities or outstanding stock purchase rights or options that could be converted into common stock.

**Stock dividend.** A pro rata distribution of additional shares of a corporation's own stock to its shareholders.

**Stock split.** A decrease in the par or stated value of the authorized stock with a proportionate increase in the number of shares authorized, issued, and outstanding.

**Treasury stock.** Shares of the corporation's own stock that have been issued and reacquired but have not been retired or reissued.

## REVIEW QUESTIONS

1. Describe the two components of corporate stockholders' equity. [LO1a]
2. What does retained earnings represent? [LO1a]
3. Name the five factors that affect the Retained Earnings account. [LO1a]
4. Name and briefly describe the significance of the important dates associated with dividends. [LO1b]
5. Differentiate between cash dividends, stock dividends, and stock splits. [LO1b]
6. Differentiate between small stock dividends and large stock dividends. [LO1b]
7. Give two reasons why a corporate board of directors may declare a stock dividend. [LO1b]
8. Why is no journal entry needed to record a stock split? [LO1b]
9. What accounting treatment is given to errors discovered in the same period in which they occurred? [LO1c]
10. What accounting treatment is given to errors discovered in a period subsequent to the period in which the errors were made? [LO1c]
11. Give six reasons why a corporation would purchase its own stock. [LO1d]
12. What is the most commonly used method of accounting for the purchase of treasury stock? [LO1d]
13. How is treasury stock reported in the balance sheet? [LO1d]
14. What account is debited or credited when treasury stock is reissued at more or less than its original cost? Under what conditions would another account be debited? [LO2a]
15. Give three reasons why restrictions may be placed on a part of retained earnings. [LO1e]
16. Differentiate between the two ways that stockholders and others may be informed that a part of retained earnings has been restricted. [LO1e]
17. Indicate the nature of each of the components in the statement of retained earnings. [LO2b]
18. Indicate the nature of each of the components in the stockholders' equity section of a balance sheet. [LO2c]
19. Name the three categories of unusual and nonrecurring transactions or events that are identified and reported separately in the income statement. [LO1f]
20. What two items of information are reported in the income statement under the category called Discontinued Operations? [LO1f]
21. Briefly explain what is meant by *intraperiod tax allocation*. [LO1f]
22. What criteria (two characteristics) must exist before a gain or loss resulting from a transaction or event can be reported in the income statement as an extraordinary item? [LO1f]
23. Where is the gain or loss resulting from an extraordinary item reported in the income statement? [LO1f]
24. What is a change in accounting principle? [LO1f]
25. What information is disclosed in the notes to the financial statements when an accounting principle is changed? [LO1f]
26. What information is reported in the income statement when an accounting principle is changed? [LO1f]
27. Name three principal uses made of earnings-per-share data. [LO2e]
28. How is earnings per share calculated when a corporation has only common stock outstanding? [LO2e]
29. Differentiate between a simple capital structure and a complex capital structure. [LO2e]
30. Differentiate between primary earnings per share and fully diluted earnings per share. [LO2e]

## ANALYTICAL QUESTIONS

31. You overheard the following from a company's stockholder: "The company has a substantial balance in its Retained Earnings account. I saw it on their balance sheet. I can't understand why they have not paid larger cash dividends in the past. Their Retained Earnings shows that they certainly have the capability." Comment on this statement. [LO1a,1b]
32. "Stock dividends are simply a way of making the stockholders think they are getting something when they really are not." Comment on this statement. [LO1b]
33. Daring Corporation acquired 500 shares of its own stock at $30 per share and later reissued them for $50 per share. The company's president indicated that he would show a $10,000 "gain" on the sale of the stock under a revenue caption in the company's income statement. Comment on this plan. [LO1d]
34. Why make an appropriation of Retained Earnings when no cash is set aside? Comment on this question. [LO1e]
35. After reading the financial statements of a well-known company, a friend said to you: "I found an obvious error in the company's statements. They indicate they have more shares of issued stock than outstanding stock, and that's impossible." Comment on your friend's statement. [LO1d,2c]
36. You overheard a fellow student say that "it really doesn't matter how a company reports the results of its income-producing activity. The only thing that's important is whether the company had a net income or net loss for the period." Comment on this statement. [LO1f]
37. Another friend said: "I don't understand why corporations report primary earnings per common share and fully diluted earnings per share. They are both computed on 'as if' assumptions concerning the conversion of certain securities and options. Since the earnings-per-share amounts are not based on the actual number of shares outstanding, they do not represent 'true' earnings-per-share amounts." Explain the purpose of these computations to your friend. [LO2e]

## IMPACT ANALYSIS QUESTIONS

*For each error described, indicate whether it overstates [O], understates [U], or does not affect [N] the indicated key figures.*

38. A 20% stock dividend was incorrectly recorded as a cash dividend. [LO1b]

    ______ Total Stockholders' Equity ______ Retained Earnings
    ______ Total Assets ______ Net Income

39. A cash dividend was declared on October 1, 198X, and the correct entry was made. When the dividend was paid on December 15, 198X, no entry was made to record the payment. [LO1b]

    ______ Total Stockholders' Equity ______ Retained Earnings
    ______ Total Assets ______ Total Liabilities

40. Treasury stock was purchased for $30 per share and resold for $35 per share. When the stock was resold, an entry was made debiting Cash, crediting Treasury Stock, and crediting Gain on Sale of Treasury Stock. [LO2a]

    ______ Total Stockholders' Equity ______ Retained Earnings
    ______ Total Assets ______ Net Income

41. Assume the same series of entries as in Question 40 except that a credit was made to Retained Earnings instead of a gain account when the treasury stock was resold. [LO2a]

    ______ Total Stockholders' Equity ______ Retained Earnings
    ______ Total Assets ______ Net Income

## EXERCISES

EXERCISE 15–1 *(Record Stock Dividends and Stock Splits)* Brookdale Corporation had 200,000 shares of $1 par value common stock outstanding when the board of directors declared a 5% stock dividend on August 16. The new shares will be issued on September 15 to the stockholders of record on August 31. The market price of the common stock on August 16 was $15.50 per share. On that same date the corporation had retained earnings of $580,000 and paid-in capital in excess of par of $670,000.

Required:

1. Prepare journal entries to record the declaration and distribution of the stock dividend. Also prepare the stockholders' equity section of the company's balance sheet (a) before the stock dividend is declared and (b) after the stock dividend is distributed.
2. Instead of the stock dividend, assume that the board of directors declared a 2-for-1 stock split on August 15. Prepare the journal entries, if any, for the declaration and distribution of the stock split. Also prepare the stockholders' equity section of the company's balance sheet after the stock split. [LO1b]

EXERCISE 15–2 *(Record Treasury Stock Transactions and Prepare Stockholders' Equity Section)* Flair Corporation had the following stockholders' equity on January 1, 19X6.

| | |
|---|---|
| Common Stock, $2 par, 200,000 shares authorized, issued, and outstanding | $ 400,000 |
| Paid-in Capital in Excess of Par Value | 600,000 |
| Retained Earnings | 320,000 |
| Total Stockholders' Equity | $1,320,000 |

During the year the company had the following treasury stock transactions.

| | |
|---|---|
| March 7 | Purchased 20,000 of its own common shares at $20 per share. |
| May 2 | Sold 4,000 of the treasury shares purchased on March 7 for $22 per share. |
| July 14 | Sold 5,000 of the treasury shares purchased on March 7 for $20 per share. |
| Sept. 9 | Sold 3,000 of the treasury shares purchased on March 7 for $18 per share. |
| Dec. 12 | Sold 2,000 of the treasury shares purchased on March 7 for $15 per share. |

Required:

1. Prepare journal entries to record the treasury stock transactions.
2. Prepare the stockholders' equity section of the company's balance sheet on December 31, 19X6. No new shares were issued during the year. Net income for 19X6 was $120,000, and cash dividends of $40,000 were declared and paid in 19X6. [LO2a,2c]

EXERCISE 15–3 *(Record Dividends and Appropriation of Retained Earnings)* The following are selected transactions of Ultra Corporation.

| | |
|---|---|
| March 5 | The board of directors declared a cash dividend of 50 cents per common share to be paid on April 15 to the stockholders of record on March 31. There are 200,000 shares of common stock outstanding. |
| April 1 | The board approved a $200,000 appropriation of retained earnings for a possible loss resulting from a pollution lawsuit. |
| April 15 | Paid the cash dividend declared on March 5. |
| June 6 | The board declared a 5% stock dividend on common stock to be distributed on July 15 to the stockholders of record on June 30. There are 200,000 shares of common stock outstanding, with a par value of $10. The shares have a market price of $30 per share on this date. |

| | | |
|---|---|---|
| July | 15 | Distributed the stock dividend declared on June 6. |
| Sept. | 1 | The pollution lawsuit was settled out of court with the company making a cash payment of $125,000 to the plaintiff. The board approved the removal of the appropriation of retained earnings. |

Required:
Prepare journal entries to record the above transactions. [LO1b,1e]

EXERCISE 15–4 *(Prepare a Statement of Retained Earnings)* While preparing financial statements at the end of the year, Oldlander Corporation discovered an error in the computation of depreciation that, in total, overstated Depreciation Expense by $85,000 in the income statements of prior years. The error was not repeated in 19X6, the current year, when the company reported net income of $120,000 and declared cash dividends of $4.20 per share on its 50,000 common shares outstanding. The company has no preferred stock, and the balance in Retained Earnings on January 1, 19X6, is $975,000.

Required:
Prepare a statement of retained earnings for the year ended December 31, 19X6. Income taxes of 40% have been subtracted from all income figures. The income tax rate must be used in determining the effect of the depreciation error. [LO2b]

EXERCISE 15–5 *(Prepare a Statement of Retained Earnings)* Southern Corporation had a retained earnings balance of $750,000 on January 1, 19X6. The following information pertains to transactions and events that occurred during 19X6.

1. A 5% common stock dividend was declared on December 1 and distributed on December 31. The company had 200,000, $5 par value common shares outstanding before the stock dividend was distributed. The stock was actively traded on the declaration date and had a market price of $14 per share.
2. Net income for the year was $580,000.
3. An error that occurred in 19X4, two years ago, was discovered on November 12. The error caused before-tax net income of that year to be understated by $60,000. The company is subject to a 40% income tax rate.
4. Cash dividends of $300,000 were declared and paid to common shareholders during the year.

Required:
Prepare a statement of retained earnings for the year ended December 31, 19X6. [LO1b,1c,2b]

EXERCISE 15–6 *(Report Corporate Income)* Western Company supplied the following information summarizing transactions and events during 19X8: net sales revenue, $350,000; cost of goods sold, $180,000; selling expenses, $60,000; administrative expenses, $20,000; and income tax expense on income from continuing operations, $36,000.

During 19X8 the company had an extraordinary gain of $84,000 after subtracting $56,000 of income tax on the gain. It also discontinued one of its business segments, selling the segment at a gain of $72,000 after subtracting $48,000 of income tax on the gain. Losses from the operations of the business segment prior to its discontinuance were $24,000 after subtracting $16,000 of tax savings related to the losses.

Required:
Prepare an income statement for Western Company for the year ended December 31, 19X8. The company had 100,000 shares of common stock outstanding throughout the year. [LO1f,2d]

EXERCISE 15–7 *(Compute Earnings per Share)* Eastern Corporation reported net income for 19X8 of $675,000. All income resulted from continuing operations and did not include any "special" items. On January 1, 19X8, the company had 200,000 shares of common stock outstanding. On July 1 the company issued 100,000 new shares of common stock. The company has no convertible securities or stock options outstanding that could cause it to issue additional shares of common stock.

On January 1, 19X9, Eastern issued 20,000 shares of 9%, $100 par value cumulative, convertible preferred stock. At the time of issuance the preferred stock did not qualify as a common stock equivalent. Each share of preferred stock is convertible into four shares of common stock. During 19X9 there were no transactions involving common stock, and the company reported net income of $1,080,000.

Required:
Compute earnings per common share for 19X8 and 19X9, including, if appropriate, primary and fully diluted earnings per share. [LO2e]

EXERCISE 15–8 *(Compute Earnings per Share)* A portion of Northern Corporation's income statement is shown below.

| | |
|---|---|
| Income before Cumulative Effect of an Accounting Change | $621,000 |
| Cumulative Effect of Change in Accounting Principle (net of taxes $72,000) | 108,000 |
| Net Income | $729,000 |

The company had 150,000 common shares and 15,000 shares of $100 par, 8% cumulative, convertible preferred stock outstanding throughout the year. Each preferred share, which did not qualify as a common stock equivalent at the time of issue, is convertible into three shares of common stock.

Required:
Compute and present (1) the primary and (2) the fully diluted earnings per share for the following sections of the income statement (round calculations where necessary):

a. Income before cumulative effect of an accounting change
b. Cumulative effect of change in accounting principle
c. Net income [LO2e]

## PROBLEMS

PROBLEM 15–1 *(Prepare Journal Entries Affecting Stockholders' Equity and Prepare a Retained Earnings Statement)* At the beginning of 19X6 Fortune Company had an Unappropriated Retained Earnings account with a balance of $280,000 and a Retained Earnings Appropriated for Contingencies account with a balance of $75,000. The following selected events and transactions occurred during 19X6.

| | |
|---|---|
| March 21 | Purchased 5,000 of its own common shares at $28 per share. |
| May 15 | The board of directors declared a cash dividend of $3 per common share to be paid on June 30 to the stockholders of record on June 5. The company has 60,000 common shares issued, 5,000 of which are held as treasury stock. |
| June 2 | The board approved the removal of the appropriation of retained earnings. |
| June 30 | Paid the cash dividend declared on May 15. |
| Aug. 5 | Sold the 5,000 shares held as treasury stock for $25 per share. The company has one paid-in capital account that resulted from issuing common shares above their par value. The account has a credit balance of $130,000. |
| Dec. 15 | The board declared a 4% stock dividend on common stock to be distributed January 15, 19X7, to the stockholders of record on December 31, 19X6. The common shares have a $10 par value and a market value of $28 per share. |
| Dec. 28 | A review of the plant asset depreciation schedule shows that an error was made in recording depreciation in 19X5. The error, which should be treated as a prior period adjustment, overstated net income in 19X5 by $70,000. The tax effect on this item is $28,000. |

| | |
|---|---|
| Dec. 31 | Closed the $210,000 credit balance in the Income Summary account to the Retained Earnings account. |

Required:

1. Prepare journal entries to record each of the transactions and events described above.
2. Prepare a statement of retained earnings for the year ended December 31, 19X6.

[LO1b,1c,1d,1e,2a,2b]

PROBLEM 15-2 *(Record Dividend Transactions and Prepare Stockholders' Equity Section)* The stockholders' equity section of Jordan Company's balance sheet as of December 31, 19X5, was as follows.

| | |
|---|---|
| Contributed Capital: | |
| Common Stock—$2 par value, 300,000 shares authorized, 250,000 shares issued and outstanding | $ 500,000 |
| Paid-in Capital in Excess of Par Value | 770,000 |
| Total Contributed Capital | $1,270,000 |
| Retained Earnings | 510,000 |
| Total Stockholders' Equity | $1,780,000 |

The following selected transactions occurred during 19X6.

| | |
|---|---|
| March 1 | Declared a cash dividend of 50 cents per common share to be paid on April 1 to the stockholders of record on March 20. |
| March 20 | Date of record for the cash dividend. |
| April 1 | Paid the cash dividend declared on March. 1. |
| May 29 | Declared a 5% stock dividend to be distributed on July 1 to the stockholders of record on June 20. The market price of the stock on this date is $8 per share. |
| June 20 | Date of record for the stock dividend. |
| July 1 | Distributed the stock dividend declared on May 29. |
| Oct. 1 | The board of directors approved a 2-for-1 stock split. |
| Nov. 30 | Declared a cash dividend of 30 cents per common share to be paid on January 1 to the stockholders of record on December 21. |
| Dec. 21 | Date of record for the cash dividend. |
| Dec. 31 | Closed the $340,000 credit balance in the Income Summary account to the Retained Earnings account. |

Required:

1. Prepare journal entries (where necessary) to record each of the above transactions.
2. Prepare the stockholders' equity section of the company's balance sheet as of December 31, 19X6.

[LO1b,2c]

PROBLEM 15-3 *(Prepare Journal Entries and Stockholders' Equity Section)* Olympic Corporation had the following stockholders' equity at the beginning of 19X6.

| | |
|---|---|
| Contributed Capital: | |
| Common Stock—$5 par value, 500,000 shares authorized, 200,000 shares issued and outstanding | $1,000,000 |
| Paid-in Capital in Excess of Par Value | 710,000 |
| Total Contributed Capital | $1,710,000 |
| Retained Earnings | 975,000 |
| Total Stockholders' Equity | $2,685,000 |

During 19X6 the corporation completed the following selected transactions.

| | |
|---|---|
| Jan. 19 | Purchased 10,000 shares of common stock at $15 per share; the stock is to be held as treasury stock. |

| | |
|---|---|
| Feb. 2 | Issued 10,000 shares of $50 par, 12% cumulative preferred stock at $55 per share. The company has authorization to issue 50,000 of these preferred shares. |
| April 14 | Sold 4,000 of the treasury shares purchased on January 19 for $18 per share. |
| Sept. 19 | Sold 2,000 of the treasury shares purchased on January 19 for $14 per share. |
| Dec. 20 | Declared a 4% stock dividend on the common stock, to be distributed on January 15, to the stockholders of record on December 30. The market price of the stock on December 20 is $15 per share. |

Required:

1. Prepare journal entries to record each of the above transactions.
2. Prepare the stockholders' equity section of the balance sheet on December 31, assuming the net income for 19X6 was $178,000 and the only cash dividends paid during the year were $55,000 to the preferred shareholders. [LO1b,1d,2a,2c]

PROBLEM 15–4 *(Prepare Journal Entries, Stockholders' Equity Section, and Retained Earnings Statement)* Hi-Life Corporation had the following stockholders' equity at the beginning of 19X7.

| | |
|---|---|
| Common Stock, $10 par value, 400,000 shares authorized, 100,000 shares issued and outstanding | $1,000,000 |
| Paid-in Capital in Excess of Par Value | 480,000 |
| Retained Earnings | 640,000 |
| Total Stockholders' Equity | $2,120,000 |

During 19X7 the corporation completed the following selected transactions.

| | |
|---|---|
| Feb. 19 | Purchased 8,000 shares of common stock at $18 per share; the stock is to be held as treasury stock. |
| June 27 | Declared a cash dividend of $1 per share payable on July 26 to the stockholders of record on July 12. |
| July 26 | Paid the cash dividend declared on June 27. |
| Sept. 18 | Sold 6,000 of the treasury shares purchased on February 19 for $20 per share. |
| Oct. 20 | Sold 2,000 of the treasury shares purchased on February 19 for $17 per share. |
| Dec. 12 | Declared a cash dividend of 50 cents per share payable on January 15 to the stockholders of record on December 30, and a 4% stock dividend distributable on January 20 to the stockholders of record on December 30. The market price of the stock on December 12 is $20 per share. |

Required:

1. Prepare journal entries to record each of the above transactions.
2. Prepare a statement of retained earnings for the year ended December 31, 19X7. Net income for 19X7 was $290,000.
3. Prepare the stockholders' equity section of the company's balance sheet on December 31, 19X7. [LO1b,1d,2a,2b,2c]

PROBLEM 15–5 *(Record Treasury Stock Transactions)* Powers Company issued all of its common stock at par and has no contributed capital other than that assigned to the common shares. During the current year the company had the following transactions pertaining to treasury stock.

| | |
|---|---|
| Jan. 18 | Purchased 25,000 of its own common shares at $12 per share. |
| April 30 | Sold 6,000 shares of the treasury stock for $14 per share. |
| May 15 | Sold 3,000 shares of the treasury stock for $12 per share. |
| July 1 | Sold 10,000 shares of the treasury stock for $11 per share. |

Oct. 9 Sold the remaining 6,000 shares of the treasury stock for $10 per share.

Required:
Prepare journal entries to record the above transactions. [LO2a]

PROBLEM 15–6 *(Prepare Journal Entries and Stockholders' Equity Section)* Alpine Corporation was organized three years ago. At the beginning of the current year, the stockholders' equity section of its balance sheet appeared as follows.

| | |
|---|---|
| Contributed Capital: | |
| Preferred Stock, $50 par value, 8% cumulative, 20,000 shares authorized, 6,000 shares issued and outstanding | $300,000 |
| Common Stock, $10 par value, 75,000 shares authorized, 15,000 shares issued, 1,000 held as treasury stock | 150,000 |
| Paid-in Capital in Excess of Par Value—Preferred | 22,000 |
| Paid-in Capital in Excess of Par Value—Common | 34,000 |
| Total Contributed Capital | $506,000 |
| Retained Earnings | 208,000 |
| Total Contributed Capital and Retained Earnings | $714,000 |
| Less: Treasury Stock at Cost | 16,000 |
| Total Stockholders' Equity | $698,000 |

Transactions affecting stockholders' equity that occurred during the current year are listed below in chronological sequence.

1. Sold and issued 1,000 shares of common stock at $16 per share.
2. Reissued 800 of the treasury shares at $18 per share.
3. Sold and issued 4,000 shares of preferred stock at $52 per share.
4. Reissued 200 of the treasury shares at $13 per share.
5. Declared a cash dividend large enough to meet the semiannual dividend preference of the preferred stock and pay common shareholders $2 per share.
6. Appropriated $60,000 of retained earnings for future plant expansion.
7. Declared a cash dividend large enough to meet the semiannual dividend preference of the preferred stock and declared a 2-for-1 common stock split.
8. Reported net income of $82,000.

Required:

1. Prepare journal entries to record each of the transactions and events described above.
2. Prepare the stockholders' equity section of the company's balance sheet as of December 31, 19X6.
3. Does the retained earnings appropriation indicate that $60,000 had been set aside for plant expansion purposes? If not, explain the purpose of the account.

[LO1b,1d,1e,2a,2c]

PROBLEM 15–7 *(Indicate Effect of Transactions on Amounts Reported in the Financial Statements)* For each of the transactions listed in the accompanying table, indicate the effect, if any, on

1. Total assets
2. Total liabilities
3. Common stock
4. Paid-in Capital accounts
5. Retained earnings
6. Total stockholders' equity

Use *I* for increases, *D* for decreases, and *NE* for no effect. The first transaction is shown as an example. [LO1b,1d,1e]

| | TOTAL ASSETS | TOTAL LIABILITIES | COMMON STOCK | PAID-IN CAPITAL | RETAINED EARNINGS | TOTAL STOCKHOLDERS' EQUITY |
|---|---|---|---|---|---|---|
| a. Declared a cash dividend | NE | I | NE | NE | D | D |
| b. Declared a 5% stock dividend (the market price of the shares exceeds the par value of the shares at this time) | | | | | | |
| c. Paid the cash dividend | | | | | | |
| d. Appropriated retained earnings for plant expansion | | | | | | |
| e. Distributed the shares in the 5% stock dividend | | | | | | |
| f. Purchased 1,000 shares of treasury stock at $10 per share | | | | | | |
| g. Sold 500 of the treasury shares for $12 per share | | | | | | |
| h. Sold 200 of the treasury shares for $9 per share | | | | | | |
| i. Implemented a 2-for-1 stock split | | | | | | |
| j. Closed the Income Summary account, which had a debit balance of $47,000 | | | | | | |

PROBLEM 15–8 *(Report Corporate Income)* The following information pertains to Gar Construction Company for the year ended December 31, 19X6.

| | |
|---|---|
| Net sales revenue | $920,000 |
| Cost of goods sold | 550,000 |
| Discontinued operations: | |
| Income from operations of discontinued segment | 80,000 |
| Loss on disposal of business segment | 50,000 |
| Loss from earthquake damage (considered to be unusual in nature and infrequent in occurrence) | 120,000 |
| Selling expenses | 150,000 |
| Cash dividends declared and paid | 45,000 |
| Loss on sale of machinery | 8,000 |
| Retained earnings appropriated for contingencies | 30,000 |
| Administrative expenses | 52,000 |

Gar Construction is subject to a 40% income tax rate, and all the amounts provided above are before the effect of income taxes. The corporation had retained earnings of $212,000 at the beginning of 19X6, none of which was appropriated. There were 10,000 common shares outstanding throughout the entire year.

Required:

1. Prepare the company's income statement for the year ended December 31, 19X6.
2. Determine the company's total ending retained earnings balance, and indicate the amounts for both appropriated and unappropriated retained earnings. [LO1e,1f,2d]

PROBLEM 15–9 *(Compute Earnings per Share)* Information pertaining to Tracy Corporation's capital stock is detailed below.

Preferred stock, 5%, $100 par value, cumulative and convertible, with 50,000 shares outstanding throughout the entire year. The stock did not qualify as a common stock equivalent when issued. Each share is convertible into five shares of common stock.

Common stock, $2 par value, with 300,000 shares outstanding at the beginning of the year. Additional shares were sold and issued during the year as follows: March 31, 60,000 shares; September 1, 30,000 shares.

Required:

Compute (1) primary earnings per share and (2) fully diluted earnings per share. Net income for the year was $676,000. [LO2e]

PROBLEM 15–10 *(Compute Earnings per Share)* Champion Corporation has a complex capital structure consisting of the following:

Preferred stock, 10%, $10 par value, cumulative and convertible with 20,000 shares outstanding throughout the entire year. Each share is convertible into three shares of common stock, and the stock qualifies as a common stock equivalent.

Preferred stock, 8%, $25 par value, cumulative and convertible with 10,000 shares outstanding throughout the entire year. Each share is convertible into four shares of common stock, and the stock did not qualify as a common stock equivalent when issued.

Common stock, $5 par value, 100,000 shares outstanding at the beginning of the year. Additional shares were sold and issued during the year as follows: July 1, 80,000 shares; October 1, 20,000 shares.

Required:

Compute (1) primary earnings per share and (2) fully diluted earnings per share. Net income for the year was $471,000. [LO2e]

PROBLEM 15–11 *(Comprehensive Problem on Corporate Income Reporting)* Information in the accounts shown below pertains to the normal ongoing operations of Diamond Company for the year ended December 31, 19X6.

| | |
|---|---|
| Net sales revenue | $1,720,000 |
| Cost of goods sold | 990,000 |
| Selling expenses | 280,000 |
| Administrative expenses | 110,000 |
| Income tax expense | 136,000 |

Other transactions and events affecting 19X6 income were as follows:

1. The company changed from an accelerated method to a straight-line method in computing depreciation. The cumulative effect of the change to the beginning of 19X6 was $72,000 before taxes. The change would increase the net income reported in the past.
2. An extraordinary loss of $110,000, before taxes, was incurred when a tornado severely damaged plant property.
3. The company discontinued the operations of one of its business segments on August 15, 19X6, and sold the unit on October 2 of the same year. The segment's operating loss for the current period was $88,000 before taxes. The gain on its sale was $35,000 before taxes.

Additional Information:

Diamond Company is subject to an income tax rate of 40% and has had 100,000 shares of common stock outstanding throughout the year.

Required:

Prepare the company's income statement for the year ended December 31, 19X6. [LO1f,2d]

## ALTERNATE PROBLEMS

PROBLEM 15–1A *(Record Dividend Transactions and Prepare Stockholders' Equity Section)* (Alternate to Problem 15–2) The stockholders' equity section of Pike Company's balance sheet as of December 31, 19X5, was as follows.

| | |
|---|---|
| Contributed Capital: | |
| Common Stock—$5 par value, 100,000 shares authorized, 60,000 shares issued and outstanding | $ 300,000 |
| Paid-in Capital in Excess of Par Value | 410,000 |
| Total Contributed Capital | $ 710,000 |
| Retained Earnings | 630,000 |
| Total Stockholders' Equity | $1,340,000 |

The following selected transactions occurred during 19X6.

| | |
|---|---|
| March 1 | Declared a cash dividend of $1 per common share to be paid on April 1 to the stockholders of record on March 20. |
| March 20 | Date of record for the cash dividend. |
| April 1 | Paid the cash dividend declared on March 1. |
| May 29 | Declared a 4% stock dividend to be distributed on July 1 to the stockholders of record on June 20. The market price of the stock on May 29 is $9 per share. |
| June 20 | Date of record for the stock dividend. |
| July 1 | Distributed the stock dividend declared on May 29. |
| Oct. 1 | The board of directors approved a 2-for-1 stock split. |
| Nov. 30 | Declared a cash dividend of 50 cents per common share to be paid on January 1 to the stockholders of record on December 31. |
| Dec. 31 | Date of record for the cash dividend. |
| Dec. 31 | Closed the $295,000 credit balance in the Income Summary account to the Retained Earnings account. |

Required:

1. Prepare journal entries (where necessary) to record each of the above transactions.
2. Prepare the stockholders' equity section of the company's balance sheet as of December 31, 19X6. [LO1b,2c]

PROBLEM 15–2A *(Prepare Journal Entries, Stockholders' Equity Section, and Retained Earnings Statement)* (Alternate to Problem 15–4) Westfield Corporation had the following stockholders' equity at the beginning of 19X7.

| | |
|---|---|
| Common Stock, $1 par value, 500,000 shares authorized, 200,000 shares issued and outstanding | $ 200,000 |
| Paid-in Capital in Excess of Par Value | 770,000 |
| Retained Earnings | 440,000 |
| Total Stockholders' Equity | $1,410,000 |

During 19X7 the corporation completed the following selected transactions.

| | |
|---|---|
| Feb. 19 | Purchased 10,000 shares of common stock at $6 per share; the stock is to be held as treasury stock. |
| June 27 | Declared a cash dividend of 20 cents per share payable on July 26 to the stockholders of record on July 12. |
| July 26 | Paid the cash dividend declared on June 27. |
| Sept. 18 | Sold 3,000 of the treasury shares purchased on February 19 for $9 per share. |
| Oct. 20 | Sold 7,000 of the treasury shares purchased on February 19 for $5 per share. |
| Dec. 12 | Declared a cash dividend of 15 cents per share payable on January 15 to the stockholders of record on December 30, and a 5% stock dividend distributable on January 20 to the stockholders of record on December 30. The market price of the stock on December 12 is $8 per share. |

Required:

1. Prepare journal entries to record each of the above transactions.
2. Prepare a statement of retained earnings for the year ended December 31, 19X7. Net income for 19X7 was $204,000.
3. Prepare the stockholders' equity section of the company's balance sheet on December 31, 19X7. [LO1b,1d,2a,2b,2c]

PROBLEM 15-3A *(Prepare Journal Entries and Stockholders' Equity Section)* (Alternate to Problem 15-6) De-Lite Corporation was organized two years ago. At the beginning of the current year, the stockholders' equity section of its balance sheet appeared as follows:

| | |
|---|---|
| Contributed Capital: | |
| Preferred Stock, $30 par value, 10% cumulative, 50,000 shares authorized, 15,000 shares issued and outstanding | $ 450,000 |
| Common Stock, $5 par value, 100,000 shares authorized, 25,000 shares issued, 2,000 held as treasury stock | 125,000 |
| Paid-in Capital in Excess of Par Value—Preferred | 120,000 |
| Paid-in Capital in Excess of Par Value—Common | 90,000 |
| Total Contributed Capital | $ 785,000 |
| Retained Earnings | 224,000 |
| Total Contributed Capital and Retained Earnings | $1,009,000 |
| Less: Treasury Stock at Cost | 18,000 |
| Total Stockholders' Equity | $ 991,000 |

Transactions affecting stockholders' equity that occurred during the current year are listed below in chronological sequence.

1. Sold and issued 5,000 shares of common stock at $11 per share.
2. Reissued 1,400 of the treasury shares at $10 per share.
3. Sold and issued 2,000 shares of preferred stock at $34 per share.
4. Reissued 600 of the treasury shares at $8 per share.
5. Declared a cash dividend large enough to meet the semiannual dividend preference of the preferred stock and pay common shareholders $1.50 per share.
6. Appropriated $75,000 of retained earnings for future plant expansion.
7. Declared a cash dividend large enough to meet the semiannual dividend preference of the preferred stock and declared a 4-for-1 common stock split.
8. Reported net income of $208,000.

Required:

1. Prepare journal entries to record each of the transactions and events described above.
2. Prepare the stockholders' equity section of the company's balance sheet as of December 31, 19X6.
3. Does the retained earnings appropriation mean that $75,000 of cash is available to begin the plant expansion? If not, explain what it does mean. [LO1b,1d,1e,2a,2c]

PROBLEM 15-4A *(Report Corporate Income)* (Alternate to Problem 15-8) The following information pertains to Better Builders Company for the year ended December 31, 19X6.

Better Builders is subject to a 40% income tax rate and all the amounts provided on page 555 are before the effect of income taxes. The corporation had retained earnings of $190,000 at the beginning of 19X6, none of which was appropriated. There were 20,000 common shares outstanding throughout the year.

| | |
|---|---|
| Net sales revenue | $615,000 |
| Cost of goods sold | 380,000 |
| Loss from tornado damage (considered to be unusual in nature and infrequent in occurrence) | 90,000 |
| Selling expenses | 102,000 |
| Cash dividends | 75,000 |
| Loss on sale of equipment | 12,000 |
| Retained earnings appropriated for contingencies | 50,000 |
| Administrative expenses | 33,000 |
| Discontinued operations: | |
| Loss from operations of discontinued segment | 12,000 |
| Gain on disposal of business segment | 36,000 |

Required:

1. Prepare the company's income statement for the year ended December 31, 19X6.
2. Determine the company's total ending retained earnings balance, and indicate the amounts for both appropriated and unappropriated retained earnings. [LO1e,1f,2d]

PROBLEM 15–5A *(Compute Earnings per Share)* (Alternate to Problem 15–9) Information pertaining to McCroy Corporation's capital stock is detailed below.

Preferred stock, 8%, $50 par value, cumulative and convertible, with 30,000 shares outstanding throughout the year. The stock did not qualify as a common stock equivalent when issued. Each share is convertible into five shares of common stock.

Common stock, $5 par value, with 200,000 shares outstanding at the beginning of the year. Additional shares were sold and issued during the year as follows: April 1, 80,000 shares; July 1, 80,000 shares; September 1, 30,000 shares.

Required:

Compute (1) primary earnings per share and (2) fully diluted earnings per share. Net income for the year was $430,000. [LO2e]

# 16 *Long-Term Liabilities*

## *Learning Objectives*

When you complete this chapter you will be able to

1. Answer the following questions:
   a. What is a long-term liability?
   b. What are the significant differences between bondholders and stockholders? How do these differences affect financing decisions?
   c. What are the characteristics of bonds? What types of bonds are issued?
   d. What is the purpose of a bond sinking fund?
   e. What is the difference between an operating lease and a capital lease?
2. Perform the following accounting functions:
   a. Account for the issuance of bonds at face value, at a discount, or at a premium, and account for incurred bond interest expense.
   b. Account for the retirement of bonds, including their conversion into common stock.
   c. Prepare entries to account for the transactions associated with a bond sinking fund.
   d. Account for a mortgage note payable.
   e. Account for an operating lease and a capital lease.

A company can acquire the funds needed for conducting its business activities and for expansion from several sources. For example, in earlier chapters we have seen (1) how cash or other assets acquired by profitable operations may be retained in the business, (2) how cash or other assets are acquired through investment by owners, and (3) how cash or other assets are acquired (financed) by incurring current and long-term liabilities.

*1a. A long-term liability has a maturity date beyond one year from the balance sheet date or the operating cycle, whichever is longer*

In this chapter we discuss the accounting when assets are acquired (financed) by incurring long-term liabilities (debt). A **long-term liability** is an obligation with a maturity date beyond one year from the balance sheet date or the operating cycle, whichever is longer. Although our emphasis will be on *bonds payable,* other long-term liabilities discussed in this chapter include *mortgages payable* and *lease obligations.*

## BONDS PAYABLE

A **bond** is an interest-bearing security representing money borrowed by a corporation. When a corporation borrows money by issuing a bond, it is obligated to pay interest and to pay the bond's principal amount at a stated future date. The *principal* of a bond (also called its *face value, par value,* or *maturity value)* is printed on the bond certificate and is the amount that the issuer must pay to the bondholder on the bond's maturity date. It is also the amount on which periodic interest payments are calculated. A bond issue is usually divided into units of individual bonds each having a face value of $1,000 or some other multiple thereof. For example, a corporation having a bond issue of $50,000,000 may divide it into 50,000 individual bonds having a face value of $1,000 each. Bond interest stated as an annual rate is generally paid semiannually or quarterly.

## FINANCING WITH BONDS AND STOCK

There are significant differences between acquiring long-term funds by issuing bonds (known as **debt financing**) and by issuing capital stock (known as **equity financing**). Each offers the issuing corporation certain advantages and disadvantages. The legal distinction between bondholders and stockholders is a major source of the differences. *Bondholders* are *creditors* of the corporation while *stockholders* are *owners.* This and other significant differences are outlined in the table on page 558.

*1b. The income tax deductibility of bond interest is an important consideration in deciding whether to raise additional funds through debt financing or through equity financing*

These differences are important when choosing between debt or equity financing. Of course, other factors such as the company's current capital stock and debt structures, the state of the economy, the nature of the company's business, and the company's perception of the marketplace for securities should also be considered. Nevertheless, one persuasive argument for using debt financing is the tax deductibility of bond interest for income tax purposes. To illustrate, assume that a corporation with 200,000 shares of common stock outstanding needs to raise $2,000,000 to finance new construction and improvements in its existing plant and equipment. Three financing alternatives are being considered:

Issuing 100,000 additional shares of *no-par common stock* at $20 per share.

Issuing 20,000 shares of 7% *cumulative preferred stock* having a par value of $100 per share at their par value.

Issuing 10%, *20-year term bonds* at their face value of $2,000,000. Management estimates that after the construction and improvement projects have been completed, the company will earn $800,000 annually before deducting interest on the bonds and income tax estimated at 40% of taxable income.

***1b. Differences between bondholders and stockholders are outlined here***

| Bonds (Bondholders) | Capital Stock (Stockholders) |
|---|---|
| Bondholders are creditors. | Stockholders are owners. |
| Bondholders receive periodic interest payments as specified in the bond indenture. Furthermore, the interest must be paid regardless of the profitability of the company. | Stockholders are paid dividends only if declared by the board of directors, and their decision is usually predicated on whether corporate earnings are sufficient to justify a dividend distribution. |
| Bondholders, as creditors, have a prior claim on corporate assets in case of liquidation. Defaulting on interest payments could force the company into bankruptcy. | Stockholders have a residual claim on corporate assets. In case of liquidation, they receive proceeds generated from asset sales only after all creditors' claims have been satisfied. |
| Bondholders do not have voting rights. When bonds are issued, corporate ownership remains the same. | Stockholders have voting rights (with preferred stockholders being an exception). If additional capital stock is issued, current ownership proportions may change and corporate earnings would be divided among a greater number of common shares. |
| Bonds are liabilities. When bonds mature, the debt must be paid or refunded with new debt. | Capital stock is owners' equity. The assets contributed by the shareholders represent the corporation's legal capital. |
| Bond interest payments are treated as a business expense for both income tax and financial reporting purposes. | Dividends paid to stockholders are not deductible expenses for either income tax or financial reporting purposes. |

Exhibit 16–1 shows the effect of each financing alternative on the company's net income and earnings per common share.

*EXHIBIT 16–1*

Three Alternative Financing Plans—Projected Net Income of $800,000

| | PLAN 1<br>Issue Common Stock | PLAN 2<br>Issue Preferred Stock | PLAN 3<br>Issue Bonds |
|---|---|---|---|
| Income before bond interest and income taxes | $800,000 | $800,000 | $800,000 |
| Less: Bond interest expense ($2,000,000 × 0.10) | — | — | 200,000 |
| Income before income taxes | $800,000 | $800,000 | $600,000 |
| Less: Federal income taxes (at 40% of income before taxes) | 320,000 | 320,000 | 240,000 |
| Net income | $480,000 | $480,000 | $360,000 |
| Less: Dividends on preferred stock | — | 140,000 | — |
| Net income available to common shareholders | $480,000 | $340,000 | $360,000 |
| Number of common shares outstanding | 300,000 | 200,000 | 200,000 |
| Earnings per share on common stock | $1.60 | $1.70 | $1.80 |

The "best" financing plan may depend on whether you are management, a shareholder, or a creditor. Under Plan 3 (issuing bonds), the company's reported net income is $120,000 lower than that of the other two plans. However, common shareholders would find the plan attractive because it results in the highest earnings-per-share figure. Plan 1 shows the highest figure for net income available to common shareholders because no bond interest is incurred and no preferred dividends need to be paid under this plan. However, earnings per common share are lower because 100,000 additional shares of common stock are issued, and they too share in the income available to common shareholders.

Plan 2 requires the payment of substantial dividends to preferred stockholders (almost 30% of net income), an amount that is not deductible for income tax purposes. As a result, this plan shows the lowest amount for income available to common shareholders and affects their earnings per share.

If the projected earnings should exceed $800,000, the spread between the earnings per share on common stock under Plan 1 and Plan 3 would become even greater. However, if the projected earnings of $800,000 does not materialize, that is, if it should be less than $800,000, then Plan 1 becomes more attractive than Plan 3. This is illustrated in Exhibit 16–2, where income before bond interest and income taxes is assumed to be $500,000 instead of $800,000.

EXHIBIT 16–2

Three Alternative Financing Plans—Projected Net Income of $500,000

| | PLAN 1 Issue Common Stock | PLAN 2 Issue Preferred Stock | PLAN 3 Issue Bonds |
|---|---|---|---|
| Income before bond interest and income taxes | $500,000 | $500,000 | $500,000 |
| Less: Bond interest expense ($2,000,000 × 0.10) | — | — | 200,000 |
| Income before income taxes | $500,000 | $500,000 | $300,000 |
| Less: Federal income taxes (at 40% of income before taxes) | 200,000 | 200,000 | 120,000 |
| Net income | $300,000 | $300,000 | $180,000 |
| Less: Dividends on preferred stock | — | 140,000 | — |
| Net income available to common shareholders | $300,000 | $160,000 | $180,000 |
| Number of common shares outstanding | 300,000 | 200,000 | 200,000 |
| Earnings per share on common stock | $1.00 | $.80 | $.90 |

Before deciding whether to use debt financing (issue bonds) or use equity financing (issue common stock), many things should be considered. The following are worth noting here:

*1b. Some factors to be considered when deciding on debt financing or equity financing are listed here*

Issuing bonds (debt) obligates the corporation to pay a fixed amount of interest periodically throughout the entire period that the bonds are outstanding. In contrast, there is no legal obligation to pay dividends on common stock.

The face value of the bond must be paid on a specified maturity date. In contrast, common stock does not have a maturity date.

Bond interest is a deductible expense in arriving at taxable income. Dividends are not treated as an expense, nor are they deductible in arriving at taxable income.

Issuing bonds may cause management to lose some control and flexibility over certain activities. For example, a bond contract called a **bond indenture** may include provisions that could under certain circumstances limit the amount the company could pay out as dividends and/or require the company to make periodic cash deposits in a fund that can only be used to pay the bondholders when the bonds mature.

In addition to the above, debt financing involves a concept known as **leverage.** When a company is able to use borrowed funds to earn a return that is greater than the cost of the borrowed funds, it is said to be favorably leveraged. Leveraging is risky in that a company can experience unfavorable leverage if the cost of its borrowed funds exceeds the return earned on them.

## CHARACTERISTICS OF BONDS

As mentioned earlier, the bond indenture constitutes the contractual agreement between the issuing corporation and its bondholders. The bond indenture sets forth the provisions of the bond issue including the principal amount, maturity date, interest rate, and interest payment dates. Other features include the rights of bondholders to convert their bonds to other corporate securities or the right of the corporation to call in the bonds before maturity.

When a corporation issues bonds, it usually sells the entire issue to an investment banker or a bond broker called an **underwriter.** The underwriter then sells the bonds to various institutions and to the public at a somewhat higher price than what it paid for the bonds. Rather than buying the bonds, underwriters will sometimes contract to sell the bonds on a commission basis. At the time the bonds are sold, the issuing corporation selects a third-party agent called a **trustee** to represent the bondholders. In most cases, the trustee is a large bank or trust company whose duty is to ensure that the bond-issuing corporation fulfills its bond indenture responsibilities.

Entities that issue bonds differ in their financial strength and needs. Therefore companies write the bond indenture to satisfy these needs while including features that make the bond attractive to investors. As a result, bonds issued in today's marketplace usually have one or more distinguishing features. Some of the more common ones are described below.

*1c. Bonds may be secured or unsecured*

Bonds may be secured or unsecured. A **secured bond** is one that gives the bondholder a claim against specific assets of the issuing corporation. These assets serve as collateral for the bond. Should the corporation default on its bond obligations, the pledged assets may be sold and the proceeds used to pay the bondholders. An **unsecured bond** (also called a **debenture bond**) is issued solely on the basis of the issuing corporation's general credit rating and financial reputation. No assets are pledged as collateral, and in case of default, bondholders are in the same position as other corporate creditors.

*1c. Bonds may be term or serial*

Bonds may be term or serial. **Term bonds** have a single, common maturity date. Thus when all the bonds within a given issue mature on the same date, they are called term bonds. In contrast, **serial bonds** mature in installments over several different dates. For example, a serial bond issue of $50,000,000 dated 1987 may provide for $5,000,000 to mature at a specified date in 1992 and another $5,000,000 to mature at a specified date in each of the following nine years through 2001.

*1c. Bonds may be registered or coupon*

Bonds may be registered or coupon. **Registered bonds** are issued in the name of the bondholders and may be transferred from one owner to another only by having the registered owner endorse the bond certificate. The corporation issuing registered bonds (or a trustee) maintains a record of the name and address of each bondholder. Interest is paid by check and is mailed to the registered owners. **Coupon bonds** (also called ***bearer bonds***) have printed coupons attached to them that indicate the amount of interest to be paid and the interest payment date. At each interest date the bondholder removes the appropriate coupon and sends it to the issuer to obtain payment or, as in most cases, presents it to a bank for payment. The issuing corporation does not keep records to identify its bondholders, and the rights of bond ownership can be transferred from one person to another simply by delivery. Thus the holder of a coupon bond is its owner, and interest will be paid to anyone who presents the appropriate coupon.

*1c. Bonds may be callable or convertible*

Bonds may be callable or convertible. Most corporate bonds are issued as **callable bonds.** This gives the issuing coporation the right to redeem them (call them in) before their scheduled maturity date. The preestablished redemption price, also known as the **call price,** is usually set at an amount slightly above the face value of the bonds. **Convertible bonds** are bonds that may be exchanged for other securities, usually for the common stock of the issuing corporation, at the option of the bondholder.

Bonds may be issued that combine more than one of the above features. For example, an issue may be for unsecured term bonds due in twenty years having interest coupons attached and convertible privileges after five years.

No matter what type of bonds are chosen for issuance, once they are issued the corporation is obligated to pay the bondholders (1) interest periodically throughout the life of the bonds and (2) the face amount of the bonds at maturity. The interest on a bond is calculated by multiplying the interest rate, specified in the bond indenture and generally written on the bond itself, times the face amount of the bond. The specified interest rate is called the **stated rate, *contract rate,*** or ***coupon rate.*** For example, a bond having a face value of $1,000 and a stated interest rate of 12% would pay a total of $120 in interest annually computed as follows: $1,000 × 12% = $120. If interest payments were to be semiannual, the amount of each semiannual payment would be $60. In this chapter we will assume that all the bonds issued have a face value of $1,000 each and pay interest semiannually.

Bond market prices are quoted as a percentage of face value. For example, the market price of a $1,000 face value bond quoted at 102 is $1,020 computed as follows: $1,000 × 102% = $1,020. While stock prices are quoted to the nearest one-eighth of a dollar, bond prices are quoted to the nearest one-eighth of a percentage point. Thus a bond quoted at 87⅛ would be selling for $871.25 ($1,000 × 87.125% = $871.25).

The market price of a given corporate bond will probably change many times during the bond's life. For some bonds, the market price may even change several times in one day. The major factors affecting the market price of a bond are the following:

The bond's interest rate as compared with the general level of interest rates on other investments.

The length of time that the bond must be held before it matures.

The credit rating of the issuing company, which represents an assessment of the company's ability to make all future interest and principal payments on a timely basis. Several agencies, such as Standard and Poor's and Moody's, develop credit-rating systems for bonds.

## ACCOUNTING FOR THE ISSUANCE OF AND THE INTEREST PAID ON BONDS PAYABLE

Once corporate management has decided on the type of bonds to issue, the amount of the issue, the interest rate, the interest payment dates, and the maturity date, and has received whatever approvals are necessary, the bond issue is authorized for sale. No formal journal entry is required for the authorization of the bond issue, but a memorandum entry describing the issue should be entered in the Bonds Payable account. The information is needed for financial reporting purposes, since all important details pertaining to the bonds are disclosed in the notes that accompany the financial statements.

The memorandum might read as follows:

> Received authorization to issue $500,000 of 10%, 5-year debenture bonds dated January 1, 1987. Interest is payable semiannually on June 30 and December 31 of each year.[1]

## Bonds Issued at Face Value

To illustrate the accounting, assume that Benbrook Corporation received authorization to issue the $500,000, 10%, 5-year debenture bonds described in the memorandum. If on January 1, 1987, the entire issue is sold at face value, the entry to record the sale is as follows:

*2a. An entry is made to record the issuance of bonds at face value*

| | | | |
|---|---|---|---|
| Jan. 1 | Cash | 500,000 | |
| | Bonds Payable | | 500,000 |
| | To record the sale of 10%, 5-year bonds at face value | | |

On June 30 the first semiannual interest payment of $25,000 is due. The interest amount is computed as follows: $\$500{,}000 \times 10\% \times \frac{6}{12} = \$25{,}000$. The following entry would record the payment of the semiannual interest:

*2a. An entry is made to record an interest payment*

| | | | |
|---|---|---|---|
| June 30 | Bond Interest Expense | 25,000 | |
| | Cash | | 25,000 |
| | To record payment of semiannual interest on the 10% bonds | | |

Twice a year, on June 30 and December 31, while the bonds are outstanding, the semiannual bond interest of $25,000 will be paid and an entry will be made to record the payment. Thus, the annual interest expense on the bonds is $50,000, and the total interest expense over the five-year life of the bonds is $250,000.

When the bonds mature on January 1, 1992, the principal will be paid and the bonds will be retired. The entry to record payment of the principal is as follows:

*2b. An entry is made to record payment of the principal of the bond at maturity*

| | | | |
|---|---|---|---|
| Jan. 1 | Bonds Payable | 500,000 | |
| | Cash | | 500,000 |
| | To record payment of the 10% bonds at maturity | | |

## Bonds Issued between Interest Payment Dates

Bonds may be issued on their interest payment date, as in the illustration above. However, since bonds may be sold on any date, it is likely that they will be sold on a date occurring between the interest payment dates. In such cases, it is custom-

[1] Although bonds are generally issued for larger amounts and longer periods of time, the amounts used here are kept small and the period of time kept short for illustrative purposes.

ary for the bond purchaser to pay the issuing company for the interest accrued on the bond since the last interest date. On the next interest payment date, the issuing company pays a full six months' interest on all bonds outstanding regardless of when the bonds were issued. Thus the accrued interest collected from the buyers when the bonds were sold is now returned to them in this payment along with the interest that has accrued since the date of their bond purchase.

To illustrate the journal entries when bonds are issued between interest payment dates, assume that the Benbrook Corporation's bond issue dated January 1, 1987, was sold at face value on April 1, 1987. The investors pay $12,500 for the three months of interest accrued since the last interest payment date (also the authorization date here) plus $500,000, the issuance price of the bond.

*2a. An entry is made to record the issuance of bonds with three months of accrued interest*

The entry to record the sale of the bonds on April 1 is as follows:

| | | | |
|---|---|---|---|
| April 1 | Cash | 512,500 | |
| | Bonds Payable | | 500,000 |
| | Bond Interest Payable | | 12,500 |
| | To record the sale of 10%, 5-year bonds at face value plus accrued interest for 3 months ($500,000 × 10% × $\frac{3}{12}$) | | |

When the interest payment is made on June 30, the total amount paid of $25,000 includes the $12,500 received from the investor on April 1 and bond interest expense of $12,500 for the three months that the bonds have been outstanding. The entry to record the interest payment on June 30 is as follows:

| | | | |
|---|---|---|---|
| June 30 | Bond Interest Payable | 12,500 | |
| | Bond Interest Expense | 12,500 | |
| | Cash | | 25,000 |
| | To record payment of semiannual interest on the 10% bonds | | |

*2a. The accrued interest sold when the bonds are issued could alternatively be credited to the Bond Interest Expense account*

As an alternative, the entry made on April 1 when the bonds were issued could have been recorded in a slightly different way. Rather than crediting the Bond Interest Payable account for the accrued interest, the same amount could have been credited to the Bond Interest Expense account. The April 1 entry would then be as follows:

| | | | |
|---|---|---|---|
| April 1 | Cash | 512,500 | |
| | Bonds Payable | | 500,000 |
| | Bond Interest Expense | | 12,500 |
| | To record the sale of 10%, 5-year bonds at face value plus accrued interest for 3 months ($500,000 × 10% × $\frac{3}{12}$) | | |

By crediting the accrued interest to the Bond Interest Expense account, we eliminate the need to split the amount of the interest payment between the accrued interest paid for by the investor and the interest accrued since the bonds were issued.

On June 30 when a full six months of interest is paid, the entry would be recorded as follows:

| | | | |
|---|---|---|---|
| June 30 | Bond Interest Expense | 25,000 | |
| | Cash | | 25,000 |
| | To record payment of semiannual interest on the 10% bonds | | |

After both the issuance entry and the first semiannual interest payment entry have been posted, the Bond Interest Expense account shows a debit balance of $12,500 representing interest expense for the three months that the bonds have been outstanding. This is shown in the T account illustrated below.

| BOND INTEREST EXPENSE | | | |
|---|---|---|---|
| 1987 | | 1987 | |
| June 30 | 25,000 | April 1 | 12,500 |

Regardless of which set of entries is used, the balance in the Bond Interest Expense account will of course be $12,500 on June 30, 1987.

## *Interest Rates and Bond Prices*

As mentioned earlier, one of the major factors affecting the market price of a bond is how the bond's stated interest rate compares with the rate prevailing in the market at the time the bonds are issued. The **market rate of interest** for a bond, sometimes called the **effective interest rate,** is the rate that borrowers are willing to pay and investors are willing to take for the use of money based on the bond's characteristics and level of risk involved.

When a corporation decides to issue bonds, it usually tries to set the stated interest rate at what it anticipates the market interest rate will be on the day the bonds are sold. If the stated interest rate and the market interest rate are equal on the day the bonds are sold, they will sell at their face value. However, because time passes while the corporation files the required data with regulatory bodies, prints the bond certificates, and publicizes the bond issue, the stated rate of interest and the market rate of interest are seldom the same on the bond issuance date. If when issued the bonds' stated interest rate is lower than the market rate, they will sell at a **discount.** The discount is the amount by which the face value of the bonds exceeds their issuance price. Conversely, if the bonds' stated interest rate is higher than the market rate, they will sell at a **premium.** The premium is the amount by which the bonds' issuance price exceeds their face value.

PRESENT VALUE When a corporation issues bonds, it incurs two obligations: (1) to pay the face amount of the bonds at maturity and (2) to pay interest at a stated rate periodically over the life of the bonds. An investor is willing to buy a bond to obtain those two streams of cash inflow (periodic interest receipts and return of principal on the maturity date). The amount and the timing of these anticipated cash flows are important when making an investment decision. For example, once we spend money to make an investment, we look for a rapid return on that investment so that we can use that money for another investment. Put another way, an amount of money received today is worth more to us than an equal amount to be received at a future date because the money received today can be invested, giving it an earnings potential.

Since money has a time value, we use present value concepts to determine the price that an investor would be willing to pay for a bond or for any investment.[2] The price an investor will pay for a bond is equal to the sum of the expected returns from the investment. This, then, is the sum of the *present value* of the bond's face amount due at maturity plus the *present value* of the series of periodic interest receipts.

[2] Those who need or would like a more detailed explanation of the concept of present value should refer to the chapter appendix. There we have expanded the discussion and used examples to show computations.

To illustrate how bond prices are determined, refer again to the data presented for the Benbrook bonds. Recall that they were $500,000, five-year debenture bonds with a stated interest rate of 10% per annum payable semiannually. If the prevailing market rate of interest for investments having similar characteristics and similar risk was also 10% (5% per semiannual period), the bonds would sell at their face value (as in our previous illustration).

The computations below show how the price of the Benbrook bonds is established.

| | |
|---|---|
| Present value of the $500,000 to be paid in a lump sum after 10 semiannual interest periods, discounted at the market rate of interest of 10% (5% per semiannual period). From Table 16–3, page 600, $500,000 × 0.6139 = | $306,950 |
| Present value of $25,000 to be paid semiannually for 10 periods, discounted at the market rate of interest of 10% (5% per semiannual period). From Table 16–4, page 601, $25,000 × 7.7217 rounded to the nearest fifty dollars = | 193,050 |
| Present value of bonds | 500,000 |

The first amount, $306,950 in the calculation, is the present value of the $500,000 that will be paid at maturity. That is, if $306,950 were invested at this time with interest accumulating at the rate of 10% compounded semiannually, the total amount accumulated at the end of five years would be $500,000. The second amount, $193,050, is the present value of the series of ten $25,000 interest payments. Note that a 10% market rate of interest compounded annually is equivalent to 5% interest per semiannual period (as used in the calculation above) and that in five years there are ten semiannual periods for bonds that pay interest semiannually.

## Bonds Issued at a Discount

*1c. Bonds will sell at a discount when the stated rate of interest is lower than the market rate of interest for investments having similar features and risks*

Bonds will sell at a discount when they have a stated rate of interest that is lower than the market rate for investments having similar features and risks.

To illustrate, assume that Benbrook Corporation's 10%, five-year bonds are issued when the market rate of interest for comparable investments is 12%. Present value analysis, shown in the schedule below, can be used to determine the price to be paid for the bonds so that its yield to an investor will be 12% (an amount equal to the market rate of interest on such investments).

| | |
|---|---|
| Present value of the $500,000 to be paid in a lump sum after 10 semiannual interest periods, discounted at the market rate of interest of 12% (6% per semiannual period). From Table 16–3, page 600, $500,000 × 0.5584 = | $279,200 |
| Present value of $25,000 to be paid semiannually for 10 periods, discounted at the market rate of interest of 12% (6% per semiannual period). From Table 16–4, page 601, $25,000 × 7.3601 rounded to nearest ten dollars = | 184,000 |
| Present value of bonds | $463,200 |

*2a. An entry is made to record the issuance of bonds at a discount*

If the bonds were issued for the $463,200, a price less than their face value, the entry to record the issue would be as follows:

| | | | |
|---|---|---|---|
| Jan. 1 | Cash | 463,200 | |
| | Discount on Bonds Payable | 36,800 | |
| | Bonds Payable | | 500,000 |
| | To record the sale of 10%, 5-year bonds at a discount | | |

If a balance sheet was prepared on this date, the information pertaining to the bonds would be shown in the Long-Term Liabilities section as follows:

| | | |
|---|---|---|
| Long-term Liabilities: | | |
| Bonds Payable—10% due January 1, 1992 | $500,000 | |
| Less: Unamortized Discount on Bonds Payable | 36,800 | $463,200 |

The $463,200 representing the difference between the $500,000 face value of the bond debt and the $36,800 unamortized bond discount is called the **carrying value** of the bond debt.

When bonds are issued at a discount, the issuer receives an amount on the sale date that is less than the amount that it must pay to the investor on the maturity date. The additional amount that must be paid at maturity increases the cost of borrowing. The idea that the bond discount represents a part of the total cost of borrowing may be best understood by using cash-flow figures from the Benbrook Corporation bond issue. The figures show that the total cost of borrowing the $463,200 that Benbrook received on the issuance date and can use for a five-year period is $286,800.

| | | |
|---|---|---|
| Cash to be paid to bondholders: | | |
| Interest payments for 5 years ($500,000 × .10 × 5 years) | $250,000 | |
| Principal at maturity | 500,000 | |
| Total cash payments | | $750,000 |
| Less: Cash received when the bonds were issued | | 463,200 |
| Total cost of borrowing | | $286,800 |

The total cost of borrowing (interest) consists of the $250,000 of regular interest payments and the $36,800 of bond discount. Therefore the bond discount increases the total interest paid on the bonds from the stated interest rate to the effective interest rate. Although the amount of the discount is not paid to the bondholders until the bonds mature, for accounting purposes it is allocated over the life of the bonds, thereby increasing the interest expense reported for each period. The allocation process is called amortization, and the two methods used to amortize the bond discount are (1) the *straight-line method* and (2) the *effective interest method.* Although the effective interest method is recommended, the straight-line method may be used if the results obtained from its use do not significantly differ from the results that would be obtained if the effective interest method were used.

*2a. The straight-line method of bond amortization allocates an equal amount of the bond discount to each interest period*

AMORTIZATION OF BOND DISCOUNT USING THE STRAIGHT-LINE METHOD Under the **straight-line amortization method,** an equal amount of discount is allocated to each interest period. In our illustration we assumed that the Benbrook bonds pay interest semiannually on June 30 and December 31. Therefore the bond discount of $36,800 is amortized over ten six-month interest periods, which is $3,680 ($36,800 ÷ 10) per period. The entry to record the first semiannual interest payment and periodic amortization of the bond discount is as follows:

*2a. An entry is made to record an interest payment and the amortization of bond discount under the straight-line method*

| | | | |
|---|---|---|---|
| June 30 | Bond Interest Expense | 28,680 | |
| | Discount on Bonds Payable | | 3,680 |
| | Cash | | 25,000 |
| | To record payment of semiannual interest and amortization of discount on the 10% bonds | | |

Note that although $28,680 of bond interest expense is recorded, only $25,000 cash is paid to the bondholders. The difference of $3,680 is credited to the Discount on Bonds Payable account. This credit reduces the debit balance of this contra-liability account and thereby increases the carrying value of the bonds by that amount. After the June 30 entry has been posted to the accounts, the carrying value of the bonds is $466,880 ($500,000 − $33,120 = $466,880), as shown below.

DISCOUNT ON BONDS PAYABLE

| 1987 | | 1987 | |
|---|---|---|---|
| Jan. 1 | 36,800 | June 30 | 3,680 |

BONDS PAYABLE

| | | 1987 | |
|---|---|---|---|
| | | Jan. 1 | 500,000 |

Benbrook's balance sheet on June 30, six months after the issuance, would show the liability for bonds payable as follows:

| | | |
|---|---|---|
| Long-term Liabilities: | | |
| Bonds Payable—10% due January 1, 1992 | $500,000 | |
| Less: Unamortized Discount on Bonds Payable | 33,120 | $466,880 |

When the straight-line amortization method is used, the Discount on Bonds Payable account will be credited for the same $3,680 in each subsequent interest period. Thus at the end of the fifth year, when the bond issue matures, the entire bond discount will have been allocated to interest expense, the balance in Discount on Bonds Payable will be zero, and the carrying value of the bonds payable will be equal to their face value of $500,000.

Although simple to apply, the straight-line method of amortization has a conceptual flaw. Because the bond-carrying value increases each interest period while the amount of bond interest expense remains the same, interest expense expressed as a percentage of the carrying value of the bond debt decreases over time under this method. If the carrying value of a debt increases each interest period, it seems logical that the interest expense charged to each successive period will also increase, not remain the same as it does when the straight-line method of amortization is used.

In 1971 the Accounting Principles Board showed its preference for the effective interest method of amortization by ruling that the straight-line method is acceptable only if the results obtained by its use are not materially different from the results that would be obtained by using the effective interest method.[3]

AMORTIZATION OF BOND DISCOUNT USING THE EFFECTIVE INTEREST METHOD Under the **effective interest amortization method,** the interest expense to be recorded each period is determined by applying a constant rate of interest to the bond-carrying value at the beginning of each period. The constant interest rate applied is the market rate for the bonds as of the date they

[3] Accounting Principles Board, "Interest on Receivables and Payables," *Opinion No. 21* (New York: AICPA, 1971), par. 15.

*EXHIBIT 16–3*

Amortization Table for Bonds Sold at a Discount — Effective Interest Method

| | (A) | (B) | (C) | (D) | (E) | (F) |
|---|---|---|---|---|---|---|
| SEMIANNUAL INTEREST PERIOD | CARRYING AMOUNT OF BONDS AT BEGINNING OF PERIOD | INTEREST EXPENSE TO BE RECORDED (COL. A × 6%) | INTEREST TO BE PAID TO BONDHOLDERS ($500,000 × 5%) | DISCOUNT TO BE AMORTIZED (COL. B − COL. C) | UNAMORTIZED DISCOUNT AT END OF PERIOD (COL. E − COL. D) | BOND-CARRYING AMOUNT AT END OF PERIOD (COL. A + COL. D) |
| Issue date | | | | | $36,800 | $463,200 |
| 6/30/87 | $463,200 | $ 27,792 | $ 25,000 | $ 2,792 | 34,008 | 465,992 |
| 12/31/87 | 465,992 | 27,960 | 25,000 | 2,960 | 31,048 | 468,952 |
| 6/30/88 | 468,952 | 28,137 | 25,000 | 3,137 | 27,911 | 472,089 |
| 12/31/88 | 472,089 | 28,325 | 25,000 | 3,325 | 24,586 | 475,414 |
| 6/30/89 | 475,414 | 28,525 | 25,000 | 3,525 | 21,061 | 478,939 |
| 12/31/89 | 478,939 | 28,736 | 25,000 | 3,736 | 17,325 | 482,675 |
| 6/30/90 | 482,675 | 28,961 | 25,000 | 3,961 | 13,364 | 486,636 |
| 12/31/90 | 486,636 | 29,198 | 25,000 | 4,198 | 9,166 | 490,834 |
| 6/30/91 | 490,834 | 29,450 | 25,000 | 4,450 | 4,716 | 495,284 |
| 12/31/91 | 495,284 | 29,716* | 25,000 | 4,716 | -0- | 500,000 |
| Totals | | $286,800 | $250,000 | $36,800 | | |

* In the last period, interest expense is equal to the semiannual interest paid to the bondholders plus the remaining balance in the bond discount column. The amount is rounded to the nearest dollar.

were issued. The bond-carrying value is their face amount less the amount of unamortized bond discount. The amount of discount to be amortized each period is the difference between the amount of interest expense to be recorded for the period (as computed in the manner described above) and the amount of interest paid to the bondholders for the period. Exhibit 16–3 shows a discount amortization schedule for Benbrook Corporation's $500,000, five-year, 10% bond issue that was dated January 1, 1987, and sold on that day for $463,200 in cash.

Examine the amortization table in Exhibit 16–3 and note the following points:

1. The interest expense to be recorded in each period (column B) is computed by multiplying the beginning-of-period carrying amount of the bond debt (column A) by 6%, the semiannual market rate of interest that prevailed when the bonds were issued. This computational process yields a gradually increasing amount of periodic interest expense.
2. The interest paid to the bondholders in each period (column C) remains *constant* at $25,000 and is computed by multiplying the face value of the bonds by the stated semiannual interest rate of 5%.
3. The discount to be amortized each period (column D) is the difference between the amount of interest expense to be *recorded* and the amount of interest to be *paid* to the bondholders on a given interest payment date.
4. The unamortized discount at the end of the period (column E) decreases from the initial amount of $36,800 to zero on the maturity date of the bonds.
5. The carrying amount of the bond debt (column F) increases from $463,200 (the amount received for the bonds when they were sold) to $500,000 (their face value at maturity).

***2a. An entry is made to record an interest payment and the amortization of bond discount under the effective interest method***

The entry to record the first semiannual interest payment and periodic amortization of bond discount is shown below. Note that the same accounts are debited and credited under the effective interest method as were debited and credited under the straight-line method. Only the dollar amounts for bond interest expense and for the discount amortized are different.

| | | | |
|---|---|---|---|
| June 30 | Bond Interest Expense | 27,792 | |
| | Discount on Bonds Payable | | 2,792 |
| | Cash | | 25,000 |
| | To record payment of semiannual interest and amortization of discount on the 10% bonds | | |

## Bonds Issued at a Premium

***1c. Bonds having a stated interest rate above the prevailing market rate for investments with similar features and risks will sell at a premium***

Bonds will sell at a premium when they have a stated rate of interest that is above the market rate for investments having similar features and risks. For example, if Benbrook's 10%, five-year bonds are issued when the market rate of interest on such investments is 9%, the company can expect to receive more than face value for the bonds. The price is one that will provide investors with a yield of 9% to maturity. Using present value analysis, the price to be paid for the bonds to yield 9% annually to maturity is $519,770, computed as follows:

| | |
|---|---|
| Present value of the $500,000 to be paid in a lump sum after 10 semiannual interest periods, discounted at the market rate of interest of 9% ($4\frac{1}{2}$% per semiannual period). From Table 16–3, page 600, $500,000 × 0.6439 = | $321,950 |
| Present value of $25,000 to be paid semiannually for 10 periods, discounted at the market rate of interest of 9% ($4\frac{1}{2}$% per semiannual period). From Table 16–4, page 601, $25,000 × 7.9127 rounded to nearest ten dollars = | 197,820 |
| Present value of bonds | $519,770 |

Discounting the present value of the expected returns from the investment at the semiannual market rate of interest indicates that the bonds would sell at a premium of $19,770 ($519,770 − $500,000). If on January 1, 1987, the bonds were sold for that amount, the entry to record the issuance would be as follows:

*2a. An entry is made to record issuance of bonds at a premium*

| | | | |
|---|---|---|---|
| Jan. 1 | Cash | 519,770 | |
| | Premium on Bonds Payable | | 19,770 |
| | Bonds Payable | | 500,000 |
| | To record the sale of 10%, 5-year bonds at a premium | | |

If a balance sheet were prepared on this date, the information pertaining to the bonds would be shown in the Long-Term Liabilities section as follows:

| | | |
|---|---|---|
| Long-term Liabilities: | | |
| Bonds Payable—10% due January 1, 1992 | $500,000 | |
| Add: Unamortized Premium on Bonds Payable | 19,770 | $519,770 |

The *carrying value* of the bond debt is $519,770, representing the face amount of the bonds plus the unamortized bond premium.

When bonds sell at a premium, the issuer receives an amount that exceeds the amount it must pay to the bondholder when the bonds mature. A bond premium, like a bond discount, is amortized over the life of the bonds. Bonds sold at a premium decrease the cost of borrowing, as shown in the computation below.

*2a. A bond premium is amortized over the life of the bonds*

| | | |
|---|---|---|
| Cash to be paid to bondholders: | | |
| Interest payments for 5 years ($500,000 × .10 × 5 years) | $250,000 | |
| Principal at maturity | 500,000 | |
| Total cash payments | | $750,000 |
| Less: Cash received when the bonds were issued | | 519,770 |
| Total cost of borrowing | | $230,230 |

The figures show that the bond premium reduced the total cost of borrowing to an amount below that which must be paid out in periodic interest payment to the bondholders ($230,230 total cost of borrowing compared with $250,000 of interest payments to bondholders). The difference representing the bond premium must be amortized over the life of the bond issue in a manner that will lower the recorded bond interest expense. As with bond discounts, bond premiums may be amortized using the straight-line method (if the results are not materially different from those of the effective interest method) or the effective interest method.

**AMORTIZATION OF BOND PREMIUM USING THE STRAIGHT-LINE METHOD** When the straight-line method is used to amortize a premium, an equal amount of the premium is allocated to each period to reduce the interest expense recorded for that period. Thus amortization per period on Benbrook's bond premium is $1,977 ($19,770 ÷ 10 interest periods). The entry made on June 30, 1987, to record the first semiannual interest payment and premium amortization is as follows:

*2a. An entry is made to record an interest payment and the amortization of bond premium under the straight-line method*

| | | | |
|---|---|---|---|
| June 30 | Bond Interest Expense . . . . . . . . . . | 23,023 | |
| | Premium on Bonds Payable . . . . . . . . . . | 1,977 | |
| | Cash . . . . . . . . . . | | 25,000 |
| | To record payment of semiannual interest and amortization of premium on the 10% bonds | | |

This entry is repeated on each interest payment date. Thus, over the five-year life of the bonds, total bond interest expense of $230,230 ($23,023 per period × 10 periods), an amount equal to the total cost of borrowing, will be recorded.

**AMORTIZATION OF BOND PREMIUM USING THE EFFECTIVE INTEREST METHOD** Under the effective interest method, the amount of premium amortized each period increases, causing the amount of interest expense to be recorded each period to decrease. Based upon Benbrook Corporation's $500,000 bond issue that sold for $519,770 on January 1, 1987, a premium amortization schedule has been prepared and is shown in Exhibit 16–4 on page 572.

Examine the amortization table in Exhibit 16–4 and note the following points:

1. The interest expense to be recorded in each period (column B) is computed by multiplying the beginning-of-period carrying amount of the bond debt (column A) by $4\frac{1}{2}$%, the semiannual market rate of interest that prevailed when the bonds were issued. This computational process yields a gradually decreasing amount of periodic interest expense.
2. The interest paid to the bondholders in each period (column C) remains *constant* at $25,000 and is computed by multiplying the face value of the bonds by the stated semiannual interest rate of 5%.
3. The premium to be amortized each period (column D) is the difference between the amount of interest expense to be *recorded* and the amount of interest to be *paid* to the bondholders on a given interest payment date.
4. The unamortized premium at the end of the period (column E) decreases from the initial amount of $19,770 to zero on the maturity date of the bonds.
5. The carrying amount of the bond debt (column F) decreases from $519,770 (the amount received for the bonds when they were sold) to $500,000 (their face value at maturity).

*2a. An entry is made to record an interest payment and the amortization of bond premium under the effective interest method*

Based upon the schedule, the entry to record the first semiannual interest payment and premium amortization is as follows:

| | | | |
|---|---|---|---|
| June 30 | Bond Interest Expense . . . . . . . . . . | 23,390 | |
| | Premium on Bonds Payable . . . . . . . . . . | 1,610 | |
| | Cash . . . . . . . . . . | | 25,000 |
| | To record payment of semiannual interest and amortization of premium on the 10% bonds | | |

## *Year-End Accrual For Bond Interest Expense*

A company will often issue bonds with periodic interest payment dates that do not coincide with its fiscal year end. In such cases, an adjustment is needed at the end of the year to accrue interest on the bonds and to amortize any related discount or premium from the last interest payment date to the fiscal year-end.

*EXHIBIT 16–4*

Amortization Table for Bonds Sold at a Premium—Effective Interest Method

| | (A) | (B) | (C) | (D) | (E) | (F) |
|---|---|---|---|---|---|---|
| SEMIANNUAL INTEREST PERIOD | CARRYING AMOUNT OF BONDS AT BEGINNING OF PERIOD | INTEREST EXPENSE TO BE RECORDED (COL. A × $4\frac{1}{2}$%) | INTEREST TO BE PAID TO BONDHOLDERS ($500,000 × 5%) | PREMIUM TO BE AMORTIZED (COL. C − COL. B) | UNAMORTIZED PREMIUM AT END OF PERIOD (COL. E − COL. D) | BOND-CARRYING AMOUNT AT END OF PERIOD (COL. A − COL. D) |
| Issue date | | | | | $19,770 | $519,770 |
| 6/30/87 | $519,770 | $ 23,390 | $ 25,000 | $ 1,610 | 18,160 | 518,160 |
| 12/31/87 | 518,160 | 23,317 | 25,000 | 1,683 | 16,477 | 516,477 |
| 6/30/88 | 516,477 | 23,241 | 25,000 | 1,759 | 14,718 | 514,718 |
| 12/31/88 | 514,718 | 23,162 | 25,000 | 1,838 | 12,880 | 512,880 |
| 6/30/89 | 512,880 | 23,080 | 25,000 | 1,920 | 10,960 | 510,960 |
| 12/31/89 | 510,960 | 22,993 | 25,000 | 2,007 | 8,953 | 508,953 |
| 6/30/90 | 508,953 | 22,903 | 25,000 | 2,097 | 6,856 | 506,856 |
| 12/31/90 | 506,856 | 22,809 | 25,000 | 2,191 | 4,665 | 504,665 |
| 6/30/91 | 504,665 | 22,710 | 25,000 | 2,290 | 2,375 | 502,375 |
| 12/31/91 | 502,375 | 22,625* | 25,000 | 2,375 | -0- | 500,000 |
| Totals | | $230,230 | $250,000 | $19,770 | | |

* In the last period, interest expense is equal to the semiannual interest paid to the bondholders less the remaining balance in the bond premium column. The amount is rounded to the nearest dollar.

To illustrate, assume the same facts as in our previous example where Benbrook Corporation's 10%, five-year bonds were issued on January 1, 1987, for $519,770. The bonds had semiannual interest payment dates of June 30 and December 31. Assume now that Benbrook's fiscal year ends on September 30. On September 30, 1987, the following adjusting entry is made to accrue three months of interest expense and to amortize three months of bond premium:

*2a. An adjusting entry is made when periodic interest dates do not coincide with a firm's fiscal year-end*

| | | | |
|---|---|---|---|
| Sept. 30 | Bond Interest Expense .......................... | 11,658 | |
| | Premium on Bonds Payable ...................... | 842 | |
| | Bond Interest Payable ...................... | | 12,500 |
| | To accrue interest and amortize premium for three months on the 10% bonds. Accrued interest: $500,000 × 10% × $\frac{3}{12}$ = $12,500. Amortization of one-half of the premium for the second interest payment period: $1,683 ÷ 2 = $842 (rounded) | | |

On December 31, 1987, the next date when interest is paid, the following entry is made:

| | | | |
|---|---|---|---|
| Dec. 31 | Bond Interest Expense.......................... | 11,659 | |
| | Premium on Bonds Payable........................ | 841 | |
| | Bond Interest Payable........................... | 12,500 | |
| | Cash.................................... | | 25,000 |
| | To record payment of semiannual interest and amortization of premium on the 10% bonds | | |

In this entry the bond interest expense and premium amortization for the three-month period since September 30 are recorded, and the liability for the bond interest accrued on September 30 is satisfied. The amount debited to the Premium on Bonds Payable is the rest of the $1,683 as shown in the second interest payment row of Exhibit 16–4 ($1,683 − $842 = $841). The amount debited to Bond Interest Expense represents the remaining interest expense that should be recorded when the second interest payment is made ($23,317 − $11,658 = $11,659).

When bonds are issued at a discount, the year-end accrual of interest and the amortization of the discount are recorded in a similar manner. Of course, the amortization of the discount would be credited to the Discount on Bonds Payable account instead of being debited to the Premium on Bonds Payable account.

## RETIREMENT OF BONDS AT MATURITY

*2b. An entry is made to record the retirement of bonds at the maturity date*

Bonds may remain outstanding until their maturity date, at which time they are retired by paying their face amount in cash. The entry to record the retirement of the Benbrook bonds paid at maturity is as follows:

| | | | |
|---|---|---|---|
| 1992 | | | |
| Jan. 1 | Bonds Payable.................................. | 500,000 | |
| | Cash ...................................... | | 500,000 |
| | To record payment of the 10% bonds at maturity | | |

This is the appropriate entry even if the bonds were originally sold at a discount or a premium. As discussed earlier, discounts or premiums are amortized over the life of the bonds and therefore have zero balances when the bonds mature.

## RETIREMENT OF BONDS BEFORE MATURITY

### Redeemed at a Call Price

Bonds may also be retired before their maturity date. You will remember that callable bonds are redeemable by the issuing corporation before maturity if it is willing to pay the call price stated in the bond indenture. If the market rate of interest declines after the bonds have been issued, the corporation may choose to issue new bonds at the current lower interest rate and use the proceeds to redeem the bonds having the higher interest rate. Even bonds not having a call provision may be redeemed and retired before maturity if the issuing corporation is willing to purchase them in the open market.

When bonds are redeemed at a price below their carrying value, the corporation realizes a gain on the early retirement of the debt. Conversely, if the price paid to redeem the bonds is greater than the carrying value of the bonds, a loss on the early retirement will be incurred. These gains or losses, if material, should be reported separately in the income statement as an extraordinary item.[4]

To illustrate the accounting for the early retirement of bonds, assume that the $500,000 Benbrook Corporation bonds issued for $519,770 are callable at 103. Assume further that the company exercises its call option on the entire issue on July 1, 1989, when the unamortized bond premium (as shown in Exhibit 16–4) was $10,960. The entry would be as follows:

*2b. An entry is made to record the early retirement of bonds recognizing an extraordinary gain or loss on the retirement*

| | | | |
|---|---|---|---|
| July 1 | Bonds Payable.................................... | 500,000 | |
| | Premium on Bonds Payable......................... | 10,960 | |
| | Extraordinary Loss on Retirement of Bonds............ | 4,040 | |
| | Cash ......................................... | | 515,000 |
| | To record retirement of the 10% bonds called at 103 | | |

If only a portion of the bonds were redeemed before maturity, only the portion of the premium relating to those bonds would be written off in the retirement entry.

### Conversion of Bonds into Common Stock

*1c. A conversion feature allows bond investors to benefit from an increase in the market value of the company's common stock*

As discussed earlier, some bonds have a convertible feature. These bonds, at the option of the holder, may be exchanged for other securities of the issuing corporation (usually its common stock). The conversion feature is of interest to some investors because they can receive fixed periodic interest and other benefits of being a corporate creditor while holding the bond and yet have an option to become a stockholder should that investment position become more attractive in the future. The conversion feature also gives an investor the opportunity to benefit from an increase in the market price of the corporation's common stock because the market price of a convertible bond will increase as the price of the related common stock increases.

---

[4] Financial Accounting Standards Board, "Reporting Gains and Losses from Extinguishment of Debt," *Statement No. 4* (Stamford, Conn., 1975), par. 8.

In accounting for the conversion of bonds to common stock, we generally use the carrying value method. Thus the carrying value of the bonds converted is the amount recorded for the stock issued, and the bond liability and related unamortized premium or discount are written off the books. As a result, no gain or loss is recognized on the transaction.

To illustrate, assume that each of the $1,000 Benbrook Corporation bonds is convertible into 25 shares of $10 par value common stock. On July 1, 1989, one-half of the bondholders elect to convert their bonds into common stock. Using Exhibit 16–4, we can determine that the unamortized bond premium on one-half of the outstanding bond debt on that date is $5,480 ($10,960 × ½). The entry to record the conversion is as follows:

*2b. An entry is made to record the conversion of bonds into common stock*

| | | | |
|---|---|---|---|
| July 1 | Bonds Payable | 250,000 | |
| | Premium on Bonds Payable | 5,480 | |
| | Common Stock | | 62,500 |
| | Paid-in Capital in Excess of Par Value | | 192,980 |
| | To record the conversion of 250 bonds into 6,250 shares of common stock; 250 bonds × 25 shares per bond = 6,250 shares | | |

The $250,000 debit to Bonds Payable eliminates that portion of the debt attributable to the bonds converted. The $5,480 debit to Premium on Bonds Payable eliminates that portion of the unamortized premium attributable to the converted bonds. The $62,500 credit to common stock is for the number of shares issued (6,250) times their par value ($10 per share). Since there is no gain or loss recognized on the transaction, the remainder (which is the excess of the carrying value of the bonds over the par value of the common stock) is assigned and credited to Paid-in Capital in Excess of Par Value.

## BOND SINKING FUND

Investors want assurance that the money needed for the payment of the bonds at maturity will be available. Accordingly, some companies establish a special fund called a **bond sinking fund** where assets can be set aside and accumulated during the life of the bonds. These accumulated assets can then be used to pay the bondholders for the bonds at maturity.

*1d. A bond sinking fund accumulates assets to pay the bondholders for the bonds at maturity*

A corporation having a bond sinking fund generally makes periodic cash deposits to the fund. These deposits are usually made to the fund's trustee (such as a bank or other financial entity), which invests the cash in income-producing securities. The periodic deposits and the earnings on the investments accumulate in the fund. The purpose is to accumulate enough assets in the fund to pay the face amount of the bonds at maturity.

To illustrate the accounting for a bond sinking fund, return to the Benbrook Corporation's $500,000, 10%, five-year bonds that were issued on January 1, 1987. Assume that (1) deposits will be made to a sinking fund trustee at the end of each year during the bond issue's life, and (2) the amount deposited will be sufficient to ensure that the $500,000 needed to retire the bonds on January 1, 1992, will be available. The trustee will invest the monies deposited in income-producing securities expected to earn about 10% per year.

By referring to an appropriate mathematical table (such as Table 16–2 on page 599) and dividing the figure shown (6.1051) for the future value of an annuity at 10% for five periods into $500,000, we can determine that annual deposits of $81,899 ($500,000 ÷ 6.1051) are sufficient to provide a fund of approximately $500,000 at the end of five years.

The schedule below shows exactly how the fund will grow to $500,000 (in rounded dollars) in five years if $81,899 is deposited at the end of each of the five years.

| END OF YEAR | (A) BALANCE IN FUND AT BEGINNING OF YEAR | (B) CASH DEPOSITED | (C) INTEREST EARNED ON FUND BALANCE AT 10% ANNUALLY (10%) × (A)* | (D) BALANCE IN FUND AT YEAR-END (A) + (B) + (C) |
|---|---|---|---|---|
| 1 | — | $81,899 | — | $ 81,899 |
| 2 | $ 81,899 | 81,899 | $ 8,190 | 171,988 |
| 3 | 171,988 | 81,899 | 17,198 | 271,085 |
| 4 | 271,085 | 81,899 | 27,108 | 380,092 |
| 5 | 380,092 | 81,899 | 38,009 | 500,000 |

* All amounts rounded.

*2c. An entry records the annual deposit in a bond sinking fund*

The entry to record the amount that will be deposited at the end of each year for five years is as follows:

| | | | |
|---|---|---|---|
| 1987 | | | |
| Dec. 31 | Bond Sinking Fund . . . . . . . . . . . . . . . . . . . . . . . . . . . . . . . . | 81,899 | |
| | Cash . . . . . . . . . . . . . . . . . . . . . . . . . . . . . . . . . . . . . . . . | | 81,899 |
| | To record annual deposit to the bond sinking fund | | |

The trustee invests the cash and reports the earnings on those investments periodically to Benbrook Corporation. If we assume that the $81,899 deposited in the sinking fund at the end of the first year earned the expected $8,190, the entry made by Benbrook to record the revenue earned on sinking fund investments during the second year is as follows:

| | | | |
|---|---|---|---|
| 1988 | | | |
| Dec. 31 | Bond Sinking Fund . . . . . . . . . . . . . . . . . . . . . . . . . . . . . . . . | 8,190 | |
| | Sinking Fund Revenue. . . . . . . . . . . . . . . . . . . . . . . . . | | 8,190 |
| | To record revenue earned on sinking fund investments | | |

Although the assets in the sinking fund are held by a trustee, they remain the property of the company that created the fund. Therefore the Bond Sinking Fund account would be reported in the Long-Term Investments section of Benbrook Corporation's balance sheet, and the Sinking Fund Revenue account would be reported as nonoperating revenue in its income statement.

*2c. An entry records the gain or loss resulting from the sale of sinking fund securities*

Sinking fund investments may be sold from time to time, in which case the trustee would reinvest the proceeds. Any gains or losses resulting from the sale of investments are recorded by increasing or decreasing the Bond Sinking Fund account. For example, if the sale of certain sinking fund investments resulted in a gain of $400 and this gain was reported on October 28, 1990, the following entry would be recorded:

| | | | |
|---|---|---|---|
| 1990 | | | |
| Oct. 28 | Bond Sinking Fund | 400 | |
| | Gain on Sale of Sinking Fund Investment | | 400 |
| | To record gain on investment in the bond sinking fund | | |

When the bonds mature, the trustee must sell the investments to obtain the cash needed to pay the bondholders. Usually the amount obtained is not equal to the amount needed. If less cash than needed is obtained, the corporation must make up the difference. If more cash than needed is obtained, the extra cash is returned to the corporation. For example, assume that after all the investments had been sold, Benbrook's trustee had cash of $500,470, an amount that exceeds the bond debt, on the day the bonds mature. The trustee would pay $500,000 to the bondholders and return the extra $470 to Benbrook. The corporation would then record payment of the bond debt and the elimination of the bond sinking fund with the following entry:

| | | | |
|---|---|---|---|
| 1992 | | | |
| Jan. 1 | Bonds Payable | 500,000 | |
| | Cash | 470 | |
| | Bond Sinking Fund | | 500,470 |
| | To record payment of bonds at maturity and transfer the excess sinking fund cash to the regular cash account | | |

## OTHER LONG-TERM LIABILITIES

Companies frequently have long-term liabilities other than bonds payable. Two of the more common — mortgage notes payable and lease obligations — are discussed in the following sections.

### Mortgage Notes Payable

Companies often use mortgage notes to finance the purchase of real estate and certain other plant assets. A **mortgage note payable** is a written promise to pay a stated amount of money at one or more specified future dates. By issuing a mortgage note, the borrower agrees to pledge specific property as collateral, thus providing further assurance (security) to the lender that the note obligation will be paid.

Mortgage note agreements typically require the borrower to make periodic payments, usually monthly, of a constant dollar amount. Each payment consists of two components: a partial reduction in the principal amount of the debt and interest on the debt. Although the amount of the periodic payment usually remains constant, the principal and interest component differ each period. At the beginning, much of the amount paid is applied to interest. However, the interest component will decrease, and the reduction of the principal component will increase with each successive payment.

*2d. Monthly payments on a mortgage note payable are allocated between interest and principal*

To illustrate, assume that a company purchases a building for $400,000 on August 1, 19X4. The company finances the transaction by issuing a 12% mortgage note requiring monthly payments of $5,000 beginning September 1, 19X4. The schedule below shows how the first four monthly payments are allocated between interest and principal.

| PAYMENT DATE | (A) PRINCIPAL BALANCE AT BEGINNING OF MONTH | (B) MONTHLY PAYMENT | (C) INTEREST FOR ONE MONTH (1%) × (A) | (D) REDUCTION IN PRINCIPAL (B) − (C) | (E) PRINCIPAL BALANCE AT END OF MONTH |
|---|---|---|---|---|---|
| Aug. 1 (issuance date) | $400,000 | — | — | — | $400,000 |
| Sept. 1 | 400,000 | $5,000 | $4,000 | $1,000 | 399,000 |
| Oct. 1 | 399,000 | 5,000 | 3,990 | 1,010 | 397,990 |
| Nov. 1 | 397,990 | 5,000 | 3,980* | 1,020 | 396,970 |
| Dec. 1 | 396,970 | 5,000 | 3,970* | 1,030 | 395,940 |

* Rounded to nearest dollar.

*2d. An entry records the monthly mortgage payment*

Based on the data in the schedule, the entry to record the September 1 payment would be as follows:

| | | | |
|---|---|---|---|
| Sept. 1 | Interest Expense . . . . . . . . . . | 4,000 | |
| | Mortgage Payable . . . . . . . . . . | 1,000 | |
| | Cash . . . . . . . . . . | | 5,000 |
| | To record monthly payment on mortgage | | |

If financial statements are prepared, the amount of principal to be paid in the next twelve months should be reported as a current liability, and the remaining amount of principal should be reported as a long-term liability.

Mortgage notes are frequently used by individuals as well as corporations. Because of their need to finance large amounts of money, however, most corporations issue long-term bonds.

## Lease Obligations

In recent years it has become popular for companies and individuals to acquire the use of property and equipment by leasing rather than buying. A **lease** is a contractual agreement in which one party conveys the right to use an asset for a specified period of time to another party in return for periodic rental payments. The two parties to a lease contract are the lessor and the lessee. The *lessor* is the owner of the asset who agrees to give the *lessee* the right to use the asset for a specified period of time. Examples of assets commonly leased are buildings, machines, automobiles, computers, and airplanes.

There are various reasons why a company would choose to lease assets:

Lease agreements usually permit 100% financing. Thus no down payment is needed, as is often the case when property and equipment are purchased on credit.

Lease payments are fully deductible for tax purposes in the year in which they are paid.

The risk of obsolescence on leased assets is shifted to the lessor.

*1e. Leases are classified as either capital leases or operating leases*

In accounting, lease transactions are classified as either *capital leases* or *operating leases.* A **capital lease** is a lease arrangement that transfers substantially all the benefits and risks of asset ownership to the lessee and is in effect an installment purchase of the leased asset. When the lease arrangement provides that the lessor retain all the benefits and risks of asset ownership, it is in effect a rental agreement and is classified as an **operating lease.**

Recognizing that the arrangements agreed to in a lease contract may vary widely, the FASB has established four criteria for determining the classification of a lease. If one or more of these criteria are met, the lease is classified as a capital lease. A lease that does not meet at least one of the four criteria that follow is classified as an operating lease:

The lease transfers ownership of the property to the lessee by the end of the lease term.

The lease contains a bargain purchase option that allows the lessee to purchase the leased property during or at the end of the lease term for a price that is less than the expected fair value of the property at the date that the lessee can first exercise the option.

The lease term is equal to 75% or more of the estimated economic life of the leased property.

The present value of the minimum lease payments at the beginning of the lease term is equal to or exceeds 90% of the fair value of the leased property.[5]

**OPERATING LEASES** Leases that do not meet at least one of the four criteria for a capital lease are classified as operating leases. With an operating lease, the lessee obtains the right to use leased property for a limited period of time and in return makes periodic payments to the lessor. The lessee accounts for the amount paid under the agreement as a rental expense. The lessee does not record the leased property as an asset and is not required to recognize obligations related to future payments as a liability on its balance sheet. However, if the amount of the obligation to make future lease rental payments is material, the FASB requires the lessee to disclose in a footnote the minimum future rental payments for each of the next five years.[6]

In accounting for an operating lease, no entry is made at the time the lease agreement is signed. As stated above, the lessee treats the lease payment as a rental expense and records the transaction as follows:

| | | | |
|---|---|---|---|
| Jan 15 | Rental Expense ........................................ | 200 | |
| | Cash ........................................ | | 200 |

**CAPITAL LEASES** Under a capital lease, the lessee is in effect acquiring an asset through an installment purchase plan. Thus the lessee records the asset being leased by debiting an asset account, and it records the related liability to the lessor by crediting a liability account. The amount of the entry is equal to the present value of the future lease payments. Each lease payment is recorded by allocating the amount paid between its interest component and its liability reduction component. In this respect, the accounting for lease payments is similar to the accounting for the payments on a mortgage note. Furthermore, since the lessee records the leased property on its books as an asset, it also depreciates the leased asset over its expected useful life.

Although accounting for leases can become complex, we show in the illustration below the basic entries made by the lessee when property is acquired under a leasing arrangement that qualifies as a capital lease. In preparing the illustration, we assume that on January 3, 1987, Altus Company signed a noncancelable five-year lease for a machine having an estimated life of eight years with no expected salvage value. The lease agreement, which provides for a bargain

[5] Financial Accounting Standards Board, "Accounting for Leases," *Statement No. 13* (Stamford, Conn., 1976), par. 7.

[6] Ibid., par. 16.

purchase option, calls for an immediate down payment of $10,000 and a series of five additional payments of $10,000, each to be made at the end of each of the five years.

The current market rate of interest is 12%, and the company would incur that same rate if it borrowed money. The leased asset and related obligation to the lessor would be recorded at $46,048. This amount represents the present value of future lease payments and is determined as follows: $10,000 down payment + ($10,000 × 3.6048) = *$46,048*. The factor of 3.6048 was obtained from Table 16–4, page 601, using a 12% rate for five periods.

*2e. Lease payments under a capital lease are allocated between their interest and principal components*

The schedule below shows how the amount of each subsequent lease payment will be allocated between its interest and principal components.

| PAYMENT DATE | (A) LEASE OBLIGATION AT BEGINNING OF PERIOD | (B) LEASE PAYMENT | (C) INTEREST EXPENSE (A) × (12%) | (D) PRINCIPAL REDUCTION (B) − (C) | (E) LEASE OBLIGATION AT END OF PERIOD |
|---|---|---|---|---|---|
| Jan. 3, 1987 | $46,048 | $10,000 | $ -0- | $10,000 | $36,048 |
| Dec. 31, 1987 | 36,048 | 10,000 | 4,326 | 5,674 | 30,374 |
| Dec. 31, 1988 | 30,374 | 10,000 | 3,645 | 6,355 | 24,019 |
| Dec. 31, 1989 | 24,019 | 10,000 | 2,882 | 7,118 | 16,901 |
| Dec. 31, 1990 | 16,901 | 10,000 | 2,028 | 7,972 | 8,929 |
| Dec. 31, 1991 | 8,929 | 10,000 | 1,071 | 8,929 | -0- |
| | | $60,000 | $13,952 | | |

Note that there is no interest associated with the first lease payment, since it was made on the first day of the lease term.

The sequence of journal entries recorded during the first year of the lease term is shown below.

| 1987 | | | |
|---|---|---|---|
| Jan. 3 | Leased Machinery | 46,048 | |
| | Lease Obligation | | 46,048 |
| | To record the leasing of a machine as a capital lease | | |
| Jan. 3 | Lease Obligation | 10,000 | |
| | Cash | | 10,000 |
| | To record initial lease payment | | |
| Dec. 31 | Lease Obligation | 5,674 | |
| | Interest Expense | 4,326 | |
| | Cash | | 10,000 |
| | To record payment of lease installments | | |
| Dec. 31 | Depreciation Expense—Leased Machinery | 5,756 | |
| | Accumulated Depreciation—Leased Machinery | | 5,756 |
| | To record depreciation on leased machinery using the straight-line method with an estimated useful life of 8 years ($46,048 ÷ 8 years) | | |

Similar entries are made at the end of each of the following four years.

For financial reporting, both interest expense and depreciation expense are shown on the income statement. The leased machinery is reported in the Plant

Asset section of the balance sheet for $46,048, less its accumulated depreciation. The amount of the related lease obligation is separated. The portion due in the current operating cycle or one year, whichever is longer, is shown as a current liability and the remainder is shown as a long-term liability.

## HIGHLIGHT PROBLEM

The long-term liabilities shown on Farley Corporation's December 31, 1987, balance sheet were as follows:

| | | |
|---|---|---|
| Long-term Liabilities | | |
| Bonds Payable—10% due January 1, 2000 | $3,000,000 | |
| Less: Unamortized Discount on Bonds Payable | 90,000 | $2,910,000 |

1. On January 1, 1988, the bonds were called at a price of 101. Semiannual interest payments were made on these bonds each June 30 and December 31.
2. On January 31, 1988, a new $4,000,000, 9%, 20-year bond issue was authorized. The entire issue was sold on January 31 at 101½ plus accrued interest. Bond interest is paid semiannually on June 30 and December 31 of each year, and the company has a calendar year-end.

Required:

1. Prepare journal entries to record the following:
   a. The retirement of the 10% bonds on January 1, 1988.
   b. The issuance of the 9% bonds on January 31, 1988.
   c. The semiannual interest payment and the amortization of the premium on June 30, 1988. (The company amortizes the premium using the straight-line method.)
   d. The semiannual interest payment and the amortization of the premium on December 31, 1988.
2. Show how the bonds would be reported in Farley's balance sheet on December 31, 1988.

## GLOSSARY OF KEY TERMS

**Bond.** An interest-bearing security representing money borrowed by a corporation.

**Bond indenture.** A bond contract specifying the terms and provisions of the bond agreement.

**Bond sinking fund.** A fund of assets (usually supervised and controlled by a trustee) accumulated to pay a specific bond issue at maturity.

**Callable bond.** A bond that at the option of the issuing corporation may be redeemed (called in) at a preestablished redemption price before its scheduled maturity date.

**Capital lease.** A lease arrangement that transfers substantially all the benefits and risks of ownership to the lessee and therefore is in effect an installment purchase of the leased property.

**Carrying value (of bonds).** The face value of a bond issue less any unamortized bond discount or plus any unamortized bond premium.

**Convertible bond.** A bond that may be exchanged for another security (usually common stock) of the issuing corporation at the option of the bondholder.

**Coupon bonds.** Unregistered bonds having attached coupons that are removed and presented to the issuer or agent to collect interest on the bonds. Also called *bearer bonds.*

**Debenture bond.** An unsecured bond.

**Debt financing.** Raising money by issuing bonds or using some other form of borrowing.

**Discount (on bonds).** The amount by which the face value of bonds exceeds their issuance price.

**Effective interest amortization method.** A method of determining the amortization of bond discount or bond premium for each period. It requires the application of a constant rate of interest to the carrying value of the bonds at the beginning of each period.

**Effective interest rate.** See *Market rate of interest.*

**Equity financing.** Raising money by issuing stock.

**Lease.** A contractual agreement in which one party (the lessor) conveys the right to use an asset for a specified period of time to another party (the lessee) in return for periodic rental payments.

**Leverage.** The use of borrowed funds to earn a return that is greater than the cost of the borrowed funds.

**Long-term liability.** An obligation that has a maturity date beyond one year from the balance sheet date or the operating cycle, whichever is longer.

**Market rate of interest.** The rate that borrowers are willing to pay and investors are willing to take for the use of money based on the securities' characteristics and level of risk involved.

**Mortgage note payable.** A written promise to pay a stated amount of money at one or more specified future dates.

**Operating lease.** A lease contract that is in effect a rental agreement. Under an operating lease, the lessee obtains the right to use the leased asset, but the lessor retains all the benefits and risks associated with the ownership of that asset.

**Premium (on bonds).** The amount by which the bonds' issuance price exceeds their face value.

**Present value of an amount.** The value today of an amount to be received or paid at a future date.

**Present value of an annuity.** The amount that would have to be invested today at a certain compound interest rate to enable the investor to receive a desired amount in a series of equal future payments over a specified time period.

**Registered bonds.** Bonds that are issued in the name of the bondholder and may be transferred from one owner to another through endorsement.

**Secured bond.** A bond that gives the bondholder a claim against specific assets of the issuing corporation.

**Serial bonds.** Bonds that mature in a series of installments over several different dates.

**Stated rate.** The rate of interest specified in the bond indenture. This rate applied to the face amount of a bond determines the annual interest on the bond. Also called ***contract rate*** or ***coupon rate.***

**Straight-line amortization method.** A method used to amortize a bond discount or bond premium that results in allocating equal amounts to each interest period.

**Term bonds.** A bond issue in which all the bonds mature on the same date.

**Trustee.** An independent third party appointed to represent the bondholders.

**Underwriter.** An investment banker or a bond broker that sells the bond issue for a commission.

**Unsecured bond.** A bond issued solely on the basis of the issuing corporation's general credit rating and financial reputation.

## REVIEW QUESTIONS

1. From what sources can a company obtain the funds needed to conduct its business activities and expand its operations? [LO1a]
2. What is a long-term liability? [LO1a]
3. What is a bond, and what two distinct obligations does a corporation that issues bonds incur? [LO1c]
4. Differentiate between bondholders (who are corporate creditors) and stockholders (who are corporate owners). [LO1b]
5. What factors other than the answers to question 4 should be considered when deciding between debt financing and equity financing? [LO1b]
6. What does it mean when we say a company is favorably leveraged? [LO1b]
7. Differentiate between an underwriter and a trustee. [LO1c]
8. Briefly describe the differences between the following:
   a. A secured bond and an unsecured bond
   b. A term bond and a serial bond
   c. A registered bond and a coupon bond
   d. A callable bond and a convertible bond [LO1c]
9. Describe three major factors affecting the market price of a bond. [LO1c]
10. How is the market price of a bond quoted? [LO1c]
11. How is the authorization of a bond issue recorded in the accounting records? [LO2a]

12. How is interest accrued on the bond since the last interest date accounted for when bonds are issued between interest dates? [LO2a]
13. What relationship between the market interest rate and the stated interest rate causes bonds to be sold at a discount? At a premium? [LO2a]
14. Describe how the price that an investor would be willing to pay for a bond is determined. [LO2a]
15. Name the two amortization methods that may be used to amortize a bond discount or a bond premium. [LO2a]
16. Which amortization method provides for an equal amount of discount to be allocated to each interest period? [LO2a]
17. Which amortization method ensures that the interest expense recorded for the period is determined by applying a constant rate of interest to the bond-carrying value? [LO2a]
18. How is the unamortized portion of bond discounts and bond premiums shown on the balance sheet? [LO2a]
19. Why is it sometimes necessary to accrue bond interest expense? [LO2a]
20. What are two ways in which outstanding bonds can be retired before their maturity dates? [LO2b]
21. Under what circumstances would a company realize a gain on the retirement of bonds? Under what circumstances would a loss be incurred? [LO2b]
22. How are material gains and losses from the early extinguishment of bond debt reported in the financial statements? [LO2b]
23. What is meant by the statement that "bonds have a convertible feature "and to what type of securities are bonds generally converted? [LO2b]
24. What is the purpose of a bond sinking fund? [LO1d]
25. What are the responsibilities of the trustee of a bond sinking fund? [LO1d]
26. How are sinking fund revenues reported in the financial statements? [LO2c]
27. What is a mortgage note payable? [LO2d]
28. Name the two components of each payment made on a mortgage note payable. [LO2d]
29. Why does the interest component of each successive mortgage note payment decrease while the reduction of the principal component increases? [LO2d]
30. What is a lease, and who are the two parties to a lease? [LO1e]
31. Differentiate between an operating lease and a capital lease. [LO1e]
32. Describe the four criteria used in determining the classification of a lease. [LO1e]

## ANALYTICAL QUESTIONS

33. Explain, without using numbers, why earnings per share might be higher when bond financing rather than equity financing is used. [LO1b]
34. Explain the following statement: "There is an inverse relationship between the market interest rate on a bond and its selling price." [LO2a]
35. "Accrued interest is in effect sold when bonds are issued between interest dates." Explain this statement. [LO2a]
36. "How can we justify creating an asset and a liability when capital leases are used? We are not actually purchasing property when we sign a lease." Respond to this question and statement. [LO1e,2e]

## IMPACT ANALYSIS QUESTIONS

*For each error described, indicate whether it would overstate [O], understate [U], or not affect [N] the indicated key figures.*

37. The corporation neglected to amortize $1,200 of bond discount during the current year. [LO2a]

_______ Net Income _______ Total Assets
_______ Total Liabilities _______ Retained Earnings

38. Bonds having a face value of $100,000 were converted to common stock having a total par value of $70,000 during the current year. The bonds were originally issued at their par value, and in the conversion entry a $30,000 gain on conversion was recorded. [LO2b]

_______ Net Income _______ Total Assets
_______ Total Liabilities _______ Total Owners' Equity

39. A lease was signed and the accountant concluded that it should be accounted for as an operating lease. However, the entry to record the first lease payment debited the Rent Expense account and credited a short-term liability account. [LO1e,2e]

_______ Net Income _______ Total Assets
_______ Total Liabilities _______ Retained Earnings

40. A lease was signed on the last day of the fiscal year and the accountant concluded that it should be accounted for as a capital lease. However, no entry was made to record the lease. [LO2e]

_______ Net Income _______ Total Assets
_______ Total Liabilities _______ Retained Earnings

## EXERCISES

EXERCISE 16–1 *(Make Computations for Bond Financing and Journal Entries for Issuance of Bonds)* Webb Corporation is considering a bond issue consisting of 500 bonds, each having a face value of $1,000.

Required:

1. Determine how much cash Webb will be able to borrow if the bonds are sold at their par value. Prepare the entry to record the bond issue.
2. Determine how much cash Webb will be able to borrow if the bonds are sold at 96% of their par value. Prepare the entry to record the bond issue.
3. Determine how much cash Webb will be able to borrow if the bonds are sold at 102% of their par value. Prepare the entry to record the bond issue. [LO2a]

EXERCISE 16–2 *(Prepare Journal Entries for Issuance of Bonds between Interest Payment Dates)* Austin Corporation issued $300,000 of 10-year, 12% debenture bonds on April 1, 19X5, at their face value plus accrued interest. Interest is payable on February 1 and August 1 of each year. Austin had a calendar year-end.

Required:

1. Prepare journal entries to record the following:
   a. Issuance of the bonds on April 1.
   b. First semiannual interest payment on August 1.
   c. Accrued interest on December 31.
   d. Second semiannual interest payment on February 1.
2. Compute the total bond interest expense for 19X5 and 19X6. [LO2a]

EXERCISE 16–3 *(Perform Accounting for Bonds Sold at a Discount—Straight-Line Method of Amortization)* On April 1, 19X5, Dateright Corporation issued $400,000, 9%, 10-year bonds for $390,640. The bonds are dated April 1, 19X5, and pay semiannual interest on April 1 and October 1. The company has a calendar year-end and uses the straight-line method to amortize the bond discount.

Required:

1. Prepare journal entries to record the following:
   a. Issuance of the bonds on April 1, 19X5.

b. Semiannual interest payment and the amortization of the discount on October 1, 19X5.

c. Accrual of bond interest and the amortization of the discount on December 31, 19X5.

2. Compute the amount of bond interest expense recorded in 19X5.
3. Compute the carrying value of the bonds on December 31, 19X5, and show how the bonds would be reported in Dateright's balance sheet on that date. [LO2a]

EXERCISE 16–4 *(Perform Accounting for Bonds Sold at a Premium—Straight-Line Method of Amortization)* On March 1, 19X5, Liteway Corporation issued $200,000, 12%, 10-year bonds for $204,800. The bonds are dated March 1, 19X5, and pay semiannual interest on March 1 and September 1. The company has a calendar year-end and uses the straight-line method to amortize the bond premium.

Required:

1. Prepare journal entries to record the following:
   a. Issuance of the bonds on March 1, 19X5.
   b. Semiannual interest payment and the amortization of the premium on September 1, 19X5.
   c. Accrual of bond interest and the amortization of the premium on December 31, 19X5.
2. Compute the amount of bond interest expense recorded in 19X5.
3. Compute the carrying value of the bonds on December 31, 19X5, and show how the bonds would be reported in Liteway's balance sheet on that date. [LO2a]

EXERCISE 16–5 *(Perform Computational Analysis on Bond Transactions)* Freehold Corporation issued $400,000 of 9% bonds on March 1, 19X5. The bonds pay interest on March 1 and September 1 of each year and mature ten years after their issuance date.

Required:

Based upon the data given, complete the table below for each of the three independent cases (Freehold uses the straight-line method to amortize bond discounts and premiums):

Case A: The bonds are issued at par

Case B: The bonds are issued at 102

Case C: The bonds are issued at 96 [LO2a]

| | CASE A | CASE B | CASE C |
|---|---|---|---|
| 1. Cash received on issuance date | _____ | _____ | _____ |
| 2. Total cash paid to bondholders through maturity date | _____ | _____ | _____ |
| 3. Total cost of borrowing over the life of the bond issue | _____ | _____ | _____ |
| 4. Bond interest expense reported for the year ended December 31, 19X5 | _____ | _____ | _____ |
| 5. Unamortized bond premium as of December 31, 19X5 | _____ | _____ | _____ |
| 6. Unamortized bond discount as of December 31, 19X5 | _____ | _____ | _____ |
| 7. Carrying value of bond liability as of December 31, 19X5 | _____ | _____ | _____ |

EXERCISE 16–6 *(Account for Bond Retirement Before Maturity by Paying Call Price)* Confort Corporation issued $600,000, 10%, 12-year callable debenture bonds on January 1, 19X0, for $588,000. Interest is payable semiannually on June 30 and December 31. Confort Corporation uses the straight-line method to amortize bond premiums and discounts. On July 1, 19X6, the bonds were called at 105 and retired.

Required:

1. Prepare the journal entry to record the interest payment and the amortization of the discount on June 30, 19X6.
2. Compute the amount of the unamortized bond discount as of the call date, and prepare the entry to record the retirement of the bonds on July 1, 19X6.
3. Give the reason or reasons why the company would choose to exercise its call option. [LO2a,2b]

EXERCISE 16–7 *(Record and Explain Bond Conversion)* Host Corporation has $500,000 of 8% convertible bonds outstanding. Each $1,000 bond is convertible into 30 shares of the company's $20 par value common stock. On July 1, 19X5, after an entry was made to record payment of the semiannual interest on the bonds and the amortization of the bond discount, all of the bonds were converted. The remaining balance in the Discount on Bonds Payable account on that date was $42,000.

Required:

1. Prepare the journal entry to record the conversion of the bonds.
2. Give the reason or reasons why convertible bonds are attractive investments. [LO2b]

EXERCISE 16–8 *(Perform Accounting for a Bond Sinking Fund)* On January 1, 19X0, Burnside Corporation issued $400,000, 11%, 5-year bonds at their face value. The bond agreement requires the corporation to make a deposit of an equal dollar amount to a fund on each December 31 for the next five years. The fund's investments are expected to earn a 10% return, and therefore the annual deposits will be $65,519.

Required:

Prepare journal entries to record the following:

1. The first deposit in the fund on December 31, 19X0.
2. The interest revenue earned on fund investments during 19X1 and 19X2. Assume that the 10% return on fund investments was achieved and that the entries are made on December 31 of each year.
3. The retirement of the bonds at maturity using the money accumulated in the fund. [LO2c]

EXERCISE 16–9 *(Prepare Schedule and Entry for Mortgage Notes Payable)* On March 1, 19X5, Riverfront Company purchased a building for $400,000. The purchase agreement called for (1) a cash down payment equal to 10% of the building's cost and (2) the signing of a 12% mortgage note with monthly payments of $5,000.

Required:

1. Prepare a schedule showing the monthly payment, the interest expense for the month, the reduction in principal, and the principal balance at the end of the month for the first four months of the note. Monthly payments begin on April 1, 19X5.
2. Prepare a journal entry to record (a) the purchase of the building on March 1, 19X5, and (b) the payment made on May 1, 19X5. [LO2d]

EXERCISE 16–10 *(Discuss and Prepare Entries for Leases)* On January 1, 19X5, Nico Corporation signed a noncancelable lease giving it the exclusive right to use a machine for seven years. The machine has a fair value of $102,228, which is equal to the present value of the future lease payments. The annual lease payment is $20,000 per year for seven years payable on January 1 of each year.

Required:

1. Determine whether the lease is an operating lease or a capital lease, and indicate the reason based upon FASB-established criteria.
2. Prepare the journal entries that Nico Corporation would make during 19X5. Assume an interest rate of 12%. The machine has a useful life of seven years with no salvage value. The company uses the straight-line method to depreciate its machinery. [LO1e,2e]

PROBLEM 16–1 *(Make Computations for Financing Alternatives)* The following items appear in the records of Rand Corporation on the current date.

| | |
|---|---|
| 10%, 15-year bonds payable | $400,000 |
| Common stock, $10 par value, 80,000 shares issued and outstanding | 800,000 |

The company is planning to expand its business activities. To do so, management has the responsibility for raising $500,000. Two alternative proposals are being considered. One consists of selling an additional 20,000 shares of common stock at $25 per share. The other consists of issuing $500,000 of 12% (the prevailing market interest rate), 10-year bonds. The expansion is expected to increase revenues, and as a result, income before bond interest and income taxes is expected to reach $600,000. The company is subject to a 40% income tax rate.

Required:

1. Compute the earnings per share for each of the alternative financing proposals stated above. In doing so, assume that the company will be able to achieve its earnings goal.
2. Discuss at least one advantage of each proposal.
3. Compute the earnings per share for each proposal, assuming the company is only able to achieve $450,000 of income before bond interest and income taxes. [LO1b]

PROBLEM 16–2 *(Perform Accounting for Bonds with Straight-Line Amortization)* Mudd Corporation, which has a fiscal year ending on December 31, issued $600,000, 11%, 10-year bonds on January 1, 1987. The bonds pay interest semiannually on June 30 and December 31. The market rate of interest on the date of issue was 12%.

Required:

1. Determine the price at which the bonds will be issued (round to the nearest dollar).
2. Prepare the journal entry to record the issuance of the bonds.
3. Prepare the journal entry to record the interest payment and related amortization (of the discount or premium) on the first two interest payment dates. The company amortizes premiums and discounts using the straight-line method.
4. Compute the total bond interest expense to be reported in the company's 1987 income statement.
5. Show how the bond liability would be reported in the company's balance sheet on December 31, 1987.
6. Prepare the journal entry to record the retirement of the bonds on their maturity date. [LO2a,2b]

PROBLEM 16–3 *(Perform Accounting for Bonds with Straight-Line and Effective Interest Amortization)* Makeit Corporation issued $400,000, 10%, 5-year bonds on January 1, 1987. The bonds pay interest semiannually on June 30 and December 31. At the time of issue, the prevailing market rate of interest was 12% and the bonds sold for $370,562. (Round all amounts to the nearest dollar.)

Required:

1. Prepare the journal entry to record the issuance of the bonds.
2. Prepare the journal entry to record the interest payment and related discount amortization on June 30, 1987, and December 31, 1989. The straight-line method is used to amortize discounts and premiums.
3. Compute the total bond interest expense to be reported in the company's 1987 income statement when the straight-line method of amortization is used. Assume that the company has a calendar year-end.

4. Prepare the journal entry to record the interest payment and related discount amortization on June 30, 1987, and December 31, 1989. Assume that the effective interest method is used.
5. Compute the total bond interest expense to be reported in the company's 1987 income statement when the effective interest method of amortization is used. [LO2a]

PROBLEM 16–4 *(Perform Accounting for Bonds with Straight-Line and Effective Interest Amortization)* Beneficial Corporation issued $500,000, 14%, 5-year bonds on March 1, 1987. The bonds pay interest semiannually on February 28 and August 31. At the time of issue, the prevailing market rate of interest was 12% and the bonds sold for $536,804. (Round all amounts to the nearest dollar.)

Required:

1. Prepare the journal entry to record the issuance of the bonds.
2. Prepare the journal entry to record the interest payment and related premium amortization on August 31, 1987, and February 28, 1990. The straight-line method is used to amortize discounts and premiums.
3. Compute the total bond interest expense to be reported in the company's year-end income statement dated February 28, 1988, when the straight-line method of amortization is used.
4. Prepare the journal entry to record the interest payment and related amortization on August 31, 1987, and February 28, 1990, assuming the effective interest method is used.
5. Compute the total bond interest expense to be reported in the company's year-end income statement dated February 28, 1988, when the effective interest method of amortization is used. [LO2a]

PROBLEM 16–5 *(Prepare Journal Entries for Bonds Issued between Interest Payment Dates with Retirement Before Maturity)* Halen Corporation received authorization to issue $300,000, 9%, 10-year callable debenture bonds early in 1985. The entire issue was dated March 1, 1985. Interest is payable semiannually on February 28 and August 31.

Required:

Prepare journal entries to record the following transactions and events:

1. The issuance of the bonds at their face value plus accrued interest on May 1, 1985.
2. The semiannual interest paid on August 31, 1985.
3. The accrual of bond interest on December 31, 1985, the company's year-end.
4. The semiannual interest paid on February 28, 1986.
5. The call and retirement on March 1, 1988, of one-half of the outstanding bonds at 103. [LO2a,2b]

PROBLEM 16–6 *(Prepare Journal Entries for Bonds Issued between Interest Payment Dates with Conversion into Common Stock)* Culture Corporation received authorization to issue $600,000, 8%, 10-year convertible bonds early in 1985. The entire issue was dated March 1, 1985. Each $1,000 bond is convertible into 40 shares of the company's $20 par value common stock. Interest is payable semiannually on February 28 and August 31.

Required:

Prepare journal entries to record the following transactions and events:

1. The issuance of the bonds at their face value plus accrued interest on June 1, 1985.
2. The semiannual interest paid on August 31, 1985.
3. The accrual of bond interest on December 31, 1985, the company's year-end.
4. The semiannual interest paid on February 28, 1986.
5. The conversion of $200,000 of the outstanding bonds to common stock on March 1, 1988.
6. The semiannual interest paid on August 31, 1988. [LO2a,2b]

PROBLEM 16–7 *(Answer Questions about and Prepare Journal Entries for Amortization Using the Effective Interest Method)* Forthright Corporation issued $300,000 of five-year bonds on January

1, 1987. Interest is payable semiannually on June 30 and December 31. Other facts pertaining to the issue are reflected in the amortization schedule shown below.

| SEMIANNUAL INTEREST PERIOD | INTEREST EXPENSE | INTEREST TO BE PAID | AMOUNT OF AMORTIZATION | BOND-CARRYING VALUE |
|---|---|---|---|---|
| Issue Date | — | — | — | $323,160 |
| 6/30/87 | $16,158 | $18,000 | $1,842 | 321,318 |
| 12/31/87 | 16,066 | 18,000 | 1,934 | 319,384 |
| 6/30/88 | 15,969 | 18,000 | 2,031 | 317,353 |
| 12/31/88 | 15,868 | 18,000 | 2,132 | 315,221 |
| 6/30/89 | 15,761 | 18,000 | 2,239 | 312,982 |
| 12/31/89 | 15,649 | 18,000 | 2,351 | 310,631 |
| 6/30/90 | 15,532 | 18,000 | 2,468 | 308,163 |
| 12/31/90 | 15,408 | 18,000 | 2,592 | 305,571 |
| 6/30/91 | 15,279 | 18,000 | 2,721 | 302,850 |
| 12/31/91 | 15,150* | 18,000 | 2,850 | 300,000 |

* Rounded.

Required:

1. Answer the following questions:
   a. Were the bonds sold at a premium or at a discount, and how was that determined?
   b. What method of amortization was used, and how was that determined?
   c. What is the stated rate of interest on the bonds? Show calculations.
   d. What is the effective rate of interest on the bonds? Show calculations.
2. Prepare journal entries to record the following:
   a. The sale of the bonds.
   b. The interest payment and amortization on June 30, 1987, and December 31, 1989.
3. Show how the bond liability would be reported in the company's December 31, 1989, balance sheet. [LO2a]

PROBLEM 16–8 *(Prepare Payment Schedule and Journal Entries for Mortgage Notes Payable)* On July 1, 1987, Moonglow Corporation purchased a building and land costing $800,000. Terms of the purchase agreement required Moonglow to make a cash down payment of 10% of the purchase price and sign a mortgage note carrying an interest rate of 15% for the balance. The mortgage note calls for monthly payments of $70,000, with the first payment due on August 1, 1987. The company's fiscal year ends on December 31.

Required:

1. Prepare a monthly payment schedule for the year ended December 31, 1987. Use column headings (as shown in the text) as follows: (1) Payment Date, (2) Principal Balance at Beginning of Month, (3) Monthly Payment, (4) Interest for One Month, (5) Reduction in Principal, and (6) Principal Balance at End of Month.
2. Prepare journal entries to (1) record the purchase on July 1 assigning three-quarters of the total cost to the building and one-quarter of the total cost to land and (2) record the first two monthly payments.
3. Indicate how the liability for the mortgage note payable would be reported on the balance sheet at December 31, 1987. [LO2d]

PROBLEM 16–9 *(Perform Lease Accounting)* On January 1, 1987, Best Company leased a conveyor from Dublin Company by signing a noncancelable ten-year lease. The lease terms call for a cash payment of $6,000 immediately, and cash payments of $6,000 to be made at the end of each year during the ten-year life of the lease. Best Company has the option to purchase the conveyor for $25 at the end of the lease term. The conveyor has been given an estimated useful life of ten years, with no residual value expected. Best uses the straight-line method of depreciation on all of its plant assets, and the market rate of interest is currently 12%. (Round all amounts to the nearest dollar.)

Required:

1. Prepare all the journal entries relating to the lease and the leased asset for 1987 and 1988 that Best Company needs to make.
2. Show the accounts and amounts pertaining to the lease and the leased asset as they would appear on Best's balance sheet on December 31, 1988, and on its income statement for the year ended December 31, 1988.
3. What criteria were met to make you realize that the lease agreement entered into on January 1, 1987, qualified as a capital lease? [LO1e,2e]

PROBLEM 16–10 *(Comprehensive Problem: Effective Interest Amortization and Early Retirement)* Seeclear Corporation issued $500,000, 10%, 5-year callable bonds on January 1, 1986. The bonds, which pay interest on June 30 and December 31 of each year, were issued at a price to yield 12%.

On July 1, 1989, one-half of the bond issue was called at 102 and the bonds were retired.

Required:

1. Compute the issue price of the bonds.
2. Prepare journal entries to record the following:
   a. The sale of the bonds on January 1, 1986.
   b. The interest payment and the amortization of the premium or discount on June 30, 1987, and December 31, 1988. The company uses the effective interest method to amortize both bond premiums and bond discounts.
   c. The retirement of one-half of the bond issue on July 1, 1989.
   d. The interest payment and the amortization of the premium or discount on December 31, 1989, and June 30, 1990.
   e. The payment of the remaining bond liability at maturity.
3. Show how the bond liability would be reported in the company's December 31, 1989, balance sheet.
4. Answer the following questions:
   a. What amount of bond interest expense is reported in 1986?
   b. What amount of bond interest expense is reported in 1990?
   c. What is the carrying value of the bonds on December 31, 1989?
   d. Would using the straight-line method of amortization result in the reporting of more or less bond interest expense in 1986 than that reported under the effective interest method? Explain.
   e. Would the total bond interest expense reported over the life of the bonds using the effective interest method be the same as, more than, or less than the amount reported under the straight-line method? Explain. [LO2a,2b]

## ALTERNATE PROBLEMS

PROBLEM 16–1A *(Make Computations for Financing Alternatives)* (Alternate to Problem 16–1) The following items appear in the records of Steurt Corporation on the current date.

| | |
|---|---|
| 12%, 15-year bonds payable | $200,000 |
| Common stock, $5 par value, 100,000 shares issued and outstanding | 500,000 |

The company is planning an expansion program estimated to have a cost of $600,000. Two alternative financing proposals are being considered. One involves selling an additional 50,000 shares of common stock at $12 per share. The other involves the issuing of $600,000 of eight-year callable bonds that will carry the current market rate of interest of 16%. Management expects the expansion program to increase revenues significantly, and it projects that income before bond interest and income taxes will reach $380,000. The company's income tax rate is 40%.

Required:

1. Compute the earnings per share for each of the alternative financing proposals stated above. In doing so, assume that the company will be able to achieve its earnings goal.
2. Discuss at least one advantage of each proposal.
3. Compute the earnings per share for each proposal, assuming the company is only able to achieve $300,000 of income before bond interest and income taxes. [LO1b]

PROBLEM 16–2A *(Perform Accounting for Bonds with Straight-Line Amortization)* (Alternate to Problem 16–2) Essex Corporation, which has a fiscal year ending on December 31, issued $300,000, 15%, 10-year bonds on January 1, 1987. The bonds pay interest semiannually on June 30 and December 31. The market rate of interest on the date of issue was 16%.

Required:

1. Determine the price at which the bonds will be issued (round to the nearest dollar).
2. Prepare the journal entry to record the issuance of the bonds.
3. Prepare the journal entry to record the interest payment and related amortization (of the discount or premium) on the first two interest payment dates. The company amortizes premiums and discounts using the straight-line method.
4. Compute the total bond interest expense to be reported in the company's 1987 income statement.
5. Show how the bond liability would be reported in the company's balance sheet on December 31, 1987.
6. Prepare the journal entry to record the retirement of the bonds on their maturity date. [LO2a,2b]

PROBLEM 16–3A *(Perform Accounting for Bonds with Straight-Line and Effective Interest Amortization)* (Alternate to Problem 16–4) Atrium Corporation issued $400,000, 15%, 5-year bonds on May 1, 1987. The bonds pay interest semiannually on April 30 and October 31. At the time of issue, the market rate of interest was 12%. (Round amounts to nearest dollar.)

Required:

1. Compute the issue price of the bonds.
2. Prepare the journal entry to record the issuance of the bonds.
3. Prepare the journal entry to record the interest payment and related amortization on October 31, 1987, and April 30, 1990. Assume that the company uses the straight-line method to amortize bond premiums and bond discounts.
4. Compute the total bond interest expense to be reported in the company's April 30, 1988, fiscal year-end income statement when the straight-line method of amortization is used.
5. Prepare the journal entry to record the interest payment and related amortization on October 31, 1987, and April 30, 1990. Assume that the effective interest method is used.
6. Compute the total bond interest expense to be reported in the company's April 30, 1988, fiscal year-end income statement when the effective interest method of amortization is used. [LO2a]

PROBLEM 16–4A *(Prepare Journal Entries for Bonds Issued between Interest Payment Dates with Conversion into Common Stock)* (Alternate to Problem 16–6) Stay-Rite Corporation received authorization to issue $800,000, 10%, 15-year convertible bonds early in 1983. The entire issue was dated February 1, 1983. Each $1,000 bond is convertible into 50 shares of the company's $12 par value common stock. Interest is payable semiannually on January 31 and July 31.

Required:

Prepare journal entries to record the following transactions and events:

1. The issuance of the bonds at their face value plus accrued interest on May 1, 1983.

2. The semiannual interest paid on July 31, 1983.
3. The accrual of bond interest on December 31, 1983, the company's year-end.
4. The semiannual interest paid on January 31, 1984.
5. The conversion of $200,000 of the outstanding bonds to common stock on February 1, 1989.
6. The semiannual interest paid on July 31, 1989. [LO2a,2b]

PROBLEM 16-5A *(Perform Lease Accounting)* (Alternate to Problem 16-9) On January 1, 1987, Dew-All Company leased a warehouse from Stayfit Company by signing a noncancelable fifteen-year lease. The lease terms call for a cash payment of $50,000 immediately, and cash payments of $50,000 to be made at the end of each year during the fifteen-year term of the lease. Dew-All Company has the option to purchase the warehouse at a bargain price at the end of the lease term. The warehouse has been given an estimated useful life of twenty years, after which no residual value is expected. Dew-All uses the straight-line method of depreciation on all of its plant assets. The market rate of interest was 10% at the time the lease was signed. (Round all amounts to the nearest dollar.)

Required:
1. Prepare all journal entries relating to the lease and the leased asset for 1987 and 1988 that Dew-All Company needs to make.
2. Show the accounts and amounts pertaining to the lease and the leased asset as they would appear on Dew-All's balance sheet on December 31, 1988, and on its income statement for the year ended December 31, 1988.
3. What criteria were met to make you realize that the lease agreement entered into on January 1, 1987, qualified as a capital lease? [LO1e,2e]

# APPENDIX TO CHAPTER 16

## The Present and Future Value of Money

The concepts of present and future values are based on the time value of money, which can be stated as follows: A dollar received today is worth more than a dollar to be received at, say, a year from today because money has a time value. Money has a time value because of its earning potential. The dollar received today can be invested to earn interest so that it will increase in value to more than one dollar in the future.[1]

The time value of money can be illustrated further by this simple example: If you were offered a choice of receiving $5,000 today or $5,000 one year from today, which offer would you accept? Of course you would choose to receive the $5,000 today. Why? Aside from the fact that you could spend it, you could invest the $5,000 to earn interest for a year and have more than $5,000 a year from today. If the money were invested at a modest annual interest rate of 6%, the $5,000 received today would be equal in value to $5,300 [$5,000 + (6% × $5,000) = $5,300] received one year from today.

In our example the $5,000 to be invested today is called the *present value.* Present value is the amount that an investor must invest now, at a given interest rate, to obtain a specified amount on a future date. Returning to our example, we know that $5,300 is the amount of money that will be available one year from today and that money is worth 6%. Therefore the present value of the $5,300 to be received one year from today is $5,000. Or put another way, today's $5,000

[1] Because of inflation and interest, current dollars are worth more than dollars to be received in the future. At this time our discussion of present and future values will be limited to the effect of interest. The discussion of inflation will be left to a future chapter.

has a future value of $5,300 one year from today. *Future value* is the amount that an investment will be worth at a specified future time if invested at a specific interest rate. Thus, to achieve a future value of $5,300, a present value of $5,000 must be invested for one year at an interest rate of 6%.

Let us try another example. Assume this time that we owe $50,000 that must be paid ten years from today. To know how much should be invested today to have the $50,000 needed to pay the debt in ten years if the invested money is expected to earn 8% interest compounded annually, we must determine the present value of the $50,000 amount. The present value of any amount, for any period of time, at any interest rate, can be determined by using a formula (as shown at the top of Table 16–3, page 600) or by using Table 16–3 itself. The table shows amounts, called *factors*, for various interest rates and for a number of different interest periods based on the present value of $1. The factor found in Table 16–3 under the 8% column for ten interest periods is 0.4632. Multiplying that amount by $50,000 establishes that the present value of the $50,000 debt is $23,160, which is the amount that should be invested today:

Amount to be invested, *or* Present value of $50,000 debt
= $50,000 × 0.4632, or $23,160

The difference between the amount of the debt and its present value is interest ($26,840 in this case).

As we continue with other illustrations, keep in mind that the time value of money concept is based on the cost of using someone else's money or the earnings that can be obtained by investing money. The cost that must be paid to use someone else's money is called *interest expense.* The amount that can be earned by investing money is called *interest revenue.*

We have already determined that the difference between present and future values is dependent on three factors: (1) the amount of the principal, (2) the interest rate, and (3) the time period.

Because the time value of money calculations are usually based on compound interest, a brief review of the principles of compound interest follows.

*Compound interest* is interest computed on both the amount of the original investment (principal) and all previously earned interest. To illustrate, assume that $1,000 is invested at 8% interest for four years and that interest is compounded annually. The computation of the interest totaling $360.49 for the four-year period is shown in the schedule below.

| (A) YEAR | (B) BEGINNING AMOUNT | (C) COMPOUND INTEREST (B) × (.08) | (D) ENDING AMOUNT |
|---|---|---|---|
| 1 | $1,000.00 | $ 80.00 | $1,080.00 |
| 2 | 1,080.00 | 86.40 | 1,166.40 |
| 3 | 1,166.40 | 93.31 | 1,259.71 |
| 4 | 1,259.71 | 100.78 | 1,360.49 |
| Total | | $360.49 | |

In computing compound interest, the amount accumulated at the end of each period is the amount used to calculate the interest earned in the following period.

Companies often invest money and borrow money on a long-term basis. This makes the concept of compound interest a major consideration when decisions are made.

To help us better understand present and future value concepts, we must consider four concepts:

1. Future value of an amount
2. Future value of an annuity (an *annuity* is a series of equal deposits or payments)
3. Present value of an amount
4. Present value of an annuity

All four concepts use a dollar as the single amount. This is because mathematical tables have been developed that show various interest rates for various time periods based on $1. Once the factor for a dollar is found in the appropriate table, the value of that factor can be used to determine the effect of any number of dollars.

## FUTURE VALUE OF AN AMOUNT

The future value of an amount is the dollar figure to which that amount will increase if it is invested for a certain number of periods at a specified interest rate. A dollar, or any other single amount of money, invested today will have a higher future value than the amount originally invested because interest will be earned. The future value of a single amount invested today can be computed by a formula:

$$FV = P(1 + i)^n$$

where

$FV$ = Future value of the amount invested
$P$ = Amount invested (often called the principal or the present value)
$i$ = Interest rate per period (the compounding period is often annual but may be semiannual, quarterly, monthly, or even daily)
$n$ = Number of periods

To illustrate the use of the future value formula with annual compounding, assume that $1,000 is invested at 12% interest for four years. The future value of the $1,000 is determined as follows:

$$\begin{aligned} FV &= \$1{,}000(1 + .12)^4 \\ &= \$1{,}000(1.12)(1.12)(1.12)(1.12) \\ &= \$1{,}573.52 \end{aligned}$$

If the $1,000 were invested for four years with interest at 12% compounded semiannually, the interest rate and the number of periods used in the future value formula would be changed to 6% and eight periods, respectively. The number of years (4) is multiplied by the number of compounding periods per year (2), giving eight periods. The annual interest rate (of 12%) is divided by the number of times compounding takes place within a year (2), giving 6%. The future value of the $1,000 in this case is $1,593.85, determined as follows:

$$\begin{aligned} FV &= \$1{,}000(1 + .06)^8 \\ &= \$1{,}593.85 \end{aligned}$$

Although the availability and wide use of hand calculators make the formula method of calculation quite simple, tables have been developed to further simplify the calculation. Table 16–1 on page 598 shows the future value of $1 for various interest rates and various time periods. Using the table to find the future value of $1,000 invested for four years at 12% interest compounded semiannually, we do the following: (1) locate the appropriate number of compounding periods (eight in this example) in the left column of the table, (2) read across to the appropriate interest rate column (6% in this example) to find the factor, and (3) multiply the amount invested by this decimal factor. Thus, using the table, the future value of $1,000 invested for four years at 12% interest compounded semiannually is $1,593.80 ($1,000 × 1.5938).

There is a slight difference between the amount obtained by formula and the amount obtained by using the table ($.05) because the decimal factor in the table was carried to only four places.

Practice using the table by trying one more example. Assume that we wanted to know how much $10,000 invested today at 8% interest compounded annually would be worth five years from today. The decimal factor found in the 8% column and 5-period row of Table 16–1 is 1.4693. Thus the $10,000 invested today would be worth $14,693 ($10,000 × 1.4693 = $14,693) five years from today because of the compound interest earned.

## FUTURE VALUE OF AN ANNUITY

An *annuity* is a series of equal deposits or payments made at the end of successive equal time periods. In calculating the future value of an annuity, we again use the compounding of interest. The future value of an annuity is the sum of all the deposits or payments plus the compound interest accumulated on each deposit or payment. For example, assume that $1,000 is invested at the end of each year for three years, with each deposit earning 10% interest compounded annually. The future value of the annuity can be determined by using this formula:

$$FV = A\left[\frac{(1+i)^n - 1}{i}\right]$$

where

$FV$ = Future value of an annuity
$A$ = Periodic amount invested or paid each period
$i$ = Interest rate per period
$n$ = Number of periods

Thus the future value of the annuity is $3,310, as determined below:

$$\begin{aligned} FV &= \$1{,}000\left[\frac{(1+.10)^3 - 1}{.10}\right] \\ &= \$1{,}000(3.31) \\ &= \$3{,}310.00 \end{aligned}$$

The same amount can be obtained by referring to Table 16–2 on page 599. The future value factor for 10% interest for three periods in Table 16–2 is 3.3100. This is the factor for three deposits or payments of $1 at 10% interest compounded annually. Thus the future value of the deposits made is $3,310.00 ($1,000 × 3.3100).

## PRESENT VALUE OF AN AMOUNT

The **present value of an amount** is the value today of an amount to be received or paid sometime in the future. Present value is the reciprocal of *future value*. Consequently, the present value of a given amount to be received or paid sometime in the future will be less than its future value. For example, assume that Julie Warner needs \$10,000 in three years. To determine how much should be invested today to accumulate to that amount in three years at an interest rate of 8% compounded annually, we can use this formula:

$$PV = FA\left[\frac{1}{(1+i)^n}\right]$$

where

$PV$ = Present value
$FA$ = Future amount
$i$ = Interest rate per period
$n$ = Number of periods

Applying the formula, we determine as shown below that \$7,938.32 is the amount that must be invested now to have the \$10,000 three years from now:

$$\begin{aligned} PV &= \$10{,}000\left[\frac{1}{(1+.08)^3}\right] \\ &= \$10{,}000(0.793832) \\ &= \$\ 7{,}938.32 \end{aligned}$$

Table 16–3 on page 600 shows the present value factors for the present value of \$1. Using this table, we find the factor of 0.7938 in the 8% column and 3-period row. Thus \$10,000 × 0.7938 is \$7,938.00 (the \$.32 difference in results is due to rounding).

## PRESENT VALUE OF AN ANNUITY

The **present value of an annuity** is the amount that would have to be invested today at a certain compound interest rate to enable the investor to receive a desired amount in a series of equal future payments over a specified time period.

For example, assume that we wanted to know how much a person must invest now if he or she wished to receive \$1,000 at the end of each year for the next five years. Given an interest rate of 10% compounded annually, the amount that must be invested now can be determined by the following formula:

$$PV = A\left[\frac{1-\frac{1}{(1+i)^n}}{i}\right]$$

where

$PV$ = Present value of an annuity
$A$ = Periodic amount to be invested or paid in each period
$i$ = Interest rate per period
$n$ = Number of periods

Using the formula, we determine that the amount that must be invested now is \$3,790.79 as follows:

$$\begin{aligned} PV &= \$1{,}000\left[\frac{1-\frac{1}{(1+.10)^5}}{.10}\right] \\ &= \$1{,}000\left[\frac{1-0.6209213}{.10}\right] \\ &= \$1{,}000(3.790787) \\ &= \$3{,}790.79 \end{aligned}$$

Using Table 16–4 on page 601, we look in the 10% column and 5-period row and find the factor 3.7908, which when multiplied by $1,000 gives us essentially the same result, or $3,790.80.

## EXERCISES FOR APPENDIX

EXERCISE A16–1 *(Determine the Future Value of an Amount)* For each of the following, determine the future value of the amount invested:

1. $5,000 to be invested for 5 years at 10% interest compounded annually
2. $5,000 to be invested for 5 years at 10% interest compounded semiannually
3. $5,000 to be invested for 5 years at 8% interest compounded quarterly

EXERCISE A16–2 *(Determine the Future Value of an Annuity)* For each of the following, determine the future value of an annuity:

1. $5,000 to be invested at the end of each year for 10 years at 8% compounded annually
2. $1,250 to be invested at the end of each 3-month period for 5 years at 8% compounded quarterly
3. $2,500 to be invested at the end of each 6 months for 10 years at 8% compounded semiannually

EXERCISE A16–3 *(Determine the Present Value of an Amount)* For each of the following, determine the present value of the amount to be received:

1. $10,000 to be received in 10 years at 10% interest compounded annually
2. $10,000 to be received in 5 years at 8% interest compounded quarterly
3. $8,000 to be received in 10 years at 12% interest compounded semiannually

EXERCISE A16–4 *(Determine the Present Value of an Annuity)* For each of the following, determine the present value of an annuity:

1. $3,000 to be paid at the end of each year for 5 years, assuming interest of 8% compounded annually
2. $3,000 to be paid at the end of each 3-months for 5 years, assuming interest of 8% compounded quarterly
3. $4,000 to be paid at the end of each 6 months for 5 years, assuming interest of 12% compounded semiannually

*TABLE 16–1*

**Future Value of a Dollar**

$FV = P(1+i)^n$

| PERIODS | 2% | 2.5% | 3% | 4% | 4.5% | 5% | 5.5% | 6% | 8% | 10% | 12% | 16% |
|---|---|---|---|---|---|---|---|---|---|---|---|---|
| 1 | 1.0200 | 1.0250 | 1.0300 | 1.0400 | 1.0450 | 1.0500 | 1.0550 | 1.0600 | 1.0800 | 1.1000 | 1.1200 | 1.1600 |
| 2 | 1.0404 | 1.0506 | 1.0609 | 1.0816 | 1.0920 | 1.1025 | 1.1130 | 1.1236 | 1.1664 | 1.2100 | 1.2544 | 1.3456 |
| 3 | 1.0612 | 1.0769 | 1.0927 | 1.1249 | 1.1411 | 1.1576 | 1.1742 | 1.1910 | 1.2597 | 1.3310 | 1.4049 | 1.5609 |
| 4 | 1.0824 | 1.1038 | 1.1255 | 1.1699 | 1.1925 | 1.2155 | 1.2388 | 1.2625 | 1.3605 | 1.4641 | 1.5735 | 1.8106 |
| 5 | 1.1041 | 1.1314 | 1.1593 | 1.2167 | 1.2461 | 1.2763 | 1.3069 | 1.3382 | 1.4693 | 1.6105 | 1.7623 | 2.1003 |
| 6 | 1.1262 | 1.1597 | 1.1941 | 1.2653 | 1.3022 | 1.3401 | 1.3788 | 1.4185 | 1.5869 | 1.7716 | 1.9738 | 2.4364 |
| 7 | 1.1487 | 1.1887 | 1.2299 | 1.3159 | 1.3608 | 1.4071 | 1.4547 | 1.5036 | 1.7138 | 1.9487 | 2.2107 | 2.8262 |
| 8 | 1.1717 | 1.2184 | 1.2668 | 1.3686 | 1.4221 | 1.4775 | 1.5347 | 1.5938 | 1.8509 | 2.1436 | 2.4760 | 3.2784 |
| 9 | 1.1951 | 1.2489 | 1.3048 | 1.4233 | 1.4861 | 1.5513 | 1.6191 | 1.6895 | 1.9990 | 2.3579 | 2.7731 | 3.8030 |
| 10 | 1.2190 | 1.2801 | 1.3439 | 1.4802 | 1.5529 | 1.6289 | 1.7081 | 1.7908 | 2.1589 | 2.5937 | 3.1058 | 4.4114 |
| 11 | 1.2434 | 1.3121 | 1.3842 | 1.5395 | 1.6229 | 1.7103 | 1.8021 | 1.8983 | 2.3316 | 2.8531 | 3.4785 | 5.1173 |
| 12 | 1.2682 | 1.3449 | 1.4258 | 1.6010 | 1.6959 | 1.7959 | 1.9012 | 2.0122 | 2.5182 | 3.1384 | 3.8960 | 5.9360 |
| 13 | 1.2936 | 1.3785 | 1.4685 | 1.6651 | 1.7722 | 1.8856 | 2.0058 | 2.1329 | 2.7196 | 3.4523 | 4.3635 | 6.8858 |
| 14 | 1.3195 | 1.4130 | 1.5126 | 1.7317 | 1.8519 | 1.9799 | 2.1161 | 2.2609 | 2.9372 | 3.7975 | 4.8871 | 7.9875 |
| 15 | 1.3459 | 1.4483 | 1.5580 | 1.8009 | 1.8353 | 2.0789 | 2.2325 | 2.3966 | 3.1722 | 4.1772 | 5.4736 | 9.2655 |
| 16 | 1.3728 | 1.4845 | 1.6047 | 1.8730 | 2.0224 | 2.1829 | 2.3553 | 2.5404 | 3.4259 | 4.5950 | 6.1304 | 10.7480 |
| 17 | 1.4002 | 1.5216 | 1.6528 | 1.9479 | 2.1134 | 2.2920 | 2.4848 | 2.6928 | 3.7000 | 5.0545 | 6.8660 | 12.4677 |
| 18 | 1.4282 | 1.5597 | 1.7024 | 2.0258 | 2.2085 | 2.4066 | 2.6215 | 2.8543 | 3.9960 | 5.5599 | 7.6900 | 14.4625 |
| 19 | 1.4568 | 1.5987 | 1.7535 | 2.1068 | 2.3079 | 2.5270 | 2.7656 | 3.0256 | 4.3157 | 6.1159 | 8.6128 | 16.7765 |
| 20 | 1.4859 | 1.6386 | 1.8061 | 2.1911 | 2.4117 | 2.6533 | 2.9178 | 3.2071 | 4.6610 | 6.7275 | 9.6463 | 19.4608 |
| 21 | 1.5157 | 1.6796 | 1.8603 | 2.2788 | 2.5202 | 2.7860 | 3.0782 | 3.3996 | 5.0338 | 7.4002 | 10.8038 | 22.5745 |
| 22 | 1.5460 | 1.7216 | 1.9161 | 2.3699 | 2.6337 | 2.9253 | 3.2475 | 3.6035 | 5.4365 | 8.1403 | 12.1003 | 26.1864 |
| 23 | 1.5769 | 1.7646 | 1.9736 | 2.4647 | 2.7522 | 3.0715 | 3.4262 | 3.8197 | 5.8715 | 8.9543 | 13.5523 | 30.3762 |
| 24 | 1.6084 | 1.8087 | 2.0328 | 2.5633 | 2.8760 | 3.2251 | 3.6146 | 4.0489 | 6.3412 | 9.8497 | 15.1786 | 35.2364 |
| 25 | 1.6406 | 1.8539 | 2.0938 | 2.6658 | 3.0054 | 3.3864 | 3.8134 | 4.2919 | 6.8485 | 10.8347 | 17.0001 | 40.8742 |
| 30 | 1.8114 | 2.0976 | 2.4273 | 3.2434 | 3.7453 | 4.3219 | 4.9840 | 5.7435 | 10.0627 | 17.4494 | 29.9599 | 85.8499 |

*TABLE 16–2*

Future Value of an Annuity of a Dollar

$$FV = A\left[\frac{(1+i)^n - 1}{i}\right]$$

| PERIODS | 2% | 2.5% | 3% | 4% | 4.5% | 5% | 5.5% | 6% | 8% | 10% | 12% | 16% |
|---|---|---|---|---|---|---|---|---|---|---|---|---|
| 1 | 1.0000 | 1.0000 | 1.0000 | 1.0000 | 1.0000 | 1.0000 | 1.0000 | 1.0000 | 1.0000 | 1.0000 | 1.0000 | 1.0000 |
| 2 | 2.0200 | 2.0250 | 2.0300 | 2.0400 | 2.0450 | 2.0500 | 2.0550 | 2.0600 | 2.0800 | 2.1000 | 2.1200 | 2.1600 |
| 3 | 3.0604 | 3.0756 | 3.0909 | 3.1216 | 3.1370 | 3.1525 | 3.1680 | 3.1836 | 3.2464 | 3.3100 | 3.3744 | 3.5056 |
| 4 | 4.1216 | 4.1525 | 4.1836 | 4.2465 | 4.2782 | 4.3101 | 4.3423 | 4.3746 | 4.5061 | 4.6410 | 4.7793 | 5.0665 |
| 5 | 5.2040 | 5.2563 | 5.3091 | 5.4163 | 5.4707 | 5.5256 | 5.5811 | 5.6371 | 5.8666 | 6.1051 | 6.3528 | 6.8771 |
| 6 | 6.3081 | 6.3877 | 6.4684 | 6.6330 | 6.7169 | 6.8019 | 6.8881 | 6.9753 | 7.3359 | 7.7156 | 8.1152 | 8.9775 |
| 7 | 7.4343 | 7.5474 | 7.6625 | 7.8983 | 8.0192 | 8.1420 | 8.2669 | 8.3938 | 8.9228 | 9.4872 | 10.0890 | 11.4139 |
| 8 | 8.5830 | 8.7361 | 8.8923 | 9.2142 | 9.3800 | 9.5491 | 9.7216 | 9.8975 | 10.6366 | 11.4359 | 12.2997 | 14.2401 |
| 9 | 9.7546 | 9.9545 | 10.1591 | 10.5828 | 10.8021 | 11.0266 | 11.2563 | 11.4913 | 12.4876 | 13.5795 | 14.7757 | 17.5185 |
| 10 | 10.9497 | 11.2034 | 11.4639 | 12.0061 | 12.2882 | 12.5779 | 12.8754 | 13.1808 | 14.4866 | 15.9374 | 17.5487 | 21.3215 |
| 11 | 12.1687 | 12.4835 | 12.8078 | 13.4864 | 13.8412 | 14.2068 | 14.5835 | 14.9716 | 16.6455 | 18.5312 | 20.6546 | 25.7329 |
| 12 | 13.4121 | 13.7956 | 14.1920 | 15.0258 | 15.4640 | 15.9171 | 16.3856 | 16.8699 | 18.9771 | 21.3843 | 24.1331 | 30.8502 |
| 13 | 14.6803 | 15.1404 | 15.6178 | 16.6268 | 17.1599 | 17.7130 | 18.2868 | 18.8821 | 21.4953 | 24.5227 | 28.0291 | 36.7862 |
| 14 | 15.9739 | 16.5190 | 17.0863 | 18.2919 | 18.9321 | 19.5986 | 20.2926 | 21.0151 | 24.2149 | 27.9750 | 32.3926 | 43.6720 |
| 15 | 17.2934 | 17.9319 | 18.5989 | 20.0236 | 20.7841 | 21.5786 | 22.4087 | 23.2760 | 27.1521 | 31.7725 | 37.2797 | 51.6595 |
| 16 | 18.6393 | 19.3802 | 20.1569 | 21.8245 | 22.7193 | 23.6575 | 24.6411 | 25.6725 | 30.3243 | 35.9497 | 42.7533 | 60.9250 |
| 17 | 20.0121 | 20.8647 | 21.7616 | 23.6975 | 24.7417 | 25.8404 | 26.9964 | 28.2129 | 33.7502 | 40.5447 | 48.8837 | 71.6730 |
| 18 | 21.4123 | 22.3863 | 23.4144 | 25.6454 | 26.8550 | 28.1324 | 29.4812 | 30.9057 | 37.4502 | 45.5992 | 55.7497 | 84.1407 |
| 19 | 22.8406 | 23.9460 | 25.1169 | 27.6712 | 29.0636 | 30.5390 | 32.1027 | 33.7600 | 41.4463 | 51.1591 | 63.4397 | 98.6032 |
| 20 | 24.2974 | 25.5447 | 26.8704 | 29.7781 | 31.3714 | 33.0660 | 34.8683 | 36.7856 | 45.7620 | 57.2750 | 72.0524 | 115.3797 |
| 21 | 25.7833 | 27.1833 | 28.6765 | 31.9692 | 33.7831 | 35.7193 | 37.7861 | 39.9927 | 50.4229 | 64.0025 | 81.6987 | 134.8405 |
| 22 | 27.2990 | 28.8629 | 30.5368 | 34.2480 | 36.3034 | 38.5052 | 40.8643 | 43.3923 | 55.4568 | 71.4027 | 92.5026 | 157.4150 |
| 23 | 28.8450 | 30.5844 | 32.4529 | 36.6179 | 38.9370 | 41.4305 | 44.1118 | 46.9958 | 60.8933 | 79.5430 | 104.6029 | 183.6014 |
| 24 | 30.4219 | 32.3490 | 34.4265 | 39.0826 | 41.6892 | 44.5020 | 47.5380 | 50.8156 | 66.7648 | 88.4973 | 118.1552 | 213.9776 |
| 25 | 32.0303 | 34.1578 | 36.4593 | 41.6459 | 44.5652 | 47.7271 | 51.1526 | 54.8645 | 73.1059 | 98.3471 | 133.3339 | 249.2140 |
| 30 | 40.5681 | 43.9027 | 47.5754 | 56.0849 | 61.0071 | 66.4388 | 72.4355 | 79.0582 | 113.2832 | 164.4940 | 241.3327 | 530.3117 |

*TABLE 16–3*
Present Value of a Dollar

$$PV = FA\left[\frac{1}{(1+i)^n}\right]$$

| PERIODS | 2% | 2.5% | 3% | 4% | 4.5% | 5% | 5.5% | 6% | 8% | 10% | 12% | 16% |
|---|---|---|---|---|---|---|---|---|---|---|---|---|
| 1 | 0.9804 | 0.9756 | 0.9709 | 0.9615 | 0.9569 | 0.9524 | 0.9479 | 0.9434 | 0.9259 | 0.9091 | 0.8929 | 0.8621 |
| 2 | 0.9612 | 0.9518 | 0.9426 | 0.9246 | 0.9157 | 0.9070 | 0.8985 | 0.8900 | 0.8573 | 0.8264 | 0.7922 | 0.7432 |
| 3 | 0.9423 | 0.9286 | 0.9151 | 0.8890 | 0.8763 | 0.8638 | 0.8516 | 0.8396 | 0.7938 | 0.7513 | 0.7118 | 0.6407 |
| 4 | 0.9238 | 0.9060 | 0.8885 | 0.8548 | 0.8386 | 0.8227 | 0.8072 | 0.7921 | 0.7350 | 0.6830 | 0.6355 | 0.5523 |
| 5 | 0.9057 | 0.8839 | 0.8626 | 0.8219 | 0.8025 | 0.7835 | 0.7651 | 0.7473 | 0.6806 | 0.6209 | 0.5674 | 0.4761 |
| 6 | 0.8880 | 0.8623 | 0.8375 | 0.7903 | 0.7679 | 0.7462 | 0.7252 | 0.7050 | 0.6302 | 0.5645 | 0.5066 | 0.4104 |
| 7 | 0.8706 | 0.8413 | 0.8131 | 0.7599 | 0.7348 | 0.7107 | 0.6874 | 0.6651 | 0.5835 | 0.5132 | 0.4523 | 0.3538 |
| 8 | 0.8535 | 0.8207 | 0.7894 | 0.7307 | 0.7032 | 0.6768 | 0.6516 | 0.6274 | 0.5403 | 0.4665 | 0.4039 | 0.3050 |
| 9 | 0.8368 | 0.8007 | 0.7664 | 0.7026 | 0.6729 | 0.6446 | 0.6176 | 0.5919 | 0.5002 | 0.4241 | 0.3606 | 0.2630 |
| 10 | 0.8203 | 0.7812 | 0.7441 | 0.6756 | 0.6439 | 0.6139 | 0.5854 | 0.5584 | 0.4632 | 0.3855 | 0.3220 | 0.2267 |
| 11 | 0.8043 | 0.7621 | 0.7224 | 0.6496 | 0.6162 | 0.5847 | 0.5549 | 0.5268 | 0.4289 | 0.3505 | 0.2875 | 0.1954 |
| 12 | 0.7885 | 0.7436 | 0.7014 | 0.6246 | 0.5897 | 0.5568 | 0.5260 | 0.4970 | 0.3971 | 0.3186 | 0.2567 | 0.1685 |
| 13 | 0.7730 | 0.7254 | 0.6810 | 0.6006 | 0.5643 | 0.5303 | 0.4986 | 0.4688 | 0.3677 | 0.2897 | 0.2292 | 0.1452 |
| 14 | 0.7579 | 0.7077 | 0.6611 | 0.5775 | 0.5340 | 0.5051 | 0.4726 | 0.4423 | 0.3405 | 0.2633 | 0.2046 | 0.1252 |
| 15 | 0.7430 | 0.6905 | 0.6419 | 0.5553 | 0.5167 | 0.4810 | 0.4479 | 0.4173 | 0.3152 | 0.2394 | 0.1827 | 0.1079 |
| 16 | 0.7284 | 0.6736 | 0.6232 | 0.5339 | 0.4945 | 0.4581 | 0.4246 | 0.3936 | 0.2919 | 0.2176 | 0.1631 | 0.0930 |
| 17 | 0.7142 | 0.6572 | 0.6050 | 0.5134 | 0.4732 | 0.4363 | 0.4024 | 0.3714 | 0.2703 | 0.1978 | 0.1456 | 0.0802 |
| 18 | 0.7002 | 0.6412 | 0.5874 | 0.4936 | 0.4528 | 0.4155 | 0.3815 | 0.3503 | 0.2502 | 0.1799 | 0.1300 | 0.0691 |
| 19 | 0.6864 | 0.6255 | 0.5703 | 0.4746 | 0.4333 | 0.3957 | 0.3616 | 0.3305 | 0.2317 | 0.1635 | 0.1161 | 0.0596 |
| 20 | 0.6730 | 0.6103 | 0.5537 | 0.4564 | 0.4146 | 0.3769 | 0.3427 | 0.3118 | 0.2145 | 0.1486 | 0.1037 | 0.0514 |
| 21 | 0.6598 | 0.5954 | 0.5375 | 0.4388 | 0.3968 | 0.3589 | 0.3249 | 0.2942 | 0.1987 | 0.1351 | 0.0926 | 0.0443 |
| 22 | 0.6468 | 0.5809 | 0.5219 | 0.4220 | 0.3797 | 0.3418 | 0.3079 | 0.2775 | 0.1839 | 0.1228 | 0.0826 | 0.0382 |
| 23 | 0.6342 | 0.5667 | 0.5067 | 0.4057 | 0.3634 | 0.3256 | 0.2919 | 0.2618 | 0.1703 | 0.1117 | 0.0738 | 0.0329 |
| 24 | 0.6217 | 0.5529 | 0.4919 | 0.3901 | 0.3477 | 0.3101 | 0.2767 | 0.2470 | 0.1577 | 0.1015 | 0.0659 | 0.0284 |
| 25 | 0.6095 | 0.5394 | 0.4776 | 0.3751 | 0.3327 | 0.2953 | 0.2622 | 0.2330 | 0.1460 | 0.0923 | 0.0588 | 0.0245 |
| 30 | 0.5521 | 0.4767 | 0.4120 | 0.3083 | 0.2670 | 0.2314 | 0.2006 | 0.1741 | 0.0994 | 0.0573 | 0.0334 | 0.0116 |

*TABLE 16–4*

Present Value of an Annuity of a Dollar

$$PV = A\left[\frac{1 - \frac{1}{(1+i)^n}}{i}\right]$$

| PERIODS | 2% | 2.5% | 3% | 4% | 4.5% | 5% | 5.5% | 6% | 8% | 10% | 12% | 16% |
|---|---|---|---|---|---|---|---|---|---|---|---|---|
| 1 | 0.9804 | 0.9756 | 0.9709 | 0.9615 | 0.9569 | 0.9524 | 0.9479 | 0.9434 | 0.9259 | 0.9091 | 0.8929 | 0.8621 |
| 2 | 1.9416 | 1.9274 | 1.9135 | 1.8861 | 1.8727 | 1.8594 | 1.8463 | 1.8334 | 1.7833 | 1.7355 | 1.6901 | 1.6052 |
| 3 | 2.8839 | 2.8560 | 2.8286 | 2.7751 | 2.7490 | 2.7232 | 2.6979 | 2.6730 | 2.5771 | 2.4869 | 2.4018 | 2.2459 |
| 4 | 3.8077 | 3.7620 | 3.7171 | 3.6299 | 3.5875 | 3.5460 | 3.5052 | 3.4651 | 3.3121 | 3.1699 | 3.0373 | 2.7982 |
| 5 | 4.7135 | 4.6458 | 4.5797 | 4.4518 | 4.3900 | 4.3295 | 4.2703 | 4.2124 | 3.9927 | 3.7908 | 3.6048 | 3.2743 |
| 6 | 5.6014 | 5.5081 | 5.4172 | 5.2421 | 5.1579 | 5.0757 | 4.9955 | 4.9173 | 4.6229 | 4.3553 | 4.1114 | 3.6847 |
| 7 | 6.4720 | 6.3494 | 6.2303 | 6.0021 | 5.8927 | 5.7864 | 5.6830 | 5.5824 | 5.2064 | 4.8684 | 4.5638 | 4.0386 |
| 8 | 7.3255 | 7.1701 | 7.0197 | 6.7327 | 6.5959 | 6.4632 | 6.3346 | 6.2098 | 5.7466 | 5.3349 | 4.9676 | 4.3436 |
| 9 | 8.1622 | 7.9709 | 7.7861 | 7.4353 | 7.2688 | 7.1078 | 6.9522 | 6.8017 | 6.2469 | 5.7590 | 5.3282 | 4.6065 |
| 10 | 8.9826 | 8.7521 | 8.5302 | 8.1109 | 7.9127 | 7.7217 | 7.5376 | 7.3601 | 6.7101 | 6.1446 | 5.6502 | 4.8332 |
| 11 | 9.7868 | 9.5142 | 9.2526 | 8.7605 | 8.5289 | 8.3064 | 8.0925 | 7.8869 | 7.1390 | 6.4951 | 5.9377 | 5.0286 |
| 12 | 10.5753 | 10.2578 | 9.9540 | 9.3851 | 9.1186 | 8.8633 | 8.6185 | 8.3838 | 7.5361 | 6.8137 | 6.1944 | 5.1971 |
| 13 | 11.3484 | 10.9332 | 10.6350 | 9.9856 | 9.6829 | 9.3936 | 9.1171 | 8.8527 | 7.9038 | 7.1034 | 6.4235 | 5.3423 |
| 14 | 12.1062 | 11.6909 | 11.2961 | 10.5631 | 10.2228 | 9.8986 | 9.5896 | 9.2950 | 8.2442 | 7.3667 | 6.6282 | 5.4675 |
| 15 | 12.8493 | 12.3814 | 11.9379 | 11.1184 | 10.7395 | 10.3797 | 10.0376 | 9.7122 | 8.5595 | 7.6061 | 6.8109 | 5.5755 |
| 16 | 13.5777 | 13.0550 | 12.5611 | 11.6523 | 11.2340 | 10.8378 | 10.4622 | 10.1059 | 8.8514 | 7.8237 | 6.9740 | 5.6685 |
| 17 | 14.2919 | 13.7122 | 13.1661 | 12.1657 | 11.7072 | 11.2741 | 10.8646 | 10.4773 | 9.1216 | 8.0216 | 7.1196 | 5.7487 |
| 18 | 14.9920 | 14.3534 | 13.7535 | 12.6593 | 12.1560 | 11.6896 | 11.2461 | 10.8276 | 9.3719 | 8.2014 | 7.2497 | 5.8178 |
| 19 | 15.6785 | 14.9789 | 14.3238 | 13.1339 | 12.5933 | 12.0853 | 11.6077 | 11.1581 | 9.6036 | 8.3649 | 7.3658 | 5.8775 |
| 20 | 16.3514 | 15.5892 | 14.8775 | 13.5903 | 13.0080 | 12.4622 | 11.9504 | 11.4699 | 9.8181 | 8.5136 | 7.4694 | 5.9288 |
| 21 | 17.0112 | 16.1845 | 15.4150 | 14.0292 | 13.4047 | 12.8212 | 12.2752 | 11.7641 | 10.0168 | 8.6487 | 7.5620 | 5.9731 |
| 22 | 17.6580 | 16.7654 | 15.9369 | 14.4511 | 13.7844 | 13.1630 | 12.5832 | 12.0416 | 10.2007 | 8.7715 | 7.6446 | 6.0113 |
| 23 | 18.2922 | 17.3321 | 16.4436 | 14.8568 | 14.1478 | 13.4886 | 12.8750 | 12.3034 | 10.3711 | 8.8832 | 7.7184 | 6.0442 |
| 24 | 18.9139 | 17.8850 | 16.9355 | 15.2470 | 14.4955 | 13.7986 | 13.1517 | 12.5504 | 10.5288 | 8.9847 | 7.7843 | 6.0726 |
| 25 | 19.5235 | 18.4244 | 17.4131 | 15.6221 | 14.8282 | 14.0939 | 13.4139 | 12.7834 | 10.6748 | 9.0770 | 7.8431 | 6.0911 |
| 30 | 22.3965 | 20.9303 | 19.6004 | 17.2920 | 16.2869 | 15.3725 | 14.5337 | 13.7648 | 11.2578 | 9.4269 | 8.0552 | 6.1772 |

# 17 Investments in Corporate Securities

### *Learning Objectives*

When you complete Part A of this chapter you will be able to

A1. Answer the following questions:
   a. What criteria are used to differentiate between temporary and long-term investments?
   b. What two methods are used to account for long-term investments in common stock? How do these methods differ?

A2. Perform the following accounting functions:
   a. Account for the purchase of, interest and dividend receipts on, and sale of temporary investments.
   b. Use the lower of cost or market method (LCM) to value temporary investments in equity securities.
   c. Account for the purchase of, the receipt or accrual of interest on, and the sale of long-term investments in bonds.
   d. Account for long-term investments in common stock using both the cost and equity methods.

When you complete Part B of this chapter you will be able to

B1. Answer the following questions:
   a. What is the purpose of consolidated financial statements? What methods does a company use to acquire a controlling interest in another company?
   b. What is the difference between the purchase and pooling-of-interests methods of accounting for a business combination?

B2. Perform the following accounting functions:
   a. Use the purchase method to prepare a consolidated balance sheet at the acquisition date and a consolidated income statement after acquisition.
   b. Use the pooling-of-interests method to prepare a consolidated balance sheet at the acquisition date and a consolidated income statement after acquisition.

In the preceding chapters we learned about the accounting practices to be followed when a company obtains funds by issuing shares of stock (equity securities) and by issuing bonds (debt securities). In this chapter we discuss the accounting practices to be followed when a company lends funds by investing in another company's debt or equity securities. The chapter is divided into two parts. In Part A we learn how to account for intercorporate investments. In Part B we discuss how an investment can lead to a parent-subsidiary relationship, and we introduce the basics of consolidated financial statements.

## PART A—Intercorporate Investments

One can invest in corporate securities by purchasing them from either the issuing corporation or other investors. Investors may be individuals, financial institutions such as banks or mutual funds, or other corporations. Our emphasis will be on intercorporate investments—that is, one corporation investing in another corporation by purchasing its bonds or stocks.

### CLASSIFICATION OF INVESTMENTS

*A1a. Temporary investments consist of readily marketable securities that are intended to be converted into cash within a year or the firm's operating cycle, whichever is longer*

Investments are classified as temporary or long-term. **Temporary investments** are reported on the balance sheet as current assets. An investment is considered temporary if the securities (1) are readily marketable and (2) are intended to be held for a relatively short period of time. *Readily marketable* means *readily salable,* which is true of securities regularly traded on the open market at a determinable market price. The criteria of intention refer to management's intent to convert the securities into cash within the operating cycle or one year, whichever is longer. Thus securities classified as temporary investments are intended as a ready source of cash if needed.

*A1a. Long-term investments consist of securities intended to be held for longer than a year or the firm's operating cycle*

Investments in securities that do not meet the criteria for investments in temporary investments are classified as **long-term investments.** These investment securities are intended to be held for longer than a year or the firm's operating cycle. Therefore they are not considered a ready source of cash for the normal operations of the business.

### TEMPORARY INVESTMENTS IN BONDS

Bonds purchased as a temporary investment are recorded in the Temporary Investments account at their cost. Cost includes the purchase price, brokerage commission, and any other costs related to the purchase. Interest earned on the bonds is recorded in a Bond Interest Revenue account. Any premiums or discounts on bonds purchased as a temporary investment are not amortized. Since the investing company is not expected to hold the securities very long, the amount of amortization would be insignificant and therefore amortization is not considered necessary. When the bonds are sold, the difference between their selling price and their cost is recognized as a gain or loss. Let us look at the situations that illustrate the accounting for the transactions and events just described.

*A2a. Bonds purchased as a temporary investment are recorded at their cost, which includes the purchase price, brokerage commission, and any other costs related to the purchase*

PURCHASE OF BONDS On October 1, 1986, Carefree Company purchased ten \$1,000 bonds. The bonds have a stated interest rate of 12% and pay interest semiannually on February 1 and August 1. The bonds were purchased at 99, plus two months of accrued interest, amounting to \$200 ($\$1,000 \times 12\% \times \frac{2}{12} = \$20$; $\$20 \times 10$ bonds $= \$200$). Commission and taxes relating to the transaction totaled \$150. The entry to record the investment is as follows:

| 1986 | | | |
|---|---|---|---|
| Oct. 1 | Temporary Investments | 10,050 | |
| | Bond Interest Receivable | 200 | |
| | Cash | | 10,250 |
| | To record the purchase of ten \$1,000 Communication Company bonds | | |

*A2a. Accrued bond interest is recorded by an adjusting entry at year-end*

ACCRUAL OF INTEREST EARNED ON BONDS By December 31, 1986, Carefree Company's year-end, three months of bond interest has been earned. This interest of \$300 ($\$10,000 \times 12\% \times \frac{3}{12} = \$300$) has been earned in 1986, but since it will not be received until February 1, 1987, the following year-end adjusting entry for bond interest earned is made:

| 1986 | | | |
|---|---|---|---|
| Dec. 31 | Bond Interest Receivable | 300 | |
| | Bond Interest Revenue | | 300 |
| | To record three months of bond interest earned on the Communication Company bonds | | |

*A2a. Interest received is recorded semiannually*

RECEIPT OF INTEREST On February 1, 1987, Carefree received a \$600 check for six months' interest on its investment in Communication Company's bonds. Of the \$600 received, \$200 represents the accrued interest purchased and recorded on October 1, 1986, when the bonds were purchased; \$300 represents the interest earned by Carefree in 1986 and recorded in the year-end adjusting entry. The remaining \$100 is the amount of interest earned during January 1987, which must be recorded as revenue. The following entry would record the receipt of the first interest payment:

| 1987 | | | |
|---|---|---|---|
| Feb. 1 | Cash | 600 | |
| | Bond Interest Receivable | | 500 |
| | Bond Interest Revenue | | 100 |
| | To record receipt of six months' interest on the Communication Company bonds | | |

The interest check received on August 1, 1987, would be recorded by debiting Cash and crediting Bond Interest Revenue for \$600.

*A2a. An entry records the sale of temporary investments (bonds) and the gain or loss on that sale*

SALE OF TEMPORARY BOND INVESTMENT Bonds purchased as a temporary investment are expected to be sold within a relatively short period of time after their purchase. If we assume that Carefree sold the Communication Company bonds on August 2, 1987, at 103 and paid a brokerage commission of \$70, its net proceeds from the sale would be \$10,230 ($\$10,000 \times 1.03 = \$10,300$; $\$10,300 - \$70 = \$10,230$). The entry to record the sale of this temporary investment is as follows:

| | | | |
|---|---|---|---|
| 1987 | | | |
| Aug. 2 | Cash | 10,230 | |
| | Temporary Investments | | 10,050 |
| | Gain on Sale of Temporary Investments | | 180 |
| | To record the sale of ten $1,000 Communication Company bonds | | |

Both the $180 gain on sale of temporary investments and the $100 of bond interest revenue are shown in Carefree Corporation's 1987 income statement.

But what if the bonds had been sold on September 1, 1987, one month after the last interest payment date? Recall that when the bonds were purchased on October 1, 1986, $200 (or two months) of interest was "purchased" because the last interest payment date was August 1, 1986. Now $100 (or one month) of interest is in effect "sold" along with the bonds. Thus the entry to record the sale of the bonds on September 1, 1987, at 103 less a brokerage commission of $70 would be as follows:

| | | | |
|---|---|---|---|
| 1987 | | | |
| Sept. 1 | Cash | 10,330 | |
| | Temporary Investments | | 10,050 |
| | Gain on Sale of Temporary Investments | | 180 |
| | Bond Interest Revenue | | 100 |
| | To record the sale of ten $1,000 Communication Company bonds plus accrued interest | | |

## TEMPORARY INVESTMENTS IN STOCK

Stocks purchased as a temporary investment are also recorded at their cost. Dividends are recorded in the Dividend Revenue account only after there has been notification that they have been declared (remember that dividends are not guaranteed, and therefore dividend revenue does not accrue like interest revenue). When shares held as a temporary investment are sold, the difference between their selling price and their cost is recognized as a gain or loss.

Accounting for transactions involving temporary investments in equity securities is illustrated below.

***A2a. Stocks purchased as a temporary investment are recorded at their cost, which includes the purchase price, brokerage commission, taxes, and any other costs associated with the purchase***

**PURCHASE OF STOCKS** Assume that on April 1, 1986, Carefree Company purchased as a temporary investment 300 shares of Ajax Company common stock at $35 per share. The brokerage commission and taxes relating to the transaction amounted to $250. The entry to record the investment is as follows:

| | | | |
|---|---|---|---|
| 1986 | | | |
| April 1 | Temporary Investments | 10,750 | |
| | Cash | | 10,750 |
| | To record the purchase of 300 shares of Ajax Company's common stock | | |

**RECEIPT OF DIVIDENDS** Assume further that on June 30, 1986, Carefree received a dividend check of $450 from Ajax. This is a dividend of $1.50 per

*A2a. An entry records dividends received as dividend revenue*

share. Carefree would record receipt of the dividend by the following journal entry:

| | | | |
|---|---|---|---|
| 1986 | | | |
| June 30 | Cash .......... | 450 | |
| | Dividend Revenue .......... | | 450 |
| | To record dividend received from Ajax Company | | |

*A2a. An entry records the sale of temporary investments (stocks) and the gain or loss on that sale*

SALE OF TEMPORARY STOCK INVESTMENT If the Ajax stock was sold on September 15 for $40 per share with the brokerage commission and taxes related to the sale amounting to $280, Carefree would receive net proceeds of $11,720 (300 × $40 = $12,000; $12,000 − $280 = $11,720). The entry to record the sale of this temporary investment is as follows:

| | | | |
|---|---|---|---|
| 1986 | | | |
| Sept. 15 | Cash .......... | 11,720 | |
| | Temporary Investments .......... | | 10,750 |
| | Gain on Sale of Temporary Investments .......... | | 970 |
| | To record the sale of 300 shares of Ajax Company stock | | |

Both the $450 of dividend revenue and the $970 gain on sale of temporary investments are shown in Carefree Corporation's 1986 income statement.

## TEMPORARY INVESTMENTS—VALUATION AND REPORTING

Securities held as temporary investments are reported in the Current Assets section of the balance sheet. Generally, they are listed immediately after the asset *cash*. This placement shows the degree of their expected liquidity. The asset most readily converted into cash is shown before assets that are less readily converted into cash.

Temporary investments in bonds or other debt securities are reported on the balance sheet at acquisition cost. Accordingly, changes in the value of debt securities are ignored while the securities are being held. However, temporary investments in stock (equity securities) are valued and reported at the lower of their aggregate cost or their aggregate market value determined on the date of the balance sheet.[1] Using the lower of cost or market approach means that certain types of changes that occur in the value of equity securities while they are being held will be recognized and entered in the accounting records.

*A2b. Under the LCM method the total cost of a firm's short-term stock investments is compared with the total market value, and the lower figure is used for balance sheet reporting*

To illustrate the application of the **lower of cost or market (LCM) method** for determining at what amount temporary investments in equity securities should be reported, assume that on December 31, 1986, Carefree Company had the securities in its short-term investment portfolio as shown in the table at the top of page 607.

The schedule compares the total (aggregate) cost and total (aggregate) market value of the company's short-term stock investments. We know that the lower of the two figures must be used when reporting them on the balance sheet. To reduce the carrying value of Carefree's temporary investments in equity securities to the lower of cost or market, a contra account called Allowance to

[1] Financial Accounting Standards Board, "Accounting for Certain Marketable Securities," Statement No. 12 (Stamford, Conn., 1975), par. 8.

| SECURITY | COST | MARKET |
|---|---|---|
| Hilltop Company common stock | $32,000 | $29,600 |
| Major Company common stock | 18,000 | 17,200 |
| Tenant Company common stock | 23,700 | 24,300 |
| Kopter Company preferred stock | 9,200 | 8,500 |
| Total | $82,900 | $79,600 |

Reduce Temporary Investments to Market Value must be established. Because the aggregate market value of Carefree's short-term stock investments is $3,300 less than its aggregate cost, a $3,300 unrealized loss has been incurred while holding the securities. Therefore the investment should be reported on the balance sheet at its lower market value of $79,600. The entry to record the unrealized loss and reduce the carrying value of the temporary investments to market is as follows:

*A2b. Under the LCM method, an entry is made to record an unrealized loss due to the market decline in a portfolio of short-term equity securities*

| 1986 | | | |
|---|---|---|---|
| Dec. 31 | Unrealized Loss on Temporary Investments . . . . . . . . . . . . | 3,300 | |
| | Allowance to Reduce Temporary Investments to Market Value . . . . . . . . . . . . . . . . . . . . . . . . . . . . . . | | 3,300 |
| | To reduce temporary investments to market | | |

The loss is recognized as unrealized because the securities have not been sold. Nevertheless the unrealized loss is reported in the income statement, thereby reducing the current period's reported net income.

The Allowance to Reduce Temporary Investments to Market Value is a contra-asset account, which is deducted from the cost of the Temporary Investments account on the balance sheet and shown as follows:

| | | |
|---|---|---|
| Current Assets: | | |
| Cash | | $51,700 |
| Temporary Investments | $82,900 | |
| Less: Allowance to Reduce Temporary Investments to Market Value | 3,300 | 79,600 |

This procedure is useful because it provides for the disclosure of both the cost and the market value of the temporary investments.

As we have demonstrated, decreases in the aggregate market value of the investment portfolio are accounted for as losses. If at the end of a later period, the market value of the investment portfolio increases, the amount of the recovery is recorded in the accounts and reported in the subsequent period's income statement.

For example, assume that financial statements are prepared three months later on March 31, 1987, when those investment securities owned by Carefree now have a market value of $80,900. This amount is still $2,000 below the securities' aggregate cost but $1,300 above their December 31, 1986, market value. The entry to record the $1,300 recovery in the market value of the temporary investments from $79,600 on December 31, 1986, to $80,900 on March 31, 1987, is shown on page 608:

*A2b. An entry is made to record the recovery of an unrealized loss on temporary investments*

| | | | |
|---|---|---|---|
| 1987 | | | |
| March 31 | Allowance to Reduce Temporary Investments to Market Value | 1,300 | |
| | Recovery of Unrealized Loss on Temporary Investments | | 1,300 |
| | To show the partial recovery of the unrealized loss on temporary investments | | |

The amount of recovery that can be recorded is limited to the amount of the unrealized loss previously recorded. This limitation makes certain that the securities will not be reported at an amount in excess of their original aggregate cost. Thus when the Temporary Investments account has been reduced to market, it may at a subsquent date be increased, but only to the extent that the balance in the account does not exceed the original cost of the securities being held.

At the end of each subsequent period, we determine losses or loss recoveries by adjusting the balance in the allowance account to an amount that will cause the temporary investments in equity securities to be reported at the lower of their cost or their market value.

## LONG-TERM INVESTMENTS IN BONDS

In Chapter 16 we discussed the accounting for bonds from the viewpoint of the issuing corporation. In the following sections we discuss the accounting for bonds from the viewpoint of the investor. As you read these sections, you will see that the issues associated with bond accounting are familiar. These include determining the appropriate amount at which to record the initial investment, the handling of any related bond discount or premium, the accrual and recording of interest earned on the bonds, and the sale of the bonds.

*A2c. Bonds purchased as a long-term investment are recorded at their cost, which includes the purchase price, brokerage commission, taxes, and any other costs related to the purchase*

**PURCHASE OF BONDS** Bonds purchased as a long-term investment are recorded at cost. Cost includes the purchase price of the bond plus the brokerage commission, taxes, and any other costs related to the purchase. Because interest on bonds accrues over time, when bonds are purchased between interest payment dates, the purchaser must also pay the interest that has accrued since the last interest payment date. The price paid for a bond will depend on how the bond's stated rate of interest compares with the market rate of interest, for investments having comparable features, on the date the bond is purchased. Because these interest rates frequently differ, the price paid for a bond will often be more than or less than its face value, resulting in bond premiums or discounts.

Our first example will illustrate the accounting for transactions and events when a bond is purchased between its interest payment dates at a discount.

Assume that on June 1, 1986, Carefree Company purchased one hundred $1,000 Hilltop Corporation bonds at 97 plus accrued interest and a broker's commission of $800. The bonds have a stated rate of interest of 9%, mature on December 31, 1990, and pay interest semiannually on June 30 and December 31. The journal entry to record the bond purchase is as follows:

*A2c. An entry to record bonds purchased at a discount is illustrated here*

| | | | |
|---|---|---|---|
| 1986 | | | |
| June 1 | Investment in Bonds | 97,800 | |
| | Bond Interest Receivable | 3,750 | |
| | Cash | | 101,550 |
| | To record the purchase of 100, 9%, $1,000 Hilltop Corporation bonds | | |

The bond purchase is recorded in the Investment in Bonds account at cost. The cost was computed as follows: 100 bonds × $1,000 × 97% = $97,000; $97,000 + commission of $800 = $97,800. Note that although the bonds were purchased for an amount below their face value, a separate discount account was not used. Premiums or discounts on bond investments are included in the Investment in Bonds account (along with commissions and other related items) so that the investment will initially be recorded at cost. Carefree also paid $3,750 for five months of interest that has accrued since the last interest payment made on December 31, 1985. The amount was debited to the Bond Interest Receivable account because Carefree expects to receive that amount, along with interest it has earned, on June 30 when the bond-issuing company (Hilltop) makes its semiannual interest payment.

*A2c. An entry is made for receipt of semiannual interest and amortization of discount*

**RECEIPT OF INTEREST** Carefree would receive its first semiannual interest check on June 30, 1986. The entry to record the receipt of the interest check and the amortization of the bond discount is as follows:

| | | | |
|---|---|---|---|
| 1986 | | | |
| June 30 | Cash | 4,500 | |
| | Investment in Bonds | 40 | |
| | Bond Interest Receivable | | 3,750 |
| | Bond Interest Revenue | | 790 |
| | To record receipt of semiannual interest and amortization of discount | | |

In this entry Cash is debited for the amount of the semiannual interest check that has been received. Investment in Bonds is debited for an amount representing amortization, as shown in the calculation below. Bond Interest Receivable is credited for the amount that Carefree paid to the seller of the bonds on June 1, 1986, and Bond Interest Revenue is credited for the amount of interest earned during the one-month holding period when the bond discount is amortized using the straight-line method.

| | |
|---|---|
| Maturity value of the bonds | $100,000 |
| Cost of the bonds | 97,800 |
| Amount to be amortized over the life of the bonds | $ 2,200 |
| Amortization per month ($2,200 ÷ 55 months = $40) | $ 40 |

Note that the difference between the cost of the long-term bond investment and its maturity value is amortized over the life of the bond. This is the period from the purchase date of the bonds to their maturity date. In our example there are fifty-five months between those dates. Recall that the straight-line method of amortization may be used when the results obtained do not differ significantly from the results that would have been obtained if the effective interest method had been used. Although both amortization methods were discussed in Chapter 16, we show only straight-line amortization here because the amounts involved are not considered to be significant.

The essentials of amortization can be summarized as follows:

> The straight-line method amortizes an equal amount of discount or premium each period. The effective interest method amortizes a different amount of discount or

premium to each period while recognizing bond interest revenue at the same rate each period.

Under either method, the amortization of a discount increases the amount of the investment account and increases the amount to be recorded as interest revenue.

Under either method, the amortization of a premium decreases the amount of the investment account and decreases the amount to be recorded as interest revenue.

On December 31 another semiannual interest payment will be received. The entry to record receipt of the interest and six months of amortization is as follows:

| | | | |
|---|---|---|---|
| 1986 | | | |
| Dec. 31 | Cash | 4,500 | |
| | Investment in Bonds | 240 | |
| | Bond Interest Revenue | | 4,740 |
| | To record receipt of semiannual interest and amortization of discount | | |

**RECEIPT OF MATURITY VALUE** If the Hilltop Corporation bonds were held until maturity, Carefree would receive a check for $100,000, their face value, and make the following entry:

| | | | |
|---|---|---|---|
| 1990 | | | |
| Dec. 31 | Cash | 100,000 | |
| | Investment in Bonds | | 100,000 |
| | To record cash received for bonds retired at maturity | | |

When bonds are purchased at a price that exceeds their face value — that is, at a premium rather than at a discount — our accounting procedures are somewhat similar.

The investment is recorded in the Investment in Bonds account at cost, and the premium is amortized over the remaining life of the bonds. There is a difference, however, in that the amount of periodic premium amortization is credited rather than debited to the investment account.

The entry reduces the balance in the Investment in Bonds account while reducing the amount of interest revenue to be recognized for the period. Because this entry is made periodically, the carrying value of the bond investment is gradually reduced and will equal the face value of the bonds on the day they mature.

To illustrate the accounting entries for transactions involving bonds purchased at a premium, assume that on June 1, 1986, Carefree Corporation purchased two hundred $1,000 Airway Corporation bonds at 102 plus accrued interest. Brokerage commission on the purchase was $1,160. The bonds have a stated rate of interest of 15%, mature on December 31, 1989 (giving them a remaining life of forty-three months to maturity), and pay interest semiannually on June 30 and December 31.

Entries to be made by Carefree for the transactions and events cited are shown on page 611 along with all the necessary explanations to help you understand the entries.

*June 1, 1986—Long-term bond investments purchased at a premium:*

| | | | |
|---|---|---|---|
| 1986 | | | |
| June 1 | Investment in Bonds. | 205,160 | |
| | Bond Interest Receivable | 12,500 | |
| | Cash. | | 217,660 |
| | To record the purchase of 200, 15%, $1,000 Airway Corporation bonds | | |

Cost of the bonds debited to the investment account = 200 bonds × $1,000 × 102% = $204,000; $204,000 + $1,160 = $205,160. Interest accrued on the bonds (5 months) debited to the receivable account = $200,000 × 15% × $\frac{5}{12}$ = $12,500.

*June 30, 1986—Receipt of semiannual interest and related amortization:*

| | | | |
|---|---|---|---|
| 1986 | | | |
| June 30 | Cash | 15,000 | |
| | Investment in Bonds | | 120 |
| | Bond Interest Receivable | | 12,500 |
| | Bond Interest Revenue | | 2,380 |
| | To record receipt of semiannual interest and amortization of premium | | |

Investment in Bonds is credited for an amount representing amortization, as shown in the calculation below.

| | |
|---|---|
| Cost of the bonds. | $205,160 |
| Maturity value of the bonds | 200,000 |
| Amount to be amortized over the life of the bonds. | $ 5,160 |
| Amortization per month ($5,160 ÷ 43 months = $120) | $ 120 |

*December 31, 1986—Receipt of semiannual interest and related amortization:*

| | | | |
|---|---|---|---|
| 1986 | | | |
| Dec. 31 | Cash | 15,000 | |
| | Investment in Bonds | | 720 |
| | Bond Interest Revenue | | 14,280 |
| | To record receipt of semiannual interest and amortization of premium | | |

## SALE OF BOND INVESTMENTS BEFORE MATURITY

Bonds acquired for investment purposes may be sold before maturity. When the sale occurs, the Cash account is debited for the amount received (proceeds of the sale), and the Investment in Bonds account is credited for the carrying value of the bonds sold. The difference between the proceeds received from the sale and the carrying value of the bonds on the date of the sale is recorded as a gain or loss on the sale. If the bond is sold between interest payment dates, the seller receives the interest accrued since the last interest date. Furthermore, because the gain or loss on the sale of long-term investments in bonds is determined by subtracting the carrying value of the bonds from the proceeds of the sale, it will be necessary to update amortization to the date of the sale. The entry to update amortization is needed to determine the carrying value of the bonds on the date of their sale and to ensure that an appropriate amount of interest revenue is recognized.

To illustrate the accounting for the sale of a long-term bond investment, assume that on October 1, 1988, Carefree Company sold the Airway Corporation bonds for $203,000 plus accrued interest of $7,500. Recall that Airway pays interest semiannually on June 30 and December 31, and therefore the $7,500 represents three months of interest accrued since the last interest payment date. Carefree records premium amortization twice a year on the dates when interest is received. Therefore premium amortization was last recorded on June 30, 1988. Because three months have passed since amortization was last recorded, an entry to update amortization is made on the date of the sale as follows:

***A2c. Amortization of premium (or discount) must be updated by an entry when long-term investments are sold***

| | | | |
|---|---|---|---|
| 1988 | | | |
| Oct. 1 | Bond Interest Revenue | 360 | |
| | Investment in Bonds | | 360 |
| | To record three months of premium amortization at $120 per month | | |

This entry causes the carrying value of the bonds to decrease to $201,800. The amount is verified in the schedule below.

| | |
|---|---|
| Carrying value on date of purchase, June 1, 1986 | $205,160 |
| Less: Premium amortized from June 1, 1986, through June 30, 1988 (25 months × $120) | 3,000 |
| Carrying value on June 30, 1988—before entry to update | 202,160 |
| Less: Premium amortized in updating entry | 360 |
| Carrying value of bonds on October 31, 1988 | $201,800 |

The entry to record the sale of the bonds is as follows:

| | | | |
|---|---|---|---|
| 1988 | | | |
| Oct. 1 | Cash | 210,500 | |
| | Investment in Bonds | | 201,800 |
| | Bond Interest Revenue | | 7,500 |
| | Gain on Sale of Investment | | 1,200 |
| | To record the sale of Airway Corporation bonds | | |

The gain on the sale is $1,200 because that is the amount by which the proceeds from the sale ($203,000) exceed the carrying value of the bonds sold ($201,800). Of course a loss will arise when the carrying value of an investment exceeds the proceeds obtained from its sale.

## ACCOUNTING FOR LONG-TERM INVESTMENTS IN COMMON STOCK

Like bonds, long-term investments in stocks are initially recorded at their cost. Accounting for stock investments after their acquisition, however, depends on the extent to which the investing company (the **investor company**) can exercise significant influence over the operating and financial policies of the company whose stock it owns (the **investee company**).

One important factor in determining whether an investor has the ability to exercise significant influence over an investee is related to what percentage of the investee's voting stock is owned by the investor.

*A1b. Two methods are used to account for long-term investments in common stock*

There are two methods of accounting for long-term investments in common stock: (1) the *cost method* and (2) the *equity method*. Each is based on the percentage of the investee's voting shares owned by the investor. Exhibit 17–1 summarizes the circumstances under which each method should be used.

EXHIBIT 17–1

Methods of Accounting for Long-Term Investments in Common Stock

| ACCOUNTING METHOD USED | DEGREE OF INFLUENCE AND STATUS OF OWNERSHIP |
|---|---|
| Cost Method | Investor lacks significant influence over the investee. Generally presumed when the investor owns less than 20% of the voting stock of an investee. |
| Equity Method | Investor has the ability to exercise significant influence over the investee. Presumed when the investor owns 20% or more of the voting stock of an investee. |

## The Cost Method

The **cost method** of accounting for long-term investments is used when the investor is unable to exercise significant influence over the investee. Under the cost method, stock purchased as a long-term investment is recorded at cost, and dividends are recognized as income when declared by the board of directors of the investee corporation. Following acquisition, long-term investments in equity securities accounted for under the cost method are required to be valued at the lower of cost or market.[2] Thus at the end of each accounting period, the aggregate market value of the long-term stock investment portfolio must be determined and compared with the aggregate cost of that portfolio. If the aggregate market value is less than the aggregate cost, the difference is debited to an account called Unrealized Loss on Long-Term Investments and is credited to an account called Allowance to Reduce Long-Term Investments to Market.

As you have probably noted, the procedure for valuing long-term investments in stock under the cost method is essentially the same as that used for valuing temporary investments in stock. There is, however, a major reporting difference. The Unrealized Loss on Long-Term Investments account is a contra-owners' equity account reported in the Stockholders' Equity section of the balance sheet, not in the income statement.

Transactions typically encountered when accounting for long-term investments in common stock involve (1) the purchase of the shares, (2) the receipt of dividends, and (3) the sale of the shares. Under the cost method, it is also necessary to apply the lower of cost or market procedure to determine at what amount the long-term investment in stock should be reported and to be able to prepare an adjusting entry if one is needed.

*A2d. Accounting for long-term investments in common stock using the cost method is illustrated here*

To illustrate the accounting for long-term investments in common stock using the cost method, assume the following:

[2] Ibid., par. 8.

On March 5, 1986, Carefree Company purchased as a long-term investment 5,000 common shares of Tri-State Inc. at $14 per share plus a broker's commission of $400. The 5,000 common shares constitute 2% of Tri-State's 250,000 outstanding common shares.

**PURCHASE OF STOCK INVESTMENT** The entry to record the purchase of the Tri-State shares is as follows:

| | | | |
|---|---|---|---|
| 1986 | | | |
| March 5 | Investment in Stock | 70,400 | |
| | Cash | | 70,400 |
| | To record the purchase of 5,000 shares of Tri-State common stock (5,000 shares × $14 + $400 = $70,400) | | |

**RECEIPT OF DIVIDENDS** On November 18, 1986, Tri-State's board of directors declared a $1.20-per-share dividend to the stockholders of record on December 1, payable on January 1, 1987. Under the cost method, dividends declared by the investee are recognized as income (revenue) by the investor. The entry to record the dividend declaration is as follows:

| | | | |
|---|---|---|---|
| 1986 | | | |
| Nov. 18 | Dividends Receivable | 6,000 | |
| | Dividend Revenue | | 6,000 |
| | To record dividends declared on Tri-State common stock | | |

Note that dividend revenue was recorded on November 18, the date the dividends were declared. On January 1, 1987, Carefree will record receipt of Tri-State's dividend by debiting the Cash account and crediting the Dividends Receivable account.

**VALUATION AT LOWER OF COST OR MARKET** Carefree's year ends on December 31. At this time the lower of cost or market method is applied to value long-term investments in stock in the same way that it was used to value temporary investments in stock. The total cost and total market value of these stock investment portfolios must be calculated. If the total market value is below total cost, the investments are reported on the balance sheet at this lower amount (total market). Carefree has only one long-term stock investment consisting of 5,000 shares of Tri-State common, which cost $70,400. If on December 31 Tri-State's common stock had a market price of $13.50, the market value of Carefree's investment would be $67,500 (5,000 shares × $13.50 = $67,500), which is $2,900 below cost. The adjusting entry needed to account for the decline in market value of the shares being held is as follows:

| | | | |
|---|---|---|---|
| 1986 | | | |
| Dec. 31 | Unrealized Loss on Long-Term Investments | 2,900 | |
| | Allowance to Reduce Long-Term Investments to Market Value | | 2,900 |
| | To reduce long-term investments to the lower of cost or market | | |

The long-term stock investment would be reported on Carefree's year-end balance sheet as follows:

| | | |
|---|---|---|
| Long-term Investments: | | |
| Investment in Stock | $70,400 | |
| Less: Allowance to Reduce Long-Term Investments to Market Value | 2,900 | $67,500 |

The unrealized loss is reported as a contra-owners' equity account in the Stockholders' Equity section of Carefree's balance sheet, as shown below.

| | | |
|---|---|---|
| Stockholders' Equity: | | |
| Common Stock | $600,000 | |
| Retained Earnings | 320,000 | |
| Total | $920,000 | |
| Less: Unrealized Loss on Long-Term Investments | 2,900 | |
| Total Stockholders' Equity | | $917,100 |

As with temporary investments in stocks, market value recoveries in subsequent periods are recognized with the amount of the recovery recorded being limited to the amount of unrealized losses recorded in the past. Although the market value of the entire stock investment portfolio can exceed its original cost, in no case can the investment be reported at an amount in excess of cost.

SALE OF STOCK INVESTMENT (Cost Method) When long-term investments in stocks accounted for under the cost method are sold, the difference between the amount received from the sale (proceeds of the sale) and the cost of the shares sold is recorded as a gain or loss. This realized gain or loss (realized because the shares have been sold) is reported in the income statement. For example, if on February 1, 1987, 2,500 of the Tri-State shares were sold for $34,000 (net of brokerage commission), the entry to record the sale would be as follows:

| | | | |
|---|---|---|---|
| 1987 | | | |
| Feb. 1 | Cash | 34,000 | |
| | Loss on Sale of Investment | 1,200 | |
| | Investment in Stock | | 35,200 |
| | To record the sale of 2,500 shares of Tri-State common stock | | |

The accounting records indicate that 5,000 Tri-State common shares had an acquisition cost of $70,400. Therefore the cost of 2,500 shares representing one-half of the total acquired is $35,200.

## The Equity Method

The **equity method** of accounting for long-term investments must be used when there is evidence that the investor has the ability to exercise significant influence over the investee. As mentioned earlier, we presume the investor has the ability to exercise significant influence over the investee when the investor owns 20% or more of the investee's voting stock.

Under the equity method, stock purchased as a long-term investment is recorded at cost, just as under the cost method. The main features distinguishing

*A1b. The equity method differs from the cost method in two ways*

the equity method from the cost method involve the manner in which the investor accounts for (1) the net income earned by the investee and (2) the cash dividends declared by the investee. How the investor accounts for these transactions and events when the equity method is used is summarized below.

1. The investor records its share of the investee's periodic net income as an *increase* in the Investment account and as *revenue* for the period. Should the investee report a loss for a period, the investor would record its share of the investee's loss as a *decrease* in the Investment account and as a *loss* for the period.
2. The investor records cash or property dividends received from the investee as a *decrease* in the Investment account and as an *increase* in the appropriate asset account.

*A2d. Accounting for long-term investments in common stock using the equity method is illustrated here*

To illustrate the equity method of accounting for long-term investments in stock, we will assume that on January 1 of the current year Carefree Company purchased 30,000 of Arc Company's 100,000 voting shares of common stock for $453,000, including brokerage commissions. With this purchase Carefree owns enough of Arc's voting stock (30%) to have a significant influence over its operating and financial policies. On December 31 of the current year, Arc reported net income of $210,000 for the year and paid a cash dividend of $100,000 (or $1 per share). Entries made by Carefree Company to record these transactions and events are noted below.

**PURCHASE OF STOCK INVESTMENT** The entry to record the purchase of 30% of Arc Company's voting common shares is as follows:

| | | | |
|---|---|---|---|
| Jan. 1 | Investment in Stock . . . . . . . . . . . . . . . . | 453,000 | |
| | Cash . . . . . . . . . . . . . . . . | | 453,000 |
| | To record the purchase of 30,000 shares of Arc Company's common stock | | |

**RECOGNITION OF INCOME** Under the equity method, Carefree recognizes its share of Arc's net income as revenue from the investment and increases its Investment account by that same amount. The investor's share is based on the percentage of voting stock owned. Therefore Carefree will record 30% of Arc Company's net income of $210,000 as follows:

| | | | |
|---|---|---|---|
| Dec. 31 | Investment in Stock . . . . . . . . . . . . . . . . | 63,000 | |
| | Investment Revenue . . . . . . . . . . . . . . . . | | 63,000 |
| | To record 30% of Arc Company's net income of $210,000 | | |

**RECEIPT OF DIVIDENDS** Under the equity method, cash and property dividends received are recorded as decreases in the Investment account. The following entry records the cash dividend of $30,000 received by Carefree (30% of Arc's total dividend of $100,000 = $30,000, or $1 per share on Carefree's 30,000 shares = $30,000):

| | | | |
|---|---|---|---|
| Dec. 31 | Cash . . . . . . . . . . . . . . . . | 30,000 | |
| | Investment in Stock . . . . . . . . . . . . . . . . | | 30,000 |
| | To record dividends received | | |

Note that stock dividends are accounted for in the same way under the equity method as under the cost method. A memorandum entry is made to indicate that additional shares of stock have been received. The share of ownership in the investee remains unchanged.

The equity method establishes the amount to be reported for long-term stock investments by focusing on changes in the investee's net assets, not on the market price of the investee's stock. Consequently, it is recognized that income earned by the investee not only increases the investee's net assets but also increases the investor's equity in those assets. On the other hand, dividends paid by the investee decrease its net assets, which also decreases the investor's equity in the investee. Thus under the equity method, changes in the investee's net assets are recorded as either increases or decreases in the investor's Investment in Stock account.

After recording those transactions that increased or decreased Carefree's investment account, it would appear as follows:

INVESTMENT IN STOCK

| | | | DEBIT | CREDIT | BALANCE |
|---|---|---|---|---|---|
| Jan. | 1 | Purchase | 453 000 | | 453 000 |
| Dec. | 31 | Net Income | 63 000 | | 516 000 |
| Dec. | 31 | Dividends | | 30 000 | 486 000 |

**SALE OF STOCK INVESTMENT (Equity Method)** When long-term investments in stocks accounted for under the equity method are sold, the gain or loss on the sale is determined by comparing the amount received from the sale (proceeds) with the carrying value of the stock on the date of the sale. For example, assume that Carefree sold 3,000 shares of Arc Company stock on January 5 of the following year for $50,000 (net of brokerage commission). The entry to record the sale is as follows:

| | | | |
|---|---|---|---|
| Jan. 5 | Cash.......................................... | 50,000 | |
| | Investment in Stock .......................... | | 48,600 |
| | Gain on Sale of Investment .................... | | 1,400 |
| | To record the sale of 3,000 shares of Arc Company stock | | |

The $48,600 recorded as a credit to the Investment in Stock account was determined as follows:

> The 3,000 shares sold represent 10% of the 30,000 shares owned prior to the sale. Thus 10% of the $486,000 balance in the investment account, or $48,600, should be removed from that account.
>
> Another approach would be to determine the carrying value of each share owned prior to the sale ($486,000 ÷ 30,000 shares = $16.20) and multiply that carrying value per share by the number of shares sold ($16.20 × 3,000 shares sold = $48,600).

If future sales of shares decrease Carefree's share of ownership in Arc to less than 20%, it would use the cost method to account for the investment.

Exhibit 17 – 2 compares the accounting for temporary stock investments and for long-term stock investments using both the cost method and the equity method. Study the data presented to observe the similarities and differences in the accounting.

*EXHIBIT 17 – 2*

Comparison of the Accounting for Temporary Investments and Long-Term Investments in Stock

| | TEMPORARY INVESTMENTS IN STOCK | LONG-TERM INVESTMENTS IN STOCK | |
|---|---|---|---|
| | | Cost Method | Equity Method |
| Balance sheet classification | Current asset | Investments | Investments |
| Common stock of another corporation (the investee corporation is purchased) | Record at cost | Record at cost | Record at cost |
| Investee corporation declares a cash dividend | Record dividend revenue and report amount as revenue in the income statement | Record dividend revenue and report amount as revenue in income statement | Record as a decrease in the investment account. No revenue recognized |
| Investee corporation's reported net income or net loss | No recognition, no entry recorded | No recognition, no entry recorded | Record investor's share of investee's reported net income or loss as an increase (net income) or decrease (net loss) in the investment account and as revenue (or loss) for the period |
| End-of-period valuation of investment account | Apply lower of cost or market method. If write-down is needed, establish a contra-asset account. Increases or decreases in the contra-account are recorded as unrealized losses or recoveries and reported in the income statement | Apply lower of cost or market method. If write-down is needed, establish a contra-asset account. Increases or decreases in the contra-account are recorded as unrealized losses or recoveries and reported in the stockholders' equity of the balance sheet | No action needed. Investment account reflects the ownership interest that the investor has in the net assets of the investee |
| Investor sells shares of investee | Compare the proceeds from the sale with the cost of the shares sold to determine the gain or loss on the sale. Report the gain or loss in the income statement | Compare the proceeds from the sale with the cost of the shares sold to determine the gain or loss on the sale. Report the gain or loss in the income statement | Compare the proceeds from the sale with the carrying value of the shares on the date of their sale to determine gain or loss. Report the gain or loss in the income statement. |

## *PART B — Consolidated Financial Statements — Purpose and Description*

When one company owns more than 50% of the voting stock of another company, a *parent and subsidiary relationship* is said to exist. The investing company is known as the **parent company,** and the investee company is known as the **subsidiary company.** For example, if Pree Company owns more than 50% of the voting stock of See Company, Pree is the parent company and See is the subsidiary.

Despite this ownership situation, both Pree and See continue to operate as separate legal entities. Each company maintains its own accounting records, and each prepares its own financial statements. Pree accounts for its majority-owned investment in See under the equity method consistent with our previous discussion. Thus Pree's investment account is periodically increased or decreased by its share of See's net income or net loss and is decreased by its share of the dividends declared by See. At the end of each fiscal year, the balance in Pree's investment account is reported in its (the parent company's) balance sheet as a long-term investment. Its share of See Company's net income or net loss is reported in its income statement.

Reporting a single amount in the parent company's balance sheet to show its investment in a subsidiary, and reporting a single amount in the parent company's income statement to show the income that resulted from its investment in the subsidiary, may not provide enough detail to satisfy financial statement users. A better approach might be to provide information about the subsidiary's assets and liabilities in the parent company's balance sheet and information about the subsidiary's revenues and expenses in the parent company's income statement. This approach is typically taken when preparing financial statements for a company that owns a **controlling interest** in the shares of the voting stock of one or more other companies. The act of combining the information from the separate financial statements of a parent company and one or more of its subsidiaries into a single set of financial statements is known as a *consolidation.* The statements produced, known as **consolidated financial statements,** report the results of operations and the financial position of the parent and its subsidiary or subsidiaries as if they were a single business entity.

***B1a. Consolidated financial statements view a parent and its controlled subsidiary as if they were a single business entity***

The mechanics of preparing consolidated financial statements is complex, and generally the discussion of this topic is deferred to more-advanced accounting courses. However, because so many large publicly held corporations consist of a parent company with one or more subsidiaries, we feel that it is important to provide a basic background for understanding and preparing consolidated financial statements.

## THE PARENT AND SUBSIDIARY RELATIONSHIP

***B1a. A parent-subsidiary relationship may be accomplished by a purchase or a pooling of interests***

The parent-subsidiary relationship arises from a "purchase" or from a "pooling of interests."

*Purchase.* A parent company can acquire a controlling interest in a subsidiary by exchanging cash, other assets, or debt for more than 50% of the subsidiary's voting stock. Control achieved in this way is accounted for as a *purchase.* In this situation, the stockholders of the subsidiary company sell their shares to the parent company and are no longer owners of either the parent or the subsidiary company.

*Pooling of interests.* A parent company can acquire a controlling interest in a subsidiary by exchanging its voting shares for 90% or more of the subsidiary's voting stock. If, in addition to this exchange of stock, certain other specific conditions are met, the parent-subsidiary relationship formed is accounted for as a *pooling of interests.* In this situation stockholders of the subsidiary company transfer their shares to the parent in exchange for shares of the parent company. Thus former stockholders of the subsidiary become stockholders of the parent.

In the following examples we will assume (1) that the acquiring company is able to exercise control over its subsidiary and (2) that their activities are similar and compatible. These conditions make it necessary for the acquiring (parent) company to prepare consolidated financial statements so that the affiliated companies report as if they are a single business entity. As we go through the illustrations, keep in mind that although the companies are said to be affiliated, each remains a separate legal entity. Each maintains its own accounting records, and each prepares its own periodic financial statements. It is the parent company that prepares consolidated financial statements to present the parent and subsidiary companies as a single business entity.

## CONSOLIDATED BALANCE SHEET AT DATE OF ACQUISITION—PURCHASE METHOD

When a controlling corporation acquires more than 50% of the voting stock of another corporation in exchange for cash, other assets, or the issuance of debt, the transaction is treated as a purchase. To illustrate how to prepare a consolidated balance sheet on the date of acquisition using the **purchase method,** assume that Pree Company is interested in acquiring a controlling interest in See Company. The individual condensed balance sheets of the two companies prepared on January 1, 1986, just prior to Pree's acquisition of See, are shown in Exhibit 17–3.

*EXHIBIT 17–3*

Preacquisition Balance Sheets

| | PREE COMPANY | SEE COMPANY |
|---|---|---|
| Assets: | | |
| Cash | $280,000 | $ 30,000 |
| Accounts Receivable (net) | 120,000 | 50,000 |
| Notes Receivable—See Company | 50,000 | — |
| Inventory | 200,000 | 90,000 |
| Plant and Equipment (net) | 300,000 | 160,000 |
| Total Assets | $950,000 | $330,000 |
| Liabilities and Stockholders' Equity: | | |
| Accounts Payable | $130,000 | $ 60,000 |
| Notes Payable—Pree Company | — | 50,000 |
| Bonds Payable | 200,000 | — |
| Common Stock | 300,000 | 100,000 |
| Paid-in Capital | 50,000 | 30,000 |
| Retained Earnings | 270,000 | 90,000 |
| | $950,000 | $330,000 |

### Purchase of 100% of Subsidiary's Stock at Book Value

Assume that on January 1, 1986, Pree Company purchased all the outstanding common stock of See Company on the open market for $220,000. This amount is equal to the book value of See Company's net assets (assets of $330,000 minus liabilities of $110,000 equals $220,000). Pree Company would record the purchase of See Company's stock as follows:

| 1986 | | | |
|---|---|---|---|
| Jan. 1 | Investment in See Company ........................ | 220,000 | |
| | Cash ........................................ | | 220,000 |
| | To record the purchase of 100% of See Company's outstanding stock | | |

After the journal entry amounts have been posted to Pree Company's accounts, its balance sheet will change as follows: (1) its Cash account balance will be $60,000 because $220,000 of cash was spent to acquire See Company's stock,

EXHIBIT 17–4

Work Sheet for a Consolidated Balance Sheet: 100% Ownership—Purchase Method

PREE COMPANY AND SUBSIDIARY
Work Sheet for a Consolidated Balance Sheet
As of Acquisition Date

| ACCOUNTS | PREE COMPANY | SEE COMPANY | ADJUSTMENTS AND ELIMINATIONS Debit | ADJUSTMENTS AND ELIMINATIONS Credit | CONSOLIDATED BALANCE SHEET |
|---|---|---|---|---|---|
| Cash | 60 000 | 30 000 | | | 90 000 |
| Accounts Receivable (net) | 120 000 | 50 000 | | | 170 000 |
| Notes Receivable—See Company | 50 000 | | | (2)50 000 | |
| Inventory | 200 000 | 90 000 | | | 290 000 |
| Investment in See Company | 220 000 | | | (1)220 000 | |
| Plant and Equipment (net) | 300 000 | 160 000 | | | 460 000 |
| Total Assets | 950 000 | 330 000 | | | 1010 000 |
| | | | | | |
| Accounts Payable | 130 000 | 60 000 | | | 190 000 |
| Notes Payable—Pree Company | | 50 000 | (2)50 000 | | |
| Bonds Payable | 200 000 | | | | 200 000 |
| Common Stock | 300 000 | 100 000 | (1)100 000 | | 300 000 |
| Paid-in Capital | 50 000 | 30 000 | (1) 30 000 | | 50 000 |
| Retained Earnings | 270 000 | 90 000 | (1) 90 000 | | 270 000 |
| Total Liabilities and Stockholders' Equity | 950 000 | 330 000 | 270 000 | 270 000 | 1010 000 |

(1) To eliminate the investment in See Company

(2) To eliminate the intercompany note receivable and note payable.

*B2a. In preparing a consolidated balance sheet at acquisition date by the purchase method, a work sheet similar to Exhibit 17–4 is often used*

and (2) it shows a $220,000 Investment account to reflect the cost of See Company's stock. When separate balance sheets of two companies are combined to develop a consolidated balance sheet, a work sheet similar to the one in Exhibit 17–4 is often prepared. The purpose of the work sheet is to aid in combining the account balances of the companies being consolidated.

In examining the work sheet, note first that it has five columns. The first two columns show the balance sheet account balances of the two companies being consolidated. The next two columns are for entering amounts to adjust or eliminate account balances. The last column shows the amounts for items that should be reported in the balance sheet of the consolidated entity.

Although the process of preparing the work sheet is essentially one of combining the balances in similar accounts, the effects of transactions between the two entities are removed from the consolidated balance sheet by elimination entries made on the work sheet. The adjusting or eliminating entries are work sheet entries only. They are not recorded in either the parent company's or the subsidiary company's books. They are used to obtain appropriate balances for items reported in the balance sheet of the consolidated entity.

Eliminating entry (1) eliminates the account Investment in See Company and all of See Company's stockholders' equity accounts. This entry must be made to avoid the double counting that would occur when the net assets of two companies are combined and to eliminate the Stockholders' Equity section of the subsidiary company. Remember that the underlying purpose of consolidated financial statements is to view the affiliated companies as a single entity.

The balance sheets of the two companies show that See Company owes $50,000 to Pree Company. This intercompany note receivable and note payable is eliminated by entry (2).

This entry was made because the combined entity does not have a receivable or a payable to any outside party for these items. By eliminating the receivable and the payable, the assets and liabilities of the combined entity are not overstated.

After the eliminating entries have been made on the work sheet, the process of consolidation involves combining the balances in each of the remaining accounts to produce the parent company's consolidated balance sheet. Using the data from the consolidated balance sheet column in Exhibit 17–4, the parent company's consolidated balance sheet can be formulated.

PREE COMPANY AND SUBSIDIARY
Consolidated Balance Sheet
January 1, 1986

| | | |
|---|---|---|
| Current Assets: | | |
| Cash | $ 90,000 | |
| Accounts Receivable (net) | 170,000 | |
| Inventory | 290,000 | |
| Total Current Assets | | $ 550,000 |
| Plant and Equipment (net) | | 460,000 |
| Total Assets | | $1,010,000 |
| Current Liabilities: | | |
| Accounts Payable | $190,000 | |
| Long-term Liabilities: | | |
| Bonds Payable | 200,000 | |
| Total Liabilities | | $ 390,000 |
| Stockholders' Equity: | | |
| Common Stock | $300,000 | |
| Paid-in Capital | 50,000 | |
| Retained Earnings | 270,000 | |
| Total Stockholders' Equity | | 620,000 |
| Total Liabilities and Stockholders' Equity | | $1,010,000 |

A consolidated income statement on the date of acquisition would be the parent company's income statement because the subsidiary's income up to the date of acquisition is not included.

## Purchase of Less Than 100% of Subsidiary's Stock at Book Value

It is unnecessary and often impossible for a company to acquire 100% of the outstanding stock of the company it would like to control. As mentioned earlier, control is presumed to exist when a company owns more than 50% of another company's voting stock. In the following illustration we will assume that the parent company purchases 80% of the subsidiary's outstanding stock. In this case, the subsidiary company has minority stockholders, who own 20% of the subsidiary's outstanding shares. They continue to have an interest in the net assets of the subsidiary, and collectively their interest is called a **minority interest.** This interest must be reported in the consolidated balance sheet at an amount equal to their percentage of ownership times the net assets of the subsidiary.

*B2a. When the parent company purchases less than 100% of the subsidiary's stock at book value, the preparation of the work sheet differs, as shown in Exhibit 17–5*

To illustrate the parent company's accounting when less than 100% of the subsidiary's outstanding stock is purchased at book value, we return to the same preacquisition data shown for the two companies in Exhibit 17–3. This time assume that Pree Company was able to purchase 80% of See Company's outstanding voting stock for $176,000. Once again, the cost of the shares purchased is equal to the book value of See Company's net assets (80% × $220,000 = $176,000). The entry made by Pree Company at the time of the purchase is as follows:

| 1986 | | | |
|---|---|---|---|
| Jan. 1 | Investment in See Company | 176,000 | |
| | Cash | | 176,000 |
| | To record the purchase of 80% of See Company's outstanding stock | | |

The work sheet for the preparation of Pree Company's consolidated balance sheet on the date of acquisition is shown in Exhibit 17–5 on page 624.

The first elimination entry in Exhibit 17–5 is handled the same way as in the preceding work sheet except that when less than 100% of the subsidiary's stock is acquired, the minority interest must be accounted for. Thus eliminating entry (1) eliminated the parent company's investment account, eliminated all of the subsidiary company's stockholders' equity account, and recognized the difference in amounts as minority interest. Since Pree Company purchased 80% of the subsidiary's stock, the minority interest in the net assets of See Company amounts to $44,000, determined as follows: 20% × $220,000 = $44,000. The minority interest is shown as a separate item on the last line of the consolidation work sheet. It is also reported as a separate item on the consolidated balance sheet, usually between liabilities and stockholders' equity. This presentation is illustrated in Pree Company's partial balance sheet shown below.

PREE COMPANY AND SUBSIDIARY
Partial Balance Sheet
January 1, 1986

| | | |
|---|---|---|
| Current Liabilities: | | |
| Accounts Payable | $190,000 | |
| Long-term Liabilities: | | |
| Bonds Payable | 200,000 | |
| Total Liabilities | | $ 390,000 |
| Minority Interest | | 44,000 |
| Stockholders' Equity: | | |
| Common Stock | $300,000 | |
| Paid-in Capital | 50,000 | |
| Retained Earnings | 270,000 | |
| Total Stockholders' Equity | | 620,000 |
| Total Liabilities and Stockholders' Equity | | $1,054,000 |

*EXHIBIT 17-5*

Work Sheet for a Consolidated Balance Sheet:
Less Than 100% Ownership—Purchase Method

PREE COMPANY AND SUBSIDIARY
Work Sheet for a Consolidated Balance Sheet
As of Acquisition Date

| ACCOUNTS | PREE COMPANY | SEE COMPANY | ADJUSTMENTS AND ELIMINATIONS Debit | ADJUSTMENTS AND ELIMINATIONS Credit | CONSOLIDATED BALANCE SHEET |
|---|---|---|---|---|---|
| Cash | 104 000 | 30 000 | | | 134 000 |
| Accounts Receivable (net) | 120 000 | 50 000 | | | 170 000 |
| Notes Receivable—See Company | 50 000 | | | (2) 50 000 | |
| Inventory | 200 000 | 90 000 | | | 290 000 |
| Investment in See Company | 176 000 | | | (1) 176 000 | |
| Plant and Equipment (net) | 300 000 | 160 000 | | | 460 000 |
| Total Assets | 950 000 | 330 000 | | | 1 054 000 |
| | | | | | |
| Accounts Payable | 130 000 | 60 000 | | | 190 000 |
| Notes Payable—Pree Company | | 50 000 | (2) 50 000 | | |
| Bonds Payable | 200 000 | | | | 200 000 |
| Common Stock | 300 000 | 100 000 | (1) 100 000 | | 300 000 |
| Paid-in Capital | 50 000 | 30 000 | (1) 30 000 | | 50 000 |
| Retained Earnings | 270 000 | 90 000 | (1) 90 000 | | 270 000 |
| Minority Interest | | | | (1) 44 000 | 44 000 |
| Total Liabilities and Stockholders' Equity | 950 000 | 330 000 | 270 000 | 270 000 | 1 054 000 |

(1) To eliminate the investment in See Company.
(2) To eliminate the intercompany note receivable and note payable.

Eliminating entry (2) eliminates the intercompany notes receivable and notes payable in the same way and for the same reasons as explained in the preceding illustration.

## *Purchase of Stock for More or Less Than Book Value*

In each of the two previous illustrations, the parent company purchased the subsidiary's stock at a price equal to the book value of the subsidiary's net assets. Although this may occur, it usually does not. The price to be paid for the subsidiary's stock will depend on the market price of those shares on the date of purchase, which will generally be more or less than their book value. Therefore let us assume now that on January 1, 1986, Pree Company paid $260,000 to purchase

*B2a. When the parent pays more than book value for its share of the subsidiary's stock, certain guidelines must be followed in consolidating the affiliated companies*

100% of See Company's outstanding stock. This is $40,000 above the stock's book value determined from the same preacquisition data found in Exhibit 17–3. In consolidating the two balance sheets, the $40,000 difference between the cost of the investment and the book value of the net assets acquired must be accounted for in an acceptable manner. The Accounting Principles Board has provided the following guidelines to be used by the parent company in allocating the cost of an acquired company to the assets acquired and liabilities assumed:

> First, all identifiable assets acquired—and liabilities assumed—should be assigned a portion of the cost of the acquired company, normally equal to their fair values at date of acquisition. Second, the excess of the cost of the acquired company over the sum of the amounts assigned to identifiable assets acquired less liabilities assumed should be recorded as goodwill.[3]

To illustrate the application of these guidelines, we will account for Pree's purchase of 100% of See's stock for $260,000. On the purchase date, Pree would record the transaction in its books as follows:

| 1986 | | | |
|---|---|---|---|
| Jan. 1 | Investment in See Company | 260,000 | |
| | Cash | | 260,000 |
| | To record the purchase of 100% of See Company's outstanding stock | | |

After the entry has been posted to the accounts, the balance in Pree Company's Cash account will be $20,000. This amount is $260,000 less than the company's preacquisition cash balance, reflecting the amount used to acquire See Company's stock. The balance in Pree's Investment account is $260,000, representing the cost of the See shares acquired. These amounts are in the work sheet shown in Exhibit 17–6. Note that this transaction has not changed the amounts shown in See Company's balance sheet. This is because its stock was purchased from its stockholders (who received the cash), not from the company itself.

There are many reasons why a company would be willing to pay more than book value to acquire the shares of another company. For our purposes, let us assume that it is because the fair market value of certain assets owned by the subsidiary is greater than their book value. Specifically, assume that Pree believes that the fair market value of See Company's plant and equipment assets exceeds their book value by $30,000, but that the fair market values of the other assets are equal to their book values. Based on these assumptions, $30,000 would be added to See Company's plant and equipment assets, and the remaining $10,000 cost in excess of book value would be attributed to goodwill. The work sheet for the preparation of the consolidated balance sheet on the date of acquisition is shown in Exhibit 17–6 on page 626.

Note that in the consolidated work sheet when the $260,000 debit balance in Pree Company's investment account (which represents the cost of the shares acquired) is eliminated against See Company's stockholders' equity (which is at

[3] Accounting Principles Board, "Business Combinations," *Opinion No. 16* (New York: AICPA, 1970), par. 87.

*EXHIBIT 17–6*

Work Sheet for a Consolidated Balance Sheet:
Purchase Cost Exceeds Book Value—Purchase Method

PREE COMPANY AND SUBSIDIARY
Work Sheet for a Consolidated Balance Sheet
As of Acquisition Date

| ACCOUNTS | PREE COMPANY | SEE COMPANY | ADJUSTMENTS AND ELIMINATIONS Debit | ADJUSTMENTS AND ELIMINATIONS Credit | CONSOLIDATED BALANCE SHEET |
|---|---|---|---|---|---|
| Cash | 20 000 | 30 000 | | | 50 000 |
| Accounts Receivable (net) | 120 000 | 50 000 | | | 170 000 |
| Notes Receivable—See Company | 50 000 | | | (2) 50 000 | |
| Inventory | 200 000 | 90 000 | | | 290 000 |
| Investment in See Company | 260 000 | | | (1) 260 000 | |
| Plant and Equipment (net) | 300 000 | 160 000 | (1) 30 000 | | 490 000 |
| Goodwill | | | (1) 10 000 | | 10 000 |
| Total Assets | 950 000 | 330 000 | | | 1010 000 |
| | | | | | |
| Accounts Payable | 130 000 | 60 000 | | | 190 000 |
| Notes Payable—Pree Company | | 50 000 | (2) 50 000 | | |
| Bonds Payable | 200 000 | | | | 200 000 |
| Common Stock | 300 000 | 100 000 | (1) 100 000 | | 300 000 |
| Paid-in Capital | 50 000 | 30 000 | (1) 30 000 | | 50 000 |
| Retained Earnings | 270 000 | 90 000 | (1) 90 000 | | 270 000 |
| Total Liabilities and Stockholders' Equity | 950 000 | 330 000 | 310 000 | 310 000 | 1010 000 |

(1) To eliminate the investment in See Company.
(2) To eliminate the intercompany note receivable and note payable.

book value), $40,000 of cost remains unassigned. The $40,000 excess cost over book equity acquired is assigned as follows:

1. Increase See Company's plant and equipment asset from its book value of $160,000 to its fair market value of $190,000 by inserting a debit of $30,000 in the adjustments column on the plant and equipment line.
2. Recognize $10,000 of purchased goodwill by adding the account title on a separate line of the consolidated work sheet and inserting a debit of $10,000 in the adjustments column on this line.

Sometimes the parent company is able to purchase the outstanding shares of the subsidiary company for less than book value. When this happens, the APB states that the excess of book value over the cost of the investment should be allocated to reduce proportionately the values assigned to noncurrent assets except long term investments in marketable securities in determining their fair values.[4]

[4] Ibid., par 91.

## CONSOLIDATED INCOME STATEMENT—PURCHASE METHOD

Following the date of acquisition, the operations of the parent and its subsidiary companies are consolidated and reported as if the two companies were a single business entity. The consolidated income statement is prepared by combining the revenue and expense accounts of the parent company and its subsidiaries. The procedure (which is illustrated in Exhibit 17–8), uses the data from Exhibit 17–7. This exhibit contains the separate condensed income statements that show Pree Company's and See Company's results of operations for the year ended December 31, 1986.

*EXHIBIT 17–7*

Condensed Income Statement
For the Year Ended December 31, 1986

| | PREE COMPANY | SEE COMPANY |
|---|---|---|
| Revenue: | | |
| Sales | $800,000 | $280,000 |
| Interest Revenue | 6,000 | — |
| Total Revenue | $806,000 | $280,000 |
| Cost and Expenses: | | |
| Cost of Goods Sold | $500,000 | $150,000 |
| Operating Expenses | 140,000 | 30,000 |
| Interest Expense | — | 6,000 |
| Income Tax Expense | 60,000 | 34,000 |
| Total Costs and Expenses | $700,000 | $220,000 |
| Net Income | $106,000 | $ 60,000 |

*B2a. In preparing a consolidated income statement by the purchase method, a work sheet similar to Exhibit 17–8 is often used*

Once again, the worksheet in Exhibit 17–8 on page 628 is used to accumulate the data needed for preparing a consolidated income statement.

The income statement accounts of both companies appear in the first two columns of the work sheet. Before the balances in these accounts can be combined to develop a consolidated income statement, certain adjustments and eliminations are required. These generally involve intercompany revenue and expense transactions, which must be eliminated so that the consolidated income statement will show the results of operations only from transactions with outside parties. Examples of intercompany transactions that must be eliminated are (1) sales and purchases of goods or services made between the affiliated companies, (2) interest revenue and interest expense resulting from receivables and payables between the affiliated companies, and (3) rent revenue and rent expense on facilities owned and used between the affiliated companies.

As you will recall, no work sheet adjustments or eliminations are ever recorded in the accounts of either company. Their purpose is to have the consolidated income statement report the results of operations for two separate companies as if they were a single entity.

In preparing the consolidated work sheet, we returned to our previous example in which Pree Company paid $260,000 for 100% of See Company's outstanding stock. We then entered amounts in the adjustments and eliminations columns to eliminate the effects of two intercompany transactions and to recognize two adjustments before we combined the individual revenue and expense accounts of the affiliated companies. Each eliminating and adjusting entry is further described in Exhibit 17–8 on page 628.

EXHIBIT 17–8
Work Sheet for a Consolidated Income Statement: Purchase Method

PREE COMPANY AND SUBSIDIARY
Work Sheet for a Consolidated Income Statement
For the Year Ended December 31, 1986

| Accounts | Pree Company | See Company | Adjustments and Eliminations Debit | Adjustments and Eliminations Credit | Consolidated Income Statement |
|---|---|---|---|---|---|
| Sales | 800 000 | 280 000 | (1) 70 000 | | 1010 000 |
| Interest Revenue | 6 000 | | (2) 6 000 | | |
| Total Revenue | 806 000 | 280 000 | | | 1010 000 |
| Cost of Goods Sold | 500 000 | 150 000 | | (1) 70 000 | 580 000 |
| Operating Expenses | 140 000 | 30 000 | (3) 3 000<br>(4) 1 000 | | 174 000 |
| Interest Expense | | 6 000 | | (2) 6 000 | |
| Income Tax Expense | 60 000 | 34 000 | | | 94 000 |
| Total Costs and Expenses | 700 000 | 220 000 | | | 848 000 |
| Total | | | 80 000 | 76 000 | |
| Net Income | 106 000 | 60 000 | | | 162 000 |

(1) To eliminate intercompany sales and purchases.
(2) To eliminate intercompany interest revenue and interest expense.
(3) To depreciate excess cost over book value assigned to plant and equipment assets.
(4) To amortize goodwill created at the time the subsidiary was acquired.

1. Pree Company sold $70,000 worth of merchandise to See Company during the year. Pree recorded the transaction as a sale, and See recorded it as a purchase.

The intercompany purchase has been eliminated through the cost of goods sold because See was able to sell all the merchandise it purchased from Pree during 1986. The eliminating entry is needed to ensure that the sales and cost of goods sold figures reported in the consolidated income statement include only amounts resulting from transactions with parties outside the affiliated group.

2. Pree Company recorded $6,000 of interest revenue and See Company recorded $6,000 of interest expense on an intercompany note receivable and note payable.

This intercompany interest revenue and interest expense has been eliminated in the work sheet. The cash paid to Pree by See is considered to be a cash transfer within the consolidated entity, since no outside party was involved. As such, it does not represent a revenue or expense item and was therefore eliminated in determining consolidated net income.

3. On the date of acquisition when Pree paid $260,000 for See's outstanding stock, the plant and equipment assets were written up by $30,000 to reflect their fair market value. One year has gone by since the acquisition, and depreciation on the $30,000 write-up must be included in the consolidated income statement for 1986. The $3,000 amount shown by entry (3) increasing the consolidated entity's operating expenses was determined by using the straight-line depreciation method with an estimated life of ten years and no residual value.

The credit portion of this entry affects the carrying value of the plant and equipment assets on the balance sheet.

4. On the date of acquisition, the remaining $10,000 of cost in excess of book value was assigned to goodwill. Since one year has gone by since the acquisition, one year of goodwill amortization must be included in the consolidated income statement for 1986. The $1,000 amount shown in the work sheet assumes that goodwill is being amortized over ten years.

The credit portion of this entry reduces the amount reported for goodwill on the balance sheet.

In examining the work sheet for a consolidated income statement, note that the $162,000 net income of the affiliated companies is $4,000 less than the aggregate net income reported by the two companies. This is due to greater consolidated expenses for plant and equipment depreciation and for goodwill amortization.

In preparing this illustration, we have made a number of simplifying assumptions about the activities of the two companies. The eliminations involved in the preparation of a consolidated income statement can often be quite complex. We have focused here on the basic concepts.

## CONSOLIDATED BALANCE SHEET AT DATE OF ACQUISITION—POOLING-OF-INTERESTS METHOD

When the parent company exchanges its voting stock for at least 90% of the subsidiary's voting stock and certain other specific conditions set forth by the APB are met, the acquisition is accounted for by the **pooling-of-interests method.** A pooling of interests involves an exchange of stock. No assets are acquired or given up by either company. The stockholders of the two combining companies become stockholders of the consolidated entity. In effect, they have pooled their ownership interests while two existing companies have merged and now report their operations as if they were a single entity.

Because only stock is exchanged in a pooling, the assets and liabilities of both companies continue to be valued at historical cost. Consequently, poolings of interest are recorded at book values. That is, the book values of the subsidiary's assets and liabilities are combined with those of the parent in preparing a consolidated balance sheet. Since the fair market values of the subsidiary's assets and liabilities are ignored, there can be no excess of cost over book value. Therefore there is no goodwill to be reported in a pooling.

To illustrate the pooling-of-interests method, assume that on January 1, 1986, instead of purchasing See Company's outstanding stock, Pree Company issued 15,000 shares of its $10 par value common stock. This stock had a market value of $18 per share and was exchanged for all of See Company's outstanding stock. Assume also that all the other conditions for a pooling of interests were met. The exchange of stock would be recorded by Pree Company as follows:

| 1986 | | | |
|---|---|---|---|
| Jan. 1 | Investment in See Company . . . . . . . . . . . . . . . . . . . . . . . . | 220,000 | |
| | Common Stock. . . . . . . . . . . . . . . . . . . . . . . . . . . . . | | 150,000 |
| | Paid-in Capital. . . . . . . . . . . . . . . . . . . . . . . . . . . . . | | 70,000 |
| | To record the issuance of 15,000 shares of $10 par value stock in exchange for all the outstanding stock of See Company | | |

Pree Company recorded the investment at $220,000, an amount equal to the book value of See Company's net assets. The investment was not recorded at its cost, which would have been $270,000 (15,000 shares × market value of $18 per share). Common Stock is credited for the par value of the 15,000 shares issued by Pree, and the Paid-in Capital is credited for the difference.

*B2b. Exhibit 17–9 shows the work sheet for preparing a consolidated balance sheet using the pooling-of-interests method*

The work sheet for the preparation of a consolidated balance sheet on the date of acquisition under the pooling-of-interests method is shown in Exhibit 17–9. Note that Pree Company's account balances have changed to reflect the above entry. The account Investment in See Company appears in Pree Company's unconsolidated balance sheet at $220,000. The Common Stock account shows a balance of $450,000, which reflects the $150,000 increase resulting from shares issued in exchange for those of See Company. The Paid-in Capital account also shows an increase of $70,000 to $120,000 as a result of the exchange of shares. Note also that Pree Company's Cash account balance remains the same at $280,000. Remember: In a pooling, no cash is used to acquire the subsidiary's stock.

EXHIBIT 17–9

Work Sheet for a Consolidated Balance Sheet: Pooling-of-Interests Method

PREE COMPANY AND SUBSIDIARY
Work Sheet for a Consolidated Balance Sheet
As of Acquisition Date

| Accounts | Pree Company | See Company | Adjustments and Eliminations: Debit | Adjustments and Eliminations: Credit | Consolidated Balance Sheet |
|---|---|---|---|---|---|
| Cash | 280 000 | 30 000 | | | 310 000 |
| Accounts Receivable (net) | 120 000 | 50 000 | | | 170 000 |
| Notes Receivable—See Company | 50 000 | | | (2)50 000 | |
| Inventory | 200 000 | 90 000 | | | 290 000 |
| Investment in See Company | 220 000 | | | (1)220 000 | |
| Plant and Equipment (net) | 300 000 | 160 000 | | | 460 000 |
| Total Assets | 1170 000 | 330 000 | | | 1230 000 |
| | | | | | |
| Accounts Payable | 130 000 | 60 000 | | | 190 000 |
| Notes Payable—Pree Company | | 50 000 | (2)50 000 | | |
| Bonds Payable | 200 000 | | | | 200 000 |
| Common Stock | 450 000 | 100 000 | (1)100 000 | | 450 000 |
| Paid-in Capital | 120 000 | 30 000 | (1)120 000 | | 30 000 |
| Retained Earnings | 270 000 | 90 000 | | | 360 000 |
| Total Liabilities and Stockholders' Equity | 1170 000 | 330 000 | 270 000 | 270 000 | 1230 000 |

(1) To eliminate the investment in See Company.
(2) To eliminate the intercompany note receivable and note payable.

Eliminating entry (1) reflects the theory underlying the pooling-of-interests method. The $220,000 debit balance in Pree Company's Investment account is eliminated because it is being replaced on the consolidated balance sheet with the net assets of See Company. In a pooling, the Investment account balance is eliminated in a specific order. The first $100,000 is eliminated against the Common Stock of the subsidiary because the shares are now owned by Pree. Next the difference between the Investment account balance and the subsidiary's Common Stock account balance is eliminated against the Paid-in Capital, leaving that account with a balance of $30,000. If the difference between the Investment account balance and the subsidiary's Common Stock account balance exceeds the balance in the Paid-in Capital account, it is eliminated against Retained Earnings. Note that the subsidiary's Retained Earnings account is not eliminated. Instead it is combined with the parent company's Retained Earnings. This seems appropriate in light of the pooling assumption that two continuing companies have pooled their interests and now report as if they had always been one company.

Eliminating entry (2) is done to eliminate the intercompany notes receivable and notes payable.

## CONSOLIDATED INCOME STATEMENT—POOLING-OF-INTERESTS METHOD

A consolidated income statement under the pooling-of-interests method is prepared in much the same way as it was under the purchase method. That is, revenue and expense accounts of the parent and its subsidiaries are combined after all intercompany transactions have been eliminated. However, major differences do exist. Recall that under the purchase method, it is often necessary to revalue specific assets acquired in the business combination to reflect their fair market value. Furthermore, the purchase method often gives rise to a consolidated goodwill because the cost of the investment often exceeds the book value of the subsidiary's net assets. Under a pooling, the subsidiary's assets are not revalued. The book values of the subsidiary's net assets are combined with those of the parent company. Consequently, there would be no goodwill recorded in the accounts.

***B2b. The work sheet for preparing a consolidated income statement by the pooling-of-interests method is shown in Exhibit 17–10***

The work sheet for the preparation of a consolidated income statement under the pooling-of-interests method is shown in Exhibit 17–10 on page 632. The data in the first two columns of the work sheet have been taken from the separate income statements of Pree and See Companies shown in Exhibit 17–7.

Since excess of cost over book value is not recorded under the pooling method, only the intercompany transactions that took place during the year must be eliminated. Two such transactions occurred. The intercompany sales and purchases of $70,000 were eliminated with entry (1) in the same way that they were under the purchase method. The intercompany interest revenue and interest expense were eliminated with entry (2) as before.

The consolidated net income of a business combination accounted for under the pooling method will usually be greater than it would have been under the purchase method for the following reasons:

EXHIBIT 17-10

Work Sheet for a Consolidated Income Statement: Pooling-of-Interests Method

PREE COMPANY AND SUBSIDIARY
Work Sheet for a Consolidated Income Statement
For the Year Ended December 31, 1986

| ACCOUNTS | PREE COMPANY | SEE COMPANY | ADJUSTMENTS AND ELIMINATIONS Debit | ADJUSTMENTS AND ELIMINATIONS Credit | CONSOLIDATED INCOME STATEMENT |
|---|---|---|---|---|---|
| Sales | 800 000 | 280 000 | (1) 70 000 | | 1010 000 |
| Interest Revenue | 6 000 | | (2) 6 000 | | |
| Total Revenue | 806 000 | 280 000 | | | 1010 000 |
| Cost of Goods Sold | 500 000 | 150 000 | | (1) 70 000 | 580 000 |
| Operating Expenses | 140 000 | 30 000 | | | 170 000 |
| Interest Expense | | 6 000 | | (2) 6 000 | |
| Income Tax Expense | 60 000 | 34 000 | | | 94 000 |
| Total Costs and Expenses | 700 000 | 220 000 | | | 844 000 |
| Net Income | 106 000 | 60 000 | | | 166 000 |

(1) To eliminate intercompany sales and purchases.
(2) To eliminate intercompany interest revenue and interest expense.

*B1b. The purchase and pooling-of-interests methods are compared here and in Exhibit 17-11*

1. Under the pooling-of-interests method, the assets of the subsidiary are not revalued in the consolidated balance sheet. Thus there will be no additional depreciation expense resulting from the write-up of depreciable assets to their fair market value in the consolidated income statements.
2. Under a pooling, no amounts are assigned to goodwill. Thus there will be no amortization expense for goodwill in the consolidated income statement.
3. Under a pooling, the parent company is permitted to include the subsidiary's net income for the entire year in the consolidated net income, even though the business combination may have occurred near year-end. Under the purchase method, only the net income earned by the subsidiary since the date of acquisition can be included in the consolidated net income.

## THE PURCHASE AND POOLING METHODS COMPARED

Exhibit 17 – 11 summarizes and compares the major features of the purchase and pooling methods.

*EXHIBIT 17 – 11*

Comparison of Purchase and Pooling Methods

| PURCHASE METHOD | POOLING-OF-INTERESTS METHOD |
|---|---|
| 1. The purchase method is used when one company (the parent) acquires a controlling interest in another company (the subsidiary) by exchanging its cash, other assets, or debt securities for more than 50% of the acquired company's outstanding voting stock. | 1. The pooling-of-interests method is used when one company (the parent) acquires a controlling interest in another company (the subsidiary) by exchanging its voting stock for 90% or more of the outstanding voting stock of the subsidiary and when certain other conditions are met. |
| 2. The parent company records the investment at cost. When a consolidated balance sheet is prepared, if the price paid by the parent for the subsidiary's stock exceeds the book value of the net assets acquired, the subsidiary's assets and liabilities are revalued to reflect their fair market value. Any remaining excess cost over the value of the subsidiary's net assets is recognized as goodwill. The assets and liabilities (less any eliminations) of the subsidiary are added, at their fair market values, to the book values of the assets and liabilities of the parent to establish the consolidated balance sheet. | 2. The parent company records the investment at an amount equal to the book value of the subsidiary's net assets. When a consolidated balance sheet is prepared, the subsidiary's assets and liabilities are not revalued regardless of the market price of the shares issued by the parent company. No goodwill is recognized. The assets and liabilities (less any eliminations) of the subsidiary are added, at their book values, to the book values of the assets and liabilities of the parent to establish the consolidated balance sheet. |
| 3. Retained earnings of the subsidiary are not combined with the retained earnings of the parent in establishing consolidated retained earnings. | 3. Retained earnings of the subsidiary are combined with the retained earnings of the parent in establishing consolidated retained earnings. |
| 4. When preparing an income statement, the revenues reported by each company (less any eliminations) are combined. Expenses (less eliminations), plus additional depreciation expense for the excess cost over book value assigned to depreciable assets, and amortization expense for the excess cost over book value assigned to goodwill, are combined. | 4. When preparing an income statement, the revenues and expenses reported by each company (less any eliminations) are combined. No excess cost over book value exists. Therefore there is no additional depreciation expense or amortization expense. |
| 5. Earnings of the subsidiary are included in consolidated net income only from the date that the acquisition occurred. | 5. Earnings of the subsidiary are included in consolidated net income for the entire year in which the acquisition occurred. |

## HIGHLIGHT PROBLEM

Prank Company and Ster Company had the following balance sheets on December 31, 1985.

| | PRANK COMPANY | STER COMPANY |
|---|---|---|
| Cash | $ 360,000 | $ 70,000 |
| Accounts Receivable (net) | 110,000 | 45,000 |
| Notes Receivable—Ster Company | 60,000 | — |
| Inventory | 140,000 | 60,000 |
| Plant and Equipment (net) | 580,000 | 135,000 |
| Total Assets | $1,250,000 | $310,000 |
| Accounts Payable | $ 150,000 | $ 80,000 |
| Notes Payable—Prank Company | — | 60,000 |
| Bonds Payable | 200,000 | — |
| Common Stock ($10 par value) | 500,000 | 100,000 |
| Retained Earnings | 400,000 | 70,000 |
| Total Liabilities and Stockholders' Equity | $1,250,000 | $310,000 |

On January 1, 1986, Prank Company purchased all the outstanding stock of Ster Company for $170,000.

Required:

1. Prepare the entry made by Prank Company when the 10,000 shares of Ster Company's stock were purchased.
2. Prepare a work sheet for a consolidated balance sheet on January 1, 1986, the date of acquisition.

## GLOSSARY OF KEY TERMS

**Consolidated financial statements.** Financial statements that show the results of operations and the financial position of two or more companies (the parent and one or more subsidiary companies) as if they were a single business entity.

**Controlling interest.** The relationship that exists when the investor is able to control the operating and financial policies of an investee company. A controlling interest is presumed to exist when the investor owns more than 50% of the outstanding voting stock of the investee.

**Cost method.** The method used when the investor cannot exercise significant influence over the investee. The investment is recorded at cost, and dividends received from the investee are recognized as revenue.

**Equity method.** The method used when the investor can exercise significant influence over the operating and financial policies of the investee. Significant influence is presumed to exist when the investor owns 20% or more of the voting stock of the investee. The investment is recorded at cost, and (1) a proportionate share of the investee's subsequent reported net income or net loss increases or decreases the investment account, and (2) dividends received subsequently from the investee decrease the investment account.

**Investee company.** A company whose stock is owned by another company.

**Investor company.** A company that owns stock in another company.

**Long-term investments.** Investments in securities that management does not intend to sell within one year or the firm's operating cycle, whichever is longer.

**Lower of cost or market (LCM) method.** The procedure for valuing a group of equity securities in the balance sheet at the lower of their aggregate cost or their aggregate market value. Used to measure the value of an investment in a group of short-term equity securities and long-term equity securities where the investor cannot exercise significant influence or control over the investee.

**Minority interest.** The interest owned in the net assets of a subsidiary company by stockholders other than those of the parent company.

**Parent company.** A company that owns a controlling interest in another company. Generally, such an interest is gained by acquiring more than 50% of another company's outstanding voting stock.

**Pooling-of-interests method.** A method of accounting for a business combination in which the parent company exchanges its voting stock for 90% or more of the subsidiary's voting stock and in which certain other specific conditions are met.

**Purchase method.** A method of accounting for a business combination in which the parent company exchanges cash, other assets, or debt for more than 50% of the subsidiary's voting stock.

**Subsidiary company.** A company owned or controlled by another company. A company that has 50% or more of its outstanding voting stock owned by another company.

**Temporary investments.** Investments in securities that are readily marketable and that management intends to convert into cash within a year or the firm's operating cycle, whichever is longer.

## REVIEW QUESTIONS

1. How do investments classified as temporary differ from those classified as long-term? [LOA1a]
2. What two criteria must be met before an investment in securities can be classified as temporary? [LOA1a]
3. For what amount is the Temporary Investments account debited when a corporation purchases short-term investments? [LOA2a]
4. When temporary investments in debt securities are sold, how is the gain or loss computed? [LOA2a]
5. What event must occur before dividends on temporary investments in equity securities can be recorded? [LOA2a]
6. How are securities held as temporary investments reported on the balance sheet? [LOA2a]
7. Differentiate between (a) the way that changes in the value of temporary investments in debt securities are handled on the balance sheet and (b) the way that changes in the value of temporary investments in equity securities are handled on the balance sheet. [LOA2b]
8. How is the account entitled "Allowance to Reduce Temporary Investments to Market Value" classified on the balance sheet? [LOA2b]
9. At what amount are long-term investments in bonds initially entered in the accounts? [LOA2c]
10. What are two important interest rates in determining the purchase price of a bond? [LOA2c]
11. When long-term bonds are purchased at a discount, how is the discount treated in the accounting records? [LOA2c]
12. Differentiate between the straight-line method and the effective interest method of amortizing bond discount. [LOA2c]
13. When long-term bonds are purchased at a premium, how is the premium treated in the accounting records? [LOA2c]
14. Differentiate between the straight-line method and the effective interest method of amortizing bond premium. [LOA2c]
15. When long-term bonds are sold prior to maturity, how is the gain or loss on the sale computed? [LOA2c]
16. Describe, in terms of degree of influence and status of ownership, the difference between the two methods of accounting for long-term investments in common stock. [LOA1b]
17. How are dividends arising from long-term investments reported in the financial statements of the investor when the cost method is used? [LOA2d]
18. How is the account entitled "Unrealized Loss on Long-Term Investments" reported in the financial statements? [LOA2d]
19. What percentage of the investee's stock must the investor own to indicate that the investor has the ability to exercise significant influence over an investee? [LOA2d]
20. When the equity method of accounting for long-term investments is used, how are the

investee's reported net income and the investee's cash dividend declaration accounted for by the investor? [LOA2d]

21. Describe a condition that would establish a parent-subsidiary relationship between two or more companies. [LOB1a]
22. What is the purpose of consolidated financial statements? [LOB1a]
23. What is the purpose of eliminating entry (1) and the purpose of eliminating entry (2) in Exhibit 17–4? [LOB2a]
24. What is meant by *minority interest*, and how does it occur? [LOB2a]
25. How does goodwill occur in the preparation of consolidated financial statements? [LOB2a]
26. When a consolidated income statement is prepared, why must intercompany revenue and expense transactions be eliminated? [LOB2a]
27. Why is no goodwill recognized when the pooling-of-interests method is used in accounting for a business combination? [LOB2b]
28. Why aren't the assets and liabilities of the acquired company reported at their fair market value when the pooling-of-interests method is used? [LOB2b]
29. Why is the consolidated net income of a business combination accounted for under the pooling method usually greater than it would have been if the combination had been accounted for as a purchase? [LOB1b]
30. Differentiate between the purchase method and the pooling-of-interests method of accounting for business combinations. [LOB1b]

## ANALYTICAL QUESTIONS

31. Management decided to classify all equity investments as long-term to avoid recognition of any unrealized losses. What is the possible effect of this decision on the income statement? [LOA1a]
32. "The lower of cost or market method is inconsistent because it does not adjust cost if the market value is higher." Comment on this statement. [LOA2b]
33. Why are bond discounts and bond premiums amortized when they relate to the purchase of long-term investments but not amortized when they relate to the purchase of temporary investments? [LOA2a,A2c]
34. "How can accountants justify the equity method of accounting for long-term stock investments in which the investment account is credited for the dividends received from the investee?" Reply to this question. [LOA1b,A2d]
35. You overhear the manager of a company assert: "Accounting for the acquisition of a controlling interest in another company by using the pooling-of-interests method rather than the purchase method is a better course of action and results in better consolidated financial statements." Comment on this statement. [LOB1a,B1b,B2b]

## IMPACT ANALYSIS QUESTIONS

*For each error described, indicate whether it would overstate [O], understate [U], or not affect [N] the indicated key figures.*

36. On April 1, 19X8, the company received an interest check for $600. Half of the $600 was for interest earned in 19X8, and half of the $600 was for interest accrued and earned in 19X7. An adjusting entry for accrued interest had been made on December 31, 19X7, for $300 and was not reversed on January 1, 19X8. However, on April 1, 19X8, an entry was made debiting cash and crediting bond interest revenue for the entire $600 amount. [LOA2a,A2c]

_______ Total Assets _______ Total Liabilities
_______ Net Income _______ Stockholders' Equity

37. At the end of the year, the aggregate market value of a short-term equity investment portfolio was less than its aggregate cost. No journal entry was made to recognize this market decline. [LOA2b]

_______ Total Assets _______ Total Liabilities
_______ Net Income _______ Stockholders' Equity

38. Company A held a controlling interest in the voting stock of Company B. Although the equity method of accounting was used, no entry was made on the books of Company A for any portion of the net income reported by Company B. [LOA2d]

_______ Total Assets _______ Total Liabilities
_______ Net Income _______ Stockholders' Equity

39. Refer to question 38. Although the equity method of accounting was used, Company A debited the investment account and credited a revenue account when Company B declared a cash dividend. [LOA2d]

_______ Total Assets _______ Total Liabilities
_______ Net Income _______ Stockholders' Equity

40. Company Par owns 100% of the common stock of Company Sub. In preparing the consolidated balance sheet, no elimination was made on the worksheet for Company Par's investment in Company Sub. [LOB2a]

_______ Total Assets on the Consolidated Balance Sheet
_______ Total Liabilities on the Consolidated Balance Sheet
_______ Total Stockholders' Equity on the Consolidated Balance Sheet

## EXERCISES

EXERCISE 17–1 *(Account for Temporary Investments in Bonds and Stocks)* During 1986 West Company made two separate investments in income-yielding securities. Information relating to these investments follows.

On March 1 West purchased 1,000 shares of Mack Company's common stock at $23 per share and paid $500 in commissions and taxes related to the purchase. Mack Company has 120,000 common shares outstanding.

On July 31 West purchased ten 9%, $1,000 bonds of Templeton Company at 98, plus one month of accrued interest. Commissions relating to the purchase totaled $300.

On December 27 West received a cash dividend of $2,000 on Mack Company stock.

On December 31 West received a check for the semiannual interest on the Templeton Company bonds.

On December 31 West sold 800 shares of the Mack Company stock at $24 per share.

Required:

1. Prepare journal entries to record each of the above transactions.
2. What accounts and amounts related to these investments would be shown in West Company's income statement?
3. Were the remaining shares of Mack Company reported in West Company's balance sheet at cost or at market? Explain. [LOA2a,A2b]

EXERCISE 17–2 *(Account for Temporary Investments in Stock)* The aggregate cost and aggregate market value of a group of equity securities being held as a temporary investment by Darling Company are shown below at two consecutive year-end dates.

| DATE | AGGREGATE COST | AGGREGATE MARKET |
|---|---|---|
| December 31, 1985 | $110,000 | $ 97,000 |
| December 31, 1986 | 110,000 | 112,000 |

Required:

1. Prepare the journal entry required at the end of each year, assuming Darling has a calendar year-end.
2. Show how the temporary investments would be reported in Darling's balance sheet on December 31, 1985. [LOA2b]

EXERCISE 17-3 *(Account for Long-Term Investments in Bonds)* On January 1, 1986, MBK Company purchased as a long-term investment eighty $1,000 face value, 9% bonds of Baron Company at 95 plus brokerage fees of $1,200. The bonds pay interest semiannually on June 30 and December 31. They mature on December 31, 1995.

Required:

Assuming MBK amortizes bond discounts and premiums using the straight-line method and that the investment will be held to maturity, answer the following questions:

1. How much cash will MBK Company receive in each of the years 1986 through 1995?
2. How much of the bond discount will be amortized in each year that the bonds are held?
3. How much will the company report as bond interest revenue on its income statement for each year that the bonds are held?
4. How much will the long-term bond investment account increase each year?
5. At what amount will the bond investment be reported in the company's December 31, 1991, balance sheet?
6. What is the net amount of cash received (total cash inflows minus total cash outflows) from this investment? [LOA2c]

EXERCISE 17-4 *(Prepare Journal Entries for Long-Term Investments in Bonds)* On June 1, 1986, Marbrad Company purchased as a long-term investment sixty $1,000 face value, 9% bonds of Kimellen Company. The bonds pay interest semiannually on February 1 and August 1. They mature on February 1, 1991. Marbrad Company's fiscal year ends on December 31. The company records bond discount and bond premium amortization on each interest payment date using the straight-line method. Amortization and accrued bond interest is also recorded at year-end with amounts rounded to the nearest dollar.

Required:

Prepare all the journal entries relating to the bond investment for 1986 and 1987 assuming that

1. The bonds were purchased at 96 plus accrued interest
2. The bonds were purchased at 103 plus accrued interest [LOA2c]

EXERCISE 17-5 *(Compute Interest Revenue and Prepare Entries for Long-Term Investments in Bonds)* On April 1, 1986, Riverton Company purchased as a long-term investment fifty $1,000, 12% bonds of Reese Company at 102 plus accrued interest and a brokerage fee of $770. The bonds pay interest semiannually on January 31 and July 31. They mature on February 1, 1996. The company amortizes bond discounts and bond premiums using the straight-line method.

Required:

1. Prepare all the journal entries made by Riverton to account for the bond investment during 1986. The company has a calendar year-end.
2. How much bond interest revenue would be reported in Riverton's income statement for the year ended December 31, 1986?
3. Prepare a journal entry to record the sale of the bonds on January 31, 1989. The bonds were sold for $51,500. [LOA2c]

EXERCISE 17-6 *(Determine the Appropriate Method and Account for Long-Term Investments in Stock)* On January 2, 1986, Cook Company purchased 20,000 shares of Disk Company's outstanding common stock as a long-term investment at $35 per share plus a broker's commission of $3,000. On December 19, 1986, Cook received a cash dividend of $2 per share from Disk Company. The Disk shares are the only securities being held as a long-term investment by Cook. Disk Company's reported net income of $280,000 was announced on

December 31, 1986. There were 200,000 common shares of Disk Company outstanding throughout 1986.

Required:

1. State the accounting method that should be used to account for this long-term investment and explain why it is used.
2. Based on your answer to requirement 1, prepare all the journal entries that would be made by Cook Company during 1986 to account for its long-term stock investment. Disk Company's common shares had a market price of $33 per share at the close of business on December 31, 1986.
3. Assume that all the facts and transactions stated in the exercise remain the same except that on January 2, 1986, Cook Company purchased 50,000 shares of Disk Company's outstanding common stock instead of 20,000 shares. State the accounting method that should be used to account for the long-term investment and give the reason for your answer.
4. Based on your answer to requirement 3, prepare all the journal entries that would be made by Cook during 1986. [LOA2d]

EXERCISE 17–7 *(Account for Long-Term Investments in Stock—Equity Method)* On January 1, 1986, Barclay Corporation purchased as a long-term investment 90,000 shares of Logan Corporation's common stock for $20 per share. After completing this transaction, Logan had a total of 300,000 common shares outstanding. Other transactions and events related to this investment are as follows:

On November 12, 1986, Logan declared and paid a dividend of $.50 per share.

On December 31, 1986, Logan reported net income of $450,000 for the year.

On December 31, 1986, Logan's common shares had a market value of $24 per share.

On January 9, 1987, Barclay sold 15,000 of Logan's shares for $25 per share less a broker's commission of $4,000.

Required:

1. Prepare all the journal entries made by Barclay Corporation to account for the transactions and events stated above.
2. Determine the balance in the investment account on January 9, 1987, after the transaction to record the sale of the 15,000 shares has been posted. [LOA2d]

EXERCISE 17–8 *(Prepare Acquisition and Elimination Entries for a Consolidated Balance Sheet—Purchase Method)* On January 2, 1986, Pax Company purchased all of Sacks Company's outstanding common shares for $170,000 in cash. On the date of acquisition, each company had the following individual balance sheets.

| | PAX COMPANY | SACKS COMPANY |
|---|---|---|
| Cash | $290,000 | $ 80,000 |
| Accounts Receivable (net) | 140,000 | 50,000 |
| Note Receivable—Sacks Company | 20,000 | — |
| Inventory | 110,000 | 60,000 |
| Plant and Equipment (net) | 370,000 | 130,000 |
| Total Assets | $930,000 | $320,000 |
| Accounts Payable | $105,000 | $ 30,000 |
| Note Payable—Pax Company | — | 20,000 |
| Bonds Payable | 200,000 | 100,000 |
| Common Stock (no par value) | 500,000 | 100,000 |
| Retained Earnings | 125,000 | 70,000 |
| Total Liabilities and Stockholders' Equity | $930,000 | $320,000 |

Required:

1. Prepare the journal entry that would be made by Pax Company to record its investment in Sacks Company.
2. Prepare the elimination entries (in general journal form) that would be made on the work sheet used to prepare a consolidated balance sheet at the date of acquisition.

[LOB2a]

EXERCISE 17–9 *(Prepare a Consolidated Income Statement—Purchase Method)* On October 1, 1986, Chain Company paid $400,000 to acquire all the outstanding stock of Link Company. The amount paid by Chain was equal to the book value of the net assets being acquired. Both companies have fiscal years that end on September 30, and their condensed income statements are shown below.

| | CHAIN COMPANY | LINK COMPANY |
|---|---|---|
| Sales | $850,000 | $310,000 |
| Interest Revenue | 30,000 | — |
| Total Revenue | $880,000 | $310,000 |
| Cost of Goods Sold | $490,000 | $150,000 |
| Operating Expenses | 260,000 | 110,000 |
| Interest Expense | 10,000 | 3,000 |
| Total Expenses | $760,000 | $263,000 |
| Net Income | $120,000 | $ 47,000 |

During the fiscal year, Chain Company sold $50,000 of merchandise to Link Company, which Link then sold to its customers. Chain also recorded $3,000 in cash from Link for interest on an intercompany note receivable and note payable.

Required:

Prepare a work sheet containing a column to show a consolidated income statement for the fiscal year ended September 30, 1987. [LOB2a]

EXERCISE 17–10 *(Prepare Acquisition and Elimination Entries for a Consolidated Balance Sheet—Pooling Method)* On April 1, 1986, Falley Company acquired all of Clay Company's outstanding common stock by issuing 20,000 of its own $10 par value common shares in exchange. On the date of the exchange, Falley's common stock was selling at $28, and Clay Company's stockholders' equity was as follows.

| | |
|---|---|
| Common Stock ($2 per share) | $ 80,000 |
| Paid-in Capital | 170,000 |
| Retained Earnings | 190,000 |
| | $440,000 |

Required:

1. Assume that the transaction met all the requirements of a pooling of interests. Prepare the journal entry made by Falley to record the exchange of shares.
2. Assume that on the date of the stock exchange, Clay Company owed $25,000 to Falley Company on a note payable. Prepare in general journal form the elimination entries that would be made on the work sheet for a consolidated balance sheet on April 1, 1986. [LOB2b]

## PROBLEMS

PROBLEM 17–1 *(Account for Temporary Bond and Stock Investments)* The following data pertain to the short-term investment securities acquired by Sterling Company during 1986.

a. Purchased five $1,000 bonds of Chaps Company at par, plus accrued interest of $50 and brokerage fees of $150.
b. Purchased 500 shares of Allied Company stock at $40 per share, plus brokerage fees of $70.
c. Received interest of $150 on the Chaps Company bonds.
d. Received a cash dividend of $2 per share on the Allied Company stock.
e. Sold 200 shares of Allied Company stock, receiving cash proceeds of $8,400.
f. Received interest of $150 on the Chaps Company bonds.
g. Purchased 200 shares of Valley Company stock at $50 per share, plus brokerage fees of $40.

At year-end the short-term stock portfolio had an aggregate market value of $23,600, and the accrued interest on Chaps Company bonds totaled $100.

Required:

1. Prepare all the journal entries that would be made by Sterling Company to account for these short-term investments during 1986.
2. Determine the amounts that would be reported in Sterling Company's income statement for the following:
   a. Bond interest revenue
   b. Dividend revenue
   c. Gain or loss on the sale of temporary investments
   d. Unrealized loss, if any [LOA2a,A2b]

PROBLEM 17–2 *(Account for Temporary Investments in Stock)* Burnside Company frequently purchases the common shares of other companies as a temporary investment. Shares held by Burnside as of April 1, 1986, are summarized below.

| COMPANY AND NUMBER OF SHARES HELD | COST |
|---|---|
| Webster Company—300 common shares | $ 9,300 |
| Lance Corporation—500 common shares | 21,600 |
| Edwards Company—200 preferred shares | 18,400 |
| Wingfoot Company—400 common shares | 14,200 |
| Total cost | $63,500 |

On August 1, 1986, Burnside sold 200 shares of the Webster Company stock, receiving cash proceeds of $6,700. During 1986 Burnside received $5,100 in cash dividends from these investments. On December 31, 1986, the investment group had the market values shown below.

| COMPANY AND NUMBER OF SHARES HELD | MARKET VALUE |
|---|---|
| Webster Company—100 common shares | $ 3,500 |
| Lance Corporation—500 common shares | 19,900 |
| Edwards Company—200 preferred shares | 17,800 |
| Wingfoot Company—400 common shares | 14,900 |
| Total market value | $56,100 |

Required:

1. Prepare journal entries to
   a. Record the sale of the Webster Company stock.
   b. Record the dividends received (this must be a summary entry—use a December 31, 1986, date).
   c. Apply the lower of cost or market rule to the temporary stock investment group. Prepare an adjusting entry if one is needed.

2. State how the temporary investments are classified on the balance sheet, and illustrate how they are reported in the December 31, 1986, balance sheet.
3. State the accounts and amounts that would be reported in the income statement for the year 1986. [LOA2a,A2b]

PROBLEM 17–3 *(Compute Interest and Prepare Entries for Long-Term Investment in Bonds)* Expressit Corporation purchased as a long-term investment fifty $1,000 face value, 12% bonds of Nightlife Company at 102 plus accrued interest on February 1, 1985. Brokerage fees on this transaction were $900. The bonds pay interest semiannually on April 1 and October 1. They mature on April 1, 1995.

On June 1, 1986, Expressit Corporation sold twenty-five of the bonds, receiving cash proceeds of $26,450, which included two months of accrued interest. Expressit Corporation uses the straight-line method of amortizing bond discounts and bond premiums and rounds amounts to the nearest dollar.

Required:

1. Prepare all the journal entries needed to account for the bond investment during the years 1985 and 1986. Expressit's fiscal year ends on December 31.
2. Determine the amount of bond interest revenue that would be reported in Expressit's income statement for the years ended December 31, 1985 and 1986.
3. Prepare the journal entry that would be made on April 1, 1995, to record maturity of the bonds.
4. On the date the bonds were originally purchased, was the prevailing market rate of interest higher or lower than 12%? How did you determine this? [LOA2c]

PROBLEM 17–4 *(Account for Long-Term Investments in Bonds)* On June 1, 1985, Page Corporation purchased as a long-term investment eighty $1,000 par value, 9%, 10-year bonds for $77,600, plus accrued interest. The bonds mature on February 1, 1995, and pay semiannual interest on January 31 and July 31.

On March 31, 1986, Page sold one-half of the bonds at their par value, plus accrued interest. Page uses the straight-line method of amortization for bond discounts and bond premiums and rounds amounts to the nearest dollar.

Required:

1. Prepare journal entries to record the following:
   a. The purchase of the bonds on June 1, 1985
   b. The semiannual interest received on July 31, 1985, and the amortization of the related bond discount (or bond premium)
   c. Accrued interest and amortization on December 31, 1985, Page Corporation's fiscal year-end
2. Prepare journal entries to record the following:
   a. The semiannual interest received on January 31, 1986, and the amortization of the related bond discount (or bond premium).
   b. The bond sale on March 31, 1986. (*Hint:* Remember to bring amortization up to date on the day of sale and to include accrued bond interest in the sale entry.)
   c. The semiannual interest received on the bonds still being held on July 31, 1986, and the amortization of the related bond discount (or bond premium) on those bonds.
   d. Accrued interest and amortization on December 31, 1986.
3. Determine the amount of bond interest revenue that would be reported in Page Corporation's income statement for the year ended December 31, 1986.
4. Illustrate how the bond investment would be reported in Page Corporation's December 31, 1986, balance sheet.
5. Prepare the journal entry that would be made on February 1, 1995, when the bonds mature. [LOA2c]

PROBLEM 17–5 *(Account for Long-Term Investments in Stock)* On January 5, 1986, Haynes Corporation purchased as a long-term investment 25,000 of the 100,000 outstanding common shares of Lee Company at $24 per share, plus brokerage commission of $3,000. Other data pertaining to the investment in Lee Company's common shares follow.

On November 20 Lee Company declared and paid a cash dividend of $1.50 per share.

On December 31 Lee Company reported net income of $160,000 for the year.

On December 31 the market price of Lee Company's stock was $22 per share.

Required:

1. What method should Haynes use to account for its long-term investment in Lee Company? Why should this method be used?
2. Prepare the journal entries that Haynes Corporation should make during 1986 to account for its investment in Lee Company.
3. Prepare the journal entry that would be made on March 31, 1987, when Haynes received $127,500 in cash for the sale of 5,000 Lee Company shares.
4. Repeat requirements 1, 2, and 3 using the same information except assume that on January 5, 1986, Haynes purchased 5,000 shares (instead of 25,000 shares) of Lee Company's stock at $26 per share, plus a broker's commission of $800. [LOA2d]

PROBLEM 17–6 *(Account for Long-Term Investments in Stock)* Bergen Company invests in the common stock of other corporations. The following transactions took place during 1985 and 1986.

| | |
|---|---|
| 1985 | |
| Jan. 1 | Bergen purchased as a long-term investment 210,000 shares of Morris Corporation at $15 per share plus a brokerage commission of $3,000. |
| Dec. 4 | Morris Corporation declared and paid a cash dividend of $.90 per share. |
| Dec. 31 | Morris Corporation reported a net income of $120,000 for the year. The market price of Morris Corporation's stock was $16.50 per share on this date. |
| 1986 | |
| Jan. 2 | Bergen sold 5,000 shares of Morris Corporation's stock, receiving cash proceeds of $79,350. (Round cost of shares sold to the nearest dollar.) |
| Dec. 5 | Morris Corporation declared and paid a cash dividend of $.70 per share. |
| Dec. 31 | Morris Corporation reported a net loss of $30,000 for the year. The market price of Morris Corporation's stock was $13.50 per share on this date. |

Required:

1. Prepare all the journal entries needed to account for the long-term stock investment during the years 1985 and 1986. Based on the percentage of shares owned, Bergen should use the cost method to account for this investment. If an entry is not needed for any of the dated items, explain why.
2. Under the cost method, what items and amounts will Bergen Company report in its income statement for the years 1985 and 1986?
3. Prepare all the journal entries needed to account for the long-term stock investment during the years 1985 and 1986. Assume this time that the equity method should be used. If an entry is needed for any of the dated items, explain why. (*Note:* On December 31, 1985, Bergen owned 40% of Morris Corporation, and on December 31, 1986, Bergen owned 30% of Morris.)
4. Under the equity method, what items and amounts will Bergen Company report in its income statement for the years 1985 and 1986? [LOA2d]

PROBLEM 17–7 *(Prepare Work Sheet for a Consolidated Balance Sheet—Puchase Method—90% Ownership)* The balance sheets of Power Company and Sands Company as of January 1, 1986, are shown on page 644.

| | POWER COMPANY | SANDS COMPANY |
|---|---|---|
| Assets: | | |
| Cash | $300,000 | $ 60,000 |
| Accounts Receivable | 120,000 | 40,000 |
| Notes Receivable—Sands Company | 50,000 | — |
| Inventory | 100,000 | 70,000 |
| Plant and Equipment (net) | 420,000 | 140,000 |
| Total Assets | $990,000 | $310,000 |
| Liabilities and Stockholders' Equity: | | |
| Accounts Payable | $130,000 | $ 20,000 |
| Notes Payable—Power Company | — | 50,000 |
| Bonds Payable | 300,000 | — |
| Common Stock ($5 par value) | 400,000 | 150,000 |
| Retained Earnings | 160,000 | 90,000 |
| Total Liabilities and Stockholders' Equity | $990,000 | $310,000 |

On January 2, 1986, Power Company purchased 27,000 shares of Sands Company's outstanding stock for $216,000.

Required:

1. Prepare the entry to record the purchase of Sands Company's stock.
2. Prepare a work sheet for a consolidated balance sheet as of January 2, 1986.
3. Prepare a consolidated balance sheet. [LOB2a]

PROBLEM 17–8 *(Prepare Journal Entry and Work Sheet for a Consolidated Balance Sheet—Purchase Method—100% Ownership)* The balance sheets of Plaza Company and Summit Company as of January 1, 1986, are shown below.

| | PLAZA COMPANY | SUMMIT COMPANY |
|---|---|---|
| Assets: | | |
| Cash | $250,000 | $ 40,000 |
| Accounts Receivable (net) | 70,000 | 25,000 |
| Notes Receivable—Summit Company | 20,000 | — |
| Inventory | 90,000 | 50,000 |
| Plant and Equipment (net) | 300,000 | 130,000 |
| Total Assets | $730,000 | $245,000 |
| Liabilities and Stockholders' Equity: | | |
| Accounts Payable | $110,000 | $ 65,000 |
| Notes Payable—Plaza Company | — | 20,000 |
| Bonds Payable | 200,000 | — |
| Common Stock ($10 par value) | 300,000 | 100,000 |
| Retained Earnings | 120,000 | 60,000 |
| Total Liabilities and Stockholders' Equity | $730,000 | $245,000 |

On January 2, 1986, Plaza Company purchased all the outstanding stock of Summit Company for $205,000. The fair market values of Summit's assets were equal to their book values except for inventory, which has a fair market value of $65,000.

Required:

1. Prepare the entry to record the purchase of Summit's stock.
2. Prepare a work sheet for a consolidated balance sheet as of January 2, 1986. [LOB2a]

PROBLEM 17–9 *(Prepare Work Sheet for a Consolidated Income Statement—Purchase Method)* Parkway Company has owned all of Sommer Company's outstanding common shares since 1983. The condensed income statements for these two companies for the year ended December 31, 1986, are presented on page 645.

| | PARKWAY COMPANY | SOMMER COMPANY |
|---|---|---|
| Revenue: | | |
| Sales | $920,000 | $480,000 |
| Interest Revenue | 18,000 | — |
| Total Revenue | $938,000 | $480,000 |
| Costs and Expenses: | | |
| Cost of Goods Sold | $590,000 | $310,000 |
| Operating Expenses | 220,000 | 90,000 |
| Interest Expense | 13,000 | 20,000 |
| Total Costs and Expenses | $823,000 | $420,000 |
| Net Income | $115,000 | $ 60,000 |

Additional Information:

a. Parkway acquired Sommer Company by purchasing all of its outstanding shares for cash. The amount paid by Parkway exceeded the book value of Sommer's net assets by $60,000. Of this excess cost, $40,000 was assigned to depreciable equipment and $20,000 to goodwill. When acquired on March 8, 1983, the equipment had a remaining life of eight years. Goodwill was given a twenty-year amortization period. Straight-line methods are to be used for depreciation and amortization, and the equipment is not expected to have a salvage value.

b. Parkway sold $70,000 of merchandise to Sommer Company during the year 1986. Sommer in turn sold all the merchandise to persons and companies other than Parkway.

c. Included in interest revenue on Parkway's income statement and interest expense on Sommer's income statement is $6,000 of interest on an intercompany note receivable and note payable.

Required:

Prepare a work sheet for a consolidated income statement for the year ended December 31, 1986. [LOB2a]

PROBLEM 17–10 *(Prepare Journal Entry and Work Sheet for a Consolidated Balance Sheet—Pooling-of-Interests Method)* On January 1, 1986, Porsche Company acquired a controlling interest in Sandler Company by exchanging 10,000 of its $5 par value common shares for all the outstanding common shares of Sandler Company. The market value of the Porsche Company shares was $25 on the date of the exchange. Balance sheets for the two companies on December 31, 1985, are shown below.

| | PORSCHE COMPANY | SANDLER COMPANY |
|---|---|---|
| Assets: | | |
| Cash | $150,000 | $ 40,000 |
| Accounts Receivable (net) | 160,000 | 30,000 |
| Notes Receivable—Sandler Company | 40,000 | — |
| Inventory | 190,000 | 75,000 |
| Plant and Equipment (net) | 380,000 | 135,000 |
| Total Assets | $920,000 | $280,000 |
| Liabilities and Stockholders' Equity: | | |
| Accounts Payable | $170,000 | $ 60,000 |
| Note Payable—Porsche Company | — | 40,000 |
| Bonds Payable | 100,000 | — |
| Common Stock ($5 par value) | 300,000 | 70,000 |
| Paid-in Capital | 110,000 | 20,000 |
| Retained Earnings | 240,000 | 90,000 |
| Total Liabilities and Stockholders' Equity | $920,000 | $280,000 |

Required:

1. Prepare the journal entry that Porsche Company would make to record the exchange of stock, assuming the transaction meets all the criteria for a pooling of interests.
2. Prepare a work sheet for a consolidated balance sheet as of January 1, 1986 (the acquisition date). [LOB2b]

PROBLEM 17–11 *(Comprehensive Problem: Temporary and Long-Term Investments)* On January 2, 1986, Keynote Company purchased as a long-term investment 15,000 of the 50,000 outstanding common shares of Landy Company at $33 per share, plus a brokerage commission of $1,500. On December 5, 1986, Landy Company declared and paid a cash dividend of $2 per share. On December 31, 1986, when the market price of Landy Company's stock was $31 per share, the company reported that its net income for 1986 was only $18,000.

On March 31, 1986, Keynote also purchased as a long-term investment twenty-five $1,000 par value, 10% bonds of Collins Company at 101 plus accrued interest. Brokerage fees related to this transaction were $600. The bonds pay interest semiannually on June 30 and December 31. They mature on January 1, 1996.

In addition, on June 12, 1986, Keynote purchased as a temporary investment 300 shares of Wicker Company's common stock at $42 per share, plus a brokerage commission of $120. On November 9, 1986, Wicker Company declared and paid a cash dividend of $4 per share. On December 31, 1986, when Wicker Company reported that its net income for the year was $280,000, the market price of its common stock was $40 per share.

Required:

1. Prepare all the journal entries made by Keynote Company to account for these three investments. Round amortization amounts to the nearest dollar. Keynote Company's year ends on December 31.
2. Show how the three investments and the revenues, gains, or losses related to the investments would be reported on the financial statements prepared by Keynote at the end of 1986. [LOA2a,A2b,A2c]

## ALTERNATE PROBLEMS

PROBLEM 17–1A *(Account for Temporary Bond and Stock Investments)* (Alternate to Problem 17–1) The following data pertain to the short-term investment securities acquired by Pureall Company during 1986.

a. Purchased ten $1,000 bonds of Block Company at par, plus accrued interest of $100 and brokerage fees of $250.
b. Purchased 300 shares of Superior Company stock at $62 per share, plus brokerage fees of $90.
c. Received interest of $300 on the Block Company bonds.
d. Received a cash dividend of $3 per share on the Superior Company stock.
e. Sold 150 shares of Superior Company stock, receiving cash proceeds of $9,200.
f. Received interest of $300 on the Block Company bonds.
g. Purchased 500 shares of Saber Company stock at $44 per share, plus brokerage fees of $80.

At year-end the short-term stock portfolio had an aggregate market value of $30,440, and the accrued interest on Block Company bonds totaled $200.

Required:

1. Prepare all the journal entries that would be made by Pureall Company to account for these short-term investments during 1986.
2. Determine the amounts that would be reported in Pureall Company's income statement for
   a. Bond interest revenue
   b. Dividend revenue

c. Gain or loss on the sale of temporary investment
d. Unrealized loss, if any [LOA2a,A2b]

PROBLEM 17–2A *(Account for Long-Term Investments in Bonds)* (Alternate to Problem 17–4) On June 1, 1985, Maple Corporation purchased as a long-term investment fifty $1,000 par value, 12%, 10-year bonds for $51,440, plus accrued interest. The bonds mature on February 1, 1995, and pay semiannual interest on January 31 and July 31.

On March 31, 1986, Maple sold one-half of the bonds for $25,350, plus accrued interest. Maple uses the straight-line method of amortization of bond discounts and bond premiums and rounds amounts to the nearest dollars.

Required:

1. Prepare journal entries to record the following:
   a. The purchase of the bonds on June 1, 1985
   b. The semiannual interest received on July 31, 1985, and the amortization of the related bond discount (or bond premium)
   c. Accrued interest and amortization on December 31, 1985, Maple Corporation's fiscal year-end
2. Prepare journal entries to record the following:
   a. The semiannual interest received on January 31, 1986, and the amortization of the related bond discount (or bond premium).
   b. The bond sale on March 31, 1986. (*Hint:* Remember to bring amortization up to date on the day of sale and to include accrued bond interest in the sale entry.)
   c. The semiannual interest received on the bonds still being held on July 31, 1986, and the amortization of the related bond discount (or bond premium) on those bonds.
   d. Accrued interest and amortization on December 31, 1986.
3. Determine the amount of bond interest revenue that would be reported in Maple Corporation's income statement for the year ended December 31, 1986.
4. Illustrate how the bond investment would be reported in Maple Corporation's December 31, 1986, balance sheet.
5. Prepare the journal entry that would be made on February 1, 1995, when the bonds mature. [LOA2c]

PROBLEM 17–3A *(Account for Long-Term Investments in Stock)* (Alternate to Problem 17–5) On January 5, 1986, Saber Corporation purchased as a long-term investment 30% of the 100,000 outstanding common shares of Dexter Company at $28 per share, plus brokerage commission of $4,000. Other data pertaining to the investment in Dexter Company's common shares follow.

On November 20 Dexter Company declared and paid a cash dividend of $1 per share.

On December 31 Dexter Company reported net income of $120,000 for the year.

On December 31 the market price of Dexter Company's stock was $27 per share.

Required:

1. What method should Saber use to account for its long-term investment in Dexter Company? Why should this method be used?
2. Prepare the journal entries that Saber Corporation should make during 1986 to account for its investment in Dexter Company.
3. Prepare the journal entry that would be made on March 1, 1987, when Saber received $158,400 in cash for the sale of 5,000 Dexter Company shares.
4. Repeat requirements 1, 2, and 3 using the same information except assume that on January 5, 1986, Saber purchased 5,000 shares (instead of 30%) of Dexter Company's stock at $30 per share, plus a broker's commission of $900. [LOA2d]

PROBLEM 17–4A *(Prepare Journal Entry and Work Sheet for a Consolidated Balance Sheet—Purchase Method—100% Ownership)* (Alternate to Problem 17–8) The balance sheets of Purity Company and Sunshine Company as of January 1, 1986, are shown on page 648.

| | PURITY COMPANY | SUNSHINE COMPANY |
|---|---|---|
| Assets: | | |
| Cash | $270,000 | $ 30,000 |
| Accounts Receivable (net) | 90,000 | 55,000 |
| Notes Receivable—Sunshine | 25,000 | — |
| Inventory | 105,000 | 45,000 |
| Plant and Equipment (net) | 350,000 | 90,000 |
| Total Assets | $840,000 | $220,000 |
| Liabilities and Stockholders' Equity: | | |
| Accounts Payable | $ 90,000 | $ 35,000 |
| Notes Payable—Purity Company | — | 25,000 |
| Bonds Payable | 100,000 | — |
| Common Stock (no par value) | 360,000 | 100,000 |
| Retained Earnings | 290,000 | 60,000 |
| Total Liabilities and Stockholders' Equity | $840,000 | $220,000 |

On January 2, 1986, Purity Company purchased all the outstanding stock of Sunshine Company for $190,000. Any excess of cost over book value will be attributed to goodwill.

Required:

1. Prepare the entry to record the purchase of Sunshine's stock.
2. Prepare a work sheet for a consolidated balance sheet as of January 2, 1986. [LOB2a]

PROBLEM 17–5A *(Prepare Journal Entry and Work Sheet for a Consolidated Balance Sheet—Pooling-of-Interests Method)* (Alternate to Problem 17–10) On January 1, 1986, Park Company acquired a controlling interest in Saunders Company by exchanging 50,000 of its par value common shares for all the outstanding common shares of Saunders Company. The market value of the Park Company shares was $28 on the date of the exchange. Balance sheets for the two companies on December 31, 1985, are shown below.

| | PARK COMPANY | SAUNDERS COMPANY |
|---|---|---|
| Assets: | | |
| Cash | $120,000 | $ 50,000 |
| Accounts Receivable (net) | 100,000 | 40,000 |
| Notes Receivable—Saunders Company | 30,000 | — |
| Inventory | 140,000 | 60,000 |
| Plant and Equipment (net) | 350,000 | 100,000 |
| Total Assets | $740,000 | $250,000 |
| Liabilities and Stockholders' Equity: | | |
| Accounts Payable | $150,000 | $ 20,000 |
| Notes Payable—Park Company | — | 30,000 |
| Common Stock ($1 par value) | 200,000 | 60,000 |
| Paid-in Capital | 280,000 | 90,000 |
| Retained Earnings | 110,000 | 50,000 |
| Total Liabilities and Stockholders' Equity | $740,000 | $250,000 |

Required:

1. Prepare the journal entry that Park Company would make to record the exchange of stock, assuming the transaction meets all the criteria for a pooling of interests.
2. Prepare a work sheet for a consolidated balance sheet as of January 1, 1986 (the acquisition date). [LOB2b]

# 18 Statement of Changes in Financial Position

## *Learning Objectives*

When you complete this chapter you will be able to

1. Answer the following questions:
   a. What are the different concepts of funds?
   b. What are the major financing and investing activities?
   c. What are the purposes of (1) a statement of changes in financial position prepared on the working capital basis and (2) a statement of changes in financial position prepared on the cash basis?
2. Perform the following accounting functions:
   a. Prepare a work sheet for a statement of changes in financial position on a working capital basis.
   b. Prepare a statement of changes in financial position on a working capital basis.
   c. Prepare a statement of changes in financial position on a cash basis.

To keep the material in the text as current as possible, we have described and illustrated in Appendix C of the book a recent proposal by the Financial Accounting Standards Board that would require a statement of cash flows for general purpose external reporting.

In previous chapters we have examined the need for and the procedures required to prepare

1. The *balance sheet,* which reports the financial position of a business entity on a specific date
2. The *income statement,* which summarizes the nature and results of a business entity's income-producing activities for a period of time
3. The *statement of retained earnings,* which summarizes the changes in a corporate entity's retained earnings during a period of time

Although each of these statements contains useful information, none of them shows, in direct summary form, the financing and investing activities of the company for a given period of time. Investors, creditors, security analysts, management, and other groups who use financial statements need information that will answer such questions as the following:

How were the new plant assets acquired during the period financed?
How were the funds used to retire long-term debt obtained?
How were the proceeds from the issuance of new stock used?
How was the acquisition of the new subsidiary company financed?
What caused the amount of long-term debt to change during the period?

The **statement of changes in financial position,** one of the four statements in a set of financial statements, is most useful in answering these and other questions. The statement of changes in financial position summarizes the financing and investing activities of a business entity, including its income-oriented operating activities. The Accounting Principles Board has recognized the need for reporting the financing and investing activities of a company. In 1971 the board issued *APB Opinion No. 19,* requiring that a statement of changes in financial position be provided as a basic financial statement for each period for which an income statement is presented.[1] In this chapter we discuss the nature of the statement of changes in financial position, demonstrate how it is prepared, and examine the kind of information it provides.

## THE CONCEPT OF FUNDS

***1a. In business, "funds" may mean cash, or cash and marketable securities, or working capital***

All firms engage in various financing and investing activities. As they do so, they generate and use funds. The term **funds** has traditionally had different meanings to different people. To some, funds are cash; to others, cash and marketable securities; to still others, **working capital**—that is, the excess of current assets over current liabilities. The **FASB** has proposed that cash and cash equivalents, defined as short-term highly liquid investments of cash in excess of immediate needs, be the acceptable definition of funds for general purpose financial reporting. For managerial internal reporting purposes, however, funds may still be defined in different ways. In this chapter, we will demonstrate how to prepare a statement of changes in financial position using both the working capital and the cash version.

[1] Accounting Principles Board, "Reporting Changes in Financial Position," *Opinion No. 19* (New York: AICPA, 1971), par. 7.

## SOURCES AND USES OF WORKING CAPITAL

*1c. The working capital basis is employed to provide information about sources and uses of working capital*

When funds are defined as working capital, the statement of changes describes both the sources and the uses of working capital and shows how working capital changed from the amount available at the beginning of the period to the amount available at the end of the period. Transactions that increase working capital are sources of working capital, and transactions that decrease working capital are uses of working capital.

Because working capital is defined as current assets less current liabilities, the amount of working capital will increase or decrease only by transactions that affect both current and noncurrent accounts. Transactions that affect only current accounts are neither sources nor uses of working capital. For example, the collection of an account receivable will increase cash and decrease accounts receivable by an equal amount. This transaction affected only current accounts and is not a source or use of working capital because the amount of working capital is the same after the transaction as it was before the transaction. For another example, consider the payment of an account payable. This transaction decreases cash and decreases accounts payable, both current accounts. Since the amount of working capital is not changed by this transaction, it is neither a source nor a use of working capital. Sources (increases) of working capital and uses (decreases) of working capital arise from many kinds of transactions and events. When transactions and events that increase working capital are viewed as *financing activities*, and when transactions and events that decrease working capital are viewed as *investing activities*, we can identify four common sources and four common uses of working capital.

### Sources of Working Capital

*1b. Firms obtain working capital from four common financing activities*

Four common **financing activities** (sources) that provide working capital are (1) current operations, (2) the sale of noncurrent assets, (3) long-term borrowing, and (4) the sale of capital stock.

CURRENT OPERATIONS An important source of working capital is that generated by a company's current operations. Because the income statement contains data about an entity's operating activities, we look to it to determine the amount of working capital provided by operations. Revenues recorded on the accrual basis usually result in an increase in a current asset, such as cash or accounts receivable. Therefore they increase working capital. Expenses recorded on the accrual basis usually result in a decrease in a current asset, such as cash, or in an increase in a current liability, such as accounts payable. Therefore they decrease working capital.

The following two entries demonstrate how current assets and current liabilities and thus working capital are affected by revenue and expense transactions:

| | | | |
|---|---|---|---|
| Revenue entry | Cash or Accounts Receivable | 500 | |
| | Sales | | 500 |
| Expense entry | Salaries Expense | 300 | |
| | Cash or Salaries Payable | | 300 |

If all revenue and expense transactions affected both a current and a noncurrent account, as in the entries above, the net income reported in the income statement would be the net source of working capital provided by operations. There are, however, revenues and expenses recognized in accounting and therefore included in the determination of net income that do not affect working capital. As a result, reported net income must be adjusted for those types of revenue and expense items to determine the amount of working capital provided by operations.

A common example of an expense that reduces net income but does not affect working capital is depreciation. Depreciation expense is recorded by debiting an expense account and crediting the contra noncurrent asset account Accumulated Depreciation. Since this entry does not affect a current account, it has no effect on working capital. Another common example of an expense that does not affect working capital is amortization expense. Also quite common are gains and losses on the sale of noncurrent assets. Because such gains and losses affect reported net income but neither provide nor use working capital, we adjust for them when calculating the amount of working capital provided by operations. This is done directly in the statement of changes itself. There depreciation and other expenses that are deducted from revenue in determining periodic net income but do not cause working capital to decrease in that same period are added back to net income in determining working capital provided by operations. Similarly and conversely, gains and other revenue items that were used in determining periodic net income but did not cause working capital to increase in that same period are deducted from net income in determining working capital provided by operations.

Thus the working capital provided by operations is: net income *plus* items that decrease net income but do not use working capital, such as depreciation, *minus* items that increase net income but do not provide working capital, such as gains on the sale of noncurrent assets.

How these items are shown in the statement of changes in financial position is illustrated in the partial statement in Exhibit 18–1.

***1b. Exhibit 18–1, a partial statement of changes, illustrates the presentation of a firm's financing activities***

*EXHIBIT 18–1*

Partial Statement of Changes in Financial Position

SELRIGHT CORPORATION
Statement of Changes in Financial Position
For the Year Ended December 31, 19X6

| | | |
|---|---|---|
| Sources of Working Capital: | | |
| Current Operations: | | |
| Net Income | $120,000 | |
| Add (or deduct) items not affecting working capital: | | |
| Depreciation and Amortization Expense | 3,200 | |
| Gain on Sale of Land | (20,000) | |
| Loss on Sale of Investments | 1,000 | |
| Working Capital Provided by Operations | | $104,200 |
| Other Sources: | | |
| Sale of Land | | 50,000 |
| Sale of Investments | | 8,000 |

**SALE OF NONCURRENT ASSET** When a plant asset, long-term investment asset, or any other noncurrent asset is sold for cash or other current asset, a company's working capital is increased by the proceeds from the sale. For example, if land having a cost of $30,000 is sold for $50,000, the entry to record the sale is as follows:

| | | | |
|---|---|---|---|
| Nov. 30 | Cash | 50,000 | |
| | Land | | 30,000 |
| | Gain on Sale of Land | | 20,000 |

The company's working capital increased by the amount of the current assets received, which in this case is $50,000, regardless of whether the noncurrent asset was sold at a gain or a loss. The $20,000 gain on the sale of the land is reported as revenue in the company's income statement and is therefore included in its net income figure. However, the amount is already reflected in the $50,000 received from the sale. Thus any gains reported in the income statement must be deducted from the net income figure in determining the amount of working capital provided by operations.

Take a moment to examine Exhibit 18–1 to see how the working capital resulting from the land sale is shown on the statement of changes. Also notice the procedure used for deducting gains on such sales from reported net income in determining working capital provided by operations.

LONG-TERM BORROWING Issuing long-term debt securities, such as notes or bonds, for cash increases working capital by the amount received at the time the debt was issued. For example, if bonds having a face value of $500,000 were sold at 105, the sale would generate cash proceeds of $525,000. The amount by which this transaction increases the current asset cash ($525,000) is the amount of working capital provided by the activity. Short-term borrowing, however, is not a source of working capital because short-term borrowing does not increase working capital. For example, if $20,000 is borrowed for a short term such as three months, the transaction increases both current assets and current liabilities by the same amount, leaving total working capital unchanged.

SALE OF CAPITAL STOCK The issuance of preferred or common stock for cash or any other current asset increases working capital because the transaction increases current assets and stockholders' equity by the same amount. Also the reissue of treasury stock for cash or any other current asset will increase working capital. Similarly, an additional investment of current assets by an individual owner or partner is a source of working capital for a single proprietorship or partnership. The issuance of stock as a stock dividend or stock split, however, does not provide working capital because the transaction affects only stockholders' equity accounts.

## Uses of Working Capital

*1b. We discuss here four major investing activities*

Four common **investing activities** that use working capital are (1) the purchase of noncurrent assets, (2) the repayment of long-term debt, (3) the purchase or retirement of capital stock, and (4) the declaration of cash dividends. Before we discuss each of these, we should also note that if a company has a net loss large enough to exceed the amounts added back for such items as depreciation, depletion, and amortization, it will have a decrease in working capital from operations.

PURCHASE OF NONCURRENT ASSETS When noncurrent assets such as buildings, machinery, or long-term investment securities are purchased in exchange for current assets or current liabilities, working capital decreases by the amount of the purchase price. For example, suppose a company purchased a $60,000 machine by paying $20,000 in cash and issuing a six-month note payable for the $40,000 balance. Its working capital would decrease by $60,000. This decrease (use) of working capital is measured by the transaction's combined effect on current assets (which were decreased) and current liabilities (which were increased).

**REPAYMENT OF LONG-TERM DEBT** When current assets are used to pay long-term debts such as bonds payable, working capital is reduced (used) by the amount of current assets used to retire the debt. For example, if cash were used to retire a long-term $100,000 bond issue at 102, cash—a current asset—would be reduced, resulting in a $102,000 use of working capital. When current assets are used to repay short-term debt, working capital is not affected because current assets and current liabilities are decreased by the same amount.

**PURCHASE OR RETIREMENT OF CAPITAL STOCK** When cash or other current assets are used to purchase capital stock that is to be retired or held as treasury stock, working capital is reduced (used) by the amount of current assets used to purchase the shares. Similarly, the withdrawal of cash or other current assets by a proprietor or partner is a use of working capital to a single proprietorship or partnership.

**DECLARATION OF CASH DIVIDENDS** The declaration of a dividend that is to be paid in cash reduces working capital and is therefore a use of working capital. Note that it is the declaration of cash dividends, not their payment, that reduces working capital. The declaration establishes the current liability dividends payable, and this causes the reduction in working capital. When cash dividends previously declared are paid, current assets and current liabilities are reduced by equal amounts, and therefore this transaction does not affect working capital.

## EXCHANGE TRANSACTIONS

Occasionally a company will have a transaction that significantly affects its financial position but not its working capital. These transactions represent financing and investing activities that must be disclosed in the statement of changes. For example, a company may acquire a building or some other noncurrent asset by issuing long-term debt such as a note or mortgage payable. Or a company could issue its stock in direct exchange for a building or other noncurrent asset. These significant exchange transactions would be shown in the statement of changes as both a source of funds (the issuance of the debt or stock), and as a use of funds (the acquisition of the building or other noncurrent assets).[2]

To illustrate, assume that a company acquires land in exchange for 20,000 shares of its $5 par value common stock having a current market price of $12 per share. This exchange transaction would be recorded as follows:

| | | |
|---|---|---|
| Land | 240,000 | |
| Common Stock | | 100,000 |
| Paid-in Capital in Excess of Par Value | | 140,000 |
| Exchanged 20,000 shares of common stock having a market value of $12 per share for land | | |

[2] Ibid., par. 8.

This transaction does not involve current assets or current liabilities and therefore has no effect on working capital. It is, however, a significant transaction that is disclosed in the statement of changes, so that statement users are made fully aware of the company's major financing and investing activities. Here the issuance of the common stock would be reported as a $240,000 source of working capital, and the land acquisition would be reported as a $240,000 use of working capital. The reporting of significant exchange transactions in this manner is known as the **all financial resources** approach of presentation in the statement of changes in financial position.

Transactions that affect only noncurrent accounts are usually exchange transactions that must be reported in the statement of changes. There are, however, two exceptions: stock dividends and stock splits. Stock dividends and stock splits affect noncurrent accounts, but are not exchange transactions, do not affect a company's assets or liabilities, and are not reported in the statement of changes.

*1b. Exhibit 18–2 diagrams major financing and investing activities using the working capital model*

The types of financing activities that provide working capital and the types of investing activities that require the use of working capital can be summarized as shown in Exhibit 18–2.

EXHIBIT 18–2
Working Capital Inflows and Outflows

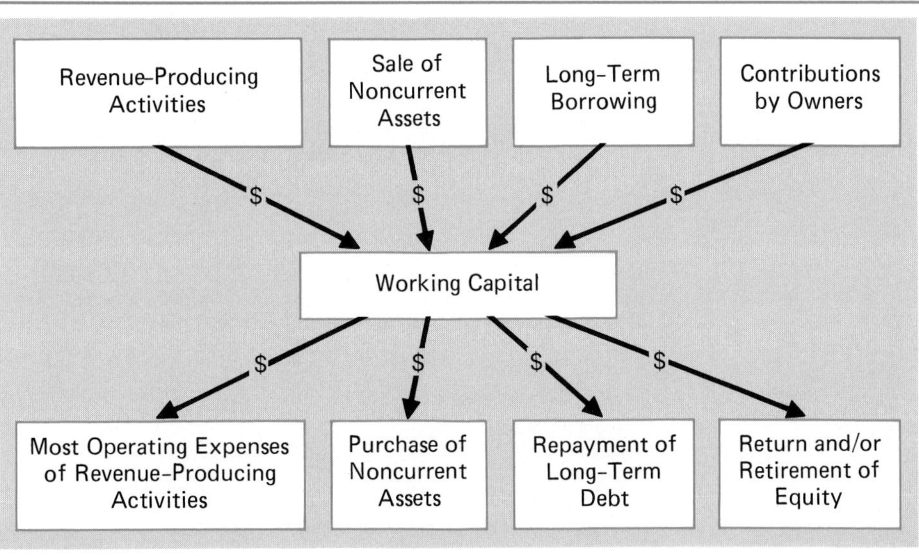


## THE STATEMENT OF CHANGES IN FINANCIAL POSITION—WORKING CAPITAL BASIS

The **working capital basis of the statement of changes in financial position** summarizes a company's long-term financing and investing activities. Specifically, it shows how much working capital was provided by the company's financing activities and how much working capital was used by its investing activities. The difference between the amount of working capital provided and the amount used is shown and designated as the increase or decrease in working capital during the period covered by the statement. In addition, when a working capital basis is used, the statement of changes in financial position is accompanied by a supporting **schedule of changes in working capital components.** This schedule shows the change in working capital for the period as well as the changes in each of the individual accounts that constitute working capital.

In Exhibit 18–3 we show a completed statement of changes in financial position for Mandy Company, along with its supporting schedule of changes in working capital components.

*EXHIBIT 18–3*

MANDY COMPANY
Statement of Changes in Financial Position
For the Year Ended December 31, 19X6

| | | |
|---|---|---|
| Sources of Working Capital: | | |
| Current Operations: | | |
| Net Income | $100,000 | |
| Add items that do not affect working capital: | | |
| Depreciation Expense | 20,000 | |
| Working Capital Provided by Operations | | $120,000 |
| Other Sources: | | |
| Proceeds from the Issuance of Bonds | $ 75,000 | |
| Proceeds from the Issuance of Common Stock | 55,000 | 130,000 |
| Total Sources of Working Capital | | $250,000 |
| Uses of Working Capital: | | |
| Declaration of Cash Dividends | $ 40,000 | |
| Purchase of Equipment | 170,000 | |
| Total Uses of Working Capital | | 210,000 |
| Increase in Working Capital | | $ 40,000 |

MANDY COMPANY
Schedule of Changes in Working Capital Components
For the Year Ended December 31, 19X6

| | DECEMBER 31 | | WORKING CAPITAL | |
|---|---|---|---|---|
| | 19X6 | 19X5 | Increase | Decrease |
| Current Assets: | | | | |
| Cash | $ 25,000 | $ 20,000 | $ 5,000 | |
| Marketable Securities | 10,000 | 15,000 | | $ 5,000 |
| Accounts Receivable | 32,000 | 40,000 | | 8,000 |
| Inventory | 60,000 | 28,000 | 32,000 | |
| Prepaid Expenses | 3,000 | 2,000 | 1,000 | |
| Total Current Assets | $130,000 | $105,000 | | |
| Current Liabilities: | | | | |
| Accounts Payable | $ 45,000 | $ 60,000 | 15,000 | |
| Taxes Payable | 7,000 | 5,000 | | 2,000 |
| Accrued Liabilities | 3,000 | 5,000 | 2,000 | |
| Total Current Liabilities | $ 55,000 | $ 70,000 | | |
| Working Capital | $ 75,000 | $ 35,000 | | |
| | | | $55,000 | $15,000 |
| Increase in Working Capital | | | | 40,000 |
| | | | $55,000 | $55,000 |

Note that the statement of changes has three main sections: the sources of working capital, the uses of working capital, and the increase or the decrease in working capital for the period. The financing activities that provided working capital are listed in the Sources of Working Capital section. Exhibit 18–3 shows that working capital of $250,000 was provided by Mandy's financing activities. The investing activities that used working capital are listed in the Uses of Working Capital section. Here we see that Mandy had two investing activities during 19X6 that used $210,000 of working capital. The difference between the totals in each of these sections is $40,000 and represents the increase in Mandy's working capital for the period.

The supporting schedule of changes in working capital components does exactly that. In other words, it shows the changes in each of the individual accounts that constitute working capital and shows the net change in working capital for the period. It too can provide useful information to the statement user. For example, we can see that Mandy has had a substantial buildup in its inventory. Reviewing the other current accounts, we can see that much of this inventory buildup was not financed by short term creditors (note that Accounts Payable and Accrued Liabilities decreased during the period) but was financed from other sources.

## Preparing the Statement of Changes in Financial Position — Working Capital Basis

*2b. Preparation of a statement of changes begins with accumulation of data*

Much of the information needed to prepare the statement of changes in financial position is obtained from the income statement, statement of retained earnings, and comparative balance sheets. When the statement of changes is based on a working capital definition of funds, we need to examine the noncurrent accounts to determine the nature of the transaction or transactions that caused the balance in a noncurrent account to change during the period. Such transactions generally affect both working capital accounts and noncurrent accounts (the noncurrent asset, noncurrent liability, and stockholders' equity accounts). Although the number of these transactions is minimal compared with that of transactions that affect operations, they represent activities that are some of the main sources and uses of funds. Examples include long-term borrowing, the sale of capital stock, the purchase of plant assets, the declaration of cash dividends, and the repayment of long-term debt. The effect that such transactions have on funds, by any of its definitions, must be reported in the statement of changes.

To illustrate the preparation of the statement of changes in financial position, we will use data of Republic Corporation. Exhibit 18–4 on page 658 contains the company's comparative balance sheet, its income statement, and its statement of retained earnings. In addition, supplementary information about transactions that affected the company's noncurrent accounts during the period is given. This information was obtained by examining ledger accounts for noncurrent assets, noncurrent liabilities, and stockholders' equity to determine why the balance in the account changed during the period.

## Steps in Preparing A Statement of Changes in Financial Position — Working Capital Basis

*2b. We use a three-step approach in preparing a statement of changes on a working capital basis*

We will use a three-step approach in preparing the statement of changes in financial position:

1. Compute the change in working capital during the period.
2. Analyze the change in each noncurrent account balance to determine the cause or causes for the change. In this process we will prepare a work sheet identifying the sources and uses of working capital for the period.
3. Prepare the statement of changes in financial position and the supporting schedule of changes in working capital components.

*Step 1:* Information for computing the change in Republic Corporation's working capital during 19X5 is taken directly from the company's comparative

*EXHIBIT 18–4*

Republic Corporation: Financial Statements and Supplementary Information

REPUBLIC CORPORATION
Comparative Balance Sheet
December 31, 19X5 and 19X4

| | 19X5 | 19X4 |
|---|---|---|
| **ASSETS** | | |
| Current Assets: | | |
| Cash | $ 32,000 | $ 20,000 |
| Marketable Securities | 6,000 | 10,000 |
| Accounts Receivable (net) | 68,000 | 65,000 |
| Inventories | 72,000 | 68,000 |
| Prepaid Expenses | 3,000 | 2,000 |
| Total Current Assets | $181,000 | $165,000 |
| Long-Term Investments | $ 41,000 | $ 30,000 |
| Plant and Equipment: | | |
| Land | $ 55,000 | $ 55,000 |
| Buildings | 165,000 | 130,000 |
| Accumulated Depreciation—Buildings | (28,000) | (21,000) |
| Equipment | 143,000 | 96,000 |
| Accumulated Depreciation—Equipment | (28,000) | (18,000) |
| Total Plant and Equipment | $307,000 | $242,000 |
| Total Assets | $529,000 | $437,000 |
| **LIABILITIES AND STOCKHOLDERS' EQUITY** | | |
| Current Liabilities: | | |
| Accounts Payable | $ 62,000 | $ 55,000 |
| Taxes Payable | 14,000 | 18,000 |
| Accrued Liabilities | 5,000 | 16,000 |
| Total Current Liabilities | $ 81,000 | $ 89,000 |
| Long-Term 12% Bonds Payable | $ 50,000 | $ 0 |
| Stockholders' Equity: | | |
| Common Stock, $5 Par Value | $220,000 | $200,000 |
| Paid-in Capital in Excess of Par Value | 66,000 | 60,000 |
| Retained Earnings | 112,000 | 88,000 |
| Total Stockholders' Equity | $398,000 | $348,000 |
| Total Liabilities and Stockholders' Equity | $529,000 | $437,000 |

REPUBLIC CORPORATION
Income Statement
For the Year Ended December 31, 19X5

| | | |
|---|---|---|
| Sales | | $635,000 |
| Cost of Goods Sold | | 456,000 |
| Gross Profit | | $179,000 |
| Operating Expenses: | | |
| Selling Expenses | $68,000 | |
| Depreciation Expense | 17,000 | |
| Administrative Expenses | 21,000 | |
| General Expenses | 12,000 | |
| Total Operating Expenses | | 118,000 |
| Income from Operations | | $ 61,000 |
| Add: Interest and Dividend Revenue | | 3,000 |
| Income before Income Taxes | | $ 64,000 |
| Income Taxes | | 28,000 |
| Net Income | | $ 36,000 |

REPUBLIC CORPORATION
Statement of Retained Earnings
For the Year Ended December 31, 19X5

| | |
|---|---|
| Retained Earnings, January 1, 19X5 | $ 88,000 |
| Add: Net Income | 36,000 |
| | $124,000 |
| Less: Dividends | 12,000 |
| Retained Earnings, December 31, 19X5 | $112,000 |

Supplementary Information:

1. Shares of another company's stock costing $11,000 were purchased as a long-term investment. No investments were sold during the year.
2. There were no transactions affecting the land account during the year.
3. A building costing $35,000 was purchased. No buildings were sold during the year.
4. Equipment costing $47,000 was purchased. No equipment was sold or discarded during the year.
5. The change in the Accumulated Depreciation—Buildings account was caused solely by the entry to record annual depreciation. The amount $7,000 was deducted on Republic's 19X5 income statement.
6. The change in the Accumulated Depreciation—Equipment account was caused solely by the entry to record annual depreciation. The amount $10,000 was deducted on Republic's 19X5 income statement.
7. Bonds payable of $50,000 were issued for cash at their face value. There were no other long-term debt transactions during the year.
8. An additional 4,000 shares of common stock were sold and issued at $6.50 a share. There were no other transactions affecting common stock during the year.

balance sheet. During 19X5 Republic Corporation's working capital increased by $24,000, as shown below.

| | DECEMBER 31 | |
|---|---|---|
| | 19X5 | 19X4 |
| Current assets | $181,000 | $165,000 |
| Current liabilities | 81,000 | 89,000 |
| Working capital | $100,000 | $ 76,000 |
| Increase in working capital during 19X5 ($100,000 − $76,000) | | $ 24,000 |

Because working capital increased by $24,000 during the year, the sources of working capital reported on the statement of changes in financial position should exceed the uses of working capital by $24,000.

*Step 2:* Next we analyze changes in the noncurrent accounts to determine whether they have resulted in a source or a use of working capital. When there are many changes to be analyzed, accountants frequently use a work sheet to help assemble and organize the information that will be needed to prepare the statement of changes in financial position. The work sheet represents a practical way to gather the information needed for the statement, but it is not a requirement. Several other methods, such as T account analysis, may also be used to gather the information.

*EXHIBIT 18-5*

REPUBLIC CORPORATION

Work Sheet for the Statement of Changes in Financial Position
For the Year Ended December 31, 19X5

| | Account Balances 12/31/X4 | Analysis of Transactions For 19X5 | | Account Balances 12/31/X5 |
|---|---|---|---|---|
| DEBITS | | | | |
| Working Capital | 76,000 | (X)24,000 | | 100,000 |
| Long-Term Investments | 30,000 | (1) 11,000 | | 41,000 |
| Land | 55,000 | | | 55,000 |
| Buildings | 130,000 | (2) 35,000 | | 165,000 |
| Equipment | 96,000 | (4) 47,000 | | 143,000 |
| Total Debits | 387,000 | | | 504,000 |
| CREDITS | | | | |
| Accumulated Depreciation—Buildings | 21,000 | | (3) 7,000 | 28,000 |
| Accumulated Depreciation—Equipment | 18,000 | | (5)10,000 | 28,000 |
| Long-Term 12% Bonds Payable | – 0 – | | (6)50,000 | 50,000 |
| Common Stock | 200,000 | | (7)20,000 | 220,000 |
| Paid-in Capital in Excess of Par Value | 60,000 | | (7) 6,000 | 66,000 |
| Retained Earnings | 88,000 | (9) 12,000 | (8)36,000 | 112,000 |
| Total Credits | 387,000 | | | 504,000 |
| Totals | | 129,000 | 129,000 | |
| | | Sources | Uses | |
| Sources of Working Capital: | | | | |
| Operations: | | | | |
| Net Income | | (8)36,000 | | |
| Add: Depreciation—Buildings | | (3) 7,000 | | |
| Depreciation—Equipment | | (5)10,000 | | |
| Issuance of Bonds Payable | | (6)50,000 | | |
| Issuance of Common Stock | | (7)26,000 | | |
| Uses of Working Capital: | | | | |
| Purchased Long-Term Investments | | | (1) 11,000 | |
| Purchased a Building | | | (2) 35,000 | |
| Purchased Equipment | | | (4) 47,000 | |
| Cash Dividends Declared and Paid | | | (9) 12,000 | |
| | | 129,000 | 105,000 | |
| Increase in Working Capital | | | (X) 24,000 | |
| | | 129,000 | 129,000 | |

The work sheet for Republic Corporation's statement of changes in financial position is shown in Exhibit 18–5. The work sheet was prepared by following these steps:

*2a. Procedures for preparing a work sheet for the statement of changes in financial position are described here*

1. The amount of working capital at the beginning of the year is entered on the first line in the first money column (far left), and the amount of working capital at the end of the year is entered on the same line in the last money column (far right). You will recall that the amounts were previously determined by preparing the working capital summary in step 1. A major purpose of the work sheet is to identify the activities that caused the $24,000 change in working capital. These include operations and other financing activities and investing activities.
2. Noncurrent balance sheet accounts are entered on the work sheet. Note that as a convenience, the noncurrent accounts having a debit balance are listed first. They are followed by the noncurrent accounts having a credit balance. The beginning-of-the-year account balances are entered in the first money column, and the end-of-the-year account balances are entered in the last money column.
3. The debit amounts in the first and last money columns are added, and the credit amounts in those columns are added to prove that the debit totals and credit totals in each column are equal.
4. The heading "Sources of Working Capital" is written on a line below the total of the credit items in the bottom portion of the work sheet. Several lines are then skipped to allow for the listing of the individual sources of working capital, and then the heading "Uses of Working Capital" is used.
5. The changes in each noncurrent account are analyzed and explained. Entries are then made in the second and third money columns titled "Analysis of Transactions." These entries do the following: (1) They reconcile the beginning-of-the-year and end-of-the-year balances in each noncurrent account, and (2) they identify the individual sources and uses of working capital, which are then listed in the bottom portion of the work sheet. The transaction analysis entries shown on this work sheet are discussed in the following section of this chapter. These analyzing entries are not entered in a journal or posted to the accounts. They are not account adjustments; they are simply work sheet entries to explain changes in each noncurrent account and to identify sources and uses of working capital.
6. After the last analyzing entry has been entered, the debits and credits in the second and third money columns headed "Analysis of Transactions" are added to prove their equality. Note that the $24,000 increase in working capital must be entered as a debit on the first line of the Analysis of Transactions section to achieve equality of debits and credits.
7. To complete the work sheet, the column headed "Sources" and the column headed "Uses" in the bottom portion of the work sheet are added. The difference between these columns represents the net change in working capital during the period under review. In our example, working capital increased by $24,000. This amount, which was entered on the top line of the work sheet, is now entered as the balancing figure in the Uses column at the bottom of the work sheet. In each case we use an (X) to designate the entry. Had the working capital decreased, the amount would have been entered as a credit to Working Capital at the top of the work sheet and as a balancing figure in the Sources column at the bottom of the work sheet.

*2a. By analyzing transactions that affect noncurrent accounts, we identify all sources and uses of working capital*

ANALYZING THE CHANGES IN NONCURRENT ACCOUNTS The major step in the preparation of the statement of changes in financial position is the analysis of transactions that caused the balances in one or more noncurrent accounts to change during the period. The analyzing entries on the work sheet shown in Exhibit 18–5 account for the changes in Republic Corporation's noncurrent accounts and identify the financing and investing activities that provided and used working capital. Explanations for these work sheet entries are presented below. They are keyed to the entries by the figures shown parenthetically in Exhibit 18–5.

1. Investments. Securities costing $11,000 were purchased as a long-term investment during the year. This transaction caused a decrease in cash, which is a use of working capital. It also caused an $11,000 increase in the balance of the Long-Term Investments account. The work sheet analyzing entry is a debit to Long-Term Investments and a credit to Uses of Working Capital: Purchased Long-Term Investments. The debit reconciles the beginning and ending balances in the Investments account. The credit identifies an investing activity that used working capital.
2. Buildings. Another building costing $35,000 was acquired during the year. The transaction caused a decrease in cash of $15,000, an increase in a current liability for a short-term note payable of $20,000, and an increase in the balance of the noncurrent account Buildings of $35,000. The amount by which the current asset cash decreased plus the amount by which the current liability notes payable increased is the amount of working capital used to make the purchase. The work sheet analyzing entry is a debit to Buildings and a credit to Uses of Working Capital: Purchased a Building. The debit reconciles the beginning and ending balances in the Buildings account. The credit identifies an investing activity that used working capital. If, instead of cash, long-term bonds were issued in exchange for the building, the transaction would have no effect on working capital. Under the all financial resources approach, however, the issuance of the long-term bonds would be entered on the work sheet as a source of working capital. The cost of the building would be shown as a use of working capital. This accords with the all financial resources approach to the presentation of the statement of changes in financial position.
3. Accumulated Depreciation—Buildings. The entry to record annual depreciation is the only amount that affected this account during this year. The entry debits the Depreciation Expense—Buildings account and credits the noncurrent account Accumulated Depreciation—Buildings. As explained previously, depreciation expense reduces net income but does not affect working capital (because no current asset is decreased and no current liability is increased by the depreciation entry). All the expense items not affecting working capital are added back to net income as a step in determining the amount of working capital provided by operations. The debit of the work sheet analyzing entry adds the depreciation taken back to net income to help establish the working capital provided by operations. The credit portion of the entry accounts for the change between the beginning and ending balances in the Accumulated Depreciation—Buildings account.
4. Equipment. Additional equipment costing $47,000 was purchased during the year. This transaction caused a decrease in cash, which is a use of working capital. It also caused a $47,000 increase in the balance in the Equipment account. The work sheet analyzing entry is a debit to Equipment and a credit to Uses of Working Capital: Purchased Equipment. The debit reconciles the beginning and ending balances in the Equipment account. The credit identifies an investing activity that used working capital.
5. Accumulated Depreciation—Equipment. The entry to record annual depreciation is the only amount that affected this account. Of course, it is analyzed and handled in the same manner as the entry to record depreciation on the building or, for that matter, any other depreciable asset. The work sheet entry's debit adds the amount of depreciation taken on the equipment back to net income to help establish the working capital provided by operations. The credit accounts for the change between the beginning and ending balances in the Accumulated Depreciation—Equipment account.
6. Long-Term Bonds Payable. A review of transactions reveals that bonds having a face value of $50,000 were issued for cash during the year. This financing activity provided working capital of $50,000 and increased the noncurrent liability account Bonds Payable by that amount. Work sheet entry (6) identifies the source of this working capital and reconciles the beginning and ending balances in the Long-Term Bonds Payable account.
7. Common Stock and Paid-in Capital in Excess of Par Value. Only one transaction affected both of these accounts: the sale and issuance of 4,000 shares of the company's $5 par value common stock at $6.50 per share. The $26,000 received from the sale increased cash, providing the company with working capital of that amount.

The work sheet entry debits Sources of Working Capital: Issuance of Common Stock. It credits both the Common Stock account and the Paid-in Capital in Excess of Par Value account. The debit identifies a financing activity that provided working capital. The credits reconcile the beginning and ending balances in the Common Stock and Paid-in Capital in Excess of Par Value accounts.

8. Retained Earnings. There were two reasons for the change in the balance of this account:
   a. Republic Corporation reported a $36,000 net income for 19X5, and, as discussed earlier, net income represents a source of working capital. Through the year-end closing process, net income also causes an increase in the noncurrent account Retained Earnings. The work sheet analyzing entry, therefore, debits reported net income to Sources of Working Capital: Net Income and credits the Retained Earnings account. The debit identifies an activity that provided working capital. The credit helps to account for the change in the Retained Earnings account balance.
   b. Cash dividends declared and paid during the year totaled $12,000. The declaration of a cash dividend decreases working capital and decreases the balance in the Retained Earnings account by an equal amount. Note that it is the declaration of the cash dividend that decreases working capital because it establishes the current liability Dividends Payable. The payment of a previously declared cash dividend is recorded by debiting Dividends Payable and crediting Cash and therefore has no effect on working capital. Work sheet entry (9) debits the Retained Earnings account and helps to account for the change in that account. It credits Uses of Working Capital: Cash Dividends Declared and Paid to identify an activity that uses working capital.

*2b. We prepare the statement of changes from the work sheet by listing the items as shown in Exhibit 18–6*

*Step 3:* After the work sheet has been completed, information about the activities that provided and used working capital can conveniently be found in the bottom part of the work sheet. The statement of changes in financial position is then prepared from that gathered information and is shown in Exhibit 18–6. Note that the operations and other financing activities provided $129,000 of working capital and that the identified investing activities used $105,000 of working capital. The increase in working capital for the year of $24,000 is shown as the final item.

Exhibit 18–6 on page 664 also includes the supporting schedule, which shows the net change that has occurred in each component of working capital during the year.

## Uses of the Statement

*1c. The statement of changes provides explanatory information that users want*

The statement of changes in financial position reports the major financing and investing activities that caused working capital to change during the accounting period. It supplements the income statement, statement of retained earnings, and balance sheet by showing the reasons for the increase or decrease in working capital. It is usually not enough for investors, creditors, and others to know simply that net working capital has increased by $24,000 during the year. They may wish to know about the company's major sources of working capital. For example, they may be interested in how much working capital was obtained from current operations, from the issuance of debt, and from the issuance of stock. This statement provides them with that information. Likewise, they may be interested in how much working capital was used to pay dividends, to purchase plant and equipment assets, and to acquire long-term investments. Again, this statement provides them with that information.

The statement of changes in financial position can also serve as a basis for planning. Our example shows that a major source of Republic's working capital

*EXHIBIT 18-6*

Statement of Changes in Financial Position

REPUBLIC CORPORATION
Statement of Changes in Financial Position
For the Year Ended December 31, 19X5

| | | |
|---|---|---|
| Sources of Working Capital: | | |
| Current Operations: | | |
| Net Income | $36,000 | |
| Add: Items that do not affect working capital: | | |
| Depreciation Expense* | 17,000 | |
| Working Capital Provided by Operations | | $ 53,000 |
| Other Sources: | | |
| Proceeds from the Issuance of Bonds | $50,000 | |
| Proceeds from the Issuance of Stock | 26,000 | 76,000 |
| Total Sources of Working Capital | | $129,000 |
| Uses of Working Capital: | | |
| Purchase of Long-Term Investments | $11,000 | |
| Purchase of a Building | 35,000 | |
| Purchase of Equipment | 47,000 | |
| Cash Dividends Declared and Paid | 12,000 | |
| Total Uses of Working Capital | | 105,000 |
| Increase in Working Capital | | $ 24,000 |

REPUBLIC CORPORATION
Schedule of Changes in Working Capital Components
For the Year Ended December 31, 19X5

| | DECEMBER 31 | | WORKING | CAPITAL |
|---|---|---|---|---|
| | 19X5 | 19X4 | Increase | Decrease |
| Current Assets: | | | | |
| Cash | $ 32,000 | $ 20,000 | $12,000 | |
| Marketable Securities | 6,000 | 10,000 | | $ 4,000 |
| Accounts Receivable | 68,000 | 65,000 | 3,000 | |
| Inventories | 72,000 | 68,000 | 4,000 | |
| Prepaid Expenses | 3,000 | 2,000 | 1,000 | |
| Total Current Assets | $181,000 | $165,000 | | |
| Current Liabilities: | | | | |
| Accounts Payable | $ 62,000 | $ 55,000 | | 7,000 |
| Taxes Payable | 14,000 | 18,000 | 4,000 | |
| Accrued Liabilities | 5,000 | 16,000 | 11,000 | |
| Total Current Liabilities | $ 81,000 | $ 89,000 | | |
| Working Capital | $100,000 | $ 76,000 | | |
| | | | $35,000 | $11,000 |
| Increase in Working Capital | | | | 24,000 |
| | | | $35,000 | $35,000 |

* Note that depreciation on the buildings and equipment is combined on the formal statement.

was generated by the issuance of long-term bonds payable. In fact, it provided $50,000, or almost 39%, of all working capital provided during the year. Since the net increase in working capital was only $24,000, we can assume that net working capital would have decreased considerably had the bonds not been issued. If we assume further that next year the company may not be able to borrow or may be reluctant to borrow, it is obvious that either its other sources of working capital will have to increase or its uses of working capital will have to decrease if the current working capital of $100,000 is to be maintained.

## THE STATEMENT OF CHANGES IN FINANCIAL POSITION—CASH BASIS

*1c. The statement of changes with funds defined as cash provides information on a company's cash flow and liquidity*

Although the working capital definition of funds has traditionally been used extensively in preparing the statement of changes in financial position, many consider the cash definition to be the better one to use. This is probably due to the influence of the **FASB**, which has stressed the needs of users for information on a company's cash flow and liquidity, and the efforts of the Financial Executives Institute, which has urged its members to adopt a format that will emphasize cash flows rather than working capital in their companies' statements of changes in financial position. As a result of this influence, the version of the statement prepared on a cash basis is likely to become increasingly popular for management's internal use and will be illustrated in the remainder of the chapter.

The format of the statement of changes in financial position has not become as standardized as that of the balance sheet and income statement. The version of the statement prepared on a cash basis shown in Exhibit 18-7, however, can be used for internal reporting purposes.

*2c. Exhibit 18–7 illustrates a statement of changes prepared on a cash basis*

EXHIBIT 18–7

LINLEY CORPORATION
Statement of Changes in Financial Position (Cash Basis)
For the Year Ended December 31, 19X3

| | | |
|---|---|---|
| Sources of Cash: | | |
| Current Operations (see Schedule) | | $ 87,000 |
| Other Sources: | | |
| Proceeds from the Issuance of Bonds | $50,000 | |
| Proceeds from the Issuance of Stock | 70,000 | 120,000 |
| Total Sources of Cash | | $207,000 |
| Uses of Cash: | | |
| Purchase of Building | $90,000 | |
| Purchase of Equipment | 60,000 | |
| Payment of Cash Dividends | 25,000 | |
| Total Uses of Cash | | 175,000 |
| Increase in Cash | | $ 32,000 |

A **cash-basis statement of changes in financial position** shows the amount of cash generated by the company's various financing activities, the amount of cash used for its various investing activities, and the resulting increase or decrease in its cash balance. The procedures for preparing a statement of changes in financial position on a cash basis are similar to those used when the statement was prepared on a working capital basis. However, since one purpose of the cash-basis statement is to explain the change in the cash balance rather than the change in working capital, the changes in all accounts, not just noncurrent accounts, must be analyzed. This of course means that the noncash working capital accounts (all current assets except cash and all current liabilities) must also be analyzed, since they represent potential sources and uses of cash.

The cash-basis statement of changes must also show changes in all financial resources (the all financial resources approach), not just changes in cash. Thus significant exchange transactions are reported as both sources and uses of cash. For example, if a long-term note payable is exchanged for equipment, the transaction is reported in the statement as if the note had been issued for cash (source of cash) and as if that cash had then been used to purchase the equipment.

### *Preparing the Statement of Changes in Financial Position—Cash Basis*

Once again the information needed to prepare the statement of changes in financial position is gathered by examining the other financial statements (comparative balance sheets, income statement, and statement of retained earnings) and by analyzing changes in ledger account balances.

To illustrate the preparation of a cash-basis statement of changes, we will use data of Linley Corporation. Exhibit 18–8 contains the company's comparative balance sheet, its income statement, statement of retained earnings, and supplementary information concerning the cash transactions that did not involve current operations.

*EXHIBIT 18–8*

Linley Corporation: Financial Statements and Supplementary Information

LINLEY CORPORATION
Comparative Balance Sheet
December 31, 19X5 and 19X4

| | 19X5 | 19X4 |
|---|---|---|
| ASSETS | | |
| Current Assets: | | |
| Cash | $ 30,000 | $ 40,000 |
| Accounts Receivable (net) | 150,000 | 110,000 |
| Inventory | 90,000 | 75,000 |
| Prepaid Expenses | 5,000 | 7,000 |
| Total Current Assets | $275,000 | $232,000 |
| Plant and Equipment: | | |
| Land | $ 30,000 | $ 30,000 |
| Buildings | 250,000 | 200,000 |
| Accumulated Depreciation—Buildings | (80,000) | (60,000) |
| Equipment | 170,000 | 106,000 |
| Accumulated Depreciation—Equipment | (50,000) | (35,000) |
| Total Plant and Equipment | $320,000 | $241,000 |
| Total Assets | $595,000 | $473,000 |
| LIABILITIES AND STOCKHOLDERS' EQUITY | | |
| Current Liabilities: | | |
| Accounts Payable | $ 96,000 | $ 90,000 |
| Salaries Payable | 900 | 1,200 |
| Taxes Payable | 12,000 | 10,000 |
| Interest Payable | 4,000 | 3,000 |
| Accrued Liabilities | 52,100 | 53,800 |
| Total Current Liabilities | $165,000 | $158,000 |
| Long-Term 10% Bonds Payable | $150,000 | $100,000 |
| Stockholders' Equity: | | |
| Common Stock, $10 Par Value | $120,000 | $ 90,000 |
| Paid-in Capital in Excess of Par Value | 15,000 | 10,000 |
| Retained Earnings | 145,000 | 115,000 |
| Total Stockholders' Equity | $280,000 | $215,000 |
| Total Liabilities and Stockholders' Equity | $595,000 | $473,000 |

LINLEY CORPORATION
Income Statement
For the Year Ended December 31, 19X5

| | | |
|---|---|---|
| Sales (net) | | $467,000 |
| Cost of Goods Sold | | 280,000 |
| Gross Profit | | $187,000 |
| Operating Expenses: | | |
| Depreciation Expense | $ 35,000 | |
| Salaries Expense | 50,000 | |
| Selling Expense | 15,000 | |
| General Expense | 6,000 | |
| Interest Expense | 12,000 | |
| Total Operating Expenses | | 118,000 |
| Income before Income Taxes | | $ 69,000 |
| Income Taxes | | 21,000 |
| Net Income | | $ 48,000 |

LINLEY CORPORATION
Statement of Retained Earnings
For the Year Ended December 31, 19X5

| | |
|---|---|
| Retained Earnings, January 1, 19X5 | $115,000 |
| Add: Net Income | 48,000 |
| | $163,000 |
| Less: Dividends | 18,000 |
| Retained Earnings, December 31, 19X5 | $145,000 |

Supplementary Information:

1. A building costing $50,000 was purchased for cash.
2. Equipment costing $64,000 was purchased for cash.
3. Bonds payable of $50,000 were issued at their face value for cash.
4. An additional 3,000 shares of $10 par value common stock were sold and issued for $35,000.
5. Cash dividends of $18,000 were declared and paid.

## Steps in Preparing a Statement of Changes in Financial Position—Cash Basis

*2c. We use a four-step approach in preparing a statement of changes on a cash basis*

We will use a four-step approach in preparing the cash-basis statement of changes in financial position:

1. Compute the change in the Cash account balance for the period.
2. Determine the amount of cash provided by operations.
3. Determine the sources and uses of cash from nonoperating financing and investing activities.
4. Prepare the statement of changes in financial position.

*Step 1:* Because this statement emphasizes the inflows and outflows of cash, the first step is to determine the change in Linley's Cash account balance. According to the comparative balance sheet shown in Exhibit 18–8, the company's cash balance decreased by $10,000 during 19X5.

*Step 2:* To determine the amount of cash provided by operations, we refer to Linley's income statement and determine (1) the amount of cash received from the revenues reported there and (2) the amount of cash paid for the expenses reported there. Because most businesses account for transactions on the accrual basis, there will be revenues and expenses included in net income that did not involve the receipt or payment of cash. Thus our accrual-based income statement figures must be converted to the cash basis to determine the amount of cash received from revenues and the amount of cash paid for expenses. The process of converting revenue and expense figures included in the determination of net income under the accrual basis of accounting to a cash basis of accounting is illustrated in the following subsections.

CASH RECEIVED FROM CUSTOMERS The relationship between the amount of revenue reported in a company's income statement for a given period and the amount of cash received from its customers during that period depends on the change in its accounts receivable. The amount of cash received from customers during the period under review can be determined by adding the beginning balance in the Accounts Receivable account to the accrual-basis sales figure shown in the income statement and subtracting the ending Accounts Receivable balance from that figure. The beginning balance of Accounts Receivable is added to the sales figure to recognize the cash collected on the receivables during the current year from credit sales reported in a prior year. The ending balance of Accounts Receivable is subtracted from the sales figure to exclude sales of the current period that have not yet been collected.

Referring to the Linley Corporation's income statement and comparative balance sheet, we find the accounts receivable and sales figures needed to determine how much cash Linley received from customers during 19X5:

| | |
|---|---|
| Sales | $467,000 |
| Add: Accounts receivable at beginning of the period | 110,000 |
| | 577,000 |
| Deduct: Accounts Receivable at end of the period | 150,000 |
| Cash received from customers | $427,000 |

The procedure for adjusting the accrual-basis sales figure to a cash-basis figure can also be shown in summary fashion as follows:

| | | |
|---|---|---|
| | + A Decrease in Accounts Receivable | |
| Net Sales | or | = Cash Received from Customers |
| | − An Increase in Accounts Receivable | |

CASH PAID FOR PURCHASES Under the accrual basis of accounting, the cost of merchandise purchased on account is recognized when the goods are purchased. On a cash basis, the cost of merchandise purchased on account is not recognized until cash is paid. Thus the relationship between the cost of goods sold reported on the income statement and the amount of cash paid for merchandise purchased during the period covered by the income statement depends on both the change in Inventory and the change in Accounts Payable (if that change resulted from merchandise purchased on account). The amount of cash paid for purchases during a given period can be calculated in two steps.

First, determine net purchases by adding the ending balance in the Inventory account to Cost of Goods Sold and deducting the beginning balance in the Inventory account from Cost of Goods Sold. The resulting figure is the amount of merchandise purchased during the year. Next, we must determine how much of the merchandise purchased during the year was paid for this year. This is done by adding the beginning balance in the Accounts Payable account to the net purchases figure and deducting the ending balance in the Accounts Payable account from that figure. We add the beginning Accounts Payable to include cash paid this year for purchases made last year, and we deduct the ending Accounts Payable to exclude an amount from purchases this year that will not be paid until next year.

Linley Corporation's cash paid for purchases during 19X5 is $289,000, computed as follows:

| | |
|---|---|
| Cost of goods sold | $280,000 |
| Add: Inventory at end of the period | 90,000 |
| | 370,000 |
| Deduct: Inventory at beginning of the period | 75,000 |
| Net purchases | 295,000 |
| Add: Accounts Payable at beginning of the period | 90,000 |
| | 385,000 |
| Deduct: Accounts Payable at end of the period | 96,000 |
| Cash paid for purchases | $289,000 |

A summarized version for determining the cash paid for purchases follows:

| | | |
|---|---|---|
| | + Increase in Inventory | |
| Cost of Goods Sold | or | = Net Purchases |
| | − Decrease in Inventory | |

| | | |
|---|---|---|
| | + Decrease in Accounts Payable | |
| Net Purchases | or | = Cash Paid for Purchases |
| | − Increase in Accounts Payable | |

**CASH PAID FOR EXPENSES** Under the accrual basis of accounting, expenses are recognized when incurred. On a cash basis, expenses are recognized when they are paid for. Thus there is a difference between the expense figures reported on the income statement and the expenses actually paid for during the period. The relationship between them depends on the changes that have occurred in two types of balance sheet accounts: prepaid expenses and accrued liabilities. The timing differences that arise between the recognition of expenses reported in the income statement and the actual cash payment for these expenses must be considered when we are converting the accrual-basis expense figures to cash-basis expense figures. Thus, to accrual-basis expenses we add the ending balance in the Prepaid Expenses account and deduct the beginning balance in that account. The ending balance of prepaid expenses is added to recognize the cash paid this year for expenses that will not be reported until next year. The beginning balance of prepaid expenses is deducted to eliminate expenses reported this year that were paid for last year. We must make a similar but opposite calculation for accrued items, since unlike prepaid expenses they are current liabilities, not current assets. Thus we add to expenses the beginning balance of accrued liabilities and deduct from expenses the ending balance of accrued liabilities. The conversion process for expenses can be summarized as follows:

| | | | | |
|---|---|---|---|---|
| | + Increase in Prepayments | | + Decrease in Accrued Liabilities | |
| Expenses (Other Than Depreciation and Amortization) | or | and/or | or | = Cash Paid for Expenses |
| | − Decrease in Prepayments | | − Increase in Accrued Liabilities | |

Referring to Lindley Corporation's comparative balance sheet, we see that prepaid expenses decreased by $2,000 and that accrued liabilities (consisting of four items—salaries payable, taxes payable, interest payable, and other accrued liabilities) show a net increase of $1,000. Therefore the amount of cash paid for expenses, including income taxes during the year 19X5, was $101,000, computed as follows:

| | | |
|---|---|---|
| Expenses reported in the income statement ($118,000 + $21,000) | | $139,000 |
| Less: | | |
| Decrease in prepaid expenses | $ 2,000 | |
| Net increase in accrued liabilities | 1,000 | |
| Depreciation expense | 35,000 | 38,000 |
| Cash paid for expenses | | $101,000 |

Note that in addition to the adjustments for prepaid expenses and accrued liabilities, depreciation expense was also subtracted in determining the amount of cash paid for expenses during 19X5. Although depreciation is an expense in determining net income, it is subtracted here because it did not require the use of cash during the current period.

The schedule below summarizes all the cash-basis information we have developed and shows the amount of cash provided by operations.

| | | |
|---|---|---|
| Cash received from customers | | $427,000 |
| Less: | | |
| Cash paid for purchases | $289,000 | |
| Cash paid for expenses | 101,000 | |
| Total cash paid | | 390,000 |
| Cash provided by operations | | $ 37,000 |

In determining the cash paid for expenses ($101,000), we could have used the alternative approach of analyzing each expense item separately instead of treating all expenses as a total. This approach provides information on the amount of cash paid for each item of expense reported in the income statement rather than for expenses as a whole. Since management may find this information useful in planning and controlling one aspect of cash outflow—specifically, that required for expense items—we will show how it works here. The schedules below simply show the adjustment, if any, that is needed to convert a specific accrual-basis expense figure to a cash-basis figure. The expense items are taken in the order in which they appear in Linley's income statement.

*Depreciation expense:*

| | |
|---|---|
| Depreciation expense per income statement | $35,000 |
| Less: Depreciation recorded | 35,000 |
| Cash paid for depreciation | $ -0- |

*Salaries expense:*

| | |
|---|---|
| Salaries expense per income statement | $50,000 |
| Add: Decrease in related accrued liability, salaries payable | 300 |
| Cash paid for salaries | $50,300 |

*Selling expense:*

| | |
|---|---|
| Selling expense per income statement | $15,000 |
| Add: Decrease in related accrued liability, other accrued liabilities | 1,700 |
| Cash paid for selling expenses | $16,700 |

*General expense:*

| | |
|---|---|
| General expense per income statement | $6,000 |
| Less: Decrease in related current asset, prepaid expenses | 2,000 |
| Cash paid for general expenses | $4,000 |

*Interest expense:*

| | |
|---|---|
| Interest expense per income statement | $12,000 |
| Less: Increase in related accrued liability, interest payable | 1,000 |
| Cash paid for interest expense | $11,000 |

*Income tax expense:*

| | |
|---|---|
| Income taxes per income statement | $21,000 |
| Less: Increase in related accrued liability taxes payable | 2,000 |
| Cash paid for income taxes | $19,000 |

A schedule like the one in Exhibit 18–9 can also be prepared just to show managers or other users the amount of cash provided by operations.

*EXHIBIT 18–9*

Schedule to Determine Cash Provided by Operations

LINLEY CORPORATION

Conversion of Income Statement Amounts from an Accrual to a Cash Basis

For the Year Ended December 31, 19X5

| | ACCRUAL-BASIS AMOUNTS (FROM INCOME STATEMENT) | ADD OR (DEDUCT) | CASH-BASIS AMOUNTS |
|---|---|---|---|
| Sales (net) | $467,000 | (40,000) | $427,000 |
| Cost of Goods Sold | 280,000 | {15,000 (6,000)} | 289,000 |
| Gross Profit | $187,000 | | $138,000 |
| Operating Expenses: | | | |
| Depreciation Expense | $35,000 | (35,000) | $ -0- |
| Salaries Expense | 50,000 | 300 | 50,300 |
| Selling Expense | 15,000 | 1,700 | 16,700 |
| General Expense | 6,000 | (2,000) | 4,000 |
| Interest Expense | 12,000 | (1,000) | 11,000 |
| Total Operating Expenses | $118,000 | | $ 82,000 |
| Income before Income Taxes | $ 69,000 | | $ 56,000 |
| Income Taxes | 21,000 | (2,000) | 19,000 |
| Net Income | $ 48,000 | | |
| Cash Provided by Operations | | | $ 37,000 |

Although we have approached it in a number of ways, the process of determining the amount of cash provided by operations (step 2 in preparing the statement of changes on a cash basis) can be summarized on page 672.

Net income
Plus: Items reducing income but not using cash (such as depreciation, amortization, and losses)
  Decreases in current assets other than cash
  Increases in current liabilities
Minus: Items increasing income but not providing cash
  Increases in current assets other than cash
  Decreases in current liabilities
Equals: Cash provided by operations

*Step 3:* We must now determine sources and uses of cash from the company's nonoperating financing and investing activities. This is done by analyzing the cause of change in each noncurrent account to determine its effect on cash, just as we did earlier to determine nonoperational sources and uses of working capital. It is assumed that the supplementary information given in Exhibit 18–8 was derived by analyzing changes in Linley Corporation's noncurrent accounts. Linley had some but not all of the common nonoperating sources of cash, which include borrowing, selling additional shares of stock, reissuing treasury stock, and selling noncurrent assets such as buildings, equipment, and investment securities. They also had some of the common nonoperating uses of cash, which include cash dividend payments, purchase of plant assets such as buildings and equipment, debt repayment, and purchase of treasury stock.

*Step 4:* After all the data obtained in the first three steps have been assembled, we can prepare a cash-basis statement of changes in financial position, as shown in Exhibit 18–10. All sources and uses of cash during the year 19X5 are identified. The resulting $10,000 decrease in cash equals the change in cash for the year, as shown in Linley's comparative balance sheet in Exhibit 18–8.

***2c. A statement of changes prepared on a cash basis is shown in Exhibit 18–10***

*EXHIBIT 18–10*

LINLEY CORPORATION
Statement of Changes in Financial Position (Cash Basis)
For the Year Ended December 31, 19X5

| | | |
|---|---|---|
| Sources of Cash: | | |
| Current Operations (see Schedule) | | $ 37,000 |
| Other Sources: | | |
| Proceeds from the Issuance of Bonds | $50,000 | |
| Proceeds from the Issuance of Stock | 35,000 | 85,000 |
| Total Sources of Cash | | $122,000 |
| Uses of Cash: | | |
| Purchase of Building | $50,000 | |
| Purchase of Equipment | 64,000 | |
| Payment of Cash Dividends | 18,000 | |
| Total Uses of Cash | | 132,000 |
| Decrease in Cash | | $ 10,000 |

## Uses of the Statement

Managers are especially interested in identifying where a company is getting its cash from and what it is using it for. This is the company's most liquid asset and the "lifeline" of the business. Information on cash sources and uses is needed to maintain control over business operations and to keep the components of working capital at appropriate levels.

## HIGHLIGHT PROBLEM

This highlight problem requires an understanding of some complex corporate transactions. Condensed information about those transactions is given as supplementary information, and you are asked to prepare the following:

1. A schedule of changes in working capital components
2. A statement of changes in financial position—working capital basis

HILLSIDE COMPANY

Condensed Financial Information
Balance Sheet Accounts and Balances

| | DECEMBER 31 19X5 | DECEMBER 31 19X4 |
|---|---|---|
| Cash | $ 19,000 | $ 15,000 |
| Accounts Receivable (net) | 56,000 | 48,000 |
| Inventory | 40,000 | 45,000 |
| Prepaid Expenses | 3,000 | 2,000 |
| Land | 60,000 | 34,000 |
| Buildings | 230,000 | 170,000 |
| Accumulated Depreciation—Buildings | (47,000) | (38,000) |
| Equipment | 145,000 | 95,000 |
| Accumulated Depreciation—Equipment | (28,500) | (30,000) |
| Patents | 8,000 | 9,000 |
| Total Assets | $485,500 | $350,000 |
| Accounts Payable | $ 42,000 | $ 46,000 |
| Salaries Payable | 4,000 | 3,000 |
| Other Accrued Liabilities | 25,200 | 29,000 |
| Bonds Payable | 100,000 | — |
| Common Stock | 170,000 | 150,000 |
| Paid-in Capital | 28,000 | 24,000 |
| Retained earnings | 116,300 | 98,000 |
| Total Liabilities and Stockholders' Equity | $485,500 | $350,000 |

HILLSIDE COMPANY

Condensed Income Statement Information
For the Year Ended December 31, 19X5

| | | |
|---|---|---|
| Sales | | $310,000 |
| Add: Gain on Sale of Equipment | | 4,000 |
| Total | | $314,000 |
| Deduct: | | |
| Cost of Goods Sold | $148,400 | |
| Depreciation—Buildings | 9,000 | |
| Depreciation—Equipment | 14,500 | |
| Amortization—Patent | 1,000 | |
| Bond Interest Expense | 10,200 | |
| Selling Expense | 47,700 | |
| Administrative Expense | 24,900 | |
| Income Tax Expense | 26,000 | |
| Loss on Sale of Land | 2,000 | |
| Total | | 283,700 |
| Net Income | | $ 30,300 |

HILLSIDE COMPANY
Retained Earnings Information
For the Year Ended December 31, 19X5

| | |
|---|---|
| Retained Earnings, January 1, 19X5 | $ 98,000 |
| Add: Net Income | 30,300 |
| | $128,300 |
| Less: Dividends Paid | 12,000 |
| Retained Earnings, December 31, 19X5 | $116,300 |

Supplementary Information about 19X5 Transactions:

1. Land costing $38,000 was purchased for cash.
2. Land that cost $12,000 when acquired was sold for $10,000 cash.
3. A new building costing $60,000 was purchased for cash.
4. Equipment that cost $30,000 when acquired was sold for $18,000 cash. The accumulated depreciation on this equipment amounted to $16,000 on the date of sale.
5. New equipment costing $80,000 was purchased for cash.
6. Depreciation expense for the year on the buildings was $9,000.
7. Depreciation expense for the year on the equipment was $14,500.
8. Amortization expense for the year on the patents was $1,000.
9. Bonds payable of $100,000 were issued for cash at their face value.
10. An additional 2,000 shares of $10 par value common stock was sold and issued at $12 per share.

## GLOSSARY OF KEY TERMS

**All financial resources.** A reporting requirement for the statement of changes in financial position in which significant exchange transactions involving noncurrent items are shown as both a source of funds and as a use of funds, however the term *funds* is defined.

**Cash basis—statement of changes in financial position.** A statement that summarizes a company's financing and investing activities during a period, showing their effects on cash.

**Financing activities.** Business activities that provide funds, such as current operations, the sale of noncurrent assets, long-term borrowing, and the sale of capital stock.

**Funds.** Liquid resources used by a business to conduct its day-to-day operations. When used in the context of the statement of changes in financial position, funds generally mean working capital, cash, or cash plus marketable securities.

**Investing activities.** Business activities that use funds such as the purchase of noncurrent assets, repayment of long-term debt, purchase or retirement of capital stock, and declaration of cash dividends.

**Schedule of changes in working capital components.** A schedule showing the change in working capital for the period, as well as the changes in each of the individual accounts that constitute working capital.

**Statement of changes in financial position.** A financial statement that identifies the sources and uses of funds and explains all the significant changes that have taken place in a company's financial position during a period. In preparing the statement, the reporting entity decides on a definition of funds and focuses its presentation accordingly.

**Working capital.** Current assets less current liabilities.

**Working capital basis—statement of changes in financial position.** A statement that summarizes a company's long-term financing and investing activities during a period, showing their effects on working capital.

## REVIEW QUESTIONS

1. What does APB Opinion No. 19 now require concerning the statement of changes in financial position? [LO1c]
2. What are the three different meanings of *funds*? [LO1a]
3. Name the four common sources from which firms obtain their working capital. [LO1a]

4. When computing the source of working capital from current operations, what types of items are added to net income? Subtracted from net income? [LO2b]
5. Name the four common uses of working capital. [LO1b]
6. Differentiate between the journal entry made when a cash dividend is declared and the journal entry made when a previously declared cash dividend is paid. [LO2b]
7. How are significant exchange transactions not affecting funds shown in the statement of changes in financial position? [LO2b]
8. What is the relationship between the amounts of sources and uses of working capital in the statement of changes in financial position and the amount of increase or decrease in the company's working capital for the period? [LO2b]
9. Describe the format of the working capital model of the statement of changes in financial position. [LO2b]
10. Describe the data needed to prepare a working capital model of a statement of changes in financial position. [LO2b]
11. Name each of the steps required to prepare a working capital model of a statement of changes in financial position. [LO2b]
12. Describe in sequence the steps required to prepare a work sheet for a working capital model of a statement of changes in financial position. [LO2a]
13. Describe the uses that can be made of a working capital model of a statement of changes in financial position. [LO1c,2b]
14. Describe two major differences between the format of a statement of changes in financial position prepared on a cash basis and a statement of changes in financial position prepared on a working capital basis. [LO1c,2b,2c]
15. What items of information are needed to determine the net cash flow from operations? [LO2c]
16. Name the four steps used to prepare a cash-basis model of a statement of changes in financial position. [LO2c]
17. When are revenues recognized under the accrual basis of accounting? Under the cash basis of accounting? [LO2c]
18. When is the cost of merchandise purchased on account recognized under the accrual basis of accounting? Under the cash basis of accounting? [LO2c]
19. When are operating expenses recognized under the accrual basis of accounting? Under the cash basis of accounting? [LO2c]
20. Why is the amount of depreciation expense deducted from accrual operating expenses as a step in computing the amount of cash paid for expenses? [LO2c]
21. Describe the uses made of the cash-basis model of a statement of changes in financial position. [LO1c,2c]

## ANALYTICAL QUESTIONS

22. Which of the three definitions of funds is the most useful? Why? [LO1a]
23. Explain why a cash-basis statement of changes in financial position is an expansion of the working-capital-basis statement. [LO1c,2b,2c]
24. "Why should I care about changes in cash and working capital? Net income and earnings per share tell me what I need to know to make an investment or financing decision." Comment on this statement. [LO1c]
25. "Both the source of cash provided by operations and the working capital provided by operations are confusing. Which is the more important measure of financial performance —these figures or net income?" Reply to this question. [LO1c]
26. "I don't understand how additional information is gained by preparing a formal statement of changes in financial position. Why not merely scan the account differences in a comparative balance sheet?" Reply to this question. [LO1c]

27. How is it possible for a company to have a net loss for the year and yet show an amount for cash or working capital provided by operations? [LO2b,2c]

## IMPACT ANALYSIS QUESTIONS

*For each error described, indicate whether it would overstate [O], understate [U], or not affect [N] the specified key figures.*

28. In analyzing the $10,000 increase in the Land account for the year, the company recorded a $10,000 use of working capital for the purchase of land in the statement of changes in financial position. Actually, $2,000 of the land was acquired in exchange for common stock. [LO2b]

    ________ Total Uses of Working Capital
    ________ Source of Working Capital Provided by Operations
    ________ Working Capital Increases Shown on the Statement of Changes in Financial Position

29. In analyzing the $5,000 decrease in the Land account for the year, the company did not record any source of working capital from the sale of land even though it was sold for cash. [LO2b]

    ________ Total Sources of Working Capital
    ________ Source of Working Capital Provided by Operations
    ________ Working Capital Increases Shown on the Statement of Changes in Financial Position

30. In preparing the statement of changes in financial position on the working capital basis, the company failed to recognize $1,000 of patent amortization. [LO2b]

    ________ Total Sources of Working Capital
    ________ Source of Working Capital Provided by Operations
    ________ Working Capital Increases Shown on the Statement of Changes in Financial Position

## EXERCISES

EXERCISE 18–1 *(Indicate Effect of Transactions on Working Capital)* For each transaction, place a check mark under the appropriate column(s) to indicate how it should be reported in a statement of changes prepared on a working capital basis. [LO2b]

| TRANSACTION | GOES IN SOURCE OF WORKING CAPITAL SECTION | GOES IN USE OF WORKING CAPITAL SECTION | DOES NOT GO IN STATEMENT |
|---|---|---|---|
| 1. Recorded depreciation expense on a building | | | |
| 2. Collected cash from accounts receivable customers | | | |
| 3. Declared and paid a cash dividend | | | |
| 4. Purchased inventory on account | | | |
| 5. Sold equipment for cash | | | |
| 6. Purchased treasury stock for cash | | | |
| 7. Settled an account payable by paying cash | | | |
| 8. Borrowed cash on a long-term note payable | | | |
| 9. Acquired land in exchange for 500 shares of common stock | | | |
| 10. Recorded amortization expense on a patent | | | |

EXERCISE 18–2 *(Determine the Appropriate Presentation of Items in the Statement of Changes)* For each of the following transactions or changes in account balances, indicate (using a check mark) in which type of statement of changes, one prepared on a cash basis or one prepared on a working capital basis, the transaction or account change should be reported. In some cases the transaction or account change may be reported in both statements if both are prepared. [LO2b,2c]

| TRANSACTION OR ACCOUNT CHANGE | SHOULD BE REPORTED IN A CASH-BASIS STATEMENT OF CHANGES | SHOULD BE REPORTED IN A WORKING-CAPITAL-BASIS STATEMENT OF CHANGES |
|---|---|---|
| 1. An increase in Accounts Receivable | | |
| 2. An increase in Accounts Payable | | |
| 3. The sale of land for cash | | |
| 4. The exchange of common stock for land | | |
| 5. Recorded depreciation on a building | | |
| 6. A decrease in prepaid expenses | | |
| 7. Cash dividends declared and paid | | |
| 8. A decrease in Inventory | | |
| 9. The purchase of long-term investment securities for cash | | |
| 10. The sale of previously acquired treasury stock | | |

EXERCISE 18–3 *(Determine Cash Paid for Purchases)* Warren Company reported its cost of goods sold as $290,400 in its 19X5 income statement. The following accounts were taken from Warren's comparative balance sheet for December 31, 19X5 and 19X4.

| | DECEMBER 31 19X5 | DECEMBER 31 19X4 |
|---|---|---|
| Cash | $30,000 | $25,000 |
| Accounts Receivable | 60,000 | 63,000 |
| Inventory | 40,000 | 37,000 |
| Accounts Payable | 52,000 | 55,000 |
| Salaries Payable | 8,000 | 6,000 |

All the accounts receivable are from customers, and all the accounts payable are from the purchase of merchandise.

Required:
Determine how much cash Warren paid for purchases of merchandise during 19X5. [LO2c]

EXERCISE 18–4 *(Determine the Amount of Cash Provided by Operations)* From the following balance sheet data, prepare a schedule to show the amount of cash provided by the company's current operations. [LO2c]

| | YEAR ENDED DECEMBER 31 | |
|---|---|---|
| | 19X5 | 19X4 |
| Assets: | | |
| Cash | $ 6,000 | $ 5,000 |
| Accounts Receivable | 11,000 | 10,000 |
| Inventory | 18,000 | 20,000 |
| Total Assets | $35,000 | $35,000 |
| Liabilities and Stockholders' Equity: | | |
| Accounts Payable | $ 3,000 | $ 4,000 |
| Accrued Liabilities | 3,000 | 6,000 |
| Capital Stock | 11,000 | 10,000 |
| Retained Earnings (cash dividends of $1,000 paid during 19X5) | 18,000 | 15,000 |
| Total Liabilities and Stockholders' Equity | $35,000 | $35,000 |

EXERCISE 18–5 *(Supply Missing Data and Source of Cash from Current Operations)* For each of the following four cases, determine the missing amount and place it in the blank. [LO2c]

| | CASE 1 | CASE 2 | CASE 3 | CASE 4 |
|---|---|---|---|---|
| Accounts Receivable, 1/1 | $10,000 | $12,000 | $14,000 | $____ |
| Accounts Receivable, 12/31 | 12,000 | ____ | 15,000 | 16,000 |
| Accounts Payable, 1/1 | 8,000 | 10,000 | 7,000 | 5,000 |
| Accounts Payable, 12/31 | 9,000 | 8,000 | 7,000 | 3,000 |
| Inventory, 1/1 | 15,000 | 12,000 | 12,000 | 9,000 |
| Inventory, 12/31 | 13,000 | 14,000 | 10,000 | 12,000 |
| Depreciation Expense for Year | 12,000 | 10,000 | 8,000 | 10,000 |
| Net Income for Year | 5,000 | 4,000 | ____ | 6,000 |
| Source of Cash from Current Operations | ____ | 12,000 | 15,000 | 11,000 |

EXERCISE 18–6 *(Supply Missing Data and Source of Working Capital from Current Operations)* For each of the following four cases, determine the missing amount and place it in the blank. [LO2b]

| | CASE 1 | CASE 2 | CASE 3 | CASE 4 |
|---|---|---|---|---|
| Working Capital, 1/1 | $10,000 | $20,000 | $ 5,000 | $____ |
| Working Capital, 12/31 | 11,000 | ____ | 3,000 | 12,000 |
| Sale of Land for Cash | 20,000 | 40,000 | 12,000 | 8,000 |
| Purchase of Equipment for Cash | 35,000 | 20,000 | 9,000 | 11,000 |
| Cash Dividends Declared and Paid | 3,000 | 10,000 | ____ | 2,000 |
| Payment on Long-Term Note Payable | 5,000 | 5,000 | 7,000 | 10,000 |
| Sale of Common Stock for Cash | 10,000 | 3,000 | 2,000 | 13,000 |
| Source of Working Capital from Current Operations | ____ | 2,000 | 7,000 | 8,000 |

EXERCISE 18–7 *(Convert Accrual-Basis Amounts to Cash-Basis Amounts)* The ledger accounts of Cole Company prepared on the accrual basis of accounting show the following amounts on the dates indicated.

| | YEAR-END | |
|---|---|---|
| | 19X6 | 19X5 |
| Accounts Receivable | $ 24,500 | $19,900 |
| Inventory | 37,200 | 39,400 |
| Prepaid Expenses | 1,000 | 1,300 |
| Accounts Payable (for merchandise purchased) | 30,000 | 31,500 |
| Salaries Payable | 1,400 | 1,200 |
| Sales (net) | 149,800 | |
| Cost of Goods Sold | 51,600 | |
| Operating Expenses (other than depreciation) | 47,200 | |
| Depreciation Expense | 14,500 | |
| Federal Income Taxes Expense | 12,800 | |

Required:
Compute each of the following:
1. The amount of cash received from customers during 19X6
2. The amount of cash paid for purchases during 19X6
3. The amount of cash paid for expenses and federal income taxes during 19X6 [LO2c]

EXERCISE 18-8 *(Prepare a Schedule of Changes in Working Capital Components)* Data taken from the comparative balance sheet of Wayside Corporation appear below.

| | 19X5 | 19X4 |
|---|---|---|
| Cash | $ 20,000 | $ 16,000 |
| Accounts Receivable | 35,000 | 38,000 |
| Inventory | 50,000 | 52,000 |
| Prepaid Expenses | 5,000 | 4,000 |
| Equipment | 90,000 | 70,000 |
| Patent | 15,000 | 10,000 |
| Total Assets | $215,000 | $190,000 |
| Accounts Payable | $ 36,000 | $ 40,000 |
| Taxes Payable | 2,000 | 1,000 |
| Salaries Payable | 1,000 | 1,000 |
| Bonds Payable (due in 19X9) | 50,000 | 50,000 |
| Common Stock | 60,000 | 60,000 |
| Paid-in Capital | 22,000 | 22,000 |
| Retained Earnings | 44,000 | 16,000 |
| Total Liabilities and Stockholders' Equity | $215,000 | $190,000 |

Required:
Prepare a schedule of changes in working capital components for the year ended December 31, 19X5. [LO2b]

## PROBLEMS

PROBLEM 18-1 *(Determine the Effect of Transactions on Working Capital)* Analyze the transactions presented below and place a check mark in the appropriate column to identify the transaction as increasing, decreasing, or having no effect on working capital. [LO2b]

| TRANSACTION | EFFECT ON WORKING CAPITAL Increase | Decrease | No Effect |
|---|---|---|---|
| 1. Purchased equipment for cash | | | |
| 2. Declared a cash dividend | | | |
| 3. Purchased treasury stock for cash | | | |
| 4. Reported net income for the year | | | |
| 5. Sold and issued additional shares of common stock for cash | | | |
| 6. Collected accounts receivable | | | |
| 7. Paid the cash dividend previously declared | | | |
| 8. Sold long-term investment securities at a price in excess of their cost | | | |
| 9. Retired long-term debt before maturity, paying cash in excess of the debt's face value | | | |
| 10. Purchased inventory for cash | | | |
| 11. Issued shares of common stock in exchange for land | | | |
| 12. Declared a stock dividend | | | |

PROBLEM 18–2 *(Prepare a Statement of Changes in Financial Position—Working Capital Basis)* Financial statement data for the Cullum Corporation are shown below.

| BALANCE SHEET DATA | 19X5 | 19X4 |
|---|---|---|
| Assets: | | |
| Cash | $ 50,000 | $ 40,000 |
| Marketable Securities | 36,000 | 15,000 |
| Accounts Receivable | 74,000 | 77,000 |
| Inventory | 115,000 | 95,000 |
| Plant and Equipment | 90,000 | 110,000 |
| Accumulated Depreciation | (25,000) | (20,000) |
| Total Assets | $340,000 | $317,000 |
| Liabilities and Stockholders' Equity: | | |
| Accounts Payable | $ 60,000 | $ 50,000 |
| Capital Stock | 200,000 | 200,000 |
| Retained Earnings | 80,000 | 67,000 |
| Total Liabilities and Stockholders' Equity | $340,000 | $317,000 |

| INCOME STATEMENT DATA | FOR 19X5 |
|---|---|
| Sales (net) | $500,000 |
| Cost of Goods Sold | 300,000 |
| Gross Profit | 200,000 |
| Operating Expenses (including depreciation) | 180,000 |
| Net Income | $ 20,000 |

Additional Data:

1. Cash dividends of $7,000 were declared and paid during the year.
2. No plant and equipment assets were purchased during the year.
3. Depreciation expense of $10,000 was recorded on the plant and equipment assets.
4. There was no gain or loss on the plant assets sold during the year.

Required:
Prepare a statement of changes in financial position on a working capital basis. A work sheet may not be necessary. Remember to include a schedule of changes in working capital components. [LO2b]

PROBLEM 18–3 *(Prepare a Statement of Changes in Financial Position—Cash Basis)* Using the data presented in Problem 18–2, prepare a cash-basis statement of changes for Cullum Corporation for the year ended December 31, 19X5. [LO2c]

PROBLEM 18–4 *(Prepare a Statement of Changes in Financial Position—Working Capital Basis)* The following represents the condensed comparative balance sheet of Success Corporation:

| | DECEMBER 31 | |
|---|---|---|
| | 19X5 | 19X4 |
| ASSETS | | |
| Cash | $18,000 | $22,000 |
| Accounts Receivable (net) | 27,000 | 29,500 |
| Long-Term Investments | 15,000 | 15,000 |
| Patents | 1,200 | 1,500 |
| Goodwill | 19,000 | 20,000 |
| Total Assets | $80,200 | $88,000 |
| LIABILITIES AND STOCKHOLDERS' EQUITY | | |
| Accounts Payable | $12,000 | $21,000 |
| Accrued Liabilities | 1,200 | 2,000 |
| Note Payable—Long-Term | 5,000 | — |
| Common Stock | 25,000 | 25,000 |
| Retained Earnings | 37,000 | 40,000 |
| Total Liabilities and Stockholders' Equity | $80,200 | $88,000 |

Supplementary Data:
1. Net income for the year was $10,000.
2. Cash dividends of $13,000 were declared and paid during the year.
3. The decrease in the Patents account is the result of annual amortization. The amortization expense appears as an operating expense in the 19X5 income statement.
4. The decrease in the Goodwill account is also the result of annual amortization reported as an operating expense in the 19X5 income statement.
5. A long-term note payable was issued for cash late in 19X5.

Required:
Prepare a statement of changes in financial position for the year ended December 31, 19X5, using a working capital basis. Include the related schedule of changes in working capital components. A work sheet is not required. [LO2b]

PROBLEM 18–5 *(Prepare a Statement of Changes in Financial Position—Cash Basis)* Using the data presented in Problem 18–4 plus the information given below, prepare a cash-basis statement of changes for Success Corporation for the year ended December 31, 19X5.
1. All the accounts payable are the result of merchandise purchases.
2. All the accrued liabilities are the result of operating expenses.
3. Sales for 19X5 totaled $90,700, and the cost of the goods related to those sales was $63,800.
4. Expenses including amortization expenses were $16,900. [LO2c]

PROBLEM 18–6 *(Prepare a Statement of Changes in Financial Position—Working Capital Basis)* A condensed comparative balance sheet for Charger Corporation on December 31, 19X5 and 19X4, is presented on page 682.

| | DECEMBER 31 | |
|---|---|---|
| | 19X5 | 19X4 |
| ASSETS | | |
| Cash | $ 19,000 | $ 12,000 |
| Accounts Receivable (net) | 43,000 | 45,000 |
| Notes Receivable | 7,000 | 11,000 |
| Inventory | 66,000 | 62,000 |
| Land (held for future site) | 20,000 | 20,000 |
| Equipment | 93,000 | 80,000 |
| Accumulated Depreciation—Equipment | (36,000) | (31,500) |
| Total Assets | $212,000 | $198,500 |
| LIABILITIES AND STOCKHOLDERS' EQUITY | | |
| Accounts Payable | $ 37,000 | $ 42,500 |
| Accrued Liabilities | 9,000 | 16,000 |
| Common stock, $100 Par Value | 100,000 | 80,000 |
| Retained Earnings | 66,000 | 60,000 |
| Total Liabilities and Stockholders' Equity | $212,000 | $198,500 |

An examination of the firm's other financial statements and its accounting records disclosed that 200 additional shares of common stock were sold at par and that the company purchased new equipment costing $13,000 during the year. Also a cash dividend of $8,000 was declared and paid during 19X5, and the net income reported on the income statement was $14,000.

Required:
Prepare a statement of changes in financial position on a working capital basis. A work sheet may not be necessary. Remember to include a schedule of changes in working capital components. [LO2b]

PROBLEM 18–7 *(Prepare a Statement of Changes in Financial Position— Working Capital Basis)* Shown below is condensed financial information on a comparative basis for Artley Company.

| | DECEMBER 31 | |
|---|---|---|
| | 19X5 | 19X4 |
| Current Assets | $250,000 | $180,000 |
| Current Liabilities | 160,000 | 70,000 |
| Working Capital | $ 90,000 | $110,000 |
| Buildings | 420,000 | 340,000 |
| Accumulated Depreciation | (150,000) | (100,000) |
| Long-Term Investments | 25,000 | 50,000 |
| Capital Stock | 180,000 | 150,000 |
| Retained Earnings | 205,000 | 250,000 |

Additional Information:

1. The 19X5 reported net income of $40,000 included a $10,000 gain on the sale of long-term investments.
2. Buildings were purchased but not sold during the year.
3. Long-term investments were sold for $35,000 cash.
4. Cash dividends declared and paid during the year totaled $85,000.
5. No-par capital stock was sold for $30,000 cash.

Required:
Prepare a statement of changes in financial position for the year ended December 31, 19X5, using a working capital basis. A schedule of changes in working capital components must of course be omitted, and a work sheet is not required. [LO2b]

PROBLEM 18–8 *(Prepare a Work Sheet and a Statement of Changes in Financial Position—Working Capital Basis)* Condensed comparative balance sheets for Bold Company are presented below.

| | DECEMBER 31 | |
|---|---|---|
| | 19X5 | 19X4 |
| ASSETS | | |
| Cash | $ 18,000 | $ 11,000 |
| Accounts Receivable (net) | 27,100 | 19,200 |
| Inventory | 21,500 | 24,300 |
| Prepaid Expenses | 2,200 | 2,000 |
| Land | 15,000 | 35,000 |
| Building | 118,000 | 98,000 |
| Accumulated Depreciation—Building | (26,000) | (20,000) |
| Total Assets | $175,800 | $169,500 |
| LIABILITIES AND STOCKHOLDERS' EQUITY | | |
| Accounts Payable | $ 30,100 | $ 19,400 |
| Accrued Liabilities | 6,300 | 5,900 |
| Bonds Payable—Long-Term | 25,000 | 40,000 |
| Capital Stock | 90,000 | 75,000 |
| Retained Earnings | 24,400 | 29,200 |
| Total Liabilities and Stockholders' Equity | $175,800 | $169,500 |

Additional Data:

1. Net income for the year was $35,900.
2. Depreciation of $6,000 was recorded during the year.
3. Bonds having a face value of $15,000 were retired at their face value during the year.
4. A wing costing $20,000 was added to the building during the year.
5. Cash dividends of $40,700 were declared and paid during the year.
6. Additional new shares of capital stock having no par or stated value were sold and issued during the year for $15,000 cash.
7. Land costing $20,000 was sold for $30,000, and the $10,000 gain on the sale was included in the $35,900 of reported net income.

Required:

1. Prepare a work sheet for a working-capital-basis statement of changes in financial position.
2. Prepare a formal statement of changes in financial position and a supporting schedule of changes in working capital components. [LO2a,2b]

PROBLEM 18–9 *(Prepare a Statement of Changes in Financial Position Using the Cash Basis)* Condensed comparative balance sheets for Calcore Corporation are presented on page 684.

Supplementary information gathered from the company's income statement, statement of retained earnings, and general ledger accounts established the following:

1. Net income for the year was $61,000.
2. Depreciation expense for the year was $22,000.
3. Long-term bonds having a face value of $25,000 were issued at face value for cash.
4. Equipment costing $95,000 was purchased during the year for cash.
5. A fully depreciated piece of equipment having an original cost of $10,000 was scrapped. Its cost and accumulated depreciation were removed from the records by a journal entry.
6. Five thousand shares of common stock were issued during the year at $2 above their par value.
7. Cash dividends declared and paid during the year totaled $32,000.

| | DECEMBER 31 19X5 | DECEMBER 31 19X4 |
|---|---|---|
| ASSETS | | |
| Cash | $ 78,000 | $ 72,000 |
| Accounts Receivable (net) | 93,000 | 84,000 |
| Inventory | 75,000 | 79,000 |
| Prepaid Expenses | 8,000 | 6,000 |
| Equipment | 275,000 | 190,000 |
| Accumulated Depreciation | (30,000) | (18,000) |
| Total Assets | $499,000 | $413,000 |
| LIABILITIES AND STOCKHOLDERS' EQUITY | | |
| Accounts Payable | $ 89,000 | $ 94,000 |
| Accrued Liabilities | 12,000 | 10,000 |
| Long-Term Bonds Payable | 100,000 | 75,000 |
| Common Stock, $5 Par Value | 150,000 | 125,000 |
| Paid-in Capital in Excess of Par Value | 70,000 | 60,000 |
| Retained Earnings | 78,000 | 49,000 |
| Total Liabilities and Stockholders' Equity | $499,000 | $413,000 |

8. Additional data obtained from the income statement are summarized as follows: net sales, $840,000; cost of goods sold, $570,000; expenses including depreciation, $209,000.
9. All the accounts payable are the result of merchandise purchases, and all the accrued liabilities are the result of operating expenses.

Required:
Prepare a statement of changes in financial position on a cash basis. [LO2c]

PROBLEM 18–10 *(Prepare a Work Sheet and a Statement of Changes in Financial Position—Working Capital Basis)* The condensed comparative balance sheet of Rex Corporation appears below.

REX CORPORATION
Comparative Balance Sheet

| | DECEMBER 31 19X5 | DECEMBER 31 19X4 |
|---|---|---|
| ASSETS | | |
| Cash | $ 60,000 | $ 54,000 |
| Accounts Receivable (net) | 93,000 | 98,000 |
| Inventory | 120,000 | 133,000 |
| Prepaid Expenses | 7,200 | 9,400 |
| Long-Term Investments | 65,000 | 40,000 |
| Land (held for future site) | 40,000 | 50,000 |
| Equipment | 270,000 | 233,000 |
| Accumulated Depreciation—Equipment | (87,000) | (73,000) |
| Total Assets | $568,200 | $544,400 |
| LIABILITIES AND STOCKHOLDERS' EQUITY | | |
| Accounts Payable | $ 78,000 | $ 91,000 |
| Notes Payable—Short-Term | 15,000 | 10,000 |
| Accrued Liabilities | 3,200 | 4,400 |
| Bonds Payable, Due in 15 Years | 60,000 | 40,000 |
| Common Stock, $10 Par Value | 280,000 | 250,000 |
| Retained Earnings | 132,000 | 149,000 |
| Total Liabilities and Stockholders' Equity | $568,200 | $544,400 |

Additional Data:

Anticipating future expansion, the firm sold 3,000 additional shares of common stock and issued additional long-term debt securities, both at par, on October 15, 19X5. Some of this money was used to purchase additional equipment and to increase the firm's holdings in long-term investments. No equipment or investments were sold during the year. Land originally costing $10,000 was sold for $15,000 during the year. The firm's income statement showed net income of $31,000. The dividend policy of the past was continued in 19X5. As a result, cash dividends of $48,000 were declared and paid to stockholders of record as of December 18, 19X5. Depreciation expense on equipment was recorded for $14,000 during the year.

Required:

1. Prepare a work sheet for a working-capital-basis statement of changes in financial position.
2. Prepare a formal statement of changes in financial position and supporting schedule of changes in working capital components. [LO2a,2b]

PROBLEM 18–11 *(Comprehensive Problem—Prepare a Statement of Changes in Financial Position on Both a Working Capital and a Cash Basis)* A comparative balance sheet for Mart Merchandising Corporation on December 31, 19X5 and 19X4, is presented below (amounts are in thousands of dollars).

| | DECEMBER 31 | |
|---|---|---|
| | 19X5 | 19X4 |
| Current Assets | | |
| Cash | $ 1,000 | $ 1,650 |
| Accounts Receivable (net) | 5,800 | 3,960 |
| Inventory | 8,100 | 7,800 |
| Prepaid Expenses | 225 | 250 |
| Total Current Assets | 15,125 | 13,660 |
| Plant and Equipment: | | |
| Land | 2,100 | 2,100 |
| Buildings | 9,150 | 8,000 |
| Accumulated Depreciation—Buildings | (1,250) | (800) |
| Equipment | 850 | 620 |
| Accumulated Depreciation—Equipment | (90) | (60) |
| Total Plant and Equipment | 10,760 | 9,860 |
| Intangible Assets | 435 | 750 |
| Total Assets | $26,320 | $24,270 |
| Current Liabilities: | | |
| Accounts Payable | $ 8,500 | $ 7,100 |
| Accrued Liabilities | 1,000 | 1,200 |
| Total Current Liabilities | 9,500 | 8,300 |
| Long-Term Bonds Payable | 2,000 | 1,000 |
| Total Liabilities | 11,500 | 9,300 |
| Stockholders' Equity: | | |
| Common Stock, $100 Par Value | 10,000 | 12,000 |
| Paid-in Capital in Excess of Par Value | 600 | 1,000 |
| Retained Earnings | 4,220 | 1,970 |
| Total Stockholders' Equity | 14,820 | 14,970 |
| Total Liabilities and Stockholders' Equity | $26,320 | $24,270 |

Additional Information:

1. All the accounts payable are the result of merchandise purchases, and all the accrued liabilities are the result of operating expenses.
2. Income statement items show the following: net sales, $29,400,000; cost of goods sold, $11,900,000; expenses other than depreciation and amortization and excluding losses if any, $14,160,000.

During 19X5 the following occurred:

1. A building addition was constructed at a cost of $1,150,000. The cash paid for this addition was obtained primarily by a new $1,000,000 bond issue that was sold at face value.
2. Some equipment acquired previously at a cost of $170,000 and having accumulated depreciation of $20,000 on the date of sale was sold for $125,000. New equipment purchased during 19X5 amounting to $400,000 was paid for in cash.
3. Depreciation expense recorded on buildings was $450,000, and depreciation expense recorded on equipment was $50,000.
4. Amortization expense of $315,000 was recorded and charged directly to the Intangible Assets account.
5. Twenty thousand shares of common stock were retired by paying $2,400,000 in cash to the shareholders. The $400,000 excess redemption price over the par value of the shares was charged to the Paid-in Capital account.
6. The only items affecting the Retained Earnings account during the year were the reported net income and the cash dividends of $250,000 that were declared and paid.

Required:

1. Prepare a work sheet for a working-capital-basis statement of changes in financial position.
2. Prepare a formal statement of changes in financial position and the supporting schedule of changes in working capital components.
3. Prepare a statement of changes in financial position on a cash basis. [LO2a,2b,2c]

## ALTERNATE PROBLEMS

PROBLEM 18–1A *(Prepare a Statement of Changes in Financial Position—Working Capital Basis)* (Alternate to Problem 18–4) A comparative balance sheet for Hold Company is shown below.

| | DECEMBER 31 19X5 | 19X4 |
|---|---|---|
| **ASSETS** | | |
| Cash | $ 18,000 | $ 14,000 |
| Accounts Receivable—(net) | 27,100 | 16,200 |
| Inventory | 21,500 | 24,300 |
| Prepaid Expenses | 2,200 | 2,000 |
| Land | 15,000 | 34,000 |
| Building | 118,000 | 99,000 |
| Accumulated Depreciation—Building | (26,000) | (20,000) |
| Total Assets | $175,800 | $169,500 |
| **LIABILITIES AND STOCKHOLDERS' EQUITY** | | |
| Accounts Payable | $ 30,100 | $ 19,400 |
| Accrued Liabilities | 6,300 | 5,900 |
| Bonds Payable—Long-Term | 25,000 | 45,000 |
| Capital Stock | 90,000 | 70,000 |
| Retained Earnings | 24,400 | 29,200 |
| Total Liabilities and Stockholders' Equity | $175,800 | $169,500 |

Additional Data:

1. Net income for the year was $27,900.
2. Cash dividends of $32,700 were declared and paid during the year.
3. Land costing $19,000 was sold for $28,000, and the $9,000 gain on the sale was included in the $27,900 of reported net income.

4. Bonds having a face value of $20,000 were retired at their face value (with $20,000 of cash) during the year.
5. A building annex costing $19,000 was purchased for cash during the year.
6. Additional new shares of capital stock having no par or stated value were sold and issued during the year for $20,000 cash.
7. Depreciation of $6,000 was recorded during the year.

Required:
Prepare a statement of changes in financial position on a working capital basis. A work sheet may not be necessary. Remember to include a schedule of changes in working capital components. [LO2b]

PROBLEM 18–2A *(Prepare a Statement of Changes in Financial Position—Cash Basis)* (Alternate to Problem 18–5) Using the data presented in Problem 18–1A plus the additional data presented below, prepare a cash-basis statement of changes for Hold Company for the year ended December 31, 19X5.

1. All the accounts payable are the result of merchandise purchases.
2. All the accrued liabilities are the result of operating expenses.
3. Sales for 19X5 totaled $203,700, and the cost of the goods related to those sales was $142,500.
4. Expenses including depreciation expense were $42,300. [LO2c]

PROBLEM 18–3A *(Prepare a Statement of Changes in Financial Position—Working Capital Basis)* (Alternate to Problem 18–6) A condensed comparative balance sheet for Fineview Corporation on December 31, 19X5 and 19X4, is presented below.

| | DECEMBER 31 19X5 | 19X4 |
|---|---|---|
| ASSETS | | |
| Cash | $ 9,000 | $ 10,000 |
| Accounts Receivable (net) | 43,000 | 44,000 |
| Notes Receivable | 17,000 | 12,000 |
| Inventory | 66,000 | 42,000 |
| Land (held for future site) | 20,000 | 20,000 |
| Equipment | 93,000 | 90,000 |
| Accumulated Depreciation—Equipment | (36,000) | (30,500) |
| Total Assets | $212,000 | $187,500 |
| LIABILITIES AND STOCKHOLDERS' EQUITY | | |
| Accounts Payable | $ 37,000 | $ 35,500 |
| Accrued Liabilities | 9,000 | 12,000 |
| Common Stock, $10 Par Value | 100,000 | 90,000 |
| Retained Earnings | 66,000 | 50,000 |
| Total Liabilities and Stockholders' Equity | $212,000 | $187,500 |

An examination of the firm's other financial statements and its accounting records disclosed that 1,000 additional shares of common stock were sold at par and that the company purchased new equipment costing $3,000 during the year. In addition, cash dividends totaling $9,000 were declared and paid during 19X5, and the net income reported on the income statement was $25,000.

Required:
Prepare a statement of changes in financial position on a working capital basis. A work sheet may not be necessary. Remember to include a schedule of changes in working capital components. [LO2b]

PROBLEM 18–4A *(Prepare a Work Sheet and a Statement of Changes in Financial Position—Working Capital Basis)* (Alternate to Problem 18–8) Condensed comparative balance sheets for Templeton Corporation on December 31, 19X5 and 19X4, are presented on page 688.

| | DECEMBER 31 | |
|---|---|---|
| | 19X5 | 19X4 |
| ASSETS | | |
| Cash | $ 9,100 | $ 11,300 |
| Accounts Receivable (net) | 21,200 | 19,800 |
| Inventory | 37,000 | 33,400 |
| Prepaid Expenses | 1,800 | 2,200 |
| Equipment | 58,000 | 41,000 |
| Accumulated Depreciation—Equipment | (13,300) | (9,600) |
| Land | 40,000 | -0- |
| Long-Term Investments | 29,000 | 38,000 |
| Total Assets | $182,800 | $136,100 |
| LIABILITIES AND STOCKHOLDERS' EQUITY | | |
| Accounts Payable | $ 17,100 | $ 19,400 |
| Note Payable—Short Term | 3,000 | 5,500 |
| Accrued Liabilities | 1,500 | 1,300 |
| Bonds Payable—Long-Term | 20,000 | -0- |
| Common Stock | 90,000 | 60,000 |
| Retained Earnings | 51,200 | 49,900 |
| Total Liabilities and Stockholders' Equity | $182,800 | $136,100 |

Additional Data:

1. Net income for the year was $29,600.
2. Depreciation of $3,700 was recorded on equipment during the year.
3. Twenty thousand dollars of face value bonds payable were issued for $20,000 cash during the year.
4. Long-term investments costing $9,000 were sold for $9,600, and the $600 gain on the sale was included in the $29,600 of reported net income.
5. New equipment costing $17,000 was purchased during the year for cash.
6. Land costing $40,000 was acquired by paying $30,000 cash and by giving $10,000 of no-par, no stated value, common stock in exchange.
7. Cash dividends of $28,300 were declared and paid during the year.
8. Additional no-par shares of common stock were sold for $20,000 during the year.

Required:

1. Prepare a work sheet for a working-capital-basis statement of changes in financial position.
2. Prepare a formal statement of changes in financial position and a supporting schedule of changes in working capital componets. [LO2a,2b]

PROBLEM 18–5A *(Prepare a Statement of Changes in Financial Position Using the Cash Basis)* (Alternate to Problem 18–9) Condensed comparative balance sheets for Corebal Corporation are presented on page 689.

Supplementary information gathered from the company's income statement, statement of retained earnings, and general ledger accounts established the following:

1. Net income for the year was $11,400.
2. Depreciation expense for the year was $31,000.
3. Equipment costing $45,000 was purchased during the year for cash.
4. A fully depreciated piece of equipment having an original cost of $15,000 was scrapped. Its cost and accumulated depreciation were removed from the records by a journal entry.
5. Five hundred shares of common stock were issued on January 8, 19X5, at $32 per share.

| | DECEMBER 31 | |
|---|---|---|
| | 19X5 | 19X4 |
| ASSETS | | |
| Cash | $ 23,500 | $ 19,700 |
| Accounts Receivable (net) | 51,300 | 60,100 |
| Inventory | 46,700 | 51,800 |
| Prepaid Expenses | 2,500 | 2,400 |
| Equipment | 180,000 | 150,000 |
| Accumulated Depreciation | (64,000) | (48,000) |
| Total Assets | $240,000 | $236,000 |
| LIABILITIES AND STOCKHOLDERS' EQUITY | | |
| Accounts Payable | $ 61,600 | $ 58,800 |
| Accrued Liabilities | 10,400 | 6,200 |
| Long-Term Bonds Payable | 50,000 | 70,000 |
| Common Stock, $10 Par Value | 20,000 | 15,000 |
| Paid-in Capital in Excess of Par Value | 55,000 | 44,000 |
| Retained Earnings | 43,000 | 42,000 |
| Total Liabilities and Stockholders' Equity | $240,000 | $236,000 |

6. Twenty thousand dollars of long-term bonds payable were retired during the year at their face value for cash.
7. Cash dividends of $5.20 per share were declared and paid during 19X5.
8. Net sales for the year were $267,800, and the related cost of goods sold was $119,200.
9. Expenses (including depreciation expense) reported on the income statement were $137,200.
10. All the accounts payable are the result of merchandise purchases, and all the accrued liabilities are the result of operating expenses.

Required:

Prepare a statement of changes in financial position on a cash basis. [LO2c]

# 19 Financial Statement Analysis

### *Learning Objectives*

When you complete this chapter you will be able to

1. Answer the following questions:
   a. How is financial statement information used by internal and external groups in making decisions about management, investment, or the granting of credit?
   b. What are some common bases for establishing standards, and how might they be used as a basis for comparison when interpreting financial ratios?
   c. How are long-term financial summaries and graphic presentation useful when analyzing and interpreting financial statement data?
2. Perform the following accounting functions:
   a. Conduct a horizontal analysis, trend analysis, and vertical analysis of comparative financial statements and discuss the benefits obtained from applying each of these analytical techniques.
   b. Compute the ratios widely used in the analysis of financial statements.
   c. Apply ratio analysis to measure and evaluate a firm's liquidity, profitability, solvency, and market strength.

In earlier chapters we have seen how a firm gathers and uses financial data to prepare its balance sheet, income statement, and statement of changes in financial position. These statements, together with their accompanying explanatory notes, are the primary means by which management communicates information about the firm's financial position, its operating performance, and its financing and investing activities to interested parties outside the firm. Although a set of financial statements provides considerable information about a firm, the statements become more informative when the user is able to recognize and understand the relationships and trends that the financial statement data can reveal. This chapter explains several analytical techniques used to uncover these relationships and trends.

## THE USE OF FINANCIAL STATEMENT DATA IN DECISION MAKING

*1a. Decision makers are either internal or external to the firm*

The basic objective of financial statements is to provide information that is useful to decision makers. These consist of two broad groups: (1) internal decision makers and (2) external decision makers. The *internal decision makers* are the company managers who have access to financial data beyond those contained in the financial statements. They use procedures and techniques discussed in this chapter, as well as those discussed in Chapters 21 through 27. The *external decision makers* include investors, potential investors, creditors, security analysts, regulatory agents, and others who make decisions about various aspects of the firm.

Although their specific interests differ, these groups of decision makers all rely heavily on financial statements as their primary source of information. Before we discuss the techniques used in financial statement analysis, we will briefly describe the information needs of some of the key decision makers and the way that financial statements are used as an aid in obtaining the needed information.

*1a. Investors want information that can be useful in predicting a company's future profitability*

INVESTMENT DECISIONS Investors are interested in earning a return on their investments from (1) dividends and (2) a subsequent increase in the market price of their investment. Since both dividends and subsequent changes in the market price of their investment are related to earnings (profits), investors want information that can be useful in predicting a company's future **profitability.** By referring to the current and past financial statements of the companies whose shares they own or are interested in buying, investors can make judgments about the adequacy of past profitability and dividend distributions. They can also determine whether any significant trends have developed in these areas. Evaluating past earnings and dividend data is often the first step in making decisions that affect the future.

*1a. Short-term creditors want to determine the company's ability to pay debts when due*

CREDIT DECISIONS Those who *sell* goods or services to a company on short-term credit terms want to know whether the company will be able to pay for the purchase when the amount is due. Those who *lend* money to a company on a short-term note want to know whether they will receive the agreed-upon interest during the period in which the note is outstanding and whether the loan will be repaid when the note comes due. These short-term creditors frequently use the borrowing company's balance sheet to determine the amount and the composition of the assets that it has available to pay for its short-term debts. Specifically, they look at the borrowing company's cash position and make judgments about its ability to generate future cash from such near-cash assets as short-term investments, accounts receivable, and inventory. They may also be interested in determining the borrower's *working capital* (the amount by which its current assets exceed its current liabilities). This analysis, generally referred to as *liquidity* analysis, is useful in establishing a company's debt-paying ability.

***1a. Long-term creditors want to determine the company's ability to pay interest and principal when due***

Long-term creditors are interested in the company's ability to pay interest during the period of time in which the long-term debt is outstanding and the principal when the debt is due. The type of financial analysis done to evaluate the ability of a company to meet its long-term obligations as they come due is generally referred to as **solvency** analysis.

**SECURITY ANALYSTS' DECISIONS** Security analysts, as advisers to investors, also use information contained in financial statements to identify firms whose stock purchase they are willing to recommend. Because their clients are interested in earning a return on their investment, security analysts want information that will help them in making predictions about profitability. Profitability is important because it affects the timing and amount of dividends to be distributed and is used to evaluate the company's operating success (or lack of it), which will ultimately affect the market price of the company's stock. A primary source of information for predicting whether an investor can expect future returns from dividends and from increases in the market price of the shares purchased is the company's past and current financial statements.

***1a. Security analysts also want information that will help them predict a company's future profitability***

***1a. Decision makers analyze financial statements to assess a company's past operational performance and current financial condition as a basis for predicting future performance***

Although certain aspects of a company's financial condition or its operational performance are more important to some decision makers than to others, generally all have an interest in the company's liquidity, solvency, and profitability. When making investment, credit, or other decisions, these decision makers frequently use financial information to

1. *Assess the company's past performance.* This is usually a good starting point for developing data that can be used to predict future performance.
2. *Assess the company's current financial condition.* An analysis of the company's current financial condition will, among other things, identify what type of assets the company owns and the dollar amount invested in each of the individual assets, the amount of debt it has, when the debt comes due, and the relationship between its debt and its owners' equity. This information is useful in making judgments about the company's short-term liquidity and its long-run solvency. It can also be useful in predicting the company's future cash flows and its profit potential.
3. *Predict the future performance of the company.* Investors are primarily interested in future earnings. Creditors are primarily interested in the ability to pay debts on a timely basis. Managers are interested in both. Recent financial statements are often good indicators for making predictions about future earnings and for determining the risk associated with generating those earnings.

## ANALYTICAL TECHNIQUES

When the financial statements of a business are analyzed, individual statement items and amounts are in themselves generally not very informative. It is the relationships between items and amounts, or groups of items and amounts, plus changes that have occurred in them that are important. For example, knowing that a company's reported net income for the year is $500,000 is not very informative unless this net income can be related to other data. Earning a net income of $500,000 might be viewed as an outstanding performance for a company having $4 million in sales but might be viewed as inadequate for a company having $20 million in sales. On the other hand, $500,000 of net income represents an improved performance if the company's net income was only $400,000 last year. The techniques of financial statement analysis are designed to uncover relationships and trends in financial statement data for use in evaluating the liquidity, solvency, and profitability of an entity.

*2a,2b. Four types of analysis widely used are horizontal, trend, vertical, and ratio*

Four widely used techniques of financial statement analysis are listed below.

1. **Horizontal analysis:** Comparative financial statements are presented side by side, and the change in corresponding items or groups of items presented on those statements is computed in dollar amounts, as a percentage, or both, over two or more years.
2. **Trend analysis:** Another type of horizontal analysis whereby the change in selected corresponding items or groups of items presented on the financial statements is computed for a number of years, usually three or more.
3. **Vertical analysis:** The dollar amount of each item presented on a financial statement is related to a relevant total on that statement and is expressed as a percentage of that total. For example, each asset item on the balance sheet would be stated as a percentage of total assets.
4. **Ratio analysis:** The dollar amounts of two items appearing in the financial statements are compared and expressed in a relationship.

Each of these techniques is examined in the following sections.

Before examining each technique, a brief note relating to calculations may be useful. Percentages and ratios are calculated by rounding to one or two decimal places. Keep in mind that the purpose of the calculation is to point out significant changes and to provide information about item relationships. This is generally accomplished by a figure carried one or two places. However, since there is no consensus on this matter, the assignment material at the end of the chapter will clearly state the requirement.

## Horizontal Analysis

Most companies prepare **comparative financial statements** in which the data for two or more successive years are presented side by side to facilitate the analysis of changes. A common starting point for analyzing the comparative data is to determine the dollar amount of increase or decrease and the percentage change from year to year in each item shown on the statement. The process is known as horizontal analysis. In Exhibits 19-1 and 19-2 on pages 694-695 we show a comparative balance sheet, a comparative income statement, and a comparative statement of retained earnings for Astor Company with dollar and percentage changes computed.

*2a. Horizontal analysis is illustrated in Exhibits 19-1 and 19-2*

In computing the increase or decrease in dollar amounts, the corresponding items are compared and the earlier period is used as the base against which the later period is compared. For example, Astor's Cash account balances were compared, and the $10,000 increase that occurred between the two successive periods (19X5 and 19X4) was listed. The amount was computed by comparing the 19X5 amount with the 19X4 base period amount to determine that the change was an increase. The increase or decrease in dollar amounts for all corresponding items is calculated, and the results are listed in the comparative statements together with their percentage increase or decrease. The percentage increase or decrease (percentage change) is computed by dividing the item's dollar change by its base-year amount. For example, Astor shows that the per-

*EXHIBIT 19–1*

Comparative Balance Sheet—Horizontal Analysis

ASTOR COMPANY
Comparative Balance Sheet
December 31, 19X5 and 19X4

| | DECEMBER 31 | | INCREASE OR (DECREASE) | |
|---|---|---|---|---|
| | 19X5 | 19X4 | Amount | Percentage |
| ASSETS | | | | |
| Current Assets: | | | | |
| Cash | $ 38,000 | $ 28,000 | $ 10,000 | 35.7 |
| Accounts Receivable—Net | 82,000 | 75,000 | 7,000 | 9.3 |
| Inventory | 127,000 | 102,000 | 25,000 | 24.5 |
| Prepaid Expenses | 8,100 | 8,900 | (800) | (9.0) |
| Total Current Assets | $255,100 | $213,900 | $ 41,200 | 19.3 |
| Plant Assets: | | | | |
| Land | $ 40,000 | $ 40,000 | $ 0 | 0 |
| Buildings | 290,000 | 250,000 | 40,000 | 16.0 |
| Equipment | 470,000 | 390,000 | 80,000 | 20.5 |
| Total | $800,000 | $680,000 | $120,000 | 17.6 |
| Less Accumulated Depreciation | (295,000) | (249,000) | 46,000 | 18.5 |
| Total Plant Assets—Net | $505,000 | $431,000 | $ 74,000 | 17.2 |
| Total Assets | $760,100 | $644,900 | $115,200 | 17.9 |
| LIABILITIES AND STOCKHOLDERS' EQUITY | | | | |
| Current Liabilities: | | | | |
| Accounts Payable | $ 96,000 | $ 81,000 | $ 15,000 | 18.5 |
| Taxes Payable | 20,000 | 18,000 | 2,000 | 11.1 |
| Accrued Liabilities | 33,000 | 37,000 | (4,000) | (10.8) |
| Total Current Liabilities | $149,000 | $136,000 | $ 13,000 | 9.6 |
| Long-Term Liabilities: | | | | |
| Bonds Payable (12%) | 200,000 | 150,000 | 50,000 | 33.3 |
| Total Liabilities | $349,000 | $286,000 | $ 63,000 | 22.0 |
| Stockholders' Equity: | | | | |
| Common Stock ($10 par value) | $200,000 | $180,000 | $ 20,000 | 11.1 |
| Paid-in Capital | 31,100 | 28,900 | 2,200 | 7.6 |
| Retained Earnings | 180,000 | 150,000 | 30,000 | 20.0 |
| Total Stockholders' Equity | $411,100 | $358,900 | $ 52,200 | 14.5 |
| Total Liabilities and Stockholders' Equity | $760,100 | $644,900 | $115,200 | 17.9 |

centage change in its Cash account balance from 19X4 to 19X5 was 35.7%. This was computed as follows:

$$\text{Percentage Change} = 100\left(\frac{\overset{\text{Amount of Change}}{\$10{,}000}}{\underset{\text{Base-Year Amount}}{\$28{,}000}}\right) = 35.7\%$$

A percentage change can be computed only when the amount reported for the item in the base year is a positive amount. When no amount is reported or when a negative amount is reported in the base year, a percentage increase or decrease cannot be computed.

Comparative statements with horizontal analysis clearly reveal the magnitude and the direction of change that occurred in corresponding financial statement items between the periods under review. The cause of the change and whether the change is favorable or unfavorable probably cannot be fully deter-

*EXHIBIT 19–2*

Comparative Income Statement and Statement of Retained Earnings—Horizontal Analysis

ASTOR COMPANY
Comparative Income Statement
For the Years Ended December 31, 19X5 and 19X4

| | YEAR ENDED | | INCREASE OR (DECREASE) | |
|---|---|---|---|---|
| | 19X5 | 19X4 | Amount | Percentage |
| Net Sales | $760,000 | $700,000 | $60,000 | 8.6 |
| Less: Cost of Goods Sold | 390,000 | 340,000 | 50,000 | 14.7 |
| Gross Profit on Sales | $370,000 | $360,000 | $10,000 | 2.8 |
| Selling Expenses | 175,000 | 162,800 | 12,200 | 7.5 |
| Administrative Expenses | 79,500 | 94,000 | (14,500) | (15.4) |
| Interest Expense | 29,000 | 22,000 | 7,000 | 31.8 |
| Total Expenses | $283,500 | $278,800 | $ 4,700 | 1.7 |
| Income before Taxes | $ 86,500 | $ 81,200 | $ 5,300 | 6.5 |
| Income Taxes | 34,500 | 33,200 | 1,300 | 3.9 |
| Net Income | $ 52,000 | $ 48,000 | $ 4,000 | 8.3 |

ASTOR COMPANY
Comparative Statement of Retained Earnings
For the Years Ended December 31, 19X5 and 19X4

| | YEAR ENDED | | INCREASE OR (DECREASE) | |
|---|---|---|---|---|
| | 19X5 | 19X4 | Amount | Percentage |
| Retained Earnings, January 1 | $150,000 | $122,000 | $28,000 | 23.0 |
| Add Net Income | 52,000 | 48,000 | 4,000 | 8.3 |
| | 202,000 | 170,000 | 32,000 | 18.8 |
| Deduct Dividends | 22,000 | 20,000 | 2,000 | 10.0 |
| Retained Earnings, December 31 | $180,000 | $150,000 | $30,000 | 20.0 |

mined without additional information. However, some conclusions can be drawn from the figures reported in Exhibits 19–1 and 19–2.

*2a. Horizontal analysis points out accounts that had the most significant changes in terms of dollars and percentages*

In analyzing the data, those accounts having large balances and those showing significant change would probably receive the most attention. Referring to Astor's balance sheet, inventory is clearly revealed as an item having a large balance compared with other current assets and one that has experienced a significant percentage change (24.5%) from 19X4 to 19X5. Additionally, equipment is prominently revealed as the plant asset with a large balance that has had a significant change in both dollars and percentage.

One of the major purposes of financial statement analysis is to point out significant changes that need explanation or further investigation. An analyst would probably be interested in whether the inventory buildup was voluntary or involuntary. It could also be important to establish how the equipment and other plant assets were financed. Did the source of funding come from operations, from the issuance of debt, from the sale of stock, or from some combination of sources?

Turning to the comparative income statement, horizontal analysis shows that from 19X4 to 19X5 net sales increased by 8.6%. This in itself would probably be viewed as favorable. However, because cost of goods sold increased by 14.7% and operating expenses increased by 1.7%, net income increased by only 8.3%, slightly below the percentage increase in net sales. Information such as this is useful in assessing management's past performance and in making judgments about where improvement in performance is needed. For example, can sales be increased by more than 8.6% in the future? Will management be able to control future costs, especially its cost of goods sold?

## Trend Analysis

*2a. Trend analysis shows changes in selected financial data for several successive years*

Trend analysis is a variation of horizontal analysis in which changes in selected financial data are shown for several successive years. To illustrate, assume that we were interested in the sales and net income trends experienced by Astor Company over the last five years. The dollar data reported by the company for these items are as follows:

| | 19X1 | 19X2 | 19X3 | 19X4 | 19X5 |
|---|---|---|---|---|---|
| Sales | $550,000 | $590,000 | $650,000 | $700,000 | $760,000 |
| Net Income | 32,000 | 35,000 | 39,000 | 48,000 | 52,000 |

The data clearly point out that the dollar amount of both sales and net income is increasing from year to year. However, expressing the relationship between the change in sales and net income in percentages may be more useful in assessing the company's performance over the five-year period. This is done by selecting a base year and dividing the amount reported for each subsequent year by the base-year amount. When data for a number of years are being analyzed, the base year may be the earliest year, as in our analysis, or each year's data may be compared with data of the immediately preceding year.

Trend percentages calculated for Astor Company, rounded to the nearest whole percent, are shown in the table below.

| | 19X1 | 19X2 | 19X3 | 19X4 | 19X5 |
|---|---|---|---|---|---|
| Sales | 100% | 107% | 118% | 127% | 138% |
| Net Income | 100 | 109 | 122 | 150 | 163 |

The trend percentages show that net income is increasing more rapidly than sales, especially in the last two years. This appears favorable. However, without determining trends in other income statement items, we can only speculate as to why this is happening. For example, the favorable trend increase in net income may be because the selling price of the company's products is increasing more than the cost to acquire them is increasing. Or it may be because the company has been able to decrease its operating expenses, or it may be that the company's revenue from sources other than sales has been increasing rapidly each year. In any case, it should be recognized that a trend percentage can only show the degree of increase or decrease in a selected item. It cannot indicate the cause for the increase or decrease.

*2a. A statement of trend percentages highlights favorable items (indicating good management) as well as problem areas*

Nevertheless, a statement showing trend percentages is useful to management because it highlights favorable items indicating that good management has taken place, as well as highlighting unfavorable items where explanations may be expected and further investigation may be required. Persons other than management having an interest in the company use trend percentages to get an overview of the company's past performance and to try to determine whether recent trends can be expected to continue in the future.

## Vertical Analysis

*2a. Vertical analysis shows the dollar amount of each item reported on a financial statement as a percentage of some relevant base amount*

Percentage analysis can also be used to show the relationship of individual items to a total in a single financial statement. This type of analysis is called vertical analysis. In vertical analysis the dollar amount of each item reported on a financial statement is shown as a percentage of some relevant amount selected from that same statement. On the balance sheet, for example, each item reported is stated as a percentage of total assets or as a percentage of total liabilities and stockholders' equity. Thus cash would be expressed as a percentage of total assets, and accounts payable as a percentage of total liabilities and stockholders' equity. In vertical analysis of the income statement, each item is stated as a

EXHIBIT 19–3

Comparative Common-Size Balance Sheet—Vertical Analysis

ASTOR COMPANY
Comparative Balance Sheet
December 31, 19X5 and 19X4

| | DECEMBER 31 | | COMMON-SIZE PERCENTAGES | |
|---|---|---|---|---|
| | 19X5 | 19X4 | 19X5 | 19X4 |
| ASSETS | | | | |
| Current Assets: | | | | |
| Cash | $ 38,000 | $ 28,000 | 5.0 | 4.3 |
| Accounts Receivable—Net | 82,000 | 75,000 | 10.8 | 11.6 |
| Inventory | 127,000 | 102,000 | 16.7 | 15.8 |
| Prepaid Expenses | 8,100 | 8,900 | 1.1 | 1.4 |
| Total Current Assets | $255,100 | $213,900 | 33.6 | 33.2 |
| Plant Assets: | | | | |
| Land | $ 40,000 | $ 40,000 | 5.3 | 6.2 |
| Buildings | 290,000 | 250,000 | 38.2 | 38.8 |
| Equipment | 470,000 | 390,000 | 61.8 | 60.5 |
| Total | $800,000 | $680,000 | 105.2 | 105.4 |
| Less Accumulated Depreciation | (295,000) | (249,000) | (38.8) | (38.6) |
| Total Plant Assets—Net | $505,000 | $431,000 | 66.4 | 66.8 |
| Total Assets | $760,100 | $644,900 | 100.0 | 100.0 |
| LIABILITIES AND STOCKHOLDERS' EQUITY | | | | |
| Current Liabilities: | | | | |
| Accounts Payable | $ 96,000 | $ 81,000 | 12.6 | 12.6 |
| Taxes Payable | 20,000 | 18,000 | 2.6 | 2.8 |
| Accrued Liabilities | 33,000 | 37,000 | 4.3 | 5.7 |
| Total Current Liabilities | 149,000 | 136,000 | 19.6 | 21.1 |
| Long-Term Liabilities | | | | |
| Bonds Payable (12%) | 200,000 | 150,000 | 26.3 | 23.3 |
| Total Liabilities | 349,000 | 286,000 | 45.9 | 44.3 |
| Stockholders' Equity: | | | | |
| Common Stock ($10 par value) | 200,000 | 180,000 | 26.3 | 27.9 |
| Paid-in Capital | 31,100 | 28,900 | 4.1 | 4.5 |
| Retained Earnings | 180,000 | 150,000 | 23.7 | 23.3 |
| Total Stockholders' Equity | 411,100 | 358,900 | 54.1 | 55.7 |
| Total Liabilities and Stockholders' Equity | $760,100 | $644,900 | 100.0 | 100.0 |

Some percentage columns do not add up to the total because of rounding.

percentage of net sales. Statements presented in this manner are often called **common-size financial statements.** Common-size statements show all items as a percentage of a common base amount, thereby expressing them only in relative terms.

*2a. Vertical analysis is illustrated in Exhibits 19–3 and 19–4*

Astor Company's comparative balance sheet with vertical analysis is shown in Exhibit 19–3 on page 697. Its comparative income statement and comparative statement of retained earnings with vertical analysis (indicating common-size percentages) are shown below in Exhibit 19–4.

EXHIBIT 19–4

Comparative Common-Size Income Statement and Statement of Retained Earnings—Vertical Analysis

ASTOR COMPANY
Comparative Income Statement
For the Years Ended December 31, 19X5 and 19X4

| | YEAR ENDED | | COMMON-SIZE PERCENTAGES YEAR ENDED | |
|---|---|---|---|---|
| | 19X5 | 19X4 | 19X5 | 19X4 |
| Net Sales | $760,000 | $700,000 | 100.0 | 100.0 |
| Less: Cost of Goods Sold | 390,000 | 340,000 | 51.3 | 48.6 |
| Gross Profit on Sales | $370,000 | $360,000 | 48.7 | 51.4 |
| Selling Expenses | 175,000 | 162,800 | 23.0 | 23.3 |
| Administrative Expenses | 79,500 | 94,000 | 10.5 | 13.4 |
| Interest Expense | 29,000 | 22,000 | 3.8 | 3.1 |
| Total Expenses | $283,500 | $278,800 | 37.3 | 39.8 |
| Income before Taxes | $ 86,500 | $ 81,200 | 11.4 | 11.6 |
| Income Taxes | 34,500 | 33,200 | 4.5 | 4.7 |
| Net Income | $ 52,000 | $ 48,000 | 6.8 | 6.9 |

ASTOR COMPANY
Comparative Statement of Retained Earnings
For the Years Ended December 31, 19X5 and 19X4

| | YEAR ENDED | | COMMON-SIZE PERCENTAGES YEAR ENDED | |
|---|---|---|---|---|
| | 19X5 | 19X4 | 19X5 | 19X4 |
| Retained Earnings, January 1 | $150,000 | $122,000 | 83.3 | 81.3 |
| Add net income | 52,000 | 48,000 | 28.9 | 32.0 |
| | $202,000 | $170,000 | 112.2 | 113.3 |
| Deduct Dividends | 22,000 | 20,000 | 12.2 | 13.3 |
| Retained Earnings, December 31 | $180,000 | $150,000 | 100.0 | 100.0 |

Vertical analysis is useful for pointing out the relative importance of a statement item to a selected total in that statement. It is also useful because it reveals significant changes that may have occurred in individual items reported in the statement from one year to the next. For example, the common-size percentages on Astor's comparative income statement (Exhibit 19–4) point out that the cost of goods sold is an important item in income determination and that its increase from 48.6% to 51.3% of net sales is the primary reason for the decrease in net income as a percentage of net sales (from 6.9% to 6.8% of net sales).

The comparative balance sheet (Exhibit 19–3) shows remarkable stability in the composition of all reported items. Both current and noncurrent assets have remained relatively stable in their relationship to total assets from 19X4 to 19X5. The percentage of total liabilities to total liabilities and stockholders' equity has, however, shown some increase (from 44.3% to 45.9%). A future examination of these percentages shows that although current liabilities decreased in proportion to their base amount, long-term liabilities increased in proportion to that base. This indicates that the company relied more heavily on long-term debt as one source of financing its growth.

The percentages generated by vertical analysis can be used to see how each dollar of net sales revenue relates to other income statement items. For example, the 19X5 common-size percentages in Astor's comparative income statement show that

1. For every dollar of net sales revenue, 51.3 cents is needed to cover the cost of the items sold
2. For every dollar of net sales revenue, 37.3 cents is needed to cover the operating expenses
3. After taxes, 6.8 cents of every net sales dollar is left for the payment of dividends and for reinvestment in the company

Other things are also more easily observed when vertical analysis is prepared. For example, although the income statement shows that selling expenses increased by $12,200 in absolute terms from 19X4 to 19X5, they actually decreased in relative terms because they represented 23.0% of sales in 19X5 compared with 23.3% of sales in 19X4.

We have shown how an individual company (Astor) uses vertical analysis. Vertical analysis is also useful when comparing the financial statement data of one company with those of another, especially if the companies are of different size. Vertical analysis makes the comparisons easier because it expresses the data in relative terms. This is also important when comparing a company with averages developed and published for the industry in which the company operates.

*2a. Vertical analysis is useful in comparing one company with another or with industry averages*

## Ratio Analysis

A **ratio** is merely a mathematical expression of the relationship that one number has to another. It is computed by dividing one of the numbers by the other. The ratio of 100 to 25 would be $100 \div 25 = 4$, often expressed as 4 to 1. This means that the first number is four times as large as the second number.

*Ratio analysis* is a technique of analysis in which the dollar amounts of selected items appearing in the financial statements are compared and expressed in a relationship. Thus a financial ratio is computed by dividing the amount of a selected financial statement item by the amount of another selected financial statement item. For example, if a company had current assets of $150,000 and current liabilities of $60,000, its ratio of current assets to current liabilities would be 2.5 to 1, computed by dividing $150,000 by $60,000. Expressing the relationship between the company's current assets and its current liabilities in ratio form (such as 2.5 to 1) makes the relationship easier to understand, easier to compare from period to period, and easier to compare with the relationship existing between these items in other companies operating in the same industry.

Given the large quantity of items included in financial statements, many different ratios can be computed and presented. The number of ratios to be computed and the types to be used depend on the information needs of the person doing the analysis.

*2b. Ratios widely used fall into four categories*

The ratios discussed in this chapter are those most frequently used by analysts. We have classified these ratios into four categories—those used to evaluate a firm's

1. Short-term debt-paying ability (liquidity)
2. Operating performance (profitability)
3. Long-term debt-paying ability (solvency)
4. Market strength

Unless otherwise indicated, computations are based on the data reported in Astor Company's financial statements shown in Exhibits 19–1 and 19–2. The discussion indicates how each ratio is calculated and how it can be used. When necessary, calculations are rounded to one decimal place.

## Ratios to Evaluate Liquidity

*2c. Four ratios used to evaluate liquidity are the current ratio, quick ratio, accounts receivable turnover, and inventory turnover*

**Liquidity** refers to a company's ability to meets its current obligations as they come due. Therefore the evaluation of liquidity focuses on the relationship between current assets and current liabilities. The ability of a company to meet its current obligations is an important factor in evaluating short-term financial strength. Companies that do not have enough cash on hand to pay bills as they come due will lose cash discounts, will run a risk of losing the right to buy on credit, and may eventually be forced into bankruptcy. Four ratios associated with the evaluation of liquidity are the current ratio, the quick ratio, receivable turnover, and inventory turnover.

*2b,2c. Current ratio = current assets ÷ current liabilities*

**CURRENT RATIO** The *current ratio*, sometimes called the *working capital ratio*, measures the relationship between total current assets and total current liabilities at a specific date. The current ratio is computed by dividing the total current assets by the total current liabilities:

$$\text{Current Ratio} = \frac{\text{Current Assets}}{\text{Current Liabilities}}$$

The current ratios for Astor Company for 19X5 and 19X4 are

19X5: \$255,100 ÷ \$149,000 = 1.7 times, or 1.7 to 1
19X4: \$213,900 ÷ \$136,000 = 1.6 times, or 1.6 to 1

Astor Company shows a slight improvement in the relationship between current assets and current liabilities. The ratio indicates that at the end of 1985 (the most current year), Astor had \$1.70 of current assets for every \$1.00 of current liabilities. It would be difficult to generalize as to what constitutes an acceptable level for this ratio. Certain types of manufacturing firms expect a low current ratio because most of their assets are "tied up" in income-producing plant assets. Other businesses, such as finance companies, which find liquidity more important, have current ratios of greater than 2 to 1. While a high current ratio will be looked upon favorably by the company's short-term creditors, others may feel that it indicates an excessive investment in current assets. For example, a company overstocked in inventory may have a high current ratio but may not be producing an adequate return on its investments. It is expected that creditors as well as other users would keep in mind the type of company under review, its past data, future goals, and other factors when making evaluations based on ratios.

**QUICK RATIO** One of the criticisms of the current ratio is that it overstates short-term liquidity by including inventory and prepaid amounts in the numerator of the calculation. One of the items, inventory, clearly is not as readily available to meet current obligations as are cash, marketable securities, and receivables. The other item, prepaid expenses, is not even intended to be converted into cash. For these reasons, inventories and prepayments are excluded in the *quick ratio* computation. Thus the quick ratio, sometimes called the *acid test ratio,* is a more stringent measure of short-term liquidity and includes only cash and the near-cash assets such as marketable securities, accounts receivable, and short-term notes receivable. The quick ratio is computed as follows:

***2b,2c. Quick ratio = (cash + marketable securities + net receivables) ÷ current liabilities***

$$\text{Quick Ratio} = \frac{\text{Cash} + \text{Marketable Securities} + \text{Net Receivables}}{\text{Current Liabilities}}$$

The quick ratio measures the company's immediate liquid position, and therefore the higher the ratio, the more liquid the company. For a number of industries, a quick ratio of 1 to 1 is considered satisfactory.

The quick ratios for Astor Company, which are computed below, are slightly lower than those of typical firms in its industry:

19X5: \$120,000 ÷ \$149,000 = .8 times, or .8 to 1
19X4: \$103,000 ÷ \$136,000 = .8 times, or .8 to 1

If carried two or more decimal places, the ratios would indicate that Astor has slightly improved the relationship between its quick assets and its current liabilities. Short-term creditors, as might be expected, generally prefer a higher quick ratio. However, because investments in cash, marketable securities, and receivables sometimes earn small returns compared with those expected to be earned from investments in long-term assets, management must minimize the proportion of capital invested in near-cash assets if it is to earn an adequate return for its owners.

**ACCOUNTS RECEIVABLE TURNOVER** The ability of a company to collect its accounts receivable affects its liquidity. The *accounts receivable turnover ratio* shows the number of times the average net accounts receivable balance was converted into cash during the year. The ratio also provides a measure of how efficient the company's credit-granting and collection activity have been. The higher the accounts receivable turnover, the most efficient the company has been in those areas. The accounts receivable turnover is computed by dividing net sales by the average net accounts receivable balance:

***2b,2c. Accounts Receivable turnover = net sales ÷ average net accounts receivable balance***

$$\text{Accounts Receivable Turnover} = \frac{\text{Net Sales}}{\text{Average Net Accounts Receivable Balance}}$$

The amounts used to compute the average net accounts receivable balance are the beginning and ending accounts receivable balances for the year. For Astor Company, the accounts receivable turnover ratios for 19X5 and 19X4 are

19X5: \$760,000 ÷ [(\$82,000 + \$75,000) ÷ 2] = 9.7 times
19X4: \$700,000 ÷ [(\$75,000 + \$73,000) ÷ 2] = 9.5 times

The higher the turnover ratio, the shorter the period of time between the sale and the cash collection. The slight increase in Astor's turnover ratio indicates that the company is converting its accounts receivable into cash at a slightly faster pace in 19X5 than it did in 19X4.

Ideally, only net credit sales should be included in the numerator. Cash sales should be excluded because they do not involve an account receivable. However, information pertaining only to credit sales may not be available, and therefore the net sales figure is necessarily used as a substitute.

For a more reliable result, the amount of the denominator should be determined by averaging the accounts receivable balances at the end of every month (or even shorter periods), rather than by averaging the end-of-the-year balances. In practice, however, we might find that the only information available on accounts receivable is the year-end balances listed in published annual reports. To determine the denominator in our 19X4 calculation, we needed Astor's net accounts receivable at the end of 19X3, which we assumed was $73,000.

*2b,2c. Receivable turnover may be converted to reflect the average number of days needed to collect receivables*

The accounts receivable turnover ratio is often more informative when converted to a statistic that reflects the average number of days it takes to collect receivables. This statistic is determined by dividing the number of days in a year by the accounts receivable turnover figure:

$$\text{Average Number of Days Needed to Collect} = \frac{\text{365 Days}}{\text{Accounts Receivable Turnover}}$$

The equation shows that 365 days, the number of days in a year, was used. Some analysts would prefer to use 360 days or calculate the actual number of business days excluding Saturdays, Sundays, and holidays if appropriate. The important thing is to be consistent in the choice so that the results over time or across an industry are comparable.

Using the equation, we find that in 19X5, Astor took an average of 37.6 days to collect its receivables, which is some improvement over its 19X4 average collection period of 38.4 days. These calculations are as follows:

19X5: 365 days ÷ 9.7 = 37.6 days
19X4: 365 days ÷ 9.5 = 38.4 days

Assuming that Astor normally allows customers 30 days to pay for items that they purchased on credit, the average days of uncollected accounts receivable (37.6 days and 38.4 days) may seem a bit high. On the other hand, if customers were given 60 days to pay, the same average days to collect would be considered favorable by most analysts. In other words, if the company's collection procedures are effective, the average days needed to collect the receivables should be approximately equal to the time allowed by the terms of the credit sales.

Creditors view receivable turnovers and average days to collect as indicators of how successful a company is in converting its receivables into cash needed for operations and debt payment. Others use the data to assess management's efficiency in credit-granting and collection policies.

**INVENTORY TURNOVER** Inventory turnover measures liquidity by determining how many times the average number of dollars invested in inventory is recovered (turned over) through sales during a period. It is considered good management to hold as little inventory as possible without losing sales and to turn that inventory over as rapidly as possible. The *inventory turnover ratio* can be used to indicate the adequacy of inventory and how efficiently it is being managed. It is computed by dividing the cost of goods sold by the average inventory balance:

*2b,2c. Inventory turnover = cost of goods sold ÷ average inventory balance*

$$\text{Inventory Turnover} = \frac{\text{Cost of Goods Sold}}{\text{Average Inventory Balance}}$$

The amounts used to compute the average inventory balance are the beginning and ending inventory account balances for the year. The inventory turnover ratios for Astor Company are

$$19X5: \$390,000 \div [(\$127,000 + \$102,000) \div 2] = 3.4 \text{ times}$$
$$19X4: \$340,000 \div [(\$102,000 + \$108,000) \div 2] = 3.2 \text{ times}$$

For purposes of calculating the 19X4 denominator, we assumed that Astor's inventory at the end of 19X3 was $108,000. Once again we would have achieved a more reliable result if end-of-the-month rather than end-of-the-year inventory balances were averaged, but this information might not be available. The 19X5 inventory turnover ratio indicates that Astor's average inventory was sold 3.4 times during the year, a turnover slightly higher than the 3.2 turns experienced in 19X4. The increased turnover is generally looked upon favorably because inventory is sold at a profit, and the more times it can be sold during a period, the more profit can be realized. On the other hand, a very high inventory turnover may indicate that the company is not maintaining a sufficient amount of goods on hand and may therefore be losing sales because the item requested is not in stock.

When assessing the inventory turnover ratio, we must keep in mind the industry that the company operates in, the company's turnover ratios in the past, and any unique aspect of its operations during the year under review. Nevertheless, a low inventory turnover ratio provides evidence that the company is keeping too much inventory on hand, which may lead to an involuntary buildup of obsolete inventory items. In inventory management careful consideration must be given to the costs (for storage space and insurance) and risks (damaged and obsolete goods) that are incurred while goods are being held against the amount of sales that may be lost if a sufficient amount of goods is not held.

***2b,2c. Inventory turnover may be converted to reflect the average number of days till inventory is sold***

Inventory turnover is often more informative when dollar amounts are converted to a time basis to show the average number of days it takes before the inventory is sold. The computation is as follows:

$$\text{Average Number of Days Needed to Sell} = \frac{\text{365 Days}}{\text{Inventory Turnover}}$$

Using the equation, we find that in terms of days Astor held its inventory about 107 days in 19X5 before it was sold and about 114 days in 19X4 before it was sold:

$$19X5: 365 \text{ days} \div 3.4 = 107.4 \text{ days}$$
$$19X4: 365 \text{ days} \div 3.2 = 114.1 \text{ days}$$

In deciding whether the result is good or bad, Astor's turnover ratio and number of days needed to dispose of its inventory should be compared with figures developed from companies in its industry or some other "norm." For a company in the jewelry business, the 107-to-114-days figure may be acceptable or may even be considered good. However, for a company in the grocery business, taking approximately 107 to 114 days to turn over an inventory would probably be considered poor and perhaps even intolerable.

## Ratios to Evaluate Profitability

*Profitability* ratios measure a company's ability to generate earnings. Companies that are well known for their financial strength have a record of sustained profitability. Ratios used to evaluate the adequacy of a company's past earnings receive considerable attention because they reveal trends and provide the basis for predicting the company's potential to generate future earnings.

Continuing profitability is of vital concern to all groups who have a financial interest in the company. Investors, for example, pay attention to current earnings and the potential for future earnings because of their interest in the market price of their investments and in the prospects for future dividend distributions. Earnings and potential earnings are also important to creditors because earnings generate cash and working capital, which ultimately affects liquidity and solvency. Management is interested in earnings because it is often used as a measurement of their performance. Furthermore, and perhaps most important, a company's long-run survival depends on its ability to generate adequate earnings.

No absolute number or single analytical test provides sufficient information to evaluate a company's earnings performance. Information needed for the evaluation can be obtained by computing several ratios known collectively as profitability ratios. These ratios, which are discussed below, consist of (1) return on sales, (2) return on total assets, (3) asset turnover, (4) return on common stockholders' equity, and (5) earnings per common share.

***2b,2c. Return on sales = net income ÷ net sales***

**RETURN ON SALES** *Return on sales,* also called *profit margin,* shows the amount of net income earned on an average dollar of sales revenue. The ratio calculated as a percentage is determined by dividing net income by net sales:

$$\text{Return on Sales} = \frac{\text{Net Income}}{\text{Net Sales}}$$

Astor Company's rates of return on sales for 19X5 and 19X4, respectively, are

19X5: $52,000 ÷ $760,000 = 6.8%
19X4: $48,000 ÷ $700,000 = 6.9%

Recall that the same calculation is made in preparing the common-size income statement shown in Exhibit 19–4.

The ratios show that in 19X5, each dollar of sales generated 6.8 cents in net income and that there has been a slight decline in the company's profitability when compared with 19X4. In other words, for every dollar in sales, the company made 6.8 cents and 6.9 cents in profit during the years 19X5 and 19X4, respectively.

In considering whether the company's rate of return on sales is satisfactory, it should be compared with other standards. For example, if the prevailing rate of return on sales for the industry in which Astor's operates is 5%, Astor's rate compares favorably. However, even when its rate compared with industry standards is high, if the company has been experiencing a declining trend in its rate over the past few years, the cause for the decline needs to be investigated.

**RETURN ON TOTAL ASSETS** *Return on total assets* measures how productively a company used all of its assets, both those provided by owners and those provided by creditors, to generate earnings. Many analysts view this ratio, sometimes called return on investment or simply ROI, as one of the more relevant tests of profitability, since it measures management's earnings performance in using all the resources available to the company.

***2b,2c. Return on total assets = net income ÷ average total assets***

Return on total assets is generally calculated by dividing net income by the average total assets employed throughout the year. Thus the formula for computing the ratio is:

$$\text{Return on Total Assets} = \frac{\text{Net Income}}{\text{Average Total Assets}}$$

Average total assets is used in the denominator to reflect the resources employed throughout the period, not those that were on hand at the beginning or at the end of the period. This figure is appropriate because the income for the period was generated by using the resources that were available throughout the period.

Astor Company's return on total assets for 19X5 and 19X4 was 7.4% and 7.7%, respectively, computed as follows:

19X5: \$52,000 ÷ [(\$760,100 + \$644,900) ÷ 2] = 7.4%
19X4: \$48,000 ÷ [(\$644,900 + \$602,500) ÷ 2] = 7.7%

The ratio shows that Astor's management earned an average of 7.4 cents on each dollar invested in the company during 19X5. The significance of this result could be better evaluated if it could be compared over a longer period of time (trend analysis) and if the same ratios for other similar companies (industry comparisons) were available. The amount of Astor's total assets at the end of 19X3 we assumed to be \$602,500.

When computing this ratio, some analysts would prefer to use income before deducting interest expense for the numerator. They would argue that the income generated by the assets should not be affected by the method used in financing the acquisition of those assets. That is without regard to whether the assets used in the business were obtained from borrowed money or from money invested by owners.

*2b,2c. Asset turnover = net sales ÷ average total assets*

ASSET TURNOVER The *asset turnover ratio* is a measure of how efficiently assets are used to generate sales revenue. It relates net sales to average total assets to show how many times in a period the assets were turned over in generating sales. The formula for the asset turnover ratio is:

$$\text{Asset Turnover} = \frac{\text{Net Sales}}{\text{Average Total Assets}}$$

Since the net sales were generated over a period of time, the average total assets employed during that same period is once again used as the denominator in order to make the relationship valid. The higher the asset turnover, the more efficiently the assets were utilized. The result is a more profitable firm, and one that is more capable of paying its obligations as they come due. The asset turnover ratios for Astor Company are computed as follows:

19X5: \$760,000 ÷ [(\$760,100 + \$644,900) ÷ 2] = 1.08 times
19X4: \$700,000 ÷ [(\$644,900 + \$602,500) ÷ 2] = 1.12 times

*2b,2c. Return on sales × asset turnover = return on total assets*

Analysts often combine the asset turnover ratio with the return on sales ratio to determine a more precise return on total assets ratio. This calculation is shown below using Astor Company's previously determined asset turnover and return and sales ratios:

Return on Sales × Asset Turnover = Return on Total Assets

19X5: 6.8% × 1.08 times = 7.34%
19X4: 6.9% × 1.12 times = 7.73%

From this analysis it becomes evident that if a company can increase its return on sales or its asset turnovers, or both, it will increase its return on total assets. In contrast, Astor's decrease in its return on total assets is attributable to both its declining return on sales and its declining asset turnover.

*2b,2c. Return on common stockholders' equity = (net income − preferred dividends) ÷ average common stockholders' equity*

**RETURN ON COMMON STOCKHOLDERS' EQUITY** This ratio is a measure of how effective a corporation has been in earning income for its owners. The ratio will show how much the company earned for each dollar invested by common shareholders. The rate of return on common stockholders' equity may be higher or lower than the rate of return achieved on total assets. The difference is caused by the company's use of leverage (trading on equity). When a company is able to earn more on borrowed funds than the cost of those funds, the return on common stockholders' equity will be higher than the return on total assets. Conversely, when the cost of borrowed funds exceeds the amount earned on those funds, the return on common stockholders' equity will be lower than the return on total assets.

The formula for computing return on common stockholders' equity is:

$$\text{Return on Common Stockholders' Equity} = \frac{\text{Net Income} - \text{Preferred Dividends}}{\text{Average Common Stockholders' Equity}}$$

Preferred dividends are subtracted from net income in the numerator to arrive at the portion of net income belonging to the common stockholders. Average common stockholders' equity is used in the denominator because it represents an approximation of the amount that common shareholders have had invested throughout the year.

Astor's rates of return on common stockholders' equity for the years 19X5 and 19X4 are computed below (with $320,700 given as the amount for Astor's common stockholders' equity for 19X3):

19X5: $52,000 ÷ [($411,100 + $358,900) ÷ 2] = 13.5%
19X4: $48,000 ÷ [($358,900 + $320,700) ÷ 2] = 14.1%

The 19X5 ratio shows that Astor has earned 13.5 cents for each dollar invested by common shareholders. Because Astor's rates of return on common stockholders' equity are higher than its rates of return on total assets in both years, we know that the company has made effective use of leverage. The percentage decrease in the company's return on common stockholders' equity (from 14.1% in 19X4 to 13.5% in 19X5) should, however, be noted and its cause investigated.

*2b,2c. Earnings per common share = (net income − preferred dividends) ÷ weighted average number of common shares outstanding*

**EARNINGS PER COMMON SHARE** This ratio is one of the most widely publicized measures of profitability. You have already studied earnings per common share in Chapter 15, where its calculation was illustrated. The basic formula is repeated here:

$$\text{Earnings per Common Share} = \frac{\text{Net Income} - \text{Preferred Dividends}}{\text{Weighted Average Number of Common Shares Outstanding}}$$

The calculation of Astor Company's earnings per share is shown below:

19X5: $52,000 ÷ 20,000 shares = $2.60
19X4: $48,000 ÷ 18,000 shares = $2.67

The number of shares outstanding was determined by dividing the amount shown for common stock in the 19X5 and 19X4 balance sheet (Exhibit 19–1) by the par value of the shares as follows:

19X5: $200,000 ÷ $10 par value = 20,000 shares
19X4: $180,000 ÷ $10 par value = 18,000 shares

Furthermore, it was assumed that the additional 2,000 shares were issued at the beginning of 19X5. You will recall that earnings per common share figures must be reported on the face of the income statement.

## Ratios to Evaluate Solvency

**Solvency** refers to the ability of a company to meet all of its financial obligations as they come due. Perhaps the best indicator for predicting whether a company can do this on a continuing basis is its profitability record over a period of recent years. Profitable companies are usually able to generate sufficient cash from operations to meet obligations as they come due. Nevertheless, three widely used ratios to test solvency focus on the company's ability to satisfy its long-term creditors. In their evaluation of a company, long-term creditors are interested in its ability to make timely interest payments on its debt and principal payments when the debt is due. Ratios to test solvency include (1) debt to equity, (2) debt to total assets, and (3) times interest earned.

***2b,2c. Ratios used to evaluate solvency include debt to equity, debt to total assets, and times interest earned***

DEBT TO EQUITY The *debt to equity ratio* measures the relationship of the company's assets provided by its creditors to the amount provided by its stockholders (through investment and retained earnings). The ratio is computed by dividing total liabilities by total stockholders' equity:

***2b,2c. Debt to equity ratio = total liabilities ÷ total stockholders' equity***

$$\text{Debt to Equity Ratio} = \frac{\text{Total Liabilities}}{\text{Total Stockholders' Equity}}$$

The calculation of Astor Company's debt to equity ratios for the years 19X5 and 19X4 follows:

19X5: $349,000 ÷ $411,100 = 84.9%
19X4: $286,000 ÷ $358,900 = 79.7%

The 19X5 ratio can be interpreted as follows: For each dollar of stockholders' equity, Astor has almost 85 cents of liabilities. Clearly, the lower the debt to equity ratio, the smaller the company's debt. This generally means that less risk is assumed by the company's creditors. A debt to equity ratio of one, or 100%, indicates that the company's owners and its creditors provided an equal amount of the company's resources. A debt to equity ratio of less than one, or 100%, like Astor's, indicates that the company's owners provided more of the company's resources than did its creditors. There is no bench mark to establish what a company's debt to equity ratio should be. In some industries, companies typically have debt to equity ratios that exceed 100%. Of course, as the ratio increases, the risk assumed by creditors increases. This is so because the creditors' margin of protection decreases as the company's total debt increases.

DEBT TO TOTAL ASSETS The *debt to total assets ratio* shows the percentage of the company's total assets that have been financed by debt. It measures the margin of safety that creditors have in case the company is liquidated. The lower the ratio, the greater the asset protection for creditors. The higher the ratio, the greater the risk concerning the company's ability to meet its obligations as they

*2b,2c. Debt to total assets ratio = total liabilities ÷ total assets*

come due. The debt to total assets ratio formula and the calculations of Astor's ratios follow:

$$\text{Debt to Total Assets Ratio} = \frac{\text{Total Liabilities}}{\text{Total Assets}}$$

19X5: $349,000 ÷ $760,100 = 45.9%
19X4: $286,000 ÷ $644,900 = 44.3%

Approximately 45% of Astor's total assets were financed by debt in each of the years 19X5 and 19X4. Conversely, approximately 55% of its assets were financed by owners during those years.

**TIMES INTEREST EARNED** Creditors, and perhaps others, want to know whether a company is currently generating earnings large enough to meet its required interest payments. Some companies have earnings that are several times larger than their interest payments. Others do not earn enough to cover their interest payments, or their coverage is marginal. To determine how many times a company could pay its interest expense from current earnings, a ratio called times interest earned is calculated. This is done by dividing income before interest and taxes by the interest expense itself.

*2b,2c. Times interest earned ratio = (net income + interest expense + income tax expense) ÷ interest expense*

The formula for the times interest earned ratio can therefore be presented as follows:

$$\text{Times Interest Earned Ratio} = \frac{\text{Net Income} + \text{Interest Expense} + \text{Income Tax Expense}}{\text{Interest Expense}}$$

Interest expense is added to net income in the numerator to show the amount of income available to pay the interest. Income tax expense is added because interest is deductible in determining income tax. The calculations of Astor Company's times interest earned ratio are as follows:

19X5 – ($52,000 + $29,000 + $34,500) ÷ $29,000 = 4.0 times
19X4 – ($48,000 + $22,000 + $33,200) ÷ $22,000 = 4.7 times

Astor's income available to meet its fixed interest obligations was approximately 4.0 times the amount of its interest expense in 19X5 and 4.7 times the amount in 19X4.

Each creditor or other user might have a different standard for judging how many times interest should be earned to provide a satisfactory margin of safety. Astor Company's figures, although not particularly high, seem to provide reasonable coverage in this area. If in the future either long-term debt is decreased or net income is increased, or both, the ratio for times interest earned will increase.

The times interest earned ratio may be criticized as a measure for assessing solvency because it uses income rather than cash flows in the numerator. As you know, income from operations is not totally equal to cash flow from operations. For this reason, cash flow information, if available, may be used in testing this aspect of a company's solvency.

### Market Test Ratios

Ratios that measure a company's performance and indicate the return earned by those who own the company's stock provide useful data for decisions. This applies especially to the decisions made by investors and by those who act as advisers to investors. As mentioned earlier, corporate investors (shareholders) earn returns on their investment from increases in the market price of their shares and from dividends. As a result, most market test ratios are based on a company's earnings, the current market price of its stock, and/or its dividend distributions. Each ratio establishes a relevant relationship between two or more of those figures. Three market test ratios widely used by investors, advisers to investors (security analysts), and others are the (1) price-earnings ratio, (2) dividend yield ratio, and (3) dividend payout ratio.

*2b,2c. Three widely used market test ratios are price-earnings, dividend yield, and dividend payout*

**PRICE-EARNINGS RATIO** The *price-earnings ratio* measures the relationship between the market price of a share of common stock and its earnings per share. The ratio is computed by dividing the market price of a share of common stock by the earnings per common share. For example, a stock selling for \$30 per share and earning \$3 per share would have a price-earnings ratio of 10 (\$30 ÷ \$3). This simply means that the company's stock is currently selling for ten times its earnings. Or put another way, it means that to buy a dollar of the company's annual earnings, an investor must pay ten times that amount.

*2b,2c. Price-earnings ratio = market price per share of common stock ÷ earnings per share of common stock*

The formula for calculating the price-earnings ratio is

$$\text{Price-Earnings Ratio} = \frac{\text{Market Price per Share of Common Stock}}{\text{Earnings per Share of Common Stock}}$$

Using Astor Company's market prices of \$15.00 and \$14.50 per share in 19X5 and 19X4, respectively, we can compute its price-earnings ratio for each of these two years:

19X5: \$15.00 ÷ \$2.60 = 5.8 times
19X4: \$14.50 ÷ \$2.67 = 5.4 times

The price-earnings ratio indicates investors' expectations regarding the future performance of the company. A company with a high price-earnings ratio shows that investors have been willing to pay several times its current earnings per share to purchase the stock. They believe the company's future performance will be good and will thereby give them a more than adequate return on their investment.

**DIVIDEND YIELD RATIO** Some investors buy common stock to receive a steady flow of cash in the form of dividends. Many of them are more interested in dividends as their form of return on investment than they are in the potential for appreciation in the market price of their shares. To these individuals the dividend yield ratio, which measures the rate of return on their stock investment, is important.

The dividend yield ratio is determined by the following formula:

*2b,2c. Dividend yield ratio = dividend per share of common stock ÷ market price per share of common stock*

$$\text{Dividend Yield Ratio} = \frac{\text{Dividend per Share of Common Stock}}{\text{Market price per Share of Common Stock}}$$

As the formula indicates, the ratio is affected by two factors: the company's dividend policy and the market price of its shares. Because the market price of a company's stock changes frequently, the dividend yield ratio, like the price-earnings ratio, is a volatile market test measurement. Astor Company's dividend yield ratios follow:

19X5: \$1.10 ÷ \$15.00 = 7.3%
19X4: \$1.11 ÷ \$14.50 = 7.7%

The dividends per share were determined by dividing the annual dividends as shown in the comparative statement of retained earnings (Exhibit 19–2) by the number of shares outstanding:

19X5 dividends of \$22,000 ÷ 20,000 shares outstanding = \$1.10 per share
19X4 dividends of \$20,000 ÷ 18,000 shares outstanding = \$1.11 per share

As already mentioned, the dividend yield ratio is more important to investors who buy shares seeking a return in the form of dividends rather than in the increasing market value of their shares. Many investors feel that if earnings are reinvested, they are better served because the company should be able to increase its profitability, which tends to increase the market value of its shares. Nevertheless, dividends do represent one form of return on investment. Thus the dividend payout ratio, which indicates the rate of return earned on the dollars invested, is useful to investors and potential investors when making comparisons with rates of return on alternative investment opportunities having similar or different risks. Furthermore, although equal and continuous dividends are not guaranteed, they are usually more certain than market value gains, making the dividend yield ratio a useful analytical technique.

*2b,2c. Dividend payout ratio = dividends to common stockholders ÷ net income available to common stockholders*

**DIVIDEND PAYOUT RATIO** This ratio shows the percentage of net income distributed by the company to its shareholders. It can be used to indicate what portion of a company's net income is distributed to its common shareholders and what portion is retained in the business. Like other ratios, it is determined only for common shareholders and is computed by dividing dividends paid to common stockholders by the net income available to common stockholders:

$$\text{Dividend Payout Ratio} = \frac{\text{Dividends to Common Stockholders}}{\text{Net Income Available to Common Stockholders}}$$

Astor Company's dividend payout ratios are as follows:

19X5: \$22,000 ÷ \$52,000 = 42.3%
19X4: \$20,000 ÷ \$48,000 = 41.7%

Note that the ratio's reciprocal will show the percentage of net income retained by the company for reinvestment. Thus in 19X5 the company returned 42.3% of its net income to its shareholders as dividends and reinvested the remaining 57.7%.

There is no rule of thumb to determine an appropriate payout ratio. The ratio varies from company to company even within a given industry. The adequacy of the dividend payout depends on the investors' objectives. As mentioned earlier, some investors prefer high dividends while others prefer to have the company reinvest its earnings in anticipation that they will benefit from the company's growth by an increase in the market price of the shares.

The purpose of all market test ratios is to provide information that will be useful to investors when selecting between alternative common stock ownership opportunities.

*2b,2c. The ratios are summarized in Exhibit 19–5*

The ratios discussed in this chapter are summarized in Exhibit 19–5.

## Interpretation of Ratios

No one ratio or group of ratios is best for assessing a company's performance or for predicting its future profitability and growth. Ratios are useful in analyzing financial statements because they conveniently summarize a mass of data in a

EXHIBIT 19–5

## Summary of Widely Used Financial Ratios

| RATIO | METHOD OF COMPUTATION | SIGNIFICANCE |
|---|---|---|
| | **Liquidity Ratios** | |
| 1. Current Ratio | $\frac{\text{Current Assets}}{\text{Current Liabilities}}$ | Measures ability to pay current debts from current assets. |
| 2. Quick Ratio | $\frac{\text{Cash + Marketable Securities + Net Receivables}}{\text{Current Liabilities}}$ | A more-stringent test of short-term liquidity. Measures ability to pay current debts from highly liquid current assets. |
| 3. Accounts Receivable Turnover | $\frac{\text{Net Sales}}{\text{Average Net Accounts Receivable Balance}}$ | Measures ability to convert receivables into cash by computing the number of collection cycles needed. |
| 4. Average Number of Days Needed to Collect | $\frac{\text{365 Days}}{\text{Accounts Receivable Turnover}}$ | Measures the effectiveness of credit-granting and collection activity by computing the average collection period in number of days. |
| 5. Inventory Turnover | $\frac{\text{Cost of Goods Sold}}{\text{Average Inventory Balance}}$ | Measures ability to sell inventory by computing the number of sales cycles needed. |
| 6. Average Number of Days Needed to Sell | $\frac{\text{365 Days}}{\text{Inventory Turnover}}$ | Measures the effectiveness of inventory management by computing the time required to sell average inventory in number of days. |
| | **Profitability Ratios** | |
| 7. Return on Sales | $\frac{\text{Net Income}}{\text{Net Sales}}$ | Measures in percentage the amount of net income earned on an average dollar of sales revenue. |
| 8. Return on Total Assets | $\frac{\text{Net Income}}{\text{Average Total Assets}}$ | Measures the rate of return earned on total assets used in operating the business. |
| 9. Asset Turnover | $\frac{\text{Net Sales}}{\text{Average Total Assets}}$ | Measures how efficiently assets are being used to generate sales revenue. |
| 10. Return on Common Stockholders' Equity | $\frac{\text{Net Income − Preferred Dividends}}{\text{Average Common Stockholders' Equity}}$ | Measures the rate of return earned by common stockholders on their investment. |
| 11. Earnings per Common Share | $\frac{\text{Net Income − Preferred Dividends}}{\text{Weighted Average Number of Common Shares Outstanding}}$ | Measures the amount of net income applicable to each share of common stock. |
| | **Solvency Ratios** | |
| 12. Debt to Equity Ratio | $\frac{\text{Total Liabilities}}{\text{Total Stockholders' Equity}}$ | Measures the relationship of assets provided by creditors to the amount provided by stockholders. |
| 13. Debt to Total Assets Ratio | $\frac{\text{Total Liabilities}}{\text{Total Assets}}$ | Measures the percentage of total assets provided by creditors. |
| 14. Times Interest Earned Ratio | $\frac{\text{Net Income + Interest Expense + Income Tax Expense}}{\text{Interest Expense}}$ | Measures ability to meet periodic interest payments from current earnings. |
| | **Market Test Ratios** | |
| 15. Price-Earnings Ratio | $\frac{\text{Market Price per Share of Common Stock}}{\text{Earnings per Share of Common Stock}}$ | Measures the amount investors are willing to pay for each dollar of corporate earnings. |
| 16. Dividend Yield Ratio | $\frac{\text{Dividends per Share of Common Stock}}{\text{Market Price per Share of Common Stock}}$ | Measures the rate of return from dividends that a shareholder is earning based on the current market price of a share of stock. |
| 17. Dividend Payout Ratio | $\frac{\text{Dividends to Common Shareholders}}{\text{Net Income Available to Common Stockholders}}$ | Measures the percentage of net income distributed to common stockholders as dividends. |

form that is more easily understood, interpreted, and compared. Their usefulness is further enhanced when they are compared with some standard. For example, a return on total assets of 8.5% is not very informative when taken by itself, but it could be judged as outstanding when compared with a standard showing an expected return of 7.0%. Some standards that might be used as a basis for comparison are

*1b. Some standards that serve as a basis for comparison of ratios are goals, historical data, and industry standards*

1. The planned outcome for the period, referred to here as goals
2. The outcome of a preceding period for the same company, referred to here as historical data
3. The outcome of a similar company or group of companies in the same industry, referred to here as industry standards

**GOALS** Many companies prepare forecasts and budgets designed to show what result is expected under prevailing conditions. If the forecasts and budgets are carefully prepared and if the company's operating environment remains relatively unchanged, it may be possible to evaluate expected future performance. Of course, prevailing or anticipated economic conditions must also be recognized.

**HISTORICAL DATA** Comparing a company's current financial data with those of a past period or number of past periods provides a basis for judging whether current performance is improving or deteriorating. It is assumed that the prior period's data represent data accumulated under similar conditions or the comparative result will not be valid.

**INDUSTRY STANDARDS** Measuring the performance of a particular company by comparing it with that of a similar company or group of companies provides an external standard for judging its performance. For the comparison to be valid, the accounting practices of the company or companies being compared must be the same, or the differences must be compensated for by the analyst.

## LONG-TERM FINANCIAL SUMMARIES

*1c. Long-term financial summaries are especially useful for detecting changes in key items*

Financial analysts, although mainly concerned with a company's current financial information, may find that their analysis can be advantageously supplemented by the use of **long-term financial summaries.** These summaries, included in annual reports, typically cover five- or ten-year periods and are especially useful for detecting changes in key items. Items of particular concern on the income statements include sales revenue, gross profit on sales, income from operations, net income, and earnings per share. On the balance sheet, interest would focus on total assets, long-term and total liabilities, and total stockholders' equity. Many summaries include other important items such as working capital, dividends per share, and selected ratios. Changes occurring in any of these items, either upward or downward, may be interpreted as signals of future trends. Of course, the critical thing is not merely being able to detect change but being able to determine the cause of the change or changes.

### Graphic Presentations

*1c. Graphic presentation is probably the best visual method for depicting trends and relationships*

The use of graphic presentations in annual reports has become quite widespread. This is probably because a graphic illustration can often show financial relationships in an eye-catching way. Many users of financial information would agree that graphs provide the best visual method for depicting trends and relationships.

An example of graphic presentations taken from an annual report of Pepsico, Inc., is shown in Exhibit 19–6.

*EXHIBIT 19–6*

Graphic Presentations

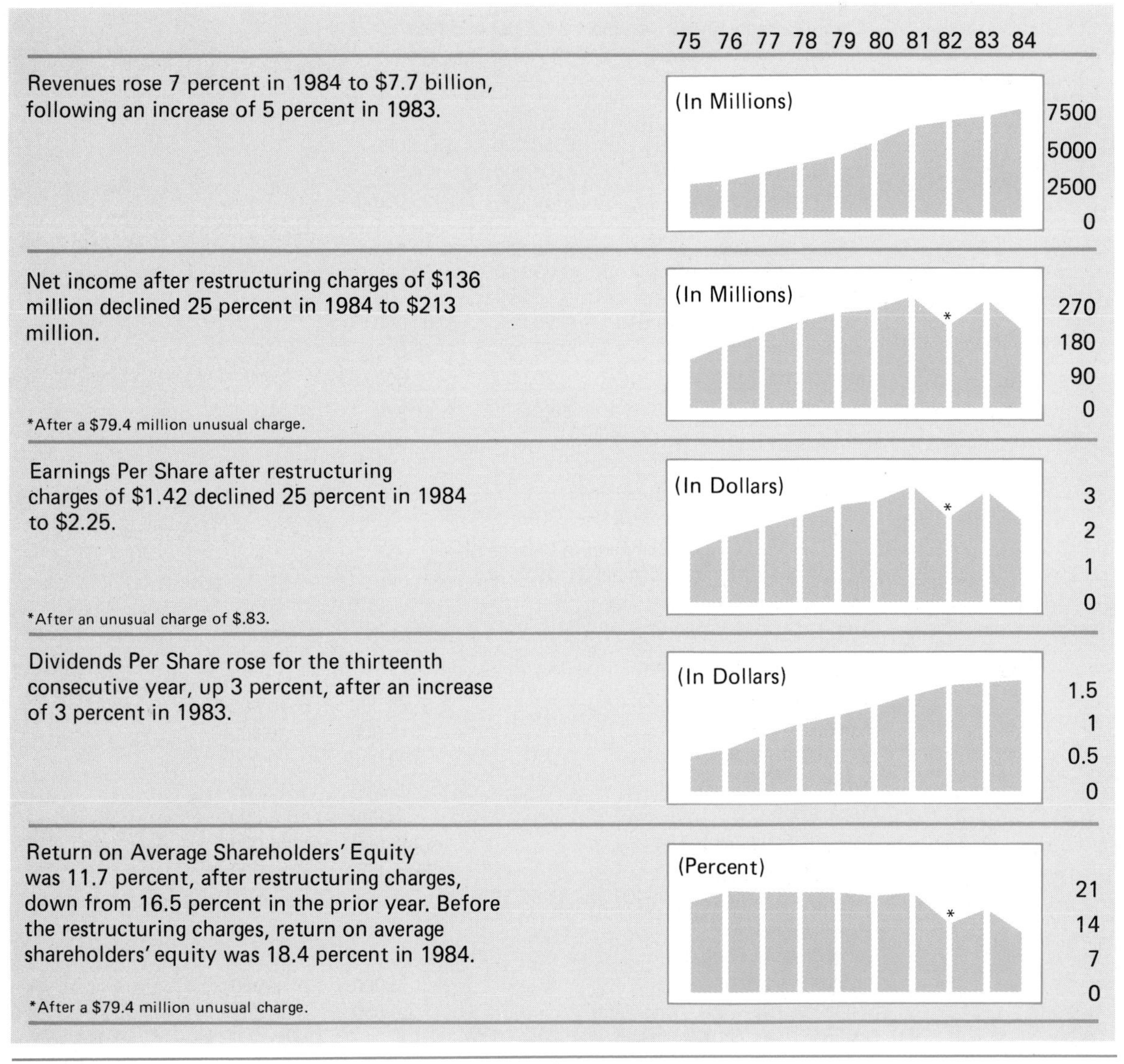

75 76 77 78 79 80 81 82 83 84
Revenues rose 7 percent in 1984 to $7.7 billion, following an increase of 5 percent in 1983.
(In Millions)
7500
5000
2500
0
Net income after restructuring charges of $136 million declined 25 percent in 1984 to $213 million.
*After a $79.4 million unusual charge.
(In Millions)
270
180
90
0
Earnings Per Share after restructuring charges of $1.42 declined 25 percent in 1984 to $2.25.
*After an unusual charge of $.83.
(In Dollars)
3
2
1
0
Dividends Per Share rose for the thirteenth consecutive year, up 3 percent, after an increase of 3 percent in 1983.
(In Dollars)
1.5
1
0.5
0
Return on Average Shareholders' Equity was 11.7 percent, after restructuring charges, down from 16.5 percent in the prior year. Before the restructuring charges, return on average shareholders' equity was 18.4 percent in 1984.
*After a $79.4 million unusual charge.
(Percent)
21
14
7
0

## HIGHLIGHT PROBLEM

The comparative income statement and balance sheet of Clark Company are shown below.

CLARK COMPANY

Comparative Income Statement
For the Years Ended December 31, 19X5 and 19X4

| | YEAR ENDED DECEMBER 31 | |
|---|---|---|
| | 19X5 | 19X4 |
| Net Sales | $350,000 | $310,000 |
| Less: Cost of Goods Sold | 200,000 | 175,000 |
| Gross Profit on Sales | $150,000 | $135,000 |
| Operating Expenses: | | |
| Selling Expenses | $ 60,000 | $ 54,000 |
| Administrative Expenses | 33,000 | 32,000 |
| Interest Expense | 5,000 | 4,000 |
| Total Operating Expenses | $ 98,000 | $ 90,000 |
| Income before Taxes | $ 52,000 | $ 45,000 |
| Less: Income Taxes | 20,000 | 18,000 |
| Net Income | $ 32,000 | $ 27,000 |

CLARK COMPANY

Comparative Balance Sheet
December 31, 19X5 and 19X4

| | DECEMBER 31 | |
|---|---|---|
| | 19X5 | 19X4 |
| ASSETS | | |
| Cash | $ 25,000 | $ 10,000 |
| Marketable Securities | 10,000 | 20,000 |
| Accounts Receivable—Net | 30,000 | 20,000 |
| Inventory | 35,000 | 40,000 |
| Prepayments | 5,000 | 2,000 |
| Plant and Equipment—Net | 145,000 | 123,000 |
| Total Assets | $250,000 | $215,000 |
| LIABILITIES AND STOCKHOLDERS' EQUITY | | |
| Accounts Payable | $ 32,000 | $ 26,000 |
| Notes Payable, Short-Term | 20,000 | 15,000 |
| Salaries Payable | 3,000 | 5,000 |
| Bonds Payable—6%, Long-Term | 60,000 | 50,000 |
| Common Stock ($10 par value) | 100,000 | 100,000 |
| Retained Earnings | 35,000 | 19,000 |
| Total Liabilities and Stockholders' Equity | $250,000 | $215,000 |

Additional Information:

| | 19X5 | 19X4 |
|---|---|---|
| Cash dividends declared and paid | $16,000 | $12,000 |
| Market price per share of common stock on December 31 | $18.00 | $14.50 |

Figures for selected items as of December 31, 19X3, were as follows:

| | |
|---|---|
| Accounts Receivable—Net | $ 16,000 |
| Inventory | 40,000 |
| Total Assets | 207,000 |
| Common Stockholders' Equity | 105,000 |

Required:

Compute the following ratios for 19X5 and 19X4 (rounded to one decimal point):

a. Current ratio
b. Quick ratio
c. Accounts receivable turnover
d. Inventory turnover
e. Return on sales
f. Return on total assets
g. Asset turnover
h. Return on common stockholders' equity
i. Earnings per share
j. Debt to equity ratio
k. Debt to total assets ratio
l. Times interest earned ratio
m. Price-earnings ratio
n. Dividend yield ratio
o. Dividend payout ratio

## GLOSSARY OF KEY TERMS

**Common-size financial statement.** A financial statement in which the amount of each item reported in the statement is expressed as a percentage of an amount of some other item reported in the same statement.

**Comparative financial statements.** Financial statements in which the data for two or more successive years are presented side by side.

**Horizontal analysis.** A technique of analysis in which dollar and percentage changes for corresponding items presented in comparative financial statements are computed.

**Liquidity.** The ability of a company to meet its current obligations as they come due.

**Long-term financial summaries.** Summaries of key financial data, frequently covering a period of five or more years.

**Profitability.** The ability of a company to generate revenues in excess of the costs it incurred to produce those revenues. In short, the ability of a company to earn income.

**Ratio.** A mathematical expression of the relationship of one number to another.

**Ratio analysis.** A technique of analysis in which the dollar amounts of selected items appearing in the financial statements are compared and expressed in a relationship.

**Solvency.** The ability of a company to meet its long-term obligations as they come due.

**Trend analysis.** A technique of analysis in which the change in selected corresponding items or groups of items presented in the financial statements is computed for a number of years, usually three or more.

**Vertical analysis.** A technique of analysis in which the dollar amount of each item presented in a financial statement is related to a relevant total on that statement and expressed as a percentage of that total.

## REVIEW QUESTIONS

1. What is the basic objective of financial statements? [LO1a]
2. From what two sources do investors earn a return on their investments? [LO1a]

3. For what three purposes do decision makers use financial statement analysis in making their investment, credit, or managerial decisions? [LO1a]
4. Describe the four techniques widely used in analyzing financial statements. [LO2a,2b]
5. What use can be made of horizontal analysis of two or more comparative financial statements? [LO2a]
6. Describe the two steps used in making trend analysis. [LO2a]
7. In what way does vertical analysis provide the statement user with number relationships that are not available elsewhere? [LO2a]
8. What four categories of ratios are discussed in this chapter? [LO2b]
9. How are the following ratios that are used to evaluate liquidity computed?
   a. Current ratio
   b. Quick ratio
   c. Receivable turnover
   d. Inventory turnover [LO2b]
10. How are the following ratios that are used to evaluate profitability computed?
    a. Return on sales
    b. Return on total assets
    c. Asset turnover
    d. Return on common stockholders' equity
    e. Earnings per common share [LO2b]
11. How are the following ratios that are used to evaluate solvency computed?
    a. Debt to equity
    b. Debt to total assets
    c. Times interest earned [LO2b]
12. How are the following market test ratios computed?
    a. Price-earnings
    b. Dividend yield
    c. Dividend payout [LO2b]
13. Name three standards that might be used when interpreting financial ratios. [LO1b]

## ANALYTICAL QUESTIONS

14. The management of Company X thought the current ratio was too high. On the other hand, the creditors of that company thought the current ratio was too low. Explain why there may be this difference of opinion. [LO1a,2b]
15. Someone makes the following statement: "The net incomes of Company A and Company B are both a million dollars. Therefore the two companies are equally profitable." Reply to this statement. [LO1a]
16. The accounts receivable turnover ratio for Company X is 5.8, and its credit terms are 30 days. Comment on the company's credit and collection policies. [LO2c]
17. Company Z has a rate of return on common stockholders' equity of 11% and a rate of return on total assets of 13%. Explain why Company Z does or does not have favorable leverage. [LO2c]
18. The company president makes the following statement: "Something is wrong with the calculation that shows an increase in the current ratio and a decrease in the working capital." Explain to the president why this is possible. [LO2b]

## IMPACT ANALYSIS QUESTIONS

*For each error decribed, indicate whether it would overstate [O], understate [U], or not affect [N] the indicated ratios.*

19. A sale of merchandise on account is recorded by debiting cash and crediting sales. [LO2b]

_______ Current Ratio _______ Quick Ratio
_______ Receivable Turnover _______ Return on Sales

20. The entry for building depreciation was omitted. [LO2b]

_______ Current Ratio _______ Quick Ratio
_______ Receivable Turnover _______ Return on Total Assets

21. An entry should have been made debiting Repairs Expense and crediting Accounts Payable. The entry was omitted. [LO2b]

_______ Return on Sales _______ Return on Common Stockholders' Equity
_______ Asset Turnover
_______ Return on Total Assets

## EXERCISES

EXERCISE 19–1 *(Perform Horizontal Analysis)* A condensed comparative balance sheet for Carson Company is shown below.

| | DECEMBER 31 | |
|---|---|---|
| | 19X5 | 19X4 |
| ASSETS | | |
| Current Assets | $ 72,400 | $ 61,800 |
| Long-Term Investments | 40,600 | 57,300 |
| Plant Assets—Net | 137,000 | 118,900 |
| Total Assets | $250,000 | $238,000 |
| LIABILITIES AND STOCKHOLDERS' EQUITY | | |
| Current Liabilities | $ 59,300 | $ 47,200 |
| Long-Term Liabilities | 40,000 | 50,000 |
| Common Stock | 100,000 | 100,000 |
| Retained Earnings | 50,700 | 40,800 |
| Total Liabilities and Stockholders' Equity | $250,000 | $238,000 |

Required:

1. Compute the changes in the balance sheet from 19X4 to 19X5 in both dollar amounts and percentages. Round percentages to one decimal place.
2. Comment on the changes revealed by the analysis. [LO2a]

EXERCISE 19–2 *(Prepare a Trend Analysis)* Selected income statement data reported by Modern Company over the past five years appear below.

| | 19X1 | 19X2 | 19X3 | 19X4 | 19X5 |
|---|---|---|---|---|---|
| Sales | $480,000 | $510,000 | $570,000 | $550,000 | $620,000 |
| Gross Profit on Sales | 250,000 | 262,000 | 287,000 | 276,000 | 320,000 |
| Operating Expenses | 180,000 | 186,000 | 193,000 | 191,200 | 212,000 |
| Net Income | 44,500 | 50,100 | 56,400 | 54,600 | 62,200 |

Required:

1. Prepare a trend analysis of the data using 19X1 as the base year. Round percentages to one decimal place.
2. In your opinion, do the trends indicate a favorable or an unfavorable situation? Explain your answer. [LO2a]

EXERCISE 19–3 *(Perform Vertical Analysis)* A condensed comparative income statement for Queen Company is shown below.

| | YEAR ENDED DECEMBER 31 | |
|---|---|---|
| | 19X5 | 19X4 |
| Sales | $600,000 | $520,000 |
| Less: Cost of Goods Sold | 350,000 | 290,000 |
| Gross Profit on Sales | $250,000 | $230,000 |
| Operating Expenses: | | |
| Selling Expenses | $120,000 | $115,000 |
| General Expenses | 26,000 | 22,000 |
| Total Operating Expenses | $146,000 | $137,000 |
| Income before Taxes | $104,000 | $ 93,000 |
| Income Taxes | 48,000 | 45,000 |
| Net Income | $ 56,000 | $ 48,000 |

Required:

1. Prepare a common-size statement for both years. Round percentages to one decimal place.
2. Comment on the changes revealed by the analysis. [LO2a]

EXERCISE 19–4 *(Perform Liquidity Analysis)* The following data have been taken from the financial statements of Newport Company.

| | 19X5 | 19X4 |
|---|---|---|
| Sales | $320,000 | $280,000 |
| Cost of Goods Sold | 190,000 | 180,000 |
| Cash | 15,000 | 13,000 |
| Marketable Securities | 20,000 | 26,000 |
| Accounts Receivable—Net | 35,000 | 31,000 |
| Inventory | 75,000 | 70,000 |
| Prepaid Expenses | 5,000 | 5,000 |
| Plant Assets—Net | 150,000 | 130,000 |
| Current Liabilities | 60,000 | 70,000 |

Required:

Compute the following ratios for each of the years 19X5 and 19X4. Round calculations to one decimal place.

1. Current ratio.
2. Quick ratio.
3. Accounts receivable turnover ratio. Assume that all sales are on account and that the net accounts receivable balance at the end of 19X3 was $29,000.
4. Average number of days needed to collect the accounts receivable.
5. Inventory turnover ratio. The average inventory balance carried during 19X4 was $72,000.
6. Average number of days for an inventory turnover. [LO2b]

EXERCISE 19–5 *(Perform Profitability Analysis)* The summarized data shown below were taken from the records of Prince Company.

| | 19X5 | 19X4 |
|---|---|---|
| Common Stock | $ 500,000 | $ 500,000 |
| Net Income | 150,000 | 142,000 |
| Net Sales | 1,800,000 | 1,650,000 |
| Preferred Dividends Paid | 8,000 | 8,000 |
| Preferred Stock | 100,000 | 100,000 |
| Retained Earnings | 355,000 | 285,000 |
| Total Assets | 1,600,000 | 1,480,000 |

Additional Information:

a. The company issued 50,000 shares of common stock when it was organized several years ago, and the shares have remained outstanding through December 31, 19X5.

b. The company's total assets at the end of 19X3 were $1,320,000.

c. The company's total common stockholders' equity at the end of 19X3 was $735,000.

Required:

Compute the following ratios for each of the years 19X5 and 19X4. Round calculations to one decimal place.

1. Return on sales
2. Return on total assets
3. Asset turnover
4. Return on common stockholders' equity
5. Earnings per share [LO2b]

EXERCISE 19–6 *(Perform Profitability, Solvency, and Market Test Analysis)* Mack and Jack, two similar companies operating in the same industry, have the following financial information on December 31, 19X5, the close of their fiscal year.

| | MACK COMPANY | JACK COMPANY |
|---|---|---|
| Total Assets—December 31, 19X5 | $1,500,000 | $800,000 |
| Average Total Assets Held During 19X5 | 1,440,000 | 770,000 |
| Total Liabilities—December 31, 19X5 | 900,000 | 480,000 |
| Net Sales | 1,850,000 | 940,000 |
| Interest Expense | 45,000 | 19,000 |
| Income Tax Expense | 120,000 | 50,000 |
| Net Income | 190,000 | 90,000 |
| Earnings per Common Share | 2.80 | 1.05 |
| Market Price per Share of Common Stock | $17\frac{1}{2}$ | $13\frac{1}{4}$ |
| Dividends per Share of Common Stock | 1.20 | .25 |

Required:

Calculate the following ratios for each company. Round calculations to one decimal place.

1. Return on sales
2. Return on assets
3. Asset turnover
4. Debt to total assets
5. Debt to stockholders' equity—there are no preferred shares outstanding
6. Times interest earned
7. Price-earnings ratio
8. Dividend yield ratio [LO2b]

EXERCISE 19–7 *(Compute Ratios and Use Ratios to Determine Missing Data)* For each of the three independent cases shown below, determine the missing amounts. Where necessary, round calculations to one decimal place. When average amounts are not available use ending balances as given. [LO2b]

| | CASE 1 | CASE 2 | CASE 3 |
|---|---|---|---|
| Average Total Assets | $190,000 | ? | $200,000 |
| Year-end Total Assets | 200,000 | $500,000 | 210,000 |
| Year-end Total Liabilities | 80,000 | 400,000 | 60,000 |
| Sales—Net | 300,000 | 900,000 | ? |
| Net Income | ? | 100,000 | ? |
| Return on Sales | 8% | ? | ? |
| Return on Assets | ? | 22.2% | 15% |
| Asset Turnover | ? | 2 | 5 |
| Debt to Equity | ? | ? | ? |

EXERCISE 19–8 *(Compute Ratios and Use Ratios to Determine Missing Data)* For each of the four independent cases shown below, determine the missing amounts. Where necessary, round calculations to one decimal place. When average amounts are not available, use ending balances as given. [LO2b]

| | CASE 1 | CASE 2 | CASE 3 | CASE 4 |
|---|---|---|---|---|
| Inventory | $10,000 | $ 12,000 | $15,000 | $ 11,000 |
| Cash | 5,000 | 4,000 | 5,000 | 9,000 |
| Net Income | 4,000 | 2,000 | ? | 5,000 |
| Current Liabilities | 6,000 | ? | 10,000 | 6,000 |
| Dividends | 1,000 | 500 | 1,000 | 2,000 |
| Common Stock | 20,000 | 25,000 | 12,000 | 25,000 |
| Paid-in Capital | 10,000 | 15,000 | 8,000 | 5,000 |
| Accounts Receivable | 7,000 | 8,000 | 10,000 | 10,000 |
| Retained Earnings | 10,000 | 15,000 | 20,000 | 10,000 |
| Total Assets | 50,000 | 80,000 | 60,000 | ? |
| Sales | 70,000 | 100,000 | 90,000 | 100,000 |
| Current Ratio | ? | 3 to 1 | ? | ? |
| Return on Assets | ? | ? | 5% | ? |
| Asset Turnover | ? | ? | ? | 2 |
| Return on Stockholders' Equity | ? | ? | 5% | ? |
| Dividend Payout | ? | ? | ? | ? |

## PROBLEMS

PROBLEM 19–1 *(Perform Horizontal and Vertical Analysis)* The comparative income statement and balance sheet of Watkins Corporation are shown on page 721.

WATKINS CORPORATION
Comparative Income Statement
For the Years Ended December 31, 19X5 and 19X4

| | 19X5 | 19X4 |
|---|---|---|
| Net Sales | $1,000,000 | $800,000 |
| Less: Cost of Goods Sold | 600,000 | 490,000 |
| Gross Profit on Sales | $ 400,000 | $310,000 |
| Operating Expenses: | | |
| Selling Expenses | $ 100,000 | $ 80,000 |
| General Expenses | 60,000 | 43,000 |
| Interest Expense | 20,000 | 12,000 |
| Total Expenses | $ 180,000 | $135,000 |
| Income before Taxes | $ 220,000 | $175,000 |
| Income Taxes | 80,000 | 65,000 |
| Net Income | $ 140,000 | $110,000 |

WATKINS CORPORATION
Comparative Balance Sheet
December 31, 19X5 and 19X4

| ASSETS | 19X5 | 19X4 |
|---|---|---|
| Current Assets: | | |
| Cash | $ 30,000 | $ 28,000 |
| Accounts Receivable—Net | 95,000 | 60,000 |
| Inventory | 100,000 | 90,000 |
| Prepaid Expenses | 10,000 | 7,000 |
| Total Current Assets | $235,000 | $185,000 |
| Plant Assets: | | |
| Land | $ 50,000 | $ 40,000 |
| Buildings | 180,000 | 150,000 |
| Equipment | 440,000 | 360,000 |
| Total | $670,000 | $550,000 |
| Less: Accumulated Depreciation | 220,000 | 185,000 |
| Total Plant Assets—Net | $450,000 | $365,000 |
| Total Assets | $685,000 | $550,000 |
| LIABILITIES AND STOCKHOLDERS' EQUITY | | |
| Current Liabilities: | | |
| Accounts Payable | $ 75,000 | $ 60,000 |
| Taxes Payable | 20,000 | 26,000 |
| Accrued Liabilities | 35,000 | 44,000 |
| Total Current Liabilities | $130,000 | $130,000 |
| Long-Term Liabilities: | | |
| Bonds Payable (10%) | 200,000 | 150,000 |
| Total Liabilities | $330,000 | $280,000 |
| Stockholders' Equity: | | |
| Common Stock ($5 par value) | $140,000 | $120,000 |
| Paid-in Capital | 105,000 | 85,000 |
| Retained Earnings | 110,000 | 65,000 |
| Total Stockholders' Equity | $355,000 | $270,000 |
| Total Liabilities and Stockholders' Equity | $685,000 | $550,000 |

Required:

1. Prepare a horizontal analysis of the income statement and balance sheet showing changes in both dollar amounts and percentages. Round calculations to one decimal place.
2. Prepare a common-size income statement and balance sheet for both years. Round calculations to one decimal place.
3. Comment briefly on any significant relationships revealed by the horizontal and vertical analyses in Requirements 1 and 2. [LO2a]

PROBLEM 19–2 *(Prepare a Trend Analysis)* A condensed comparative income statement and a financial summary of selected data pertaining to Royal Corporation appear below.

| | 19X1 | 19X2 | 19X3 | 19X4 | 19X5 |
|---|---|---|---|---|---|
| Net Sales | $445,000 | $480,000 | $560,000 | $610,000 | $700,000 |
| Cost of Goods Sold | 330,000 | 352,000 | 411,000 | 452,000 | 490,000 |
| Gross Profit on Sales | 115,000 | 128,000 | 149,000 | 158,000 | 210,000 |
| Expenses | 101,800 | 114,000 | 133,800 | 141,900 | 189,200 |
| Net Income | $ 13,200 | $ 14,000 | $ 15,200 | $ 16,100 | $ 20,800 |

Financial summary of selected data:

| | 19X1 | 19X2 | 19X3 | 19X4 | 19X5 |
|---|---|---|---|---|---|
| Total Assets | $832,500 | $887,400 | $944,200 | $997,800 | $1,350,000 |
| Total Liabilities | 390,200 | 493,100 | 491,600 | 488,200 | 612,300 |
| Earnings per Share | .66 | .70 | .76 | .82 | 1.04 |
| Dividends per Share | .40 | .40 | .42 | .45 | .50 |
| Market Price per Share | 6.50 | 6.25 | 7.00 | 7.75 | 9.50 |

Required:

1. Prepare a trend analysis of the data using 19X1 as a base year. Round percentages to two decimal places.
2. Comment on any significant relationships, both favorable and unfavorable, revealed by the trend analysis. [LO2a]

PROBLEM 19–3 *(Perform Ratio Analysis)* Condensed comparative financial statements of Highlow Corporation are shown below.

HIGHLOW CORPORATION
Comparative Income Statement
For the Years Ended December 31, 19X5 and 19X4
($000 omitted)

| | 19X5 | 19X4 |
|---|---|---|
| Net Sales | $32,000 | $29,500 |
| Less: Cost of Goods Sold | 18,400 | 17,200 |
| Gross Profit on Sales | $13,600 | $12,300 |
| Selling Expenses | $ 7,900 | $ 7,600 |
| Administrative Expenses | 2,800 | 2,200 |
| Interest Expense | 500 | 400 |
| Income Tax Expense | 800 | 700 |
| Total Expenses | $12,000 | $10,900 |
| Net Income | $ 1,600 | $ 1,400 |

HIGHLOW CORPORATION
Comparative Balance Sheet
December 31, 19X5 and 19X4
($000 omitted)

| ASSETS | 19X5 | 19X4 |
|---|---|---|
| Current Assets: | | |
| Cash | $ 450 | $ 420 |
| Accounts Receivable—Net | 1,900 | 1,680 |
| Inventory | 2,450 | 2,130 |
| Total Current Assets | $ 4,800 | $ 4,230 |
| Plant Assets—Net | 9,600 | 9,170 |
| Total Assets | $14,400 | $13,400 |
| LIABILITIES AND STOCKHOLDERS' EQUITY | | |
| Current Liabilities: | | |
| Accounts Payable | $ 1,480 | $ 2,000 |
| Accrued Liabilities | 1,200 | 1,100 |
| Total Current Liabilities | $ 2,680 | $ 3,100 |
| Long-Term Bonds Payable | 5,000 | 4,400 |
| Total Liabilities | $ 7,680 | $ 7,500 |
| Stockholders' Equity: | | |
| Preferred Stock (10%, $50 par value) | $ 300 | $ 300 |
| Common Stock ($2 par value) | 500 | 500 |
| Paid-in Capital—Common Stock | 3,900 | 3,900 |
| Retained Earnings | 2,020 | 1,200 |
| Total Stockholders' Equity | $ 6,720 | $ 5,900 |
| Total Liabilities and Stockholders' Equity | $14,400 | $13,400 |

Additional Information:

| | 19X5 | 19X4 |
|---|---|---|
| Preferred Dividends, Declared and Paid | $ 30,000 | $ 30,000 |
| Common Dividends, Declared and Paid | 750,000 | 700,000 |
| Market Price per Share of Common Stock on December 31 | 33.50 | 29.00 |

Required:
Rounding all calculations to one decimal place, prepare the following ratios for 19X5.

1. To assess the company's liquidity:
   a. Current ratio
   b. Quick Ratio
   c. Accounts receivable turnover, including average number of days needed to collect
   d. Inventory turnover, including average number of days needed to sell
2. To assess the company's profitability:
   a. Return on sales
   b. Return on total assets
   c. Asset turnover
   d. Return on common stockholders' equity
   e. Earnings per share
3. To assess the company's long-term solvency:
   a. Debt to equity
   b. Debt to total assets
   c. Times interest earned
4. To conduct a market test:
   a. Price-earnings ratio

b. Dividend yield ratio

c. Dividend payout ratio [LO2b]

PROBLEM 19–4 *(Determine the Effect of Transactions on Ratios)* Selected transactions of Claymore Company are listed in the first column of the table below.

| TRANSACTION | RATIO |
|---|---|
| 1. Issued common stock for cash | Return on common stockholders' equity |
| 2. Declared a cash dividend on common stock | Current ratio |
| 3. Sold merchandise for cash | Quick ratio |
| 4. Purchased merchandise on account | Current ratio |
| 5. Borrowed cash by issuing a long-term note payable | Return on total assets |
| 6. Borrowed cash by issuing long-term bonds payable | Debt to equity |
| 7. Sold merchandise on account | Accounts receivable turnover |
| 8. Puchased short-term marketable securities for cash | Quick ratio |
| 9. Recorded depreciation expense on plant assets | Return on sales |
| 10. Wrote off an uncollectible account receivable against the credit balance in the Allowance for Uncollectible Accounts account | Quick ratio |
| 11. Used cash to retire bonds payable before their maturity date—there was no gain or loss to be recognized | Return on total assets |
| 12. Acquired treasury stock for cash | Earnings per share |

Required:
For each transaction, indicate whether it will increase, decrease, or have no effect on the ratio listed in the column directly across from it. The company uses the perpetual inventory method. [LO2b]

PROBLEM 19–5 *(Perform Ratio Analysis)* The summarized data shown below were compiled by Universal Company.

| | 19X2 | 19X3 | 19X4 | 19X5 |
|---|---|---|---|---|
| Total Current Assets, 12/31 | $ 47,000 | $ 52,000 | $ 59,000 | $ 66,000 |
| Total Current Liabilities, 12/31 | 30,000 | 34,000 | 35,000 | 33,000 |
| Accounts Receivable, 1/1 | 12,000 | 14,000 | 18,000 | 17,400 |
| Accounts Receivable, 12/31 | 14,000 | 18,000 | 17,400 | 17,800 |
| Inventory, 1/1 | 20,000 | 24,000 | 25,000 | 21,000 |
| Inventory, 12/31 | 24,000 | 25,000 | 21,000 | 27,000 |
| Net Sales | 136,000 | 175,000 | 182,000 | 190,000 |
| Cost of Goods Sold | 88,000 | 110,000 | 116,000 | 123,500 |

Required:
1. Compute the current ratio for each of the four years, rounding this and all other calculations in the problem, except those dealing with days, to two decimal places. In your opinion, does the company's current ratio seem to be adequate? Suppose the company changed its method of inventory valuation from LIFO to FIFO in 19X4, a year in which the cost of the items it purchases was increasing due to inflation. Would your opinion change? Explain.
2. Compute the accounts receivable turnover for each year.
3. Compute the average number of days needed to collect the accounts receivable.
4. Comment on how well the company is managing its credit and collection policies.
5. Compute the inventory turnover for each year.
6. Compute the average number of days needed for an inventory turnover.
7. Comment on how well the company is managing its inventory. [LO2b,2c]

PROBLEM 19–6 *(Use Ratios and Percentages to Compute Dollar Amounts Missing in Financial Statements)* The condensed and incomplete financial statements of Techtronics Corporation are as follows.

| TECHTRONICS CORPORATION | |
|---|---|
| Condensed Income Statement | |
| For the Year Ended December 31, 19X5 | |
| Net Sales | 100% |
| Cost of Goods Sold | 33% |
| Gross Profit on Sales | 67% |
| Operating Expenses | 50% |
| Interest Expense | 3% |
| Income before Taxes | 14% |
| Income Taxes | 5% |
| Net Income | 9% |
| Earnings per Common Share | ? |

| TECHTRONICS CORPORATION | |
|---|---|
| Condensed Balance Sheet | |
| December 31, 19X5 | |
| *Assets:* | |
| Current Assets | $40,000 |
| Plant Assets—Net | ? |
| Total Assets | ? |
| *Liabilities:* | |
| Current Liabilities | ? |
| Long-Term Liabilities | ? |
| Total Liabilities | 65,000 |
| *Stockholders' Equity:* | |
| Common Stock—$2 par value | ? |
| Retained Earnings | ? |
| Total Stockholders' Equity | ? |
| Total Liabilities and Stockholders' Equity | ? |

Additional Information:

a. Gross profit on sales amounted to $100,500.

b. The current ratio is 2.5 to 1.

c. The debt to total assets ratio is 65%.

d. There were 12,500 shares of common stock outstanding throughout the entire year.

Required:

1. Determine dollar amounts for all the items listed in the condensed income statement. Show supporting computations.
2. Determine dollar amounts for all the items listed in the condensed balance sheet. Show supporting computations. [LO2b]

PROBLEM 19–7 *(Perform Ratio Analysis)* The following financial data pertaining to Delta Corporation were obtained from financial reports and other sources.

| ITEM | 19X5 |
|---|---|
| Net Sales | $700,000 |
| Cost of Goods Sold | 500,000 |
| Current Assets, 12/31 | 210,000 |
| Quick Assets, 12/31 | 90,000 |
| Total Assets, 12/31 | 520,000 |
| Current Liabilities, 12/31 | 130,000 |
| Total Liabilities, 12/31 | 202,000 |
| Net Income | 44,900 |
| Interest Expense | 8,000 |
| Income Tax Expense | 16,200 |
| Total Stockholders' Equity, 12/31 | 318,000 |
| Preferred Stock—10%, $25 par value | 125,000 |
| Common Stock—$2 par value | 60,000 |
| Preferred Dividends, Declared and Paid | 12,500 |
| Common Dividends, Declared and Paid | 15,000 |
| Market Price per share of Preferred Stock, 12/31 | 28.00 |
| Market Price per share of Common Stock, 12/31 | 5.50 |

Additional Information:

| | |
|---|---|
| Average total assets during 19X5 | $508,000 |
| Average accounts receivable (net) during 19X5 | 80,500 |
| Average inventory balance during 19X5 | 113,500 |
| Average common stockholders' equity during 19X5 | 309,800 |

No preferred shares or common shares were issued during 19X5.

Required:

Selecting items from the data given, compute Delta Corporation's following ratios for 19X5. Round calculations to one decimal place.

1. Current ratio
2. Quick ratio
3. Accounts receivable turnover and number of days on average needed for a turnover
4. Inventory turnover and number of days on average needed for a turnover
5. Return on sales
6. Return on total assets
7. Asset turnover
8. Return on common stockholders' equity
9. Earnings per share
10. Debt to equity
11. Debt to total assets
12. Times interest earned
13. Price-earnings ratio
14. Dividend yield ratio
15. Dividend payout ratio

[LO2b]

PROBLEM 19–8 *(Use Ratios to Compute Missing Items in Financial Statements)* The incomplete financial statements of Rutherford Corporation appear on page 727.

| RUTHERFORD CORPORATION<br>Income Statement<br>For the Year Ended December 31, 19X5 | |
|---|---|
| Net Sales | ? |
| Cost of Goods Sold | ? |
| Gross Profit on Sales | ? |
| Operating Expenses: | |
| Selling Expenses | ? |
| Administrative Expenses | $12,000 |
| Interest Expense | ? |
| Total Expenses | ? |
| Income before Taxes | ? |
| Income Taxes | ? |
| Net Income | $30,000 |
| Earnings per Common Share | ? |

| RUTHERFORD CORPORATION<br>Balance Sheet<br>December 31, 19X5 | |
|---|---|
| ASSETS | |
| Current Assets: | |
| Cash | ? |
| Accounts Receivable—Net | ? |
| Inventory | ? |
| Total Current Assets | $216,000 |
| Plant Assets—Net | ? |
| Total Assets | 400,000 |
| LIABILITIES AND STOCKHOLDERS' EQUITY | |
| Current Liabilities: | |
| Accounts Payable | ? |
| Long-Term Liabilities: | |
| Bonds Payable | ? |
| Total Liabilities | ? |
| Stockholders' Equity: | |
| Common Stock—$1 par value | ? |
| Retained Earnings | ? |
| Total Stockholders' Equity | ? |
| Total Liabilities and Stockholders' Equity | ? |

Additional Information:

a. The return on sales is 5%.
b. Income taxes are 40% of income before taxes.
c. The times interest earned ratio is 6.0 times.
d. The current ratio is 3.0 to 1.
e. The quick ratio is 1.5 to 1.
f. The inventory turnover ratio is 4.8 times, and the balance in the inventory account at the beginning of the period was $92,000.
g. The accounts receivable turnover ratio is 8.0 times, and the net accounts receivable balance on January 1, 19X5, was $77,000.
h. The debt to total assets ratio is 60%.
i. The debt to equity ratio is 150%.
j. Selling expenses are 40% of the amount shown for gross profit on sales.
k. There were 60,000 shares of common stock outstanding throughout the entire year.

Required:
Use the additional information given in items a through k to complete Rutherford's financial statements. Show supporting computations. [LO2b]

PROBLEM 19–9 *(Perform Ratio Analysis of Two Companies)* The condensed balance sheet and income statement for Rye Company and for Wheat Company for the year ended December 31, 19X5, appear below.

| | RYE COMPANY | WHEAT COMPANY |
|---|---|---|
| Cash | $ 13,400 | $ 35,200 |
| Marketable Securities | 15,000 | — |
| Accounts Receivable—Net | 83,000 | 33,100 |
| Inventory | 73,600 | 37,700 |
| Plant and Equipment | 135,000 | 149,000 |
| Accumulated Depreciation | (90,000) | (25,000) |
| Total | $230,000 | $230,000 |
| Accounts Payable | $ 59,000 | $ 44,000 |
| Salaries Payable | 10,000 | 8,000 |
| Other Accrued Liabilities | 6,000 | 3,000 |
| Long-Term Debt—10% | 70,000 | 20,000 |
| Common Stock—$10 Par Value | 50,000 | 50,000 |
| Retained Earnings | 35,000 | 105,000 |
| Total | $230,000 | $230,000 |

| | RYE | WHEAT |
|---|---|---|
| Net Sales | $300,000 | $310,000 |
| Cost of Goods Sold | 175,000 | 190,000 |
| Gross Profit on Sales | $125,000 | $120,000 |
| Operating Expenses | 90,000 | 80,000 |
| Income before Taxes | $ 35,000 | $ 40,000 |
| Income Taxes | 15,000 | 17,000 |
| Net Income | $ 20,000 | $ 23,000 |

Additional Information:

| | RYE | WHEAT |
|---|---|---|
| a. Accounts receivable at beginning of the year totaled | $ 79,000 | $ 33,500 |
| b. Inventory at beginning of the year totaled | 73,200 | 35,300 |
| c. Assets at beginning of the year totaled | 220,000 | 218,000 |
| d. Stockholders' equity at beginning of the year totaled | 73,000 | 95,000 |
| e. Interest expense included in this year's income statement totaled | 4,500 | 1,200 |
| f. Dividends declared and paid during 19X5 were | 8,000 | 5,000 |
| g. Market price per share of common stock on December 31, the end of each company's fiscal year, was | 20 | $36\frac{1}{2}$ |

Required:
Rounding all calculations to two decimal places, prepare the following ratios for both companies.

1. To assess their liquidity:
   a. Current ratio
   b. Quick ratio
   c. Accounts receivable turnover, including average number of days needed to collect
   d. Inventory turnover, including average number of days needed to sell

2. To assess their profitability:
   a. Return on sales
   b. Return on total assets
   c. Asset turnover
   d. Return on common stockholders' equity
   e. Earnings per share
3. To assess their long-term solvency:
   a. Debt to equity
   b. Debt to total assets
   c. Times interest earned
4. To conduct a market test:
   a. Price-earnings ratio
   b. Dividend yield ratio
   c. Dividend payout ratio
5. In your opinion, which of the two companies had a better operating performance in 19X5? Which company is doing a better job of trading on equity (leverage)? Explain. [LO2b,2c]

PROBLEM 19–10 *(Comprehensive Problem: Ratio Analysis)* The condensed comparative financial statements of Yankee Corporation are shown below. All figures are in thousands of dollars.

YANKEE CORPORATION
Comparative Income Statement
For the Years Ended December 31, 19X5 and 19X4

| | 19X5 | 19X4 |
|---|---|---|
| Net Sales | $22,000 | $19,800 |
| Less: Cost of Goods Sold | 12,500 | 11,300 |
| Gross Profit on Sales | $ 9,500 | $ 8,500 |
| Selling Expenses | $ 4,400 | $ 4,310 |
| Administrative Expenses | 2,600 | 2,150 |
| Interest Expense | 350 | 300 |
| Income Tax Expense | 850 | 690 |
| Total Expenses | $ 8,200 | $ 7,450 |
| Net Income | $ 1,300 | $ 1,050 |

*(Continued on page 730)*

YANKEE CORPORATION
Comparative Balance Sheet
December 31, 19X5 and 19X4

| ASSETS | 19X5 | 19X4 |
|---|---|---|
| Current Assets | | |
| Cash | $ 360 | $ 330 |
| Accounts Receivable—Net | 2,400 | 2,260 |
| Inventory | 2,700 | 2,780 |
| Prepaid Expenses | 40 | 30 |
| Total Current Assets | $ 5,500 | $ 5,400 |
| Plant Assets—Net | 8,100 | 7,300 |
| Total Assets | $13,600 | $12,700 |
| LIABILITIES AND STOCKHOLDERS' EQUITY | | |
| Current Liabilities | | |
| Accounts Payable | $ 3,620 | $ 3,470 |
| Accrued Liabilities | 1,200 | 1,540 |
| Total Current Liabilities | $ 4,820 | $ 5,010 |
| Long-Term Bonds Payable | 3,500 | 3,200 |
| Total Liabilities | $ 8,320 | $ 8,210 |
| Stockholders' Equity | | |
| Preferred Stock—10%, $50 Par Value | $ 100 | $ 100 |
| Common Stock—$15 Par Value | 3,000 | 3,000 |
| Paid-in Capital | 760 | 760 |
| Retained Earnings | 1,420 | 630 |
| Total Stockholders' Equity | $ 5,280 | $ 4,490 |
| Total Liabilities and Stockholders' Equity | $13,600 | $12,700 |

Additional Information:

| | 19X5 | 19X4 | 19X3 |
|---|---|---|---|
| Preferred Dividends Declared and Paid | $ 10,000 | $ 10,000 | $ 10,000 |
| Common Dividends Declared and Paid | 500,000 | 460,000 | 400,000 |
| Market Price per Share of Common Stock, 12/31 | 42.50 | 37.00 | 34.50 |
| Total Assets, 12/31 | 13,600,000 | 12,700,000 | 12,100,000 |
| Total Common Stockholders' Equity, 12/31 | 5,180,000 | 4,390,000 | 3,850,000 |
| Net Accounts Receivable Balance, 12/31 | 2,400,000 | 2,260,000 | 2,040,000 |
| Inventory Account Balance, 12/31 | 2,700,000 | 2,780,000 | 2,920,000 |

Required:
Rounding all calculations to two decimal places:

1. Prepare the following ratios as a basis for assessing the company's liquidity for both 19X5 and 19X4.
   a. Current ratio
   b. Quick ratio
   c. Accounts receivable turnover, including average number of days needed to collect
   d. Inventory turnover, including average number of days needed to sell
2. Prepare the following ratios as a basis for assessing the company's profitability for both 19X5 and 19X4.
   a. Return on sales
   b. Return on total assets
   c. Asset turnover

d. Return on common stockholders' equity
e. Earnings per share

3. Prepare the following ratios as a basis for assessing the company's long-term solvency for both 19X5 and 19X4.
   a. Debt to equity
   b. Debt to total assets
   c. Times interest earned
4. Prepare the following ratios as a basis for conducting a market test analysis for both 19X5 and 19X4.
   a. Price-earnings ratio
   b. Dividend yield ratio
   c. Dividend payout ratio
5. Evaluate the results obtained and answer the following questions:
   a. Did the company's short-term liquidity position change? Was it a favorable or an unfavorable change? Explain.
   b. Did the company's performance pertaining to profitablity change? Was the change favorable or unfavorable? Indicate how you reached your conclusion. Be specific.
   c. In the year 19X5, was leverage working to the advantage of the common stockholders? Indicate how you reached your conclusion. Be specific. [LO2b,2c]

## ALTERNATE PROBLEMS

PROBLEM 19–1A *(Perform Horizontal and Vertical Analysis)* (Alternate to Problem 19–1) The comparative income statement and balance sheet of Visi Corporation are shown below:

VISI CORPORATION
Comparative Income Statement
For the Years Ended December 31, 19X5 and 19X4

| | 19X5 | 19X4 |
|---|---|---|
| Net Sales | $2,000,000 | $1,500,000 |
| Less: Cost of Goods Sold | 1,400,000 | 900,000 |
| Gross Profit on Sales | $ 600,000 | $ 600,000 |
| Operating Expenses: | | |
| Selling Expenses | $ 215,000 | $ 270,000 |
| General Expenses | 140,000 | 150,000 |
| Interest Expense | 25,000 | 15,000 |
| Total Expenses | $ 380,000 | $ 435,000 |
| Income before Taxes | $ 220,000 | $ 165,000 |
| Income Taxes | 90,000 | 72,000 |
| Net Income | $ 130,000 | $ 93,000 |

*(Continued on page 732)*

VISI CORPORATION
Comparative Balance Sheet
December 31, 19X5 and 19X4

| ASSETS | 19X5 | 19X4 |
|---|---|---|
| Current Assets: | | |
| Cash | $ 70,000 | $ 60,000 |
| Accounts Receivable—Net | 140,000 | 160,000 |
| Inventory | 190,000 | 210,000 |
| Prepaid Expenses | 15,000 | 10,000 |
| Total Current Assets | $ 415,000 | $ 440,000 |
| Plant Assets: | | |
| Land | $ 70,000 | $ 50,000 |
| Buildings | 985,000 | 815,000 |
| Equipment | 1,055,000 | 680,000 |
| Total | $2,110,000 | $1,545,000 |
| Less: Accumulated Depreciation | 925,000 | 785,000 |
| Total Plant Assets—Net | $1,185,000 | $ 760,000 |
| Total Assets | $1,600,000 | $1,200,000 |
| LIABILITIES AND STOCKHOLDERS' EQUITY | | |
| Current Liabilities: | | |
| Accounts Payable | $ 330,000 | $ 250,000 |
| Accrued Liabilities | 160,000 | 110,000 |
| Total Current Liabilities | $ 490,000 | $ 360,000 |
| Long-Term Debt | 270,000 | 150,000 |
| Total Liabilities | $ 760,000 | $ 510,000 |
| Stockholders' Equity: | | |
| Common Stock ($5 par value) | $ 250,000 | $ 200,000 |
| Paid-in Capital | 180,000 | 160,000 |
| Retained Earnings | 410,000 | 330,000 |
| Total Stockholders' Equity | $ 840,000 | $ 690,000 |
| Total Liabilities and Stockholders' Equity | $1,600,000 | $1,200,000 |

Required:

1. Prepare a horizontal analysis of the income statement and balance sheet showing changes in both dollar amounts and percentages. Round calculations to one decimal place.
2. Prepare a common-size income statement and balance sheet for both years. Round calculations to one decimal place.
3. Comment briefly on any significant relationships revealed by the horizontal and vertical analyses in Requirements 1 and 2. [LO2a]

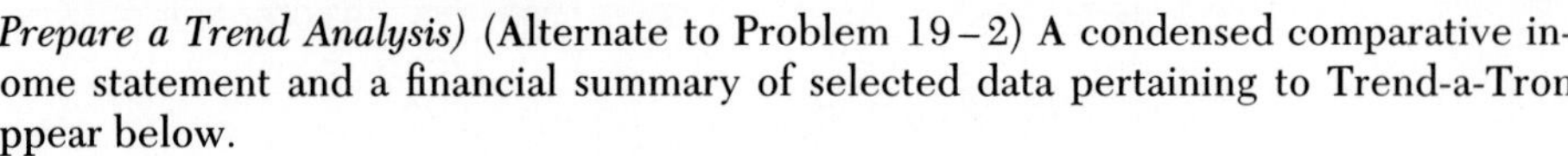

PROBLEM 19–2A *(Prepare a Trend Analysis)* (Alternate to Problem 19–2) A condensed comparative income statement and a financial summary of selected data pertaining to Trend-a-Tron appear below.

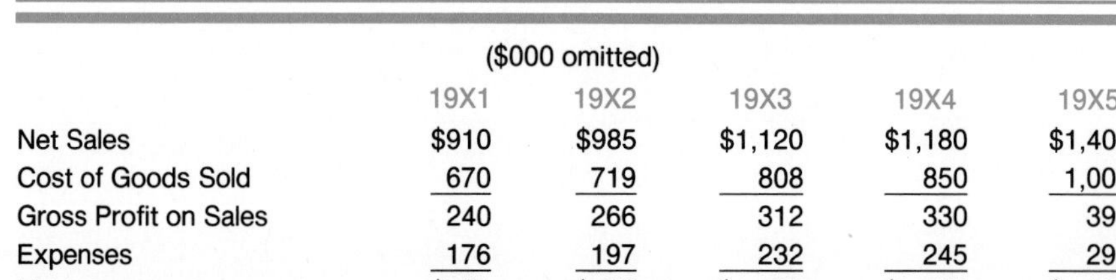

($000 omitted)

| | 19X1 | 19X2 | 19X3 | 19X4 | 19X5 |
|---|---|---|---|---|---|
| Net Sales | $910 | $985 | $1,120 | $1,180 | $1,400 |
| Cost of Goods Sold | 670 | 719 | 808 | 850 | 1,005 |
| Gross Profit on Sales | 240 | 266 | 312 | 330 | 395 |
| Expenses | 176 | 197 | 232 | 245 | 294 |
| Net Income | $ 64 | $ 69 | $ 80 | $ 85 | $ 101 |

Financial summary of selected data:

| | ($000 omitted—except per share amounts) 19X1 | 19X2 | 19X3 | 19X4 | 19X5 |
|---|---|---|---|---|---|
| Total Assets | $1,245 | $1,315 | $1,420 | $1,500 | $1,660 |
| Total Liabilities | 790 | 800 | 810 | 840 | 880 |
| Earnings per Share | 1.71 | 1.80 | 2.01 | 2.05 | 2.33 |
| Dividends per Share | .35 | .38 | .40 | .42 | .50 |
| Market Price per Share | 17.00 | 18.25 | 20.50 | 21.00 | 24.50 |

Required:

1. Prepare a trend analysis of the data using 19X1 as a base year. Round percentages to two decimal places.
2. Comment on any significant relationships, both favorable and unfavorable, revealed by the trend analysis. [LO2a]

PROBLEM 19–3A *(Perform Ratio Analysis)* (Alternate to Problem 19–3) Condensed comparative financial statements for Crescent Corporation are shown below.

CRESCENT CORPORATION
Comparative Income Statement
For the Years Ended December 31, 19X5 and 19X4
($000 omitted)

| | 19X5 | 19X4 |
|---|---|---|
| Net Sales | $1,870 | $1,590 |
| Less: Cost of Goods Sold | 750 | 634 |
| Gross Profit on Sales | $1,120 | $ 956 |
| Selling Expenses | $ 570 | $ 498 |
| Administrative Expenses | 220 | 200 |
| Interest Expense | 80 | 70 |
| Income Tax Expense | 100 | 62 |
| Total Expenses | $ 970 | $ 830 |
| Net Income | $ 150 | $ 126 |

*(Continued on page 734)*

CRESCENT CORPORATION

Comparative Balance Sheet
December 31, 19X5 and 19X4
($000 omitted)

| ASSETS | 19X5 | 19X4 |
|---|---|---|
| Current Assets: | | |
| Cash | $ 150 | $ 90 |
| Accounts Receivable—Net | 330 | 278 |
| Inventory | 390 | 302 |
| Total Current Assets | $ 870 | $ 670 |
| Plant Assets—Net | 1,080 | 940 |
| Total Assets | $1,950 | $1,610 |
| LIABILITIES AND STOCKHOLDERS' EQUITY | | |
| Current Liabilities: | | |
| Accounts Payable | $ 314 | $ 274 |
| Accrued Liabilities | 104 | 92 |
| Total Current Liabilities | $ 418 | $ 366 |
| Long-Term Bonds Payable | 800 | 600 |
| Total Liabilities | $1,218 | $ 966 |
| Stockholders' Equity: | | |
| Preferred Stock (10%, $100 par Value) | $ 20 | $ 20 |
| Common Stock ($5 par value) | 500 | 500 |
| Paid-in Capital—Common Stock | 110 | 110 |
| Retained Earnings | 102 | 14 |
| Total Stockholders' Equity | $ 732 | $ 644 |
| Total Liabilities and Stockholders' Equity | $1,950 | $1,610 |

Additional Information:

| | 19X5 | 19X4 |
|---|---|---|
| Preferred Dividends, Declared and Paid | $ 2,000 | $ 2,000 |
| Common Dividends, Declared and Paid | 60,000 | 50,000 |
| Market Price per Share of Common Stock on December 31 | 12.50 | 10.25 |

Required:

Rounding all calculations to one decimal place, prepare the following ratios for 19X5.

1. To assess the company's liquidity:
   a. Current ratio
   b. Quick ratio
   c. Accounts receivable turnover, including average number of days needed to collect
   d. Inventory turnover, including average number of days needed to sell
2. To assess the company's profitability:
   a. Return on sales
   b. Return on total assets
   c. Asset turnover
   d. Return on common stockholders' equity
   e. Earnings per share
3. To assess the company's long-term solvency:
   a. Debt to equity
   b. Debt to total assets
   c. Times interest earned
4. To conduct a market test:
   a. Price-earnings ratio
   b. Dividend yield ratio
   c. Dividend payout ratio [LO2b]

PROBLEM 19–4A *(Determine the Effect of Transactions on Ratios)* (Alternate to Problem 19–4) Selected transactions of Boxwood Corporation are listed in the first column of the table below.

| TRANSACTION | RATIO |
|---|---|
| 1. Sold inventory on account | Current ratio |
| 2. Declared a cash dividend on preferred stock | Quick ratio |
| 3. Sold damaged inventory at cost | Earnings per share |
| 4. Issued long-term bonds for cash | Debt to total assets |
| 5. Received cash representing interest on a long-term note receivable | Return on total assets |
| 6. Reinstated an account receivable previously written off against the Allowance for Uncollectible Accounts account | Current ratio |
| 7. Sold inventory for cash | Inventory turnover |
| 8. Declared and paid a cash dividend on common stock | Dividend yield |
| 9. Retired bonds at maturity with a cash payment | Debt to equity |
| 10. Acquired treasury stock for cash | Return on sales |
| 11. Collected on accounts receivable | Accounts receivable turnover |
| 12. Recorded amortization expense on a patent | Return on sales |

Required:

For each transaction, indicate whether it will increase, decrease, or have no effect on the ratio listed in the column directly across from it. The company uses the perpetual inventory method. [LO2b]

PROBLEM 19–5A *(Use Ratios and Percentages to Compute Dollar Amounts Missing in Financial Statements)* (Alternate to Problem 19–6) The condensed and incomplete financial statements of Dean Corporation are as follows.

| DEAN CORPORATION<br>Condensed Income Statement<br>For the Year Ended December 31, 19X5 | |
|---|---|
| Net Sales | 100% |
| Cost of Goods Sold | 42% |
| Gross Profit on Sales | 58% |
| Operating Expenses | 42% |
| Interest Expense | 3% |
| Income before Taxes | 13% |
| Income Taxes | 6% |
| Net Income | 7% |
| Earnings per Common Share | ? |

| DEAN CORPORATION<br>Condensed Balance Sheet<br>December 31, 19X5 | |
|---|---|
| Assets: | |
| Current Assets | $ ? |
| Plant Assets—Net | ? |
| Total Assets | 80,000 |
| Liabilities: | |
| Current Liabilities | 20,000 |
| Long-Term Liabilities | ? |
| Total Liabilities | ? |
| Stockholders' Equity: | |
| Common Stock—$1 par value | ? |
| Retained Earnings | ? |
| Total Stockholders' Equity | ? |
| Total Liabilities and Stockholders' Equity | ? |

Additional Information:

a. Interest expense during 19X5 totaled $3,000.
b. The current ratio is 1.5 to 1.
c. The debt to total assets ratio is 60%.
d. There were 20,000 shares of common stock outstanding throughout the entire year.

Required:

1. Determine dollar amounts for all the items listed in the condensed income statement. Show supporting computations.
2. Determine dollar amounts for all the items listed in the condensed balance sheet. Show supporting computations. [LO2b]

# 20 Accounting Principles and the Effects of Changing Prices

### Learning Objectives

When you complete this chapter you will be able to

1. Answer the following questions:
   a. Why are generally accepted accounting principles needed?
   b. How did generally accepted accounting principles develop, and what organizations have influenced their development?
   c. What is the Financial Accounting Standards Board's Conceptual Framework Project, and what is its purpose?
   d. What are the objectives of financial reporting, and what qualitative characteristics make accounting information useful?
   e. How are the assumptions, principles, and conventions collectively known as generally accepted accounting principles defined? What are some illustrations of their application?
   f. What are the types and effects of price changes?
   g. What are the FASB requirements for financial reporting and changing prices?
2. Perform the following accounting functions:
   a. Apply the percentage-of-completion and installment methods of revenue realization.
   b. Use constant dollar accounting to restate the historical costs reported in the conventional balance sheet and income statement for changes in the general price level.
   c. Use current cost accounting to restate the historical costs reported in the conventional balance sheet and income statement for specific price-level changes.

This chapter has two major purposes. First, we need a broad overview of the accounting concepts, assumptions, and practices collectively known as generally accepted accounting principles. Although previous chapters have identified the principles used to account for specific items in the financial statements, we will benefit from discussions of *all* the principles used to record, classify, and report financial data. After studying this section of the chapter, we will have a better understanding of why and how we do things in accounting.

Second, we need to study the effect of changing prices on financial measurement and reporting. Even though the impact of inflation on our daily lives changes through the years, inflation itself will be a fact of life for some time to come. It is important that we learn about the effect of changing prices on financial measurement and reporting and how this effect can be accounted for in financial statements.

Therefore we will discuss generally accepted accounting principles in the first section of this chapter and the effect of changing prices on financial measurement and reporting in the second section.

## THE NEED FOR GENERALLY ACCEPTED ACCOUNTING PRINCIPLES

As pointed out in previous chapters, many groups use financial statements (investors, managers, financial analysts, etc.). However, accountants attempt to satisfy the needs of these various groups by preparing a set of general-purpose financial statements. Therefore it is important that the information contained in these financial statements have the following characteristics:

***1a. GAAP are needed so that financial statement information will be reliable, complete, and understandable***

The information should be reliable.

The information should be complete.

The information should be understandable.

To possess these characteristics, financial statements must be prepared in a way that allows them to be compared (1) with the same company's financial statements of prior accounting periods and (2) with the financial statements of other companies for the same accounting period. Financial statements will have these characteristics only if they are developed from guidelines that come from a common set of assumptions, concepts, and practices called **generally accepted accounting principles *(GAAP)*.**

Without these common principles, companies could prepare financial statements by using whatever measurement processes they chose. For example, one company might report its inventory at cost while another company reported its inventory at market price. Such inconsistency would distort the comparability of each company's operating results over a given accounting period and the financial position of each company at the end of an accounting period. In short, the existence of generally accepted accounting principles establishes order in financial reporting that otherwise might not exist.

## THE DEVELOPMENT OF GENERALLY ACCEPTED ACCOUNTING PRINCIPLES

Generally accepted accounting principles were not developed for the purpose of requiring all companies to measure and report their financial activity in exactly the same manner. Within the broad set of principles, alternative ways of measuring financial transactions do exist. In previous chapters, for example, we have studied different ways to determine depreciation for an accounting period and different ways to determine the cost of inventory at the end of an accounting period. No two companies operate in the same manner, and therefore when given alternatives most companies should select a procedure that seems most appropriate for measuring a given transaction or set of transactions.

*1b. Some GAAP have developed from experience, custom, usage, and practical necessity*

Some generally accepted accounting principles "have developed on the basis of experience, custom, usage, and, to a significant extent, practical necessity."[1] These principles attain the status of "generally accepted" because the accounting profession considers them to be the best possible practice for achieving the objectives of financial reporting. Other generally accepted accounting principles have acquired their status through substantial authoritative support of the accounting profession.

Many organizations have contributed to the development of generally accepted accounting principles. Among the most influential are the following (all of which have been discussed in previous chapters):

*1b. Development of GAAP has been influenced by the AICPA, FASB, and SEC*

The American Institute of Certified Public Accountants (AICPA)
The Financial Accounting Standards Board (FASB)
The Securities and Exchange Commission (SEC)

Although the publications of all three organizations are regarded as authoritative support for accounting principles, the Financial Accounting Standards Board currently establishes generally accepted accounting principles in the private sector of the accounting profession. For this reason, we will use five pronouncements of this organization to discuss the conceptual framework that serves as an evaluator of current and future accounting standards. This discussion will be followed by explanations of the concepts and practices that underlie what are currently considered to be generally accepted accounting principles.

## THE CONCEPTUAL FRAMEWORK AS AN EVALUATOR OF CURRENT AND FUTURE ACCOUNTING STANDARDS

*1c. The Conceptual Framework Project aims to provide a structure of broad fundamentals for financial accounting*

The Conceptual Framework Project was developed by the Financial Accounting Standards Board to serve as a structure of broad fundamentals for financial accounting. The FASB itself refers to the project as a "constitution" that can be used to evaluate current standards and serve as the basis for future standards. So far, six statements of concepts have been produced, each of which is summarized in the following subsections.

### Statement of Financial Accounting Concepts No. 1

*1d. The Framework Project's first statement of concepts identifies the objectives of financial reporting*

The Statement of Financial Concepts No. 1 was published in 1978 and is entitled "Objectives of Financial Reporting by Business Enterprises." Basically it confirms the role of usefulness in financial reporting and states that financial reporting should provide the following:

Information that is useful to present and potential investors and creditors and other users in making rational investment, credit, and similar decisions.

Information that is useful in assessing the amounts, timing, and uncertainty of prospective net cash inflows to the related enterprise.

---

[1] Accounting Principles Board, "Basic Concepts of Accounting Principles Underlying Financial Statements of Business Enterprises," *Statement No. 4* (New York: AICPA, 1970), par. 139.

Information about economic resources (assets) of an enterprise, the claims to those resources (liabilities and owners' equity), and the effects of transactions, events, and circumstances that change resources and claims to those resources.

Information about an enterprise's financial performance during a period, with primary focus on measures of earnings and its components.

Information that is useful in assessing an enterprise's liquidity and solvency.

Information about how management of an enterprise has discharged its stewardship responsibility to owners (stockholders) for the use of enterprise resources entrusted to it.

## Statement of Financial Accounting Concepts No. 2

*1d. The second statement of concepts identifies the qualitative characteristics that make accounting information useful*

The Statement of Financial Accounting Concepts No. 2 was published in 1980 and is entitled "Qualitative Characteristics of Accounting Information." It identifies the following as qualitative characteristics that make accounting information useful:

*Understandability*, which is the quality of information that enables reasonably informed users to perceive its significance.

*Relevance*, which is the capacity of information to make a difference in a decision and to help users to make predictions about the outcome of past, present, and future events, or confirm or correct prior expectations.

*Reliability*, which is the quality of information that gives assurance that it is reasonably free of error and bias and faithfully represents what it is supposed to represent.

*Comparability*, which is the quality of information that enables the user to identify similarities and differences among events and conditions, and includes the notion that an enterprise's accounting practices will be consistently applied.

## Statement of Financial Accounting Concepts No. 3 (Superseded by No. 6)

## Statement of Financial Accounting Concepts No. 4

*1d. The fourth statement identifies the objectives of financial reporting by nonbusiness organizations*

The Statement of Financial Accounting Concepts No. 4 was published in 1980 and is entitled "Objectives of Financial Reporting by Nonbusiness Organizations." It establishes the objectives of financial reporting by such nonbusiness organizations as (1) human services, (2) churches, (3) foundations, and (4) nonprofit hospitals.

A separate statement was considered necessary because nonbusiness organizations engage in certain types of transactions that seldom occur in business enterprises. For example, nonbusiness organizations frequently receive contributions and grants.

## Statement of Financial Accounting Concepts No. 5

*1d. The fifth statement provides guidance on what items should be reported in the financial statements and how their value should be measured*

The Statement of Financial Accounting Concepts No. 5 was published in 1984 and is entitled "Recognition and Measurement in Financial Statements of Business Enterprises." It sets forth guidance on what information should be included in financial statements and when that information should be included. Basically the current financial reporting practices are reaffirmed, with allowances for certain gradual and evolutionary changes. A shift toward more use of current market values is a possibility.

### Statement of Financial Accounting Concepts No. 6

The Statement of Financial Accounting Concepts No. 6 was published in 1985 and is entitled "Elements of Financial Statements." It identifies and defines ten elements directly related to measuring the performance and financial status of both business enterprises and not-for-profit organizations. According to the FASB, the elements of financial statements are the building blocks with which financial statements are constructed—the classes of items that financial statements constitute.

Exhibit 20–1 contains a listing of these interrelated elements. Note that many of these terms are used throughout the book. **Comprehensive income,** as used here, includes all changes in net assets resulting from transactions, events, and circumstances other than investments by or distributions to owners.

*1d. The sixth statement identifies and defines ten elements of financial statements*

EXHIBIT 20–1

Elements of Financial Statements

Seven Elements That Relate to Both Business Enterprises and Not-for-Profit Organizations:

**1.** Assets
**2.** Liabilities
**3a.** Equity (business enterprises)
**b.** Net Assets (not-for-profit organizations)
**4.** Revenues
**5.** Expenses
**6.** Gains
**7.** Losses

Three Elements That Relate to Business Enterprises Only:

**1.** Investments by Owners
**2.** Distributions to Owners
**3.** Comprehensive Income

### A Concluding Note on the Conceptual Framework Project

The statements of financial accounting concepts summarized above do not *necessarily* represent, at the current time, the concepts and practices that constitute generally accepted accounting principles. Eventually, however, these statements may have an impact on financial reporting, and some of the ideas expressed may change the way financial statements are constructed.

## GENERALLY ACCEPTED ACCOUNTING PRINCIPLES CURRENTLY USED

Let us now focus on what is considered, at the present time, to be generally accepted accounting principles. For purposes of our discussion, we will divide these principles into the following categories:

Underlying assumptions
Basic principles
Modifying conventions

Each of these will be explained in the three following subsections.

## Underlying Assumptions

*1e. Assumptions underlying GAAP are explained and their use illustrated here*

Assumptions generally relate to things that are taken for granted. Thus the underlying assumptions that we discuss will provide the framework for the generally accepted accounting principles that are currently used.

ENTITY ASSUMPTION The **entity assumption** states that information is accumulated for a specific unit called an entity. An **accounting entity** is an economic unit that controls resources and engages in economic activities. The activities of the accounting entity are recorded separately from the personal activities of its owners.

Remember from earlier chapters that the following journal entry is made when a person invests a sum of money, say $5,000, in a business that is organized as a single proprietorship or partnership:

| | | |
|---|---|---|
| Cash | 5,000 | |
| Abbot, Capital | | 5,000 |
| To record investment of cash in the business | | |

This transaction that simply transfers money from one bank account to another may be viewed as a decrease in Abbot's personal cash and an increase in the cash held by a company that he owns or in which he is a part owner. Under law (unless the business was organized as a corporation), no distinction is made between the assets and liabilities of a business and those of the owners. Thus, under law the cash in either bank account may be used to pay business debts. However, in accounting, where the entity assumption is used, the assets and liabilities of any business, regardless of organization form, are considered to be separate from those of the owners. Therefore, Abbot's business-related investment transaction is accounted for separately as in the entry above.

GOING CONCERN ASSUMPTION The **going concern assumption** states that an entity will continue to operate in the future unless there is evidence to the contrary, and that it will remain in operation for a period sufficiently long enough to carry out its plans and commitments. The going concern assumption is sometimes called the **continuity assumption.**

Let us again use an accounting transaction to illustrate this assumption. Suppose that we purchase some equipment for $8,000 cash and make the following journal entry:

| | | |
|---|---|---|
| Equipment | 8,000 | |
| Cash | | 8,000 |
| To record the purchase of equipment for cash | | |

The above entry is the correct way to record that transaction because the cost of the equipment is $8,000. Let us now suppose, however, that a year later someone appraises the current market value of that equipment at $10,000. The following entry would be *incorrect:*

| | | |
|---|---|---|
| Equipment | 2,000 | |
| Gain on Reappraisal of Equipment | | 2,000 |
| To record the equipment at current market value | | |

Since it is the intent of the business to use the equipment rather than sell it, increasing its carrying amount provides little or no useful information to users of the company's financial statements. Allowing entries like the one shown on page 742 could also open the door to significant bias in the financial statements.

The going concern assumption also supports accounting treatment such as the following:

The systematic allocation of a plant asset's cost over its estimated useful life because the company is expected to stay in business during the time period designated in the useful life

The classification of prepaid expenses as assets in the balance sheet because the company is expected to operate long enough to benefit from those prepaid expenses in future accounting periods

However, if there is evidence that an entity will not stay in business for the foreseeable future, the going concern assumption should be abandoned. In this case, the financial statements should report assets at their net realizable value and liabilities at amounts currently needed for their settlement.

TIME PERIOD ASSUMPTION The **time period assumption,** sometimes called the **periodicity assumption,** assumes that the life span of a firm can be divided into a series of arbitrary short time periods and that the firm's economic activities can be appropriately related to those time periods.

Although financial statements are usually prepared for periods covering twelve consecutive months (annually), many businesses prepare them for shorter periods, such as a quarter of a year or a month. The need for reports covering relatively short time periods creates certain measurement problems.

To illustrate, let us take the purchase of equipment discussed in the going concern concept. If the equipment was expected to last ten years and we could wait that long to prepare an income statement, no measurement problem would exist. The $8,000 cost of the equipment would be written off as an expense, and our ten-year income statement would show an expense of $8,000. However, when preparing annual income statements, we must assign part of the equipment's $8,000 cost to each of the ten years that the equipment is expected to be used. One way to make this cost assignment is to prepare the following journal entry in each of the next ten years:

| | | |
|---|---|---|
| Depreciation Expense | 800 | |
| Accumulated Depreciation—Equipment | | 800 |
| To record depreciation on equipment | | |

This entry assigns one-tenth of the $8,000 cost as an expense in each of the next ten years' income statements, and thus it satisfies the time period assumption. Bear in mind, however, that depreciation expense is a measurement based upon estimates. Users of financial statements should be aware of the nature of these reported amounts when making decisions.

MONETARY UNIT ASSUMPTION Information contained in financial statements is usually presented in quantified form, making it necessary to have an agreed-upon measuring unit. The **monetary unit assumption** holds that money is the appropriate measuring unit. Thus money serves as the common denominator for measuring and reporting an entity's economic activity.

The monetary unit (dollars in the United States) is reported in the financial statements as if its value remained constant over time. Assume, for example, that these two journal entries are made in 19X6 and 19X7, respectively:

| | | |
|---|---|---|
| 19X6 | | |
| Land .................................................. | 40,000 | |
| Cash ............................................ | | 40,000 |
| To record the purchase of land | | |
| 19X7 | | |
| Land .................................................. | 40,000 | |
| Cash ............................................ | | 40,000 |
| To record the purchase of land | | |

In each year land was recorded at its cost when purchased. If no other land purchases were made, the balance sheet prepared at the end of 19X7 would show land at $80,000 regardless of the fact that each block of land might have been purchased when the dollars used to buy them had different values. Later in this chapter we will show how to prepare price-level adjusted financial statements that account for the differences in the value of the dollars that are spent at different times.

## Basic Principles

*1e. Basic accounting principles are explained and their use illustrated here*

Basic accounting principles have a pervasive effect on when and how an entity records its economic activity. This, in turn, affects the form and content of financial statements. We will discuss each of these basic principles in the next six subsections.

OBJECTIVITY PRINCIPLE Simply stated, the **objectivity principle** means that accounting information should be free from bias and based on verifiable evidence. Such evidence can take the form of contracts, invoices, bank checks, and observations. Objectivity does not mean, however, that accounting information can be prepared without estimates and judgments. Information is said to be objective and verifiable when similar measurements generating similar results would be developed by two or more competent persons examining the same data.

Objective data is sometimes hard to attain. To demonstrate what we mean, go back, once again, to the equipment purchase first used in the discussion of the going concern assumption. It is reasonable to assume that one person might estimate the useful life of the equipment at ten years (calling for yearly depreciation of $800), and another person might estimate the useful life of the equipment at eight years (calling for yearly depreciation of $1,000). However, it would be rare for one person to estimate a useful life of five years and for another person to estimate a useful life of fifty years on the same equipment.

COST PRINCIPLE This principle states that the cost incurred at the time the transaction occurs is the basis for initially recording goods and services acquired by an enterprise. Cost incurred is measured by the amount of cash or cash equivalent given to acquire the goods or services in an exchange transaction between two unrelated parties.

We have shown how the **cost principle** is applied in a number of places throughout the text. The cost principle is closely adhered to because it provides amounts that are clearly objective and easily verified.

REVENUE REALIZATION PRINCIPLE One of the major measurement problems of income determination is deciding when revenue should be recognized. The **revenue realization principle** states that revenue should be recognized as earned when the following occurs:

The earnings process is complete or is virtually complete.
An exchange transaction has taken place.

For most business activities, these two conditions are met at the time goods are sold or services are rendered (the point-of-sale method of revenue recognition). For example, revenue from the sale of goods is recognized as earned when title to the goods passes from the seller to the buyer.

Occasionally, however, we must make exceptions to the point-of-sale method of revenue recognition. We will look at two of these exceptions.

*Installment Method:* Some businesses, especially retailers selling home furnishings and appliances, often make sales on an installment basis. The installment sale agreement usually requires that the purchaser make a down payment and agree to pay the remainder of the purchase price in specified amounts at stated intervals over an extended period. The seller may retain title to the property until final payment is received or make arrangements for its repossession if the purchaser defaults on the payments.

Although the agreed-upon conditions under which an installment sale is made may differ substantially from those of other sales, it should ordinarily be accounted for in the same manner as any other sale made on account. Thus revenue for the entire sales price should be recognized at the time the sale occurs, even though the cash will be received in installments. However, there is an exception. In cases where collection of the receivable is not reasonably assured, the recognition of revenue at the point of sale is inappropriate and the *installment method of accounting* may be used.

***2a. The installment method recognizes two portions of each cash collection: (1) a partial recovery of cost, (2) gross profit on the sale***

The **installment method** recognizes a portion of each cash collection as (1) a partial recovery of the cost of the item sold and (2) revenue—that is, gross profit on the sale. For example, suppose the gross profit rate on an installment sale is 40%. As cash collections are received, forty cents of each dollar collected is recognized as gross profit and sixty cents is recognized as a recovery of the cost of the item sold.

To illustrate, assume that in 19X5 a retailer had installment sales totaling \$400,000 and the cost of the items sold amounted to \$240,000. The retailer's gross profit rate is 40% [(\$400,000 − \$240,000) ÷ \$400,000]. Assume also that collections of installment accounts receivable were to be made over three years as follows: first year, \$140,000; second year, \$160,000; third year, \$100,000. The amount of revenue (gross profit) from installment sales recognized in each year is based on the cash collections as computed below.

| YEAR | AMOUNT OF CASH COLLECTED | | GROSS PROFIT RATE | | GROSS PROFIT ON INSTALLMENT SALES |
|---|---|---|---|---|---|
| 1 | \$140,000 | × | 40% | = | \$ 56,000 |
| 2 | 160,000 | × | 40% | = | 64,000 |
| 3 | 100,000 | × | 40% | = | 40,000 |
| Total | \$400,000 | | | | \$160,000 |

Installment sale contracts generally provide for interest payments, in addition to regular installment payments. The amount of each payment representing interest would be recorded and reported by the seller as Interest Revenue. Interest payments have been ignored here to simplify the example. Our purpose is to illustrate that under the installment method, recognition of revenue (gross profit) is delayed until a cash payment is received.

*Percentage-of-Completion Method:* Many companies earn revenues by engaging in construction projects that may take several years to complete. For example, the construction of an office complex, hospital, or oceangoing ship usually takes longer than one year. How much revenue should be recognized and what treatment should be given to the costs incurred during the construction period?

If the point-of-sale method of revenue recognition were followed, net income or net loss on a long-term construction project could not be determined until the project had been completed. Income statements prepared during the construction period would not clearly show the profit-directed activities of the company and as a result would have little or no decision usefulness. Thus an alternative method of recognizing revenue on long-term construction projects, the **percentage-of-completion method,** is often used. The underlying idea is that when the total cost to complete a construction project and the extent of progress toward its completion can be estimated with reasonable reliability, it is preferable to recognize revenue over the project's life instead of waiting until the project has been completed.

*2a. The percentage-of-completion method recognizes revenue over a construction project's life*

The amount of revenue, expense, and gross profit to be recognized in each accounting period is determined on the basis of the estimated percentage of the contract that has been completed during the period. If it is estimated that 20% of the project has been completed in a particular period, then 20% of the expected total revenue from the project would be recognized. The percentage of completion is usually estimated by comparing incurred construction costs with an estimate of the total costs to be incurred on the project. Estimates of completion can also be obtained by consulting with architects, engineers, or other personnel qualified to judge the progress made toward the completion of the project.

To illustrate the procedure, assume that Mercury Construction Company signed a contract to build a hospital wing at a price of $20,000,000. The project is expected to take three years to complete, and its estimated construction costs are $15,000,000. Estimated gross profit on the project is therefore $5,000,000. The following schedule shows the actual costs incurred and the amount of gross profit realized each year.

| YEAR | (A) ACTUAL COST INCURRED | (B) PERCENTAGE OF WORK COMPLETED (A) ÷ ($15,000,000) | (C) GROSS PROFIT RECOGNIZED FOR THE YEAR ($5,000,000) × (B) |
|---|---|---|---|
| 1 | $ 3,000,000 | 20% | $ 1,000,000 |
| 2 | 7,500,000 | 50% | 2,500,000 |
| 3 | 4,700,000 | * | 1,300,000† |
| | $15,200,000 | | $ 4,800,000 |

* Balance required to complete the contract.
† Remaining gross profit (actual gross profit on project less gross profit recognized in first two years).

The percentage of work completed in the first two years was determined by dividing the actual cost incurred by the estimated total cost of the project.

Because it is assumed that incurred costs represent a reliable method for determining progress toward completion of the project, 20% ($3,000,000 ÷ $15,000,000) of the $5,000,000 estimated gross profit was recognized in year 1. Similarly, 50% of the then-estimated total cost was incurred in year 2, and therefore 50% of the estimated gross profit was recognized in year 2. Note that year 3, the year in which construction was completed, was handled differently. In year 3 the total actual construction cost of $15,200,000 is known, and therefore the actual total profit on the project is $4,800,000 ($20,000,000 − $15,200,000). Since the gross profit recognized in years 1 and 2 totaled $3,500,000, only the remaining gross profit of $1,300,000 ($4,800,000 − $3,500,000) can be recognized in year 3. In other words, the gross profit recognized in year 3 is an amount equal to the actual gross profit on the project less the cumulative amount of gross profit recognized in years 1 and 2.

The percentage-of-completion method involves subjective estimates that affect the amount of reported gross profit and the determination of net income. Nevertheless, the method is widely used. Financial statements prepared under the percentage-of-completion method are considered more relevant in depicting the profit-directed activities of an entity and are therefore more useful than the statements would be if none of the revenue were recognized until the long-term project had been completed.

Note that in our example we expected profit in each year of construction. If at the end of any accounting period, construction cost estimates indicate that a loss should be expected on a project in progress, the entire loss should be recognized immediately.

MATCHING PRINCIPLE The **matching principle** holds that the best measure of net income is achieved when expenses for a particular period are matched with the revenue earned during that period.

We use the *realization principle* to determine when revenue should be recognized and reported in the income statement. We use the *matching principle* to determine when costs should be recognized as expenses so that they can be reported in the income statement for the period in which the related revenues were recognized. Three general guidelines are used for recognizing expenses:

Associating cause and effect
Systematic and rational allocation
Immediate recognition

*Associating Cause and Effect:* Costs that have contributed to the earning of revenues should be reported as expenses. Sometimes there is a direct association of expenses with revenues. This means that as certain revenues are recognized, certain costs that relate directly to the revenue-generating process can be identified. For example, when a retailer sells an appliance costing $480 to a customer for $600, the cost of the appliance can be directly associated with the revenue produced by its sale. The $480 cost is matched with the $600 revenue for purposes of determining net income.

*Systematic and Rational Allocation:* Some costs are incurred to acquire assets that are expected to provide benefits for more than one year. The costs of these assets cannot be clearly related to specific revenues and cannot be directly associated with specific accounting periods, yet we know that the assets contribute to revenues over their useful life. We match the costs of these assets with revenue by allocating them to expenses over time periods in a systematic and rational manner. The depreciation of plant assets and the amortization of certain intangible assets are examples of a systematic and rational method for allocating the cost of an asset to the periods expected to benefit from their use.

*Immediate Recognition:* Some costs are recognized as expenses as incurred. These are (1) costs that cannot be directly related to or associated with recognized revenue or (2) costs for which a systematic and rational allocation is not possible because future benefits are uncertain or cannot be objectively measured. Examples of such costs include salaries of officers and supervisors, advertising, and research and development. They are charged to expense as incurred.

CONSISTENCY PRINCIPLE To improve the comparability of accounting information from one period to the next, accountants observe the consistency principle. The **consistency principle** holds that an entity must use the same accounting practices to measure and report its activities from one accounting period to the next.

Because the consistency principle applies to an individual entity, the user of a given firm's financial statements can assume that the same methods and practices were used from year to year. If the consistency principle were not observed, real changes in a firm's financial position or its profitability might be hard to detect.

The consistency principle does not, however, prohibit a company from changing from one accounting method to another if there is a good reason for doing so. Changes in conditions, circumstances, or assumptions often are cited to justify a change. The Accounting Principles Board requires that changes be justified on the basis that the use of the new method is preferable. Furthermore, when a company changes from one accounting method to another, it must disclose the nature of and justification for the change as well as its effect on net income in the financial statements of the period in which the change is made.

FULL DISCLOSURE PRINCIPLE The **full disclosure principle** means that all the accounting information that is believed to be significant to a user in understanding the financial status of an entity must be reported in its financial statements and their accompanying notes. To comply with the disclosure principle, the accountant must follow authoritative pronouncements and must use professional judgment in deciding what information will be useful in making economic decisions.

Full disclosure does not mean that information must be presented in great detail. For example, accountants combine individual customer account balances into a single summarized figure of Accounts Receivable when presenting these data on the balance sheet. Similarly, cash deposited in several bank accounts would be combined and presented as a single Cash figure on the balance sheet. Excessive detail in financial statements may impede rather than promote understandability. As a result, some summarization of reported information is desirable. Of course, all material facts relevant to users should be disclosed in the body of the financial statements or in the accompanying notes to those statements if the goal of full disclosure is to be achieved.

## Modifying Conventions

*1e. Modifying conventions—exceptions to strict application of accounting principles—include materiality, conservatism, and industry practices*

In measuring and reporting financial information, accountants often face practical considerations that cause them to depart from a strict application of accounting principles. These departures are based on modifying conventions. **Modifying conventions** are exceptions to accounting principles based on practical reasons and are discussed in the following three subsections.

MATERIALITY **Materiality** refers to the relative importance or magnitude of an item or event. Deciding whether an item or event is material requires considerable judgment. Because of differences in circumstances, an item judged to be material for one company may not be judged material for another. Both the size and the nature of the item and its relationship to the size and the nature of other items must be considered in making materiality judgments. For example, a $10,000 error in reporting expenses for a company that reports net income of $250,000,000 would probably be viewed as immaterial because it would not be expected to influence the decisions made by users of that statement. However, the same error would probably be material to a company reporting net income of $90,000. On the other hand, an amount resulting from an illegal transaction, such as a bribe payment, would represent a material event for all companies regardless of the amount involved.

To illustrate materiality, assume that a company purchased a pencil sharpener for $7.50 and that it had an expected useful life of five years. Strict adherence to accounting principles would require that it be recorded in the accounts as an asset and depreciated over its useful life. Under the straight-line method, annual depreciation of $1.50 would be recognized. This would be the proper treatment under the matching principle, but would it be practical? Most companies would choose to avoid the cost of maintaining depreciation records for this immaterial amount and would charge the $7.50 cost of the pencil sharpener to an expense account at the time that it was purchased.

The test of materiality is whether the accounting treatment given to the item or event will affect the decisions made by users of the financial statements. In general, an item or event is said to be material if there is a reasonable expectation that knowledge of it would influence the decisions made by informed users of the financial statements.

CONSERVATISM Accounting measurements are made in an attempt to generate fair and reliable financial reports. These measurements often require the making of judgments, assumptions, and estimates in an environment of uncertainty. In dealing with the pervasive uncertainties of accounting measurements, accountants apply the convention of conservatism. The **conservatism convention** holds that when faced with uncertainty and doubt as to which accounting measurement alternative to use, the one least likely to overstate assets and income for the current period should be selected. It describes the tendency of accountants to be cautious or moderate when making measurement decisions that involve judgments, assumptions, and estimates.

The attitude of conservatism is apparent in many areas of accounting. For example, the lower of cost or market basis is used to measure the value of marketable securities and inventory. Here if the market value of the asset is less than its cost, a loss is recognized and reported in that period, even though the asset has not been sold. If market value exceeds cost, however, the gain is not recognized or reported until the period in which the asset is sold.

Conservatism is a useful modifying convention but should be applied only in situations where there is uncertainty and doubt. Overly zealous application can lead to abuses that produce incorrect and misleading financial statements. Examples of overly zealous application would be an attempt to use conservatism as a reason for delaying the recognition of revenues to future periods and charging costs more likely to benefit future periods to the current period.

INDUSTRY PRACTICES Accounting measurements and reporting practices are sometimes modified to recognize the peculiar nature of some industries and businesses. These modifications of basic accounting principles are applied in practice to increase the usefulness of accounting information reported by companies operating in industries having unique characteristics. For example, banks and investment companies often report investment securities at market value. This industry practice is a clear departure from the cost principle. Because these securities constitute most of the companies' assets, and are traded frequently, many believe that reporting them at market value provides more useful information. Furthermore, the industry's practice of recognizing and reporting unrealized holding gains on these securities in their income statement is an exception to the revenue realization principle.

Exceptions to strict adherence to accounting principles are not many, but variations do exist in the insurance, mutual fund, agricultural, meatpacking, and public utility industries. For example, public utility companies report plant assets before current assets on their balance sheets to emphasize the capital-intensive nature of their business.

The **industry practices convention** holds that the unique characteristics of an industry may make modifications of accounting principles necessary in order to provide the most useful accounting information.

## THE EFFECTS OF CHANGING PRICES

### General Discussion

*1f. Price changes over time make the dollar an inconsistent unit of measure*

The conventional financial statements described in earlier chapters have for many years served the needs of the business and financial community by providing information that is useful in making rational economic decisions. However, they are based on historical cost, with the implicit assumption that the dollar as a unit of measure remains stable or constant over time. The fact that a significant upward movement in prices has been occurring for more than two decades means that the **purchasing power** of the dollar (the amount of goods and services that can be bought with the dollar) has declined instead of remaining constant. The nature of the problem is illustrated in the following two examples.

1. Assume that in 19X0 a company purchased as an investment a tract of land costing $60,000. Five years later, in 19X5, the land was sold for $80,000. Under conventional accounting practices, based on historical cost and the assumption that the dollar as a unit of measure is stable, the $80,000 received in payment represents two elements:

A $60,000 return of the asset's cost

A $20,000 gain on the sale

The $20,000 gain would be reported in the company's 19X5 income statement and would be reflected in that period's net income.

If the purchasing power of the dollar remained constant during the five-year period that the land was held, the company's monetary gain, represented by the increase in the number of dollars, would be the same as its purchasing-power gain. That is, the company has $20,000 more than it started out with, and each dollar has the same purchasing power in 19X5 that it had in 19X0 when the land was purchased.

On the other hand, if, while the land was held, the price level (discussed shortly) rose from 100 to 150, how should the gain be measured? Conventional accounting recognizes the gain of $20,000 (gain measured in number of dollars).

However, in dollars of constant purchasing power, the company would need \$90,000 at current price levels to get back the purchasing power it had when the land investment was made (\$60,000 × 150/100 = \$90,000). Measured in terms of purchasing power, the company experienced a \$10,000 loss on its 19X5 transaction. Many would contend that this measurement procedure more accurately reflects the result of the land sale transaction.

2. Historical cost financial statements often consist of aggregated amounts of dollars from different years. For example, the costs of assets purchased in different years are combined and shown as one aggregate amount on the balance sheet. To illustrate the problems associated with this practice, assume that a company purchased equipment costing \$100,000 in 19X1 when the price level was 100. In 19X2, when the price level was 110, the company purchased additional equipment costing \$100,000. In 19X3, when the price level was 120, it made another equipment purchase costing \$100,000. Based on the 19X3 price level, it would take \$120 to purchase the same amount of goods and services that could have been purchased in 19X1 for \$100. Yet under conventional accounting, the company would record each purchase transaction at acquisition cost and report Equipment of \$300,000 in its 19X3 balance sheet. Dollars from different years, which in this case are specifically different dollars in terms of purchasing power, are combined and shown in total in the conventional financial statements.

To the extent that conventional accounting does not deal with changing prices, alternative practices must be introduced. We can best understand these practices by first considering the nature and types of price changes.

## Nature and Types of Price Changes

*1f. Price levels may exhibit a sustained increase (inflation) or a sustained decrease (deflation)*

**A price change** is an increase or decrease in the price of a good or service. The amount of goods or services that can be purchased with a given amount of currency (dollars) changes over time. When the overall level of prices for goods and services throughout our economy is increasing, the purchasing power of the dollar decreases. Periods of sustained increases in the overall level of prices are known as periods of **inflation.** Periods of sustained decreases in the overall level of prices, which result in increasing the purchasing power of the dollar, are known as periods of **deflation.**

Price changes are of two types: (1) general price-level changes and (2) specific price-level changes.

*1f. General price-level changes refer to changes in the weighted average price of all goods and services in the economy*

GENERAL PRICE-LEVEL CHANGES **General price-level changes** are changes in the weighted average price of all goods and services in the economy. These changes are measured by using a general price-level index prepared by the federal government. Several different price indexes are constructed by the government, each based on a predetermined sample group or "market basket" of goods and services.

We can more readily understand the process by constructing our own price index. Suppose we want to measure the change in the overall prices for a group of goods, identified as items A, B, C, and D, for the period between January 1 and December 31 as shown on page 752.

The illustration shows that prices for the predetermined market basket of goods A, B, C, and D increased by an average of about 7% between the beginning and the end of the year. Consequently, the purchasing power of the dollar in terms of the amount of items A, B, C, and D that can be purchased has decreased by about 7% for the year. The prices of individual items changed in different

| ITEM | PRICE PER UNIT JANUARY 1 | PRICE PER UNIT DECEMBER 31 | PERCENTAGE CHANGE IN MARKET PRICE OF INDIVIDUAL ITEMS |
|---|---|---|---|
| A | $ 4.00 | $ 4.60 | +15% |
| B | 9.00 | 9.92 | +10% |
| C | 5.50 | 5.17 | − 6% |
| D | 9.75 | 10.54 | + 8% |
| Total | $28.25 | $30.23 | |
| | PRICE INDEX JANUARY 1 | PRICE INDEX DECEMBER 31 | |
| | 100 | 107 (= $30.23/$28.25) | |

directions and at different rates. However, if the group represents a typical market basket of items purchased by an individual or business, the 7% average fairly reflects the decrease in the purchasing power of the dollar over the specified time period.

Two widely used general price-level indexes, both constructed by the government, are the *Consumer Price Index* published monthly by the Bureau of Labor Statistics and the *Gross National Product Implicit Price Deflator Index* published quarterly by the U.S. Department of Commerce.

*1f. Specific price-level changes refer to changes in the price of a specific good or service or a specified narrow grouping of goods or services*

SPECIFIC PRICE-LEVEL CHANGES **Specific price-level changes** are changes in the prices of a specific good or service or a specified narrow grouping of goods and services. Prices for specific items may change at a different rate or even in a different direction from the general level of prices in the economy. For example, in a given year the prices of health-care services may be rising at a rate of 15%, thereby exceeding the rise in the general price level, while the price of hand-held calculators may be decreasing by 10%.

## TWO APPROACHES TO ACCOUNTING FOR THE EFFECTS OF CHANGING PRICES

In an attempt to develop a method of accounting for the effects of changing prices on amounts reported in financial statements, several approaches have been suggested. The two that are receiving the most attention are (1) constant dollar accounting and (2) current cost accounting. Each of these will be discussed in the next two subsections.

### Constant Dollar Accounting

The historical cost amounts reported in conventional financial statements are restated for changes in the purchasing power of the dollar by using a general price-level index. Under **constant dollar accounting** all financial statement amounts are stated in dollars of common purchasing power, thereby obtaining a uniform or constant measuring unit. The conversion to dollars of common purchasing power is accomplished by using a conversion formula whereby a historical cost amount is multiplied by the index of the year we are converting to and divided by the index of the year we are converting from.

*2b. The use of constant dollar accounting is illustrated here*

To illustrate the process, assume that land costing $50,000 was purchased in December 1975 when the general price-level index was 166.3. The general price-level index nine years later, on December 31, 1984, was 311.1. Using these indexes, we can convert the original cost of the land to 1984 end-of-the-year dollars of purchasing power as follows:

$$\text{Historical Cost} \times \frac{\text{Index of the Year Being Converted to}}{\text{Index of the Year Being Converted from}} = \text{Restated Amount in 1984 Dollars}$$

$$\$50{,}000 \times \frac{311.1}{166.3} = \$93{,}535.78$$

Land would be reported on the December 31, 1984, constant dollar balance sheet at its restated amount of $93,536 (rounded). The restated amount does not represent the current market value of the land or the cost to purchase the same parcel of land at the end of 1984, because the adjustment did not reflect specific price-level changes occurring in real estate. These could have changed in a direction and pattern entirely different from the general price change. The restatement does show that $50,000 spent at the end of 1975 had, when it was spent, the general purchasing power equivalent to that of $93,536 at the end of 1984.

Let us look at another example to further illustrate the use of index numbers to restate historical cost dollars to current dollars. Assume that the data below pertain to a company's holdings of the noncurrent asset equipment.

| YEAR ACQUIRED | ACQUISITION COST | CPI–U INDEX (ROUNDED) |
|---|---|---|
| 1965 | $10,000 | 95 |
| 1969 | 20,000 | 110 |
| 1975 | 20,000 | 161 |
| 1984 | 10,000 | 311 |
| | $60,000 | |

If the constant dollar financial statements were prepared on December 31, 1984, the acquisition costs of these assets would be restated in terms of 1984 dollars as follows.

| | | | | | | |
|---|---|---|---|---|---|---|
| 1965: | 311/95 | × | $10,000 | = | $ 32,737 |
| 1969: | 311/110 | × | 20,000 | = | 56,545 |
| 1975: | 311/161 | × | 20,000 | = | 38,634 |
| 1984: | 311/311 | × | 10,000 | = | 10,000 |
| Restated in terms of 1984 end-of-year dollars | | | | | $137,916 |

In the conventional financial statements, the company would report the equipment at its historical cost of $60,000. In the constant dollar financial statements, the equipment would be reported in terms of 1984 year-end dollars as $137,916.

When preparing constant dollar financial statements, it is important to distinguish between monetary and nonmonetary items because they are treated differently.

MONETARY ITEMS **Monetary items** are assets or liabilities that represent the right to receive or the obligation to pay a fixed number of dollars in the future regardless of the change in the price level. Monetary assets include cash, accounts receivable, notes receivable, interest receivable and most investments in preferred stock and bonds. Most liabilities are monetary items and include accounts, notes, interest, and bonds payable. Monetary items are reported only on the balance sheet. Because monetary items represent claims to a fixed dollar amount, no restatement is necessary. The amounts reported for monetary items on the conventionally prepared balance sheet are the same as those reported on the constant dollar balance sheet.

However, the holding of monetary items over time while the general purchasing power of the dollar changes will result in a *purchasing power gain or loss.* For example, holding cash during a period of rising prices causes a **purchasing power loss** because the cash will buy fewer goods and services as more and more time passes. On the other hand, the holder of a monetary liability during a period of rising prices experiences a **purchasing power gain** because the dollars needed in the future to repay the debt will have less purchasing power than the dollars originally borrowed. The results will of course reverse during periods of falling prices (deflation).

The computation of purchasing power gains and losses is illustrated in the following two examples.

*Example 1—Purchasing Power Loss:* Assume that on January 1, 1984, a company had a cash balance of $25,000, which was held throughout the year. If the general price-level index increased during the year from 298 to 311, the company would, as a consequence of holding the monetary asset Cash, experience a purchasing power loss of $1,091, computed as follows.

| | |
|---|---|
| Number of dollars needed to maintain the original purchasing power of cash ($25,000 × 311/298) | $26,091 |
| Actual number of dollars held at end of the year | 25,000 |
| Purchasing power loss | $ 1,091 |

*Example 2—Purchasing Power Gain:* Assume that on January 1, 1984, the company became obligated for a note payable of $40,000, and the note remained outstanding throughout the year. The purchasing power gain from having the monetary liability Note Payable for the full year is $1,745, computed as follows:

| | |
|---|---|
| Number of year-end dollars representing the same purchasing power as the amount owed on January 1, 1984 ($40,000 × 311/298) | $41,745 |
| Number of dollars actually owed on December 31, 1984 | 40,000 |
| Purchasing power gain | $ 1,745 |

As we will see in a later illustration, the net gain or loss from holding monetary items is reported as an element of constant dollar net income.

NONMONETARY ITEMS **Nonmonetary items** are assets and equities that do not represent claims to a fixed number of dollars in the future. All the items that are not monetary in nature are classified as nonmonetary items. Examples of nonmonetary items include inventories, investments in common stock of other companies, plant assets, intangibles, capital stock, and retained earnings. Nonmonetary items are reported on the balance sheet along with monetary items. All revenues, expenses, gains, and losses reported on the income statement are nomonetary items.

No purchasing power gain or loss is recognized from holding nonmonetary items. Their historical cost amounts reported in conventional financial statements are, however, restated to dollars of uniform or constant purchasing power. This is done to recognize the effect of changes in the general price level from the time the items were originally acquired to the constant dollar restatement date.

**PREPARING A CONSTANT DOLLAR BALANCE SHEET** When preparing a constant dollar balance sheet, we must distinguish between monetary and nonmonetary items because they are treated differently. Monetary items are not restated. However, the net purchasing power gain or loss resulting from holding monetary items is recognized in the constant dollar balance sheet as an adjustment to owners' equity. Nonmonetary items are restated in terms of constant dollars for the constant dollar balance sheet.

To illustrate, assume that Windsor Company was organized on January 1, 19X2, when the general price index was 100. Assume also that common stock was issued, and all inventories and land were acquired on that date. The company's conventional balance sheet on January 1, 19X2, is shown below.

WINDSOR COMPANY
Balance Sheet
January 1, 19X2

| ASSETS | |
|---|---|
| Cash | $ 10,000 |
| Inventory | 30,000 |
| Land | 60,000 |
| Total Assets | $100,000 |
| STOCKHOLDERS' EQUITY | |
| Common Stock | $100,000 |
| Total Stockholders' Equity | $100,000 |

For purposes of this illustration, assume that no other transactions occurred during the year. By the end of the year, the general price index was 120. Since no transactions occurred during the year the company's conventional balance sheet as of December 31, 19X2, would be the same as its January 1, 19X2, balance sheet. Its constant dollar balance sheet as of December 31, 19X2, however, would appear as shown at the top of page 756. (For illustrative purposes, the restatement computations are shown in parentheses next to the amounts.)

Note two important things about the restatement of historical cost amounts for general price-level changes:

Restatement for general price-level changes is not a departure from the historical cost principle but is a departure from the stable monetary unit assumption.

Restated amounts show changes in the purchasing power of the monetary unit over time.

**PREPARING A CONSTANT DOLLAR INCOME STATEMENT** When preparing a constant dollar income statement, all revenues and expenses are restated

WINDSOR COMPANY
Constant Dollar Balance Sheet
December 31, 19X2

| ASSETS | | |
|---|---|---|
| Cash | $ 10,000 | (Monetary asset already stated in constant dollars. No restatement.) |
| Inventory | 36,000 | (Nonmonetary asset restated in constant dollars: $30,000 × 120/100) |
| Land | 72,000 | (Nonmonetary asset restated in constant dollars: $60,000 × 120/100) |
| Total Assets | $118,000 | |
| STOCKHOLDERS' EQUITY | | |
| Common Stock | $120,000 | (Nonmonetary item restated in constant dollars: $100,000 × 120/100) |
| Retained Earnings (deficit) | (2,000) | (Purchasing power loss on net monetary items: $10,000 of cash × 120/100 less $10,000) |
| Total Stockholders' Equity | $118,000 | |

to end-of-the-year constant dollars by use of a price-level index. The net purchasing power gain or loss on monetary items is then computed. This amount is added to or subtracted from the income or loss before the purchasing power gain or loss to determine the constant dollar net income or loss.

To illustrate, assume that Windsor Company has operated for five years since its inception and its conventional income statement for the year ended December 31, 19X6, is as follows.

WINDSOR COMPANY
Income Statement
For the Year Ended December 31, 19X6

| | | |
|---|---|---|
| Sales | | $100,000 |
| Less: Cost of Goods Sold | | 45,000 |
| Gross Profit on Sales | | $ 55,000 |
| Selling and Administrative Expenses | $20,000 | |
| Depreciation Expense | 10,000 | |
| Total Expenses | | 30,000 |
| Income before Income Taxes | | $ 25,000 |
| Income Taxes | | 10,000 |
| Net Income | | $ 15,000 |

Additional information follows:

1. Sales revenue was earned and expenses (except depreciation) were incurred evenly throughout the year.
2. Inventory items were purchased evenly throughout the year. The company uses the first-in, first-out inventory method, and there was no significant difference between the beginning and ending inventory amounts.
3. Equipment was acquired in 19X3 when the general price index was 125. The equipment is being depreciated under the straight-line method, using an estimated useful life of ten years and no salvage value.

4. The following 19X6 general price indexes are assumed for purposes of this illustration:
Average price index during 19X6—155
Year-end price index 19X6—160

*2b. A constant dollar income statement is illustrated here*

Windsor Company's constant dollar income statement for the year ended 19X6, with restatement computations shown parenthetically, would appear as follows.

| WINDSOR COMPANY<br>Constant Dollar Income Statement<br>For the Year Ended December 31, 19X6 | | | |
|---|---|---|---|
| Sales | | $103,226 | (Made evenly throughout the year. Restated in constant dollars: $100,000 × 160/155) |
| Less: Cost of Goods Sold | | 46,452 | (Goods purchased evenly throughout the year. Restated in constant dollars: $45,000 × 160/155) |
| Gross Profit on Sales | | $ 56,774 | |
| Selling and Administrative Expenses | $20,645 | | (Incurred evenly throughout the year. Restated in constant dollars: $20,000 × 160/155) |
| Depreciation Expense | 12,800 | | (Equipment purchased in 19X3 when the price index was 125. Restated in constant dollars: $10,000 × 160/125) |
| Total Expenses | | 33,445 | |
| Income before Taxes | | $ 23,329 | |
| Income Taxes | | 10,323 | (Incurred evenly throughout the year. Restated in constant dollars: $10,000 × 160/155) |
| Income before Purchasing Power Loss | | $ 13,006 | |
| Purchasing Power Loss | | (4,130) | (Amount assumed in illustration. A result of holding monetary assets during a period of rising prices) |
| Constant Dollar Net Income | | $ 8,876 | |

There is obviously a considerable difference between Windsor Company's conventionally determined net income of $15,000 and its constant dollar net income of $8,876. There are two major reasons for the difference: (1) the restatement of Depreciation Expense, which shows the cumulative effect of rising prices since the depreciable equipment was acquired, and (2) the purchasing power loss resulting from holding monetary assets during a period of rising prices (inflation). Should inflation persist, the restated Depreciation Expense will become even higher in future years. For example, if next year's price index is 170 instead of 160, Depreciation Expense would be restated at $13,600 ($10,000 × 170/125) in the company's income statement for the year ended December 31, 19X7. On the other hand, if next year the sum of purchasing power gains resulting from holding monetary liabilities exceeds the purchasing power losses resulting from holding monetary assets, the company will show a purchasing power gain.

## Current Cost Accounting

The objective of current cost accounting is to report amounts in the financial statements that reflect the effects of specific price changes. Under **current cost accounting,** historical cost amounts reported in the conventional financial statements are restated and reported at their current cost. The effect of specific price-level changes on items reported in conventional financial statements depends on the amount and direction of the change in specific prices of the firm's assets and liabilities and on the type of assets and liabilities that the firm holds.

CURRENT COSTS IN THE FINANCIAL STATEMENTS Assets are reported at their **current cost**—the amount that the company would have to pay currently to acquire them in their present condition. Liabilities are reported at the amounts that the company would have to pay currently to satisfy them. Once again, a distinction is made between *monetary* and *nonmonetary* assets and liabilities. Monetary assets and monetary liabilities have already been stated at current amounts in the conventional balance sheet and therefore do not need to be restated when preparing a current cost balance sheet. Nonmonetary assets such as inventory and plant assets must be restated to reflect their current cost on the date that the current cost balance sheet is prepared. Several sources of information can be consulted when determining the current cost of a specific nonmonetary asset. For example, the current cost of inventory can be determined on the basis of price quotations for the items held in the inventory obtained from the suppliers of those items or from the suppliers' current price catalog. Another approach would be for the company to develop a specific price index for the inventory items whose current cost is being measured. The current cost of land can be determined by referring to prices currently being quoted in the marketplace for similar parcels of land or by obtaining appraisals. Vehicles, machines, and similar plant assets frequently have a used asset market that can be consulted to determine their current cost.

*2c. The use of current cost accounting is illustrated here*

In the process of restating the historical costs of nonmonetary items to current costs, holding gains and losses are determined. For example, assume that on January 1, 1987, a company purchased land for $45,000 and that its current cost on December 31, 1987, is $50,000. On the current cost balance sheet, the land would be reported at $50,000. The current cost income statement for the year ended December 31, 1987, would show an unrealized holding gain of $5,000, which represents the increase of the current cost over the historical acquisition cost of the land. The $5,000 holding gain is called unrealized because the land has not been sold. If the land is subsequently sold for $50,000, the company's current cost income statement for that period would show a realized holding gain of $5,000.

It is important that we understand how holding gains and losses are reported in current cost financial statements. An increase in the current cost of an asset being held is recognized as a **holding gain,** whereas a decrease in the current cost of an asset being held is recognized as a **holding loss. Realized holding gains or losses** are computed when a nonmonetary asset is sold or consumed in operations (that is, when its original cost is changed to expense).

To illustrate the procedure involved in holding gains and losses, assume that Hilltop Company began operations on January 1, 1987, by issuing common stock for cash of $50,000. It used some of the proceeds to acquire 10,000 units of inventory at $3 per unit for a total acquisition cost of $30,000. During 1987 the company had the following transactions:

Sold 8,000 units @ $8 per unit—$64,000
Incurred operating expenses (all paid in cash)—$25,000

Assume further that by April 1, 1987, before any inventory was sold, its current replacement cost increased to $3.50 per unit and remained at that cost until December 31, 1987, the end of the company's accounting period. Under the current cost approach to accounting, gross profit on sales is determined by deducting from revenue the cost of the goods sold at the amount required to replace the inventory items at the time that they were sold. Operating income is then determined by deducting from gross profit the operating expenses at the amount incurred when the expense occurred. Hilltop's current operating income under current cost accounting would be $11,000, computed as follows.

| | | |
|---|---|---|
| Sales | $64,000 | |
| Cost of Goods Sold | 28,000 | (8,000 units at a replacement cost of $3.50 at the time the units were sold) |
| Gross Profit on Sales | $36,000 | |
| Operating Expenses | 25,000 | (at amount incurred when expenses occurred) |
| Operating Income | $11,000 | |

Hilltop would then report a realized holding gain of $4,000, which is the difference between the current cost of the merchandise sold (as computed in the current cost income statement) and the original cost of merchandise sold [$28,000 − $24,000 (8,000 units sold × the original cost of $3 per unit) = $4,000]. The gain is called a holding gain because it relates to an increase in the current cost of an asset (inventory) occurring during the period in which the asset was held by the company. If the current cost of the inventory had decreased, the amount calculated would be called a realized holding loss.

**Unrealized holding gains or losses** are also recognized under current cost accounting. Increases in the current cost of nonmonetary assets that are still on hand at year-end result in unrealized holding gains. Conversely, when the current cost of nonmonetary assets on hand at year-end decreases below their acquisition cost, an unrealized holding loss is recognized. Since the current cost of Hilltop's ending inventory, consisting of 2,000 units, has increased by fifty cents per unit above its acquisition cost, the company has experienced an unrealized holding gain of $1,000 (2,000 units × $.50 per unit = $1,000).

Holding gains and losses are shown separately from the company's operating income. For comparative purposes, we show items and amounts reported in Hilltop's conventional income statement and current cost income statement side by side below.

| CONVENTIONAL INCOME STATEMENT | | CURRENT COST INCOME STATEMENT | |
|---|---|---|---|
| Sales | $64,000 | Sales | $64,000 |
| Cost of Goods Sold (8,000 × $3.00) | 24,000 | Cost of Goods Sold (8,000 × $3.50) | 28,000 |
| Gross Profit on Sales | $40,000 | Gross Profit on Sales | $36,000 |
| Operating Expenses | 25,000 | Operating Expenses | 25,000 |
| Operating Income | $15,000 | Operating Income | $11,000 |
| Realized Holding Gain | — | Realized Holding Gain (8,000 × $.50) | 4,000 |
| Unrealized Holding Gain | — | Unrealized Holding Gain (2,000 × $.50) | 1,000 |
| Net Income | $15,000 | Net Income | $16,000 |

Thus the net income reported in the current cost income statement exceeds the net income reported in the conventional income statement by $1,000. The amount will be included in the Retained Earnings account on the December 31 current cost balance sheet, shown below. The Inventory account will also show its current replacement cost of \$7,000 (2,000 units × \$3.50) instead of its acquisition cost of \$6,000 (2,000 units × \$3.00).

HILLTOP CORPORATION
Current Cost Balance Sheet
December 31, 19X7

| ASSETS | | EQUITIES | |
|---|---|---|---|
| Cash* | \$59,000 | Common Stock | \$50,000 |
| Inventory | 7,000 | Retained Earnings | 16,000 |
| Total Assets | \$66,000 | Total Equities | \$66,000 |

* \$50,000 on common stock sale − \$30,000 spent on inventory + \$64,000 assumed to be collected on sales − \$25,000 for operating expenses = \$59,000.

Proponents of current cost financial statements feel that the current cost balance sheet provides a more realistic indication of the current value of assets and liabilities than do conventional balance sheets based on historical costs. Furthermore, they would argue that the separation of business income into operating income, realized holding gains or losses, and unrealized gains or losses is useful to statement readers in assessing the impact of changing prices on the earnings of a firm. Opponents of current cost accounting question the reliability of current cost amounts used in the preparation of statements for a given firm and voice concern about the comparability of current cost data among firms.

## CURRENTLY REQUIRED DISCLOSURES OF THE EFFECTS OF CHANGING PRICES

In 1979 the Financial Accounting Standards Board issued Statement No. 33, which addressed the disclosure and reporting of certain supplementary information about the effects of changing prices. The requirements set forth in the statement apply only to large publicly held companies that have either (1) inventories and property, plant, and equipment (before deducting accumulated depreciation) amounting to more than \$125 million or (2) total assets amounting to more than \$1 billion (after deducting accumulated depreciation). In November 1984 the board issued Statement No. 82 as an amendment of Statement 33, which eliminated the requirement for supplementary information on a constant dollar basis while maintaining the disclosure requirements of certain current cost information. In any case, note that the information required is to be presented as supplementary information to the conventional (historical cost based) financial statements and does not affect the measurement or reporting of items in the historical cost statements, which remain the primary statements. The major supplementary disclosures required* include the following:

*1g. The FASB requires five major disclosures of the effects of changing prices*

1. Income from continuing operations for the current fiscal year on a current cost basis.
2. The current cost amounts of inventory and property, plant, and equipment at the end of the current fiscal year.

* As we go to print, the FASB has under consideration a proposal that would make these supplementary disclosures optional.

3. Increases or decreases for the current fiscal year in the current cost amounts of inventory and property, plant, and equipment, net of inflation. (We have referred to these increases and decreases as holding gains and losses.)
4. For each of its five most recent fiscal years, schedules and notes should disclose the current cost amounts for
   a. Net sales and other operating revenues
   b. Income from continuing operations
   c. Income per common share from continuing operations
   d. Increases or decreases in the current cost amounts of inventory and property, plant, and equipment net of inflation
5. Other five-year summary data that should be disclosed include
   a. Purchasing power gain or loss on monetary items
   b. Cash dividends declared per common share
   c. Market price per common share at fiscal year-end

An example of these disclosures as made by PepsiCo, Inc., in its 1984 annual report is reproduced in the accompanying tables.

Statement of Earnings Adjusted for the Effects of Inflation—for the Year Ended December 29, 1984 (in thousands except per share amounts)

| | AS REPORTED IN THE PRIMARY FINANCIAL STATEMENTS (HISTORICAL COST) | ADJUSTED FOR CHANGES IN SPECIFIC PRICES (CURRENT COST) |
|---|---|---|
| Net sales | $7,698,678 | $7,698,678 |
| Cost of sales, excluding depreciation | $3,065,935 | $3,076,000 |
| Depreciation and amortization | 244,798 | 307,521 |
| Other operating expenses, net | 3,692,747 | 3,692,747 |
| Net interest expense | 120,825 | 120,825 |
| Provision for restructuring | 220,000 | 220,000 |
| Provision for income taxes | 147,701 | 147,701 |
| | $7,492,006 | $7,564,794 |
| Income from continuing operations | $ 206,672 | $ 133,884 |
| Per common share | $ 2.19 | $ 1.43 |
| Purchasing power gain on net monetary liabilities | | $ 61,648 |
| Effect of changes in general price level and specific prices on inventories and property, plant and equipment during the year: | | |
| Increase in general price level | | $ 96,867 |
| Decrease in specific prices (current costs)* | | 126,267 |
| Excess of increase in general price level over decrease in specific prices | | $ 223,134 |

* At December 29, 1984 current cost of inventory was $469,503 compared to $451,781 at historical cost. The current cost of property, plant and equipment, net of accumulated depreciation, was $2,645,512 compared to $2,163,013 at historical cost.

Five-Year Comparison of Selected Supplementary Financial Data Adjusted for the Effects of Inflation (in thousands of average 1984 dollars except per share amounts)

| | 1984 | 1983 | 1982 | 1981 | 1980 |
|---|---|---|---|---|---|
| Net sales | $7,698,678 | $7,470,556 | $7,327,251 | $7,199,034 | $6,703,520 |
| Current Cost Information: | | | | | |
| Income from continuing operations | $ 133,884* | $ 211,236 | $ 132,278† | $ 219,603 | $ 207,013 |
| Per common share | $ 1.43* | $ 2.25 | $ 1.43† | $ 2.40 | $ 2.27 |
| Excess of increase in general price level over the change in specific prices | $ 223,134 | $ 123,861 | $ 121,937 | $ 157,224 | $ 115,562 |
| Net assets | $2,353,303 | $2,556,267 | $2,512,964 | $2,583,667 | $2,573,512 |
| Other information: | | | | | |
| Purchasing power gain on net monetary liabilities | $ 61,648 | $ 47,745 | $ 47,819 | $ 107,933 | $ 132,025 |
| Cash dividends declared per common share | $ 1.665 | $ 1.668 | $ 1.700 | $ 1.622 | $ 1.589 |
| Market price per common share at year end | $ 41.29 | $ 39.21 | $ 36.18 | $ 40.20 | $ 31.30 |
| Average consumer price index (1967 = 100) | 311.1 | 298.4 | 289.1 | 272.4 | 246.8 |

* After $121,300 in after-tax charges ($1.26 per share) related to a series of restructuring actions (see Note 2 to Consolidated Financial Statements).
† After a $79,400 charge ($.83 per share) related to a reduction in the net assets of foreign bottling operations. This charge was without tax benefit (see Note 2 to Consolidated Financial Statements).

## HIGHLIGHT PROBLEM

Lassale Company's financial statements prepared in accordance with generally accepted accounting principles are shown below.

LASSALE COMPANY
Balance Sheet
December 31, 19X7

| | | | |
|---|---|---|---|
| Cash | $ 30,000 | Accounts Payable | $ 15,000 |
| Inventory | 20,000 | Common Stock | 60,000 |
| Land | 50,000 | Retained Earnings | 25,000 |
| Total Assets | $100,000 | Total Liabilities and Stockholders' Equity | $100,000 |

LASSALE COMPANY
Income Statement
For the Year Ended December 31, 19X7

| | |
|---|---|
| Sales | $90,000* |
| Less: Cost of Goods Sold | 50,000* |
| Gross Profit on Sales | $40,000 |
| Selling and Administrative Expenses | 30,000* |
| Income before Income Taxes | $10,000 |
| Income Taxes | 3,000* |
| Net Income | $ 7,000 |

* Made or incurred evenly throughout the year.
Data concerning general price-level indexes at various times:

Beginning of the year 19X7—145 On date land was purchased—130
End of the year 19X7—160 On date common stock was issued—110
Average for the year 19X7—150

Required:

1. Using the data presented and assuming that (1) inventory was purchased evenly throughout the year and (2) a purchasing power loss of $900 was computed during the year, prepare the following:
   a. A constant dollar balance sheet at December 31, 19X7
   b. A constant dollar income statement for the year ended December 31, 19X7
2. Where applicable, show how the amounts were computed by making parenthetical notations in the statements.

## GLOSSARY OF KEY TERMS

**Accounting entity.** An economic unit that controls resources and engages in economic activities.

**Comprehensive income.** As used by the Financial Accounting Standards Board in Concepts Statement No. 3, comprehensive income includes all the changes in net assets resulting from transactions, events, and circumstances other than investments by or distributions to owners.

**Conservatism convention.** A modifying convention that holds that when faced with uncertainty and doubt as to which accounting measurement alternative to use, the one least likely to overstate assets and income for the current period should be selected.

**Consistency principle.** A principle that holds that an entity must use the same accounting practices to measure and report its activities from one accounting period to the next.

**Constant dollar accounting.** The restatement, in dollars of constant purchasing power, of historical cost amounts reported in conventional financial statements for changes in the purchasing power of the dollar using a general price-level index.

**Continuity assumption.** Alternate term for *going concern assumption.*

**Cost principle.** The principle that states that the cost incurred at the time the transaction occurs is the basis for initially recording goods and services acquired by an enterprise. Cost is measured by the amount of cash or cash equivalent given to acquire goods or services in an exchange transaction between two unrelated parties.

**Current cost.** The amount that would have to be paid currently to acquire an asset in its present condition.

**Current cost accounting.** The restatement of historical cost amounts reported in conventional financial statements on the basis of current cost.

**Deflation.** A sustained decrease in prices in general, accompanied by a rise in the purchasing power of money.

**Entity assumption.** The assumption that information is accumulated for a specific economic unit called an entity. In accounting, the business activities of an entity are separated from the personal activities of its owners.

**Full disclosure principle.** An accounting principle designed to ensure that all information believed to be significant to a user in understanding the financial status of an entity will be reported in the financial statements and their accompanying notes.

**General price-level changes.** Changes in the weighted average price of all goods and services in the economy.

**Generally Accepted Accounting Principles (GAAP).** A common set of assumptions, concepts, and practices that accountants follow in preparing external financial statements.

**Going concern (continuity) assumption.** The assumption that an entity will continue to operate in the future unless there is evidence to the contrary, and that it will remain in operation long enough to carry out its plans and commitments.

**Holding gain.** An increase in the current cost of an asset being held.

**Holding loss.** A decrease in the current cost of an asset being held.

**Industry practices convention.** The modifying convention that holds that the unique characteristics of an industry may make modifications of accounting principles necessary in order to provide the most useful accounting information.

**Inflation.** A sustained increase in prices in general, accompanied by a decline in the purchasing power of money.

**Installment method.** A revenue recognition procedure in accounting for certain installment sales under which gross profit is recognized in proportion to the amount of cash collected on the installment account receivable.

**Matching principle.** The accounting principle that states that the best measure of net income is achieved by matching against the revenues earned during the period the expenses incurred in generating the revenues. The principle is fundamental to the accrual basis of accounting.

**Materiality.** The relative importance or magnitude of an item or event. A modifying convention in accounting that recognizes that some deviation from strict adherence to GAAP for immaterial items and amounts may be justified by practicality.

**Modifying conventions.** Exceptions to accounting principles based on practical reasons.

**Monetary items.** Assets and liabilities that represent claims to a fixed number of dollars in the future regardless of the change in the price level.

**Monetary unit assumption.** The assumption that money is the appropriate measuring unit and thus serves as the common denominator for measuring and reporting an entity's economic activity.

**Nonmonetary items.** Assets and liabilities that do not represent claims to a fixed number of dollars in the future.

**Objectivity principle.** The principle that states that accounting information should be free from bias and based on verifiable evidence.

**Percentage-of-completion method.** A revenue recognition procedure in accounting for long-term construction projects under which gross profit is recognized in proportion to an estimate of the progress made toward the project's completion during the period.

**Periodicity assumption.** Alternate term for *time period assumption.*

**Price change.** An increase or decrease in the price of a good or service.

**Purchasing power.** The amount of goods and services that can be purchased with a dollar (or other unit measurement of money).

**Purchasing power gain.** The gain that results from holding monetary assets during a period of declining prices or monetary liabilities during a period of rising prices.

**Purchasing power loss.** The loss that results from holding monetary assets during a period of rising prices or monetary liabilities during a period of declining prices.

**Realized holding gains and losses.** Holding gains or losses relating to nonmonetary assets that have been sold or consumed in operations as an expense.

**Revenue realization principle.** The principle in accounting that states that revenue should be recognized as earned when the earnings process is complete or virtually complete and an exchange transaction has taken place.

**Specific price-level changes.** Changes in the prices of a specific good or service or a specified narrow group of goods or services.

**Time period (periodicity) assumption.** An assumption that a firm's life span can be divided into a series of arbitrary short time periods and that the firm's economic activities can be appropriately related to those time periods.

**Unrealized holding gains and losses.** Holding gains or losses relating to nonmonetary assets that are still on hand and have not been sold or consumed in operations as an expense.

## REVIEW QUESTIONS

1. Name three characteristics that information contained in the financial statements should have. [LO1a]
2. Name three organizations that have contributed to the development of generally accepted accounting principles. [LO1b]
3. What are the qualitative characteristics that make accounting information useful? [LO1d]
4. What three elements, identified in Concepts Statement No. 3, relate to measuring the financial position of an enterprise? [LO1c]
5. What seven elements, identified in Concepts Statement No. 3, relate to the reporting of changes in the financial position of an enterprise? [LO1c]
6. What is meant by the entity assumption, and why is it important? [LO1e]
7. What is meant by the going concern assumption? What accounting practices receive their justification and support from this assumption? [LO1e]
8. Of what significance to accounting is the time period assumption? [LO1e]

9. What problem is created by applying the monetary unit assumption when the purchasing power of the dollar is declining? [LO1e]
10. As it relates to accounting information, what is meant by the objectivity principle? [LO1e]
11. What reason is given to justify adherence to the cost principle? [LO1e]
12. What two criteria should generally be met before revenue is recognized as earned in a given period? [LO1e]
13. What two methods can be used to recognize revenue on long-term construction projects? [LO2a]
14. What is meant by the matching principle? Identify three guidelines used for recognizing expenses. [LO1e]
15. What is meant by the consistency principle? [LO1e]
16. What is meant by the full disclosure principle? [LO1e]
17. How is the materiality convention applied in accounting practice? [LO1e]
18. What is meant by the conservatism convention, and how does it affect the amounts reported in financial statements? [LO1e]
19. Differentiate between general price-level changes and specific price-level changes. [LO1f]
20. What two approaches might be used to account for the effects of changing prices on amounts reported in the financial statements? [LO2b,2c]
21. What is the objective of constant dollar accounting? [LO2b]
22. What is meant by the term *monetary items?* Give three examples of monetary items. [LO2b]
23. How does a purchasing power gain occur? How does a purchasing power loss occur? [LO2b]
24. What is meant by the term *nonmonetary items?* Give three examples of nonmonetary items. [LO2b]
25. What is the objective of current cost accounting? [LO2c]
26. Differentiate between unrealized holding gains or losses and realized holding gains or losses. [LO2c]
27. What types of supplementary disclosures to the conventional financial statements are required by FASB Statement No. 33. [LO1g]

## ANALYTICAL QUESTIONS

28. A company's financial officer said that in preparing financial statements, he often found it necessary to "trade off between reliability and relevance." Comment on the meaning and significance of the financial officer's remark. [LO1d]
29. A user of financial information reported by a large publicly held company stated: "I wonder if this information is accurate. You know there are no laws stipulating how accounting information is to be measured or reported as there are for information reported on federal income tax returns." Respond to this statement by explaining the nature and authoritative support for generally accepted accounting principles. [LO1e]
30. There are many proponents and many opponents of current cost financial statements. Give the reasons frequently presented by those who advocate current cost financial information to support its decision usefulness. Also give the major reasons for questioning the information contained in current cost statements. [LO2c]
31. A friend asked, "What is the relevance of distinguishing between monetary and nonmonetary items in accounting for the effects of changes in the general price level?" Develop a response to your friend's question. [LO2b]

32. On page 46 of Allied Corporation's 1984 annual report, the following sentence is directly under the title *Supplementary Information Regarding Inflation and Changing Prices:* "Management cautions users of this information that the data is of limited value for decision making purposes." It of course gives its reasons for this statement. In terms of your knowledge of current cost accounting, indicate why you think the sentence is appropriate or, in your own words, refute the statement. [LO1g,2c]

## IMPACT ANALYSIS QUESTIONS

*For each error described, indicate whether it would overstate [O], understate [U], or not affect [N] the specified key figures.*

33. Company B sells merchandise on the installment basis. During the year it had $20,000 of installment sales that called for a 10% down payment of $6,000 a year for the next three years. There is a serious question as to whether all the installments will be collected. The company recorded the transaction by crediting Sales for the entire $20,000 and debiting a receivable. It then debited Cost of Goods sold for $15,000 and credited Inventory for that amount.

_______ Total Owners' Equity _______ Gross Profit [LO2a]

34. Company B is a construction contractor. During the year the company contracted for a building that would have a selling price of $100,000 and a total estimated cost, over a three-year period, of $80,000. Even though it was apparent that the percentage-of-completion method should be used, the company decided to wait until the project was completed before it recognized any profit. During the year the costs accumulated on the project were $25,000.

_______ Total Owners' Equity _______ Gross Profit [LO2a]

35. In preparing a constant dollar balance sheet, Company C used a year end price index of 120 to restate inventory. The price index that should have been used was 110.

_______ Inventory on the Constant Dollar Balance Sheet
_______ Total Assets on the Constant Dollar Balance Sheet
_______ Retained Earnings on the Constant Dollar Balance Sheet [LO2b]

36. In preparing a current cost income statement, Company D computed Cost of Goods Sold by using the historical cost of inventory, which is $5. The replacement cost of the inventory before any of it was sold was $6.

_______ Sales on the Current Cost Income Statement
_______ Cost of Goods Sold on the Current Cost Income Statement
_______ Gross Profit on Sales on the Current Cost Income Statement [LO2c]

## EXERCISES

EXERCISE 20-1 *(Indicate Violation of Assumptions, Principles, and Conventions of Accounting)* For each lettered situation described below, indicate which accounting assumption, principle, or convention (if any) has been violated. Your choice should be made from the following: entity, going concern, objectivity, (historical) cost, matching, consistency, full disclosure, materiality, conservatism.

a. A new pencil sharpener acquired for the bookkeeping department of a large company at a cost of $20 was recorded as a plant asset and is being depreciated over a useful life of seven years.

b. A relatively large company did not indicate the method it uses in computing depreciation expense, nor did it mention in its published annual report that it plans to dispose of a major segment of its business within the next few months.

c. The owner of a small business used a company check to pay for shrubs to be planted at her personal residence, and the amount was recorded as a business expense.

d. Land acquired by a company a few years ago for $10,000 has appreciated in value. The company reported the land on its balance sheet at $15,000, reflecting the land's estimated sales price, and included the increase in value on its current income statement.

e. No depreciation expense was recorded for the current period because the company's management felt the expense would reduce reported net income below the amount expected for the period.

f. Because several methods for determining depreciation are acceptable, the company changes methods every year or so in order to achieve what management believes to be the appropriate effect of net income. The method used during a given period is disclosed in the notes that accompany the financial statements.

g. A company having items of inventory on hand that cost $60,000 determined that some of the items were damaged and others were obsolete. Accordingly, the inventory was reported on the balance sheet at $46,000, and a $14,000 loss appeared on the current income statement.

h. Land was donated to a company by the municipality where the company is located. Just prior to donation, the land had a fair market value of $25,000 as determined by an independent real estate appraiser. However, the company's management believed the land was worth much more than $25,000 and recorded it in the accounting records at $40,000. [LO1e]

EXERCISE 20–2 *(Match Accounting Assumptions, Principles, and Conventions)* Match the items in column A with the proper descriptions in column B.

*Column A*

| | |
|---|---|
| 1. Full Disclosure | 7. Entity |
| 2. Going Concern | 8. Conservatism |
| 3. Matching | 9. Objectivity |
| 4. Time Period | 10. Monetary Unit |
| 5. Revenue Realization | 11. Consistency |
| 6. Materiality | 12. Cost |

*Column B*

**a.** It is used to discourage undue optimism in measuring and reporting assets and net income.

**b.** It relates to the relative size of dollar amounts and/or relative importance of an item or event.

**c.** It states that in accounting for transactions and events, an entity's business activity is separated from the personal activity of its owner(s).

**d.** An assumption relied on in the recording and reporting of an entity's business activity that would be inappropriate for an entity facing bankruptcy.

**e.** The valuation basis to be used when goods and services are acquired by an ongoing entity.

**f.** The earnings process is determined to be complete or virtually complete, and an exchange transaction has taken place.

**g.** It requires that all material accounting information believed to be significant to a user in understanding the financial status of an entity be reported in its financial statements and their accompanying footnotes.

**h.** It is used as the appropriate common denominator for measuring and reporting an entity's economic activity.

**i.** An assumption that the life of an entity can arbitrarily be subdivided into periods of time for reporting purposes.

j. A company should use the same accounting methods and practices from one period to another.

k. All costs and expenses related to the generation of revenue are recognized when the revenue is recognized.

l. Accounting information should be free from bias and based on verifiable evidence. [LO1e]

EXERCISE 20–3 *(Indicate Recognition of Accounting Assumptions, Principles, and Conventions)* For each accounting method and/or practice stated below, indicate the assumption, principle, or convention that is being observed.

a. Expenditures for each asset under a certain amount, and in terms of relative size considered minor, are expensed as incurred rather than capitalized.

b. Sales revenue is recorded only after the earnings process is considered complete and an exchange has taken place.

c. The company's business activity is separated from the activities of its owners in the recording and reporting process.

d. The company communicates financial information to interested parties by preparing quarterly and annual financial statements.

e. Inventories are reported in the company's balance sheet at their cost or market value, whichever is lower.

f. Care is taken to ensure that all relevant and significant information affecting net income and financial status is revealed in the financial statements and accompanying notes.

g. Accounting methods and practices once adopted are not arbitrarily changed from one period to another.

h. When assets are purchased, they are initially recorded in the accounts at the amount of cash or cash equivalent given to acquire them.

i. Expenses incurred in generating revenue are recognized in the same period in which the revenue is recognized.

j. When faced with uncertainty as to which accounting measurement alternative to use, the company selects the one least likely to overstate income and assets for the current period. [LO1e]

EXERCISE 20–4 *(Apply Percentage-of-Completion Method)* Britt Construction Company recognizes gross profit on long-term construction projects as the work progresses. Information pertaining to one of its long-term construction projects is given in the schedule below.

| | |
|---|---|
| Contract price | $20,000,000 |
| Estimated cost | $14,000,000 |
| Years to complete | 4 years |

Actual costs incurred:

| YEAR | COST INCURRED |
|---|---|
| 1 | $ 2,800,000 |
| 2 | 4,200,000 |
| 3 | 3,500,000 |
| 4 | 3,450,000 |
| Total | $13,950,000 |

Required:
Compute the amount of gross profit that should be recognized in each year of the contract. [LO2a]

EXERCISE 20-5 *(Compute Purchasing Power Gain or Loss)* Starlite Company held a cash fund of $20,000 throughout the year 1985. The company also became obligated for a note payable of $15,000 on January 2, 1985, and the note remained outstanding throughout the year. Assume the Consumer Price Index used to determine purchasing power gain or loss on monetary items was 311 on January 1, 1985, and 325 on December 31, 1985.

Required:
Compute Starlite Company's purchasing power gain or loss from holding monetary items during 1985. (Round the amount to the nearest dollar.) [LO2b]

EXERCISE 20-6 *(Prepare Conventional and Constant Dollar Balance Sheet)* Baron Company was organized on January 2, 1985, at which time it issued stock in exchange for (1) land valued at $58,000 and (2) cash of $42,000. No transactions occurred during the year. However, the Consumer Price Index changed from 311 on January 2, 1985, to 325 on December 31, 1985.

Required:

1. Prepare a conventional (historical cost) balance sheet.
2. Prepare a constant dollar balance sheet, rounding amounts to the nearest dollar. [LO2b]

EXERCISE 20-7 *(Prepare Conventional and Constant Dollar Income Statement)* Morgan Company was organized on January 1, 1985, at which time it issued capital stock in exchange for cash of $75,000. The company sells its products on a cash-and-carry basis. Summarized data pertaining to the company's activities during 1985 are shown below.

| | |
|---|---|
| Merchandise purchased (at cost) | $310,000 |
| Merchandise inventory (at FIFO cost) | 70,000 |
| Sales (incurred evenly) | 420,000 |
| Operating expenses (incurred evenly) | 130,000 |
| Cost of equipment | 8,000 |
| Depreciation expense (amount not included in operating expenses) | 1,000 |
| Income taxes (incurred evenly) | 22,000 |

Additional Data:

1. The 1985 general price indexes (assumed) are:
   Average price index during 1985—318
   Year-end price index—325
2. Merchandise was purchased evenly throughout the year.
3. Equipment was purchased early in 1985 when the price index was 314.
4. A $2,800 purchasing power gain resulting from holding net monetary liabilities during 1985 was computed.

Required:

1. Prepare a conventional income statement for the year ended December 31, 1985.
2. Prepare a constant dollar income statement for the year ended December 31, 1985. (Round amounts to the nearest dollar.) [LO2b]

EXERCISE 20-8 *(Compute Realized and Unrealized Holding Losses)* On January 28, 1987, Cellular Company purchased 10,000 units of a high-technology item at $8.80 per unit. On February

15, 1987, before any of the units were sold, the price to replace them dropped to $8.25 and remained at that level throughout the rest of the year. On December 31, 1987, the end of Cellular's accounting period, 2,200 units remained in inventory.

Required:

1. Compute Cellular's cost of goods sold using (a) conventional accounting and (b) current cost accounting.
2. Compute the amount of the company's (a) realized holding loss and (b) unrealized holding loss as determined under current cost accounting. [LO2c]

EXERCISE 20-9 *(Prepare Conventional and Current Cost Income Statement and Compute Holding Gains or Losses)* Olden Company was organized on January 1, 1987, at which time it issued 25,000 of its $5 par value common shares in exchange for land of $45,000 and cash of $80,000. On January 3, 1987, Olden purchased 30,000 units of inventory at $20 per unit. During the year the company sold 26,000 units of inventory at an average price of $30 per unit. In addition, the company incurred cash operating expenses of $184,000 for the year. On December 31, 1987, Olden determined the current cost amounts for the following items by using appraised values and various suppliers' catalogs.

| | |
|---|---|
| Land | $ 55,000 |
| Cost of Goods Sold | 574,600 |
| Operating Expenses | 184,000 |
| Inventory | 22.75 (per unit) |

Required:

1. Prepare a conventional (historical cost) income statement for the year ended December 31, 1987. Disregard federal income taxes.
2. Determine the company's realized holding gain or loss on the units sold and its unrealized holding gain or loss on the units remaining in inventory.
3. Prepare a current cost income statement for the year ended December 31, 1987. Disregard federal income taxes. [LO2c]

## PROBLEMS

PROBLEM 20-1 *(Determine Accounting Principles)* You have been asked to review the accounting records of Fleetwood Company prior to closing the revenue and expense accounts as of December 31, the company's year-end. The following information concerning transactions and events has come to your attention during the review.

1. On March 5 of the current year, Fleetwood purchased land from a company in financial distress by paying cash of $40,000. Fleetwood's management believed that the land would have cost $55,000 if the seller had not been in dire need of cash and that the land could easily be sold for that amount. Consequently, the following entry was made on the date of the purchase:

| | | |
|---|---|---|
| Land | 55,000 | |
| Cash | | 40,000 |
| Gain on Bargain Purchase | | 15,000 |

2. The company uses the accrual basis of accounting, and you noted the following:
   a. An examination of insurance policies confirmed that the $1,800 paid for insurance premiums on September 1 of the current year provided coverage for six months. The Prepaid Insurance account has a balance of $1,800.
   b. Administrative salaries are $16,000 a month. Salaries earned in December were

paid on January 2 of the following year, but no accrual entry was recorded on December 31 of the current year.

3. On December 29 of the current year, Fleetwood signed a contract under which it agreed, at the customer's request, to ship merchandise to the customer after January 3 but no later than January 10. Fleetwood required a $3,000 cash advance on the contract and the money was received on December 29, at which time the following entry was made:

| | | |
|---|---|---|
| Cash | 3,000 | |
| Accounts Receivable | 27,000 | |
| Sales | | 30,000 |

4. The president of Fleetwood used a company check to purchase a power lawn mower that was delivered to his home and is to be used solely on his personal premises. The following entry was made on the date of purchase:

| | | |
|---|---|---|
| General Expense | 420 | |
| Cash | | 420 |

5. Inventory on hand at December 31 of the current year had a cost of $108,000, and that amount appeared in the Inventory account. The year-end market price of the inventory (its replacement cost) is only $96,000.
6. During the current year Fleetwood borrowed $25,000 on a short-term interest-bearing note. The note plus interest was paid on December 30 and the following entry was made:

| | | |
|---|---|---|
| Note Payable | 25,850 | |
| Cash | | 25,850 |

7. Fleetwood uses the straight-line method to compute depreciation on its buildings and the sum-of-the-years'-digits method to compute depreciation on its equipment. Although different methods are used for computing depreciation on different plant assets, the methods have been consistently applied since the company began operating, and the depreciation amount has been computed accurately. The depreciation entry recorded on December 31 of the current year was as follows:

| | | |
|---|---|---|
| Depreciation Expense | 54,000 | |
| Accumulated Depreciation—Buildings | | 20,000 |
| Accumulated Depreciation—Equipment | | 34,000 |

8. Fleetwood is being sued for $100,000 by a customer. No entry regarding this matter has been made. You have established that the company does not plan to mention it in any published financial reports, although management believes it is "reasonably possible" for the customer to win the suit.

Required:

1. For each transaction or event described above, determine which generally accepted accounting principle or principles (if any) have been violated, and briefly explain your answer.
2. For each numbered item resulting in a violation of GAAP, prepare the journal entry needed to adjust or correct the accounts. Next to the entry, indicate the item being adjusted or corrected by using the item's number. [LO1e]

PROBLEM 20-2 *(Determine Accounting Principles)* In measuring and reporting its business activities, Broadland Company has followed the accounting practices described below.

1. Land is recorded at acquisition cost and reported at that amount in the balance sheet even when its appraised value is higher.

2. The collection of cash for services to be performed in the next accounting period is initially recorded by debiting the Cash account and crediting an appropriately titled current liability account.
3. Depreciation expense is determined by using the straight-line method in certain years and by using the sum-of-the-years'-digits method in other years. This is done in order to achieve a reasonably consistent amount of net income from year to year.
4. No journal entry or mention is ever made of pending lawsuits against the firm, even when the amount involved in a given suit is significant and it is almost certain that the plaintiff will win in the courts.
5. Damaged and obsolete inventory is written off as a loss at the time that financial statements are prepared.
6. All plant assets are reported in the balance sheet at cost less accumulated depreciation, even though the market value of some plant assets is less than the amount reported.
7. The cost of insurance premiums is recorded and reported as insurance expense, even though some of the premium cost provides coverage for a period of time after the balance sheet date.
8. Controls have been instituted in an attempt to keep personal transactions of the company's owners separate from the activities of the business. In the few instances where personal transactions occur, they are accounted for by debiting an owner's Drawings account.
9. A policy has been established whereby minor expenditures of less than $5,000 relating to an asset's acquisition or its use are debited directly to an expense account.

Required:
For each of the practices described in items 1 through 9 above, indicate whether you agree or disagree with the accounting practice followed. State the assumptions, principles, or conventions that provide the basis for your position. [LO1e]

PROBLEM 20–3 *(Determine Revenue Realized on Installment Sales)* Rocket Kook Company sells compressors for air-conditioning units. On November 6, 1985, a relatively large compressor costing $2,000 was sold for $3,500. The customer made a down payment of $500 and agreed to pay the balance in fifteen equal monthly payments beginning on December 31, 1985.

Required:
Determine the amount of gross profit that should be recognized on the installment sale in 1985, 1986, and 1987, assuming the following:
1. The company is reasonably sure that the full sales price will be collected from the customer, and it therefore accounts for the transaction in the same manner as it does for other credit sale transactions.
2. The company is not reasonably sure that the full sales price will be collected from the customer, and it therefore uses the installment method of accounting. Carry the gross profit rate two decimal places and round amounts to the nearest dollar. [LO2a]

PROBLEM 20–4 *(Determine Revenue Realized on Long-Term Construction Projects)* Broadland Construction Company signed three contracts during 1985. One contract calls for the construction of a shopping center, another for an office complex, and the third for indoor parking facilities. All construction is on the same land site, is to begin immediately, and is expected to take three years. The following information pertains to each of the projects.

| CONTRACT | CONTRACT PRICE | ESTIMATED TOTAL COST | ACTUAL COSTS INCURRED—1985 | ACTUAL COSTS INCURRED—1986 | ACTUAL COSTS INCURRED—1987 |
|---|---|---|---|---|---|
| Office Complex | $5,000,000 | $3,500,000 | $ 630,000 | $1,295,000 | $1,570,000 |
| Shopping Center | 8,000,000 | 5,800,000 | 1,160,000 | 2,204,000 | 2,448,000 |
| Parking Facility | 3,600,000 | 2,500,000 | 250,000 | 1,625,000 | 633,000 |

The projects were completed on time in late 1987. Broadland's accounting department has been able to estimate total construction costs with reasonable accuracy in the past. It did not change its estimate of total construction costs on these three projects during the entire construction period.

Required:

1. Prepare a schedule showing the amount of gross profit that would be recognized on each project and in total in each of the three years—1985, 1986, and 1987—assuming that:
   (a) Revenue is recognized by the point-of-sale method (no income is recognized until the projects have been completed).
   (b) Revenue is recognized by the percentage-of-completion method.
2. Explain which revenue recognition method you consider most appropriate in this situation. [LO2a]

PROBLEM 20-5 *(Prepare Constant Dollar Balance Sheet)* The conventional balance sheet prepared for Globe Company on December 31, 1986, appears below.

GLOBE COMPANY
Balance Sheet
December 31, 1986

| ASSETS | | |
|---|---|---|
| Cash | | $ 25,000 |
| Accounts Receivable | | 38,000 |
| Inventory | | 52,000 |
| Land | | 60,000 |
| Plant and Equipment | $140,000 | |
| Less: Accumulated Depreciation | 30,000 | |
| | | 110,000 |
| Total Assets | | $285,000 |
| LIABILITIES AND STOCKHOLDERS' EQUITY | | |
| Accounts Payable | | $ 66,000 |
| Notes Payable | | 25,000 |
| Capital Stock | | 100,000 |
| Retained Earnings | | 94,000 |
| Total Liabilities and Stockholders' Equity | | $285,000 |

Additional Information:

1. Inventory items were purchased evenly throughout the year.
2. Land costing $60,000 was acquired on December 29, 1984.
3. All plant and equipment assets were acquired on January 3, 1983.
4. The company was organized on January 1, 1983, at which time capital stock was issued for cash.
5. Constant dollar retained earnings have been computed at $101,604.
6. Consumer Price Index data (figures assumed for purposes of this problem) are as follows:

| | |
|---|---|
| December 31, 1982—258 | December 31, 1985—303 |
| December 31, 1983—281 | Year average, 1986—311 |
| December 31, 1984—292 | December 31, 1986—315 |

Required:

Prepare a constant dollar balance sheet as of December 31, 1986. (Round amounts to the nearest dollar.) [LO2b]

PROBLEM 20-6 *(Prepare Constant Dollar Income Statement)* A conventional income statement prepared for Drexel Company for the year ended December 31, 1987, appears below.

DREXEL COMPANY
Income Statement
For the Year Ended December 31, 1987

| | | |
|---|---|---|
| Sales | | $163,000 |
| Less: Cost of Goods Sold | | 106,600 |
| Gross Profit on Sales | | $ 56,400 |
| Selling and Administrative Expenses | $29,000 | |
| Depreciation Expense | 13,000 | |
| Total Expenses | | 42,000 |
| Income before Income Taxes | | $ 14,400 |
| Income Taxes | | 6,600 |
| Net Income | | $ 7,800 |

Additional Information:

1. Sales were for cash. All expenses except for depreciation, but including income taxes, were paid for in cash.
2. Inventory items were purchased evenly throughout the year.
3. Selling and administrative expenses were incurred and paid evenly throughout the year.
4. Depreciation expense is computed on equipment acquired in January 1985 and is being depreciated under the straight-line method using an estimated useful life of twelve years and no salvage value.
5. Income taxes were incurred and paid evenly throughout the year.
6. A purchasing power loss of $2,372 that resulted from holding monetary items was computed for the year. Information relating to the company's only monetary items is as follows:

| MONETARY ASSET | | MONETARY LIABILITY | |
|---|---|---|---|
| Cash balance, January 1, 1987 | $ 13,800 | Note payable, January 1, 1987 | $ 0 |
| Add cash collections from sales | 163,000 | Add note issued October 1, 1987 | 10,000 |
| Subtotal | $176,800 | | $10,000 |
| Deduct cash payment for cost of goods sold, selling and administrative expenses, and income taxes | 142,200 | | |
| Cash balance, December 31, 1987 | $ 34,600 | | |

7. Consumer Price Index data (figures assumed for purposes of this problem) are as follows:

| | |
|---|---|
| December 31, 1984—150 | October 1, 1987—195 |
| December 31, 1985—170 | Year average, 1987—190 |
| December 31, 1986—180 | December 31, 1987—200 |

Required:

1. Prepare a constant dollar income statement for the year ended December 31, 1987. (Round amounts to the nearest dollar.)
2. Prepare a schedule, in good form, to verify the purchasing power loss of $2,372 computed for the year 1987. [LO2b]

PROBLEM 20–7 *(Prepare Constant Dollar Financial Statements)* The conventionally prepared income statement for the year 1987 and the conventionally prepared balance sheet at December 31, 1987, for Mentor Company are presented below.

MENTOR COMPANY
Income Statement
For the Year Ended December 31, 1987

| | | |
|---|---|---|
| Sales | | $740,000 |
| Less: Cost of Goods Sold | | 408,400 |
| Gross Profit on Sales | | $331,600 |
| Selling and Administrative Expenses | $192,500 | |
| Depreciation Expense | 19,300 | |
| Total Expenses | | 211,800 |
| Income from Operations | | $119,800 |
| Add: Interest Revenue | | 6,100 |
| Income before Income Taxes | | $125,900 |
| Income Taxes | | 57,600 |
| Net Income | | $ 68,300 |

MENTOR COMPANY
Balance Sheet
December 31, 1987

| | | |
|---|---|---|
| ASSETS | | |
| Cash | | $ 41,200 |
| Accounts Receivable—Net | | 82,400 |
| Inventory | | 96,500 |
| Long-Term Investments—Bonds | | 60,700 |
| Land—Held for Future Site | | 52,000 |
| Plant and Equipment | $188,000 | |
| Less: Accumulated Depreciation | 115,200 | 72,800 |
| Total Assets | | $405,600 |
| LIABILITIES AND STOCKHOLDERS' EQUITY | | |
| Accounts Payable | | $ 58,400 |
| Notes Payable (due in 1990) | | 20,000 |
| Capital Stock | | 200,000 |
| Retained Earnings | | 127,200 |
| Total Liabilities and Stockholders' Equity | | $405,600 |

Additional Information:

1. The company was organized on February 1, 1982, at which time the capital stock was issued and the plant and equipment assets were purchased.
2. The land was purchased on March 1, 1985, for cash.
3. The long-term investments consist of municipal bonds, which were purchased on June 30, 1985, for cash.
4. Inventory items were purchased evenly throughout the year. The company uses the first-in, first-out inventory method. There was no significant difference between the beginning and ending inventory amounts.
5. Sales and interest revenues were earned evenly throughout the year.
6. Expenses except for depreciation were incurred evenly throughout the year.
7. A purchasing power loss of $3,900, the result of holding monetary items, was computed for the year.

8. Consumer Price Index data (figures assumed) on various dates are as follows:

| | |
|---|---|
| February 1, 1982—150 | December 31, 1987—230 |
| March 1, 1985—190 | Year Average, 1987—220 |

Required:

1. Prepare a constant dollar income statement for the year ended December 31, 1987.
2. Prepare a constant dollar balance sheet at December 31, 1987. *Note:* Enter a balancing amount for Retained Earnings to achieve equality between total assets and total liabilities and stockholders' equity. All amounts in Requirements 1 and 2 should be rounded to the nearest dollar. [LO2b]

PROBLEM 20-8 *(Prepare Current Cost Financial Statements)* Rockford Company was organized on January 5, 1987, and sold $300,000 of capital stock for cash on that date. The following day the company purchased 25,000 units of inventory at $8 per unit and a land site costing $50,000. After operating for the year ending December 31, 1987, the company issued the following condensed financial statements.

ROCKFORD COMPANY
Balance Sheet
December 31, 1987

| | |
|---|---|
| Cash | $218,000 |
| Accounts Receivable | 37,000 |
| Inventory (5,000 units @ $8) | 40,000 |
| Land | 50,000 |
| Total Assets | $345,000 |
| Accounts Payable | $ 15,000 |
| Capital Stock | 300,000 |
| Retained Earnings | 30,000 |
| Total Liabilities and Stockholders' Equity | $345,000 |

ROCKFORD COMPANY
Income Statement
For the Year Ended December 31, 1987

| | |
|---|---|
| Sales (20,000 units @ $15) | $300,000 |
| Cost of Goods Sold (20,000 units @ $8) | 160,000 |
| Gross Profit on Sales | $140,000 |
| Operating Expenses | 90,000 |
| Income from Operations before Taxes | $ 50,000 |
| Income Taxes | 20,000 |
| Net Income | $ 30,000 |

The relevant current cost amounts pertaining to certain items appearing in the preceding financial statements are as follows:

| | |
|---|---|
| Cash—as reported | $218,000 |
| Accounts receivable—as reported | 37,000 |
| Inventory—based on suppliers' catalogs | 10.50 (per unit) |
| Land—based on appraisal | 55,000 |
| Accounts payable—as reported | 15,000 |
| Capital stock—as reported | 300,000 |
| Sales—as reported | 300,000 |
| Cost of goods sold—per calculation | 210,000 |
| Operating expenses—as reported | 90,000 |
| Income taxes—as reported | 20,000 |

Required:

1. Prepare a current cost income statement for the year ended December 31, 1987.
2. Prepare a current cost balance sheet at December 31, 1987. [LO2c]

PROBLEM 20–9 *(Prepare Conventional and Current Cost Financial Statements)* Worldwide Company was organized on January 3, 1987, at which time 25,000 shares of its $10 par value stock were issued at $12 per share. The summary below describes the activities, events, and circumstances occurring during the year ended December 31, 1987.

1. On January 5 the company purchased 40,000 units of inventory at a cost of $6 per unit.
2. On March 3 the company had its first sale, consisting of 10,000 units, for which it received cash of $20,000 and an account receivable for $80,000. On this date the company established that the replacement cost of units sold had increased to $7 per unit.
3. During the remainder of the year, 24,000 additional units of inventory were sold at $10.25 per unit. Although no other units were purchased to replace the items sold, the replacement cost remained constant at $7 per unit throughout the year.
4. On April 10 land costing $60,000 was purchased for cash.
5. Operating expenses of $68,000 were incurred during the year.
6. Federal income tax expense for the year totaled $29,000 and was paid in cash.
7. At December 31 the company had accounts receivable of $87,000 and accounts payable of $6,000.
8. By referring to the selling price of similar land sites, the company established that its land had a current value of $70,000 at year-end.

Required:

1. Prepare a conventional income statement for the year ended December 31, 1987, and a conventional balance sheet as of December 31, 1987.
2. Prepare a current cost income statement for the year ended December 31, 1987, and a current cost balance sheet as of December 31, 1987. [LO2c]

## ALTERNATE PROBLEMS

PROBLEM 20–1A *(Determine Accounting Principles)* (Alternate to Problem 20–1) You have been asked to review the accounting records of Raidit Company prior to closing the revenue and expense accounts as of December 31, the company's year-end. The following information concerning transactions and events has come to your attention during the review.

1. On March 2 of the current year, Raidit purchased a machine at an auction sale for $25,000. In making comparisons, the company concluded that a similar machine would have cost $29,000 if purchased from middlemen suppliers rather than at auction. Consequently, the following entry was made on the date of the purchase:

| | | |
|---|---|---|
| Machine | 29,000 | |
| Cash | | 25,000 |
| Gain on Bargain Purchase | | 4,000 |

2. The company uses the accrual basis of accounting, and you noted the following:
   a. The asset account Office Supplies has a balance of $3,200 on December 31. The cost of supplies actually on hand at that date was $900.
   b. No interest has been accrued on a $25,000, 12%, six-month note payable, dated October 1 of the current year.
3. The president of Raidit used a company check to pay for carpeting that was delivered and installed in her home. The president's home is used solely for personal purposes. The following entry was made on the date the carpeting was purchased:

| | | |
|---|---|---|
| General Expense | 2,800 | |
| Cash | | 2,800 |

4. On December 22 of the current year, Raidit agreed to manufacture a piece of equipment for one of its customers. The agreement stated that work would begin on January 2 of the following year, that the item would be completed in two weeks, and that the customer would pay for the item by making a $3,000 down payment now and $12,000 when the item was delivered. The entry made on December 22 was as follows:

| | | |
|---|---|---|
| Cash | 3,000 | |
| Accounts Receivable | 12,000 | |
| Sales | | 15,000 |

5. Inventory on hand at December 31 of the current year had a cost of $214,000, and that amount appeared in the Inventory account. The year-end market price of the inventory (its replacement cost) is only $196,000.
6. During the current year, Raidit collected in full on its $15,000 short-term interest-bearing note receivable. When the check was received, Raidit recorded the transaction as follows:

| | | |
|---|---|---|
| Cash | 15,600 | |
| Note Receivable | | 15,600 |

7. Raidit uses the straight-line method to compute depreciation on its buildings and the declining-balance method to compute depreciation on its equipment. Although different methods are used for computing depreciation on different plant assets, the methods have been consistently applied since the company began operating, and the depreciation amount has been computed accurately. The depreciation entry recorded on December 31 of the current year was as follows:

| | | |
|---|---|---|
| Depreciation Expense | 88,000 | |
| Accumulated Depreciation—Buildings | | 26,000 |
| Accumulated Depreciation—Equipment | | 62,000 |

8. Raidit is being sued for $200,000 by a customer who is claiming damages for personal injury allegedly caused by a defective product. No entry regarding this matter has been made because company attorneys have been discussing the case with the customer and feel confident that the case can soon be settled out of court for half the amount, or $100,000.

Required:

1. For each transaction or event described above, determine which generally accepted accounting principles (if any) have been violated, and briefly explain your answer.
2. For each numbered item resulting in a violation of GAAP, prepare the journal entry needed to adjust or correct the accounts. Next to the entry, indicate the item being adjusted or corrected by using the item's number. [LO1e]

PROBLEM 20–2A *(Determine Accounting Principles)* (Alternate to Problem 20–2) In measuring and reporting its business activities, Phillips Company has followed the accounting practices described below.

1. All minor expenditures for office equipment are charged to an expense account as incurred.
2. The petty cash fund is frequently used to pay for personal expenses. When the fund is replenished, the Miscellaneous Expense account is debited for the aggregate amount of these personal disbursements.
3. The company owns many assets, which are reported in its balance sheet. Two of the assets, land and inventories, have consistently been measured and valued as follows:
   a. Land—reported at current market value
   b. Inventories—reported at LIFO cost or market value, whichever is lower
4. Damaged and obsolete inventory items are written down from cost to expected realizable value and are sold at auction for prices close to established realizable values.

5. Financial statements are prepared at the end of each twenty-eight-day period and for the current year. The year ends on December 27.
6. The company uses the accrual basis of accounting. However, it does not recognize as an expense of the current period salaries earned by administrative employees that are payable in the next accounting period. The justification given for this practice is that administrative work involves planning for future periods.
7. The company changed from the declining-balance method of computing depreciation to the straight-line method this year. Because of this change in depreciation method, salvage values were estimated for all depreciable assets and for the first time were used in the computation of depreciation.
8. No journal entry or mention was made of a pending lawsuit against the firm. The amount involved is significant, and it is almost certain that the plaintiff will be successful in the courts.

Required:
For each of the practices described in items 1 through 8 above, indicate whether you agree or disagree with the accounting practice followed. State the assumptions, principles, or conventions that provide the basis for your position. [LO1e]

PROBLEM 20–3A *(Determine Revenue Realized on Long-Term Construction Projects)* (Alternate to Problem 20–4) Makeit Company began construction on three separate long-term projects during 1985. Each project was completed in late 1987. The following information pertains to the contracts and the projects for the years 1985, 1986, and 1987.

| CONTRACT | CONTRACT PRICE | ESTIMATED TOTAL COST |
|---|---|---|
| 1 | $11,200,000 | $ 9,000,000 |
| 2 | 5,600,000 | 4,800,000 |
| 3 | 18,000,000 | 15,000,000 |

Actual costs incurred for contracts 1, 2, and 3, respectively, during the years of construction are as follows:

| | ACTUAL COSTS INCURRED | | |
|---|---|---|---|
| CONTRACT | 1985 | 1986 | 1987 |
| 1 | $2,250,000 | $ 5,400,000 | $1,420,000 |
| 2 | 864,000 | 1,776,000 | 2,130,000 |
| 3 | 3,300,000 | 5,700,000 | 6,040,000 |
| Total | $6,414,000 | $12,876,000 | $9,590,000 |

Makeit Company's accounting department has been able to estimate total construction costs on a project with reasonable accuracy in the past. It did not change its estimate of costs on any of these three projects during the construction period.

Required:
1. Prepare a schedule showing the amount of gross profit that would be recognized on each project and in total in each of the three years—1985, 1986, and 1987.
   a. Revenue is recognized by the point-of-sale method (no income is recognized until the projects have been completed).
   b. Revenue is recognized by the percentage-of-completion method.
2. Explain which revenue recognition method you consider most appropriate in this situation. [LO2a]

PROBLEM 20–4A *(Prepare Constant Dollar Financial Statements)* (Alternate to Problem 20–7) The conventionally prepared income statement for the year 1987 and the conventionally prepared balance sheet at December 31, 1987, for Metro Company are presented below.

METRO COMPANY
Income Statement
For the Year Ended December 31, 1987

| | | |
|---|---|---|
| Sales | | $570,000 |
| Less: Cost of Goods Sold | | 292,300 |
| Gross Profit on Sales | | $277,700 |
| Selling and Administrative Expenses | $155,300 | |
| Depreciation Expense | 16,200 | |
| Total Expenses | | 171,500 |
| Income from Operations | | $106,200 |
| Add: Interest Revenue | | 4,600 |
| Income before Income Taxes | | $110,800 |
| Income Taxes | | 36,600 |
| Net Income | | $ 74,200 |

METRO COMPANY
Balance Sheet
December 31, 1987

| | | |
|---|---|---|
| ASSETS | | |
| Cash | | $ 36,700 |
| Accounts Receivable—Net | | 78,200 |
| Inventory | | 49,600 |
| Long-Term Investments—Bonds | | 72,500 |
| Land—Held for Future Site | | 60,900 |
| Plant and Equipment | $243,000 | |
| Less: Accumulated Depreciation | 97,200 | 145,800 |
| Total Assets | | $443,700 |
| LIABILITIES AND STOCKHOLDERS' EQUITY | | |
| Accounts Payable | | $ 28,400 |
| Notes Payable (due in 1992) | | 66,000 |
| Capital Stock | | 280,000 |
| Retained Earnings | | 69,300 |
| Total Liabilities and Stockholders' Equity | | $443,700 |

Additional Information:

1. The company was organized on January 15, 1982, at which time the capital stock was issued and the plant and equipment assets were purchased.
2. The land was purchased on April 15, 1985, for cash.
3. The long-term investments consist of municipal bonds, which were purchased on July 1, 1985, for cash.
4. Inventory items were purchased evenly throughout the year. The company uses the first-in, first-out inventory method. There was no significant difference between the beginning and ending inventory amounts.
5. Sales and interest revenues were earned evenly throughout the year.

6. Expenses except for depreciation were incurred evenly throughout the year.
7. A purchasing power gain of $1,400, the result of holding monetary items, was computed for the year.
8. Consumer Price Index data (figures assumed) on various dates are as follows:

| | |
|---|---|
| January 15, 1982–140 | December 31, 1987—210 |
| April 15, 1985—170 | Year average, 1987—200 |

Required:

1. Prepare a constant dollar income statement for the year ended December 31, 1987.
2. Prepare a constant dollar balance sheet at December 31, 1987. Round amounts to the nearest dollar. *Note:* Enter a balancing amount for Retained Earnings to achieve equality between total assets and total liabilities and stockholders' equity. [LO2b]

PROBLEM 20–5A *(Prepare Current Cost Financial Statements)* (Alternate to Problem 20–8) Rockaway Company was organized on January 3, 1987, and sold $200,000 of capital stock for cash on that date. The following day the company purchased 50,000 units of inventory at $3.20 per unit and a land site costing $27,000. After operating for the year ending December 31, 1987, the company issued the following condensed financial statements.

ROCKAWAY COMPANY
Balance Sheet
December 31, 1987

| | |
|---|---|
| Cash | $142,300 |
| Accounts Receivable | 27,500 |
| Inventory (10,000 units @ $3.20) | 32,000 |
| Land | 27,000 |
| Total Assets | $228,800 |
| Accounts Payable | $ 12,000 |
| Capital Stock | 200,000 |
| Retained Earnings | 16,800 |
| Total Liabilities and Stockholders' Equity | $228,800 |

ROCKAWAY COMPANY
Income Statement
For the Year Ended December 31, 1987

| | |
|---|---|
| Sales (40,000 units @ $5.50) | $220,000 |
| Cost of Goods Sold (40,000 units @ $3.20) | 128,000 |
| Gross Profit on Sales | $ 92,000 |
| Operations Expense | 64,000 |
| Income from Operations before Taxes | $ 28,000 |
| Income Taxes | 11,200 |
| Net Income | $ 16,800 |

The relevant current cost amounts pertaining to certain items appearing in the preceding financial statements are as follows:

| | |
|---|---|
| Cash—as reported | $142,300 |
| Accounts Receivable—as reported | 27,500 |
| Inventory—based on suppliers' catalogs | 3.50 (per unit) |
| Land—based on appraisal | 31,000 |
| Accounts Payable—as reported | 12,000 |
| Capital Stock—as reported | 200,000 |
| Sales—as reported | 220,000 |
| Cost of Goods Sold—per calculation | 140,000 |
| Operating Expenses—as reported | 64,000 |
| Income Taxes—as reported | 11,200 |

Required:

1. Prepare a current cost income statement for the year ended December 31, 1987.
2. Prepare a current cost balance sheet at December 31, 1987. [LO2c]

# 21 *Accounting for Manufacturing Companies*

### *Learning Objectives*

When you complete this chapter you will be able to

1. Answer the following questions:
   a. What is the difference between accounting for manufacturing firms and accounting for merchandising firms?
   b. What is the difference between product costs and period costs, and how does this difference relate to accounting for manufacturing costs?
   c. What are the components of the three inventories in a manufacturing company?
   d. What are the components of the three elements of manufacturing costs?
2. Perform the following accounting functions:
   a. Demonstrate the flow of costs in a manufacturing company.
   b. Prepare financial statements in summary form for a manufacturing company.

We have learned about the accounting for operations of both merchandising and service companies. We now turn to those of a manufacturing company.

What is it about the operations of a manufacturing company that is different and leads to a difference in the way we do our accounting?

## DIFFERENCES BETWEEN MANUFACTURING AND MERCHANDISING COMPANIES

*1a. A merchandising company sells the products that it buys*

A **merchandising company,** as we have seen, sells to its customers the same products that it buys from its suppliers. It does not change the physical form or the nature of these products. Department stores, furniture retailers, and stereo and TV discounters are typical examples of merchandising companies. They buy from wholesalers or manufacturers, and they sell to consumers.

*1a. A manufacturing company sells finished goods that it has produced from raw materials*

A **manufacturing company** performs operations to produce finished goods from raw materials and sells these finished goods to customers. Garment makers, furniture manufacturers, and TV and stereo manufacturers are typical examples of manufacturing companies.

Manufacturing companies buy raw materials from industrial suppliers or other manufacturers. For example, a furniture company buys lumber, glue, nails, screws, hinges, paint, and varnish from wholesalers or manufacturers of these items. The company then makes expenditures to convert these raw materials into completed chairs, tables, bureaus, desks, and other items of furniture, which it sells to retail merchandising companies.

## HOW ACCOUNTING DIFFERS BETWEEN MANUFACTURING AND MERCHANDISING COMPANIES

*1a. The manufacturing company's conversion costs make the difference in the way we account for its operations*

The manufacturing company's **conversion costs**—its expenditures to convert the raw materials it buys into the finished goods it sells—make the difference in the way we account for the company's operations. This difference shows up in the assignment of dollar amounts to inventory and cost of goods sold.

In a merchandising company this assignment is more straightforward. The cost of goods sold and the cost of goods that are in inventory at the beginning and the end of the accounting period are usually stated as the initial purchase cost of those goods. All other costs (except those that remain attached to items classified

EXHIBIT 21-1

Partial Income Statement of Oldfield Furniture Outlet—A Merchandising Company

| | | |
|---|---|---|
| Sales | | $100,000 |
| Cost of Goods Sold: | | |
| Inventory, 1/1/X8 | $10,000 | |
| Purchases | 60,000 | |
| Cost of Goods Available for Sale | $70,000 | |
| Less: Inventory, 12/31/X8 | 5,000 | 65,000 |
| Gross Profit on Sales | | $ 35,000 |
| Operating Expenses: | | |
| Supplies Used | $ 3,000 | |
| Depreciation on Building | 10,000 | |
| Salaries Expense | 15,000 | |
| Miscellaneous Expense | 5,000 | 33,000 |
| Net Income | | $ 2,000 |

as assets) are stated as operating expenses. Such expenses include, for example, supplies used and depreciation on buildings.

Look at Exhibit 21 – 1, which is part of an income statement for a merchandising company. Note the clear distinction there between the costs entered above the line "Gross Profit on Sales" and those entered below the line.

For a manufacturing company, on the other hand, the dollar amounts assigned to inventory and to costs of goods sold must take account of conversion costs. A furniture manufacturer, for example, makes expenditures not only for raw materials but also for the wages of employees and costs of machinery to convert these raw materials into chairs, tables, and other items of furniture. The *cost of goods sold* is

> The cost of the raw materials *plus*
>
> The cost of converting them into finished products that have been sold.

The *cost of inventory* is

> The cost of the raw materials *or*
>
> The cost of raw materials plus the cost of whatever operations have been performed to convert the raw materials into unsold finished goods—or sometimes into goods that are only partly finished at the inventory date.

In accounting for conversion costs, a furniture manufacturer makes an important distinction. Costs such as salaries of manufacturing employees and depreciation of manufacturing equipment are assigned as *costs of the products*—chairs, tables, and so on. On the other hand, clerical salaries and depreciation on nonmanufacturing equipment are assigned as *operating expenses.*

This distinction usually makes the accounting for inventory and cost of goods sold more complex in a manufacturing than in a merchandising company. The extra effort of performing this accounting is undertaken because it yields information that is useful in managing the company's operations efficiently and making them profitable.

Thus some of the difference between accounting for merchandising companies and accounting for manufacturing companies can be seen by comparing Exhibit 21 – 1 (a partial income statement of a merchandising company) with Exhibit 21 – 2 (a partial income statement of a manufacturing company). Note

*EXHIBIT 21 – 2*

Partial Income Statement of Oldfield Manufacturing, Inc.—
A Manufacturing Company

| | | |
|---|---|---|
| Sales | | $100,000 |
| Cost of Goods Sold: | | |
| Finished Goods Inventory, 1/1/X8 | $10,000 | |
| Cost of Goods Manufactured | 60,000 | |
| Cost of Goods Available for Sale | $70,000 | |
| Less: Finished Goods Inventory, 12/31/X8 | 5,000 | 65,000 |
| Gross Profit on Sales | | $ 35,000 |
| Operating Expenses: | | |
| Supplies Used | $ 3,000 | |
| Depreciation on Building | 10,000 | |
| Salaries Expense | 15,000 | |
| Miscellaneous Expense | 5,000 | 33,000 |
| Net Income | | $ 2,000 |

that the difference is in the Cost of Goods Sold section. A manufacturing company adds to its beginning inventory of finished and unsold products the cost of manufacturing new products during the period. The company then subtracts its ending inventory of finished and unsold products, and the result is cost of goods sold.

In this and the next chapter we will learn how to perform the accounting for inventory and cost of goods sold for a manufacturing company.

## PRODUCT AND PERIOD COSTS— A NECESSARY COST CLASSIFICATION

A **cost** is the economic sacrifice made to acquire goods or services or to attain an objective. To produce financial statements for manufacturing companies that are useful to management, cost information must be properly arranged or classified. One necessary classification is the timing of the costs, which determines when the costs will become income statement accounts. For the purpose of preparing financial statements for manufacturing companies, therefore, all costs are considered to be either product or period.

***1b. Product costs add value to the items produced and are "attached" to any product the company makes***

**Product costs** are costs associated with the manufacturing process that add value to the items produced. Accountants assign product costs to the Cost of Goods Sold section of the income statement and to the Inventory section of the balance sheet. These costs are "attached" (figuratively speaking) to any product made by the company. Costs attached to a product will not appear in the income statement until that product has been sold.

Merchandising companies afford only a few examples of costs that are assigned to inventory or cost of goods sold. The major component of such costs is the invoice price of merchandise purchased and sold. Sometimes a portion of transportation and other related costs is added.

Manufacturing companies acquire materials in a "raw" state and transform them physically into new items to be sold to customers. The production process entails many kinds of product costs, such as the following:

Materials that constitute a part of, or are associated with, the finished product
Labor that is associated both directly and indirectly with the production process
Utilities on the buildings or parts of buildings devoted to the production process
Depreciation on plant and equipment assets used in production
Salaries and wages of employees who work in the manufacturing process

Accountants assign such costs either to cost of goods sold or to inventory by using a concept called *cost per unit.* As a simple example, assume the following:

| | |
|---|---|
| Total Manufacturing Cost for the Year | $10,000 |
| Number of Units Manufactured for the Year (assume no inventory from the prior year) | 5,000 |
| Cost per Unit ($10,000 ÷ 5,000 units) | $ 2.00 |

This $2 unit cost is "attached" to each manufactured item. Thus the assignment of the $10,000 to cost of goods sold and to inventory depends on how many units are sold and how many remain on hand at year-end. If 4,000 of the 5,000 manufactured units were sold, the product cost of $10,000 would be divided as follows:

| | |
|---|---|
| Cost of Goods Sold: 4,000 × $2 = | $ 8,000 |
| Inventory: 1,000 × $2 = | 2,000 |
| Total Manufacturing Cost Assigned | $10,000 |

In actual practice the determining of cost per unit is much more complicated than in this illustration. Chapter 22 gives a detailed explanation of unit cost calculations.

*1b. Period costs appear in the income statement based on the passage of time and are usually shown as operating expenses*

**Period costs** appear in the income statement on the basis of the passage of time rather than movement of manufactured units. Such costs, since they are not associated with the manufacturing process, are usually shown as operating expenses. Examples of period costs include commissions, delivery, depreciation on selling and clerical facilities, and salaries of selling and clerical employees.

Note that such accounts as depreciation, salaries, utilities, repairs, and taxes can be either product or period costs, depending on whether they are associated with the manufacturing process. Sometimes a company has a cost like utilities on both the plant and office operations. In this case the part of the utilities cost on the plant is a product cost, and the part of the utilities cost on the office is a period cost.

At this point we can think of product costs of a manufacturing company as belonging in the Cost of Goods Sold section of the income statement. Also, we can consider period costs of a manufacturing company as belonging in the Operating Expenses section of the income statement.

## INVENTORIES IN A MANUFACTURING COMPANY

**Product costing** can be defined generally as the recordkeeping process that establishes the cost of purchased or manufactured merchandise and assigns that cost to the income statement (under cost of goods sold) or to the balance sheet (under inventory).

*1c. Inventories in a manufacturing company can be divided into three categories: direct materials, work in process, and finished goods*

Product costing is necessary for formulating the financial statements of manufacturing companies. The inventories and their costs in a manufacturing company can be divided into three categories:

**Direct materials inventory**—the acquisition cost of materials not yet placed in the manufacturing process

**Work in process inventory**—the cost of direct materials together with related conversion costs of goods still in the production process

**Finished goods inventory**—the cost of direct materials together with related conversion costs of completely processed goods that are on hand available for sale

Exhibit 21–3 presents abbreviated financial statements of a merchandising and a manufacturing company so that you can compare the way they list their inventories. Note that the cost of goods manufactured in a manufacturing company is comparable to cost of purchases in a merchandising company. Note also that a manufacturing company keeps three separate categories of inventory costs on its balance sheet. A merchandising company needs only one.

EXHIBIT 21–3
Inventory Differences Between Merchandising and Manufacturing Companies

Income Statement

| Merchandising Company | | | Manufacturing Company | | |
|---|---|---|---|---|---|
| Sales | | $514,000 | Sales | | $514,000 |
| Cost of Goods Sold: | | | Cost of Goods Sold: | | |
| Inventory of Merchandise, 1/1 | $ 42,000 | | Inventory of Finished Goods, 1/1 | $ 42,000 | |
| Cost of Purchases | 285,000 | | Cost of (Finished) Goods Manufactured | 285,000 | |
| Cost of Goods Available for Sale | $327,000 | | Cost of Goods Available for Sale | $327,000 | |
| Inventory of Merchandise, 1/31 | 45,000 | | Inventory of Finished Goods, 1/31 | 45,000 | |
| Cost of Goods Sold | | $282,000 | Cost of Goods Sold | | $282,000 |
| Gross Profit on Sales | | $232,000 | Gross Profit on Sales | | $232,000 |

Balance Sheet

| Merchandising Company | | Manufacturing Company | |
|---|---|---|---|
| Current Assets: | | Current Assets: | |
| Inventory of Merchandise | $ 45,000 | Inventory of Direct Materials | $ 12,000 |
| | | Inventory of Work in Process | 40,000 |
| | | Inventory of Finished Goods | 45,000 |

## ELEMENTS OF MANUFACTURING COSTS

*1d. Manufacturing costs are divided into three elements: direct materials, direct labor, and manufacturing overhead*

To achieve the objective of product costing, a manufacturing company must compute the cost of the items produced. This computation requires recognizing the three elements of manufacturing cost:

Direct materials
Direct labor
Manufacturing overhead

**Direct materials** (sometimes called **raw materials**) refers to all materials that become an intrinsic part of, and can readily and practically be associated with, the finished product.

Those materials that are indirectly associated with the finished product are classified as **indirect materials.** Rivets, tacks, glue, thread, and grease provide examples of the latter category.

**Direct labor** consists of the labor effort applied by the worker upon materials either by physical contact or through the medium of a machine to transform them into finished products.

Any labor that cannot be associated directly with the finished products or is not performed directly upon the material being converted into finished products is classified as **indirect labor.** The costs of inspectors, general helpers, supervisors, cleaners, and other such laborers belong in the indirect category.

**Manufacturing overhead** (sometimes called **overhead**) consists of all manufacturing costs except direct materials and direct labor that are connected with the production of a product.

It is impractical to trace manufacturing overhead costs to individual units of a product. These costs are incurred jointly to benefit a group of products. Unlike direct materials and direct labor, which can be readily and directly associated with a specific finished product, manufacturing overhead costs must be related indirectly to finished products through some equitable assignment. (These assignment methods are discussed in Chapter 22.)

Among the many types of manufacturing costs identified as manufacturing overhead are the following:

Indirect materials and indirect labor
Factory property taxes and fire insurance
Factory light, heat, and power
Factory repairs and maintenance
Depreciation of factory equipment and machinery
Depreciation of factory buildings

## THE FLOW OF COSTS

The process of collecting, summarizing, and classifying data in a manufacturing company is the same as that in a merchandising company. The major difference is that a manufacturing company needs more accounts to collect such data.

### Cost Attachment

As we have seen, it is convenient and has become traditional to classify the three elements of manufacturing cost as direct materials, direct labor, and manufacturing overhead. Direct materials and direct labor are called **prime costs.** Direct labor and manufacturing overhead are referred to as *conversion costs.*

Manufacturing companies require three inventory accounts because the materials pass through three stages of production. At any point in time, the materials are

In a preproduction "raw" state,
Partially completed, or
Finished and ready for sale to customers.

The relationships between the three elements of manufacturing costs and the three inventory accounts are shown in Exhibit 21–4.

*XHIBIT 21–4*

elationship Between Elements of Manufacturing Costs and Inventory Accounts

| DIRECT MATERIALS | | WORK IN PROCESS | | FINISHED GOODS | | COST OF GOODS SOLD | |
|---|---|---|---|---|---|---|---|
| Beginning balance | | Beginning balance | | Beginning balance | | | |
| Purchases | Usage ⟶ | Direct materials | Completed ⟶ and transferred | Completed and transferred | Sold ⟶ | Sold | |
| | | Direct labor | | | | | |
| | | Manufacturing overhead | | | | | |

When finished goods are transferred (sold) to company customers, all three elements of manufacturing costs will ultimately appear in the Cost of Goods Sold section of the income statement. However, at the end of any given accounting period:

Some materials will be acquired but not placed in production.
Some production will be partially completed.
Some production will be completed and unsold.
Some production will be completed and sold to the company's customers.

When the balance sheet and income statement are prepared, some manufacturing cost is "attached" to

The direct materials inventory
The work in process inventory
The finished goods inventory
Cost of goods sold.

Thus the term **cost attachment** is used when referring to the flow of manufacturing costs.

## An Illustration of Cost Attachment

As an example, let us consider a company that manufactures chairs, tables, and other furniture (we could just as easily use steel, coal, or automobiles as an example).

Wood, paint, and other items are the direct materials.

Direct labor is the portion of the workers' payroll incurred directly converting the direct materials into finished products.

Manufacturing overhead consists of the indirect costs, such as supervision, supplies, utilities, machine repairs, indirect materials, and indirect labor.

The company has no beginning inventory of direct materials, work in process, or finished goods.

The company purchases $1,000 of direct materials; $400 of the direct materials is used in the production process, and $600 is left in the Direct (or Raw) Materials Inventory account at the end of the accounting period.

The company incurs $1,500 on direct labor, all of which is used in the production process (there is no such thing as an inventory of direct labor).

The company uses $2,000 of manufacturing overhead in the production process.

At the end of the accounting period, the company has used $200 of direct materials, $600 of direct labor, and $900 of manufacturing overhead on the production of furniture that is partially completed. The Work in Process Inventory account has a total balance of $1,700 ($200 + $600 + $900).

At the end of the accounting period, the company has used $100 of direct materials, $500 of direct labor, and $600 of manufacturing overhead on the production of furniture that is fully completed and unsold. The Finished Goods Inventory account has a total balance of $1,200 ($100 + $500 + $600).

At the end of the accounting period, the company has used $100 of direct materials, $400 of direct labor, and $500 of manufacturing overhead on the production of furniture that is fully completed and sold to customers. The Cost of Goods Sold account has a total balance of $1,000 ($100 + $400 + $500).

*2a. The assignment of manufacturing costs is illustrated in Exhibits 21–5 and 21–6*

Exhibit 21–5 shows the assignment of the three elements of manufacturing cost to the three inventory accounts and to cost of goods sold. Exhibit 21–6 shows the same cost assignment in general ledger T-account form.

The amount of manufacturing cost assigned to each inventory account and to cost of goods sold depends on the number of units that pass through each production stage and the number of units sold during the accounting period. Chapter 22 explains these cost assignments in greater depth.

*EXHIBIT 21-5*
Cost Attachment

| | TOTAL AMOUNT SPENT | = | DIRECT MATERIALS INVENTORY ACCOUNT | + | WORK IN PROCESS INVENTORY ACCOUNT | + | FINISHED GOODS INVENTORY ACCOUNT | + | COST OF GOODS SOLD ACCOUNT |
|---|---|---|---|---|---|---|---|---|---|
| Direct materials | $1,000 | | $600 | | $ 200 | | $ 100 | | $ 100 |
| Direct labor | 1,500 | | — | | 600 | | 500 | | 400 |
| Manufacturing overhead | 2,000 | | — | | 900 | | 600 | | 500 |
| | $4,500 | = | $600 | + | $1,700 | + | $1,200 | + | $1,000 |

*EXHIBIT 21-6*
Cost Attachment

| DIRECT MATERIALS | | WORK IN PROCESS | | FINISHED GOODS | | COST OF GOODS SOLD | |
|---|---|---|---|---|---|---|---|
| 1,000 | 400 → | → 400 | 2,200 → | → 2,200 | 1,000 → | → 1,000 | |
| | | 1,500 | | | | | |
| | | 2,000 | | | | | |
| 600 Ending Balance | | 1,700 Ending Balance | | 1,200 Ending Balance | | 1,000 Ending Balance | |

## *FINANCIAL REPORTING BY MANUFACTURING COMPANIES*

The different flow of costs in a manufacturing company (in contrast to a merchandising company) creates more detail in its financial statements. In addition to three inventory accounts in the balance sheet, the Cost of Goods Sold section of the income statement is supported by a separate statement of cost of goods manufactured.

To explain the financial statements prepared by a manufacturing company, we continue the illustration of cost attachment started in the preceding section. The following facts are assumed:

The Direct Materials Inventory account has a $200 balance at the beginning of the accounting period, representing the direct materials unassigned to production at the end of the last period.

The company purchased $1,000 of direct materials during the period.

The Work in Process Inventory account has an $1,800 balance at the beginning of the accounting period, representing the sum of direct materials, direct labor, and manufacturing overhead used on partially finished production at the end of the previous period.

A total of $600 of direct materials was put into production during the current period.

Amounts totaling $1,500 for direct labor and $2,000 for manufacturing overhead were spent on production during the current accounting period.

The Finished Goods Inventory account has a $1,000 balance at the beginning of the accounting period, representing the sum of direct materials, direct labor, and manufacturing overhead used on completed and unsold production at the end of the previous period.

Production totaling $4,200 of direct materials, direct labor, and manufacturing overhead was completed during the current accounting period and added to the finished goods inventory.

Cost of goods sold for the current accounting period was $4,000.

## The Income Statement and Balance Sheet

*2b. Financial statements for a manufacturing company are illustrated in Exhibits 21–7 and 21–8*

The income statement and balance sheet, assuming the described transactions, are illustrated in Exhibits 21–7 and 21–8.

EXHIBIT 21–7
Income Statement for a Manufacturing Company

CASCADE COMPANY
Income Statement
For the Year Ended December 31, 19X6

| | | |
|---|---|---|
| Sales | | $7,000 |
| Cost of Goods Sold: | | |
| Finished Goods Inventory, 1/1/X6 | $1,000 | |
| Cost of Goods Manufactured | 4,200 | |
| Cost of Finished Goods Available for Sale | $5,200 | |
| Finished Goods Inventory, 12/31/X6 | 1,200 | 4,000 |
| Gross Profit on Sales | | $3,000 |
| Operating Expenses: | | |
| Salaries | $1,000 | |
| Rent | 200 | |
| Advertising | 200 | |
| Utilities | 100 | |
| Depreciation | 800 | |
| Insurance | 200 | 2,500 |
| Net Income | | $ 500 |

EXHIBIT 21–8
Balance Sheet for a Manufacturing Company

CASCADE COMPANY
Balance Sheet
December 31, 19X6

ASSETS

| | | | |
|---|---|---|---|
| Current Assets: | | | |
| Cash | | $ 4,200 | |
| Accounts Receivable | | 3,700 | |
| Merchandise Inventories: | | | |
| Direct Materials | $ 600 | | |
| Work in Process | 1,700 | | |
| Finished Goods | 1,200 | 3,500 | |
| Prepaid Insurance | | 400 | |
| Total Current Assets | | | $11,800 |
| Long-Term Assets: | | | |
| Equipment | | $18,000 | |
| Less: Accumulated Depreciation | | 2,800 | |
| Total Long-term Assets | | | 15,200 |
| Total Assets | | | $27,000 |

LIABILITIES AND OWNER'S EQUITY

| | | |
|---|---|---|
| Current Liabilities: | | |
| Accounts Payable | $ 9,000 | |
| Salaries Payable | 300 | |
| Total Current Liabilities | | $ 9,300 |
| Owner's Equity: | | |
| S. Field, Capital | | 17,700 |
| Total Liabilities and Owner's Equity | | $27,000 |

### The Statement of Cost of Goods Manufactured

For manufacturing companies, accountants prepare a separate schedule supporting the cost of goods manufactured during the current accounting period. This schedule, called the statement of cost of goods manufactured, gives details of the three elements of manufacturing costs incurred during that accounting period and represents the cost of the inventory added to the beginning-of-period finished goods.

Exhibit 21–9 is an example of such a statement.

EXHIBIT 21–9

CASCADE COMPANY
Statement of Cost of Goods Manufactured
For the Year Ended December 31, 19X6

| | |
|---|---|
| Direct Materials: | |
| Inventory, 1/1/X6 | $ 200 |
| Add: Purchases for the year | 1,000 |
| Direct Materials available for use | $1,200 |
| Less: Inventory, 12/31/X6 | 600 |
| Direct Materials used | $ 600 |
| Direct Labor | 1,500 |
| Manufacturing Overhead | 2,000* |
| Total Current Cost of Production | $4,100 |
| Add: Work in Process Inventory, 1/1/X6 | 1,800 |
| Total Manufacturing Costs | $5,900 |
| Less: Work in Process Inventory, 12/31/X6 | 1,700 |
| Cost of Goods Manufactured | $4,200 |

* Sometimes all the individual manufacturing overhead items are listed. For example:

| | | |
|---|---|---|
| Manufacturing Overhead: | | |
| Indirect Labor | $1,000 | |
| Factory Supplies | 1,000 | $2,000 |

## ADDITIONAL COMMENTS ON ACCOUNTING FOR MANUFACTURING COSTS

Many amounts that appear in the financial statements illustrated in this chapter are supported by detailed records, some of which we will describe in the next chapter. Taken together, the illustrations and examples in this chapter depict, in a general way, accounting for manufacturing companies. In Chapter 22 we will further explain the accounting for manufacturing companies by distinguishing between job order costing and process costing.

## HIGHLIGHT PROBLEM

Selected accounts of Global Company are shown below. Some represent product costs and others represent period costs.

Required:
Prepare a statement of cost of goods manufactured for the year ended September 30, 19X6. All manufacturing overhead items should be shown separately.

| | |
|---|---:|
| Advertising Expense | $ 5,500 |
| Depreciation—Factory Building | 2,200 |
| Depreciation—Factory Machinery | 3,400 |
| Direct Labor | 83,200 |
| Factory Supplies Used | 9,400 |
| Factory Utilities | 5,600 |
| Federal Income Taxes | 22,000 |
| Finished Goods Inventory (Beginning) | 53,000 |
| Finished Goods Inventory (Ending) | 46,000 |
| Work in Process Inventory (Beginning) | 28,500 |
| Work in Process Inventory (Ending) | 19,500 |
| Indirect Labor | 17,200 |
| Insurance—Factory | 2,100 |
| Insurance—Office | 1,900 |
| Maintenance Expense—Factory | 4,300 |
| Purchases of Direct Materials | 51,000 |
| Office Salaries | 17,000 |
| Office Supplies Expense | 1,100 |
| Direct Materials Inventory (Beginning) | 12,000 |
| Direct Materials Inventory (Ending) | 15,000 |

## GLOSSARY OF KEY TERMS

**Conversion costs.** Expenditures to convert raw materials into finished goods. Direct labor and manufacturing overhead.

**Cost.** The economic sacrifice made to acquire goods or services or to attain an objective.

**Cost attachment.** Figuratively, the attaching of manufacturing costs to units. If the units are uncompleted or completed and unsold, the attached costs show up in the balance sheet. If the units are sold, the attached costs show up in the income statement.

**Direct labor.** The labor effort applied by the worker upon materials, either through physical contact or through the medium of a machine, to transform them into finished products.

**Direct materials.** All materials that become an intrinsic part of, and can be readily and practically associated with, the finished product.

**Direct materials inventory.** The acquisition cost of materials not yet placed in the manufacturing process.

**Finished goods inventory.** The cost of direct materials together with related conversion costs of completely processed goods that are on hand and available for sale.

**Indirect labor.** Any labor that cannot be associated directly with the finished products or is not performed directly upon the material being converted into finished products.

**Indirect materials.** Materials that are indirectly associated with the finished product. Many manufacturing supply items are indirect materials.

**Manufacturing company.** A company that buys raw materials, converts them into finished goods, and sells the finished goods to customers.

**Manufacturing overhead.** All manufacturing costs except direct materials and direct labor that are connected with the production of a product. Unlike direct materials and direct labor, manufacturing overhead is indirectly associated with a specific product.

**Merchandising company.** A company that sells to its customers the same products that it buys from its suppliers. Department stores and furniture companies are examples.

**Overhead.** Alternate term for *manufacturing overhead.*

**Period costs.** Costs that appear in the income statement on the basis of the passage of time rather than movement of manufactured units. Such costs are classified in the Operating Expenses section of the income statement.

**Prime costs.** Direct materials and direct labor.

**Product costing.** The recordkeeping process that establishes the cost of purchased or manufactured merchandise and assigns that cost to the income statement or to the balance sheet.

**Product costs.** Costs associated with the manufacturing process that add value to the items produced. When such costs appear in the income statement, they are classified in the Cost of Goods Sold section.

**Raw materials.** Alternate term for *direct materials.*

**Work in process inventory.** The cost of direct materials together with related conversion costs of goods still in the production process.

## REVIEW QUESTIONS

1. Differentiate between a merchandising company and a manufacturing company. [LO1a]
2. What does the cost of goods sold consist of in a manufacturing company? What does the cost of inventory consist of in a manufacturing company? [LO1a]
3. Differentiate between the dollar amounts that go into (1) the Cost of Goods Sold section of the income statement of a merchandising company and (2) the Cost of Goods Sold section of the income statement of a manufacturing company. [LO1a]
4. Differentiate between product costs and period costs. [LO1b]
5. Where are product costs assigned in the financial statements? Where are period costs assigned in the financial statements? [LO1b]
6. Give five examples of product costs. Give four examples of period costs. [LO1b]
7. What is product costing? [LO1c]
8. Name and describe the composition of the three inventories in a manufacturing company. [LO1c]
9. Differentiate between direct materials and indirect materials. [LO1d]
10. Differentiate between direct labor and indirect labor. [LO1d]
11. What is manufacturing overhead? Give six examples of manufacturing overhead. [LO1d]
12. Differentiate between prime costs and conversion costs. [LO2a]
13. Why do manufacturing companies require three inventory accounts? [LO2a]
14. Name the four accounts to which some manufacturing costs are "attached" when the balance sheet and income statement are prepared. [LO2a]
15. In financial statements of a manufacturing company, what separate statement supports the Cost of Goods Sold section of the income statement? [LO2b]
16. Describe the contents of a statement of cost of goods manufactured. [LO2b]

## ANALYTICAL QUESTIONS

17. Why must all manufacturing costs be assigned either to cost of goods sold or to an inventory account when financial statements are prepared? [LO1a,2b]
18. "What difference does it make whether a cost is classified as a product or a period cost? Eventually all costs go through the income statement." Respond to this question and explanation. [LO1b,2b]
19. "It is the conversion process that creates more inventory accounts in a manufacturing company than in a merchandising company." Explain the meaning of this statement. [LO1a,1c,1d]
20. Why are some manufacturing costs referred to as conversion costs? [LO2a]
21. If the Work in Process Inventory account is higher at the end of the period than at the beginning of the same period, would the cost of goods manufactured be higher or lower than the current cost of production? Why? [LO2b]

## IMPACT ANALYSIS QUESTIONS

*For each error described, indicate whether it would overstate [O], understate [U], or not affect [N] the specified key figures.* [LO2b]

22. The ending inventory of direct materials was overstated.

| | | | |
|---|---|---|---|
| ______ | Total Assets | ______ | Cost of Goods Sold |
| ______ | Net Income | ______ | Cost of Goods Manufactured |

23. Direct labor charges were understated.

| | | | |
|---|---|---|---|
| ______ | Current Cost of Production | ______ | Cost of Goods Sold |
| ______ | Net Income | ______ | Cost of Goods Manufactured |

24. The beginning inventory of direct materials was understated.

| | | | |
|---|---|---|---|
| ______ | Current Cost of Production | ______ | Cost of Goods Sold |
| ______ | Net Income | ______ | Cost of Goods Manufactured |

25. The ending inventory of finished goods was understated.

| | | | |
|---|---|---|---|
| ______ | Total Assets | ______ | Cost of Goods Sold |
| ______ | Current Cost of Production | ______ | Cost of Goods Manufactured |

26. Manufacturing overhead was overstated.

| | | | |
|---|---|---|---|
| ______ | Total Cost of Production | ______ | Cost of Goods Sold |
| ______ | Net Income | ______ | Cost of Goods Manufactured |

## EXERCISES

EXERCISE 21-1 *(Determine Missing Amounts in Statements of Cost of Goods Manufactured)* In each of the following cases, supply the missing amount in the blanks.

| | 1 | 2 | 3 |
|---|---|---|---|
| Indirect Materials | $ 5,000 | $ 8,000 | $10,000 |
| Direct Materials Inventory, 1/1 | 20,000 | 22,000 | 25,000 |
| Purchases of Direct Materials | 30,000 | 36,000 | 40,000 |
| Depreciation on Factory Building | 2,000 | 3,000 | 5,000 |
| Direct Labor | 6,000 | 5,000 | ______ |
| Work in Process Inventory, 12/31 | 31,000 | ______ | 45,000 |
| Direct Materials Inventory, 12/31 | 19,000 | 21,000 | 23,000 |
| Work in Process Inventory, 1/1 | 29,000 | 35,000 | 40,000 |
| Utilities on Factory Building | 3,000 | 5,000 | 8,000 |
| Cost of Goods Manufactured | ______ | 50,000 | 64,000 |

[LO2b]

EXERCISE 21-2 *(Determine Missing Amounts in Schedules of Cost of Goods Sold)* In each of the following cases, supply the missing amount in the blanks.

| | 1 | 2 | 3 |
|---|---|---|---|
| Direct Materials Used | $30,000 | $25,000 | $ 35,000 |
| Direct Labor | 40,000 | 22,000 | 40,000 |
| Manufacturing Overhead | 45,000 | ______ | 34,000 |
| Work in Process Inventory, 1/1 | 10,000 | 15,000 | 18,000 |
| Work in Process Inventory, 12/31 | 15,000 | 16,000 | 19,000 |
| Finished Goods Inventory, 1/1 | 25,000 | 21,000 | 21,000 |
| Finished Goods Inventory, 12/31 | 28,000 | 19,000 | ______ |
| Cost of Goods Sold | ______ | 75,000 | 110,000 |

[LO2b]

EXERCISE 21-3 *(Determine Missing Amounts in an Income Statement)* In each of the following items, find the unknowns, designated by blanks.

| | |
|---|---|
| Sales | $100,000 |
| Direct Materials Used | 29,000 |
| Direct Labor | 10,000 |
| Operating Expenses | 25,000 |
| Manufacturing Overhead | ______ |
| Gross Profit on Sales | ______ |
| Finished Goods Inventory, 1/1 | -0- |
| Finished Goods Inventory, 12/31 | -0- |
| Direct Materials Inventory, 1/1 | 1,000 |
| Direct Materials Inventory, 12/31 | 10,000 |
| Work in Process Inventory, 1/1 | -0- |
| Work in Process Inventory, 12/31 | -0- |
| Purchases of Direct Materials | ______ |
| Cost of Goods Manufactured | ______ |
| Net Income (Loss) | 1,000 |

[LO2b]

EXERCISE 21–4 *(Prepare a Statement of Cost of Goods Manufactured and a Schedule of Cost of Goods Sold)* From the Eldred Manufacturing Company's adjusted trial balance of December 31, 19X9, the following account balances have been calculated.

| | |
|---|---|
| Direct Materials Inventory, 1/1/X9 | 75,000 |
| Work in Process Inventory, 1/1/X9 | 21,200 |
| Finished Goods Inventory, 1/1/X9 | 50,000 |
| Purchases | 182,000 |
| Direct Labor | 125,000 |
| Indirect Labor | 40,000 |
| Heat, Light, and Power | 35,000 |
| Insurance | 6,000 |
| Factory and Machine Maintenance | 8,000 |
| Factory Supplies | 6,000 |
| Depreciation—Factory Building | 9,000 |
| Depreciation—Equipment | 23,000 |
| Property Taxes—Equipment | 3,600 |

In addition, direct materials costing $187,000 were used, the cost of goods manufactured for the year 19X9 was $440,000, and the cost of goods sold was $430,000.

Required:

1. A statement of cost of goods manufactured for the year 19X9. Show one total figure for manufacturing overhead.
2. A schedule of cost of goods sold for the year 19X9 [LO2b]

EXERCISE 21–5 *(Calculate Cost of Goods Sold from Incomplete Data)* From the following information, determine the cost of goods sold for 19X8. Assume the first year of operation.

| | |
|---|---|
| Direct Materials Purchased and Used in 19X8 | $25,000 |
| Direct Labor Used in 19X8 | 15,000 |
| Manufacturing Overhead in 19X8 | 20,000 |
| Work in Process Inventory, 12/31/X8 | 5,000 |
| Finished Goods Inventory, 12/31/X8 | 18,000 |

[LO2b]

## PROBLEMS

PROBLEM 21–1 *(Determine Cost Classifications)* In each of the ten blanks below, indicate whether the cost is a product cost or a period cost by writing product or period in the blank.

| | |
|---|---|
| 1. Direct materials that become a part of the finished product | ____ |
| 2. Hourly labor traced to the product | ____ |
| 3. Factory building utilities | ____ |
| 4. Hourly factory labor not traced to the product | ____ |
| 5. Salaried supervisory factory labor | ____ |
| 6. Commissions on sales | ____ |
| 7. Repairs to delivery trucks | ____ |
| 8. Taxes on factory building | ____ |
| 9. Indirect materials that do not become a part of the finished product | ____ |
| 10. Delivery expense | ____ |

[LO1b]

PROBLEM 21–2 *(Attach Costs to Proper Accounts)* Quesattach Company had the following transactions during its first year of operations.

1. Purchased $2,000 of direct materials.
2. Spent and used $3,000 and $4,000 of direct labor and manufacturing overhead, respectively.
3. Used $1,400 of direct materials in production.
4. The year-end work in process inventory consisted of $800 of direct materials, $1,000 of direct labor, and $1,500 of manufacturing overhead.
5. The year-end finished goods inventory consisted in part of $1,200 of direct labor and $1,600 of manufacturing overhead.
6. Total cost of goods sold for the year was $2,000.

Required:

Place the correct amounts in the blanks in the table below. Use Exhibit 21–5 as a guide.

[LO2a]

| | TOTAL | DIRECT MATERIALS INVENTORY | WORK IN PROCESS INVENTORY | FINISHED GOODS INVENTORY | COST OF GOODS SOLD |
|---|---|---|---|---|---|
| Direct Materials | $____ | $____ | $____ | $____ | $____ |
| Direct Labor | ____ | ____ | ____ | ____ | ____ |
| Manufacturing Overhead | ____ | ____ | ____ | ____ | ____ |

PROBLEM 21–3 *(Compute Various Manufacturing Cost Amounts)* The following amounts were taken from the records of the Island Manufacturing Company.

| | |
|---|---|
| Direct Material Purchases | $210,000 |
| Direct Labor | 305,000 |
| Manufacturing Overhead | 170,000 |
| Direct Material Inventories: | |
| Beginning | 43,000 |
| Ending | 37,500 |
| Work in Process Inventories: | |
| Beginning | 27,400 |
| Ending | 38,200 |
| Finished Goods Inventories: | |
| Beginning | 51,000 |
| Ending | 47,400 |

Required:

Compute (and show computations for) the following:

1. Current cost of production
2. Total manufacturing costs
3. Cost of goods manufactured
4. Cost of goods sold [LO2b]

PROBLEM 21-4 *(Prepare Statements and Calculate Inventory)* W. T. Dohr Company manufactures and sells an electric fan. The following data were taken from the company's books and other records as of January 1, 19X9 and December 31, 19X9.

| | JAN. 1, 19X9 | DEC. 31, 19X9 |
|---|---|---|
| Inventory of Direct Materials | $35,600 | $ 25,600 |
| Inventory of Work in Process | 18,000 | 25,300 |
| Inventory of Finished Goods | 66,000 | ? |
| Sales Returns | | 22,000 |
| Plant and Machinery | | 712,000 |
| Sales | | 1,584,000 |
| Direct Labor | | 350,000 |
| Power and Light—Factory | | 20,000 |
| Insurance—Factory | | 3,000 |
| Purchase Returns—Direct Materials | | 6,200 |
| Depreciation of Office Equipment | | 16,800 |
| Factory Superintendent's Salary | | 29,000 |
| Small Tools Expense—Factory | | 2,500 |
| Factory Supplies Used | | 17,200 |
| Machine Royalty Rentals | | 51,000 |
| Miscellaneous Manufacturing Overhead | | 8,500 |
| Indirect Labor | | 113,000 |
| Purchases of Direct Materials | | 452,700 |
| Depreciation of Plant and Machinery | | 51,500 |
| Repairs to Plant and Machinery | | 11,100 |
| Sales Allowances | | 2,200 |
| Property Taxes—Factory | | 21,000 |
| Factory Workmen's Compensation Insurance | | 12,000 |

Required:

1. Prepare a statement of cost of goods manufactured for the year 19X9.
2. Submit figures to find the cost of the inventory of finished goods on December 31, 19X9. Cost of Goods Sold for the year is $1,130,000.
3. Prepare a schedule of the cost of goods sold for the year 19X9.

(*Hint:* A decision must be made as to which accounts to use. Individual manufacturing overhead accounts must also be identified.) [LO2b]

PROBLEM 21-5 *(Prepare a Statement of Cost of Goods Manufactured)* Bryan Manufacturing Company manufactures and sells a small electric motor. The following data were taken from the company's books and other records as of January 1, 19X9 and December 31, 19X9.

| | JAN. 1, 19X9 | DEC. 31, 19X9 |
|---|---|---|
| Inventory of Direct Materials | $16,000 | $ 18,500 |
| Inventory of Work in Process | 12,500 | 18,500 |
| Inventory of Finished Goods | 24,000 | ? |
| Sales @ $30 each | | 533,250 |
| Sales Returns | | 4,500 |
| Cost of Goods Sold | | 370,125 |
| Direct Labor | | 140,000 |
| Factory Expenses, Miscellaneous | | 7,000 |
| Indirect Labor | | 42,000 |
| Purchases, Direct Materials | | 162,500 |
| Depreciation of Plant and Equipment | | 19,000 |
| Heat, Light, and Power—Factory | | 21,000 |
| Indirect Materials | | 16,000 |

Required:
Prepare a statement of cost of goods manufactured for the year 19X9. Individual manufacturing overhead accounts must be identified and listed. [LO2b]

PROBLEM 21–6 *(Prepare Three Statements)* The following amounts were taken from the books and records of the Denver Rug Company as of December 31, 19X8.

| | |
|---|---:|
| Cash | $ 10,000 |
| Accounts Receivable | 15,000 |
| Inventory, Direct Materials, 1/1/X8 | 3,000 |
| Inventory, Work in Process, 1/1/X8 | 2,000 |
| Inventory, Finished Goods, 1/1/X8 | 4,000 |
| Inventory, Direct Materials, 12/31/X8 | 6,000 |
| Inventory, Work in Process, 12/31/X8 | 1,000 |
| Inventory, Finished Goods, 12/31/X8 | 2,000 |
| Depreciation of Plant and Equipment | 5,000 |
| Direct Labor | 25,000 |
| Indirect Labor | 3,000 |
| Factory Supplies Used | 3,000 |
| Light, Heat, and Power—Factory | 4,000 |
| Repairs to Machinery | 600 |
| Sales Salaries | 9,500 |
| S. Denver, Capital, 1/1/X8 | 101,800 |
| Sales | 120,000 |
| Sales Returns | 1,700 |
| Purchases, Direct Materials | 60,000 |
| Purchase Discounts | 1,200 |
| Transportation-in—Direct Materials | 1,500 |
| Plant and Equipment | 100,000 |
| Accumulated Depreciation of Plant and Equipment | 15,000 |
| Shipping Expenses | 1,200 |
| Advertising | 500 |
| Administrative Salaries | 8,000 |
| Office Expenses | 1,000 |
| Accounts Payable | 20,000 |

Required:
Prepare the following:

1. Statement of cost of goods manufactured for the year ended December 31, 19X8.
2. Income statement for the year ended December 31, 19X8. Show clearly the determination of the cost of goods sold.
3. Balance sheet as of December 31, 19X8. [LO2b]

PROBLEM 21–7 *(Prepare a Statement of Cost of Goods Manufactured)* Michigan Manufacturing Company manufactures and sells product A. The following amounts were taken from its books and records as of December 31, 19X8.

| | |
|---|---|
| Inventory of Direct Materials, 1/1/X8 | $ 12,000 |
| Inventory of Work in Process, 1/1/X8 | 14,000 |
| Inventory of Finished Goods, 1/1/X8 | 10,000 |
| Inventory of Direct Materials, 12/31/X8 | 16,000 |
| Inventory of Work in Process, 12/31/X8 | 8,000 |
| Inventory of Finished Goods, 12/31/X8 | 18,000 |
| Sales | 444,000 |
| Purchases of Direct Materials | 246,000 |
| Direct Labor | 100,000 |
| Indirect Labor | 10,000 |
| Property Taxes—Factory | 2,000 |
| Depreciation of Plant and Machinery | 18,000 |
| Light, Heat, and Power—Factory | 6,000 |
| Repairs to Machinery | 1,000 |
| Payroll Taxes—Factory | 6,000 |
| Factory Supplies Used | 4,000 |
| Delivery Expense | 2,000 |
| Payroll Taxes—Office | 3,400 |

Required:

Prepare a statement of cost of goods manufactured for the year ended December 31, 19X8. Individual manufacturing overhead accounts must be identified and listed.

[LO2b]

PROBLEM 21–8 *(Prepare Two Statements)* The following amounts were taken from the books and records of the M.B.K. Company at the close of its fiscal year, July 31, 19X8.

| | AUG. 1, 19X7 | JULY 31, 19X8 |
|---|---|---|
| Inventories: | | |
| Direct Materials Inventory | $ 30,500 | $ 42,400 |
| Work in Process Inventory | 19,200 | 14,000 |
| Finished Goods Inventory | 66,500 | 68,000 |
| Other Information: | | |
| Sales | | $517,000 |
| Direct Labor | | 112,000 |
| Indirect Labor | | 41,200 |
| Direct Materials Used | | 95,000 |
| Office Expense | | 800 |
| Sales Returns | | 3,700 |
| Depreciation—Factory | | 7,300 |
| Telephone Expense—Office | | 3,400 |
| Depreciation—Delivery Equipment | | 4,200 |
| Sales Commissions | | 39,600 |
| Advertising | | 18,400 |
| Utilities* | | 24,000 |
| Delivery Expense | | 17,300 |
| Factory Supplies Used | | 16,100 |
| Administrative Salaries | | 12,000 |
| Office Salaries | | 18,100 |
| Insurance Expense† | | 6,800 |
| Total Current Cost of Production | | 307,100 |
| Direct Materials Purchased | | 106,900 |
| Depreciation—Office Equipment | | 900 |
| Rental Expense‡ | | 16,000 |
| Repairs—Factory | | 1,600 |
| Repairs—Office | | 400 |

* Utilities expense is divided as follows: 80% to manufacturing, 20% to operating expense.
† Insurance expense is divided as follows: 75% to manufacturing, 25% to operating expense.
‡ Rental expense is divided as follows: 60% to manufacturing, 40% to operating expense.

Required:

1. Prepare a statement of cost of goods manufactured for the year ended July 31, 19X8. Individual manufacturing overhead accounts must be identified and listed.
2. Prepare an income statement for the year ended July 31, 19X8. [LO2b]

## ALTERNATE PROBLEMS

PROBLEM 21-1A *(Prepare a Statement of Cost of Goods Manufactured)* (Alternate to Problem 21-5) The Capital Manufacturing Company manufactures and sells baseballs. Its inventory accounts at the beginning of the year had the following balances:

| | |
|---|---:|
| Direct Materials | $16,000 |
| Work in Process | 61,000 |
| Finished Goods | 28,000 |

During the year the following costs and expenses were incurred:

| | |
|---|---:|
| Purchases of Direct Materials | $115,000 |
| Direct Labor | 52,000 |
| Sales Salaries | 47,000 |
| Administrative Salaries | 22,000 |
| Indirect Labor | 14,000 |
| Rental Expense—Factory | 24,000 |
| Rental Expense—Office | 6,000 |
| Depreciation Expense—Factory | 3,200 |
| Depreciation Expense—Office | 1,400 |
| Utilities—Factory | 5,600 |
| Utilities—Office | 2,200 |
| Supplies—Office | 800 |
| Supplies—Factory | 6,700 |

The inventory accounts revealed the following balances at year-end:

| | |
|---|---:|
| Direct Materials | $19,000 |
| Work in Process | 53,000 |
| Finished Goods | 12,000 |

Required:

Prepare a statement of cost of goods manufactured for the year ended August 31, 19X5. Individual manufacturing overhead accounts must be identified and listed. [LO2b]

PROBLEM 21-2A *(Prepare Three Statements)* (Alternate to Problem 21-6) The adjusted trial balance (except for the inventories) for the Zero Company on June 30, 19X5, the end of its fiscal year, is presented below.

ZERO COMPANY
Adjusted Trial Balance
June 30, 19X5

| | | |
|---|---|---|
| Cash | 55,000 | |
| Accounts Receivable | 89,400 | |
| Direct Materials Inventory, 7/1/X4 | 12,500 | |
| Work in Process Inventory, 7/1/X4 | 15,000 | |
| Finished Goods Inventory, 7/1/X4 | 11,100 | |
| Factory Machinery | 196,000 | |
| Accumulated Depreciation—Machinery | | 59,500 |
| Nonfactory Equipment | 61,400 | |
| Accumulated Depreciation—Equipment | | 24,600 |
| Accounts Payable | | 37,100 |
| Accrued Expenses Payable | | 12,200 |
| A. Zero, Capital | | 238,900 |
| Sales | | 543,000 |
| Direct Materials Purchases* | 106,700 | |
| Direct Labor | 153,500 | |
| Manufacturing Overhead (total) | 94,900 | |
| Selling Expenses (total) | 87,200 | |
| Administrative Expenses (total) | 32,600 | |
| | 915,300 | 915,300 |

* Assume that the periodic inventory method is used and that a separate account is used for purchases.

Inventories at June 30, 19X5, were as follows:

| | |
|---|---|
| Direct materials inventory | $15,100 |
| Work in process inventory | 9,800 |
| Finished goods inventory | 13,400 |

Required:
1. Prepare a statement of cost of goods manufactured for the year ended June 30, 19X5.
2. Prepare an income statement for the year ended June 30, 19X5.
3. Prepare a balance sheet as of June 30, 19X5. [LO2b]

PROBLEM 21–3A *(Prepare a Statement of Cost of Goods Manufactured)* (Alternate to Problem 21–7) The following items were taken from the books and records of the Better-Way Manufacturing Company as of December 31, 19X5, its year-end.

| | |
|---|---|
| Direct Materials Inventory (Beginning) | $ 19,000 |
| Direct Materials Inventory (Ending) | 16,000 |
| Work in Process Inventory (Ending) | 14,000 |
| Work in Process Inventory (Beginning) | 10,000 |
| Finished Goods Inventory (Beginning) | 21,000 |
| Finished Goods Inventory (Ending) | 16,000 |
| Sales | 380,000 |
| Direct Materials Purchased | 82,000 |
| Direct Labor | 99,000 |
| Indirect Labor | 15,000 |
| Heat, Light, and Power—Factory | 12,000 |
| Machinery Repairs | 3,000 |
| Machinery Depreciation | 4,000 |
| Factory Building Repairs | 2,000 |
| Factory Building Rent | 9,000 |
| Factory Supplies Used | 7,000 |
| Selling Expenses | 78,000 |
| Administrative Expenses | 35,000 |

Required:
From the information given above, prepare a statement of cost of goods manufactured for the year ended December 31, 19X5. Individual manufacturing overhead accounts must be identified and listed. [LO2b]

PROBLEM 21–4A *(Prepare Two Statements)* (Alternate to Problem 21–8) The following amounts, presented alphabetically, were taken from the December 31, 19X8, trial balance of the Oxcam Company.

| | |
|---|---|
| Accounts Payable | $ 25,500 |
| Accounts Receivable | 54,280 |
| Accumulated Depreciation—Equipment | 36,070 |
| Advertising | 12,200 |
| Bad Debts Expense | 1,100 |
| B. Oxcam, Capital | 199,315 |
| Cash | 26,645 |
| Delivery Expense | 6,900 |
| Depreciation—Equipment | 9,100 |
| Direct Labor | 84,200 |
| Direct Materials Inventory, 1/1/X8 | 15,360 |
| Direct Materials Purchased | 70,500 |
| Equipment | 232,000 |
| Factory Insurance | 9,300 |
| Factory Rent | 7,200 |
| Factory Supplies | 13,900 |
| Finished Goods Inventory, 1/1/X8 | 10,500 |
| Work in Process Inventory, 1/1/X8 | 7,400 |
| Indirect Labor | 10,700 |
| Interest Expense | 800 |
| Notes Payable | 35,000 |
| Office Salaries | 12,200 |
| Officers' Salaries | 25,000 |
| Prepaid Insurance | 5,300 |
| Salaries Payable | 8,200 |
| Sales | 437,600 |
| Sales Salaries | 47,800 |
| Selling Expenses | 18,400 |
| Stationery and Postage | 2,300 |
| Utilities—Factory | 23,400 |

Additional Information:

The beginning direct materials inventory was 80% of the ending direct materials inventory. The ending finished goods inventory was 10% below the beginning finished goods inventory, and the ending work in process inventory increased by $12\frac{1}{2}$% over the beginning work in process inventory. The cost of utilities is divided as follows: 80% to manufacturing and 20% to operating expense.

Required:

1. Prepare a statement of cost of goods manufactured. Individual manufacturing overhead accounts must be identified and listed.
2. Prepare an income statement.

(*Hint:* Balance sheet accounts must be identified.) [LO2b]

# 22 Cost Accounting Systems

## *Learning Objectives*

After you complete this chapter you will be able to

1. Answer the following questions:
   a. What is the difference between job order costing and process costing?
   b. What control records are used in job order accounting?
   c. What are the cost flows in a job order costing system?
   d. What is a predetermined overhead rate, and what are its components?
   e. What are the cost flows in a process costing system?
   f. What are equivalent units of production, and when are they used?
2. Perform the following accounting functions:
   a. Account for direct materials, direct labor, and manufacturing overhead in a job order costing system.
   b. Calculate the predetermined overhead rate.
   c. Account for direct materials, direct labor, and manufacturing overhead in a process costing system.
   d. Prepare a cost-of-production report.
   e. Calculate equivalent units of production.

In this chapter we take a closer look at product costing and, in particular, two product costing methods: job order costing and process costing. We will start with a general discussion of the difference between the two. Then we will examine the accounting for both methods.

## HOW JOB ORDER COSTING DIFFERS FROM PROCESS COSTING

Both job order and process costing accomplish the same basic results — the costs of manufactured products are collected, reported, and used in a variety of ways, including preparation of periodic financial statements. The method used by a particular company will depend upon the nature of its manufacturing operation.

**Job order costing** is a method of product costing whereby costs are accumulated by jobs. It is appropriate when it is desirable and possible to distinguish each unit or group of units throughout the production process. In terms of industries, job order costing is:

Very adaptable to the construction industry because each contract represents a separate project (job), and costs can easily be collected on such a basis.

Usable for locomotive or aircraft production because these industries produce physically separate and identifiable units.

Applicable to printing, foundry, or furniture-making processes in which a single production order covers identical or similar products.

*1a. Job order costing accumulates product costs for each job*

Job order costing is used by companies that have a number of high-dollar items, whose products are manufactured according to customers' orders or specifications, and where the identity of each job is kept separately. The three product costs are assigned and accumulated separately for each job currently in production.

Direct materials used and direct labor are *identified* with and *charged* to the specific job on which they were incurred.

Manufacturing overhead, which cannot be traced directly to the production of a specific item, is *estimated* and *assigned* or *applied* to each job.

In job order costing, unit costs are computed by using the following formula:

$$\frac{\text{Total Manufacturing Costs of the Finished Job}}{\text{Number of Units Produced for the Finished Job}}$$

*1a. Process costing accumulates product costs for each processing department*

**Process costing** is a method of product costing whereby costs are accumulated by processing departments or processing centers, and a unit cost is calculated for each department or cost center each month. It is appropriate when the company has a large number of low-dollar items, where the manufacturing process occurs continuously and routinely, and when standardized items are mass produced. The items are not produced according to customer specifications. Sometimes at the time of production the customers' identity is unknown. Such industries as cement, flour, coal, automobile, textile, steel, chemical, and oil refining use process costing.

In process costing the producing departments (such as cutting, assembling, and finishing) collect the product costs that we need to prepare the financial statements. A producing department (sometimes called a cost center) performs a specific step or operation in the completion of the product.

In process costing the *time period*, rather than the job, is the basis for measurement of unit costs. At the end of a month, quarter, or other period, unit costs for process costing are computed by using the following formula:

$$\frac{\text{Total Manufacturing Costs for the Period}}{\text{Number of Units Produced for the Period}}$$

## CONTROL RECORDS FOR JOB ORDER COSTING

*1b. Important control records in job order costing are requisitions, time tickets, and job cost sheets*

All costing systems require records and documentation. In job order costing some of the most important records consist of:

Requisitions used for direct materials.
Time tickets used for direct labor.
Job cost sheets used to accumulate all manufacturing costs charged to each job.

### Control of Direct Materials Costs

*1b. The materials requisition form shows direct materials issued to production*

Direct materials costs derive from direct materials issued to production on the basis of a **materials requisition form.** The materials requisition form in Exhibit 22–1 shows that $2,000 of materials have been issued for use on a specific job numbered 9474. These materials are direct because they can be identified with a specific job. *Indirect materials,* such as supplies, cannot be identified with a specific job and are classified as manufacturing overhead.

Note that the materials requisition shows information concerning the description, quantity, unit cost, and total cost of materials requisitioned for use on Job No. 9474. This is one of several forms that serve as documents and provide information concerning each event or transaction involved in the production process.

EXHIBIT 22–1

Materials Requisition Form

MATERIALS REQUISITION

Requisition No. 4128 Date 12/1/X9
Job. No. 9474
Department No. 71
Authorized by MBK

| Description | Quantity | Unit Cost | Total Cost |
|---|---|---|---|
| Piping Assembly | 500 | $4.00 | $2,000 |

### Control of Direct Labor Costs

*1b. Labor time tickets are the basis for computing direct and indirect labor costs*

The procedure for charging direct labor costs to specific jobs is similar to that for direct materials costs. Factory employees enter their hours on a source document called a **labor time ticket.** A labor time ticket is shown in Exhibit 22–2. Note that this ticket shows daily labor information for a specific employee (identified as No. 317). The cost of the labor has been assigned to Job No. 9474. The labor time tickets of all employees are collected and sent to the accounting department. There they are summarized and classified as *direct labor costs* or *indirect labor costs.*

Direct labor costs are chargeable *directly* to a job. Indirect labor costs, since they cannot be traced to any one job, are charged to manufacturing overhead. For example, the wages of workers who actually cut, assemble, and finish the furniture products (for a furniture manufacturer) are charged to direct labor. Supervisors' salaries and wages for other work incidental to the production process are assigned to indirect labor.

EXHIBIT 22–2

Labor Time Ticket

| | | | |
|---|---|---|---|
| | | Ticket No. | 3741 |
| Work Performed | Assembly | Employee No. | 317 |
| Job No. | 9474 | Date | 12/5/X9 |
| Time Started | 9:00 | | |
| Time Stopped | 5:00 | | |
| Total Hours | 8 | | |
| Rate per Hour | $10 | Total Cost | $80 |

## Job Cost Sheet

*1b. Job cost sheets accumulate the costs of each job*

The costs of each job are accumulated on a document known as a **job cost sheet.** The job cost sheet is the primary control document used to account for all manufacturing costs in a job order costing system. A separate sheet is kept for each job. The sheet provides an itemized listing and a summary of all direct materials, direct labor, and manufacturing overhead charged to a specific job.

An example of a job cost sheet is shown in Exhibit 22–3. We see that direct materials used and direct labor were charged directly to the specific job on which they were incurred. Manufacturing overhead was charged by using a reliable basis of allocation to assign or apply some of the total manufacturing overhead to this specific job.

Exhibit 22–3 shows that the items produced for Allison Brothers under Job Order No. 9474 had a total cost of $26,400. This amount includes the following:

$8,000 for materials, as documented by material requisition forms
$8,600 for direct labor, as shown on labor time tickets
$9,800 of allocated manufacturing overhead

The job cost sheet in Exhibit 22–3 shows the cost to produce one unit ($26,400 ÷ 4,400 = $6), the selling price ($61,600), and the gross profit on sales ($35,200).

Job cost sheets are prepared when a sales order is received and production begins. The items will be manufactured according to a customer's orders or specifications. Therefore production will generally begin when the sales department has confirmed with the customer all aspects of the sale, such as selling price, quantity, and shipping dates.

In addition to serving as a convenient document to summarize all manufacturing costs incurred on a specific job, the job cost sheets function as subsidiary

EXHIBIT 22–3
Job Cost Sheet

| Customer | Allison Brothers | Job Order Number | 9474 |
|---|---|---|---|
| Specifications | Attached | Date Ordered | 10/18/X9 |
| Blueprint | Attached | Date Commenced | 12/1/X9 |
| Description | Widget 226A4 | Date Completed | 12/13/X9 |
| Quantity | 4400 | Date Shipped | 12/15/X9 |

Direct Materials

| Date | Department | Requisition | Amount |
|---|---|---|---|
| 12/1 | 71 | 4128 | $2,000 |
| 12/1 | 72 | 4129 | 4,000 |
| 12/1 | 73 | 4210 | 2,000 |
| | | Total | $8,000 |

Direct Labor

| Date | Department | Operation | Amount |
|---|---|---|---|
| 12/1–6 | 71 | 112 | $1,400 |
| 12/6–10 | 72 | 231 | 4,200 |
| 12/10–13 | 73 | 317 | 3,000 |
| | | Total | $8,600 |

Manufacturing Overhead

| Date | Department | Basis | Amount |
|---|---|---|---|
| 12/6 | 71 | Machine Hrs. | $3,500 |
| 12/13 | 72 | D.L. Hrs. | 4,800 |
| 12/13 | 73 | D.L. Cost | 1,500 |
| | | | $9,800 |

Summary

| | |
|---|---|
| Direct Materials | $ 8,000 |
| Direct Labor | 8,600 |
| Manufacturing Overhead | 9,800 |
| Total Manufacturing Cost | $26,400 |
| Units Produced | 4,400 |
| Unit Cost | $ 6.00 |
| Selling Price | $61,600 |
| Manufacturing Cost | 26,400 |
| Gross Profit | $35,200 |

ledgers during and after the manufacturing process. The job cost sheets for all unfinished jobs serve as a subsidiary ledger for the Work in Process Inventory account.

The total of *all* costs shown on the job cost sheets of unfinished jobs should equal the *debit* balance in the Work in Process Inventory account at the end of the accounting period.

When a job is completed, the job cost sheet is transferred to the subsidiary ledger for finished goods.

The total of *all* costs shown on the job cost sheets of finished and unsold jobs should equal the *debit* balance in the Finished Goods Inventory account. When the finished goods are shipped to the customer, the total cost of the job is charged to the Cost of Goods Sold account. The job cost sheet is then transferred to a cost of goods sold subsidiary ledger.

The total of all costs on the job cost sheets of finished and sold jobs should equal the *amount* shown in the Cost of Goods Sold account.

Exhibit 22–4 contains information pertaining to six jobs of the Dart Manufacturing Company. Each job is supported by a job cost sheet showing the three elements of manufacturing cost.

> Jobs 1 and 2 are in process; their cumulative cost of $11,100 equals the debit balance in the Work in Process Inventory account.

EXHIBIT 22–4

Jobs of Dart Manufacturing Company in Various Stages

| | JOB NO. 1 | JOB NO. 2 | JOB NO. 3 | JOB NO. 4 | JOB NO. 5 | JOB NO. 6 |
|---|---|---|---|---|---|---|
| Direct Materials | $1,000 | $2,500 | $3,000 | $ 5,800 | $2,200 | $2,900 |
| Direct Labor | 1,500 | 2,300 | 1,800 | 5,200 | 3,000 | 3,000 |
| Manufacturing Overhead | 1,200 | 2,600 | 1,200 | 6,000 | 2,100 | 2,800 |
| | $3,700 | $7,400 | $6,000 | $17,000 | $7,300 | $8,700 |
| Work in Process | $11,100 | | | | | |
| Finished Goods Inventory | | | $23,000 | | | |
| Cost of Goods Sold | | | | | $16,000 | |

Jobs 3 and 4 are finished but unshipped; their cumulative cost of $23,000 equals the debit balance in the Finished Goods Inventory account.

Jobs 5 and 6 are finished and shipped; their cumulative cost of $16,000 is transferred to the Cost of Goods Sold account.

## A COST FLOW ILLUSTRATION OF JOB ORDER COSTING

*1c. Exhibit 22–5 depicts the flow of manufacturing costs*

To understand job order costing we need to understand the jobs' cost flows and the accumulation of the data required for financial statements. Manufacturing cost flows were briefly discussed in Chapter 21 and are depicted in Exhibit 22–5. In the following sections we will demonstrate the techniques needed to

EXHIBIT 22–5

Manufacturing Cost Flows

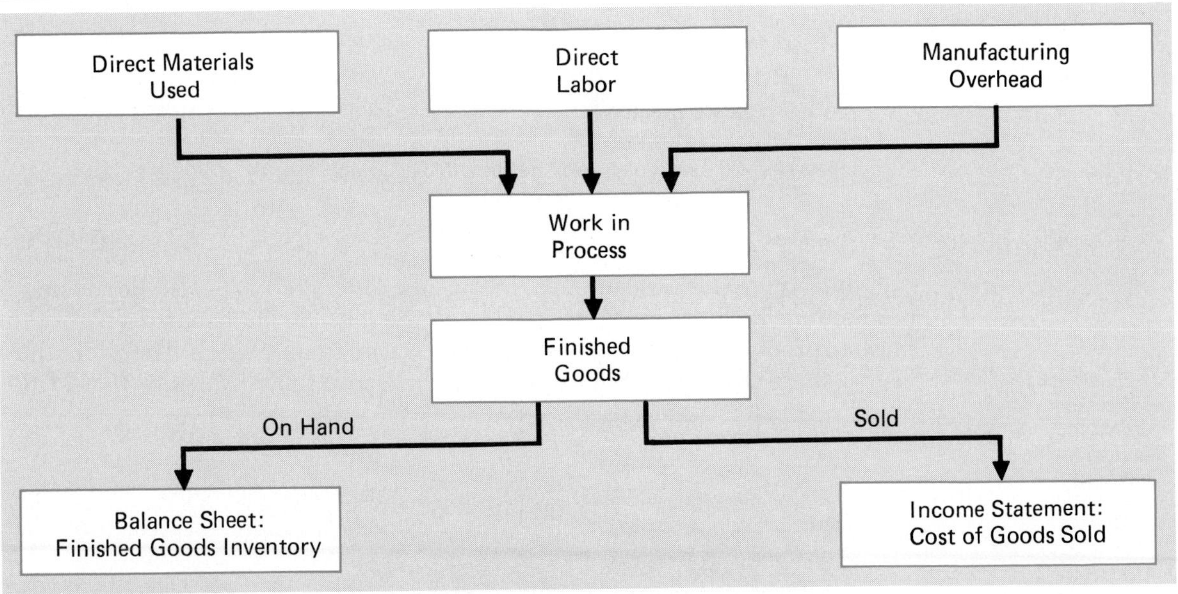

account for these cost flows by preparing journal entries and posting selected ledger accounts. We will assume the use of the perpetual inventory system. Thus debits and credits made to raw materials, work in process, and finished goods will be made to accounts entitled Raw Materials Inventory, Work in Process Inventory, and Finished Goods Inventory.

## ACCOUNTING FOR MATERIALS COSTS

Generally, materials are acquired through orders issued by a purchasing agent or someone with similar authority. Suppose that Dart Manufacturing Company purchased $50,000 of materials to be used both directly and indirectly in the manufacturing process. The entry to record this purchase would be as follows:

| | | |
|---|---|---|
| Raw Materials Inventory | 50,000 | |
| Accounts Payable | | 50,000 |
| To record raw materials purchased | | |

*1c,2a. In job order costing, costs of materials are accumulated in Raw Materials Inventory*

In Chapter 21 we kept the illustrations simple and straightforward by assuming that all materials inventory consisted of direct materials. However, we will now assume that both direct and indirect materials are accumulated in the same account, which we will refer to as *Raw Materials Inventory.*

Materials are kept in a warehouse or storeroom until issued for use in production upon receipt of authorized materials requisition forms. Assume that $15,000 of materials classified as direct have been requisitioned for use on Job No. 172. These materials can be traced to and become a part of the finished product on this job. (Wood for furniture products is an example.)

*1c,2a. Issuance of direct materials is debited to Work in Process Inventory*

The following entry would record the issuance of direct materials to production:

| | | |
|---|---|---|
| Work in Process Inventory | 15,000 | |
| Raw Materials Inventory | | 15,000 |
| To record the issuance of direct materials to production | | |

*1c,2a. Issuance of indirect materials is debited to Manufacturing Overhead*

*Indirect materials* (supplies, lubricants, glue, etc.) may also be needed in production. Such materials are used in *all* the jobs, do not become a part of the finished product, and cannot be practically traced to any *one* job. Therefore these materials are charged to manufacturing overhead as follows (assume that $1,000 of indirect materials are used):

| | | |
|---|---|---|
| Manufacturing Overhead | 1,000 | |
| Raw Materials Inventory | | 1,000 |
| To record the issuance of indirect materials to production | | |

## ACCOUNTING FOR LABOR COSTS

The procedures for charging labor costs to production are similar to those used for materials costs. Labor costs are also classified as direct or indirect, depending upon our ability to trace the cost to a specific job.

*1c,2a. Direct labor costs are debited to Work in Process Inventory*

Recall that manufacturing labor costs are accumulated by using time tickets for each employee. The tickets are summarized to calculate the total labor costs applicable to each job. Assume that direct labor costs attributable to Job No. 172 are $10,000 and are recorded as follows:

| | | |
|---|---|---|
| Work in Process Inventory . . . . . . . . . . . . . . . . . . . . . . . . . . . . . . . . . . | 10,000 | |
| Wages Payable. . . . . . . . . . . . . . . . . . . . . . . . . . . . . . . . . . . . . . . | | 10,000 |
| To record direct labor costs on Job No. 172 | | |

*1c,2a. Indirect labor costs are debited to Manufacturing Overhead*

*Indirect labor* includes the wages of employees who work in the production process, but not on a specific job. Examples would include wages earned by maintenance, custodian, and supervisory employees. If $2,000 of indirect labor costs were used in production, the following journal entry would record these costs:

| | | |
|---|---|---|
| Manufacturing Overhead. . . . . . . . . . . . . . . . . . . . . . . . . . . . . . . . . . . . | 2,000 | |
| Wages Payable. . . . . . . . . . . . . . . . . . . . . . . . . . . . . . . . . . . . . . . | | 2,000 |
| To record indirect labor costs incurred in production | | |

## ACCOUNTING FOR MANUFACTURING OVERHEAD

*1c,2a. Other manufacturing overhead costs are debited as a sum to Manufacturing Overhead and credited to specific accounts*

Assume that Dart Manufacturing Company incurred the following manufacturing overhead costs in addition to the indirect materials and indirect labor costs already recorded:

| | |
|---|---|
| Repairs (on account) | $ 300 |
| Utilities (on account) | 1,200 |
| Insurance (on account) | 600 |
| Property taxes (accrued) | 900 |
| Depreciation on factory equipment | 3,000 |

The journal entry to record these costs would be as follows:

| | | |
|---|---|---|
| Manufacturing Overhead. . . . . . . . . . . . . . . . . . . . . . . . . . . . . . . . . . . . | 6,000 | |
| Accounts Payable ($300 + $1,200 + $600) . . . . . . . . . . . . . . . | | 2,100 |
| Property Taxes Payable. . . . . . . . . . . . . . . . . . . . . . . . . . . . . . . | | 900 |
| Accumulated Depreciation . . . . . . . . . . . . . . . . . . . . . . . . . . . . | | 3,000 |
| To record manufacturing overhead costs incurred | | |

As indicated earlier, manufacturing overhead is incurred for the general benefit of all production activity and cannot be identified with particular jobs. Therefore a procedure must be developed to *assign* manufacturing overhead to jobs on some reasonable basis. The procedure uses a *predetermined manufacturing overhead rate.*

## Predetermined Manufacturing Overhead Rate

A **predetermined overhead rate** is a rate calculated at the beginning of the accounting period and is used to assign the manufacturing overhead to the cost of the individual jobs. For example, if the rate is $2 per direct labor hour, each job is charged with $2 times the number of direct labor hours spent on that particular job. Because we can easily determine the number of direct labor hours spent on any one job, assigning manufacturing overhead becomes a mathematical process once the predetermined manufacturing rate is derived. This rate is determined by using the following three-step process.

*1d,2b. A predetermined overhead rate is determined in a three-step process*

1. Select a productive activity that has some relationship to the incurrence of manufacturing overhead. For example, management might perceive or identify a correlation between the number of direct labor hours spent in production and the amount of manufacturing overhead incurred. Other activities frequently used include:
   The number of machine hours, and
   The amount of direct labor costs.
2. At the beginning of the accounting period, make estimates of:
   The level of activity (number of direct labor hours, for example) for the period, and
   The total manufacturing overhead to be incurred for the same period.
3. Find the predetermined manufacturing overhead rate by dividing:
   The estimated manufacturing overhead by
   The estimated level of activity.

   The equation is

$$\text{Predetermined Overhead Rate} = \frac{\text{Estimated Manufacturing Overhead for the Period}}{\text{Estimated Level of Activity for the Period}}$$

If the company budgets $160,000 of manufacturing overhead costs and also budgets 20,000 direct labor hours during the accounting period, the predetermined manufacturing overhead rate is $8 per direct labor hour, computed as follows:

$$\frac{\$160{,}000}{20{,}000} = \$8$$

As each job is finished, its manufacturing overhead is determined by multiplying the actual direct labor hours by the predetermined overhead rate. For example, if Job No. 172 required 500 direct labor hours, it would be charged with $4,000 of manufacturing overhead, determined as follows:

$$500 \text{ direct labor hours} \times \$8 = \$4{,}000$$

Thus $4,000 is charged to Job No. 172 by entering that amount in the manufacturing overhead section of the Job No. 172 job cost sheet.

*1c,2a. At the end of the accounting period, the predetermined overhead rate is used to determine the amount of manufacturing overhead charged to Work in Process*

At the end of the accounting period, all the actual direct labor hours are multiplied by the predetermined overhead rate to determine how much manufacturing overhead is charged to the Work in Process account. For example, if a total of 1,100 direct labor hours were used on *all jobs* during the accounting period, the following journal entry would be made:

| | | |
|---|---|---|
| Work in Process Inventory (1,100 × $8) | 8,800 | |
| Manufacturing Overhead | | 8,800 |
| To record applied overhead to the Work in Process account for the year | | |

In addition, a total of $8,800 would be charged to the individual jobs. The *total* debit to Work in Process for manufacturing overhead must match the *total* manufacturing overhead applied to *all* the individual jobs.

By using a predetermined overhead rate, we can calculate the total job cost when the job is complete even if that completion date occurs before the end of the accounting period. Refer again to Exhibit 22–3 on page 810. Note that the $9,800 was computed when the job was completed on December 13, 19X9. Thus the company knew before the end of the period that the gross profit on Job No. 9474 would be $35,200, the difference between the selling price of $61,600 and the total manufacturing cost of $26,400.

## Overapplied and Underapplied Manufacturing Overhead

Ideally, the total dollar amount of manufacturing overhead applied to all the jobs during the accounting period will be the same as the manufacturing overhead actually incurred during that same period. However, it rarely is. Instead,

> *Actual* overhead incurred is different from the *estimated* overhead, and/or
>
> The *actual* level of activity (such as the number of direct labor hours worked) differs from the *estimated* activity level.

For example, the predetermined overhead rate might be $8 based on the following data:

$$\frac{\text{Estimated Manufacturing Overhead}}{\text{Estimated Direct Labor Hours}} = \frac{\$40{,}000}{5{,}000} = \$8$$

If 5,000 direct labor hours were used but the actual manufacturing overhead for the period was $41,000, the Manufacturing Overhead account would appear as follows:

| MANUFACTURING OVERHEAD | |
|---|---|
| 41,000 (Actual) | 40,000 (Applied) |

On the other hand, if the actual manufacturing overhead for the period was $40,000 but the actual direct labor hours used were 5,100, the Manufacturing Overhead account would appear as follows:

| MANUFACTURING OVERHEAD | |
|---|---|
| 40,000 (Actual) | 40,800 (Applied) |

In both cases the debit to manufacturing overhead for actual expenditures is different from the credit to manufacturing overhead.

Here are two "rules of thumb" that we can use for determining whether manufacturing overhead has been underapplied or overapplied:

> If the amount of manufacturing overhead applied is less than the actual overhead costs, the Manufacturing Overhead account will have a *debit balance,* and the amount of this balance will be **underapplied manufacturing overhead.**
>
> If the amount of manufacturing overhead applied exceeds the actual overhead costs, the Manufacturing Overhead account will have a *credit balance,* and the amount of this balance will be **overapplied manufacturing overhead.**

### Disposing of the Manufacturing Overhead Balance

*1c,2a. At year-end the balance in Manufacturing Overhead is disposed of by a journal entry*

Since it is almost certain that there will be either a debit or a credit balance in the Manufacturing Overhead account at the end of the accounting period, we are now faced with the question of how to dispose of this balance. There are two generally acceptable methods, both accomplished at year-end by a journal entry:[1]

Close the account by allocating its balance among the Work in Process, Finished Goods, and Cost of Goods Sold accounts. The theory of this allocation is that the overapplied or underapplied manufacturing overhead relates to all three of these accounts.

Close the account by transferring its balance to the Cost of Goods Sold account. This is the more simple and practical way to dispose of the account balance, especially if the amount is small. We will use this method by accumulating the actual manufacturing overhead ($1,000 for indirect materials, plus $2,000 for indirect labor, plus $6,000 for other = $9,000). We will then subtract the applied manufacturing overhead of $8,800 to derive an underapplied manufacturing overhead of $200 ($9,000 − $8,800). The following journal entry is made:

| | | |
|---|---|---|
| Cost of Goods Sold | 200 | |
| Manufacturing Overhead | | 200 |
| To close out underapplied manufacturing overhead to Cost of Goods Sold | | |

## ACCOUNTING FOR THE COMPLETION OF JOB ORDERS

*1c,2a. The cost of completed job orders is transferred from Work in Process Inventory to Finished Goods Inventory*

When a job order is completed, the items produced are transferred from the factory to the finished goods warehouse. The cost of the items determined from the completed job cost sheet is also transferred from the Work in Process Inventory account to the Finished Goods Inventory account.

For example, assume that Dart Company completed jobs with cost sheets totaling $18,000. The following entry would show the transfer of these jobs from Work in Process to Finished Goods:

| | | |
|---|---|---|
| Finished Goods Inventory | 18,000 | |
| Work in Process Inventory | | 18,000 |
| To record the transfer of completed production to finished goods | | |

## ACCOUNTING FOR THE SALE OF FINISHED GOODS

*1c,2a. The cost of finished goods sold is debited to Cost of Goods Sold*

Because Dart Company uses a perpetual inventory for finished goods, it needs two journal entries to record a sale. One entry recognizes the revenue from the sale; the other accounts for the cost of the items sold.

Assume that the company sold finished goods costing $14,000 on account for $20,000. The journal entries to record these transactions are as follows:

| | | |
|---|---|---|
| Accounts Receivable | 20,000 | |
| Sales | | 20,000 |
| To record sales on account | | |
| Cost of Goods Sold | 14,000 | |
| Finished Goods Inventory | | 14,000 |
| To record the cost of goods sold | | |

[1] The account balance is usually held open at the end of each month during the year.

## JOB ORDER COSTING—POSTING TO THE ACCOUNTS

*1c,2a. Exhibit 22–6 reviews the journalizing and posting of costs in job order costing*

By examining Exhibit 22–6 on pages 818–819, you can review the journal entries illustrated so far and also see how these entries are posted to their respective ledger accounts.

## JOB ORDER COSTING—JOURNAL ENTRIES AND THE COST OF INDIVIDUAL JOBS

*1c,2a. The accumulation of costs of individual jobs at the time journal entries are made is illustrated here*

We will now illustrate how the costs of individual jobs are accumulated at the same time that the journal entries are made. The following are selected transactions of Mellon Company for one month. Note the way in which this material is presented.

Summaries of the transactions are given, and where appropriate, the cost of the individual jobs is shown.

The underlying source document or documents for the transaction are identified.

The appropriate entry is made in general journal form. Assume that there are no beginning inventories for raw materials, work in process, or finished goods.

1. Materials costing $30,000 were purchased on account.

   Source documents: Purchase invoices and receiving reports

| Entry: | | | |
|---|---|---|---|
| Raw Materials Inventory | | 30,000 | |
| | Accounts Payable | | 30,000 |

2. Materials were requisitioned for use. A summary showed direct and indirect materials as follows:

| | |
|---|---|
| Job Order No. 91 | $12,000 |
| Job Order No. 92 | 9,000 |
| Job Order No. 93 | 1,000 |
| Indirect materials | 2,000 |
| Total | $24,000 |

   Source documents: Materials requisition forms

| Entry: | | | |
|---|---|---|---|
| Work in Process Inventory | | 22,000 | |
| Manufacturing Overhead | | 2,000 | |
| | Raw Materials Inventory | | 24,000 |

3. A summary of the month's factory time tickets showed the following:

| | |
|---|---|
| Job Order No. 91 | $ 8,000 |
| Job Order No. 92 | 7,500 |
| Job Order No. 93 | 1,200 |
| Indirect labor | 400 |
| Total | $17,100 |

*EXHIBIT 22–6*

Summary of Journal Entries for Dart Manufacturing Company Using Job Order Costing

| Entry | Debit | Credit |
|---|---|---|
| 1. Raw Materials Inventory | 50,000 | |
| Accounts Payable | | 50,000 |
| 2. Work in Process Inventory | 15,000 | |
| Raw Materials Inventory | | 15,000 |
| 3. Manufacturing Overhead | 1,000 | |
| Raw Materials Inventory | | 1,000 |
| 4. Work in Process Inventory | 10,000 | |
| Wages Payable | | 10,000 |
| 5. Manufacturing Overhead | 2,000 | |
| Wages Payable | | 2,000 |
| 6. Manufacturing Overhead | 6,000 | |
| Accounts Payable | | 2,100 |
| Property Taxes Payable | | 900 |
| Accumulated Depreciation | | 3,000 |
| 7. Work in Process Inventory | 8,800 | |
| Manufacturing Overhead | | 8,800 |
| 8. Cost of Goods Sold | 200 | |
| Manufacturing Overhead | | 200 |
| 9. Finished Goods Inventory | 18,000 | |
| Work in Process Inventory | | 18,000 |
| 10. Accounts Receivable | 20,000 | |
| Sales | | 20,000 |
| 11. Cost of Goods Sold | 14,000 | |
| Finished Goods Inventory | | 14,000 |

*EXHIBIT 22–6 (Cont'd)*

Summary of Cost Flows for Dart Manufacturing Company

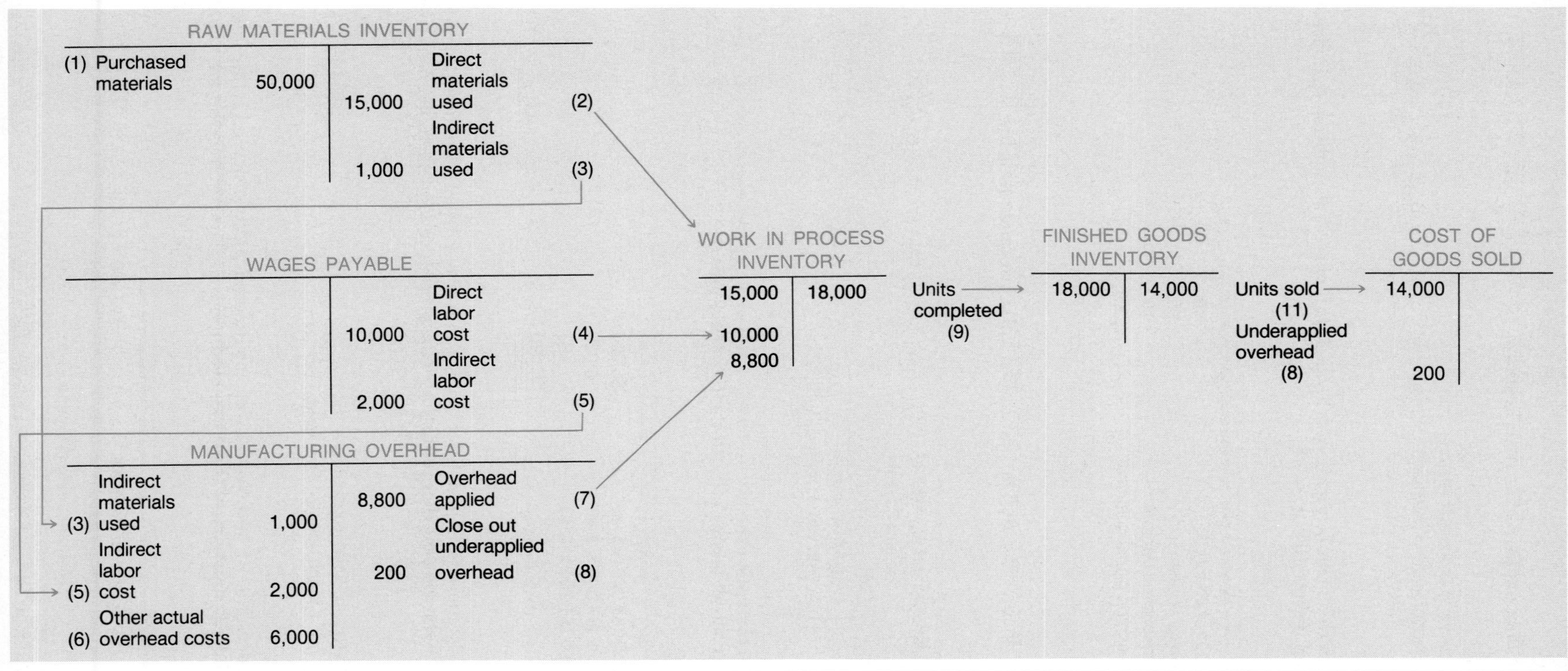

Source documents: Labor time tickets

| Entry: Work in Process Inventory | 16,700 | |
|---|---|---|
| Manufacturing Overhead | 400 | |
| Wages Payable | | 17,100 |

4. The month's manufacturing overhead costs incurred, in addition to indirect materials and indirect labor, were:

| | |
|---|---|
| Repairs (on account) | $ 400 |
| Utilities (paid in cash) | 900 |
| Insurance (expired portion) | 700 |
| Depreciation on plant equipment | 2,200 |
| Total | $4,200 |

Source documents: Repair and utility bills, insurance policies, and depreciation schedules

| Entry: Manufacturing Overhead | 4,200 | |
|---|---|---|
| Accounts Payable | | 400 |
| Cash | | 900 |
| Prepaid Insurance | | 700 |
| Accumulated Depreciation | | 2,200 |

5. Manufacturing overhead costs were applied at a predetermined overhead rate of $.40 per direct labor *dollar* to the following jobs:

| | |
|---|---|
| Job No. 91 ($8,000 × $.40) | $3,200 |
| Job No. 92 ($7,500 × $.40) | 3,000 |
| Job No. 93 ($1,200 × $.40) | 480 |
| Total | $6,680 |

Source documents: Schedules showing summary of direct labor hours incurred and schedule showing the determination of the predetermined manufacturing overhead rate

| Entry: Work in Process Inventory | 6,680 | |
|---|---|---|
| Manufacturing Overhead | | 6,680 |

6. Job Orders No. 91 and No. 92 were completed and transferred to finished goods inventory. A summary of the completed job cost sheets shows the following:

| | | |
|---|---|---|
| Job No. 91 | Direct materials | $12,000 |
| | Direct labor | 8,000 |
| | Manufacturing overhead | 3,200 |
| | Total | $23,200 |

| | | |
|---|---|---|
| Job No. 92 | Direct materials | $ 9,000 |
| | Direct labor | 7,500 |
| | Manufacturing overhead | 3,000 |
| | Total | $19,500 |

Source documents: Job order cost sheets

| | | |
|---|---|---|
| Entry: Finished Goods Inventory | 42,700 | |
| Work in Process Inventory | | 42,700 |

7. All the units completed on Job Order No. 91 were sold on account and shipped to customers. The cost of Job Order No. 91 is $23,200 (as per the above analysis), and the selling price is $29,000.

   Source documents: Job order cost sheets, sales invoices, and shipping orders

| | | |
|---|---|---|
| Entry: Accounts Receivable | 29,000 | |
| Sales | | 29,000 |
| Entry: Cost of Goods Sold | 23,200 | |
| Finished Goods Inventory | | 23,200 |

After all the above transactions were recorded and posted, Cost of Goods Sold, Finished Goods Inventory, and Work in Process Inventory would have the following debit balances:

| Cost of Goods Sold: | |
|---|---|
| Job No. 91: | |
| Direct Materials | $12,000 |
| Direct Labor | 8,000 |
| Manufacturing Overhead | 3,200 |
| Total | $23,200 |

| Finished Goods Inventory: | |
|---|---|
| Job No. 92: | |
| Direct Materials | $ 9,000 |
| Direct Labor | 7,500 |
| Manufacturing Overhead | 3,000 |
| Total | $19,500 |

| Work in Process Inventory: | |
|---|---|
| Job No. 93: | |
| Direct Materials | $ 1,000 |
| Direct Labor | 1,200 |
| Manufacturing Overhead | 480 |
| Total | $ 2,680 |

## A COMMENT ABOUT PRODUCING DEPARTMENTS AND SERVICE DEPARTMENTS

Before finishing our discussion of job order processing, we need to briefly distinguish between producing departments and service departments. **Producing departments** make the product manufactured by the company. The number and type of departments depend on the size of the company and the items it produces.

For example, the makers of furniture might have as a minimum three departments:

Cutting department
Assembling department
Finishing department

All items of furniture pass through each of these departments, and each department adds its own direct materials, direct labor, and manufacturing overhead.

On the other hand, **service departments** provide auxiliary services, such as repairs, engineering, supplies, and recording.

Because service departments do not make the products, *all* of their costs are classified as overhead and allocated to the producing departments. The producing departments, in turn, allocate service department overhead *and* their own overhead to the products produced by the various jobs.

Failure to make all of these overhead allocations would result in understated product costs.

## A GENERAL MODEL OF PROCESS COSTING

We have seen that process costing is appropriate for assigning costs to manufactured products that:

Move through a series of *continuous processes.*
Have a *homogeneous* principal product.
Are produced in *mass.*

**A process** is a step in manufacturing a product. In a process costing system the costs of direct materials, direct labor, and manufacturing overhead are charged to processing departments rather than to specific job orders. A record of these manufacturing costs and the physical output in units should be maintained by each processing department (such as the cutting, assembling, and finishing departments). These records must be kept for each accounting period during which unit costs are calculated and financial statements are prepared. Such processes occur every month.

In a job order costing system, one Work in Process account is often maintained as a control account for individual jobs. However, in a process costing system, *each* department typically maintains its own Work in Process account to collect the production costs of each stage of production.

A wide variety of processes could be used in manufacturing operations that have several production stages. Here are two possibilities:

Direct materials could be issued only to the department that performs the initial production operations (the cutting department, for example). From that point, direct labor and manufacturing overhead costs are used in both the initial and remaining departments.

Direct materials could be issued to several departments along the production route. For example, in a furniture-making operation that requires cutting, assembling, and finishing, wood might be issued to the cutting department, and metal and other furniture components issued to the assembling department. Direct labor and manufacturing overhead costs would be used in all the departments.

*1e. Exhibit 22–7 depicts the flow of manufacturing costs in a process costing system*

Using the second possibility as the example, Exhibit 22–7 shows the flow of manufacturing costs in a process costing system.

EXHIBIT 22–7
Flow of Manufacturing Costs—Process Costing

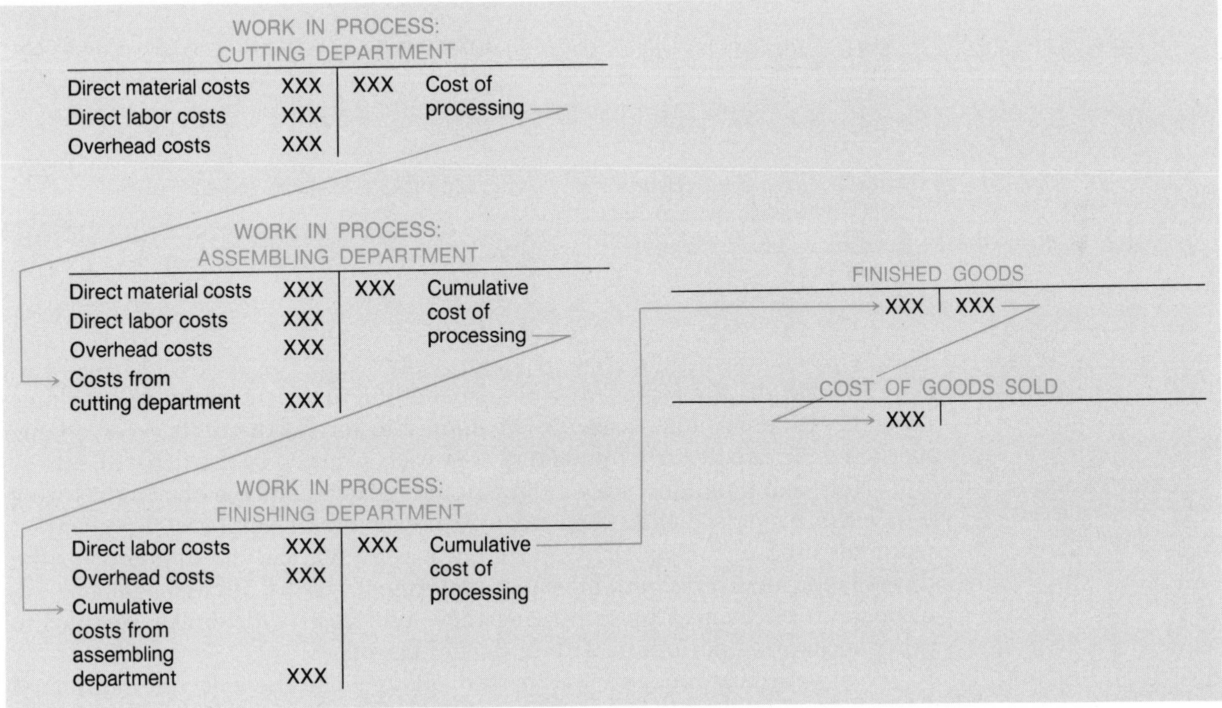


## THE COST-OF-PRODUCTION REPORT

*1e,2c. The cost-of-production report provides information vital to process costing*

In process costing, the **cost-of-production report** shown in Exhibit 22–8 is a control document that serves much the same purpose as the job order cost sheet used in a job order costing system. This report, which is prepared periodically, provides information vitally needed in process costing. Specifically:

It shows the units that each department is accountable for and their disposition. For example, the cutting department was responsible for 8,000 units of product. The cost-of-production report shows that the units were worked on in this department during January. All units were transferred to the assembling department.

It shows the manufacturing costs charged to each department and their disposition. The cost-of-production report shows that the cutting department was charged with $28,000 of manufacturing costs during January. The entire amount was transferred to the assembling department, since all 8,000 units on which the $28,000 was incurred were also transferred to the Assembling Department.

It may be used as a source for the calculation of unit cost. The production report shows that the cost of each completed unit is $6.75 (total accumulated costs of $54,000 ÷ 8,000, the number of completed units, = $6.75).

EXHIBIT 22–8

COST-OF-PRODUCTION REPORT
For the Month of January 19X9

| | CUTTING | | ASSEMBLING | | FINISHING | |
|---|---|---|---|---|---|---|
| **Quantity Schedule (Units):** | | | | | | |
| Started in Process | 8,000 | | | | | |
| Received in Department | | | 8,000 | | 8,000 | |
| Transferred to Next Department | 8,000 | | 8,000 | | | |
| Transferred to Finished Goods | | | | | 8,000 | |
| | TOTAL COST | UNIT COST | TOTAL COST | UNIT COST | TOTAL COST | UNIT COST |
| **Departmental Costs:** | | | | | | |
| Direct Materials | $16,000 | $2.00 | $ 2,000 | $ .25 | –0– | –0– |
| Direct Labor | 8,000 | 1.00 | 4,000 | .50 | $12,000 | $1.50 |
| Manufacturing Overhead | 4,000 | .50 | 2,000 | .25 | 6,000 | .75 |
| Total Departmental Costs | $28,000 | $3.50 | $ 8,000 | $1.00 | $18,000 | $2.25 |
| Cost Transferred into Department | | | 28,000 | 3.50 | 36,000 | 4.50 |
| Total Cost Accumulated | $28,000 | $3.50 | $36,000 | $4.50 | $54,000 | $6.75 |
| Cost Transferred to Next Department | $28,000 | $3.50 | $36,000 | $4.50 | | |
| Cost Transferred to Finished Goods | | | | | $54,000 | $6.75 |

In addition, the report provides data helpful to management in controlling costs. Each department manager is responsible for (1) the units received and worked on in the department, and (2) the costs charged to the department.

*2c,2d. The cost-of-production report is analyzed here*

Note that the report shows unit cost figures for each type of manufacturing cost within each producing department. For example, the unit cost for the direct materials used in the cutting department was $2.00, and the unit cost for the direct labor incurred in the finishing department was $1.50. Management can evaluate performances by comparing these unit costs with similar amounts in other accounting periods or with budgeted figures.

Note also that the costs are "passed" along when the units are transferred from the cutting department to the assembling department, and then again when the units are transferred from the assembling department to the finishing department. The $54,000 transferred to Finished Goods Inventory represents

$28,000 of manufacturing costs incurred by the cutting department on the 8,000 units it worked on

$8,000 of manufacturing costs incurred by the assembling department on the same 8,000 units it worked on

$18,000 of manufacturing costs incurred by the finishing department on the same 8,000 units it worked on

If units were uncompleted in any department, some of the costs would be assigned to that department's Work in Process account.

*1e,2c. Journal entries for process costing are illustrated here*

Here are the journal entries that would be made:

| a. | | | |
|---|---|---|---|
| | Work in Process—Cutting | 16,000 | |
| | Work in Process—Assembling | 2,000 | |
| | Raw Materials Inventory | | 18,000 |
| | To show the issuance of direct materials to the cutting and assembling departments | | |

b.

| | | |
|---|---|---|
| Work in Process—Cutting | 8,000 | |
| Work in Process—Assembling | 4,000 | |
| Work in Process—Finishing | 12,000 | |
| Wages Payable | | 24,000 |
| To show the incurrence of direct labor by the cutting, assembling, and finishing departments | | |

c.

| | | |
|---|---|---|
| Manufacturing Overhead—Cutting | 4,000 | |
| Manufacturing Overhead—Assembling | 2,000 | |
| Manufacturing Overhead—Finishing | 6,000 | |
| Accounts Payable | | 7,500* |
| Prepaid Expenses | | 1,500* |
| Accumulated Depreciation | | 3,000* |
| To show the incurrence of manufacturing overhead by the cutting, assembling, and finishing departments | | |

* Assumed amounts.

Because it will result in a simpler illustration and because predetermined overhead rates have already been discussed, we will assume that all the manufacturing overhead incurred can be charged directly to the various producing departments.

d.

| | | |
|---|---|---|
| Work in Process—Cutting | 4,000 | |
| Work in Process—Assembling | 2,000 | |
| Work in Process—Finishing | 6,000 | |
| Manufacturing Overhead—Cutting | | 4,000 |
| Manufacturing Overhead—Assembling | | 2,000 |
| Manufacturing Overhead—Finishing | | 6,000 |
| To show the direct charge of manufacturing overhead incurred to the Work in Process accounts for all three producing departments | | |

e.

| | | |
|---|---|---|
| Work in Process—Assembling | 28,000 | |
| Work in Process—Cutting | | 28,000 |
| To show the cutting department's cost of the 8,000 units transferred from the cutting to the assembling department during the accounting period | | |

f.

| | | |
|---|---|---|
| Work in Process—Finishing | 36,000 | |
| Work in Process—Assembling | | 36,000 |
| To show the cutting and assembling departments' costs of the 8,000 units transferred from the assembling to the finishing department during the accounting period | | |

g.

| | | |
|---|---|---|
| Finished Goods Inventory | 54,000 | |
| Work in Process—Finishing | | 54,000 |
| To show the cutting, assembling, and finishing departments' costs of the 8,000 units transferred from the finishing department to finished goods inventory | | |

*EXHIBIT 22–9*

Summary of Cost Flow—Process Costing

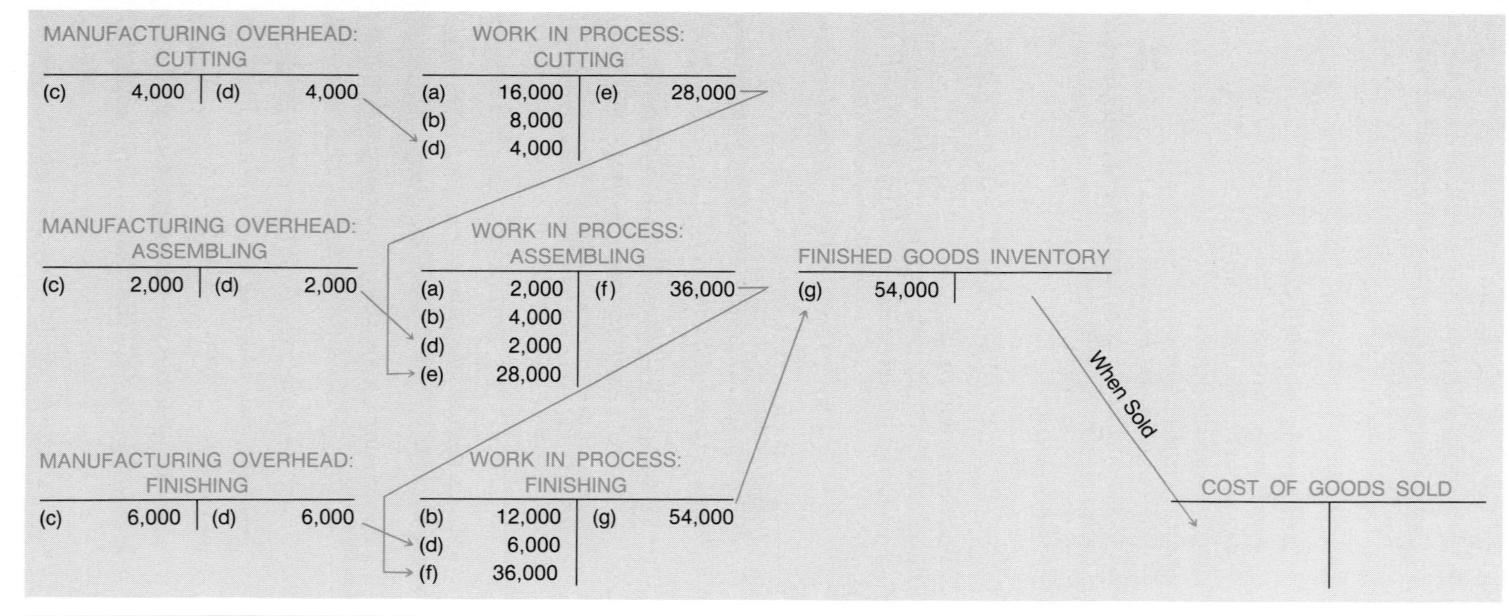

*1e,2c. Exhibit 22–9 reviews the posting of costs in a process costing system*

Exhibit 22–9 shows the posted amounts for the previous entries *a* through *g*. The arrows indicate the cost flows to the Work in Process accounts, the Finished Goods account, and eventually to the Cost of Goods Sold account. The amount that is transferred from Finished Goods Inventory to Cost of Goods Sold would depend on how many of the 8,000 units were sold during the accounting period. In this illustration we are assuming that each of the producing departments starts and finishes the same 8,000 units during the period—an unlikely assumption, but one that you will find useful for this illustration.

## A MORE COMPLEX MODEL OF PROCESS COSTING—EQUIVALENT UNITS OF PRODUCTION

In the preceding illustration we assumed that the company had no beginning or ending work in process inventories. Therefore all units manufactured during the period were both started and completed during the same period.

*1f. Equivalent units of production are used when uncompleted units must be accounted for as Work in Process Inventory*

When a manufacturing process is continuous, however, it is common to have units partially complete at the end of an accounting period. These uncompleted units must be accounted for as Work in Process Inventory. As a result, we must change the way productive output is determined in a department. In measuring output, we count each completed unit as a whole unit. Each unfinished unit is counted as a part of a whole unit, the part being estimated on a percentage-of-completion basis.

Once the productive output is determined, manufacturing costs can be allocated between

Units *completed* and *transferred out* (to another department or to finished goods) and

Units still in *process* within the department (representing ending Work in Process Inventory).

To make this allocation of manufacturing costs when we assume that we have uncompleted units at the end of the accounting period, we must use a concept called *equivalent units of production.*

### Equivalent Units of Production

*1f. Equivalent units measure the work completed on unfinished units in terms of the work necessary to produce finished units*

When production is partially completed at the end of an accounting period, it becomes necessary to state that production on the basis of the equivalent work that it would take to fully complete a smaller amount of production. For example, we assume that if we have done one-fourth of the work necessary to complete 4,000 units, it is equivalent to all the work necessary to complete 1,000 units. If 4,000 units are one-fourth complete at the end of an accounting period, this is equivalent to starting and completing 1,000 units. An **equivalent unit,** therefore, is a physical unit stated in terms of its equivalence to a finished unit.

The number of equivalent units produced during a period is equal to:

The number of units *completed* during the period, plus

An amount for the *partially completed* units that represents a restatement of these units as equivalent whole units.

This restatement is accomplished by applying an estimated percentage-of-completion factor to the unfinished units. Here are several examples of such restatements.

| PHYSICAL UNIT | PERCENTAGE OF WORK COMPLETED | EQUIVALENT UNITS |
|---|---|---|
| 1,000 | 50% | 500 |
| 1,600 | 25% | 400 |
| 2,500 | 20% | 500 |

Let us now look at how to compute equivalent units and account for the cost of production when there is an inventory of unfinished production at the end of an accounting period. We will leave additional complicating factors for a more advanced accounting course.

### Accounting for the Cost of Completed and Uncompleted Production

*2e. Calculation of equivalent units of production is illustrated here*

Let us assume the following facts about the cutting department.

At the beginning of the accounting period, there is no inventory of Work in Process (for this illustration, we assume that all production was started in this period).

During the period, 20,000 units were started in production.

By the end of the period, 14,000 units were completed.

The other 6,000 units had 30% of their manufacturing work done on them, and therefore 30% of their manufacturing costs applied to them at the end of the period.

The following manufacturing costs were incurred during the period:

| | |
|---|---|
| Direct Materials | $23,700 |
| Direct Labor | 15,800 |
| Manufacturing Overhead | 7,900 |
| Total | $47,400 |

Our first task is to compute the equivalent units of production during the accounting period. This computation is shown below.

| | UNITS TO BE ACCOUNTED FOR | | PERCENTAGE OF WORK COMPLETED DURING THE PERIOD | | EQUIVALENT UNITS OF PRODUCTION |
|---|---|---|---|---|---|
| Number of units started and completed | 14,000 | × | 100% | = | 14,000 |
| Number of units uncompleted | 6,000 | × | 30% | = | 1,800 |
| | | | | | 15,800 |

The *total* unit cost of production is computed as follows:

Total manufacturing costs of $47,400
Divided by the equivalent units of 15,800
Equals a unit cost of $3

We can now prepare a cost-of-production report that shows how to account for the manufacturing costs of $47,400—that is, which part of the costs should be "attached" to the 14,000 units completed and sent to the assembling department and which part of the costs should be "attached" to the cutting department's ending Work in Process Inventory of 6,000 units.

*2d. Exhibit 22–10 is a cost-of-production report using equivalent units of production*

The cost-of-production report is shown in Exhibit 22–10. Note the difference between this format and the one in Exhibit 22–8, which does not contain equivalent units of production.

EXHIBIT 22–10

COST-OF-PRODUCTION REPORT
Cutting Department
For the Month of October 19X6

| | | |
|---|---|---|
| Units to Be Accounted For: | | |
| Units started and completed during month (14,000 units × 100% completion) | | 14,000 |
| Units uncompleted at month-end (6,000 units × 30% completion) | | 1,800 |
| Equivalent units of production during month | | 15,800 |
| Costs to Be Accounted For: | | |
| Direct materials | $23,700 | |
| Direct labor | 15,800 | |
| Manufacturing overhead | 7,900 | |
| Total | | $47,400 |
| Unit Cost of Production ($47,400/15,800) | | $ 3.00 |
| Costs Accounted For as Follows: | | |
| Completed and transferred to assembling department (14,000 units × $3.00) | | $42,000 |
| Uncompleted and in process (6,000 units × 30% = 1,800 units × $3.00) | | 5,400 |
| Total | | $47,400 |

This cost-of-production report shows that $42,000 should be debited to the Work in Process account of the assembling department and credited to the Work in Process account of the cutting department (the debit would be to Finished Goods Inventory if the cutting department was the last operation and the 14,000 units were transferred to the finished goods stock). The report also shows that the Work in Process account of the cutting department should have a debit balance of $5,400 at the end of the period.

*2c. Journal entries for process costing using equivalent units are illustrated here*

The following journal entries would be made for the entire month's operations:

| | | Debit | Credit |
|---|---|---|---|
| a. | Work in Process—Cutting | 23,700 | |
| | Raw Materials Inventory | | 23,700 |
| | To show the requisition of direct materials by the cutting department | | |

| | | Debit | Credit |
|---|---|---|---|
| b. | Work in Process—Cutting | 15,800 | |
| | Wages Payable (or Cash) | | 15,800 |
| | To show the incurrence of direct labor by the cutting department | | |

| | | Debit | Credit |
|---|---|---|---|
| c. | Manufacturing Overhead | 7,900 | |
| | Cash | | 4,900* |
| | Prepaid Expenses | | 1,000* |
| | Accumulated Depreciation—Equipment | | 2,000* |

* Assumed amounts.

d.

| | | |
|---|---|---|
| Work in Process—Cutting | 7,900 | |
| Manufacturing Overhead | | 7,900 |
| To show the charging of manufacturing overhead to the cutting department | | |

e.

| | | |
|---|---|---|
| Work in Process—Assembling | 42,000 | |
| Work in Process—Cutting | | 42,000 |
| To show the cost of the transfer of 14,000 units from the cutting to the assembling department | | |

To summarize, accounting for manufacturing costs in a process costing system becomes a bit more complicated when some units are completed during the period and some remain unfinished at the end of the period. Calculation of equivalent units is the most realistic way to account for such costs.

## HIGHLIGHT PROBLEM

Careful Company uses a job order cost system to account for its production costs. Each job represents a special customer order and is given a job number. At the end of the job, the total production costs are accumulated, a unit cost is derived, and the job is sold to the customer at a markup of 25%, based on unit cost. The following information is available for all jobs worked upon.

1. Direct materials requisitioned for use, $50,000.
2. Indirect materials requisitioned for use, $3,000.
3. Direct labor accrued, $60,000 (6,000 hours).
4. Indirect labor accrued, $2,000.
5. Other manufacturing overhead for the period, $15,000 (assume cash was paid).
6. Careful Company applies its manufacturing overhead to production on the basis of direct labor hours. At the beginning of the current accounting period, the following estimates were made:
   Estimated direct labor hours for the period, 70,000
   Estimated manufacturing overhead for the period, $210,000
7. All the jobs were completed, and the units were transferred to the finished goods storeroom.
8. The units for the jobs were sold.

Required:

1. Compute the company's predetermined manufacturing overhead rate.
2. Prepare all the necessary journal entries for the above transactions, including the application of manufacturing overhead and the closing of underapplied or overapplied manufacturing overhead to Cost of Goods Sold.

## GLOSSARY OF KEY TERMS

**Cost-of-production report.** A control document that is prepared for each processing department and summarizes the units for which the department is accountable, the disposition of the units, the manufacturing costs charged to the department, and the disposition of the costs.

**Equivalent unit.** A physical unit stated in terms of its equivalence to a finished unit.

**Job cost sheet.** A control document that provides a detailed listing of the amount of manufacturing costs charged to a specific job.

**Job order costing.** A method of product costing whereby costs are accumulated by jobs. This method is used in industries where it is desirable and possible to distinguish each unit or group of units throughout the production process.

**Labor time ticket.** A source document showing daily information for the amount of time an employee spent on a specific job. Used as a basis for charging direct labor costs to a job and/or assigning indirect labor costs to manufacturing overhead.

**Materials requisition form.** A source document used to request materials needed for production and to identify the cost of the materials so that they can be charged to production.

**Overapplied manufacturing overhead.** The amount by which manufacturing overhead applied to the jobs exceeds the actual amount of manufacturing overhead costs for a period.

**Predetermined overhead rate.** A rate calculated at the beginning of the accounting period and used to assign the manufacturing overhead to the cost of the individual jobs. The rate is computed by dividing estimated manufacturing overhead for the period by an estimated activity level for the period.

**Process.** A step in manufacturing a product.

**Process costing.** A method of product costing whereby costs are accumulated by processing departments or processing centers, and a unit cost is calculated for each department or cost center each month. This method is used in industries where production occurs continuously and routinely, and when mass-produced standardized items are made.

**Producing departments.** Departments that make the product manufactured by the company.

**Service departments.** Departments that provide auxiliary services but do not make the products manufactured by the company.

**Underapplied manufacturing overhead.** The amount by which manufacturing overhead applied to the jobs is less than the actual amount of manufacturing overhead costs for a period.

## REVIEW QUESTIONS

1. Name three types of industries that probably use job order costing, and give the reasons why they do. [LO1a]
2. When is the use of process costing appropriate? [LO1a]
3. What is the purpose of a materials requisition form? [LO1b]
4. Differentiate between direct labor costs and indirect labor costs. [LO1b,2a]
5. What is the purpose of a labor time ticket? [LO1b]
6. What is the purpose of a job cost sheet? [LO1b]
7. What three subsidiary ledgers can be used in connection with the job cost sheets? [LO1b]
8. Describe the cost flows in a job order costing system as shown in Exhibit 22–5. [LO1c]
9. What account is debited when either direct materials or indirect materials are acquired? [LO2a]
10. What account is debited when direct materials are issued to production? [LO2a]
11. What account is debited when indirect materials are issued to production? [LO2a]
12. What account is debited when direct labor costs are incurred? [LO2a]
13. What account is debited when indirect labor costs are incurred? [LO2a]
14. What account is debited when manufacturing overhead costs are incurred? [LO2a]
15. Why is it necessary to use a predetermined overhead rate to assign manufacturing overhead to jobs? [LO1d]
16. Explain the three-step process by which the predetermined manufacturing overhead rate is computed. [LO1d,2a,2b]
17. What account is debited when manufacturing overhead is allocated to the jobs through the predetermined overhead rate? [LO2a]
18. State the two reasons why there will usually be overapplied or underapplied overhead at the end of the accounting period. [LO1d,2a,2b]
19. Describe the two methods that can be used to dispose of the manufacturing overhead account balance at the end of the accounting period. [LO2a]

20. What account is debited when units being worked on are completed? [LO2a]
21. What two entries are made when completed units are sold? [LO2a]
22. In process costing, what does the term *process* refer to? [LO1a]
23. Describe two types of processes that could be used in manufacturing operations that have several production stages. [LO1e]
24. Describe the flow of costs in the process costing diagram shown in Exhibit 22–7. [LO1e]
25. What three major types of information are shown in a cost-of-production report? [LO2d]
26. What type of journal entry is made when goods are transferred from one department to another in a process costing system? [LO2c]
27. Under what production conditions are equivalent units of production used? [LO1f]

## ANALYTICAL QUESTIONS

28. "Both job order costing and process costing accomplish basically the same goals." Explain this statement. [LO1a]
29. Why is manufacturing overhead an indirect cost in job order costing? [LO2a]
30. "Underapplied or overapplied overhead means that errors were made in the recording process." Comment on this statement. [LO2a]
31. Why is there likely to be more than one Work in Process Inventory account in a process costing system? [LO1e]
32. Why is it usually necessary to calculate equivalent units of production when accounting for production costs in a process costing system? [LO1f]
33. "It is improper to use equivalent units to account for production costs in a process costing system." "There are no tangible batches of units that exist." Comment on these two statements. [LO1f,2e]

## IMPACT ANALYSIS QUESTIONS

*For each error described, indicate whether it would overstate [O], understate [U], or not affect [N] the key figures.* [LO2a]

34. The cost of the direct materials transferred to production was stated as $10,000 when it should have been stated as $12,000.
    _______ Debits made to Work in Process Inventory
    _______ Debits made to Raw Materials Inventory
    _______ Debits made to Manufacturing Overhead
35. The cost of the indirect materials transferred to production was stated as $1,200 when it should have been stated as $1,000.
    _______ Debits made to Work in Process Inventory
    _______ Debits made to Raw Materials Inventory
    _______ Debits made to Manufacturing Overhead
36. Five thousand dollars of manufacturing labor was incorrectly classified as direct labor instead of indirect labor.
    _______ Debits made to Work in Process Inventory
    _______ Debits made to Raw Materials Inventory
    _______ Debits made to Manufacturing Overhead
37. The predetermined overhead was incorrectly calculated at $2.00 per hour instead of $1.50 per hour.
    _______ Debits made to Work in Process Inventory

_______ Debits made to Raw Materials Inventory
_______ Debits made to Manufacturing Overhead

38. The cost of production completed and sent to finished goods was incorrectly calculated at $20,000 instead of $25,000. Some of the units of production were sold. There was no beginning inventory of finished goods.

_______ Ending balance in Work in Process Inventory
_______ Ending balance in Finished Goods Inventory
_______ Cost of Goods Sold

## EXERCISES

EXERCISE 22–1 *(Supply Missing Data for a Job Cost Sheet)* From the following data, fill in the missing amounts in the blanks.

| | CASE 1 | CASE 2 | CASE 3 |
|---|---|---|---|
| Department No. 1: | | | |
| Direct Materials | $1,000 | _____ | $ 3,000 |
| Direct Labor | 1,500 | $ 2,000 | 1,500 |
| Manufacturing Overhead | 2,100 | 3,000 | 1,500 |
| Department No. 2: | | | |
| Direct Materials | 800 | 2,500 | 2,500 |
| Direct Labor | 600 | 2,100 | 2,200 |
| Manufacturing Overhead | 1,200 | 2,000 | 2,300 |
| Total Units Produced and Sold | _____ | 1,000 | _____ |
| Unit Cost | 6.00 | _____ | 13.00 |
| Selling Price (Total Dollars) | _____ | 15,000 | 18,000 |
| Gross Profit | 800 | 2,900 | 5,000 |

[LO2a]

EXERCISE 22–2 *(Journalize Job Order Costing Transactions)* Merriwell Company uses a job order cost system. The following data summarize the operations related to production for November, the first month of operations.

a. Materials purchased on account, $10,500.
b. Materials requisitioned for use: direct, $6,000; indirect, $2,000.
c. Labor costs incurred: direct, $9,000; indirect, $1,000.
d. Manufacturing overhead costs incurred: on accounts payable, $9,500; for depreciation of factory machinery, $1,500.
e. Manufacturing overhead applied to production using a predetermined rate of $10 per direct labor hour (1,300 direct labor hours were incurred during November).
f. Total cost of jobs completed and transferred to finished goods, $28,000.
g. Sales for the month, all on account:

| | |
|---|---|
| Selling price | $35,000 |
| Cost | 20,000 |

h. Balance in the Manufacturing Overhead account was closed to the Cost of Goods Sold account.

Required:

1. Prepare journal entries to record the above activity.
2. Determine the balances in the Raw Materials, Work in Process, and Finished Goods Inventory accounts as of November 30. [LO2a]

EXERCISE 22–3 *(Prepare Journal Entries from Financial Statement Data)* At the end of Z Company's initial year of operations, sections of its income statement and balance sheet appeared as follows.

*Partial income statement*

| | | |
|---|---|---|
| Sales | | $100,000 |
| Cost of Goods Sold: | | |
| Finished Goods Inventory, 1/1 | — | |
| Plus: Cost of Goods Manufactured | $60,000 | |
| | $60,000 | |
| Less: Finished Goods Inventory, 12/31 | 8,000 | 52,000 |
| Gross Profit | | $ 48,000 |

*Balance sheet: Inventories section:*

| | | |
|---|---|---|
| Raw Materials | $ 7,000 | |
| Work in Process | 10,000 | |
| Finished Goods | 8,000 | |
| Total Inventories | | $25,000 |

Listed below are four accounts as they appeared in Z Company's ledger after only part of the postings had been completed.

| RAW MATERIALS INVENTORY | | WORK IN PROCESS INVENTORY | |
|---|---|---|---|
| 20,000 | | 27,000 | |

| FINISHED GOODS INVENTORY | | MANUFACTURING OVERHEAD | |
|---|---|---|---|
| | 52,000 | | 30,000 |

Required:
Prepare the journal entries needed to create the figures in the partial income statement and balance sheet. Assume that no indirect materials or indirect labor was used and that there was no underapplied or overapplied overhead. [LO1c,2a]

EXERCISE 22–4 *(Prepare Journal Entries from Financial Statement Data)* Shown below is a partial list of ledger account balances at the end of two accounting periods.

| | 19X8 | 19X9 |
|---|---|---|
| Raw Materials Inventory | $ 20,000 | $ 22,000 |
| Work in Process Inventory | 25,000 | 21,000 |
| Finished Goods Inventory | 40,000 | 45,000 |
| Cost of Goods Sold | 250,000 | 270,000* |

* Includes underapplied overhead closed to Cost of Goods Sold.

Additional Information for 19X9:

1. Direct materials purchased on account, $80,000
2. Cost of goods manufactured, $270,000
3. Underapplied overhead for the year, $5,000
4. Direct labor costs incurred, $75,000
5. Indirect materials issued to production, $10,000

Required:
Make all the necessary journal entries for manufacturing activities in 19X9. Assume that cash was spent for manufacturing overhead expenditures. [LO1c,2a]

EXERCISE 22–5 *(Compute Predetermined Overhead Rates.)* Melmore Company determines its manufacturing overhead rate by relating its year's estimated manufacturing cost to some reliable estimate of production activity. Selected information follows.

a. Estimated manufacturing overhead costs for the year, $224,000
b. Estimated direct labor costs for the year, $336,000

c. Estimated direct labor hours for the year, 56,000
d. Direct labor hours incurred in March, 5,000
e. Direct labor costs incurred in March, $30,000

Required:
1. Compute Melmore's predetermined overhead rate based on direct labor hours.
2. Compute Melmore's predetermined overhead rate based on direct labor costs.
3. Compute the total amount of manufacturing overhead applied to job orders in March using the predetermined overhead rate per direct labor hour.
4. Compute the total amount of manufacturing overhead applied to job orders in March using the predetermined overhead rate per direct labor costs. [LO2a,2b]

EXERCISE 22-6 *(Process Costing—Make Computations for the Flow of Units through Two Departments)* Royal Company manufactures a product that passes through two processing departments prior to completion. Data concerning the flow of units appear below.

| | DEPT. I | DEPT. II |
|---|---|---|
| Beginning inventory (in units) | 5,000 | 3,000 |
| Units started (or transferred in) | 50,000 | ______ |
| Total units to be accounted for | ______ | ______ |
| Ending inventory (in units) | ______ | 8,000 |
| Units completed and transferred out | 40,000 | ______ |

Required:
Determine the numbers that should appear in each of the above blanks.

Data concerning the flow of units for the same company but for a different accounting period appear below.

| | DEPT. I | DEPT. II |
|---|---|---|
| Beginning inventory (in units) | 15,000 | ______ |
| Units started (or transferred in) | ______ | 50,000 |
| Total units to be accounted for | ______ | 54,000 |
| Ending inventory (in units) | 3,000 | ______ |
| Units completed and transferred out | ______ | 46,000 |

Required:
Determine the numbers that should appear in each of the above blanks. [LO2c]

EXERCISE 22-7 *(Make Computations of Equivalent Units and Account for Production Costs)* The following information pertains to the mixing department of a certain firm that manufactures Product X. There were no uncompleted units at the beginning of the accounting period.

Total units accounted for during the period, 46,000
Units uncompleted at the end of the period, 12,000
Estimated percentage of completion of unfinished units is 60%

The following costs were incurred during the period:

| | |
|---|---|
| Direct materials | $20,000 |
| Direct labor | 10,000 |
| Manufacturing overhead | 7,080 |

Required:
1. Determine the equivalent units of production for the period. Round the calculations to two decimal places.

2. Determine the costs "attached" to the units completed and forwarded to the next department.
3. Determine the costs "attached" to the units unfinished in the mixing department at the end of the period. [LO2c,2d,2e]

## PROBLEMS

PROBLEM 22–1 *(Perform Job Order Costing with Journal Entries)* Excell Company uses a job order cost system. The following balances appeared in the inventory accounts on October 1, 19X6.

| | |
|---|---|
| Raw Materials Inventory | $ 8,000 |
| Work in Process Inventory | 12,000 |
| Finished Goods Inventory | 15,000 |

Data pertaining to the month of October are as follows:

1. Raw materials purchased on account, $65,000.
2. Raw materials issued to production, $58,000; $8,000 of these materials were indirect.
3. Factory wages incurred, $75,000, of which $5,000 was charged as indirect. Ten thousand direct labor hours were used.
4. Manufacturing overhead is allocated or applied at $7.50 per direct labor hour.
5. Manufacturing overhead charges totaled $64,900 as follows:

| | |
|---|---|
| Rent (paid in cash) | $25,000 |
| Utilities (on account) | 20,600 |
| Repairs (on account) | 700 |
| Insurance (expired portion) | 2,600 |
| Depreciation on factory equipment | 16,000 |

6. Jobs completed and transferred to finished goods, $175,000.
7. Jobs with a cost of $160,000 were sold on account for $250,000.

Required:

1. Prepare journal entries to record the transactions. Do not close out the overapplied or underapplied manufacturing overhead.
2. Determine the ending balances in the Raw Materials, Work in Process, and Finished Goods Inventories accounts.
3. Compute the amount of overapplied or underapplied manufacturing overhead as of October 31, 19X6. [LO2a]

PROBLEM 22–2 *(Predetermined Overhead Rate—Supply Missing Data)* In each of the following three cases, place the appropriate amounts in the blanks.

| | CASE | | |
|---|---|---|---|
| | 1 | 2 | 3 |
| Estimate of Manufacturing Overhead Cost | $10,000 | $20,000 | $40,000 |
| Estimate of Activity Level | ____ | 5,000 | ____ |
| Overhead Rate | $____ | $____ | $ 8.00 |
| Actual Activity Level | 6,000 | ____ | ____ |
| Applied Overhead | $12,000 | $____ | $39,000 |
| Actual Manufacturing Overhead Cost | $11,000 | $25,000 | $____ |
| Under- (Over-) applied Overhead | $____ | $ 1,000 | $ (1,000) |

[LO2a,2b]

PROBLEM 22–3 *(Prepare Journal Entries for Job Order Costing)* The Baker Manufacturing Company maintains a job order cost system. The following transactions occurred during the first year of operations.

a. Purchased $295,000 of raw materials on account.
b. During the year, $270,000 of raw materials were issued as direct materials, and $720,000 of direct labor was used.
c. In addition, $25,000 of raw materials were issued as indirect materials. Indirect laborers earn $75,000, and the factory superintendent earns $5,000.
d. Manufacturing overhead incurred exclusive of material issues and factory payroll costs:

| | |
|---|---|
| Power (paid in cash) | $30,000 |
| Depreciation on Plant and Equipment | 95,000 |
| Maintenance (paid in cash) | 25,000 |
| Insurance (paid in cash) | 15,000 |
| Taxes (paid in cash) | 10,000 |
| Miscellaneous (paid in cash) | 5,000 |

e. Manufacturing overhead applied was $288,000.
f. During the year, all the 6,000 units that were started were completed.

Required:

Record the transactions in general journal form, including the closing of underapplied or overapplied overhead. [LO2a]

PROBLEM 22–4 *(Prepare Job Order Journal Entries and Determine Balances)* The W Company uses a job order cost system. The following data pertain to the company's first month of operations.

a. Raw materials requisitioned and used as follows:

| | |
|---|---|
| Job. No. 1 | $4,200 |
| Job. No. 2 | 3,600 |
| Job. No. 3 | 4,500 |

b. Direct labor costs incurred as follows:

| | |
|---|---|
| Job. No. 1 | $6,400 |
| Job. No. 2 | 5,000 |
| Job. No. 3 | 7,200 |

c. Manufacturing overhead is applied to production at the rate of 75% of direct labor cost.
d. Actual manufacturing overhead incurred and paid in cash during the month amounted to $14,000.
e. Jobs No. 1 and No. 2 were completed during the month and sold on account at a markup of 20% based on the cost of the jobs.

Required:

1. Prepare entries in journal form to record the above transactions. (Setting up and posting to Work in Process T accounts for each job would be helpful.)
2. Determine the amount of the overapplied or underapplied manufacturing overhead for the month. Do not make a journal entry to close out the account.
3. Determine the balance that should appear in the Work in Process account at the end of the month. [LO2a]

PROBLEM 22-5 *(Prepare Journal Entries from Statement)*

ATLAS CORPORATION

Statement of Cost of Goods Manufactured
For the Year Ended December 31, 19X5

| | | |
|---|---|---|
| Raw materials: | | |
| Beginning raw materials inventory | $15,000 | |
| Raw materials purchased | 84,500 | |
| Cost of materials available for use | $99,500 | |
| Less: Ending raw materials inventory | 18,000 | |
| Cost of raw materials used | | $ 81,500 |
| Direct labor | | 118,700 |
| Manufacturing overhead: | | |
| Indirect labor | $19,100 | |
| Utilities | 7,400 | |
| Factory maintenance | 1,900 | |
| Factory supplies | 3,000 | |
| Factory insurance | 1,600 | |
| Depreciation—factory building | 2,100 | |
| Depreciation—machinery and equipment | 4,400 | |
| Property taxes | 800 | |
| Total manufacturing overhead | | 40,300 |
| Current manufacturing costs | | $240,500 |
| Add: Work in process inventory, January 1, 19X5 | | 33,600 |
| | | $274,100 |
| Deduct: Work in process inventory, December 31, 19X5 | | 28,700 |
| Cost of goods manufactured | | $245,400 |

Required:

Prepare all the journal entries that would pertain to this statement. Assume that all manufacturing overhead except the two depreciation accounts were paid for in cash. Also assume that there was no overapplied or underapplied overhead. [LO1c,2a]

PROBLEM 22-6 *(Compute Inventory Account Balances)* From the following data, compute the value of the (a) work in process inventory, (b) finished goods inventory, and (c) cost of goods sold. Assume no beginning-of-year amount for each account.

| | |
|---|---|
| Direct Materials Cost for Job No. 101 | $25,000 |
| Direct Labor Cost for Job No. 101 | $16,000 |
| Manufacturing Overhead Cost for Job No. 101 | $19,000 |
| Direct Materials Cost for Job No. 102 | $18,000 |
| Direct Labor Cost for Job No. 102 | $26,000 |
| Manufacturing Overhead Cost for Job No. 102 | $31,000 |
| Direct Materials Cost for Job No. 103 | $20,000 |
| Direct Labor Cost for Job No. 103 | $21,000 |
| Manufacturing Overhead Cost for Job No. 103 | $27,000 |
| No. of Units to Be Produced for Job No. 101 | 1,500 |
| No. of Units to Be Produced for Job No. 102 | 1,500 |
| No. of Units to Be Produced for Job No. 103 | 1,700 |
| No. of Units Finished for Job No. 101 | 1,200 |
| No. of Units Finished for Job No. 102 | 1,200 |
| No. of Units Finished for Job No. 103 | 1,400 |
| No. of Units Sold from Job No. 101 | 1,000 |
| No. of Units Sold from Job No. 102 | 800 |
| No. of Units Sold from Job No. 103 | 1,100 |

[LO2a]

PROBLEM 22-7 *(Prepare Cost-of-Production Report)* From the following data, prepare a cost-of-production report for the month. Use Exhibit 22-8 as a guide.

1. Production starts in Department A, goes to Department B, and then to finished goods. Departments A and B started and completed 10,000 units of production during the month. No production was in process at the beginning or end of the month.
2. The following manufacturing costs were incurred in each department during the year.

| | A | B |
|---|---|---|
| Direct Materials | $100,000 | $ 50,000 |
| Direct Labor | 80,000 | 60,000 |
| Manufacturing Overhead | 90,000 | 100,000 |
| Total | $270,000 | $210,000 |

[LO2c,2d]

PROBLEM 22–8 *(Prepare Journal Entries for Process Costing)* Take the manufacturing cost data from Problem 22–7 and prepare journal entries for the following transactions (assume that a separate Work in Process Inventory account is maintained for each department).

a. The issuance of direct materials to production.
b. The direct labor costs incurred.
c. The manufacturing overhead costs incurred and applied (assume all incurred amounts are paid in cash).
d. The transfer of costs from Department A to Department B.
e. The transfer of costs from Department B to finished goods inventory. [LO2c]

PROBLEM 22–9 *(Compute Equivalent Units, Make Cost Calculations, and Prepare Journal Entries)*

| | |
|---|---|
| Units started in Department A during the month (no units were on hand at the beginning of the month) | 4,000 |
| Costs incurred during the month: | |
| Direct materials | $ 9,120 |
| Direct labor | 12,350 |
| Manufacturing overhead | 7,790 |

During the month, 3,200 units were completed and the remaining 800 units are 75% complete.

Required:

1. Determine the equivalent units of production.
2. Determine the total unit cost of production.
3. Determine the total dollar cost attached to the 3,200 completed units.
4. Determine the total dollar cost attached to the 800 units unfinished at the end of the month.
5. Prepare all the necessary journal entries, assuming that cash was paid for overhead. Assume that the completed units are transferred to finished stock. Use only one Work in Process account and call it "Work in Process Inventory—A." [LO2c,2d,2e]

PROBLEM 22–10 *(Compute Equivalent Units, Prepare a Cost-of-Production Report, and Prepare Journal Entries)* Metro Company uses a process costing system and makes a single product (with a single production process) known as Metric. During September 19X5, 36,000 units of Metric were started and completed (no units were on hand at the beginning of September). Remaining in process and uncompleted on September 30 were 1,200 units, 75% complete. During September, the following manufacturing costs were incurred:

| | |
|---|---|
| Direct materials | $147,600 |
| Direct labor | 184,500 |
| Manufacturing overhead | 95,940 |

Required:

1. Compute the equivalent units of production for the month of September 19X5.
2. Prepare a cost-of-production report for September.
3. Prepare all the necessary journal entries for the department, assuming that cash was paid for overhead. Assume that completed units are transferred to finished stock. Use only one Work in Process account and call it "Work in Process Inventory—Metric." [LO2c,2d,2e]

## ALTERNATE PROBLEMS

PROBLEM 22–1A *(Prepare Job Order Journal Entries)* (Alternate to Problem 22–1) The following accounts appeared in the ledger of the Wilson Manufacturing Company at the end of May 19X5.

| | |
|---|---|
| Raw Materials Inventory | $ 6,300 |
| Work in Process Inventory | 18,200 |
| Finished Goods Inventory | 12,800 |

The following summarized data relate to the firm's production activities during the month of June 19X5.

a. Materials purchased on account, $21,700.

b. Wage costs incurred:

| | |
|---|---|
| Direct labor | $36,900 |
| Indirect labor | 9,200 |

c. Direct materials requisitioned for use on all job orders, $19,500.

d. Monthly depreciation on factory building and equipment, $1,800.

e. Manufacturing overhead is applied to production at the rate of 75% of direct labor cost.

f. Other manufacturing overhead expenses incurred during the month:

| | |
|---|---|
| On account | $14,200 |
| Depreciation on factory equipment | 1,600 |

g. Goods unfinished at the end of the month amounted to $12,400; all other goods were transferred to finished stock.

h. Finished goods sold on credit, $97,000 (the retail price—the cost of goods sold must be computed).

i. Finished goods remaining on hand, $21,400.

Required:

1. Prepare journal entries to record the above transactions. Do not close out the overapplied or underapplied manufacturing overhead.
2. Determine the ending balances in the Raw Materials, Work in Process, and Finished Goods Inventory accounts.
3. Compute the amount of overapplied or underapplied manufacturing overhead as of June 30, 19X5. [LO2a]

PROBLEM 22–2A *(Prepare Journal Entries for Job Order Costing)* (Alternate to Problem 22–3) The following transactions occurred during the first year of operations.

a. Purchased $73,500 of raw materials on account.

b. Manufacturing wages incurred during the period totaled $83,200. Of this amount, $77,000 represented the cost of direct labor.

c. Manufacturing overhead costs incurred on account during the period, $39,300.

d. Depreciation on factory machinery, $640.

e. Manufacturing overhead applied, $46,200.

f. Materials requisitioned for production, $57,900—all of which were direct materials cost.

g. All the 8,200 units that were started were completed.

Required:

Record the transactions in general journal form, including the closing of underapplied or overapplied overhead. [LO2a]

PROBLEM 22–3A *(Prepare Job Order Journal Entries)* (Alternate to Problem 22–4) The Hammond Manufacturing Corporation uses a job order cost system. The following information summarizes the firm's factory operations for its first month of business.

a. Materials purchased on account, $66,000.

b. Materials requisitioned for production:

| | |
|---|---|
| Job Order No. 1 | $28,000 |
| Job Order No. 2 | 16,000 |
| Job Order No. 3 | 11,000 |
| Indirect Materials | 6,000 |

c. Labor cost for the month totaled $80,000 and was distributed as follows:

| | |
|---|---|
| Job Order No. 1 | $40,000 |
| Job Order No. 2 | 20,000 |
| Job Order No. 3 | 15,000 |
| Indirect Labor | 5,000 |

d. Other manufacturing overhead costs incurred on account during the month totaled $65,000.

e. Overhead was applied at the rate of 80% of direct labor cost.

f. Job Orders No. 1 and No. 2 were completed, and the goods were transferred to the finished stock storeroom.

g. All the completed goods (Job Orders No. 1 and No. 2) were sold on account for a retail price of $195,000.

Required:

1. Prepare entries in general journal form to record the above transactions. (Setting up and posting to Work in Process T accounts for each job would be helpful.)
2. Determine the amount of the overapplied or underapplied manufacturing overhead for the month. Do not make a journal entry to close out the account.
3. Determine the balance that should appear in the Work in Process account at the end of the month. [LO2a]

PROBLEM 22–4A *(Compute Equivalent Units, Prepare a Cost-of-Production Report, and Prepare Journal Entries)* (Alternate to Problem 22–10) The Noel Company manufactures a single product known as Zipp. Production and cost reports in summarized form are presented below (no units were on hand at the beginning of February 19X8).

During the month of February, 23,200 units were started and completed and transferred to finished stock.

Remaining in process on February 28 were 6,000 units, 20% complete.

The following manufacturing costs were incurred during February:

| | |
|---|---|
| Direct materials | $34,160 |
| Direct labor | 43,920 |
| Manufacturing overhead | 20,252 |

Required:

1. Compute the equivalent units of production for February.
2. Prepare a cost-of-production report for February.
3. Prepare all the necessary journal entries for the department, assuming that cash was paid for overhead. Assume that completed units are transferred to finished stock. Use only one Work in Process account and call it "Work in Process Inventory—Zipp."

[LO2c,2d,2e]

# 23 Cost-Volume-Profit Analysis

## *Learning Objectives*

When you complete this chapter you will be able to

1. Answer the following questions:
   a. What is cost-volume-profit analysis, and what questions does it answer?
   b. What is the difference between fixed costs, variable costs, and mixed (semivariable) costs?
   c. What techniques are available for estimating the behavioral patterns of costs?
   d. What is the income equation, and how is it used in cost-volume-profit analysis?
   e. What is a break-even graph and what is its purpose? What are the components of a break-even graph?
   f. What is the contribution margin approach, and how can it be used in cost-volume-profit analysis?
   g. How can the contribution margin approach be used in income statement reporting?
2. Perform the following accounting functions:
   a. Construct a graph of a variable cost, a fixed cost, and a mixed (semivariable) cost.
   b. Estimate the fixed and variable components of costs by constructing a scatter diagram and/or by using the high-low approach.
   c. Use the income equation approach to perform cost-volume-profit analysis.
   d. Use the contribution margin approach to perform cost-volume-profit analysis.
   e. Use the contribution margin approach to prepare income statements.

Because of the effect on potential net income, it is important that managers know what costs to expect under planned levels of activity. Such knowledge helps them to develop operating strategies and make short-run decisions in planning for future net income. The cost-volume-profit analysis discussed in this chapter will provide the necessary knowledge.

## WHAT COST-VOLUME-PROFIT ANALYSIS IS

*1a. Cost-volume-profit analysis answers a number of questions*

**Cost-volume-profit analysis** is a set of techniques used to determine how sales, costs, and net income are affected by changes in business activity. An understanding of this analysis helps management to answer the following questions:

At what volume or level of activity (often expressed in sales dollars or units of sales) does a company neither earn a net income nor incur a net loss?

How many sales dollars are needed to earn a desired amount of net income?

How will increased advertising and product promotion expenses affect net income and sales volume?

How will net income be affected if plant capacity is expanded, thus increasing fixed manufacturing overhead costs?

How will total sales volume be affected if unit selling prices are increased? Decreased?

Cost-volume-profit analysis is useful in answering the above questions because the analysis is based on the relationships among

Costs

Volume (such as sales revenue, sales volume, and production volume)

Net income or profit (generally expressed as a planned or targeted amount)

However, before we can use cost-volume-profit methods effectively, we must understand the behavioral patterns of costs—that is, the difference between fixed and variable costs. We must also understand the methods that are available to separate costs into their fixed and variable components. This separation allows management to estimate total costs at various levels of activity.

Once we have acquired this knowledge, we will discuss various techniques for applying cost-volume-profit analysis.

## BEHAVIORAL PATTERNS OF COSTS

*1b. In their behavioral pattern, costs may be fixed, variable, or mixed (semivariable)*

The **behavioral pattern of a cost** indicates how much, if any, the dollar amount of that cost will vary with a certain type of activity. An accurate assessment of a cost's behavioral pattern allows managers to predict whether that cost will increase, decrease, or remain the same as a result of their decisions and/or other events.

FIXED COSTS **Fixed costs** are costs that are not expected to change as the level or volume of activity changes.

Managers have valuable information if they can predict which costs will remain the same as the result of certain decisions or events. Rent, depreciation, insurance, and supervisory salaries are examples of costs that are usually fixed.

*2a. A fixed cost is graphed in Exhibit 23–1*

The behavioral pattern of a fixed cost is shown graphically in Exhibit 23–1. Note that the vertical axis shows the dollar amount of supervision costs, while the horizontal axis depicts the level of activity expressed in machine hours. Note also that the repair cost line itself is horizontal, depicting an unchanged dollar cost at different activity levels.

EXHIBIT 23–1
Graph of a Fixed Cost

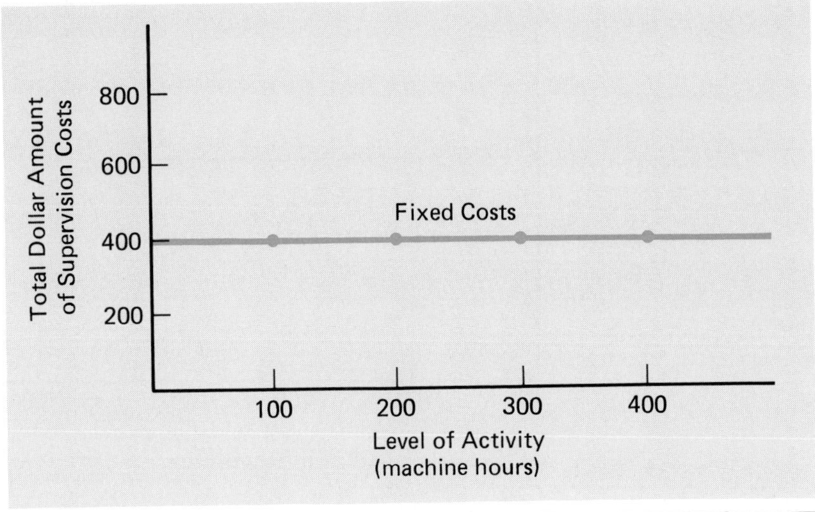


VARIABLE COSTS **Variable costs** are costs that are expected to change in direct proportion to the change in a given level or volume of activity.

For example, assume that repair costs on factory machinery are expected to increase $2 for every hour that production equipment is operated. The estimated dollar amount of repair costs for a given time period is computed as follows:

| | |
|---|---|
| Estimated Number of Machine Hours | 5,000 |
| × Estimated Repair Costs per Hour | $ 2 |
| = Estimated Dollar Amount of Repair Costs | $10,000 |

The knowledge that a certain cost's behavioral pattern is variable, together with an accurate estimate of the rate of such variability, is valuable information for managers. Methods for estimating the rate of variability are discussed later in the chapter.

*2a. A variable cost is graphed in Exhibit 23–2*

The graph in Exhibit 23–2 shows the behavioral pattern of a variable cost. Note that like Exhibit 23–1, the vertical axis shows the dollar amount of repair costs, while the horizontal axis depicts the level of activity expressed in machine hours. An activity level of 100 machine hours produces $200 of repair costs, an activity level of 200 machine hours produces $400 of repair costs, and so forth. As can be seen, the $2 per-machine-hour cost remains the same at all indicated levels of activity.

MIXED (SEMIVARIABLE) COSTS **Mixed (semivariable) costs** are costs that vary in relation to the change in an activity level, but the variance is not directly proportionate.

While some dollar portion of the cost remains constant with alternative activity levels, another part of the same cost varies in direct proportion to alternative activity levels. Thus a mixed (semivariable) cost has both a fixed and a variable portion.

EXHIBIT 23–2

Graph of a Variable Cost

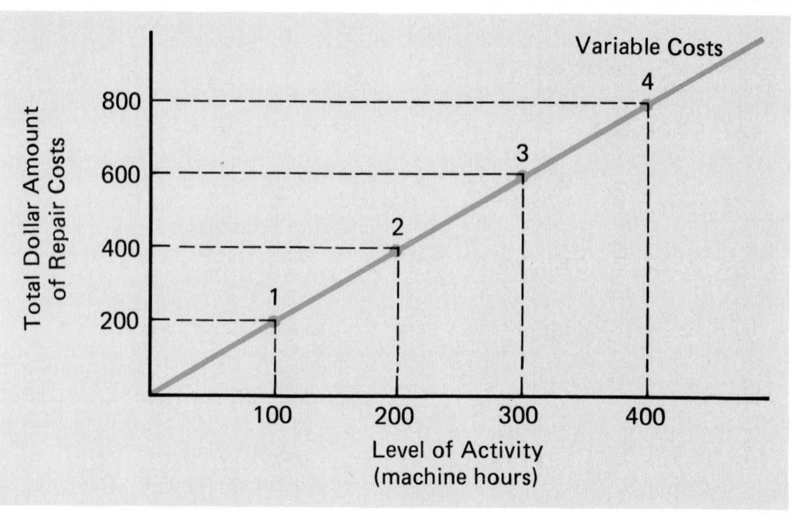


Machinery repairs and utilities are examples of costs that are sometimes mixed. However, many costs can be fixed, variable, or mixed, depending on the circumstances of a given company's operations.

*2a. A mixed cost is graphed in Exhibit 23–3*

The graph in Exhibit 23–3 shows the behavioral pattern of a mixed cost. The point where the cost line originates on the vertical axis ($400) represents the *fixed portion* of the total cost. The slope of the cost line ($2 per machine hour) shows the *variable rate.* Thus, at an activity level of 100 machine hours, the company expects a cost of $600 ($400 fixed added to $200 variable).

EXHIBIT 23–3

Graph of a Mixed Cost

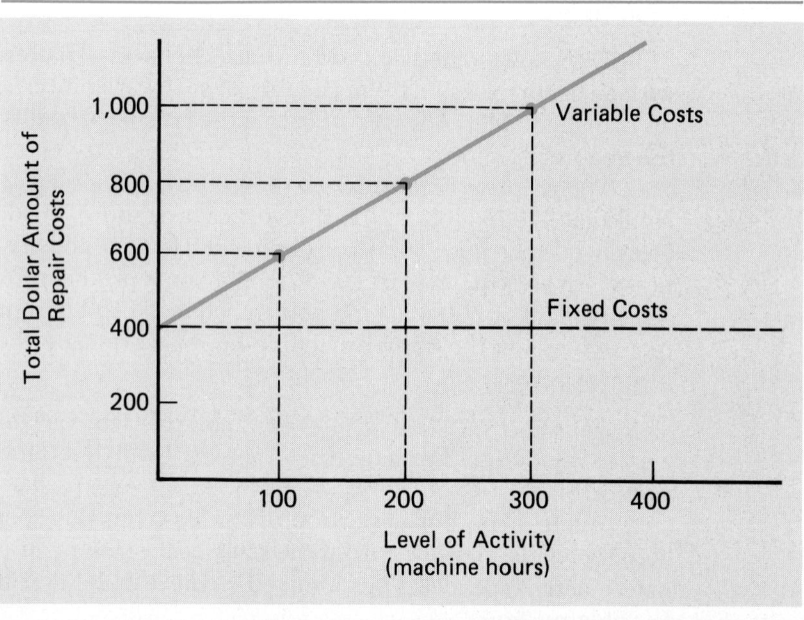

*2a. Graphed patterns of fixed and variable costs are valid only over a specific relevant range of company activity*

RELEVANT RANGE The described behavioral patterns of fixed and variable costs are valid only over a limited range of company activity called the **relevant range.** The range of activity or volume depends on a particular company's operating characteristics.

A fixed cost is expected to remain constant over the relevant range of company activity. Conversely, a variable cost is expected to change in relation to a change in the level of some company activity over the relevant range. The rate of variability is assumed to be constant for the purpose of accounting analyses.

The graph in Exhibit 23–4 shows the concept of relevant range. This graph shows the relevant range between 100 and 300 machine hours of activity. The level of activity could also be expressed in terms of units of sales or units of production. Within this range, it is assumed that the $400 fixed portion of utility costs remains constant and that the variable rate of $2 per machine hour stays the same.

EXHIBIT 23–4

Graph of Relevant Range

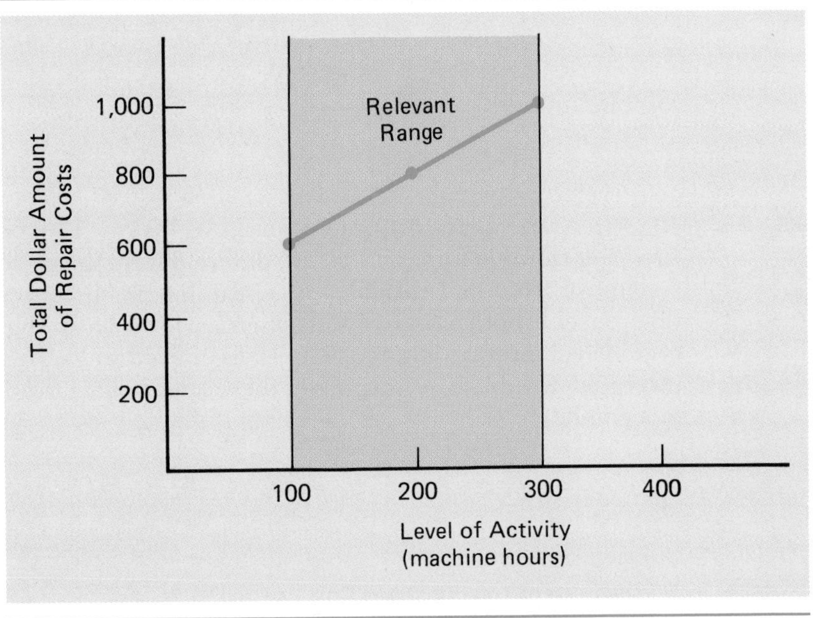


*2a. A step-fixed cost is graphed in Exhibit 23–5*

STEP-FIXED COSTS **Step-fixed costs** increase or decrease in discrete steps when activity reaches certain specific levels. Exhibit 23–5 illustrates a cost of this type. The cost remains the same until activity reaches the level of a higher plateau (100, 200, 300, or 400). At that point, the cost makes a discrete increase to a larger dollar figure and remains at that amount until the level of activity reaches another plateau. The sudden cost change probably results from the management's decision. For example, one type of cost that has this behavioral pattern might be an expenditure for part-time clerical help.

Although experience may show that some costs behave in a step-fixed fashion, the company could treat them as mixed costs. The difference between the two methods of treating costs is probably small enough that the practical advantage of using the mixed rather than the step-fixed treatment outweighs the disadvantage of lost accuracy.

*EXHIBIT 23–5*
Graph of a Step-Fixed Cost

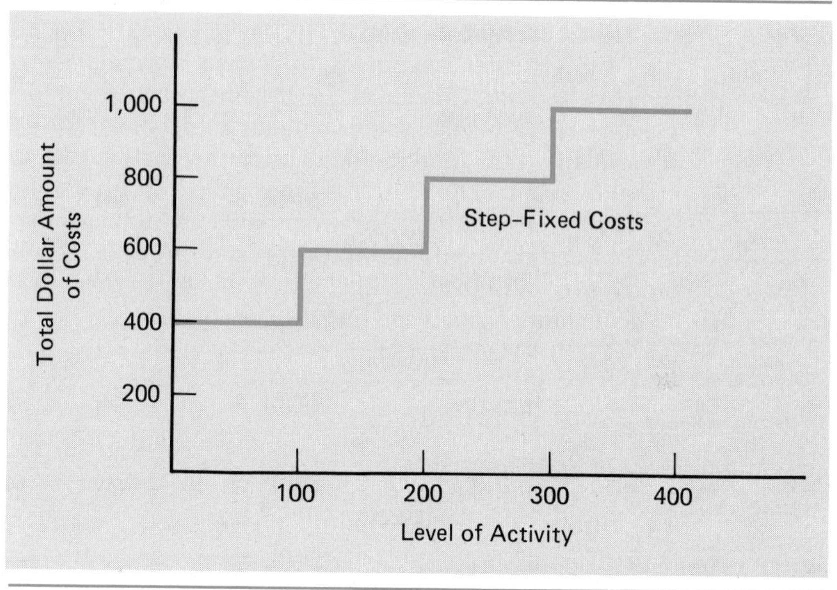


***2a. Cost behavioral patterns differ between those of total costs and those of costs per unit***

FIXED AND VARIABLE COSTS PER UNIT The behavioral patterns of *fixed and variable costs per unit* are different from the patterns of the total dollar amount of fixed and variable costs. Exhibit 23–6 expresses these behavioral differences in both narrative and numerical form, and it shows that in the absence of sufficient information, the definitions of fixed and variable costs can be misinterpreted. Exhibit 23–7 expresses these same behavioral differences in the form of a graph.

*EXHIBIT 23–6*
Comparisons of Total Cost and Cost per Unit

| TYPE OF COST | WHEN EXPRESSED AS TOTAL COST | WHEN EXPRESSED AS COST PER UNIT |
|---|---|---|
| Fixed Costs | Remains constant as level of activity changes | Changes as level of activity changes |
| Variable Costs | Changes as level of activity changes | Remains constant as level of activity changes |
| | 100 UNITS OF PRODUCTION | 200 UNITS OF PRODUCTION |
| Fixed Costs (total) | $400 | $400 |
| Variable Costs (total) | $200 (100 × $2.00) | $400 (200 × $2.00) |
| Fixed Costs (per unit) | $4.00 (400 ÷ 100) | $2.00 (400 ÷ 200) |
| Variable Costs (per unit) | $2.00 (200 ÷ 100) | $2.00 (400 ÷ 200) |

EXHIBIT 23–7
Behavioral Differences Between Total Costs and Costs per Unit

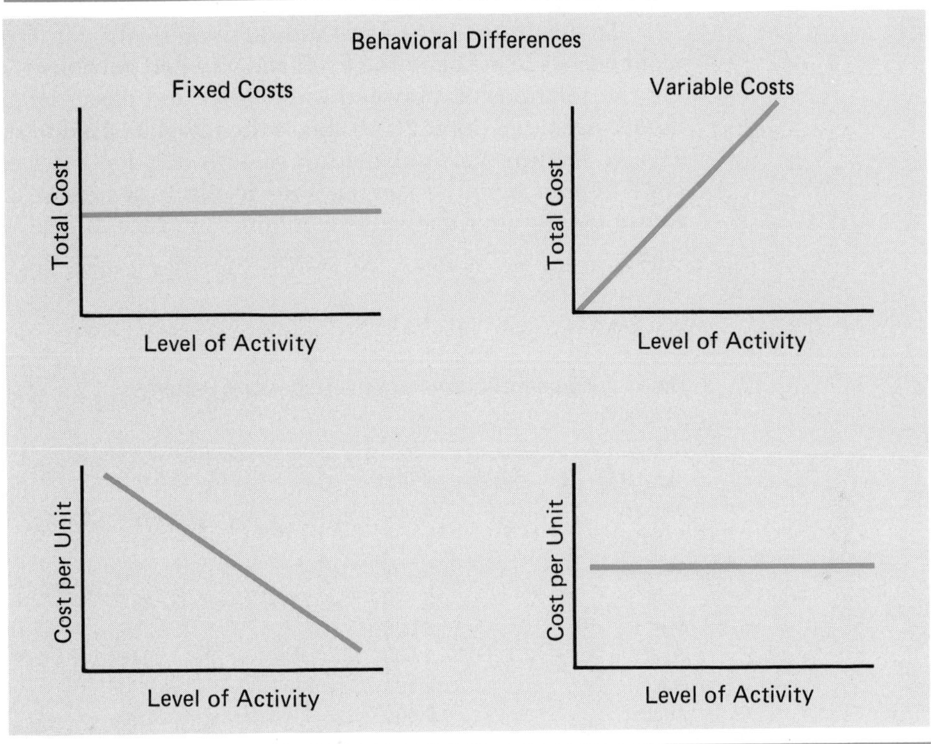


## ESTIMATING THE BEHAVIORAL PATTERNS OF COSTS

We now know the difference between fixed, variable, and mixed costs. In this section we will explain how to estimate the behavioral patterns of costs and how to separate costs into their fixed and variable components.

Generally, either of two techniques can be used to estimate the behavioral patterns of costs: *judgmental identification* or *numerical analysis.*

### Judgmental Identification of Behavioral Patterns

*1c. Behavioral patterns of costs can be identified by using judgment and past experience*

By applying judgment and past company experience, each cost can be identified as fixed, variable, or mixed. For example, such accounts as taxes, supervision, and depreciation could easily be judged as fixed.

However, **judgmental identification** has definite limitations, once the obvious fixed costs are selected. On the one hand, the rate of change of variable costs might be difficult to determine without studies of some type. On the other hand, separating the fixed and variable portions of mixed costs could be difficult without applying numerical processes to these costs.

### Numerical Analysis of Behavioral Patterns

*1c. Behavioral patterns of costs can be identified by using numerical analysis*

In general, **numerical analysis** separates costs into their fixed and variable components by calculating relationships between historical cost data and activity. Many complex numerical techniques are available for separating costs into their fixed and variable components. We will confine our explanations of numerical analyses to two relatively simple ones—the visual inspection of a scatter diagram and the high-low method.

To illustrate the two methods of numerical analysis, assume that a department wishes to estimate the fixed and variable portions of repair costs by studying the relationship between these costs and direct labor hours for a twelve-month period. Exhibit 23–8 shows the raw data used to study this relationship. Twelve months were selected to smooth out the effect of abnormal operating conditions or rapidly changing price levels. In some cases, it might be necessary to use twenty-four or thirty-six months in order to derive a more useful set of data.

*EXHIBIT 23–8*

Data for Numerical Analysis of the Behavioral Patterns of Costs

| MONTH | DIRECT LABOR HOURS | REPAIR COSTS |
|---|---|---|
| January | 4,500 | $ 335 |
| February | 4,300 | 315 |
| March | 3,700 | 280 |
| April | 3,300 | 285 |
| May | 3,000 | 250 |
| June | 2,800 | 245 |
| July | 2,700 | 230 |
| August | 2,500 | 220 |
| September | 2,800 | 240 |
| October | 3,100 | 260 |
| November | 3,800 | 300 |
| December | 3,500 | 275 |
| Total | | |

*1c,2b. Cost behavior can be plotted in a scatter diagram*

VISUAL INSPECTION OF A SCATTER DIAGRAM After collecting the data in Exhibit 23–8, the company constructs a **scatter diagram.** This diagram depicts the relationship between two variables—in this case, direct labor hours and repair costs. Each of the twelve points plotted on the diagram represents the repair costs associated with the direct labor hours for a particular month.

Exhibit 23–9 shows the scatter diagram made from the data in Exhibit 23–8.

Since the points on the scatter diagram are clustered, it seems that there is a positive relationship between direct labor hours and repair costs. That is, the change in repair costs seems to be explained by the change in direct labor hours. When using scatter diagrams, however, you should be careful about their implications. Clustered points on the diagram do not necessarily denote a cause-and-effect relationship between the two variables. If management believes that a causal relationship should exist between two variables (direct labor hours and repair costs, for example), a scatter diagram can (1) help prove or disprove this belief and (2) indicate in the form of a graph the approximate correlation between the variables. If the plotted points are too scattered, a straight line through them is of no benefit in estimating the fixed and variable portion of the cost.

However, the points in Exhibit 23–9 are sufficiently clustered so that we

*EXHIBIT 23–9*

Scatter Diagram Relating Repair Costs with Direct Labor Hours

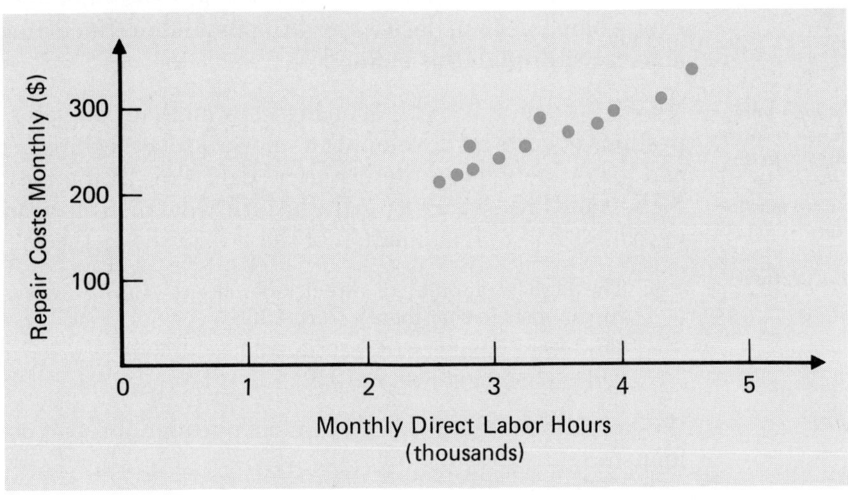


***1c,2b. A trendline is drawn through the points on a scatter diagram by visual inspection***

can draw a straight line, called a **trendline,** through these points and use this straight line as a basis for estimating the fixed and variable portions of repair costs. The **visual inspection method** is used to draw the trendline. That is, the trendline is drawn in a "freehand manner" so that it will go as close as possible through the center of the plotted points.

Exhibit 23–10 shows the scatter diagram in Exhibit 23–9 with a trendline added to it. Note that the trendline is positioned so that some of the plotted points are above the line and some of them are below the line.

Examination of Exhibit 23–10 shows that the slope of the trendline intersects the repair costs line (the vertical axis) at approximately $90. Thus $90 is the

*EXHIBIT 23–10*

Scatter Diagram and Line Fitted by Visual Inspection Relating Repair Costs with Direct Labor Hours

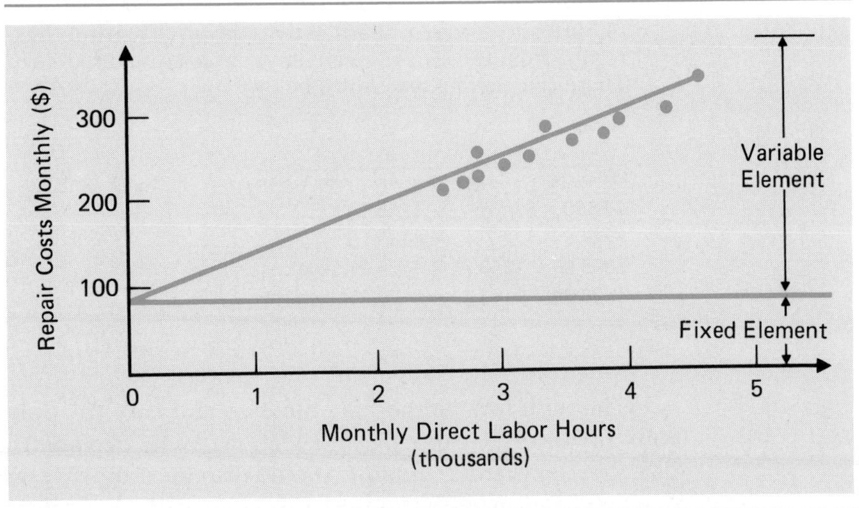

estimated fixed portion of repair costs, and the slope of the trendline is the estimated variable portion of repair costs.

The visual inspection method is of course subjective. In many cases, however, companies can derive approximate, but useful, estimates of fixed and variable costs through this method.

*1c,2b. The high-low method shows relationships between the highest and the lowest activity levels in the historical data and the costs associated with these levels*

HIGH-LOW METHOD The **high-low method** estimates the fixed and variable portions of costs by developing numerical relationships between (1) the highest and lowest activity in the historical data and (2) the costs associated with the highest and lowest activity in the historical data. To illustrate, we will use the data in Exhibit 23–8. Examination of these data shows the following:

> The highest number of direct labor hours (4,500) occurred in January, and the repair costs in that month were $335.
>
> The lowest number of direct labor hours (2,500) occurred in August, and the repair costs in that month were $220.

We can estimate the fixed and variable portions of repair costs by following these four steps:

1. Calculate the difference between the highest and lowest number of direct labor hours.
2. Calculate the difference between the repair costs at the highest and lowest number of direct labor hours. These differences are shown below.

| ACTIVITY | DIRECT LABOR HOURS | REPAIR COSTS |
|---|---|---|
| High | 4,500 | $335 |
| Low | 2,500 | 220 |
| Difference | 2,000 | $115 |

3. Divide the difference in repair costs by the difference in direct labor hours. This arithmetic produces the following variable rate per direct labor hour:

$$\$115/2{,}000 = \$.0575$$

4. Multiply the variable rate by the number of direct labor hours at both the highest (4,500) and lowest (2,500) activity levels. Then subtract the two multiplication results from the two respective repair costs, and the final figure is the fixed cost. These calculations are shown below.

$4,500 × $.0575 = $258.75
$2,500 × $.0575 = $143.75
$335.00 − $258.75 = $ 76.25 fixed cost
$220.00 − $143.75 = $ 76.25 fixed cost

The high-low method is objective and easy to apply. This technique has limits, however, because of the selection of only two points in the historical data. Also, the user of this technique should disregard any extremely high or low levels of activity because unusual operating conditions have probably caused these extreme activity levels.

## APPLICATION OF COST-VOLUME-PROFIT ANALYSIS

At this point we will apply our knowledge of fixed and variable costs to cost-volume-profit analysis. We will do so first by examining the *income equation* and its various applications.

### The Income Equation

*1d,2c. The income equation is stated here, and its use is illustrated by an example*

To develop the income equation, we must first separate total costs into their fixed and variable components using the techniques explained in the earlier part of the chapter. Once this separation is performed, we express the **income equation** as the following relationship of net income to sales revenue, fixed costs, and variable costs:

Sales Revenue = Variable Costs + Fixed Costs + Net Income

This same equation is often expressed in income statement format as follows:

Sales Revenue − Variable Costs − Fixed Costs = Net Income

To illustrate the income equation, we will use the following hypothetical facts. Tandy Company manufactures one product, a specialized golf putter. Each putter sells for $50. Fixed costs are estimated at $8,000 per month. Variable costs are estimated at $30 per unit (we often express fixed costs in total dollars and variable costs in dollars per unit, per hour, and the like).

Letting $x$ represent the number of putters expected to be sold, we compute the net income at the expected sales volume by using the income equation as follows:

| Sales Revenue | − Variable Costs | − Fixed Costs | = Net Income |
|---|---|---|---|
| $50x | − $30x | − $8,000 | = Net Income |

Total sales revenue is calculated by multiplying the selling price per unit by the number of units sold. Total variable costs are determined by multiplying the variable costs per unit by the number of units sold. Total fixed costs remain constant.

To complete the computation and determine the net income, we take the number of putters the company plans to sell. Assume 600. We then substitute 600 for $x$ in the income equation.

| Sales Revenue | − Variable Costs | − Fixed Costs | = Net Income |
|---|---|---|---|
| $50 × 600 | − $30 × 600 | − $8,000 | = Net Income |
| $30,000 | − $18,000 | − $8,000 | = $4,000 |

We can now show how net income is affected by changes in costs, volume, and revenues. As we proceed through the examples, note how cost-volume-profit analysis provides the answers to managers' questions listed in the first section of the chapter.

### Break-Even Computations

*1d. Knowledge of the break-even point is useful in cost-volume-profit analysis*

The **break-even point** is the volume of activity where total revenues cover both fixed and variable costs and where there is no net income or net loss. Management often finds it useful to know this volume.

The break-even point can be expressed in units of sales or sales dollars.

Using the Tandy Company data, the break-even point in units is calculated as follows:

| | | |
|---|---|---|
| Sales Revenue | = Variable Costs | + Fixed Costs |
| $50x$ | $= 30x$ | + \$8,000 |
| $20x$ | = \$8,000 | |
| $x$ | = 400 units | |

The break-even point is expressed in sales dollars by multiplying the break-even point in units (400) by the selling price per unit (\$50):

400 units × \$50 per unit = \$20,000

By preparing the summarized income statement for Tandy Company shown in Exhibit 23–11, we can verify the results of our break-even analysis.

*EXHIBIT 23–11*

Income Statement at the Break-Even Point

| | | |
|---|---|---|
| Sales (400 units @ \$50 per unit) | | \$20,000 |
| Costs: | | |
| Variable (400 units @ \$30 per unit) | \$12,000 | |
| Fixed | 8,000 | |
| Total costs | | 20,000 |
| Net Income | | \$ -0- |

## *Target Net Income*

*1d. We can compute the number of units that must be sold to yield a target net income*

Knowledge of the break-even point leads to a calculation that management may be more interested in knowing—the number of units that must be sold to earn a desired or target net income. **Target net income** can be expressed as a fixed amount of net income or as a percentage of sales.

Assume that the price remains at \$50 and that the costs respond predictably to activity changes. The following computations show how many units of sales are needed to earn a net income of \$10,000:

| | | | |
|---|---|---|---|
| Sales Revenue | = Variable Costs | + Fixed Costs | + Net Income |
| $50x$ | $= 30x$ | + \$8,000 | + \$10,000 |
| $20x$ | = \$18,000 | | |
| $x$ | = 900 units (putters) | | |

The following summarized income statement verifies our analysis.

| | | |
|---|---|---|
| Sales (900 units @ \$50 per unit) | | \$45,000 |
| Costs: | | |
| Variable (900 units @ \$30 per unit) | \$27,000 | |
| Fixed | 8,000 | |
| Total costs | | 35,000 |
| Net Income | | \$10,000 |

Assume that Tandy Company sets target net income at 20% of revenues. The break-even calculations would produce the following results:

| | | | |
|---|---|---|---|
| Sales Revenue | = Variable Costs | + Fixed Costs | + Net Income |
| $50x$ | $= 30x$ | + $8,000 | + 20% of $50x$ |
| $50x$ | $= 30x$ | + 8,000 | $+ 10x$ |
| $10x$ | = $8,000 | | |
| $x$ | = 800 units (putters) | | |

Again, we can verify our analysis by preparing this summarized income statement:

| | | |
|---|---|---|
| Sales (800 units @ $50 per unit) | | $40,000 |
| Costs: | | |
| Variable (800 units @ $30 per unit) | $24,000 | |
| Fixed | 8,000 | |
| Total costs | | 32,000 |
| Net Income (20% of sales) | | $ 8,000 |

## Estimating Net Income at a Given Sales Level

*1d. We can calculate net income at a given sales level*

Break-even analysis can also be used to calculate net income at a given sales level. For example, if Tandy Company wished to know how much profit would be earned on the sale of 1,000 putters, the following analysis would be made using the income equation:

| | | | |
|---|---|---|---|
| Sales Revenue | = Variable Costs | + Fixed Costs | + Net Income |
| $50 × 1,000 | = $30 × 1,000 | + $8,000 | + Net Income |
| $50,000 | = $30,000 | + $8,000 | + $12,000 |

## Margin of Safety

The **margin of safety** is the amount by which sales may decrease before a loss is incurred. At sales of 800 units, Tandy Company's margin is $20,000, the difference between the $40,000 of revenue generated from sales of 800 units and the $20,000 of revenue generated at the break-even point of 400 units.

The margin of safety can also be expressed as 400 units (800 − 400 to break even) or as 50% of sales ($20,000 of revenue at the break-even point ÷ $40,000). The higher the margin of safety, the better the company's financial position.

## Use of a Break-Even Graph

*1e. A break-even graph is illustrated in Exhibit 23–12*

Cost-volume-profit analysis may also be shown in graph form, as in Exhibit 23–12. This **break-even graph** not only shows the break-even point but also provides a visual basis for evaluating the relationships among sales, costs, and net income at varying levels of activity. The graph's horizontal axis shows volume in units; the vertical axis shows dollars of sales and costs. The dotted lines are provided to help distinguish between total costs and fixed costs.

The straight revenue line is drawn from the zero point of the axis at a selling price of $50 per unit (note that $35,000 of sales corresponds to 700 units of volume). A uniform selling price is assumed. The straight total cost line is drawn from the $8,000 point on the vertical axis at a variable cost per unit of $30 (note that $20,000 of total cost − $8,000 of fixed cost = $12,000 of variable costs, which corresponds to 400 units of volume). The variable cost per unit is assumed to be uniform. The straight fixed cost line is drawn horizontally from the $8,000 point on the vertical axis. Fixed costs are assumed to be constant.

EXHIBIT 23–12
Break-Even Graph

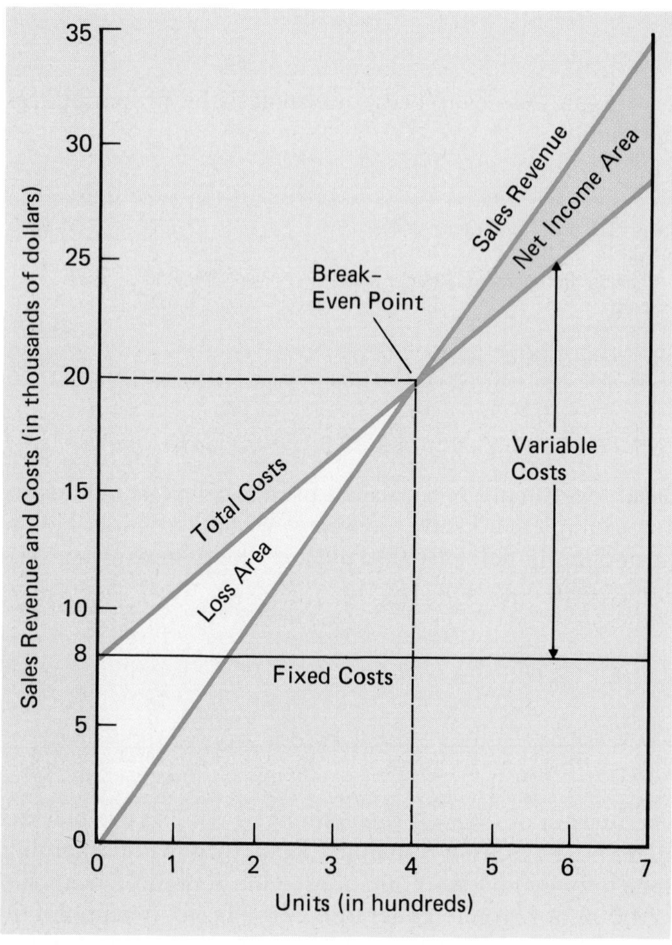


Note that the total cost line, consisting of fixed and variable costs, intersects the sales revenue line at the break-even point. At this point, the sales and total costs are equal at a volume of 400 units. All volume above this break-even point yields a profit; all volume below this break-even point yields a loss.

## EXPANSION OF COST-VOLUME-PROFIT ANALYSIS TO THE CONTRIBUTION MARGIN APPROACH

With the income equation approach as a background for learning the elements of break-even analysis, we now turn to the *contribution margin approach,* which will be used in the remainder of the chapter.

### The Contribution Margin per Unit Approach

**Contribution margin** is defined as the excess of sales revenue over all variable costs. **Contribution margin per unit** is the excess of the sales price of one unit over the variable cost of one unit. Knowledge of contribution margin is useful because this figure represents the amount available to cover fixed costs and to contribute toward generating net income.

Using the Tandy Company data from previous pages, we can compute both the contribution margin per unit and the contribution margin:

> Contribution margin per unit is $20 (the sales price of $50 less the variable costs per unit of $30).
>
> With sales of 600 units, the contribution margin is $12,000 (sales of $30,000 less variable costs of $18,000). At this level of activity, contribution margin fully covers fixed costs of $8,000 and provides $4,000 of net income.
>
> With sales of 400 units, the contribution margin is $8,000 (sales of $20,000 less variable costs of $12,000). At this level of activity, there is no net income or net loss. Sales are $20,000 and total costs are also $20,000 ($12,000 variable and $8,000 fixed).

*1f,2d. Use of the contribution margin per unit approach is illustrated here*

To illustrate the contribution margin per unit approach to break-even analysis, we will again use the Tandy Company data and apply the following formula to determine the number of units Tandy needs to sell to break even:

$$\text{Break-even Point in Units} = \frac{\text{Fixed Costs}}{\text{Contribution Margin per Unit}} = \frac{\$8{,}000}{\$20} = 400 \text{ units}$$

Each additional putter sold over 400 increases net income by $20, the amount of the contribution margin per unit. If 410 putters are sold, we can make the following analysis:

410 units − 400 units = 10 units
× $20 contribution margin per unit
= *$200* of net income

This analysis can be verified by showing the following income statement for the sale of 410 putters (note, however, the relative ease of the above analysis).

| | | |
|---|---|---|
| Sales (410 units @ $50 per unit) | | $20,500 |
| Costs: | | |
| Variable (410 units @ $30 per unit) | $12,300 | |
| Fixed | 8,000 | |
| Total costs | | 20,300 |
| Net Income | | $ 200 |

## Contribution Margin Ratio Approach

*1f,2d. The contribution margin ratio is computed by dividing the contribution margin by sales*

The contribution margin ratio (or contribution margin percentage) is another method for analyzing the relationships among costs, volume, and net income. The **contribution margin ratio** is the contribution margin divided by sales. Using the same Tandy Company data, we derive the following:

$$\text{Contribution Margin Ratio} = \frac{\text{Sales} - \text{Variable Costs}}{\text{Sales}} = \frac{\$20{,}000 - \$12{,}000}{\$20{,}000} = 40\%, \text{ or } .40$$

By dividing the contribution margin ratio into total fixed costs, we can calculate the break-even point in sales dollars:

$$\text{Break-even Point in Sales Dollars} = \frac{\text{Fixed Costs}}{\text{Contribution Margin Ratio}} = \frac{\$8,000}{.40} = \$20,000$$

Note that we can calculate the same $20,000 by multiplying the $50 sales price by the 400 units needed to break even. Note also that the contribution margin ratio does not change as sales volume goes up or down.

Break-even analysis in sales dollars is particularly useful to companies that sell multiple products. Such companies need break-even information about sales dollars.

## USING THE CONTRIBUTION MARGIN APPROACH TO PREDICT THE EFFECT OF REVENUE AND COST CHANGES ON NET INCOME

Frequently, both planned and unplanned activities cause a change in a company's revenues and costs. In this section we will keep other factors constant and show how individual changes in

Selling price,
Fixed costs, and
Variable costs

affect net income. In addition, we will demonstrate how multiple changes affect net income.

Here are some of the original Tandy Company data that we will use:

| | | |
|---|---|---|
| Selling price per unit | $50 | |
| Variable costs per unit | 30 | |
| Contribution margin per unit | 20 | |
| Total fixed costs | | $8,000 |
| Break-even point | | 400 (putters) |
| Sales volume needed to earn a target net income of $10,000 | | 900 (putters) |

### Changing the Selling Price

*1f,2d. We can use the contribution margin approach to calculate the effect of a change in selling price*

Before any final pricing decisions are made, managers should understand the probable effect that proposed changes in selling prices will have on net income. In some situations, small increases and decreases in selling prices have no effect on the number of units sold. In other situations, a price increase lowers volume and a price decrease has the opposite effect.

By using cost-volume-profit analysis, we can calculate what should happen to both the break-even point and the net income when selling prices are altered. Assume that Tandy Company has sold an average of 800 putters per accounting period. Its average net income was $8,000, determined as follows:

| | | | |
|---|---|---|---|
| Sales Revenue | − Variable Costs | − Fixed Costs | = Net Income |
| $50 × 800 | − $30 × 800 | − $8,000 | = Net Income |
| $40,000 | − $24,000 | − $8,000 | = $8,000 |

The company is considering a 10% price increase from $50 to $55. Contribution margin would increase from $20 to $25 (the new selling price of $55 minus the same variable costs per unit of $30). Assuming that both the variable costs per unit and the fixed dollar costs remain constant, the new break-even point in units is calculated as follows:

$$\text{Break-even Point in Units} = \frac{\text{Fixed Costs}}{\text{Contribution Margin per Unit}} = \frac{\$8{,}000}{\$25} = 320 \text{ units}$$

With the increased selling price, 320 rather than 400 units would cover both variable and fixed costs. Of more use to management, however, might be the knowledge of how many units must be sold at $55 per unit to maintain the same $8,000 of net income earned in previous periods. We can calculate the necessary number of units using the contribution margin approach:

$$\text{Sales in Units for \$8,000 of Net Income} = \frac{\text{Fixed Costs} + \text{Net Income}}{\text{Contribution Margin per Unit}} = \frac{\$8{,}000 + \$8{,}000}{\$25} = 640 \text{ units}$$

The knowledge that a $5 increase in the selling price could lower volume from 800 to 640 units and still maintain an $8,000 profit is valuable information for management. If unit sales went below 640, net income would be lower than $8,000, given our assumptions of break-even analysis.

Suppose that management wishes to estimate the effect of a 10% price reduction ($50 to $45), which would cause a 15% increase in volume (800 units to 920 units). The following analysis shows the new break-even point in units and the new net income.

*New break-even point:*

$$\frac{\$8{,}000}{\$15 \text{ (new contribution margin per unit)}} = 534 \text{ units (rounded)}$$

*New net income at 920 units:*

| Sales Revenue | − Variable Costs | − Fixed Costs | = Net Income |
|---|---|---|---|
| $45 × 920 | − $30 × 920 | − $8,000 | = Net Income |
| $41,400 | − $27,600 | − $8,000 | = $5,800 |

While sales revenue would go up by $1,400 ($41,400 − $40,000), net income would decrease by $2,200 ($8,000 − $5,800). The $5 price reduction would not be offset by the sale of 120 additional units. The break-even point would also go up from 400 to 534 units. Given our break-even analysis assumptions, management would be well advised to avoid the price reduction unless volume can be increased by more than 120 units.

### Change in Fixed Costs

Normally, fixed costs are expected to remain constant within the relevant range. In certain situations, however, management may intentionally increase fixed costs in an attempt to generate more sales. A sales promotion campaign is an example.

Assume that management wishes to estimate the effect of an increase in fixed costs on:

The break-even point in units.
The number of units of sales that will generate a target net income of $10,000.

A schedule of original data before the change in fixed costs and the revised data after the change in fixed costs is shown below.

| | ORIGINAL DATA | FIXED COSTS INCREASE OF $500 |
|---|---|---|
| Sales price per unit | $50 | $50 |
| Variable cost per unit | $30 | $30 |
| Contribution margin per unit | $20 | $20 |
| Total fixed costs | $8,000 | $8,500 |
| Break-even point in units | 400 | (unknown) |
| Sales in units to earn target net income of $10,000 | 900 | (unknown) |

*1f,2d. We can use the contribution margin approach to calculate the effect of a change in fixed costs*

To calculate the new break-even point in units and the new sales in units necessary to earn the target net income, we will use the contribution margin approach. The analysis is shown below.

$$\text{Break-even Point in Units} = \frac{\text{Fixed Costs}}{\text{Contribution Margin per Unit}}$$

$$= \frac{\$8{,}500}{\$20} = 425 \text{ units}$$

$$\text{Sales in Units to Earn } \$10{,}000 = \frac{\$8{,}500 + \$10{,}000}{\$20} = 925 \text{ units}$$

Because each putter sold contributes $20, an additional *25* putters must be sold to cover the *$500* increase in fixed costs. To maintain the same target net income of $10,000, 25 more putters must be sold. A *6.25%* increase in fixed costs ($\frac{\$500}{\$8{,}000}$) must be accompanied by a *2.8%* increase in putter sales ($\frac{25}{900}$) to maintain the target net income of $10,000.

## Change in Variable Costs

*1f,2d. We can use the contribution margin approach to calculate the effect of a change in variable costs*

Suppose management considers making a production change that should reduce variable costs by $5 per unit (increasing the contribution margin per unit from $20 to $25). Using the original data, we can calculate the new break-even point in units and the new unit sales necessary to maintain the target net income of $10,000:

$$\text{Break-even Point in Units} = \frac{\$8{,}000}{\$25} = 320 \text{ units}$$

$$\text{Sales in Units to Earn } \$10{,}000 = \frac{\$8{,}000 + \$10{,}000}{\$25} = 720 \text{ units}$$

Each putter sold will now contribute $25 rather than $20. Therefore only 320 putters must be sold to break even. Likewise, only 720 putters must be sold to keep the target net income. An increase in the contribution margin will lower both the break-even point and the number of units necessary to maintain a given target net income of $10,000.

### Multiple Changes

In practice, it is common for more than one variable to change at the same time. For example, assume that Tandy Company believes that

A $5 increase in its selling price (from $50 to $55) would raise net income

At the same time, a proposed production change would lower variable costs per unit by $5 (from $30 per unit to $25 per unit)

The new contribution margin would be $30 ($55 − $25)

In addition, a promotion campaign would increase fixed costs by $500

*1f,2d. Contribution margin lets us calculate the effect of multiple changes*

Using the contribution margin approach, the following schedule shows the impact of the three changes on the break-even point in units and on the number of unit sales necessary to keep the target net income of $10,000:

| | WITH ORIGINAL DATA | DATA WITH CHANGES |
|---|---|---|
| Break-even Point in Units | = $8,000 / $20 | = $8,500 / $30 |
| | = 400 units | = 284 units (rounded) |
| Sales in Units to Earn $10,000 | = $18,000 / $20 | = $18,500 / $30 |
| | = 900 units | = 617 units (rounded) |

## CONTRIBUTION MARGIN APPROACH TO INCOME STATEMENT REPORTING

The contribution margin approach to cost-volume-profit analysis not only is useful for break-even computations but also provides better income statements for managers. We will demonstrate this by comparing the income statement format typically used for reporting to stockholders and other outside groups with the type that uses the contribution margin approach and emphasizes the behavioral patterns of costs.

*1g,2e. Use of the contribution margin approach in income statement reporting is illustrated here*

To illustrate, we take the data of Ortley Company, which has completed its first year of operations. The company manufactures a specialized harmonica. Because the harmonicas are manufactured only upon receipt of a customer's order, the company does not keep a finished goods inventory. Also assume that there is no work in process inventory at year-end.

| | |
|---|---|
| Sales for the year (in units) | 1,000 |
| Selling price per unit | $ 100 |
| Cost of goods sold | $60,000 |
| Operating expenses | $30,000 |

Exhibit 23–13 shows how the data are presented in summary form in an income statement intended for use by parties external to the company's management.

*EXHIBIT 23–13*

Income Statement Using the Cost of Goods Sold and Operating Expense Format

| | |
|---|---|
| Sales | $100,000 |
| Cost of Goods Sold | 60,000 |
| Gross Profit | $ 40,000 |
| Operating Costs (or Expenses) | 30,000 |
| Net Income | $ 10,000 |

This income statement arranges costs according to their functional classifications. Thus all fixed and variable manufacturing costs are shown as Cost of Goods Sold. Likewise, all fixed and variable selling and administrative costs are shown as Operating Costs (or Expenses).

*1g,2e. An income statement can be cast in a contribution margin format*

However, for the purpose of cost-volume-profit analysis, the income statement shown in Exhibit 23–14 has more appropriate classifications. The contribution margin format is used by placing all variable costs in one category and all fixed costs in another (the amounts of fixed costs and variable costs are assumed).

*EXHIBIT 23–14*

Income Statement Using the Contribution Margin Format

| | | |
|---|---|---|
| Sales (1,000 units @ $100 per unit) | | $100,000 |
| Less: Variable Costs: | | |
| Variable Cost of Goods Sold | $40,000 | |
| Variable Operating Costs | 15,000 | 55,000 |
| Contribution Margin (1,000 units @ $45 per unit) | | $ 45,000 |
| Less: Fixed Costs: | | |
| Fixed Cost of Goods Sold | $20,000 | |
| Fixed Operating Costs | 15,000 | 35,000 |
| Net Income | | $ 10,000 |

In Exhibit 23–14 all variable costs are subtracted from sales to derive contribution margin. Then all fixed costs are subtracted to arrive at net income. The contribution margin calculation is a major difference between the Exhibit 23–13 and Exhibit 23–14 formats. Without additional detail, contribution margin cannot be determined from the data in Exhibit 23–13.

The income statement that emphasizes cost behavior and contribution margin calculation is used for internal reporting purposes only. Published financial statements contain summary income statements similar to the one shown in Exhibit 23–13.

## ASSUMPTIONS UNDERLYING COST-VOLUME-PROFIT ANALYSIS

We will end the explanation of cost-volume-profit analysis by listing its major assumptions. It is important that these assumptions be mentioned because they prevent the application of cost-volume-profit analysis to *all* "real world" situations.

All costs can be reliably separated into their variable and fixed components.

Unless the problem situation states otherwise, fixed costs will remain the same at all levels of volume within the relevant range.

Unless the problem situation states otherwise, variable costs per unit (or per hour, etc.) will remain the same at all levels of volume within the relevant range.

Unless the problem situation states otherwise, the selling price per unit will remain the same.

The number of units produced is equal to the number of units sold, or there will be no significant change in the beginning and ending finished goods inventories.

## HIGHLIGHT PROBLEM

Summarized data of Longley Company are shown below.

| | |
|---|---:|
| Sales (10,000 units @ $200 per unit) | $2,000,000 |
| Fixed Costs | 540,000 |
| Variable Costs | 1,400,000 |
| Net Income | 60,000 |

Required:

Using the contribution margin approach:

1. Compute Longley's contribution margin per unit and contribution margin percentage.
2. Compute the break-even point in units and sales dollars.
3. Determine the volume in units and sales dollars required to earn a target net income of $96,000.
4. Determine the new break-even point in units and sales dollars if fixed costs are increased by $18,000.

## GLOSSARY OF KEY TERMS

**Behavioral pattern of a cost.** The characteristic of a cost that indicates how much, if any, the dollar amount of that cost will vary with a certain type of activity.

**Break-even graph.** A graph that shows the break-even point and provides a visual basis for evaluating the relationships among sales, costs, and net income at varying levels of activity.

**Break-even point.** The volume of activity where total revenues cover both fixed and variable costs and where there is no net income or net loss.

**Contribution margin.** The excess of sales revenue over all variable costs.

**Contribution margin per unit.** The excess of the sales price of one unit over the variable cost of one unit.

**Contribution margin ratio.** The contribution margin divided by sales.

**Cost-volume-profit analysis.** A set of techniques used to determine how sales, costs, and net income are affected by changes in business activity.

**Fixed costs.** Costs that are not expected to change as the level or volume of activity changes.

**High-low method.** A method of estimating the fixed and variable portions of costs. Using this method, we develop numerical relationships between the highest and the lowest activity in the historical data and the costs associated with those levels of activity.

**Income equation.** The basic equation in which net income is represented in terms of revenue, variable costs, and fixed costs as follows: Sales Revenue = Variable Costs + Fixed Costs + Net Income, or Sales Revenue − Variable Costs − Fixed Costs = Net Income.

**Judgmental identification.** The identifying of behavioral patterns of costs by applying judgment and past company experience. No numerical analyses are made.

**Margin of safety.** The amount by which sales may decrease before a loss is incurred. Used as a measurement of risk.

**Mixed costs.** Costs that vary in relation to the change in an activity level, but the variance is not directly proportionate.

**Numerical analysis.** The separation of costs into their fixed and variable components by calculating relationships between historical cost data and activity.

**Relevant range.** The range of activity or volume over which the behavioral patterns of fixed and variable costs described in this chapter are valid.

**Scatter diagram.** A diagram of the relationship between two variables. In this chapter the two variables are direct labor hours and repair costs.

**Semivariable costs.** An alternate term for *mixed costs*.

**Step-fixed costs.** Costs that increase or decrease in discrete steps when activity reaches certain specific levels.

**Target net income.** The level of net income desired by management for a given period of time.

**Trendline.** A straight line drawn or calculated through points on a scatter diagram and used as a basis for estimating the fixed and variable portions of a cost.

**Variable costs.** Costs that are expected to change in direct proportion to the change in a given level or volume of activity.

**Visual inspection method.** The drawing of a trendline in a "freehand manner" so that it goes as close as possible through the center of the plotted points on a scatter diagram.

## REVIEW QUESTIONS

1. What questions can cost-volume-profit analysis help management to answer? [LO1a]
2. Cost-volume-profit analysis is based on the relationships among three variables. Name these variables. [LO1a]
3. On the graph of a fixed cost shown in Exhibit 23–1, why is the fixed cost line horizontal? [LO1b]
4. On the graph of a variable cost shown in Exhibit 23–2, why is the variable cost line a straight line drawn out of the origin of the graph? (The *origin* is the point where there is zero cost and zero level of activity.) [LO1b]
5. On the graph of a mixed (semivariable) cost shown in Exhibit 23–3, why is the mixed cost line a straight line drawn out of the vertical axis of the graph? (Why is the line drawn from the point that represents a $400 repair cost?) [LO1b]
6. Differentiate between the shape of the cost line in Exhibit 23–3 and the shape of the cost line in Exhibit 23–5. [LO1b]
7. In what ways are the behavioral patterns of fixed and variable costs per unit different from the patterns of the total dollar amounts of fixed and variable costs? (Use Exhibits 23–6 and 23–7 in answering this question.) [LO1b]
8. Differentiate between judgmental identification of behavioral patterns of costs and numerical analysis of behavioral patterns of costs. [LO1c]
9. Differentiate between the following two techniques of determining the behavioral patterns of costs: (a) the visual inspection of a scatter diagram and (b) the high-low method. [LO1c]
10. When the plotted points on a scatter diagram are clustered, what relationship seems to exist between the two variables on the scatter diagram? [LO1c]
11. Why is the high-low method more objective than the visual inspection of a scatter diagram? [LO1c]
12. Describe the income equation in the two ways that it is described in the chapter. [LO1d]
13. What is the break-even point? [LO1d]
14. What is target net income? [LO1d]
15. What is the margin of safety? [LO1d]
16. What is shown on the horizontal axis of a break-even graph? On the vertical axis? [LO1e]
17. Where is the break-even point located on a break-even graph? [LO1e]
18. Differentiate between contribution margin and contribution margin per unit. [LO1f]
19. Describe the formula for determining the break-even point in units when the contribution margin approach is used. [LO1f]
20. Describe the formula for determining the break-even point in sales dollars when the contribution margin approach is used. [LO1f]

21. When all other factors remain the same, state what happens to the break-even point in units when the following changes take place: (a) the selling price decreases, (b) the fixed costs increase, (c) the variable costs per unit decrease. [LO1f]
22. What are the multiple changes in cost-volume-profit analysis? [LO1f]
23. Describe the difference between an income statement that uses the cost of goods sold and operating expense format and an income statement that uses the contribution margin format. [LO1g]
24. Name the five assumptions of cost-volume-profit analysis. [LO1a,1d,1f]

## ANALYTICAL QUESTIONS

25. Why is it essential to divide costs into their fixed and variable components before cost-volume-profit analysis can be used? [LO1a,1b]
26. Under what conditions is the use of the visual inspection technique likely to produce reliable estimates of the fixed and variable components of costs? (Relate your answer to the cluster of the plotted points on a scatter diagram.) [LO1c]
27. Differentiate between the income equation and contribution margin approaches to computing the break-even point. Explain why both approaches result in the same computations. [LO1d,1f]
28. What advantages does the use of a break-even graph have over a numerical illustration of break-even analysis? [LO1e]
29. Comment on this statement: "The assumptions underlying cost-volume-profit analysis are so broad that they severely limit the usefulness of this type of analysis." [LO1a,1d,1f]

## IMPACT ANALYSIS QUESTIONS

*For each change described, indicate whether the change would increase [I], decrease [D], or not affect [N] the specified key figures. (In each case assume that all other variables remain the same.)* [LO2c,2d]

30. Selling price per unit is increased.
    ______ Break-even Point in Units ______ Net Income
    ______ Contribution Margin per Unit
31. Selling price per unit is decreased.
    ______ Break-even Point in Units ______ Net Income
    ______ Contribution Margin per Unit
32. Variable cost per unit is decreased.
    ______ Break-even Point in Units ______ Net Income
    ______ Contribution Margin per Unit
33. Variable cost per unit is increased.
    ______ Break-even Point in Units ______ Net Income
    ______ Contribution Margin per Unit
34. Fixed costs are increased.
    ______ Break-even Point in Units ______ Net Income
    ______ Contribution Margin per Unit
35. Fixed costs are decreased.
    ______ Break-even Point in Units ______ Net Income
    ______ Contribution Margin per Unit
36. Decrease in the number of units sold.
    ______ Break-even Point in Units ______ Net Income
    ______ Contribution Margin per Unit

37. Increase in the number of units sold.

_______ Break-even Point in Units _______ Net Income

_______ Contribution Margin per Unit

## EXERCISES

EXERCISE 23–1 *(Determine Behavioral Cost Patterns)* Assume the following cost and activity observations for a year.

| MONTH | INDIRECT LABOR COST | ACTIVITY—DIRECT LABOR COST |
|---|---|---|
| January | $1,200 | $4,600 |
| February | 900 | 4,000 |
| March | 1,000 | 4,200 |
| April | 1,000 | 4,400 |
| May | 1,800 | 6,200 |
| June | 1,900 | 6,800 |
| July | 1,100 | 4,400 |
| August | 1,800 | 6,600 |
| September | 1,600 | 6,600 |
| October | 1,800 | 6,400 |
| November | 1,200 | 4,400 |
| December | 800 | 3,000 |

Required:

1. Calculate the fixed and variable portions of indirect labor using the high-low technique.
2. Draw a scatter diagram and plot the twelve sets of cost and activity observations. Fit a trendline to the diagram using the visual inspection method. [LO2b]

EXERCISE 23–2 *(Analyze a Break-even Graph)* The following break-even graph shows the revenue and cost lines.

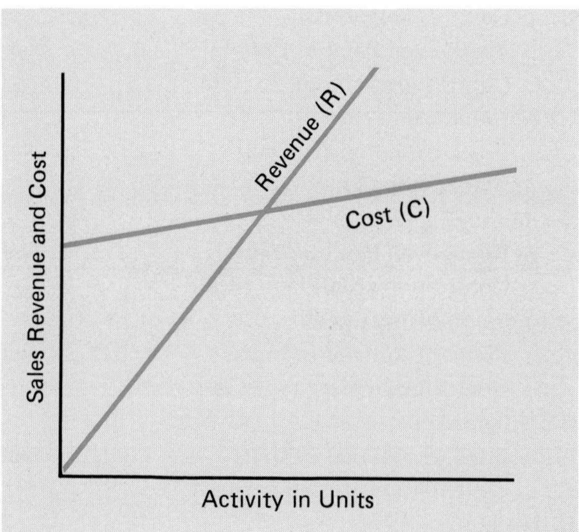


Required:

Match up the following by placing the correct letter in the blank.

_____ 1. The selling price per unit goes up. a. The break-even point increases.

_____ 2. The variable cost per unit goes down. b. The break-even point decreases.

_____ 3. The fixed dollar cost goes up. c. The break-even point remains the same.
_____ 4. The volume of activity goes up.
_____ 5. The variable cost per unit goes up.
_____ 6. The fixed dollar cost goes down. [LO1e,2c,2d]

EXERCISE 23–3 *(Perform Cost-Volume-Profit Analysis and Analyze Changes in Variables)* City Company produced 50,000 units of a single product. Other data pertaining to the company's activity follow.

Sales, 50,000 units at a price of $10 per unit
Variable manufacturing costs, $4 per unit
Variable selling costs, $2 per unit
Fixed manufacturing costs for the year, $90,000
Fixed selling costs for the year, $30,000

There were no beginning or ending inventories.

Required:
Using the income equation approach, answer the following questions:

1. What is the company's break-even point in units and sales dollars?
2. How many units must be sold to earn a target net income of $120,000?
3. How many units must be sold to earn a target net income of 10% of sales?
4. What is the safety margin in units if 50,000 units are sold? [LO2c]

EXERCISE 23–4 *(Perform Cost-Volume-Profit Analysis)*

Required:
Using the contribution margin approach, calculate the amounts that should appear in the blanks for each of the four independent situations shown below.

| | CASE 1 | CASE 2 | CASE 3 | CASE 4 |
|---|---|---|---|---|
| Sales revenue | $90,000 | _____ | $25,000 | $135,000 |
| Variable costs | _____ | $18,000 | _____ | $ 90,000 |
| Contribution margin per unit | $ 2 | $ 15 | _____ | _____ |
| Fixed costs | $22,000 | _____ | $20,000 | $ 30,000 |
| Net income | _____ | $10,000 | $(6,000) | $ 15,000 |
| Number of units sold | 18,000 | 1,200 | 5,000 | 9,000 |

[LO2d]

EXERCISE 23–5 *(Perform Cost-Volume-Profit Analysis and Prepare an Income Statement)* Whereon Company manufactures a single product called Eron. The company's accountant prepared the following statement at the end of the fiscal year.

| WHEREON COMPANY | | |
|---|---|---|
| Income Statement for Year Ended December 31, 19X8 | | |
| Sales Revenue | | $800,000 |
| Cost of Goods Sold: | | |
| Variable Costs | $500,000 | |
| Fixed Costs | 50,000 | 550,000 |
| Gross Profit | | $250,000 |
| Selling and Administrative Costs: | | |
| Variable Costs | $ 25,000 | |
| Fixed Costs | 45,000 | 70,000 |
| Net Income | | $180,000 |

Required:

1. Using the contribution margin approach, determine the company's break-even point in sales dollars.

2. Prepare a net income statement for 19X9, assuming that the volume of operations is 90% of the 19X8 volume. Use the contribution margin format. (*Hint:* Remember the behavioral pattern of fixed costs in the relevant range. Assume that the level of operations for both 19X8 and 19X9 is in the relevant range.) [LO2d,2e]

EXERCISE 23–6 *(Perform Cost-Volume-Profit Analysis and Prepare an Income Statement Using the Contribution Margin Approach)*

Required:

1. Using the contribution margin approach, determine the amounts that should appear in the blanks below.

| | |
|---|---|
| Sales | $100,000 |
| Variable Manufacturing Costs | 39,000 |
| Variable Selling and Administrative Costs | 16,000 |
| Fixed Manufacturing Costs | 30,000 |
| Fixed Selling and Administrative Costs | 9,000 |
| Contribution Margin (Dollars) | _____ |
| Break-even Point (in Sales Dollars) | _____ |

[LO2d,2e]

2. Prepare an income statement using the contribution margin approach.

## PROBLEMS

PROBLEM 23–1 *(Graph the Behavioral Pattern of Costs)* The three described costs have the following behavioral patterns.

a. For every machine hour used, repair costs increase by $.75.
b. Supervision costs of $200 do not change as the machine hour level of activity changes.
c. The fixed portion of repair costs is $100. For every machine hour used, repair costs increase by $1.50.

Required:

Using increments of 100, 200, 300, and 400 machine hours (as shown in the chapter graphs), construct a graph of

1. The variable cost
2. The fixed cost
3. The mixed cost [LO2a]

PROBLEM 23–2 *(Identify Behavioral Pattern of Cost)* Assume the following cost and activity observations for each month throughout a year.

| MONTH | REPAIR COSTS | ACTIVITY—MACHINE HOURS |
|---|---|---|
| January | $ 700 | 1,000 |
| February | 800 | 1,200 |
| March | 500 | 800 |
| April | 900 | 1,200 |
| May | 1,300 | 2,000 |
| June | 1,200 | 1,800 |
| July | 1,300 | 1,800 |
| August | 1,500 | 2,200 |
| September | 1,600 | 2,200 |
| October | 1,000 | 1,400 |
| November | 900 | 1,400 |
| December | 800 | 1,000 |

Required:

1. Calculate the fixed and variable portions of repair costs by using the high-low technique.
2. Draw a scatter diagram and plot the twelve sets of cost and activity observations. Fit a trendline to the diagram using the visual inspection method. [LO2b]

PROBLEM 23–3 *(Perform Cost-Volume-Profit Analysis)* Shown below is information relating to the only product sold by Garwood Company.

| | |
|---|---|
| Sales price per unit | $ 60 |
| Variable costs per unit | $ 44 |
| Fixed costs per year | $120,000 |

Required:

Using the income equation approach, calculate the following, showing all computations.

1. The break-even point in sales dollars.
2. The net income if 25,000 units are sold.
3. The number of units that must be sold to earn a target net income of $420,000.
4. The margin of safety in units if 15,000 units are sold. [LO2c]

PROBLEM 23–4 *(Perform Cost-Volume-Profit Analysis)* Westway Company sells a single product for $50 per unit. Variable costs are $35 per unit and fixed costs are $30,000.

Required:

Using the income equation approach, calculate the following, showing all computations.

1. Break-even point in sales dollars.
2. Break-even point in units.
3. Volume in units needed to earn a target net income of $50,000.
4. Volume in units needed to earn a target net income equal to 20% of sales revenue.
5. The margin of safety in units if 3,000 units are sold. [LO2c]

PROBLEM 23–5 *(Perform Cost-Volume-Profit Analysis)* Frome Manufacturing Company prepared the following data:

Expected sales revenue for the year, $8,000,000
Expected variable costs for the year, 60% of sales revenue
Expected fixed costs for the year, $2,000,000

Required:

Using the contribution margin approach, calculate the following, showing all computations.

1. Expected net income for the coming year.
2. Break-even point in sales dollars.
3. If a planned move to expand facilities increases fixed costs by $200,000, calculate (a) a new break-even point in sales dollars and (b) the sales needed to earn a target net income of $2,000,000. [LO2d]

PROBLEM 23–6 *(Perform Cost-Volume-Profit Analysis)* The Winslow Company compiled the following data pertaining to its operations for the past year.

Sales, 30,000 units @ $10 per unit
Variable manufacturing costs, $6 per unit
Variable operating costs, $1 per unit
Fixed manufacturing costs, $30,000
Fixed operating costs, $10,000

Required:

Using the contribution margin approach, calculate the following (classify each requirement separately).

1. Net income earned last year.
2. Sales volume needed to attain a target net income of $80,000.
3. The net income expected if sales volume increases 10% because of an advertising campaign that increases fixed operating costs by $9,000.
4. The number of units that would have to be sold (if selling price remains at $10 per unit) to earn a target net income of $50,000. Assume that variable manufacturing costs increase by 15%, and variable operating costs increase by 10%. [LO2d]

PROBLEM 23–7 *(Perform Cost-Volume-Profit Analysis with Several Products)* Potter Company manufactures and sells three products. Data relating to each product appear below.

| | AERCO | BEVCO | CALCO |
|---|---|---|---|
| Sales price per unit | $10.00 | $18.00 | $6.00 |
| Variable costs per unit | $ 7.00 | $12.00 | $3.50 |
| Sales in units | 15,000 | 10,000 | 40,000 |

Required:
Using the contribution margin approach, calculate the following, showing all computations. For each product, assume separate fixed costs of $105,000.
1. Net income for each product based on the units sold
2. Break-even point in units for each product [LO2d]

PROBLEM 23–8 *(Net Income Changes Using Cost-Volume-Profit Analysis)* Springfield Manufacturing Company produces number-learning games for children. Pertinent budget data for the coming year are as follows.

| | |
|---|---|
| Sales | 100,000 units |
| Selling price | $1.00 per unit |
| Variable costs | $ .40 per unit |
| Fixed costs | $54,000 |

In anticipation of the various questions that might be raised at the next meeting of the financial committee, the budget director has computed the net income or loss that would be realized under different conditions. (*Hint:* Solving this problem might require the use of both the income equation and contribution margin approaches.)

Required:
What estimated net income or loss would the budget director have associated with each of the following changes? (Consider each change separately.)
1. A 20% increase in volume of units sold
2. A 20% decrease in volume of units sold
3. A $.05 increase in unit variable costs
4. A $.05 decrease in unit variable costs
5. A 10% increase in fixed costs
6. A 10% decrease in fixed costs
7. A 10% decrease in unit selling price and a 20 percent increase in volume of units sold
8. A 10% increase in unit selling price and a 20 percent decrease in volume of units sold
9. A $.10-per-unit decrease in variable costs and a $16,000 increase in fixed costs [LO2c,2d]

PROBLEM 23–9 *(Use the Contribution Margin Approach to Prepare an Income Statement)* Shown below is per unit information relating to a product sold by Jordon Company. The company produced and sold 12,000 units during the year.

| | |
|---|---|
| Sales price per unit | $200 |
| Variable manufacturing costs per unit | 85 |
| Variable operating costs (expenses) per unit | 45 |
| Fixed manufacturing costs per unit | 13 (at 12,000 units) |
| Fixed operating costs (expenses) per unit | 5 (at 12,000 units) |

Required:

1. Prepare an income statement for the year ended December 31, 19X6, using the cost of goods sold and operating expense format.
2. Prepare an income statement for the year ended December 31, 19X6, using the contribution margin format. [LO2e]

PROBLEM 23–10 *(Comprehensive Problem)* Powell Company manufactures a single product, which sells for $12 per unit. The company's variable cost per unit has been relatively high at $10 per unit. The company has also incurred fixed costs of $50,000 during the current year.

Required:

Part I. Using the income equation approach, calculate the following showing all computations.

a. The company's break-even point in units and in sales dollars
b. The net income or net loss if the company had sales of 20,000 units during the year
c. The number of units that the company must sell to earn a target net income of $25,000

Part II. Assume that the company increases the selling price to $15 per unit. Variable costs per unit decrease to $9 per unit. Fixed costs increase by $12,000. Using the contribution margin approach, calculate the company's new

a. Contribution margin per unit and contribution margin ratio
b. Break-even point in units and in sales dollars
c. Net income or net loss if 20,000 units were sold
d. Number of units that must be sold to earn a target net income of $25,000

Part III. Using the costs from Part II and assuming that 20,000 units are sold, prepare an income statement using the contribution margin approach. [LO2c,2d,2e]

## ALTERNATE PROBLEMS

PROBLEM 23–1A *(Identify Behavioral Pattern of Cost)* (Alternate to Problem 23–2) The budget department of Wildwood Country Club is currently engaged in preparing a fixed and variable expense analysis for its flexible budget. The following table shows the cost of electricity and sales revenue for each of the past twelve months.

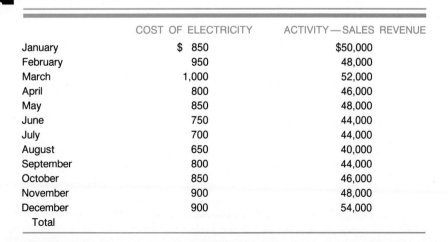

| | COST OF ELECTRICITY | ACTIVITY—SALES REVENUE |
|---|---|---|
| January | $ 850 | $50,000 |
| February | 950 | 48,000 |
| March | 1,000 | 52,000 |
| April | 800 | 46,000 |
| May | 850 | 48,000 |
| June | 750 | 44,000 |
| July | 700 | 44,000 |
| August | 650 | 40,000 |
| September | 800 | 44,000 |
| October | 850 | 46,000 |
| November | 900 | 48,000 |
| December | 900 | 54,000 |
| Total | | |

Required:

1. Calculate the fixed and variable costs of electricity using the high and low points method.
2. Draw a scatter diagram and plot the twelve sets of cost and activity observations. Fit a trendline to the diagram using the visual inspection method. [LO2b]

PROBLEM 23–2A *(Perform Cost-Volume-Profit Analysis)* (Alternate to Problem 23–3) Information concerning a product manufactured by Rutherford Company appears below.

| | |
|---|---|
| Selling price per unit | $ 60 |
| Variable costs per unit | $ 44 |
| Fixed costs per year | $120,000 |

Required:

Using the income equation, calculate the following, showing all computations.

1. The number of units and the sales volume to break even
2. The margin of safety in units if the company sells 10,000 units during the current year
3. The number of units that must be sold to earn a target net income of $100,000
4. The net income if 20,000 units are sold [LO2c]

PROBLEM 23–3A *(Perform Cost-Volume-Profit Analysis)* (Alternate to Problem 23–6) Using the contribution margin approach, calculate the amounts that should appear in the blanks for each independent situation shown below. The selling price is $20 per unit in all situations.

| | CASE 1 | CASE 2 | CASE 3 |
|---|---|---|---|
| Sales revenue | $200,000 | $ ____ | $____ |
| Variable costs | $120,000 | $ ____ | $90,000 |
| Contribution margin | $ ____ | $120,000 | $60,000 |
| Fixed costs | $ ____ | $ 50,000 | ____ |
| Net income | $ 30,000 | $ ____ | $10,000 |
| Number of units sold | ____ | 15,000 | ____ |
| Break-even point (in units) | ____ | ____ | 6,250 |

[LO2d]

PROBLEM 23–4A *(Perform Cost-Volume-Profit Analysis with Several Products)* (Alternate to Problem 23–7) The following is a statement of a company for one month for its three products.

| | PRODUCT W | PRODUCT X | PRODUCT Y |
|---|---|---|---|
| Sales price per unit | $10.00 | $5.00 | $5.00 |
| Variable costs per unit | $ 6.00 | $3.50 | $2.50 |
| Sales in units | 10,000 | 8,000 | 6,000 |
| Fixed costs | $10,000 | $10,000 | $10,000 |

Required:

1. Using the contribution margin approach, compute the net income for each product based on the units sold.
2. Compute the break-even point in units for each product. [LO2d]

PROBLEM 23–5A *(Use the Contribution Margin Approach to Prepare an Income Statement)* (Alternate to Problem 23–9) Estes Company developed the following information relating to its activities during the year ended December 31, 19X6.

| | |
|---|---|
| Sales revenue | $500,000 |
| Variable manufacturing costs | 335,000 |
| Variable selling and administrative costs (expenses) | 58,000 |
| Fixed manufacturing costs | 25,000 |
| Fixed selling and administrative costs (expenses) | 32,000 |

Required:

Prepare income statements for 19X6 using (a) the cost of goods sold operating expense format and (b) the contribution margin format. The company produced and sold 5,000 units. [LO2e]

# 24 *Budgeting— Static and Flexible*

### *Learning Objectives*

When you complete this chapter you will be able to

1. Answer the following questions:
   a. What is the general nature of budgeting? What benefits are derived from budgeting? What are the types of budgets?
   b. What are the components of a master budget? How is each component used?
   c. What are flexible budgets? How do they differ from static budgets?
   d. How can flexible budgets be used as a planning guide and a control device?
2. Perform the following accounting functions:
   a. Prepare each budget in a master budget.
   b. Prepare a flexible budget.

The budget in any organization provides a basic tool for better planning and control of that organization's activities. On the one hand, budgeting gives managers the chance to anticipate the effects of a given set of events on the organization and its resources. On the other hand, the budget can become a bench mark against which to measure events as they occur. If handled properly, budgets can also provide positive motivation for company employees.

## WHAT A BUDGET IS AND DOES

A **budget** is a detailed plan that shows how an entity expects to acquire and use its resources over some specified period of time. A budget may be prepared for the entity as a whole or for various segments of its operations. The process of preparing a budget, called **budgeting,** is important to those who are charged with the responsibility for planning and directing a company's operations efficiently and effectively.

***1a. Budgeting provides five major benefits***

The preparation of budgets requires time and effort. However, the investment should be worthwhile because of the following major benefits that budgets provide:

*Planning.* The preparation of a budget forces management to "look ahead" and establish specific goals for its future operations.

*Performance evaluation.* A company's budget is a quantitative statement of management's objectives and expectations. Thus a budget provides expected (budgeted) data against which actual results can be compared.

*Coordination.* Many diverse activities are required in the operations of a business. In large companies these activities include purchasing, production, sales, credit extension, and collections. These activities are generally carried out by separate departments within the company, each under the direction of a manager. A budget helps management to integrate and coordinate the activities of each department to help attain company goals.

*Communication.* In large organizations budget planning provides a desirable method for department managers to become aware of how their activity can aid in achieving overall company goals. In addition to budgets for various business activities, companies prepare comprehensive (master) budgets, which provide a means for communicating the business plan for the whole organization.

*Motivation.* A budget establishes organizational goals and can be a positive influence in motivating managers and other employees toward achieving these goals. For budgets to be a positive motivating factor in achieving goals, the following are essential:

Employees must accept the budgetary process as necessary for attaining company goals.

Employees whose performance will be measured and evaluated against budget data should actively participate in the development of the data.

The goals established should be realistic and attainable.

## HOW THE BUDGETING PROCESS STARTS

The budgeting process usually starts with the decisions of top management on broad policy goals for the period. In some firms, the estimates and opinions of lower-level managers aid in setting goals. In others, the goals will be transmitted from upper to lower levels of management. Under either circumstance, the setting of income and/or sales goals by top management should be the initial step in formulating the budget.

## THE BUDGET COMMITTEE

Responsibility for the budget process sometimes rests with a **budget committee.** This committee, in turn, is directed by a member of the committee designated as the **budget director.** The upper-level management, accounting department, and other major line and staff functions are usually represented. The budget director often comes from the accounting or financial area. This committee, along with upper management, may be responsible for establishing the procedures, gathering and coordinating all the data, and preparing the final budget.

Planning and resource allocation is important to the committee, since the budget's objectives consist of setting the levels of activity and planning for the acquisition and use of company resources. With experience and time, a firm's management can develop a set of standardized operating procedures for the budgeting process. A formalized budget manual is sometimes prepared and used as a guide and policy tool to aid all those involved in creating the budget.

## THE BUDGET PERIOD

Although budgets can be prepared for any time period, they are usually prepared for one year, which is short enough to make reasonably reliable estimates concerning future operating activities. One year also allows management to budget for its full accounting period.

The annual budgets are often subdivided into shorter time periods, such as months or quarters of the year. For example, a cannery that pays cash to its suppliers for materials purchased (raw fruits and vegetables) may have to wait several months before its finished goods are converted into cash. As a result, the company may need to borrow money at the beginning of the period to pay its suppliers. These loans are repaid as the goods are sold and the receivables collected. To forecast the amount of loan money needed, management must prepare a detailed cash-flow schedule to cover the time period of the cash shortage.

## STATIC AND FLEXIBLE BUDGETS

In this chapter we discuss both static and flexible budgets. A **static budget** is a set of projected figures developed for a specific level of anticipated activity. Static budgeting may be appropriate for a company's master budget, as illustrated in the first part of this chapter. A **flexible budget** is a set of projected figures developed for several levels of anticipated activity. Flexible budgets are useful for planning and controlling manufacturing overhead costs within departments, as illustrated later in this chapter.

## THE MASTER BUDGET

*1b. A master budget is a comprehensive set of integrated budgets. Its main categories are operating budgets and financial budgets*

A **master budget** is a comprehensive set of integrated budgets that collectively express the planned activities for the entire organization for the budget period. The number and the arrangement of the budgets included in the master budget depend on the company's size, activity (manufacturing or nonmanufacturing), and needs. Sometimes the master budgets are divided into two categories:

> **Operating budgets,** which show detailed descriptions of the planned revenues, expenses, and other operating items for the coming year

**Financial budgets,** which show the anticipated sources and uses of cash and other resources and establish the ending balances in these resources

Master budgets can also be subdivided as follows:

Operating Budgets:
- Sales budget
- Production budget
- Direct materials purchases budget
- Direct labor budget
- Manufacturing overhead budget
- Cost of goods sold budget
- Other operating budgets
- Forecasted (projected) income statement

Financial Budgets:
- Accounts receivable budget
- Accounts payable budget
- Cash budget
- Forecasted (projected) balance sheet

These budgets cannot be prepared independently. The level of sales activity, for example, will have a direct effect on production. The anticipated number of units to be produced will in turn affect direct materials, direct labor, and manufacturing overhead costs. All of these costs affect the cash budget and ultimately the financial statements. Keep these relationships in mind as we illustrate the separate budgets and schedules that are a part of the master budget.

## *ILLUSTRATION OF A MASTER BUDGET*

To illustrate the preparation of a master budget, we will refer to data available to the management of R.M.S. Company. Exhibit 24–1 contains a schedule of the estimated manufacturing costs and estimated unit costs for Products A, B, and C. Much of this material will be used to develop the other budgets.

*EXHIBIT 24–1*

R.M.S. COMPANY
Unit Costs for Products A, B, and C

| DIRECT MATERIALS | | PRODUCT A | | PRODUCT B | | PRODUCT C | |
|---|---|---|---|---|---|---|---|
| Item | Price | Quantity | Amount | Quantity | Amount | Quantity | Amount |
| 101 | $3.00 | 2 | $ 6.00 | 4 | $12.00 | 4 | $ 12.00 |
| 102 | 2.50 | 2 | 5.00 | 3 | 7.50 | 3 | 7.50 |
| 103 | 3.50 | 1 | 3.50 | 1 | 3.50 | | |
| 104 | 5.50 | | | | | 2 | 11.00 |
| 105 | 6.50 | | | | | 1 | 6.50 |
| Total Direct Materials | | | $14.50 | | $23.00 | | $ 37.00 |
| | | Hours | | Hours | | Hours | |
| Direct Labor ($4.00 hourly rate) | | 5.5 | 22.00 | 8.5 | 34.00 | 16.5 | 66.00 |
| Manufacturing Overhead ($2.00 per direct labor hour) | | 5.5 | 11.00 | 8.5 | 17.00 | 16.5 | 33.00 |
| Unit Manufacturing Cost | | | $47.50 | | $74.00 | | $136.00 |

Exhibit 24–1 shows the following for Product A:

Direct materials for item 101 are expected to cost $3.00 per unit. The company is budgeting two units of item 101 to produce a finished unit of Product A. Therefore the expected cost of using item 101 to produce a unit of Product A is $6.00. Product A also uses two units of item 102 at an anticipated cost of $2.50 per unit (totaling $5.00), and one unit of item 103 at an anticipated cost of $3.50. Adding the three costs together ($6.00 + $5.00 + $3.50), we see that the total direct materials cost expected for Product A is $14.50.

The company is assuming a $4.00 hourly rate for direct labor and 5.5 hours of direct labor to produce a finished unit of Product A. Therefore the expected direct labor cost for Product A is $22.00 ($4.00 × 5.5 direct labor hours).

Manufacturing overhead is estimated at $2.00 per direct labor hour, making the overhead cost for Product A $11.00 ($2.00 × 5.5 direct labor hours).

The total estimated cost for one finished unit of Product A is *$47.50,* determined as follows: direct materials cost $14.50 + direct labor cost $22.00 + manufacturing overhead cost $11.00 = $47.50.

The estimated costs of Product B ($74.00) and Product C ($136.00) are also shown in Exhibit 24–1. The costs were determined in the same way as those of Product A.

Using the data shown in Exhibit 24–1, as well as other data, we can now develop each budget in the master budget.

## The Sales Budget

***1b. A sales budget is based upon sales forecasts. It is used as a basis for preparing other budgets***

The first and perhaps most important step in the budget process is making a realistic and reliable sales forecast. **A sales forecast** is an estimate of the sales expected throughout the budget period. Forecasted sales information is important because it provides the basis for preparing the sales budget, estimating cash receipts, and compiling various expense budgets. The forecast must consider the

EXHIBIT 24–2

R.M.S. COMPANY
Forecasted Sales Budget
For Year Ending December 31, 19X1

| SALES IN UNITS: | | | | | |
|---|---|---|---|---|---|
| Product | QTR. 1 | QTR. 2 | QTR. 3 | QTR. 4 | ANNUAL |
| A | 1,000 | 1,500 | 2,000 | 3,000 | 7,500 |
| B | 1,500 | 2,000 | 3,000 | 4,000 | 10,500 |
| C | 600 | 800 | 800 | 1,000 | 3,200 |
| SALES IN DOLLARS: | | | | | |
| Product | QTR. 1 | QTR. 2 | QTR. 3 | QTR. 4 | ANNUAL |
| A at $70 | $ 70,000 | $105,000 | $140,000 | $210,000 | $ 525,000 |
| B at $110 | 165,000 | 220,000 | 330,000 | 440,000 | 1,155,000 |
| C at $180 | 108,000 | 144,000 | 144,000 | 180,000 | 576,000 |
| Total | $343,000 | $469,000 | $614,000 | $830,000 | $2,256,000 |
| NET SALES SCHEDULE: | QTR. 1 | QTR. 2 | QTR. 3 | QTR. 4 | ANNUAL |
| Gross Sales | $343,000 | $469,000 | $614,000 | $830,000 | $2,256,000 |
| Less: Discounts and Allowances; 2% of gross | 6,860 | 9,380 | 12,280 | 16,600 | 45,120 |
| Net Sales | $336,140 | $459,620 | $601,720 | $813,400 | $2,210,880 |

expected demand for the company's product and other factors. Obviously, sales forecasting is uncertain and may require some changes during the budget period.

*2a. A sales budget is illustrated in Exhibit 24–2*

R.M.S. Company's sales budget is shown in Exhibit 24–2. Like all budgets, the sales budget is structured in a format most useful to management. For our illustration, we show:

Forecasted unit sales by product and for each quarter in the budget period.

Forecasted gross sales revenue by product and for each quarter in the budget period.

Forecasted net sales revenue for each quarter in the budget period.

Note that sales budget information will be used in preparing other budgets. For example, unit sales information will be used to prepare the production budget (Exhibit 24–3). The sales revenue figures will be used to prepare the charge sales section of the accounts receivable budget (Exhibit 24–8) and the revenue section of the forecasted income statement (Exhibit 24–11).

## The Production Budget

*1b. The sales budget is used as the basis for the production budget*

Once the sales budget has been prepared, the company can determine the number of units that must be produced in each budget period. Production requirements take into account the expected sales for the period, the amount of units in the beginning inventory, and the desired number of units in the ending inventory. Production requirements can therefore be stated as follows:

Desired Ending Inventory of Finished Goods
+ Forecasted Unit Sales
= Total Unit Requirements
− Beginning Inventory of Finished Goods
= Units to Be Produced

EXHIBIT 24–3

R.M.S. COMPANY
Production Budget
For Year Ending December 31, 19X1 (in units)

| PRODUCT A | QTR. 1 | QTR. 2 | QTR. 3 | QTR. 4 | ANNUAL |
|---|---|---|---|---|---|
| Desired Closing Inventory | 1,000 | 1,300 | 1,600 | 500 | |
| Plus: Forecasted Sales | 1,000 | 1,500 | 2,000 | 3,000 | 7,500 |
| Total Unit Requirement | 2,000 | 2,800 | 3,600 | 3,500 | |
| Less: Opening Inventory | 600 | 1,000 | 1,300 | 1,600 | |
| Production Requirement | 1,400 | 1,800 | 2,300 | 1,900 | 7,400 |
| **PRODUCT B** | **QTR. 1** | **QTR. 2** | **QTR. 3** | **QTR. 4** | **ANNUAL** |
| Desired Closing Inventory | 900 | 1,100 | 2,100 | 600 | |
| Plus: Forecasted Sales | 1,500 | 2,000 | 3,000 | 4,000 | 10,500 |
| Total Unit Requirement | 2,400 | 3,100 | 5,100 | 4,600 | |
| Less: Opening Inventory | 700 | 900 | 1,100 | 2,100 | |
| Production Requirement | 1,700 | 2,200 | 4,000 | 2,500 | 10,400 |
| **PRODUCT C** | **QTR. 1** | **QTR. 2** | **QTR. 3** | **QTR. 4** | **ANNUAL** |
| Desired Closing Inventory | 400 | 400 | 600 | 300 | |
| Plus: Forecasted Sales | 600 | 800 | 800 | 1,000 | 3,200 |
| Total Unit Requirement | 1,000 | 1,200 | 1,400 | 1,300 | |
| Less: Opening Inventory | 300 | 400 | 400 | 600 | |
| Production Requirement | 700 | 800 | 1,000 | 700 | 3,200 |

The number of desired units in ending inventory is an important decision determined by management. Maintaining some level of finished goods inventory is necessary to meet the expected sales for the first part of the subsequent period.

*2a. A production budget is illustrated in Exhibit 24–3*

Exhibit 24–3 shows the production budget for R.M.S. Company by product and by quarter, expressed entirely in units.

## The Direct Materials Purchases Budget

*1b. The production budget becomes a basis for the direct materials purchases budget*

After the production requirements have been determined, the direct materials purchases budget can be prepared. Budgeted purchases of materials are based on anticipated production and direct material inventories.

The desired amount of direct materials purchases can be determined in a manner similar to that used for budgeted units of production in Exhibit 24–3. The calculation is as follows:

Desired Ending Inventory of Direct Materials
+ Direct Materials Needed for Production
= Total Requirement for the Period
− Beginning Inventory of Direct Materials
= Unit Purchases Required

*2a. A direct materials purchases budget is illustrated in Exhibit 24–4*

The budgeted schedule of direct materials purchases for R.M.S. Company is shown in Exhibit 24–4. It summarizes the costs on a quarterly basis and in total for each of the five types of materials (101 through 105). Since information from other budgets must be used to calculate the budgeted direct materials costs for each type of material for each quarter, an explanation is needed. Referring to Exhibit 24–1, which shows the unit data, we find that two, four, and four units of material 101 are needed to produce a finished unit of Products A, B, and C, respectively. The production budget (Exhibit 24–3) shows that for the first quarter of the year, the production requirements for Products A, B, and C are 1,400, 1,700, and 700 units, respectively. Putting these sets of figures together, we determine the following usage requirement for material 101 for the first quarter of 19X1, as shown in Exhibit 24–4.

| PRODUCT | NUMBER OF 101 UNITS FOR A FINISHED UNIT | PRODUCTION REQUIREMENTS | TOTAL FOR 101 |
|---|---|---|---|
| A | 2 | 1,400 | 2,800 |
| B | 4 | 1,700 | 6,800 |
| C | 4 | 700 | 2,800 |
| | | | 12,400 |

The first-quarter cost for material 101 is shown in Exhibit 24–4 as $38,400 and was determined as follows.

| | |
|---|---|
| Desired ending inventory of direct materials (assumed) | 1,600 units |
| Direct materials needed for production (per above) | 12,400 units |
| Total direct materials needed for the period | 14,000 units |
| Less: Beginning inventory of direct materials (assumed) | 1,200 units |
| Unit purchases required | 12,800 units |
| Budgeted cost of units purchased (12,800 × $3 per unit for material 101 as taken from Exhibit 24–1) | $38,400 |

EXHIBIT 24–4

R.M.S. COMPANY
Direct Materials Purchases Budget
For Year Ending December 31, 19X1

| MATERIAL | QTR. 1 | QTR. 2 | QTR. 3 | QTR. 4 | ANNUAL |
|---|---|---|---|---|---|
| 101 | $38,400 | $ 49,500 | $ 71,400 | $ 48,900 | $208,200 |
| 102 | 25,750 | 33,250 | 47,250 | 33,000 | 139,250 |
| 103 | 11,200 | 14,700 | 21,350 | 15,400 | 62,650 |
| 104 | 7,700 | 9,350 | 10,450 | 8,250 | 35,750 |
| 105 | 4,550 | 5,850 | 5,525 | 4,550 | 20,475 |
| Total | $87,600 | $112,650 | $155,975 | $110,100 | $466,325 |

The other amounts in Exhibit 24–4 for each material for each quarter are computed in the same way.

## The Direct Labor Budget

*1b,2a. The direct labor budget is based upon the unit cost schedule and the production budget and is illustrated in Exhibit 24–5*

The direct labor budget is shown in Exhibit 24–5 and is developed by referring to the unit cost schedule (Exhibit 24–1) and the production budget (Exhibit 24–3). The budgeted direct labor cost of $134,800 for quarter 1 in Exhibit 24–5 is computed as follows:

> The 7,700 hours needed to manufacture Product A are computed by multiplying the 5.5 estimated direct labor hours needed to manufacture one unit of Product A (from Exhibit 24–1) times the 1,400 units of production required for Product A (from Exhibit 24–3).
>
> The 14,450 hours needed to manufacture Product B are computed the same way as the 7,700 hours shown above.
>
> The 11,550 hours needed to manufacture product C are computed the same way as the 7,700 hours shown above.
>
> The 33,700 total direct labor hours needed in quarter 1 are multiplied by $4 (the direct labor hourly rate for Product A as taken from Exhibit 24–1) to derive $134,800.

The amounts for quarters 2, 3, and 4 in Exhibit 24–5 are computed in the same way as the $134,800 for quarter 1 in Exhibit 24–5.

EXHIBIT 24–5

R.M.S. COMPANY
Direct Labor Budget
For Year Ending December 31, 19X1

| | DIRECT LABOR HOURS (DLH) | | | | |
|---|---|---|---|---|---|
| PRODUCT | Qtr. 1 | Qtr. 2 | Qtr. 3 | Qtr. 4 | Annual |
| A | 7,700 | 9,900 | 12,650 | 10,450 | 40,700 |
| B | 14,450 | 18,700 | 34,000 | 21,250 | 88,400 |
| C | 11,550 | 13,200 | 16,500 | 11,550 | 52,800 |
| Total Hours | 33,700 | 41,800 | 63,150 | 43,250 | 181,900 |
| Total Dollars ($4 × DLH) | $134,800 | $167,200 | $252,600 | $173,000 | $727,600 |

## The Manufacturing Overhead Budget

*1b,2a. The manufacturing overhead budget is based on budgeted production and is illustrated in Exhibit 24–6*

The manufacturing overhead costs estimated to meet production requirements are shown in Exhibit 24–6. The four quarterly amounts for manufacturing overhead applied ($67,400 for quarter 1, $83,600 for quarter 2, $126,300 for quarter 3, and $86,500 for quarter 4) are computed as follows:

> The budgeted direct labor hours for each quarter as taken from Exhibit 24–5 (33,700, 41,800, 63,150, and 43,250) are multiplied by the $2 manufacturing overhead rate taken from Exhibit 24–1.

The upper part of Exhibit 24–6 shows the quarterly budget for manufacturing overhead costs that are expected to be incurred during the period. Note that the *annual* budget for manufacturing costs to be incurred during the period ($363,800) is divided by the *annual* budgeted direct labor hours (181,900) to derive the annual manufacturing overhead rate of $2. Thus no underapplied or overapplied manufacturing overhead is budgeted for the year. However, underapplied and overapplied manufacturing overhead amounts are budgeted for each quarter. Remember from Chapter 22 that the manufacturing overhead rate is computed on an annual basis.

*EXHIBIT 24–6*

R.M.S. COMPANY
Manufacturing Overhead Budget
For Year Ending December 31, 19X1

| | | | QTR. 1 | QTR. 2 | QTR. 3 | QTR. 4 | ANNUAL |
|---|---|---|---|---|---|---|---|
| Supervision Salaries | | | $24,000 | $26,000 | $ 29,000 | $26,000 | $105,000 |
| Indirect Labor | | | 12,500 | 15,600 | 23,800 | 16,100 | 68,000 |
| Social Security Taxes | | | 8,100 | 10,200 | 14,900 | 9,800 | 43,000 |
| Compensation Insurance | | | 3,800 | 4,900 | 7,300 | 5,000 | 21,000 |
| Factory Supplies | | | 3,100 | 3,900 | 5,900 | 4,100 | 17,000 |
| Utilities | | | 3,300 | 4,100 | 5,500 | 3,900 | 16,800 |
| Maintenance and Repair | | | 2,900 | 4,000 | 4,500 | 3,600 | 15,000 |
| Equipment Rental | | | 7,000 | 7,000 | 9,000 | 9,000 | 32,000 |
| Property Tax | | | 3,000 | 3,000 | 3,000 | 3,000 | 12,000 |
| Depreciation | | | 6,000 | 6,000 | 7,000 | 7,000 | 26,000 |
| Property Insurance | | | 2,000 | 2,000 | 2,000 | 2,000 | 8,000 |
| Total | | | $75,700 | $86,700 | $111,900 | $89,500 | $363,800 |
| PERIOD | NO. DLH | MANUFACTURING OVERHEAD RATE | | | | | |
| Qtr. 1 | 33,700 | $2.00 | 67,400 | | | | |
| Qtr. 2 | 41,800 | $2.00 | | 83,600 | | | |
| Qtr. 3 | 63,150 | $2.00 | | | 126,300 | | |
| Qtr. 4 | 43,250 | $2.00 | | | | 86,500 | |
| Annual | 181,900 | $2.00 | | | | | 363,800 |
| (Underapplied) Overapplied Mfg. Overhead | | | ($ 8,300) | ($ 3,100) | $ 14,400 | ($ 3,000) | $ -0- |

## The Cost of Goods Sold Budget

*1b,2a. We multiply unit cost by expected unit sales to prepare the cost of goods sold budget, which is illustrated in Exhibit 24–7*

The cost of goods sold budget is shown in Exhibit 24–7. To determine the cost of goods sold, we must take unit cost data from Exhibit 24–1 and expected unit sales from Exhibit 24–2 and multiply them together on a quarter-by-quarter basis. For example: the unit cost of Product A is *$47.50*, which is multiplied by the *1,000* expected unit sales for Product A for the first quarter (to obtain *$47,500*, which is Product A's estimated cost of goods sold for quarter 1, as shown in Exhibit 24–7).

EXHIBIT 24–7

R.M.S. COMPANY
Cost of Goods Sold Budget
For Year Ending December 31, 19X1

| PRODUCT | QTR. 1 | QTR. 2 | QTR. 3 | QTR. 4 | ANNUAL |
|---|---|---|---|---|---|
| A | $ 47,500 | $ 71,250 | $ 95,000 | $142,500 | $ 356,250 |
| B | 111,000 | 148,000 | 222,000 | 296,000 | 777,000 |
| C | 81,600 | 108,800 | 108,800 | 136,000 | 435,200 |
| Total | $240,100 | $328,050 | $425,800 | $574,500 | $1,568,450 |

This same procedure is repeated for each quarter for each of the three products, A, B, and C. We will not repeat all twelve of these calculations. The analysis below, however, does show how the total estimated cost of goods sold is derived for each product in Exhibit 24–7.

| | BUDGETED SALES (IN UNITS) | BUDGETED COST PER UNIT | COST OF GOODS SOLD |
|---|---|---|---|
| Product A | 7,500 | $ 47.50 | $ 356,250 |
| Product B | 10,500 | 74.00 | 777,000 |
| Product C | 3,200 | 136.00 | 435,200 |
| | | | $1,568,450 |

## Other Operating Budgets

*1b. A company may also prepare selling and administrative expense budgets*

In addition to the operating budgets already shown, a company could also prepare the following:

A selling expense budget
An administrative expense budget

A selling expense budget is a list of the expected selling expenses during the period and is generally prepared with the sales budget. Expenses like sales commissions, advertising, and travel would be included in a selling expense budget.

An administrative expense budget would include a list of all the expected operating expenses except those that were included in the selling expense budget. An administrative expense budget would consist of items like office supplies expense and legal expenses.

## Accounts Receivable and Accounts Payable Budgets

Budgets of accounts receivable and accounts payable are not necessary but are highly desirable if a company wishes to make forecasts of changes in important current asset and current liability accounts.

*1b. An accounts receivable budget helps management project trends in sales and collections*

Exhibit 24–8 summarizes the budgeted changes in accounts receivable for the year. By preparing this schedule, management can project trends in sales and collections. These trends can be used to make vital decisions, such as a change in collection policies.

*2a. The accounts receivable budget in Exhibit 24–8 is explained here*

A brief explanation of the accounts receivable budget in Exhibit 24–8 follows.

The opening balance in the first quarter is an assumed figure.

The opening balance in quarter 2 is the closing balance in quarter 1 ($33,614).

The opening balance in quarter 3 is the closing balance in quarter 2 ($45,962).

The opening balance in quarter 4 is the closing balance in quarter 3 ($60,172).

The charge sales in each quarter are taken from the sales budget (Exhibit 24–2).

The collections for each quarter are based on management's judgment and a desire that the closing balances for each quarter be 10% of the charge sales for that quarter ($33,614 is 10% of $336,140, and so on).

EXHIBIT 24–8

R.M.S. COMPANY
Accounts Receivable Budget
For Year Ending December 31, 19X1

| | QTR. 1 | QTR. 2 | QTR. 3 | QTR. 4 |
|---|---|---|---|---|
| Opening Balance | $ 80,000 | $ 33,614 | $ 45,962 | $ 60,172 |
| Charge Sales (net) | 336,140 | 459,620 | 601,720 | 813,400 |
| Total | $416,140 | $493,234 | $647,682 | $873,572 |
| Less Collections from: | | | | |
| Previous Quarter | 80,000 | 33,614 | 45,962 | 60,172 |
| Current Quarter | 302,526 | 413,658 | 541,548 | 732,060 |
| Total Collections | $382,526 | $447,272 | $587,510 | $792,232 |
| Closing Balance | $ 33,614 | $ 45,962 | $ 60,172 | $ 81,340 |

*1b. An accounts payable budget helps management to project changes in important current liability accounts*

Exhibit 24–9 contains an accounts payable budget shown in the same format as the accounts receivable budget. An explanation of Exhibit 24–9 follows.

*2a. The accounts payable budget in Exhibit 24–9 is explained here*

The opening balance in the first quarter is an assumed figure.

The opening balance in quarter 2 is the closing balance in quarter 1 ($22,530).

The opening balance in quarter 3 is the closing balance in quarter 2 ($27,890).

The opening balance in quarter 4 is the closing balance in quarter 3 ($41,393).

The direct materials additions for each quarter are taken from the direct materials purchases budget (Exhibit 24–4).

The manufacturing overhead additions for each quarter come from the manufacturing overhead budget (with property tax, depreciation, and property insurance excluded) (Exhibit 24–6).

The quarterly additions for selling expenses, administrative expenses, and machinery are assumed figures.

The cash payments for each quarter are based on management's desire that the closing balances for each quarter be 10% of the total current charges for that quarter ($22,530 is 10% of $225,300, and so on).

EXHIBIT 24–9

| R.M.S. COMPANY<br>Accounts Payable Budget<br>For Year Ending December 31, 19X1 | QTR. 1 | QTR. 2 | QTR. 3 | QTR. 4 |
|---|---|---|---|---|
| Opening Balance | $ 21,400 | $ 22,530 | $ 27,890 | $ 41,393 |
| Current Additions: | | | | |
| Direct Materials | $ 87,600 | $112,650 | $155,975 | $110,100 |
| Manufacturing Overhead | 64,700 | 75,700 | 99,900 | 77,500 |
| Selling Expenses | 46,300 | 62,850 | 78,750 | 57,600 |
| Administrative Expenses | 26,700 | 27,700 | 29,300 | 31,300 |
| Machinery | — | — | 50,000 | — |
| Total Current Charges | $225,300 | $278,900 | $413,925 | $276,500 |
| Total | $246,700 | $301,430 | $441,815 | $317,893 |
| Cash Payments | 224,170 | 273,540 | 400,422 | 290,243 |
| Closing Balance | $ 22,530 | $ 27,890 | $ 41,393 | $ 27,650 |

## The Cash Budget

*1b. A cash budget should be prepared at least on a quarterly basis*

Even if a master budget was not prepared, a company should prepare a cash budget at least on a quarterly basis. Cash is the most "liquid" asset on the balance sheet and must be budgeted carefully. If it is not, a company may find that it does not have enough cash to meet payroll and other short-term expenditures.

*2a. The cash budget illustrated in Exhibit 24–10 is explained here*

The cash budget shown in Exhibit 24–10 presents the expected inflow and outflow of cash for the budget period. This budget (like the accounts receivable and accounts payable budgets) needs the following explanation.

The opening balance for the first quarter is an assumed figure.
The opening balance for quarter 2 is the closing balance for quarter 1 ($162,036).
The opening balance for quarter 3 is the closing balance for quarter 2 ($101,808).
The opening balance for quarter 4 is the closing balance for quarter 3 ($44,836).
The cash receipts for each quarter come from the Total Collections section of the accounts receivable budget (Exhibit 24–8).

EXHIBIT 24–10

| R.M.S. COMPANY<br>Cash Budget<br>For Year Ending December 31, 19X1 | QTR. 1 | QTR. 2 | QTR. 3 | QTR. 4 |
|---|---|---|---|---|
| Opening Balance | $135,000 | $162,036 | $101,808 | $ 44,836 |
| Receipts | 382,526 | 447,272 | 587,510 | 792,232 |
| Total Available | $517,526 | $609,308 | $689,318 | $837,068 |
| Disbursements: | | | | |
| Accounts Payable | $224,170 | $273,540 | $400,422 | $290,243 |
| Accrued Wages | 131,320 | 163,960 | 244,060 | 180,960 |
| Accrued Interest | — | 15,000 | — | 15,000 |
| Income Taxes Payable | — | 55,000 | — | — |
| Accrued Property Taxes | — | — | — | 29,000 |
| Dividends Payable | — | — | — | 25,000 |
| Total Disbursements | $355,490 | $507,500 | $644,482 | $540,203 |
| Closing Balance | $162,036 | $101,808 | $ 44,836 | $296,865 |

The cash disbursements for accounts payable for each quarter come from the Cash Payments section of the accounts payable budget (Exhibit 24–9).

The rest of the disbursements for each quarter are assumed figures. In an actual budgeting situation, these amounts would be determined by an analysis of expected transactions relating to the accounts (interest payments every six months, for example).

## Forecasted Financial Statements

*1b,2a. Last in the master budget are the forecasted income statement and forecasted balance sheet explained here and illustrated in Exhibits 24–11 and 24–12*

The final schedules in the master budget are the forecasted income statement and the forecasted balance sheet. The forecasted income statement in Exhibit 24–11 shows the company's anticipated revenues and expenses for the year, assuming all the activity was carried out as planned. The forecasted balance sheet in Exhibit 24–12 shows the company's anticipated financial position at year-end, assuming all the activity was also carried out as planned. Many of the amounts on the forecasted financial statements are determined from previous budgets that we have prepared. Other amounts are based on management's estimates or on obligations that cannot be avoided. For example, the quarterly payments for interest expense are based on the company's long-term debt.

Many uses can be made of forecasted financial statements. As a planning device, management can ascertain whether special attention should be given to potentially troublesome areas. As an example, R.M.S. Company may be satisfied with the quarterly projections in the forecasted income statement that show net income increasing from a negative $4,760 in the first quarter to $127,500 in the fourth quarter. On the other hand, the company may be dissatisfied with the quarterly projections in the forecasted balance sheet that indicate cash will decrease from $162,036 at the end of the first quarter to $44,836 at the end of the third quarter. Although the cash projection at the end of the fourth quarter is $296,865, management may wish to take action to prevent a temporary cash shortage.

Management can also use forecasted financial statements as a control device by comparing them with the actual financial statements at the end of each quarter and the end of the year. If some major differences occur, the company will investigate the reasons for these differences and take corrective action. As an

EXHIBIT 24–11

R.M.S. COMPANY
Forecasted Income Statement
By Quarters for the Year 19X1

| | QTR. 1 | QTR. 2 | QTR. 3 | QTR. 4 | ANNUAL |
|---|---|---|---|---|---|
| Net Sales | $336,140 | $459,620 | $601,720 | $813,400 | $2,210,880 |
| Less: Cost of Goods Sold | 240,100 | 328,050 | 425,800 | 574,500 | 1,568,450 |
| Gross Margin, Unadjusted | $ 96,040 | $131,570 | $175,920 | $238,900 | $ 642,430 |
| (Underapplied) Overapplied Manufacturing Overhead | (8,300) | (3,100) | 14,400 | (3,000) | -0- |
| Gross Margin, Adjusted | $ 87,740 | $128,470 | $190,320 | $235,900 | $ 642,430 |
| Selling Expenses | 53,550 | 70,100 | 86,000 | 64,850 | 274,500 |
| Administrative Expenses | 31,450 | 32,450 | 34,050 | 36,050 | 134,000 |
| Net Income from Operations | $ 2,740 | $ 25,920 | $ 70,270 | $135,000 | $ 233,930 |
| Interest Expense | 7,500 | 7,500 | 7,500 | 7,500 | 30,000 |
| Net Income | $ (4,760) | $ 18,420 | $ 62,770 | $127,500 | $ 203,930 |

EXHIBIT 24-12

R.M.S. COMPANY
Forecasted Balance Sheet
By Quarters for the Year 19X1

| | QTR. 1 | QTR. 2 | QTR. 3 | QTR. 4 |
|---|---|---|---|---|
| ASSETS | | | | |
| Current Assets: | | | | |
| Cash | $ 162,036 | $ 101,808 | $ 44,836 | $ 296,865 |
| Accounts Receivable | 33,614 | 45,962 | 60,172 | 81,340 |
| Inventories: | | | | |
| Raw Materials | 11,850 | 18,200 | 11,825 | 10,975 |
| Finished Goods | 168,500 | 197,550 | 313,000 | 108,950 |
| Prepaid Insurance | 12,000 | 8,000 | 4,000 | -0- |
| Total Current Assets | $ 388,000 | $ 371,520 | $ 433,833 | $ 498,130 |
| Property, Plant, and Equipment: | | | | |
| Land | $ 30,000 | $ 30,000 | $ 30,000 | $ 30,000 |
| Buildings | 360,000 | 360,000 | 360,000 | 360,000 |
| Equipment | 650,000 | 650,000 | 700,000 | 700,000 |
| Total | $1,040,000 | $1,040,000 | $1,090,000 | $1,090,000 |
| Less: Accumulated Depreciation | 261,750 | 273,500 | 286,250 | 299,000 |
| Net Property, Plant, and Equipment | $ 778,250 | $ 766,500 | $ 803,750 | $ 791,000 |
| Total Assets | $1,166,250 | $1,138,020 | $1,237,583 | $1,289,130 |
| LIABILITIES | | | | |
| Current Liabilities: | | | | |
| Accounts Payable | $ 22,530 | $ 27,890 | $ 41,393 | $ 27,650 |
| Accrued Wages, Taxes, and Interest | 28,230 | 31,220 | 54,510 | 17,300 |
| Income Taxes Payable | 52,620 | 6,830 | 38,215 | 101,965 |
| Total Current Liabilities | $ 103,380 | $ 65,940 | $ 134,118 | $ 146,915 |
| Long-Term Debt: | | | | |
| Bonds Payable | 500,000 | 500,000 | 500,000 | 500,000 |
| Total Liabilities | $ 603,380 | $ 565,940 | $ 634,118 | $ 646,915 |
| STOCKHOLDERS' EQUITY | | | | |
| Capital Stock | $ 400,000 | $ 400,000 | $ 400,000 | $ 400,000 |
| Retained Earnings | 162,870 | 172,080 | 203,465 | 242,215 |
| Total Stockholders' Equity | $ 562,870 | $ 572,080 | $ 603,465 | $ 642,215 |
| Total Liabilities and Stockholders' Equity | $1,166,250 | $1,138,020 | $1,237,583 | $1,289,130 |

example, assume that the actual December 31, 19X1, balance sheet shows cash at $50,000 below and accounts receivable at $50,000 above their forecasted amounts. When we investigate, we may find that collection policies were responsible for these serious differences. In this case, the company might change its credit terms.

## WHAT FLEXIBLE BUDGETS ARE—AND WHY

*1c. Flexible budgets project costs at several possible levels of activity*

Management may occasionally need to budget costs at several possible levels of activity rather than at the one level of activity shown in the earlier sections of the chapter. If so, management can use the flexible-budgeting techniques explained in this section of the chapter.

Here is an example of what we mean about the need for flexible budgeting: Assume that a company budgets repair costs at $1,000 and estimates that 5,000 machine hours will be used for the next month, April. Assume also that in April the actual repair costs and number of machine hours used were $1,200 and

5,300, respectively. It would be improper to charge the department supervisor or some other operating official with a $200 budget variance ($1,200 − $1,000) because the $1,200 was spent at a 5,300-machine-hour level. Instead a repair costs budget should be devised that is based on the actual machine hours used. The operating supervisor could then be asked to account for significant differences between the actual repair costs and an appropriate budget, given the actual number of machine hours used.

A budget based on this latter concept is called a flexible budget and helps us in the planning and control of manufacturing overhead costs. We can construct a flexible budget by developing formulas for fixed, variable, and mixed costs that can be used at any expected level of activity within the relevant range. (Fixed, variable, and mixed costs and the relevant range were discussed in Chapter 23.)

*2b. Steps in constructing a flexible budget are explained here, and the flexible budget data is illustrated in Exhibit 24-13*

Flexible budgets must be constructed with care. If they are not, too much time will be spent looking for insignificant budget deviations, or too little time will be spent looking for important budget deviations. To construct useful flexible budgets, each department can use these general guidelines:

> Determine the type of activity that should be used to budget the manufacturing overhead costs in that department. For some departments that make heavy use of machinery, machine hours might be appropriate. For other departments that make extensive use of labor, direct labor hours might be proper.
>
> Take the manufacturing overhead costs that are used in that department and determine the behavioral pattern of each cost. The techniques for dividing costs into fixed, variable, and mixed are explained in Chapter 23.
>
> Construct flexible budget data that can be used to budget manufacturing costs at an activity level within the relevant range.

To illustrate, assume that the assembling department of a manufacturing company decides that direct labor hours is the appropriate type of activity to use to budget its manufacturing overhead costs. Through judgmental identification or some numerical analysis, the department concludes that its manufacturing overhead accounts have the following behavioral patterns:

> Indirect materials is a *variable* cost and is expected to change $.02 for every direct labor hour used in the department.
>
> Indirect labor is a *mixed* cost; $720 of the cost is fixed, and the variable part of the cost is expected to change $.04 for every direct labor hour used in the department.
>
> Repairs is a *mixed* cost; $200 of the cost is fixed, and the variable part of the cost is expected to change $.01 for every direct labor hour used in the department.

EXHIBIT 24-13
Flexible Budget Data

| ACCOUNT | FIXED DOLLAR AMOUNT | VARIABLE RATE PER DIRECT LABOR HOUR |
|---|---|---|
| Indirect Materials | $ — | $.02 |
| Indirect Labor | 720 | .04 |
| Repairs | 200 | .01 |
| Utilities | 130 | .08 |
| Property Taxes | 140 | — |
| Insurance | 90 | — |
| Supervision | 800 | — |
| Depreciation | 600 | — |
| | $2,680 | $.15 |

Utilities is a *mixed* cost; $130 of the cost is fixed, and the variable part of the cost is expected to change $.08 for every direct labor hour used in the department.

Property taxes, insurance, supervision, and depreciation are all *fixed* costs and are expected to remain the same regardless of the number of direct labor hours used in the department.

We now have the data to construct flexible budgets at varying levels of direct labor hour activity. Exhibit 24–13 shows these compiled data, which we will apply in the next two subsections to illustrate how flexible budgets can be used for planning and control.

### Use of Flexible Budgeting for Planning

To illustrate how flexible budgeting can be used to plan operations for the coming period, assume that the assembling department considers 4,000, 5,000, and 6,000 direct labor hours to be levels of activity that the department might attain during the next period. Exhibit 24–14 contains the flexible budget data in Exhibit 24–13 applied to 4,000, 5,000, and 6,000 direct labor hours.

EXHIBIT 24–14

Planned Flexible Budget Amounts for Assembling Department

| ACCOUNT | FIXED DOLLAR AMOUNT | VARIABLE RATE PER DIRECT LABOR HOUR | DIRECT LABOR HOURS 4,000 | 5,000 | 6,000 |
|---|---|---|---|---|---|
| Indirect Materials | — | $.02 | $ 80 | $ 100 | $ 120 |
| Indirect Labor | 720 | .04 | 880 | 920 | 960 |
| Repairs | 200 | .01 | 240 | 250 | 260 |
| Utilities | 130 | .08 | 450 | 530 | 610 |
| Property Taxes | 140 | — | 140 | 140 | 140 |
| Insurance | 90 | — | 90 | 90 | 90 |
| Supervision | 800 | — | 800 | 800 | 800 |
| Depreciation | 600 | — | 600 | 600 | 600 |
| | | | $3,280 | $3,430 | $3,580 |

*1d. Application of flexible budget data to planning is illustrated here*

An examination of Exhibit 24–14 shows that if 4,000 direct labor hours are used, the budget for indirect materials is $80 (4,000 direct labor hours × $.02). However, if 5,000 direct labor hours are used, the budget for indirect materials is $100 (5,000 direct labor hours × $.02). The budget for each account for 4,000, 5,000, and 6,000 direct labor hours can be computed by applying the flexible budget data to the number of direct labor hours.

Let us assume that we wish to know what the budget for an account would be if we planned to use 4,500 direct labor hours. Simply apply the flexible budget data to 4,500 hours and we have the answer. For example, at 4,000 direct labor hours, indirect labor is budgeted at $880 [$720 + ($.04 × 4,000 hours)]. Therefore, at 4,500 direct labor hours, indirect labor is budgeted at $900 [$720 + ($.04 × 4,500 hours)].

Thus we are able to compute a budget for any account for any anticipated activity level by applying the flexible budget data to the number of direct labor hours that we plan to use.

## Use of Flexible Budgeting for Control

*1d. Application of flexible budget data to control is illustrated here*

To illustrate the use of flexible budget data for control purposes, let us assume that the assembling department uses 5,000 direct labor hours during the period. The department budgets and spends, for each manufacturing overhead account, the amounts shown in Exhibit 24–15.

*EXHIBIT 24–15*

End-of-Period Budget Report

| ACCOUNT | BUDGET @ 5,000 DIRECT LABOR HOURS | ACTUAL SPENDING @ 5,000 DIRECT LABOR HOURS | DIFFERENCES |
|---|---|---|---|
| Indirect Materials | $ 100 | $ 120 | $ (20) |
| Indirect Labor | 920 | 930 | (10) |
| Repairs | 250 | 350 | (100) |
| Utilities | 530 | 500 | 30 |
| Property Taxes | 140 | 140 | — |
| Insurance | 90 | 90 | — |
| Supervision | 800 | 800 | — |
| Depreciation | 600 | 600 | — |
| | $3,430 | $3,530 | $(100) |

Looking at Exhibit 24–15, we now have a basis for evaluating the differences between the actual amounts spent for each manufacturing overhead account and the budget for each manufacturing overhead account. The differences are important because we are comparing spending at 5,000 direct labor hours with "what we should have spent" at 5,000 direct labor hours.

Management will investigate any differences in Exhibit 24–15 that it considers too large. A variety of reasons could account for these differences. For example:

Inefficient spending practices could have occurred.

Obsolete machines could have been used.

Special efforts could have been made to conserve costs.

In addition, faulty budgeting techniques could have been used. If so, the spending differences in Exhibit 24–15 are not very important. For flexible budgeting to be effective in controlling costs, care must be taken in constructing the flexible budget data shown in Exhibit 24–13.

Also note from examining Exhibit 24–15 that there are no differences between actual and budgeted fixed costs. This may not be unusual, since fixed costs are usually the easiest to predict.

Finally, note that data similar to those in Exhibit 24–15 can be constructed for the actual spending and the budget at any level of direct labor hours in the relevant range.

## HIGHLIGHT PROBLEM

The finishing department of Flex Company uses flexible budgeting for its manufacturing overhead accounts. The behavioral patterns of accounts are determined to be as follows:

1. Machine repairs has a $300 fixed element and varies $.10 per direct labor hour.

2. Indirect materials is variable at $.05 per direct labor hour.
3. Utilities is variable at $.10 per direct labor hour.
4. Indirect labor has a $500 fixed element and varies $.05 per direct labor hour.
5. Supervision is fixed at $1,000.
6. Depreciation is fixed at $2,000.

Required:
Prepare a flexible budget for the finishing department using the model in Exhibit 24–14. Calculate flexible budget amounts for 1,000, 2,000, and 3,000 direct labor hours.

## GLOSSARY OF KEY TERMS

**Budget.** A detailed plan that shows how an entity expects to acquire and use its resources over some specified period of time.

**Budgeting.** The process of preparing a budget.

**Budget committee.** A group responsible for the budget process. Upper-level management, the accounting department, and other major line and staff functions are usually represented.

**Budget director.** A member of the budget committee who directs its activity.

**Financial budgets.** A subset of the master budget that includes budgets and schedules showing the anticipated sources and uses of cash and other resources and the ending account balances in these resources.

**Flexible budget.** A set of projected figures prepared for several levels of anticipated activity.

**Master budget.** A comprehensive set of integrated budgets that collectively express the planned activities for the entire organization for the budget period.

**Operating budgets.** A subset of the master budget that includes budgets and schedules showing detailed descriptions of the planned revenues, expenses, and other operating items for the coming year.

**Sales forecast.** An estimate of the sales expected throughout the budget period.

**Static budget.** A set of projected figures prepared for a specific level of anticipated activity.

## REVIEW QUESTIONS

1. What is a budget? [LO1a]
2. Name the five major benefits provided by budgets. [LO1a]
3. What is the function of a budget committee? A budget director? [LO1a]
4. What is the typical period of time covered by a budget? Why? [LO1a]
5. Differentiate between a static budget and a flexible budget. [LO1c]
6. What is a master budget? Into what two categories are master budgets sometimes divided? [LO1b]
7. Name the budgets and schedules that constitute the master budget in this chapter. [LO1b]
8. In what situation will management need to use the flexible-budgeting techniques explained in the chapter? [LO1c]
9. Describe the guidelines that each department can use to construct useful flexible budgets. [LO1c,2b]
10. How can flexible budgets be used for planning? [LO1d]
11. How can flexible budgets be used for control? [LO1d]

## ANALYTICAL QUESTIONS

12. The manager of a small supply store is uneasy about the time and effort that would be involved in preparing a comprehensive budget. She thinks it might be more than she could afford, particularly in relation to possible benefits. Reply to this manager's concern. [LO1a]

13. Some companies that do not use a comprehensive budget may, however, prepare a cash budget. Explain why this is true. [LO1b]
14. "Comparing actual manufacturing overhead costs with a static budget could be similar to comparing quantities of different types of commodities." Explain the meaning of this statement. [LO1c]
15. "How is it possible for flexible budgets to be used for both planning and control purposes? It seems that planning and control are two different concepts." Reply to this question and comment. [LO1d]

## IMPACT ANALYSIS QUESTIONS

*For each error described, indicate whether it would overstate [O], understate [U], or not affect [N] the specified key figures.* [LO2a]

16. When budgeting sales for the coming year, the company used a lower and outdated sales price. Some of the sales will be cash sales.
    _____ Budgeted Sales _____ Budgeted Accounts Receivable
    _____ Budgeted Production _____ Budgeted Cash
17. When budgeting credit sales for the coming year, the company failed to consider the sales discounts. Some of the sales will be collected.
    _____ Budgeted Sales _____ Budgeted Accounts Receivable
    _____ Budgeted Production _____ Budgeted Cash
18. When preparing the cash budget, depreciation expense was included in the Cash Disbursements section.
    _____ Opening Cash Balance _____ Closing Cash Balance
    _____ Cash Receipts _____ Cash Disbursements
19. When preparing the cash budget, credit sales were used rather than cash collections from customers. The amount of credit sales will be higher than the amount of cash collections.
    _____ Opening Cash Balance _____ Closing Cash Balance
    _____ Cash Receipts _____ Cash Disbursements

## EXERCISES

EXERCISE 24–1 *(Prepare a Sales Budget)* The Marx Company prepares a sales budget for two of its products, Alt and Malt. Marketing managers have reviewed actual sales data for the previous year and have employed forecasting techniques that were successful in the past to make the following projections: Product Alt sales in units will increase 10%; Product Malt sales in units will increase 6%.

Actual sales data from last year (19X5) were:

Alt—480 units, $9,600

Malt—510 units, $15,300

Selling prices for both products will be increased at the beginning of the budget period by 15% and 10% for Alt and Malt, respectively. The percentage of each product's sales occurring in a given quarter of 19X6 is estimated as follows:

| | QTR. 1 | QTR. 2 | QTR. 3 | QTR. 4 |
|---|---|---|---|---|
| Alt | 20% | 30% | 20% | 30% |
| Malt | 25 | 15 | 25 | 35 |

Required:

Prepare a sales budget for 19X6 showing unit and dollar sales by quarter and in total. Exhibit 24–2 can be used as a model. Show your computations. [LO2a]

EXERCISE 24–2 *(Prepare a Direct Materials Purchases Budget)* Springfield Company will begin operating on January 1 of the current year with no beginning inventory. The company has asked for help in preparing a materials purchases budget using the following estimates and other data.

| MONTH | ESTIMATED PRODUCTION USAGE IN UNITS |
|---|---|
| January | 10,000 |
| February | 12,000 |
| March | 16,000 |
| April | 18,000 |

Each unit of product requires three pounds of direct materials anticipated to cost $7 per pound. The company buys the materials on account. The company has set the following policy concerning inventory level: Materials inventory at the end of each month will be maintained at 10% of the following month's usage requirement.

Required:

Prepare a direct materials purchases budget for the first quarter showing the costs for each month and in total. Exhibit 24–4 can be used as a guide. Show your computations. [LO2a]

EXERCISE 24–3 *(Prepare a Direct Labor Budget)* Use Springfield Company's estimated production data (from Exercise 24–2). The company uses five direct labor hours to produce one unit of product. The direct labor rate is $8 per hour. All monthly direct labor wage costs are paid on the first day of the following month.

Required:

Prepare a direct labor budget showing the costs for each month and in total. Exhibit 24–5 can be used as a guide. Show your computations. [LO2a]

EXERCISE 24–4 *(Prepare an Accounts Receivable Budget)* The following quarterly data are available for Quesby Company for the year. The opening balance in quarter 1 is $7,000.

| | QTR. 1 | QTR. 2 | QTR. 3 | QTR. 4 |
|---|---|---|---|---|
| Desired Opening Inventory of Finished Goods (units) | 1,000 | 800 | 700 | 800 |
| Production Requirement (units) | 1,500 | 1,200 | 1,300 | 1,700 |
| Desired Closing Inventory of Finished Goods (units) | 800 | 700 | 800 | 1,000 |
| Selling Price | $20 | $20 | $20 | $20 |
| Discount on Charge Sales | 2% | 2% | 2% | 2% |
| Desired Closing Balance of Accounts Receivable | 15% of net charge sales | 15% of net charge sales | 15% of net charge sales | 15% of net charge sales |

Required:

Prepare an accounts receivable budget by quarters. Exhibit 24–8 can be used as a model. Show your computations. (Assume that in each quarter the dollar amount of collections from the previous quarter is equal to the opening balance, as per Exhibit 24–8.) [LO2a]

EXERCISE 24–5 *(Prepare an Accounts Payable Budget)* The following journal entries represent anticipated transactions by the Prepbug Company during the coming year. Assume uniform quarterly amounts. The opening balance in quarter 1 is $8,000.

| | | |
|---|---|---|
| Direct Materials Inventory | 100,000 | |
| Cash | | 20,000 |
| Accounts Payable | | 80,000 |
| Manufacturing Overhead | 80,000 | |
| Cash | | 10,000 |
| Accounts Payable | | 60,000 |
| Accumulated Depreciation | | 10,000 |
| Selling Expenses | 70,000 | |
| Cash | | 50,000 |
| Accounts Payable | | 20,000 |
| Administrative Expenses | 60,000 | |
| Cash | | 40,000 |
| Accounts Payable | | 20,000 |

In each quarter the company desires to keep the closing balance of accounts payable at 5% of the current additions.

Required:
Prepare an accounts payable budget by quarters. Exhibit 24–9 can be used as a model. Show your computations. [LO2a]

EXERCISE 24–6 *(Compute the Cash Receipts of a Cash Budget)* Dudley Company had sales of $90,000 and $120,000 for November 19X5 and December 19X5, respectively. Sales for the first three months of 19X6 are forecasted as follows.

| | |
|---|---|
| January | $100,000 |
| February | 110,000 |
| March | 130,000 |

All sales are made on credit terms, with collections consistently following the pattern described below:

40% of the sales amount is collected in the month of sale.

50% is collected in the month following the sale.

8% is collected in the second month following the sale.

2% is uncollected due to either credits granted or bad debts, or a combination of both.

The company believes the pattern will continue during the first half of 19X6. At that point it will be studied to determine if changes have occurred.

Required:
Compute the cash receipts of the cash budget for January, February, and March 19X6. Show your computations. [LO2a]

EXERCISE 24–7 *(Determine Amounts for Completed Flexible Budget Data and Prepare a Budget Report)* The following table contains completed flexible budget data.

| ACCOUNT | FIXED DOLLAR AMOUNT | VARIABLE RATE PER MACHINE HOUR | MACHINE HOURS 10,000 | 15,000 | 20,000 |
|---|---|---|---|---|---|
| Repairs | $____ | $____ | $3,000 | $3,750 | $4,500 |
| Utilities | ____ | ____ | 2,100 | 2,150 | 2,200 |
| Indirect Labor | ____ | ____ | 3,000 | 4,000 | 5,000 |

Required:

1. For each of the six blanks in the table, calculate the appropriate amount. Show your calculations.
2. Prepare an end-of-period budget report using Exhibit 24–15 as a guide. Prepare the report for 10,000 machine hours and assume that the following amounts were spent at 10,000 machine hours: repairs, $3,250; utilities, $2,500; and indirect labor, $2,700. [LO2b]

## PROBLEMS

PROBLEM 24–1 *(Compute Unit Costs for Two Company Products)* Design Company makes two products, X and Y. Each product is made with the following two types of direct materials:

Material A costs $2 per unit. It takes three units of material A to make one unit of Product X, and five units of material A to make one unit of Product Y.

Material B costs $5 per unit. It takes four units of material B to make one unit of Product X, and six units of material B to make one unit of Product Y.

The direct labor hourly rate is $8 per hour. It takes four hours of direct labor to make one unit of Product X, and it takes five hours of direct labor to make one unit of Product Y.

The manufacturing overhead rate is $5 per direct labor hour.

Required:

Prepare a report of unit costs for Products X and Y. Use Exhibit 24–1 as a model. [LO2a]

PROBLEM 24–2 *(Prepare a Sales Budget)* Destiny Company produces two products, Beta and Zeta. Last year (19X7) each of the products sold the following number of units at the following sales prices.

Beta—10,000 units at $50 per unit. Thirty percent of the sales were made in the first quarter, 15% were made in the second quarter, 25% were made in the third quarter, and 30% were made in the fourth quarter.

Zeta—8,000 units at $40 per unit. Thirty-five percent of the sales were made in the first quarter, 20% were made in the second quarter, 20% were made in the third quarter, and 25% were made in the fourth quarter.

Destiny Company estimates that in 19X8 the following will occur as compared with last year.

The selling price of Beta will increase by 10%. However, the total number of units sold in 19X8 will be reduced by 5%. The company estimates that the percentage of sales in each quarter in 19X8 will be the same as the quarterly percentages last year.

The selling price of Zeta will decrease by 5%. Therefore the total number of units sold in 19X8 will increase by 10%. The company estimates that the percentage of sales in each quarter in 19X8 will be the same as the quarterly percentages last year.

Required:

Prepare a sales budget for the year 19X8. Use Exhibit 24–2 as a model. [LO2a]

PROBLEM 24–3 *(Prepare a Production Budget)* Rule Company is budgeting its production needs in units for each quarter of 19X8 and is using the following data for its only product, Alpha.

The opening inventory for quarter 1 of 19X8 is 500 units.

In 19X7 the sales in units for each quarter were 2,000 units in quarter 1, 2,500 units in quarter 2, 2,500 units in quarter 3, and 3,000 units in quarter 4. Rule Company expects the unit sales in each quarter of 19X8 to be 20% higher than the unit sales in the same quarter of 19X7.

The closing inventory for quarter 1 of 19X8 is expected to contain twice as many units as the opening inventory for quarter 1 of 19X8.

The closing inventories for quarters 2, 3, and 4 of 19X8 are expected to be 600 units, 700 units, and 800 units, respectively.

Required:

Prepare a production budget for the year 19X8. Use Exhibit 24–3 as a model. Show your computations. [LO2a]

PROBLEM 24–4 *(Prepare a Direct Materials Purchases Budget)* Crude Company wishes to budget the dollar amount of direct materials purchases for its three types of materials for each of the four quarters of 19X9. The company sells two products, Alpha and Beta. Each product requires all three types of materials, Dee, Kee, and Zee. The following data are available.

The company plans to produce 1,000, 1,500, 2,000, and 2,500 units of product Alpha in quarters 1, 2, 3, and 4, respectively.

The company plans to produce 500, 700, 900, and 1,200 units of product Beta in quarters 1, 2, 3, and 4, respectively.

It takes two units of material Dee, three units of material Kee, and four units of material Zee to make one unit of product Alpha.

It takes three units of material Dee, three units of material Kee, and five units of material Zee to make one unit of product Beta.

The beginning material inventories in quarter 1 are as follows: material Dee, 500 units; material Kee, 600 units; and material Zee, 700 units.

The desired ending inventories in quarters 1, 2, 3, and 4 are as follows.

| | NO. OF UNITS |
|---|---|
| Quarter 1: | |
| Material Dee | 550 |
| Material Kee | 650 |
| Material Zee | 750 |
| Quarter 2: | |
| Material Dee | 600 |
| Material Kee | 700 |
| Material Zee | 800 |
| Quarter 3: | |
| Material Dee | 600 |
| Material Kee | 700 |
| Material Zee | 800 |
| Quarter 4: | |
| Material Dee | 300 |
| Material Kee | 400 |
| Material Zee | 500 |

The unit cost of each of the materials is as follows.

| | COST PER UNIT |
|---|---|
| Material Dee | $5 |
| Material Kee | $6 |
| Material Zee | $7 |

Required:

Prepare a direct materials purchases budget for the year 19X9. Use Exhibit 24–4 as a model. Show your computations. [LO2a]

PROBLEM 24–5 *(Prepare a Direct Labor Budget)* Cope Company desires to budget, for each quarter of 19X8, the number of direct labor hours required to produce each of its three products and the total direct labor dollars for each quarter of 19X8. The following data are available.

For the entire year, 50,000 direct labor hours will be required to produce product Gamma. Of these hours, 25% will be used in quarter 1, 20% in quarter 2, 30% in quarter 3, and 25% in quarter 4.

For the entire year, 40,000 direct labor hours will be required to produce product Hamma. Of these hours, 25% will be used in each of the four quarters.

For the entire year, 60,000 direct labor hours will be required to produce product Kamma. Of these hours, 35% will be used in quarter 1, 25% in quarter 2, 20% in quarter 3, and 20% in quarter 4.

The direct labor hourly rate is $5 per hour.

Required:

Prepare a direct labor budget for the year 19X8. Use Exhibit 24–5 as a model. Show your computations. [LO2a]

PROBLEM 24–6 *(Prepare a Manufacturing Overhead Budget)* Use the direct labor hour data from Problem 24–5 and prepare a manufacturing overhead budget using Exhibit 24–6 as a model. Show your calculations. The following additional data are available for preparing the budget.

The manufacturing overhead rate is $4 per hour.

Supervision salaries for the year are expected to be $200,000 spread evenly for each of the four quarters.

Indirect labor for the year is expected to be $120,000, of which 25% is expected in quarter 1, 20% in quarter 2, 30% in quarter 3, and 25% in quarter 4.

Factory supplies for the year are expected to be $36,000, of which 30% is expected in quarter 1, 25% in quarter 2, 25% in quarter 3, and 20% in quarter 4.

The other manufacturing overhead costs for the year (25% for each quarter, which will be referred to as miscellaneous) are expected to be an amount that will make the total budgeted manufacturing overhead costs for the entire year 19X8 the same as the budgeted manufacturing overhead applied. (There is no budgeted underapplied or overapplied manufacturing overhead for the year, but there is budgeted underapplied or overapplied manufacturing overhead for each quarter.) [LO2a]

PROBLEM 24–7 *(Prepare a Cost of Goods Sold Budget)* Kappa Company is planning to prepare a budget of cost of goods sold by product and by quarter for the year 19X9. The following data are available.

The estimated unit cost of product Kapu is $50.

The estimated unit cost of product Tapu is $45.

The estimated unit cost of product Hono is $48.

The expected unit sales for the entire year for product Kapu are 8,000, of which 24% are expected in quarter 1, 26% in quarter 2, 28% in quarter 3, and 22% in quarter 4.

The expected unit sales for the entire year for product Tapu are 9,000, of which 27% are expected in quarter 1, 23% in quarter 2, 29% in quarter 3, and 21% in quarter 4.

The expected unit sales for the entire year for Product Hono are 10,000, of which 25% are expected to be sold in each of the four quarters.

Required:

Prepare a cost of goods sold budget for the year 19X9. Use Exhibit 24–7 as a model. Show your computations. [LO2a]

PROBLEM 24–8 *(Prepare an Accounts Receivable Budget)* Hana Company is gathering data to compile an accounts receivable budget for the year 19X7. The budget will show, by quarters and in total, opening balances for accounts receivable, charge sales, collections, and closing balances for accounts receivable. The following data are used.

The opening balance in quarter 1 is $50,000.

The total charge sales for the year are expected to be $700,000, of which 23% are expected in quarter 1, 25% in quarter 2, 32% in quarter 3, and 20% in quarter 4.

The closing balances in each quarter are expected to be 5% of the charge sales for that quarter.

Hana Company anticipates that some of its collections in each quarter will come from sales in the previous quarter and some from sales in the current quarter. It estimates that collections in each quarter from the previous quarter's sales will be an amount equal to 90% of the opening balances for that quarter. For example, collections in quarter 1 from the previous quarter's sales will be $45,000 (90% of the opening balance of $50,000 in quarter 1). The rest of the collections for each quarter will come from the current quarter's sales.

Required:

Prepare an accounts receivable budget for the year 19X7. Use Exhibit 24–8 as a model. Show your computations. [LO2a]

PROBLEM 24–9 *(Prepare an Accounts Payable Budget)* Carmel Company plans to make an accounts payable budget for the year 19X9 that will show, by quarter and in total, opening balances of accounts payable, current additions, cash payments, and closing balances of accounts payable. The following data are used.

The opening balance in quarter 1 is $25,000.

The company anticipates that it will charge the following amounts for the entire year and that 25% of the year's charges will be incurred in each quarter:

Direct materials, $120,000

Manufacturing overhead, $80,000

Selling expenses, $60,000

Administrative expenses, $30,000

The closing balance in quarter 1 will be 10% of the current additions for that quarter.

The closing balance in quarter 2 will be 12% of the current additions for that quarter.

The closing balance in quarter 3 will be 12% of the current additions for that quarter.

The closing balance in quarter 4 will be 10% of the current additions for that quarter.

Required:

Prepare an accounts payable budget for the year. Use Exhibit 24–9 as a model. Show your computations. [LO2a]

PROBLEM 24–10 *(Prepare a Cash Budget)* The following refers to transactions and other data of Hurtz Company.

1. Actual sales for January and February were $120,000 and $150,000, respectively. Collection patterns, which are expected to remain consistent during the budget period, are 50% collected in the month of sale, 30% collected in the next month, 18% collected in the following month, and 2% uncollectible.
2. Budgeted sales for March are $200,000.
3. Cash balance on March 1 is $27,000.
4. Materials purchased in February were $80,000. Budgeted materials purchases for March are $100,000. Payment patterns are as follows: 40% paid in the month of purchase, and 60% paid in the month following the purchases. No return or discount privileges are granted.
5. Budgeted direct labor costs for March are $30,000. Past direct labor costs have been paid as incurred.
6. Budgeted manufacturing overhead for March is $68,000 and includes depreciation expense of $3,000. All past costs accrued and incurred have been paid.
7. Budgeted selling and administrative expenses for March are $16,000, including depreciation expense of $1,000. All past costs accrued and incurred have been paid.

Required:

Prepare a cash budget for the month of March. Exhibit 24–10 can be used as a model, although the format will not be exactly the same. Show your computations. [LO2a]

PROBLEM 24–11 *(Construct Flexible Budget Amounts)* After studying the behavioral pattern of several overhead accounts, Company A derived the following data.

| ACCOUNT | FIXED DOLLAR AMOUNT | VARIABLE RATE PER DIRECT LABOR HOUR |
|---|---|---|
| Indirect Materials | $ — | $.05 |
| Indirect Labor | 1,000 | .10 |
| Repairs | 500 | .07 |
| Taxes | 2,000 | — |
| Depreciation | 3,000 | — |
| | $6,500 | $.22 |

Required:

1. Construct a diagram like the one in Exhibit 24–14, showing the budget for each account and the total budget at activity levels of 1,000, 2,000, and 3,000 direct labor hours.
2. Explain how these data could be used for planning and control purposes. [LO2b]

PROBLEM 24–12 *(Determine Amounts for Completed Budget Data and Prepare Budget Report)* The following table contains completed flexible budget data.

| ACCOUNT | FIXED DOLLAR AMOUNT | VARIABLE RATE PER MACHINE HOUR | MACHINE HOURS 10,000 | 15,000 | 20,000 |
|---|---|---|---|---|---|
| Repairs | $____ | $____ | $4,000 | $4,750 | $5,500 |
| Utilities | ____ | ____ | 1,100 | 1,150 | 1,200 |
| Indirect Labor | ____ | ____ | 2,000 | 3,000 | 4,000 |

Required:

1. Place the appropriate amounts in the six blanks of the table. Show your calculations.
2. Prepare an end-of-period budget report using Exhibit 24–15 as a guide. Prepare the report for 15,000 machine hours, and assume that the following amounts were spent at 15,000 machine hours: repairs, $5,000; utilities, $950; and indirect labor, $4,350.
3. Discuss how management might determine whether the variances in Requirement 2 are too large. [LO2b]

PROBLEM 24–13 *(Comprehensive Review Problem)*[1] As chief budget officer of Smith, Inc., you are given the responsibility for preparing the forecasted balance sheet and the forecasted income state-

SMITH, INC.
Balance Sheet
December 31, 19X8

| ASSETS | | LIABILITIES | |
|---|---|---|---|
| Current Assets: | | Current Liabilities: | |
| Cash | $ 10,000 | Accounts Payable | $ 18,000 |
| Accounts Receivable | 15,000 | Accrued Salaries Payable | 1,000 |
| Inventory: | | Total Current Liabilities | $ 19,000 |
| Raw Materials | 10,000 | | |
| Finished Goods | 20,000 | | |
| Prepaid Rent | 1,000 | | |
| Total Current Assets | $ 56,000 | | |
| Plant Assets: | | Stockholders' Equity: | |
| Equipment | $100,000 | Capital Stock | $ 40,000 |
| Less: Accumulated Depreciation | 27,000 | Retained Earnings | 70,000 |
| Net Equipment | $ 73,000 | Total Stockholder's Equity | $110,000 |
| Total Assets | $129,000 | Total Liabilities and Stockholders' Equity | $129,000 |

[1] This problem requires a careful reading of the problem data and the chapter material.

ment. Smith, Inc., buys unfinished widgets and finishes them. You have been provided with the company's actual balance sheet as of December 31, 19X8, and the various budget schedules. Reproduced below are the balance sheet and the quarterly figures for the various budgets.

Forecasted Sales Budget for Quarter Ending March 31, 19X9

| PRODUCT | QUANTITY | SELLING PRICE | GROSS SALES* | DISCOUNTS AND ALLOWANCES | NET SALES |
|---|---|---|---|---|---|
| Widget | 10,000 | $15 | $150,000 | $5,000 | $145,000 |

* All sales are credit sales.

Production and Purchase Requirements Budget for Quarter Ending March 31, 19X9

| | FINISHED WIDGETS | UNFINISHED WIDGETS |
|---|---|---|
| Desired Ending Inventory | 2,000 units | 3,500 units |
| Period Requirement | 10,000 units | 9,500 units |
| Total Requirement | 12,000 units | 13,000 units |
| Less: Opening Inventory | 2,500 units | 2,500 units |
| Unit Requirement for Quarter | 9,500 units | 10,500 units |
| Unit Cost per Unfinished Widget | | × $4 |
| Dollar Purchase Requirement for Raw Materials | | $42,000 |

Manufacturing Overhead for Quarter Ending March 31, 19X9

| ACTUAL COSTS | AMOUNT |
|---|---|
| Indirect Wages, Salaries, and Fringes | $ 9,000 |
| Supplies | 500 |
| Utilities | 500 |
| Rent | 6,000 |
| Depreciation | 3,000 |
| Total | $19,000 |
| Applied Overhead (4,750 Direct Labor Hours at $4 per hour) | 19,000 |
| Overapplied (Underapplied) Overhead | $ -0- |

Selling and Administrative Expense Budgets for Quarter Ending March 31, 19X9

| | AMOUNT |
|---|---|
| Various Selling Expenses | $25,000 |
| Administrative Expenses: | |
| Salaries | $13,000 |
| Depreciation on Office Equipment | 2,000 |
| Total Administrative Expenses | $15,000 |

Cost—Widget for Quarter Ending March 31, 19X9

| | |
|---|---|
| Raw Material: Unfinished Widget (1 unit at $4 per unit) | $4.00 |
| Direct Labor ($\frac{1}{2}$ hour at $4 per hour) | 2.00 |
| Manufacturing Overhead ($4 per hour) | 2.00 |
| Cost per Unit | $8.00 |

Cash Budget for Quarter Ending March 31, 19X9

| | |
|---|---|
| Opening Balance | $ 10,000 |
| Collections from Accounts Receivable | 140,000 |
| New 10%, 10-year debentures issued 3/31/X9 | 20,000 |
| Total Available | $170,000 |
| Disbursements: | |
| Accounts Payable—Raw Materials | $ 42,000 |
| Direct Labor | 19,500 |
| Overhead—Manufacturing | 15,000 |
| Selling and Administrative Expenses | 38,000 |
| Prepaid Rent | 1,000 |
| Equipment Additions | 25,000 |
| Cash Dividend | 10,000 |
| Total Disbursements | $150,500 |
| Closing Balance | $ 19,500 |

Additional Information:

Rent amounts to $6,000 per quarter, and $1,000 is paid in advance. Supplies and utilities costs incurred during the period will be paid by the end of the period.

Required:

Prepare in good form the forecasted income statement for the quarter ended March 31, 19X9, and the forecasted balance sheet as of March 31, 19X9. [LO2a]

## ALTERNATE PROBLEMS

PROBLEM 24–1A *(Prepare a Sales Budget)* (Alternate to Problem 24–2) Fate Company produces two products, Beet and Heat. Last year (19X7) each of the products sold the following number of units at the following sales prices.

Beet—12,000 units at $40 per unit. Thirty-two percent of the sales were made in the first quarter, 18% were made in the second quarter, 20% were made in the third quarter, and 30% were made in the fourth quarter.

Heat—9,000 units at $50 per unit. Thirty-one percent of the sales were made in the first quarter, 24% were made in the second quarter, 23% were made in the third quarter, and 22% were made in the fourth quarter.

Fate Company estimates that in 19X8 the following will occur as compared with last year.

The selling price of Beet will increase by 15%. However, the total number of units sold in 19X8 will be reduced by 7%. The company estimates that the percentage of sales in each quarter in 19X8 will be the same as the quarterly percentages last year.

The selling price of Heat will decrease by 8%. Therefore the total number of units sold in 19X8 will increase by 12%. The company estimates that the percentage of sales in each quarter in 19X8 will be the same as the quarterly percentages last year.

Required:

Prepare a sales budget for the year 19X8. Use Exhibit 24–2 as a model. [LO2a]

PROBLEM 24–2A *(Prepare a Production Budget)* (Alternate to Problem 24–3) Kule Company is budgeting its production needs in units for each quarter of 19X8 and is using the following data for its only product, Lambda.

The opening inventory for quarter 1 of 19X8 is 600 units.

In 19X7 the sales in units for each quarter were 2,500 units in quarter 1, 2,000 units in quarter 2, 2,000 units in quarter 3, and 3,500 units in quarter 4. Kule Company expects the unit sales in each quarter of 19X8 to be 10% higher than the unit sales in the same quarter of 19X7.

The closing inventory for quarter 1 of 19X8 is expected to contain twice as many units as the opening inventory for quarter 1 of 19X8.

The closing inventories for quarters 2, 3, and 4 of 19X8 are expected to be 500 units, 600 units, and 700 units, respectively.

Required:

Prepare a production budget for the year 19X8. Use Exhibit 24–3 as a model. Show your computations. [LO2a]

PROBLEM 24–3A *(Prepare a Direct Labor Budget)* (Alternate to Problem 24–5) Mope Company desires to budget, for each quarter of 19X8, the number of direct labor hours required to produce each of its three products and the total direct labor dollars for each quarter of 19X8. The following data are available.

For the entire year, 40,000 direct labor hours will be required to produce product Slama. Of these hours, 20% will be used in quarter 1, 25% in quarter 2, 25% in quarter 3, and 30% in quarter 4.

For the entire year, 50,000 direct labor hours will be required to produce product Yama. Of these hours, 25% will be used in each of the four quarters.

For the entire year, 70,000 direct labor hours will be required to produce product Lamma. Of these hours, 25% will be used in quarter 1, 35% in quarter 2, 25% in quarter 3, and 15% in quarter 4.

The direct labor hourly rate is $6 per hour.

Required:

Prepare a direct labor budget for the year 19X8. Use Exhibit 24–5 as a model. Show your computations. [LO2a]

PROBLEM 24–4A *(Prepare an Accounts Receivable Budget)* (Alternate to Problem 24–8) Bana Company is gathering data to compile an accounts receivable budget for the year 19X7. The budget will show, by quarters and in total, opening balances for accounts receivable, charge sales, collections, and closing balances for accounts receivable. The following data are used.

The opening balance in quarter 1 is $60,000.

The total charge sales for the year are expected to be $800,000, of which 21% are expected in quarter 1, 29% in quarter 2, 28% in quarter 3, and 22% in quarter 4.

The closing balances in each quarter are expected to be 10% of the charge sales for that quarter.

Bana Company anticipates that some of its collections in each quarter will come from sales in the previous quarter and some from sales in the current quarter. It estimates that collections in each quarter from the previous quarter's sales will be an amount equal to 80% of the opening balances for that quarter. For example, collections in quarter 1 from the previous quarter's sales will be $48,000 (80% of the opening balance of $60,000 in quarter 1). The rest of the collections for each quarter will come from the current quarter's sales.

Required:

Prepare an accounts receivable budget for the year 19X7. Use Exhibit 24–8 as a model. Show your computations. [LO2a]

PROBLEM 24–5A *(Construct Flexible Budget Amounts)* (Alternate to Problem 24–11) After studying the behavioral pattern of several overhead accounts, Company A derived the following data.

| ACCOUNT | FIXED DOLLAR AMOUNT | VARIABLE RATE PER DIRECT LABOR HOUR |
|---|---|---|
| Indirect Materials | $ — | $.10 |
| Indirect Labor | 2,000 | .04 |
| Repairs | 500 | .08 |
| Taxes | 3,000 | — |
| Depreciation | 4,000 | — |
| | $9,500 | $.22 |

Required:

1. Construct a diagram like the one in Exhibit 24–14, showing the budget for each account and the total budget at activity levels of 2,000, 3,000, and 4,000 direct labor hours.
2. Explain how these data can be used for planning and control purposes. [LO2b]

# 25 Standard Costs

## *Learning Objectives*

After you complete this chapter you will be able to

1. Answer the following questions:
   a. What are standard costs, and what are the different types of standard costs?
   b. What different uses can management make of standard costs?
   c. What is a standard cost variance, and what is the difference between favorable and unfavorable standard cost variances?
   d. How are the two direct materials and the two direct labor standards set?
   e. How are the fixed and variable portions of the manufacturing overhead rate determined?
   f. How are standard cost variances classified in the financial statements?
2. Perform the following accounting functions:
   a. Calculate the standard cost variances for direct materials, direct labor, and manufacturing overhead.
   b. Prepare journal entries to incorporate standard costs into the general ledger accounts.

In Chapter 22 we described how actual manufacturing costs are assigned to manufactured products. These data on manufacturing costs are useful because they show management what actually happened. To make judgments about performance, however, management must compare what happened with what should have happened. Once the actual costs of production are determined, management needs a recognized standard against which performance can be measured.

## WHAT STANDARD COSTS ARE

*1a. Standard costs are predetermined estimates of costs that "should be" incurred*

In a manufacturing firm, predetermined cost estimates are sometimes used for direct materials, direct labor, and manufacturing overhead. **Standard costs** are predetermined estimates of the costs that should be incurred to produce a unit of product or perform an operation under planned conditions. Standard costs are "should be" costs that serve as a benchmark against which actual performance can be evaluated.

For example, assume that the standard cost of a product has been set at $3.00 per unit and that the current actual cost to produce it is $3.30. Since management *planned* its costs at $3.00 per unit, the figures show that the company missed the "targeted costs" by $.30 per unit. This $.30 might be a significant amount. If so, the factors responsible for the excess cost must be determined so that appropriate corrective action can be taken. This action is in keeping with management's responsibility to *control* costs.

Standard costing is not another cost accounting system. It is a method whereby predetermined costs are used to enter data in the records of either a job order or a process cost system. Standard costing provides data that management can use to *plan and control costs* and *evaluate performance.*

Standard costing is not limited to manufacturing businesses. It is also used for planning, control, and performance evaluation in nonmanufacturing businesses such as banks, hospitals, hotels, and restaurants. In this chapter we will confine our explanation of standard costing to manufacturing companies.

## STANDARD, ESTIMATED, AND BUDGETED COSTS

*1a. Standard costs differ from estimated and budgeted costs*

Although it might appear that standard, estimated, and budgeted costs are the same, some dissimilarity exists. An **estimated cost** is corrected automatically when it differs from an actual cost. On the other hand, a standard cost normally is not changed unless there is conclusive evidence that it was established incorrectly. A **budgeted cost** represents a total dollar figure, whereas a standard cost is usually expressed as a per unit cost.

Consider the following example. A company anticipates a need for 100 units of direct materials to produce one finished unit. The company sets a production goal for the month of 200 finished units. If the standard cost of one unit of direct materials is set at $10, the standard cost of producing one finished unit will be calculated as follows:

| | |
|---|---|
| Standard price of one unit of direct materials | $ 10 |
| × Number of units of direct materials to produce one finished unit | 100 |
| = Standard direct materials cost of one finished unit | $1,000 |

We can calculate the budgeted materials cost of producing the 200 finished units by applying an additional step:

| | |
|---|---|
| Standard direct materials cost of one finished unit | $ 1,000 |
| × Number of finished units set as a goal | 200 |
| = Budgeted direct materials cost of finished production | $200,000 |

For our purposes in this chapter we will describe standard costs in terms of units, hours, pounds, and the like.

## LEVELS OF STANDARDS

*1a. Standards may be either ideal or attainable*

A standard may be set at either an *ideal* or an *attainable* level.

**Ideal standards** are set by assuming maximum efficiency and minimum cost. They act as a goal that employees strive toward but seldom attain. For example, a college student may set a 4.0 grade-point ratio as a standard for performance. Some students will be able to achieve this high standard, but others may be discouraged when their performance falls short. Discouragement may occur even when highly motivated and above-average students (or workers) make constant and concerted efforts to attain the ideal standards but fall short of achieving them.

**Attainable standards** are set by assuming that actual performance will be efficient but not perfect. As such, they provide allowances for such things as machinery breakdowns, scheduling problems, and worker fatigue.

Attainable standards are realistic expectations of what would occur under efficient operating conditions. For purposes of cost control, attainable standards are preferable to ideal standards.

Once cost standards are developed, they should be reviewed periodically and, when necessary, revised. For example, if the prices paid for materials, labor, or manufacturing overhead change, the standard costs should also be changed.

## MANAGEMENT'S USES OF STANDARD COSTS

Standard costs may be used for a number of purposes, including:

Cost control
Budget preparation
The recording of transaction entries
Motivational goals

### Uses for Cost Control

*1b. Management may use standard costs to keep costs within tolerable limits*

**Cost control** refers to the appraisal processes and actions taken to keep costs within tolerable limits as prescribed by management. Cost control does not necessarily mean reducing costs. There are tolerances between standard and actual costs. For instance, the head of the cutting operation in a furniture manufacturing company might set a 3% tolerance in the number of hours allotted to a certain operation. The manager of the assembling operation could allow a 5% tolerance in another type of operation.

Any large differences (variances) between standard and actual costs should be investigated to determine what caused them and what corrective action can be taken to keep them from recurring. Standard costs, if carefully set, often provide better guidelines for evaluating performance than a comparison of current and prior periods' actual costs. Such a comparison, in fact, could be misleading. For example, it would not be useful to compare two sets of figures from two different accounting periods if both sets of figures resulted from operating inefficiencies.

## Uses for Budget Preparation

***1b.** Standard costs can be used in preparing component budgets of the master budget*

Standard costs can be used when preparing certain component budgets of the master budget (see Chapter 24). For example, the direct materials, direct labor, and manufacturing overhead budgets can be developed from a production budget using standard costs. Standard costs are also used for preparing the selling expense and general and administrative expense budgets contained within the master budget.

## Uses for Recording of Transaction Entries

***1b.** Some costs affecting Inventory and Cost of Goods Sold accounts can be stated in standard dollars*

When standard costs are used, some costs affecting the three inventory accounts and the Cost of Goods Sold account are stated in standard rather than actual dollars. Standard costs are used to record the direct materials, direct labor, and manufacturing overhead as production takes place. However, financial reporting and preparation of tax returns do require the use of actual costs. When financial statements are prepared, the differences between the standard and the actual costs can be accounted for through a process described later in the chapter.

## Uses for Motivational Goals

***1b.** Standard costs may be used to motivate employees to perform more efficiently*

The use of standards may make employees more cost and time conscious and motivate them to seek more efficient ways of carrying out their assignments. To motivate employees toward accomplishing desirable goals, management may set standards that are demanding, yet attainable. For example, the average number of hours needed to perform an operation may be one hundred. However, management may set the standard at a demanding ninety-five hours. It is hoped that employees will strive to achieve this goal, thereby reducing the cost of the operation.

Another example is to lower the standard cost of obtaining a unit of direct materials. Theoretically, the purchasing agent is encouraged to search for materials that cost less than the former standard cost.

Managers should be cautious, however, in using standards to motivate employees. They should not assume that motivational standards have the same effect on everybody. Nor do motivational standards operate in the same way for everybody or have the same purpose as standards designed to provide effective cost control.

## STANDARD COST VARIANCES

*1c. When actual costs are above or below the standard, we have an unfavorable or a favorable standard cost variance*

The difference between a standard cost and an actual cost is called a **variance.** There is a **favorable variance** when an actual cost is less than a standard cost. When an actual cost exceeds a standard cost, there is an **unfavorable variance.**

To be useful in cost control, variances must be isolated. Once this is done, we can analyze and use them to appraise individual performance, determine responsibility, and take corrective action. Management usually concentrates on large variances that require detailed investigation and corrective action.

In the remainder of this chapter we will discuss the development of standard costs for a manufacturing operation. We will also calculate and explain the significance of variances and demonstrate how they can be integrated into a company's accounting records.

## STANDARD COSTS AND VARIANCES FOR DIRECT MATERIALS

Two factors must be considered when determining the standard direct materials cost of a product:

The standard quantity of materials that should be used
The standard price that should be paid for those materials

### Direct Materials Quantity Standards

*1d. Direct materials quantity standards are based on specifications prepared by production personnel*

The amount of direct materials needed for one unit of product is generally obtained from material specifications prepared by product engineers and other production personnel. The specifications depend on company policy and may be based on an assumption of ideal performance or attainable performance.

Once the direct materials quantity standard is set, future usage of materials at amounts more than or less than standard causes a quantity variance. Larger variances are expected if ideal performance standards are used.

### Direct Materials Price Standards

The direct materials price standard is set by estimating the amount that should be paid for each type of material used in manufacturing a product. Determining a standard price can be difficult because it requires a prediction of prices during the next accounting period.

*1d. Direct materials price standards are based on forecasts by purchasing and accounting personnel*

Setting material price standards requires coordination between the purchasing and accounting departments. If a large inventory of materials is carried, the price paid for this inventory is available and can be used as the price standard.

In the absence of large inventories, the purchasing and accounting department personnel must use any available information to forecast prices. Consideration can be given to:

The prices quoted by suppliers.
The availability of discounts.
The cost of transportation.

Because of the difficulty in setting them, direct materials price standards should be periodically reviewed for possible revisions. If a major price change occurs during the accounting period, an immediate revision should be made.

### Direct Materials Variances

To be useful for implementing cost control measures, the total direct materials variance must be divided into its component parts. These parts are the *quantity variance* and the *price variance.*

To illustrate, assume that Able Company has established the following standard cost for the direct materials of one finished unit of Product X:

Direct Materials (1 pound @ $10.00 per pound)

*2a. The total direct materials variance and the quantity and price variances are illustrated in this section*

During January the company completed 3,500 units of finished Product X. It purchased and used 3,520 pounds of direct materials costing $9.75 per pound. The actual and standard direct materials costs for the 3,500 units of Product X are as follows.

| | QUANTITY | UNIT PRICE | AMOUNT |
|---|---|---|---|
| Actual direct materials cost | 3,520 pounds | $ 9.75 | $34,320 |
| Standard direct materials cost (3,500 finished units × 1 pound = 3,500 pounds) | 3,500 pounds | 10.00 | 35,000 |
| Total direct materials variance (favorable) | | | $ 680 |

The schedule shows a favorable direct materials variance of $680—the actual direct materials cost is less than the standard direct materials cost. But the $680 favorable variance alone does not explain whether the variance is attributable to price, quantity, or a combination of both. The causes of the favorable price variance are determined by isolating the **direct materials quantity variance** and the **direct materials price variance,** as shown below.

| | | |
|---|---|---|
| Direct materials quantity variance: | | |
| Actual quantity | 3,520 pounds | |
| Standard quantity | 3,500 pounds | |
| Difference (unfavorable) | 20 pounds | |
| Times standard price | × $ 10 | |
| Total quantity variance (unfavorable) | | $200 |
| Direct materials price variance: | | |
| Actual price | $ 9.75 per lb. | |
| Standard price | 10.00 per lb. | |
| Difference (favorable) | $ .25 per lb. | |
| Times actual quantity | × 3,520 | |
| Total price variance (favorable) | | $880 |
| Total direct materials variance (favorable) | | $680 |

The direct materials variances can also be expressed by formula and computed as follows.

| | | | |
|---|---|---|---|
| Direct materials quantity variance (unfavorable) | = Difference between actual quantity used and standard quantity (3,520 − 3,500) | × Standard cost per unit × $10 | = $200 |
| Direct materials price variance (favorable) | = Difference between actual materials price and standard materials price ($9.75 − $10.00) | × Actual quantity used × 3,520 | = $880 |
| Total direct materials variance (favorable) | | | $680 |

The $200 unfavorable variance was caused by using *20* pounds more than standard. On the other hand, the $880 favorable variance resulted from a unit price that was *$.25* below standard. With this information, management must decide whether the variances are large enough to investigate. If the variances are sufficiently large, responsibility must be determined and corrective action implemented.

Investigation frequently reveals nonapparent causes. For example, the $880 favorable price variance appears to indicate purchasing department efficiency because materials were purchased below the standard price. However, inferior material may have been purchased and may have caused inefficient workmanship, resulting in the use of 20 pounds above standard and an unfavorable quantity variance of $200.

Many companies need timely information and prefer to recognize the direct materials price variance when materials are purchased. Timely information for materials purchases is crucial. Therefore our examples and end-of-chapter exercises and problems will assume the computation of materials price variances when materials are purchased. They will also assume, for simplicity, that the same amounts of materials are purchased and used.

## STANDARD COSTS AND VARIANCES FOR DIRECT LABOR

As with direct materials costs, two factors must be considered when determining the standard direct labor cost of a product: (1) the standard amount of time (hours of labor) allowed to complete a product and (2) the standard wage rate that should be paid for that labor.

### The Direct Labor Time Standard

***1d. The direct labor time standard may be based on time and motion studies and may be either ideal or attainable***

The *direct labor time standard* (also called the *direct labor efficiency standard*) can be difficult to establish. Companies often use time and motion studies to determine the standard time needed to perform each labor operation.

Direct labor time standards, like direct material quantity standards, can be set by using either ideal performance or attainable performance. Ideal performance is a "tight" standard, achieved only under the most favorable circumstances. Attainable performance considers allowable imperfections of employees and machines.

The type of standard performance chosen (ideal or attainable) is important. Each type requires a different analysis of the variance. For motivational and cost control purposes, the standard should be rigorous enough to require near maximum effort.

### The Direct Labor Rate Standard

***1d. The direct labor rate standard may be set by agreements, contracts, or labor market conditions***

The *direct labor rate standard* is often the amount actually paid the employees and is sometimes determined by collective bargaining agreements and labor contracts. Without a labor contract, conditions such as supply and demand determine the amount paid for labor. Within the same company, employees often receive different rates based on such factors as seniority and skills. Companies can set an average standard labor rate for a specific operation, although the rate paid to individual employees working on that operation may vary.

Direct labor rate standards should be maintained on a current basis. If they are not, it is difficult to establish responsibility for variances.

## Direct Labor Variances

To be most useful in controlling costs, direct labor variances must also be isolated and divided into labor *time* and labor *rate* variances.

To illustrate the procedure, assume the following direct labor standard for processing one unit of Product X:

Direct Labor (5 hours @ $3.90 per hour)

*2a. The total direct labor variance and the time and rate variances are illustrated in this section*

During January Able Company completed 3,500 units of Product X using 17,600 direct labor hours at an average cost of $4.00 per hour. The actual and standard direct labor costs for the 3,500 completed units of Product X can be summarized as follows.

| | HOURS | HOURLY RATE | AMOUNT |
|---|---|---|---|
| Actual direct labor cost | 17,600 | $4.00 | $70,400 |
| Standard direct labor cost (3,500 finished units × 5 hours = 17,500 hours) | 17,500 | 3.90 | 68,250 |
| Total direct labor variance (unfavorable) | | | $ 2,150 |

The total variance of $2,150 is unfavorable because the actual direct labor cost exceeds the standard direct labor cost. However, the $2,150 does not show how much of the variance was caused by excessive *hours* over standard or excessive *rate* over standard. These causes can be shown by isolating the $2,150 into the portion that represents the **direct labor time variance** and the portion that represents the **direct labor rate variance,** as shown below.

| | | |
|---|---|---|
| Direct labor time variance: | | |
| Actual time | 17,600 hours | |
| Standard time | 17,500 hours | |
| Difference (unfavorable) | 100 hours | |
| Times standard rate | × $3.90 | |
| Total labor time variance (unfavorable) | | $ 390 |
| Direct labor rate variance: | | |
| Actual rate | $4.00 per hour | |
| Standard rate | 3.90 per hour | |
| Difference (unfavorable) | $ .10 per hour | |
| Times actual time | × 17,600 hours | |
| Total labor rate variance (unfavorable) | | 1,760 |
| Total direct labor variance (unfavorable) | | $2,150 |

The direct labor variances can also be computed by formula, as shown on page 912. The methods are the same as those used to calculate the direct materials quantity and price variances. Here the terms *time* and *rate* are used instead of *quantity* and *price*.

| | | | | |
|---|---|---|---|---|
| Direct labor time variance (unfavorable) | = Difference between actual hours worked and standard hours (17,600 − 17,500) | × Standard rate per hour $3.90 | = | $ 390 |
| Direct labor rate variance (unfavorable) | = Difference between actual wage rate and standard wage rate ($4.00 − $3.90) | × Actual hours worked × 17,600 | = | $1,760 |
| Total direct labor variance (unfavorable) | | | | $2,150 |

The unfavorable time variance of $390 was caused by actual usage of *100* hours in excess of the standard established for the number of units produced. The unfavorable rate variance of $1,760 was caused by an actual average rate *$.10* in excess of the standard set for this type of operation.

These variances should be explained if they are considered *significant.* If production supervisors are held responsible for control of direct labor hours, they should explain this excessive use of 100 hours. The labor rate variance also needs explanation. If the $.10 rate variance was the result of a union contract or another type of wage increase granted by management, the standard labor rate of $3.90 should be revised.

However, the unfavorable rate variance may have occurred because different employees with different wage rates were used in the labor operation. Perhaps employees with higher-skill levels or more seniority were used. Once again, responsible personnel, such as production supervisors, should explain why these different employees were used.

## STANDARD COSTS FOR MANUFACTURING OVERHEAD

### The Standard Overhead Rate

*1e. The illustration given in this section is used to determine the two components of manufacturing overhead rate*

When we first discussed the concept of a predetermined overhead rate in Chapter 22, we assumed one level of activity. We calculated predetermined overhead rate by dividing the total expected overhead costs by the budgeted activity level. For example, if total overhead costs were budgeted at $200,000 at an activity level of 25,000 machine hours, the predetermined overhead rate per machine hour would be $8.00 ($200,000 ÷ 25,000).

To understand the two standard manufacturing overhead variances, we must use (1) the behavioral patterns of cost developed in Chapter 23 and (2) the flexible budget techniques developed in Chapter 24. Recall from Chapter 23 that fixed costs remain constant in total dollars over a relevant range of activity. However, the total dollars of variable costs change in direct proportion to the change in the level of activity.

We now need to look at a flexible budget for Able Company shown in Exhibit 25–1. The budget uses standard direct labor hours to measure the level of production activity for the year 19X8. The activity range is from 17,500 to 25,000 hours during the period. The budget shows four activity levels expressed as a percentage of maximum capacity and ranging from 70% to 100%.

EXHIBIT 25–1

ABLE COMPANY
Manufacturing Overhead Flexible Budget
For the Year 19X8

| | | | | |
|---|---|---|---|---|
| Percentage of normal capacity | 70% | 80% | 90% | 100% |
| Units of production | 3,500 | 4,000 | 4,500 | 5,000 |
| Standard direct labor hours | 17,500 | 20,000 | 22,500 | 25,000 |
| Budgeted Manufacturing Overhead: | | | | |
| Variable costs: | | | | |
| Indirect materials | $ 7,000 | $ 8,000 | $ 9,000 | $10,000 |
| Indirect labor | 8,750 | 10,000 | 11,250 | 12,500 |
| Power and light | 3,500 | 4,000 | 4,500 | 5,000 |
| Maintenance | 1,750 | 2,000 | 2,250 | 2,500 |
| Total variable costs | $21,000 | $24,000 | $27,000 | $30,000 |
| Fixed costs: | | | | |
| Supervisory salaries | $ 8,000 | $ 8,000 | $ 8,000 | $ 8,000 |
| Rent—building | 5,000 | 5,000 | 5,000 | 5,000 |
| Depreciation—machines | 6,200 | 6,200 | 6,200 | 6,200 |
| Insurance | 800 | 800 | 800 | 800 |
| Total fixed costs | $20,000 | $20,000 | $20,000 | $20,000 |
| Total Manufacturing Overhead | $41,000 | $44,000 | $47,000 | $50,000 |

Using the information from Exhibit 25–1, we can now calculate the total standard overhead rate per direct labor hour at any of the four levels of activity. These calculations are shown in the schedule below.

| | | | | |
|---|---|---|---|---|
| Percentage of total capacity | 70% | 80% | 90% | 100% |
| Total budgeted manufacturing overhead (A) | $41,000 | $44,000 | $47,000 | $50,000 |
| Total budgeted standard direct labor hours (B) | 17,500 | 20,000 | 22,500 | 25,000 |
| Total standard overhead rate per direct labor hour (A/B) | $ 2.34 | $ 2.20 | $ 2.09 | $ 2.00 |

Note that the standard overhead rate is lower if we use a higher level of activity to calculate the rate. The reason is that fixed manufacturing overhead remains the same at all four levels of activity. Thus we have four possible overhead rates, depending on the percentage of total capacity that management chooses to use as its "normal" level of operations. We will assume that Able Company expects an 80% level of activity during 19X8 and thus uses a manufacturing overhead rate of $2.20 ($44,000 budgeted manufacturing overhead ÷ 20,000 budgeted standard direct labor hours).

We can also divide the total standard manufacturing overhead rate of $2.20 into its fixed and variable components, as shown below.

*1e. The fixed and variable portions of manufacturing overhead rate are illustrated here*

$$\text{Fixed overhead rate per direct labor hour} = \frac{\text{Total fixed overhead costs}}{\text{Standard direct labor hours}} = \frac{\$20{,}000}{20{,}000} = \$1.00$$

$$\text{Variable overhead rate per direct labor hour} = \frac{\text{Total variable overhead costs}}{\text{Standard direct labor hours}} = \frac{\$24{,}000}{20{,}000} = \$1.20$$

In the next section we will see how this overhead rate information is used to calculate the two manufacturing overhead variances.

## MANUFACTURING OVERHEAD VARIANCES

To illustrate the two manufacturing overhead variances, assume that Able Company experienced some unexpected work stoppages during 19X8 and operated at 70% rather than 80% of capacity. At 70% of capacity, the company produced only 3,500 units rather than the 4,000 that would have been produced at 80% of capacity. According to Exhibit 25–1, the standard number of direct labor hours allowed to produce 3,500 units was 17,500. Thus the total manufacturing overhead variance is computed as follows (the amount of actual manufacturing overhead is assumed).

*2a. Computation of the total standard cost variance for manufacturing overhead is illustrated here*

| | | |
|---|---|---|
| Overhead applied (the amount debited to Work in Process and credited to overhead): (17,500 standard direct labor hours × $2.20 standard overhead rate) | | $38,500 |
| Actual overhead: | | |
| Variable | $21,700 | |
| Fixed | 20,000 | 41,700 |
| Total overhead variance (unfavorable) | | $ 3,200 |

The total manufacturing overhead variance of $3,200 consists of a manufacturing overhead volume variance and a manufacturing overhead controllable variance, as explained in the following subsections.

### Manufacturing Overhead Volume Variance

The **manufacturing overhead volume variance** (sometimes referred to simply as the **volume variance**) is the difference between

The manufacturing overhead budgeted at the actual production level achieved and
The manufacturing overhead applied to production (the amount debited to Work in Process and credited to Manufacturing Overhead).

If Able Company produced 3,500 units during 19X8, the volume variance would be calculated as follows.

*2a. Illustrated here is a computation for manufacturing overhead volume variance*

| | |
|---|---|
| Manufacturing overhead budgeted at the actual production level achieved (70% and 3,500 units from Exhibit 25–1) | $41,000 |
| Manufacturing overhead applied to production (the amount debited to Work in Process and credited to overhead): $2.20 (the total overhead rate used by Able in 19X8) × 17,500 hours (the standard number of direct labor hours for the 3,500 units produced at the 70% capacity used by Able in 19X8) | 38,500 |
| Volume variance (unfavorable) | $ 2,500 |

What does a $2,500 unfavorable volume variance actually mean? It means that factory operations did not reach the operating level expected, resulting in underutilization of fixed manufacturing overhead costs. Remember from Exhibit 25–1 that our normal operating level of activity is 80% of capacity and 4,000 units. During 19X8 we operated, instead, at 70% of capacity and produced 3,500 units. We simply "did not get our money's worth" out of the $20,000 of fixed costs that must be incurred at all operating levels shown in Exhibit 25–1.

Management should investigate the cause of the variance if the amount is large enough to warrant investigation. However, the volume variance is not controllable at the departmental operating level. The variance is caused by the fact that we operated at 70% rather than 80% of capacity. As such, it is either controllable by top management or uncontrollable.

We may wish to use an alternate calculation of the volume variance, as shown below.

| | |
|---|---|
| Normal productive capacity in direct labor hours (for 4,000 units) | 20,000 hours |
| Standard direct labor hours for actual production of 3,500 units | 17,500 hours |
| Difference | 2,500 hours |
| Standard fixed overhead rate | $ 1 |
| Volume variance (unfavorable) | $2,500 |

This calculation shows us that the volume variance is strictly related to fixed manufacturing overhead. By falling 500 units below our normal operating level (4,000 units − 3,500 units), we also fell 2,500 standard direct labor hours below our normal operating level (20,000 standard direct labor hours − 17,500 standard direct labor hours). Thus the unfavorable volume variance is this 2,500 standard direct labor hours times the standard fixed overhead rate.

If we had operated at more than 80% of capacity during 19X8, the volume variance would have been favorable. This is because the number of units produced would have been in excess of 4,000, and the standard direct labor hours for actual production would have been in excess of 20,000 direct labor hours.

## Manufacturing Overhead Controllable Variance

The **manufacturing overhead controllable variance** (sometimes called the **controllable variance**) is the difference between

The manufacturing overhead actually incurred and
The manufacturing overhead budgeted at the actual production level achieved.

Able Company incurred $41,700 of overhead costs during 19X8 when its factory operated at 70% of capacity. The controllable variance is calculated as follows.

*2a. Illustrated here is a computation for manufacturing overhead controllable variance*

| | |
|---|---|
| Manufacturing overhead incurred | $41,700 |
| Manufacturing overhead budget for the actual production level achieved (from Exhibit 25–1) | 41,000 |
| Controllable variance (unfavorable) | $ 700 |

The controllable variance of $700 can be explained in this way: We should have incurred $41,000 of overhead, given that we actually operated at 70% of capacity and actually produced 3,500 units. Instead we incurred $41,700, or $700 too much.

If the actual manufacturing overhead incurred is more than the manufacturing overhead budget for the actual production level achieved, the controllable variance is *unfavorable,* meaning that we incurred too much overhead costs.

If the actual manufacturing overhead incurred is less than the manufacturing overhead budget for the actual production level achieved, the controllable variance is *favorable,* meaning that we "saved" overhead costs.

Both unfavorable and favorable controllable variances should be investigated if the amounts are considered excessive. The causes of excessive unfavorable or favorable variances include the following:

Purchase of overhead items at supposedly "bargain" prices

Inefficient or efficient use of overhead resources

Poor techniques that result in an unreliable overhead budget and make it appear that actual overhead spending is too large or too small

## STANDARD COSTS IN THE ACCOUNTS

Some companies might use standards only to control costs and make periodic reports to management. Others might also incorporate standard costs directly into their accounts. By doing so, the financial statements used for internal purposes reflect inventory and cost of goods sold figures that are representative of what costs "should have been."

There are several ways to incorporate standard costs into the accounts. One way is to charge direct materials, direct labor, and manufacturing overhead to the Work in Process Inventory account at standard costs. Units transferred to Finished Goods Inventory and to Cost of Goods Sold would also be recorded at standard costs. This means that differences between standard and actual costs are recorded in variance accounts.

Unfavorable variances (actual costs exceed standard costs) are recorded as *debits.*

Favorable variances (standard costs exceed actual costs) are recorded as *credits.*

To illustrate, we will use the Able Company data given earlier in the chapter.

### The Entry for the Purchase of Direct Materials

*2b. Journal entries to incorporate standard costs into general ledger accounts are illustrated here*

Able Company purchased and used 3,520 pounds of direct materials at $9.75 per pound (the standard cost is $10.00 per pound). The entry to record the purchase is as follows:

| | | |
|---|---|---|
| Raw Materials Inventory (3,520 × $10.00) | 35,200 | |
| Materials Price Variance (3,520 × $.25) | | 880 |
| Accounts Payable (3,520 × $9.75) | | 34,320 |
| To record the purchase of direct materials and the setting up of the materials price variance | | |

### The Entry for the Usage of Direct Materials

To produce the number of finished units, 3,520 pounds of direct materials were needed (the standard is 3,500 pounds). The entry to record the materials requisitioned for use is as follows:

| | | |
|---|---|---|
| Work in Process Inventory (3,500 × $10.00) | 35,000 | |
| Materials Quantity Variance (20 × $10.00) | 200 | |
| Raw Materials Inventory (3,520 × $10.00) | | 35,200 |
| To record the issuance of direct materials to production and the setting up of the materials quantity variance | | |

### The Entry for the Usage of Direct Labor

During the period Able Company used 17,600 direct labor hours (the standard is 17,500 direct labor hours). The actual direct labor rate was $4.00 per hour (the standard direct labor rate is $3.90 per hour). The entry to record the direct labor cost and distribute it to the Work in Process Inventory and the variance accounts appears below.

| | | |
|---|---|---|
| Work in Process Inventory (17,500 × $3.90) | 68,250 | |
| Labor Time Variance (100 × $3.90) | 390 | |
| Labor Rate Variance (17,600 × $.10) | 1,760 | |
| Wages Payable (17,600 × $4.00) | | 70,400 |
| To record direct labor for January and to set up the labor time variance and the labor rate variance | | |

### The Entries for Manufacturing Overhead

Able Company incurred $41,700 of manufacturing overhead costs during the period. To simplify the illustration, the journal entry to show actual manufacturing overhead contains a credit to an account called Various Credits.

| | | |
|---|---|---|
| Manufacturing Overhead | 41,700 | |
| Various Credits | | 41,700 |
| To record the actual overhead incurred in January | | |

The journal entry to apply the overhead production is shown below and is based on the following data:

| | |
|---|---|
| Normal productive capacity expressed in standard direct labor hours | 20,000 |
| Standard direct labor hours allowed for actual production | 17,500 |
| Total standard overhead rate | $ 2.20 |
| Fixed standard overhead rate | $ 1.00 |
| Manufacturing overhead budgeted for actual production | $41,000 |

| | | |
|---|---|---|
| Work in Process Inventory (17,500 × $2.20) | 38,500 | |
| Overhead Volume Variance (2,500 × $1.00) | 2,500 | |
| Overhead Controllable Variance ($41,700 − $41,000) | 700 | |
| Manufacturing Overhead | | 41,700 |
| To apply overhead to production and to set up the overhead volume variance and the overhead controllable variance | | |

## The Entry to Transfer the Cost of Completed Units to Finished Goods Inventory

At the end of the period when all units are completed, the following entry is made:

| | | |
|---|---|---|
| Finished Goods Inventory | 141,750 | |
| Work in Process Inventory | | 141,750 |
| To record the transfer of completed goods to finished goods inventory at standard costs ($35,000 for direct materials, $68,250 for direct labor, and $38,500 for manufacturing overhead) | | |

## The Entry to Close the Variance Accounts

Variance accounts are frequently debited and credited during the year, reflecting the fact that in some months the variances are favorable and in others they are unfavorable. However, variance accounts are usually closed at the end of the year rather than at the end of each month.

For illustrative purposes, we will assume that all variance accounts calculated in this chapter are closed to the Cost of Goods Sold account at the end of the yearly accounting period. The following journal entry is made:

| | | |
|---|---|---|
| Materials Price Variance | 880 | |
| Cost of Goods Sold | 4,670 | |
| Materials Quantity Variance | | 200 |
| Labor Time Variance | | 390 |
| Labor Rate Variance | | 1,760 |
| Overhead Volume Variance | | 2,500 |
| Overhead Controllable Variance | | 700 |
| To close the standard cost variance accounts | | |

EXHIBIT 25–2

ABLE COMPANY
Income Statement Showing Disposition of Standard Cost Variances
For the Year 19X8

| | | |
|---|---|---|
| Sales | | $262,500 |
| Cost of Goods Sold—at Standard | | 141,750 |
| Gross Profit—at Standard | | $120,750 |
| Less Variances from Standards:* | | |
| Direct Materials Price | $ (880) | |
| Direct Materials Quantity | 200 | |
| Direct Labor Time | 390 | |
| Direct Labor Rate | 1,760 | |
| Manufacturing Overhead Volume | 2,500 | |
| Manufacturing Overhead Controllable | 700 | |
| Total Variances—Unfavorable | | 4,670 |
| Gross Profit | | $116,080 |
| Operating Expenses: | | |
| Selling | $57,500 | |
| General and Administrative | 23,900 | |
| Total Operating Expenses | | 81,400 |
| Net Income | | $ 34,680 |

* Parentheses mean that the variance is favorable. The other variances are unfavorable.

## THE FINANCIAL STATEMENT CLASSIFICATION OF STANDARD COST VARIANCES

*1f. Exhibit 25–2 shows how standard cost variances might be classified in an income statement*

Although variances are not generally reported to groups outside the company, they are often disclosed on periodic income statements prepared for management. Exhibit 25–2 shows how such variances might be disclosed in Able Company's income statement. Assume that all 3,500 finished units were sold at $75 each, providing revenue of $262,500. Assume no beginning or ending inventories. Selling expenses and general and administrative expenses are also assumed.

## HIGHLIGHT PROBLEM

Data concerning standards for Lilly Company appear below.

| PRODUCT COST STANDARDS: | |
|---|---|
| Direct materials | 5 lbs. @ $.80 per lb. |
| Direct labor | 2 hrs. @ $5.00 per hr. |
| Manufacturing overhead | 2 hrs. @ $2.50 per hr. |

| SELECTED FLEXIBLE BUDGET DATA: | | |
|---|---|---|
| Standard Direct Labor Hours | 50,000 | 50,400 |
| Variable overhead | $ 80,000 | $ 80,640 |
| Fixed overhead | 45,000 | 45,000 |
| Total budgeted overhead | $125,000 | $125,640 |

The normal production level measured in direct labor hours is 50,000. Therefore the fixed and variable components of the overhead rate, as well as the total overhead rate, are shown below:

| | |
|---|---|
| Variable overhead | $ 80,000 ÷ 50,000 = $1.60 |
| Fixed overhead | 45,000 ÷ 50,000 = .90 |
| Total overhead | $125,000 ÷ 50,000 = $2.50 |

*Actual production and cost data for the month of January:*

Finished units completed—25,200.

Direct materials—130,000 pounds were purchased on account for $101,400. All of the pounds were used in production.

Direct labor—all wages of $248,490 for 50,200 hours worked were paid in cash.

Manufacturing overhead costs incurred—$126,200.

Required:

1. Compute the direct materials quantity and price variances.
2. Compute the direct labor time and rate variances.
3. Compute the total manufacturing overhead variance.
4. Compute the manufacturing overhead volume and controllable variances.
5. Prepare journal entries to record the purchase of direct materials and the flow of costs through the Work in Process account to the Finished Goods account for
   a. Direct materials
   b. Direct labor
   c. Manufacturing overhead (credit the account called Various Credits for the actual manufacturing overhead costs)

## GLOSSARY OF KEY TERMS

**Attainable standards.** Standards that can be achieved by efficient, but not perfect, performance.

**Budgeted cost.** A total dollar figure rather than a per unit cost.

**Cost control.** The appraisal processes and actions taken to keep costs within tolerable limits as prescribed by management.

**Controllable variance.** The same as the manufacturing overhead controllable variance.

**Direct labor rate variance.** The difference between the standard direct labor rate and the actual direct labor rate multiplied by the actual number of direct labor hours worked.

**Direct labor time variance.** The difference between the standard number of direct labor hours allowed for production and the actual number of direct labor hours worked multiplied by the standard direct labor rate per hour.

**Direct materials price variance.** The difference between the standard direct materials price per unit and the actual direct materials price per unit multiplied by the actual quantity of direct materials purchased or used.

**Direct materials quantity variance.** The difference between the standard quantity of direct materials allowed for production and the actual quantity of direct materials used multiplied by the standard price of the direct materials.

**Estimated cost.** A cost that is automatically corrected when it differs from an actual cost.

**Favorable variance.** A variance that occurs when the actual cost is less than the standard cost.

**Ideal standards.** Standards that are set by assuming maximum efficiency and minimum cost.

**Manufacturing overhead controllable variance.** The difference between the manufacturing overhead actually incurred and the manufacturing overhead budgeted at the actual production level achieved.

**Manufacturing overhead volume variance.** The difference between the manufacturing overhead budgeted at the actual production level achieved and the manufacturing overhead applied to production (debited to Work in Process and credited to Manufacturing Overhead).

**Standard costs.** Predetermined estimates of the costs that should be incurred to produce a unit of product or perform an operation under planned conditions.

**Unfavorable variance.** A variance that occurs when the actual cost exceeds the standard cost.

**Variance.** The difference between a standard cost and an actual cost.

**Volume variance.** The same as the manufacturing overhead volume variance.

## REVIEW QUESTIONS

1. What are standard costs? [LO1a]
2. Differentiate between standard, estimated, and budgeted costs. [LO1a]
3. Differentiate between ideal standards and attainable standards. Which ones are better for cost control purposes? [LO1a]
4. Name the four uses that management can make of standard costs. [LO1b]
5. What is a favorable variance? An unfavorable variance? [LO1c]
6. What two factors must be considered when determining the standard direct materials cost of a product? [LO1d]
7. Describe how the two direct materials variances are calculated. [LO2a]
8. What two factors must be considered when determining the standard direct labor cost of a product? [LO1d]
9. Describe how the two direct labor variances are calculated. [LO2a]
10. Describe how to calculate the variable components of the total standard manufacturing overhead rate. [LO1e]
11. Describe how the two manufacturing overhead variances are calculated. [LO2a]
12. Which standard cost variances are recorded as debits? Which ones as credits? [LO2b]

13. Describe the journal entries made when the following events take place:
    a. Direct materials are purchased at less than the standard price.
    b. Direct materials are used in a larger quantity than the standard.
    c. More direct labor hours are used than the standard, and the direct labor rate is higher than the standard.
    d. Actual manufacturing overhead incurred is more than the amount applied to production. Both manufacturing overhead variances are unfavorable. [LO2b]
14. How might standard cost variances be classified in financial statements? [LO1f]

## *ANALYTICAL QUESTIONS*

15. Under what conditions could the use of ideal standards be useful? [LO1a]
16. "We always set our materials standards two to three percent lower than the current prevailing market price of the various materials we purchase." Comment on why a company would use a policy of this type. [LO1b]
17. Comment on the following statement: "Standard costs that are set too tight or too loose are not useful for motivational purposes." [LO1b]
18. Explain why the following statement is true: "A favorable variance can be a matter of management concern." [LO1c]
19. Comment on the following statement: "The manufacturing overhead volume variance relates to fixed manufacturing costs and is uncontrollable." [LO2a]
20. Why is it desirable to divide the total direct materials variance and the total direct labor variance into two variances each? [LO2a]

## *IMPACT ANALYSIS QUESTIONS*

*For each error described, indicate whether it would overstate [O], understate [U], or not affect [N] the specified key figures.*

21. The actual cost of direct materials purchased was incorrectly calculated at $5.50 per unit instead of at $5.40 per unit. The standard is $5.00 per unit.

    ________ Direct Materials Price Variance
    ________ Direct Materials Quantity Variance [LO2a]

22. The actual number of direct materials units put into production was miscalculated at 5,200 instead of 5,100. The standard number of direct materials units was 5,000.

    ________ Direct Materials Price Variance
    ________ Direct Materials Quantity Variance [LO2a]

23. The entry to show the purchase of direct materials omitted the unfavorable materials price variance.

    ________ Raw Materials Inventory
    ________ Accounts Payable (or Cash) [LO2b]

24. The entry to apply manufacturing overhead to production was omitted.

    ________ Work in Process Inventory
    ________ Manufacturing Overhead [LO2b]

## *EXERCISES*

EXERCISE 25-1 *(Compute Direct Materials and Direct Labor Variances)* Royal Couple Company uses a standard cost system. The company's standard cost data for direct materials and direct labor are as follows.

| | STANDARD COSTS—PER UNIT |
|---|---|
| Direct materials | 2 lbs. @ $5 per lb. |
| Direct labor | 4 hrs. @ $6 per hr. |

During the period the company produced 3,000 units of product and incurred actual costs as follows.

Direct materials—$30,855, using 6,050 pounds
Direct labor—$71,390 for 11,800 hours worked

Required:
Calculate the following standard cost variances:
1. Direct materials price
2. Direct materials quantity
3. Direct labor time
4. Direct labor rate [LO2a]

EXERCISE 25–2 *(Compute Manufacturing Overhead Volume and Controllable Variances)* Allway Company uses standard costs and makes a single product. The company's normal production for the month is 50,000 direct labor hours. Manufacturing overhead costs are budgeted on the basis of direct labor hours. The monthly overhead budget based on 50,000 direct labor hours is as follows.

| | |
|---|---|
| Fixed costs | $ 50,000 |
| Variable costs | 75,000 |
| Total overhead | $125,000 |

During the month, the number of standard direct labor hours for production achieved was 48,000. The number of direct labor hours actually used was 45,000, and the company incurred the following manufacturing overhead costs.

| | |
|---|---|
| Fixed costs | $ 50,000 |
| Variable costs | 69,600 |
| | $119,600 |

Required:
Calculate the following cost variances:
1. Manufacturing overhead volume
2. Manufacturing overhead controllable [LO2a]

EXERCISE 25–3 *(Complete the Data for Direct Materials Variances)* For each of the following independent cases, determine the missing amounts. For standard cost variances, indicate whether the variance is favorable (F) or unfavorable (U).

| | CASE 1 | CASE 2 | CASE 3 |
|---|---|---|---|
| Actual materials price | $ 3.10 | $ 4.90 | $ ____ |
| Standard materials price | $ ____ | $ 5.00 | $ 6.00 |
| Actual number of materials units purchased and used | 1,000 | ____ | 2,500 |
| Standard number of materials units used | ____ | 2,000 | 2,300 |
| Materials price variance | $100 U | ____ | $250 U |
| Materials quantity variance | $300 F | $1,000 U | $____ |

[LO2a]

EXERCISE 25–4 *(Complete the Data for Direct Labor Variances)* For each of the following independent cases, determine the missing amounts. For standard cost variances, indicate whether the variance is favorable (F) or unfavorable (U).

| | CASE 1 | CASE 2 | CASE 3 |
|---|---|---|---|
| Actual labor rate | $ 5.00 | $ 6.00 | $ 7.20 |
| Standard labor rate | $ 5.20 | $ 6.10 | $ 7.00 |
| Actual number of labor hours | ____ | 3,000 | ____ |
| Standard number of labor hours | 1,500 | 3,100 | ____ |
| Labor rate variance | $ 340 F | $ 300 F | $ 400 U |
| Labor time variance | $1,040 U | $ ____ | $2,100 U |

[LO2a]

EXERCISE 25–5 *(Prepare a Flexible Budget and Calculate the Fixed and Variable Portions of the Overhead Rate)* Lonely Hearts Manufacturing Company has established relevant range cost estimates of 8,000 to 12,000 direct labor hours. The cost estimates within the range are as follows.

| | |
|---|---|
| Fixed costs | $24,000 |
| Variable costs (per direct labor hour) | |
| Indirect materials | $ .30 |
| Indirect labor | .90 |
| Power and light | .50 |
| Maintenance | .20 |

Required:

1. Prepare a flexible budget for 8,000, 10,000, and 12,000 direct labor hours (use Exhibit 25–1 as a model).
2. Calculate the fixed and variable overhead rate per direct labor hour assuming the normal level of productive activity is 10,000 direct labor hours.
3. Calculate the fixed and variable overhead rate per direct labor hour assuming the normal level of productive activity is 8,000 direct labor hours. [LO1e]

EXERCISE 25–6 *(Incorporate Standard Costs into the Accounts)* The standard cost variance accounts of Honeydo Chore Company as they appear at year-end are shown below.

| | |
|---|---|
| Labor rate variance—favorable | $2,800 |
| Labor time variance—unfavorable | 1,100 |
| Materials price variance—unfavorable | 2,500 |
| Materials quantity variance—unfavorable | 900 |
| Overhead controllable variance—favorable | 1,700 |
| Overhead volume variance—unfavorable | 2,400 |

The following transactions occurred during the year.

1. Direct materials were purchased for $52,500. The standard price of the direct materials purchased was $50,000.
2. All the purchased materials were used in production. The standard amount of materials that should have been used for actual production was $49,100.
3. The actual direct labor cost was $38,300. The standard direct labor cost for actual production was $40,000.
4. Actual manufacturing overhead incurred was $30,700. The manufacturing overhead applied to production was $30,000.

Required:
Prepare journal entries for all the transactions for the year relating to direct materials, direct labor, and manufacturing overhead, including the entry to close the Standard Cost Variance accounts. Credit the Various Credits account for the entry showing the manufacturing overhead incurred. [LO2b]

EXERCISE 25–7 *(Prepare an Income Statement with Cost Variances)* The following data for 19X8 are taken from the records of Exacto Computer Company.

| | |
|---|---|
| Administrative expenses | $ 53,000 |
| Cost of goods sold (at standard) | 600,000 |
| Direct labor rate variance—unfavorable | 3,200 |
| Direct labor time variance—favorable | 1,800 |
| Direct materials price variance—favorable | 900 |
| Direct materials quantity variance—unfavorable | 2,300 |
| Manufacturing overhead controllable variance—favorable | 1,400 |
| Manufacturing overhead volume variance—favorable | 2,600 |
| Sales | 820,000 |
| Selling expenses | 94,000 |

Required:
Prepare an income statement in a format that can be used by internal management. Use the format shown in the chapter and disclose all cost variances. [LO1f]

## PROBLEMS

PROBLEM 25–1 *(Compute Materials Price and Quantity Variances)* The following data are available to the management of Carson Company.

| | |
|---|---|
| Standard materials price | $3 per gallon |
| Standard quantity of materials per finished unit | 8 gallons |
| Normal monthly production of finished units | 80,000 units |
| Actual price of materials purchased | $3.10 per gallon |
| Actual quantity of materials purchased and used | 638,000 gallons |
| Actual monthly production of units | 78,500 units |

Required:
1. Compute the materials quantity and price variances. Indicate whether the variances are favorable (F) or unfavorable (U).
2. Discuss the possible causes for the standard cost variances. [LO2a]

PROBLEM 25–2 *(Compute Labor Time and Rate Variances)* The K.B.M. Wheat Company produces a single product and has developed the following direct labor standards.

| | |
|---|---|
| Standard direct labor hours per unit of output | $2\frac{2}{3}$ hrs. |
| Standard direct labor rate per hour | $5.00 |

During the month of June the company produced 3,000 units of product using 8,100 direct labor hours at an average direct labor rate of $5.03 per hour.

Required:
1. Compute the direct labor time and rate variances for the month. Indicate whether the variances are favorable (F) or unfavorable (U).
2. Discuss who would usually be held responsible for these standard cost variances and how they might be controlled. [LO2a]

PROBLEM 25–3 *(Compute Materials, Labor, and Overhead Variances)* Muddy Banks Company has set 100,000 units as its normal productive capacity for the year. Standard costs per finished unit are as follows:

Direct materials, 3 pounds @ $1.00 per pound
Direct labor, 2 hours @ $4.00 per direct labor hour
Variable overhead, $1.00 per direct labor hour
Fixed overhead, $0.25 per direct labor hour

During the year 96,000 units were produced. Actual data for the year are as follows.

| | |
|---|---|
| Direct materials purchased and used | 300,000 lbs. @ $.98 per lb. |
| Direct labor costs | 192,400 hrs. @ $4.10 per hr. |
| Variable overhead costs incurred | $196,200 |
| Fixed overhead costs incurred | $ 48,000 |

Required:
Compute the following variances and indicate whether they are favorable (F) or unfavorable (U):

1. Materials quantity and price
2. Labor time and rate
3. Overhead volume and controllable [LO2a]

PROBLEM 25–4 *(Calculate Amounts and Record Journal Entries for Materials and Labor Variances)* Information pertaining to Departments A and B of Zoro Company, as well as information for the total operations, is listed below.

1. The company produced 20,000 units of output during the period.
2. It takes Department A two units of direct materials to produce one unit of output. Department B needs three units of direct materials to produce one unit of output.
3. It takes Department A one-half hour to produce one unit of output. It takes Department B one-quarter hour to produce one unit of output.
4. Each department had the following data for the period.

| | DEPARTMENT A | DEPARTMENT B |
|---|---|---|
| Actual number of units of materials purchased and used | 41,000 | 58,000 |
| Actual unit price of materials | $5.25 | $8.20 |
| Standard unit price of materials | $5.00 | $8.50 |
| Actual number of direct labor hours worked | 8,000 | 6,000 |
| Standard labor rate per hour | $8.00 | $9.00 |
| Actual labor rate per hour | $7.70 | $9.10 |

Required:

1. Compute the materials price and quantity variances for each department. Indicate whether the variances are favorable or unfavorable.
2. Compute the labor time and rate variances for each department. Indicate whether the variances are favorable or unfavorable.
3. Prepare journal entries to record the following:
   a. Purchase of direct materials for Department A
   b. Purchase of direct materials for Department B
   c. Issuance of direct materials to production from Department A
   d. Issuance of direct materials to production from Department B
   e. Direct labor payroll for Department A
   f. Direct labor payroll for Department B [LO2a, 2b]

PROBLEM 25-5 *(Compute Materials Price and Quantity Variances)* During the month of April a company purchased 3,020 pieces of item Z of direct materials for the production of X.

The standard cost of item Z is $1.00 per unit. The actual cost of item Z is $1.02 per unit.

On April 1 there was no inventory of item Z on hand, nor were any units of item Z issued to production during April.

Required:

Part I

a. If the company recognizes a materials price variance when the items are purchased, what is the materials price variance?

b. If the company recognizes a materials price variance when the items are issued to production, what is the materials price variance?

c. Discuss the advantages and disadvantages of the two practices described in A and B above.

Part II

During April all of the 3,020 pieces of item Z were issued to production, and 3,000 units of Product X were produced. The materials quantity standard for one unit of Product X is as follows:

1 piece of item Z for every finished unit of Product X

Compute the materials quantity variance and indicate whether it is favorable or unfavorable. [LO2a]

PROBLEM 25-6 *(Compute Materials, Labor, and Overhead Variances)* The following information was developed for Holmes Company.

Standard costs per finished unit:

Direct materials, 2 units @ $3 per unit

Direct labor, 1 hour @ $5 per hour

Manufacturing overhead, $3 ($1 variable and $2 fixed) applied on the basis of direct labor hours (the normal level of activity is 5,000 direct labor hours)

Actual input, output, and cost figures for the period:

Direct materials purchased and used during the period, 10,200 units @ $2.97 per unit

Direct labor hours worked, 5,140

Direct labor costs, $26,214

Actual manufacturing overhead costs incurred: $15,800, of which $10,000 represents fixed overhead costs

Number of units produced, 5,000

Required:

1. Compute the materials quantity and price variances. Indicate whether the variances are favorable or unfavorable.
2. Compute the direct labor time and rate variances. Indicate whether the variances are favorable or unfavorable.
3. Compute the manufacturing overhead volume and controllable variances. Indicate whether the variances are favorable or unfavorable. [LO2a]

PROBLEM 25-7 *(Compute Materials, Labor, and Overhead Variances, Prepare Journal Entries, and Prepare Income Statement)* Standard cost data per finished unit for Mason Company's standard cost system appear below.

| ELEMENTS OF COST | STANDARDS |
|---|---|
| Direct materials | 2 lbs. @ $5 per lb. |
| Direct labor | 1 hr. @ $7 per hr. |
| Manufacturing overhead | $4 per hr. |

Manufacturing overhead rates are based on a flexible budget. Normal capacity is

8,000 direct labor hours. The total budgeted manufacturing overhead for 8,000 direct labor hours divided into its variable and fixed components is as follows.

| | TOTAL | PER LABOR HOUR |
|---|---|---|
| Variable manufacturing overhead | $20,000 | $2.50 |
| Fixed manufacturing overhead | 12,000 | 1.50 |
| Total | $32,000 | $4.00 |

Actual production and cost data for May are as follows:

1. There was no beginning or ending work in process inventory, nor any beginning or ending finished goods inventory.
2. During May, 7,980 units were completed.
3. During May, 15,600 pounds of direct materials costing $77,376 were purchased on account and used.
4. Direct labor costs of $55,600 were paid in cash during the month.
5. The number of direct labor hours worked during the month was 8,000.
6. Total overhead costs were $35,000, of which $12,000 represents fixed overhead.

Required:

Part I

a. Compute the materials quantity and price variances.

b. Compute the labor time and rate variances.

c. Compute the total manufacturing overhead variance.

d. Compute the manufacturing overhead volume and controllable variances.

Part II

Prepare journal entries to record the purchase of materials and the flow of all manufacturing costs through the Work in Process account to the Finished Goods account, including the closing of the variance accounts. (Use the journal entries in the chapter as models. Do not record the entries for sales.)

Part III

Prepare an income statement in which the cost of goods sold is reported at standard cost and all variance accounts and amounts are disclosed. Additional information follows:

a. During the month all finished units were sold on account for $287,280.

b. Selling expenses incurred were $55,860.

c. General and administrative expenses incurred were $23,940. [LO1f,2a,2b]

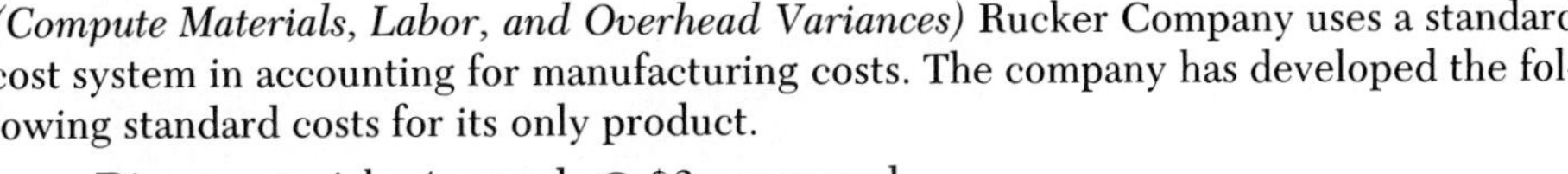

PROBLEM 25–8 *(Compute Materials, Labor, and Overhead Variances)* Rucker Company uses a standard cost system in accounting for manufacturing costs. The company has developed the following standard costs for its only product.

Direct materials, 4 pounds @ $2 per pound

Direct labor, 2 hours @ $6 per hour

Variable manufacturing overhead, $2 per direct labor hour

Fixed manufacturing overhead, $90,000 ÷ normal capacity of 30,000 direct labor hours = $3

During January, 15,050 units were produced. Other data pertaining to the company's monthly operations follow.

1. Direct materials purchased and used, 62,000 pounds @ $1.95 per pound
2. Actual direct labor hours worked, 30,000 hours @ $6.05 per hour
3. Actual overhead costs incurred, $121,700

Required:

1. Compute the materials quantity and price variances.
2. Compute the labor time and rate variances.
3. Compute the manufacturing overhead volume and controllable variances. [LO2a]

PROBLEM 25–9 *(Compute All Manufacturing Cost Variances and Prepare Journal Entries)* Famous Company uses a standard cost system in accounting for the manufacturing costs of one product. Normal capacity is 10,000 direct labor hours per year. The standard costs are as follows.

Direct materials, 5 gallons @ $2.00 per gallon

Direct labor, 1 hour @ $5.50 per hour

Variable manufacturing overhead, $2 per direct labor hour

Fixed manufacturing overhead, $15,000 ÷ 10,000 direct labor hours = $1.50 per direct labor hour

Other data pertaining to the year are as follows:

1. Gallons of materials purchased on account and used, 60,000 @ $2.02 per gallon.
2. Actual direct labor costs of production, $54,060.
3. Actual direct labor hours used, 10,200.
4. Actual variable overhead costs, $20,500.
5. Actual fixed overhead costs, $14,800.
6. There were no beginning or ending work in process inventories, nor any beginning or ending finished goods inventories.
7. Units produced, 10,000.
8. Units sold on account, 6,000 @ $35 per unit.
9. Units sold for cash, 3,200 @ $33 per unit.

Required:

1. Compute the materials quantity and price variances.
2. Compute the labor time and rate variances.
3. Compute the total manufacturing overhead variance.
4. Compute the manufacturing overhead volume and controllable variances.
5. Prepare journal entries to record the purchase of direct materials and the flow of all manufacturing costs through the Work in Process, Finished Goods, and Cost of Goods Sold accounts, including the closing of the standard cost variances. Also record the entry for sales. [LO2a,2b]

## ALTERNATE PROBLEMS

PROBLEM 25–1A *(Compute Materials Price and Quantity Variances)* (Alternate to Problem 25–1) The following data are available to the management of Cannon Company.

| | |
|---|---|
| Standard materials price | $4 per gallon |
| Standard quantity of materials per finished unit | 7 gallons |
| Normal production of finished units | 90,000 units |
| Actual price of materials purchased | $3.90 per gallon |
| Actual quantity of materials purchased and used | 640,000 gallons |
| Actual production of units | 88,500 units |

Required:

1. Compute the materials quantity and price variances. Indicate whether the variances are favorable (F) or unfavorable (U).
2. Discuss the possible causes for the standard cost variances. [LO2a]

PROBLEM 25–2A *(Compute Labor Time and Rate Variances)* (Alternate to Problem 25–2) The L.V.V. Corn Company produces a single product and has developed the following direct labor standards.

| | |
|---|---|
| Standard direct labor hours per unit of output | $3\frac{2}{3}$ hrs. |
| Standard direct labor rate per hour | $6.00 |

During the month of June the company produced 3,300 units of product using 9,100 direct labor hours at an average direct labor rate of $5.93 per hour.

Required:

1. Compute the direct labor time and rate variances for the month. Indicate whether the variances are favorable (F) or unfavorable (U).
2. Discuss who would usually be held responsible for these standard cost variances and how they might be controlled. [LO2a]

PROBLEM 25–3A *(Calculate Amounts and Record Journal Entries for Materials and Labor Variances)* (Alternate to Problem 25–4) Information pertaining to Departments X and Y of Boro Company, as well as information for the total operations, is listed below.

1. The company produced 30,000 units of output during the period.
2. It takes Department X three units of direct materials to produce one unit of output. Department Y needs four units of direct materials to produce one unit of output.
3. It takes Department X one-quarter hour to produce one unit of output. It takes Department Y one-half hour to produce one unit of output.
4. Each department had the following data for the period.

| | DEPARTMENT X | DEPARTMENT Y |
|---|---|---|
| Actual number of units of materials purchased and used | 91,000 | 118,800 |
| Actual unit price of materials | $6.25 | $9.20 |
| Standard unit price of materials | $6.50 | $9.50 |
| Actual number of direct labor hours worked | 9,000 | 14,000 |
| Standard labor rate per hour | $7.00 | $8.00 |
| Actual labor rate per hour | $6.70 | $7.90 |

Required:

1. Compute the materials price and quantity variances for each department. Indicate whether the variances are favorable or unfavorable.
2. Compute the labor time and rate variances for each department. Indicate whether the variances are favorable or unfavorable.
3. Prepare journal entries to record the following:
   a. Purchase of direct materials for Department X
   b. Purchase of direct materials for Department Y
   c. Issuance of direct materials to production from Department X
   d. Issuance of direct materials to production from Department Y
   e. Direct labor payroll for Department X
   f. Direct labor payroll for Department Y [LO2a,2b]

PROBLEM 25–4A *(Compute Materials, Labor, and Overhead Variances)* (Alternate to Problem 25–6) The following information was developed for Combs Company.

Standard Costs per Finished Unit:

Direct Materials, 3 units @ $2 per unit

Direct labor, 1 hour @ $6 per hour

Manufacturing overhead, $4 ($2 variable and $2 fixed) applied on the basis of direct labor hours (normal activity level is 5,000 direct labor hours)

Actual input, output, and cost figures for the period:

Direct materials purchased and used during the period, 9,200 units @ $2.03 per unit

Direct labor hours worked, 3,600

Direct labor costs, $21,960

Actual manufacturing overhead costs incurred, $22,800, of which $10,000 represents fixed overhead costs

Number of units produced, 3,200

Required:

1. Compute the materials quantity and price variances. Indicate whether the variances are favorable or unfavorable.
2. Compute the direct labor time and rate variances. Indicate whether the variances are favorable or unfavorable.
3. Compute the manufacturing overhead volume and controllable variances. Indicate whether the variances are favorable or unfavorable. [LO2a]

PROBLEM 25–5A *(Compute Materials, Labor, and Overhead Variances, Prepare Journal Entries, and Prepare Income Statement)* (Alternate to Problem 25–7) Standard cost data per finished unit for Saxon Company's standard cost system appear below.

| ELEMENTS OF COST | STANDARDS |
|---|---|
| Direct materials | 2 lbs. @ $4 per lb. |
| Direct labor | 1 hr @ $6 per hr. |
| Manufacturing overhead | $5 per hr. |

Manufacturing overhead rates are based on a flexible budget. Normal capacity is 7,000 direct labor hours. The total budgeted manufacturing overhead for 7,000 direct labor hours divided into its variable and fixed components is as follows.

| | TOTAL | PER LABOR HOUR |
|---|---|---|
| Variable manufacturing overhead | $21,000 | $3.00 |
| Fixed manufacturing overhead | 14,000 | 2.00 |
| Total | $35,000 | $5.00 |

Actual production and cost data for May are as follows.

1. There was no beginning or ending work in process inventory, nor any beginning or ending finished goods inventory.
2. During May, 9,000 units were completed.
3. During May, 16,000 pounds of direct materials costing $65,600 were purchased on account and used.
4. Direct labor costs of $52,030 were paid in cash during the month.
5. The number of direct labor hours worked during the month was 8,600.
6. Total overhead costs were $47,000, of which $14,000 represents fixed overhead.

Required:

Part I

a. Compute the materials quantity and price variances.

b. Compute the labor time and rate variances.

c. Compute the total manufacturing overhead variance.

d. Compute the manufacturing overhead volume and controllable variances.

Part II

Prepare journal entries to record the purchase of materials and the flow of all manufacturing costs through the Work in Process account to the Finished Goods account, including the closing of the variance accounts. (Use the journal entries in the chapter as models. Do not record the entries for sales.)

Part III

Prepare an income statement in which the cost of goods sold is reported at a standard cost and all variance accounts and amounts are disclosed. Additional information follows:

a. During the month all finished units were sold on account for $330,000.

b. Selling expenses incurred were $54,860.

c. General and administrative expenses incurred were $21,940. [LO1f,2a,2b]

# 26 Responsibility Accounting and Decentralization Concepts

### *Learning Objectives*

After you complete this chapter you will be able to

1. Answer the following questions:
   a. What is the rationale for decentralization, and what is the relationship between decentralization and responsibility accounting?
   b. What are company segments, and how can segment data be used by management?
   c. What is a responsibility center, and what are the distinctions among the three types of responsibility centers?
   d. What is transfer pricing? What are the reasons why companies have transfer pricing? What are the two basic methods of determining transfer prices?
2. Perform the following accounting functions:
   a. Prepare income statements for company segments.
   b. Compute the rate of return.
   c. Compute the residual income.
   d. Compute the profit margin on sales and the asset turnover.

Any business enterprise that engages in complex operations, sells a variety of products, and operates in several territories will find it necessary to build some form of decentralization into its organizational structure. **Decentralization** is an organizational arrangement in which personnel in company **segments**—product lines, divisions, territories, or other organizational units—are given some form of decision-making autonomy in operating these segments. This autonomy could range from complete authority to set prices or decide production quotas to some type of tightly supervised authority to make certain decisions. For example, product line managers might be allowed to use their own discretion in replacing assets, or centralized policies of asset purchases might be employed.

## THE RATIONALE FOR DECENTRALIZATION

***1a. Decentralization may be desirable or necessary for a number of reasons***

Why may a company find it desirable or perhaps necessary to use decentralization concepts?

First of all, company operations may be so widely spread out and diversified that centralized decision making would create an *inefficient* organizational structure. In this case, many key decisions should be made by managers closer to the problems. For instance, territorial managers may have better information than the central office on the best types of products to sell in their area.

Decentralization *relieves* top management of daily operating problems, thereby allowing them time to direct their attention to broader company issues, such as long-range planning.

Decentralization provides *training* in decision making for segment managers, so that they can absorb more responsibility as they advance within the organizational structure.

Decentralization can promote more *efficient performance* and innovative ideas from segment managers because of the incentive that freedom of action provides them.

Decentralization provides a basis for *appraising* the performance of many company personnel. If top management entrusts product line managers or department heads with assets and gives them wide latitude on operating policies, top management can also hold them accountable for certain standards of performance within their segments.

## DECENTRALIZATION AND RESPONSIBILITY ACCOUNTING

The combining of decentralized responsibility with accountability for results is the basis of responsibility accounting. **Responsibility accounting** is a reporting system that subdivides the organizational structure of a company into various responsibility centers. A **responsibility center** is a segment that is assigned particular tasks and provided with resources to carry out these tasks. These centers are established wherever top management believes it is important to accumulate and measure costs, revenues, or profits.

***1a. Responsibility accounting requires responsibility center autonomy***

Because the manager of each responsibility center is held accountable for results and is evaluated accordingly, the center must be granted some degree of autonomy. When centers operate with a high degree of autonomy, the company is said to be decentralized. Managers at all levels have the authority to make operating decisions in their areas of responsibility. In contrast, a centralized organization is one in which segment managers have little decision-making authority. Decisions for all levels of operations are made by top management.

Even when decentralized, however, it is unlikely that companies will allow their segments to operate, in all respects, as separate organizations. Companies have goals (such as earning a satisfactory return on investments), and they will use decentralization policies designed to encourage goal consistency. As used in this context, **goal consistency** refers to actions and policies by segment managers that accomplish both their goals and those of the company as a whole. A sound system of decentralization should result in a greater degree of goal consistency.

In the following section we will describe how segment data are used by management. In the remainder of this chapter we will discuss two areas where various forms of decentralization are practiced and where inevitable goal consistency problems arise: *rates of return* and *transfer pricing.*

## MANAGEMENT USES OF SEGMENT ANALYSIS

*1b. Segments are organizational elements of a company*

A company's financial health depends on its management's ability to make intelligent decisions. Many of these decisions relate to financial matters or policies of the entire company, such as which lines of business to pursue or how to select the top officers. Others, however, being more detailed in nature, relate to different segments of the company. In fact, some segment decisions might be among the most important made by the firm, such as the opening or closing of a key product line.

### Types of Segments

Depending on its size and complexity, a company could have several combinations of segments.

If the products pass through several *production stages,* each stage would be classified as a segment, such as a *department.* In previous chapters we have used as examples the cutting, assembling, and finishing departments of a furniture manufacturer. Many of the decisions applicable to these types of segments relate to cost control and the use of budgets and standards.

The firm might sell more than one *product.* In such a case, the organizational arrangements would probably include a separate segment for each product and a separate product manager as well.

The firm might sell its product(s) in more than one *area* of the town, state, or country. Markets of this type would call for segmentation of the firm into *territories* or *divisions* (or perhaps other names). Several different types of products could be sold within each territory or division.

### Types of Decisions Using Segment Data

*1b. Segment analysis can be useful for a wide variety of management decisions*

Company segments are normally operated by department heads, product line supervisors, territorial managers, and so on. These individuals make, participate in, or are affected by a wide variety of decisions. For example:

The price of the products

The segments that will be opened, continued in operation, or closed

The commitment of resources to the various segments

The rewards or lack of rewards based on segment financial results

All the aforementioned decisions can be made with the help of quantitative tools provided by segment analysis and illustrated in the next section.

## SEGMENT REPORTING FORMATS

Segment income statements can be formulated and reported in at least two ways. One method uses the format for annual reporting to stockholders and other parties "external" to management. The other method follows a style more useful for management decision making. We will discuss each type in turn and explain why the latter style provides better tools for segment analysis.

### Cost of Goods Sold and Operating Expense Format

Assume the existence of four products—A, B, C, and D. Exhibit 26–1 uses a product line income statement arranged according to the Cost of Goods Sold and Operating Expense format (illustrated in Chapter 23 with only one product). All the amounts are assumed.

EXHIBIT 26–1

Income Statement by Product Line
Cost of Goods Sold and Operating Expense Format

| | TOTAL | A | B | C | D |
|---|---|---|---|---|---|
| Selling Prices | $ — | $ 40 | $ 18 | $ 42 | $ 14 |
| Units Sold | 16,189 | 3,175 | 1,720 | 6,894 | 4,400 |
| Sales | $509,108 | $127,000 | $ 30,960 | $289,548 | $ 61,600 |
| Cost of Goods Sold | 288,000 | 65,000 | 23,000 | 150,000 | 50,000 |
| Gross Profit | $221,108 | $ 62,000 | $ 7,960 | $139,548 | $ 11,600 |
| Operating Expenses | 188,000 | 34,646 | 18,391 | 85,046 | 49,917 |
| Net Income | $ 33,108 | $ 27,354 | $(10,431) | $ 54,502 | $(38,317) |

In general, Exhibit 26–1 provides little if any information helpful in making the types of segment decisions referred to earlier. Specifically, the limited usefulness of these data is caused by the fact that they are arranged improperly for the purpose of providing management with the tools needed to aid in important segment decisions. The costs have not been divided into the categories that would enable management to tell

How such costs react to *volume* changes

Whether the costs are *direct* or *indirect* to the individual product lines

In addition, misleading ideas of profitability can often result from a review of this type of segment income statement. As we will show next, it is not necessarily true that the discontinuance of Products B and D will result in improved total net income of $10,431 and $38,317, respectively.

### Contribution Margin and Segment Margin Format

*1b,2a. The contribution margin/segment margin format can provide income statement information useful to managers*

Within the format of the segment income statement, cost data can be arranged in two ways to provide important information to managers:

First, cost data can be arranged according to the *behavioral patterns* of the costs (as discussed in Chapter 23). Data of this sort are vital for management to assess the profit impact of decisions designed to change the company's volume of production and/or sales.

Second, cost data can be arranged according to whether the costs are *direct* or *indirect* to the segment in question (product line, territory, etc.). **Direct costs** (costs that can be traced directly to the segment) will react in one way to certain decisions (such as closing a product line). **Indirect costs** (costs that cannot be traced directly to the segment and must be allocated to it) will react in another way.

In formulating a segment income statement, we will assume that variable costs can be directly traced to each product. We will also assume that some fixed costs can be directly traced to products and are referred to as direct traceable costs. Other fixed costs are assumed to be common or joint to the entire company and are referred to as indirect common costs. Medium or large firms would probably have costs of both types.

The income statement in Exhibit 26–2 follows the patterns described in the two preceding paragraphs. It also shows the selling prices, variable costs per unit, and number of units sold. Like Exhibit 26–1, the amounts in Exhibit 26–2 are assumed.

*EXHIBIT 26–2*

Income Statement by Product Line
Contribution Margin and Segment Margin Format

| | TOTAL | A | B | C | D |
|---|---|---|---|---|---|
| Selling Prices | $ — | $ 40 | $ 18 | $ 42 | $ 14 |
| Variable Costs | $ — | $ 16 | $ 12 | $ 20 | $ 15 |
| Units Sold | 16,189 | 3,175 | 1,720 | 6,894 | 4,400 |
| Sales | $509,108 | $127,000 | $ 30,960 | $289,548 | $ 61,600 |
| Less: Variable Costs | 275,320 | 50,800 | 20,640 | 137,880 | 66,000 |
| Contribution Margin (in dollars) | $233,788 | $ 76,200 | $ 10,320 | $151,668 | $ (4,400) |
| Contribution Margin (as a percentage of sales)* | — | 60% | 33% | 52% | — |
| Less: Direct Traceable Costs | 65,000 | 15,000 | 12,500 | 20,000 | 17,500 |
| Segment Margin | $168,788 | $ 61,200 | $ (2,180) | $131,668 | $(21,900) |
| Less: Indirect Common Costs† | 135,680 | 33,846 | 8,251 | 77,166 | 16,417 |
| Net Income | $ 33,108 | $ 27,354 | $(10,431) | $ 54,502 | $(38,317) |

* Rounded to nearest whole percentage.
† Allocated by relative sales dollar for ease of analysis. For example, Product A is allocated $33,846 [$135,680 ($127,000 ÷ $509,108)].

By examining Exhibit 26–2, we can see that Product B has earned a *$10,320* contribution margin that has helped to cover the firm's $65,000 direct costs and $135,680 indirect costs. If Product B were discontinued and the total indirect common costs of the company remained the same, the increased net income would amount to only $2,180 (Product B's negative segment margin) because these indirect common costs would be reallocated to the other products. Exhibit 26–3 demonstrates this point. We are assuming that the reallocation of the $135,680 of indirect common costs is made on the basis of the remaining sales

*EXHIBIT 26–3*

Discontinuance of Product B

| | TOTAL | A | C | D |
|---|---|---|---|---|
| Sales | $478,148 | $127,000 | $289,548 | $ 61,600 |
| Variable Costs | 254,680 | 50,800 | 137,880 | 66,000 |
| Contribution Margin | $223,468 | $ 76,200 | $151,668 | $ (4,400) |
| Direct Costs | 52,500 | 15,000 | 20,000 | 17,500 |
| Segment Margin | $170,968 | $ 61,200 | $131,668 | $(21,900) |
| Indirect Costs | 135,680 | 36,038 | 82,163 | 17,479 |
| Net Income | $ 35,288 | $ 25,162 | $ 49,505 | $(39,379) |

of Products A, C, and D. For example, Product A is allocated $36,038 [$135,680($127,000 ÷ $478,148)].

The change in net income ($33,108 to $35,288) from dropping Product B is the amount of Product B's negative segment margin ($2,180). Care must be taken to avoid drawing incorrect inferences from the net income figures of a segment income statement.

Finally, we must understand that the change in a company's total net income as the result of a dropped product can be determined only after careful analysis of such factors as the following:

The effect of a dropped product on other products' sales.

The shifting of costs from one product to another. For example, some or all of Product B's direct traceable costs might be transferred to other lines (e.g., a position change for a supervisor).

The amount of indirect common costs, if any, that will be saved.

However, a contribution margin and segment margin income statement does provide managers with useful information about the effect of a dropped product on net income.

## DIFFERENT SEGMENT INCOME STATEMENT DATA FOR DIFFERENT DECISIONS

*1b. Reporting of contribution margin amounts helps managers allocate advertising or research funds*

Let us continue our discussion of the contribution margin and segment margin income statement by considering the different sets of figures that will provide managers with the most satisfactory guidelines for a particular decision. For example, the *contribution margin* amounts provide managers with some information on how to allocate advertising or research funds to the various products. Since contribution margin represents the difference between sales and variable costs, it is a good indicator of net income changes that result from increases or decreases in volume when fixed costs remain the same.

An examination of Exhibit 26–2 shows that for this accounting period, the contribution margin as a percentage of sales was the following for each product:

Product A: 60% ($76,200/$127,000)
Product B: 33% ($10,320/$30,960)
Product C: 52% ($151,668/$289,548)

If these percentages were expected to remain the same in the next accounting period, a good case could be made for using resources that increase the volume of sales of Product A. Every additional dollar of sales revenue generated by Product A generates $.60 of contribution margin, and if fixed costs do not change, $.60 of net income.

*1b. Segment margin information helps managers in deciding whether to retain or close out a product line*

On the other hand, if management must decide whether to retain or close out a product line, the **segment margin** probably provides a more appropriate figure than either the contribution margin or the net income. The segment margin includes the direct traceable costs of that segment. Some examples are:

The depreciation on equipment used for only one product.

The salary of a product supervisor.

In many situations, these types of costs are more likely to be eliminated by dropping a product. Indirect common costs, such as executive salaries and certain types of company overhead, are less likely to be eliminated by dropping a product.

For example, assume that a small portion of a department store is used to sell a special style of shoes. The store hires a manager and purchases equipment solely for the purpose of maintaining this product line. After a year, top management assesses the profitability of this operation for the purpose of deciding on its retention.

The net income of the shoe department, from which allocated indirect common costs have already been deducted, would certainly be a misleading figure to use for this decision. Practically none of the total store's indirect common costs would be eliminated by closing the shoe department. However, the cost of the manager and the equipment would probably be eliminated, along with the department's sales and variable costs. In this case, top management should look to the segment margin as an indicator of the change in net income caused by dropping this shoe operation.

## ALLOCATION OF INDIRECT COMMON COSTS IN SEGMENT INCOME STATEMENTS

Some prefer to draw "double lines" under the segment margin amounts and not allocate the indirect common costs at all. By reproducing a portion of Exhibit 26–2, we can see the reporting results of this viewpoint:

| | TOTAL | A | B | C | D |
|---|---|---|---|---|---|
| Segment Margin | $168,788 | $61,200 | $(2,180) | $131,668 | $(21,900) |
| Indirect Common Costs | 135,680 | | | | |
| Net Income | $ 33,108 | | | | |

Others believe that by omitting allocated indirect common costs, product line managers might ignore such costs. Managers would be more "cost control conscious" if they knew that part of such costs would be allocated and charged to their product. However, if indirect common costs are allocated to each segment, the following techniques are commonly used:

> The relative number of square feet of occupied facilities could be used to allocate certain depreciation and rental costs.
>
> The number of employees could be used to allocate executive salaries and payroll costs.
>
> The volume of sales, in either units or dollars, could be used to allocate advertising and research costs.

All costs that can be identified as direct should be reported as such, thus minimizing the need to make allocations.

## RESPONSIBILITY CENTERS

If a company practices decentralization, it also has responsibility centers. A *responsibility center*, as we have seen, is an organizational unit within a company that is assigned particular tasks and provided with resources to carry out these tasks. Each center has an organizational structure and is headed by a superintendent, manager, division chief, or other supervisory person. The head of the center oversees the center's activities, is responsible for its performance, and is evaluated accordingly.

A responsibility center can be a department, a product line, a plant, a service center, a territory, or a division. There are three basic types of responsibility centers: *cost* centers, *profit* centers, and *investment* centers.

## Cost Centers

*1c. For cost centers, we accumulate and report only costs incurred. The manager controls and must account for these costs*

A **cost center** is an organizational unit whose structure and tasks are designed in such a manner that management considers it necessary only to accumulate and report costs incurred by the unit. In a cost center the manager has control over and is held accountable for the costs incurred by the unit. Cost centers do not generate revenues from the sale of products or services. Therefore the manager of a cost center is not responsible for earnings (profits) or investments.

Examples of cost centers include service departments such as maintenance, payroll, supply, billing, and purchasing. Such centers or units provide goods and services to other segments of the company and are not expected to produce revenues.

Because cost centers do not produce revenues and profits, their financial accountability must be determined in other ways. For example, the efficiency of a cost center might be judged in part on how closely its actual expenditures compare with budgeted figures.

## Profit Centers

*1c. For profit centers we accumulate revenues and costs and report profits and losses. The manager controls costs and revenues and is accountable for profits*

A **profit center** is an organizational unit whose structure and tasks are designed in such a manner that management considers it necessary to accumulate revenues and costs and to report profits or losses. In a profit center the manager has control over both costs and revenues and is held accountable for the profit earned by the unit.

In some cases, the profit center may generate revenues by selling goods and services to the public or to other companies. For example, the clothing department of a retail store sells its product to the general public. A steel manufacturing firm may sell its product to another manufacturing firm, such as an auto maker.

In other cases, management might "create" a profit center by internally pricing the goods and services provided by a responsibility center to other company segments. These sales are often referred to as intracompany, that is, sales made within the company. For example, a component part of a manufactured item such as those produced in the aerospace industry may be sold between divisions of the company. Also, the services rendered by a company's computer center may be sold to other divisions within the same company. This internal pricing procedure is called *transfer pricing* and will be discussed later in this chapter.

## Investment Centers

*1c. The manager of an investment center is responsible for revenues, costs, and the return earned on assets used*

An investment center is the most complete form of a responsibility center. An **investment center** is an organizational unit in which management is responsible not only for the revenues and costs but also for the return earned on the assets used by the unit.

A specific grocery store operated by a chain store organization often operates as an investment center. In an investment center the manager is accountable for revenues and costs and is evaluated on the basis of rate of return earned on its specified assets. In an investment center the manager generally operates the unit with a high degree of autonomy. Sometimes the responsibility unit is run like a separate smaller business rather than as a part of a larger unit.

## METHODS OF EVALUATING PERFORMANCE IN A RESPONSIBILITY CENTER

In a decentralized organization managers of responsibility centers have the freedom to make decisions concerning their segments. Responsibility accounting helps top management by defining a segment manager's area of responsibility and by evaluating how well the segment has performed.

A *cost center's* performance is evaluated, in part, by comparing its actual costs with its predetermined standard or budgeted costs.

A *profit center's* performance is evaluated, in part, by comparing contribution margin income statements with budgets to determine whether sales and cost objectives have been met.

An *investment center's* performance is evaluated, in part, by analyzing contribution margin income statements and the rate of return it is able to generate on its specified assets.

In the following section we will discuss rate of return as a means of evaluating the performance of an investment center.

## RATE OF RETURN

### A Basic Rate of Return Computation

*2b. Rate of return = net income ÷ average assets. A computation is illustrated in Exhibit 26–4*

One way to measure the performance of investment centers (which in the following illustrations are described as product lines) is to calculate their rates of return.

The **rate of return** (also called *return on investment*) is calculated by using the following equation:

$$\text{Rate of Return} = \frac{\text{Net Income}}{\text{Average Assets}}$$

To illustrate rates of return for company segments, we will use hypothetical data for Reese Company, which operates with three product lines. Exhibit 26–4 shows the appropriate financial data for each product line and for the company.

EXHIBIT 26–4

Rates of Return for the Company and for Each Product Line

| | | PRODUCT LINE | | |
|---|---|---|---|---|
| | COMPANY | A | B | C |
| Net Income (taken from the published financial statements) | $ 10,000 | $ 4,000 | $ 3,000 | $ 3,000 |
| ÷ Average Assets (taken from the published financial statements)* | $100,000 | $32,000 | $36,000 | $32,000 |
| = Rate of Return | 10.0% | 12.5% | 8.3% | 9.4% |

* *Average assets* are the total assets at the beginning of the accounting period plus the total assets at the end of the accounting period divided by 2.

If product line rates of return are compared among themselves, Product A is the most profitable. Comparing rates of return among product lines may be misleading, however, because each line may operate differently.

The rates of return for the present period could be compared with those of the prior period. For example, if Products A, B, and C showed rates of return in the previous period of 11.0%, 7.0%, and 8.0%, respectively, the performance appraisal for each product line would be positive. But a flaw may lie in this appraisal method if the rates of return for the last period were considered to be poor.

## Residual Income

To avoid some of the appraisal problems we have just discussed, an appraisal method called **residual income** could be used. Under this method, each product line's net income is compared with a minimum acceptable amount, computed by multiplying the product line's asset figure by some percentage. Any excess of net income over this "acceptable" amount is referred to as residual income and is considered a measure of superior performance. Conversely, any net income that is less than this "acceptable" amount is regarded as a measure of unacceptable performance.

*2c. Computation of residual income is illustrated in Exhibit 26–5*

To illustrate, assume that 10% is the minimum acceptable rate of return for each product line. Exhibit 26–5 shows the residual income for each product line.

*EXHIBIT 26–5*

Residual Income

| | PRODUCT LINE | | |
|---|---|---|---|
| | A | B | C |
| Average Assets | $32,000 | $36,000 | $32,000 |
| × Minimum Acceptable Rate of Return | 10% | 10% | 10% |
| = Minimum Acceptable Net Income | 3,200 | 3,600 | 3,200 |
| − Actual Net Income | 4,000 | 3,000 | 3,000 |
| = Residual Income | $ 800 | $ (600)* | $ (200)* |

* Parentheses indicate a negative residual income.

On the basis of the figures shown here, the performance of product line A would be considered superior, while that of product lines B and C would be considered inadequate.

## Subdividing the Rate of Return

*2d. Rate of return can be subdivided into profit margin on sales and asset turnover*

Sometimes the reason for a superior or inferior rate of return for a segment can be seen more clearly by subdividing the rate into two additional parts.

> The **profit margin on sales** is the net income divided by the net sales and is a measure of operating performance (the number of dollars of net income earned for every dollar of net sales).
>
> The **asset turnover** is the net sales divided by the average assets and is a measure of asset utilization (the number of times assets were converted into sales).

By multiplying the two factors together, we derive the rate of return, as shown below.

$$\text{Profit Margin on Sales} \times \text{Asset Turnover} = \text{Rate of Return}$$

$$\frac{\text{Net Income}}{\text{Net Sales}} \times \frac{\text{Net Sales}}{\text{Average Assets}} = \frac{\text{Net Income}}{\text{Average Assets}}$$

To illustrate with numbers, assume the following data for an investment center.

| | |
|---|---:|
| Net sales | $500,000 |
| Net income | 50,000 |
| Average assets | 250,000 |

*2b. Computation of rate of return for an investment center is illustrated here*

The rate of return generated by the investment center is 20%, calculated as follows:

$$\frac{\text{Net Income}}{\text{Net Sales}} \times \frac{\text{Net Sales}}{\text{Average Assets}} = \text{Rate of Return}$$

$$\frac{\$50{,}000}{\$500{,}000} \times \frac{\$500{,}000}{\$250{,}000} = 20\%$$

$$10\% \times 2 = 20\%$$

Thus we can see that if the rate of return is too low for an investment center, it can be improved in two ways:

By increasing the profit margin on sales. This would require an *increase* in sales or a *decrease* in expenses.

By increasing the asset turnover. This would require an *increase* in sales or a *decrease* in the amount of assets utilized in generating the sales.

# TRANSFER PRICING

## The Need for Transfer Pricing

Decentralization can also be practiced by using a concept called transfer pricing. **Transfer pricing** is the setting of an "internal" price that one responsibility center charges another for goods sold to it or services rendered to it.

There are many examples of transfer pricing in the business world. One of them is the price charged by a company's responsibility center for a manufactured component part sold to another responsibility center of the same company (batteries for automobiles are an example).

The responsibility center that makes and sells this component part is sometimes called the **selling unit.**

The responsibility center that buys this component part is sometimes called the **buying unit.**

*1d. Transfer pricing is used for several reasons*

Company managers use transfer pricing for the following reasons:

To provide a better basis for appraising the performance of segment managers. A transfer price creates revenue for the selling unit and creates expenses for the buying unit.

To provide segment managers with further incentives to perform more efficiently because of the freedom of action that transfer pricing grants them. In many cases, selling and buying units are allowed to negotiate a transfer price between them.

To institute policies designed to encourage goal consistency between the segment managers and the company. A good transfer pricing policy can encourage segment managers to maximize the net income of their own segments without decreasing the overall net income of the company.

## Transfer Pricing Methods

*1d. The cost method of transfer pricing is easy to apply, but the market method has the advantage of simulating the competitive environment*

THE COST METHOD OF TRANSFER PRICING Management may decide to calculate transfer prices by adding a dollar or percentage markup to the selling unit's cost of the manufactured item or the cost of the service. The **cost method of transfer pricing** is easy to apply, but from a motivational standpoint it has one distinct disadvantage. Because the full cost will be recovered by the selling unit through the transfer price, there is little incentive for the selling unit to be cost-efficient.

The use of a budgeted or standard cost for the transfer price may overcome this motivational problem. Under the budgeted or standard cost method, the transfer price would consist of the budgeted or standard cost plus a markup, regardless of the amount of the selling unit's actual cost.

THE MARKET METHOD OF TRANSFER PRICING If management wished to create profit centers that operated in a manner similar to a separate company functioning in a competitive environment, it could use the **market method of transfer pricing.** Generally, this type of transfer price is based on one of the following criteria:

If the product or service furnished by the selling unit is also sold outside the company, the transfer price is the amount charged to customers.

The selling units and buying units within the company could negotiate a market price.

There are many interesting and complex problems associated with the formulation and administration of transfer prices. However, we will leave these complexities to a more-advanced course.

## HIGHLIGHT PROBLEM

The management of Rate Company was not satisfied with the rate of return on investment in recent years. To obtain a better understanding of why the return was low, the controller was asked to analyze it. The controller was told to estimate the return for the current year if certain variables changed.

The pertinent data for the past year are as follows:

| | |
|---|---|
| Net Sales | $200,000 |
| Average Assets | 100,000 |
| Net Income | 10,000 |

Required:

1. For the past year, calculate the (a) profit margin on sales, (b) asset turnover, and (c) rate of return.
2. Calculate the rate of return for the current year if (a) net income is 10% higher than last year's and (b) average assets are 5% lower than last year's.

## GLOSSARY OF KEY TERMS

**Asset turnover.** Net sales divided by average assets.

**Buying unit.** A responsibility center that buys goods or services from another responsibility center and pays a transfer price for the goods or services.

**Cost center.** An organizational unit whose structure and tasks are designed in such a manner that management considers it necessary only to accumulate and report costs incurred by the unit.

**Cost method of transfer pricing.** The setting of a transfer price by adding a dollar or percentage markup to the cost of the selling unit's goods or services.

**Decentralization.** An organizational arrangement in which personnel in product lines, divisions, territories, or other company segments are given some form of decision-making autonomy in operating these segments.

**Direct costs.** Costs that can be traced directly to the segment in question.

**Goal consistency.** Actions and policies by segment managers that accomplish both their goals and those of the company as a whole.

**Indirect costs.** Costs that cannot be traced directly to the segment in question and must be allocated to the segment.

**Investment center.** An organizational unit in which management is responsible not only for revenues and costs but also for the return earned on the assets used by the unit.

**Market method of transfer pricing.** A transfer price based on some type of market-price determination. The market price could be the price that the company's customers pay for similar goods or services, or the price could be negotiated between the buying and selling units.

**Profit center.** An organizational unit whose structure and tasks are designed in such a manner that management considers it necessary to accumulate revenues and costs and to report profits or losses.

**Profit margin on sales.** Net income divided by net sales.

**Rate of return.** Net income divided by average assets. Also called *return on investment.*

**Residual income.** The difference between net income and a minimum acceptable figure; this figure is computed by multiplying the segment's average assets by some percentage.

**Responsibility accounting.** A reporting system that subdivides the organizational structure of a company into various responsibility centers.

**Responsibility center.** An organizational unit or segment within a company that is assigned particular tasks and provided with resources to carry out these tasks.

**Segment margin.** The difference between the contribution margin and direct traceable costs.

**Segments.** Organizational elements of a company such as a department, product line, territory, or division.

**Selling unit.** A responsibility center that sells goods or renders services to another responsibility center and charges a transfer price for the goods or services.

**Transfer pricing.** The setting of an "internal" price that one responsibility center charges another for goods sold to it or services rendered to it.

## REVIEW QUESTIONS

1. Give five reasons why companies find it desirable or necessary to use decentralization concepts. [LO1a]
2. What is the basis of responsibility accounting? [LO1a]
3. Describe three types of segments that a company might have. [LO1b]
4. Name four types of decisions that heads of company segments might make, participate in, or be affected by. [LO1b]
5. Differentiate between the formats of the two following types of segment income statements: (a) the cost of goods sold and operating expense format and (b) the contribution margin and segment margin format. [LO1b,2a]
6. What information does the contribution margin for each company segment provide to managers? [LO1b,2a]
7. What information does the segment margin for each company segment provide to managers? [LO1b,2a]

8. Why do some hold that indirect common costs should be allocated to segments when segment income statements are prepared? [LO1b,2a]
9. Name three commonly used techniques for allocating indirect common costs to segments when segment income statements are prepared. [LO1b,2a]
10. What is a responsibility center? [LO1c]
11. Describe the differences among the organizational structures and responsibilities of (a) cost centers, (b) profit centers, and (c) investment centers. [LO1c]
12. How is the performance of a cost center evaluated? A profit center? An investment center? [LO1c]
13. What is the equation for the rate-of-return computation? [LO2b]
14. Explain how residual income is computed. [LO2c]
15. Explain how to calculate (a) profit margin on sales and (b) asset turnover. [LO2d]
16. Differentiate between the responsibility center called the selling unit and the responsibility center called the buying unit. [LO1d]
17. Give three reasons why company managers would use transfer pricing. [LO1d]
18. Differentiate between the cost basis and the market basis of transfer pricing. [LO1d]
19. Name two types of costs that could be used when the cost basis of transfer pricing is used. [LO1d]

## *ANALYTICAL QUESTIONS*

20. Why would you encourage some degree of decentralization but would oppose total decentralization (assuming it is possible to achieve total decentralization). [LO1a]
21. "There is too much emphasis placed on contribution and segment margin analysis. In the long run, all segments must earn a net income and cover indirect costs to be considered profitable." Comment on this statement. [LO1b,2a]
22. "If the techniques for allocating common costs to segments are arbitrary, why allocate them at all?" Respond to this question. [LO1b,2a]
23. Explain why the discontinuance of a segment with a net loss would not necessarily increase the firm's net income or decrease the firm's net loss. [LO1b,2a]
24. Indicate why, in your opinion, each of the following segments should or should not be treated as an investment center:
    a. The product line of a manufacturing firm
    b. The supply room of a bookstore
    c. The cafeteria of a department store
    d. The computer center of a manufacturing firm [LO1c]
25. "Rates of return are more meaningful if they are divided into their component parts." Comment on this statement. [LO2d]
26. "Transfer pricing is somewhat 'artificial' because the prices are only internal to the company." Comment on this statement. [LO1d]

## *IMPACT ANALYSIS QUESTIONS*

*For each error described, indicate whether it would overstate [O], understate [U], or not affect [N] the specified key figures.*

27. Company A has three product lines—Alpha, Beta, and Gamma. Segment income statements are made by using the contribution margin and segment margin format. In assigning direct costs to each product line, some sales commissions were incorrectly assigned to Alpha instead of Beta.

_______ Alpha Net Income _______ Beta Net Income
_______ Gamma Net Income _______ Total Net Income [LO2a]

28. Company B computes profit margin on sales, asset turnover, and rate of return. The net income was incorrectly computed at $10,000 instead of $8,000; all the other figures were correct.

_______ Profit Margin on Sales
_______ Asset Turnover
_______ Rate of Return [LO2b,2d]

29. Company C computes profit margin on sales, asset turnover, and rate of return. The average assets were incorrectly computed at $100,000 instead of $90,000; all the other figures were correct.

_______ Profit Margin on Sales
_______ Asset Turnover
_______ Rate of Return [LO2b,2d]

30. Company D computes profit margin on sales, asset turnover, and rate of return. The sales were incorrectly computed at $50,000 instead of $55,000; all the other figures were correct.

_______ Profit Margin on Sales
_______ Asset Turnover
_______ Rate of Return [LO2b,2d]

31. Company E has three product lines—Kappa, Lambda, and Omega. Segment income statements are made using the contribution margin and segment margin format. In allocating indirect costs to each product line, the company incorrectly classified a cost as indirect and allocated it according to sales. The sales of Kappa, Lambda, and Omega were $10,000, $20,000, and $30,000, respectively. The cost should have been classified as direct, and one-third of the cost should have been assigned to each product line.

_______ Kappa Net Income _______ Lambda Net Income
_______ Omega Net Income _______ Total Net Income [LO2a]

## EXERCISES

EXERCISE 26–1 *(Allocate Indirect Common Costs)* Slater Company provided the following data arranged by product lines A, B, and C, respectively.

| | | PRODUCTS | | |
|---|---|---|---|---|
| | OVERALL COMPANY | A | B | C |
| Sales Price | $ — | $ 20 | $ 25 | $ 30 |
| Units Sold | 8,800 | 5,000 | 2,000 | 1,800 |
| Segment Margin | $4,000 | $2,000 | $1,500 | $ 500 |
| Indirect Common Costs | $3,000 | ? | ? | ? |

1. The manager of product line A prefers to allocate indirect common costs according to the relative sales prices of the products.
2. The manager of product line B prefers to allocate indirect common costs according to the relative sales dollar of the products.
3. The manager of product line C prefers to allocate indirect common costs according to the relative number of units of each product sold.

Required:

1. Allocate the indirect common costs according to the methods suggested by each product line manager. Determine the net income under each method.
2. Which method do you believe is preferable? Why? [LO1b,2a]

EXERCISE 26–2 *(Supply Missing Data for Segments)* Compute the missing data in the following tabulations.

| | CASE A | CASE B | CASE C |
|---|---|---|---|
| Sales Price | $ 10 | $ — | $ 5 |
| Units Sold | — | 200 | — |
| Sales | 2,000 | 4,000 | 5,000 |
| Variable Costs | — | 1,500 | — |
| Contribution Margin ($) | — | 2,500 | — |
| Contribution Margin (percentage of sales) | 40% | — | 20% |
| Direct Traceable Costs | 500 | — | — |
| Segment Margin | — | — | 300 |
| Indirect Common Costs | 100 | 1,000 | — |
| Net Income | — | 1,000 | 100 |

[LO2a]

EXERCISE 26–3 *(Compute Segment Amounts)* The management of Formost Company has asked you to help them analyze the performance of one of their product lines. The following data, representing a given period of time and pertaining to the product line, were given to you.

| | |
|---|---|
| Unit Sales Price | $ 100 |
| Unit Variable Costs | 60 |
| Direct Traceable Costs | 900,000 |
| Allocated Indirect Common Costs | 420,000 |

The product line's average assets were $2,900,000; 42,000 units of product were sold during the period.

Required:
Determine the contribution margin, segment margin, net income, and residual income for the product line assuming the company regards a 12% return as the minimum acceptable rate for the line. Comment on whether the performance of the product line is acceptable or unacceptable. [LO2a,2c]

EXERCISE 26–4 *(Compare Rates of Return)* The following amounts appear on the books of Divisions A, B, and C.

| | A | B | C |
|---|---|---|---|
| Average Assets | $20,000 | $25,000 | $30,000 |
| Sales | 50,000 | 60,000 | 70,000 |
| Expenses | 48,000 | 57,000 | 66,100 |
| Net Income | 2,000 | 3,000 | 3,900 |

Someone says to you: "The major purpose of the above schedule is to see who made the most money. It's obvious that Division C is the best. They made $3,900. It's similar to comparing three different companies."

Required:
1. Divide the rates of return for each division into their two component parts.
2. Comment on the statement that Division C is best. [LO2b,2d]

EXERCISE 26–5 *(Supply Missing Rate-of-Return Data)* Provide the missing data in the following tabulation.

| | DIVISION | | |
|---|---|---|---|
| | X | Y | Z |
| Sales | $300,000 | $225,000 | $ — |
| Net Income | $ 24,000 | $ 22,500 | $ — |
| Average Assets | $ — | $ 90,000 | $50,000 |
| Profit Margin on Sales | — | — | 6% |
| Asset Turnover | — | — | 3 |
| Rate of Return | 10% | — | — |

[LO2b,2d]

## PROBLEMS

PROBLEM 26–1 *(Prepare an Income Statement That Shows Contribution Margin, Segment Margin, and Net Income)* Using the following segment income statement and additional information, prepare a statement that shows the contribution margin, segment margin, and net income for each product line.

| | PRODUCT TOTAL | A | B | C |
|---|---|---|---|---|
| Selling Prices | $ — | $12.00 | $14.00 | $ 6.80 |
| Units Sold | 2,000 | 400 | 600 | 1,000 |
| Sales | $20,000 | $4,800 | $8,400 | $6,800 |
| Cost of Goods Sold | 14,000 | 3,200 | 4,800 | 6,000 |
| Gross Profit | $ 6,000 | $1,600 | $3,600 | $ 800 |
| Operating Expenses (Costs) | 4,000 | 800 | 2,200 | 1,000 |
| Net Income | $ 2,000 | $ 800 | $1,400 | $ (200) |

Additional Information:

1. Of the $14,000 cost of goods sold, $8,000 is variable.
2. Of the $4,000 operating expenses (costs), $3,000 is fixed.
3. Of the $9,000 fixed costs (combination of fixed cost of goods sold and fixed operating expenses), $4,200 is direct and traceable to the product lines in the following percentages:
   a. Forty percent of the $4,200 belongs to product A.
   b. Forty percent of the $4,200 belongs to Product B.
   c. Twenty percent of the $4,200 belongs to Product C.
4. The rest of the fixed costs are allocated according to the relative sales dollar.
5. Assume that the variable costs are traceable and that the variable cost ratios are the same for each product line as they are in total (for example, if the total variable costs are 45% of total sales, then each product's variable costs are 45% of each product's sales).

[LO2a]

PROBLEM 26–2 *(Compute Contribution Margin and Net Income for Two Segments)* Worldwide Company has two identifiable segments: Atlas and Baldwin. Shown below are data applicable to these segments.

| | ATLAS SEGMENT | BALDWIN SEGMENT |
|---|---|---|
| Sales | $300,000 | $440,000 |
| Variable Costs | $6 per unit | $4 per unit |
| Direct Traceable Costs | 60,000 | 135,000 |
| Allocated Common Costs | 36,500 | 53,500 |

Atlas sells its product for $10 per unit, and Baldwin sells its product for $8 per unit.

Required:

1. Compute the contribution margin in dollars and as a percentage of sales for each segment.
2. Compute the net income for each segment.
3. Compute the overall net income for the company. Express the company's overall income as a percentage of sales.
4. Evaluate the two segments using (a) contribution margin dollars and percentages and (b) net income figures as a percentage of sales.
5. Are the evaluations of the two segments in Requirement 4 different? If so, why? If not, why not? [LO2a]

PROBLEM 26–3 *(Prepare Segment Income Statements After Dropping a Product Line)* Assume the following income statements for three divisions.

| | TOTAL | PRODUCT A | PRODUCT B | PRODUCT C |
|---|---|---|---|---|
| Sales | $10,000 | $5,000 | $3,000 | $2,000 |
| Variable Costs | 6,000 | 3,500 | 1,600 | 900 |
| Contribution Margin | $ 4,000 | $1,500 | $1,400 | $1,100 |
| Direct Traceable Costs | 2,500 | 1,000 | 500 | 1,000 |
| Segment Margin | $ 1,500 | $ 500 | $ 900 | $ 100 |
| Indirect Common Costs | 1,000 | 500 | 300 | 200 |
| Net Income | $ 500 | — | $ 600 | $ (100) |

Required:

1. Restructure the income statement for each division assuming the following changes. Consider each change separately.
   a. Product line A is dropped. There is no effect on the sales or variable costs of the other product lines. The direct traceable costs of A are eliminated, but there is no change in the indirect common costs.
   b. Product line C is dropped. There is no effect on the sales or variable costs of the other product lines. The direct traceable costs of product line C are eliminated, but there is no change in the indirect common costs.
   c. Indirect common costs are reduced by 20%, and the remainder of the indirect common costs are allocated in the same way.
2. Comment on why the changes in Requirements 1a, 1b, and 1c occurred. [LO2a]

PROBLEM 26–4 *(Determine the Fairness of Allocation Methods)* Company X has three divisions—A, B, and C. Each division sells a different product, generates its own outside sales, and has its own production and sales personnel. However, the divisions have certain indirect common costs. Company X has traditionally shown its income statement in the following manner.

| | | DIVISION | | |
|---|---|---|---|---|
| | TOTAL | A | B | C |
| Sales | $100,000 | $50,000 | $30,000 | $20,000 |
| Cost of Sales: | | | | |
| Variable Manufacturing Costs | 40,000 | 20,000 | 12,000 | 8,000 |
| Fixed Manufacturing Costs | 30,000 | 15,000 * | 9,000 * | 6,000 * |
| | 70,000 | 35,000 | 21,000 | 14,000 |
| Gross Profit | $ 30,000 | $15,000 | $ 9,000 | $ 6,000 |
| Operating Expenses: | | | | |
| Sales Salaries (B's) | $ 8,000 | $ 4,000 | $ 2,400 | $ 1,600 |
| Sales Commissions (A's and C's)** | 9,000 | 4,500 | 2,700 | 1,800 |
| Depreciation (Common) | 10,000 | 5,000 | 3,000 | 2,000 |
| Executive Salaries (Common) | 15,000 | 7,500 | 4,500 | 3,000 |
| Other (separate and fixed for A) | 3,000 | 1,500 | 900 | 600 |
| | $ 45,000 | $22,500 | $13,500 | $ 9,000 |
| Net Income | $ (15,000) | $ (7,500) | $ (4,500) | $ (3,000) |

* Traceable in these amounts.
** $6,429 is traceable to A; $2,571 is traceable to C.

The company lost $15,000. This loss appears to have been distributed as fairly as possible. Do you believe this is true based on your review of the data for Company X? Support your answer with revised income statement data and a brief explanation. [LO1b,2a]

PROBLEM 26–5 *(Compute Rates of Return for Segments)* Selected data for two divisions of Waverly Company are shown below.

| | EASTERN DIVISION | WESTERN DIVISION |
|---|---|---|
| Net Sales | $500,000 | $300,000 |
| Net Income | 40,000 | 30,000 |
| Average Assets | 200,000 | 100,000 |
| Stockholders' Equity | 70,000 | 50,000 |

Required:

1. Compute the rate of return for each division.
2. From the data available, which division seems to have the better performance? Indicate why by subdividing the rates of return into profit margin on sales and asset turnover. [LO2b,2d]

PROBLEM 26–6 *(Compute Rates of Return and Residual Income)* Assume the following data for each division of Zenith Company.

| | A | B | C |
|---|---|---|---|
| Sales | $10,000 | $20,000 | $25,000 |
| Number of Units Sold | 1,000 | 5,000 | 10,000 |

1. The variable costs per unit of Products A, B, and C, respectively, are $6.00, $3.00, and $1.50.
2. The total fixed costs amount to $10,000, of which 60% are direct traceable costs to the product lines in the following way: 20% of the 60% is traceable to A; 50% of the 60% is traceable to B; 30% of the 60% is traceable to C.
3. The balance of the fixed costs are indirect common costs and are allocated on the basis of relative dollar sales.

Asset information for Zenith Company follows:

The average assets of the company are $40,000, of which $8,000 belongs to Product A, $12,000 to Product B, and $20,000 to Product C.

Required:

1. Compute rates of return for each division.
2. Compute the residual income for each division using (a) a 30% minimum rate of return and (b) a 20% minimum rate of return.
3. Based on the above results, which division showed the best performance? [LO2b,2c]

PROBLEM 26–7 *(Compute Residual Income)*

1. Compute the residual income for the following departments assuming a minimum rate of 14%, 12%, and 10%.

| DEPT. | AVERAGE ASSETS | NET SALES | NET INCOME | 14% RESIDUAL INCOME | 12% RESIDUAL INCOME | 10% RESIDUAL INCOME |
|---|---|---|---|---|---|---|
| A | $100,000 | $60,000 | $12,000 | $_____ | $_____ | $_____ |
| B | 50,000 | 32,000 | 4,000 | $_____ | $_____ | $_____ |
| C | 60,000 | 30,000 | 6,000 | $_____ | $_____ | $_____ |
| D | 80,000 | 54,000 | 9,000 | $_____ | $_____ | $_____ |

2. Compare and comment briefly on the results of each set of residual incomes. [LO2c]

PROBLEM 26–8 *(Subdivide Rates of Return)* Take the data from Problem 26–7 and do the following:

1. Compute the profit margin on sales for each department.
2. Compute the asset turnover for each department. [LO2b,2d]

## ALTERNATE PROBLEMS

PROBLEM 26–1A *(Prepare an Income Statement That Shows Contribution Margin, Segment Margin, and Net Income)* (Alternate to Problem 26–1) Using the following segment income statement and additional information, prepare a statement that shows the contribution margin, segment margin, and net income for each product line.

| | TOTAL | A | B | C |
|---|---|---|---|---|
| Selling Prices | $ — | $12.00 | $14.00 | $ 6.80 |
| Units Sold | 2,000 | 400 | 600 | 1,000 |
| Sales | $20,000 | $4,800 | $8,400 | $6,800 |
| Cost of Goods Sold | 15,000 | 3,800 | 5,000 | 6,200 |
| Gross Profit | $ 5,000 | $1,000 | $3,400 | $ 600 |
| Operating Expenses (Costs) | 4,000 | 800 | 2,200 | 1,000 |
| Net Income | $ 1,000 | $ 200 | $1,200 | $ (400) |

Additional Information:

1. Of the $15,000 cost of goods sold, $8,000 is variable.
2. Of the $4,000 operating expenses (costs), $2,000 is fixed.
3. Of the $9,000 fixed costs (combination of fixed cost of goods sold and fixed operating expenses), $4,200 is direct and traceable to the product lines in the following percentages:
   a. Fifty percent of the $4,200 belongs to Product A.
   b. Twenty-five percent of the $4,200 belongs to Product B.
   c. Twenty-five percent of the $4,200 belongs to Product C.
4. The rest of the fixed costs are allocated according to the relative sales dollar.
5. Assume that the variable costs are traceable and that the variable costs per unit are the same for each product line as they are in total (for example, if the total variable costs per unit are $5.00, then the variable costs per unit are $5.00 each for Product Lines A, B, and C). [LO2a]

PROBLEM 26–2A *(Prepare Segment Income Statements After Dropping a Product Line)* (Alternate to Problem 26–3) Assume the following income statements for three divisions.

| | TOTAL | A | B | C |
|---|---|---|---|---|
| Sales | $10,000 | $5,000 | $3,000 | $2,000 |
| Variable Costs | 6,200 | 3,500 | 1,600 | 1,100 |
| Contribution Margin | $ 3,800 | $1,500 | $1,400 | $ 900 |
| Direct Traceable Costs | 2,400 | 400 | 1,100 | 900 |
| Segment Margin | $ 1,400 | $1,100 | $ 300 | $ — |
| Indirect Common Costs | 1,000 | 500 | 300 | 200 |
| Net Income | $ 400 | $ 600 | — | $ (200) |

Required:

1. Restructure the income statement for each division assuming the following changes. Consider each change separately.
   a. Product line A is dropped. There is no effect on the sales or variable costs of the other product lines. The direct traceable costs of A are eliminated, but there is no change in the indirect common costs.
   b. Product line C is dropped. There is no effect on the sales or variable costs of the other product lines. The direct traceable costs of product line C are eliminated, but there is no change in the indirect common cost.
   c. Indirect common costs are reduced by 30% and the remainder of the indirect common costs are allocated in the same way.
2. Comment on why the changes in Requirements 1a, 1b, and 1c occurred. [LO2a]

PROBLEM 26–3A *(Compute Rates of Return for Segments)* (Alternate to Problem 26–5) Selected data for two divisions of Vaverly Company are shown below.

| | NORTHERN DIVISION | SOUTHERN DIVISION |
|---|---|---|
| Net Sales | $400,000 | $200,000 |
| Net Income | 80,000 | 25,000 |
| Average Assets | 400,000 | 150,000 |
| Stockholders' Equity | 50,000 | 40,000 |

Required:

1. Compute the rate of return for each division.
2. From the data available, which division seems to have the better performance? Indicate why by subdividing the rates of return into profit margin on sales and asset turnovers. [LO2b,2d]

PROBLEM 26–4A *(Compute Residual Income)* (Alternate to Problem 26–7)

1. Compute the residual income for the following departments assuming a minimum rate of 11%, 13%, and 15%.

| DEPT. | AVERAGE ASSETS | NET INCOME | 11% RESIDUAL INCOME | 13% RESIDUAL INCOME | 15% RESIDUAL INCOME |
|---|---|---|---|---|---|
| A | $200,000 | $25,000 | $_____ | $_____ | $_____ |
| B | 40,000 | 5,000 | $_____ | $_____ | $_____ |
| C | 55,000 | 5,400 | $_____ | $_____ | $_____ |
| D | 75,000 | 9,500 | $_____ | $_____ | $_____ |

2. Compare and comment briefly on the results of each set of residual incomes. [LO2c]

# 27 Capital Budgeting

## Learning Objectives

After you complete this chapter you will be able to

1. Answer the following questions:
   a. What is capital budgeting? What is its importance?
   b. What is the difference between the present value of an amount and the present value of an annuity?
   c. How are the concepts of economic life of an asset and cash inflows related to the capital budgeting techniques presented in this chapter?
2. Perform the following accounting functions:
   a. Calculate the present value of an amount and the present value of an annuity.
   b. Calculate the cash inflows after tax that affect capital budgeting decisions.
   c. Compute the accounting rate of return, payback, discounted rate of return, and excess present value.

Organizations use many types of resources in conducting their day-to-day business affairs. Examples include cash; inventory; property, plant, and equipment; skilled labor; and managerial talent. Some of these resources are expected to last long periods of time, and care must be taken in planning their acquisition. Otherwise large sums of money may be spent without proper benefits. The use of capital budgeting techniques can help companies make more-informed decisions on the long-term commitment of resources.

## WHAT CAPITAL BUDGETING IS

*1a. Capital budgeting is the study of the feasibility of long-term investments. It is important because of the length of such investments*

**Capital budgeting** has been defined in a number of ways. For our purposes, we can describe it as the study of the feasibility of long-term investments.

Research projects, long advertising campaigns, and purchase of equipment are a few examples of long-term investments. In each case, the company is committing significant amounts of resources in exchange for benefits that it hopes will accrue over long periods of time. Mistakes in making these types of commitments can have a more-lasting adverse effect than the improper purchase of some inventory or the ill-advised extension of credit to certain customers.

Capital budgeting decisions require the answer to a fundamental question: Are the potential *benefits* of making the long-term investment expected to be more than or less than the *cost* of the resources needed to make the investment?

Both the benefits and the costs can be measured qualitatively or quantitatively. In our models, however, we will confine our measurements to dollar amounts. We will also make other assumptions, such as the following:

The proposed investment is a depreciable asset, such as equipment. Other types of long-term investments, such as research and advertising, could be illustrated, but they would not include the impact of depreciation, which we wish to describe.

The proposed investment is purchased immediately for cash. Although long-term investments are often purchased with notes or bonds, we will assume that our illustrated cash outlay is the dollar equivalent of borrowing money at a certain interest rate.

The expected benefits of making the long-term investment are measured as cash inflows (net income before depreciation expenses) to be received for several years.

Bear in mind that the models in this chapter are introductory illustrations of capital budgeting.

## CONCEPTS THAT UNDERLIE CAPITAL BUDGETING

Before illustrating our capital budgeting methodology, we need to discuss in the next three subsections some important underlying concepts:

The concept of present value
The concept of economic life of an asset
The concept of cash inflows after tax

## Present Value

The concept of **present value** is the idea that money has a time value and what is to be received or paid immediately is worth more than what is to be received or paid at some future date.[1]

*1b,2a. We calculate the present value of an amount from Table 27–1*

THE PRESENT VALUE OF AN AMOUNT Look at Table 27–1, which is used to calculate the **present value of an amount** (the present value of a single sum of money to be received or paid in the future). Using $1 as an illustrative amount, note that the leftmost column contains *periods* (1, for example) and the other columns have *values* for the appropriate *rate-of-return percentages* (.962 under 4%, for example). The periods could represent various lengths of time, but because capital budgeting is the study of long-term investment feasibilities, yearly periods are assumed.

*TABLE 27–1*

Present Value of $1.00

| PERIODS | 4% | 6% | 8% | 10% | 12% | 14% | 16% | 18% | 20% | 22% | 24% | 30% | 40% |
|---|---|---|---|---|---|---|---|---|---|---|---|---|---|
| 1 | .962 | .943 | .926 | .909 | .893 | .877 | .862 | .847 | .833 | .820 | .806 | .769 | .714 |
| 2 | .925 | .890 | .857 | .826 | .797 | .769 | .743 | .718 | .694 | .672 | .650 | .592 | .510 |
| 3 | .889 | .840 | .794 | .751 | .712 | .675 | .641 | .609 | .579 | .551 | .524 | .455 | .364 |
| 4 | .855 | .792 | .735 | .683 | .636 | .592 | .552 | .516 | .482 | .451 | .423 | .350 | .260 |
| 5 | .822 | .747 | .681 | .621 | .567 | .519 | .476 | .437 | .402 | .370 | .341 | .269 | .186 |
| 6 | .790 | .705 | .630 | .564 | .507 | .456 | .410 | .370 | .335 | .303 | .275 | .207 | .133 |
| 7 | .760 | .665 | .583 | .513 | .452 | .400 | .354 | .314 | .279 | .249 | .222 | .159 | .095 |
| 8 | .731 | .627 | .540 | .467 | .404 | .351 | .305 | .266 | .233 | .204 | .179 | .123 | .068 |
| 9 | .703 | .592 | .500 | .424 | .361 | .308 | .263 | .225 | .194 | .167 | .144 | .094 | .048 |
| 10 | .676 | .558 | .463 | .386 | .322 | .270 | .227 | .191 | .162 | .137 | .116 | .073 | .035 |
| 11 | .650 | .527 | .429 | .350 | .287 | .237 | .195 | .162 | .135 | .112 | .094 | .056 | .025 |
| 12 | .625 | .497 | .397 | .319 | .257 | .208 | .168 | .137 | .112 | .092 | .076 | .043 | .018 |
| 13 | .601 | .469 | .368 | .290 | .229 | .182 | .145 | .116 | .093 | .075 | .061 | .033 | .013 |
| 14 | .577 | .442 | .340 | .263 | .205 | .160 | .125 | .099 | .078 | .062 | .049 | .025 | .009 |
| 15 | .555 | .417 | .315 | .239 | .183 | .140 | .108 | .084 | .065 | .051 | .040 | .020 | .006 |
| 16 | .534 | .394 | .292 | .218 | .163 | .123 | .093 | .071 | .054 | .042 | .032 | .015 | .005 |
| 17 | .513 | .371 | .270 | .198 | .146 | .108 | .080 | .060 | .045 | .034 | .026 | .012 | .003 |
| 18 | .494 | .350 | .250 | .180 | .130 | .095 | .069 | .051 | .038 | .028 | .021 | .009 | .002 |
| 19 | .475 | .331 | .232 | .164 | .116 | .083 | .060 | .043 | .031 | .023 | .017 | .007 | .002 |
| 20 | .456 | .312 | .215 | .149 | .104 | .073 | .051 | .037 | .026 | .019 | .014 | .005 | .001 |
| 21 | .439 | .294 | .199 | .135 | .093 | .064 | .044 | .031 | .022 | .015 | .011 | .004 | .001 |
| 22 | .422 | .278 | .184 | .123 | .083 | .056 | .038 | .026 | .018 | .013 | .009 | .003 | .001 |
| 23 | .406 | .262 | .170 | .112 | .074 | .049 | .033 | .022 | .015 | .010 | .007 | .002 | — |
| 24 | .390 | .247 | .158 | .102 | .066 | .043 | .028 | .019 | .013 | .008 | .006 | .002 | — |
| 25 | .375 | .233 | .146 | .092 | .059 | .038 | .024 | .016 | .010 | .007 | .005 | .001 | — |
| 30 | .308 | .174 | .099 | .057 | .033 | .020 | .012 | .007 | .004 | .003 | .002 | — | — |
| 40 | .208 | .097 | .046 | .022 | .011 | .005 | .003 | .001 | .001 | — | — | — | — |

In looking at Table 27–1, assume that we wish to know the present value of the right to receive or the burden to pay $1 in three years at a rate of return of 8%. We look in the *period column* and find 3, and then we look across that *row* until we find the value under the 8% column, .794. The present value of $1 to be received or paid in three years at an 8% rate is $.794.

The present value of any amount can be calculated by multiplying that

[1] Chapter 16 contains discussions and illustrations of present value and future value concepts. This brief section is presented to reinforce your understanding of present value concepts, particularly as they relate to capital budgeting decisions. Tables 27–1 and 27–2, the present value tables used in this chapter, are condensed versions of the present value tables used in Chapter 16.

amount by the value in the appropriate period row and percentage column. Referring to the previous example, the present value of \$500 to be received or paid in three years at an 8% rate is \$397 (.794 × \$500). Stated another way, if we had \$397 and invested it at an 8% rate of return (compounded yearly), it would amount to \$500 at the end of three years. We can prove this concept with the following illustration.

| YEAR | INVESTMENT AT BEGINNING OF YEAR | RATE OF RETURN | INVESTMENT AT END OF YEAR (ROUNDED) |
|---|---|---|---|
| 1 | \$397 | 8% | \$429 (397 × 1.08) |
| 2 | 429 | 8% | 463 (429 × 1.08) |
| 3 | 463 | 8% | 500 (463 × 1.08) |

*1b,2a. We use Table 27–2 to calculate the present value of an annuity*

THE PRESENT VALUE OF AN ANNUITY Table 27–2 is used to calculate the **present value of an annuity** (the present value of a series of equal amounts to be received or paid for a certain number of periods in the future). As in Table 27–1, the leftmost column contains periods (2, for example), and the other columns have values for the appropriate rates of return (1.886 under 4%, for example). We can also use periods of one year.

In looking at Table 27–2, assume that we wish to know the present value of the right to receive or the burden to pay \$1 at the end of each of the next three

*TABLE 27–2*

Present Value of an Annuity of \$1.00

| PERIODS | 4% | 6% | 8% | 10% | 12% | 14% | 16% | 18% | 20% | 22% | 24% | 30% | 40% |
|---|---|---|---|---|---|---|---|---|---|---|---|---|---|
| 1 | 0.962 | 0.943 | 0.926 | 0.909 | 0.893 | 0.877 | 0.862 | 0.847 | 0.833 | 0.820 | 0.806 | 0.769 | 0.714 |
| 2 | 1.886 | 1.833 | 1.783 | 1.736 | 1.690 | 1.647 | 1.605 | 1.566 | 1.528 | 1.492 | 1.457 | 1.361 | 1.224 |
| 3 | 2.775 | 2.673 | 2.577 | 2.487 | 2.402 | 2.322 | 2.246 | 2.174 | 2.106 | 2.042 | 1.981 | 1.816 | 1.589 |
| 4 | 3.630 | 3.465 | 3.312 | 3.170 | 3.037 | 2.914 | 2.798 | 2.690 | 2.589 | 2.494 | 2.404 | 2.166 | 1.849 |
| 5 | 4.452 | 4.212 | 3.993 | 3.791 | 3.605 | 3.433 | 3.274 | 3.127 | 2.991 | 2.864 | 2.745 | 2.436 | 2.035 |
| 6 | 5.242 | 4.917 | 4.623 | 4.355 | 4.111 | 3.889 | 3.685 | 3.498 | 3.326 | 3.167 | 3.020 | 2.643 | 2.168 |
| 7 | 6.002 | 5.582 | 5.206 | 4.868 | 4.564 | 4.288 | 4.039 | 3.812 | 3.605 | 3.416 | 3.242 | 2.802 | 2.263 |
| 8 | 6.733 | 6.210 | 5.747 | 5.335 | 4.968 | 4.639 | 4.344 | 4.078 | 3.837 | 3.619 | 3.421 | 2.925 | 2.331 |
| 9 | 7.435 | 6.802 | 6.247 | 5.759 | 5.328 | 4.946 | 4.607 | 4.303 | 4.031 | 3.786 | 3.566 | 3.019 | 2.379 |
| 10 | 8.111 | 7.360 | 6.710 | 6.145 | 5.650 | 5.216 | 4.833 | 4.494 | 4.192 | 3.923 | 3.682 | 3.092 | 2.414 |
| 11 | 8.760 | 7.887 | 7.139 | 6.495 | 5.988 | 5.453 | 5.029 | 4.656 | 4.327 | 4.035 | 3.776 | 3.147 | 2.438 |
| 12 | 9.385 | 8.384 | 7.536 | 6.814 | 6.194 | 5.660 | 5.197 | 4.793 | 4.439 | 4.127 | 3.851 | 3.190 | 2.456 |
| 13 | 9.986 | 8.853 | 7.904 | 7.103 | 6.424 | 5.842 | 5.342 | 4.910 | 4.533 | 4.203 | 3.912 | 3.223 | 2.468 |
| 14 | 10.563 | 9.295 | 8.244 | 7.367 | 6.628 | 6.002 | 5.468 | 5.008 | 4.611 | 4.265 | 3.962 | 3.249 | 2.477 |
| 15 | 11.118 | 9.712 | 8.559 | 7.606 | 6.811 | 6.142 | 5.575 | 5.092 | 4.675 | 4.315 | 4.001 | 3.268 | 2.484 |
| 16 | 11.652 | 10.106 | 8.851 | 7.824 | 6.974 | 6.265 | 5.669 | 5.162 | 4.730 | 4.357 | 4.033 | 3.283 | 2.489 |
| 17 | 12.166 | 10.477 | 9.122 | 8.022 | 7.120 | 6.373 | 5.749 | 5.222 | 4.775 | 4.391 | 4.059 | 3.295 | 2.492 |
| 18 | 12.659 | 10.828 | 9.372 | 8.201 | 7.250 | 6.467 | 5.818 | 5.273 | 4.812 | 4.419 | 4.080 | 3.304 | 2.494 |
| 19 | 13.134 | 11.158 | 9.604 | 8.365 | 7.366 | 6.550 | 5.877 | 5.316 | 4.844 | 4.442 | 4.097 | 3.311 | 2.496 |
| 20 | 13.590 | 11.470 | 9.818 | 8.514 | 7.469 | 6.623 | 5.929 | 5.353 | 4.870 | 4.460 | 4.110 | 3.316 | 2.497 |
| 21 | 14.029 | 11.764 | 10.017 | 8.649 | 7.562 | 6.687 | 5.973 | 5.384 | 4.891 | 4.476 | 4.121 | 3.320 | 2.498 |
| 22 | 14.451 | 12.042 | 10.201 | 8.772 | 7.645 | 6.743 | 6.011 | 5.410 | 4.909 | 4.488 | 4.130 | 3.323 | 2.498 |
| 23 | 14.857 | 12.303 | 10.371 | 8.883 | 7.718 | 6.792 | 6.044 | 5.432 | 4.925 | 4.499 | 4.137 | 3.325 | 2.499 |
| 24 | 15.247 | 12.550 | 10.529 | 8.985 | 7.784 | 6.835 | 6.073 | 5.451 | 4.937 | 4.507 | 4.143 | 3.327 | 2.499 |
| 25 | 15.622 | 12.783 | 10.675 | 9.077 | 7.843 | 6.873 | 6.097 | 5.467 | 4.948 | 4.514 | 4.147 | 3.329 | 2.499 |
| 30 | 17.292 | 13.765 | 11.258 | 9.427 | 8.055 | 7.003 | 6.177 | 5.517 | 4.979 | 4.534 | 4.160 | 3.332 | 2.500 |
| 40 | 19.793 | 15.046 | 11.925 | 9.779 | 8.244 | 7.105 | 6.234 | 5.548 | 4.997 | 4.544 | 4.166 | 3.333 | 2.500 |

years at a rate of 8%. We look in the period 3 *column* and look across that *row* until we find the *value* under the 8% column, 2.577. The present value of an annuity of $1 to be received or paid at the end of each of the next three years is $2.577.

The present value of any annuity can be calculated by multiplying that annuity by the value in the appropriate period row and percentage column. Referring to the example above, the present value of a series of $500 amounts to be received or paid at the end of each of the next three years at an 8% rate is $1,289 (2.577 × $500 and rounded). Stated another way, if we had $1,289 and invested it at an 8% rate of return (compounded yearly), we could withdraw $500 at the end of each of the next three years. We can prove this concept with the following illustration.

| YEAR | INVESTMENT AT BEGINNING OF YEAR | RATE OF RETURN | INVESTMENT AT END OF YEAR | AMOUNT TAKEN OUT BY INVESTOR | REMAINING INVESTMENT AT END OF YEAR |
|---|---|---|---|---|---|
| 1 | $1,289 | 8% | $1,392 (1,289 × 1.08) | $500 | $892 |
| 2 | 892 | 8% | 963 (892 × 1.08) | 500 | 463 |
| 3 | 463 | 8% | 500 (463 × 1.08) | 500 | — |

Capital budgeting decisions can be made without using present value concepts, and later in the chapter we will study models that omit them. Many believe, however, that present value concepts should be used to study the feasibility of long-term investments realistically. According to this view, when we pay out funds now to acquire long-term investments, we should take into account the present value of future benefits that accrue from making these long-term investments.

## Economic Life of an Asset

The **physical life** of an asset is the length of time it will physically operate. The **economic life** of an asset is the length of time it will provide service benefits to a given user or users.

For example, an automobile may function for ten or fifteen years before it is incapable of operation. The original purchaser of that automobile, however, may keep it for five years and decide that a newer model is more useful. Therefore five years is the economic life to that particular user.

***1c. In capital budgeting, an asset's expected benefits must be related to its expected economic life***

For evaluating the feasibility of long-term investments (capital budgeting), a company should carefully consider expected *economic life*. The decision to buy $100,000 of equipment, for example, would certainly depend in part on whether benefits of $30,000 a year are expected for three or five years.

In our examples we will assume that the expected economic life of the investment is the same as the depreciable life for income tax purposes. Recent accelerated cost recovery methods enacted by Congress do give purchasers of certain assets the opportunity to write them off quickly. We will classify accelerated cost recovery, however, as a special case and, for purposes of simplicity, omit it from our models.

## Cash Inflows After Tax

*1c,2b. Cash inflows may be translated into after-tax cash inflows*

Long-term investments are often made with tax-deductible outlays. Also, benefits that will flow to the company as a result of acquiring the investment (which we will refer to as **cash inflows** or incremental net income before depreciation expense) are subject to income tax charges. For these reasons, many capital budgeting decisions must consider the income tax effects of resulting transactions.

Any benefit taxed at a 45% rate, for example, is worth only 55% of its original amount. Note the following illustration.

| | |
|---|---:|
| Cash inflows resulting from long-term investment | $100,000 |
| Less: 45% tax paid | 45,000 |
| After-tax cash inflows (55%) | $ 55,000 |

Likewise, any outlay that is tax deductible at a 45% rate has a burden equal to 55% of its original amount. Again, note the following illustration.

| | |
|---|---:|
| Outlay for long-term investment | $200,000 |
| Less: 45% income tax deduction | 90,000 |
| After-tax burden (55%) | $110,000 |

In the case of a depreciable asset, the tax deductibility of the investment will raise the **cash inflows after tax** (the cash inflows of an investment less the tax paid on these inflows) by lowering their tax charges. This is an example of the income tax effects of depreciation.

To illustrate, assume the following facts relating to a capital budgeting decision to purchase a long-term depreciable investment:

The cost of the depreciable investment is *$180,000.*
The estimated economic life of the investment is *five* years.
The yearly depreciation allowed for tax purposes is *$36,000* ($180,000 ÷ 5 years).
The expected benefits (cash inflows) from acquiring the investment are *$50,000* a year for the five-year economic life of the investment.
The expected tax rate for the five-year period is *45%.*

If no tax-deductible depreciation was allowed on the investment, the yearly cash inflows after tax would be as follows:

| | YEAR | | | | |
|---|---:|---:|---:|---:|---:|
| | 1 | 2 | 3 | 4 | 5 |
| Cash inflows | $50,000 | $50,000 | $50,000 | $50,000 | $50,000 |
| 45% tax | 22,500 | 22,500 | 22,500 | 22,500 | 22,500 |
| After-tax cash inflows | $27,500 | $27,500 | $27,500 | $27,500 | $27,500 |

The tax deductibility of the investment, however, raises the after-tax cash inflows as shown below.

| | YEAR | | | | |
|---|---|---|---|---|---|
| | 1 | 2 | 3 | 4 | 5 |
| Cash inflows | $50,000 | $50,000 | $50,000 | $50,000 | $50,000 |
| Less: Depreciation deductions* | 36,000 | 36,000 | 36,000 | 36,000 | 36,000 |
| Amount on which tax is paid | $14,000 | $14,000 | $14,000 | $14,000 | $14,000 |
| 45% tax | 6,300 | 6,300 | 6,300 | 6,300 | 6,300 |
| After-tax cash inflows | $43,700 | $43,700 | $43,700 | $43,700 | $43,700 |

* Cost of $180,000 ÷ 5 years = $36,000 depreciation.

The difference between the $43,700 after-tax cash inflows with depreciation deductions and the $27,500 after-tax cash inflows without depreciation deductions is *$16,200.* This figure ($36,000 × 45%) is the yearly tax benefit of depreciation of the investment.

If the proposed long-term investment is not a depreciable asset (land, for example), the tax-effect of depreciation is not a consideration in the decision.

## ILLUSTRATIONS OF CAPITAL BUDGETING TECHNIQUES

We now have the material we need to describe a variety of capital budgeting techniques. Four of the most commonly used ones are the following:

Accounting rate of return
Payback
Discounted rate of return
Excess present value

The first two listed techniques *do not* require the use of present value concepts. The last two *do* require it, together with information from Tables 27–1 and 27–2. Also, in our explanation of capital budgeting techniques we will assume that the cash inflows after taxes have already been computed.

For purposes of illustration, let us use the following data:

The cost of the anticipated investment is *$100,000.*

The estimated economic life is *five years.*

The estimated salvage value of the asset at the end of five years is *$10,000.* The salvage value is the resale price after our use of the asset has ended.

The **minimum acceptable rate of return** that the company will accept for investments of this type is *10%.* This means that if the anticipated cash inflows after taxes during the economic life of the asset do not produce a rate of return of 10% or more, the investment will not be feasible. The minimum acceptable rate of return is sometimes called **cost of capital** and represents the long-term average cost of acquiring money. If the anticipated investment is not expected to produce a rate of return that is at least as large as the cost of acquiring the money to make the investment, it is not generally considered feasible. Because the minimum acceptable rate of return considers present value, it will be used to illustrate only the *discounted rate of return* and *present value* methods.

The anticipated cash inflows after taxes are *$25,200* a year for five years.

The anticipated average net income (from the income statement) is *$7,200* a year for five years.

## Accounting Rate of Return

The **accounting rate of return,** also known as the **average rate of return,** is calculated by dividing the anticipated average net income per year by the average amount of the investment.

*2c. Computation of accounting rate of return is illustrated here*

Thus the rate in our example is 14.4%, illustrated as follows.

$$\text{Accounting Rate of Return} = \frac{\text{Anticipated Average Net Income per Year}}{\text{Average Investment}}$$

$$\text{Accounting Rate of Return} = \frac{\$7{,}200}{\$50{,}000\ (\$100{,}000/2)} = 14.4\%$$

Sometimes the total investment cost is used ($100,000 in this illustration). If so, the accounting rate of return is decreased ($7,200 ÷ $100,000 = 7.2%).

The accounting rate of return might be useful in providing the company with an approximate comparison of various projects (project one shows a rate of 14.4%, project two shows a rate of 17.0%, and so forth). The method has two limitations, however.

The first is that the net income may *not* be the same each year.

The second, and more serious, is the failure of the method to consider *present value.* In our data the net income is expected to accrue over the next five years, whereas the investment must be paid for at the present time.

## Payback

The payback method of measuring the feasibility of long-term investments has traditionally been used and has some popularity because of its simplicity. **Payback** is the cost of the investment divided by the anticipated after-tax cash inflows per year.

*2c. Use of a formula for payback is illustrated here*

Taking amounts from our data, we obtain the following:

$$\text{Payback} = \frac{\text{Investment}}{\text{Anticipated After-Tax Cash Inflows per Year}}$$

$$\text{Payback} = \frac{\$100{,}000}{\$25{,}200} = 3.97 \text{ (or about 4 years)}$$

As you can see, payback shows the estimated length of time to "recapture" the investment, or "get your money back." In itself, the payback factor means little. It should be compared with payback factors for other proposed investments and/or a minimum acceptable payback period. If the company sets a minimum period of three years, for example, the proposed investment may not be feasible because the estimated payback is almost four years.

Payback is a convenient method of determining the approximate length of time required to recoup or recapture the investment. Like the accounting rate of return, however, it has definite limitations. In addition to its failure to consider present value, the payback method ignores returns on the investment after the payback period is over. In our example, the payback period is approximately four years, but the total estimated life of the investment is five. Companies need a basis for determining the profitability of the investment during its entire estimated life.

In the next two subsections we examine techniques that overcome the limitations of accounting rate of return and payback. These techniques consider both the present value and the entire profitability of the investment.

## Discounted Rate of Return

The **discounted rate of return** (also called the **time-adjusted rate of return** or the **discounted cash flow**) is the rate that equates the present value of the after-tax cash inflows with the cost of the investment. Put another way, it is the actual rate of return the cash inflows earn on the investment, correctly considering the concept of present value.

***2c. The technique for computing discounted rate of return is illustrated here***

We can illustrate this method by using some of the data common to all four capital budgeting methods described in this chapter:

The cost of the investment is *$100,000.*

The anticipated after-tax cash inflows for *five years* are *$25,200* a year. (For purposes of simplicity, we will ignore salvage value in this explanation.)

The percentage that discounts the present value of these inflows to $100,000 is the discounted or time-adjusted rate earned on the investment. To find this rate, we classify the $25,200 cash inflow as a five-year annuity (remember the present value discussions) and refer to Table 27–2. The following steps are used:

Compute the payback factor ($100,000 ÷ $25,200 = *3.97*).

Find the 5-period row of Table 27–2 (to correspond to a five-year life of the investment).

Look across the 5-period row of Table 27–2 until the nearest factor to 3.97 is reached (the nearest factor is *3.993*).

Look up that column to the percentage, which is the approximate discounted or time-adjusted rate of return (*8%*).

This technique is illustrated in the sketch below, which is derived from Table 27–2:

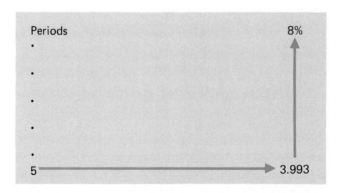

If the cost of the investment is $100,000 and the anticipated after-tax cash inflows for five years are $33,333 a year, the discounted rate of return is about 20%, calculated as follows:

$$\text{Payback} = \frac{\$100{,}000}{\$33{,}333} = 3$$

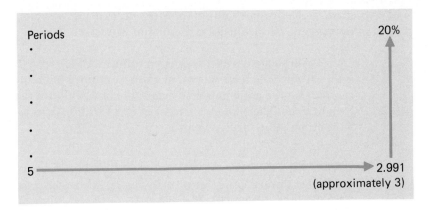

The approximate accuracy of the discounted rate of return can be proved by calculating the present value of $25,200 a year for five years at 8%:

$25,200 × 3.993 (the present value of an annuity of $1 for 5 years)
= *$100,624* (approximately $100,000)

The calculation of the discounted rate of return becomes more complicated if the after-tax cash inflows are uneven for each year of the economic life ($26,000 in year 1, $24,000 in year 2, and so forth). Because the theory is the same, we will not present a full explanation of this technique. An approximate estimate of the discounted rate of return can be made, however, if we use an average yearly cash inflow for the economic life. We can also make an estimate by calculating the present value of each of the cash inflows of the individual years for different percentages on a trial-and-error basis. The percentage that comes closest to discounting all the present values to the cost of the asset is the percentage that is closest to the discounted rate of return. Computer programs can also be written to find the discounted rate of return for uneven cash inflows.

What useful information do we now have when we calculate an 8% discounted or time-adjusted rate of return? By comparing 8% with the cost of capital (the minimum acceptable rate of return), we decide whether or not the investment appears to be attractive.

If the cost of capital is *above 8%,* normally we *would not* make the investment unless there were other reasons to do so. If the cost of capital is *below 8%,* normally we *would* make the investment unless there were reasons not to do so. If the cost of capital is *8%, other factors* would probably weigh very heavily in the decision.

It is possible, of course, that the company would acquire the investment if the cost of capital were higher than the discounted rate of return on the expected cash inflows. Good reasons should exist, however, for making an investment that promises an 8% rate of return when the cost of obtaining these funds is more than 8%.

## Excess Present Value

Instead of or in addition to calculating a discounted rate of return, the company can calculate the present value of the after-tax cash inflows at the cost-of-capital percentage. The resulting figure is compared with the cost of the investment, and the difference is referred to as **excess present value.**

*2c. Computation of excess present value helps a company decide whether to acquire an investment*

If the present value of the after-tax cash inflows is *higher* than the cost of the investment, the acquisition should be made unless there are other reasons not to do so. If the present value of the after-tax cash inflows is *lower* than the cost of the investment, the acquisition should not be made unless there are other reasons to do so.

To illustrate the excess present value method, we will work with the data we used earlier, which are shown in a different form in Exhibit 27–1. We will also assume that the anticipated salvage value of $10,000 at the end of five years is of benefit to us. Therefore we will treat this $10,000 as a cash inflow and calculate its present value for five years.

*EXHIBIT 27–1*

The Excess Present Value Method of Evaluating Depreciable Asset Investment Decisions—Five-Year Life

| | (1) END OF YEAR | (2) CASH INFLOW AFTER TAX | (3) PRESENT VALUE 10% (FROM TABLE 27–1) | (4) PRESENT VALUE (2) × (3) |
|---|---|---|---|---|
| Cost | 0 | $ — | — | ($100,000) |
| Inflow | 1 | 25,200 | .909 | 22,907 |
| Inflow | 2 | 25,200 | .826 | 20,815 |
| Inflow | 3 | 25,200 | .751 | 18,925 |
| Inflow | 4 | 25,200 | .683 | 17,212 |
| Inflow | 5 | 25,200 | .621 | 15,649 |
| Salvage value | 5 | 10,000 | .621 | 6,210 |
| Excess present value (positive) | | | | $ 1,718 |

The same approximate results can be calculated in the following way:

| | |
|---|---|
| Cost | ($100,000) |
| Present value of annuity of after-tax cash inflows for 5 years at 10% ($25,200 × 3.791—from Table 27–2) | 95,533 |
| Present value of the amount of the salvage value at the end of 5 years ($10,000 × .621—from Table 27–1) | 6,210 |
| Excess present value (difference in rounding) | $ 1,743 |

Would the company acquire this investment? The present value of the inflows is $101,717, and the cost is only $100,000. The **profitability index,** which is the present value of the cash inflows after tax divided by the investment cost, is approximately 1.017 ($101,717 ÷ $100,000). In all likelihood, the company would use several quantitative and qualitative guides to make the investment decision, one of which would be a study similar in concept to that illustrated in Exhibit 27–1. Given all the subjective variables in the capital budgeting models (cash inflows, cost of capital, estimated salvage value, and so forth), it is unlikely that the company would acquire the asset *merely* because there is an excess present value of $1,717. The information in Exhibit 27–1 is valuable, however, and provides a good reason to make the investment.

A valuable use of the excess present value method is its versatility. The company can change any one or more of the assumptions and make alternative calculations.

*2c. The effects of changes in assumptions on the excess present value are illustrated in Exhibit 27–2*

To illustrate the effect of changes in assumptions, Exhibit 27–2 presents the same data as in Exhibit 27–1 except that

The after-tax cash inflows are $26,000 a year

The economic life is *four years*

The salvage value is *$20,000*

*EXHIBIT 27–2*

The Excess Present Value Method of Evaluating Depreciable Asset Investment Decisions—Four-Year Life

| | (1) END OF YEAR | (2) CASH INFLOW AFTER TAX | (3) PRESENT VALUE 10% (FROM TABLE 27–1) | (4) PRESENT VALUE (2) × (3) |
|---|---|---|---|---|
| Cost | 0 | $ — | — | ($100,000) |
| Inflow | 1 | 26,000 | .909 | 23,634 |
| Inflow | 2 | 26,000 | .826 | 21,476 |
| Inflow | 3 | 26,000 | .751 | 19,526 |
| Inflow | 4 | 26,000 | .683 | 17,758 |
| Salvage value | 4 | 20,000 | .683 | 13,660 |
| Excess present value (negative) | | | | ($ 3,946) |

Note that in Exhibit 27–2 we calculated a negative excess present value. Therefore if the data in Exhibits 27–1 and 27–2 were the sole basis for making the investment decision (we would not always expect it to be), the company would

Acquire the asset based on the results in *Exhibit 27–1*

Not acquire the asset based on the results in *Exhibit 27–2*

## THE USE OF CAPITAL BUDGETING TECHNIQUES IN THE BUSINESS WORLD

The capital budgeting techniques illustrated in this chapter are more simple and straightforward than those normally used by medium-sized and large companies that spend thousands (or millions) of dollars annually on long-term investments. The concepts used in the business world are basically the same, however.

Anticipated *future benefits* are quantified in some way and are compared with the *cost* of the investment. These quantitative guidelines are combined with qualitative considerations to make the final capital budgeting decision.

Many assumptions are made in the capital budgeting models. Users should be aware of this and should calculate results using a variety of reasonable assumptions.

## HIGHLIGHT PROBLEM

The president of Expand Company has been presented with the following data concerning a proposed investment in new earth-digging equipment:

1. The cost (to be paid in cash immediately) is $50,000.
2. The estimated economic life is four years.

3. The estimated salvage value at the end of four years is $2,000.
4. The equipment will be depreciated over a four-year period on a straight-line basis.
5. The cost of capital (minimum acceptable rate of return) is 12%.
6. The company anticipates a tax rate of 45% during the four-year life.
7. The anticipated cash inflows before tax are $20,000 a year for four years.
8. The anticipated average net income is $4,400 for the next four years.

Required:

1. Calculate the after-tax cash inflows for each year of the four-year period.
2. Calculate the following (consider salvage value only in *d*):
   a. The accounting rate of return
   b. The payback
   c. The discounted rate of return (ignore salvage value)
   d. The excess present value

## GLOSSARY OF KEY TERMS

**Accounting rate of return.** The anticipated average net income per year divided by the average amount of the investment. In this chapter the term means the same as *average rate of return.*

**Average rate of return.** In this chapter the term means the same as *accounting rate of return.*

**Capital budgeting.** The study of the feasibility of long-term investments.

**Cash inflows.** The anticipated incremental net income, before depreciation expense, that will flow to a company as the result of acquiring a long-term investment.

**Cash inflows after tax.** The cash inflows of an investment less the tax paid on these inflows.

**Cost of capital.** The long-term average cost of acquiring money. In this chapter it means the same as *minimum acceptable rate of return.*

**Discounted cash flow.** As used in this chapter, the term means the same as *discounted rate of return.*

**Discounted rate of return.** The rate of return that equates the present value of the after-tax cash inflows with the cost of the investment. In this chapter the term is also called *time-adjusted rate of return* or *discounted cash flow.*

**Economic life.** The length of time an asset will provide service benefits to a given user or users.

**Excess present value.** The difference between the present value of the after-tax cash inflows at the cost-of-capital percentage and the cost of the investment.

**Minimum acceptable rate of return.** In this chapter the term means the same as *cost of capital.*

**Payback.** The cost of the investment divided by the anticipated after-tax cash inflows per year.

**Physical life.** The length of time an asset will physically operate.

**Present value.** The idea that money has a time value and what is to be received or paid immediately is worth more than what is to be received or paid at some future date.

**Present value of an amount.** Present value of a single sum of money to be received or paid at some future date (for example, the present value of $10,000 to be received or paid at the end of three years).

**Present value of an annuity.** Present value of a series of equal amounts to be received or paid for a certain number of periods in the future (for example, the present value of $10,000 to be received or paid at the end of each of the next three years).

**Profitability index.** The present value of the cash inflows after tax divided by the investment cost.

**Time-adjusted rate of return.** In this chapter the term means the same as *discounted rate of return.*

## REVIEW QUESTIONS

1. What is capital budgeting? [LO1a]
2. Capital budgeting decisions require the answer to a fundamental question. What is the question? [LO1a]
3. Name three important underlying concepts of capital budgeting methodology. [LO1a]

4. Differentiate between the present value of an amount and the present value of an annuity. [LO1b]
5. Describe how to use Table 27–1 to find the present value of $1 for three periods at 10%. [LO1b,2a]
6. Describe how to use Table 27–2 to find the present value of an annuity of $1 for four periods at 12%. [LO1b,2a]
7. Differentiate between the physical life of an asset and the economic life of an asset. [LO1c]
8. Why is the economic life of an asset an important factor in the capital budgeting decision? [LO1c]
9. Give two examples of the income tax effect of transactions that affect the capital budgeting decision. [LO1c,2b]
10. Why will the cash inflows after tax be more with an investment that has tax-deductible depreciation than with an investment that does not have tax-deductible depreciation? [LO1c,2b]
11. Which two capital budgeting techniques do not use present value concepts? Which two capital budgeting techniques do use present value concepts? [LO2c]
12. What is the formula for the accounting rate of return? [LO2c]
13. Describe two limitations of the accounting rate of return. [LO2c]
14. What is the formula for the payback method? [LO2c]
15. Give two limitations of the payback method. [LO2c]
16. Differentiate between the discounted rate-of-return method and the excess present value method. [LO2c]
17. Describe the four-step method of finding the discounted rate of return. [LO2c]
18. After finding the discounted rate of return, how do we decide whether the investment appears to be attractive? [LO2c]
19. After the present value of the after-tax cash inflows has been computed, what decision criteria are used to decide whether the investment should be made? [LO2c]

## ANALYTICAL QUESTIONS

20. In what way does capital budgeting differ from other forms of budgeting discussed in the text? [LO1a]
21. A review of Table 27–1 shows that the factors become smaller as we move across the period rows and down the percentage columns. Explain why this is true. [LO1b,2a]
22. "An asset has one physical life but can have two or more economic lives." Explain why this statement is true. [LO1c]
23. Explain the following statement: "If the tax rate is 40%, the after-tax burden of a tax-deductible outlay is only 60%." [LO1c,2b]
24. "If the discounted rate of return is higher than the cost of capital, the excess present value will be positive." Explain why this is true. [LO2c]

## IMPACT ANALYSIS QUESTIONS

*For each error described, indicate whether it would overstate [O], understate [U], or not affect [N] the positive excess present values* [LO2c]

25. The minimum acceptable rate of return used to calculate the present value of the cash inflows after tax is 8% instead of 10%.

    _______ Excess Present Value

26. The present value of the salvage value was ignored in the calculation of excess present value. (It was considered in calculating the depreciable amount of the asset.)

    ______ Excess Present Value

27. Cash inflows after tax of $10,000 a year instead of $9,000 a year were used to calculate the excess present value. All the other calculations were correct.

    ______ Excess Present Value

## EXERCISES

EXERCISE 27–1 *(Calculate Present Values of Amounts)*

1. Use Table 27–1 to make the following calculations:
   a. The present value of $500 for five years at 12%
   b. The present value of $500 for five years at 14%
   c. The present value of $500 for six years at 12%
2. Why is the present value less in 1b than in 1a? (Discuss rather than refer to table factors.)
3. Why is the present value less in 1c than in 1a? (Discuss rather than refer to table factors.) [LO2a]

EXERCISE 27–2 *(Calculate Present Values of Annuities)*

1. Use Table 27–2 to make the following calculations:
   a. The present value of an annuity of $1,000 a year for four years at 10%
   b. The present value of an annuity of $1,000 a year for four years at 12%
   c. The present value of an annuity of $1,000 a year for five years at 10%
2. Why is the present value less in 1b than in 1a? (Discuss rather than refer to table factors.) [LO2a]

EXERCISE 27–3 *(Calculate After-Tax Cash Inflows)* Using the following data, calculate the after-tax cash inflows for each year using each of these two assumptions:

1. The investment is not depreciable.
2. The investment is depreciable and the straight-line method is used.

Here are the data to be used for each of the two assumptions:

1. The cost of the asset is $70,000.
2. The estimated salvage value of the asset is $10,000.
3. The estimated economic life of the asset is four years.
4. The expected cash inflows (before tax) are $25,000 a year.
5. The expected tax rate for the four years is 46%. [LO2b]

EXERCISE 27–4 *(Compute Accounting Rate of Return and Payback)* Armstrong Company is considering the purchase of several hauling trucks, which it estimates will produce $15,000 per year in cash inflows after tax. The total cost of the trucks is $50,000, and no salvage value is anticipated.

Required:

1. Calculate the accounting rate of return. (Use the original investment cost.)
2. Calculate the payback.
3. The president of Armstrong indicates that after the company "recoups" its money on the trucks, everything should be "clear profit." Comment on this viewpoint. [LO2c]

EXERCISE 27–5 *(Compute Discounted Rate of Return)* Careful Pipe Company is considering an investment in new pipe-fitting equipment that will supposedly last five years and save wages of employees who previously did the jobs manually (thus producing cash inflows after tax). The proposed cost of the equipment is $200,000, with no salvage value. Currently, it costs the company 10% to obtain its funds. If the asset is purchased, straight-line depreciation will be used.

Required:

1. Calculate the discounted rates of return that would be earned if
   a. Cash inflows after tax of $60,000 a year are produced.
   b. Cash inflows after tax of $70,000 a year are produced.
   c. Cash inflows after tax of $80,000 a year are produced.
2. In which of the above cases, if any, would the investment be feasible (considering only the quantitative factors)? Give reasons for your answers. [LO2c]

EXERCISE 27–6 *(Compute Excess Present Values)* Using the same data given in Exercise 27–5:

1. Calculate the excess present values for cases 1a, 1b, and 1c in Exercise 27–5.
2. Indicate whether the positive excess present values correspond to positive investment decisions made in cases 1a, 1b, and 1c in Exercise 27–5. [LO2c]

## PROBLEMS

PROBLEM 27–1 *(Calculate Present Values)*

1. Calculate the present value of each of these amounts:
   a. $500 due in four years at 8%
   b. $2,000 due in five years at 12%
   c. $3,000 due in six years at 14%
2. Prove, with an analysis similar to the one in the chapter, that the present value of $500 due in four years at 8% can be invested now at 8% and will amount to $500 in four years.
3. Calculate the present value of each of these annuities:
   a. $500 at the end of each of four years at 8%
   b. $2,000 at the end of each of five years at 12%
   c. $3,000 at the end of each of six years at 14%
4. Prove, with an analysis similar to the one in the chapter, that the present value of an annuity of $2,000 a year for five years at 12% can be invested now at 12% and will produce an annuity of $2,000 a year for five years. [LO1b,2a]

PROBLEM 27–2 *(Compare Present Value of an Amount and an Annuity)* In attempting to show someone the difference between the present value of an amount and the present value of an annuity, you decide to use the following approach:

a. The present value of an annuity of $600 for five years at 12% is calculated.
b. The present value of an annuity of $600 for four years at 12% is calculated.
c. The result obtained in item b is subtracted from the result obtained in item a.
d. The present value of $600 due in five years at 12% is calculated and compared with the result obtained in item c. The two results are about the same (allowing for rounding differences).

Required:

1. Perform the calculations in items a, b, c, and d above.
2. Explain why the results in item d are about the same as those in item c. [LO1b,2a]

PROBLEM 27–3 *(Compare After-Tax Benefits of Depreciable and Nondepreciable Investments)* Consider Company is studying the alternatives of investing $20,000 in (1) new microcomputers to be used in maintaining inventory records or (2) land to be used for a parking lot. In the first case, it is estimated that $5,000 per year can be saved in clerical expenses and storage costs (these would be cash inflows before tax). Depreciation per year using the straight-line method would be $4,000. In the second case, it is estimated that $7,500 per year can be generated in parking lot revenues (these would be cash inflows before tax).

The controller is pointing out to the investment committee that the tax benefit of depreciation on the microcomputers must be considered before making a decision on use of the funds. To emphasize this point, she prepared an analysis of after-tax cash inflows for both alternatives assuming 38%, 40%, 42%, and 44% tax rates.

Required:

1. Compute the cash inflows after tax per year of both alternatives using each of the four tax rates.
2. Comment on the comparative results obtained in Requirement 1. [LO1c,2b]

PROBLEM 27-4 *(Calculate After-Tax Cash Inflows Using Different Tax Rates)* Think-out Company is considering the purchase of new toy-making equipment and needs an analysis of the effects of taxes on cash inflows. Jim Percept, the chief accountant, started the following four-part analysis but was unable to complete it because of illness.

| | CASE | | | |
|---|---|---|---|---|
| | 1 | 2 | 3 | 4 |
| Cash inflows (before tax) from acquisition of equipment | $ 30,000 | $ 30,000 | $ 30,000 | $ 30,000 |
| Cost of the equipment | $100,000 | $100,000 | $100,000 | $100,000 |
| Estimated life of the equipment | 4 years | 4 years | 4 years | 4 years |
| Estimated salvage value | $ 5,000 | $ 5,000 | $ 5,000 | $ 5,000 |
| (Depreciation method is straight-line in all four cases) | | | | |
| Tax rate | 40% | 45% | 42% | 38% |
| Cash inflows (after tax) | $ ____ | $ ____ | $ ____ | $ ____ |

Required:

1. Calculate the correct amount for each blank and place these amounts in the blanks.
2. Comment on the differences caused by alternative tax rates. [LO1c,2b]

PROBLEM 27-5 *(Calculate Accounting Rates of Return and Paybacks)*

Required:

1. Based on the data given below, place the correct amount in each of the blanks.
2. Indicate in what way these calculations are deficient in making the investment decision.

| | CASE | | | |
|---|---|---|---|---|
| | 1 | 2 | 3 | 4 |
| Investment cost | $50,000 | $60,000 | $70,000 | $40,000 |
| Estimated life | 5 years | 4 years | 7 years | 4 years |
| Estimated cash inflows after tax each year | $13,000 | $20,000 | $13,000 | $14,000 |
| Estimated average net income each year | $ 6,000 | $ 8,000 | $ 5,000 | $ 7,000 |
| Accounting rate of return (Use the original investment cost) | ____ | ____ | ____ | ____ |
| Payback | ____ | ____ | ____ | ____ |

[LO2c]

PROBLEM 27-6 *(Compute Alternate Discounted Rates of Return)* Complete Company is considering borrowing $100,000 at 8% and making one of three alternative investments for four years:

1. Upgrade the computer terminals and printers. Although no increased revenues can automatically be anticipated, the company is convinced that saved salaries, repairs, and so forth, will produce $40,000 a year in cash inflows after tax for the four-year period.

2. Purchase ten additional cars for sales personnel. The company believes that $35,000 per year in cash inflows after tax can be generated for four years by expansion of territorial coverage.
3. Buy new manufacturing equipment which the company believes will produce $36,000 per year in cash inflows after tax for four years.

The tax rate is 45%, and straight-line depreciation will be used.

Required:

1. Calculate the discounted rate of return on each of the three alternative proposals.
2. Based solely on the calculations in Requirement 1, indicate which proposals, if any, should be considered. [LO2c]

PROBLEM 27-7 *(Calculate Several Excess Present Value Amounts)* In each of the following three cases, place the correct amounts in the blanks and complete the calculation of the excess present value. Each case has different (1) estimated lives, (2) estimated salvage values, and (3) present value percentages.

| 1. | END OF YEAR | CASH INFLOW AFTER TAX | PRESENT VALUE 10% | PRESENT VALUE |
|---|---|---|---|---|
| Cost | 0 | | | ($100,000) |
| Inflow | 1 | $30,000 | ____ | ____ |
| Inflow | 2 | 30,000 | ____ | ____ |
| Inflow | 3 | 30,000 | ____ | ____ |
| Inflow | 4 | 30,000 | ____ | ____ |
| Salvage value | 4 | 8,000 | ____ | ____ |
| Excess present value | | | | $ ____ |

| 2. | END OF YEAR | CASH INFLOW AFTER TAX | PRESENT VALUE 8% | PRESENT VALUE |
|---|---|---|---|---|
| Cost | 0 | | | ($100,000) |
| Inflow | 1 | $25,000 | ____ | ____ |
| Inflow | 2 | 25,000 | ____ | ____ |
| Inflow | 3 | 25,000 | ____ | ____ |
| Inflow | 4 | 25,000 | ____ | ____ |
| Inflow | 5 | 25,000 | ____ | ____ |
| Salvage value | 5 | 5,000 | ____ | ____ |
| Excess present value | | | | $ ____ |

| 3. | END OF YEAR | CASH INFLOW AFTER TAX | PRESENT VALUE 12% | PRESENT VALUE |
|---|---|---|---|---|
| Cost | 0 | | | ($100,000) |
| Inflow | 1 | $35,000 | ____ | ____ |
| Inflow | 2 | 35,000 | ____ | ____ |
| Inflow | 3 | 35,000 | ____ | ____ |
| Inflow | 4 | 35,000 | ____ | ____ |
| Salvage value | 4 | 10,000 | ____ | ____ |
| Excess present value | | | | $ ____ |

[LO2c]

PROBLEM 27–8 *(Use Three Capital Budgeting Techniques)* Search Company is considering a long-term investment in new dry-cleaning equipment that would cost $40,000, last five years, and produce $12,000 a year in cash inflows after tax.

Straight-line depreciation would be used, and the tax rate would be 40%. No salvage value is anticipated. The cost of obtaining funds (cost of capital) is 8%.

Required:

1. Calculate the payback.
2. Calculate the discounted rate of return.
3. Calculate the excess present value.
4. If all qualitative factors were favorable, would the investment be made?
5. Would the investment be made if the cost of capital was 18%? Why or why not?

[LO2c]

PROBLEM 27–9 *(Comprehensive Problem on Calculation of Excess Present Values Using Several Assumptions)* Value Company's investment committee is engaged in debate about the feasibility of a long-term investment in new delivery trucks. The committee members agree that the trucks would cost $60,000 and last five years, but they disagree about other factors. Here is a summary of the position taken by each member.

Mr. Josh believes that the new trucks could produce $22,000 of cash inflows after tax each year. He maintains that the trucks could be sold for $10,000 at the end of five years and that a loan from the bank could be obtained for 10%.

Ms. Koch believes that the new trucks could produce $15,000 of cash inflows after tax each year. She also maintains that the trucks could only be sold for $6,000 at the end of five years and that the bank would charge 12% for a loan of this type.

Mr. Arbitrate agrees with Mr. Josh's cash inflow projections and estimate of salvage value. However, he agrees with Ms. Koch's estimate of the interest the bank will charge.

Everyone agrees that the interest rate on a bank loan is the best available estimate of the cost of capital.

Required:

1. Calculate the three excess present values using the assumptions made by each of the three members of the committee. Which set of assumptions would result in favorable decisions to invest? Unfavorable decisions?
2. *(Optional question)* If you were not sure of the assumptions made by the committee members, what could you do to gain additional information as to their validity?

[LO2c]

## ALTERNATE PROBLEMS

PROBLEM 27–1A *(Calculate Present Values)* (Alternate to Problem 27–1)

1. Calculate the present value of each of these amounts:
   a. $700 due in four years at 10%
   b. $800 due in five years at 12%
   c. $1,500 due in six years at 14%
2. Prove, with an analysis similar to the one in the chapter, that the present value of $800 due in five years at 12% can be invested now at 12% and will amount to $800 in five years.
3. Calculate the present value of each of these annuities:
   a. $700 at the end of each of four years at 10%
   b. $800 at the end of each of five years at 12%
   c. $1,500 at the end of each of six years at 14%
4. Prove, with an analysis similar to the one in the chapter, that the present value of an annuity of $800 a year for five years at 12% can be invested now at 12% and will produce an annuity of $800 a year for five years. [LO1b,2a]

PROBLEM 27–2A *(Compare After-Tax Benefits of Depreciable and Nondepreciable Investments)* (Alternate to Problem 27–3) Cautious Company is studying the alternatives of investing $30,000 in (1) new equipment to crunch widgets or (2) land to be used for a parking lot. In the first case, it is estimated that $6,000 per year can be saved in repair expenses. (These are cash inflows before tax.) Depreciation per year using the straight-line method would be $5,000. In the second case, it is estimated that $8,000 per year can be generated in parking lot revenues. (These are cash inflows before tax.)

The chief accountant is pointing out to the president that the tax benefit of depreciation on the widget crunch equipment must be considered before making a decision on the use of the funds. To emphasize this point, he prepared an analysis of after-tax cash inflows for both alternatives assuming 40%, 42%, 44%, and 46% tax rates.

Required:

1. Compute the cash inflows after tax per year of both alternatives using each of the four tax rates.
2. Comment on the comparative results obtained in Requirement 1. [LO1c,2b]

PROBLEM 27–3A *(Calculate Accounting Rates of Return and Paybacks)* (Alternate to Problem 27–5)

Required:

1. Based on the data given below, place the correct amount in each of the blanks.
2. Indicate in what way these calculations are deficient in making the investment decision.

| | CASE | | | |
|---|---|---|---|---|
| | 1 | 2 | 3 | 4 |
| Investment cost | $40,000 | $45,000 | $50,000 | $54,000 |
| Estimated life | 4 years | 5 years | 5 years | 6 years |
| Estimated cash inflows after tax each year | $14,000 | $13,000 | $15,000 | $12,000 |
| Estimated average net income each year | $ 6,000 | $ 5,000 | $ 7,000 | $ 4,000 |
| Accounting rate of return (Use the original investment cost) | _____ | _____ | _____ | _____ |
| Payback | _____ | _____ | _____ | _____ |

[LO2c]

PROBLEM 27–4A *(Compute Alternate Discounted Rates of Return)* (Alternate to Problem 27–6) Contemplate Company is considering borrowing $80,000 at a 10% interest rate and making one of three alternative investments for five years:

1. Upgrade the computer equipment and produce $20,000 of cash inflows after tax each year for the five-year period.
2. Purchase eight additional delivery trucks that will produce $18,000 of cash inflows after tax each year in additional sales for five years.
3. Buy new manufacturing equipment that will produce $19,000 of cash inflows after tax each year for five years.

The tax rate is 40%, and straight-line depreciation will be used.

Required:

1. Calculate the discounted rate of return on each of the three alternative proposals.
2. Based solely on the calculations in Requirement 1, indicate which proposals, if any, should be considered. [LO2c]

PROBLEM 27–5A *(Calculate Several Excess Present Value Amounts)* (Alternate to Problem 27–7) In each of the following three cases, place the correct amounts in the blanks and complete the calculation of the excess present value. Each case has different (1) estimated lives, (2) estimated salvage values, and (3) present value percentages.

| 1. | END OF YEAR | CASH INFLOW AFTER TAX | PRESENT VALUE 8% | PRESENT VALUE |
|---|---|---|---|---|
| Cost | 0 | | | ($100,000) |
| Inflow | 1 | $35,000 | _____ | _____ |
| Inflow | 2 | 35,000 | _____ | _____ |
| Inflow | 3 | 35,000 | _____ | _____ |
| Inflow | 4 | 35,000 | _____ | _____ |
| Salvage value | 4 | 10,000 | _____ | _____ |
| Excess present value | | | | $_____ |

| 2. | END OF YEAR | CASH INFLOW AFTER TAX | PRESENT VALUE 10% | PRESENT VALUE |
|---|---|---|---|---|
| Cost | 0 | | | ($100,000) |
| Inflow | 1 | $30,000 | _____ | _____ |
| Inflow | 2 | 30,000 | _____ | _____ |
| Inflow | 3 | 30,000 | _____ | _____ |
| Inflow | 4 | 30,000 | _____ | _____ |
| Inflow | 5 | 30,000 | _____ | _____ |
| Salvage value | 5 | 8,000 | _____ | _____ |
| Excess present value | | | | $_____ |

| 3. | END OF YEAR | CASH INFLOW AFTER TAX | PRESENT VALUE 12% | PRESENT VALUE |
|---|---|---|---|---|
| Cost | 0 | | | ($100,000) |
| Inflow | 1 | $40,000 | _____ | _____ |
| Inflow | 2 | 40,000 | _____ | _____ |
| Inflow | 3 | 40,000 | _____ | _____ |
| Inflow | 4 | 40,000 | _____ | _____ |
| Salvage value | 4 | 12,000 | _____ | _____ |
| Excess present value | | | | $_____ |

[LO2c]

# 28 *Income Taxes and Business Decisions*

### *Learning Objectives*

When you complete this chapter you will be able to

1. Answer the following questions:
   a. What is tax planning? How does tax avoidance differ from tax evasion?
   b. What are the four classifications of taxable entities?
   c. What are the major components used in determining the amount of an individual's income tax liability?
   d. How does the determination of taxes for a corporation differ from that for an individual?
   e. In what ways do income taxes affect business decisions?
2. Perform the following accounting functions:
   a. Compute the tax liability for an individual based on the material contained in this chapter.
   b. Compute the tax liability for a corporation based on the material contained in this chapter.

From our own experience, we all realize that income taxes can be a significant expenditure for both individuals and businesses. For example, some individuals and many corporations pay 23% or more of their taxable income to the government in income taxes. For this reason, it is important that taxpayers try to plan their financial affairs to minimize the amount of their tax liability.

This chapter explains some of the major provisions of the federal income tax law as they pertain to individuals and corporations, and it describes several ways in which income taxes affect business decisions. Because income tax laws are detailed and complex, we must limit our discussion to a sampling of the basic provisions of the law. If you want to pursue the subject in greater depth, many books and courses devoted entirely to federal income taxes are available, and we encourage you to seek them out. In the meantime, keep in mind that tax laws are often changed, and you should examine the current law when planning strategies to minimize your legal tax liability.

## TAX PLANNING

*1a. Tax planning means planning one's affairs in a manner that will minimize one's tax liability*

Because income tax payments are often a significant expenditure, it is natural to expect taxpayers to plan their financial affairs in a manner that will minimize their tax liability. In the words of Judge Learned Hand, "[T]here is nothing sinister in so arranging one's affairs as to keep taxes as low as possible. . . . [N]obody owes any duty to pay more than the law demands." **Tax planning** involves the arrangement of a taxpayer's affairs in such a way as to incur the lowest possible tax liability. Its goals are to pay the least amount of tax at the latest possible time. To achieve these goals, the taxpayer must evaluate the tax consequences of alternative courses of action.

For almost every business decision, there are alternative courses of action. For example, deciding whether to purchase or lease a business vehicle is a decision that will have an effect on **taxable income**—the amount of income to which the appropriate tax rate is applied to determine the entity's gross **tax liability** (the total amount of taxes that must be paid on the entity's taxable income for the year). For assets other than automobiles, there may be other alternative courses of action to be evaluated. For example, should the resource in question be acquired by paying for it in cash, by offering securities instead of cash in exchange, by leasing it, or perhaps by self-constructing it? Furthermore, once acquired, another decision must be made concerning whether the resource should be depreciated by using the straight-line method or an accelerated method. The selection will affect the amount of income tax liability, not only in the year the choice is made but also in a number of subsequent years.

Tax planning involves evaluating each alternative course of action in terms of its tax consequences and selecting the one that will result in the lowest legal tax liability.

## TAX AVOIDANCE AND TAX EVASION

*1a. Tax avoidance is legal minimization of tax liability; tax evasion is the fraudulent understatement of taxable income*

When discussing taxes, a clear distinction must be made between tax avoidance and tax evasion. **Tax avoidance** is achieved by arranging a taxpayer's financial affairs and transactions, within the legal confines of the tax statutes, in a manner that will minimize tax liability. In contrast, **tax evasion** is the deliberate understatement of taxable income by failing to report income received or by claiming fraudulent deductions. For example, taxes are evaded when taxable income such as interest, dividends, tips, and gains on security sales is not reported. Tax evasion is of course illegal, and the tax code stipulates that it is punishable by fine and imprisonment.

## TAX ACCOUNTING METHODS

The **Internal Revenue Code** (a compilation of all current federal income tax laws passed by Congress) generally gives the taxpayer the option of using either the cash basis or the accrual basis of accounting to determine taxable income (except when inventories are a significant factor in the determination of net income, the accrual basis must be used for purchases and sales). Also, corporations or partnerships with a corporate partner that have gross receipts in excess of $5 million cannot use the cash method of accounting for tax purposes.

## CLASSIFICATIONS OF TAXABLE ENTITIES

***1b. Taxable entities include (1) individuals, (2) corporations, (3) estates, (4) trusts***

There are four classifications of taxable entities: (1) individuals, (2) corporations, (3) estates, and (4) trusts. Each must file a tax return and pay taxes on taxable income.

Single proprietorships and partnerships are not treated as separate taxable entities under the law. Instead the owner of a proprietorship includes the income or loss from the business on his or her individual tax return. Partners include their share of the partnership's income or loss in their respective individual tax returns.

A corporation is a separate taxable entity and must file a tax return and pay taxes on its taxable income. Also, when the corporation distributes some of its after-tax income to its stockholders as a dividend, the amount must be included as income in the stockholder's individual tax return. This taxing of corporate income when earned, and again when distributed to the recipient (the stockholder), has often been referred to as the "double taxation" of corporate income.

Estates and trusts are also separate taxable entities. They file specific types of tax returns and pay tax in accordance with the tax law.

## TAX REFORM

As indicated earlier, tax laws are often changed. In 1986, however, one of the most massive overhauls the tax system had seen in the previous fifty years was passed by Congress. The Tax Reform Act of 1986 is designed to decrease the perception of unfairness in our tax laws. It is a very modified form of a flat tax, since it increases the tax base and decreases tax rates. The new Act is revenue neutral. It generates the same total tax revenue over a six-year period beginning in 1987 as the previous tax laws would have generated. In general, individuals will pay less of this tax and corporations will pay more under the Act. However, specific individuals and corporations will be affected differently. An individual who previously took advantage of large tax deductions and tax credits which were eliminated under the Act may suffer a total tax increase, despite the lowering of the tax rates. Although many tax deductions and tax credits were eliminated by the Act, tax considerations continue to be an important part of economic decision making.

## INCOME TAX ON INDIVIDUALS

The federal government provides forms and instructions for the computation and filing of income taxes. Although the sequential listing of specific material in the income tax form changes from time to time, the general approach for determin-

*EXHIBIT 28–1*

Formula for Determining an Individual's Tax Liability

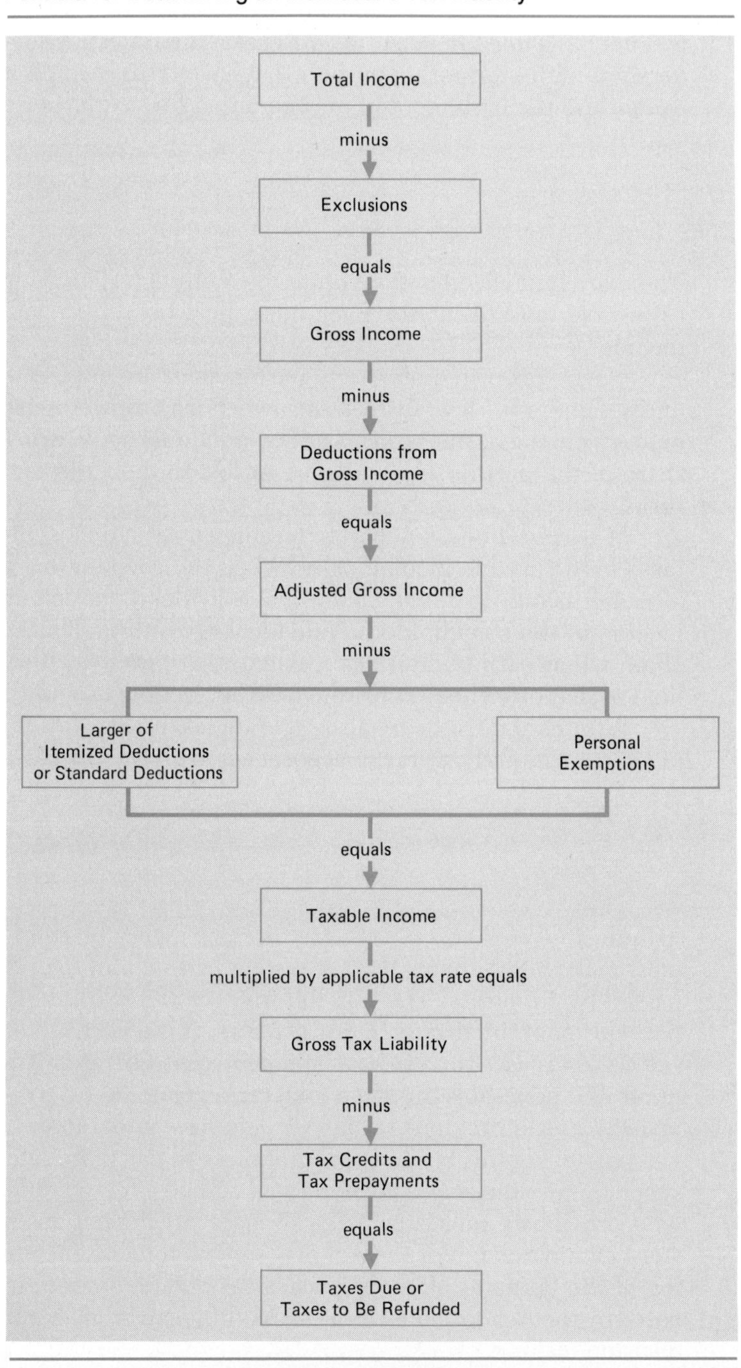

*1c. The formula for determining an individual's tax liability is shown in Exhibit 28-1*

ing an individual taxpayer's tax liability can be shown by the formula in Exhibit 28-1. The various components appearing in the formula are discussed in the following sections.

### Total Income

**Total income** includes all income from whatever sources derived. However, as the formula in Exhibit 28-1 shows, not all income is included in taxable gross income. Some income items can be excluded in arriving at gross income that is income subject to tax. An example of an income item that would be included in total income and excluded in arriving at gross income is interest earned on state and municipal bonds.

### Exclusions

**Exclusions** are income items specifically excluded from total income by law, Treasury regulations, or court decisions. Thus all income items are included in gross income unless there is a provision in the tax law that permits excluding the item. Examples of income items to be excluded are shown in Exhibit 28-2.

### Gross Income

**Gross income** for tax purposes is total income less allowable exclusions. Exhibit 28-2 contains examples of items included in gross income.

Items that are fully excludable from gross income, such as interest on state and municipal bonds, are reported on the tax return only for disclosure purposes. As of January 1, 1987, gains from the sale of all assets, including capital assets, are

*EXHIBIT 28-2*

Examples of Inclusions in Gross Income and Exclusions from Gross Income

| ITEMS INCLUDED IN GROSS INCOME | ITEMS EXCLUDED FROM GROSS INCOME |
|---|---|
| Wages, salaries, bonuses, commissions, and any other remuneration from employer | Interest on state and municipal bonds |
| Tips for services rendered | Gifts, inheritance, and bequests received |
| Unemployment compensation | Life insurance proceeds in most cases |
| Portions of pensions and annuities representing income | Scholarships to the extent spent on tuition or course-required equipment |
| Portions of Social Security benefits | Portion of pensions and annuities representing a return of invested capital |
| Interest on savings account | Veteran payments in most cases |
| Rents and royalties | Accident and disability benefits |
| Severance and vacation pay | Child support received |
| Prizes and gambling gains | |
| Income from a business operated as a single proprietorship | |
| Allocated share of partnership income | |
| Alimony received | |
| Dividends | |
| Gains from the sale of real estate, securities, and other property | |

fully included in income reported on the tax return. The tax treatment of capital gains and capital losses is discussed in more detail later in this chapter.

## Deductions from Gross Income

Note that in Exhibit 28–1, **deductions** from gross income are subtracted from gross income to determine the **adjusted gross income.** These deductions are generally of a business nature and consist of business expenses and other expenses incurred in generating income from such items as rents and royalties. The calculation of adjusted gross income is important to the individual because it becomes the basis for certain personal deductions in computing taxable income. The adjusted gross income provides a more equitable base for certain other calculations than that provided by gross income. For example, a taxpayer who generates a high gross income may have incurred many business expenses while producing that gross income.

Deductions from gross income allowed in determining adjusted gross income include the items discussed below. Some are self-explanatory and are therefore merely listed.

**TRADE AND BUSINESS DEDUCTIONS** Ordinary and necessary expenses attributable to a taxpayer's trade or business are deductible. These expenses consist of such items as cost of goods sold, salaries to employees, rent, advertising, depreciation, and business meals and entertainment. While all other ordinary and necessary trade or business expenses are fully deductible, the deduction for business meals and entertainment is limited to 80% of such expenses. Deductible business expenses are subtracted from business revenues to determine the business net income, which is then included in the taxpayer's adjusted gross income.

**CONTRIBUTION TO RETIREMENT PLANS** Taxpayers may establish their own retirement funds by depositing amounts with financial institutions. The Economic Recovery Tax Act of 1981 allows taxpayers to establish retirement funds known as **individual retirement accounts,** or simply **IRAs.** A taxpayer is permitted to contribute as much as \$2,000 a year (\$2,250 if married to a nonworking spouse) to the plan. The amount contributed is deducted from gross income in determining adjusted gross income. Thus a taxpayer whose tax rate is 20% can save \$400 in taxes by investing \$2,000 in an IRA. In addition, earnings on IRA contributions are not taxed until distributed. Amounts paid to an IRA provide for annuities that are paid to the taxpayer beginning as early as age 59½.

As of January 1, 1987, individuals not covered by employer-sponsored pension plans can continue to fully deduct IRA contributions up to the annual limits. However, the deduction may be limited or completely denied to individuals covered by pension plans, depending on their adjusted gross income level. Married individuals with adjusted gross income of less than \$40,000 and single individuals with adjusted gross income of less than \$25,000 can still take the full deduction, even though they are covered by a pension plan. However, the maximum deduction is phased out between \$40,000 and \$50,000 of adjusted gross income, if married and filing jointly, and between \$25,000 and \$35,000, if single. Those covered by pension plans and with income above these levels are not entitled to an IRA deduction. These individuals can still fund an IRA on a nondeductible basis, and earnings on such accounts will not be taxed until actually distributed.

Self-employed individuals are also allowed to deduct annual contributions made to a retirement plan called a **Keogh plan.** These plans are subject to the same rules as corporate pension plans. Annual additions to a defined contribution Keogh plan are limited to the lesser of $30,000 or 25% of compensation.

ALIMONY Alimony payments are deductible by the payer in arriving at adjusted gross income. Alimony payments are, however, taxable to the recipient. Child support payments are not deductible by the payer, nor taxable to the recipient.

LOSSES FROM SALES OR EXCHANGES OF PROPERTY Losses from the sale or exchange of business or investment property (property acquired or used to produce income) are deductible in arriving at adjusted gross income. On the other hand, losses from the sale or exchange of personal property (such as a personal home or automobile) are not deductible.

PASSIVE BUSINESS AND RENTAL LOSSES In an effort to curb **tax shelter** investments (investments largely motivated by the tax losses they generate which offset other income and hence decrease taxes), Congress recently disallowed or limited the deduction of passive business and rental losses. Losses from any partnership or other business in which the taxpayer does not materially participate are limited to the taxpayer's income from such businesses. Thus anyone who invests in a business but does not participate in its operations on a regular, continuous, and substantial basis is unable to use such losses to offset other income.

In addition, all losses from rental activities are subject to the loss-limitation rule, regardless of whether the taxpayer participates in managing the property. Under a special exception, taxpayers may use up to $25,000 of losses from rental real estate activities in which they actively participate to offset other income. This rental real estate loss exception is phased out for high-income taxpayers.

For investments made before the enactment of the Tax Reform Act of 1986, these loss limitation rules are phased in. A limited percentage of the losses that would be disallowed under these rules is deductible during the transition period. These percentages are 65% in 1987, 40% in 1988, 20% in 1989, and 10% in 1990.

## *Deductions from Adjusted Gross Income*

As shown in Exhibit 28–1, an individual taxpayer is permitted two types of deductions from adjusted gross income: (1) itemized deductions or the standard deduction and (2) personal exemptions.

Most taxpayers are allowed to subtract an amount known as the **standard deduction** from adjusted gross income in computing taxable income. The amount of this standard deduction depends on the taxpayer's filing status. The standard deduction amounts for the most recent and upcoming years are as follows:

| TAXPAYER'S FILING STATUS | STANDARD DEDUCTION | | |
|---|---|---|---|
| | 1986 | 1987 | 1988 |
| Married persons filing a joint return and qualifying surviving spouses | $3,670 | $3,760 | $5,000 |
| Unmarried persons qualifying as head of household | 2,480 | 2,540 | 4,400 |
| Single persons | 2,480 | 2,540 | 3,000 |

In 1989 and later years, the 1988 standard deduction level will be adjusted annually for inflation by applying changes in the Consumer Price Index (CPI).

As of January 1, 1987, taxpayers who are elderly or blind receive an additional standard deduction of $600 if they are married, and $750 if they are single. This addition to the standard deduction replaces the additional personal exemption allowed to the elderly and blind under previous law.

The age addition to the standard deduction is available to a taxpayer and/or spouse who is 65 years of age or older on the last day of the taxable year. For a married couple filing jointly where both individuals are 65 years of age or older, the addition would be $1,200. Similarly, the sight deduction addition is available to a taxpayer and/or spouse who is blind at the end of the taxable year. For example, assume that Alex and Beth are filing a 1988 joint return. Alex is 72 years old and blind, and Beth is 68 years old and has normal vision. The couple would be entitled to a standard deduction computed as follows:

| | |
|---|---|
| Standard deduction for married couple filing jointly | $5,000 |
| Alex: Age deduction addition ($600) and sight deduction addition ($600) | 1,200 |
| Beth: Age deduction addition ($600) | 600 |
| Total standard deduction | $6,800 |

Neither the age nor the sight deduction addition is available for dependents of the taxpayer. They only apply to the taxpayer and/or spouse.

Rather than taking the standard deduction, the taxpayer may elect to subtract **itemized deductions** from adjusted gross income in computing taxable income. The taxpayer will usually subtract itemized deductions if this total is larger than the applicable standard deduction. Itemized deductions consist mostly of personal expenses and employee business expenses.

Taxpayers are responsible for proving the validity of their itemized deductions. Therefore adequate records should be maintained, and all the documents needed to verify and support the deductions should be kept.

The tax laws specify the items that qualify as deductions for personal and employee business expenses. The major categories of these expenses that may be itemized and deducted from adjusted gross income are discussed in the following paragraphs.

**MEDICAL AND DENTAL EXPENSES** Unreimbursed medical and dental expenses of the taxpayer and his or her family are deductible to the extent that they exceed 7.5% of adjusted gross income. This category includes the fees paid to hospitals and doctors, the cost of medical insurance, the cost of prescription drugs and insulin, and the amounts paid for medical appliances such as crutches and wheelchairs.

**TAXES** Many state and local taxes are deductible. Examples of deductible taxes include real estate taxes, personal property taxes, state and local income taxes, and general sales taxes. Federal taxes and certain state and local taxes are not deductible. Examples of nondeductible taxes include gift and inheritance taxes; taxes on gasoline, tobacco, and alcoholic beverages; and most licensing fees, such as drivers' licenses, marriage licenses, and pet licenses. State and local general sales taxes became nondeductible as of January 1, 1987.

**INTEREST** Generally mortgage interest on a first and a second home is deductible. Interest paid on loans backed by the appreciated value of a home is deductible only if the loan proceeds are used for home improvements, educational tuition, or medical expenses. The deduction for consumer interest, which includes interest paid on credit cards, car loans, or boat loans, is being phased out. The phase-out disallows a percentage of consumer interest deduction each year, according to the following schedule: 1987—35%; 1988—60%; 1989—80%; 1990—90%; and 1991 and later years—100%.

Interest paid on loans to finance investments is deductible. However, the deduction is limited to the amount of the taxpayer's dividend and interest income. Any investment interest that is disallowed due to this limit is subject to the phase-out schedule above.

CHARITABLE CONTRIBUTIONS Subject to certain limitations, contributions of money and property made to religious, charitable, educational, and other qualifying nonprofit organizations are deductible. Contributions to relatives, friends, or other individuals are not deductible.

CASUALTY AND THEFT LOSSES The uninsured portion of certain property losses resulting from a casualty or theft in excess of $100 for each loss is deductible only to the extent that the total of all such losses for the year exceeds 10% of adjusted gross income. For example, assume that a taxpayer having an adjusted gross income of $30,000 incurred two casualty losses of $4,000 and $500, respectively, during the year. The taxpayer would be entitled to a casualty loss deduction of $1,300 computed as follows:

| | | |
|---|---|---|
| First casualty loss: | $4,000 − $100 = | $3,900 |
| Second casualty loss: | $ 500 − $100 = | 400 |
| Casualty losses in excess of $100 per loss | | $4,300 |
| Less: 10% of adjusted gross income (.10 × $30,000) = | | 3,000 |
| Casualty loss deduction | | $1,300 |

Casualty losses must result from sudden, unexpected, or unusual events such as fire, storm, flood, earthquake, automobile accident, or theft.

MOVING EXPENSES Self-employed individuals and employees may deduct unreimbursed moving expenses incurred in connection with beginning employment or changing job locations. To qualify for deducting moving expenses, a taxpayer must move a sufficient distance and keep the new job for a sustained time period. Starting in 1987, moving expenses became an itemized deduction.

BUSINESS EXPENSES OF AN EMPLOYEE Employees may deduct certain expenses incurred in connection with their employment. Qualifying expenses include the following:

1. *Travel*—employment-related travel expenses including transportation and the cost of meals and lodging when incurred by the employee while away from home overnight.
2. *Transportation*—employment-related transportation expenses including the cost of using the employee's automobile and the cost of public transportation. However, costs incurred by an employee in commuting between home and work are not deductible.
3. *Outside salesperson's expenses*—expenses incurred in soliciting business for an employer while away from the employer's place of business. These expenses include travel and transportation, telephone, postage, and telegrams.

Note that employers may reimburse their employees for the expenses outlined above. In such cases, employees may deduct only that portion of their expenses not reimbursed by the employer. Furthermore, if the reimbursement exceeds their expenses, the employee must include the excess amount in his or her gross income.

Once the total qualifying unreimbursed employee business expenses are determined, this total must be combined with other expenses related to producing income discussed below. The combined total is then deductible as an itemized deduction only to the extent that it exceeds 2% of a taxpayer's adjusted gross income.

**EXPENSES RELATED TO PRODUCING INCOME** Included in this category are allowable expenses related to the production of income or to the management of income-producing property that are not included in the employee business expenses listed above. Examples include union dues, uniforms and protective clothing costs, dues to professional organizations, subscriptions to professional journals, certain employment agency fees, safe deposit box rentals related to investments in income-producing properties, and fees paid for income tax advice and for the preparation of tax returns. These expenses are combined with the above employee business expenses and are deductible to the extent that they exceed the 2% floor.

## *Personal Exemptions*

In addition to itemized deductions or the standard deduction, a taxpayer is allowed a second kind of deduction from adjusted gross income called a **personal exemption.** One exemption is allowed for the taxpayer and another for his or her spouse when a joint return is filed, and one additional exemption is allowed for each person who qualifies as a dependent. To qualify as a dependent, a person must satisfy all of the following requirements:

1. Be closely related to the taxpayer or have lived in the taxpayer's home for the entire year
2. Have received over one-half of his or her support from the taxpayer during the year
3. If married, does not file a joint return with his or her spouse
4. Had less than $1,080 of gross income during the year
5. Be a citizen or resident of the United States or a resident of Canada or Mexico

The $1,080 limitation on gross income (requirement 4) does not apply to children of the taxpayer who are either under 19 years of age at the end of the taxable year or who have been full-time students at an educational institution for at least five months of the year.

The taxpayer is allowed a deduction for each personal exemption claimed. The amount of this deduction per exemption claimed is as follows:

| YEAR | DEDUCTION PER PERSONAL EXEMPTION |
|---|---|
| 1986 | $1,080 |
| 1987 | 1,900 |
| 1988 | 1,950 |
| 1989 | 2,000 |

EXHIBIT 28-3
1986 and 1988 Tax Rate Schedules

SCHEDULE X—SINGLE TAXPAYERS

For the 1986 Taxable Year

| *If taxable income is:* | *The tax is:* |
|---|---|
| Not over $2,480 | No tax. |
| Over $2,480 but not over $3,670 | 11% of the excess over $2,480. |
| Over $3,670 but not over $4,750 | $130.90, plus 12% of the excess over $3,670. |
| Over $4,750 but not over $7,010 | $260.50, plus 14% of the excess over $4,750. |
| Over $7,010 but not over $9,170 | $576.90, plus 15% of the excess over $7,010. |
| Over $9,170 but not over $11,650 | $900.90, plus 16% of the excess over $9,170. |
| Over $11,650 but not over $13,920 | $1,297.70, plus 18% of the excess over $11,650. |
| Over $13,920 but not over $16,190 | $1,706.30, plus 20% of the excess over $13,920. |
| Over $16,190 but not over $19,640 | $2,160.30, plus 23% of the excess over $16,190. |
| Over $19,640 but not over $25,360 | $2,953.80, plus 26% of the excess over $19,640. |
| Over $25,360 but not over $31,080 | $4,441.00, plus 30% of the excess over $25,360. |
| Over $31,080 but not over $36,800 | $6,157.00, plus 34% of the excess over $31,080. |
| Over $36,800 but not over $44,780 | $8,101.80, plus 38% of the excess over $36,800. |
| Over $44,780 but not over $59,670 | $11,134.20, plus 42% of the excess over $44,780. |
| Over $59,670 but not over $88,270 | $17,388.00, plus 48% of the excess over $59,670. |
| Over $88,270 | $31,116.00, plus 50% of the excess over $88,270. |

For the 1988 Taxable Year

| *If taxable income is:* | *The tax is:* |
|---|---|
| Not over $17,850 | 15% of taxable income. |
| Over $17,850 but not over $43,150 | $2,677.50, plus 28% of the excess over $17,850. |
| Over $43,150 but not over $89,560 | $9,761.50, plus 33% of the excess over $43,150. |
| Over $89,560 | 28% of taxable income. |

SCHEDULE Y—MARRIED TAXPAYERS FILING JOINT RETURNS AND QUALIFYING WIDOWS AND WIDOWERS

For the 1986 Taxable Year

| *If taxable income is:* | *The tax is:* |
|---|---|
| Not over $3,670 | No tax. |
| Over $3,670 but not over $5,940 | 11% of the excess over $3,670. |
| Over $5,940 but not over $8,200 | $249.70, plus 12% of the excess over $5,940. |
| Over $8,200 but not over $12,840 | $520.90, plus 14% of the excess over $8,200. |
| Over $12,840 but not over $17,270 | $1,170.50, plus 16% of the excess over $12,840. |
| Over $17,270 but not over $21,800 | $1,879.30, plus 18% of the excess over $17,270. |
| Over $21,800 but not over $26,550 | $2,694.70, plus 22% of the excess over $21,800. |
| Over $26,550 but not over $32,270 | $3,739.70, plus 25% of the excess over $26,550. |
| Over $32,270 but not over $37,980 | $5,169.70, plus 28% of the excess over $32,270. |
| Over $37,980 but not over $49,420 | $6,768.50, plus 33% of the excess over $37,980. |
| Over $49,420 but not over $64,750 | $10,543.70, plus 38% of the excess over $49,420. |
| Over $64,750 but not over $92,370 | $16,369.10, plus 42% of the excess over $64,750. |
| Over $92,370 but not over $118,050 | $27,969.50, plus 45% of the excess over $92,370. |
| Over $118,050 but not over $175,250 | $39,525.50, plus 49% of the excess over $118,050. |
| Over $175,250 | $67,553.50, plus 50% of the excess over $175,250. |

For the 1988 Taxable Year

| *If taxable income is:* | *The tax is:* |
|---|---|
| Not over $29,750 | 15% of taxable income. |
| Over $29,750 but not over $71,900 | $4,462.50, plus 28% of the excess over $29,750. |
| Over $71,900 but not over $149,250 | $16,264.50, plus 33% of the excess over $71,900. |
| Over $149,250 | 28% of taxable income. |

## SCHEDULE Y—MARRIED TAXPAYERS FILING SEPARATE RETURNS

### For the 1986 Taxable Year

| *If taxable income is:* | *The tax is:* |
|---|---|
| Not over $1,835 | No tax. |
| Over $1,835 but not over $2,970 | 11% of the excess over $1,835. |
| Over $2,970 but not over $4,100 | $124.85, plus 12% of the excess over $2,970. |
| Over $4,100 but not over $6,420 | $260.45, plus 14% of the excess over $4,100. |
| Over $6,420 but not over $8,635 | $585.25, plus 16% of the excess over $6,420. |
| Over $8,635 but not over $10,900 | $939.65, plus 18% of the excess over $8,635. |
| Over $10,900 but not over $13,275 | $1,347.35, plus 22% of the excess over $10,900. |
| Over $13,275 but not over $16,135 | $1,869.85, plus 25% of the excess over $13,275. |
| Over $16,135 but not over $18,990 | $2,584.85, plus 28% of the excess over $16,135. |
| Over $18,990 but not over $24,710 | $3,384.25, plus 33% of the excess over $18,990. |
| Over $24,710 but not over $32,375 | $5,271.85, plus 38% of the excess over $24,710. |
| Over $32,375 but not over $46,185 | $8,184.55, plus 42% of the excess over $32,375. |
| Over $46,185 but not over $59,025 | $13,984.75, plus 45% of the excess over $46,185. |
| Over $59,025 but not over $87,625 | $19,762.75, plus 49% of the excess over $59,025. |
| Over $87,625 | $33,776.75, plus 50% of the excess over $87,625. |

### For the 1988 Taxable Year

| *If taxable income is:* | *The tax is:* |
|---|---|
| Not over $14,875 | 15% of taxable income. |
| Over $14,875 but not over $35,950 | $2,231.25, plus 28% of the excess over $14,875. |
| Over $35,950 but not over $113,300 | $8,132.25, plus 33% of the excess over $35,950. |
| Over $113,300 | 28% of taxable income. |

## SCHEDULE Z—UNMARRIED HEADS OF HOUSEHOLD

### For the 1986 Taxable Year

| *If taxable income is:* | *The tax is:* |
|---|---|
| Not over $2,480 | No tax. |
| Over $2,480 but not over $4,750 | 11% of the excess over $2,480. |
| Over $4,750 but not over $7,010 | $249.70, plus 12% of the excess over $4,750. |
| Over $7,010 but not over $9,390 | $520.90, plus 14% of the excess over $7,010. |
| Over $9,390 but not over $12,730 | $854.10, plus 17% of the excess over $9,390. |
| Over $12,730 but not over $16,190 | $1,421.90, plus 18% of the excess over $12,730. |
| Over $16,190 but not over $19,640 | $2,044.70, plus 20% of the excess over $16,190. |
| Over $19,640 but not over $25,360 | $2,734.70, plus 24% of the excess over $19,640. |
| Over $25,360 but not over $31,080 | $4,107.50, plus 28% of the excess over $25,360. |
| Over $31,080 but not over $36,800 | $5,709.10, plus 32% of the excess over $31,080. |
| Over $36,800 but not over $48,240 | $7,539.50, plus 35% of the excess over $36,800. |
| Over $48,240 but not over $65,390 | $11,543.50, plus 42% of the excess over $48,240. |
| Over $65,390 but not over $88,270 | $18,746.50, plus 45% of the excess over $65,390. |
| Over $88,270 but not over $116,870 | $29,042.50, plus 48% of the excess over $88,270. |
| Over $116,870 | $42,770.50, plus 50% of the excess over $116,870. |

### For the 1988 Taxable Year

| *If taxable income is:* | *The tax is:* |
|---|---|
| Not over $23,900 | 15% of taxable income. |
| Over $23,900 but not over $61,650 | $3,585.20, plus 28% of the excess over $23,900. |
| Over $61,650 but not over $123,790 | $14,155, plus 33% of the excess over $61,650. |
| Over $123,790 | 28% of taxable income. |

Beginning in 1990, the 1989 personal exemption deduction will be adjusted annually for changes in the Consumer Price Index. Also, as of 1988 the exemption deduction is partially or completely eliminated for certain high-income taxpayers. For married couples filing jointly, this elimination begins when taxable income exceeds $149,250.

## Computing the Gross Tax Liability

*2a. Computation of tax liability for an individual is explained here*

Adjusted gross income minus itemized deductions or the standard deduction and minus allowable personal exemptions equals *taxable income.* Once the taxpayer's taxable income is determined, the **gross tax liability** can be computed by using a **tax rate schedule.** The schedule to be used in determining the taxpayer's gross tax liability depends on the taxpayer's filing status and the amount of taxable income. Tax rate schedule are provided for

1. Single taxpayers
2. Married taxpayers filing joint returns and qualifying widows and widowers
3. Married taxpayers filing separate returns
4. Unmarried taxpayers who qualify as heads of household

The four tax rate schedules are shown in Exhibit 28–3.

## Tax Rate Schedules

In 1986 there were fourteen tax rate brackets (fifteen for singles), ranging from 11% to 50%. As a result of the 1986 Tax Reform Act, these rate brackets were compressed into just two tax rates for 1988: 15% and 28%. The 1986 and 1988 tax rate schedules for each filing status are shown in Exhibit 28–3.

In 1986 the standard deduction was known as the zero bracket amount, and it was built into the tax rate schedules instead of being deducted in computing taxable income. Thus the 1986 rate schedules do not show any tax until taxable income exceeds the 1986 zero bracket amounts. As mentioned earlier, beginning in 1987 the standard deduction is subtracted in computing taxable income. Thus the 1987 and 1988 rate schedules begin with any taxable income greater than zero.

Also beginning in 1988, the benefits of the 15% tax rate are phased out for high-income taxpayers. This phase out is accomplished by applying a 33% tax rate to a specified income range ($71,900 to $149,250 for married couples filing jointly). Once these taxpayers reach certain taxable income levels ($149,250 for married couples filing jointly), a flat 28% effective tax rate is applied to all of their taxable income.

The 1987 tax rates are a blend of the 1986 and 1988 tax rate schedules. The 1987 blended rates for married couples filing jointly and single taxpayers are shown in Exhibit 28–4 on page 986.

To illustrate the use of the tax rate schedules, assume that Carole and Bill Kool file a 1987 joint tax return. Their adjusted gross income is $50,600 and their itemized deductions are $8,620. They have one young child. Their taxable income is $36,280 and gross tax liability of $6,398 would be computed as follows:

| | | |
|---|---|---|
| Adjusted gross income | | $50,600 |
| Less: The larger of itemized deductions or | $8,620 | |
| the standard deduction | 3,760 | (8,620) |
| Less: Personal exemptions (3 × $1,900) | | (5,700) |
| Taxable income | | 36,280 |
| Tax on first $28,000 of taxable income | | 4,080 |
| Tax on remaining taxable income ($36,280 − $28,000 = $8,280 × 28%) | | 2,318 |
| Gross tax liability | | $ 6,398 |

*EXHIBIT 28–4*
Partial 1987 Tax Rate Schedule

SCHEDULE Y—MARRIED TAXPAYERS FILING JOINT RETURNS AND QUALIFYING WIDOWS AND WIDOWERS
For the 1987 Taxable Year

| *If taxable income is:* | *The tax is:* |
|---|---|
| Not over $3,000 | 11% of taxable income. |
| Over $3,000 but not over $28,000 | $330, plus 15% of the excess over $3,000. |
| Over $28,000 but not over $45,000 | $4,080, plus 28% of the excess over $28,000. |
| Over $45,000 but not over $90,000 | $8,840, plus 35% of the excess over $45,000. |
| Over $90,000 | $24,590, plus 38.5% of the excess over $90,000. |

SCHEDULES X—SINGLE TAXPAYERS
For the 1987 Taxable Year

| *If taxable income is:* | *The tax is:* |
|---|---|
| Not over $1,800 | 11% of taxable income. |
| Over $1,800 but not over $16,800 | $198, plus 15% of the excess over $1,800. |
| Over $16,800 but not over $27,000 | $2,448, plus 28% of the excess over $16,800. |
| Over $27,000 but not over $54,000 | $5,304, plus 35% of the excess over $27,000. |
| Over $54,000 | $14,754, plus 38.5% of the excess over $54,000. |

The tax rate schedules show the progressive nature of income tax rates. A **progressive tax** is one in which the tax rate increases as the amount of taxable income increases. In our example, the 28% rate, which was the highest rate applied to the couple's taxable income, is often called the taxpayer's marginal tax rate because it is applied to the last increment of taxable income. However, the effective or average tax rate for this couple would be lower because their lower income levels were taxed at lower rates. Their effective or average tax rate is in fact between 17% and 18%, determined as follows:

$$\$6,398/\$36,280 = 17.635\%$$

## *Tax Credits and Prepayments*

After the taxpayer has computed the gross tax liability, the next step is to subtract any tax credits and prepayments to determine **net tax liability.**

**Tax credits** are direct dollar-for-dollar reductions in the amount of a taxpayer's computed gross tax liability. There is a major distinction to be made between tax credits and tax deductions. Deductions are subtracted from adjusted gross income to determine taxable income. Thus deductions reduce the amount to which the tax rate is applied when determining the gross tax liability. By comparison, tax credits are direct dollar-for-dollar reductions in the gross tax liability. Because tax credits reduce the amount of tax liability dollar for dollar, they are more beneficial to the taxpayer than an equal dollar amount of deductions. For example, if we assume a marginal tax rate of 28%, an additional tax deduction of $200 reduces the tax liability by $56 ($200 × 28%). However, a tax credit of $200 reduces the tax liability by the full $200.

Some examples of tax credits available to a taxpayer are outlined below. Generally, all tax credits are subject to specified limitations, as well as requirements that can become quite complex. For these reasons and because tax rules are subject to frequent changes, we have limited our comments to an overview of the more common tax credits.

### Child Care Credit

A credit against the tax liability may be claimed by taxpayers who incur child or dependent care expenses in order to work or seek employment. The credit is a specified percentage, ranging from 20% to 30%, of the expenses incurred up to a limit. Expenses on which the credit is based are limited to $2,400 for one child and $4,800 for two or more children.

### Earned Income Credit

A credit against the tax liability is allowed to persons who have a child living with them for the year and who have earned income and an adjusted gross income of less than $10,000. The amount of the credit is determined by referring to an earned income credit table provided by the government and is limited to a maximum of $550. It is referred to as a refundable credit because if the amount of the credit reduces the tax liability below zero, the negative amount is paid (refunded) to the taxpayer.

As of January 1, 1988, the earned income credit will be substantially expanded to offset the erosion in its value resulting from inflation over the past decade. The maximum credit will be $800, and it will be phased out for workers earning between $9,000 and $17,000.

### Other Credits

Under specified conditions and within certain limits, there are tax credits available to the elderly, for income taxes paid to a foreign government, and for the installation of certain renewable energy devices.

Before 1986, an investment tax credit was allowed for the purchase of certain property to be used in the taxpayer's trade or business or for the production of income. This credit was an example of how the tax law could be used to encourage business investment in an effort to raise the level of economic activity. Although the investment credit is not currently allowed, it is a credit that has been repealed and reenacted often. Hence this credit may again become a part of our tax laws in the future.

In addition to tax credits, any tax prepayments made by the taxpayer are also deducted from the gross tax liability to determine either the amount of unpaid taxes due or the refund claimed at the time the tax return is filed. For most individuals the tax year ends on December 31, and their tax return is due three and one-half months later on April 15. During the tax year, employers have withheld income taxes from the wages and salaries paid to their employees. As discussed in Chapter 12, the amount withheld depends on the employee's earnings and the number of withholding allowances claimed by the employee. The employer must report the amount withheld to the employee on form W-2 on or before January 31 for a preceding calendar year.

Self-employed taxpayers and taxpayers who received income beyond a certain amount that is not subject to withholding must estimate their tax for the year and file a **Declaration of Estimated Tax** by April 15 of each year. The estimated tax, less any amounts expected to be withheld, is paid in four quarterly installments to the Internal Revenue Service, with the first installment due on April 15. Both the income tax withholdings and the estimated tax payments are tax prepayments. These prepayments, along with tax credits, are subtracted from the gross tax liability to determine the amount that must be paid or the refund claimed when the tax return is filed.

## OTHER TAX CONSIDERATIONS

We have now concluded our discussion of all the components contained in the general formula. Other tax considerations, however, may significantly affect the amount of the tax liability: (1) the alternative minimum tax, (2) capital gains and losses, and (3) inflation.

### Alternative Minimum Tax

The alternative minimum tax may apply to a taxpayer who has tax preference items. The tax laws give special treatment to certain kinds of income and allow special deductions for certain kinds of expenses. These items are known as tax preference items.

To ensure that taxpayers who benefit from tax preference items pay at least a minimum amount of tax, the alternative minimum tax law was enacted.

The alternative minimum tax is calculated in three steps as follows:

1. First add certain of the tax preference items to the taxpayer's adjusted gross income to determine the "alternative" taxable income.
2. Subtract from the "alternative" taxable income the amount that is exempt from the alternative minimum tax. The amounts are $40,000 for a married couple filing a joint return, $30,000 for a single person, and $20,000 for a married person filing a separate return.
3. Multiply the remaining amount (the amount by which the "alternative" taxable income exceeds the exempt amount) by 21%.

The amount computed as the alternative minimum tax is the taxpayer's gross liability only if it exceeds the taxpayer's regular tax liability.

The exemption in step 2 above is phased out for high-income taxpayers. *High-income taxpayers* are defined here as joint filers with "alternative" taxable income greater than $150,000 and single filers with "alternative" taxable income greater than $112,500. The effect of the phase-out is to apply roughly a 26% tax rate to the "alternative" taxable income of these individuals.

### Capital Gains and Losses

One of the unique features of the tax law since 1921 has been the special treatment given to gains and losses related to the sale or exchange of certain assets called capital assets. **Capital assets** are defined in the Internal Revenue Code as any item of property except (1) inventories, (2) trade accounts and notes receivable, (3) real property and depreciable property used in a trade or business, and (4) copyrights and certain other intangible property. Examples of capital assets most commonly owned by individuals are stock and bond investments, a personal residence, household furnishings, an automobile, gems and jewelry, precious metals, and coin and stamp collections. Under certain conditions specified by the tax law, real and depreciable property used in a trade or business may also qualify as capital assets.

The sale of a capital asset generally results in a gain or loss. A **capital gain** occurs when the proceeds from the sale exceed the basis of the asset sold. A **capital loss** occurs when the proceeds from the sale are less than the basis of the asset sold. The **basis** of a purchased asset is generally its cost or its cost less any depreciation previously allowed or allowable in computing taxable income. In some cases, the determination of basis can be difficult, especially for assets acquired in ways other than by purchase, such as a gift or an inheritance.

Once determined, a gain or loss from the sale or exchange of a capital asset is classified as either long-term or short-term based on the length of time that the asset was held before being sold or exchanged. If the asset was held longer than six months, the gain or loss is classified as long-term. Otherwise it is short-term.

Under previous tax law, gains from the sale of long-term capital assets were given special tax treatment. The taxpayer was able to exclude 60% of such long-term gains from gross income in arriving at adjusted gross income. For assets sold after December 31, 1986, this exclusion is no longer available.

However, for the 1987 taxable year, long-term capital gains are still given somewhat favorable treatment. The top tax rate applied to capital gains is held at 28% in 1987, even though the top individual rate is 38.5%. For a married couple filing jointly in 1987, the regular marginal tax rate exceeds 28% when taxable income exceeds $45,000. This can be seen in Exhibit 28–4. Thus married taxpayers with total taxable income less than or equal to $45,000 include their capital gain income with their other income and use the regular rate schedules to determine their tax liability. However, married taxpayers with taxable income greater than $45,000 determine the tax on their capital gain income separately.

In 1988 the top individual tax rate will be 28%. Thus there will be no distinction in the tax treatment of capital gain income and other income. The definition of capital assets and long-term versus short-term holding periods has been retained in the tax laws. This is to make it easier for lawmakers to reinstate a preferential rate for long-term capital gains if there is a future increase in the regular tax rates.

If the taxpayer's transactions in capital assets during the year result in a net capital loss, the deductibility of the loss in any one year is limited. The amount of loss that can be deducted in any one year is limited to $3,000. The net capital loss in excess of $3,000 can be carried forward and deducted in future tax years subject to the same $3,000 annual limitations.

## Inflation

For a number of years, taxpayers have complained that the effect of inflation has moved them into increasingly higher brackets without receiving any additional purchasing power. This has commonly been referred to as "bracket creep." In 1981 Congress adopted several changes to the law, which became effective in 1985. One of these changes provides for a system of tax indexing. The purpose of indexing is to equalize, or at the very least limit, the effect that inflation will have on a taxpayer's tax liability. Under indexing, three tax formula items—(1) the tax brackets, (2) the personal exemption, and (3) the zero bracket amount or the standard deduction—will be adjusted annually for inflation by applying the changes in the Consumer Price Index (CPI). The Tax Reform Act of 1986 raises each of these three items over the next few years. When these legislative increases end (1988 for the tax brackets and standard deduction and 1989 for the personal exemption), annual adjustments for inflation will resume in the following year.

For example, if the Consumer Price Index rose by 5% between 1989 and 1990, the personal exemption would increase from $2,000 to $2,100 ($2,000 × 5% = a $100 increase). Similar calculations would be made to increase the standard deduction and to establish revised tax brackets. Note that at the present time, the indexing provision does not apply to corporations.

## DETERMINATION OF TAX LIABILITY—AN ILLUSTRATION

Now that we have completed our discussion of income tax for individuals, let us review the determination of a taxpayer's tax liability using a comprehensive illustration.

Assume that Carole and Bill Kool, a married couple having two children who qualify as dependents, are filing a joint return in 1988. Carole Kool, a systems consultant, has her own business. During the tax year, she received $90,000 in gross consulting fees and incurred $42,000 of business expenses. Her voucher of estimated federal income tax was filed quarterly, with payments totaling $6,400. In addition, she contributed $2,000 to a qualified individual retirement account, since she did not have an employer-provided pension plan.

*EXHIBIT 28-5*

Determination of Tax Liability for Carole and Bill Kool—Joint Return

| | | |
|---|---|---|
| Gross income: | | |
| Gross fees from Carole Kool's consulting business | $90,000 | |
| Less: Expenses incurred in the business | 42,000 | $48,000 |
| Bill Kool's salary | | 50,000 |
| Dividends received | | 1,240 |
| Interest on savings account | | 590 |
| Interest on municipal bonds of which $620 is excluded | | — |
| Total gross income for tax purposes | | $99,830 |
| Deductions from gross income: | | |
| Net capital loss: $6,000 capital loss plus $1,000 capital gain equals $5,000 net capital loss, limited to $3,000 | $ 3,000 | |
| Contribution to individual retirement account | 2,000 | |
| Total deductions | | 5,000 |
| Adjusted gross income | | $94,830 |
| Deductions from adjusted gross income: | | |
| Larger of itemized deductions ($17,230) or standard deduction ($5,000) | $17,230 | |
| Personal exemptions (4 × $1,950) | 7,800 | |
| Total deductions from adjusted gross income | | 25,030 |
| Taxable income | | $69,800 |
| Computation of Federal Income Tax Using Tax Schedule Y Shown in Exhibit 28-3: | | |
| Tax on $29,750 | $ 4,463 | |
| Tax on $40,050 ($69,800 − $29,750) at 28% | 11,214 | |
| Gross tax liability | | $15,677 |
| Less: Tax credits and prepayments | | |
| Child care credit: ($6,000 limited to $4,800) × 20% | $ 960 | |
| Federal income taxes withheld | 7,630 | |
| Estimated federal income tax payments | 6,400 | 14,990 |
| Net tax liability due | | $ 687 |

Bill Kool earned $50,000 during the year working as an accountant and had $7,630 withheld from his salary for federal income taxes.

The Kools earned $590 interest on their savings account and $620 interest on municipal bonds. Dividends received on jointly owned stock investments totaled $1,240. During the year they sold stock purchased several years ago, incurring a loss of $6,000 on the transaction. They also sold stock purchased two months prior to the sale, realizing a $1,000 gain on the transaction.

The Kools have allowable itemized deductions for medical expenses, taxes, interest, charitable contributions, dues to professional organizations, professional journals, and safe deposit box rental totaling $17,230. This total is after subtracting any floor amounts. The Kools also paid $6,000 in child care expenses, which qualify for a 20% child care credit.

The tax due when the Kools file their return is $687, as shown in Exhibit 28–5.

The information in Exhibit 28–5 is presented in condensed form. In practice, the information would be reported in more detail and on official tax forms and supporting schedules provided by the government.

## PARTNERSHIPS

Partnerships are not considered taxable entities for income tax purposes. The tax law treats a partnership as a conduit through which taxable income flows to the partners. Each partner must file a personal tax return that includes his or her share of the partnership's net income or loss. Unlike a proprietorship, a partnership is required to file a separate annual tax return. However, since a partnership is not required to pay a tax on its income, the return is for information purposes only. It shows the computation of net income or loss and the share of net income or loss allowable to each partner.

The partnership return includes a schedule that segregates items of income, expenses, and credits by type. The segregated items include ordinary income and items of income and expense subject to limitations or special tax treatment, such as capital gains and losses, tax-exempt interest, and charitable contributions. Each partner reports his or her respective share of the these items as if received or paid personally in the appropriate categories on his or her personal tax return. Thus the entire partnership income is taxed to the partners regardless of whether it is left in the business or distributed to the partners.

## INCOME TAX ON CORPORATIONS

A corporation is a separate taxable entity that must file a tax return and pay taxes. Certain corporations, such as banks and insurance companies, are subject to special tax regulations. For corporations not given special tax treatment (which we call general business corporations), taxable income is determined in much the same way as net income is determined for corporate financial reporting. A corporation's taxable income is determined by subtracting allowable business expenses from the revenues and gains included in gross income.

*1d. The formula for computation of corporate income tax is shown in Exhibit 28–6*

The computation of corporate taxable income and tax liability can be shown by the formula in Exhibit 28–6. Comparing this formula with the one for individuals in Exhibit 28–1, note the following differences:

*EXHIBIT 28-6*

Formula for Determining the Corporate Tax Liability

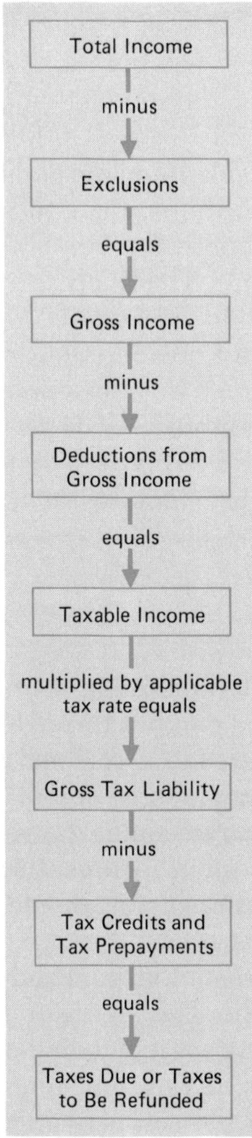


There is no adjusted gross income step in the calculation of taxable income for a corporation. The concept of adjusted gross income is not applicable to a corporation.

There is no deduction for personal exemptions for a corporation.

There are no itemized deductions and no standard deduction for a corporation.

Despite these differences, the concept of determining taxable income remains the same in that all income is taxable unless specifically excluded by tax law. Expenses are deducted only to the extent that they qualify under the tax law.

Although the concept is the same, there are several differences in determining the amount to be included or excluded in each component of taxable income. We have already indicated that corporations in contrast with individuals make no distinction between gross income and adjusted gross income, do not itemize personal deductions or use a standard deduction, and do not have deductions for personal exemptions. Other differences can make corporate taxation a complex matter. So we will limit our study to the following major differences: (1) the dividends received deduction, (2) the treatment of capital gains and losses, (3) the net operating loss deduction, and (4) charitable contributions.

**DIVIDENDS RECEIVED DEDUCTION** All the dividends received by a corporation on its investments in shares of stock of other corporations are included in gross income. However, the corporation may subtract 80% of such dividends received from domestic corporations as a special deduction from gross income. Thus only 20% of dividend income is taxable to the receiving corporation. As of January 1, 1987, dividends are included in full in the taxable income of individuals. Individuals had previously been able to exclude $100 ($200 for married couples filing a joint return) of dividends received from domestic corporations.

**CAPITAL GAINS AND LOSSES** As in the case of individuals, capital gains and losses of corporations are classified as long-term or short-term according to the time the capital asset was held before being sold. Previously the total net long-term capital gain was included in taxable income but was taxed at a maximum rate of 28%, even though the top corporate rate was 46%. As of 1988, capital gain income will be taxed with all other corporate income at the applicable regular tax rates. The top corporate tax rate at this time will be 34%.

Capital losses cannot be deducted from ordinary income; they can only be used to offset capital gains. However, if in a given year there is a net capital loss, the amount can be carried back and deducted from the net capital gains of the three preceding years. The remaining amount, if any, can be carried forward five years following the loss year and can be used to reduce any net capital gains of these years. Note that loss carrybacks and carryforwards can only be used to reduce capital gains, not ordinary income. When a capital loss is carried back, the tax liability for that year is recalculated, and a refund claim for the difference between the original tax and the revised tax is filed.

**NET OPERATING LOSS DEDUCTION** A corporation is entitled to offset the losses of a particular year against the income of other years. Losses may be carried back to the three preceding years beginning with the earliest. The tax liability for those years is recalculated, and a refund claim for the difference between the original tax and the revised tax is filed. Any unused loss can be carried forward successively to the next fifteen years following the loss year and deducted in determining taxable income. A corporation may also elect to forgo the carryback and only carry the loss forward.

**CHARITABLE CONTRIBUTIONS** A corporation may deduct charitable contributions. However, the amount of this deduction is limited to 10% of taxable income computed before deducting any contributions and the special 80% dividend received deduction. Contributions in excess of the 10% limitation in any given year may be carried forward to the five succeeding years, subject to the 10% limitation in each of those years.

### *Determining the Corporate Tax Liability*

*2b. Computation of tax liability for a corporation is explained here*

The corporate income tax is also progressive. The rate structure was changed in the Tax Reform Act of 1986. The new corporate rate structure is effective as of July 1, 1987. Both rate schedules are shown in Exhibit 28–7 on page 994. Since the new tax rates are effective as of July 1, 1987, corporate taxpayers will actually use a rate schedule that is a "blend" of the two schedules above to

*EXHIBIT 28–7*

Corporate Income Tax Rate Schedules

| EFFECTIVE BEFORE JULY 1, 1987 | |
|---|---|
| Taxable Income | Tax Rate |
| Up to $25,000 | 15% |
| Over $25,000 but does not exceed $50,000 | 18% |
| Over $50,000 but does not exceed $75,000 | 30% |
| Over $75,000 but does not exceed $100,000 | 40% |
| Over $100,000 | 46% |
| EFFECTIVE AS OF JULY 1, 1987 | |
| Taxable Income | Tax Rate |
| Up to $50,000 | 15% |
| Over $50,000 but does not exceed $75,000 | 25% |
| Over $75,000 | 34% |

compute their 1987 tax liability. The top blended tax rate in 1987 will be 40%, an average of 46% and 34%.

The benefits of the lower tax rates are phased out for high-income corporations, as they are for individuals. In 1988, corporations earning more than $100,000 will pay an additional 5% tax on income over that amount until their total tax liability is equal to a flat 34% of taxable income. This occurs at taxable income levels of $335,000 or higher.

To illustrate the use of the corporate tax rate schedules, assume that a corporation has taxable income of $115,000 in 1988. The gross tax liability of $28,100 is computed as follows:

| | |
|---|---|
| Tax on first $50,000 of taxable income at 15% rate | $ 7,500 |
| Tax on next $25,000 of taxable income at 25% rate | 6,250 |
| Tax on next $40,000 of taxable income at 34% rate | 13,600 |
| Additional tax on taxable income $100,000 at 5% rate | 750 |
| Total tax on $115,000 of taxable income | $28,100 |

Although the most popular tax credit used by corporations, the investment tax credit, has currently been repealed, corporations still qualify for certain other tax credits. One of the favorite tax credits of technology corporations is the research and development tax credit. This credit is equal to 20% of the increase in research and experimentation expenses. The increase is computed as the current year expenditures less the average amount of research expenditures in the three preceding taxable years.

Corporations are not subject to withholding. They are required to pay estimated taxes in quarterly installments.

## CORPORATE TAX ILLUSTRATION

Exhibit 28–8 illustrates the determination of the tax liability when a number of the distinguishing features of the corporate tax system are involved. For this

*EXHIBIT 28–8*

Determination of Tax Liability for Logistics Corporation

| | | |
|---|---|---|
| Gross income: | | |
| Sales less cost of goods sold | | $350,000 |
| Dividends received from domestic corporations | | 30,000 |
| Net long-term capital gains | $ 50,000 | |
| Less: Net capital loss carryforward | (8,000) | 42,000 |
| Total gross income | | $422,000 |
| Deductions: | | |
| Business expenses excluding charitable contributions of $25,000 | $185,000 | |
| Charitable contributions limited to 10% of $237,000 ($422,000 − $185,000) | 23,700 | |
| Dividends received deduction, 80% of $30,000 | 24,000 | |
| Total deductions | | 232,700 |
| Taxable income | | $189,300 |
| Computation of federal income tax | | |
| Tax on first $50,000 at 15% | $ 7,500 | |
| Tax on next $25,000 at 25% | 6,250 | |
| Tax on next $114,300 at 34% | 38,862 | |
| Tax on excess over $100,000 ($89,300) at 5% | 4,465 | |
| Gross tax liability | | $ 57,077 |
| Less: Tax credits | | |
| Research and development credit ($10,000 × 20%) | | 2,000 |
| Total tax liability | | $ 55,077 |

example, assume that Logistics Corporation had a gross profit of $350,000 in 1988 based on sales of $750,000, and a cost of goods sold of $400,000.

Other information pertaining to the company was assembled and reported as follows:

| | |
|---|---|
| Business expenses including charitable contributions of $25,000 | $210,000 |
| Dividends received from domestic corporations | 30,000 |
| Net long-term capital gains on the sale of capital assets | 50,000 |
| Unused net capital loss carryforward from the preceding year | 8,000 |
| Increase in research and development expenses over previous three-year average | 10,000 |

Assuming the company made tax payments of $13,500 quarterly, it would have a net tax liability of $1,077 [$55,077 − ($13,500 × 4) = $1,077], which would be paid when the tax return is filed.

## TAX PLANNING AND BUSINESS DECISIONS

Income taxes are recognized as a major factor when evaluating alternative courses of action. An important consideration when selecting among alternatives is which alternative action will result in the lowest tax liability. Planning events and transactions in such a way that the tax liability is reduced or minimized is a perfectly legal and beneficial activity. Some major areas where income taxes can be minimized or reduced by planned transactions and events are discussed below.

**USING THE MARGINAL TAX RATE** When considering the tax effect of a proposed course of action, it is important that the taxpayer's marginal tax rate rather than average tax rate be used. The **marginal tax rate** is the tax rate applied to the next dollar of taxable income. To illustrate, assume that on the last day of the 1988 taxable year an individual had taxable income of $22,000. Also assume that the taxpayer computed this amount using the standard deduction of $3,000, since itemized deductions were also equal to $3,000. In accordance with a single person's tax rate schedule shown in Exhibit 28 – 3, the taxpayer has a marginal tax rate of 28%. If just before year-end the taxpayer makes a $1,000 cash contribution to charity, he or she would now have itemized deductions greater than the standard deduction by $1,000. Taxable income would change to $21,000. The tax effect of this contribution is shown below.

| | BEFORE CONTRIBUTION | AFTER CONTRIBUTION |
|---|---|---|
| Taxable income | $22,000 | $21,000 |
| Tax on first $17,850 of taxable income | 2,678 | 2,678 |
| Tax on remaining taxable income | | |
| $22,000 – $17,850 = $4,150 × 28% | 1,162 | |
| $21,000 – $17,850 = $3,150 × 28% | | 882 |
| Gross tax liability | $ 3,840 | $ 3,560 |

The $1,000 contribution gave the taxpayer $1,000 of additional itemized deductions, which in turn reduced taxable income by $1,000 and income taxes by $280. Note also that the tax savings is at the taxpayer's marginal tax rate ($1,000 × 28% = $280). In terms of cash outflow, making the $1,000 cash contribution increased the taxpayer's cash outflow by only $720 ($1,000 cash outflow for contribution less $280 reduced cash outflow for taxes = $720 of net cash outflow).

This analysis can be applied to the amount of any deduction when the marginal tax rate is known. For example, it can be said that the net cost of a $6,000 state income tax payment is $4,320 for a taxpayer having a marginal tax rate of 28%.

## *Form of Business Organization*

*1e. The impact of federal income tax may affect the selection of entity form*

One of the first and most important decisions a person or persons must make is whether to operate the business as a single proprietorship, a partnership, or a corporation. Such factors as pride of individual ownership, ability to raise capital, and desire to limit liability will enter into the decision. Another factor to be considered when selecting the entity form is the impact of the federal income tax. Provisions of the tax law vary greatly with the form of a business. Some of the major provisions having tax consequences are as follows.

If the business is a proprietorship or a partnership, business income must be reported on the personal income tax return of the owner or owners and taxed at rates ranging from 15% to 28% in 1988. If the business is incorporated, the corporation is a separate entity and must report and pay an income tax ranging from 15% to 34% of its 1988 income.

In determining taxable income, corporations may deduct, as a business expense, the salaries paid to owners (stockholders) who work for the corporation, but they cannot deduct the dividends paid to the owners (stockholders). Both the salaries and the dividends paid are taxable income to the individual stockholders receiving them. On the other hand, salaries paid to a proprietor or a partner are considered to be an allocation of income and are therefore not deductible as a business expense in determining taxable income.

To illustrate the impact of taxes on the form of business organization, assume that Tom Darling starts a business in 1988 that he expects will produce an average annual business income of $70,000. He plans to withdraw $40,000 a year from the business. The combined corporate and individual taxes under the corporate and single proprietorship form of business organizations are summarized below.

| | FORM OF BUSINESS ORGANIZATION | |
|---|---|---|
| | Corporation | Proprietorship |
| Business income | $70,000 | $70,000 |
| Salary to Tom Darling | 40,000 | — |
| Taxable income | $30,000 | $70,000 |
| Corporate tax: 15% × $30,000 | 4,500 | — |
| Net income | $25,500 | $70,000 |
| Combined corporate and individual tax: | | |
| Corporate tax—from above | $ 4,500 | |
| Individual tax* | | |
| On Tom Darling's salary | 4,841 | |
| On Tom Darling's share of business income | | 13,241 |
| Total tax | $ 9,341 | $13,241 |

* From the tax rate schedule in Exhibit 28–3, assuming a joint return and a combined total of $8,900 for deductions and personal exemptions.

Under these assumptions, the corporate form reduces Tom Darling's 1988 tax liability by $3,900 ($13,241 − $9,341). By incorporating, the combined tax on the corporation and on Darling personally will be $9,341. As a sole proprietor, Darling would pay a personal tax of $13,241. This advantage resulted because $30,000 of earnings was not withdrawn from the corporation and was taxed at the corporate tax rate of 15%. However, this undistributed amount is taxed in the current year as additional income subject to the individual tax rate of 28% when the business is operated as a single proprietorship. The $3,900 tax savings is $30,000 × 13% (28% − 15%).

If part or all of the $25,500 after-tax net income retained in the corporation is subsequently distributed as a dividend, it will be taxed to the recipient—Tom Darling in this case—as ordinary income. This indicates that Darling can only get money out of the corporation in the form of salaries or dividends, and in either case it would then be taxable as ordinary income. The advantage gained from the corporate form of business organization is that Darling can postpone individual income tax payments on the portion of the earnings retained in the business.

## Timing of Transactions

*1e. The impact of federal income tax may affect the timing of transactions*

The timing of transactions can be crucial in tax planning. A cash-basis taxpayer may be able to plan some revenue receipts and expense payments to minimize taxes in the current year. For example, a taxpayer can plan to make certain charitable contributions in the year in which his or her other allowable deductions exceed the standard deduction to receive the greatest tax benefit from the amount contributed. If the charitable contribution is made in a year in which total itemized deductions, including the contribution, do not exceed the standard deduction, the donation will not result in any tax benefit. Furthermore, a business that uses the cash basis of accounting may be able to defer receipt from a revenue-producing activity until next year, thereby reducing the taxable income of the current year. This technique would be especially useful when the company's taxable income for the year was nearing the upper limits of a given bracket of taxable income. Another technique to accomplish the same purpose is to time certain discretionary cash expenditures. That is, those expenditures planned for early next year might best be made near the end of the current year if the company is seeking to minimize its taxes in the current year.

The timing of transactions will be especially important in the next few years as the tax changes legislated in the Tax Reform Act of 1986 become effective. For example, a taxpayer planning to purchase an automobile might want to consider the phase-out of the consumer interest deduction. Purchasing the automobile as soon as possible may result in a greater percentage of the interest on the loan being deductible.

## HIGHLIGHT PROBLEM

Mary Ann and Mark Roth are married, have two dependent children, and plan to file a joint return. Both Mary Ann and Mark are under 65 years of age and have good vision. Mary Ann is a marriage counselor with a private practice. Mark is a marketing manager for a large pharmaceutical company. The couple have assembled the following information for the 1988 tax year:

| | |
|---|---:|
| Revenue from Mary Ann's practice | $82,600 |
| Expenses of Mary Ann's practice | 47,200 |
| Mark's salary | 42,500 |
| Interest earned on savings | 620 |
| Dividends from jointly held investments in securities | 1,210 |
| Interest earned on municipal bonds | 550 |
| Medical and dental expenses | 420 |
| Mortgage interest on residence | 5,100 |
| Interest on car loan | 570 |
| Property taxes on residence | 4,200 |
| Sales tax | 630 |
| Charitable contributions | 450 |
| Capital gain income from the sale of stock | 1,800 |
| Contribution to an individual retirement account by Mary | 2,000 |
| Income tax withheld from Mark's salary | 6,800 |
| Estimated tax payments | 6,400 |

Required:

Determine the amount of income tax the Roths must pay when their return is filed or the amount of refund due. Use the appropriate tax rate schedule shown in Exhibit 28–3.

## GLOSSARY OF KEY TERMS

**Adjusted gross income.** Gross income less ordinary and necessary business expenses and other deductions permitted by law.

**Basis.** Generally, the cost of a purchased asset or cost less any depreciation previously allowed or allowable in computing taxable income.

**Capital assets.** Any item of property except (1) inventories, (2) trade accounts and notes receivable, (3) real property and depreciable property used in a trade or a business, and (4) copyrights and certain other intangible property.

**Capital gain.** The excess of the proceeds from the sale of a capital asset over the cost basis of the capital asset.

**Capital loss.** The excess of the cost basis of a capital asset over the proceeds from the sale of a capital asset.

**Deductions.** Items that reduce the amount of income subject to income taxes

**Estimated tax voucher.** A form that self-employed taxpayers and taxpayers with income not subject to withholding who anticipate owing taxes on such income must submit by April 15 of each year. The amount of the estimated tax is paid in quarterly installments, with the first installment due on April 15.

**Exclusions.** Income items that are omitted (excluded) from taxable gross income because, in accordance with tax law, the items are not subject to tax.

**Gross income.** For tax purposes, total income less allowable exclusions.

**Gross tax liability.** Taxable income multiplied by the applicable tax rate. The total amount of taxes that must be paid on the entity's taxable income for the year.

**Individual retirement accounts (IRAs).** A plan under which a taxpayer pays into a personal retirement fund as much as $2,000 a year ($2,250 if married to a nonworking spouse) with the right to deduct the amount from gross income in determining adjusted gross income. This deduction is limited for workers covered by employer-sponsored pension plans or earning above certain levels.

**Internal revenue code.** A compilation of all the current federal income tax laws passed by Congress.

**Itemized deductions.** Personal and employee business expenses that can be deducted from adjusted gross income in computing taxable income.

**Keogh plan.** A retirement plan available for self-employed taxpayers.

**Marginal tax rate.** The tax rate applied to the next dollar of taxable income.

**Net tax liability.** The amount of tax after the tax credits and prepayments have been deducted. The amount that is due when the tax return is filed.

**Personal exemption.** A deduction from adjusted gross income for each exemption claimed by the taxpayer. A separate exemption is allowed for a taxpayer, the taxpayer's spouse, and each dependent. The exemption amount is $1,900, $1,950, and $2,000 for 1987, 1988, and 1989, respectively.

**Progressive tax.** A tax in which the tax rate increases as the amount of taxable income increases.

**Standard deduction.** A specified amount that can be subtracted from adjusted gross income in computing taxable income. The 1988 standard deduction amounts are $5,000 for married taxpayers filing a joint return and $3,000 for single taxpayers. Taxpayers who are elderly or blind receive an additional standard deduction amount of $600 if they are married, and $750 if they are single. Taxpayers deduct the larger of their applicable standard deduction or allowable itemized deductions in computing taxable income.

**Taxable income.** The amount of income to which the appropriate tax rate is applied in determining an entity's gross tax liability.

**Tax avoidance.** The arrangement of a taxpayer's financial affairs and transactions, within the legal confines of the tax statutes, in a manner that will minimize tax liability.

**Tax credits.** Direct dollar-for-dollar reductions in the amount of a taxpayer's computed gross tax liability.

**Tax evasion.** The deliberate understatement of taxable income by failing to report income received or by claiming fraudulent deductions.

**Tax planning.** The arrangement of a taxpayer's affairs in such a way as to incur the lowest possible tax liability.

**Tax rate schedule.** Any of the four schedules prepared for (1) single taxpayers, (2) married taxpayers filing joint returns, (3) married taxpayers filing separate returns, and (4) heads of households.

**Tax shelter.** An investment largely motivated by the tax losses it generates which can be used by the taxpayer to offset other income and hence reduce taxes.

**Total income.** All income from whatever sources derived.

## REVIEW QUESTIONS

1. What is *tax planning?* [LO1a]
2. Differentiate between *tax avoidance* and *tax evasion.* [LO1a]
3. What two tax accounting methods can be used to determine taxable income? [LO1c]
4. Name the four classifications of taxable entities. [LO1b]
5. What was the broad purpose of the Tax Reform Act of 1986? How were the tax base and tax rates affected? [LO1c]
6. Name the components in Exhibit 28–1 that constitute the formula for determining an individual taxpayer's tax liability. [LO1c,2a]
7. Differentiate between *exclusions* and *deductions.* [LO1c,2a]
8. Name six types of expenses that qualify as itemized deductions. [LO1c,2a]
9. What is a *personal exemption?* [LO1c,2a]
10. What are *tax credits?* [LO1c,2a]
11. What are *capital gains* and *losses?* [LO1c,2a]
12. How is a partnership's net income or loss treated on the personal tax return of each partner? [LO1c,2a]
13. How is a corporation's taxable income determined? [LO1d,2b]
14. What are the three differences between the tax liability formula for individuals shown in Exhibit 28–1 and the tax liability formula for corporations shown in Exhibit 28–6? [LO1c,1d,2a,2b]
15. Describe three major areas where income taxes can be minimized or reduced by planned transactions and events. [LO1e]

## ANALYTICAL QUESTIONS

16. A friend of yours makes this statement: "There is no reason to take on this extra work. If I did, it would increase my taxable income by $1,000 and put me in a higher tax bracket." Comment on this statement. [LO1c,2a]
17. A friend of yours makes this statement: "I plan to make a large donation to my favorite charitable organization. Since the donation is tax deductible, I will receive all the money back anyway." Comment on this statement. [LO1c,2a]
18. A friend of yours makes this statement: "I was told that I should use my marginal tax rate when considering the tax consequences of my business decisions. What does this mean?" Reply to this question. [LO1e]
19. A friend of yours makes this statement: "The Tax Reform Act of 1986 was revenue neutral. Therefore it should have no effect on the amount of taxes I will have to pay." Comment on this statement. [LO1c,2a]
20. A friend of yours makes this statement: "I am indifferent between a $200 tax credit and a $200 tax deduction." Comment on this statement. [LO1c,2a]

## IMPACT ANALYSIS QUESTIONS

*For each error described, indicate whether it would incorrectly overstate [O], incorrectly understate [U], or not affect [N] the specified key figures.* [LO2a]

21. Mr. Omit neglected to include $300 of dividends on his current year's tax return. He is single.

_______ Gross Income _______ Adjusted Gross Income
_______ Taxable Income _______ Exemptions

22. Mr. Comit took all of the $3,000 of medical costs he incurred as a medical deduction rather than excluding 7.5% of his adjusted gross income.

_______ Gross Income _______ Adjusted Gross Income
_______ Taxable Income _______ Exemptions

23. Ms. Omit neglected to take $2,000 of depreciation on her business property.

_______ Gross Income _______ Adjusted Gross Income
_______ Taxable Income _______ Exemptions

## EXERCISES

For the exercises and problems in this chapter, all calculations should be rounded to the nearest dollar. Calculations of an individual taxpayer's tax liability should be based on the tax rate schedules in Exhibits 28–3 and 28–4 (see pages 983, 984 and 986). Calculations for a corporation should be based on the tax rate schedules in Exhibit 28–7 (see page 994).

EXERCISE 28–1 *(Classify Items in Determining an Individual's Tax Liability)* For each item listed in 1 through 15 below, write the letter that identifies how each item would be treated in determining an individual's tax liability.

A. An exclusion from total income to determine gross income
B. A deduction from gross income to determine adjusted gross income
C. A deduction from adjusted gross income to determine taxable income
D. A tax credit deductible from the gross tax liability

In making your determination, ignore amount limitations specified by the tax law.

1. Payments to an individual retirement account if an individual is not covered by a pension plan
2. Medical expense payments not covered by insurance
3. Interest received on an investment in municipal bonds
4. Interest payments on a home mortgage
5. Unreimbursed job-related moving expenses
6. Payment for subscriptions to professional journals
7. Social Security benefits
8. Property tax payments on a personal residence
9. Alimony payments
10. Uninsured loss from automobile accident
11. Employment-related child care expenses
12. Gifts received
13. Unemployment compensation
14. Business-related travel expenses of an employee
15. Child support received

EXERCISE 28–2 *(Compute Gross Tax Liability for Individuals)* Using the tax rate schedules that apply, compute the 1986 and 1988 gross tax liability for each of the following. [LO2a]

| STATUS OF TAXPAYER | TAXABLE INCOME |
|---|---|
| 1. Single taxpayer | $20,000 |
| 2. Single taxpayer | 90,000 |
| 3. Married taxpayers filing a joint return | 20,000 |
| 4. Married taxpayers filing a joint return | 90,000 |
| 5. Married taxpayer filing a separate return | 20,000 |
| 6. Married taxpayer filing a separate return | 90,000 |
| 7. Unmarried head of household | 20,000 |
| 8. Unmarried head of household | 90,000 |

EXERCISE 28–3 *(Compute Gross Tax Liability for a Corporation)* CSC Corporation has gross income of $275,000 and deductions from gross income of $120,000 for both 1986 and 1988. Compute its gross tax liability for each of these two years. [LO2b]

EXERCISE 28–4 *(Compute Standard Deduction)* Sam and Cindy Argo file a joint 1988 tax return. Sam is 67 years of age and Cindy is 62. They have one dependent child, who is blind. Compute their applicable 1988 standard deduction. [LO1c,2a]

EXERCISE 28–5 *(Compute Casualty Loss Deduction)* Ronnie Roberts had an uninsured loss of $900 as a result of a car accident and an uninsured loss of $3,500 as a result of fire damage to his home. His adjusted gross income for the year was $18,000. Compute Ronnie's allowable casualty loss deduction. [LO1c,2a]

EXERCISE 28–6 *(Compute Allowable Itemized Deductions)* Tom and Sandy Lewis provide you with the following information concerning their 1988 personal and employee business expenses:

| | |
|---|---|
| Medical and dental expenses | $1,750 |
| State income taxes | 1,250 |
| Home mortgage interest | 3,100 |
| Consumer interest | 800 |
| Charitable contributions | 725 |
| Employment-related travel expenses | 500 |
| Dues to professional organizations | 200 |

Their adjusted gross income is $20,000. Compute their total allowable itemized deductions after any applicable limits. [LO1c,2a]

EXERCISE 28–7 *(Compute Research and Development Credit)* Arklane Technological Corporation incurred research and development expenses as follows:

| YEAR | RESEARCH AND DEVELOPMENT EXPENSES |
|---|---|
| 1985 | $32,000 |
| 1986 | 40,000 |
| 1987 | 51,000 |
| 1988 | 59,000 |

Calculate its 1988 tax credit for these expenses.

EXERCISE 28–8 *(Compute Tax for a Single Taxpayer)* Loretta Lott is single and has no dependents. She has assembled the following information for preparing her 1988 tax return:

| | |
|---|---|
| Total income | $57,000 |
| Income taxes withheld from salary | 9,800 |
| Itemized deductions | 3,700 |
| Payments to an individual retirement account (Loretta is not covered by a pension plan) | 2,000 |
| Exclusions from total income | 4,000 |

Required:

Determine the following:

1. Gross income
2. Adjusted gross income
3. Taxable income
4. Gross tax liability
5. Amount of tax remaining to be paid or the amount of refund claimed [LO2a]

EXERCISE 28–9 *(Compute Tax for a Married Couple Filing a Joint Return)* John and Mary Arnone are married and have one dependent child. They have assembled the following information for preparing their 1988 tax return:

| | |
|---|---:|
| John's salary | $43,500 |
| Gifts and inheritances | 14,700 |
| Interest on savings account | 1,300 |
| Dividends on jointly owned investments | 600 |
| Deductions from gross income | 3,200 |
| Itemized deductions | 4,800 |
| Income taxes withheld from John's salary | 6,100 |

Required:

Determine the following:

1. Gross income
2. Adjusted gross income
3. Taxable income
4. Gross tax liability
5. Amount of tax remaining to be paid or the amount of refund claimed
6. The couple's average tax rate [LO2a]

EXERCISE 28–10 *(Compute Gross Tax Liability for a Corporation)* Olympic Catering Corporation assembled the following summary information:

| | |
|---|---:|
| Net sales | $850,000 |
| Cost of goods sold | 500,000 |
| Operating expenses | 120,000 |
| Dividend income received from other corporations | 14,000 |
| Long-term capital gain on sale of investment | 36,000 |
| Dividends paid to stockholders | 42,000 |

Required:

Compute the gross tax liability for Olympic Catering Corporation for 1988. [LO2b]

EXERCISE 28–11 *(Determine Tax Consequences of Form of Business Organization)* Sally Hill owns and operates a clothing boutique. In 1987, the business was organized as a single proprietorship and had taxable income of $30,000. During the year, Sally withdrew $25,000 cash for her personal use. The business is growing rapidly, and Sally is considering whether it would be beneficial from an income tax point of view to incorporate. The business is Sally's only source of income. She anticipates that with increased sales, the business will have a net income of $50,000 before deducting $30,000 that she would withdraw as a salary for services performed. Sally is single with no dependents and does not itemize personal deductions.

Required:

1. Using the amounts anticipated for 1988 and assuming the business is incorporated, determine the combined corporate and individual income tax liability.
2. Assuming the business remains organized as a single proprietorship, determine Sally's individual income tax liability.
3. How much more or less would Sally pay in total taxes if the business is incorporated? [LO1e,2a,2b]

## PROBLEMS

PROBLEM 28–1 *(Compute Tax for a Single Taxpayer)* Donald Price is single and has no dependents. He has assembled the following information for use in preparing his 1988 tax return:

| | |
|---|---|
| Donald's salary as an employee (supervisor) for an aerospace company | $48,000 |
| Interest on bank savings account | 2,300 |
| Dividends on investments in stock | 1,800 |
| Nonreimbursed moving expenses related to change in residence required by job relocation | 3,700 |
| Interest on auto loan | 620 |
| Real property tax | 835 |
| Contributions to organized charities (no political contributions included) | 520 |
| Sales tax | 890 |
| Net long-term capital gains from sale of securities | 9,200 |
| Net short-term capital gains from sale of securities | 730 |
| Hospital and doctors' bills paid | 3,180 |
| Hospital and medical insurance premiums paid | 640 |
| Dental expenses paid | 910 |
| Drugs and medicines (all bills paid) | 180 |
| Federal income tax withheld from salary | 12,200 |
| Inheritance received | 6,000 |
| Music lesson fees paid | 1,300 |
| Casualty loss—automobile accident: total loss $4,800, reimbursed by insurance coverage | 4,200 |

Required:
Compute Donald Price's
1. Adjusted gross income
2. Taxable income
3. Gross tax liability
4. Amount of tax remaining to be paid or the amount of refund claimed [LO2a]

PROBLEM 28–2 *(Compute Tax for a Married Couple)* Seth and Kathy Murray are married and file a joint 1988 tax return. They support their two children, one of whom is a full-time college student. They also provide full support for Kathy's mother, who is 66 years old and lives with them.

Seth is employed by a local television station and received a salary of $52,000 for the current year. Kathy is self-employed in a single proprietorship offering dancing lessons for a fee. She received fee revenues of $61,000 from her business and paid $28,000 in expenses to operate the business during the current year. The couple kept records throughout the year and assembled the following information:

| | |
|---|---|
| Federal income tax withheld from Seth's salary | $10,200 |
| Estimated tax payments made | 6,400 |
| Interest on bank savings account | 910 |
| Interest on municipal bonds | 630 |
| Dividends on jointly held investments in stock | 820 |
| Real estate taxes on personal residence | 2,440 |
| Sales tax | 570 |
| Cash contributed to organized charities | 390 |
| Interest paid on personal residence mortgage | 3,380 |
| Interest paid on automobile loan | 760 |
| Uninsured portion of casualty loss resulting from automobile accident | 500 |
| Cash gift received by Kathy Murray | 1,200 |
| Net long-term capital gains from the sale of jointly owned securities | 4,600 |
| Net short-term capital losses from the sale of jointly owned securities | 800 |
| Hospital and doctors' bills paid | 2,100 |
| Hospital and medical insurance premiums paid | 920 |
| Dental expenses paid | 4,780 |
| Drugs and medicines (all bills paid) | 560 |
| Safe deposit box rental | 120 |
| Payments made by Kathy Murray to a Keogh plan | 3,300 |

Required:

Compute the Murrays'

1. Adjusted gross income
2. Taxable income
3. Gross tax liability
4. Amount of tax remaining to be paid or the amount of refund claimed [LO2a]

PROBLEM 28–3 *(Compute Gross Tax Liability for a Corporation)* The 1988 records of Mountain Magic Corporation contained the following data:

| | |
|---|---|
| Net sales | $925,000 |
| Beginning inventory | 90,500 |
| Ending inventory | 92,800 |
| Net purchases | 412,400 |
| Selling expenses | 290,600 |
| General expenses | 115,200 |
| Dividend income on long-term investments | 36,900 |
| Dividends paid to stockholders | 40,000 |
| Long-term capital gains | 27,700 |
| Short-term capital losses | 9,300 |
| Operating loss carryforward from previous years | 52,100 |

Required:

Compute the gross tax liability for Mountain Magic Corporation for 1988. [LO2b]

PROBLEM 28–4 *(Determine Tax Consequences of Form of Business Organization)* Ralph Wanzer is considering the option of incorporating his business. He asks whether incorporating would be beneficial from a tax point of view and provides the following data taken from the 1988 business records:

| | |
|---|---|
| Net sales | $430,000 |
| Cost of goods sold | 260,000 |
| Operating expenses | 90,000 |

The operating expenses do not include Ralph's withdrawals of $31,000, which he believes is a reasonable amount to consider as a salary for services performed under the corporate form of business organization. The business is Ralph's only source of income. He is single, has no dependents, and does not itemize deductions on his personal income tax return.

Required:

1. Prepare a schedule that shows the net income of the business if it is organized as a corporation and as a single proprietorship.
2. Prepare a schedule that shows the combined income tax liability if the business is incorporated and the tax liability on Ralph Wanzer's share of business income under the single proprietorship form of organization. [LO1e,2a,2b]

PROBLEM 28–5 *(Determine Tax Consequences of Form of Business Organization)* Chris Leeder has operated the Holiday Ski Shop as a single proprietorship for the past five years. During that period sales revenue has increased slightly each year, and net income before taxes has averaged $60,000. Chris has been withdrawing $55,000 from the business, her only source of income, to pay for personal living expenses. She is single, has no dependents, and does not itemize deductions when filing her tax return.

Based on a careful analysis of data, Chris has concluded that net income should exceed the five-year average by 10% during the coming tax year (1988). During the analysis of expected revenues and operating expenses, it occurred to Chris that she might be able to achieve a tax benefit by incorporating her business.

Required:

1. Assuming the business will be incorporated at the beginning of 1988, prepare a schedule to compare the net income of the business operated as a corporation with that operated as a single proprietorship. If incorporated, Chris would be paid an annual salary of $55,000, an amount considered fair for the services she will perform.
2. Prepare a schedule showing the following in comparative form:
   a. The corporate tax liability combined with the tax liability of Chris Leeder's salary of $55,000
   b. The tax liability on Chris Leeder's share of the business income if the business continues to operate as a single proprietorship
3. Prepare a schedule showing the corporate tax liability combined with Chris Leeder's tax liability. Assume that she is paid a salary of $55,000 and also receives $8,000 per year in dividends from the corporation. [LO1e,2a,2b]

PROBLEM 28–6 *(Compute Tax for a Married Couple)* Larry and Judy Wise are married and have three dependent children. They also provide full support for Larry's father, who is 67 years of age and lives in their home. Information assembled for use in preparing their 1988 joint tax return is as follows:

| | |
|---|---:|
| Larry's salary | $42,000 |
| Judy's salary | 35,000 |
| Interest on bank savings | 880 |
| Interest on municipal bonds | 510 |
| Dividends on jointly held investments in stock | 940 |
| Real estate taxes on personal residence | 3,100 |
| Sales tax | 620 |
| Interest paid on personal residence mortgage | 3,840 |
| Interest paid on automobile loan | 490 |
| Cash contributed to organized charities | 480 |
| Unreimbursed employment-related travel expense | 1,050 |
| State lottery winnings | 500 |
| Cash gift received by Judy Wise | 2,000 |
| Net capital gains from the sale of jointly owned securities | 1,300 |
| Net capital losses from the sale of jointly owned securities | 4,800 |
| Uninsured portion of casualty loss resulting from automobile accident | 660 |
| Dues to professional organizations | 540 |
| Hospital and medical insurance premiums paid | 870 |
| Hospital and doctors' bills paid | 3,950 |
| Dental expenses paid | 3,370 |
| Drugs and medicines (all bills paid) | 590 |
| Safe deposit box rental | 150 |
| Payments to an individual retirement account (Judy Wise) | 2,000 |
| Employment-related child care expenses for one child (assume 20% credit) | 2,600 |
| Taxes withheld from Larry's and Judy's salary | 10,500 |

Required:
Compute the Wises'
1. Adjusted gross income
2. Taxable income
3. Gross tax liability
4. Amount of tax remaining to be paid or the amount of refund claimed [LO2a]

PROBLEM 28–7 *(Compute Tax for a Single Taxpayer)* Billy James is single and has no dependents. He has assembled the following information for use in preparing his 1988 tax return:

| | |
|---|---:|
| Billy's salary | $85,000 |
| Interest on mutual fund investment | 3,200 |
| Loss from non-real estate tax shelter investment | 10,000 |
| Loss from rental real estate activities that Billy manages | 27,000 |
| Contribution to an individual retirement account (Billy is covered by a pension plan) | 2,000 |
| Undistributed earnings on previous contributions to an individual retirement account | 560 |
| Interest paid on credit card balances | 720 |
| Interest paid on personal residence mortgage | 3,275 |
| Cash contributed to organized charities | 1,300 |
| Safe deposit box rental | 125 |

Required:
Compute items 1 through 4 for Billy James.
1. Gross income
2. Adjusted gross income
3. Taxable income
4. Gross tax liability [LO2a]

## ALTERNATE PROBLEMS

PROBLEM 28–1A *(Compute Tax for a Single Taxpayer)* (Alternate to Problem 28–1) Art Jarvits is single and has no dependents. He has assembled the following information for use in preparing his 1988 tax return:

| | |
|---|---:|
| Art's salary as an employee of a steel company | $21,300 |
| Interest on bank savings account | 320 |
| Dividends on investments in stock | 90 |
| Gifts received in cash | 400 |
| Interest on auto loan | 510 |
| Charitable contributions | 100 |
| Sales tax | 240 |
| Payment to individual retirement account (Art is covered by a pension plan) | 2,000 |
| Interest on credit card balances | 60 |
| Uninsured portion of casualty loss resulting from automobile accident | 400 |
| Union dues | 315 |
| Special work uniforms and protective clothing | 320 |
| Federal income tax withheld from salary | 3,400 |

Required:
Compute the amounts called for in items 1 through 4 below for Art Jarvits.
1. Adjusted gross income
2. Taxable income
3. Gross tax liability
4. Amount of tax remaining to be paid or amount of refund claimed [LO2a]

PROBLEM 28–2A *(Compute Gross Tax Liability for a Corporation)* (Alternate to Problem 28–3) The records of Leisure Trends Corporation contained the following data:

| | |
|---|---:|
| Net sales | $570,000 |
| Beginning inventory | 49,200 |
| Ending inventory | 47,500 |
| Net purchases | 294,300 |
| Marketing expenses | 137,600 |
| General expenses | 62,400 |
| Dividend income on long-term investments | 12,000 |
| Dividends paid to stockholders | 25,000 |
| Long-term capital gains | 6,000 |
| Short-term capital losses | 9,000 |
| Operating loss carryforward from previous years | 13,200 |

Required:
Compute the 1988 gross tax liability for Leisure Trends Corporation. [LO2b]

PROBLEM 28–3A *(Determine Tax Effects of Form of Business Organization)* (Alternate to Problem 28–5) Susan Brooks has decided to start her own design business and is concerned about how the form of organization will affect her income tax liability. She anticipates annual net income of $30,000 before taxes and before deducting the amount she intends to withdraw from the business. If operated as a single proprietorship, Susan will make personal withdrawals of $20,300 per year. If operated as a corporation, the $20,300 will be paid to Susan as a salary for managerial services performed. Susan is single, has no dependents, and does not itemize deductions on her personal income tax return.

Required:

1. Prepare a schedule that shows, on a comparative basis, the net income of the business if it is organized as a single proprietorship and as a corporation.
2. Prepare a schedule that shows the combined 1988 income tax liability if the business is incorporated and the 1988 tax liability on Susan's share of business income if the business is organized as a single proprietorship.
3. Prepare a schedule showing the 1988 corporate tax liability combined with Susan's tax liability. Assume that she is paid a salary of $20,300 and also receives $6,000 per year in dividends from the corporation. [LO1e,2a,2b]

PROBLEM 28–4A *(Compute Tax for a Single Taxpayer Filing as Head of Household)* (Alternate to Problem 28–7) Mary Sawall is single but qualifies to file as a head of household. She has two dependents. Mary assembled the following information for use in preparing her 1988 tax return:

| | |
|---|---:|
| Mary's salary | $17,000 |
| Child support payments received | 2,400 |
| Inheritance received | 3,650 |
| Alimony received | 1,200 |
| Interest on personal residence mortgage | 890 |
| Interest on car loan | 760 |
| Charitable contributions | 600 |
| Real estate taxes on personal residence | 900 |
| Federal income tax withheld from Mary's salary | 1,000 |

Required:

Compute the amounts called for in items 1 through 4 below for Mary Sawall.

1. Adjusted gross income
2. Taxable income
3. Gross tax liability
4. Amount of tax remaining to be paid or amount of refund claimed [LO2a]

# A Solutions to Highlight Problems

## Chapter 1

| JERRY'S GAME GALLERY | | | |
|---|---|---|---|
| Balance Sheet | | | |
| Current Date | | | |
| ASSETS | | LIABILITIES | |
| Cash | $ 12,000 | Accounts Payable | $ 18,000 |
| Accounts Receivable | 31,000 | Mortgage Payable | 25,000 |
| Equipment | 27,000 | Total Liabilities | $ 43,000 |
| Building | 40,000 | OWNER'S EQUITY | |
| | | J. Garamond, Capital | 67,000 |
| Total Assets | $110,000 | Total Liabilities and Owner's Equity | $110,000 |

By knowing the relationship that exists among assets, liabilities, and owner's equity you were able to determine that J. Garamond had a capital balance of $67,000.

1.

GENERAL JOURNAL PAGE 1

| DATE | | ACCOUNT TITLE AND EXPLANATION | POST. REF. | DEBIT | CREDIT |
|---|---|---|---|---|---|
| 19X1 Oct. | 1 | Cash | 1 | 25 000 | |
| | | Judy Hart, Capital | 30 | | 25 000 |
| | | Judy Hart invested cash in her business | | | |
| | 1 | Rent Expense | 51 | 400 | |
| | | Cash | 1 | | 400 |
| | | Paid monthly rent | | | |
| | 4 | Office Equipment | 10 | 6 000 | |
| | | Cash | 1 | | 2 000 |
| | | Accounts Payable | 20 | | 4 000 |
| | | Purchased office equipment. Paid one-third cash and promised to pay the balance | | | |
| | 9 | Cash | 1 | 800 | |
| | | Fees Earned | 40 | | 800 |
| | | Earned and collected fee for completed work | | | |
| | 13 | Cash | 1 | 700 | |
| | | Accounts Receivable | 3 | 700 | |
| | | Fees Earned | 40 | | 1 400 |
| | | Completed work and received one-half payment and promise to receive the balance soon | | | |
| | 24 | Accounts Payable | 20 | 2 000 | |
| | | Cash | 1 | | 2 000 |
| | | Paid one-half of amount due for office equipment purchased on October 4 | | | |
| | 27 | Cash | 1 | 300 | |
| | | Accounts Receivable | 3 | | 300 |
| | | Received partial payment for work completed and billed on the thirteenth | | | |
| | 30 | Salaries Expense | 50 | 700 | |
| | | Cash | 1 | | 700 |
| | | Paid part-time employees' salary | | | |
| | 31 | Utilities Expense | 55 | 200 | |
| | | Cash | 1 | | 200 |
| | | Paid monthly utility bill | | | |
| | 31 | Judy Hart, Drawings | 31 | 500 | |
| | | Cash | 1 | | 500 |
| | | Judy withdrew cash for personal use | | | |

2 and 3.

GENERAL LEDGER

CASH — ACCT. NO. 1

| DATE | | EXPLANATION | POST. REF. | DEBIT | CREDIT | BALANCE |
|---|---|---|---|---|---|---|
| 19X1 | | | | | | |
| Oct. | 1 | | 1 | 25 000 | | 25 000 |
| | 1 | | 1 | | 400 | 24 600 |
| | 4 | | 1 | | 2 000 | 22 600 |
| | 9 | | 1 | 800 | | 23 400 |
| | 13 | | 1 . | 700 | | 24 100 |
| | 24 | | 1 | | 2 000 | 22 100 |
| | 27 | | 1 | 300 | | 22 400 |
| | 30 | | 1 | | 700 | 21 700 |
| | 31 | | 1 | | 200 | 21 500 |
| | 31 | | 1 | | 500 | 21 000 |

ACCOUNTS RECEIVABLE — ACCT. NO. 3

| DATE | | EXPLANATION | POST. REF. | DEBIT | CREDIT | BALANCE |
|---|---|---|---|---|---|---|
| 19X1 | | | | | | |
| Oct. | 13 | | 1 | 700 | | 700 |
| | 27 | | 1 | | 300 | 400 |

OFFICE EQUIPMENT — ACCT. NO. 10

| DATE | | EXPLANATION | POST. REF. | DEBIT | CREDIT | BALANCE |
|---|---|---|---|---|---|---|
| 19X1 | | | | | | |
| Oct. | 4 | | 1 | 6 000 | | 6 000 |

ACCOUNTS PAYABLE — ACCT. NO. 20

| DATE | | EXPLANATION | POST. REF. | DEBIT | CREDIT | BALANCE |
|---|---|---|---|---|---|---|
| 19X1 | | | | | | |
| Oct. | 4 | | 1 | | 4 000 | 4 000 |
| | 24 | | 1 | 2 000 | | 2 000 |

JUDY HART, CAPITAL — ACCT. NO. 30

| DATE | | EXPLANATION | POST. REF. | DEBIT | CREDIT | BALANCE |
|---|---|---|---|---|---|---|
| 19X1 | | | | | | |
| Oct. | 1 | | 1 | | 25 000 | 25 000 |

JUDY HART, DRAWINGS ACCT. NO. 31

| DATE | | EXPLANATION | POST. REF. | DEBIT | CREDIT | BALANCE |
|---|---|---|---|---|---|---|
| 19X1 Oct. | 31 | | 1 | 500 | | 500 |

FEES EARNED ACCT. NO. 40

| DATE | | EXPLANATION | POST. REF. | DEBIT | CREDIT | BALANCE |
|---|---|---|---|---|---|---|
| 19X1 Oct. | 9 | | 1 | | 800 | 800 |
| | 13 | | 1 | | 1 400 | 2 200 |

SALARIES EXPENSE ACCT. NO. 50

| DATE | | EXPLANATION | POST. REF. | DEBIT | CREDIT | BALANCE |
|---|---|---|---|---|---|---|
| 19X1 Oct. | 30 | | 1 | 700 | | 700 |

RENT EXPENSE ACCT. NO. 51

| DATE | | EXPLANATION | POST. REF. | DEBIT | CREDIT | BALANCE |
|---|---|---|---|---|---|---|
| 19X1 Oct. | 1 | | 1 | 400 | | 400 |

UTILITIES EXPENSE ACCT. NO. 55

| DATE | | EXPLANATION | POST. REF. | DEBIT | CREDIT | BALANCE |
|---|---|---|---|---|---|---|
| 19X1 Oct. | 31 | | 1 | 200 | | 200 |

4.

| HART COMPANY<br>Trial Balance<br>October 31, 19X1 | | |
|---|---|---|
| Cash | $21,000 | |
| Accounts Receivable | 400 | |
| Office Equipment | 6,000 | |
| Accounts Payable | | $ 2,000 |
| Judy Hart, Capital | | 25,000 |
| Judy Hart, Drawings | 500 | |
| Fees Earned | | 2,200 |
| Salaries Expense | 700 | |
| Rent Expense | 400 | |
| Utilities Expense | 200 | |
| | $29,200 | $29,200 |

## Chapter 3

| | Date | Account | Debit | Credit |
|---|---|---|---|---|
| a. | Nov. 30 | Office Supplies Expense | 110 | |
| | | Office Supplies | | 110 |
| | | To record office supplies used during the month of November. | | |
| b. | 30 | Insurance Expense | 100 | |
| | | Prepaid Insurance | | 100 |
| | | To record insurance expense for the month of November. | | |
| c. | 30 | Depreciation Expense—Building | 200 | |
| | | Accumulated Depreciation—Building | | 200 |
| | | To record depreciation for the month of November. | | |
| d. | 30 | Depreciation Expense—Office Equipment | 100 | |
| | | Accumulated Depreciation—Office Equipment | | 100 |
| | | To record depreciation for the month of November. | | |
| e. | 30 | Unearned Commissions | 300 | |
| | | Commissions Earned | | 300 |
| | | To record commissions earned during the month of November. | | |
| f. | 30 | Interest Expense | 150 | |
| | | Interest Payable | | 150 |
| | | To record accrued interest expense for November. | | |
| g. | 30 | Salaries Expense | 600 | |
| | | Salaries Payable | | 600 |
| | | To record accrued salary expense for November. | | |

## Chapter 4

| ACCOUNTS | ADJUSTED TRIAL BALANCE | | INCOME STATEMENT | | BALANCE SHEET | |
|---|---|---|---|---|---|---|
| | Debit | Credit | Debit | Credit | Debit | Credit |
| Cash | 3,000 | | | | 3,000 | |
| Notes Receivable | 4,000 | | | | 4,000 | |
| Accounts Receivable | 2,000 | | | | 2,000 | |
| Prepaid Insurance | 800 | | | | 800 | |
| Vehicles | 16,300 | | | | 16,300 | |
| Accounts Payable | | 4,000 | | | | 4,000 |
| R. Stewart, Capital | | 20,000 | | | | 20,000 |
| R. Stewart, Drawings | 2,000 | | | | 2,000 | |
| Commission Revenue | | 21,500 | | 21,500 | | |
| Salaries Expense | 12,400 | | 12,400 | | | |
| Advertising Expense | 3,000 | | 3,000 | | | |
| Rent Expense | 1,500 | | 1,500 | | | |
| Utilities Expense | 800 | | 800 | | | |
| Insurance Expense | 100 | | 100 | | | |
| Depreciation—Vehicles | 200 | | 200 | | | |
| Accumulated Depreciation—Vehicles | | 200 | | | | 200 |
| Salaries Payable | | 400 | | | | 400 |
| Interest Receivable | 50 | | | | 50 | |
| Interest Revenue | | 50 | | 50 | | |
| | 46,150 | 46,150 | 18,000 | 21,550 | | |
| Net Income | | | 3,550 | | | 3,550 |
| | | | 21,550 | 21,550 | 28,150 | 28,150 |

Requirement 1 — A Work Sheet

CHEEPER AUDIO & VIDEO
Work Sheet
For the Year Ended December 31, 19X1

| | Trial Balance | | Adjustments | | Income Statement | | Balance Sheet | |
|---|---|---|---|---|---|---|---|---|
| | Debit | Credit | Debit | Credit | Debit | Credit | Debit | Credit |
| Cash | 7 900 | | | | | | 7 900 | |
| Accounts Receivable | 17 200 | | | | | | 17 200 | |
| Merchandise Inventory | 10 400 | | | | 10 400 | 9 600 | 9 600 | |
| Prepaid Rent | 1 000 | | | (b) 500 | | | 500 | |
| Equipment | 36 000 | | | | | | 36 000 | |
| Accumulated Depreciation—Equipment | | 6 000 | | (c) 1 800 | | | | 7 800 |
| Accounts Payable | | 7 500 | | | | | | 7 500 |
| Taxes Payable | | 1 100 | | | | | | 1 100 |
| M. Cheeper, Capital | | 50 000 | | | | | | 50 000 |
| M. Cheeper, Drawings | 17 000 | | | | | | 17 000 | |
| Sales | | 188 000 | | | | 188 000 | | |
| Sales Return and Allowances | 2 100 | | | | 2 100 | | | |
| Sales Discounts | 3 500 | | | | 3 500 | | | |
| Purchases | 107 600 | | | | 107 600 | | | |
| Purchase Returns and Allowances | | 2 800 | | | | 2 800 | | |
| Purchase Discounts | | 3 700 | | | | 3 700 | | |
| Transportation - In | 2 000 | | | | 2 000 | | | |
| Salaries Expense | 30 600 | | (d) 700 | | 31 300 | | | |
| Rent Expense | 5 500 | | (b) 500 | | 6 000 | | | |
| Advertising Expense | 13 800 | | | | 13 800 | | | |
| Insurance Expense | 1 600 | | | | 1 600 | | | |
| Utilities Expense | 2 900 | | | | 2 900 | | | |
| | 259 100 | 259 100 | | | | | | |
| Depreciation Expense | | | (c) 1 800 | | 1 800 | | | |
| Salaries Payable | | | | (d) 700 | | | | 700 |
| | | | 3 000 | 3 000 | 183 000 | 204 100 | | |
| Net Income | | | | | 21 100 | | | 21 100 |
| | | | | | 204 100 | 204 100 | 88 200 | 88 200 |

Requirement 2—Income Statement

CHEEPER AUDIO & VIDEO
Income Statement
For the Year Ended December 31, 19X1

| | | | | |
|---|---|---|---|---|
| Revenue: | | | | |
| Gross Sales | | | | $188,000 |
| Less: Sales Returns and Allowances | | | $ 2,100 | |
| Sales Discounts | | | 3,500 | 5,600 |
| Net Sales | | | | $182,400 |
| Cost of Goods Sold: | | | | |
| Merchandise Inventory, Jan. 1, 19X1 | | | $10,400 | |
| Purchases | | $107,600 | | |
| Less: Purchase Returns and Allowances | $2,800 | | | |
| Purchase Discounts | 3,700 | 6,500 | | |
| Net Purchases | | $101,100 | | |
| Add: Transportation-In | | 2,000 | | |
| Net Cost of Purchases | | | 103,100 | |
| Cost of Goods Available for Sale | | | $113,500 | |
| Less: Merchandise Inventory, Dec. 31, 19X1 | | | 9,600 | |
| Cost of Goods Sold | | | | 103,900 |
| Gross Margin on Sales | | | | $ 78,500 |
| Operating Expenses: | | | | |
| Salaries Expense | | | $ 31,300 | |
| Rent Expense | | | 6,000 | |
| Advertising Expense | | | 13,800 | |
| Insurance Expense | | | 1,600 | |
| Utilities Expense | | | 2,900 | |
| Depreciation Expense | | | 1,800 | |
| Total Operating Expenses | | | | 57,400 |
| Net Income | | | | $ 21,100 |

Requirement 3—Closing Entries

| Date | Account | Debit | Credit |
|---|---|---|---|
| Dec. 31 | Merchandise Inventory | 9,600 | |
| | Sales | 188,000 | |
| | Purchase Returns and Allowances | 2,800 | |
| | Purchase Discounts | 3,700 | |
| | Income Summary | | 204,100 |
| | To record the ending inventory and to close the temporary accounts having credit balances. | | |
| Dec. 31 | Income Summary | 183,000 | |
| | Merchandise Inventory | | 10,400 |
| | Sales Returns and Allowances | | 2,100 |
| | Sales Discounts | | 3,500 |
| | Purchases | | 107,600 |
| | Transportation-In | | 2,000 |
| | Salaries Expense | | 31,300 |
| | Rent Expense | | 6,000 |
| | Advertising Expense | | 13,800 |
| | Insurance Expense | | 1,600 |
| | Utilities Expense | | 2,900 |
| | Depreciation Expense | | 1,800 |
| | To remove the beginning inventory and to close the temporary accounts having debit balances. | | |
| Dec. 31 | Income Summary | 21,100 | |
| | M. Cheeper, Capital | | 21,100 |
| | To close the Income Summary account. | | |

| | | | |
|---|---|---|---|
| Dec. 31 | M. Cheeper, Capital | 17,000 | |
| | M. Cheeper, Drawings | | 17,000 |
| | To close the Drawings account. | | |

## Chapter 6

| | |
|---|---|
| July 1 | Cash Payments Journal |
| 2 | Purchases Journal |
| 2 | Cash Payments Journal |
| 3 | Sales Journal |
| 4 | Cash Receipts Journal |
| 8 | Purchases Journal |
| 8 | Sales Journal |
| 10 | Cash Payments Journal |
| 12 | General Journal |
| 12 | Cash Receipts Journal |
| 15 | Cash Payments Journal |
| 16 | Cash Receipts Journal |
| 16 | Cash Payments Journal |
| 18 | General Journal |
| 19 | General Journal |
| 22 | Sales Journal |
| 24 | Cash Receipts Journal |
| 25 | Purchases Journal |
| 29 | Cash Payments Journal |
| 31 | Cash Payments Journal |

## Chapter 7

REGAL COMPANY

Bank Reconciliation

September 30, 19X7

| | | |
|---|---|---|
| Balance per books | | $4,230 |
| Add: Proceeds of note collected from J. Harris | | 200 |
| | | $4,430 |
| Deduct: NSF check of R. Evans | $260 | |
| Bank service charge | 10 | 270 |
| Adjusted cash balance | | $4,160 |
| Balance per bank statement | | $5,260 |
| Add: Deposit in transit as of September 30 | | 180 |
| | | $5,440 |
| Deduct: Outstanding checks no. 57 | $370 | |
| no. 60 | 910 | 1,280 |
| Adjusted cash balance | | $4,160 |

JOURNAL ENTRIES

| | | | |
|---|---|---|---|
| Sept. 30 | Cash | 200 | |
| | Notes Receivable | | 200 |
| | To record the collection of the J. Harris note receivable by the bank | | |
| 30 | Accounts Receivable, R. Evans | 260 | |
| | Cash | | 260 |
| | To record a receivable from R. Evans in the amount of the NSF check returned by the bank | | |

| | | Debit | Credit |
|---|---|---|---|
| 30 | Service Charge | 10 | |
| | Cash | | 10 |
| | To record the bank service charge | | |

Note that the accounting records could be adjusted by one compound entry such as the following:

| | | Debit | Credit |
|---|---|---|---|
| Sept. 30 | Accounts Receivable, R. Evans | 260 | |
| | Service Charge | 10 | |
| | Notes Receivable | | 200 |
| | Cash | | 70 |
| | To record the effect of September's bank reconciliation items | | |

## Chapter 8

### Part I

| | | Debit | Credit |
|---|---|---|---|
| March 15 | Notes Receivable | 8,000 | |
| | Accounts Receivable, F. Bates | | 8,000 |
| | To record a 90-day, 12% note received from F. Bates | | |
| April 14 | Cash | 8,034 | |
| | Notes Receivable | | 8,000 |
| | Interest Revenue | | 34 |
| | To record discounting F. Bates 90-day, 12% note with 60 days left at 15%. Cash proceeds computed as follows: | | |

| | |
|---|---|
| Maturity value of note | \$8,240 |
| Discount (\$8,240 × .15 × 60/360) | 206 |
| | \$8,034 |

| | | Debit | Credit |
|---|---|---|---|
| June 13 | Accounts Receivable, F. Bates | 8,250 | |
| | Cash | | 8,250 |
| | To record payment of the maturity value of a discounted note dishonored by the maker F. Bates, plus a protest fee of \$10 | | |

### Part II

| | | Debit | Credit |
|---|---|---|---|
| Dec. 31 | Uncollectible Accounts Expense | 3,400 | |
| | Allowance for Uncollectible Accounts | | 3,400 |
| | To increase the Allowance account to its required balance | | |
| Feb. 2 | Allowance for Uncollectible Accounts | 400 | |
| | Accounts Receivable, D. Letters | | 400 |
| | To write off an uncollectible account | | |
| March 9 | Allowance for Uncollectible Accounts | 200 | |
| | Accounts Receivable, L. Helms | | 200 |
| | To write off an uncollectible account | | |
| March 16 | Accounts Receivable, D. Letters | 400 | |
| | Allowance for Uncollectible Accounts | | 400 |
| | To reinstate a customer's account previously written off | | |
| March 16 | Cash | 400 | |
| | Accounts Receivable, D. Letters | | 400 |
| | To record collection of customer's account | | |

## Chapter 9

Sales:

| | | |
|---|---|---|
| Jan. 12 | 100 units @ $120 | $12,000 |
| Feb. 9 | 80 units @ $125 | 10,000 |
| March 15 | 110 units @ $130 | 14,300 |
| | 290 units | $36,300 |

Cost of Goods Available for Sale in units and dollars:

| | | |
|---|---|---|
| Beginning Inventory | 70 units @ $ 85 | $ 5,950 |
| Jan. 8 purchase | 50 units @ 90 | 4,500 |
| Feb. 2 purchase | 100 units @ 92 | 9,200 |
| Feb. 19 purchase | 60 units @ 94 | 5,640 |
| March 3 purchase | 80 units @ 95 | 7,600 |
| March 12 purchase | 40 units @ 98 | 3,920 |
| March 27 purchase | 80 units @ 100 | 8,000 |
| | 480 units | $44,810 |

1. FIFO Cost-Flow Assumption
Ending Inventory—Consists of the most recent costs:

| | |
|---|---|
| 70 units remaining from the purchase on March 3 @ $95 | $ 6,650 |
| 40 units from the purchase on March 12 @ $98 | 3,920 |
| 80 units from the purchase on March 27 @ $100 | 8,000 |
| 190 units Total Ending Inventory | $18,570 |

Cost of Goods Sold—Consists of the earliest costs:

| | |
|---|---|
| Cost of Goods Available for Sale | $44,810 |
| Less: Ending Inventory | 18,570 |
| Cost of Goods Sold | $26,240 |

Gross Margin on Sales:

| | |
|---|---|
| Sales | $36,300 |
| Less: Cost of Goods Sold | 26,240 |
| Gross Margin on Sales | $10,060 |

2. LIFO Cost-Flow Assumption
Ending Inventory—Consists of the earliest costs:

| | |
|---|---|
| 70 units from the beginning inventory @ $85 | $ 5,950 |
| 50 units from the purchase on Jan. 8 @ $90 | 4,500 |
| 70 units remaining from the purchase on Feb. 2 @ $92 | 6,440 |
| 190 units Total Ending Inventory | $16,890 |

Cost of Goods Sold—Consists of the most recent costs:

| | |
|---|---|
| Cost of Goods Available for Sale | $44,810 |
| Less: Ending Inventory | 16,890 |
| Cost of Goods Sold | $27,920 |

Gross Margin on Sales:

| | |
|---|---|
| Sales | $36,300 |
| Less: Cost of Goods Sold | 27,920 |
| Gross Margin on Sales | $ 8,380 |

3. Weighted Average Cost-Flow Assumption
Ending Inventory—Consists of the average cost per unit:

| | |
|---|---|
| Cost of Goods Available for Sale | $44,810 |
| Number of Units Available for Sale | 480 |
| Average Cost per Unit ($44,810 ÷ 480) | $ 93.354 |
| Ending Inventory (190 units @ $93.354) | $17,737 (rounded) |

Cost of Goods Sold—Consists of the average cost per unit:

| | |
|---|---|
| Cost of Goods Available for Sale | $44,810 |
| Less: Ending Inventory | 17,737 |
| Cost of Goods Sold | $27,073 |

Gross Margin on Sales:

| | |
|---|---|
| Sales | $36,300 |
| Less: Cost of Goods Sold | 27,073 |
| Gross Margin on Sales | $ 9,227 |

## Chapter 10

a. Straight-Line Method

$$\frac{\$165{,}000 - \$15{,}000}{5 \text{ years}} = \$30{,}000 \text{ of depreciation expense for each year of the asset's expected useful life}$$

Depreciation Schedule:

| YEAR | DEPRECIATION EXPENSE | ACCUMULATED DEPRECIATION | CARRYING VALUE |
|---|---|---|---|
| Date of Purchase | $ — | $ — | $165,000 |
| 19X4 | 30,000 | 30,000 | 135,000 |
| 19X5 | 30,000 | 60,000 | 105,000 |
| 19X6 | 30,000 | 90,000 | 75,000 |
| 19X7 | 30,000 | 120,000 | 45,000 |
| 19X8 | 30,000 | 150,000 | 15,000 |

b. Sum-of-the-Years'-Digits Method

$$1 + 2 + 3 + 4 + 5 = 15, \text{ or } 5\left(\frac{5+1}{2}\right) = 15$$

Depreciation Schedule:

| YEAR | FRACTION USED | | COST LESS RESIDUAL VALUE | DEPRECIATION EXPENSE | ACCUMULATED DEPRECIATION | CARRYING VALUE |
|---|---|---|---|---|---|---|
| Date of Purchase | | | $150,000 | $ — | $ — | $165,000 |
| 19X4 | 5/15 | × | 150,000 | 50,000 | 50,000 | 115,000 |
| 19X5 | 4/15 | × | 150,000 | 40,000 | 90,000 | 75,000 |
| 19X6 | 3/15 | × | 150,000 | 30,000 | 120,000 | 45,000 |
| 19X7 | 2/15 | × | 150,000 | 20,000 | 140,000 | 25,000 |
| 19X8 | 1/15 | × | 150,000 | 10,000 | 150,000 | 15,000 |

c. Double-Declining Method

$$100\% \div 5 \text{ years} = 20\% \times 2 = 40\% \text{ rate}$$

Depreciation Schedule:

| YEAR | COMPUTATION USING A FIXED RATE (40% × CARRYING VALUE) | DEPRECIATION EXPENSE | ACCUMULATED DEPRECIATION | CARRYING VALUE |
|---|---|---|---|---|
| Date of Purchase | | $ — | $ — | $165,000 |
| 19X4 | 40% × $165,000 | 66,000 | 66,000 | 99,000 |
| 19X5 | 40% × 99,000 | 39,600 | 105,600 | 59,400 |
| 19X6 | 40% × 59,400 | 23,760 | 129,360 | 35,640 |
| 19X7 | 40% × 35,640 | 14,256 | 143,616 | 21,384 |
| 19X8 | | 6,384* | 150,000 | 15,000 |

* Amount necessary to reduce asset's carrying value to $15,000.

d. Units-of-Production Method

$$\frac{\$165{,}000 - \$15{,}000}{300{,}000 \text{ units}} = \$.50 \text{ per unit}$$

Depreciation Schedule:

| YEAR | PRODUCTION IN UNITS | DEPRECIATION EXPENSE | ACCUMULATED DEPRECIATION | CARRYING VALUE |
|---|---|---|---|---|
| Date of Purchase | | $ — | $ — | $165,000 |
| 19X4 | 40,000 × .50 | 20,000 | 20,000 | 145,000 |
| 19X5 | 30,000 × .50 | 15,000 | 35,000 | 130,000 |
| 19X6 | 70,000 × .50 | 35,000 | 70,000 | 95,000 |
| 19X7 | 60,000 × .50 | 30,000 | 100,000 | 65,000 |
| 19X8 | 100,000 × .50 | 50,000 | 150,000 | 15,000 |

## Chapter 11

A1.

*Computer:*

| | | | |
|---|---|---|---|
| 19X6 | | | |
| July 1 | Depreciation Expense—Computer | 2,000 | |
| | Accumulated Depreciation—Computer | | 2,000 |
| | To record depreciation to date of trade-in | | |
| July 1 | Computer (new) | 30,000 | |
| | Accumulated Depreciation—Computer | 14,000 | |
| | Loss on Disposal of Plant Asset | 3,000 | |
| | Computer (old) | | 25,000 |
| | Cash | | 22,000 |
| | To record the exchange of an old computer for a new one having a similar use | | |

*Copier:*

| | | | |
|---|---|---|---|
| Dec. 31 | Depreciation Expense—Copier | 2,000 | |
| | Accumulated Depreciation—Copier | | 2,000 |
| | To record annual depreciation | | |
| Dec. 31 | Copier (new) | 17,500 | |
| | Accumulated Depreciation—Copier | 10,000 | |
| | Copier (old) | | 12,500 |
| | Cash | | 15,000 |
| | To record the exchange of an old copier for a new one having a similar use | | |

| | | | | |
|---|---|---|---|---|
| A2. | Dec. 31 | Depreciation Expense—Computer | 3,000 | |
| | | Accumulated Depreciation—Computer | | 3,000 |
| | | To record the partial year's depreciation on computer | | |
| B1. | 19X6 | | | |
| | April 1 | Patents | 90,000 | |
| | | Cash | | 90,000 |
| | | To record the purchase of a patent | | |
| | June 30 | Leasehold Improvements | 57,000 | |
| | | Cash | | 57,000 |
| | | To record payment for improvements to leased building | | |
| | Aug. 31 | Trademarks | 120,000 | |
| | | Cash | | 120,000 |
| | | To record the purchase of a trademark | | |

| | | | | |
|---|---|---|---|---|
| B2. | Dec. 31 | Amortization Expense—Patent | 6,750 | |
| | | Patents | | 6,750 |
| | | To record patent amortization using an estimated life of ten years ($90,000 ÷ 10 years = $9,000 × $\frac{3}{4}$ of a year = $6,750) | | |
| | Dec. 31 | Amortization Expense—Trademarks | 1,000 | |
| | | Trademarks | | 1,000 |
| | | To record amortization of trademarks using a useful life of forty years ($120,000 ÷ 40 years = $3,000 × $\frac{1}{3}$ of a year = $1,000) | | |
| | Dec. 31 | Amortization Expense—Leasehold Improvements | 3,000 | |
| | | Leasehold Improvements | | 3,000 |
| | | To record amortization of leasehold improvements using a useful life of 9.5 years ($57,000 ÷ 9$\frac{1}{2}$ years = $6,000 × $\frac{1}{2}$ of a year = $3,000) | | |

## Chapter 12

| | | | | |
|---|---|---|---|---|
| 1a. | Jan. 15 | Cash | 11,400 | |
| | | Discount on Notes Payable | 600 | |
| | | Notes Payable | | 12,000 |
| | | To record borrowing on a six-month $12,000 note discounted at 10% | | |
| 1b. | Jan. 31 | Cash | 159,000 | |
| | | Sales | | 150,000 |
| | | Sales Tax Payable | | 9,000 |
| | | To record January sales and the related sales taxes | | |
| 1c. | Jan. 31 | Product Warranty Expense | 1,000 | |
| | | Product Warranty Liability | | 1,000 |
| | | To record estimated product warranty costs on January sales | | |
| 1d. | Jan. 31 | Sales Salaries Expense | 24,000 | |
| | | Office Salaries Expense | 6,000 | |
| | | Employees Federal Income Taxes Payable | | 4,800 |
| | | Employees State Income Taxes Payable | | 900 |
| | | FICA Taxes Payable | | 2,100 |
| | | Medical Insurance Payable | | 560 |
| | | Union Dues Payable | | 230 |
| | | Salaries Payable | | 21,410 |
| | | To record the payroll for the month of January | | |
| 1e. | Jan. 31 | Payroll Tax Expense | 3,150 | |
| | | FICA Taxes Payable | | 2,100* |
| | | State Unemployment Taxes Payable | | 810** |
| | | Federal Unemployment Taxes Payable | | 240*** |
| | | To record payroll taxes for the month of January | | |

* (.07 × $30,000 = $2,100)
** (.027 × $30,000 = $810)
*** (.008 × $30,000 = $240)

| | | | | |
|---|---|---|---|---|
| 1f. | Jan. 31 | Interest Expense | 50* | |
| | | Discount on Notes Payable | | 50* |
| | | To accrue interest on bank note for January | | |

* $600 ÷ 6 months = $100 per month × $\frac{1}{2}$ = $50

2. $33,150

| Gross Salaries | + | Payroll Taxes | = | Total Payroll Expense |
|---|---|---|---|---|
| $30,000 | + | $3,150 | = | $33,150 |

## Chapter 13

1. Division of Net Income

| | Alexis | Bramble | Costa | Total |
|---|---|---|---|---|
| Salary Allowances to Partners | $15,000 | $12,000 | $10,000 | $37,000 |
| Remaining Income ($75,000 − 37,000 = $38,000) divided 4:2:4 | 15,200 | 7,600 | 15,200 | 38,000 |
| Total | $30,200 | $19,600 | $25,200 | $75,000 |

2. Partners' Capital

ABC PARTNERSHIP
Statement of Partners' Capital
For the Year Ended December 31, 19X5

| | ALEXIS | BRAMBLE | COSTA | TOTAL |
|---|---|---|---|---|
| Capital Balances, January 1, 19X5 | $ 92,000 | $ 85,000 | $ 76,000 | $253,000 |
| Add: Net Income | 30,200 | 19,600 | 25,200 | 75,000 |
| Total | $122,200 | $104,600 | $101,200 | $328,000 |
| Less: Withdrawals | 24,200 | 15,600 | 27,200 | 67,000 |
| Capital Balances, December 31, 19X5 | $ 98,000 | $ 89,000 | $ 74,000 | $261,000 |

3. Journal Entries

| 19X6 | | | |
|---|---|---|---|
| Jan. 1 | Cash | 275,000 | |
| | Gain or Loss from Realization of Assets | 40,000 | |
| | Noncash Assets | | 315,000 |
| | To record the sale of assets | | |
| Jan. 1 | Alexis, Capital | 16,000 | |
| | Bramble, Capital | 8,000 | |
| | Costa, Capital | 16,000 | |
| | Gain or Loss from Realization of Assets | | 40,000 |
| | To divide the loss on the sale of assets according to the income-sharing ratio | | |
| Jan. 1 | Liabilities | 94,000 | |
| | Cash | | 94,000 |
| | To record payment of liabilities | | |
| Jan. 1 | Alexis, Capital | 82,000 | |
| | Bramble, Capital | 81,000 | |
| | Costa, Capital | 58,000 | |
| | Cash | | 221,000 |
| | To record distribution of remaining cash to partners | | |

## Chapter 14

### Requirement 1—Journal Entries

| Date | | Account and Explanation | Debit | Credit |
|---|---|---|---|---|
| Jan. | 5 | Cash | 240,000 | |
| | | Preferred Stock | | 200,000 |
| | | Paid-in Capital in Excess of Par Value—Preferred | | 40,000 |
| | | Issued 2,000 shares of $100 par value preferred stock for $120 per share | | |
| | 15 | Land | 18,000 | |
| | | Common Stock | | 15,000 |
| | | Paid-in Capital in Excess of Stated Value—Common | | 3,000 |
| | | Issued 3,000 shares of $5 stated value common stock in exchange for land | | |
| Feb. | 1 | Subscriptions Receivable—Common | 80,000 | |
| | | Common Stock Subscribed | | 50,000 |
| | | Paid-in Capital in Excess of Stated Value—Common | | 30,000 |
| | | Received subscriptions for 10,000 shares of $5 stated value common stock at $8 per share | | |
| | 1 | Cash | 40,000 | |
| | | Subscriptions Receivable—Common | | 40,000 |
| | | Collected one-half payment for subscriptions to 10,000 common shares | | |
| March | 1 | Cash | 20,000 | |
| | | Subscriptions Receivable—Common | | 20,000 |
| | | Collected one-fourth payment for subscriptions to 10,000 common shares | | |

### Requirement 2—Stockholders' Equity Section of the Balance Sheet

| | |
|---|---|
| Contributed Capital: | |
| Preferred Stock, $100 par value, 9% cumulative and nonparticipating, 50,000 shares authorized, 12,000 shares issued and outstanding | $1,200,000 |
| Common Stock, $5 stated value, 200,000 shares authorized, 103,000 shares issued, 10,000 shares subscribed to and 103,000 shares outstanding | 515,000 |
| Common Stock Subscribed | 50,000 |
| Paid-in Capital in Excess of Par Value—Preferred | 120,000 |
| Paid-in Capital in Excess of Stated Value—Common | 333,000 |
| Total Contributed Capital | $2,218,000 |
| Retained Earnings | 860,500 |
| Total Stockholders' Equity | $3,078,500 |

### Requirement 3—Book Value Per Share

| | |
|---|---|
| Total Stockholders' Equity | $3,078,500 |
| Allocated to Preferred Stock: | |
| Call price (12,000 shares × $120) | 1,440,000 |
| Common Stockholders' Equity | $1,638,500 |

$$\text{Book Value per Share of Preferred Stock} = \frac{\$1,440,000}{12,000 \text{ shares}} = \$120.00$$

$$\text{Book Value per Share of Common Stock} = \frac{\$1,638,500}{113,000 \text{ shares}} = \$14.50$$

Two things in the calculation should be noted:

1. The paid-in capital in excess of par value on the preferred stock is not allocated to the preferred stock equity. This is because the amount will not be returned to the preferred shareholders should their stock be called or should the corporation be terminated.
2. The common shares subscribed is allocated to the common stock equity. This is because the Common Stock Subscribed account is also a stockholders' equity account. The stock has not been fully paid for and therefore the stock certificates have not been issued but will be as soon as final payment on the subscription is received.

Requirement 4—Questions

a. $9 per share (9% × par value of $100 per share)
b. $108,000 ($9 per share × 12,000 shares outstanding)
c. 38,000 unissued preferred shares (50,000 authorized shares minus 12,000 issued shares)

## Chapter 15

GOLDEN CORPORATION
Income Statement
For the Year Ended December 31, 19X6

| | | |
|---|---|---|
| Sales Revenue | | $270,000 |
| Operating Expenses: | | |
| Cost of goods sold | $105,000 | |
| Selling expenses | 29,000 | |
| Administrative expenses | 18,000 | |
| Loss from labor strike | 12,000 | |
| Interest expense | 4,000 | 168,000 |
| Income from Continuing Operations before Taxes | | $102,000 |
| Income Tax Expense | | 40,800 |
| Income from Continuing Operations | | $ 61,200 |
| Discontinued Operations: | | |
| Operating loss of discontinued segment (net of tax savings, $6,000) | $ (9,000) | |
| Gain on disposal of segment (net of taxes $4,000) | 6,000 | (3,000) |
| Income before Extraordinary Items | | $ 58,200 |
| Extraordinary Item: Loss from expropriated property (net of tax savings, $16,000) | | (24,000) |
| Net Income | | $ 34,200 |
| Primary Earnings per Common Share: | | |
| Income from continuing operations | | $ 2.56 |
| Discontinued operations | | (.15) |
| Income before extraordinary item | | $ 2.41 |
| Extraordinary loss | | (1.20) |
| Net income | | $ 1.21 |
| Fully Diluted Earnings per Common Share: | | |
| Income from continuing operations | | $ 2.04 |
| Discontinued operations | | (.10) |
| Income before extraordinary item | | $ 1.94 |
| Extraordinary loss | | (.80) |
| Net income | | 1.14 |

Explanation of per share amounts:

In computing primary earnings per share, the net income applicable to common stock is \$24,200 (net income of \$34,200 less preferred dividend requirement of \$10,000). The weighted average number of common shares outstanding is 20,000. Thus primary earnings per share is \$1.21 (\$24,200 ÷ 20,000 = \$1.21).

In computing fully diluted earnings per share, it is assumed that the preferred shareholders converted their shares into common shares as of the beginning of the year. Net income of \$34,200 is applicable to common stock. However, after assumed conversion, the weighted average number of common shares outstanding is 30,000 [20,000 + (2 × 5,000)]. Thus fully diluted earnings per share is \$1.14 (\$34,200 ÷ 30,000 common shares assumed to be outstanding).

## Chapter 16

| | Date | Account | Debit | Credit |
|---|---|---|---|---|
| 1a. | 1988 | | | |
| | Jan. 1 | Bonds Payable | 3,000,000 | |
| | | Extraordinary Loss on Retirement of Bonds | 120,000 | |
| | | Discount on Bonds Payable | | 90,000 |
| | | Cash | | 3,030,000 |
| | | To record retirement of the 10% bonds called at 101 | | |
| 1b. | Jan. 31 | Cash | 4,090,000 | |
| | | Bonds Payable | | 4,000,000 |
| | | Premium on Bonds Payable | | 60,000 |
| | | Bond Interest Payable | | 30,000 |
| | | To record the issuance of 9%, 20-year bonds at $101\frac{1}{2}$ plus accrued interest | | |
| 1c. | June 30 | Bond Interest Expense | 148,745 | |
| | | Bond Interest Payable | 30,000 | |
| | | Premium on Bonds Payable | 1,255 | |
| | | Cash | | 180,000 |
| | | To record payment of semiannual interest (\$4,000,000 × .09 × $\frac{6}{12}$ = \$180,000) and amortization of premium (\$60,000 × $\frac{5}{239}$ = \$1,255 [rounded]) | | |
| 1d. | Dec. 31 | Bond Interest Expense | 178,494 | |
| | | Premium on Bonds Payable | 1,506 | |
| | | Cash | | 180,000 |
| | | To record payment of semiannual interest (\$4,000,000 × .09 × $\frac{6}{12}$ = \$180,000) and amortization of premium (\$60,000 × $\frac{6}{239}$ = \$1,506 [rounded]) | | |

2.

| Long-Term Liabilities: | | |
|---|---|---|
| Bonds Payable—9% due January 1, 2008 | \$4,000,000 | |
| Add: Unamortized Premium on Bonds Payable | 57,239 | \$4,057,239 |

## Chapter 17

1. Jan. 1 Investment in Ster Company ........................... 170,000
   Cash ........................................ 170,000
   To record the purchase of 100% of Ster Company's outstanding stock

2. Work Sheet for a Consolidated Balance Sheet

PRANK COMPANY AND SUBSIDIARY
Work Sheet for a Consolidated Balance Sheet
As of Acquisition Date

| Accounts | Prank Company | Ster Company | Adjustments and Eliminations Debit | Adjustments and Eliminations Credit | Consolidated Balance Sheet |
|---|---|---|---|---|---|
| Cash | 190 000 | 70 000 | | | 260 000 |
| Accounts Receivable (net) | 110 000 | 45 000 | | | 155 000 |
| Notes Receivable—Ster Company | 60 000 | | | (2) 60 000 | — |
| Inventory | 140 000 | 60 000 | | | 200 000 |
| Investment in Ster Company | 170 000 | — | | (1) 170 000 | — |
| Plant and Equipment (net) | 580 000 | 135 000 | | | 715 000 |
| Total Assets | 1250 000 | 310 000 | | | 1330 000 |
| | | | | | |
| Accounts Payable | 150 000 | 80 000 | | | 230 000 |
| Notes Payable—Prank Company | | 60 000 | (2) 60 000 | | — |
| Bonds Payable | 200 000 | | | | 200 000 |
| Common stock ($10 par value) | 500 000 | 100 000 | (1) 100 000 | | 500 000 |
| Retained Earnings | 400 000 | 70 000 | (1) 70 000 | | 400 000 |
| Total Liabilities and Stockholder's Equity | 1250 000 | 310 000 | 230 000 | 230 000 | 1330 000 |

(1) To eliminate the investment in Ster Company.
(2) To eliminate the intercompany note receivable and note payable.

## Chapter 18

HILLSIDE COMPANY
Schedule of Changes in Working Capital Components
For the Year Ended December 31, 19X5

| | DECEMBER 31 | | WORKING CAPITAL | |
|---|---|---|---|---|
| | 19X5 | 19X4 | Increase | Decrease |
| Current Assets: | | | | |
| Cash | $ 19,000 | $ 15,000 | $ 4,000 | |
| Accounts Receivable | 56,000 | 48,000 | 8,000 | |
| Inventory | 40,000 | 45,000 | | $ 5,000 |
| Prepaid Expenses | 3,000 | 2,000 | 1,000 | |
| Total Current Assets | $118,000 | $110,000 | | |
| Current Liabilities: | | | | |
| Accounts Payable | $ 42,000 | $ 46,000 | 4,000 | |
| Salaries Payable | 4,000 | 3,000 | | 1,000 |
| Other Accrued Liabilities | 25,200 | 29,000 | 3,800 | |
| Total Current Liabilities | $ 71,200 | $ 78,000 | | |
| Working Capital | $ 46,800 | $ 32,000 | | |
| | | | $20,800 | $ 6,000 |
| Increase in Working Capital | | | | 14,800 |
| | | | $20,800 | $20,800 |

HILLSIDE COMPANY
Statement of Changes in Financial Position
For the Year Ended December 31, 19X5

| | | |
|---|---|---|
| Sources of Working Capital: | | |
| Current Operations: | | |
| Net Income | $ 30,300 | |
| Add (or deduct) items that do not affect working capital: | | |
| Depreciation Expense | 23,500 | |
| Amortization Expense | 1,000 | |
| Loss on Sale of Land | 2,000 | |
| Gain on Sale of Equipment | (4,000) | |
| Working Capital Provided by Operations | | $ 52,800 |
| Other Sources: | | |
| Proceeds from the Issuance of Bonds | $100,000 | |
| Proceeds from the Issuance of Stock | 24,000 | |
| Proceeds from the Sale of Land | 10,000 | |
| Proceeds from the Sale of Equipment | 18,000 | 152,000 |
| Total Sources of Working Capital | | $204,800 |
| Uses of Working Capital: | | |
| Cash Dividends Declared and Paid | $ 12,000 | |
| Purchase of Land | 38,000 | |
| Purchase of a Building | 60,000 | |
| Purchase of Equipment | 80,000 | |
| Total Uses of Working Capital | | 190,000 |
| Increase in Working Capital | | $ 14,800 |

| | 19X5 | 19X4 |
|---|---|---|
| a. Current Ratio | | |
| 105,000 ÷ 55,000 | 1.9 to 1 | |
| 92,000 ÷ 46,000 | | 2.0 to 1 |
| b. Quick Ratio | | |
| 65,000 ÷ 55,000 | 1.2 to 1 | |
| 50,000 ÷ 46,000 | | 1.1 to 1 |
| c. Accounts Receivable Turnover | | |
| 350,000 ÷ 25,000 | 14 times | |
| 310,000 ÷ 18,000 | | 17.2 times |
| d. Inventory Turnover | | |
| 200,000 ÷ 37,500 | 5.3 times | |
| 175,000 ÷ 40,000 | | 4.4 times |
| e. Return on Sales | | |
| 32,000 ÷ 350,000 | 9.1% | |
| 27,000 ÷ 310,000 | | 8.7% |
| f. Return on Total Assets | | |
| 32,000 ÷ 232,500 | 13.8% | |
| 27,000 ÷ 211,000 | | 12.8% |
| g. Asset Turnover | | |
| 350,000 ÷ 232,500 | 1.5 times | |
| 310,000 ÷ 211,000 | | 1.5 times |
| h. Return on Common Stockholders' Equity | | |
| 32,000 ÷ 127,000 | 25.2% | |
| 27,000 ÷ 112,000 | | 24.1% |
| i. Earnings per Share | | |
| 32,000 ÷ 10,000 shares | $3.20 | |
| 27,000 ÷ 10,000 shares | | $2.70 |
| j. Debt to Equity | | |
| 115,000 ÷ 135,000 | 85.2% | |
| 96,000 ÷ 119,000 | | 80.7% |
| k. Debt to Total Assets | | |
| 115,000 ÷ 250,000 | 46.0% | |
| 96,000 ÷ 215,000 | | 44.7% |
| l. Times Interest Earned | | |
| 57,000 ÷ 5,000 | 11.4 times | |
| 49,000 ÷ 4,000 | | 12.3 times |
| m. Price-Earnings Ratio | | |
| 18.00 ÷ 3.20 | 5.6 times | |
| 14.50 ÷ 2.70 | | 5.4 times |
| n. Dividend Yield Ratio | | |
| 1.60 ÷ 18.00 | 8.9% | |
| 1.20 ÷ 14.50 | | 8.3% |
| o. Dividend Payout Ratio | | |
| 16,000 ÷ 32,000 | 50% | |
| 12,000 ÷ 27,000 | | 44.4% |

## Chapter 20

LASSALE COMPANY
Constant Dollar Balance Sheet
December 31, 19X7

| | | |
|---|---|---|
| Cash | $ 30,000 | (Monetary asset—No restatement) |
| Inventory | 21,333 | (Nonmonetary asset restated in constant dollars: $20,000 × 160/150) |
| Land | 61,538 | (Nonmonetary asset restated in constant dollars: $50,000 × 160/130) |
| Total Assets | $112,871 | |
| Accounts Payable | $ 15,000 | (Monetary liability—No restatement) |
| Common Stock | 87,273 | (Nonmonetary item restated in constant dollars: $60,000 × 160/110) |
| Retained Earnings | 10,598 | (Balancing amount—Total constant dollar assets less constant dollar amounts for accounts payable and common stock: $112,871 − the sum of $15,000 + $87,273 = $10,598) |
| Total Liabilities and Stockholders' Equity | $112,871 | |

LASSALE COMPANY
Constant Dollar Income Statement
For the Year Ended December 31, 19X7

| | | |
|---|---|---|
| Sales | $96,000 | (Made evenly throughout the year. Restated in constant dollars: $90,000 × 160/150) |
| Less: Cost of Goods Sold | 53,333 | (Goods purchased evenly throughout the year. Restated in constant dollars: $50,000 × 160/150) |
| Gross Profit on Sales | $42,667 | |
| Selling and Administrative Expenses | 32,000 | (Incurred evenly throughout the year. Restated in constant dollars: $30,000 × 160/150) |
| Income before Income Taxes | $10,667 | |
| Income Taxes | 3,200 | (Incurred evenly throughout the year. Restated in constant dollars: $3,000 × 160/150) |
| Income before Purchasing Power Loss | $ 7,467 | |
| Purchasing Power Loss | (900) | (Amount provided in problem—In practice, computed on the basis of net monetary items held during the year. Holding monetary assets during a period of inflation causes a loss in purchasing power and owing monetary liabilities during a period of inflation causes a gain in purchasing power) |
| Constant Dollar Net Income | $ 6,567 | |

## Chapter 21

GLOBAL COMPANY
Statement of Cost of Goods Manufactured
For the Year Ended September 30, 19X6

| | | |
|---|---|---|
| Direct Materials: | | |
| Inventory, 10/1/X5 | | $ 12,000 |
| Add: Purchases | | 51,000 |
| Cost of Direct Materials Available for Use | | $ 63,000 |
| Less: Inventory, 9/30/X6 | | 15,000 |
| Direct Materials Used | | $ 48,000 |
| Direct Labor | | 83,200 |
| Manufacturing Overhead: | | |
| Indirect Labor | $17,200 | |
| Factory Supplies Used | 9,400 | |
| Factory Utilities | 5,600 | |
| Factory Insurance | 2,100 | |
| Maintenance Expense—Factory | 4,300 | |
| Depreciation—Factory Building | 2,200 | |
| Depreciation—Factory Machinery | 3,400 | |
| Total Manufacturing Overhead | | $ 44,200 |
| Total Current Cost of Production | | $175,400 |
| Add: Work in Process Inventory, 10/1/X5 | | 28,500 |
| Total Manufacturing Costs | | $203,900 |
| Less: Work in Process Inventory, 9/30/X6 | | 19,500 |
| Cost of Goods Manufactured | | $184,400 |

## Chapter 22

1.

$$\frac{\$210{,}000}{70{,}000} = \$3 \text{ per direct labor hour}$$

2.

| | | |
|---|---|---|
| Work in Process Inventory | 50,000 | |
| Raw Materials Inventory | | 50,000 |
| To show the requisition of direct materials to production | | |
| Manufacturing Overhead | 3,000 | |
| Raw Materials Inventory | | 3,000 |
| To show the requisition of indirect materials to production | | |
| Work in Process Inventory | 60,000 | |
| Wages Payable | | 60,000 |
| To show the accrual of direct labor | | |
| Manufacturing Overhead | 2,000 | |
| Wages Payable | | 2,000 |
| To show the accrual of indirect labor | | |
| Manufacturing Overhead | 15,000 | |
| Cash | | 15,000 |
| To show the incurrence of other manufacturing overhead | | |
| Work in Process Inventory | 18,000 | |
| Manufacturing Overhead | | 18,000 |
| To show the application of manufacturing overhead to production (6,000 direct labor hours × $3 per hour) | | |

| | | |
|---|---|---|
| Finished Goods Inventory | 128,000 | |
| Work in Process Inventory | | 128,000 |
| To show the transfer of completed units to finished goods | | |
| Accounts Receivable (or Cash) | 160,000 | |
| Sales | | 160,000 |
| To record the sale of the completed units ($128,000 × 1.25) | | |
| Cost of Goods Sold | 128,000 | |
| Finished Goods Inventory | | 128,000 |
| To record the cost of the completed units sold | | |
| Cost of Goods Sold | 2,000 | |
| Manufacturing Overhead | | 2,000 |
| To close out the manufacturing overhead account | | |

## Chapter 23

1. Contribution Margin per Unit

| | |
|---|---|
| Selling price per unit | $200 |
| Less: Variable costs per unit ($1,400,000 ÷ 10,000 units) | 140 |
| Contribution margin per unit | $ 60 |

1. Contribution Margin Percentage

$\$60 \div \$200 = 30\%$, or .30

2. Break-even Point in Units

$$\frac{\$540{,}000}{\$60} = 9{,}000 \text{ units}$$

2. Break-even Point in Sales Dollars

$$\frac{\$540{,}000}{.30} = \$1{,}800{,}000$$

3. Volume in Units to Earn $96,000

$$\frac{\$540{,}000 + \$96{,}000}{\$60} = 10{,}600 \text{ units}$$

3. Volume in Sales Dollars to Earn $96,000

$$\frac{\$540{,}000 + \$96{,}000}{.30} = \$2{,}120{,}000$$

4. Break-even Point in Units after Change in Total Fixed Costs

$$\frac{\$558{,}000}{\$60} = 9{,}300 \text{ units}$$

4. Break-even Point in Sales Dollars after Change in Total Fixed Costs

$$\frac{\$558{,}000}{.30} = \$1{,}860{,}000$$

## Chapter 24

| ACCOUNT | FIXED DOLLAR AMOUNT | VARIABLE RATE PER DIRECT LABOR HOUR | DIRECT LABOR HOURS 1,000 | 2,000 | 3,000 |
|---|---|---|---|---|---|
| Machine Repairs | $ 300 | $.10 | $ 400 | $ 500 | $ 600 |
| Indirect Materials | — | .05 | 50 | 100 | 150 |
| Utilities | — | .10 | 100 | 200 | 300 |
| Indirect Labor | 500 | .05 | 550 | 600 | 650 |
| Supervision | 1,000 | — | 1,000 | 1,000 | 1,000 |
| Depreciation | 2,000 | — | 2,000 | 2,000 | 2,000 |
| | | | $4,100 | $4,400 | $4,700 |

## Chapter 25

1. Direct Materials Quantity Variance
Actual quantity used (130,000) minus standard quantity allowed (126,000) = 4,000 × standard cost per pound ($.80) = *$3,200* (unfavorable)

1. Direct Materials Price Variance
Actual price [$.78 ($101,400/130,000)] minus standard price ($.80) = $.02 × actual quantity purchased (130,000) = *$2,600* (favorable)

2. Direct Labor Time Variance
Actual hours (50,200) minus standard hours allowed [50,400 (25,200 units × 2 hours per unit)] = 200 × standard rate per hour ($5.00) = *$1,000* (favorable)

2. Direct Labor Rate Variance
Actual rate [$4.95 ($248,490/50,200 hours)] minus standard rate ($5.00) = $.05 × actual hours (50,200) = *$2,510* (favorable)

3. Total Manufacturing Overhead Variance
Actual overhead incurred ($126,200) minus overhead applied [$126,000 (50,400 × $2.50)] = *$200* (unfavorable)

4. Manufacturing Overhead Volume Variance
Overhead applied ($126,000) minus overhead budgeted for actual productive level achieved ($125,640 for 50,400 standard direct labor hours) = *$360* (favorable), or 400 direct labor hours (50,400 standard direct hours for actual productive level achieved − 50,000 direct labor hours for normal production) × $.90 (the fixed standard overhead rate) = *$360* (favorable)

4. Manufacturing Overhead Controllable Variance
Overhead incurred ($126,200) minus overhead budgeted for actual productive level achieved ($125,640) = *$560* (unfavorable)

5. Journal Entries

| | | |
|---|---|---|
| Raw Materials Inventory | 104,000 | |
| Materials Price Variance | | 2,600 |
| Accounts Payable | | 101,400 |
| To record the purchase of direct materials | | |

| | | |
|---|---|---|
| Work in Process Inventory | 100,800 | |
| Materials Quantity Variance | 3,200 | |
| Raw Materials Inventory | | 104,000 |
| To record the issuance of direct materials | | |

| | | |
|---|---|---|
| Work in Process Inventory | 252,000 | |
| Labor Time Variance | | 1,000 |
| Labor Rate Variance | | 2,510 |
| Wages Payable | | 248,490 |
| To record direct labor for January | | |
| Manufacturing Overhead | 126,200 | |
| Various Credits | | 126,200 |
| To record the actual overhead incurred | | |
| Work in Process Inventory | 126,000 | |
| Overhead Controllable Variance | 560 | |
| Overhead Volume Variance | | 360 |
| Manufacturing Overhead | | 126,200 |
| To apply overhead to production (50,400 standard hours allowed × $2.50 standard overhead rate) | | |

## Chapter 26

1a.
$10,000 ÷ $200,000 = 5%

1b.
$200,000 ÷ $100,000 = 2 times

1c.
5% × 2 = 10%, or $10,000 ÷ $100,000 = 10%

2a.
$11,000 ÷ $100,000 = 11%

2b.
$10,000 ÷ $95,000 = 10.5%

## Chapter 27

1.

| | |
|---|---|
| Cost of the asset | $50,000 |
| Less: Salvage value | 2,000 |
| Depreciable amount | $48,000 |
| Depreciation deduction for each year ($48,000 ÷ 4 years) | $12,000 |
| Cash inflows before tax | $20,000 |
| Depreciation deduction | 12,000 |
| Amount on which tax is paid | $ 8,000 |
| Tax ($8,000 × 45%) | $ 3,600 |
| Cash inflows after tax ($20,000 − $3,600) | $16,400 |

2a.

$$\frac{\$4,400}{\$50,000} = 8.8\%$$

2b.

$$\frac{\$50,000}{\$16,400} = 3.0 \text{ years (rounded)}$$

2c. 3.0 Payback Factor
Factor in Table 27–2 is 3.037, which is the present value of a $1 annuity for four years at 12%. Therefore 12% is the approximate discounted rate of return.

2d.

| | |
|---|---|
| Cost | ($50,000) |
| Present value of annuity of cash inflows after tax for 4 years at 12% (3.037 × $16,400) | 49,807 |
| Present value of the amount of the salvage value at the end of 4 years (.636 × $2,000) | 1,272 |
| Excess present value (positive) | $ 1,079 |

## Chapter 28

| | | |
|---|---|---|
| Gross income: | | |
| Revenue from Mary Ann's practice | $82,600 | |
| Less: Expenses of Mary Ann's practice | 47,200 | $35,400 |
| Mark's salary | | 42,500 |
| Interest | | 620 |
| Dividends | | 1,210 |
| Capital gain income: | | 1,800 |
| Total gross income | | $81,530 |
| Deductions from gross income: | | |
| IRA contribution | | 2,000 |
| Adjusted gross income | | $79,530 |
| Less: Itemized deductions | | |
| Medical and dental expenses ($420) | | |
| Less: 7.5% × AGI = $5965 | 0 | |
| Mortgage interest | $ 5,100 | |
| Interest on car loan ($570 × 40%) | 228 | |
| Property taxes | 4,200 | |
| Charitable contributions | 450 | 9,978 |
| Less: Personal exemptions (4 × $1,950) | | 7,800 |
| Taxable income | | $61,752 |
| Calculation of gross tax liability: | | |
| Taxes on $29,750 | $ 4,463 | |
| Taxes on excess over $29,750 | 8,961 | 13,424 |
| Less: Taxes paid | | |
| Taxes withheld | $ 6,800 | |
| Estimated taxes | 6,400 | 13,200 |
| Net tax liability | | $ 224 |

# B PepsiCo, Inc. 1985 Annual Report

## Report of Chief Financial Officer

To Our Shareholders:

Management is responsible for the integrity and objectivity of the financial statements and related notes. To meet this responsibility, we maintain a system of internal control, supported by formal policies and procedures and an internal audit program designed to monitor and report on the adequacy of and compliance with our internal controls, policies and procedures. We believe the established system of internal control provides reasonable assurance that assets are safeguarded, transactions are recorded in accordance with our policies and the financial information is reliable.

The financial statements have been prepared in conformity with generally accepted accounting principles applied on a consistent basis, and include amounts based upon our estimates and judgments, as required. The financial statements have been audited by certified public accountants who have expressed their opinion, presented below, with respect to the fairness of the statements. Their examination included a review of the system of internal control and tests of transactions to the extent they considered necessary to render their opinion.

The Audit Committee of the Board of Directors is composed of non-employee directors. The Audit Committee meets on a regular basis with management, our internal auditors and certified public accountants to review audit plans, results and recommendations, as well as the effectiveness of our system of internal control.

Both our certified public accountants and internal auditors have free access to the Audit Committee.

Michael H. Jordan
Executive Vice President
and Chief Financial Officer

## Report of Certified Public Accountants

Board of Directors and Shareholders
PepsiCo, Inc.

We have examined the accompanying consolidated statement of financial condition of PepsiCo, Inc. and subsidiaries at December 28, 1985 and December 29, 1984, and the related consolidated statements of income, changes in financial condition and shareholders' equity for each of the three years in the period ended December 28, 1985, appearing on pages 36, 38, 40 and 42 through 51. Our examinations were made in accordance with generally accepted auditing standards and, accordingly, included such tests of the accounting records and such other auditing procedures as we considered necessary in the circumstances.

In our opinion, the statements mentioned above present fairly the consolidated financial position of PepsiCo, Inc. and subsidiaries at December 28, 1985 and December 29, 1984, and the consolidated results of operations and changes in financial position for each of the three years in the period ended December 28, 1985, in conformity with generally accepted accounting principles applied on a consistent basis during the period.

Arthur Young & Company

277 Park Avenue
New York, New York
February 4, 1986

# Consolidated Statement of Income

(in thousands except per share amounts)
PepsiCo, Inc. and Subsidiaries
Years ended December 28, 1985 (fifty-two weeks), December 29, 1984 (fifty-two weeks) and December 31, 1983 (fifty-three weeks)

| | 1985 | 1984 | 1983 |
|---|---|---|---|
| **Net Sales** | **$8,056,662** | $7,451,106 | $6,899,884 |
| **Costs and Expenses** | | | |
| Cost of sales | **3,148,261** | 2,974,458 | 2,821,816 |
| Marketing, administrative and other expenses | **4,171,339** | 3,763,974 | 3,537,556 |
| Interest expense | **195,378** | 205,099 | 175,232 |
| Interest income | **(96,382)** | (86,117) | (53,614) |
| | **7,418,596** | 6,857,414 | 6,480,990 |
| **Income From Continuing Operations Before Refranchising Credit (Charge) and Income Taxes** | **638,066** | 593,692 | 418,894 |
| Refranchising credit (charge) | **25,900** | (156,000) | – |
| **Income From Continuing Operations Before Income Taxes** | **663,966** | 437,692 | 418,894 |
| Provision for federal and foreign income taxes | **243,885** | 162,677 | 140,602 |
| **Income From Continuing Operations** | **420,081** | 275,015 | 278,292 |
| **Discontinued Operations** | | | |
| Income (loss) from discontinued operations (net of income tax provision (benefit) of $6,716, $(61) and $359 in 1985, 1984 and 1983, respectively) | **9,609** | (47,468) | 5,819 |
| Gain (loss) from disposals (net of income tax provision (benefit) of $28,760 and $(500) in 1985 and 1984, respectively) | **114,000** | (15,000) | – |
| | **123,609** | (62,468) | 5,819 |
| **Net Income** | **$ 543,690** | $ 212,547 | $ 284,111 |
| **Net Income (Loss) Per Share** | | | |
| Continuing operations | **$4.51** | $2.90 | $2.95 |
| Discontinued operations | **1.32** | (.65) | .06 |
| **Net Income** | **$5.83** | $2.25 | $3.01 |
| Average shares outstanding used to calculate earnings per share | **93,567** | 95,827 | 95,480 |

See accompanying notes

# Management's Review—Results of Continuing Operations

**Net sales** increased eight percent to $8.1 billion in 1985, following an eight percent increase in 1984. The increase in 1985 was driven primarily by volume gains in our domestic soft drinks, domestic restaurants and foreign snack foods businesses and small price increases in all segments. Volume gains primarily reflect the impact of new products, new restaurants and strong diet soft drink growth. The increase in 1984 sales reflected strong growth in the restaurants and snack foods segments and the domestic soft drinks business.

**Cost of sales** rose at a slower pace than net sales, six percent in 1985 and five percent in 1984. The 1985 increase reflected increased volume in all segments and higher ingredient costs in the domestic soft drinks segment due to both a diet formula change to 100 percent NutraSweet brand sweetener in early 1985 and a mix shift to higher cost diet drinks and new juice-based Slice. This increase was moderated by lower food and ingredient costs in the restaurants and snack foods segments, respectively. The 1984 increase primarily resulted from increased volume and higher ingredient costs in the soft drinks and snack foods segments. (The impact of inflation on PepsiCo's operations is discussed in the Information on the Effects of Inflation on page 52.)

**Marketing, administrative and other expenses** increased 11 percent in 1985 following a six percent increase in 1984, reflecting the continued development and expansion of all three of PepsiCo's segments. Marketing expenses increased 13 percent in 1985, following a 15 percent increase in 1984. The increase in 1985 was primarily due to higher levels of competitive spending in domestic soft drinks and increased promotional spending for new products in all segments. Also contributing to the increase in marketing, administrative and other expenses were increased fixed costs, primarily due to new restaurant openings, and one-time charges recorded in the fourth quarter of 1985. A $16 million charge was recorded by Frito-Lay related to packaged cookies, and a $12 million charge was recorded related to the planned move to a new soft drinks headquarters in Somers, N.Y. The 1984 increase was attributable to competitive spending and new product introductions in all three segments.

Net foreign currency translation gains, which are included in marketing, administrative and other expenses, arise principally from the favorable impact of devaluation on local currency borrowings of PepsiCo's foreign operations. In 1985 the gains were $32 million compared to $53 million in 1984 and $17 million in 1983. The reduction in 1985 from 1984 is primarily attributable to the Philippines, where losses were sustained in 1985 compared to gains in 1984. The increase in 1984 over 1983 was a result of losses experienced in Venezuela in 1983, increased gains in Brazil and Argentina in 1984 and gains in the Philippines in 1984 compared to a small loss in 1983.

**Net interest expense** (after deducting interest income) decreased 17 percent to $99 million in 1985, following a two percent decrease in 1984. International net interest expense decreased 17 percent. The decrease was primarily attributable to a reduction in foreign currency borrowings, particularly in Brazil and Mexico, and lower interest rates in the Philippines. These borrowings had previously financed the now refranchised foreign bottling operations. Domestic net interest expense also decreased 17 percent. This was principally due to increased interest income from short-term investments and the North American Van Lines receivable. Commercial paper interest expense increased as a result of higher commercial paper borrowings used primarily to finance the share repurchase program and the acquisition of the Allegheny Pepsi-Cola Bottling Company. The two percent decrease in 1984 was due to lower net domestic borrowing costs, which more than offset increased foreign currency borrowing costs. The foreign borrowings were used, in part, to hedge foreign investments in certain Latin American countries and the Philippines against devaluations.

**Income from continuing operations before refranchising credit (charge) and income taxes** increased seven percent in 1985, following a 42 percent increase in 1984. Nineteen eighty-five results reflected increases in all three segments, led by restaurants, international soft drinks and international snack foods. Results were moderated by the two one-time charges and reduced foreign currency gains. Excluding the one-time charges in 1985, results were up 12 percent. The significant increase in 1984 was the result of a turnaround in foreign soft drinks and snack foods operations and continued growth in domestic snack foods and restaurants operations.

**Refranchising credit (charge)** relates to the refranchising of several company-owned foreign bottling operations (the Refranchising Program). In 1984 a charge of $156 million was recorded to cover the estimated costs of the Refranchising Program. In 1985 the Refranchising Program was substantially completed, and, as a result of more favorable results than originally estimated, a $26 million credit was recorded. (See Notes to Consolidated Financial Statements on page 43 for a detailed discussion of the Refranchising Program.)

**Provision for federal and foreign income taxes** on income from continuing operations was 36.7 percent in 1985, compared to 37.2 percent in 1984 and 33.6 percent in 1983. The lower rate in 1983 reflected one-time U.S. tax benefits from legal reorganizations and tax elections involving certain company-owned foreign bottling operations. Excluding the impact of the Refranchising Program, the provision for taxes was 36.5 percent in 1985 compared to 43.2 percent in 1984. The lower rate in 1985 was caused by a higher percentage of foreign income taxed at rates below the statutory federal rate of 46 percent and reduced foreign losses without tax benefit. For tax purposes, foreign income includes 50 percent of the income arising from the sale in the U.S. domestic market of Pepsi-Cola concentrate that is manufactured in Puerto Rico under tax incentive grants.

**Income from continuing operations** of $420 million in 1985 was up 53 percent from $275 million in 1984, which decreased one percent from $278 million in 1983. **Income per share** from continuing operations of $4.51 increased 56 percent from $2.90 in 1984. Nineteen eighty-four income per share declined two percent from the $2.95 reported in 1983. Income from continuing operations before the effects of the Refranchising Program and the one-time charges was $420 million in 1985, up 25 percent from $337 million in 1984, which increased 21 percent from $278 million in 1983. The related earnings per share was $4.51 in 1985, up 27 percent from $3.55 in 1984, which was up 20 percent from $2.95 in 1983. Nineteen eighty-five per share amounts were favorably affected by PepsiCo's repurchase of 7.3 million shares. (See Notes to Consolidated Financial Statements on page 45 for additional information.)

For a discussion of the results of operations of PepsiCo's business segments, see pages 24, 28 and 32.

# Consolidated Statement of Financial Condition

(in thousands except share amounts)
PepsiCo, Inc. and Subsidiaries
December 28, 1985 and December 29, 1984

| | 1985 | 1984 |
|---|---|---|
| **Assets** | | |
| **Current Assets** | | |
| Cash | **$ 25,738** | $ 27,501 |
| Short-term investments | **886,527** | 784,684 |
| Receivable from sale of North American Van Lines | **375,540** | – |
| Notes and accounts receivable, less allowance: 1985–$30,382; 1984–$30,663 | **648,659** | 587,373 |
| Inventories | **380,096** | 340,689 |
| Prepaid expenses, taxes and other current assets | **477,984** | 232,998 |
| Net assets held for disposal | **–** | 289,593 |
| | **2,794,544** | 2,262,838 |
| **Long-term Receivables and Other Investments** | **232,251** | 254,184 |
| **Property, Plant and Equipment** | **2,571,773** | 2,115,981 |
| **Goodwill** | **185,716** | 163,904 |
| **Other Assets** | **76,876** | 79,497 |
| | **$5,861,160** | $4,876,404 |
| **Liabilities and Shareholders' Equity** | | |
| **Current Liabilities** | | |
| Notes payable (including current installments on long-term debt and capital lease obligations) | **$ 344,137** | $ 280,796 |
| Accounts payable | **621,993** | 487,451 |
| Federal and foreign income taxes | **123,609** | 117,736 |
| Other accrued taxes | **64,746** | 63,414 |
| Other current liabilities | **681,234** | 622,658 |
| | **1,835,719** | 1,572,055 |
| **Long-term Debt** | **1,035,571** | 536,076 |
| **Capital Lease Obligations** | **127,097** | 133,565 |
| **Other Liabilities and Deferred Credits** | **211,391** | 162,732 |
| **Deferred Income Taxes** | **813,700** | 618,600 |
| **Shareholders' Equity** | | |
| Capital stock, par value 5¢ per share; authorized 135,000,000 shares; issued: 1985–95,898,068; 1984–95,164,331 shares | **4,795** | 4,758 |
| Capital in excess of par value | **282,453** | 251,915 |
| Retained earnings | **2,061,442** | 1,678,912 |
| Cumulative translation adjustment | **(40,931)** | (49,426) |
| Cost of repurchased shares: 1985–8,191,905; 1984–1,256,768 | **(470,077)** | (32,783) |
| | **1,837,682** | 1,853,376 |
| | **$5,861,160** | $4,876,404 |

See accompanying notes

# Management's Review—Financial Condition

PepsiCo continues to maintain a strong overall financial condition as shown in its Consolidated Statement of Financial Condition at the end of 1985 and 1984. A discussion of the significant items relating to PepsiCo's financial condition and liquidity follows:

**Short-term investments** consist primarily of marketable securities held offshore. This portfolio has grown significantly in recent years as the result of strong operating cash flows and increased soft drink concentrate manufacturing activity in Puerto Rico where a sizeable amount of these investments are held. Funds domiciled in Puerto Rico can be repatriated as a dividend at management's discretion upon payment of a modest tollgate tax. In addition, PepsiCo has invested approximately $200 million in 1985 in secured pools of short-term third party receivables.

The $376 million **Receivable from sale of North American Van Lines** was subsequently collected in full on its scheduled due date in January 1986.

Current **Notes and accounts receivable** primarily represent amounts due from Pepsi-Cola franchised bottlers and Frito-Lay customers. Collection experience continues to be favorable.

**Inventories** consist primarily of raw materials and finished goods relating to the soft drinks and snack foods segments. The days sales in inventory decreased modestly in 1985.

The 1985 increase in **Prepaid expenses, taxes and other current assets** primarily represents the $160 million temporary investment in the Allegheny Pepsi-Cola Bottling Company. Also included in the account is $194 million and $176 million of the current portion of deferred income taxes, in 1985 and 1984, respectively.

**Net assets held for disposal** in 1984 represented the net assets of Wilson Sporting Goods and North American Van Lines, which were sold in 1985.

PepsiCo increased its net investment in **Property, plant and equipment** by $456 million, a 22 percent increase from 1984, reflecting its strong commitment to its businesses. While investment continued in all business segments, the fast-growing restaurants segment has accounted for the largest percentage of capital additions for the last several years.

The increase in **Goodwill** is attributable to a number of small franchised bottler and restaurant acquisitions, partially offset by amortization.

**Notes payable** increased $63 million in 1985 principally due to the reclassification from long-term debt of $150 million of 10⅛ percent Notes maturing in 1986 reduced by the retirement of $100 million of 8¼ percent Notes.

**Accounts payable** consist primarily of trade payables for raw materials and services in all segments. The increase in 1985 over 1984 is the result of general growth of the business.

**Other current liabilities** primarily represent accruals for employee compensation and compensation related costs, advertising and marketing programs, insurance costs, accrued interest on borrowings and the net liability from the Refranchising Program. (See Notes to Consolidated Financial Statements on page 43 for additional information.)

**Long-term debt** represents PepsiCo's borrowings with maturity dates one or more years in the future. The 1985 increase in long-term borrowings was primarily caused by the issuance of $603 million of commercial paper, used to finance the share repurchase program and the acquisition of the Allegheny Pepsi-Cola Bottling Company (see Notes to Consolidated Financial Statements on page 45 for additional information), reduced by the reclassification of $150 million of 1986 maturities to notes payable. The commercial paper has been classified as long-term as it is PepsiCo's intention to refinance these borrowings on a long-term basis during 1986.

**Deferred income taxes** increased by $195 million, primarily related to the tax attributes associated with tax lease transactions ($114 million) and depreciation ($41 million).

**Shareholders' equity** decreased $16 million during the year. The decrease is principally attributable to PepsiCo repurchasing 7.3 million shares for $458 million and $161 million of cash dividends, substantially offset by 1985's net income. (See the Consolidated Statement of Shareholders' Equity on page 42 for additional information.)

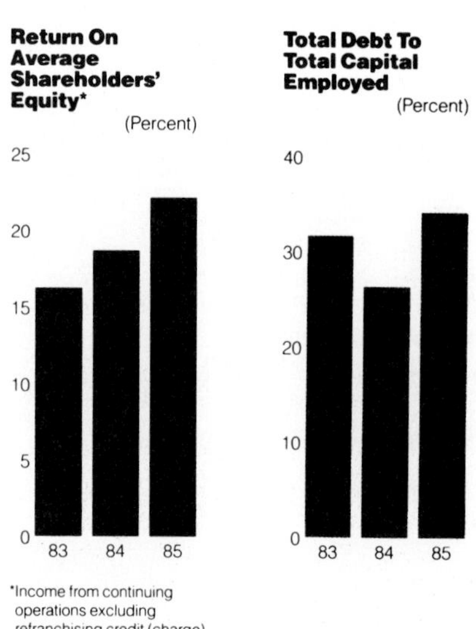


Based on income from continuing operations before the refranchising credit (charge), the return on average shareholders' equity was 22.0 percent in 1985 compared to 18.5 percent and 16.2 percent in 1984 and 1983, respectively. The increase in 1985 is due to the significant increase in income coupled with the impact of the share repurchase program. After the refranchising credit (charge), return on average shareholders' equity was 22.8 percent and 15.1 percent in 1985 and 1984, respectively.

PepsiCo's ratio of total debt (including capital lease obligations) to capital employed (which is total debt, deferred income taxes, other liabilities and deferred credits and shareholders' equity) increased to 34.5 percent in 1985 from 26.5 percent in 1984, reflecting the borrowings used to finance the share repurchases and the Allegheny Pepsi-Cola Bottling Company acquisition. The 1984 ratio, the lowest in over five years, reflected a net decrease in borrowings of $125 million during 1984 and strong growth in internally generated capital. In 1983 the ratio was 31.7 percent.

# Consolidated Statement of Changes in Financial Condition

(in thousands)
PepsiCo, Inc. and Subsidiaries
Years ended December 28, 1985 (fifty-two weeks), December 29, 1984 (fifty-two weeks) and December 31, 1983 (fifty-three weeks)

| | **1985** | 1984 | 1983 |
|---|---|---|---|
| **Cash was Generated by (Used for):** | | | |
| Continuing Operations: | | | |
| Income | **$ 420,081** | $ 275,015 | $ 278,292 |
| Depreciation and amortization | **290,819** | 249,604 | 232,852 |
| Deferred income taxes | **81,100** | 121,300 | 60,200 |
| Refranchising (credit) charge | **(14,900)** | 62,000 | – |
| Changes in operating working capital accounts (see details below) | **(68,694)** | 186,600 | (9,004) |
| Other non-cash charges and credits, net | **95,840** | 85,360 | 107,894 |
| **Cash generated by continuing operations** | **804,246** | 979,879 | 670,234 |
| Discontinued operations: | | | |
| Cash generated by (used for) discontinued operations | **16,507** | (63,211) | 30,001 |
| Wilson restructuring charge | **–** | 59,300 | – |
| Other, net | **(15,147)** | 2,872 | (29,755) |
| **Cash generated by (used for) discontinued operations** | **1,360** | (1,039) | 246 |
| Investment activities: | | | |
| Purchases of property, plant and equipment | **785,896** | 555,802 | 503,352 |
| Receivable from sale of North American Van Lines | **375,540** | – | – |
| Proceeds from sale of North American Van Lines | **(368,950)** | – | – |
| Allegheny Pepsi-Cola acquisition | **160,000** | – | – |
| Proceeds from the sale of Wilson Sporting Goods | **(134,100)** | – | – |
| Proceeds from sales of property, plant and equipment | **(49,459)** | (42,210) | (42,910) |
| Miscellaneous, net | **15,605** | 26,828 | (89,997) |
| **Cash used for investment activities** | **784,532** | 540,420 | 370,445 |
| Financing activities: | | | |
| Increase in long-term debt | **689,930** | 41,356 | 62,257 |
| Purchase of capital stock | **(458,171)** | – | – |
| Reductions of long-term debt and capital lease obligations | **(220,527)** | (197,849) | (135,363) |
| Cash dividends | **(161,054)** | (154,624) | (151,271) |
| Deferred income taxes arising from tax leases | **114,035** | 115,584 | 105,347 |
| Increase in notes payable | **63,341** | 5,501 | 87,372 |
| Issuance of capital stock | **51,452** | 11,306 | 5,903 |
| **Cash generated by (used for) financing activities** | **79,006** | (178,726) | (25,755) |
| **Resulting in:** | | | |
| Increase in cash and short-term investments during the year | **$ 100,080** | $ 259,694 | $ 274,280 |
| **Details of Changes in Operating Working Capital Accounts Which Generated (Used) Cash:** | | | |
| Notes and accounts receivable | **$ (61,286)** | $ (45,005) | $ 1,732 |
| Inventories | **(39,407)** | (80,951) | 17,410 |
| Prepaid expenses, taxes and other current assets | **(125,096)** | 17,844 | (43,433) |
| Accounts payable | **134,542** | 130,489 | (74,766) |
| Other current liabilities | **24,910** | 106,958 | 39,531 |
| Federal and foreign income taxes payable | **5,397** | 58,898 | 34,662 |
| Other accrued taxes | **(7,754)** | (1,633) | 15,860 |
| | **$ (68,694)** | $ 186,600 | $ (9,004) |

See accompanying notes

# Management's Review— Changes in Financial Condition

As reflected in PepsiCo's Statement of Changes in Financial Condition, the internal generation of funds from operations continues to be a significant financial strength of PepsiCo. On a cumulative basis, cash provided by continuing operations has been sufficient to fund record capital expenditures and dividends for the past three years.

**Cash Generated by Continuing Operations vs. Purchases of P.P.&E. and Dividends Paid**

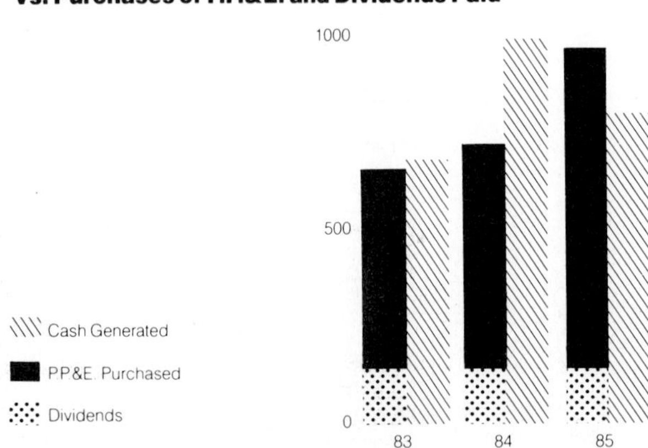


Continuing operations are PepsiCo's principal source of cash, averaging almost $900 million a year for the last two years. Cash from operations is income adjusted for changes in non-cash working capital and items that affect accounting income for a given year, but do not produce cash receipts or payments in the same year; for example, depreciation, deferred income taxes and the refranchising (credit) charge.

**Cash generated by continuing operations** totaled $804 million in 1985, an 18 percent decrease from 1984. The decrease reflected the $145 million increase in **Income from continuing operations**, which was more than offset by a $77 million decrease associated with the **Refranchising (credit) charge** and a $255 million decrease in the amount of cash generated from **Operating working capital**. The significant decrease in cash generated from operating working capital from continuing operations was attributable to a smaller increase in other current liabilities in 1985 than was experienced in 1984 coupled with the changes in federal and foreign income taxes payable and prepaid taxes. In 1984 cash generated by continuing operations increased 46 percent from 1983, reflecting increases in non-cash charges and a reduction in operating working capital.

**Investment activities** represent the investment and generation of cash from the purchase or sale, respectively, of capital assets and business units.

PepsiCo's principal investment activity over the past three years has been the **Purchase of property, plant and equipment** in support of its continuing businesses. These investments form the cornerstone of PepsiCo's strategy to invest in its businesses to provide for consistent earnings growth in the future. Total spending in 1985 of $786 million was led again by the restaurants segment, reflecting continued additions of company-owned stores and the upgrading of existing stores.

Also, 1985 investment activities reflect the cash effects of PepsiCo's strategic restructuring actions begun in 1984. The divestitures of both the transportation segment and Wilson Sporting Goods were completed and the **Receivable from the sale of North American Van Lines** was collected in early 1986.

Finally, PepsiCo acquired the **Allegheny Pepsi-Cola Bottling Company** for the purpose of refranchising it to other Pepsi-Cola bottlers to strengthen its bottler system.

**Financing activities** represent PepsiCo's management of its capital structure to achieve a balance between debt and equity that is appropriate in terms of its cash flow and business requirements. When external financing is required, and within the constraints of maintaining a strong credit rating, it is generally PepsiCo's policy to use debt rather than equity due to the favorable impact on the overall cost of capital.

PepsiCo's capital structure was significantly affected by financing activities in 1985 as compared to the previous two years. During 1985 PepsiCo's Board of Directors approved programs to repurchase up to 9.7 million shares of PepsiCo Capital Stock. Through December 28, 1985, 7.3 million shares of PepsiCo's **Capital Stock** were repurchased at an aggregate cost of $458 million. When completed, PepsiCo will have repurchased approximately 10 percent of total outstanding shares. In evaluating share repurchase, PepsiCo compares economic returns, the impact on corporate performance and after-tax benefits to shareholders with the alternatives of higher dividends or other investment opportunities.

The share repurchase programs and the acquisition of the Allegheny Pepsi-Cola Bottling Company gave rise to financing needs that were satisfied principally by the issuance of $603 million of commercial paper. The use of short-term instruments to satisfy these requirements was supported by the very attractive short-term rates prevailing for most of the year. The commercial paper issued has been classified as **Long-term debt** because it is PepsiCo's intent to refinance these borrowings on a long-term basis during 1986.

At December 28, 1985 and February 28, 1986, PepsiCo had unused credit facilities aggregating $1.52 billion, providing it with domestic and international credit availability and support for the issuance and long-term classification of commercial paper, $603 million, which is currently outstanding. The existing credit facilities, PepsiCo's portfolio of short-term investments (net of any taxes that may arise as a result of repatriation) and its existing, unused debt capacity provide it with the capital resources to finance the approximately $970 million of commitments associated with the pending acquisitions of MEI Corporation and the franchise beverage business of The Seven-Up Company.

Over the past three years, PepsiCo has generated an average of over $100 million of cash from the deferral of income taxes relating to its investment in **Tax leases**. PepsiCo's $429 million investment in tax leases in 1981 and 1982 has generated cash benefits of $709 million on a cumulative basis, $362 million of which represents temporary cash savings. These cash savings will begin to reverse in 1986, and will require cash outlays, based on the current federal tax rate, of $1 million in 1986, $15 million in 1987, $18 million in 1988, $22 million in 1989, $26 million in 1990 and $280 million in the years 1991 through 2005.

PepsiCo paid **Cash dividends** of $161 million in 1985, while retaining sufficient resources and financial flexibility to provide for future earnings growth.

PepsiCo has consistently demonstrated its ability to maintain a strong financial condition, to invest for its future through internal expansion and external acquisition, and provide an attractive return to its shareholders.

# Consolidated Statement of Shareholders' Equity

(in thousands except per share amounts)
PepsiCo, Inc. and Subsidiaries
Years ended December 28, 1985 (fifty-two weeks), December 29, 1984 (fifty-two weeks) and December 31, 1983 (fifty-three weeks)

| | Capital Stock | | | | Capital in Excess of Par Value | Retained Earnings | Cumulative Translation Adjustment | Total |
|---|---|---|---|---|---|---|---|---|
| | Issued | | Repurchased | | | | | |
| | Shares | Amount | Shares | Amount | | | | |
| Shareholders' Equity, December 25, 1982 | 94,916 | $4,746 | (1,542) | $ (40,219) | $242,154 | $1,489,797 | $(46,013) | $1,650,465 |
| 1983 Net income | | | | | | 284,111 | | 284,111 |
| Cash dividends declared (per share–$1.62) | | | | | | (151,358) | | (151,358) |
| Shares reissued to TRASOP | | | 116 | 3,024 | 886 | | | 3,910 |
| Payment of compensation awards and exercise of stock options | 53 | 2 | | | 1,640 | | | 1,642 |
| Conversion of debentures | 17 | 1 | | | 350 | | | 351 |
| Translation adjustments (net of income taxes of $25,900) | | | | | | | 5,037 | 5,037 |
| Shareholders' Equity, December 31, 1983 | 94,986 | 4,749 | (1,426) | (37,195) | 245,030 | 1,622,550 | (40,976) | 1,794,158 |
| 1984 Net income | | | | | | 212,547 | | 212,547 |
| Cash dividends declared (per share–$1.665) | | | | | | (156,185) | | (156,185) |
| Shares reissued to PAYSOP | | | 169 | 4,412 | 2,484 | | | 6,896 |
| Payment of compensation awards and exercise of stock options | 170 | 9 | | | 4,237 | | | 4,246 |
| Conversion of debentures | 8 | | | | 164 | | | 164 |
| Translation adjustments (net of income taxes of $18,700) | | | | | | | (8,059) | (8,059) |
| Amount included in refranchising charge (net of income taxes of $44,500) | | | | | | | (391) | (391) |
| Shareholders' Equity, December 29, 1984 | 95,164 | 4,758 | (1,257) | (32,783) | 251,915 | 1,678,912 | (49,426) | 1,853,376 |
| 1985 Net income | | | | | | 543,690 | | 543,690 |
| Cash dividends declared (per share–$1.755) | | | | | | (161,160) | | (161,160) |
| Shares reissued to PAYSOP | | | 76 | 3,946 | 478 | | | 4,424 |
| Payment of compensation awards and exercise of stock options | 156 | 8 | 25 | 1,316 | 5,500 | | | 6,824 |
| Conversion of debentures | 578 | 29 | 299 | 15,615 | 24,560 | | | 40,204 |
| Translation adjustments (net of income taxes of $100) | | | | | | | 8,495 | 8,495 |
| Share repurchases | | | (7,335) | (458,171) | | | | (458,171) |
| **Shareholders' Equity, December 28, 1985** | **95,898** | **$4,795** | **(8,192)** | **$(470,077)** | **$282,453** | **$2,061,442** | **$(40,931)** | **$1,837,682** |

See accompanying notes

# Notes to Consolidated Financial Statements

## Summary of Significant Accounting Policies

Principles of Consolidation. The consolidated financial statements include the accounts of PepsiCo, Inc. and its subsidiaries (all of which are wholly-owned), except for those held as temporary investments, which are accounted for under the cost method. The financial statements and accompanying notes have been reclassified for discontinued operations. All significant intercompany accounts and transactions have been eliminated.

Short-term Investments. Short-term investments are stated at cost, which approximates market, and include time deposits of $269 million and $481 million at year-end 1985 and 1984, respectively, and secured interests in pools of short-term discounted third-party receivables of $203 million in 1985.

Inventories. Inventories are valued at the lower of cost (computed on the average, first-in, first-out or last-in, first-out method) or net realizable value.

Property, Plant and Equipment. Property, plant and equipment, including capital leases, are stated at cost. Depreciation is calculated principally on a straight-line basis over the estimated useful lives of the respective assets.

Goodwill. Goodwill represents the excess of cost over identifiable net assets of companies acquired. Goodwill is amortized over appropriate periods not exceeding 40 years. Amortization was $8 million in 1985, $10 million in 1984 and $8 million in 1983.

Marketing Costs. Costs of advertising and other marketing and promotional programs are charged to expense during the year, generally in relation to sales, and except for materials in inventory and prepayments, are substantially expensed by the end of the year in which the costs are incurred.

Income Taxes. Deferred income taxes arise from the deferral of investment tax credits, which are amortized over the estimated useful lives of the related assets, and from timing differences between financial and tax reporting, principally financing transactions, foreign exchange translation and depreciation.

Taxes that would result from dividend distributions by foreign subsidiaries to the U.S. parent are provided to the extent dividends are anticipated. All other undistributed earnings of subsidiaries operating outside the United States have been reinvested indefinitely and no provision has been made for additional taxes that might be payable with regard to such earnings in the event of remittance.

Net Income Per Share. Net income per share is computed by dividing net income (adjusted for interest expense related to convertible debentures) by the average number of shares and share equivalents outstanding during each year. The conversion of all convertible debentures would not result in a material dilution.

## Refranchising Credit (Charge)

In 1984, PepsiCo recorded a $156 million before-tax and $62 million after-tax ($.65 per share) charge for the refranchising of several company-owned foreign bottling operations (the Refranchising Program). This charge was comprised of a $24 million before-tax and $11 million after-tax charge for estimated losses from operations expected to be incurred during the course of the Refranchising Program and a $132 million before-tax and $51 million after-tax charge for estimated net losses upon disposition of the various operations.

Subsequent to the initiation of the Refranchising Program, charges applied to the operating loss reserve totaled $26 million before-tax and $16 million after-tax. Net losses actually incurred to December 28, 1985 upon the disposition of operations refranchised totaled $27 million before-tax (net of a cumulative translation adjustment gain of $50 million) and $3 million after-tax. As of December 28, 1985 all but one of the company-owned foreign bottling operations in the Refranchising Program have been refranchised. As a result of more favorable results than originally estimated from the 1985 refranchisings, the reserve has been reduced and a $26 million before-tax and $15 million after-tax ($.16 per share) credit has been recorded. This credit is reflected in the Consolidated Statement of Income under the caption "Refranchising credit (charge)." The balance of the reserve, $72 million, represents the estimated amount required to complete the Refranchising Program and to provide for other obligations and contingencies related to the completed refranchisings.

In 1985 refranchisings were completed in Belgium, Brazil, Canada, the Philippines and South Africa. In 1984, a refranchising was completed in Mexico.

The remaining net assets of the company-owned foreign bottling operations in the Refranchising Program are carried, net of accruals for future operating and disposition related losses, in the Consolidated Statement of Financial Condition under the caption "Other current liabilities." The net liability arising from the Refranchising Program as of December 28, 1985 and December 29, 1984 is detailed below:

| | 1985 | 1984 |
|---|---|---|
| | (in thousands) | |
| Current assets | $14,308 | $ 47,318 |
| Current liabilities | 21,249 | 39,696 |
| Net current assets | (6,941) | 7,622 |
| Property, plant and equipment | 23,919 | 78,888 |
| Other non-current assets | 4,406 | 11,602 |
| Non-current liabilities | 1,974 | 2,001 |
| Net non-current assets | 26,351 | 88,489 |
| Net assets | 19,410 | 96,111 |
| Less: | | |
| Accrued future operating and disposition related losses | 72,300 | 160,606[a] |
| Net liability for refranchising | $52,890 | $ 64,495 |

[a] Represents the year-end balance of the approximately $201 million of accruals established at the outset of the Refranchising Program in 1984. The accruals were reduced by approximately $45 million of balance sheet translation gains transferred from the "Cumulative translation adjustment" account, resulting in a $156 million before-tax charge to 1984 earnings.

### Discontinued Operations

In 1985 PepsiCo sold its Wilson Sporting Goods operation (Wilson). The proceeds from the sale of $134 million consisted of cash and $42 million (face amount) of Wilson 10 percent cumulative preferred stock, valued at $13 million. The loss on the sale of $41 million before-tax and $18 million after-tax ($.19 per share), includes provisions for certain obligations of Wilson assumed by PepsiCo in connection with the sale, and is reflected in the Consolidated Statement of Income under the caption "Gain (loss) from disposals." Of the loss, $12 million before-tax and $9 million after-tax ($.09 per share) was recorded in the fourth quarter, primarily to reflect the currently estimated fair market value of the Wilson preferred stock. The sale proceeds are subject to adjustments arising from the audit of Wilson's balance sheet as of the closing date, which is not yet complete. If PepsiCo and the purchaser are unable to agree upon the adjustments related to Wilson's balance sheet, the contract provides that the differences will be settled by an independent accounting firm agreed upon by the parties. Management believes any change will not have a material adverse effect on PepsiCo's business or financial condition.

PepsiCo has extended Wilson a $10 million line of credit, expiring December 31, 1986. As of February 1986 the line of credit remains unused. PepsiCo is contingently liable as of December 28, 1985 for $14 million of various obligations of Wilson, including $9 million of short-term letters of credit, which decreased to $3 million in February 1986. The letters of credit expire in August 1986.

In 1984 PepsiCo adopted a plan to sell its transportation segment, which was comprised of North American Van Lines, Inc. (NAVL) and Lee Way Motor Freight, Inc. (Lee Way).

The sale of NAVL was completed in 1985 for a $369 million interest-bearing deferred payment due January 2, 1986. On that date, $376 million, including accrued interest, was received. The sale resulted in a gain of $194 million before-tax and $139 million after-tax ($1.49 per share), and is reflected in the Consolidated Statement of Income under the caption "Gain (loss) from disposals."

The sale of Lee Way was completed in 1984 and produced a loss of $16 million before-tax and $15 million after-tax ($.16 per share). This loss is reflected in the Consolidated Statement of Income under the caption "Gain (loss) from disposals." In 1985 PepsiCo made payments and incurred costs under certain guarantees that existed at, or were entered into in connection with, the sale of Lee Way. The purchaser of Lee Way merged into Lee Way in 1985, shortly before filing for bankruptcy. The merged company is now in liquidation. PepsiCo has filed a claim to recover the amounts paid or payable under the guarantees, but any significant recovery is uncertain. As a result, an additional charge of $10 million before-tax and $7 million after-tax ($.08 per share) was recorded in the fourth quarter of 1985. This loss is reflected in the Consolidated Statement of Income under the caption "Gain (loss) from disposals."

The results of operations of NAVL, Wilson and Lee Way are recorded in the Consolidated Statement of Income under the caption "Income (loss) from discontinued operations" and include results of operations through the dates in 1985 and 1984 on which the sales of the respective operations were recorded in the financial statements. Also included under this caption is the $64 million before-tax and $59 million after-tax ($.62 per share) Wilson restructuring charge recorded in 1984, primarily resulting from the write-off of $54 million (without tax benefit) of Wilson's goodwill. The results of NAVL, Wilson and Lee Way are as follows:

| | 1985 | 1984 | 1983 |
|---|---|---|---|
| | | (in thousands) | |
| Net sales and operating revenues | $422,240 | $ 976,888 | $996,052 |
| Costs and expenses | 404,802 | 957,546 | 988,052 |
| Net interest expense | 1,113 | 2,871 | 1,822 |
| Wilson restructuring charge | – | 64,000 | – |
| | 405,915 | 1,024,417 | 989,874 |
| Income (loss) before income taxes | 16,325 | (47,529) | 6,178 |
| Income tax provision (benefit) | 6,716 | (61) | 359 |
| Income (loss) from discontinued operations | $ 9,609 | $ (47,468) | $ 5,819 |

The net assets of Wilson and NAVL are carried at their historical cost in the Consolidated Statement of Financial Condition under the caption "Net assets held for disposal" at December 29, 1984 as follows (in thousands):

| | |
|---|---|
| Current assets | $405,688 |
| Current liabilities | 217,566 |
| Net current assets | 188,122 |
| Property, plant and equipment | 145,887 |
| Other non-current assets | 52,529 |
| Non-current liabilities | 96,945 |
| Net non-current assets | 101,471 |
| Net assets held for disposal | $289,593 |

### Acquisitions

In May 1985 PepsiCo purchased the Allegheny Pepsi-Cola Bottling Company (Allegheny) for $160 million in cash. Allegheny was acquired with the intent of refranchising the operations to other purchasers. Accordingly, the acquisition has been accounted for as a temporary investment under the cost method and is included in the Consolidated Statement of Financial Condition under the caption "Prepaid expenses, taxes and other current assets."

In December 1985 PepsiCo agreed to purchase the soft drink business of MEI Corporation (MEI) for $590 million in cash. The transaction is subject to various conditions, including approval by the shareholders of MEI. MEI is PepsiCo's third largest independent bottler. This acquisition will be accounted for by the purchase method and is expected to be completed in the second quarter of 1986.

In January 1986 PepsiCo agreed to purchase the domestic and international franchise beverage businesses of The Seven-Up Company (Seven-Up) from Philip Morris Incorporated (Philip Morris) for $380 million cash. The transaction is subject to various governmental approvals. Upon transfer of the international business, PepsiCo is obligated to pay the full purchase price, and assume all the risks of ownership, for both the international and domestic Seven-Up businesses, even though governmental approvals for the transfer of the domestic business may not have been received. If, after transfer of the international business, sale of the domestic Seven-Up business to PepsiCo is prohibited under the antitrust laws or if PepsiCo so requests, then Philip Morris is obligated to use its best efforts to sell the domestic business on the same terms and conditions as the proposed sale and to remit the net proceeds to PepsiCo. Management believes that none of the foregoing alternatives will have a material adverse affect on PepsiCo's business or financial condition. This acquisition will be accounted for by the purchase method.

Also, in January 1986 PepsiCo agreed to acquire A & M Food Services, Inc. (A & M) in exchange for PepsiCo Capital Stock. The number of shares of PepsiCo Capital Stock to be received by stockholders of A&M will be between 584,000 and 741,000. The transaction is subject to various conditions, including approval by the shareholders of A & M. A & M is Pizza Hut's largest franchisee. This acquisition will be accounted for by the purchase method and is expected to be completed in the second quarter of 1986.

### Share Repurchases

During 1985 PepsiCo announced plans to repurchase up to 9.7 million shares of PepsiCo's Capital Stock. These shares are to be used to fund outstanding convertible securities, employee stock plans and for other corporate purposes.

As of December 28, 1985 PepsiCo had purchased 7.3 million shares at an aggregate purchase price of $458 million and had commitments to purchase 260,000 shares at an aggregate purchase price of $18 million. As of February 4, 1986 PepsiCo had purchased 9 million shares at an aggregate purchase price of $572 million and had commitments to purchase 57,000 shares at an aggregate purchase price of $4 million.

### Inventories

Inventories at December 28, 1985 and December 29, 1984 are summarized as follows:

| | 1985 | 1984 |
|---|---|---|
| | (in thousands) | |
| Finished goods | $163,311 | $140,482 |
| Raw materials, supplies and in-process | 223,132 | 208,323 |
| Total (approximates current cost) | 386,443 | 348,805 |
| Excess of current cost over LIFO cost | (6,347) | (8,116) |
| | $380,096 | $340,689 |

Inventories valued at cost, computed on the last-in, first-out (LIFO) method comprised 57 percent of inventories at December 28, 1985 and December 29, 1984.

### Property, Plant and Equipment

Property, plant and equipment at December 28, 1985 and December 29, 1984 are summarized as follows:

| | 1985 | 1984 |
|---|---|---|
| | (in thousands) | |
| Land | $ 250,671 | $ 217,811 |
| Buildings | 1,015,068 | 809,513 |
| Machinery and equipment | 2,361,762 | 1,934,954 |
| Capital leases | 170,901 | 172,535 |
| Bottles and cases | 25,048 | 23,785 |
| | 3,823,450 | 3,158,598 |
| Less accumulated depreciation and amortization | 1,251,677 | 1,042,617 |
| | $2,571,773 | $2,115,981 |

## Notes Payable and Long-term Debt

Notes payable and long-term debt (less current maturities) at December 28, 1985 and December 29, 1984 are summarized below:

| | 1985 | 1984 |
|---|---|---|
| | (in thousands) | |
| **Notes Payable** | | |
| 10⅛% notes due 1986 | $150,000 | $ – |
| 8¼% notes due 1985 | – | 100,000 |
| Current maturities on other long-term debt and capital lease obligations | 25,284 | 17,789 |
| Other notes payable, primarily to foreign banks | 168,853 | 163,007 |
| | $344,137 | $280,796 |

| | 1985 | 1984 |
|---|---|---|
| | (in thousands) | |
| **Long-term Debt (less current maturities)** | | |
| Commercial paper (7.97% weighted average interest rate) | $ 603,000 | $ – |
| 10⅛% notes due 1986 | – | 150,000 |
| Zero coupon serial debentures, $850 million face value due 1988-2012 (13.91% semiannual yield to maturity) | 89,361 | 78,014 |
| 13% notes, 50 million Australian dollars, due 1990 (After interest rate swap: Variable interest based on 90-day Australian Bank Bill rate–19.6% at year-end) | 34,456 | – |
| Zero coupon notes, $100 million face value due 1992 (14.42% semiannual yield to maturity) | 42,758 | 37,213 |
| Zero coupon notes, $125 million face value due 1994 (14.08% semiannual yield to maturity) | 41,112 | 35,896 |
| 5¼% bearer bonds, 130 million Swiss francs, due 1995 (After exchange agreement: $50 million principal at maturity, 10.96% semiannual yield to maturity) | 47,773 | – |
| 8% convertible subordinated debentures due 1996 | 40,088 | 73,184 |
| Other (11.9% weighted average interest rate) | 137,023 | 161,769 |
| | $1,035,571 | $536,076 |

The original issue discounts associated with the zero coupon issues listed above are being amortized over the lives of the issues on a yield-to-maturity basis. For tax purposes, the original issue discounts are deductible on a straight-line basis over the lives of the issues, thus reducing the effective costs of these transactions.

At the option of the holder, the convertible subordinated debentures are primarily convertible at a rate of approximately 26 shares for each $1,000 of principal. At December 28, 1985, 1.1 million shares were reserved for issuance upon conversion of the debentures.

During 1985 PepsiCo issued Swiss francs (SFr.) 130 million of 5¼ percent Bearer Bonds, due March 1995. Simultaneously with the issuance of the SFr. Bonds, PepsiCo entered into a currency exchange agreement. The debt issuance and related agreement created a U.S. dollar liability in the amount of $50 million at maturity with a semiannual yield to maturity of 10.96 percent.

Also in 1985 PepsiCo issued Australian dollar 50 million of 13 percent Guaranteed Notes due 1990. Subsequent to the issuance of the notes, PepsiCo entered into an interest rate swap converting the fixed interest rate to a variable interest rate based on the 90-day Australian Bank Bill rate which at year-end 1985 was 19.6 percent.

During 1984 PepsiCo issued $104 million Deutsche mark denominated bearer bonds yielding 7¼ percent, due February, 1994. A major portion of the bond proceeds were used to purchase higher yielding notes of the West German Government that produce cash flows sufficient to meet the interest and principal payments of the bearer bonds. PepsiCo defeased the bonds by depositing the Deutsche mark denominated government notes in an irrevocable trust established for the sole purpose of servicing the bearer bonds. This defeasance resulted in a $2 million ($.02 per share) gain, after related expenses and taxes. The bearer bonds and promissory notes of the West German Government offset each other in the Consolidated Statement of Financial Condition.

At December 28, 1985 PepsiCo had unused credit facilities aggregating $1.52 billion, providing it with domestic and international credit availability and support for the issuance of commercial paper. Of the total, approximately $17 million represents lines of credit and $1.5 billion represents revolving credit agreements covering maximum potential borrowings maturing January 2, 1991. These unused credit facilities of $1.52 billion provide PepsiCo the ability to refinance short-term borrowings and currently support the classification of $603 million of commercial paper as long-term debt, since it is PepsiCo's intent to refinance this commercial paper during 1986 on a long-term basis.

Maturities of long-term debt (excluding capital lease obligations) are as follows: 1986-$165 million; 1987-$6 million; 1988-$46 million; 1989-$14 million; and 1990-$43 million. The debt agreements to which PepsiCo is a party include various restrictions, none of which is presently significant to PepsiCo.

Interest capitalized as an additional cost of property, plant and equipment was $13 million in 1985, $8 million in 1984 and $7 million in 1983.

In February 1986 PepsiCo issued Australian dollar 75 million of 14⅛ percent notes due in 1989. Concurrently with the issuance, PepsiCo has committed to enter into a currency exchange agreement. The debt issuance and related agreement create a U.S. dollar liability in the amount of $51 million at maturity with a floating interest rate based upon the AA Federal Reserve Composite Commercial Paper rate.

### Employee Stock Option and Ownership Plans

The shareholder-approved 1979 Incentive Plan (the Plan) provides long-term incentives to certain key employees through the granting of performance shares, stock options, stock appreciation rights (SARs) and incentive stock units. Under the Plan a maximum of 4.6 million shares of PepsiCo Capital Stock may be purchased or paid pursuant to grants by the Compensation Committee of the Board of Directors (the Committee) at prices not less than 100 percent of the fair market value at the date of grant. The Committee is composed of outside directors.

Performance shares and an equal number of stock options have been awarded to senior management employees. Each stock option represents the right to purchase one share of PepsiCo Capital Stock. The Committee sets the period during which an option may be exercised; however, none are exercisable until four years after the option is granted and may not have a term longer than 10 years from date of grant. Stock option activity for the years 1983 through 1985 was as follows:

| | Option Exercise Prices | Shares Under Option |
|---|---|---|
| Balance, December 25, 1982 | $23.88 to $43.06 | 978,526 |
| **1983** | | |
| Granted | – | – |
| Exercised | $28.31 | (22,175) |
| Cancelled or surrendered for SARs | – | (211,259) |
| Balance, December 31, 1983 | $23.88 to $43.06 | 745,092 |
| **1984** | | |
| Granted | $37.00 | 526,590 |
| Exercised | $23.88 and $24.13 | (158,082) |
| Cancelled or surrendered for SARs | – | (237,129) |
| Balance, December 29, 1984 | $23.88 to $43.06 | 876,471 |
| **1985** | | |
| Granted | $34.69 | 1,488 |
| Exercised | $23.88 | (101,548) |
| Cancelled or surrendered for SARs | – | (103,395) |
| Balance, December 28, 1985 | $34.69 to $43.06 | 673,016 |

At December 28, 1985 no options for shares were exercisable. Also at year-end 1985, 3,245,613 shares were reserved for issuance under the Plan. In January 1986, 278,349 options were issued at an exercise price of $69.25 per share.

Each performance share is equivalent to one share of PepsiCo Capital Stock. Performance shares are not paid unless PepsiCo achieves earnings per share growth targets established by the Committee for the four-year period following the award. Upon a determination by the Committee that a performance share has been earned, the holder receives the lesser of the fair market value of one share of Capital Stock at the date of award or the fair market value of one share of Capital Stock at the end of the award period. The performance share is paid in cash or Capital Stock or a combination thereof as determined by the Committee. During 1982 and 1984, 1,008,224 performance shares were awarded, of which 694,252 and 804,136 shares were outstanding at December 28, 1985 and December 29, 1984, respectively. In January 1986, 278,349 performance shares were awarded.

Stock appreciation rights (SARs) permit the holder of a stock option to surrender an exercisable option for an amount equal to the appreciation between the option price and the fair market value of Capital Stock on the date the SAR is exercised or expires. The amount is paid in cash or Capital Stock or a combination thereof. SARs expire on the same dates as the related options. In January 1984, 141,352 SARs were granted; and as of December 28, 1985, none was outstanding. In January 1986, 85,385 SARs were granted.

Incentive stock units (Units) are awarded by the Committee as incentives to middle management employees. Each Unit entitles the holder to receive the value of a share of Capital Stock without payment of any amounts to PepsiCo or satisfaction of any performance objectives. Each Unit is valued at the fair market value of the Capital Stock at the end of each vesting period. Currently, 30 percent of each award vests at the end of two years, an additional 30 percent vests at the end of four years, and the remainder vests at the end of six years. Payment of the Units is made in cash or Capital Stock or a combination thereof as determined by the Committee. From 1979 to 1985, 645,497 Units were awarded, of which 233,894 were outstanding at December 28, 1985.

The estimated cost of all awards under the Plan is charged to expense over the applicable terms of the awards. The cost was $19 million in 1985, $11 million in 1984 and $13 million in 1983.

Effective January 1, 1981, PepsiCo established a Tax Reduction Act Stock Ownership Plan (TRASOP) for the benefit of most employees. Beginning January 1, 1983, this plan was changed as a result of the Tax Reform Act of 1982, to a Payroll-based Employee Stock Ownership Plan (PAYSOP). Under these plans, PepsiCo may make a tax creditable contribution of either cash or Capital Stock to a trust on behalf of participating employees. During 1985 and 1984, PepsiCo contributed 75,540 and 169,147 shares, respectively, to the employee trust.

### Income Taxes

U.S. and foreign income (loss) from continuing operations before federal and foreign income taxes were as follows:

| | 1985 | 1984 | 1983 |
|---|---|---|---|
| | (in thousands) | | |
| U.S | $440,528 | $ 503,592 | $509,730 |
| Foreign | 197,538 | 90,100 | (90,836) |
| | 638,066 | 593,692 | 418,894 |
| Refranchising credit (charge) | 25,900 | (156,000) | – |
| | $663,966 | $ 437,692 | $418,894 |

The provision for federal and foreign income taxes on continuing operations is comprised of the following:

| | 1985 | 1984 | 1983 |
|---|---|---|---|
| | (in thousands) | | |
| Current: | | | |
| Federal | $ 82,132 | $ 135,609 | $ 77,408 |
| Foreign | 6,453 | 13,568 | 12,294 |
| Deferred (principally federal) | | | |
| Current | 74,200 | (107,800) | (9,300) |
| Non-current | 81,100 | 121,300 | 60,200 |
| | $243,885 | $ 162,677 | $140,602 |

The provision for state income taxes, which is included in marketing, administrative and other expenses, was $7 million in 1985, $13 million in 1984 and $26 million in 1983.

The differences between the effective and statutory federal income tax rate on continuing operations are comprised of the following:

| | 1985 | 1984 | 1983 |
|---|---|---|---|
| Statutory federal rate | 46.0% | 46.0% | 46.0% |
| Investment tax credits | (2.9) | (3.8) | (3.5) |
| Losses on refranchising of foreign bottling operations taxed at an aggregate rate different than the statutory federal rate | (0.2) | (5.1) | (4.0) |
| Earnings and losses of foreign operations taxed at an aggregate rate different than the statutory federal rate | (5.7) | (1.2) | (6.0) |
| Other-net | (0.5) | 1.3 | 1.1 |
| Effective rate | 36.7% | 37.2% | 33.6% |

The effective tax rate on earnings from discontinued operations was 41.1 percent in 1985, zero percent in 1984 and 5.8 percent in 1983. The difference between the effective and the statutory federal income tax rate for 1985 and 1983 is principally due to the amortization of investment tax credits. For 1984 the difference is principally due to the write-off of Wilson goodwill without tax benefit. In 1985 the net before-tax gain of $143 million on the disposal of NAVL and Wilson and the additional costs related to the 1984 sale of Lee Way resulted in an income tax expense of $29 million. The effective tax rate of 20 percent is due to the lower capital gain tax rate and the effect of permanent differences between the book and tax basis of the Capital Stock sold. The $16 million before-tax loss on the disposal of Lee Way in 1984 generated $500,000 of tax benefit due to the difference in the book and tax basis of the Capital Stock sold and the treatment of the sale as a capital loss.

The current portion of deferred federal income taxes of $194 million in 1985 and $176 million in 1984 was included in the Consolidated Statement of Financial Condition under the caption "Prepaid expenses, taxes and other current assets."

Federal and foreign income taxes payable consists of the following:

| | 1985 | 1984 |
|---|---|---|
| | (in thousands) | |
| Federal | $ 96,810 | $ 92,673 |
| Foreign | 26,799 | 25,063 |
| | $123,609 | $117,736 |

Deferred income tax expense on continuing operations arises from the following items:

| | 1985 | 1984 | 1983 |
|---|---|---|---|
| | (in thousands) | | |
| Excess of tax over financial statement expense related to depreciable assets (including capital leases) | $ 40,900 | $ 38,400 | $31,400 |
| Excess of tax over financial statement expense related to financing transactions | 6,100 | 21,500 | 22,200 |
| Net financial statement effect related to refranchising | 55,000 | (51,600) | – |
| Deferral of investment tax credit benefits | 13,700 | 4,700 | 3,800 |
| Prefunded employee benefits | 31,300 | – | – |
| Other-net | 8,300 | 500 | (6,500) |
| | $155,300 | $ 13,500 | $50,900 |

Deferred income taxes payable include:

| | 1985 | 1984 |
|---|---|---|
| | (in thousands) | |
| Deferred taxes–tax leases | $361,500 | $247,500 |
| Deferred taxes–other | 372,700 | 305,300 |
| Deferred investment tax credits | 79,500 | 65,800 |
| | $813,700 | $618,600 |

In 1981 and 1982, PepsiCo invested $429 million in tax leases. This investment, reduced by realized tax credits and tax savings from accelerated depreciation deductions, is principally included in the Consolidated Statement of Financial Condition under the caption "Long-term Receivables and Other Investments." The balance of the investment at year-end 1985 and 1984 was $74 million and $78 million, respectively. As a result of these investments, actual current taxes payable for 1985, 1984 and 1983 were reduced by approximately $114 million, $116 million and $119 million, respectively. Certain of the tax benefits that arise from these investments are temporary and will be repaid in future years over the lives of the leases. The benefits of the tax leases are not included in the provision for federal and foreign income taxes in the Consolidated Statement of Income.

Unremitted earnings of subsidiaries operating outside the United States that have been, or are intended to be, permanently reinvested, on which taxes have not been provided, aggregated approximately $314 million at December 28, 1985 and $214 million at December 29, 1984. These unremitted earnings are exclusive of amounts that if remitted in the future would result in little or no tax under current tax laws.

In 1985 PepsiCo reached an administrative settlement with the Internal Revenue Service regarding proposed tax deficiencies of $100 million for the years 1973 through 1978. The proposed deficiencies dealt with the reallocation to the U.S. parent company of a portion of the income of foreign soft drink concentrate manufacturing subsidiaries operating primarily in Puerto Rico and Ireland under tax incentive grants. The settlement was for significantly less than the proposed deficiencies and had no effect on 1985 results of operations.

### Leases

PepsiCo and its subsidiaries have noncancellable commitments for rental of restaurant facilities, office space, plant and warehouse facilities, transportation equipment and other personal property under both capital and operating leases. Certain franchised restaurants are leased and a portion have been subsequently subleased to franchisees. Lease commitments on capital and operating leases expire at various dates to 2031. An analysis of leased property under capital leases by major classes at December 28, 1985 and December 29, 1984 is summarized as follows:

| | 1985 | 1984 |
|---|---|---|
| | (in thousands) | |
| Buildings | $168,060 | $168,842 |
| Machinery and equipment | 2,841 | 3,693 |
| | 170,901 | 172,535 |
| Less accumulated amortization | 72,885 | 68,818 |
| | $ 98,016 | $103,717 |

The following is a schedule of future minimum lease commitments and sublease receivables under all noncancellable leases:

| | Commitments | | Sublease Receivables | |
|---|---|---|---|---|
| | Capital | Operating | Direct Financing | Operating |
| | (in thousands) | | | |
| 1986 | $ 25,097 | $ 63,053 | $ (7,891) | $ (7,601) |
| 1987 | 24,416 | 51,433 | (7,778) | (7,323) |
| 1988 | 23,226 | 41,762 | (7,492) | (6,776) |
| 1989 | 21,310 | 37,137 | (7,176) | (6,386) |
| 1990 | 20,184 | 34,473 | (6,829) | (5,841) |
| Later years | 126,418 | 250,269 | (61,582) | (48,614) |
| Total minimum lease commitments (receivables) | $240,651 | $478,127 | $(98,748) | $(82,541) |

The present value of minimum lease payments for capital leases amounts to $137 million after deducting $2 million for estimated executory costs (taxes, maintenance and insurance) and $102 million representing imputed interest. The present value of minimum sublease receivables amounts to $42 million after deducting $57 million of unearned interest income. Total rental expense for all operating leases for years ended December 28, 1985, December 29, 1984 and December 31, 1983 was $117 million, $110 million and $108 million, respectively. Total rental income from all operating subleases for years ended December 28, 1985, December 29, 1984 and December 31, 1983 was $16 million, $15 million and $15 million, respectively.

### Employee Benefit Plans

PepsiCo and its subsidiaries have several non-contributory pension plans covering substantially all domestic employees (mostly non-union). The total pension expense for all plans was approximately $37 million, $41 million and $36 million in 1985, 1984 and 1983, respectively, which includes amortization of unfunded past service cost over 30 years for certain defined benefit plans. In accordance with recommendations received from its actuary, PepsiCo changed actuarial cost methods in 1985 for its pay-related plans from the frozen initial liability cost method to the projected unit credit method. Over a period of years, the change is expected to better match pension expense to benefit obligations. The effect of this change was to reduce pension expense by approximately $7 million in 1985.

A comparison of accumulated plan benefits and plan net assets for PepsiCo's domestic defined benefit plans is presented below:

| | January 1 | |
|---|---|---|
| | 1985 | 1984 |
| | (in thousands) | |
| Actuarial present value of accumulated plan benefits: | | |
| Vested | $303,338 | $268,795 |
| Non-vested | 87,009 | 77,285 |
| | $390,347 | $346,080 |
| Net assets available for plan benefits | $469,017 | $433,360 |

PepsiCo changed its funding policy in 1985 from making annual contributions equal to amounts accrued for pension expense to making annual contributions equal to the minimum statutory requirement. As a result, $15 million of the 1984 accrued pension expense has not been currently funded and PepsiCo does not currently expect to fund $18 million of the 1985 accrued pension expense. These amounts are included in the Consolidated Statement of Financial Condition under the caption "Other Liabilities and Deferred Credits."

The rate of return used in determining the actuarial present value of accumulated plan benefits was seven percent for both 1985 and 1984.

In December 1985 the Financial Accounting Standards Board issued Statement of Financial Accounting Standards No. 87, Employers' Accounting for Pensions. None of the provisions of this statement are required to be adopted until fiscal years beginning after December 15, 1986, however, PepsiCo estimates that when adopted, they will have a favorable effect on consolidated income from continuing operations. The estimated impact may be affected by future events, the outcomes of which are not known at this time.

PepsiCo and its subsidiaries provide certain health care and life insurance benefits for retired non-union employees. Substantially all of PepsiCo's employees, including employees in certain foreign countries, may become eligible for those benefits if they reach retirement age while still working for PepsiCo. The cost of retiree health care benefits is recognized as an expense as claims are incurred. PepsiCo recognizes the cost of providing retiree life insurance by expensing the annual insurance premiums for these benefits. The domestic expenditures for retired employees under these programs for the years ended December 28, 1985, December 29, 1984 and December 31, 1983 were $4 million, $3 million and $2 million, respectively. Foreign expenditures under these programs were insignificant.

### Contingencies

PepsiCo and its subsidiaries are involved in various litigated matters, but management believes that the resolution of these matters will not have a material effect on PepsiCo's business or financial condition. PepsiCo intends to prosecute or defend vigorously, as the case may be, all such matters.

At December 28, 1985 PepsiCo and its subsidiaries were contingently liable under direct and indirect guarantees aggregating $51 million.

### Business Segments

In 1985 PepsiCo's business segments, formerly referred to as beverages, food products and food service, were renamed soft drinks, snack foods and restaurants to more clearly reflect the products and services of each business.

The soft drinks segment primarily manufactures and markets Pepsi-Cola and its allied brands. The snack foods segment primarily produces salty snacks. The restaurants segment primarily includes the operations of Pizza Hut and Taco Bell.

Sales between segments were not significant, and no single customer accounted for more than 10 percent of sales. Other than North America, no geographic area accounted for more than 10 percent of sales.

Soft drinks amounts for 1985 and part of 1984 exclude the results of company-owned foreign bottling operations in the Refranchising Program. In addition, the 1985 and 1984 soft drinks operating profits exclude a $26 million credit and a $156 million charge, respectively, related to the Refranchising Program described on page 43.

Operating profits exclude net corporate expenses and net interest expense of $221 million, $222 million and $209 million in 1985, 1984 and 1983, respectively.

The operating profits of each business segment include the foreign exchange gains and losses generated by their respective foreign operations. Operating profits in the soft drinks segment have excluded the net foreign exchange gains related to the local currency borrowings of the company-owned bottling operations in the Refranchising Program since that program was initiated in the second quarter of 1984. Foreign exchange gains included in consolidated operating profits were $32 million, $53 million and $17 million in 1985, 1984 and 1983, respectively. Segment operating profits included total research and development expenses of $66 million, $49 million and $40 million in 1985, 1984 and 1983, respectively.

Corporate identifiable assets are principally short-term investments, investment in tax leases, administrative office buildings, the receivable from the sale of North American Van Lines and the investment in the Allegheny Pepsi-Cola Bottling Company.

The following summarizes PepsiCo's business segment information:

| | 1985 | 1984 | 1983 |
|---|---|---|---|
| | | (in millions) | |
| Net Sales: | | | |
| Soft drinks | $3,128.5 | $2,908.4 | $2,940.4 |
| Snack foods | 2,847.1 | 2,709.2 | 2,430.1 |
| Restaurants | 2,081.1 | 1,833.5 | 1,529.4 |
| Total continuing operations | $8,056.7 | $7,451.1 | $6,899.9 |
| Foreign portion | $ 951.9 | $ 963.9 | $1,128.6 |
| Operating Profits: | | | |
| Soft drinks | $ 263.9 | $ 246.4 | $ 126.2 |
| Snack foods | 401.0 | 393.9 | 347.7 |
| Restaurants | 194.0 | 175.2 | 154.3 |
| Total segments | $ 858.9 | $ 815.5 | $ 628.2 |
| Foreign portion | $ 66.7 | $ 35.5 | $ (99.1) |
| Capital Spending: | | | |
| Soft drinks | $ 160.7 | $ 83.6 | $ 93.7 |
| Snack foods | 286.3 | 188.9 | 180.2 |
| Restaurants | 331.0 | 252.5 | 217.9 |
| Corporate | 7.9 | 30.8 | 11.6 |
| Total continuing operations | $ 785.9 | $ 555.8 | $ 503.4 |
| Foreign portion | $ 67.3 | $ 36.4 | $ 42.4 |
| Identifiable Assets: | | | |
| Soft drinks | $1,318.6 | $1,038.9 | $1,249.0 |
| Snack foods | 1,487.1 | 1,254.5 | 1,110.1 |
| Restaurants | 1,326.7 | 1,020.7 | 825.9 |
| Corporate | 1,728.8 | 1,277.0 | 882.7 |
| Total continuing operations | $5,861.2 | $4,591.1 | $4,067.7 |
| Foreign portion | $1,054.3 | $ 687.5 | $ 945.8 |
| Depreciation and Amortization Expense: | | | |
| Soft drinks | $ 69.2 | $ 71.1 | $ 84.9 |
| Snack foods | 107.7 | 93.6 | 81.9 |
| Restaurants | 109.2 | 75.7 | 58.0 |
| Corporate | 4.7 | 9.2 | 8.1 |
| Total continuing operations | $ 290.8 | $ 249.6 | $ 232.9 |
| Foreign portion | $ 25.3 | $ 36.8 | $ 51.7 |

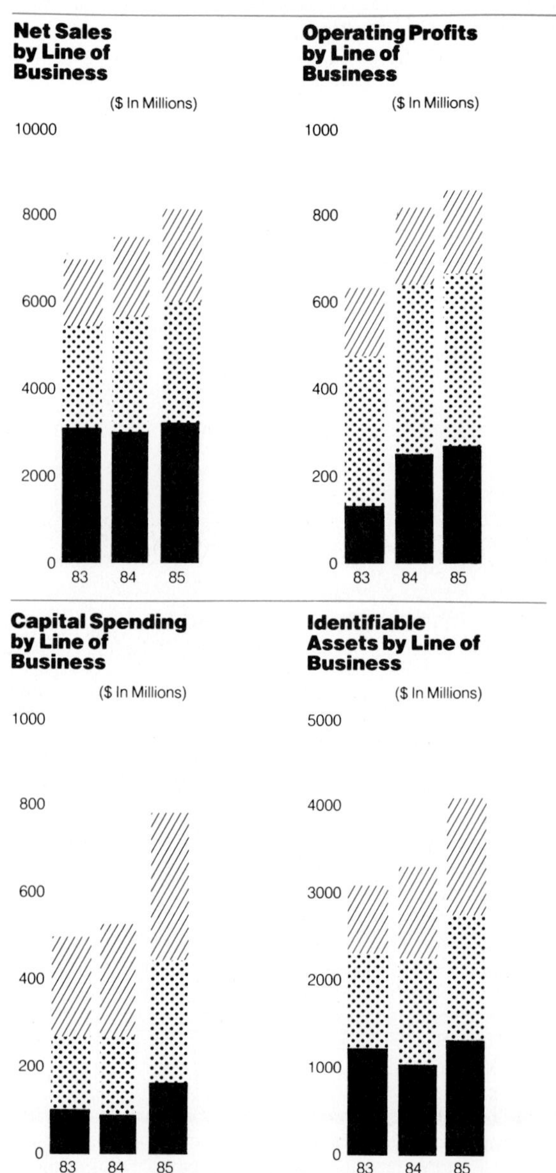

# Information on the Effects of Inflation (Unaudited)

In accordance with the Statement of Financial Accounting Standards No. 33 as amended, the information presented on this page has been provided under the current cost method in an attempt to measure the impact of inflation on PepsiCo's operations.

The current cost method attempts to measure the effects of specific price changes by reflecting the cost to replace existing property, plant and equipment and inventory with identical property, plant and equipment and inventory today. The amounts were estimated in a number of ways, including direct pricing and indexing.

Also presented is a comparison of the increase in current cost based on specific prices of property, plant and equipment and inventory with the amount of such increase in the general price level. General price level is measured by the movement in the U.S. Consumer Price Index for all Urban Consumers.

PepsiCo's 1985 adjusted financial results reflect a $66 million decrease in income from continuing operations and an increase in net assets of $375 million, which are principally attributable to the cumulative impact of inflation on PepsiCo's property, plant and equipment. The effective tax rate is increased from the historical financial statements because the provision for income taxes is not adjusted for current cost purposes, yet it is compared to reduced pre-tax income.

Since PepsiCo had net monetary liabilities during the year, a net gain in purchasing power of $57 million resulted, which should be viewed as part of the overall impact of inflation on operations.

The five-year comparison of financial data restated into average 1985 dollars, depicts that sales have grown each year, as have reported sales. Income from continuing operations when adjusted for inflation, although always lower than reported earnings, reflects the trends in PepsiCo's reported earnings.

**Statement of Earnings Adjusted for the Effects of Inflation For the Year Ended December 28, 1985**

(dollars in thousands except per share amounts, unaudited)

| | As Reported in the Primary Financial Statements (Historical Cost) | Adjusted for Changes in Specific Prices (Current Cost) |
|---|---|---|
| Net sales | $8,056,662 | $8,056,662 |
| Cost of sales, excluding depreciation | 3,080,326 | 3,082,686 |
| Depreciation and amortization | 282,405 | 346,100 |
| Other operating expenses, net | 3,956,869 | 3,956,869 |
| Net interest expense | 98,996 | 98,996 |
| Refranchising credit | (25,900) | (25,900) |
| Provision for income taxes | 243,885 | 243,885 |
| | 7,636,581 | 7,702,636 |
| Income from continuing operations | $ 420,081 | $ 354,026 |
| Per share | $ 4.51 | $ 3.81 |
| Effective income tax rate | 37% | 41% |
| Purchasing power gain on net monetary liabilities | | $ 57,193 |
| Effect of changes in general price level and specific prices on inventories and property, plant and equipment during the year: | | |
| Increase in general price level | | $ 58,353 |
| Decrease in specific prices (current costs) [a] | | 79,968 |
| Excess of increase in general price level over decrease in specific prices | | $ 138,321 |

[a] At December 28, 1985 current cost of inventory was $385,020 compared to $380,096 at historical cost. The current cost of property, plant and equipment, net of accumulated depreciation, was $2,961,561 compared to $2,571,773 at historical cost.

**Five-Year Comparison of Selected Supplementary Financial Data Adjusted for the Effects of Inflation**

(dollars in thousands of average 1985 dollars except per share amounts, unaudited)

| | 1985 | 1984 | 1983 | 1982 | 1981 |
|---|---|---|---|---|---|
| Net sales $ | 8,056,662 | 7,749,150 | 7,480,323 | 7,263,936 | 7,158,935 |
| **Current Cost Information:** | | | | | |
| Income from continuing operations $ | 354,026[a] | 209,189[b] | 231,519 | 131,789[c] | 223,478 |
| Per share $ | 3.81[a] | 2.22[b] | 2.46 | 1.42[c] | 2.44 |
| Excess of increase in general price level over the change in specific prices $ | 138,321 | 232,059 | 128,815 | 126,814 | 163,513 |
| Net assets $ | 2,212,666 | 2,387,073 | 2,568,276 | 2,613,483 | 2,687,014 |
| **Other Information:** | | | | | |
| Purchasing power gain on net monetary liabilities $ | 57,193 | 51,274 | 50,676 | 48,422 | 108,927 |
| Cash dividends declared per share $ | 1.755 | 1.732 | 1.735 | 1.768 | 1.687 |
| Market price per share at year-end $ | 71.25 | 42.94 | 40.78 | 37.63 | 41.81 |
| Average consumer price index (1967 = 100) | 322.2 | 311.1 | 298.4 | 289.1 | 272.4 |

[a] Income from continuing operations in 1985 is net of a $14,900 ($.16 per share) credit related to an adjustment of the reserve for the refranchising of several company-owned foreign bottling operations.

[b] Income from continuing operations in 1984 is net of a $62,000 ($.65 per share) charge related to the refranchising of several company-owned foreign bottling operations.

[c] Income from continuing operations in 1982 is net of a $79,400 ($.83 per share) reduction in the net assets of foreign bottling operations without tax benefit.

# Selected Financial Data

PepsiCo, Inc. and Subsidiaries
(dollars in thousands except per share amounts, unaudited)

| | | 1985 | 1984 | 1983 | 1982[c] | 1981 |
|---|---|---|---|---|---|---|
| **Summary of Operations** | | | | | | |
| Net sales | $ | **8,056,662** | 7,451,106 | 6,899,884 | 6,492,380 | 6,025,261 |
| Cost of sales and operating expenses | | **7,319,600** | 6,738,432 | 6,359,372 | 5,881,603 | 5,454,352 |
| Net interest expense | | **98,996** | 118,982 | 121,618 | 114,409 | 111,893 |
| | | **7,418,596** | 6,857,414 | 6,480,990 | 5,996,012 | 5,566,245 |
| Income from continuing operations before unusual credits (charges) and income taxes | | **638,066** | 593,692 | 418,894 | 496,368 | 459,016 |
| Unusual credits (charges) | | **25,900**[a] | (156,000)[b] | – | (79,400)[d] | – |
| Income from continuing operations before income taxes | | **663,966** | 437,692 | 418,894 | 416,968 | 459,016 |
| Federal and foreign income taxes | | **243,885** | 162,677 | 140,602 | 213,467 | 190,146 |
| Income from continuing operations | $ | **420,081** | 275,015 | 278,292 | 203,501 | 268,870 |
| Income per share from continuing operations | $ | **4.51**[a] | 2.90[b] | 2.95 | 2.18[d] | 2.92 |
| Average shares and equivalents outstanding | # | **93,567** | 95,827 | 95,480 | 94,904 | 93,060 |
| Cash dividends declared | $ | **161,160** | 156,185 | 151,358 | 147,127 | 129,944 |
| Per share | $ | **1.755** | 1.665 | 1.620 | 1.580 | 1.420 |
| **Year-End Position** | | | | | | |
| Total assets | $ | **5,861,160** | 4,876,404 | 4,421,079 | 4,005,390 | 3,883,057 |
| Long-term debt [e] | $ | **1,162,668** | 669,641 | 799,765 | 843,901 | 804,597 |
| Shareholders' equity | $ | **1,837,682** | 1,853,376 | 1,794,158 | 1,650,465 | 1,556,264 |
| Per share | $ | **20.95** | 19.74 | 19.18 | 17.68 | 16.99 |
| Shares outstanding | # | **87,706** | 93,908 | 93,561 | 93,374 | 91,605 |
| **Statistics and Ratios** | | | | | | |
| Return on average shareholders' equity [f] | % | **22.0** | 18.5 | 16.2 | 17.6 | 18.3 |
| Return on revenues [f] | % | **5.0** | 4.5 | 4.0 | 4.4 | 4.5 |
| Long-term debt [e] to total capital employed [g] | % | **26.6** | 18.7 | 23.6 | 28.3 | 27.0 |
| Total debt to total capital employed [g] | % | **34.5** | 26.5 | 31.7 | 34.6 | 40.7 |
| Employees | # | **150,000** | 150,000 | 154,000 | 133,000 | 120,000 |
| Shareholders | # | **72,000** | 62,000 | 60,000 | 48,000 | 49,000 |

[a] The unusual credit in 1985 related to an adjustment of the reserve for the refranchising of several company-owned foreign bottling operations ($14,900 after-tax or $.16 per share).

[b] The unusual charge in 1984 related to the refranchising of several company-owned foreign bottling operations ($62,000 after-tax or $.65 per share).

[c] In 1982 PepsiCo adopted the Statement of Financial Accounting Standards (SFAS) No. 52 on foreign currency translation. Prior year results have not been restated for SFAS 52.

[d] The unusual charge in 1982 related to a reduction in net assets of foreign bottling operations ($.83 per share). The charge was without tax benefit.

[e] Long-term debt includes capital lease obligations.

[f] The return on average shareholders' equity and return on revenues are calculated using income from continuing operations before unusual credits (charges) and after income taxes.

[g] Total capital employed is total debt, shareholders' equity, deferred income taxes and other liabilities and deferred credits.

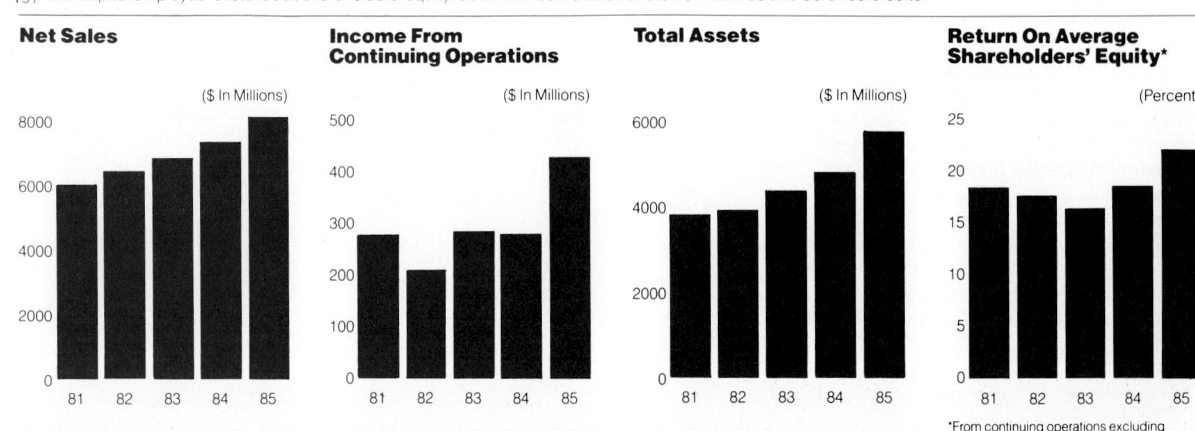


*From continuing operations excluding unusual credits and charges

# Quarterly Financial Data and Information on Capital Stock

(in thousands, except per share amounts and stock prices, unaudited)

| | First Quarter (12 weeks) | | Second Quarter (12 weeks) | | Third Quarter (12 weeks) | | Fourth Quarter (16 weeks) | | Full Year (52 weeks) | |
|---|---|---|---|---|---|---|---|---|---|---|
| | **1985** | 1984 | **1985** | 1984 | **1985** | 1984 | **1985** | 1984 | **1985** | 1984 |
| Net Sales | **$1,626,893** | 1,552,072 | **1,937,512** | 1,815,831 | **2,071,752** | 1,886,894 | **2,420,505** | 2,196,309 | **8,056,662** | 7,451,106 |
| Gross profit from continuing operations $ | **982,589** | 931,322 | **1,180,554** | 1,085,161 | **1,267,314** | 1,136,534 | **1,477,944** | 1,323,631 | **4,908,401** | 4,476,648 |
| Income from continuing operations $ | **60,529** | 47,479 | **119,295** | 30,334[d] | **135,304** | 111,632 | **104,953**[a] | 85,570 | **420,081** | 275,015 |
| Income (loss) from discontinued operations $ | **2,311** | (326) | **136,998**[c] | (72,880)[e] | **—** | 6,661 | **(15,700)**[b] | 4,077 | **123,609** | (62,468) |
| Net income (loss) $ | **62,840** | 47,153 | **256,293** | (42,546) | **135,304** | 118,293 | **89,253** | 89,647 | **543,690** | 212,547 |
| Income (loss) per share: | | | | | | | | | | |
| Continuing operations $ | **.64** | .51 | **1.25** | .32[d] | **1.45** | 1.17 | **1.17**[a] | .90 | **4.51** | 2.90 |
| Discontinued operations $ | **.02** | (.01) | **1.47**[c] | (.76)[e] | **—** | .07 | **(.17)**[b] | .05 | **1.32** | (.65) |
| Net income (loss) per share $ | **.66** | .50 | **2.72** | (.44) | **1.45** | 1.24 | **1.00** | .95 | **5.83** | 2.25 |
| Dividends per share[f] $ | **.420** | .405 | **.445** | .420 | **.445** | .420 | **.445** | .420 | **1.755** | 1.665 |
| Market price of Capital Stock[f]: | | | | | | | | | | |
| High $ | **52¾** | 38⅜ | **60⅛** | 43 | **60½** | 45 | **75⅜** | 45⅝ | **75⅜** | 45⅝ |
| Low $ | **40⅝** | 34½ | **50½** | 36¼ | **55¼** | 40½ | **57⅜** | 39⅞ | **40⅝** | 34½ |
| Close $ | **51⅝** | 36½ | **59** | 42⅜ | **58⅞** | 42⅜ | **71¼** | 41⅞ | **71¼** | 41⅞ |

[a] Income from continuing operations in the fourth quarter of 1985 includes a $14,900 after-tax credit ($.16 per share) related to an adjustment of the reserve for the refranchising of several company-owned foreign bottling operations.

[b] Income (loss) from discontinued operations in the fourth quarter of 1985 includes an additional $8,600 after-tax loss ($.09 per share) from the sale of Wilson Sporting Goods and a $7,100 after-tax charge ($.08 per share) from the sale of Lee Way Motor Freight, Inc.

[c] Income (loss) from discontinued operations in the second quarter of 1985 includes a $139,000 after-tax gain ($1.49 per share) from the sale of North American Van Lines, Inc. and a $9,300 after-tax loss ($.10 per share) from the sale of Wilson Sporting Goods.

[d] Income from continuing operations in the second quarter of 1984 includes a $62,000 after-tax charge ($.65 per share) related to the refranchising of several company-owned foreign bottling operations.

[e] Income (loss) from discontinued operations in the second quarter of 1984 includes a $59,300 after-tax charge ($.62 per share) related to the restructuring of Wilson Sporting Goods and a $15,000 after-tax loss ($.16 per share) from the sale of Lee Way Motor Freight, Inc.

[f] The Capital Stock of PepsiCo, Inc. is traded on the New York and Midwest Stock Exchanges. The quarterly dividend was increased six percent in May 1985 from 42 cents per share to 44½ cents per share. In May 1984 the quarterly dividend was increased four percent from 40½ cents per share to 42 cents per share. As of February 21, 1986, the approximate number of holders of record of Capital Stock was 71,000.

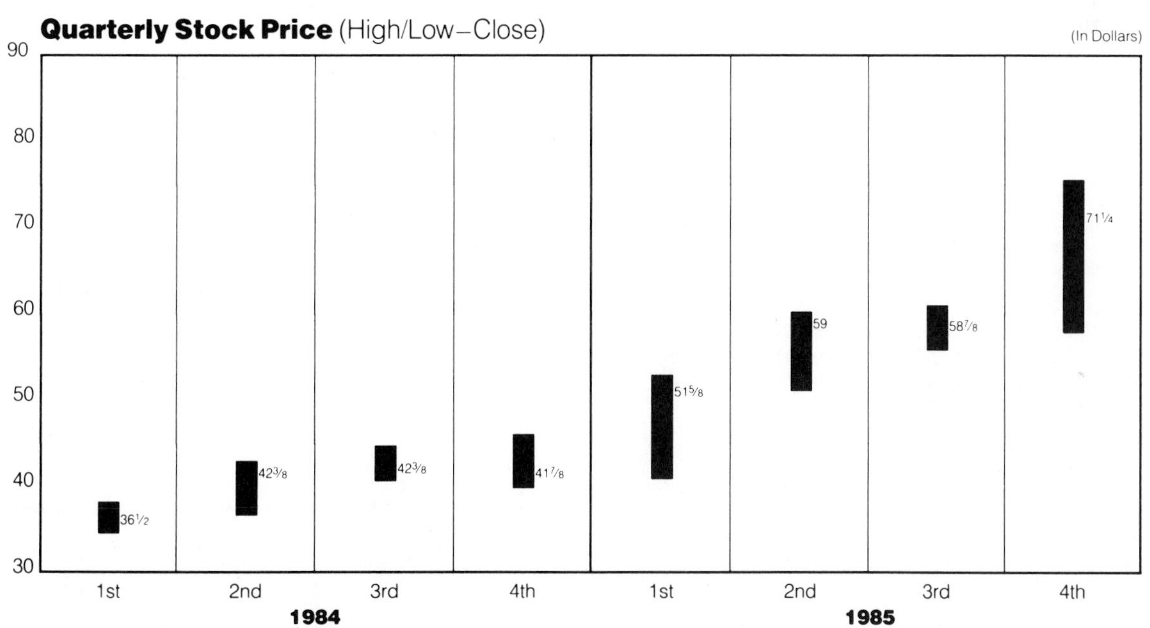

# Shareholder Information

### Capital Stock
Shares of PepsiCo Capital Stock are traded on the New York and Midwest Stock Exchanges (Symbol: PEP).

On February 21, 1986 there were 85,556,306 outstanding shares of capital stock held by approximately 71,000 shareholders of record. The number of shareholders of record includes the many institutions that represent the interests of thousands of beneficial holders.

### Dividends
PepsiCo's goal is to provide shareholders with the highest return achievable consonant with operating and business goals. PepsiCo has consistently paid cash dividends and expects to continue this policy.

Cash dividends are declared quarterly. PepsiCo's dividend is at an annual rate of $1.78.

### Dividend Reinvestment Plan
The Dividend Reinvestment Plan for PepsiCo stockholders is being offered by Manufacturers Hanover Trust Company, our transfer agent.

Shareholders may direct that all or part of quarterly cash dividends be invested in PepsiCo Capital Stock and may elect to supplement dividend reinvestments with voluntary cash payments. PepsiCo pays all brokerage and administrative costs associated with the Plan.

### Double Dividend Taxation
PepsiCo pays taxes on the earnings that produce shareholder dividends. Most of our shareholders also pay taxes on the same dividends. If you believe that this double taxation is inequitable, you may wish to write to your congressman.

### Publications
In addition to the Annual Report, interim reports are mailed to shareholders and include financial results, news of the company and other notices. The First Quarter Report includes highlights of the Annual Meeting. Shareholders also receive notice of the Annual Meeting, proxy statement and proxy.

Many of our divisions publish information booklets about their histories and their products. These are available from the divisions on request.

**Copies of PepsiCo's Form 10-K and 10-Q Reports to the Securities and Exchange Commission may be obtained without charge from the Manager of Shareholder Relations, PepsiCo, Inc., Purchase, New York 10577.**

### Annual Meeting
The Annual Meeting of Shareholders will be held at the offices of the corporation, Purchase, New York at 10 a.m. (EDT), Wednesday, May 7, 1986. Proxies for the meeting will be solicited by management in a separate Proxy Statement. This report is not part of such a proxy solicitation.

### Transfer Agent
Manufacturers Hanover Trust Company, 450 West 33rd Street, New York, New York 10001.

### Shareholder Inquiries
Correspondence concerning your dividend reinvestment account, dividend payments or address changes should be addressed to:

Manufacturers Hanover Trust Company
Security Holder Relations, P.O. Box 24935, Church Street Station, New York, New York 10249, (212)613-7147.

Please mention PepsiCo, Inc. and include your name, as shown on your stock certificate, address and telephone number in all correspondence.

For additional assistance or information please contact:

Manager of Shareholder Relations, PepsiCo, Inc., Purchase, New York 10577, (914)253-3055.

### Financial Information
Security analysts and representatives of financial institutions requiring information are invited to contact:

Jerry Hostetter, Director, Investor Relations, (914)253-3035.

### Certified Public Accountants
Arthur Young & Company, 277 Park Avenue, New York, New York 10172.

This Annual Report contains many of the valuable trademarks owned and used by PepsiCo and its subsidiaries and affiliates in the United States and internationally to distinguish products and services of outstanding quality. NutraSweet is a registered trademark of The NutraSweet Company. 7UP is a registered trademark of The Seven-Up Company.



Design: Eisenman & Enock, Inc.
Printing: National Bickford Foremost
Photography: Paul Chauncey, Philip Jones Griffiths, Grant Peterson, Ben Rosenthal, Stephen Wilkes

# C Statement of Cash Flows

For a number of years, general-purpose external financial statements have included statements of changes in financial position similar to those illustrated in Chapter 18. The format of these statements was flexible, and the focus could be on any of the following:

Cash
Cash and temporary investments
Quick assets (cash, temporary investments, receivables minus current liabilities)
Working capital (current assets minus current liabilities)

This flexibility was due to different companies having different objectives in presenting a statement of changes in financial position. For some companies, it was important that stockholders, creditors, and other groups outside management read a statement that showed the major sources and uses of working capital. Other companies believed that these groups would be better served by reading a statement that showed the major sources and uses of cash.

In recent years, however, the significance of cash flow has become increasingly important to business enterprises, as indicated by *FASB Concepts Statement No. 5*. According to *FASB No. 5*, a complete set of financial statements for a period should show cash flows during that period. It has now become apparent that investors, creditors, and others need information about an entity's cash receipts and cash disbursements during a period. By having information of this sort available to them, and with the help of information in the company's other financial statements, they should be able to assess the following:

1. The entity's ability to generate positive future net cash flows
2. The entity's ability to meet its obligations and pay dividends, and its needs for external financing
3. The reasons for differences between net income and associated cash receipts and payments
4. Both the cash and the noncash aspects of the entity's investing and financing transactions during the period

## DISCUSSION OF THE STATEMENT OF CASH FLOWS

### General Requirements

To help meet the needs referred to above, the FASB has issued a proposed standard called "Statement of Cash Flows." When a company issues a set of financial statements that shows both financial position and results of operations, a statement of cash flows will be provided for each period for which the results of operations are shown. For example, if the accounting period is from January 1, 1987, to December 31, 1987, and the income statement covers that period, a statement of cash flows that covers that same period should also be issued. For purposes of reporting to parties external to management, the statement of cash flows replaces the statement of changes in financial position. However, for purposes of reporting to management and other internal parties, a company may use the traditional statement of changes in financial position in either the working capital version or the cash version (both of which are examined in Chapter 18).

Even though some flexibility in format is allowed (as illustrated later in this appendix), the FASB requires that the statement of cash flows contain the three following classifications:

1. Operating activities
2. Investing activities
3. Financing activities

In addition, the statement should report the effects of important noncash investing and financing transactions.

Another important aspect of the statement of cash flows is that it will not contain the term *funds.* Instead the term *cash* or, if appropriate, *cash* and *cash equivalents* will be used. The term *cash equivalents* refers to investments of cash in excess of immediate needs, that is, investments in short-term highly liquid assets such as treasury bills, commercial paper, and money market funds. Therefore the old concept of funds will now be used in one of the following ways:

1. If the entity does not own short-term highly liquid investments, the statement of cash flows will show cash receipts and cash payments for a period divided into those that affect
   a. Operating transactions
   b. Investing transactions
   c. Financing transactions
   
   The statement will also show the effects of important investing and financing transactions that do not directly affect cash.
2. If the entity does own short-term highly liquid investments, the statement of cash flows will show transactions that affect the composite figure for cash and cash equivalents for a period (no cash purchases or sales of short-term highly liquid investments will be shown) divided into those that affect
   a. Operating transactions
   b. Investing transactions
   c. Financing transactions
   
   The statement will also show the effects of important investing and financing transactions that do not directly affect cash and cash equivalents.

## DISCUSSION OF OPERATING, INVESTING, AND FINANCING ACTIVITIES

Although we illustrate several types of cash flow statements later in this appendix, it will be beneficial at this point to discuss the general content of each of the three major sections of the cash flow statement. We will henceforth refer to these three sections as *activities.*

**OPERATING ACTIVITIES** All transactions and other events that are not investing or financing activities belong in this section of the statement. They consist of transactions and other events that are a part of income and include the following:

1. Cash receipts (inflows) from sales of goods and services, from interest, and from dividends
2. Cash payments (outflows) for acquisitions of inventory and for salaries, taxes, interest, and other expenses

INVESTING ACTIVITIES For the most part, all transactions that involve loans, noncash equivalent securities, and long-term productive assets belong in this section. In general, they include the following:

1. Cash receipts (inflows) from loans, sales of debt or equity securities of other entities, and dispositions of property, plant, and equipment
2. Cash payments (outflows) to make loans, to acquire debt or equity securities of other entities, and to acquire property, plant, and equipment

FINANCING ACTIVITIES Generally, all transactions with owners and creditors belong in this section. There are some exceptions, such as the payment of accounts payable incurred to purchase inventory and the payment of wages payable. These two transactions are operating activities. Financing activities include the following:

1. Cash receipts (inflows) from the issuance of capital stock and from bonds, mortgages, notes, and other short- or long-term debts
2. Cash payments (outflows) for dividends, purchases of treasury stock, and payment of debt

## *ILLUSTRATIONS OF STATEMENTS OF CASH FLOWS*

The FASB has suggested a number of optional reporting formats for the formal statement of cash flows. In this section we will first collect the data in work sheet form and then report it in three illustrations, each following an option permitted by the FASB. The data have been taken from Exhibit 18–8 (pages 666–67 of Chapter 18), and the financial statements from that exhibit are reproduced as Exhibit C–1. As already noted, we will later make some changes in the data to allow us to illustrate a noncash transaction.

## *SUMMARY OF TRANSACTIONS AND OTHER EVENTS FOR LINLEY CORPORATION*

1. Linley's sales for the year were $467,000, and its accounts receivable increased by $40,000 during the year. This means that cash received from customers was $40,000 less than sales for the year.
2. Linley's cost of goods sold for the year was $280,000, its inventory increased by $15,000 during the year, and its accounts payable increased by $6,000 during the year. This means that cash paid to suppliers was $9,000 more ($15,000 − $6,000) than cost of goods sold for the year.
3. Linley's depreciation expense for the year was $35,000. Since depreciation is a noncash expense, no cash was expended.

*EXHIBIT C-1*

Linley Corporation: Financial Statements and Supplementary Information

LINLEY CORPORATION

Comparative Balance Sheet

December 31, 19X5 and 19X4

| | 19X5 | 19X4 |
|---|---|---|
| *ASSETS* | | |
| Current Assets: | | |
| Cash | $ 30,000 | $ 40,000 |
| Accounts Receivable (net) | 150,000 | 110,000 |
| Inventory | 90,000 | 75,000 |
| Prepaid Expenses | 5,000 | 7,000 |
| Total Current Assets | $275,000 | $232,000 |
| Plant and Equipment: | | |
| Land | $ 30,000 | $ 30,000 |
| Buildings | 250,000 | 200,000 |
| Accumulated Depreciation—Buildings | (80,000) | (60,000) |
| Equipment | 170,000 | 106,000 |
| Accumulated Depreciation—Equipment | (50,000) | (35,000) |
| Total Plant and Equipment | $320,000 | $241,000 |
| Total Assets | $595,000 | $473,000 |
| LIABILITIES AND STOCKHOLDERS' EQUITY | | |
| Current Liabilities: | | |
| Accounts Payable | $ 96,000 | $ 90,000 |
| Salaries Payable | 900 | 1,200 |
| Taxes Payable | 12,000 | 10,000 |
| Interest Payable | 4,000 | 3,000 |
| Accrued Liabilities | 52,100 | 53,800 |
| Total Current Liabilities | $165,000 | $158,000 |
| Long-Term 10% Bonds Payable | $150,000 | $100,000 |
| Stockholders' Equity: | | |
| Common Stock, $10 Par Value | $120,000 | $ 90,000 |
| Paid-in Capital in Excess of Par Value | 15,000 | 10,000 |
| Retained Earnings | 145,000 | 115,000 |
| Total Stockholders' Equity | $280,000 | $215,000 |
| Total Liabilities and Stockholders' Equity | $595,000 | $473,000 |

LINLEY CORPORATION

Income Statement

For the Year Ended December 31, 19X5

| | | |
|---|---|---|
| Sales (net) | | $467,000 |
| Cost of Goods Sold | | 280,000 |
| Gross Profit | | $187,000 |
| Operating Expenses: | | |
| Depreciation Expense | $ 35,000 | |
| Salaries Expense | 50,000 | |
| Selling Expense | 15,000 | |
| General Expense | 6,000 | |
| Interest Expense | 12,000 | |
| Total Operating Expenses | | 118,000 |
| Income before Income Taxes | | $ 69,000 |
| Income Taxes | | 21,000 |
| Net Income | | $ 48,000 |

LINLEY CORPORATION

Statement of Retained Earnings

For the Year Ended December 31, 19X5

| | |
|---|---|
| Retained Earnings, January 1, 19X5 | $115,000 |
| Add: Net Income | 48,000 |
| | $163,000 |
| Less: Dividends | 18,000 |
| Retained Earnings, December 31, 19X5 | $145,000 |

4. Linley's salaries expense for the year was $50,000, and its salaries payable decreased by $300 during the year. This means that cash paid to employees was $300 more than salaries expense for the year.
5. Linley's selling expense for the year was $15,000, and its accrued liabilities decreased by $1,700 during the year. This means that cash paid for selling expenses was $1,700 more than selling expense for the year.
6. Linley's general expense for the year was $6,000, and its prepaid expenses decreased by $2,000 during the year. This means that cash paid for general expenses was $2,000 less than general expenses for the year.
7. Linley's interest expense for the year was $12,000, and its interest payable increased by $1,000 during the year. This means that cash paid for interest was $1,000 less than interest expense for the year.
8. Linley's income taxes expense for the year was $21,000, and its taxes payable increased by $2,000 during the year. This means that cash paid for taxes was $2,000 less than income taxes expense for the year.
9. The $50,000 increase in buildings during the year was caused by the cash purchase of an additional building.
10. The $64,000 increase in equipment during the year was caused by the cash purchase of additional equipment.
11. The combined $20,000 increase in the accumulated depreciation for buildings and the $15,000 increase in the accumulated depreciation for equipment was caused by the recording of $35,000 of depreciation expense shown on the income statement.
12. The $50,000 increase in bonds payable during the year was caused by the following:
    a. Bonds payable of $60,000 were issued at their face value for cash. (This transaction is for a different amount than that shown in Chapter 18.)
    b. Bonds payable of $10,000 were retired by the issuance of additional common stock. (This transaction is added to those shown in Chapter 18.)
13. The combined increase of $30,000 in common stock during the year and the increase of $5,000 in paid-in capital in excess of par value during the year were caused by the following:
    a. An additional 2,000 shares of $10 par value common stock were sold and issued for $25,000. (This transaction is for a different amount than that shown in Chapter 18.)
    b. An additional 1,000 shares of $10 par value common stock were issued to retire $10,000 of bonds payable. (This transaction is added to those shown in Chapter 18.)
14. The $30,000 increase in retained earnings during the year was caused by the following:
    a. Net income of $48,000 was earned.
    b. Cash dividends of $18,000 were declared and paid.

## WORK SHEET FOR STATEMENT OF CASH FLOWS

We will now illustrate a work sheet (Exhibit C–2). This work sheet can be used to prepare the statements of cash flows shown later in Exhibits C–3 and C–4. The third illustrated version in Exhibit C–5 is an expansion of the first two and will be explained later.

EXHIBIT C–2

LINLEY CORPORATION
Work Sheet for the Statement of Cash Flows
For the Year Ended December 31, 19X5

| | Account Balances 12/31/X4 | Analysis of Transactions For 19X5 | | Account Balances 12/31/X5 |
|---|---|---|---|---|
| DEBITS | | | | |
| Cash | 40,000 | | (X)10,000 | 30,000 |
| Accounts Receivable (net) | 110,000 | (1)40,000 | | 150,000 |
| Inventory | 75,000 | (1)15,000 | | 90,000 |
| Prepaid Expenses | 7,000 | | (1) 2,000 | 5,000 |
| Land | 30,000 | | | 30,000 |
| Buildings | 200,000 | (2)50,000 | | 250,000 |
| Equipment | 106,000 | (3)64,000 | | 170,000 |
| Total Debits | 568,000 | | | 725,000 |
| CREDITS | | | | |
| Accumulated Depreciation—Buildings | 60,000 | | (4)20,000 | 80,000 |
| Accumulated Depreciation—Equipment | 35,000 | | (4)15,000 | 50,000 |
| Accounts Payable | 90,000 | | (5) 6,000 | 96,000 |
| Salaries Payable | 1,200 | (5) 300 | | 900 |
| Taxes Payable | 10,000 | | (5) 2,000 | 12,000 |
| Interest Payable | 3,000 | | (5) 1,000 | 4,000 |
| Accrued Liabilities | 53,800 | (5) 1,700 | | 52,100 |
| Long-Term 10% Bonds Payable | 100,000 | (6)10,000 | (7)60,000 | 150,000 |
| Common Stock | 90,000 | | { (8)20,000<br>(6)10,000 } | 120,000 |
| Paid-in Capital in Excess of Par Value | 10,000 | | (8) 5,000 | 15,000 |
| Retained Earnings | 115,000 | (9)18,000 | (10)48,000 | 145,000 |
| Total Credits | 568,000 | 199,000 | 199,000 | 725,000 |
| Cash Flows from Operating Activities | | | | |
| Net Income | | (10)48,000 | | |
| Depreciation | | (4)35,000 | | |
| Net Increase in Current Assets Other Than Cash | | | (1)53,000 | |
| Net Increase in Current Liabilities | | (5) 7,000 | | |
| Cash Flows from Investing Activities | | | | |
| Purchase of Building | | | (2)50,000 | |
| Purchase of Equipment | | | (3)64,000 | |
| Cash Flows from Financing Activities | | | | |
| Proceeds from Selling Bonds | | (7)60,000 | | |
| Proceeds from Selling Common Stock | | (8)25,000 | | |
| Payment of Dividends | | | (9)18,000 | |
| Common Stock Issued to Retire Long-Term Bonds | | (6)10,000 | (6)10,000 | |
| | | 185,000 | 195,000 | |
| Decrease in Cash | | (X)10,000 | | |
| | | 195,000 | 195,000 | |

## STATEMENT OF CASH FLOWS— INDIRECT WITH SEPARATE SCHEDULES

If preparers desire to do so, they can present the statement of cash flows in a manner that shows cash flow from operating activities "indirectly" and includes separate supporting schedules. Basically, this is the method traditionally shown in most statements of changes in financial position; a reconciliation is made between net income on the income statement and net cash flow from operating activities.

Exhibit C–3 illustrates the "indirect" method using the data from the work sheet in Exhibit C–2.

EXHIBIT C–3

LINLEY CORPORATION
Statement of Cash Flows (Indirect and Supporting Schedule)
For the Year Ended December 31, 19X5

| | | |
|---|---|---|
| Net Cash Flow from Operating Activities | | $ 37,000 |
| Cash Flows from Investing Activities: | | |
| Purchase of Building | (50,000) | |
| Purchase of Equipment | (64,000) | |
| Net Cash Used by Investing Activities | | (114,000) |
| Cash Flows from Financing Activities: | | |
| Proceeds from Selling Bonds | 60,000 | |
| Proceeds from Selling Common Stock | 25,000 | |
| Payment of Dividends | (18,000) | |
| Net Cash Provided by Financing Activities | | 67,000 |
| Net Increase (Decrease) in Cash | | $(10,000) |
| Schedule reconciling earnings to net cash flow from operating activities: | | |
| Net Income | $48,000 | |
| Noncash Expenses, Revenues, Losses, and Gains included in Income: | | |
| Depreciation on Building and Equipment | 35,000 | |
| Net Increase in Current Assets Other Than Cash | (53,000) | |
| Net Increase in Current Liabilities | 7,000 | |
| Net Cash Flow from Operating Activities | | $ 37,000 |
| Schedule of Noncash Investing and Financing Activities: | | |
| Common Stock Issued to Retire Long-Term Bonds | | $ 10,000 |

## STATEMENT OF CASH FLOWS— INDIRECT WITHOUT SEPARATE SCHEDULES

Preparers can also present the statement of cash flows in a manner that shows cash flow from operating activities "indirectly" and includes all the necessary items in the body of the statement rather than including supporting schedules. This method is shown in Exhibit C–4.

EXHIBIT C–4

| LINLEY CORPORATION<br>Statement of Cash Flows (Indirect Without Supporting Schedules)<br>For the Year Ended December 31, 19X5 | | |
|---|---|---|
| Net Cash Flow from Operating Activities: | | |
| Net Income | $48,000 | |
| Noncash Expenses, Revenues, Losses, and Gains Included in Income: | | |
| Depreciation on Building and Equipment | 35,000 | |
| Net Increase in Current Assets Other Than Cash | (53,000) | |
| Net Increase in Current Liabilities | 7,000 | |
| Net Cash Flow from Operating Activities | | $ 37,000 |
| Cash Flows from Investing Activities: | | |
| Purchase of Building | (50,000) | |
| Purchase of Equipment | (64,000) | |
| Net Cash Used by Investing Activities | | (114,000) |
| Cash Flows from Financing Activities: | | |
| Proceeds from Selling Bonds | 60,000 | |
| Proceeds from Selling Common Stock | 35,000 | |
| Less: Common Stock Used to Retire Long-Term Bonds | (10,000) | |
| Cash Proceeds from Selling Common Stock | 25,000 | |
| Payment of Dividends | (18,000) | |
| Net Cash Provided by Financing Activities | | 67,000 |
| Net Increase (Decrease) in Cash | | $(10,000) |

## STATEMENT OF CASH FLOWS—DIRECT WITH SEPARATE SCHEDULE

Some preparers may prefer to present net cash flows from operating activities in a "direct" way by showing cash provided by operating activities and cash disbursed for operating activities. In every other respect, the format of the statement is like the one shown in Exhibit C–3 and has a separate supporting schedule of noncash investing and financing activities.

The data to prepare cash flows from investing activities and cash flows from financing activities can be obtained from the work sheet in Exhibit C–2. However, to prepare the cash flows from operating activities, we should refer to Exhibit 18–9 in Chapter 18, which is reproduced as Exhibit C–5.

Note that in Exhibit C–5 the conversion of accrual-basis amounts to cash-basis amounts allows us to easily list the items that constitute cash provided by operating activities and cash disbursed for operating activities. The following analysis can be used to explain the list:

1. Cash received from customers is derived by taking the sales of $467,000 and subtracting the $40,000 increase in accounts receivable during the year ($467,000 − $40,000 = $427,000).

*EXHIBIT C–5*

Schedule to Determine Cash Provided by Operations

LINLEY CORPORATION
Conversion of Income Statement Amounts from an Accrual to a Cash Basis
For the Year Ended December 31, 19X5

| | ACCRUAL-BASIS AMOUNTS (FROM INCOME STATEMENT) | ADD OR (DEDUCT) | CASH-BASIS AMOUNTS |
|---|---|---|---|
| Sales (net) | $467,000 | (40,000) | $427,000 |
| Cost of Goods Sold | 280,000 | { 15,000<br>(6,000) } | 289,000 |
| Gross Profit | $187,000 | | $138,000 |
| Operating Expenses: | | | |
| Depreciation Expense | $ 35,000 | (35,000) | $ -0- |
| Salaries Expense | 50,000 | 300 | 50,300 |
| Selling Expense | 15,000 | 1,700 | 16,700 |
| General Expense | 6,000 | (2,000) | 4,000 |
| Interest Expense | 12,000 | (1,000) | 11,000 |
| Total Operating Expenses | $118,000 | | $ 82,000 |
| Income Before Income Taxes | $ 69,000 | | $ 56,000 |
| Income Taxes | 21,000 | (2,000) | 19,000 |
| Net Income | $ 48,000 | | |
| Cash Provided by Operations | | | $ 37,000 |

2. Cash paid to suppliers is derived by taking the cost of goods sold of $280,000, adding the $15,000 increase in inventory during the year, and subtracting the $6,000 increase in accounts payable during the year ($280,000 + $15,000 − $6,000 = $289,000).
3. Since depreciation is a noncash expense, there is no cash paid out for this item, and it does not appear in the cash flows from operating activities (note that when the indirect method is used, depreciation expense is added to net income).
4. Cash paid to employees is derived by taking the salaries expense of $50,000 and adding the $300 decrease in salaries payable during the year ($50,000 + $300 = $50,300).
5. Cash paid for selling expense is derived by taking the selling expense of $15,000 and adding the $1,700 decrease in accrued liabilities during the year ($15,000 + $1,700 = $16,700).
6. Cash paid for general expense is derived by taking the general expense of $6,000 and subtracting the $2,000 decrease in prepaid expenses during the year ($6,000 − $2,000 = $4,000).
7. Cash paid for interest is derived by taking the interest expense of $12,000 and subtracting the $1,000 increase in interest payable during the year ($12,000 − $1,000 = $11,000).
8. Cash paid for taxes is derived by taking the income taxes expense of $21,000 and subtracting the $2,000 increase in taxes payable during the year ($21,000 − $2,000 = $19,000).

We now have the data to prepare a statement using the direct method of reporting cash flows from operating activities. Such a statement is shown in Exhibit C–6.

EXHIBIT C-6

| LINLEY CORPORATION | | |
|---|---|---|
| Statement of Cash Flows (Direct and Supporting Schedules) | | |
| For the Year Ended December 31, 19X5 | | |
| Cash Flows from Operating Activities: | | |
| Cash Received from Customers | $427,000 | |
| Cash Provided by Operating Activities | | $427,000 |
| Cash Paid to Suppliers | 289,000 | |
| Cash Paid to Employees | 50,300 | |
| Cash Paid for Selling Expense | 16,700 | |
| Cash Paid for General Expense | 4,000 | |
| Cash Paid for Interest | 11,000 | |
| Cash Paid for Taxes | 19,000 | |
| Cash Disbursed for Operating Activities | | 390,000 |
| Net Cash Flow from Operating Activities | | 37,000 |
| Cash Flows from Investing Activities: | | |
| Purchase of Building | (50,000) | |
| Purchase of Equipment | (64,000) | |
| Net Cash Used by Investing Activities | | (114,000) |
| Cash Flows from Financing Activities: | | |
| Proceeds from Selling Bonds | 60,000 | |
| Proceeds from Selling Common Stock | 25,000 | |
| Payment of Dividends | (18,000) | |
| Net Cash Provided by Financing Activities | | 67,000 |
| Net Increase (Decrease) in Cash | | $ (10,000) |
| Schedule of Noncash Investing and Financing Activities: | | |
| Common Stock Issued to Retire Long-Term Bonds | | $ 10,000 |

## SUMMARY

We have demonstrated the rationale for and the methods of preparing a statement of cash flows, which for general-purpose external reporting may replace the traditional statement of changes in financial position. The statement of cash flows emphasizes receipts and disbursements of cash classified by operating activities, investing activities, and financing activities. For general-purpose external reporting, a company may no longer have the option of using either a working capital version or a cash version, and the term *funds* may be replaced by the terms *cash* or *cash* and *cash equivalents.*

We also illustrated the following three formats for reporting a statement of cash flows:

1. Reporting the cash flow from operating activities indirectly by using a separate schedule to reconcile net income to net cash flow from operating activities. Noncash investing and financing activities are reported in a separate schedule.
2. Reporting the cash flow from operating activities indirectly by reconciling net income to net cash flow from operating activities within the body of the statement. Noncash investing and financing activities are also reported within the body of the statement.
3. Reporting cash flow from operating activities directly by showing, within the body of the statement, cash provided by operating activities and cash disbursed for operating activities. Noncash investing and financing activities are reported in a separate schedule.

We should point out, however, that while the statement of cash flows may be required for general-purpose external reporting, the traditional statement of changes in financial position can still be used for internal management purposes. As illustrated in Chapter 18, either the working capital version or the cash version is acceptable for internal use.

# INDEX

## A

## O



## P

**Problem 15–3** Total Contributed Capital, $2,387,600
**Problem 15–4** Retained Earnings, December 31, 19X7, $708,000
**Problem 15–5** No Key Figure
**Problem 15–6** Total Contributed Capital, $731,000
**Problem 15–7** No Key Figure
**Problem 15–8** Net Income, $42,000
**Problem 15–9** Primary Earnings per Common Share, $1.20
**Problem 15–10** Weighted Average Number of Shares Outstanding, 145,000
**Problem 15–11** Net Income, $149,400
**Problem 15–1A** Total Stockholders' Equity, $1,512,600
**Problem 15–2A** Retained Earnings, December 31, 19X7, $496,000
**Problem 15–3A** Total Contributed Capital, $908,800
**Problem 15–4A** Net Income, $13,200
**Problem 15–5A** Primary Earnings per Common Share $1.00

### Chapter 16

**Exercise 16–1** (2), $480,000
**Exercise 16–2** Bond Interest Expense 19X5, $27,000
**Exercise 16–3** Carrying Value of Bonds, $391,342
**Exercise 16–4** Bond Interest Expense 19X5, $19,600
**Exercise 16–5** No Key Figure
**Exercise 16–6** Unamortized Discount, $5,500
**Exercise 16–7** No Key Figure
**Exercise 16–8** No Key Figure
**Exercise 16–9** May 1, Interest Expense, $3,586
**Exercise 16–10** December 31, Interest Expense, $9,867 (rounded)
**Problem 16–1** (1) Earnings per Share Plan 2, $3.75
**Problem 16–2** Present Value of Bonds, $565,587
**Problem 16–3** Interest Expense Reported in 1987, $45,888
**Problem 16–4** Interest Expense Reported for Year Ended 2/28/88, $64,249
**Problem 16–5** No Key Figure
**Problem 16–6** (6) Bond Interest Expense, $16,000
**Problem 16–7** Carrying Value of Bonds, $310,631
**Problem 16–8** Interest Expense—September 1, $8,237.50
**Problem 16–9** Interest Expense for the Year Ended 12/31/88, $3,836
**Problem 16–10** Present Value of Bonds, $463,203
**Problem 16–1A** (1) Earnings per Share Plan 2, $1.56
**Problem 16–2A** Present Value of Bonds, $285,257
**Problem 16–3A** Interest Expense Reported for Year Ended 4/30/88, $51,168
**Problem 16–4A** (6) Bond Interest Expense, $30,000
**Problem 16–5A** Interest Expense for the Year Ended 12/31/88, $36,834

### *Appendix to Chapter 16*

**Exercise A–16–1** (2) $8,144.50
**Exercise A–16–2** (1) $72,433.00
**Exercise A–16–3** (3) $2,494.40
**Exercise A–16–4** (2) $49,054.20

### Chapter 17

**Exercise 17–1** Gain on Sale of Temporary Investments, $400
**Exercise 17–2** Carrying Value of Temporary Investments, $97,000
**Exercise 17–3** (6) Net Cash Received, $74,800
**Exercise 17–4** No Key Figure
**Exercise 17–5** Bond Interest Revenue Reported for 1986, $4,365
**Exercise 17–6** No Key Figure
**Exercise 17–7** Investment Account Balance, $1,575,000
**Exercise 17–8** No Key Figure
**Exercise 17–9** Consolidated Revenue, $1,137,000
**Exercise 17–10** Paid-in Capital—April 1, Credited $240,000
**Problem 17–1** Gain on Sale of Temporary Investments, $372
**Problem 17–2** Carrying Value of Temporary Investments, $56,100
**Problem 17–3** Bond Interest Revenue for 1985, $5,329
**Problem 17–4** Bond Interest Revenue for 1986, $4,655 (Rounded)
**Problem 17–5** (4) Loss on Sale of Investments, $20,800
**Problem 17–6** (2) Gain on Sale of Investments, $4,279
**Problem 17–7** Minority Interest, $24,000
**Problem 17–8** Consolidated Balance Sheet, Total Assets, $795,000
**Problem 17–9** Consolidated Net Income, $169,000
**Problem 17–10** Consolidated Balance Sheet, Total Assets, $1,160,000
**Problem 17–11** Income Statement—Total Revenue, $8,409
**Problem 17–1A** Loss on Sale of Temporary Investments, $145
**Problem 17–2A** Bond Interest Revenue for 1986, $3,657 (Rounded)
**Problem 17–3A** (4) Gain on Sale of Investments, $7,500
**Problem 17–4A** Consolidated Balance Sheet, Total Assets, $875,000
**Problem 17–5A** Consolidated Balance Sheet, Total Assets, $960,000

### Chapter 18

**Exercise 18–1** No Key Figure
**Exercise 18–2** No Key Figure
**Exercise 18–3** Net Purchases, $293,400
**Exercise 18–4** Net Income, $4,000
**Exercise 18–5** No Key Figure
**Exercise 18–6** No Key Figure
**Exercise 18–7** No Key Figure
**Exercise 18–8** Increase in Working Capital, $3,000
**Problem 18–1** No Key Figure
**Problem 18–2** Total Sources of Working Capital, $45,000
**Problem 18–3** Current Operations, $2,000
**Problem 18–4** Increase in Working Capital, $3,300
**Problem 18–5** Total Sources of Cash, $9,000
**Problem 18–6** Total Uses of Cash, $21,000
**Problem 18–7** Working Capital Provided by Operations, $80,000
**Problem 18–8** Total Sources of Working Capital, $76,900
**Problem 18–9** Current Operations, $73,000
**Problem 18–10** Total Uses of Working Capital, $110,000
**Problem 18–11** Total Sources of Working Capital, $4,465
**Problem 18–1A** Working Capital Provided by Operations, $24,900
**Problem 18–2A** Total Sources of Cash, $75,700
**Problem 18–3A** Total Uses of Working Capital, $12,000
**Problem 18–4A** Total Sources of Working Capital, $92,300
**Problem 18–5A** Current Operations, $63,200

### Chapter 19

**Exercise 19–1** Total Assets, 5.0%
**Exercise 19–2** Sales 19X5, 129.2%
**Exercise 19–3** Net Income 19X5, 9.3%
**Exercise 19–4** Days to Collect Receivables, 19X5—37.6 Days
**Exercise 19–5** Earnings per Share, 19X5, $2.84
**Exercise 19–6** Asset Turnovers, Mack Company 1.3 Times
**Exercise 19–7** Case 1 Return on Assets, 12.6%
**Exercise 19–8** Case 2 Return on Stockholders' Equity, 3.6%
**Problem 19–1** Net Income 19X5, 14.0%
**Problem 19–2** Net Sales 19X5, 157.30%
**Problem 19–3** Quick Ratio, .9 to 1
**Problem 19–4** No Key Figure
**Problem 19–5** Accounts Receivable Turnover, 19X2, 10.46
**Problem 19–6** Current Liabilities, $16,000
**Problem 19–7** Return on Sales, 6.4%
**Problem 19–8** No Key Figure
**Problem 19–9** Debt to Total Assets, Rye Company 63.04%
**Problem 19–10** Earnings per Share, 19X5, $6.45
**Problem 19–1A** Net Income 19X5, 6.5%
**Problem 19–2A** Net Sales 19X5, 153.85%
**Problem 19–3A** Return on Common Stockholders' Equity, 22.2%
**Problem 19–4A** No Key Figure
**Problem 19–5A** Cost of Goods Sold, $42,000

### Chapter 20

**Exercise 20–1** No Key Figure
**Exercise 20–2** No Key Figure
**Exercise 20–3** No Key Figure
**Exercise 20–4** Gross Profit in Year 4, $1,550,000
**Exercise 20–5** Purchasing Power Loss, $225
**Exercise 20–6** Constant Dollar Total Assets, $102,611
**Exercise 20–7** Constant Dollar Net Income, $30,381
**Exercise 20–8** Current Cost—Cost of Goods Sold, $64,350
**Exercise 20–9** Current Cost—Net Income, $87,000
**Problem 20–1** No Key Figure
**Problem 20–2** No Key Figure
**Problem 20–3** Gross Profit 1986, $1,029
**Problem 20–4** 1(b) Gross Profit 1987, $1,859,000
**Problem 20–5** Total Assets, $314,697
**Problem 20–6** Constant Dollar Net Income, $2,190
**Problem 20–7** Total Assets, $459,760
**Problem 20–8** Current Cost Net Income, $47,500
**Problem 20–9** Current Cost Net Income, $61,000
**Problem 20–1A** No Key Figure
**Problem 20–2A** No Key Figure
**Problem 20–3A** 1(b) Gross Profit 1987, $1,810,000
**Problem 20–4A** Total Assets, $533,409
**Problem 20–5A** Current Cost Net Income, $23,800

### Chapter 21

**Exercise 21–1** No Key Figure
**Exercise 21–2** No Key Figure
**Exercise 21–3** No Key Figure
**Exercise 21–4** Direct Materials Inventory, 12/31/X9, $70,000
**Exercise 21–5** No Key Figure
**Problem 21–1** No Key Figure
**Problem 21–2** No Key Figure
**Problem 21–3** Cost of Goods Sold, $683,300
**Problem 21–4** Cost of Goods Manufactured, $1,139,000
**Problem 21–5** Cost of Goods Manufactured, $399,000
**Problem 21–6** Cost of Goods Manufactured, $98,900
**Problem 21–7** Cost of Goods Manufactured, $395,000
**Problem 21–8** Net Income, $74,500
**Problem 21–1A** Cost of Goods Manufactured, $225,500
**Problem 21–2A** Cost of Goods Manufactured, $357,700